Nikolai Demidov

At the time of his death, Konstantin Stanislavsky considered Nikolai Demidov to be "his only student, who understands the System." Demidov's incredibly forward-thinking processes not only continued his teacher's pioneering work, but also solved the problems of an actor's creativity that Stanislavsky never conquered.

Despite being one of the original teachers of the Stanislavsky system, Demidov's name was little known either in his native Russia or the wider world until the turn of the twenty-first century. Since then, his extensive works have been published in Russian but are yet to find their way to the English-speaking world. His sophisticated psychological techniques, stimulation of creativity, and methods of developing the actors themselves are now gaining increasing recognition.

Nikolai Demidov: Becoming an Actor-Creator brings together Demidov's five volumes on actor training. Supplementary materials, including transcriptions of Demidov's classes, and notes make this the definitive collection on one of Russian theatre's most important figures.

Nikolai Demidov (1884–1953) was co-founder of the Moscow Art Theatre School, and one of the original teachers of Stanislavski's system. Demidov's radical approach saw him ostracized from Moscow and his role in Russian actor training largely wiped from the history books. The efforts of his celebrated pupils – including Maria Knebel, Boris Livanov, and Margarita Laskina – have seen his work gradually return to recognition.

Andrei Malaev-Babel is an actor, director and scholar, a graduate of the Vakhtangov Theatre Institute in Moscow. He serves as Head of Acting at the FSU/Asolo Conservatory for Actor Training, and on the board of the Michael Chekhov Association. He is the editor of *The Vakhtangov Sourcebook* and author of *Yevgeny Vakhtangov: A Critical Portrait*.

Margarita Laskina is a noted Russian theatre scholar. She served as Aleksandrinsky Theatre's literary manager and editor-in-chief for the Leningrad Television. As assistant to Nikolai Demidov, she learned directly from the teacher, and as keeper of the Demidov archive, she edited his fundamental four-volume *Heritage* (2004–2009).

Figure 1　Nikolai Demidov, Moscow, 1951

Nikolai Demidov

Becoming an Actor-Creator

Edited by Andrei Malaev-Babel and Margarita Laskina

Translated by Andrei Malaev-Babel with Alexander Rojavin and Sarah Lillibridge

Routledge
Taylor & Francis Group

LONDON AND NEW YORK

First published 2016 by Routledge

2 Park Square, Milton Park, Abingdon, Oxon, OX14 4RN
605 Third Avenue, New York, NY 10017

Routledge is an imprint of the Taylor & Francis Group, an informa business

First issued in paperback 2020

British Library Cataloguing-in-Publication Data
A catalogue record for this book is available from the British Library

Library of Congress Cataloguing-in-Publication Data
Names: Demidov, N.V. (Nikolaæi Vasil§evich), 1884–1953, author. |
    Malaev-Babel, Andrei, editor translator. | Laskina, M. N.
    (Margarita Nikolaevna), editor.
Title: Nikolai Demidov : becoming an actor-creator / edited by
    Andrei Malaev-Babel and Margarita Laskina ; translated by
    Andrei Malaev-Babel with Alexander Rojavin and Sarah
    Lillibridge.
Description: Milton Park, Abingdon, Oxon ; New York : Routledge,
    2016. | Includes bibliographical references and index.
Identifiers: LCCN 2015044135 | ISBN 9781138776494 (hardback) |
    ISBN 9781315621685 (ebook)
Subjects: LCSH: Acting. | Theater—Production and direction.
Classification: LCC PN2061.D443 2016 | DDC 792.02/8—dc23
LC record available at http://lccn.loc.gov/2015044135

ISBN: 978-1-138-77649-4 (hbk)
ISBN: 978-0-367-73700-9 (pbk)

Typeset in Bembo Std
by Swales & Willis Ltd, Exeter, Devon, UK

All these books are but a modest wreath on my father's unknown tomb. Early in my childhood he planted in my soul the golden seeds of artistic truth. Thanks to him alone I could perceive correctly what I heard from all my voluntary and involuntary teachers. This solitary, phenomenally pure and proud man, this enormous natural talent, remained in the shadows only because he was deprived of those human shortcomings required to build a career and obtain fame in the theatre world. When it comes to other art forms, artists like him meet their appreciation after death – for what remains after them; in our art, however, we leave nothing behind.

Nikolai Demidov

Contents

Contents

Contents

Figures

Acknowledgements

This book would not have been possible without contributions and support from many generous individuals. At Routledge, we would like to acknowledge Talia Rogers, Ben Piggott and Kate Edwards.

Florida State University and its Council on Research and Creativity (COFRS) generously supported this book. We are thankful to them, and to those individuals, who spoke in favor of the COFRS award, or who supported the application process: Provost Sally McRorie; Dean of the College of Fine Arts Peter Weishar; Dr. C. Cameron Jackson, Director of the FSU School of Theatre; Professors Kris Salata and Daniel Sack; as well as the School of Theatre's business administrator Lauren Snyder. We would also like to thank Gary K. Ostrander, Vice President for Research and Lezlee Richerson, Research Development Coordinator.

Special thanks go to Professor Sergei Tcherkasski (St. Petersburg State Theatre Arts Academy, Russia), for his support of this book. Our gratitude also goes to Lyudmila Shulga of the Irkutsk Theatre School, and Vlada Milovskaya of St. Petersburg's *Vokrug Da Okolo* Creative Laboratory, for their work on transcribing the Demidov lectures and notes. We are indebted to the Moscow theatre director and photographer Sergei Tuptalov for restoring some of the illustrations to this book.

Dr. Laskina is eternally grateful to the author of this book, Nikolai Demidov, for his lessons, and for his advice of "slow reading." It allowed her to delve deeper into Demidov's brilliant thoughts.

She would like to thank her co-editor and translator, Andrei Malaev-Babel, who remained creative, yet precise in his work of translating Demidov, and who feels "the soul" of Demidov's pedagogical method. Above all, she is thankful to Professor Malaev-Babel for granting Demidov's school an international life.

She is grateful to God for being able to complete this work.

Last, but not least, Dr. Laskina will always remain thankful to destiny for bringing her together with her husband Oleg Okulevich (1921–2006) – a brilliant actor and Demidov's closest student. Although he is no longer with us, she continues to seek his advice daily.

Andrei Malaev-Babel would like to acknowledge his wife, Lisa Eveland Malaev, who dedicated numerous hours to proofreading his translations and writings, and managed to maintain a healthy sense of humor in facing the self-sacrificing Russian visionaries and their lofty ideas. He also wants to thank his mother Lidiya and his son Nicholai for their patience and support during this all-consuming project. He is forever grateful to the memory of his grandmother, a brilliant construction engineer, teacher and author Antonina Pirozhkova (1909–2010) for tirelessly cultivating his creativity. He is also grateful for the provident influence his late grandfather, the writer Isaac Babel (1894–1940), has had on his entire life, and on that of his family.

His deep gratitude goes to Steven Ross Eveland for his kindness, generosity of spirit and editing advice.

He is thankful to Marina Tsapovetskaya and Tatyana Sinelnikova of the St. Petersburg State Theatre Library, for their invaluable assistance in his research. He also would like to acknowledge Marfa Bubnova, Director of the Moscow Art Theatre's Museum for her help and advice.

Professor Malaev-Babel's is also grateful to his chief co-translator Alexander Rojavin for taking this project so close to his heart, and contributing so many hours of inspired and dedicated labor to the Demidov collection. He would like to thank his other co-translator, Sarah Lillibridge, for her dedication. His special gratitude goes to Svetlana Tikhonov for her generous help with translation and research.

Professor Malaev-Babel is extremely fortunate to be collaborating with Dr. Margarita Laskina – a pioneer of the Demidov research and publication, and a living link to the master himself. He would like to acknowledge the generosity and expertise of Pavel Dmitriev, Curator of St. Petersburg Philharmonia's Music Library, for his editorial contribution to the four-volume *Demidov Heritage* Russian collection. Without Mr. Dmitriev's support, he would not have been able to advance as far in his Demidov research. Last but not least, Professor Malaev-Babel would like to thank his colleagues and students at the Florida State University/ Asolo Conservatory for Actor Training and at the New College of Florida. He learns from them daily.

Special thanks to the Florida State University's Council on Research and Creativity for their support through the COFRS grant award.

A Note on the Text

This collection contains the fundamental works of one of the most outstanding figures of Russian theatre pedagogy, Nikolai Vasilyevich Demidov (1884–1953). A close collaborator of Konstantin Stanislavsky, Demidov pioneered the "organic acting technique" belonging to the art of "genuine creative living onstage." This volume is designed for students and teachers of theatre schools, but also for anyone seriously interested in the art of the theatre and the actor. It includes Demidov's five major books, in an abridged format. (Cuts in the text are not specified.) The Glossary of Terms and Exercises further clarifies key Demidov terms and techniques, and it offers guidance for practical exercises, which are essential to the mastering the organic technique.

In translating Demidov, we tried to remain faithful to the author's original language and style. The colloquial nature of Demidov's writings was preserved by the translators. All emphases in quoted materials have been added by the author, Demidov.

The names of students, and those of the "etude characters," are kept as original Russian names. This might present a certain challenge for some readers. On the other hand, we felt it was important to set the Demidov classroom in his native Russia, in the period between the early 1920s to late 1940s – rather than introducing English and/or contemporary equivalents. This is why we preserved Demidov's use of masculine "he" (instead of "they" or "he or she") when generally referring to an actor.

The third book, *The Art of Living Onstage*, presented special challenges, as it is rich in dialogues between the teacher and his students. In order to better set off these dialogues from narration, we introduced the use of bulleted dialogue – specifically for this book. This device is not used in the other four books.

Nikolai Demidov

A Creative Biography

From the Editors

Konstantin Stanislavsky (1954: 8), in his Introduction[1] to *An Actor's Work* extends "sincere gratitude" to Nikolai Vasilyevich Demidov for helping him with the "creation of this book." "He gave me," Stanislavsky writes, "valuable guidance, materials, and examples to illustrate my points, he critiqued my book, and exposed my mistakes." *Guidance?! To Stanislavsky himself!? Mistakes?! Surely not grammatical mistakes!* What did Stanislavsky mean? And who is this individual who dared point out to Stanislavsky his mistakes?

This is how Stanislavsky (2009a: 460) himself portrays Demidov in a document circa 1926:

> This is a man full of genuine love for the art, and a selfless enthusiast. From the time we met [in 1907], . . . he continuously helped me develop the rich and complex subject of the actor's creativity. At the moment, I think he is one of the few who knows the "system" theoretically and practically.
>
> For four years he worked in my Opera Studio as a director and a teacher.
>
> For two years he headed the Art Theatre's School, where he led (after Sulerzhitsky and Vakhtangov) educational work and training based on the 'system.'

"I've known N. V. Demidov through our mutual work for approximately 30 years," says Stanislavsky (2009b: 487) in yet another document (circa 1937). "He is an extremely valuable artist and is my closest associate in teaching and research."

In fact, by the end of his life, Demidov had 40 years of hard work behind him as a teacher of theatre, a director, and persistent researcher of the actor's creativity – the man who succeeded penetrating the very depths of the creative process and discovering its strings. Is this not the highest achievement for a man, a scholar, but also an artist? Decades of pedagogical practice alone don't bring about such results. It is, in fact, an artistic achievement – the fruit of a gifted artist's intuition.

The decades of Demidov's research and practice resulted in a series of written texts. His thoughts are surprisingly deep, original and . . . modern. Composed 60, even 80 years ago, these texts manage to transcend the present and take us into the future.

The other founder of the Moscow Art Theatre, Vladimir Nemirovich-Danchenko (1858–1943), echoed Stanislavsky in highly praising Demidov's work and its immense creative potential. As early as the 1920's, Nemirovich (2009: 462) had the insight to describe Demidov as "an authority in the psychology of stage art, who is continuously moving forward, *discovering many new ways that will enrich future theatre schools and the theory and practice of creative psychology* [emphasis added]."

Then how is it possible that, for so many years, the name of Nikolai Demidov remained Russian theatre's best kept secret? The answer to this inherent question is finally being supplied by time, the theatre of the future, unbiased analyses of archives, and, presently, by Demidov's own works.

★★★

The roots of Demidov's love for theatre and his practical knowledge of the stage can be traced to his childhood and young adulthood. He was born on December 8, 1884 (November 25, according to the old calendar) in the town of Ivanovo-Voznesensk, to the family of Vasily Viktorovich Demidov (1825–1908). A bright and talented individual in many respects, including as an actor, Vasily Demidov was the founder of Ivanovo-Voznesensk's Popular Theatre. He was a self-taught man, and his phenomenal artistic growth was a tribute to his own efforts. In his Popular Theatre, he was simultaneously an actor, director, and administrator. He wrote several plays on the everyday life of common people. Staged in this theatre, his

Figure 2   Vasily Demidov, August 1904. Courtesy of Margarita Laskina.

plays were published and acclaimed by the famed Russian playwright Alexander Ostrovsky (1823–1886). In the city of Ivanovo, there is still a street named after Vasily Demidov.

Vasily had three sons; among them his youngest, Nikolai, actively and passionately participated in his father's theatre. He later insisted that his theatre tastes and his point of view on the art were largely formed under his father's influence. "He planted in my soul," Demidov (p. v) writes about his father, "the golden seeds of artistic *truth*" [emphasis added].

In parallel with his theatre work, the young Demidov was seriously involved in athletics. Having reached record results in heavy weight lifting, he organized the Ivanovo-Voznesensk chapter of the St. Petersburg Athletic Society, where he developed and taught his own system of training. Notably, Demidov's system included moral education of athletes. It is also important to note that Demidov and his brother Konstantin (1869–1941) resorted to the teachings of yogis – both for sports and stage art. The results of their mutual experiments, carefully recorded by Nikolai, were presented to Stanislavsky as early as 1911. Demidov's records are currently kept in Moscow, at the Stanislavsky section of the Moscow Art Theatre's Archive (Fund 3, inventory 44, item No. 59).

In 1907, upon completing high school, Demidov moved to Moscow and was accepted to the Moscow University's Medical School (with a focus on psychiatry). Here in Moscow, Demidov was attracted to theatre with renewed force – especially to the Moscow Art Theatre. His close friendship with the MAT director Leopold Sulerzhitsky[2] (1872–1916) allowed Demidov to

Figure 3   Nikolai Demidov – *Meditation*, 1915–1916. Courtesy of Margarita Laskina.

Figure 4   Leopold Sulerzhitsky, Konstantin Stanislavsky and Nikolai Demidov, Kislovodsk, Caucuses, 1910. Courtesy of Margarita Laskina.

enter the inner world of the Moscow Arts Theatre, and to find a valid pretext for personal closeness to Stanislavsky.

The 25-year-old medical student, fascinated by the theatre arts, interested Stanislavsky. In fact, Stanislavsky's respect for Demidov was so high that he entrusted Demidov with his son Igor's physical and moral education. Igor Alekseyev (1894–1974) and Demidov kept their friendship for years to come. For several years, Demidov traveled with Stanislavsky's family on summer trips to France, Caucasus, Crimea, Shafranovo village (in Bashkiria), and Lubimovka Estate (just outside of Moscow). During these trips, he constantly discussed with Stanislavsky the nature of acting; at Stanislavsky's request, he helped him collect scientific material on this topic. Demidov suggested to Stanislavsky to pay close attention to yoga practices (see Tcherkassky 2013: 14).

The company of doctor Demidov was a great asset to Stanislavsky who, during these years, was forming his "system" of actor training. Extremely timely for Stanislavsky was Demidov's training in natural sciences and philosophy, as well as his talent for teaching and passion for research. A truly uncommon addition to all these qualities was Demidov's practical knowledge of theatre, from early childhood. Already in 1911, Demidov began to assist Stanislavsky in his work with actors.

From 1913, upon graduation from the University, Demidov practiced at Dmitry Pletnyev's Clinic, where the legendary guru Pyotr Badmaev (1851–1920) introduced him to Tibetan medicine. At the same time, Demidov continued to deepen his knowledge of yoga philosophy and practices, and he studied homeopathy. In 1919, however, Stanislavsky convinced Demidov to leave the medical profession and dedicate himself entirely to theatre.

For four years, Demidov helped Stanislavsky with the Opera Studio at the Bolshoi Theatre, serving as director and coach on the production of *Eugene Onegin*. In 1921, Demidov organized the 4th studio at MAT, which he continued to head until 1925. Demidov's reputation as the leading authority on the "system" secured him invitations to teach acting at the Proletkult

Figure 5 Demidov (center) with Stanislavsky's family (to Demidov's left – Igor Alekseyev, to his right – Konstantin Stanislavsky), Shafranovo estate, summer 1917. Courtesy of Margarita Laskina.

Theatre. In addition to that, he was invited to the newly established Georgian Studio in Moscow, and to the National Institute of the Spoken Word.

In 1922, the MAT troupe embarked on a two-year tour of Europe and the US. Before departing on the trip, Stanislavsky insisted that Demidov assume the leadership of the Moscow Art Theatre School. With Sulerzhitsky and Vakhtangov (1883–1922) both dead, Demidov remained the only original teacher of the "system," who commanded Stanislavsky's trust and respect.

Stanislavsky and Demidov served the same artistic God – the theatre of "experiencing," i.e. the theatre of genuine life onstage. According to their deep-seated convictions, such a school of theatre was unparalleled in its force and depth of impact. This ideal united them in the pursuit of a common goal: " . . . to find a way to *truly live onstage – as the world's greatest actors did in their finest moments*" (p. 141).

But how does one reach this state of creativity at the heart of every gifted actor's art? How does one achieve this unrestrained freedom and inspire the workings of the creative subconscious, organic transformation and genuine life onstage?

"The subconscious through the conscious, the involuntary through the voluntary" – such was the way of the "system," as stated by Stanislavsky (1954: 24).

Analyzing "the creative state of the actor," Stanislavsky extracted its defining "elements": "attention," "object," "task," "communication," and others. He suggested that the actor could be trained to control each of these "elements" separately, while their future integration would lead to the sound creative state.

In one of his books, Demidov speaks of his early years of teaching at the MAT. In that time, he was training students strictly in accordance with the Stanislavsky "system," i.e. training each of the elements individually. In doing so, he ran into an insurmountable problem. It took a tremendous effort to achieve freedom and spontaneity (involuntariness) in a rehearsal, and they were lost the very next day. In the following day's rehearsal, he had to start this work again from

Figure 6 Three original teachers of the Stanislavsky System: Leopold Sulerzhitsky (standing), Yevgeny Vakhtangov (sitting, in white hat) and Nikolai Demidov (standing), Yevpatoria, Crimea, 1915. Courtesy of Margarita Laskina.

scratch. At best, the actors would try to repeat and fixate the external manifestations of their "yesterday's" emotional state. Therefore, they would arrive at an outcome totally opposite to what was expected – at "presenting the role" (as Stanislavsky called it). As such, Stanislavsky's (1954: 25) objective – "live a role, i.e. experience the character's emotions every time the role is repeated"—was not achieved. (Stanislavsky himself faced the same problem, as Demidov witnessed.) Of course, such a state of affairs satisfied neither Stanislavsky nor Demidov.

Practice itself brought Demidov to question the fruitfulness of the "system's" purely analytical method (i.e. the dissection of the integral creative process into individual "elements"). Demidov observed that the students trained in separate "elements" resembled the unfortunate centipede from the fable: one day, the centipede started considering how each of its 40 legs worked, and it forgot how to walk. Demidov began to seek the root of the mistake, and he came up with the following answer: "*by rationally dividing into elements the indivisible creative process, we murdered the main thing: spontaneity and the involuntary nature of life onstage, i.e. we murdered the creative process itself*" [emphasis added] (p. 163).

Demidov asked:

> Is it not possible to structure the training itself, from the very first steps, in such a way so as, first of all, to set the actor on the path of this "natural creative state," and second, *make this state so familiar and organic that it would always be present onstage with the actor*? (Demidov 2009: 68; emphasis added)

This is when Demidov realized the necessity of the *synthesizing approach* for actor training, *in contrast to the analytical one.*

According to Demidov, actor training should begin with the cultivation of uninhibited freedom, as it is the true essence of the art:

The foundation being built out of this freedom – so firmly as to become the actors' second nature, their only way to exist onstage – such a foundation allows us to later affix to it the analysis and rationality of a commonly accepted approach to a role. Moreover, even in those cases when a certain measure of the imperative (command and order) is affixed – even then it does not extinguish the most important aspects of an actor's creative process – its freedom and spontaneity. In many cases, this will even prove to be fruitful and necessary. (p. 156)

While trying to answer these questions in theory, Stanislavsky, nevertheless, did not practice the *nurturing* of the student-actor. Instead he worked with actors as a director, in the process of preparing a specific role for the stage. By contrast, Demidov, as a born researcher and teacher, considered his main objective to unearth a student's natural talent. He worked almost exclusively to cultivate a genuine actor-artist, an independent creator possessing the ability to truly live onstage in the process of transformation – each and every time, for each and every rehearsal and performance. (Moreover, Demidov observed that this quality was characteristic of all distinguished actors of all times.)

While following the path of "synthesis" in actor training, Demidov created his "etude technique" which helps uncover and develop the student's specific gift as an actor. If etudes are properly facilitated, in accordance with Demidov's method, the creative state of the actor awakens, ripens, and grows freely. Demidov's etudes are training exercises that cultivate *the creativity of the actor* – a genuine actor, in fact, rather than the "improviser of text," or an "actor-director," who "constructs" the etude from the inside. Both of these tendencies, by the way, are quite common in the Stanislavsky-based etude work until this day.

Needless to say, the new method was not formed right away. It was slowly perfected and enhanced by Demidov over time, throughout his many years of teaching.

However, when Demidov (p. 483) merely mentioned to Stanislavsky a possibility of "training the actors in a different, completely new way – he [Stanislavsky] was surprised and dismayed: what does this mean? Does this mean without 'tasks?!' Without 'objects?!' . . . and without any 'elements' at all? How is this possible? . . . He resisted. He did not want to hear this, was outwardly upset and decisively *blocked the idea* at all costs" [emphasis added].

From that moment, Demidov begins to encounter obstacles in his way – and they keep multiplying.

In 1925, the school of MAT was closed and Demidov found himself "outside of the MAT." The Georgian Studio was moved from Moscow to Tiflis. The MAT's 4th Studio transformed into the Realistic Theatre, and Demidov resigned. The educator from God . . . ("Our school, prepared by Demidov, most likely hosts God in it" – said Stanislavsky (1999: 167)). This educator from God is suddenly denied any type of teaching practice, and simply finds himself unemployed.

However, in 1926 – according to Demidov himself – he begins his scientific-literary work. Demidov starts collecting materials for his series of books on the creative work of the actor. In these books, he integrates and arranges his new discoveries - into a sound system.

The forced unemployment did not last long (even though it was felt strongly in a mundane, material sense). Soon Alexander Tairov (1885–1950) invited Demidov to the Kamerny Theatre to teach and direct in his company's "experimental workshop." In Tairov's (2009:461) opinion, Demidov was *"a rare teacher-educator, with ability to awaken in the actor a love for true art, and teach him true mastery of the internal technique"* [emphasis added].

Demidov had to accept Tairov's offer, even though he did not share Tairov's views on theatre. He participated in the staging of Eugene O'Neill's *Desire Under the Elms* (premiered in

Figure 7 Nikolai Demidov, 1914–1915. Courtesy of Margarita Laskina.

1926; this production created a stir in Russia and abroad). In addition to his work as a director, Demidov conducted classes in actor training for the Tairov troupe.

In 1928, however, Demidov received an invitation from Nemirovich-Danchenko to join him at his Musical Theatre. Demidov left the Kamerny in a wink. Once again, he was suddenly overwhelmed with teaching: in parallel with Nemirovich's theatre, he taught acting to the Moscow Conservatory's opera students. He also began experimenting with acting for the radio at the Research Institute of Radio Broadcasting and Television. He taught a course titled "Directing Technique – Theory and Practice" for the Soviet Union's leading film studio, Mosfilm. Such was the list of Demidov's teaching activities in the late 1920s and early 1930s, and it is still incomplete.

Students and actors preserved the warmest memories of Demidov – wherever he taught. For example, in October of 1930 the Moscow Conservatory students sent Demidov the following address:

> You worked hard and tirelessly . . . You never forced your opinion onto students. You were always concerned with the development of our own individualities. Patiently and in a friendly manner you managed to find in each of us our inherent artistic self. You

masterfully instilled in everyone the foundation of a sound creative state for the stage. You cultivated our artistic taste and taught us to hate stereotypes in art, and the vulgar "theatrical market."

Because of your attentive and delicate care, even a small spark of talent and abilities began to flare . . .

You taught us to work independently, and now we feel the strength to facilitate our own work – rather than merely wait for the director's orders and passively execute his tasks . . . If it weren't for the habit of independent thought, experimentation, and creativity instilled by you, we would not have found what is most important . . . (Demidov 2009: 463–464)

In the meantime, Demidov dreamed of creating a troupe of actors trained, from the very start, according to his technique. For that purpose, one of Demidov's students, Elena Morozova (?–1947), gathered a group of young theatre enthusiasts. For a period of four months, she worked with them two to three times a week – under Demidov's supervision and according to his method. After this short period of time, the young people appeared to be well prepared to rehearse a play. For a traditional theatre school, such a readiness was unheard of – so early into the training process. The work of the group was demonstrated to Stanislavsky. The results he saw stunned him. Stanislavsky, who previously rejected Demidov's proposal to train actors in a new way, now even gave permission to feature his name as one of the founding members of Demidov's new venture – the Creative Studio Theatre.

Stanislavsky saw firsthand the fruitfulness of Demidov's ideas, and their relationship was revived. At that time, Stanislavsky was preparing for publication his new book, *An Actor's Work*. Once more, he sought Demidov's help – as the book's editor. Demidov agreed to assist Stanislavsky in completing the manuscript, as he transferred the artistic directorship of the Creative Studio Theatre to one of his colleagues. For two and a half years, he fully immersed himself in the new project. Simultaneously, Stanislavsky engaged Demidov at his Opera Theatre as a director-teacher. Once again, a period of close collaboration between Demidov and Stanislavsky began: at the theatre, in rehearsals, and at home, while working on the book.

Stanislavsky's description of this work is already familiar to us: ". . . He gave me valuable guidance, materials, and examples to illustrate my points, he critiqued my book, and exposed my mistakes." Demidov tried to convince Stanislavsky about the necessity of the synthesizing approach in the actor training method. He offered synthesis as an alternative to the rational and analytical approach. This approach, embedded in the system, failed to deliver desired results for both of them, and Demidov was ready to share his own findings. It appears that Stanislavsky knew the validity of Demidov's ideas (he saw it first hand), however, he was unable to "cross out" what he had already written. He simply lacked time to begin everything anew. Restructuring his system would take years of new research (a journey already completed by Demidov). In the meantime, all publishing deadlines had expired – the book had to be completed. Stanislavsky needed the money from his American publisher in order to pay for his ailing son Igor's treatment abroad. What could be done?

"He [Stanislavsky] thoroughly reconsidered and revised everything he wrote in his book," [emphasis added] Demidov recalls (Fund 59 of the St. Petersburg State Theatre Library. The Demidov Archive [uncatalogued]).[3] Stanislavsky even wrote the additional, final chapter XVI, dedicated to the role of the subconscious in an actors' creativity. In this chapter, he stated:

Figure 8 Stanislavsky and Demidov in rehearsal, Moscow, 1935. Courtesy of Margarita Laskina.

> In total opposition to some teachers, I believe that students, beginners . . . should . . . *be led immediately toward the subconscious*. This *should be done in the earliest stages* . . . . Beginners should know *at the very start*, albeit in isolated moments, the happiest of moods an actor can have as he is being *creative*. [emphasis added] (Stanislavsky 2008: 330–331)

In his Introduction, Stanislavsky [1954: 6] highlighted that "one should pay special attention" to chapter XVI, "as it contains the essence of creativity and of the entire system."

Unfortunately, the rest of the book contradicted the conclusions in chapter XVI. The system as a whole offered a completely different path . . . Stanislavsky felt this, and he became nervous . . . In a letter to his brother, he complained:

> . . . I am stuck on a couple of chapters, cannot make a move backward or forward . . . . I already fear that I will have to redo what has already been written. I must admit, I got myself into some messy business. I started something unachievable and now I am paying for it. I do not know how I will find a way. I do not sleep well. I am exhausted – trying to do the impossible. (Stanislavsky 1961: 412)

Stanislavsky is already convinced that, in fact, one should develop a normal creative state in actors from the very start of training. But *how? How* does one lead them *"immediately toward the subconscious"? How* does one do it *"in the earliest stages"*? This question remains open for Stanislavsky and his "system." His book only covers the so-called "lures" for the creativity. Meanwhile the "keys" to this problem were already in Demidov's hands – in the etude technique he developed.

In September of 1935, the ultimate argument took place between Stanislavsky and Demidov. According to Stanislavsky (as quoted by Demidov [2009:485] in his letter to Nemirovich-Danchenko), their "creative paths divided" . . . For some time they still worked together; however, when the book was given to the publisher, Demidov was no longer listed as the editor . . . there was only an acknowledgement of him for his help, as quoted earlier.

Their "creative paths divided," and Demidov, just as in the late 1920s, found himself in "exile." "Faithful followers of the system," the ones that built their prosperity around it, crossed out Demidov's name from the history and practice of theatre for many years to come.

After Stanislavsky's death in 1938, the attitude towards Demidov becomes more intolerable. In fact, it borders on persecution: his name was completely eliminated from the history of the MAT and from the Russian theatre history at large. Demidov was fired from the Maly Theatre's Shchepkin School, where he was teaching in the late 1930s and early 1940s. One year after Stanislavsky's death, Demidov quit the Stanislavsky Opera Theatre, quoting, in his resignation letter, a misalignment of his creative views with those of the theatre's leadership.

When, in the early 1940s, Demidov submitted the manuscript of one of his books on the new method (*The Art of Living Onstage*) to the *Iskusstvo* publishers, he faced a slew of grave "internal reviews" swarming with accusations of "idealism," "mysticism," "lack of proper ideological orientation," etc. All accusations were, of course, consistent with the Soviet dogmas of the time. One of the authors of such a review accused Demidov of "creeping empiricism," "agnosticism," "intuitivism," "physiologism," and of being a proponent of the "free-run theory." He ended his review, written in the style of "report to the authorities," with far-reaching conclusions: "If the author of this 'system' is teaching anything to anyone, it is critical to step in and end these teaching activities at once" (Fund 59).

Even under such difficult circumstances, Demidov continued his work. In 1940, a group of his students graduated from the Glazunov School of Music and Theatre. Approximately at the same time (in 1939 and 1940), Demidov recruited two groups of students for the Maly Theatre's School. On the eve of the war with Nazi Germany, Demidov directed Gorky's drama *The Last Ones* in a production featuring these students alongside the Glazunov School graduates. The Gorky production was intended to lay a foundation for a new, young theatre, but . . . the war shattered all of Demidov's plans.

At the end of 1942 the government of the Karelo-Finnish Soviet Republic invited Demidov to head the Finnish National Theatre in Petrozavodsk. Demidov accepted, despite the wartime challenges. At the time, the Finnish Theatre had to work in Belomorsk after being evacuated from Petrozavodsk. After a few months of special training with a newly created troupe, Demidov produces *Nora* – a performance based on Ibsen's *A Doll's House*. The local press, along with the experts that arrived from Moscow, acclaimed the production. Irja Viitanen (?–1944), the actress who played the title role in the play, was equated to the great Russian tragic actress Komissarzhevskaya (1864–1910). In Moscow, in the Russian Theatre Society's section of national theatres, theatre critic Georgy Shtain (1911–?) gave a report on Demidov's production. Demidov was commissioned to Moscow to speak on the methods he used at the Finnish Theatre. After Demidov's talk, it had been decided to show the production in Moscow. And . . . as fate has it, in the autumn of 1944, the wonderful Nora, Irja Viitanen, tragically committed suicide. With her death, Finnish Theatre's *Nora* also ceased to exist.

Figure 9 Demidov in rehearsal, with his students – Ester Volodarskaya (1918–1995) (to his left) and Vladimir Bogachev (to his right), Moscow, 1941. Courtesy of Margarita Laskina.

Shortly after the end of the World War II, in 1945, Demidov (his heart beginning to weaken in the northern climate) transferred the artistic directorship of the Karelo-Finnish National Theatre to the directorial board and returned to Moscow. There, he served as the artistic director of the touring Studio theatre. Then, once again, it was time for a new journey, to the northern island of Sakhalin – now as the artistic director of the Regional Theatre of the Soviet Army in the city of Yuzhno-Sakhalinsk. However, two years of work in Sakhalin did not do any good for Demidov's health. His heart "revolted," and Demidov had to go back to the main land. The city of Ulan-Ude, the Buryat-Mongol National Theatre and its drama studio was

Demidov's last "mission field." Throughout his life in exile, Demidov furthered his research into the actor's creative process. Carefully, step-by-step, he tested his pedagogical, practical, and scholarly findings, his vast experience summarized in his writings.

Serious heart problems and, eventually, a heart attack forced Demidov to return to Moscow. Often bedridden, he dedicated the last three years of his life to his five books. Simultaneously, he attempted to break through "the wall" built around him – in order to publish at least one of the books. Unfortunately, the "opposition" was too strong. He offended the all-powerful "devotees of the 'system,'" and encroached on their territory.

The only formal accomplishment of his last three years was Demidov's participation in the so-called "debate" on the "Stanislavsky System." It took place in 1950 and 1951 in the *Soviet Art* newspaper. In it, on January 27, 1951, Demidov published the article titled "The Stanislavsky System and Actor Cultivation." It was a "lone voice crying in the wilderness . . ." The "debate" was quickly terminated.

"One way or the other, sparing a catastrophe, I will complete the work I began. I feel what a bullet must feel once it's been fired at a target: it can no longer be stopped, and there is no other way." Demidov (2009: 484) wrote these words at the end of the 1930s in a letter to the Moscow Art Theatre's star Ivan Moskvin (1874–1946). To his very last day, Demidov remained dedicated to his work. He felt the pure necessity to give people all he was able to discover in his study of the creative process. He was convinced that the future of theatre lies with the school of "experiencing" – this traditionally Russian approach. Inherently human, it will live as long as humanity itself. To this end, Demidov remained the same "selfless enthusiast," "a man full of genuine love for the art," as Stanislavsky described him.

Nikolai Vasilyevich Demidov passed away on September 8, 1953. Only death was able to stop his work. "Don Quixote . . ." were his last words.

★★★

Figure 10   Demidov with the graduates of the Buryat-Mongol Theater's Studio, Ulan-Ude, 1949. Courtesy of Margarita Laskina.

The extensive Demidov archive contains, in addition to other documents, manuscripts of three completed books, and also materials prepared for his fourth and fifth books. Demidov sorted these materials, according to themes.

In his first book, *The Art of the Actor: Its Present and Future*, Demidov established the creative standards of the theatre art, while analyzing the reasons behind their decline. Moreover, in his first book Demidov revealed the potentialities of the actor's art, including those of the theatre of the future. The reader should pay particular attention to this book, as Demidov's thought and methodology would be impossible to grasp without the clear understanding of his ideals.

The next book, *Actor Types*, is dedicated to the analysis of the differences in the quality of an actor's giftedness (as opposed to its quantity). Demidov was the first to connect the quality of an actor's talent with the Ancient Greek physician Hippocrates' teaching on the four types of human temperaments. By doing so, he extracted four types of actors: affective, emotionally-willful, imitator, and rationalist. Moreover, Demidov noticed that each of these actor types requires their own methods of training and cultivation, on behalf of a teacher, as well as different directorial techniques.

The third book – *The Art of Living Onstage* – is dedicated to Demidov's specific method of early actor cultivation, based on his signature "etudes technique." One must note that Demidov's early etudes are not dedicated to an actor's work on a role, but rather meant to cultivate an actor's specific creative qualities.

The significance of Demidov's "etude technique," as the foundation of the actor training, is difficult to overestimate. By virtue of their synthesis, Demidov's etudes cultivate a *sustainable* actor's creative state. They encompass the basic tasks of "training and drill." By doing so, the etudes develop and maintain the "psychological technique" of the theatre of experiencing. Due to a specific methodology of these etudes, an actor's most essential *qualities* are *developed* and trained from the very first lesson. These qualities are: freedom and involuntariness of life onstage, a skill of *not interfering* with one's tangible perception of the environment and imaginary circumstances; the ability to freely "green-light," i.e. *not to impede one's first, spontaneous reaction*. "There, in the first reaction, lies the *source of creative imagination and faith*," wrote Demidov (p. 293).

These etudes also facilitate the initial "shift" toward organic *transformation*. Actors who learn not to interfere with this shift, as observed by Demidov, develop a new *sense of self*. They begin to feel themselves as someone else, while the circumstances of this imaginary new life "transform them."

Moreover, Demidov's etudes automatize the creative state: upon entering the stage, the actors are automatically ready to create. In addition to that, the actors trained in the Demidov approach are able to maintain the process of life onstage and, if necessary, adjust it.

These are the basics of the technique inherent to an actor of the "theatre of experiencing."

But the basics alone are not enough for the actor-creator. Genuine ARTISTIC endeavors are impossible without constant *striving* towards the *ideal*; lofty achievements – without *mastering the skills of the "higher psychological technique."*

All outstanding actors of the "affective type" (or tragedians) utilized such methods, and they continue to do so – consciously or subconsciously. Demidov's pedagogical practices set an objective – to uncover these heightened techniques and to study their nature, to discover their laws, and to master them.

Much of this has been thought through by Demidov, and practically tested. His two completed manuscripts record some of his findings on the "higher psychological technique." The bulk of these discoveries, however, can be found in the materials for the next two books: *The Artist's Creative Process Onstage* and *Psychotechnique of the Affective Actor*.

These materials include, in part, some fully completed chapters, but also Demidov's notes that chronicle the travels of his thoughts. He called them his "travel finds." Demidov recorded his finds on separate pieces of paper, and he collected them into separate folders – by topics.

These materials did not amount to a coherent presentation. To assemble them in two books was not easy – even with the help of preliminary plans sketched by Demidov. Apparently, Demidov himself faced the difficulty of organizing his last two books.

In the Introduction to *The Artist's Creative Process Onstage*, he wrote:

> In order to make a complicated (and indescribable) process more comprehensible and tangible, it is necessary, firstly, to examine it from different sides. Secondly, it is necessary to extract individual laws from it, one by one, and to describe them as if they exist independently and separately (which in reality is not true, of course). These ideas and notions, by their very nature, nuzzle together, endlessly shaping and permeating one another. Yet we have to put them into a certain order, with each step in the sequence conclusively linked. (p. 425)

It is clear that the process of creating the fourth and fifth books, was still underway. However, the available materials in the Demidov archive are so new, intriguing and important that it was essential to make them available to readers. So many people of theatre can benefit from them: teachers and students, actors, directors, theatre critics, as well as scholars of the actor's art. Not to mention the broader audience – anyone faced with questions about the development of one's creative abilities.

The reader is bound to discover that the literary "texture" of the last two books differs from the previous three. The "colloquial" nature of these texts will not come as a surprise to the reader. The informal way of presenting problems is inherent to Demidov's literary style as a whole. It helps him to demystify even the most complex issues. The reader is, at times, caught up in a confidential talk with the author; at other times, in a dispute with an invisible opponent. At times, the reader comes to witness Demidov's dialogue with himself, as he continues to question his own conclusions, in search for the truth.

Demidov's presentation can become even less formal due to the emotional intensity of some of his texts. Periodically, it pours out in a passionate dramatic monologue, imbued with his sincere love for theatre, and for the art of the actor. Demidov's heart was bleeding over the unfortunate state of theatre art, and he deeply cared about its future. The problems Demidov felt so deeply remain current – it feels as if his texts were written today.

The "unfinished" nature of Demidov's final two books allows us to literally follow the curve of his thought, as he delves deeper into his topics. A multifaceted and an independently minded thinker, Demidov never believed that the results achieved by his study of the creative laws are the ultimate truth. He believed in the progress of science. "There will be new knowledge," Demidov wrote in the preface to his book, *The Art of Living Onstage*, "and, in its light, our present knowledge perhaps will seem ignorant" (p. 144).

The reader will notice that *The Artist's Creative Process Onstage* often references the following book: *Psychotechnique of the Affective Actor*. At the same time, both books contain references to new methods and exercises that are not featured in either of the texts. The completed Demidov heritage was supposed to include new book sections, such as *Scene Study* and *Directing*, and new titles, such as *Reflexology*, etc. Fortunately, the preliminary writings for these new sections and books survived in the Demidov archive. They contain the "unidentified" terms and exercises referenced in the two final volumes.[4] This allowed the editors to compile an extensive Glossary of Terms and Exercises. The reader is encouraged to consult the Glossary on all subjects and terms, especially those referenced in the last two books. In addition to exercises outlined throughout this collection, the Glossary can also be used as a guide for further practical work. It contains over 30 new exercises connected with the higher spheres of the actor's creativity.

Of special interest in the final two books is Demidov's pioneering study on character facilitation – the most private and "intimate" aspect of the actors' work. This includes the formation of the subconscious embryo of the role, and its development. Among other problems featured in the book are those connected with a specific relationship between the character and the actor. The technique of "psychological breath" stands out among other "aerial stunts" of the actor's creative process. Based on the "guild secrets" of the great nineteenth- and twentieth-century tragedians, this method is indispensable for work on Shakespeare and other classics. It is integrally linked with Demidov's discoveries in the area of subconscious (non-analytical) perception – those means allowing the creative impression to reach the deepest layers of the actor's psyche.

★★★

In his studies, Demidov relied primarily on his deep understanding of Stanislavsky's teachings on the school of "experiencing." He admired Stanislavsky's quest to discover the laws of the actor's art and master the process of creative living onstage. He equated Stanislavsky's work to heroism, and always considered Stanislavsky to be his teacher.

One of the challenges in bringing Demidov to the English-speaking reader lies with the variations on the Stanislavsky System terminology. Since the time when the first English publications of Stanislavsky's writings appeared in the 1920s, different translators and teachers offered various translations of the same terms. For the sake of consistency, and to bring the terminology closer to our contemporary time, editors and translators decided to feature Stanislavsky terms as they appear in the unabridged translations of Stanislavsky's major works created by Jean Benedetti and published by Routledge in 2008. The only exception is stipulated in the Glossary of Terms.

Prior to meeting Stanislavsky, Demidov was deeply influenced by his father, who guided him through his early theatrical endeavors. "Thanks to him alone I could perceive correctly what I heard from all my voluntary and involuntary teachers," – Demidov (p. v) wrote about his father. One should also remember the importance of Demidov's early practices in the application of yoga and other spiritual practices to acting. In these experiments, conducted around 1910–1912, Demidov often played the role of assistant to his brother Konstantin – in the future, a noted Russian actor.

To understand the process of actors' creativity, and to reveal its laws, one has to look up to the highest creative achievements in the realm of acting. As such, Demidov's attention was constantly drawn to the works of the luminaries of theatrical art – the great tragic actors, such as Russia's Pavel Mochalov (1800–1848) and Maria Yermolova (1853–1928), Italy's Eleonora Duse (1858–1924), Tommaso Salvini (1829–1915), and Ernesto Rossi (1827–1896), and England's David Garrick (1717–1779). Ira Aldridge (1807–1867), American and British actor (of African-American descent), known for his Shakespearian roles, was of special interest to Demidov, due to Aldridge's rare talent of combining inspiration and intellect, passion and restraint. Among Demidov's contemporaries, Alexander Moissi (1879–1935), a German actor, Albanian by descent, served as a close focus of Demidov's observations. Last, but not least, Demidov studied the work of MAT's own outstanding actors – Leonid Leonidov (1873–1941), Ivan Moskvin, Mikhail Tarkhanov (1877–1948), and others.

Furthermore, Demidov was deeply interested in the so called flashes of "inspiration," as described by the genius artists, writers and poets, such as Praxiteles (4th century BC), Leonardo da Vinci (1452–1519), Raphael (1483–1520), Michelangelo (1475–1564), Johann Wolfgang von Goethe (1749–1832), Alexander Pushkin (1799–1837), Honoré de Balzac (1799–1850), Fyodor Tyutchev (1803–1873), Nikolai Gogol (1809–1852), Fyodor Dostoevsky (1821–1881), Lev Tolstoy (1828–1910), Oscar Wilde (1854–1900) and Anton Chekhov (1860–1904), as well as great composers and musicians – Wolfgang Amadeus Mozart (1756–1791), Ludwig van Beethoven (1770–1827) Niccolò Paganini (1782–1840) and Pyotr Tchaikovsky (1840–1893).

The scope of Demidov's research also encompasses the process of scientific creativity, especially, the moments of "epiphany," as experienced by eminent scientists, such as physicist Isaac Newton (1643–1727), chemist Dmitri Mendeleev (1834–1907), rocket scientist Konstantin Tsiolkovsky (1857–1935), inventors James Watt (1736–1819) and Thomas Edison (1847–1931), physician Hermann von Helmholtz (1821–1894), mathematician Carl Friedrich Gauss (1777–1855), and others.

Demidov's heartfelt friendship with the Moscow Art Theatre director, a remarkable theatre educator and the founder of the 1st Studio of MAT, Leopold Sulerzhitsky, became a life-giving source for Demidov's work. Demidov and Sulerzhitsky shared common ideals in the areas of theatre art and education.

A graduate, with honors, of the Moscow University's School of Medicine, Demidov received a solid foundation in the fields of physiology, psychology, and psychiatry. This knowledge ultimately helped him in his research of the creative process.

The field of physiology was rapidly developing in Russia in Demidov's time. Demidov closely followed the highly influential teachings of the Russian physiologist and psychologist Ivan Sechenov (1829–1905), and those of his followers Nikolai Vvedensky (1852–1922) and Ivan Pavlov (1849–1936).

Of considerable importance to Demidov's work was his personal acquaintance (through Sulerzhitsky) with the influential Russian physiologist Alexei Ukhtomsky (1875–1942). Ukhtomsky's (2002: 112) teaching, "The nature of our being can be created and cultivated," was the impetus and the leading principle behind all of Demidov's work. After Ukhtomsky, Demidov constantly argued that human nature can be perfected and, therefore, a theatre teacher can and should help the student develop his existing acting skills to meet his talent, or even genius. Needless to say, Demidov was well aware of Ukhtomsky, in 1911, introducing the notion of *dominant*, a certain "chord" of constant influence that causes sustained excitation of certain areas of the brain. Apparently, this concept was later developed in Demidov's teachings on the need to create and strengthen certain "automatisms" in the actor. As a result of such "automatisms," an appropriately trained actor, when entering the stage, is automatically ready for the creative act to commence – this readiness triggered by the evoking of a sustainable creative state (see Book 5: chapter 5, *Unity*, chapter 6, *The Subconscious Nature of Creativity*, and chapter 7, *Automatisms*).

From Sulerzhitsky, Demidov also received a personal introduction to George (Georgy) Gurdjieff (1866–1949) and his colleague Thomas de (Foma) Hartmann (1885–1956). A noted psychologist, philosopher, and magician, Gurdjieff was popular in Russia in the beginning of the twentieth century for his psychological experiments with hypnosis, meditation, and the method of self-regulation. Demidov closely followed the work of Gurdjieff and Hartmann.

An attentive reader will find in Demidov's works numerous links to the teachings of historically significant psychologists, physiologists, psychiatrists, and philosophers. Among those – the American psychologist and philosopher William James (1842–1910), known for his insistence on the close connection between a person's external physical actions and internal psychological state. (Demidov suggested that James' teachings inspired the famous American motto: "Smile!" According to James, we don't smile because we are happy, but rather we are happy because we smile.) Russian translations of James' *Psychology* (issued in 1911), and his *Introduction to Philosophy* (1923), undoubtedly influenced the development of Demidov's views on creativity. In these two works, James stresses the important role played by instincts in our psychological processes.

German psychiatrist Ernst Kretschmer (1888–1964) believed that imposed action stops all natural processes (see Kretschmer's *Hysteria, Reflex, and Instinct*, 1923). Kretschmer's conclusions are quite consistent with Demidov's views. Demidov was also interested in the works of French neuropsychologist Pierre Janet (1859–1947). His *L'automatisme psychologique* (*On Psychic Automatism*, 1889) suggests the possibility of one's complete transformation into a different persona. Demidov believed that a physiological probability of such a transformation, albeit pathological, points out to a real chance to achieve an equally immersive *creative* transformation.

The original theory of the "set" (*ustanovka*) was introduced by the Russian-Georgian psychologist Dimitri Uznadze (1886–1950). His theory asserted the existence of certain connectivity and manageability of all processes of perception, memory, imagination, etc., originating in the subconscious mind of a man – a certain "set" that defines a given individual's reaction. This theory is echoed in Demidov's works. Moreover, Demidov creatively developed Uznadze's theory in light of his own understanding of this phenomenon, in its application to an actor's art (see Book 5, chapter 5, *Unity*).

The same can be said of the Austrian philosopher Rudolf Steiner's (1861–1925) teachings. Steiner's works, including his 1894 book *The Philosophy of Freedom*, became popular in Russian theatre circles in the 1920s. Direct references to Steiner had been found in Demidov's archive. Chapter 6 of *The Art of the Actor* features the subchapter titled "The Ability to Marvel and Venerate." Notes found in the Demidov archive indicate that this subchapter had been written under the direct influence of Steiner's ideas. Some of Demidov's contemporaries, such as the Russian actor Michael Chekhov (1891–1955) were fascinated by eurhythmy – "the art of visible speech" – an integral part of Steiner's teachings. Demidov was also familiar with Steiner's concepts of eurhythmy and speech formation. He creatively developed these ideas by Steiner in his own method of the "literal pronunciation of words." Demidov had been clearly attracted to the futuristic aspects of Steiner's anthroposophical teachings. What connected him with Steiner (and with Chekhov) the most, was their desire to reach the highest manifestations of human spirituality, and their faith in the hidden, subconscious human potential. Needless to say, Demidov never mentioned Steiner in his books – for purely "political" reasons.

The influence of Yevgeny Vakhtangov is felt in Demidov's work on the subconscious perception. Vakhtangov's own highly developed intuition was a result of persistent practices, some of them based in yogic principles. Demidov's technique of "submerging text, circumstances or tasks into the subconscious" is based partly on Vakhtangov's experiments with the subconscious perception of tasks. Among Vakhtangov's productions, Demidov admired his tragic masterpiece *The Dybbuk*, staged by Vakhtangov in 1922 at the Moscow Habima Studio (the future National Theatre of Israel).

So many philosophers and scholars attracted Demidov's attention, it would be presumptuous to attempt analyzing all these connections in a short introductory article. Nevertheless, several other names must be mentioned. Demidov's works reference German psychotherapist Emil du Bois-Reymond (1818–1896), French psychologist Maurice de Fleury (1860–1931), Russian psychoanalyst Nikolai Dahl (1860–1939), as well as Russian philosopher, author of *Genius and Creativity*, Semyon Gruzenberg (1876–1938). A slogan borrowed from the English poet Edward Young (1683–1765) – "Too low they build who build beneath the stars" (Young 1854: 157) – became Demidov's personal motto. He must have derived it from the works by Helena Blavatsky (1831–1891), an influential occultist, author, and world traveler. Demidov's frequent advice to all those who have dedicated themselves to the arts, was borrowed from Blavatsky's *The Voice of the Silence*.[5] This advice was to keep "the body agitated, mind tranquil, the Soul as limpid as a mountain lake" (Blavatsky 1909: 339).

A deep analysis of Demidov's writings in the light of those basic teachings available in his time – such is the future task of researchers, physiologists, and psychologists. These scholars, especially those of them dealing with the issue of creativity, will discover many such correlations, just as they will find in Demidov the foreshadowing of contemporary scientific studies.

For the purposes of this article, it would suffice to note that Demidov always remained a uniquely original and independent thinker. When referring to scientific opinions, he was mostly seeking to confirm his own practical insights. In other instances, he used those concepts and premises unacceptable to him in order to further develop his own, unique point of view.

In comparison to what had been achieved by Stanislavsky, Demidov made a decisive step forward by discovering the new "synthesizing" way to master the actor's creative process (as opposed to the "analytical" path of the "Stanislavsky system"). As early as the 1920s, Demidov offered a method that allowed the actor to train the automatism of freedom and organic life onstage, and thus be able to create onstage – instantly, without dissecting the creative process into separate elements. At that time, the idea of *unity*, as a newest stage in the study of creativity, had been thick in the air, and on the minds of scientists from various fields. This was true, for example, of medicine – a science closest to Demidov. Thus homeopathy, as well as allopathic medicine (both practiced by Demidov), viewed a patient's body as a whole – rather than focusing their treatment on isolated diseases.

As it turns out, the most important discoveries occur at the intersection of various sciences. For example, physical chemistry, biophysics; but also psychology, physiology, and pedagogy can no longer do without each other. In the meantime, the science of art is also in dire need of professional help from other scholarly fields. Demidov's desire to find a scientific basis for his practical discoveries and hypotheses is then nothing but his desire to progress on this new path.

This is why Demidov sought not only theoretical but also personal contacts with physiologists and psychologists. In a letter to Nemirovich-Danchenko, Demidov wrote that he shared the content of his (then yet unpublished) book, *The Art of Living Onstage*, with several modern scientists, professors of psychology:

> I read them some of the chapters of my book, and they said: "This is terribly interesting, compelling and new . . . or will be 5 years from now – in the present day psychology we see only the seeds of what you explain quite definitely and practically." One of them said, "publish it soon, or you hold my work back: I will need to reference your book."
>
> *(Demidov 2009: 486)*

Demidov modestly does not mention the names of these psychologists, but it is possible that it could be Ukhtomsky and Lev Vygotsky (1896–1934), with both of whom Demidov was personally acquainted. Vygotsky taught at the Kamerny Theatre's "experimental workshops" alongside Demidov (in 1926–1928.) At that time, Vygotsky had just finished working on his book, *The Psychology of Art* (completed in 1925).[6] However, both books – Demidov's *The Art of Living on Stage*, and Vygotsky's *The Psychology of Art* – saw the light only in 1965, when both authors were long gone. This may explain the absence of alleged links to Demidov in Vygotsky's works, and vice versa.

The Demidov archive preserves his letters, circa 1952, to the physiologists Anatoly Ivanov-Smolensky (1895–1982) and Lev Fyodorov (1891–1952), where he requests a meeting, and offers to collaborate on a study of an actor's creativity, in light of the teachings of Pavlov. Unfortunately, Lev Fyodorov, who used to work under Pavlov and was one of the founders of the Institute for Experimental Medicine, died just two months after receiving Demidov's letter.

Demidov's own death was followed by a long period of struggle, on the part of his students, to publish *The Art of Living Onstage*. In the meantime, the so-called "internal reviewers" spared no efforts trying to block this publication. Fortunately, several Russian scientists actively interfered on behalf of Demidov's work. Among them, Professor Boris Teplov (1896–1965), an outstanding psychologist, the founder of the school of Differential psychology, and a member of the Academy of Science. He wrote:

> It seems to me that Demidov's book as a whole is an interesting and creative development of Stanislavsky's ideas . . . The merit of the author is that he is not limited to merely "preserving" Stanislavsky's legacy, . . . but rather seeks to further develop and enrich it.

> The great achievement of Demidov is "the first spontaneous reaction doctrine," as I would call it. His chapters *The Significance of the First Reaction*, *The First Reaction as a Source of Imagination and Faith* and *On the Development of Imagination*, attract attention due to the subtlety of psychological analysis.
>
> *(Fund 59)*

Upon detailed analysis of Demidov's book, Teplov concluded that "the basic theoretical principles at the foundation of the Demidov curriculum should be recognized as scientifically valid and valuable" (Fund 59).

In 1965, 12 years after Demidov's death, with the help of his widow Yekaterina Knishek-Demidova (1885–1968) and his students – Vladimir Bogachev (1921–1984), Fyodor Sokolov (1911–2001), Oleg Okulevich (1921–2006), and Margarita Laskina – an abridged version of Demidov's *The Art of Living Onstage* was finally published in Moscow. The book was introduced by two celebrated students of Demidov's – the Moscow Art Theatre star Boris Livanov (1904–1972), and Maria Knebel (1898–1985) – one of the most influential Russian theatre teachers and scholars, who taught at the State Institute of Theatre Arts (GITIS).

Theater specialists and scholars did not respond to this publication, out of fear of violating the Stanislavsky system monopoly, and offending its powerful proponents. The influential TEATR Magazine took three years to review the book. When the review finally appeared, it belonged to professor Solomon Gellershtein (1896–1967) – an important psychologist and biologist, and Vygotsky's closest associate in creating the school of psychotechnique. Gellershtein wrote:

> *In this book we find true signs of foresight into ways in which the future science must research the creative process* [emphasis added]. It demonstrates an unusual (for a director and theatre scholar) breadth of vision and depth of psychological approach to the analysis of creativity. To witness this, it is sufficient to read the chapters on the subconscious mind, on imaginary actions, on entering the creative state ... on those qualities necessary for creativity, on preparing conditions for free, spontaneous reaction, on the unity of perception and action with the dominant role of perception, on the ratio of voluntary and involuntary, and so on.
>
> *(Gellershtein 1968:77–78)*

The 1965 edition of Demidov's book instantly sold out and became a rarity. In 1967 Yekaterina Knishek, Demidov's only heir, transferred the enormous Demidov archive to his favorite student Oleg Okulevich and his wife Margarita Laskina, who was also Demidov's assistant. In doing so, Knishek fulfilled Demidov's own will, entrusting Okulevich and Laskina with the laborious task of sorting the archive, and preparing it for publication. However, further attempts to publish Demidov's books remained fruitless for decades to come. "The Initiative Group" comprised of students and followers of the Demidov School, continued the fight, trying to bring awareness to Demidov's theatrical heritage. They printed *"samizdat"* publications of articles on Demidov, and fragments of his works.

Many of Demidov's students, directors, actors and teachers, remained faithful to his lessons. Among them, MAT's Mikhail Yanshin (1902–1976), Sergei Blinnikov (1891–1969), Vladimir Gribkov (1902–1960) and Anna Andreyeva-Babakhan (1923–1997), Vakhtangov Theatre's Nikolai Plotnikov (1897–1979), Buryat Drama Theatre's Fyodor Sakhirov (1928–1915), Kirov Theatre's Nikolai Pechkovsky (1896–1966), Bolshoi Theatre's Elena Kruglikova (1907–1982) and Valentina Naydakova of the East-Siberian Academy of Culture and Art. Among Demidov's students, Oleg Okulevich deserves special mention – not only as a keeper of the Demidov archive, but also as an outstanding artist. Having deeply absorbed Demidov's lessons, Okulevich went on to create a gallery of classical characters, such as Hamlet, Othello, Raskolnikov, Ivan the Terrible, Boris Godunov, and many others. He performed at St. Petersburg's leading stages, such as Lenkom, Lensovet and Komissarzhevskaya Theatres. Okulevich also took his art to the Russian provinces – in search of artistic freedom, substantial roles, and audiences hungry

Figure 11   Oleg Okulevich as Boris Godunov, Pskov, 1973–1974. Courtesy of Margarita Laskina.

for genuine art. In a way, he continued the tradition of the traveling tragedians of the old – Demidov's favorites.

This prolonged effort to publish Demidov's literary heritage finally came to fruition at the dawn of the twenty-first century. Beginning in 2002, the State Theatre Library in St. Petersburg, while accepting Demidov's archives for safekeeping, organized the publication of his *Creative Heritage* in four volumes (Margarita Laskina, ed.). This publication featured all five of Demidov's books, his articles, fragments from his correspondence, and other biographic and creative materials. The first volume of the Demidov *Heritage* came out in 2004, while the final, fourth volume was released on Demidov's 125th anniversary, in December 2009.

★★★

Nikolai Demidov's legacy – Russian theatre's best-kept secret – is swiftly spreading and influencing the theatre world. In Russia today, the Demidov School is featured at its top-five theatre schools, such as the St. Petersburg State Academy of Theatre Arts (SPgGATI) and the Russian University of Theatre Arts (GITIS/RATI) in Moscow. One of the foremost Russian teachers of acting, Veniamin Filshtinsky[7] (2006: 139), refers to the Demidov School as "pedagogy of the future."

In the US, at Florida State University's Asolo Conservatory for Actor Training (one of America's top 10 graduate schools for actors and one of the top 25 in the English-speaking world), Demidov's methods have been utilized extensively since 2008. Since then, the Conservatory's work with the Demidov technique has been shared with observers and visitors from institutions such as Peter Brook's CICT/Théâtre des Bouffes du Nord and the University of Windsor's School of Dramatic Art (Ontario, Canada). Lectures and workshops in the Demidov Technique have been presented at forums and institutions, including The Royal Academy of Dramatic Art (RADA), The Royal Central School of Speech & Drama, The University of Exeter, Rose Bruford College and its Stanislavski Center (UK); Association for Theatre in Higher Education (ATHE), University/Resident Theatre Association (URTA) and Stanford University (US), as well as the Stanislavski Institute (Brazil).

The experience of the FSU/Asolo Demidov-based training also inspired interest in Russia. Extensive master classes in the US-based Demidov curriculum have been presented for actors, directors and teachers at the St Petersburg State Academy of Theatre Arts. Some 100 years after Stanislavsky's innovations began to bridge Russian and Western theatre, the legacy of his close collaborator and successor Nikolai Demidov also begins to transcend cultural barriers. Due to its immense creative potential, it promises to foster international dialogue and exchange between theatre practitioners, scholars, teachers and students. As the interest toward Demidov grows internationally, one can hope that the Demidov School, with its origins in the renowned Russian theatrical tradition, will earn a prominent place in contemporary theatrical practices – both in Russia and around the world.

★★★

It would be wise to point the reader's attention to the essential prerequisite of succeeding with the Demidov School. Its methodology can be applied exclusively under the condition that *the teacher herself masters the "psychological technique."* Demidov shared his teaching practices with the reader, suggesting an entire series of pedagogical and self-cultivating techniques to which one must pay utmost attention.

There is another important stipulation. The psychological "transparency" acquired by actors who master Demidov's technique inevitably reveals either the depth of their soul

Figure 12 Nikolai Demidov, Moscow, 1951. Courtesy of Margarita Laskina.

onstage, or its primitive and crude nature. As such, the question of the student-actors' spiritual development arises – seeing that the depth of soul and its inner significance are the prerequisites for the birth of an artist.

Margarita Laskina, PhD
Andrei Malaev-Babel
Head of Acting,
FSU/Asolo Conservatory for Actor Training
Translated by Svetlana Tikhonov

Notes

1 Curiously omitted from all English-language editions of Stanislavsky's book, also known as *An Actor Prepares*.
2 Demidov and Sulerzhitsky met at the Athletic School, run by Vladislav Pytliasinsky (1863–1933) – a famous Russian athlete and wrestler, and a world champion.
3 Further referred to as "Fund 59."
4 It is also possible that some of these materials were meant for *The Artist's Creative Process Onstage* and *Psychotechnique of the Affective Actor*. As mentioned earlier, at the time of his death Demidov was still working on the structure of these two books.
5 According to Blavatsky, her book was comprised of unknown texts of Buddhist and pre-Buddhist origin.
6 Vygotsky was also specifically interested in actors' creativity, as evident from his article titled "On the Problem of the Psychology of the Actor's Creative Work." Completed in 1932, it was not published until 1936.
7 Stanislavski Award Laureate, Chair of the Department of Acting and Professor of the St. Petersburg State Academy of Theater Arts.

Book One

The Art of the Actor

Its Present and Future

Translated by Alexander Rojavin and Andrei Malaev-Babel

Introduction

Nature, to be commanded, must be obeyed.

Francis Bacon

When Mochalov acted, the following often happened: the curtain would fall, and only then did the audience notice that they were on their feet. To a man.[1] How did it happen? When did they get up? How long had they been standing?

Nobody knows!

Have you ever seen anything similar in our theatres? If somebody even tries to stand, you'll be the first to make him sit back down so that he doesn't get in your way, doesn't ruin your view. And this isn't because everyone has become a disciple of order, but simply because we haven't had the opportunity to become so immersed in the theatre. We can't even imagine such abandon.

Have people become different? Colder? Not at all. All you have to do is go to some sort of contest—let's say soccer—and you'll see such abandon that you won't believe your eyes! No. There's no need to blame the public. It's quite capable of forgetting everything there is to forget. All it needs is a *reason* to forget. If it's capable of forgetting itself because of their sympathies and dedication to some soccer team, then it's quite capable of forgetting itself for Ferdinand and Louise (from Schiller's *Intrigue and Love*), for Hamlet, Othello, or Lear.

It doesn't even take all that much: all it takes is for Ferdinand, Louise, and the others to become as familiar and dear as these, truth be told, total strangers – enormous, charismatic guys trying to hammer a ball into each other's goal. The requirements aren't that great. But all the same, although we do feel some excitement, we still watch somewhat half-heartedly how Louise signs the terrible letter orchestrated by the evil Wyrm, how, without suspecting a thing, she drinks the poison . . .

"But what will come of it?" some orthodox disciples of theatre ask with indignation. "If the audience will behave themselves like this, then what will come of it!? What kind of a theatre *is* that?! It'll be chaos! Bedlam!"

Not true! That's when theatre will become what it should be: a mighty, incomparable educational tool . . . The greatest of artistic delights, which combines into one the writer, musician, designer, costumer, carpenter, electrician, and, finally, the actor himself, playing the most wondrous of all instruments: his own human soul!

Is this not the most perfect of all art forms? Is it not the strongest and most comprehensible?

Having opened a book, you'll only see words written in a consistent, standard font on dead paper, but here you'll hear the tremulous, live speech, you'll see the flickering of eyes, you'll delve into the souls of the suffering, loving heroes . . . They affect you with the music of their voices, with their magnetic power, and they enthrall you . . . And here are the results:

> No quill, no brush will ever depict even a cheap imitation of what we have seen and heard here. All these sarcasms, directed at poor Ophelia, at the queen, and finally at the king himself; all these curt phrases spoken by Hamlet sitting on the bench next to Ophelia's chair as the play was being performed – it all breathed with an invisible, but palpable force – like that of an oppressive nightmare. The audience's blood grew cold, and everyone – people of different ranks, characters, inclinations, education, tastes, ages, and sexes – fused into a single, enormous mass, brought to life by one thought, one single feeling. With their mouths open, with enchanted eyes, with bated breath, everyone gazed at this short, black-haired man, pale as death, casually half-lounging on the bench.

> Heated applause would start up and end unfinished; hands raised to clap were lowered again from enervation; people stopped the hands of others; strangers forbade other strangers to express their delight – and nobody thought this was strange. (From Vissarion Belinsky's [1811-1848] article: *'Hamlet,' Shakespeare's drama. Mochalov as Hamlet* [Belinsky 1953: 321].)

Does theatre understand its own power? Does the actor know this strength inside of him? He has to know. He *must* know! Art isn't a job for the uncaring, especially the art of the actor.

Figure 13 Pavel Mochalov as Baron Meinau in the Maly Theatre's performance of Kotzebue's *Misanthropy and Repentance*. An oil painting by an unknown artist, based on Vladimir Karapalpakov's drawing circa 1837. Courtesy of Alyona Shchukina.

Whether he wants it or not, his art has an effect: it elevates thoughts, feelings and morals up to the stratosphere, or lowers them to the abyss of mediocrity, pettiness, lies, insignificance, and vice.

Since you've set upon this work, then at least know what sort of work it is.

It isn't simple, nor is it peaceful. You hold in your hands deadly things: explosives and fire. Like it or not – you're a Grenadier. You have no choice, no excuses. It's out of the question.

When an actor puts out his fire by means of apathy, of sloth and thoughtlessness; when he quenches his torch in the swamp of mundane worries and life; when he spills the precious explosives along the way, or uses them to fertilize his garden – is he not an embezzler and a criminal?

Some 30–50–100 years will pass, and television will come to every apartment, in every corner of the world . . . As evening comes, every family will eagerly sit in front of their television . . . That's when theatre will have its victory! That's when we'll be able to spread our wings, show what we are capable of! To the whole world! Without any exaggerations: go ahead, act – the entire world, all of humanity is watching! What more can you ask for?!

Only . . . by then, what will you, the actor, be able to show "all of humanity"? How can you impress them? In 100 years, are we really intending to feed people the same primitive art that we're feeding them now? What are we counting on? Humanity's boundless patience? This sort of theatre won't be passed down through the generations. It doesn't deserve it. What will be passed down are acrobatic numbers, ballet, vocal recitals, music, and, evidently . . . film.

No, actor, you don't know the strength of your art, and you fail to see its beautiful, glorious future.

It might seem that this is all just irresponsible fantasizing. Not at all. Only reality, only practice. The aforementioned moments with Mochalov happened, didn't they? They did. Were there other, similar ones? Hundreds, thousands! Each one of us has observed glimpses of talented acting. Although much weaker than the mighty explosions and flights of Mochalov, they were nevertheless of a similar nature. You're watching a show, and suddenly, you're caught up in the moment, and you've forgotten that this is theatre. A second has passed, and you've come to your senses. You did, but what does that prove? It happened, right? Then it's possible? Then this second can be prolonged?

And you, actor! Haven't you ever seen these flashes of enlightenment, when, all of a sudden, you got this inkling – that's "IT" . . . *this* is "IT!" . . . Of course you have! It's for these moments that you threw yourself into theatre in the first place.

Not at all for what you ultimately found in it . . .

So, these seconds, these fleeting moments aren't fantasy; they are completely real. And never mind that you're not in power to control them. We'll observe them, think about it, and then contrive a way to catch the elusive firebird.

Are we up to this task? Maybe it's not even worth trying, and we're just deluding ourselves with false hopes.

We've all had minutes, and if not minutes, then at least seconds of "inspiration," when we were "on fire," when we were "at our best." And so we hope (at first) for these seconds to visit us more often and last longer. That's all. And the problem isn't that we're so bold to hope, but that we give up so easily.

I can already hear someone objecting: "art isn't science. It's impossible to approach art as straightforwardly and narrowly! Art is a field of specific giftedness: of Talent. Art is . . ."

In a word, it's a forbidden zone that is accessible only to extraordinary individuals.

However, in practice, that's not how it happens at all: art is the domain not just of thousands, but tens, if not hundreds of thousands of people. This is easily confirmed – just ask the unions.

What does that mean? That these are all great, chosen talents? Unique in their giftedness? No. There are very few talents. More often, you see *ability*. Greater ones, lesser ones, different kinds . . . In the proper, favorable environment, they can develop and shine. In unfavorable ones, they fade and deform . . . Not talent, not genius, but ability – is what makes up the greater portion of those who constitute the force of our art.

Be it good or bad, but it's a fact. This is why it's necessary to tirelessly learn to make the most of the abilities, to *develop* them and *not to suppress* them.

And what if we were seeking our talent, or even genius?! What's wrong with that?!!

Note

1 See page 616.

1

Reasons for the Fall of the Art of the Actor

Enthusiasm for a Production

It must be that the path of any progress, especially the one in art, isn't a straight and simple path, but is winding, going up and down, with many possible losses and discoveries.

Let's speak about an art form that is more closely related with acting – singing.

In Greece, in Italy, there was always great singing. The climate predisposed people to it. They sang well, and they called it simply: singing – *canto*.

But, little by little, the maestros of vocal work came to the point when they started trying to achieve a certain kind of sound. A sound that is, put frankly, magical. A singer trained in this art would go onstage, sing a single note – some "A-a-a-a-a . . . !" and it immediately pierced the listener's very heart. It would instantly melt all the ice, unlock every secret chest or lockbox and, out of nowhere, tears would start flowing of their own volition.

The singer didn't sing about soul-rending suffering, he didn't tell an intricate tale of sorrow, longing, or happiness . . . he sang about something very simple or even less than that: he would just let out a single uncomplicated vocalization – "A" – and nobody was able not to dissolve in that sound. Nobody could hold back a flood of emotions and feelings, and the flood would come – unexpected, stormy, vivifying, and cleansing . . .

This amazing sound opened up all of the listener's depths as a result of some sort of specific resonance . . . It would give rise to delight and inspiration . . . from the depths of their souls, all of their best qualities would rise, clean, wholesome, and they would come up as tears, sighs, heightened senses, and a feeling of immense joy . . .

This sort of singing wasn't simply called *canto*, but *bel canto* – beautiful singing.

Now, when you watch old Italian operas of that time – you're seized by bewilderment, you don't know what to think.

Here "he" comes onstage, and, as it was done back then, stands right at the proscenium, facing the audience, incessantly sings about his love for "her." The melody is primitive, the words even more so . . . He'll sing a little, sing some more, and leave. "She" comes out. Stands to face the audience in the exact same spot and incessantly sings the same thing about her own love for "him" . . . "He" comes out yet again, and now they sing together, but they're still facing the audience (so that they're heard better), and, without looking at each other, sing about their love. "I love you, you love me, we love each other. . ." etc. 30–40 pages of this unoriginal and uncomplicated outpouring of love.

The audience used to melt from delight.

But . . . take a breath before making fun of them. Let's keep investigating.

Given the power of the vocal art, the singers didn't need to concern themselves with making the melody richer or more complex, especially since any such complications didn't reflect well on what was most important: the ease and perfection of *bel canto*. So, singers not only didn't look for new, richer melodies, but on the contrary, met any novelty with protests.

However, as beautiful as the singing may have been, music didn't stand in one spot, it developed. Impressive composers stepped out onto the field, like Glück [1714–1787], who demanded that singers perform more complex melodies, that librettists write more complex stories. This all got in the singers' way. Singers probably could have found a way to resolve their differences with composers and come to a consensus, but that would have taken too much effort. And what for? Their singing was still very popular and easily put bread on the table!

This is how the war between musicians and singers began. The musicians demanded that the music that they wrote be performed – the singers resisted. And if they performed new operas, then they performed them their own, more convenient, way. The war was heated and difficult for both sides. Music won. Progress won.

And *bel canto*, the magical *bel canto*, unable to keep pace with progress, was forced to cede its primacy to the new ruling force.

The fault lies not with singing itself, of course, but with the singers who were unable to adapt themselves to both art forms. And so, *bel canto* started to wither . . . Additionally, its masters – singers and vocal maestros – the "alchemists" of the art, were dying one by one, carrying their magical sounds with them into the grave.

Musicians weren't concerned in the least: now, singers performed all of their requests without complaints, and the music – complex, rich, sometimes genius music – ruled supreme.

Gradually, the theatrical structure of opera was also perfected, and it reached the heights of psychological musical dramas and comedies.

Now, it's become the norm that everything is SUNG in opera – phone conversations, business discussions, invitations to "have a seat," "take a walk," "see you later, alligator!" etc.

We haven't had the good fortune to hear *bel canto*, but imagine that today, in the middle of our dramatic vocal performance, i.e. operas, you'd hear the singer let out this hitherto unheard (by you), delightful sound – "Stop, stop!" you'd want to yell, "Stop moving around that furniture, doing whatever it is you're doing, and babbling on about your nonsense! I just heard something that made my heart flip . . . Do it again! Sing that sound again! It tore through the eternal darkness like a ray of light . . . Having heard it, I can't hear or see your previous gimmicks and showing off . . ."

That's what you would say.

And the ridiculous, empty librettos of old Italian operas instantly become understandable. And really, wouldn't a storyline, action, and psychological webs only take away from what's important?

Then, after you had gotten enough of this godly sound, maybe you would want to return to the best that exists in our operas today. But once you've heard *bel canto*, you can't do without it. You would want to combine that vocal wonder with today's best. But . . . it no longer exists. It is lost. A miraculous art form is lost, and can we truly find it? We probably can. We just need to apply enough willpower and know how to search.

But for now, it's gone. The trace has gone cold. The greatest support for this assertion is that you can hear "*bel canto*" everywhere, third-rate singing teachers tell their students about *bel canto*. And why not? Nobody knows the true *bel canto*.

Everybody uses this term simply to describe a sound that is more or less beautiful. And they say: "now this is *bel canto*." Well, that's that then, time to reap laurels.

Now, let's ask ourselves a question: why *isn't* anyone looking for it? The *Italians*, after all, looked for it and found it. The answer to this question is simple: they found it because nothing was distracting them; they didn't have more interesting librettos, complex staging, all they had was singers and their singing. And the public loved the opera. And so, the restless souls that must search, must perfect everything that they touch – they accidentally started running into some specific, unprecedented, electric, calling sound – it would echo for a moment and be gone the next. What's the matter? They began experimenting, searching furiously. They observed it, overheard it from nature, and transformed it into a "technique."

But today, you won't even think about searching for something UNPRECEDENTED. Why bother? Our age asks for something different. Today, you need for the singers to produce a musical phrase, to relay a THOUGHT, to accurately convey the psychological pattern of an aria or romance; they have to "grasp" the personality of their "character." And, of course, they have to sing correctly and rhythmically, and possess a beautiful, strong, technically adept voice.

This is how, in search for the new, we get carried away, and lose our interest in the old, even if it's valid . . . This isn't true of everyone, of course. This "rule" only applies to average, not particularly capacious minds. It's possible that there might have been at some point a singer who was able to combine music, thought, character, and *bel canto* in one, but he died, and his miracle-doing died with him.

★★★

Now, let's get back to our own topic – dramatic theatre.

The same thing happened to it. Mochalov's brilliant flights, Yermolova's inspired acting, or Duse's boundless authenticity and depth – that is our dramatic theatrical magic. Our *bel canto*. It could be seen in our old theatres, and, apparently, it wasn't so rare. It was beautiful – true art, perfection of an actor's artistic powers. But everything that surrounded it was so tasteless, helpless, and detestable that there was only one way to bear it: try not to notice it. These amateur, talentless actors with whom the touring star would often have to share the stage, these extras, found on the street to play a crowd, these set pieces – three, four identical "box sets" for any show, and much, much more! . . . The audience forgave all this for the moments of delight that they got from the brilliant actors' performance. They were used to this strange interweaving of mediocrity with greatness, a den of iniquity – and a temple of art. They couldn't imagine it any other way.

But then, the Meiningen Company[1] showed up, and it became abundantly clear that the crowd had to act, that every man in the crowd is an actor, not a dead extra; that it would be better if the stage had set design that complemented each play and each act – set design that gave the impression of the place that was assumed by the author, not the omnipresent standard "box sets" and "forest landscapes"; that it would be better if a play were organized, according to the playwright's wishes, by a single person – the director – than if it were organized on the run, by whomever had an idea at the time.

33

However, the Meiningen Company made one grave mistake. Paying such great significance to the set, props, costumes, makeup, they turned the actors into . . . things. Necessary, important things, but still just things. For the director Chronegk, an actor was simply a medium, an executor of his will. For every actor, Chronegk and his assistants thought everything through to such an extent that the actors didn't have anything left to do – just go according to the director's plan and vision. Willingly or not, they gave themselves completely over to the director's will. Meanwhile, he, enthused by his new idea, trained and drilled them until they performed their roles exactly as he told them. In this manner, they turned into a mass of obedient marionettes. Creative freedom, live, spontaneous moments, explosions of passion that we've grown used to in our own actors – this was all out of the question.

The progressive aspects of the Meiningen Company's art could not leave our directors uninterested, and a new stream poured into theatre. The directors' new main concern became the creation of a harmonious show.

The Meiningen Company brought with them something entirely new: the ensemble. Complete coordination between the actors.

Although, not all ensembles are made equal.

Having understood the value of an ensemble, our innovating directors couldn't fail to notice the Meiningen Company' main weakness: the mechanical style of their acting and its soullessness. In order to avoid making the same mistake, they started treating their actors differently. Together with the actors, they not only thought through every scene, every moment and every line of their role, or searched for and found the truest and most expressive actions. They also wanted the actor to be full of truth, so that he not only understood every moment of his role, but felt it too. So that he was as natural as in life. Special techniques were developed to this end. A whole system of techniques.

It seemed that everything was progressing along properly: both sides of the show and the roles, external and internal, were reaching the necessary heights. But the director's chief concern was still the creation of a show. And this concern (possibly subconsciously) created a hard line of action: everything was done for the show. The actor was only a single part of the show. Regardless of however much the directors helped him, how they supported him – in the end, he was still shut in and denied artistic freedom.

This sort of directorial custody, and more importantly: the compulsive fixation of anything that was found during rehearsals – however collaboratively – led to the actors' freedom being shackled. This killed their spontaneity. Everything is thought-through and pre-decided; all you have to do is repeat your actions and words in exactly the same way (with once and for all established intonations). What kind of *spontaneity and involuntariness*, i.e. what sort of *truth* is there to even speak of? To make everything *seem* like the truth – create the impression of the truth – that's possible. But that's it. That is, not the truth, but the appearance of truth. And that's what happened.

As for freedom of creativity and any sort of onstage "improvisations" on the part of the actor – that became not only unnecessary, but detrimental and dangerous. These improvisations might, accidently, coincide with the director's pattern of the scene, but what if they don't? What if they break it? What will your partner do then? "Improvise" too? Where will that lead the show? And why did we have the tens and hundreds of rehearsals, then? Why did we have the hundreds and thousands of great ideas?

Even if actors were to act on inspiration, like Mochalov or Yermolova, little good would come of it – the higher they would rise, the more they'd ruin the show's structure with their flight.

This is how completely new demands began to arise for the actor, gradually and unnoticeably. And with them, came a new school. It demanded not the truth from the actor, not freedom, not inspiration, but the ability to accurately and believably perform actions that were found in rehearsals beneath the watchful gaze of the director's vision; actions, blocking, a.k.a. *mise-en-scenes*, and even intonations.

And if we call the Meiningen Company' ensemble an ensemble of marionettes, then our ensemble became an ensemble of verisimilar actors.

What is this? Is this progress? Of course it's progress, without a doubt. The most important thing in the theatre should be the show – a holistic performance, not random, individual parts. In this respect, everything was developing correctly. At the same time, is it right to sit and watch the actors lose all their freedom to create in front of the audience; inspiration lose its place in theatre; authenticity and truth be replaced by verisimilitude; the actor forced to second and then third place with regards to importance, and turned into an executor of the director's will?

If this is how things will progress going forward, then it isn't long before our dramatic wonderworking sinks into oblivion, just like the magical Italian *bel canto*.

But how do we combine the harmonious, unified production with artistic freedom, even improvisation onstage?

The Director: His Excessive Power and Ignorance

There have been theatrical collectives that have successfully been formed by very strong actors who did not need the help of a director: they grasped the play and the roles very well on their own; additionally, they helped each other out with advice, and everything worked out. The director took on the roles of rehearsal administrator and general organizer.

There are examples of brilliant touring actor-directors. Like, for example, Ira Aldridge, who travelled across most of Russia's provinces [in the late 1850s and early 1860s], performing his roles alongside both professional Russian actors and amateurs. And the plays were such that they needed a director: *Othello, King Lear, Macbeth, Hamlet*, etc. He staged the shows himself, directed them, taught, patiently explained everything, and didn't give up. This was necessary for him, at least because, otherwise, the incompetent amateurs and actors would have gotten in his way onstage. Additionally, he knew, understood, and loved Shakespeare so much, that he couldn't allow for him to be played poorly and untruly.

Imagine a director so talented, enlightened, and charismatic, who is, on top of that, a brilliant, unsurpassed performer – appearing among actors and amateurs who long for art. It's easy to imagine the power his newfound troupe accords him.

And such directors – lawmakers, leaders, and absolute monarchs – weren't the only ones of their kind. They existed when the theatre was headed by Garrick, Stanislavsky and Nemirovich-Danchenko, and Sulerzhitsky (not well-known, but of the same category of directors). Under their leadership, the theatre would produce highly artistic works, full of harmony, and oneness of thought, power, and poetry.

The general level of these people's development and talent surpassed those of the troupe members to such an extent, that the actors felt themselves as no more than students in the hands of great artists. They unquestioningly heeded and obeyed, not because their "masters" demanded their obedience, but because they were enthralled and captivated by their directors' talents. And the wise, keen, and astute director – knowing what lies in an actors' souls – didn't abuse them, but artfully awakened the actors' dormant powers of creativity and fantasy . . . he didn't scare them, didn't break them, but inspired them and led them to the simple and true path (which, without such an intervention, would be difficult) – a path of stage playing.

To a lesser – to a significantly lesser – extent, some of their students, who inherited the greatest part of their skills and knowledge, did the same thing. The history of theatre will name other similar artists as well. It's not my job to list them all. Even though there haven't been that many. Their high culture and enormous creative strength gave these directors hitherto unheard of power. They became the absolute monarchs of theatre. Moreover, the power of their personalities, and the success of their work, were such that their influence expanded far beyond the walls of their personal theatres: they elevated the director's authority so high that the director is now, *without exception, considered the most important player* in any theatre.

He doesn't always elevate the theatre to great heights – not everybody can become a great person at will – but he always uses the *privileges* that come with the territory: he is a dictator, invested with absolute power, and a lawmaker.

But if he is weak in one respect or another, then his power and unlimited freedom lead to pitiful results. For the most part, these directors have powerful personalities. Maybe even aggressive ones. And the less they know, the less talent they possess, the more aggressive they happen to be.

On account of their insensitivity to the actors and lack of expertise, their demands of the performers are most often unnatural and evoke overt and silent protests on the parts of the actors. In order to preserve their dignity and authority, they are forced to use extreme measures: this is how it will be! No protests, discussion, or questions! . . . I'm the director, I know everything, and I *am* everything!

Given such leadership and directorial practices, there is no point in expecting the actors to act well. Which is exactly what comes to pass. The actors are occupied by executing various "assignments" which have been given to them by the director, and which are at severe odds with their own creative desires. Therefore, creativity, intuition, and freedom are all out of the question.

For the most part, these people pile on mistake after mistake with regards to staging and interpretation of a play. This happens because of a desire to make a show more flashy, sharp, and topical, and for other similar motives, which would never seduce a real artist. And so, the director starts employing various tricks, like mobile set pieces, deafening sound design, a thousand people onstage at a time, playing *Hamlet* in tuxedos, exploiting the audience's lesser instincts – feeding them pornography and vulgar farce, etc.

You might protest: how can this be? What about the public, the audience? They won't go to such a show. Of course they will! And they'll drag you along with them. They'll *enjoy* it.

Leisurely critics will say that there are new discoveries, brave artistic choices on the part of the director here . . . Only a true theatre expert sees the hopelessness of this kind of a show and its impeding effects on the development and growth of the art form. Others don't notice it. Especially since directors of this kind are very adept at perfecting a show's external attributes – the blocking, the opulence . . . Everything is clean, smooth, exact, like a clock, everything is without snags and so dynamic that there is no opportunity to even think. There is no room for an average audience member to evaluate whether it's good or bad.

Unless you come another time, once you already know the show, once you've seen all the tricks . . . then you might notice all the patches and thread and holes – it's not the same this time around! But their goal isn't to make the show good a second or especially a third time. It just has to be a success once.

The audience that comes to the theatre is always in a state that is advantageous for the director and actor.

They believe in advance. They already expect something wonderful, worthy of attention.

This state is supported by the theatre's atmosphere: hundreds of people have come together, leaving their business behind. They've all sat down, expectant . . .

And if the actors onstage are speaking in a certain artificial manner, not quite normally, if they're moving and gesturing somewhat strangely and unnaturally, then . . . maybe that's how it should be? There's no other way? Otherwise, it wouldn't be the theatre!? And the audience tries to adapt itself to what's happening onstage.

Soon, the audience grows used to the unnaturalness, is drawn into it, and (if the text is written well) is taken by the play. Any blanks that are left are filled in by the audience, what's bad isn't picked up on. The play ends, and the audience is fully convinced that everything happened onstage exactly as it was supposed to. The audience is pleased.

The audience members thank the actors, give them their curtain call, applaud them. Sometimes the actor deserves the applause, but how many times is it undeserved!!! The audience is applauding themselves! The audience was *doing half of the work for the actors*.

The Director: Time Pressures and Other Objective Reasons

Now let's imagine an honest and gifted director and theatre manager, a person of integrity. He's enthusiastic about his job, he loves it, lives for it . . . it would seem that that's all anyone really needs.

But he encounters his first obstacle, which turns out to be much more serious that it seemed from afar. This obstacle is the actor. The person who's supposed to supply the most pleasure and redemption is what turns out to be the main obstacle. Either the actor isn't prepared properly or experienced, and literally needs to be carried; or he's too experienced and has a wagonload of bad habits, bad taste, and is also so spoiled in terms of egotism that it's impossible to tear through all this trash; or the actor is simply talentless and ended up onstage as a result of a misunderstanding or pulled strings . . . In a word, the actor "doesn't get it," no matter how hard you work him!

Given the desire, it's possible to make an actor do wonders. It's possible to not just lead him along, but even completely remake him. Remake his whole acting apparatus. But for this, you need a combination of three exceptional conditions.

The first: the ability to do this.

Aside from tact and desire, in order to do this, you also need an appropriate "school" with a multitude of tried-and-true methods. But where is it? What you *have* learned has failed to be useful or has turned out to be fruitless theory, or, conversely, such an abusive practical approach that you had to abandon it. And so you're left with nothing. You won't get far with amateur work.

The second condition: you need energy. Fanatical levels of energy and patience. A painter applies the paints he needs, comes back to it another day – they're still there, he can just continue. But with a live person, with an actor, it's much more difficult: today, you manage to get him to where you need him, but tomorrow, nothing is left, all the "paint" has faded, slid off, gotten mixed together . . . The actor tries to evoke yesterday's emotions, but they're gone, and he's forced to hastily repeat rough external expressions of yesterday's feelings: yesterday's poses, gestures, smiles, intonations . . . i.e. starved, bloodless form.

And the third necessary condition: time.

In order to create something authentic and truly deserving of being called a "work of art," you typically need months upon months. Even if you're an experienced and skilled director and pedagogue. In order to make good theatre, you need whole years. A week, a month isn't enough to remake people or develop talent. But in this field – you're on a time crunch, the show must go up!

And so, all virtuous intentions are put off until "later," while in the meantime, you're forced to employ much more simple methods, all in order to not delay the show's premiere.

These simpler methods are well-known: *dressage*, giving line readings to the actor, "drilling," and other atrocities, which have nothing in common with directing or pedagogy or art. If you don't have a temperament — scream as loudly as you can, clench your fists, strain yourself until you turn red! Stomp your feet, punch the wall!

Are you emotionless and nothing affects you? So what! Don't feel anything. Just smile, show your teeth and speak like this — delicately, drawlingly — repeat after me.

Not like that! Again!.. Again!.. Again!.. This is how an actor is trained, just like a canary is trained to sing like a nightingale.

They'll train him, drill him, then dress him, and put him in make-up. Now fire away! Lay out what's been knocked into you.

I've often talked with directors about this difficult situation. Many of them complain that while working this way from year to year, day to day, they lose their sense of the truth and artistic perfection. Despite all previous aspirations, they turn into craftsmen, production workers, and hacks, out of necessity and habit . . .

And that when they look at craftsmanly shows like the ones they make, they like them. Previously, they would disdainfully turn away from such "art," but now . . . they're used to it . . . and it's no big deal . . . as if that's how it should be.

"But what to do? What should be done?" they would ask. "Schedules . . . time crunches . . . the actors' lack of readiness . . . their inertia . . . And my own lack of ability . . . and you sink lower and lower . . . on a daily basis! . . ."

There's only one piece of advice to give here (which is what you do): under no conditions should you allow yourself to sink, you constantly have to support the artist in you. If you cannot bring your show to complete perfection, then take one or two scenes and bring them to the state of complete perfection. Spend as much time and strength as you can on them. Then the fire of creativity won't die in you, despite the fact that all other work will be deadly for you. Maintain life in yourself all the time, don't let your heart stop. Else you'll die and not even notice it. There are many such cases. Sad cases.

The Director: Subjective Reasons (Dilettantism, Professional Craftsmanship, Charlatanism)

There probably isn't and has never been a director who didn't start with the highest of dreams, lofty speculations about art, creativity, truth, and perfection of form.

But it's one thing to dream about a beautiful end result, and another to know the path there and have the strength to reach it.

The craftsman-professional knows that if he doesn't meet some minimal expectations, then his "craft" "won't sell." This knowledge is not only useful, it's *vital* for the artist as well.

For example, quiet, incomprehensible speech onstage, unbelievably long pauses — these are mistakes that are made by young and inexperienced actors, as well as talented ones. The craftsman-professional would be indignant. He'd say that an actor's first job is to speak loudly. Everything must be heard, understood, and seen! And would he be wrong? He'll be wrong with regards to something else. Volume for volume's sake isn't the answer — the true problem lies in *the actor's improper creative state or in the wrong interpretation of the scene.* Fix this, and everything will be loud enough and understandable. If instead you require an actor to be loud — he might do as you ask, but this will consume all of his attention. He won't have time to live in the circumstances of the character, and his chief concern will be only to speak louder.

Or here's another example. An actor drags the show out, pauses, slows everything down . . . It's necessary to get rid of the root of the problem, which is either in his incorrect internal technique – his brakes, his **preoccupation** – or in the fact that he doesn't understand the scene's circumstances; fix this, and everything will be just fine. But a craftsman only knows one thing, he'll just keep yelling: "Faster, faster, don't slow down! Tempo, tempo! Rhythm, rhythm! Pulse, pulse!"

Craftsmanship and professionalism aren't bad because they require volume, clarity, expressivity, or speed and rhythm from an actor – they're bad because, first of all, they approach everything very primitively, and secondly, because they despise any kind of *pursuits*. Searching, testing, altering – in a word, everything that identifies a true, demanding artist, they commonly consider to be simply *lack of skill and inexperience*.

They're so used to following recipes and stencils that they don't ever have to search – they already know everything: everything is established by tradition. This is why a craftsman-professional can stage any play in a month or less. Searching for hidden depths or secrets in a play . . . Digging deep . . . refining the details of the characters' personalities . . . and on top of all of this, helping each actor find qualities that are necessary for his role . . . Why? What is all that for? It's all just fads and inventions . . . That's what happens when someone doesn't understand the "job." "In practice," everything is much easier and simpler, all you need is experience and skill! And what is there to do for more than a month, anyway?! Read the play, cast it, have a read-through, then "block" the actors (show them where to stand), and the job's done. For "deeper" work, you can show the actors what "intonations" to use when speaking their lines. Then everything is truly done, the job is over. If the actor plays poorly even then, then it means that the actor is bad: everything has been showed to him, explained – all that's left is to repeat it and that's it . . .

If this kind of director is given the opportunity to work on a show not for a month (as he's used to), but for a year, then he'll be faced with a dead end: he won't be able to do anything more! All that will be left is to endlessly repeat the same things over and over, mechanize it so that everything flies off the tongue.

These craftsmen-professionals are, for the most part, the ones who call for quick deadlines. An artist won't do this: he always needs more time. He always has more to do, because his ideal is always looming ahead of him.

There exists a more sophisticated kind of craftsmanship. You won't even immediately understand that it doesn't involve a drop of creative juices – just arithmetic and mechanics.

While acting in the finale of the first act of *Poverty Is No Vice*, a shoddy craftsman behaves very simply and primitively. Ostrovsky's [1917: 90] play says:

> Mitya. *(Walks towards the door and takes the letter out of his pocket)* What can she have written? I'm frightened! – My hands tremble! – Well, what is to be will be – I'll read it. *(Reads)* "And I love you. Liubov Tortsova." *(Clutches his head and runs away.)*

And he does everything exactly as written: approaches the door, takes out the letter, makes his hands shake, says the words, skims over the letter, and, without properly reading what exactly is written in there, hastily tries to depict some superlatively powerful emotion on his face – be it horror or joy – grabs his head, and runs out of the door to some other unclear place for some unclear reason. This happens in less than 5–6 seconds.

An actor who works by the truth – one who is immersed in the play's circumstances – does everything differently. Starting with the fact that he won't immediately grab the letter. Liubim Tortsov is in the room – if not for him, the letter would have been read long ago. Finally, the guest finishes his didactic tales and falls asleep. But you have to check whether he's really fallen asleep – otherwise, you might take out the letter, and he'll see you. And for some time, Mitya will cautiously observe the guest and check on his breathing. Meanwhile, his hand seems to be reaching for the letter of its own volition . . . it's in the pocket . . . the breast pocket. He's asleep! Tip-toeing, so as not to make any noise, not to wake him up, but quickly – he goes to the door, farther away from Liubim and closer to "her" – after all, she called, she sent an invitation to go upstairs. Mitya rips the letter from his pocket and suddenly stops, afraid of something: "What could she have written?" He twirls the letter (or rather, the note) in his hand, investigates it from outside: "I'm frightened!" But he cannot wait – his hands have begun to unfold the paper and, from excitement, do not heed him. Without granting it any significance, consumed by the anticipation of what's in the letter, he blurts out: "My hands tremble!" It's obvious that he's not expecting anything good, probably thinks that it's a rejection. The letter is opened.

His hand gives a jerk as if to hold the letter up, but suddenly it recoils! And his head too suddenly leans back from the letter. It turns away, afraid that it might read something awful. He stands for a second or two, refusing to read it, but then he makes up his mind: "Well, what is to be will be – I'll read it." He brings the letter to his face and leans forward to better grasp its content.

The same agitation that froze his hands as they unfolded the letter, now clouds his eyes, as they struggle to make out the words. And his lips mechanically speak: "And I . . . love . . . you . . . Liubov . . . Tortsova . . ." He reads it . . . He freezes . . . doesn't understand anything . . . Looks at it again . . . something clicks . . . he understands, and in his surprise, he feels fear – horrible fear!

Even his hand jerks away from the letter, as if burned! Ow! A man stands there with widened eyes, and is seemingly not thinking at all – he's frozen in horror . . . Then he gradually calms . . . slowly holds up the letter, his face lightens up . . . reads it again . . . now he understands everything in its entirety . . . his expression is unclear: he might be about to laugh, or maybe cry . . . he grabs his head (one hand still holding the letter), squeezes it, but his eyes are staring forward, not seeing anything. Then . . . the thought of "her" – she's upstairs . . . he looks up and flies to her.

A craftsman of verisimilitude will do everything in practically same way: he'll observe, and listen to Liubim to check that he's really fallen asleep, after which he'll tip-toe to the door, and hesitate in exactly the same manner and order: should he or shouldn't he read the letter? He'll make up his mind, read it, not understand it at first, then start to think . . . first, he'll be afraid – there's something too big about it – it doesn't fit, then he'll digest it, and finally believe his luck . . .

Everything will be the same. At least, the movements are identical. Identical to how things would look in life: the same "logic and sequence," everything is accurate. But one thing will be missing: authentic emotion and some imperceptible subtle movements of the face, eyes, hands, the whole body . . . the thing that you can't fake and which is so enthralling in the art of the actor.

But . . . for an audience that isn't too demanding, this is enough. And people will say: "He's so realistic! He's experiencing the emotions so truly!!" And if the whole show is so assiduously staged as well, and there is such coherence between the rest of the theatre workers (the set and costume designer, the composer, the sound designer, etc.), and everything is surrounded by an opulent exterior, as if by an astounding, blinding, golden frame that can cause the painting itself to start shining like the real thing (unless you take a good look at it) . . .

If, on top of all of this, there is also a dazzling advertising campaign, then success is guaranteed. And the director is triumphant.

You can employ whatever praise you will when talking about these people: practical, realistic doers, deft, inventive, and whatever else you want.

From the point of view of the progress of art, theatre leaders who support this approach destroy what's most important in theatre.

They make imitation, forgery – a cornerstone. No matter what significant results they achieve, they are mere charlatans. When it comes to art – they are demolishers; they destroy its very foundation.

Some of their names might even pop up in the annals of theatre history . . . not for long, of course, but still, it's possible – life is a great comedy.

What conclusion can we draw from all of this? That the director is *bad* for theatre? Is that it?

The theatre needs an incorruptible artist, a good, talented director who is well-versed in his job – as we need oxygen. And the actor needs him like oxygen too. He's the leader, the inspiring force, the soul of a show. But a bad director, mediocre, ungifted, a usurper, a dilettante, a charlatan is harmful. Harmful for theatre, harmful for the audience (encouraging a bad taste), and most of all, harmful for the actor.

He's the one whom theatre has to thank that the art of the actor is dwindling, that the actor's significance and position have shrunk to the level of a pitiful marionette. This is the beginning. If a proper school of directing isn't established soon, then the actor will be completely murdered. The only people who will take the stage will be those who respond well to *dressage*. Obedient puppets.

On the Actor's Responsibility and Heroism

You think the director is the only one guilty of the professional craftsmanship? What about the actor?

The actor is where this all begins. Although the director is now everything, he's a relative newcomer. Before him, the actor was everything. The actor is the one who first noticed (he couldn't help noticing) this advantageous quality of the theatrical stage – the ability to enthrall the audience, to stoke their imagination, their creativity, and eclipse their critical gaze. He noticed it and immediately took advantage of this intriguing mechanism. The director is simply his worthy heir and successor.

Say what they will about the "good ol' days," praise them or degrade them as they may, we can say only one thing with total conviction: back then, actors weren't blocked off or embellished (as they are now) by directors' magic tricks, the "ensemble," and staging. Even the sets were very primitive: an interior room, the woods, a hut – they were only useful insofar as to let the audience understand more or less where everything was happening ("in a house," "in the woods," "in a palace") and not be confused. The heart of the matter was the acting. Which is why its good qualities, as well as its shortcomings, were more evident. An actor's strengths and weaknesses weren't dimmed by anything. And, willingly or not, he had to show everything he was capable of. He was the crux of theatre. He was what people came to see.

He knew this and thought: I am the show! He saw that, in practice, that was the truth, and decided: I am the theatre!

Responsibility caused him to rise up, which turned him into a hero . . . And if his soul hid the fire of talent, then it was stoked. If the actor's soul was exceptionally deep, then the fire raged like a forest fire, like an indomitable storm.

And, seeing these flares, the audience of the "good ol' days" understood: this is art!

Audiences that had seen such actors had very clear criteria: what is "real" and what is fake.

Today, the actor is put in calmer and more comfortable conditions. He doesn't come out "one on one" against the whole audience. Now, he is only a part of a great and complex theatrical machine, just a single soldier out of the full forces. Pretty often, he doesn't even know what his commander – the director – has in store for him, and simply does what he's told. And the audience has grown used to this as well, no longer watching just the actor, but the whole show – the "staging," the general ensemble of acting, attained by the "director's" assiduous work . . . Everything is put together, everything is hitched very well . . . The actor is, of course, a part of it, but only as a single ingredient. Sometimes, not even the main one.

This new way of things has completely changed the actor's psychology. He no longer takes responsibility for the show (to say nothing of responsibility for theatre or for art!). He has become calmer . . . there is no longer a need for flares . . . and talent, whose little fire is quietly moldering in his soul's depths, will molder all the way to the grave. What need is there to flare up? Who needs saving?!

Not to mention that an actor might get himself into trouble by performing heroic fits. A show is now so tightly regulated that if you step over your bounds, you might botch the most important thing – the director's cunningly woven "pattern."

The audience has grown used to such shows and has lost the old criteria of judging acting ("real" and "fake," great and small), they've acquired new criteria: "an interesting show," "a boring show," useful, harmful, properly reflecting the author, improperly – distorting him.

This is how the demands of the audience and experts have changed.

There is one more circumstance in the actor's life and work that has drastically changed when compared with the "good ol' days" and has had enormous consequences.

The thing is that there used to be very few theatres; they survived entirely on the box office proceeds, nobody helped them. Nobody respected actors, people considered them to be outcasts, freeloaders, buffoons . . . There was little that was attractive about the profession. Only those who had an enormous desire to go there would ultimately go into theatre. People would go there to test themselves, as if to a trial. They would go there after throwing caution to the winds. These people's whole lives were a constant feat. A feat and a battle. A battle against the poverty, barbarism, and mediocrity of the crowd, against the vices of their unworthy colleagues, and, finally, against their own lack of skill. Many couldn't take it, stepped out; many fell, crushed by vices and life.

This is how, through natural selection, talents and heroes were chosen! Of course they were heroes! One man goes out, alone against hundreds of audience members . . . Alone, respected by none, despised, he goes out . . . Armed with what? Only with his bared heart. And he conquers them all in this battle. If you don't emerge victorious – pack your bags and off with you to another town.

How much love, endurance, and heroism was necessary in order to live like this? And how much fire and talent did you need to constantly emerge as the victor!

Note

1 A German theatrical company, formed in the late 1860s by Georg II, Duke of Saxe-Meiningen. It was directed by Ludwig Chronegk (1837–1891), and it toured extensively in Europe, and in Russia (in 1885 and 1890).

2
Truth

It might seem suspicious: Mochalov, Yermolova, Duse . . . all deceased . . . isn't that a sign of senescence?

Those who are old and senile always think that, in the old times, in their time, everything was better. And the author is sighing on every page: "The good old days! That's when we had art. It's not the same anymore – art is gone."

No, that's not how I think, my dear young colleagues. I don't believe that art existed and then vanished. On the contrary, I think that art as a stable achievement has yet to truly exist. There have been individual flights; there have been Praxiteleses, Raphaels, Paganinis, Mozarts, Beethovens, Garricks, Mochalovs, Yermolovas, Aldridges . . . They flew over the world like a shimmering comet, shone through our darkness, and hid again, leaving only bewilderment in their wake.

True, after every comet, art could not stay in the same place, it would shift. But this shift would be incredibly small. And it would affect only the most basic laws of art. For example, in the West, after Garrick (and for us, it was after Mochalov), it became tasteless to play tragedies with the help of false declamation, howling, and striking poses.

There arose a need for *truth, authenticity*, and *naturalness*. It's a shift, but it's still a long way from the blinding truth of Mochalov, Garrick, Yermolova, and that of others.

That you should be *truthful* in a tragedy – people understood this. Only, they failed to note one other thing: in addition to simplicity, true tragedians also have *power*. It is a very rare quality. Here, at any rate, it was missing. And when the theatres were in pursuit of truth and naturalness, while some of them declared any sort of pathos as harmful and started playing tragedy in an everyday manner, "simply" – then there was much confusion. The elevated, high essence of tragedy crumbled, and we were left with a mundane drama, and in places, it was even something like a casual conversation over a cup of tea . . . This "simplicity" disappointed everyone's expectations. It didn't come through.

At that point, others, without thinking about it, and only seeing that nothing was coming of the "simplicity," ran in the other direction: as far away as possible from mundanity. Without knowing or finding the springs of great passions, they completely crossed out any sort of "truth" they may have had, and, in the search of tragedy, started howling, yelling, running across the stage with clenched fists, with bulging veins . . . even scarier and worse than those who ran and howled before them. But they didn't convince anybody with this either, didn't save tragedy, and didn't open the gates to the secrets of art.

Finally, a third group, without overthinking things, began to copy the tragedians. They liked their power, unbridledness, the storm of passions . . . they felt that the actors that affected them opened up onstage to their very core, that they lived and trembled with their bare souls . . . In their simplicity, they decided that it was enough to not tie themselves down with anything, to give themselves unlimited freedom, then to agitate, shake, fire themselves up, and . . . their "gut" will speak.

That's what they did. But this resulted in some unsightly pathology: either raving madness or intoxication with debauchery – furniture would break, costumes would rip, they would get bruises, broken bones, blood would spill, and it was unpleasant to view all of this.

Maybe their "gut" turned out to be unattractive – not like those of the great tragedians, or maybe they didn't do what they should have . . . but these keys also failed to unlock the heavenly gates to inspiration.

This is how the appearance of a genius goes by almost for nothing, leaving only confusion in the heads of "specialists."

The genii themselves most likely were privy to these secrets. At least, when they had to, they could always summon up heightened creativity in their favorite roles, which would irresistibly affect the audience.

Each one of them had his own techniques and methods. Some of these methods even reached us, but most of them vanished without a trace. Partly because these methods are very intimate and tied to the actor's personal life, and, naturally, he didn't want to tell everybody about them . . . Partly because they didn't know how to describe them. They did *something*, they pushed some button, they turned something on inside themselves – but what *exactly*, they didn't know.

Truth in art . . . there are so many arguments and misinterpretations around this word: *truth*.

A perfect work happens only when a master artist imbues it with his soul, only when he becomes carried away by it, when he melds with it.

In a word, when, in the moments of creation, the thing he is creating is the *truth* for him.

In his journal, Lev Tolstoy wrote that what he writes is good only when his inkwell contains blood, and not ink; when, dipping the quill, he writes with his blood. Anything written in ink is dry, boring, and deserves to be destroyed.[1]

In this way, truth is not the goal of art. Truth isn't the goal of the master. His goal is the creation of a perfect work of art, which presents humanity with a new idea or a new joy, or inspires new deeds and works.

Truth is only a method. A method with whose help a master enters the realm of true art. Not even a method, really, but more specifically: *the foundation of a method*. The method consists of the means, which help the master enter this realm.

However, when you listen to an actor or a director – supporters of the art of experiencing (or read their works) – it turns out that their whole goal (and the goal of their art) is to be truthful.

Tolstoy needs "blood" in his inkwell in order for his writings to be effective and vivid. For the same reason, the actor needs authenticity and sincerity – so that his creation (i.e. his acting) immersed people, affected them, evoked trust, and, in general, was a complete work of art.

We should add that there are different kinds of truths. This is best shown in painting. A portrait in which the costume's every thread is shown, every little detail of the ring, and in which the person's personality is accurately conveyed, his eyes sparkle with thought, a familiar smile crosses his lips – this sort of portrait can be authentic truth. Next to this is a caricature portrait, a cartoon, cobbled together by several miserly, but sharp, strokes; this could be such keen and vivid truth, it could say so much about a person, that no realistic portrait could ever hope to say as much.

It's the same in theatre: on one hand, realistic comedy, drama, or tragedy; on the other – vaudeville, caricatures, allusions, sketches, and jokes. Both can be full of truth.

Beauty Is not Relative

"Beauty," "truth," "the real" . . . But how can we discuss all this? Is it really concrete enough, completely set in stone once and for all? People might not agree with each other – we all have different concepts of beauty, truth, etc. It turns out that this problem isn't just complex, but impossible to solve.

However, it only seems complex and impossible.

"Beauty," "authenticity," "truth" – these aren't relative at all – they are *functions of a person's internal development*. "Beauty," "authenticity," "artfulness," etc. aren't the same for everyone at the same time, this is true. They are conditional. But they're only conditional on a person's internal development: a low level of development leads to very small demands; a higher development results in stricter demands.

People might say: but what about Praxiteles, Phidias?[2] Two thousand years ago, they created such beauty that is unattainable even today. Aren't things the other way around? Isn't art being lost? No. Loss isn't the issue here – the simple fact is that Phidias is Phidias, and Praxiteles is Praxiteles. Not everybody sculpted in their time as they did. They were unique. A genius always outpaces his contemporaries so much that either nobody understands him, and he is cast out, or he is deified. Praxiteles and Phidias outpaced humanity's art by two, maybe even three thousand years – that's all there is to it. For centuries, humanity looks at a genius's mesmerizing work, is awed by it, copies it, imitates it, but *how* it's made, by what means? – that remains a mystery.

That's how Praxiteles and Phidias stand before us for 2,000 whole years, while the vast majority of our sculptures do their work as if there never was a Phidias, or a Praxiteles, or a Michelangelo, or a Canova.

Painters paint as if there never was a Raphael, or a Leonardo, or a Rembrandt.

And there is nothing surprising or shameful about this: neither paintings nor sculptures reveal the secrets to their making and magic. The artist breathed into them a part of his soul . . . But **how** did he do this? And how to get such a soul? Nobody can say. Rather, they might say a whole lot, but nobody's said what's important so far.

To us, a genius' works of art seem like perfection, but to the artist that made them, they seem like pitiful attempts to capture what was in his imagination.

We're inclined to interpret this **self-appraisal** as modesty. It isn't modesty at all – it's just that his understanding of perfection is so much higher and stricter than ours. From his point of view, our understanding of it is childish.

That's how it is. And the problem isn't at all that "beauty," "perfection," "authenticity," "truth," "artfulness," and all such concepts are relative, but that many of us do not make the demands that we should make based on what has *already been shown* to humanity through many beautiful things. It's time to judge art not by low standards, based on what you see every day, but by high standards, based on what the genii have shown us.

Let's take an example that is close and palpable from the theatre.

Stanislavsky spent his whole life fighting against falsities onstage, against "cliché acting," "craftsmanship" . . . his whole life, he promoted "authentic experiencing" and "truth" onstage. He searched for paths to this end. He achieved that truth, and he led others to it.

You would think that his students and followers should have taken up this most important of his pursuits and developed it further . . . After all, every student begins where his teacher ends. The teacher has dug a hole, fertilized it, planted the seeds – all that's left is to let it grow and reap the harvest. (And then, if you can, keep planting.) If you can't do even this, then of course you're a bad student. But in practice, students not only don't surpass the teacher – they are incapable of getting into their heads what he tries to hammer into them on a daily basis over the course of many years. The teacher's great thoughts don't fit inside their small skull. In order to receive them, they cut them down, swallow them, and digest them in a reduced form. The words remain the same: "truth," "life," "experiencing," but their meaning is so far removed from the meaning relayed to them by their teacher that it's completely unrecognizable.

So read this – these are practically the last lines of the last page of the last book that were written by an old Stanislavsky [1954: 375] – the result of a lifetime of teaching: "I've worked in the theatre for a long time, hundreds of students have passed through my hands, but I can call *only a few of them* my followers who understood the heart of what I dedicated my life to."

If you take a look now at the works of some "pupil" of his, as well as the works of those who declare themselves his true believers, if you listen to their self-confident speeches, you'll be amazed: how much they've mutated the simplest, most obvious of ideas. And the most important thing—the *truth*, which is what dominated their teacher's life. The very same truth we observe during the world's very best actors' very best minutes, is the saddest part of their work . . . Their "truth" is as far removed from what their teacher wanted as paper flowers are from authentic roses and orchids.

Truth and Naturalism

Go ahead, listen to any discussion of a show. People of all levels of expertise get together – "experts," connoisseurs, the most ordinary of people – and . . . they discuss it. They discuss everything: the faithfulness or lack thereof of the interpretation, the positivity or negativity of the characters, the dragging or excessive speed of the rhythm, what should be underlined more, what should be mitigated . . . What *don't* they discuss, what details *don't* they go over – while they should be discussing something completely different!

I don't remember after what battle Napoleon called his artillery commander and sternly asked him why the artillery remained silent despite his orders. The commander replied: "Your Majesty, there were 63 serious reasons for it." "Name them! In detail!" "Reason number one: there was no powder." "Enough! Explain the other 62 reasons later . . . some other time."

Same thing here. Most often, you shouldn't be discussing character interpretations, but how the actors aren't acting well – how they ape around and say empty words "a la truth" (i.e. also ape around, only not as insolently and crudely). The first of the 63 reasons deserves to be discussed – the other 62 are merely consequences of the first. But almost nobody ever does. The main engine – an actor's internal powder – is almost never taken into account. So when actors don't have any powder at all, it goes unnoticed. Everything is in place, after all: the interpretation, characters, rhythm, etc. . . .

However, if, for some unknown reason, an actor's giftedness suddenly shines through onstage, and the truth is let out, then it is a pleasant surprise, which is noted and rewarded. Even for this one flare-up, some inaccuracies in performing the "director's vision" are forgiven.

But in general . . . this isn't that important. It's more of an accident . . . cute pranks of an actor's capricious nature.

In this way, truth is steadily being pushed out of our theatres. As for "sober-minded" professionals – it's almost completely out of their reach. Although, they're not very concerned about it and have even come up with an excuse: the truth is good only for simple things, but in tragedies, heroics, romanticism – you won't get by with just truth; you need breadth, temperament, power . . .

They think that the truth is good for sweeping the floor, shining shoes, drinking tea, knitting stockings, and other similar activities. When a keen, sensitive, and demanding artist achieves truth before their very eyes, they are, at first, surprised and don't believe their eyes; then they become embarrassed, but only for a single, very short moment; being "practical" individuals, the last thing they see is the beauty, power, and grandeur of the work of art. Instead, they pay attention to the danger it presents . . . the danger to their own success. A danger: what if people will start demanding more of them? Everything, every little thing is real! It's incomprehensible . . . How can this be? Life! And no mistakes . . . Nothing wrong to point out . . . What should I do? . . . And it's so powerful, so mighty . . . Life? Wait a second! That! That's what I should point out!

Suddenly happy, they let out a tireless howl: it's naturalism! It's ignoring the foundations of art! What use is there that it's life? Art demands that life in it be cleansed! The truth of life, mundaneness, everyday existence – that's not the domain of art!

Most often, they like to invoke the claim that art isn't a photograph, but *transfiguration*. At this point, they typically bring up a painter as an example: like Shishkin [1832–1898] – he's not an artist, he's a copier. He copies nature. His pines are just pines, so they don't say anything either to your intellect or to your heart. Art should be full of ideas. It should call you to something, teach you, it should explain nature, life, people!

All this is true. But in order to execute its charge, can art be built on a foundation of falsities and imitation? Can it be perfect if its own creator doesn't live with its ideas and its truth?

After all, what does it mean – to convey nature exactly? Let's take the same pine. To draw a living pine, present it on canvas exactly as it is in the woods is hardly possible – you have to be more than genius in order to do that. You would have to paint a *real pine!* And paint it in such a way that you could feel the flow of its juices, so that rays of sunlight would glimmer and dance among its needles, so that it would (just barely perceptibly) sway from the wind, so that the air, infused with its scent, would swirl around it. It would have to live, breathe, grow warm and cool. . .

That's how a pine is in the woods. That's its *nature*.

Have you ever seen a tree drawn like that?

Of course, in order to paint all this, the painter needs to feel quite a lot, think a lot of things through, keenly feel his own connection to nature. And then, if such a painting existed, it would evoke thousands of thoughts in the viewers and reveal eternal truths and awaken the most lethargic of souls.

Not many people feel nature, not by far – just leave the city on a nice summer day and what will you see? Everywhere, crowds of people sit on the grass, eat, drink, play guitars . . . Loners read, whittle . . . but none of them really see the nature . . .

But if such an everyman were to look once, twice, three times at the magically painted pine, then he'll see what he didn't see in the forest, what had been closed off to him. He'll see wondrous life in it, the beauty . . . he'll feel the breath of nature, the harmony, the power . . . Mundane concerns will leave him, and, possibly for the first time in his life, having gotten away from his everyday worries, he'll ponder the continuity of life . . . the inviolable laws of eternity; his heart will shudder, and – in response to the millions of voices of nature – a new, hitherto untouched string will vibrate in his soul.

If only landscapes were so "naturalistic!" If only portraits were so naturalistic that blood would pulse beneath the warm skin, that thoughts would wander behind people's eyes, that eyelashes, lips, fingers would quiver from the feelings running through them, that shadows would flicker across their faces, along with the life of imagination and a kaleidoscope of desires . . .

He who is afraid of "naturalism" cannot see, cannot hear – what is most important in nature and life is hidden from him.

I think that there's nothing new here. Wasn't it said long ago:

> Nature is not what you think of it:
> She's not a mold, not a mask –
> She is made of soul, and of freedom
> She's got love, she's got a tongue.
> *(Tyutchev [1966: 81])*

Nature is complex, nearly beyond a painter's power. This is why he paints it "approximately," in passing, in general terms or suggestions. He'll sense something in it that is, at the moment, vibrating in tune with his own soul, and he'll try to convey this "language of nature" with the help of sketches, spots of color . . . This is better, of course, than making a "mold" or a "mask," but it's far from the heights of the art of painting.

In exactly the same manner, in the art of the actor, you see how directors begin *searching for the truth* with the best intentions . . . But anyone can begin – after a few steps, they become tangled in the impenetrable labyrinth of an actor's complex psychology. They exercise their wits, give their imagination free rein, make things up – this doesn't help. Then they launch into an argument, spouting smart terms, telling various anecdotes from their life in theatre . . . "Here's how real actors used to act. And what are *you* doing?" They personally demonstrate to the actor how to do it . . . but they do it poorly and only confuse the actor even more.

Before you know it, everything has turned into craftsmanship, and the truth is hidden somewhere far, far away, no closer than the other hemisphere.

More about Naturality and Naturalism

There was a time (after the Meiningen Company) when theatres were very interested in naturality. When it was applied to large productions with a horde of people, it was very satisfying; when this pursuit of exactness in depicting everyday life and psychological and behavioral accuracy was carried over to simpler plays, they would turn out poorly. Mundanity and naturalness would take the forefront and would block out a play's essence, its internal workings. They would block it for both, the audience and the actors – the actors would get bogged down in small "tasks," performing mundane details; this would lead them away from internal psychological action.

This lack of success frightened the experimenters so much that they ran in the opposite direction – they started looking for truth where there's no "nature" and mundanity at all. They started working on symbolism, schematism, impressionism.

And so, in this time of worshipping decadence and symbolism, Stanislavsky left for Belgium to meet with Maeterlinck [1862–1949] – they were getting ready to put on his *Blue Bird*. This meeting is described very picturesquely, poetically, but with humor, in Stanislavsky's first book, *My Life in Art*. Yet it excludes one conversation they had concerning the very essence of Maeterlinck's art.

In a friendly exchange, when the artists' souls opened up to one another, and they spoke about what was most precious and secret, Stanislavsky, wishing to do something nice, said: "You know, in Russia you are considered the greatest symbolist alive!"

Instead of melting in joy, Maeterlinck turned red and grumbled in frustration: "Fools!" "What do you mean, fools! Who are fools? Why?" "How am I a symbolist? I'm an *ultra-naturalist of heightened emotions.*"

I'm not the only one who's heard this story – Stanislavsky loved telling it.

Maeterlinck's words contain the full, exhaustive solution to this issue of naturalism.

Naturalism on its own isn't something invented, artificial, and certainly not unnatural – it's not bad at all. But the question is: what kind of naturalism? Naturalism of what? Things? Everyday life? Blowing one's nose? Or one's internal life? Or, even more so – heightened emotions?

And who are Duse, Garrick, Yermolova, if not naturalists of great human passions, the deepest possible human emotions?

So what does this mean? Long live naturalism?

If the term's meaning has mutated from prolonged use and naturalism is now understood as over-naturalness, then this can hardly be changed. It'll stay like this. Proclaiming, "Long live over-naturalness!" would, of course, be absurd. But, "Long live nature!" That's sacrosanct.

Nature has everything. Look at the same pine – is it not symbolic? But is it not realistic at the same time? And impressionistic? And naturalistic? Etc., etc.

It has everything, you just have to know how to look.

Nature has everything. All of our "isms" are taken from it, from nature. And there are at least as many that we haven't taken yet, if not more.

Why is it, then, that painters paint the same pine differently? Some do it symbolically, others schematically, others realistically, etc. Because where are the people that could fit everything in themselves? Each artist sees in the pine only what is closest to him. One sees one thing, another sees another, and a third sees something different. Some 25th person who has nothing to do with art will come – he'll see suitable material for his new hut and cut it down . . . It'll turn out that the pine was simply lumber. Isn't that right? That's part of the pine as well. Only, in order to see that part of it, you don't have to be an artist – you just have to be a carpenter or a lumberjack . . .

Nature has everything . . . If somebody manages to see one thing in it and conveys that image in a painting – he's a painter. If somebody sees and conveys two qualities, then he's twice over a painter.

A real great work of art has all "isms" at the same time in harmonic convergence. Take Raphael, Michelangelo, Leonardo – are they not realistic? Or naturalistic? And symbolic too? Impressionistic? Etc., etc.

Naturally, they did not think about this, about all of these "isms" – these are discoveries of a later time. They knew only one thing: nature and truth. They saw it, felt it, and created it. And as we already said – it has everything!

Notes

1 Editors could not locate the source for the Tolstoy quote.
2 Renowned sculptors of Ancient Greece.

3

Truth, As It Is *Commonly* Understood (*Pseudoexperiencing*)

The Truth Isn't Limited only to Emotion: Directly Summoning Emotions

In the depths of their souls, the overwhelming majority of actors, regardless of which school they belong to, are supporters of the creative process onstage, i.e. *experiencing*. Even if they don't understand this themselves, even if they consider themselves to be cold and proficient "masters of form," when they are carried away onstage, when their blood starts boiling, when their heart starts pounding, and their voice sounds with resonating strength – they hardly fault themselves for it. This is understandable: the more skilled an actor is, the more he feels his connection with the audience, and the more they affect him, as he affects them. This is one of the laws of art onstage.[1] Those who *openly* consider themselves to be supporters of truth employ various means in trying to evoke truthfulness, sincerity, and experiencing in themselves while onstage.

But not all of them manage to succeed. For them, successful moments onstage are merely accidental. Their great misfortune is that they don't know: what *is* truth, really? They often mistake something else for truth and experiencing. Something very close and similar, but not it at all.

Instead of seriously and truly accepting all the circumstances of a character and then growing agitated, joyful or desperate from *that*, actors usually try to summon up whatever emotion they deem necessary at a given point *out of nowhere*, without paying any attention to "circumstances."

The issue here is that they obviously consider emotions to be most important. **In their minds**, emotion equals *experiencing*. Emotion is truth. Since a person has emotions, he's obviously *living*. And since he's living, it's obviously the truth. You can't say that this deduction doesn't hold any water. However, things aren't so simple: *emotion is inevitably a part of truth, but it's only a **part***. Aside from just feeling, we also think, care about things, want something. And we orient ourselves nearly every minute – comprehending the circumstances or facts with which life surrounds us, or the words that people are saying to us. And lots more.

In life, that's how it works. Why should we think that it's simpler and more primitive in art? Isn't it the other way around? If I have to take care of things in life based on all of my known and very well-known circumstances, then in art, things should be much more complex. Because onstage, I'm not just me, but somebody else as well: Chatsky in Griboyedov's *Woe From Wit*, or Boris in Ostrovsky's *The Storm*, or Iago in *Othello*. Why is that simpler? Each one of them has his own circumstances, his own personality, and his own needs. And I know very, very little about them. I have to find all of those out, search for them. And it's not enough to find them – I then have to make them my own circumstances: as if Boris is me, and his life's circumstances are my own. Then I'll start having the necessary emotions and desires and actions in response to whatever happens to me in the play. Otherwise, I'll feel and do nothing.

Every great actor consciously or subconsciously understood this, consciously or subconsciously found a path to the truth in his role (and not just to "emotion"). But that's a small amount of people. The others searched and still search for *emotions*. That's all they care about.

How is it that they evoke them? For the most part, very simply. We learn this "art" as children: kids play about, liven up – a strict teacher enters the classroom, and they immediately pull themselves together and pretend that they weren't messing around . . . they put on an air of seriousness, concern . . . Or, you can't upset someone who's sick, so everybody tries to put on a happy, carefree mien – everybody smiles, jokes, keeps telling him that he looks well, he'll get better soon, but as soon as they leave, the mask drops away. Everyone looks at everybody else significantly: "Yeah, things aren't looking good . . ."

Pay attention to this, and you'll find, for better or for worse, that we spend a fair bit of our 24 hours occupied with this "acting." Only when we're completely alone, at home, in our room, when we don't have to deal with anything or be embarrassed before anyone, are we truly ourselves. Otherwise, we're always straining just a little bit, constantly ready to assume an air of strictness, seriousness, concern, amiability, simple-mindedness, and even foolishness, and whatever you want, as needed . . . It's become second nature to us . . . This is the precious experience that the actor uses. His "technique" is ready, and he doesn't see the need in any special school. The playwright writes, "angrily," and without further ado, the actor puts on an air of "anger," yells out whatever lines he's supposed to, in this state, and everything works out great. Same thing for "joyfully" – he smiles, skips, beams at everyone . . . there's your "joy."

Depicting Emotions ("Acting Emotions")

What is an emotion, essentially? Emotion is a reaction. Why did I become sad? Because my friend is very sick, God forbid he'll pass away – he would leave behind his widow and orphaned children, as well as his important, unfinished work . . . all things considered, who would I go to for advice and to bare my soul?

In reality, of course, none of this is true – I don't have a friend who's dying (maybe I don't even have any friends) – it's just a colleague, another actor is playing "my friend who's dying." Because of this, I have no feeling of grief, and it won't come on its own. You can use your memory to summon up something resembling grief for a brief second. You can even give it free reign, and it might carry you away, but not for long and not deeply: because it has no fuel . . . And it evaporates. You have to hold on to it! But how? And the actor grabs on to what he can: the appearance of emotion – a sad expression, a bowed head, sighs, a subdued voice, slower speech, seriousness and grimness in his gaze . . .

51

This doesn't come naturally to him and instead takes up most of his attention. He has no time to think about his friend, his family, everything that he actually would be thinking about if this were to happen in real life (about comforting his wife, about getting another, better doctor, etc., etc.) – his mind is occupied with keeping his mask from flying off . . . This is called "acting an emotion." Not feeling emotions, but "acting emotions."

Earthlight

There's no need to talk about "acting emotions," i.e. depicting emotions by external means – it's obvious that this doesn't involve real emotions, experiencing, or truth. But what about actual emotions that we call up at will? What about them?

Let's suppose that I want to feel sadness. In order to do this, my face and eyes adopt a sad expression, I assume the appropriate pose, I start speak slower, more elongatedly . . . and my spirits drop, everything around me seems to appear in a different, more somber light. How is this not emotion? How is this not truth?

In order to fully and properly understand that this isn't emotion, but only the reflection of emotion, we should look to the story of the so-called James-Lange Theory.

Some 40–50 years ago, the American psychologist William James gave a presentation about a very paradoxical theory on emotions. Before him, people thought that emotion (feeling) existed in the following manner: the first stage – a person has an impression (a person sees or hears something); stage two – this impression is decoded and comprehended (for example, upon seeing a scary wild animal that we come across while alone in the forest, we comprehend the horror of not having any way out); then stage three – as a result of this decoding, an emotion wells up (in this case, fear); and the final stage, stage four – we have a physiological reaction (we pale, can't move, our hair stands, etc.).

With the help of very clever experiments and deft deductions James [1893: 375–376] showed that everything happens in a completely different order – the exact opposite, actually: upon seeing the animal, we stop (all of our voluntary actions are slowed) completely involuntarily and reflexively, *without yet understanding the horror of our situation*, the blood leaves our face, our hair stands, and *these physiological changes* cause the feeling of fear.

And only then do we comprehend that we're in danger with no way out.

Because of this, if you manage to artificially create all of these physiological conditions, then *the feeling of fear will well up*.

So what do we have here? Is this not true? When we want to throw off some heavy feeling or boredom, do we not force ourselves to smile, jump up, straighten our backs, wave our arms around, or sing? And, for the most part, this gets the job done.

James' sensational discovery created a lot of noise. And in the psychologist's motherland, this discovery spread so well and garnered so much attention, that in some towns, city officials started hanging a poster in streetcars: "Smile!"

Its meaning and purpose were as follows: in order to evoke a joyful and perky state, you have to create a series of physiological conditions that exist when one is perky and joyful. What is the main and most constant manifestation of joy? Smiling. Concordantly, if we smile, we'll be taken by joy, and we'll feel happy.

And so, the city fathers, concerned about the cheerful disposition of their citizens, gave them a universal aid to achieve it. Those absent-minded citizens, who need constant reminders, received them through posters.

However, fascination with this discovery wasn't long; in practice, it turned out that evoking all of these physiological conditions was a far more complex procedure than it initially seemed.

It turned out that it was utterly impossible to create the majority of physiological conditions – go ahead and turn pale, right here on the spot! Or make your hair stand up on your head, or make this gland (which you've never even heard of!) wiggle around!

And without these conditions precisely so, the required emotion would not be summoned. Something would rise up that remotely resembled an emotion – a reflection of an emotion.

So, this theory didn't come through in practice. And, regardless, by that point, more exact and painstaking research made an appearance. And it turned out that all of these conditions that occur during a given emotion are caused not because of what the first theory or the second theory said – in reality, *everything happens simultaneously*, like a single, complex process.

As soon as a person sees a scary beast, he begins to feel fear, his hair stands up on his head, and he comprehends that he has no way out – all at the same time. And there's only one reason: he *saw* a beast! i.e. he *perceived* an impression.

And without genuine perception, there is not and cannot be fully-fledged emotion. Such is the real mechanism behind our emotions.

However, just as people in their daily lives are satisfied with a much simpler approach, so are actors on the stage. Regardless of whether they know about James' theory, when they want to summon one emotion or another, they use the same centuries-old methods, force themselves to dance and leap when they need to be happy, and grimace when they want to be in the throes of sorrow.

We should be fair: they do get some feeling. But what kind of feeling?

The sun illuminates the earth and the moon. The half of the surface, which is facing the sun, is illuminated, while the opposite half is not. However, when we see just a slender sickle in the sky and the greater part of the moon's surface (that's facing us) is in darkness, we still see that the darkness isn't absolute, that some light is still hitting it.

What is this light? It turns out that this is light reflected from the Earth – it is sunlight, but indirect sunlight, reflected from the Earth. It's called "earthlight."

Actors believe this sort of "earthlight" feeling to be the actual feeling itself.

Even though an actor might argue or protest, if he got his "feeling" without genuine perception, then it's just the "earthlight" of a feeling. It isn't a feeling. It will never be enough to inspire us to undertake any sort of move or action. Besides, we know that *we summoned up this "feeling" ourselves*. So we're trying to pull ourselves up by our bootstraps . . .

This isn't emotion, the actor is deceived. His deception is understandable – he *wants* to be deceived . . . It's advantageous to him. Otherwise, he'll have to come to terms with the fact that he acts poorly and that his school is good for nothing. And that's not pleasant for anybody.

Besides, you can call the audience as a witness: they like it, they say that it's the truth, that it's real experiencing, that it's high art – we should listen to them.

"Buzzzzzz . . ."

Another actor will say: "Of course, maybe some actors are simply "searching for emotions," "acting emotions," or "depict" them with gestures, physicality, tone of voice, as if they're agitated, as if they're truly feeling emotions onstage. I don't do this, I really am agitated, and I don't feel that I'm "acting" – rather, I become wholly affected by these emotions."

You'll take a look at this actor in action, and you'll see that he really is agitated. But what kind of agitation is it? It deserves some attention.

Let's take a doctor who has to daily inspect one hundred patients in only three hours in a row daily. What does he condition himself to do? He conditions himself to search for and find only the roughest signs of sickness. How could he give in to details and subtleties? He ignores them. They disappear for him. Because if they don't disappear, then how could he ever get through such an amount of patients?

An actor who is not given enough rehearsal time, finds himself in essentially the same situation. How can he search for the details, the tints and undertones of one character or another, of this emotion or that? Let's assume that he plays "leading men." Every month or two, a new "leading man." God grant that you're able to memorize the lines and figure out what's going on in the play. As for love – what is there to spend a long time pondering? You must "beautifully," "passionately," "with abandon" speak the "enticing words of love" and "monologues" – and that's pretty much it. The actor practices, gets experience, "perfects" everything. Years pass, and he's able to act out any love scene on the spot. If he has to, he doesn't even need rehearsals: just a prompter. Will this be an authentic slice of life? Of course not. Do you think there exists some sort of stencil for any given emotion, and especially love?

There's a simple device – the electric bell. Press the button: buzzzzzz – and that's it. It doesn't care who presses it, when, or where – it has only one response: buzzzzzz . . . It doesn't matter if the button is pressed by some beauty's delicate hand or the hardened hand of a digger, if the person is sick and dying or strong and full of life, if he's happy or miserable, if he's a fool or the smartest man alive – if the button is pressed: buzzzzzz . . . and nothing more. The actor who becomes used to summoning up what he calls "experiencing" turns into an analogous simple machine. Because it's not experiencing at all, it's just a standard actor's approach where he fires himself up – regardless of reason; it doesn't make a difference if it's because of love, hatred, joy, or grief – it can be whatever you want – the actor's always ready to fire himself up.

This seeming experiencing and presence of emotion is merely peripheral. Rather, it's nervousness, a state of being strung-up. Imagine a person who is too nervous – somebody neurotic. When he gets offended – he becomes nervous, starts twitching, fidgeting in his chair, and biting his nails . . . Somebody makes him happy, compliments him – he becomes nervous in a different way, but he gets nervous again, nonetheless: his laughter is too loud, ready to turn into tears at any moment, his running around the room is too frantic . . . you wish that he would sit down and keep calm.

The actor develops a similar professional nervousness. Regardless of the "experiencing" that's required of him, the button is pressed, something shudders in his chest – buzzzzzz – and everything is good to go. The nervousness is conveyed to the audience. The audience sees that the actor is "emotional," he is "experiencing." As they watch him act, the audience involuntarily presumes that the actor's emotions are caused by the content of the words that he is currently saying. They don't see any other possible reason. While, in reality, the words are delivered completely mechanically. He acts and speaks in a state of some insanity, of unhealthy excitement. We can't require any clarity of thought from him in this state. Even jurisprudence doesn't punish a crime that was committed in a state of psychological abnormality; it lessens the severity of the punishment if the suspect wasn't in his right mind. How, then, can we demand from an actor who has strained his psyche so much, to give us meaning, truth, authentic creativity, i.e. a harmonious and simultaneous union and coherence of all higher human qualities?

In these moments of artificial self-excitement, the actor is nearly "out of his mind." He doesn't possess himself as he should. He interprets this state as emotion, as temperament, as "experiencing." In reality, this is just a typical strained psyche, and in this state, the actor is shallow and primitive, just like that electric bell.

A Motor Storm[2]

This is something that is more powerful, and is the next level of the light strain described above. This is neurosis. It is very popular and it is held in high regard among actors. When an actor enters a state of neurosis, he is quite pleased and, for the most part, brags about how he acted so well today that he doesn't remember a thing, that his eyes grew dark, that his head spun, that he didn't see anything or anyone, that he broke something along the way, in the heat of the moment, and rammed into something himself, sacrificing everything for art . . . The actor considers this to be inspiration. He believes that some higher power possessed him, and he gave himself over to it.

Have you ever seen a bird accidentally fly through your window? Upon seeing you and growing scared, the poor bird, instead of sitting down for a few seconds, orienting itself, and calmly flying out the way it flew in, begins to fly around, bumping into cupboards, pictures, and curtain rods. It zooms around the room, freaks out at the sight of anything, launches itself at every window but the open one, rams into the panes, the mirrors. If it doesn't die from all of these hits, then maybe it'll finally fly out the right window. At that point, it's probably thinking that it was saved by this flurry of movement, that without it, she would have perished. And it was so difficult to get out! It almost died of fear!! If not for its resourcefulness, deftness, and courage, it would have surely died! What a silly bird! Psychologists call this state a *motor storm*.

Motor storms are very widespread; we can see them especially among insects. Flies, bumblebees, moths – when you try to capture them, they zoom around with dizzying speed, instantly and unexpectedly changing direction; it's almost impossible to catch them in this state. They are also in the throes of a motor storm. Even when you've stopped your chase long ago, they continue to zoom from place to place until the storm dies down on its own. For them, such a form of defense is practical. They cannot consciously orient themselves and choose the right path; so, nature has equipped them with motor storms. But when a person uses this same strategy, and in the middle of a fire, instead of leaving through the front door, throws himself out the third-story window, and instead of taking his most precious belongings, he saves a broom, a chair, and an empty bottle from the fire – then that's shameful, that's a sickness, it's too much of a return to the past, to our ancestors.

Actors who cultivate in themselves (and even worse, in their students) the ability to enter these motor storms, this most primitive of reactions that a living being can possess, also go as far as to return too deeply to the past. They feverishly clench their fists, grinding their teeth, raise their shoulders as high as they go to the point that it's painful, almost to the point of breaking . . . breathe sporadically . . . In this state of extreme strain, which denies them the ability to think and feel, they zoom around the stage, break everything in sight, howl in an inhuman voice . . .

This kind of acting leaves some audience members – unstable and neurotic ones – with a strong impression. And not just an impression, but also a physical reaction: they become infected with this form of seizure and are almost ready to join the madmen onstage.

This sort of jaw-dropping acting can be typically observed in powerful dramatic and, naturally, tragic parts.

"Verisimilitude"

You can call a "motor storm" "experiencing" in quotes. As a counterbalance, you have a different kind of "experiencing," no less deserving of quotes, but nobody's dared to raise a hand against it yet.

At the foundation of the MAT's school lie the principles of authenticity and live creativity. This is the school of experiencing. True, not the same experiencing that would carry away truly great actors – Mochalov, Yermolova, and the whole constellation of our miracle workers. Here, they don't rely on inspiration, talent, free creativity. Hundreds of rehearsals are spent analyzing plays, dissecting each scene, searching for the right rhythms, hunting for expressive forms, and, finally, "justifying" – turning everything into the truth, bringing every bit of a role "to life," every line, every word, every *mise-en-scene*. These distinctive and clever methods allow for those actors who are more gifted to immerse themselves in the circumstances of their characters' lives. Guided by the great directorial and pedagogical experience and talent, they begin to live onstage – live with their characters' interests, feelings, and passions. They transform into those characters.

The weaker representatives of the MAT, however, couldn't handle the main requirements of the school's founders. (This applies to MAT's weaker directors and pedagogues as much as to the actors.) In the pursuit of lifelikeness and verisimilitude, they failed to pick up on what's most important. Instead, they tried to do everything so "simply," "naturally," "like in life." Gradually, without noticing it themselves, they grew closer and closer to the most pitiful and pale of "verisimilitudes."

It goes from bad to worse. The fear of "overacting," of playing something falsely, is so great in these people, that *underacting* isn't even considered a mistake. Underacted today, underacted tomorrow – and it becomes ingrained.

Such a case unfolded before my own eyes – a student asked his teacher's permission to take on Franz's final scene in Schiller's *The Robbers*. She gave it to him. Another day, I asked him: why did you take such a difficult scene?"

"I doesn't seem so difficult to me," he replied. "I tried it, and it went fine." "Ok, and how does it go? How do you play it?" "Here's how I envision everything: nighttime . . . horrors . . . I hear whispers of some kind, ruffling, as if someone's looking at me, but the someone isn't human, but something strange . . . I'm scared. I call over a priest . . . he tells me about retribution beyond the grave . . . about hell . . . it turns out my crimes are the worst of all: I killed my father, my brother . . . I understand now that the whispers and ruffling – someone's come for me . . . from beyond the veil . . . Satan's servants . . . And all of a sudden, there really is a noise, screaming, the castle is surrounded, it's under siege . . . that means that they're here for me . . . there really are fires in the window . . . if they were human, I'd meet them with my sword, but this . . . there's no way out . . . and I . . . kill myself!"

The young man's passionate tale convinced me. He explained everything so well, felt the enemy forces that he was powerless against so clearly. He understood everything in this scene so truly, and it excited him so much, that I thought: hey, maybe he really will do it! . . . He may not manage to repeat it, but he could probably do it once . . .

A few days later, he showed this scene to his teacher.

He was quite agitated before the showing, and this agitation helped him: it served as a good springboard to Franz's agitation and fear. The whole scene with the holy father was, contrary to expectations, actually quite good. The teacher sat with a surprised expression on her face and was even somewhat confused: how can this young, inexperienced student, without any help, play . . . Schiller! He's doing it, there's almost nothing to correct! This is unbelievable! This is outrageous! . . . This doesn't happen . . .

After the father left, Franz is speaking to the old servant, Daniel, and, according to Schiller's directions, he is supposed to start losing his wits. In that part, the actor was so immersed in the role that it became slightly eerie. Despite his inexperience, he acted well. All who were present grew quiet, and watched him with bated breath. He looked in the direction Daniel left long after Daniel was gone . . . Then he turned to us . . . He saw us and didn't see us . . . it looked like Daniel was still in front of him, and, turning to us and mysteriously and pointlessly smiling, he asked: "You want to say 'to hell?'"[3] he winked at us and whispered, as if entrusting us with a secret: "You're right, I'm already feeling something like it. . ." While hearing some sounds, and still smiling, he addressed the place where the sounds came from with quiet joy: "Could these songs, this hissing be yours, you serpents of the underworlds?.." And suddenly, hearing the real sound of robbers assaulting the castle—screams, noise, thuds against a distant door—he felt real danger. Reality became muddled in with hallucinations, and he started whispering or yelling things out in panic and horror: "They're coming here . . . breaking my doors. . ." He dashed from the windows to the door, from the door to the walls, looked at something above him . . . it seemed like he wanted to climb up the wall, then he would dash around the room again . . . he whipped out his sword, as if he wanted to kill himself . . . he grew afraid – threw it aside . . . He would run up to it again, then back away again: "Wherefore is this deadly blade frightening me?"

Then he grew still – he listened . . . "the door is creaking. . ." he fell down . . . "There's no salvation!" It's as if he sprouted roots . . . he couldn't move . . . he shut his eyes . . . and then, he lost it. Evidently, he looked at himself from the outside, and this interrupted the properly working process inside him. Up to this point, he heard all of the menacing sounds, screams, pounding on the door, the burst open door, but here, having looked at himself from the outside – he lost everything – he saw that he is an actor, that people are watching him . . . But what is there to look at? . . . There is all this agitation inside . . . but what is it about? What for? . . . And everybody's watching, waiting . . . inside, there's just emptiness and horror . . . What is there to do? . . . I have to do *something?!* . . . I can't just end the scene! I must do something quick . . . or they'll notice I am lost, and laugh at me. Come what may! – and the actor immediately whipped up a familiar motor storm: he clenched his fists, hunched his shoulders up to his ears, popped his eyes, and zoomed around the room . . . Then he tore a cord off of his hat (as per the stage directions) – "You take pity on me, at least!" – and with lightening speed – just to be done with everything as quickly as possible – he pretended that he hung himself . . . on some imaginary nail or window rod . . . and he fell . . . dead . . . .

"There, I thought so!" the teacher said triumphantly. "I allowed you to take on this scene so that you could understand how far beyond your reach it is. And that's just what happened."

"Why were you running around with clenched fists, not seeing everything around you? You should have been searching, looking for a way to save yourself 'from them' – so do that: look for salvation. In order to do that, you have to be able to see. You want to hang yourself? If you had really wanted to end your life with the help of that cord, what would you do?" He was silent, he was still agitated from the scene itself and from the unexpected failure in the last moment . . . She wouldn't relent: "Well? Tell me!" "I don't know," he mumbled incomprehensibly, not fully understanding what she wanted from him. But she already got on her hobby-horse, and, feeling that she was at the height of her power and wisdom, she began explaining: "Before hanging yourself on that cord, you would have first tested it to make sure that it could bear your weight – go ahead, try it. Well? Could it? It could. Now, look for a place to tie it to. Why did you immediately go to that window rod – you would have first searched for something better: a hook, a chandelier, a lamp . . ."

And so on and so forth. He was doused in cold water, even ridiculed . . . He thought that the most important part was his flight, his inspiration. But nobody even noticed that. Which must mean that it's unnecessary, and what *is* necessary is . . . the truth. His fire died out. He lost faith in himself. His teacher's words, regardless of how correct they seemed, couldn't concern everything that he did before us that day, but her triumphant tone confused him. For now, the actor understood only one thing: he didn't do anything right, and that's not how it's done!

And so he started methodically and pointedly, without any inspiration, organizing his suicide: he started checking the strength of the cord, looked for an appropriate hook, tied the cord
to it, checked it again, and, in a word – did everything "realistically."

Except that nothing was left of Schiller, Franz, the insanity and the demons . . .

But since a figure of authority said that it was much better, more true now – the poisonous
seed had taken root – that *this* was good, that it would do.

But this isn't good either! And step by step, case by case, an actor develops a habit of being
cautious, stopping himself when he should and when he shouldn't, stepping on the brakes, and,
aside from this: accepting not all of the circumstances that currently surround the character
onstage, but only a part of them, and only insignificant ones at that. As a result – it's boring,
uninteresting, pale. What's wrong?! What's wrong is that *it's not truth at all – it's all false*. That's
all that's wrong.

Inspiration, excitement, self-abandonment . . . the actor shouldn't be punished for all this,
but encouraged and taught to use it. Should we really persecute an actor who, because of his
inexperience, couldn't handle the flood of emotions, got scared, looked at himself from the
outside, lost equilibrium, began to rush, and lost it?

You should be overjoyed because of his strength as an actor, not his accidental breakdown.
An actor who is denied the ardor of his imagination . . . what is he? An electric lamp with a
burned out filament. What is it good for? The trash.

So it's thrown out.

Shallow, Verisimilar Idle Talk (Deceptive Simplicity)

Old and experienced actors often amaze everyone with their simplicity, the naturality of
their behavior onstage. They move so freely, speak so easily. Without any actorly pushing and
delivery. You look at him and think: he's so simple, so natural! Just like in life! However, one
shouldn't overrate this simplicity. It is by no means evidence of an actor's complete organic
immersion in a role. It's simply the unflappable calm of a craftsman-professional, simply the
dulling of his receptiveness. What does his "mastery" constitute? Well, it manifests itself
entirely in this acquired dulling of his soul. Judge for yourself – is this *truth*?

This "simplicity" can be observed not only among very old and experienced actors, old
sea-dogs – young ones also sometimes deftly catch on to this *carelessness* onstage, this *aplomb
of an empty soul*. The earlier they catch on to this and the more artfully they do it, the farther
away they get from truth, experiencing, and naturality.

Notes

1 See Book Five, chapter 13, *The Actor and the Audience*.
2 The term and concept of "motor storm" [Bewegungssturm] are borrowed by Demidov from
   Kretschmer's *Hysteria, Reflex, and Instinct*. This terms has also been translated into English as "instinctive
   flurry."
3 Here and further, Demidov quotes Schiller 1802: 139–140.

4

The Intangibility of Truth

Why Is it so Difficult to Find Truth?

When falling into a "motor storm," an ignorant actor with an unstable nervous system believes that he is "experiencing." A craftsman who causes himself to feel generic nervous agitation by means of "Buzzzzzz" also thinks that what he's feeling is "emotion," i.e. he is experiencing. A more cultured actor in the hands of more or less knowledgeable pedagogues doesn't make this mistake. If he chances to enter a "motor storm" or if he happens to "step on it" out of insecurity – and experience by means of "Buzzzzzz" – then he'll mark it down as a failure. But few are capable of making the last step and jumping over from verisimilitude to truth. The step is so subtle that many actors who have spent their whole lives onstage (even on a good stage) don't even suspect that they never rose above mere verisimilitude. And when this kind of actor is dunked into truth and he breathes in the new, unfamiliar air, the result is always the same: bewilderment, surprise, joy, and fear. He looks around, as if to check if everything's the same as it was . . . looks inside himself . . . remembers the experience he just lived through and, for the most part, says: "Well, this is something else entirely! . . . And it's so wonderful! Yes! . . . This is truth – can't argue with that! . . . "

Why is this so? Why were he and others like him so deceived? Why did they take the shadow of truth as truth itself? The audience is deceived – that's obvious. But why is the *actor himself* also deceived?

There's nothing simpler. This is how it must be. Look at the counterintuitive situation that the stage puts the actor in: hundreds of eyes are looking at me. And they came in order to look at me. They paid money! So what am I supposed to show them? How can I surprise them? I have to turn into another person. As if I'm not me, but somebody else – some kind of "him." The actors surrounding me aren't actors either – they're either my brother, or my mother, or my father, or my wife . . . The audience (which I can see very clearly and know that they're all here, looking at me), I'm not supposed to see. Or, at least, I have to pretend that I don't see them. And along with my colleague actors, I'm supposed to play out a whole story in front of them. And I have to truly immerse myself in a role, feel emotions, live. But the words aren't my own – they're foreign . . . I know them all beforehand . . . And the actions, the turns of events are also all predetermined . . . (which never happens in life). And the stage isn't a stage – it's a room, a forest, a field, a castle, a palace . . . And time isn't time either, it's just simple fiction – in some 10 minutes, more than 10 years come to pass – whole lifetimes . . .

There is so much that is counterintuitive here, and it doesn't all just string together into one long chain, but they increase exponentially! And you get a whole mountain of these completely incoherent demands and situations. Go ahead, try to swim your way out of it, try to look for the truth! Only a diabolical mind could have come up with such a machine, not a human one. It's full of lies and only lies, and yet they say: give us the truth! Don't be false!

Is it any wonder when, in the middle of this hellish mess, something that remotely resembles life or the truth flickers by – suddenly, for example, it'll seem like I became angry or very sad because of some chimerical reason – is it any wonder that this will seem like a miracle – a sunny day amidst impenetrable darkness. And so you think: there's that truth!

I once had to be present during one exceedingly torturous rehearsal, when both, director and actor, were wearing themselves out, trying to find authentic truth. The director was unsatisfied regardless of what the actor did. He wanted to achieve perfection. "I don't believe you!" "That's not truth!" "Look for truth!" he would demand. And so, the actor, tormented by his failures, had had more than enough of his own failures, the director, and theatre. "What!" he finally screamed, "What do you want from me!? You put me in a furnace, threw me in a fire and you want me to breathe normally in here . . . enjoy myself! . . . Who do I look like? Daniel and the three youths?!"

A lot of actors perceive the atmosphere of the stage to be so hostile and alien. And when something seems *obviously improbable*, then, out of nowhere, an invisible, but very real psychological wall instantly rises up between me and what I wanted to achieve, what seemed so close and easily attainable. This wall is a braking system. And it's so insurmountable that it seems futile to even attempt to try and live in this *inaccessible* environment normally, as we do every hour, every minute!

What exactly should you do? In essence, the conditions are counterintuitive, *unnatural* . . . Involuntarily adapting himself to them, the actor searches for counterintuitive methods and counterintuitive paths. He tries to make it seem *"as if he's living . . ."* He tries to pretend that he's feeling emotions, agitation, tries to pretend that he's interested in what is happening onstage, that he's listening to his partners . . . His face, his voice, his body try to portray the person he's playing ("the character").

What else can you do in these counterintuitive conditions if not squeeze out of yourself this counterintuitive "experiencing?" Everybody is familiar with it. People say: "theatrical gestures," "theatrical declamations." In pathology and psychiatry textbooks, you can find expressions like this: "The patient (who's suffering from some illness) is exhibiting exaggerated, theatrical behavior." It's quite sad for someone who loves and understands theatre to read something like this. But there's nothing to be done – a fact is a fact.

Actors who are practitioners of this "exaggerated, theatrical behavior" must value it and find it so interesting, significant, and beautiful, that they utilize it in life as well; especially when they're surrounded by strangers. You can immediately make one out in a crowd – he stands out – you can't go wrong: he's "an actor!"

More fastidious and serious actors understand the absurdity of such behavior, in life and on the stage. They keep away from it. They search for *authentic truth* onstage.

What is required for authentic truth? It turns out that you have to completely recondition yourself. You have to retune all of your reflexes! Yes, yes! No more, no less. In the exceedingly unnatural conditions of the stage, the actor involuntarily and reflexively develops unnatural behavior. This is a rule. But this behavior is good for nothing – it's fake, it's apery, it's untrue.

And so you have to search *how to live naturally in unnatural conditions*. Live naturally when every part of you and nature itself are protesting, revolting, refusing to accept any admonition . . .

There are only two ways out: either a certain, special giftedness, which, when an actor presents himself before an audience, feels itself as it's supposed to and does everything as the situation calls for. Or consciously developing these qualities. In the first case, you get the impression that the person has found his way into his natural habitat. Like a duck: he walked and walked along the shore, awkwardly hobbled from one foot onto the other, but once he entered the water – he came to life: he swims, he dives, he gambols about! Nothing can stop him!

If, however, you don't have any such obvious giftedness—it's a pity, of course, a great pity—but there's no need to panic – you have to gradually, step by step, develop it. Maybe not to the same level, but to a sufficient one. One way or another, but for the most part, you have to stubbornly, patiently, painstakingly *retune your natural reflexes*.

Or, so as to use ordinary vocabulary instead of the difficult language of psychology – you have to look at everything counterintuitive on the stage so that it not only didn't get in your way, paralyzed you, but on the contrary – inspired you and gave you strength; so that it didn't distract you, but on the contrary – helped you concentrate on the surrounding circumstances; so that it didn't constrict you, but on the contrary – freed you, liberated you, granted you bravery and freedom. Such bravery and freedom that you wouldn't feel in your ordinary life.

5

On Artistry and the Artist

The level of art's perfection is manifold. The greatest concepts, the most elevated intentions can manifest themselves so weakly and helplessly that they won't just fail to reach the art's intended goal, but on the contrary, they'll lessen and discredit the given elevated and noble idea, turning it into something crass.

Next to this: an artist who has taken a small, modest idea can sometimes become so involved with its execution, with the artistic process itself, that, in these creative moments, he broadens and outgrows himself. In broadening himself, he involuntarily broadens the idea, and it outgrows all its preliminary boundaries and becomes enormous.[1] And in this sense, the power of art lies not so much in its themes as much as in the perfection of execution.

Much has been written about the goals of art, the goals of various works of art. Everywhere, you'll find discussions about whether a character has been correctly understood and interpreted (a character or an event) from one and another and a third point of view. Significantly less attention is dedicated to the excellence of the work's execution, to the reason behind the actor's power or helplessness, his technique, the origins of his creative powers, the rules of the creative process, the methods of stimulating it or the reasons behind its stagnation and distortion. It's almost as if these topics aren't even worth discussing, they're all self-evident.

People who write this probably really think it's all self-evident, simple, and well-known, undeserving of discussion. That's why they write so easily and with such careless confidence . . .

I have to bitterly admit that our art form is defenseless. Somebody who isn't an expert will never allow himself to discuss whether a bridge is properly built, whether a train is properly constructed, if a surgery was done well – only in theatre is everything clear and obvious to everyone. I mean, really: people walk about the stage, sit, speak – what's so complicated about it? What is there to "get?" And who doesn't consider himself to be an expert in theatre? Anyone, whoever they may be, will go see a show and already considers it his right and even his duty to "dissect," "criticize," authoritatively expound his condemnations and exaltations, give his advice: this should be done like this, not like *this!*

However, this topic is so painful for a theatre worker that it's better to avoid it altogether for fear that it might lead us far, far away from our path.

And our chosen path is to discuss the process of an actor's creativity (and not just an actor's, but that of any performer: a singer, a storyteller, a reader, a musician, even a lector or an orator) – of its soundness or lack thereof.

Let's discuss this.

On Perfection

Experts say that as long as you hear the violin in the violinist's hands – no matter how much the music astounds you – his playing was far from perfect. It's when *the violin disappears* and you begin to hear hitherto unheard, magical sounds, the sighs of some grieving or endlessly joyful soul – that's when the *real thing* begins. Is this art? If we derive it from the word "art-fulness," then probably not – this isn't artfulness anymore, this is a step father – beyond it, *beyond artfulness*. There is a good word for it, though it's not new: **artistry**. This is a step into the realm of artistry.

I had the chance to see the *Sistine Madonna* in Dresden. It hangs on its own in a relatively small room. When I entered, it took my breath away: a woman is soaring right at me through the moving, undulating air . . . Her clothing is windblown and is vacillating slightly, her chest is breathing, her face changes between being flushed and not, her eyes sparkle and pierce you to your core . . .

No! No! It's just a painting! – I came to my senses. And yet, no matter how long I gazed at it, I didn't see a "painting." I saw a person. A person whose presence instilled such peace and calm in me that after two hours had imperceptibly slipped by, it seemed as if my soul had become clear and transparent, like a mountain lake.

That's true art. The art of a real *artist*. What's the essence, the secret of a work of art's extraordinary power and magnetism?

There are many secrets, and the primary one is truth. Truth is like the day, like an open field, like a river – you can't doubt it. You believe it and dissolve in its calmness and harmoniousness. But it can also amaze and thrill, like a stormy sea, like a thunderstorm, like human passions . . .

The Life-Giving Oneness

There was a time when I would often gaze upon the paintings of old Italian masters. At first, when your attention is still scattered, you only see shortcomings, convention, naiveté . . . But the more you look – you grow calm, you stop paying attention to external wrinkles and you're taken hold of by a singularly calm feeling of fulfillment and satisfaction. This especially happened with Raphael's paintings (it might be that I didn't yet learn how to look at other masters). You might be looking at *The Marriage of the Virgin*, and gradually, though you like one thing, something else, and a third thing, you're enraptured by **one** holistic, main quality that exists in the painting, that exists in the artist's soul.

This *one thing* makes the painting come to life. Moreover, it makes it a living creature with its own soul and its own laws of existence. And you unwittingly obey these laws. And just like that, every initial hindrance has disappeared . . . Many things seemed conventional, naïve, or even ignorant, but here, you see that it's the other way around – everything suddenly appears to have such strict, joyous consistency and, most importantly, an elevated, artistic calm! **The "life-giving oneness," the "soul-granting oneness"** . . . I don't know what to call it, but it contains the very magic of a work of art. Without it, it's dead, even if it's done with great artfulness.

The Liveliness of a Work of Art

Is a bird's corpse the form of a bird? It's just the form of a corpse. A bird is alive, and anything living breathes, pulsates, and a living creature's form is mobile and flickering. It's never in a single spot.

I saw the Mona Lisa in the Louvre. She didn't astound me in any way: she's ugly, eyebrowless, almost slant-eyed . . . I walked around the museum, and on my way out, stopped by again. What happened?! . . . Either the lighting changed, or something . . . But why isn't she smiling? She smiled then, but now, she's not . . . And her eyes aren't slanted . . . She's watching me with blame in her eyes, with pity . . .

I came another day directly to her. With snide curiosity, she looked right in my eyes . . . she's cunning . . . purses her lips so as not to laugh . . . As if to say, "look at how I puzzled you yesterday!" I looked at her for a long time, from every which way – learned her, memorized her – she won't fool me again!

I come back in some two hours – the smile is still there. But it's completely different – it's mournful . . . her eyes are serious and are looking past me; she's not interested in me at all . . .

What is the meaning of all this? It's like a hallucination!

Again, again, and again I would come . . . For a whole week. Every time, there was something different, something new. Now she's a friend, now an enemy, a sister, a mother, a stranger, or a secret lover . . . Of course there was different lighting, of course my own mood changed . . . But why don't the other paintings change? Why are they frozen, immobile, and don't react to anything? But this one, like a magical mirror, reflects my thoughts, my feelings, my life. I was afraid to speak of it – people might make fun of me: fantasizer, dreamer, "mystic" . . .

However, I was lucky – fate brought me together with one very prominent European painter. Carefully, gingerly, I swung the conversation in the direction of this painting that was making my head spin in circles . . . Seeing that my conversation partner also had a specific attitude towards it, one thing led to another, and I told him everything that had happened to me. He listened to me attentively and seriously. When I finished, he was quiet. Quiet and contemplative. It looked like he was crestfallen and let down. "Could it be," I thought, "that he's angry at me? Look at this ignoramus coming to me with his 'impressions.'"

Finally, I gathered my courage and said, "Of course, it might be that I don't get it . . . it's just my own . . . but still . . . what's going on here? There's some secret to this . . . You're a specialist – you have to know, right?"

Without uttering a word, he jumped up, ran around the room, made his entire mane of luscious hair stand on end, and, stopping before me, roared: "Hell only knows! Hell only knows how the devil did it! She's bloody alive! She moves, but how, what, and why – you try and figure it out – go ahead! They say that in his time, there were dark rumors that he sold his soul for his Lisa's eyes! It's a legend, obviously, but it means that those eyes haunted people back then too . . ."

That's when I realized that it wasn't just some silly fantasy on my part. If such a renowned artist was so distressed by this mysterious wonder, then you not only *can* talk about it, but *must*. Some might laugh, but not everybody, not by far. Of course, it's easier to laugh than to painstakingly rack your brains about something. I write for those who are capable of taking this seriously.

This is how you should interpret Hamlet! No, *that's* how you should interpret Hamlet! *No* – *that's* how you should interpret Hamlet!! And people fight about it and spend tons of paper writing about it . . . But Hamlet is alive, like Mona Lisa. And she'll smile invitingly to one person, laugh at another, sorrowfully gaze at another, and will simply turn away from a fourth. And so they argue. They think that she has the same effect on everyone that she had on them. But the most curious part is that it'll be different for *them* every day too. And it's all because Hamlet and Mona Lisa are alive. It's impossible to shove Hamlet into one concrete, constant form – isn't it the same thing as forcefully stopping someone's heart or preventing them from breathing?

When you want to establish an unshakable form or when you want to nail down the exact meaning of a work of art, it's no different from murder. In the hands of these people, it's no longer form, but necrosis – form's corpse; instead of the secret of living content – it's just a dry specimen.

Even when you don't try to capture all of a work of art's content and only try to convey the most important parts (you would think that this, at least, would be possible), but it still turns out that the form is too slippery, and it melts away. You almost had it! But you look at it: it's already dead. You'll never catch it, just as you will never catch Lisa-Gioconda's smile. Today, it's about one thing, tomorrow, about something else, and the day after – it's not even there. And this is all because a true work of art has a strange and hitherto incomprehensible attribute: it has the ability to *change* before our very eyes. Like a living being, it changes along with us, retunes itself to our feelings, thinks, grows ill, overcomes its illness, grows old, grows young again . . . In a word: it lives! And only one thing is for sure: it never dies. You can break it, tear it, destroy it altogether, but it itself will not die. Wanting to change something, you can ruin it with an inexperienced hand or poor performance, but it will never deteriorate on its own.

There are few such true, "living" works of art . . . very few. Few and far between. There are a bit more "semi-living" ones – they begin to breathe and move when another artist (performer) imbues it with a part of his "I." But for the most part, the world is full of "semi-dead" ones and completely dead ones. We have a long way to go before they vanish – for now, they're still littering . . . And looking at them, new trash finds its way into the world, slipping through every crack . . .

A Living Work of Art in Theatre

If, in painting and sculpting, an artist strives for his dead material to "come to life" – and achieves this in his best works – then it would seem that in theatre this would be completely unnecessary, seeing as the material here isn't dead, neither paint nor stone, but a real, live human – the actor. And, in this way, the main part of the work is already done by nature itself. All that's left to do is utilize its gifts.

In practice, the opposite happens: directors, and the actors themselves, try to deprive their material of any freedom, spontaneity, fluidity, and mobility that are inherent to living beings. They establish once and for all the interpretation of each scene and each character. They create concrete blockings, they have fixed speech patterns: every phrase, every word is said with a certain, eternally set intonation; they firmly prescribe the rhythm and tempo of every scene. And, if the show goes like clockwork and follows the metronome, this is considered the height of achievement. Between all this, what good is there? Transforming living, creative material into dead, speaking marionettes doesn't deserve that much praise.

Only works that you can watch countless times without end, that enthrall you more and more, make you dig deeper and deeper, and seem newer and newer are true artistry.

To this end, it's necessary for a show to be somehow new each time, like a living being. And it can't not be new if the actors are correctly trained and cultivated and *live and create onstage* every time, without chasing down the concrete, memorized "form" and director's vision; and they worry not about glorified verisimilitude, but about authentic truth, nothing but truth. And truth, like life, is *inimitable*. It's repeatable only in broad terms, but not in exact details. The ubiquitous hunt for *exact repetition* is what drives our theatres farther and farther away from true artistry. Away from the enthralling and irresistible authentic life, which we've seen in the best actors' best roles in the best minutes of their work.

These actors weren't always on top either. So what? Should we be flustered by the fact that not all of Leonardo's paintings were as magically alive as Lisa, that although Raphael has many wonderful paintings, not all can stand up to the Sistine Madonna?

The bar should be set by masterpieces, not by shoddy work.

Why is that directors and actors, instead of utilizing the ability to *live* that's been granted to them by nature, they mute it and tie it up, limiting themselves to *dressage* and rote memorization.

Simply because the ability to live isn't everything. It's just the *material* from which a work of art is made. Material, which needs to be set in the right direction. If we recall everything that was said about the artificiality of the stage environment, it will become quite clear that the ability to live (as we live in life) doesn't fulfill all the requirements for *life onstage before an audience*. Here, you need a unique and special psychological technique.

Some particularly gifted people are granted a significant part of this technique from childhood. But they are few in number. The majority of people require a special, complex course of training and cultivation. Without it, their ability to "live" in the unnatural conditions of the stage turns into verisimilitude and boredom, i.e. falsehood.

This leads to a simple and more "practical" conclusion: *destroy* this ability in the interest of avoiding any problems, switch it off and, by doing so, transform yourself into a machine, a wind-up doll, or a record player. This, at least, won't let you down.

Of course, when an actor is unable *to live onstage creatively*, nothing is left except to look for a truer and more expressive form of behavior onstage. Search, find, and fixate this form; memorize it, nail it down. If the form is expressive, tasteful, and is executed with additives that somewhat resemble the truth (there's a special expression for this: if the form is "justified"), then the show might even seem true and alive for two-three performances.

But it's necessary to understand that the effect of such art is rather limited. And the future of theatre doesn't lie with it.

The future of theatre lies with another acting technique (I assume a psychological-internal technique), as well as with another directing technique and aspirations.

The role has to be nurtured and grown in such a way that it could change any day, depending on the given actor's inner state and those of his partners. The show and its atmosphere should be entirely dependent on the actors: given one group of performers, it goes one way, given another (in the same theatre), it should be different. Most importantly, it's vital to create a show's form so that it could change every day! So the show doesn't stagnate, doesn't become a cliché (i.e. didn't mechanize), but develops, grows, becomes richer and more and more multilayered, keener and keener, more perfect in its truth and liveliness.

A Work of Art and Eternal Ideas

When he took to writing *Don Quixote*, above all, Cervantes wanted to ridicule the romances which he despised. He started writing a foolish and hapless person, a dimwitted fantasizer who completely lost his wits from reading this pompous literature. That's whom he started writing . . . And what happened next?

It just so happened that he wrote a great, eternal human figure. *Don Quixote*, as it turned out, was not so much a satirical piece as it was a psychological and philosophical one. Merging with the figure of the unfortunate Don Quixote and becoming immersed in him, Cervantes discovered one of the most touching and beautiful qualities of the human spirit in the pages of his satirical novel: the ability to believe in beautiful chimeras; the ability to completely give in to them, serve them with your whole life, heart, body, and soul 'til the grave. In every great scientist, researcher, inventor, poet – Don Quixote sits inside every one of these benefactors of humanity.

Is it not a chimera that prompts Columbus to embark on his thoughtless adventure? Any rational Sancho Panza could only be amazed and laugh at his foolishness, impracticality, and childlike naïveté: honey, why don't you sit at home and mind your own business! And is that not what ultimately happened to this seer and genius, much as it did to the Knight of the Rueful Countenance? Persecution, sickness, and death in poverty!

And what about scientists, inventors, who dedicate decades of hard work and invest all their capital, their whole lives and those of their families into their work? Are they not Don Quixotes? And it's rare when one of them reaps the fruits of their labor. For the most part, they are persecuted, ridiculed, and other, craftier, "practical," "realistic" people reap the fruits grown by their hands and minds. To the narrow-minded and "practical," do they not seem like half-witted Don Quixotes, and their efforts like battling windmills?

And don't we all have a part of Don Quixote who battles in us against our Sancho Panza?

In this way, a true artist who takes the smallest, most topical material and gets carried away, gives his imagination free reign, and . . . creates a masterpiece. In doing so, he not only crosses beyond the borders of his preliminary intentions, but also manages to capture ideas of the eternal.

In conclusion, I would like to remind actors, as well as directors, to guard themselves against the dangerous thought that artistry can only be found in the great, the powerful, the titanic – in tragedy. Is La Gioconda [Mona Lisa] something titanic? It's simply a portrait of a young woman. That's it. And just look at what it turned into!

Similarly, in theatre, there's no need to chase only "large canvas," "eternal universal figures," like Hamlet, Shylock, Macbeth, Lear, Joan of Arc, etc. A small, roadside flower can be as beautiful as a magnificent rose of Lebanon. At any rate, no artificial roses made of paper, wire, or rags go hand-in-hand with it, no matter how colorful or large they might be . . . It – it is a highly artistic, unsurpassed work of nature – a miracle of perfection. They – they are a pitiful attempt at deception by means of crude imitation.

*You should only take on what's manageable. And **bring it to perfection***. *Such is the path of artistry.*

Note

1 See *A Work of Art and Eternal Ideas*. Pages 66-67.

6
The Artist
His Chief Qualities

For the creation of such perfect works of art, one probably needs certain qualities? It's doubtful that any person can create such perfection simply because he has the desire to. There's a good reason why such perfect works are so rare.

So what are these qualities?

The question doesn't seem to be very difficult, and there's no need to think too long: a painter needs to have an affinity and ability to paint; a musician should have the same with regards to playing an instrument, having a good ear, etc. However, it's not so simple. These particular qualities are enough to become a decent worker in your sphere, and maybe even a professional. But that's it. Being a professional and even a renowned painter, sculptor, pianist, writer, poet, actor – this doesn't mean being able to create perfect works of art. In a word: it doesn't mean being an *artist*.

For the creation of works of art, you have to be *gifted and developed in a certain way*. It is necessary to speak about both separately.

Giftedness

An artist's giftedness cannot be exhausted by a single quality that is useful and vital for his profession. Giftedness that is capable of leading somebody to the creation of works of art is *inevitably* the combination of a great amount of different qualities, unique ones, as well as general, common ones. Whether a person can be an artist in a given sphere hinges only on the harmonic union of all of these qualities.

It's interesting that among all of the necessary qualities, unique ones (the ability to draw, play a musical instrument, write or rhyme easily, change personas onstage, etc.) are not always the most important ones. A genius who graced humanity with some great work of art often had to make a titanic effort *to overcome his inability in his chosen sphere of art* . . . This may be strange, but it's true.

We know that on his first attempt to deliver a speech in front of an audience, the greatest orator of his time, Demosthenes, was ridiculed. He was tongue-tied, his voice was so weak that he was barely audible, he bore himself in such a manner that it caused everyone to laugh.

It was the same with many great actors who, before attaining some glory, first had to overcome their physical shortcomings—a weak voice, speech defects, an inflexible, disobedient body—or psychological deficits, like stuttering, stage fright, the inability to easily feel emotions (so necessary for an actor), inhibited nature, etc. Obviously, some other abilities have greater weight.

The Ability to Marvel and Venerate

The first prerequisite for being an artist is one's ability *to see and sense the beautiful and grand*. At the sight of beauty, an artist has very distinctive feelings. He forgets himself, he completely gives over to the power of these feelings. An environment of beauty is the natural environment of an artist, and he flings the gates of his soul wide open for it, forgetting everything else in the world.

Seeing and feeling beauty means marveling at it. Seeing and feeling beauty means venerating it. A person who doesn't see the beautiful and doesn't understand the sublime can never be an artist. He is an everyman.

When Stanislavsky walked into a room, some people continued their babbling until they were shut up by others. Others would instantly cease speaking and would immediately become serious and expectant . . . These were the ones who understand whom they were dealing with. It would awaken the best and most significant in them and would replace the lesser, the mundane.

One of my acquaintances, a notable musician, told me about the performance of the [American born] Italian wunderkind Willy Ferrero [1906–1954] in Moscow in 1913–1914. Some details of his performance are astounding and I'll attempt to recount them.

The grand stage of the Moscow Conservatory's Great Hall is filled with music stands. The Bolshoi Theatre's orchestra is there in full. The musicians are in their places, it's a full house.

An elderly man comes out onstage. In his hands is a child, some 8–10 years of age (I don't remember for sure), and he's wearing short pantaloons, stockings, and a little velvet coat. His father carries him, threading through the musicians. The boy, not paying any attention to anything, is messing around with his father, getting in his way and distracting him. He's bothering him, covering his eyes, tugging on his tie, messing up his hair, and laughs triumphantly when his father bumps into something and almost drops his burden. Apparently, he is not concerned about his performance at all, or is, at least, not worrying about it. The applause from the audience does nothing to interrupt the touching family scene – the child is occupied by messing around with his father.

Finally, they make it to the conductor's stand. The father sets the child down on a tall stool and offers him the conductor's baton . . . The boy, still fooling around, grabs the baton and threatens his father, as if with a rapier. The father laughs as well and, deflecting the hits, catches the "rapier."

Willy's eyes fall to the score . . . and something happens that is so strange . . . so eerie . . . and significant, that the audience, like a single person, instantly fell silent – froze – stopped breathing . . .

I don't remember what was going to be performed exactly, I only know that it was something serious, deep, and grand – not something that a conductor of his age should have been able to handle.

So, the boy's eyes fall on the score . . . Evidently, he reads the first lines, instantly stops . . . The careless eyes of a child disappear somewhere into his depths and are replaced by the frightening, strict gaze of a person who has lived for many, many centuries . . . The gaze was directed not at the score, not at the musicians, but somewhere past them all . . . at the world that was probably streaming past him at the moment . . .

69

Slowly passing over the whole orchestra with his imperious and otherworldly gaze, the little sorcerer raised his baton and . . . began . . . "I cannot begin to tell you what happened," my acquaintance said, "but it was . . . godly. Not only have I never heard anything like it, I never thought that I'd *ever* hear it . . . Nearly ten years have passed, and I can still hear it in my ears . . . in my ears, my heart, my every cell . . ."

What did this genius child see in the notes? What awoke in him a wizard and sorcerer? Visions of beauty and power? The same visions that were had the genius composer when he was creating this masterpiece?

The Soul's Depth, Capacity

I have two friends: Verochka and Sonechka. They're both seven years old. And so, two weeks ago, they were struck by misfortune: they were coming back from a Christmas party, and right next to their home, some boys attacked them and took all of their presents away: toys, fruits, sweets . . .

Sonechka cried for a bit, was upset for a bit, but when she was promised that she'd be bought new toys, she calmed down and forgot about it all.

Verochka had a different reaction. She was offended. Deeply, deeply offended. She has faced the evil that exists in the world for the first time. The toys weren't the issue, they were forgotten. She remembers only the boy's eyes, his insolent, self-satisfied laughter . . . She had experienced evil, injustice, and abuse . . . And when I met her eyes, I was hit by such bottomless, hopeless sorrow, that my heart dropped.

There are artists with a similarly piercing gaze. As if he's looking at everything from the mists of time, out of his inherited experience, and sees lots of things that are hidden from everyone else.

Those are the true great artists, capable of capturing all of life in a single gaze; capable of sensing endless suffering behind a single, small pain, and in the smallest of joys, they can see the promise of such great, boundless joy in humanity's future.

Some look at a puddle and see only a puddle and their own reflection. Another sees in it the reflected sky, the sun, and he embraces the whole world, earth and heaven. This person will not think Tyutchev's [1966: 75] sweet dream is weird:

"The hour of inexpressible longing!..
Everything is in me, and I'm in everything!.."

There is little left after Mochalov, the king of all tragedians. A few opening pages survived of his manuscript, *Thoughts about the Actor's Art*. And here's what Mochalov [2000:373] writes: "The soul's depth and an ardent imagination are two qualities that make up the greater part of talent."

The soul's depth! Well what do you know!

Everybody has a different soul depth, width, and capacity. There are tiny, little streams – semi-rivers – and there are rivers . . . and then there are rivers like Volga, the Amazon, the Ob, the Mississippi . . . One shouldn't flatter oneself – not everybody can be a great or even a moderate river. If it's not there, it's not there. But there's no need to lose faith in oneself very easily either. It won't do to neglect a small river or a stream. Look after it, dam it up, and it will turn watermills for you, supply you with light and warmth. So size isn't the only issue here. Though, naturally, size is size. And true scope and depth is a possibility only for big rivers. So what? If there is no depth, girth, volume, and great capacity, then there's no hope of creating something grand, something perfect? Naturally.

Still, it's a shame. You want to create perfect things . . . and not just "feasible" things, like comedies – you want to act Shakespeare, Schiller, Calderon, Hugo.

If the desire exists, then does that not mean that your soul responds to these thoughts, images, and passions? But when I try it, nothing good comes out, it's weak. Comedies, I can do, but dramas, to say nothing of tragedies – I just wilt. It's repulsive to profane and ruin tragedies . . . I must really have a shallow stream.

However, let's remember that we all have many centuries of inherited experience through the embryonic cell. And it's not so easy to measure the depth of any of our souls. Therefore, it will be better to think of it like this: everybody has depth of soul; but for some, the gates leading to it are closed, stuffed, walled up, and have a pile of trash on top of them. If you try to get through to these forbidden doors and open them, it turns out that not all of us are such poor beggars. The only question is: **how**? How do you get to them and open them? Is there some "technique?"

I've said it before, I'll say it now, and I'll keep saying it: yes, **there is.** **All my books are the first steps towards grasping these and other realms of human psychology that were hitherto considered unapproachable.**

The Ideal

A person who is so sensitive to beauty, and has great depth, to boot, along with a vast reach – can he be satisfied by creating something not quite mediocre, not quite significant?

Of course not. Only perfection! Anything that he creates that is ordinary, mediocre is only a disappointment for him, nothing but shame. But, truth be told, many people start with this, regardless of who they may be: writers, painters, musicians, or actors – many of them initially see great heights, and they desire to create perfect things. Then a selection process happens. Some – facing their lack of readiness, or the limits of their giftedness, or some detrimental external factors – sooner or later grow tired of fighting and give up their preliminary positions. Others **remain true to their ideal and move forward, regardless of the cost** . . .

A rare few refuse to lose sight of their initial, far-away ideals 'til the end of their days. A rare few. But among the great artists, there is not a one who doesn't belong to this rare few.

Admittedly, the ideal always remains unachievable. With regards to his Sistine Madonna, Raphael would admit to a circle of friends and students that it was only a weak semblance of what he envisioned in his mind. That's how it should be. *The ideal should significantly exceed our abilities.* And God help us when our abilities exceed our ideal. Then we have nothing to strive for, we can do anything, know everything. That is when art dies. Even worse – that is when crassness takes over: "I am a great master, I'm a genius. Whatever I make cannot be weak. You don't like it? You don't understand it! You're not mature enough. Or it's just jealous slander."

To have an ideal and not lose it means to be endlessly stubborn in one's striving towards a goal. I had no luck with one thing or another. So what that I had no luck? One day, I will! Not today – tomorrow, in a month, in a year! Most importantly: tirelessly and indefatigably strive, strive, and keep striving.

And this applies to everything. When people would ask Newton how he managed to discover the law of universal gravitation, he would respond: "Quite simply – I ceaselessly thought about it over the course of 20 years."[1] When people would tell Edison how he was a genius, he would object: "Genius is one percent inspiration, ninety-nine percent perspiration" [As quoted in Rosanoff 1932: 406].

Why do the so-called might-have-beens and "unappreciated genii" fail? Because of a lack of obstinacy and dedication, or as Balzac put it wonderfully – a lack of courage[2]. They make splendid projections, decisively begin their work, bravely overcome the first obstacle, and then, step by step – they grow cold, bored, and leave their work unfinished. They fail at it altogether, and waste their life for nothing. An ideal does not loom before them, it doesn't pull them to it, as the north pulls a compass needle – tirelessly, ceaselessly, always. No matter how hard you try to throw it off, it returns again and again to its line. What do our theatre schools (and all art schools) have to do? First of all, they have to **magnetize** the compass needle of every student's soul. So that it didn't spin every which way, but constantly pointed towards its ideal.

From the very first steps, we have to adamantly ingrain in the minds and hearts of our students *the ideal of perfection that exceeds all of their abilities*. Ingrain it and constantly sustain it . . . If possible, their whole lives! The following heroic slogan should enter their souls like mother's blood and milk:

> Too low they build
> Who build beneath the stars.

"Listen!" they'll say to me. "This is extremism! This is all or nothing!" Exactly. Why are you so afraid of that word?

All things considered, what *is* extremism in this instance? It is no more and no less than *the foreshadowing of your possibilities*. And since I feel the possibility to achieve it – only weak-willed, frail souls, only those who have lost all of their energy can refuse to try to realize this achievement.

The Mission

"The image of perfection," "the ideal," "extremism," "courage" . . . This all sounds very pretty . . . but could it be that there is . . . a bit of an obsession here, some not-quite-healthy fanaticism? To spend 17 years to create a perfect painting (as Leonardo did with Mona Lisa) . . . rewrite finished novels, novellas 12 times (as Balzac) . . . burn your manuscripts (as Gogol) . . . destroy your statues (and not just any statues – statues hewn by the hand of Michelangelo himself!) . . . Certainly – it's noble, magnanimous, self-sacrificing . . . But it seems a bit too exaggerated and impractical.

Especially since it doesn't even matter: "the ideal is unattainable" – so why should I bang my head against a wall? From stubbornness? "Damn it all – I still want to!"? Or maybe from defiance? "If it's impossible, then I'll just show everyone that it *is* possible!" Or from a disposition to gamble? "Others couldn't do it, but maybe I'll get lucky, maybe I'll be able to." Or maybe the process itself is attractive? "It's all too good, it's presented very invitingly in my imagination! . . . and it turns out very weak, powerless. I have to keep trying: maybe I *will* catch hold of something. At least some small part!" And that's how the work sucks you in: the more you work, the more you achieve – the more shortcomings and imperfections you see . . . There is no stopping now: you've given it too much – you have to finish it, see it through to the end!

All of these reasons have a place and a time – one more so, another less so, depending on the person's character. But there is one more: *nobody is capable of becoming a real artist if he didn't feel to some extent that his life and talent belong to all of humanity, and that everything that nature has given him is given to him for humanity.*

As soon as a person understands this – in that happy and significant moment, everything changes for him. Up to that point, he created things either for the "market," or for a small circle of connoisseurs, or for himself, for his own delight.

Humanity! And not just the one that exists right now, but the one in the future too . . . You would think that this thought can overwhelm you, but the fear and confusion lasts for just a moment, and they're followed by such a big high. New instincts awaken . . . you gain new strength . . . Everything that you've done up to that point seems inconsequential and weak . . . You only want to create something absolute, only perfection . . .

Out of all the artists in the world, not one feels his responsibility before humanity more keenly than the actor. This is because humanity is right there, right in front of him. It isn't imaginary – it's quite real. Be there a lot of it or a little – it doesn't matter; it's right there. Can you hear it breathing? It's not here in its entirety – only a part is – but it's right here: humanity.

Go out to it. It's waiting for you! Do you have anything to say to it? What do you want to inspire in it? What do you want to protect it from? What do you want to interest it in? Go and do it.

Sow the seeds of your service into the centuries. Such is your mission.

The Enthusiasm of Youth

Before us is a class of recently accepted students. Whether it's a theatre school, a conservatory or a school of ballet, whether there are 10, 20, or 30 of them – it doesn't matter. They have just been selected out of hundreds. They're the best. It cannot be accidental; they must have sufficient potentials to be here.

Speak with them. Carefully, in a friendly manner, approach that young man . . . this young lady of 17 . . . Many hundreds of times have I spoken with these youths, and it's almost always the same: it's almost always the same timid, but full of enthusiasm, lines: "The theatre excites me . . . to act, to be onstage and next to the stage – I feel like there's nothing better! It's sacred! . . . I want to act . . . act well, act beautifully . . . Once or twice in my life, I acted (or recited, or sang) so well that I felt that it was 'IT!' It was *the real thing,,*' it was good!.. I felt that there, in the moment, I was an artist. I know that I *can*, that I *have* the right, that I *must* . . ."

Of course, students don't speak so smoothly. More often, they don't even know why exactly they went onstage. And only by helping them with various leading questions can you get their secret thoughts and desires out of them. Yet it isn't childishness, it isn't sentimentality, and it isn't hysteria. They're led by a good instinct. And right now, they might be more mature than they will be later, in some 10–15 years. By then, the fire in their eyes might go out, and they'll be 80–100 years old.

And how is it sentimentality when, for the most part, they break their lives for the sake of theatre, when, in a material sense, some have to live in poverty and near starvation? As for "hysteria," that's not even worth mentioning: our eyes are so trained that, during the auditions, we instantly note unhealthy psychological constitution. We don't accept those. If one accidentally does get through, then he won't have time for hysteria or psychopathy here – you won't be fooling anyone with those.

Just look at how full of enthusiasm the young students, who just came to school, are! How much faith! – in the teachers, in the future, and in their talent! They're full of endless energy, they're burning with enthusiasm. It's what electrifies their embryonic qualities to the point that they shine as brightly as those of polished talent.

How badly we need to seize hold of this wondrous youthful enthusiasm! It's the path! It's the *secret*! And it might be one of the most important secrets with whose help we could quickly get to the repository of talent and let it flow forth like a great river . . .

But here come the experienced elders, oracles of art – the pedagogues . . . and with their first words, they begin to quench the fire in the students' eyes, destroy their faith, and scare off talent. "Everything that you're doing," they pontificate, "is no good; it's all amateur work, clichés, play-acting. You're just material that, one day, either will turn into something or won't. And the first thing you need to do is get rid of all your previous habits. Clean it all out until you're like a blank sheet of paper." Step by step, these career grave-diggers take from the youths everything with which they lived, all of their inspiration. For whole years, and sometimes for the whole lives, their enthusiasm would be lost, as would their faith and . . . talent. Alas, but it is so! A few manage to clamber out of this pit, but others, with the helping hand of their skilled instructors, perish, drown in the carrion of their so-called "high art."

You can't quench the fire!

You have to be able to accompany the student in being delighted in his achievements, his talent. You have to *not notice*, or, at least, not show that you notice his shortcomings. *You have to see only his merits*, and direct the student's exaltation, hopes, and expectations (but never self-admiration – you'll only ruin everything with that) at them. Then these merits will quickly go forward and displace any and all shortcomings, assuming they were there. As for enthusiasm and the fire in their eyes, it is necessary for it to burn brighter. Then, miracles are possible.

Then – it's strange to say – 17-year-old girls will be able to be played by 17-year-old girls, as opposed to 30- and 50-year-olds, as is the norm right now. Then, Romeo might be 18–19 years old. In our current state, we cannot even imagine how beautiful that could be.

We have to train our eye, and our "scent" in order to see through to the core, and to "smell out" where all of this talent is springing from? We have to find a way to help it break through to the surface.

The Enthusiasm of Maturity

Naturally, there are those who hang on to this youthful ability to get carried away and burn up with enthusiasm, but for the most part, age gives rise to another type of enthusiasm. It no longer has the blindness and inexperience of youth. It knows full well all the difficulties and almost insurmountability of some obstacles, knows equally well its own shortcomings and limitations. And still, despite everything—or maybe *because* of all this, *inflamed* by these obstacles – it throws itself into the fray.

And here, the work itself interests the actor more and more . . . new thoughts and projects come to mind, he becomes truly immersed in his work, a dream rears its head, an ideal – and he can no longer tear himself away from his work and leave it alone – not until he finishes it. Every new obstacle turns into a new step. From the outside, this might seem like madness, irrationality . . . Any success seems accidental and "lucky." But life – it is afraid of audacity and willpower; it parts like the sea and gives this brave hero space to maneuver.

This "love for the impossible," this "yearning of the heart," the categorical principle "despite everything!," this need for "boundlessness," and the ability to "cross boundaries" regardless of which boundaries we're talking about; this extraordinary "stubbornness" *is **the enthusiasm of maturity***. This quality can give birth not just to an artist, but to more than that: a guiding light, a law-maker, and great creator in art, science, life . . . It is the path to greatness, that of a hero, a genius.

More on this later.

A Special Mind

Aside from the several described extraordinary qualities that bear witness to the special sensitivity and morality of an artist's emotional and volitive make-up, there are qualities that concern his intellect. Specifically his mind. A mind that is well-tuned for the chosen profession.

Any work demands its own ***special mind*** and special abilities. Ignoring big work, let's look at something simple: cleaning a room, setting a table – you need a "special mind" for that too. Observe people; you'll see a very noticeable difference: one spends a long time doing it and still does it poorly, while another does it quickly and beautifully.

It's the same for us in the art of the actor: you have to act well and truly. Not philosophize about your role, but *act*. There are those who can speak very well and intelligently about their roles, but whose acting is rather mediocre. Then there are those who can't discuss their roles at all (and seem to be very narrow-minded in life too), but then they go out onstage, and everything that they do seems so well thought-out, so true, profound, and "logical." In all appearance, their work stems not from careful calculations or intellect, but from the conclusions of deeper and more hidden layers of their consciousness.

By the way, here are a few words about this from Mochalov [2000: 373] himself (from his unfinished manuscript about the actor's art):

> I've often heard how such and such actor has a very *theatrical mind*. In my opinion, this expression isn't about an artist who can *discuss* his art well or intelligently, but about his *truthful* or *smart acting*. I think that even experience doesn't always result in the right to be called a smart *actor*. Lots of examples support this. There are actors who have been around for many years, to whom nature has granted a sound mind, who have had a good education—an important benefit for an actor—and who sometimes meet the expectations of the most demanding audience, but who, despite all of this, cannot be called *an actor with a theatrical mind*. This is why I suppose that we can attribute this faculty to the list of qualities that, when united in different proportions, are called *talent*.
>
> I think that having the means to easily comprehend a character's personality, veracity of action, and the ability to hide the cumbrance of the concurrent moral work is what is called a *theatrical mind*.

And furthermore: " . . .I am sending you the beginning of the article and am confident that you won't refuse to help me finish this speculation. We still have a lot to talk about: about the smart actor who deeply perceives all the great moments of his situation with his soul . . ."

Which means that the smart is actor is the one who "*deeply perceives* all the great moments of his situation *with his soul* . . ." He deeply perceives it **with his soul, not his intellect**.

Of course, it's better to understand with your intellect than with nothing at all, meaninglessly babbling away the playwright's words. But this understanding cannot be compared with the "*deep understanding with your soul*," which is inherent to a natural actor. No matter how complex intellectual understanding may seem, it's primitive; no matter how deep it may seem, for an actor, it's shallow; no matter how emotional it might seem, it's soulless.

Talent

Aside from the aforementioned qualities which discern an artist and a great person, every specialization requires its own specific giftedness. For the most part, *it* is what is called "*talent*." And it's worth mentioning that this word is woefully misused. If somebody has even a modicum of abilities, people instantly say that it's talent.

Talent is a rarity – only one out of several hundred of those who are just capable.

I am very grateful to James Fenimore Cooper [1789–1851], who used such simple and comprehensible words to explain talent to me in my youth, and for evoking in me such a reverent attitude towards the word "talent," as well as causing me to ponder it so thoroughly.

Other than a variety of things that he did well, his well-known hero, the Pathfinder (also known as Leatherstocking), would never miss a rifle shot. And so, some simple-minded everyman asks him to teach him. The Pathfinder responds that you cannot teach just anybody to shoot – you need talent.

What do you mean, you can't! Then how do soldiers who can't shoot at all ultimately become expert sharpshooters?

Expert . . . What do you mean, expert? Of course you can teach somebody to hit a coin at 50–60 paces. But is that truly marksmanship? Hitting a thrown potato, that's better. Or hitting it in the middle or barely grazing it, that's almost good. Hitting a swallow mid-flight isn't too bad either, and hitting two swallows with one bullet when they intersect in the air, that's very good.[3]

At the time, I was very interested in marksmanship, and this . . . knocked me off my feet. So that's what it means to shoot well!? And that's what talent is! Use one bullet . . . to hit two swallows . . . when they intersect . . . would you even have enough time to think it through . . . could you even see anything? Could you really have such accuracy? Predict so well? . . . It's just estimation, a sixth sense, foreboding, instinct . . . inspiration! . . . You probably really can't learn it after all. You have to be born with it!

Whether there truly were such marksmen is neither here nor there. There probably were – life exceeds the expectations of the most unruly fantasy. And what's the point of criticizing? So what if we say that there weren't, aren't, and can never be? What do we have to gain from that? In this case, the most important thing is to understand the nature of talent, its difference from ordinary abilities, understand that the talent of a marksman, a juggler, a violinist, a painter is something greater than ordinary abilities – it's something that surpasses ordinary abilities to such an extent that it seems extraordinary, fantastical. While learning and training, enhancing his skills, a person of average abilities achieves greater and greater results and, finally, reaches some ceiling. This limit he cannot surpass, and this ceiling is essentially the same for everyone. However, talent drastically separates itself, shoots into the lead and achieves such results that are unattainable for the rest even with the persistent and longest training.

But is there some way that we can approach talent, at least to understand what it really is? Let's even look at the Pathfinder's marksmanship: estimation, instinct, inspiration . . . Be that as it may. But can there be something analogous for us, for regular people?

For example, you're walking out of town next to a railway . . . far ahead is a telegraph post . . . Almost unexpectedly for yourself, you pick up a rock and – bam! – right in the middle of the post! And it was so easy that it's as if you could hit it anywhere, any time – there's nothing difficult about it. There is "something" that is put into action. Or rather, something in yourself that you give free rein – it acts, and you look on and egg it on: "Good, good! . . . Go!!"

What is this "thing?" It's complex, this thing: this is visual estimation, an intuitive feel of the distance between you and the post, the weight of the rock, the strength, arc, and speed with which you throw the rock, complete physical freedom and effortlessness, foresight, faith, instinct . . . there's a lot in it. And at the same time, all the strings that are tied to this – and there can be hundreds of others too – all meet up in some single center, from which everything is regulated. You just have to not get in its way. You yourself feel that if you don't get in its way, it works for you, but if you do push it in the wrong direction or have doubts, hold it up, then everything falls apart – the rock whooshes past without finding its mark!

Everybody has had a moment or an accident like this. If not with throwing a rock, then with a jump, a fall, holding your balance, etc. But this has involved not just physical movements – in a minute of difficulty, you'll get the thought: "*This* is what I have to do! *This* is the right course of actions!" But you'll waver, begin to doubt . . . And only later: "Damn it, I really was on to something, that's what should have done, and now . . . now look at what I got! . . ."

Glimmers . . . moments . . .suddenly, something flashes in the darkness . . . lights everything up! – everything is clear, it's all visible, I can do anything! . . . – and it disappears.

There can be more than just momentary glimmers: it'll take hold of you and zoom away. As if something has awoken in you: it dreamt away, and suddenly it woke up and got to work. Some wondrous engine, a control apparatus. Not for long, of course, just a few minutes – but it's still no longer just a glimmer – it's a whole enlightenment. If this happens to an actor, a musician, then they say: he's on fire, he's inspired.

> Today, indeed, success
> Did crown my every movement, every word:
> I yielded freely to my inspiration;
> The words flowed forth, as thought it was the heart,
> And not the timid memory, gave them birth.
> *(Pushkin [1936: 444],*
> The Stone Guest, *Laura's lines)*

What are these glimmers? And why do you feel everything so keenly, and regulate it even more keenly? Your sensitivity in these moments is so acute that you know everything, see everything, and can do anything. Just believe in yourself and don't get in your own way.

I once conversed with one of the greatest jugglers in the world – Kara [Michael Steiner (1867–1939)]. He essentially said the following: "In order to juggle four balls, all you really need is simple, well-focused attention. But when you juggle five or more, your consciousness *can no longer keep up*; your eyes don't catch every ball on its own. They only see them *all at once*, as a system, as a sort of living organism moving in the air. And your hands, obeying not your consciousness, but your *instinct*, enter this living organism, this flying system of balls, on their own. I act essentially involuntarily: my hands catch the balls and throw them *on their own, without my intellectual interjections*. As soon as I try to inject my intellect, instantly, the system is thrown off, and one of the balls hits the ground. (It must be said that he could juggle with up to ten balls. This was a dizzying sight – you look, and you can't believe your eyes; it seemed that the balls slowly flowed around the artist's head like a halo, while his hands practically disappeared. They flickered so quickly – you couldn't even see them.) Up to five balls – that's ordinary work. But add some more, and it becomes special . . . I throw some sort of switch in myself . . . I activate it, and something else enters the fray. *It* is what controls my movements.

What is this 'it?'

I don't know. Something is inside of me . . . And sometimes, it seems that *the balls themselves* are causing my hands to accommodate them and keep up with them."

Does an actor have something similar?

Ordinary acting, which consists partly of emersion and even self-abandon, and partly of self-observation and self-awareness, is what we usually see in the performance of an ordinary, good, so-called capable actor. It's acting that resembles juggling three or four balls, maximum. But as soon as an actor steps into a play's "system of life" with his whole essence, with his whole "I," the play's circumstances take hold of him, and he "acts essentially involuntarily," "without intellectual interjections," obeying the laws of the play. This acting resembles juggling five balls, where everything is done "on its own," where it's not the actor that's "working" in the play, but the play that's causing the actor to think, feel, and act in accordance with its flow. It "guides" the actor as Kara's balls guide his hands.

This happens very rarely and does not last for long. But it does happen. And when it does, it is no longer simple actor's work – it's its highest step. It's the manifestation of an artist. This doesn't happen to everyone; it's a sign of a special giftedness; it is **talent**.

But it's interesting to know for sure: do only a few have a monopoly on talent, or is talent something that can be grown and developed from barely perceptible signs? Of course, lacking any special abilities, it's unwise to throw yourself into a job, especially if it's as subtle as art. However, let's turn our attention once more to circus life. In it, we can find facts that answer the question about the origin and development of talent.

In my youth, I gravitated to the circus more than to any other place. I would sneak into rehearsals, acquaint myself with the artists. One dark September morning, I witnessed the following scene behind the curtains of a provincial circus: a trapeze was hung from the roof. The ropes were so long that the trapeze bar was almost touching the ground. A chair stood on the bar with its back legs. A plain girl in a poor, very worn dress sat on the chair and held on to the ropes with her hands. While she was holding the ropes, she sat, but as soon as she let them go, she would lose her balance and grab hold of them again. She did this the whole time: regains her balance, lets go of one, then the other rope, sits this way for one to two seconds, and immediately grabs them again. Once, she managed to grab hold of only one rope – the other got away: the chair slipped off, and she would've fallen to her death if her trapeze was not hung so close to the ground. The chair was promptly returned to its spot, and the girl got onto it once more.

I left. While walking, I asked my gymnast friends: who is she?

"That's Stesha . . . she's training."

"Stesha . . . Stepanida? . . . And what, has she been at it for a long time?"

"No, about a month and a half . . ."

A group of partner acrobats overtook us. Rehearsal spots were few, and they were hurrying to get to the arena. One of them yelled out with a severe foreign accent: "Herzog, the pillows! Quiiiiickly!"

My fascination with the circus gave way to something else: university, science, theatre . . . but my love for it remained. Circus, once a year – I can't live without it!

One time, I was there, enjoying all kinds of wonders . . . an elegant young woman jumps out in blue tights, easily flies up the rope ladder to the roof of the circus, and gets on the trapeze. They raise a chair up for her. She puts the chair onto the trapeze bar with its back legs. Sits in it. Gets her balance, hanging on to the ropes, then lets them go, and sits there as if it were no big deal, not holding on to anything.

The trapeze bar is hung up by ropes. It's mobile and in order to remain sitting, you have to make barely perceptible balancing movements – this is true without a chair, and it's especially true with one. The acrobat sits calmly, but the trapeze swings slightly from her balancing movements. The swinging is sometimes so significant that it feels as if the chair should slip off any second . . . But the trapeze starts swinging more and more widely – she is evidently swinging it. Obviously she must be making some imperceptible movements. She sits on her chair, which is balancing only on its back legs – she sits without holding on to anything and is swinging the trapeze more and more widely . . . I look into my binoculars and froze: her eyes! . . . austere, imperious, horrific, fierce . . . She's looking somewhere beyond all that is visible . . . Frightful, merciless . . . full of deathly, icy calmness . . .

If she loses her power and calmness for a single second – it's over!

At full speed, she gets on to her chair . . . Stands on it with her feet . . . Swings on it while standing . . . Then stands on it on her hands – swings in this position . . . You can't watch it without your heart stopping! How can you do that? How can you get to the point that you're able to do that? . . .

I don't remember what else she did . . .

The trapeze swings more and more quietly . . . it stops, and the acrobat slides down the rope headfast. The circus was in an uproar, it called the wonder-worker back onstage almost ten times. I asked for a program from my neighbor: "Balancing on the trapeze – Mademoiselle Herzog?" Does that mean Stesha? "Herzog, quiiiiickly, pillows!" So that's who they were calling seven years ago? She must have been some sort of servant for these acrobats.

Again I look into my binoculars . . . Yes, yes, it's her! It's the very same "plain girl." But many years of work, daily gamble with danger, risk, an unbending desire, success, awareness of her power – all of this made her face significant, uniquely beautiful, and nearly unrecognizable.

That's what hard work leads to. That's how instincts and abilities are trained and retrained. That's how you develop senses that normal people aren't even aware of to the limit. Is there not something here that resembles the Pathfinder or the juggler, Kara? Because "well-focused attention" isn't enough here, as it is with three or four balls. This more closely resembles ten balls, and in deadly conditions, no less.

Yet energy, patience, and hard work overcame all this!

Little Something about Genius

Many people might think the demands of the artist that are presented here are so great that only a genius can fulfill them. And many have been used as example: Raphael, Leonardo, Duse, Balzac, Mochalov, Michelangelo, Yermolova – geniuses. This must mean that only a genius can become an artist, right?

Let's not be afraid of taking our thoughts to their logical conclusion: in order to create a great work of art whose power will last entire centuries and will even increase with time; in order to turn everything in your field (art, science, life) on its head; in order to overcome your weaknesses and shortcomings; and in order to achieve such a technique, i.e. deftness, sensitivity, and confidence that would match Stesha's technique in her own field . . . in order to do all this, you need to strain all the highest qualities of an artist, and that's a genius.

A genius!?! Yes, a genius. What is there to be afraid of? Is the word scary? If you saw what Stesha was doing under the circus roof and looked deeper (through binoculars) at her frightful, otherworldly eyes, you would, without any hesitation, say that she was a genius in those moments. And that's how it is.

What is a genius?

Many different things, depending on your point of view.

From an *objective* point of view, judging by the fruits of his labor: he is the creator of great works, the discoverer of new principles, the finder of new paths, an infallible predictor of the future. In this way: 1) he creates objectively great works of perfection that are needed by humanity; 2) nothing ever grows old in his creations; quite the opposite – with time, everything becomes closer and closer to the heart of humanity, deeper and deeper, more and more comprehensible. If this concerns science and inventions – it's like Watt's steam engine – the principle doesn't age. Watt's old machine is laughable and pathetic, but its principle is still the same.

How and why does he discover the *new*?

Having arrived at the *brink* of perfection, he doesn't stop, but goes further and **crosses over the brink**. From there, new vistas and new paths open up – that is inevitable.

Do his contemporaries adequately evaluate his work?

Stepping too far, he is, for the most part, incomprehensible to his contemporaries, and they perceive him as insane, a madman, and a dangerous trouble-maker.

If we judge not by his works, but by his psychological makeup and by the process of his work, then (from an objective point of view), a genius is the harmonic union of many psychological qualities that are vital for the creation of great works of art, science, etc. And if he's missing some of them, the genius, in the face of everything, acquires them. If he doesn't have perseverance – he gets perseverance; if he doesn't have technique – he gets technique too.

Singular flights of inspiration, brilliant ideas that aren't worked through or realized – that's not genius; that's typical dilettantism. A genius won't be able to hold back from being on fire, from stealing time away from life – he *needs* to get to the end, to reach the conclusion of his work.

Genius isn't just a special giftedness, it's not just talent; first and foremost, it's inner significance, enormous seriousness, and an understanding of the importance of your work.

We've often had to hear about one person or another: "He's so gifted! He's simply a genius! But it's a shame that he's lazy – he could be so great." People who talk that way do not understand the heart of things. If he's lazy, if he doesn't do anything in his sphere, then he's absolutely not a genius.

A genius impresses everyone with his capacity for hard work and obstinacy so much that some people even thought that that was his main distinctive quality. Some would say: "Genius is patience;" others: "Genius is concentration." However, you can't reduce such a complex concept like genius to a single phrase, no matter how witty it may be – it isn't complete, and so it's mistaken.

The glimmer of giftedness is a luckily thrown stone, a timely and deft jump or blow, a striking word, a lightning bolt of a brilliant thought – this can happen to anyone. And maybe it really is the glimmer of higher capabilities. It is *potential* letting you know about its existence. If we had a different attitude towards it, it might even transform into talent. And, if combined with some of the aforementioned qualities, they could even reach the same enormous level that was had by Mochalov, for example.

Some might say: "Alright, buddy, now you've said it! If you're really planning to turn every actor into Mochalov and every actress into Yermolova, then you're a naïve man, or a fantasizer or psychotic . . . Your elevator doesn't go all the way to the top floor . . . And there's no point in reading you any further!"

And yet, you'll keep on reading. Maybe not today-tomorrow, but you'll open the book – it's interesting: what else did this madman babble on about?

But there is no madness here. First of all, there's no point in turning every actor into Mochalov. Though there is gold in the sand of any river, any river at all, in order to get even a kopeck's worth, you'd have to spend so much time and effort that the kopeck will ultimately have cost you a thousand or even more rubles.

As for the possibility to become a great actor (of Mochalov's creative type, of course) – recall Stesha's initial, helpless, unpromising exercises, and then their triumphant conclusion.

Besides, everybody thinks, for some reason, that Mochalov's inspiration appeared immediately, all of a sudden – out of the blue! Consider the fact that his father was an actor, that, as a sensitive and malleable child, he lived among actors in the thick of the theatre, that he was at rehearsals and performances daily . . . All of these conditions are so conducive to the creation and development of enthusiasm – you could not ask for better environment. There was no school that could have helped him develop his talent, but there wasn't one that could cause any damage. In general, you would act like you wanted, at your own risk. You answer for everything. This brought great responsibility, and the boldness and heroism that galvanized all of your strength, physical and psychological.

It was the same with Yermolova. Her father was a prompter, and she would sit next to him in his prompter's booth as a child, looking at all the wonders of the theatrical environment. From there, she saw the power of great actors close-up, and heard the audience's breath and applause behind her. And home – more discussions about theatre.

Add to all of this "soul's depth and ardent imagination," as well as "an actor's mind" that perfectly grasps the play and every single one of a character's lines – that's probably more than enough conditions for an artist's inspiration.

Memoirists write:

> When Mochalov appeared onstage and started acting, it was as if an electric spark passed through the whole theatre, and there wasn't a limit to the great artist-tribune's power – the power that he used to take the hearts of the audience far, far away from their worldly cares into an elevated sphere of his own passionate whims. Then, watching with bated breath the mighty vibrations of the brilliant actor's soul, the other actors and the audience would unite in uncontrollable ecstasy. [Kizevetter 1925: 117–118]

Inspiration did not always come. Mochalov had no keys to it. Sometimes, for one reason or another, his power vanished. Then he would fall into helpless anger. He would try to excite himself by any means possible – to heat up his indifferent, apathetic soul . . . He would run around the stage, scream, wave his hands, beat his thighs . . . he felt disgraced, ashamed . . . But he couldn't do anything. As for psychological technique – he didn't have it. Back at his time, people saw the technique in elaborating a role to its subtlest "intonations," finding all possible appropriate poses and vivid expressions of one's body and face. (They still see it this way, not wanting to go forward, continuing to spin in circles.)

None of this suited Mochalov's creative type. He avoided all of this deadening analytical and imitative methods . . .

Yermolova, however, did have the key to her soul, i.e. she possessed technique in our understanding of the word. Apparently she possessed it in great measure. She *did not have* any failures.

Enlightenment and inspiration, in art or in science, never comes on its own, out of the blue. It's always the result of enormous preliminary, preparative work – although it maybe subconscious. Only a dilettante or mediocrity, which is deprived of all proper (I'll allow myself to put it like this) *creative instincts*, doesn't feel this relationship between hard work and inspiration. In the pitiful simplicity of its soul, it demands that the holy spirit pays it a visit for no reason whatsoever . . . just because it seemed convenient today.

What is a genius from his own, subjective point of view?

At the start, he thinks himself an ordinary person, just one who is fascinated by one idea or interesting occupation. He is only surprised that everybody around him is blind to it and is completely apathetic to this most interesting of things. And he's confused – why do they put in so much effort and time into trifles? Could this all really be so important: dressing well, eating good food, going out, getting together and talking about random nonsense; and when there's nothing to babble about – playing cards, dancing? . . . Are these all really worthwhile ways of passing the time?

But his surprise doesn't last for long. His weight is so great when compared with that of his surrounding environment that he drops to the very bottom and remains alone until somebody forcefully drags him to the surface.

What alienates the genius from the crowd most of all are his moments of inspiration.

> In my mind, it's as if a bright light flashed, and it *illuminated everything*. I saw horde of ideas, bright and vivid, with such force and in such quantity that my heart was seized by awe and confusion. It was as if I were inebriated by the onslaught of thoughts and sensations. My heart pulsed with greater strength, squeezing my chest, tightening my breath. I settled down on the grass under a tree next to the road and sat there for half an hour . . . (Jean-Jacques Rousseau [1920: 196])

Voluntarily or otherwise, a person who experiences such "sudden inspiration" inevitably has a different attitude towards himself. He considers himself "chosen," "marked by fate," "a messenger from heaven," "a prophet." This feeling of "power that stems not from humans" is so distinct and so constant for anyone who has experienced moments of inspiration that they all speak of it.

"I work, sitting at a piano with closed eyes, and I reproduce what someone is whispering in my ear from the outside" (E.T.A. Hoffman [1971: 53]).

"*Whence* and *hour* they come I know not, nor can I force them." (Mozart [as quoted in *Musical Times* 1891: 19]).

The Italian tragedian Ernesto Rossi [as quoted in Lapshin 1923: 114] called himself "an instrument that's being played by some other being."

For an artist, inspiration is the object of all his hopes. "If only I had some inspiration. Without inspiration, nothing will happen" (Dostoevsky [1985: 312]).

For some, the knowledge that they're not quite ordinary people, that they're "marked by fate," "chosen ones," causes them to have a serious attitude towards their work and themselves. Michelangelo [as quoted in Francisco d'Ollanda 1903: 320], for example, said: ". . . it is not sufficient merely to be a great master in painting and very wise, but I think that it is necessary for the painter to be very good in his mode of life, or even, if such were possible, a saint, so that the Holy Spirit may inspire his intellect."

Yermolova also considered her work and the stage to be something sacred.

Others, however, feeling themselves to be "chosen ones," would decide that they could do anything, and that laws didn't apply to them – they would live in the fast lane, and perish in the process, depriving humanity of themselves.

Yet others still, because of their weakness and lack of principles, would try to reconcile one with the other: both, heightened moments of artistic inspiration, and their own little passions. They would delude themselves with false hopes that they would be able to reconcile the irreconcilable. Taking a look at their life and work, you see how much more beautiful their life could have become, and how much deeper their art could have been – more universal and powerful. This applies to literature, painting, music, and theatre.

Notes

1 Editors could not locate the source of the Newton quote.
2 On November 23, 1846, Balzac (1900b: 742) wrote to Madam Hanska: "Nature gives talent, but it is for man to put it to work and bring it to sight by force of will, perseverance, and courage."
3 See James Fenimore Cooper's novel *The Pathfinder, or The Inland Sea*, chapter 11.

7

The Path of the Artist

Subconscious, Reflexes, Automatic Functions

"A force of art," "sacred power," "divine logos," "the fire of inspiration" . . .

Fire . . . imagine the horror and confusion with which the cavemen, our ancestors regarded it. They shuddered, worshipped it, as a higher being – as a God! . . . Centuries have passed, and it moves our trains, ships, takes us through the air, blows up mountains, spins the wheels of our factories, lights up and warms our cities, our modest apartments, and, finally, lights our cigarettes. Such is the power of human vision.

And our own "fire," the one that is hidden inside us – flash of genius, inspiration, intuition, talent – what is it? Let's try track down and catch this heavenly fire by its tail. Sometimes it's very small – is there a way to make it bigger? If it's weak, can we fuel it? It shows up whenever it deigns to – is there a way to summon it at any time that we need it? It goes wherever the wind blows – it's impossible to direct . . . Is there a way to wield it and make it our instrument?

Stesha Herzog . . . What happened to her? How could she make herself over like that? And what goes into the makeover?

First of all, under the influence of proper training, certain *qualities* of hers were enhanced to their limits – qualities which were hitherto in embryonic states (as they usually are for us, ordinary people). The most important one was an exact sense of balance. Poke any one of us – in her place, we would feel a loss of balance only once it's too late and there's no more opportunity to equalize – once we're already falling. It was the same for her in the beginning of her training – when she would grab the ropes having felt the immanent fall, rather than the coming loss of balance. Now, however, it's impossible to imagine the acuity with which she feels the slightest, most insignificant deviation from balance. Besides, she's acquired and developed a *technique*. A *technique* of finding and maintaining balance. It is made up of trained and retrained *reflexes*, which coordinate all of a body's movements with regards to keeping it balanced. Under the influence of proper training, the acuity of her perception, as well as her technique, reached the highest level of development and polish. She now feels the slightest deviation from balance. Moreover, her refined nervous system perceives certain signs *that are noticeable only to her,* and it *foresees* the imminent hazard of losing balance. And she reflexively takes the appropriate measures in advance.

Can we conclude that her perception and technique lie within the realm of consciousness and reason? Of course not. Could she really keep track of tens or even hundreds of minuscule physical, psychological, and physiological signals by means of "well-focused attention?" Could she judge and evaluate everything with her cold intellect, logically concluding how to act?

This isn't a case of three or four, or even five or six balls – there are more. On top of everything, there's the very real danger of dying . . . In this case, you have to, like Kara, you have to join this "mobile system," become one of its parts, and just try "not to get in its way." In that case, the reflexes developed through lengthy training will kick in and begin doing their familiar job. The balance will then maintain itself *almost on its own*. As a result of her enormous and stubborn work, Stesha's equilibristics became reflexive – that's indubitable. At the same time, it's safe to say that she gained not just one reflexive apparatus, but many – each one keener than the previous one, and each one with its own specialty. Aside from these, there is one central apparatus to which all the strings are connected.

We should address the meaning of reflexes specifically.

The greater part of the processes that are ongoing in us lie beyond our consciousness, and we don't even suspect that they exist – they occur reflexively.

And I might add that so-called unconditioned reflexes are more simple and straightforward, while conditioned reflexes are more complex and subtle. They can be so complex and so subtle that sometimes, it's impossible to tell whether it's a conscious human act or just a reflex, i.e. a physiological response to an external stimulus.

Why is nature so structured that much of our actions have nothing to do with our consciousness, and are committed wholly without our influence or even awareness?

It makes an enormous amount of sense. If things were different, there would not only be dearth of scientific, artistic, and other discoveries, but we simply would not be able to exist. Let's take our simplest action as an example – walking. Recall how much attention, effort, and willpower a child needs to take his first steps – he doesn't yet have the required skills, the necessary habits. But keep in mind that his mother has already led him by the hand, so he already has experience putting one foot in front of the other, and all things considered, he has already been on a few walks. But still, taking the first independent step is a scary thing. First, he holds on to a chair, then his bed, and shuffles his feet with their support . . . What is all this for? In order to develop the skills, in order to ingrain the habit in himself, and in order to *condition reflexes*. They would move his legs, maintain his balance, regulate the force and strain of his leg muscles and others, and in general coordinate all parts of his body in a single action – walking. It's the same for all our other actions – at first, they're done timidly and captiously. They're still completely undiscovered, and they must be executed with our utmost conscious attention. Time has to pass before they are done "out of habit," i.e. reflexively, as if on their own – they then unload unnecessary cares from our consciousness.

This is one boon that reflexivity bestows upon us. But there is another, which is no less valuable.

With repetition, an automatic movement becomes lighter and lighter, smoother and smoother, faster and faster – it becomes more and more perfect. During his first days of pedestrian adventures, a child is barely able to stand on his own two feet; but soon, he begins to walk quite easily; then he runs, jumps, dances, and can reach the point of being able to dance while standing on a galloping horse, or on a tight rope just beneath a circus's roof. That is he can do such complex and difficult things he could never have managed via a conscious effort, without the help of reflexes. In this manner, numerous things would be impossible without reflexes. This includes our lives, our personal development, and all of our progress in its vast and expansive scope (beginning with its mundane side and ending with extraordinary philosophical achievements). Even our consciousness can develop and sharpen only because our reflexive apparatus exists and functions.

Firstly, this apparatus relieves our consciousness of an indescribable and unmanageable work. Secondly, it makes the material that our consciousness receives more complete, exact and comprehensive. Seeing as consciousness barely sticks its nose into this smooth reflexive act, the act becomes more and more mechanical. It becomes easier and easier, it flows more and more quickly, and its accuracy becomes more and more perfect. Ultimately, it reaches nearly instantaneous speed. The consciousness, seeing that it has nothing more to do here, completely removes itself from the equation, and the machine functions quite well on its own.

★★★

Many professions require certain remarkable qualities, be it exceptional pitch, a sharp eye, an outstanding sense of touch, good visual estimation, or manual dexterity. How can you acquire them if you don't have them?

Why do you think that you don't have them? For some reason, it's the norm to think that a person's senses are extraordinarily poor, that animals have significantly sharper senses than humans. For example, people would say: can you really compare a human's eyesight with that of an eagle, who can see a rabbit or a mouse from a height of two-three kilometers when he's circling the earth in search of prey? Or a human's sense of hearing with that of a bat, who, without having any eyes, flies around in the darkness, doesn't bump into anything, not even the slightest obstacle – only with the use of its ears?

This is all true, but still, we should take a closer look at the situation.

Are our senses as bad as they seem given our shallow acquaintance with them? . . . For example, while taking a walk, we recall an old friend "for some reason." "Strange," we think, "why did he pop up all of a sudden?" But everything turns out to be quite simple: that very friend or someone who looked a lot like him was walking on the other side of the street, and *out of the corner of my eye, without giving it a second thought,* I saw him, but didn't realize it. The sensation made it past all my guard posts and snuck by, like contraband, into the darkness where all sensations lie in wait – into the part of our "I" that we used to call our "subconscious," then our "unconscious," then our "sphere."

And here are other, more striking, instances: all of a sudden, an actor starts complaining in a rehearsal. There is seemingly no good reason for it, but he's complaining, whining, can't control himself . . .

For the most part, this is what happens: in the back of an empty and dark theatre, an ill-wishing colleague is whispering into his neighbor's ears about all of the actor's misses. The actor, without even suspecting it, *hears everything.* He can't put his finger on what's tripping him up . . . He only senses that something *is* tripping him up; very badly! His role has yet to take shape; he's ready to be angry with himself and fault himself every single minute, and here, his esteemed colleague is also fueling the fire . . .

The ill-wisher can even be silent, but the actor not only hears him, he *sees* him too. It doesn't matter that it's dark – he sees every smile, every grimace, every gesture, every shake of the head . . . He sees, hears, and senses everything so well because onstage, he's in a state of *searching, waiting, listening to himself* – in a state of keen sensitivity and complete openness. Consciously and subconsciously, he catches every rustle, every half-formed thought; he responds to every impression, and he is hundreds of times more sensitive than in his ordinary, casual state.

People might say that science acknowledges only what a subject truly sees and hears, only what his ears and eyes legitimately pick up, i.e. what his conscious marks as visible and audible. But why is that the case? Why should we only use one's conscious impressions as a criteria of what's visible or audible? Evidently, lots of things that we see, hear, and perceive in general do not reach our consciousness. The threshold between conscious and subconscious perception is, by all accounts, very high, and subtle impressions cannot jump over it, so they remain subconscious.

There is an intriguing phenomenon – "somnambulism." A subject who suffers from it, without waking, gets up from his bed, approaches the window with closed eyes, climbs out the window, goes up the cornice without opening his eyes, gets to the roof, and calmly, confidently, walks around the roof, which was hitherto host only to cats and sparrows, and even they had their eyes open. He'll walk for a bit and, satisfied, returns to his bed in the same manner, and calmly keeps on sleeping.

Apparently, this balancing act doesn't take anything out of him and holds no danger for him whatsoever. But wake him up during one of these walks, and he'll be as helpless on his roof as he is supposed to be in his normal, waking state. Why, then, does he walk so confidently in his somnambulant state? How does he see? His eyes are closed! And how is he as balanced as a circus performer?

It's amazing! Yes, amazing. It's a shame, only, that people aren't amazed enough by it.

Maybe we have some other sense that we don't know of yet – it's what gives us the ability to see without our eyes? This is, of course, also a possibility. Why *shouldn't* there be another sense? Maybe, without even being aware of it, we possess some "cat's eye." Maybe. Our "conscious sight" is very limited. We know its boundaries. As for the boundaries *of our whole sight* – we don't fully know them yet. But they are, evidently, very broad. It makes sense that much of what we see slips by our consciousness and goes to the deeper layers of our psyche and physiology. And what about our tactile and auditory perception? For example, I have a friend who sees poorly not just in darkness, but even in semi-darkness. He gets around using *his hearing*. He "hears" the road. Using his hearing, he can walk down a path better and more bravely than those of us who see. To hear him say it, every rock has its own sound. Maybe we too "hear" the road, without even suspecting it.

So, we have no right to complain about our poverty. The issue is that we don't know how to make these perceiving organs, and all the automated reflexes in our bodies, obey our wills. Truth be told, they behave rather independently and aren't at all inclined to heeding us.

Let's assume that this "circus-like" automatism, as well as any mobile automatism is possible – there's no need to deny it. But is automatism possible for processes that involve *thought*?

People whose lives are inextricably entwined with nature have an amazing quality. For example, an Eskimo goes tens of kilometers away from his home and spends several days in search of meat; we would, of course, get lost – there's snow everywhere, semi-darkness or full darkness. But when he has to return, he goes straight for his home without deviating from his course once. And he is always infallible.

True, many animals, like the horse, also have this apparatus. It always knows where its home is. And it will infallibly return to its stall – just stay out of its way. However, the apparatus doesn't become worse because animals have it too.

How does it work? Psychologists think that it has to do with an amazing memory. Animals (or people) subconsciously remember every turn, every step that they make, and an internal counter keeps track of it all, marking down every detail into its records. Just ask yourself at any moment where your house is, where you came from – and you immediately get an answer: over there. And it will be as accurate an answer as that of the most precise land-surveyor that didn't miss a single movement and marked everything down. So it's not that a person or an animal can feel tens of leagues away where their home is, but that the whole road away from their home, they have an automatic counter-surveyor keeping track of everything.

And now, knowing that in the depths of our psyche we have such an accurate apparatus, let's try to investigate what happened when the wonder of all wonders was brought to light – Maxwell's magnetic field equation.

For James Clerk Maxwell [1831–1879] the mathematician, an expert in his field, it's as natural and habitual to make mathematical deductions as walking is for a human or a horse. Maxwell sets up a problem and solves it, using rules and deductions that are normal for a mathematician. Everything is going smoothly. Suddenly, for some reason, an error is made.

If a horse or a person keeps track of every step, every turn, then it's difficult to imagine that Maxwell's inner "counter" and "surveyor" didn't note this error.

There's a mistake . . . but you have to get to the right result!

And his brilliantly developed deductive mechanisms *turn everything around on their own*. It's necessary to get off the wrong path . . . And at the first opportunity, these mechanisms take the first step to do this: they make a second mistake – but now, it's *necessary* for their goal. Then a third . . . a fourth . . . a fifth, and . . . they get back on to the right path.

The result seems miraculous. But is there anything miraculous about it? Where's the divine intervention? Maxwell got to the right result, despite the mistakes in his calculations. But not because he foresaw, *predicted this result*, or intentionally (though subconsciously) made the mistakes necessary to get this result. Everything is much simpler. *It's all because of his automated mechanisms that have been developed and honed to such a sharp state over many decades.*

And so we've left the automatic functions of our motor apparatus, and have come to automated thought processes.

Add emotions to all of this, and you'll step into the realm of artistic creativity.

And at this point, Mozart's confession [as quoted in *Musical Times* 1891: 19–20] that "the creative process happens in him as if "in a pleasing, lively dream" and that "he can not force it" won't surprise you. And there will be nothing mysterious about Rossi calling himself "an instrument that's being played by some other being."

For now, we not only cannot wield these automatic actions – we do not even suspect that they exist. And so, one person thinks that it's a muse whispering to him, another thinks it's a demon, a third – his genie, a fourth – his dead Beatrice, a fifth – simply "somebody at his side," etc.

Obviously, you have to be as healthy and well-balanced as Goethe and, while being a poet, also possessing the cold perception of a scientist; then . . . Here's what he told Eckermann [1850: 251]:

> In such a somnambulistic condition, it has often happened that I have had a sheet of paper lying before me all on one side, and I have not discovered it till all has been written, or I have found no room to write any more. I have possessed many such sheets written crossways, but they have been lost one after another, and I regret that I can no longer show any proofs of such poetic abstraction.

Somnambulism, i.e. automatic functions – that's what Goethe saw with his perceptive eye behind the act of artistic creation.

★★★

Just look at the state of helpless ignorance that we find ourselves in when faced with our own automatic functions! For the most part, they function to our advantage, but sometimes to our detriment – we can only look on and be amazed. But what's the point if we cannot control it? Unless the point is that nature itself exclaims: "Look at me! Take me, use me! You shouldn't be ignoring me!" Kara and Stesha learned to evoke their automated functions and give in to them. They give in to them and, with their help, do extraordinary things.

Maxwell didn't give himself over – his automated functions did the extraordinary on their own.

It sometimes happens that a scientist spends years searching for a solution, wandering back and forth . . . He gives in to his sound instinct, then he'll stop listening to it; he'll aid his automated functions' work, then he'll get in their way. Finally . . . the solution falls into his lap when he least expects it . . . That's what happened with Mendeleev's Table. His search lasted for a long time . . . Finally, the tormented scientist was so tired that he bent his head over his desk, fell asleep, and saw in a dream his periodic system of elements in its complete form. His consciousness grew tired and refused to work, but his automated functions, liberated from the oversight of intellect, finished the job and showed their work: "that's how it's done!"

Hermann von Helmholtz's [as quoted in Koenigsberger 1906: 209] observations about his "epiphanies" are curious:

I must first have turned my problem over and over in all directions, till I can see its twists and windings in my mind's eye, and run through it freely, without writing it down; and it is never possible to get to this point without a long period of preliminary work. And then, when the consequent fatigue has been recovered from, there must be an hour of perfect bodily recuperation and peaceful comfort, before the kindly inspiration rewards one. Often it comes in the morning on waking up, according to . . . Goethe (as Gauss [1777–1850] also noticed . . .) It came most readily, as I experienced in Heidelberg, when I went out to climb the wooded hills in sunny weather.

In this way, Helmholtz not only acknowledges the existence of these automatic functions (as did all others who observed themselves), but he even relies on them most of all. He himself just does preparatory work.

The experience of most scientists, inventors, thinkers, literary scholars was such: a long preparatory period – then a minute of "epiphany," "inspiration," and a third period – processing the results of this inspiration. Almost all of them say that, first of all, you have to amass enough material, think it through, wrestle with it adequately, and only then will you see things clearly: you'll have the answer to the problem.

However, judging from the fact that our automated abilities of perception and our automatic memories are so great that we can't even imagine, we can assume that the arduous amassment of material and the following contemplation can also be outsourced to our automated functions. Or maybe, everything is already gathered inside? . . . Maybe there's already a solution there? Maybe the reason that I choose to grapple with a problem is because I *already have* the materials and solution inside me? . . . After all, the great mathematician, Carl Friedrich Gauss [as quoted in Arber 1954: 47], did say the strange words: "I have had my results for a long time: but I do not yet know how I am to arrive at them."

"The throes of creation" are considered inevitable, vital; people think that without them, not a single true work of art can be made, just as a child cannot be born without throes. But is this a law? That remains to be seen. After all, giving birth isn't painful for everyone.

It's more probable that "the throes of creation" stem from an inability to properly utilize one's psychological apparatus. It's time, it's been time for a long time, to learn how to better get into the hidden laboratories and workshops of our soul. Get into them and control their processes.

It's not the automatic functions' fault that sometimes, we get in their way, that we don't consider their heightened sensitivity and promptness, that we have a disdainful attitude towards their signals and impulses, and that we pay for that – we deprive ourselves of the greatest helpers that we could ever want.

Technique

We have a very primitive and essentially inaccurate understanding of the power that lies in training, in work on self, and in hard work in general . . .

Let's just think about Stesha – what? Did she have an obvious specific talent for balance? Doesn't really seem that way. I saw her for the first time after a month and a half of stubborn training, and she had nothing to show for it – on the contrary, she gave off a rather hopeless impression: the girl was wasting her time.

And then! Her talents awoke. And how!

Let somebody whose main talent is balance, but who doesn't spend as much time practicing, try to go up against her. Despite his giftedness, he'll seem ridiculous and pitiful in his dilettantish helplessness next to her.

How is she different from him?

This has already been explained: the exceptional level of development of certain *qualities* that we usually possess in a state of very early development (we don't need any more for life). The most important one: a honed sense of balance. Aside from this, the keenest and subtlest of **techniques**. The technique of maintaining balance.

An innate talent has qualities and technique from birth. But they're capricious, accidental – they show up and disappear. Sometimes they show up in full, sometimes only in part; they depend on thousands of unknown reasons. In the meantime, in Stesha's case, they're all obedient instruments in the hands of the human ruler. They have been turned into mighty workhorses.

There is no doubt that in time – probably in the near future – the actor who has innate talent, is experienced enough, and leaves a big enough impression on us will seem weak and pitiful next to the new type of actor. This new actor would have developed specific *qualities and the **technique*** *of creative emotional experiencing and transformation* (he has done so in accordance with scientific evidence, as well as the newly discovered rules of his art form).

So what, does this mean that you don't need talent, and just need well-developed qualities and a technique?

If you think about it, talent is nothing if not a given quality that has been combined with a specific technique – skills that have formed during the process of ***proper work on yourself***. This union is what we call talent.

Now, a question: what is *proper work on yourself*?

Let's begin with the fact that Stesha's training *could not be improper*. Otherwise, the acrobat would have fallen and broken her neck. All the time, every second, every instant she has an infallible and exact criteria of the correctness of her work: if I'm sitting, it's correct; if I'm falling, it's incorrect. An actor, however, doesn't have such a reliable, sentinel method of checking. He might be acting falsely, he might be faking, and he can very easily not even notice it (and in fact, it's more pleasant not to notice it!). He has not only lost his "balance" – he's already "lying on the floor," and yet he thinks that what he's doing couldn't be better. This completely disorients him. And, working so *improperly*, it's no wonder that he trains such *improper* skills.

And this is the main reason behind why it's so difficult to become a decent actor – let alone true, real and fantastic one.

What does it mean to work properly? How can we recognize it? And not just almost properly, but absolutely properly! Everything depends on this absoluteness.

First of all, you need a **proper school** for this, a proper path, found and developed by experts in the field.

Secondly, you need an exceptionally **perceptive teacher** whose eagle eye won't miss a single mistake.

Thirdly, you need the teacher to have great **sensitivity and pedagogical tact**; otherwise, seeing only mistakes with eagle eye and constantly pointing them out, he may frighten the student and kill in him any desire to work. His perception should pick up not only mistakes, but the student's successes, abilities and talents as well (even though they are sometimes hidden so deeply that it's as if they're not even there). If, however, there is no such teacher, then the student himself needs to have a certain internal instrument – something like a bubble level that would instantly indicate a tip in a wrong direction. Have this sort of instrument and constantly listen to it. In fact, this device might come in handy even given a proper instructor. Then again, a good teacher should first of all concern himself with *developing* it in a student.

Fourthly, you need to have an extraordinary **capacity for work**. The teacher can only direct the student. The most important thing, however, is independent homework. This work can be ardent and inspired, but you should rely not on ardent work, but on daily, systematic, everyday work – relentless and calm, without driving yourself to the point of utter exhaustion . . . Like the swinging of a pendulum, the flow of a river, or the rising and setting of the sun.

Actor's Psycho-technique

The word "technique" is very popular among actors. You often hear: "he's a technical actor." This means: he's acting mechanically, he's not immersed, he's not a part of what's happening onstage, he's just adeptly deceiving everyone – faking "experiencing" and "emotional life." This ability to deceive people via external means – movements, facial expressions, drilled in intonations – is what actors like to call "technique."

Aside from this crude, external technique, there also exists an **internal technique** – a psycho-technique. And, if an actor trained by the theatre of "presentation" can have an external technique without an internal one, then it must be noted that an actor trained by the theatre of "experiencing" has an internal technique that is inextricable from the external one – the psycho-technique and physio-technique are one. On one hand, an actor should have astounding sensitivity and responsivity to any word or impression received from his partners onstage, as well as the ability to give in to any thought. On the other hand, he should possess a highest level of freedom and obedience of every muscle of the body, face, throat, breathing, etc. In such a case, his reactions would never be delayed, while all of his feelings, thoughts and internal movements – reflected on his face, voice, pose, hand movements, leg movements, and on his whole body . . . In a word, everything would be visible and audible.

However, unfortunately, such harmonic development can be witnessed very rarely. For the most part, actors don't have an internal technique at all, and that's why they use the infamous "external technique."

Where can you get a real psycho-technique? They don't teach it in theatres or in theatre schools. There, they teach so-called "acting mastery": they speak about truth and sincerity and other good things . . . but it all stays on the level of "theory." There, the goal isn't to bring the actor into a creative state, and certainly not to inspiration. Instead of teaching *the art of living creatively onstage*, they more or less teach actors to imitate life, reflect it by external means. Don't you know – such a means are better suited for "professional work" onstage – they never betray you, don't depend on your emotions, are always at your disposal, and are very easy to develop. And so, most often, you see how well the "body" is trained instead of the "soul." But authentic, enthralling, enchanting beauty is on the inside. It can exist even given an ugly exterior. It shines through your eyes, it can be heard in the music of the voice, it can be seen in slight shadows that flicker across the face, in barely perceptible movements of the head, shoulders, hands, fingers . . .

The *creative technique* inevitably involves an *internal* technique. For an actor of the theatre of experiencing, it plays an especially important role. Everything can be there: voice, a beautiful exterior, intelligence, a fiery heart, but if there's no internal technique that allows you to utilize it, then nothing can be accomplished. And regardless of how good his talent is, how good his external and internal attributes are (an advanced intellect, a powerful and easily affected emotionality, high morals, etc.) – if he doesn't have an *internal technique*, a technique of the *soul*, any success the actor might ever have will be only dilettantish, accidental gifts. Only once you have an advanced technique and developed qualities can you start thinking about free artistic creativity. Without an advanced internal technique, an actor cannot play anything big in the sphere of drama or comedy. To say nothing of tragedy.

No matter how obvious the necessity to acquire an internal technique is, there are few things that an actor treats lighter than this. He thinks that it's all just trifles, nothing too important. And, naturally, he bumps into the first wall.

One very intelligent director that is very curious about his field was once lamenting the quagmire that our theatrical art form is in. He said: "They are unable to create bright, new art, only because *they have nothing to say.*" He's wrong, this director. The reason is different. The reason is that the technique *is improper.* Yes, yes! However strange that may seem. There's always something to say. At any minute and for any person.

And here are some facts for you: the most common and widely accessible art is that of the reader. Person X is reading *War and Peace* – he's immersed, he grows angry, he laughs, and even cries . . . Why? Because, engaged by the author, he perceives everything so realistically that it seems that it's all happening right before him . . . He reacts with exceptional power to the things that resonate with his soul. If you're sympathetic or immersed, then something touched you, something's grazed your wounds or some deep, secret desires. That means that you have something in your soul that you could say on the subject. So: there's always *something* to say. You just have to unbridle your natural responsiveness.

And if a reader can give himself over to the author, then the actor and the director have to do that to an even greater degree. The actor should abandon himself entirely and wholly immerse himself in the personality and life of the character . . . But usually, neither the actor, nor the director *immerses himself* to that necessary degree in the play or the character; they *do not feel* it as deeply and tangibly as they should, and they *do not give themselves over.* And not because they don't want to, because it's beneath them, but because ***it's not so easy.***

Thousands of obstacles and barriers emerge on the path to this natural responsiveness. It turns out that many, many *qualities* are missing. When reading the play, the reader had enough imagination and was involved enough with it, but he tried to transform into an actor-performer – into a character – the imagination turned out to be inadequate, and the involvement . . . it's completely gone. Other than insufficient qualities, there is also a dearth of *technique.* When he was reading, everything was immersive, but here . . . nothing is breaking through – he's closed off, grown cold and stale . . . And if something does break through – there are new obstacles: he isn't brave enough to give himself over – he's closed up, put on the brakes . . . So, it turns out that everything is there: there are things to say, there's a desire to say them, but since there's no internal technique, nothing can be done.

When an actor becomes involved in a role, when it's dear to his soul, then, for the most part, this evokes a proper internal technique. But it's crucial to note: this technique will last for one show – with repetitions, this accidental technique doesn't come, and becomes worse and worse each time. Why was the first show so good? Because this actor still had an internal charge, he didn't discharge it yet. But he uses it all up on the first show, "acts it out" of himself, and ends up empty. It's a kind of catharsis.

The first show went so well because of how new it was, because it was still unexpected . . . In the second, third shows, and beyond, the newness disappears, immersion follows, and bringing up the rear is . . . creativity. As for technique, internal technique – it's not even there! And so the actors start to abuse form and forcefully evoke emotions in themselves, and the farther they go, the more they do it.

What should they do instead? What would save everything? To begin with – psycho-technique; then – psycho-technique; and finally – psycho-technique!

If you have a proper, reliable internal technique and developed acting skills, then the actor's creative capabilities will be woken up by the work itself. And even if he begins coldly and without any involvement, he'll still inevitably get into the role. And once he's in, the character's interests and life will inevitably grab and immerse the actor. As for something to *say* – that's always there. If not in his consciousness – then somewhere deeper.

A little more exactly and concretely: what sort of qualities does an actor need? What sort of technique? And how can an actor develop them both?

This whole series of books is an attempt to offer a serious and practical answer to these questions.

How Did Technique Emerge in Theatre?

An actor who has chosen the path of sincerity and experiencing onstage cannot do without an internal technique: it's the third bell, and – please, demonstrate your skills for us! Show us how you can transform into another person; and once you've done that, show us how well you can suffer, rejoice, love, hate, think, want, act, and *live his life* in general.

Every actor begins by wanting to act for real – well, like a true artist, i.e. live onstage. But the majority soon deviates from this difficult path to the well-trodden path of craftsmanship and external imitation of art. We won't speak of this majority. As for the minority – these lone individuals have always sought reliable approaches to their inspiration, they've experimented, found some things, lost them again, and then, finally, the best of them found some more or less reliable internal mechanisms and went on to amaze the world with their art. What they did to get there and how they did it is essentially unknown. In Russia, Mikhail Shchepkin [1788–1863] was the first who began to search for universal paths and rules to mastery over an actor's proper artistic state. According to hearsay, he was able to suggest a lot of things to actors and would help them a lot, but nothing remains beyond Shchepkin's [1984: 197] general notes, like "step, so to speak, into the character's shoes," beyond a few bits of advice like that.

In more recent times, Stanislavsky set about doing this much more systematically and has opened many more doors. He was a *director*, and that with great, authentically artistic demands. His goal was a perfect *show*. Without perfect acting, there cannot be a perfect show. And he demanded perfect acting from all his performers. Yet even the best actors aren't always sufficiently inspired – let alone the less talented ones. This is why he started searching for concrete paths to the state of creative inspiration.

Many of the found methods seemingly reached their goals and, given enough time, it would have been possible to reach satisfactory results – if not for production deadlines. They wouldn't allow extensive, assiduous work and training. And so faster methods were needed – methods that could allow actors to perform almost truthfully without inspiration or flights of fantasy. This verisimilitude didn't satisfy Stanislavsky, of course, but there was no other way. Besides, some of the more talented performers in the show were sometimes able to go from verisimilitude to truth thanks to their gift. And all this, along with a well-thought-through show structure (as well as the audience's theatrical self-deception) gave off the impression of perfection. And whether he liked it or not, Stanislavsky was forced to constrain himself with this seeming perfection.

The main principle that Stanislavsky proclaimed at first was: "Through the conscious to the *subconscious*." He tried to hold to it. But in order to see this principle through to its realization, he needed specially and properly trained actors. Such actors he did not have – simply because no one had come up with a school that could develop them at the time. And without it, there were constant breakdowns and disappointments. In rehearsal, an actor who has been brought to the proper state by all possible means would act, and he'd act well. But tomorrow, that state being gone, you have to start all over.

And so, he had to constantly break his principle "through the conscious to the subconscious." It ultimately fell victim to the need for a show to be created very quickly, as well as to the lack of readiness on the part of the actors (they were as of yet unable to work according to this principle, that is close to the mark, or at least creative). This resulted in the actor's work steadily entering the field of *reason and analysis* – into a field that is much more accessible to an actor. As for the relationship between creativity and the *subconscious* – it was left undiscovered.

For now, here's what things look like: creative abilities exist; they're seemingly related to the "subconscious"; they work, but they work without paying any attention to our desires. Inspiration will descend upon us one instant and be gone the next. An artist will go onstage one moment and feel himself as the character whom he's made up as, with the name by which people call him, with the past and the life that the author gave him – and the next moment, everything just listed will seem foreign, false . . . Everything gets in his way, it all trips him up – from the fireman in the wing to the coughing in the audience and the stupid light that's mercilessly hitting him right in the eye . . .

"But on other occasions," the actor says, surprised, "this whole complex of unnaturalness did not get in my way. Thousands of eyes were still staring at me, spotlights and floodlights all shining on me like ten thousand candles; I still used words that weren't my own – and sometimes they were even in verse! – and I still had to bare my soul before everyone as I never would in real life. Nevertheless, this whole complex of unnaturalness is what caused some switch to go off inside me; some recesses of my soul opened, and fire, passion, eternal grief fountained out . . . The feelings were stronger than I could ever imagine. I couldn't tell if it were me or someone else inside me . . .

At first, it's frightening and horrifying, but then you gradually get used to this unprecedented, unusual, and seemingly "abnormal" state . . .

Same thing with the "character": at first, the transformation into a character would happen only accidentally, almost without my help, and it seemed difficult and even scary . . . Now I can do it at will, and even with some abandon: you let some other personality into you – any at all – it pushes my own out of the way, speaks with my mouth, thinks with my brain, walks with my feet. And you can only observe it from afar and muse: "Look at what he does! . . ."

And so, time and practice awaken and solidify in us our own delicate and, at the same time, bold "*technique*" of owning your personal creative process.

The Actor's Automatic Functions

As a result of 40 years of working in theatre and theatre schools – first as an actor, and then as director and teacher – the author has developed a unified and principled internal acting technique. Or rather, it developed on its own.

For the first 10–15 years, being under the spell of Konstantin Stanislavsky, my thoughts would inevitably circle around the ideas that he would proclaim and bring to life.[1] But little by little, practical experience started leading me other places too. Especially since, looking at Stanislavsky, it was easy to see in him and in his work an extremely contradictory union of two mutually destructive points of departure: at times, he was spontaneous and free – at others, he was governed by intellectual reasoning, dry, deliberative, and even mechanical.

The idea that the technique of an actor's creative experiencing lies in the working of **automatic functions** didn't come immediately. In the beginning, everything concerned our usual ideas about the subconscious.

When an actor in a rehearsal became immersed, forgot himself, and acted very well, the director (the author of this book), who was typically observing the actor very carefully and *empathizing* with him, felt wavering and doubts in the actor. Worrying that the actor would lose his balance, he involuntarily said to the actor (while in his beneficent creative state): "Good, good! . . . that's right . . . don't be afraid!" And the actor, uplifted by these words, started acting even better, even more bravely. Afterwards, after the scene ended, the actor would always recall that everything was going great, but suddenly some alien thought flickered through his mind, or maybe he "looked at himself from the outside," and was suddenly in danger of "losing it." The director's words of approval put him on the right track, and he "became immersed" again, and he was "in the zone."

When you "become immersed" – the director would explain – that's the most important part. You just have to believe in it, to give yourself over to it – it won't ever fail you. And so, the director acquired a new habit: in difficult and dangerous moments, he would whisper a few words to the actor, something like, "go ahead, give it a green light," "don't worry, just let it happen!" "yes, that's correct . . . don't get in its way . . . let it act on its own!" The actor, in his turn, acquired the habit of giving in to various internal inclinations and urges that emanated from the author, his partners, or the director's words.

In this way, there gradually developed a new direction, a whole new principle of the internal technique.

At first, nobody had any questions about the nature and origins of this "IT." And really: does it even matter on a practical level what it is? It just has to work. And it works pretty well . . . It gives such unexpected qualities, such power, and such emotional explosions . . . Maybe it's the subconscious? – Maybe. It doesn't concern me. I just need it to work. In this way, this "it" first became a *weapon*, and only once we got enough facts and experience did everything become connected. And it became clear that in many, very many cases, the issue isn't with some unclear and murky subconscious, but with distinct and indisputable automated functions.

In a word, our automated functions are just the environment to which we adapt to a greater or lesser degree; then, we discover that we can bend them to our will and turn them into our instruments. Then we grow brave, we try to use them, and we even pick up. And the third period: while using them, we begin to study them. After that, we should expect the fourth period (and there are already hints of it at this point): by using the automated functions and adapting to them, we inevitably change ourselves – new *qualities* develop in us. In our experience, in our creative work with actors, this attitude towards automated functions yielded tangible fruits.

As a result of frequent observations and accidental experiments, we have found the following approaches to our automatic functions, in regards to acting:

1   Learn a skillful way of assigning them tasks.
2   Learn to set them in motion, while skillfully evoking their work.
3   Learn to obey them and give in to them. We make lots of mistakes in life and in work, because we don't listen to the signals our automatic functions give us, and we act in opposition to them.
4   Learn to govern them while in the middle of the processes. The slightest incompetent intervention stops or distorts the functions' work.
5   Learn to strengthen a certain automatic function, if it is working timidly and weakly.
6   Retrain them if they're not working in the direction they should.
7   Create them if they don't exist, but are necessary.

★★★

One's interest in the automatic functions cannot be limited by the narrow field of the actor's art. Of course, this interest will grow larger and encompass all spheres of human activity.

It's impossible to imagine the things we could do with advanced knowledge in this phenomenon. It will likely exceed our most fervent fantasies, just as our progress exceeds the bravest fantasies of cavemen. Drawing a parallel to the history of tools and machines, we can only say that once humanity steps onto this path, it will enter a new era of existence. The discovery of tools (and therefore all of our technology and science) was the first era, and this will be the second. The new era will open up before us such new worlds and new opportunities that anything described in mystical tomes will appear as lazy handicraft and child's play . . .

Note

1   Demidov is being somewhat modest when he states this here, and in other places. A careful study of Demidov's archive shows that, from the first day of his collaboration with Stanislavsky, Demidov introduced independent ideas, connected with the heightened state of an actor's creativity. Moreover, he continued to develop and teach this techniques to his students – sometimes "under the guise" of the Stanislavsky System. While using the system's terms, he nevertheless would put completely original meanings into these terms, and he would offer his own exercises and methods.

8

The Path to Becoming an Artist

The Path of Technique

How rampant are mistakes in theatre school auditions. They happen at every step. The recruiters, taken with one attribute that's useful for an actor – how somebody looks, or their excitability and emotionality, or their spontaneity and childlike naïveté, or their charm, or something else – decide that the examinees are talented. The naturally gifted youths think the same thing about themselves. But this is a woeful mistake.

In order to be an actor, it's not enough to have a single exceptional attribute. You *must* have (or get) several – each must merge with the others, each must enhance the others.

In order to be an artist, as we've already said, a person needs to have multiple unique qualities that harmonically play off of each other, and that ultimately result in a specific talent or an acquired proper technique.

Quality and technique (i.e. being a master of your creative apparatus, and of these qualities) become so entangled with one another (and they even grow out of each other) that they become indivisible. They develop together, and they function together, while you can't even tell where one ends and the other begins.

In this manner, you can develop quite a few qualities that have hitherto been in an embryonic state (because they are simply very rarely used) – for example, exceptionally *sensitive and acute perceptivity* related to the requirements of a given profession. Along with this, your physical and psychological apparatus acquires extraordinary responsiveness to impressions that originate from the realm beyond the conscious. And, finally, you get a sort of *"passivity"* – giving yourself over to the slightest of processes on which the essence of a given art form's technique is centered. As Kara said: "I essentially act involuntarily: my hands catch the balls and throw them *on their own, without my intellectual interjections.* As soon as I try to inject my intellect, instantly, the system is thrown off, and one of the balls hits the ground."

In this way, everything – quality and technique – becomes a single whole during its process: a certain acute state of working, in which technique at times turns into quality, and vice versa.

Once a person has gotten this new ability, it greatly influences his further development. A whole new world of sensations opens up before him. He sees everything with fresh eyes – more keenly, more deeply, more acutely, and more accurately. He thinks and wants in a new manner . . . He is a different person entirely. And he has additionally acquired the highest intellectual and moral qualities of an artist.

But!!! . . .

I must insert this addendum! I'd like to sear it in with letters made of fire: *only the right* work on your technique can lead you to full and wondrous results.

Here's how things work: if an actor's work is *incorrect*, then it ruins the actor's creative apparatus (destroying or damaging all of his sound instincts), as well as his soul's intellectual, moral, and aesthetic make-up. Nothing perverts an actor's view of his art as much as an incorrect technique – all of these "Buzzzzzz," "motor storms," "simplicity" without a living nucleus inside, "depictionism," "delivering the text to the audience," etc., etc . . . the whole rescuing collection of a craftsman's techniques. *It* is what instills ideas in an actor that his art is nothing more than a simple craft. And the more that an actor works incorrectly and veers from a true path, then the cruder he grows, and the more foolish he becomes with regard to his work. The more he loses any sensitivity to beauty, to its subtleties and nuances, then the farther he moves away from the high ideal that may have, at one point, flickered in his mind, in the beginning of his path.

Now, if he reads or hears anything about a higher mission of serving humanity via his art, then he's probably only capable of making fun of it. These strings no longer reverberate within him – they're torn.

"Broken Outer Shell"

Egoism, being stuck in the world of your own petty interests is always a very big obstacle to creating significant works of art. After all, it's nothing other than crudeness and pettiness of the soul; it's the removal of the great, big world from your life – a wall between you and a limitless horizon, a wall that keeps you confined within your own mundane little doghouse.

If this is your actor, and you are forced to give him big roles, then no matter how hard you work, how much you try to "unlock" him, you will never get to the depths of his souls, and you will never get any compensation for your efforts. In the darkest depths, there probably *is* something—every person has it—but it must be so far away, so deep, under such heavy locks, behind very thick walls, that there is no possibility of ever reaching it.

For a time, you'll lose sight of your actor . . . Later, you'll run into him and won't be able to recognize him: is it really the same man? So sensitive, so softened . . . like wax. You'll think, "Who is this, what great master managed to get through to his soul?" It turns out that the master is life – simple, everyday, life. It slapped him around as it had to, flayed him a few times, turned him inside out, and this opened up new windows inside him. He started to see and understand what would earlier evoke only boredom and scorn. And we know of so many cases when misfortune would give birth to a poet, and, having been "broken," a hitherto silent heart would find its passionate and inspired tongue.

However, catastrophes and misfortunate do not always mellow an egoist out and widen his horizon. Sometimes, after all the trials, he only becomes more embittered, more narrow-minded, and more egoistic. There are many egoists in the world, and it's a benevolent deed to break their outer shell.

But there is another kind of person too: they give off the impression of being most evil, egoistic, ungrateful, and crude – but in reality, they are completely different. Life has run them down, tortured, and embittered them to such an extent that they no longer see anything else in it, or want anything else from it.

I remember one such case from my childhood.

One day, in the suburban neighborhood where I lived, a shaggy, gaunt, angry, wretched little dog showed up. It would respond to any affection with threatening growling and a gaze full of such scorn that, even though the dog was small, you would become uncomfortable. You couldn't come near it – it wouldn't let you. If you threw it a bite of something, you'd have to remove yourself far away, and only then would it creep up to it while looking around, grab it, and quickly, without chewing, choking on it, swallow it whole. It would immediately run away, looking around to check if anyone was hounding it, if anyone was throwing stones at it or threatening it with a stick. Then, for some reason, it disappeared; it must have run off somewhere.

However, it turned out that it didn't – it was found in the woods beneath a bush. They thought it was dead, but upon closer inspection, saw that it was breathing. There was blood in a few spots – it didn't look like a fight, more like gun rifle wounds . . . it evidently crawled there to die . . . Eyes closed, barely breathing . . . They brought it some water in a dish – it sensed it, stuck its tongue into the cool water a few times – it seemed like it was coming around . . . They figured they would feed it – not likely! It howled, moaned in pain, and all the while, it keeps crawling, pained, wounded – just to get away from the people. They were forced to leave food for it and then leave. More or less, one day after another, our patient began to get better.

And one day, I decided to try to tame it. I came to its favorite regular spot, didn't come close to it, but sat farther away on a stump. But so that I could see her. I sat there in silence – it didn't leave – just continued to lie where it lay. I called it over – it continued to lie. Once more I called it, and again – it wouldn't move. I called it for a long time – said various affectionate words, but I didn't approach it myself – I was just sitting there, calling and waiting, calling and waiting . . . And suddenly and I see: she's looking, looking at me from afar, and suddenly, she made a small movement towards me – something must have stirred in its little heart . . . And I just keep sitting . . . calling . . . waiting . . . And it began to crawl. On its stomach. It crawled . . . howling pitifully and looking into my eyes: just don't beat me! Don't deceive me! . . . It shook all over when I petted it, closed its eyes and still waited . . . for a blow.

But I just petted it and kept saying: "Well, Dikan'ka, Dikarochka,[1] why are you afraid, you silly little dog? . . . Well?.. Well?.." She would shake, howl . . . she covered her face with her paws . . . finally, she calmed down, and I saw that tears were flowing from her eyes . . .

Afterwards, she was joyful, tender, devoted, playful, everyone's favorite, a frisky little dog with wonderful, transparent eyes, with a sense of humor. And only sometimes, in dreams, would she be returned to the nightmare of her past. She would moan, howl, obviously see visions of someone chasing her, beating her, choking her . . . Then you would call her, wake her up . . . She would get up, quietly walk through all the rooms, look around, smell everything familiar, as if checking whether she was in a dream . . . she would bump into your hand, you'd pet her. And after verifying that it wasn't anything real, she would go back to her bedding, heavily tumble onto it, make herself comfortable for a long time, and then you could hear how she would sigh deeply in relief many, many times – she was recovering from the frightening vision. Gradually, she would calm down and would quietly, peacefully begin to sleep.

Haven't you ever met people with a similarly tender and easily wounded soul? They seem crude, angry, dull, with such a hard "shell" that seems impenetrable. In reality, they don't have any shell at all and have never had one. People and life have made them so angry, scornful, closed off . . . They've tightened up, curled into a ball, and expect nothing but the worst . . . But to us, it seems as if they're villains and egoists at their core, incapable of seeing, hearing, understanding. Is beating them the right thing to do? Wouldn't it be better to show them affection? How many years might they be waiting for such affection? And you – once you see their true essence through the gloomy exterior – will *want* to show them affection. You won't even be able to hold back from showing it, from caressing them, warming them, encouraging them . . . Indulge . . . Don't hold back . . . Don't hold it back, yes, yes.

Conclusion

Not everybody who gets onto the path of the artist inevitably reaches a great conclusion to his work. Many people, unable to withstand the difficulties, and growing weary, leave this thorny, though glorious path . . . It's an especial shame when this happens to those who seem to begin their path as true champions: self-sacrificing, strict, virtuous, and seemingly with limitless energy. But . . . success, the delight of the audience, fans – alas, even they would become susceptible to them, and their previous beneficial doubts would be unnoticeably put to bed. They would become more agreeable, more condescending with regard to their demands of themselves; further efforts would seem unnecessary, and they would find their way onto a simpler, easier path. Everything would be done just for today, to meet the needs of their "generous" patrons.

But in losing their connection to eternity, they lost the ability to create anything for eternity. In short, they left the path of the artist. Their ideals, their sense of purpose, their strict demands didn't last for long. In actuality, it turned out that they were just disguised everymen and careerists. As soon as they got what they wanted, they stopped trying.

"No, enough!" many might be yelling. "We're tired of this hopeless extremism. Nothing's good enough for him – just give him more, more, and more!" This is true . . . For a first acquaintance, it's probably a bit too much . . . You're tired – take a break.

And . . . let's be quite candid with one another: don't exaggerate – I'm not calling for some unprecedented super-heroism, and I'm not requiring that everyone tirelessly attempt things that are out of their reach – I see things much more simply: I think that every one of us is either a volunteer or a deserter. And there cannot be anything in between.

An everyman or a slouch is a deserter. After all, everybody sees (as long as they don't forcefully ignore it) how much work there is to be done, and that everybody can do his part.

If you receive an idea, but become frightened, and turn away from it – you're a deserter.

Something flickers in your heart – you get up to do some good, necessary deed, but . . . prudence, deliberation – you're a deserter.

There's no need for any back-breaking feats. You just have to work, to create. But create *no less than what you can*. Create honestly and persistently. If you're tired – take a break, but don't seek a reason to desert.

Note

1 Translator's note: In Russian "Dikan'ka" and "Dikarochka" are both affectionate, diminutive names made up and derived from the word "dikiy" – "wild."

Book Two

Actor Types

Translated by Alexander Rojavin and Andrei Malaev-Babel

Actor Types

Any actor who has worked on a stage knows from experience that it's difficult for him to work with one director, but easy with another. One hinders, the other helps. The one – any advice that he gives seems foreign, unnecessary, it strains the actor's nature. The other is the opposite: anything he says is always welcome, everything is useful. It's as if his advice is the very thing that was missing – hoist those sails high and bring it home, no slacking off.

The solution to this riddle may be very simple: perhaps one is talented, the other is mediocre?

But the thing is that that's not the case. Both are talented. This one doesn't suit one actor, but give him another, and he does wonders.

Any director who has worked enough in his life has probably experienced the same thing. With one actor, everything meshes like clockwork, with another, it's like they're speaking different languages: you try to bare your soul to him, while he armors up, sets himself in his ways, complains, gets angry, and seems useless and talentless.

As a result of my personal directorial and pedagogical successes and failures, victories and defeats, willingly or no, I've established categories: it's easy for me to work with actors of a certain type – we easily understand each other, but with actors of *another* type, I can't make anything good happen, no matter how I try. He might even act relatively well, but that's not enough, it's not worth wasting time and effort for such "achievements."

When all is said and done, in my mind, actors can be broken down into four completely defined groups. And, before beginning to work on a play, I would first try to identify them, evaluate each – what type of a gift does he possess, which group does he belong to? Then, I would act accordingly. It's evident that the main divisor happens to be *the difference in their creative constitution*.

Let's try to show this difference with a simple, mundane example.

Imagine a birch grove, a small field, it's summer, good weather, sunny . . . A person comes and starts taking it all in. He sees everything, notices everything: every tree, every blade of grass – doesn't miss a thing . . . There's a woodpecker jumping along an old birch's trunk, as if dancing a folk dance . . . he stops and starts whacking away, as if with a hammer, with his long beak, bringing up a cloud of dust and dirt . . . There're half a dozen little ants dragging along some beetle, each one clutching it and trying to pull it in a different direction, only they're getting in each other's way, funny little buggers . . . And the-e-ere! A hawk is circling in the blue, just like an airplane . . . and the clouds, the clouds – what do they look like right now? Like a herd, like crowds of people – they roll over one another, subduing, consuming each other . . .

Upon his return home, this person has lots to tell. Thousands of things turned his attention towards them, nothing got past him. And it all left such an impression on him that he won't just retell it – he will, without a doubt, demonstrate it, show it all in movement, in action . . . how the little insect crawled along, how curiously the birch's trunk bent, how the mosquito ever so delicately emitted its song . . . And he'll show the woodpecker so funnily, how it banged away at the birch, that you'll keel over from laughter, and you'll muse to yourself – how is it that I didn't notice that myself, how it's so amusing, so funny?!

Another will come and will immediately start gathering berries, mushrooms . . . he'll weave himself a wreath from the flowers . . . he'll climb a tree, he'll sing, scream . . . He'll chase a butterfly . . . There's a river down the hill – he'll go take a swim and will start "doctoring" himself in a hurry: he'll tan, do some stretches, breathe deeply . . . he'll build a little dam or a bridge across the river, he'll start fishing – if he doesn't have any gear with him, his bare hands will do . . . He'll get together some kindling and start a fire. He'll remember some verses from Pushkin's *Gypsies* . . . he'll make some tea, eat some snacks, maybe drink a little shot – he's handy, he'd bring a little rucksack, maybe a backpack . . .

And he'll come home with arms full of little trophies: an armful of flowers, mushrooms in his hat, a necklace of lilies around his neck, and in the little satchel made out of his handkerchief – a hedgehog!

A third will come and . . . he won't run anywhere, but his soul will blaze up from joy, from the single, overwhelming feeling of happiness at life that is filling him to the brim . . . Calming down a bit, he'll look around, but even then, looking up at the sky, he won't be racking his brains over what that little cloud looks like and what can a hawk make out on the ground from such heights; in the sky, he'll see a never-ending multitude of worlds, eternity, and he'll get lost in them so completely that all earthly things will disappear for him.

Then he'll see the clouds, and the hawk . . . the clouds will seem alive to him: they speak to him . . . call to him . . . intimidate . . . promise . . . warn . . . The hawk, a barely visible dot in the blue sky will spark a thirst in him for limitless freedom . . . What can be more beautiful and intoxicating for a person than freedom – for he, who was born to think and create?! He hears the sound of nature everywhere and sees life and thought in everything . . . The wind shook up some branches – that's the birch welcoming him . . .

He'll come home, and . . . he has nothing to tell. "How excellent! Wonderful! Delightful!" That's all that you'll hear from him. And if you do manage to make him tell something, then he'll recount such things that if you, enticed by his stories, actually go there, then you'll only wonder: where did he get all of these ideas from? What wonders are there, what secrets, and beauties? Birches are birches, the sky is the same, mosquitoes are no different . . .

Here are three different people, perceiving their surroundings and giving themselves to them in completely different ways.

They are all fiery and acutely sensitive in their own ways, imagination plays a big role for all of them, they are all capable of being fascinated by something, to give themselves to their impulses, their feelings, and their fantasies. And this is exactly that which makes people suitable for art, especially the art of the actor. But however great the difference is in their perception of nature and in their reactions and impressions, the difference in their creative work is equally great.

We'll speak about each of them separately.

The First Type: THE IMITATOR

His main quality: an extraordinary impressionability to the external – to form.

Form is his preferred element.

He greedily and keenly notices not just the general, but all the little things and details as well. He captures them with an even greater distinctiveness. He does not just see and hear them – he feels them with his entire being. This characteristic of his propels him to constantly be showing, demonstrating, copying, presenting something, because in a conversation, he is not satisfied with just words.

If we were to speak about an actor, then these are the qualities that inevitably lead to mimicry, imitation; this type of actor can be called the *actor-imitator*. This distinguished ability to sense the very essence of the external expressions of the imitated persona, even something physical of his, inherent only to him, this ability to almost *reconstruct* himself into him is an inconceivable phenomenon. At a loss for other words, you can say only one thing: it's genius.

And how easily can this genius, using his wonderful gift, repeat Mochalov's or somebody else's inspired acting? But, alas . . . experience has shown that the imitator is only an imitator. After a few minutes, his acting reveals something false in it, some discrepancy between his inner character and the character which he took upon himself . . . The reason is in the superficiality: a tragic role requires prolonged internal concentration, and in this respect, the imitator is utterly helpless.

I remember one of the greatest of our actors (Mikhail [Michael] Chekhov) told me once that an actor must undoubtedly have, as he said, an "ape instinct" (a desire to mimic, to "ape"). For a few years, that bothered me . . . How could that be? If someone does not have this instinct, then is he not an actor?

Now, there is no mystery for me: the presence of an "ape instinct" in an actor points indubitably to only one thing – to the presence of the gift of imitation, but it says nothing of any great acting abilities. Sometimes, it is quite the opposite.

Not at all am I about to conclude that this here is a "talent" that is beneath human dignity and points to nothing but atavism – a return to the deep past, and the only ones who should be proud of it are apes. Not at all. In my opinion, it is a shame to waste any ability. How can it be bad that it's appeared again? Only, it shouldn't push out of the way something more important. On the contrary: we must grasp it, enrich it, combine it with other abilities, send it through the wringer of human thought, and then wield it in full.

The Second Type: THE EMOTIONAL ACTOR

He is not so much interested by the observation of various manifestations and curiosities of life as he is by simply *living* it, without overthinking and not losing any time: to act, react, give himself to his desires, combat obstacles, create, and in general, meld with his surroundings, enter them, get lost in them.

If this kind of person is an actor, then he will not have the need to "imitate" or copy somebody, anybody on a stage. What would that be for? It's uncharacteristic for him. It's significantly more pleasant for him to dive into the thick of a character's life circumstances. And once he's already there, the circumstances will swirl him around, and *life* will begin. If he isn't able to immediately enter a character's life circumstances and, as Shchepkin said, "step into the character's shoes," then he'll still aim to do just that, for such is his creative nature.

As a result, the following happens: "In his execution, the characterless colonel lives onstage with a piercing veracity, and for many minutes, you are ready to believe that it's not the actor in front of you, but the colonel himself, one moment charming in his boundless kindness, but another – disgustingly weak-willed" (Written by critic S. [1891: 127] in the *Artist* Magazine about Stanislavsky as Colonel Rostanev in *Foma* – an adaptation of Dostoevsky's *The Village of Stepanchikovo*).

The Third Type: THE AFFECTIVE ACTOR

This one isn't an observer or an admirer of form either. He too feels the need to *live*. However, in opposition to the second type, which so easily responds to external impressions and, in a way, fuses with his surroundings, this one is chiefly concerned with his *internal life*. It is as if he is removed from the external; he is in the power of his inner world.

He perceives the external world, of course. But very selectively: that which directly touches his inner world, he perceives distinctly, vividly – often, much more distinctly and vividly than it is in real life, but that which has no direct relationship with his inner world, he perceives diffusely, as if through a fog – in a way, it does not reach him.

This is why, overall, his impression of life does not coincide with reality – it is subjective (nothing can be done about this) – this is exactly how he *saw* and *heard* it. And he probably heard and saw it not because he is foolish and cannot interpret various events in life, but because a given fact of life (although it might be unimportant on its own) tugs on his deepest heartstrings, his secret thoughts, passions . . . It is enough for a fact to *remind* him of something even vaguely resembling what had occurred – a vivid feeling flares up and consumes his entire soul.

Add to this that his inner world is exceedingly sensitive and easily wounded, all it takes is a slight touch – and such a storm rises up that he himself turns into a frail vessel, which is harassed by the waves of his own insurgent sea. This is why he is called *affective*. (Affect is the condition of psychological excitement, which *reshapes the flow of calm human thought*. And the person becomes wholly under the will of utterly unbound feelings.)

In the depths of the affective actor's soul, there are always explosive masses, which are just waiting for the opportunity to explode. That's why, sometimes, for a seemingly insignificant reason, a person can become a raging fire, a storm.

Examples of this type: Mochalov, Aldridge, Mitrofan Ivanov-Kozelsky [1850–1898], Yermolova, Duse, Polina (Pelageya) Strepetova [1850–1903], Komissarzhevskaya. In other arts: Dante, Michelangelo, Schiller, Beethoven, Dostoevsky, and others.

★★★

Now, let's return to our birch grove and observe a newcomer. He comes with a small bundle and a thermos on a strap across his shoulder, looks around, calmly picks the most comfortable place, tries the grass – it's dry – and sits on it. Not without some pleasure does he assert that it's very picturesque, pleasant, and quiet. One can calmly sit, think, rest from the loud city. He takes off his tie, suit jacket, lies on the grass. The sky . . . clouds . . . a hawk . . . can it really see from such a distance? Clouds . . . beautiful . . . wonderful . . . fantastic . . . It's understandable, of course, that cavemen saw real monsters and spirits in them . . . And it's evident, it's like they're alive: they roll over one another, bump into each other . . . they breathe, caress one another, crush, consume . . . But in reality, they're just water vapor and snow. And it's not beautiful or comfortable up there – it's deathly cold, probably . . . the wind!

Various thoughts and worries start creeping into his head . . . He stops them: what for?! for what purpose?! Your brain needs to rest too! He feels the desire to take a swim – the river is so clear, so clean, minnows gambol around the bottom . . . But . . . is there any point to it? Swimming is nice when it's systematic, but just like this, you could even catch a cold. A shabby, old birch is hanging over the river . . . Maybe he should climb up on it, sit over the water? . . . But who knows, it might break – you'd crash into the water! Before heading home, he takes out a sandwich and an apple, eats, drinks some hot, sweet tea from his thermos, and, leisurely, goes to the train. At the station, he buys a small bouquet from a little boy for his sister and returns home in a timely manner.

Here's a man who can't not impress with his equilibrium, his harmony . . . . It is impossible to call him a coarse, insensitive man – he admired the beauty and poetry of the place, deeply and with great pleasure did he breathe the out-of-town air, full of the aroma of flowers and ozone. *And* he didn't forget about his sister: he brought her a little bouquet so that she could put it in a vase and feel the expanse of the fields. He is neither cold, nor dry. But his feelings are under his control – he allows himself to feel as much as is necessary. Given the chance, he is not averse to making a joke, maybe even having a lark, but everything in moderation, of course. He is just, objective . . . Yes, *objective* is the word. For he is to the side from everything, evaluates everything from the outside – this is why he is objective. The most important thing that rules over everything in him is a sensible practicality and self-possession.

Will such a well-balanced person devote himself to the ephemeral activity of an actor? Hardly. It's not really serious, and isn't even interesting. To act in some amateur production – that might do, might be useful for experience, to try it out. But to turn such a futile activity into the most important job in your life? That's not respectable. Though, of course, if it's well-paid . . . After all, not everything in life is exciting! And, heaven knows, sitting in your office all day long isn't a delight either, and yet, you have to. Finally, you don't *have* to love your profession and dedicate all of your thoughts to it! There's a family to think about, and your own needs and personal interests. If so . . . why not try it out? Especially since friends and acquaintances all approve – they say I acted at least as well as the others.

It's a bit inconvenient, though, that I can't lose my mind onstage as genuine actors must – I'm a bit embarrassed. Worst comes to worst, I can probably avoid the crazy roles. No need to stick my neck out. Calm, composure, a civilized nature, the ability to control yourself, good manners – all this is also important in theatre . . . God gave me intelligence, and I have plenty of willpower . . .

Tell me, don't we know actors like this – cold, even-tempered and rational? Instead of softness and tenderness, they have only the external signs of these feelings: a smile, musical, "velvety" notes in their voice . . . Instead of strength and temper – physiologically strained excitement, yelling, and *trembling* in their voice. Instead of honesty and truth – pleasantness and restraint . . . and ostentatious attentiveness . . . Do we not know such actors? There are many of them. Even moderately well-known and famous ones. This is the fourth type. We'll call him: the RATIONALIST.

Rationality and the Stage

So, imagine that such an individual will "dedicate" himself to art! What's more, to the art of an actor!

This is a person who is sober and "realistic," but on stage, the exact opposite must be true – everything is unreal, everything consists of fantasies and dreams! Nevertheless, this cold person (or rather, a dullard in disguise) goes into this hostile world of the actor's creativity. He goes there and leaves only in a few very rare cases.

How could this be? He doesn't have the most important thing: the ability to start a fire in his soul at a single thought, at a single word – he has no imagination.

Yes, he has none of these things. But he doesn't need them. Most of the time, he acclimates wonderfully and finds his place there. Moreover, he sometimes founds whole schools, entire movements in this art . . . he starts revolutions, of a kind. Why experience emotions onstage? It's enough to deftly play it *as if* you're feeling emotions . . . You'll get away with everything scot free. Especially if you are exceptionally cunning at forging emotions.

Emotional Attributes: Their "Structure" and Development. Perception and Reaction

In order to better understand the "structure" of a creative soul, of a creative apparatus, let's begin by investigating the main qualities of the psychological apparatus (the soul) of an infant. Schematically, they consist of the ability to feel, that is to perceive, and the ability to react, that is to respond to these perceptions. Reactions manifest themselves either as actions (movements) or as thoughts, or more commonly as both. Just as an infant's senses are primitive, so are his reactions: a "strange man" has picked him up – he starts worrying, squirming, makes a face, screams, starts pushing him away, tearing away . . . His mother comes in, takes him – he calms down, smiles, vocalizes his joy, grabs her nose with his little hand, her eyes . . .

Now, everything depends on the further development of these abilities – perception and reaction. If perception becomes more refined and sharp, then reaction will similarly sharpen and become more complex. If, however, the ability to perceive halts in its development or if something constantly gets in the way of the process of perception, then reactions will also be poor and primitive.

The ability to perceive can stop in its development on its own, or something can stop it from without. For example, at the sight of pretty scenes of nature, a child might react loudly with screaming, running, jumping, clapping – such is his involuntary reaction. However, if he is restrained, stopped, or if someone categorically forbids these "foolish" manifestations of joy, then his ability to perceive will steadily fade – since I can't be so happy, then there must be nothing to be happy about. An automatic braking system will form. Every subsequent time, this brake will function more and more strongly, and the ability to perceive will begin to fade and atrophy.

It follows from this discussion that a well-developed perception enhances a person's abilities to think and act. The more refined his ability to perceive and experience, the more refined are his thoughts, and so the more refined are his actions.

Both abilities, perception and reaction, are imbued in each living creature, and especially in a human. Similarly imbued is the ability to develop them. If exercised correctly, they can be developed and sharpened to a very high degree. But similarly, without any exercise, or for some other reason, they can stop developing at any stage, even at the very beginning.

Emotionality and Its Various Forms

In everyday language, the word "emotion" means "feeling." Emotionality is sensitivity, responsiveness, impressionability. That's how it probably is in reality: emotionality is sensitivity. Only it's necessary to keep in mind that a sense or a feeling is a complex concept. Emotionality encapsulates almost everything: feelings, immediate physiological reactions to them, thought processes, the organism's acclimation to these changes, and its responsive action . . . If we were to accurately and literally translate the Latin word moveo, then it would mean "I move." In psychological terms, the word "emotion" means exactly this complex process – a feeling, accompanied by highly complex movements inside the organism.

To one extent or another, everybody is imbued with emotionality. The degree to which we are all imbued with emotionality is different for each of us: some are very sensitive and responsive, others are less so. Emotionality, just as any ability, can be developed. But here too, one person is predisposed to developing it, another is less so.

But the degree of emotionality is the not the only difference – there are different kinds of emotionality as well. For example, in his first months of life, any infant will squirm, or push away, or maybe even lash out if you bring something unsavory or unpleasant to his mouth, and any infant, as has been said, will reach out, smile, if he sees his mother, who is desirable . . . This is to say that each infant is necessarily impulsive and instantly responds with an action to what he sees or hears or perceives in some other way. To bring this closer to our subject, each one actively participates in the life that surrounds him, or which, at least, comes in contact with him.

This is one kind of emotionality.

Similarly, in one's childhood, as soon as the infant starts to clearly see and hear, he'll start involuntarily mimicking what happens around him with his voice, hands, his whole body. This is how he learns the world, how he attempts to understand it. Everybody, in their childhood, is a little copycat, a little monkey that mimics everything. To bring this closer to our subject – everyone has the emotionality of *an imitator*.

And, finally, each and every one of us is capable to one extent or another to hide in himself the feeling of being hurt, of pain, longing, hope, joy, and hope . . . And every one of us can, because of something seemingly insignificant, suddenly unleash this hidden torrent of joy or tears and suffering. Which is to say that everybody has a small, dark corner of *affectivity*.

From these three kinds of emotionality (and maybe from some others that have yet to be observed and identified), an actor's individuality is formed.

One can imagine this sort of path and order of development: one of the three qualities – by virtue of predisposition or by virtue of some external force – develops, strengthens, and refines, while the others lag behind or maybe even stop. They stop altogether, maybe even after the very first steps. As a result, we get one or another emotional type: the actively-emotional, the imitator, or the affective. But they are all necessarily *emotional*. Only each one is uniquely different. Their art is fueled by their emotionality. Emotionality *is* that electrical energy that causes the metal wire of their creative lamp to light up.

Rationality (Reasoning): A Lack of Emotional Development

The fourth visitor of the birch grove is contemplative, practical, reserved. Although he has some emotionality, he has it in rather small quantities. The other three are almost like children, capable of forgetting themselves in their enthusiasm and capable of committing foolish acts, but this one apparently outgrew them by many years. Such calmness! Such reserve! Look at him: harmony and perfection! Where did he grow into such a sober and mature person?

Do not be fooled, however: this isn't maturity, it's underdevelopment. His growth has stopped. Rather, his entire emotional side has stopped. He only seems mature and smart, but it's the reverse that's true.

Imagine yourself in the company of a smart child. He might not just be smart – he is a philosopher, if you will. He deliberates a lot, tries to understand everything . . . Even now, he sits, silently and attentively listening to the adults' conversation . . . Why are they laughing? There is decidedly nothing funny here! What idiots! And this happens often! – more and more, he begins to earnestly despise adults. But really: he understands all the words, it's all clear to him – there is decidedly nothing funny there.

One can think: such seriousness, such concentration, he must be so gifted! But the reality is simply that his sphere of understanding is still remarkably poor. He does understand the words, but he is incapable of comprehending the complexity of events, the whole artful design of human relationships, the humor of what is going on. He likewise cannot pick up on the barely perceptible tinges and hues in the meanings of the words, how meaning changes depending on word order, differences in intonation. He cannot, because he doesn't know anything, not a single thing. But he thinks he knows everything.

This path of conclusions is the same one that is taken by any ignorant person, regardless of whether he is a child or an adult. Nobody makes judgments so dogmatically and categorically as the ignoramus, and nobody imagines himself such a know-it-all as the ignoramus. On the contrary, in fact, only the most highly developed and well-learned can be adequately careful and cautious in their judgments.

As his worldview widens, this very child begins to understand life and people and language more acutely, and bit by bit turns into that which he hinted at from an early age – that is, a philosopher who acutely feels life and thought and art. This example is taken from real life. This boy is now just that, a young man who is able to pick up on life's nuances and humor on the level of man far beyond his years, with an expansive intellectual reach, and with a very cautious approach to making judgments.

However, with our "sage" (the birch grove's fourth visitor), things turned out differently. His ability to make judgments (his reasoning) continued its development somewhat, but as for his emotional capabilities, they either stopped or abruptly fell behind in development. He isn't really fascinated by nature. Why? Only because he does not really see it. He looks at the birches and sees . . . only trees with white bark and green leaves. Another step in this direction, and he'll see only wood for the fireplace . . . His senses are not developed, not sharpened, and so his imagination remains silent.

This kind of person comes to a museum, looks at a painting, and thinks: this woman is rather well drawn . . . realistic . . . just like in life. Looks at the guide and, finding out that it's Raphael's Sistine Madonna, is surprised: really? What's the big deal? It's drawn pretty well, sure. But still . . .

He sees nothing.

Process and Result

Throughout the history of acting, there have been predominantly two directions. One seeks to *depict* life, the other to *experience* it (onstage).

Let's look at both directions close-up.

Puppet theatre can leave a big impression, maybe even bigger than that left by a human performance. Why? Because I, as an audience member, know ahead of time that everything here is conventional. I know that those are dead puppets in front of me, and so I am not awaiting any miracles (the puppets coming alive). My imagination endows them with the qualities of *seemingly* living beings. In a word, the same thing happens here which also happens with children during their games: they too "bring to life" dead objects and imbue them with any attribute that they want.

Let's keep going – a step higher. Let's look into the theatre where actors do not worry about artistic truth onstage, who don't even worry about believability, but are satisfied by nearly and roughly depicting the emotions that the characters ought to feel: they smile when they want to depict happiness, furrow their brows and clench their fists when they need to depict anger, etc . . . They scream when they need to play a dramatic scene, and make their voices sweet when the scene should be, in their minds, lyrical . . . In a word, they act like puppets, only with a better developed mechanism.

A single minute will pass before I, an audience member, will understand the simple mechanics of their "art," and, if it's not my cup of tea, I'll leave; if I want to stay, then soon, I'll start fleshing out their acting, which is to say that I'll start doing the same thing I would in a puppet theatre: I will experience their emotions and imagine *in their place.*

Let's step to the next level. We'll buy a ticket to a theatre where their acting isn't so garish and primitive. Here, the actors are more nuanced . . . Everything on stage is almost "real," all of their movements across the stage, their mimicry, all of their actions are staged according to the "logic of feelings." Everything seems very much like what we're used to seeing in real life, everything is "*realistic.*"

But still, we won't be deceived *only if we don't allow ourselves* to be deceived; we'll sense the false notes, we'll figure out that it's all just a skilled forgery. Oh well! At least the forgery is skillfully done. Now we can more easily give in to our fantasies and flesh out the sharp external falsification of the "masters" of this refined marionette art.

These refined marionettes walk around, talk . . . and everything is so microscopically worked out, with such "taste," with such a "sense of moderation" that soon, you forget and begin to believe that they really do feel, desire, think; in a word – they live as the characters should live . . .

But then one of the actors accidentally snags his foot on a rug, trips, and hits his hand hard on a table. He's in pain, his face grows red, he bites his lip . . . But he's still on his path and continues his "acting." But now, involuntarily, his body responds to some impulses that he can't control: his hand is in pain, his face twitches, he involuntarily touches the hurting spot . . . his body undergoes a process in spite of his will . . . This process has not been pre-established, and it happens on its own – as nature wills it, against the prescriptions of his craft. The marionette has come to life. It fought with this life, wanted to quench it, but life was stronger and never gave up.

Up to that point, the marionette was concerned only with executing drilled movements, delivering lines learned in a specific manner, and filling them with "verisimilar" "emotions." After he hits his hand, this concern doesn't diminish, it only grows greater: the pain broke his concentration, and he had to divert some energy towards ignoring the pain. But ignore it or not, the pain is still closer to the person than the learned semi-mechanical "acting."

And aside from his conscious, forced actions on the stage, the actor now has an *involuntary process* going on inside him: "It's painful . . . aching . . . could I have fractured the bone? . . . OK, I press it, now it's more painful . . . it even radiates to my shoulder and . . . my head's spinning . . . God damn that stupid carpet! . . . I need to get off-stage! . . . I need a doctor . . ."

There's the authenticity, there's life! Involuntary, natural.

It doesn't happen because we will it to, but of its own volition. We don't feel joy, sorrow, annoyance because we *want* to, because we *willed* ourselves to, but because such are the conditions of our life, such is our *being*. *Being* governs our consciousness, not the other way around.

And so, one actor, endowed with a prolific imagination, is capable of becoming so caught up in the circumstances of the play that he accepts them as his own and perceives them as if they truly were happening. In response to this, an involuntary response occurs: *life*. (An author's text and the director's notes (if only they are sensible) not only don't hinder the actor, but help him, like a well-tread path helps a pedestrian. It leads him.)

Another actor, incapable of such flights of fantasy, remains solely in the circumstances of his own personal life. For him, life onstage in the guise of another being is incomprehensible – he can only depict it with external gestures.

Let's say that there is a whole group of these depictors on the stage. There's even no need to look too hard – we can instantly see what they're doing, how they're living, these people who are acting up a little bit of something – they're primarily trying to show as accurately and expressively as possible whatever they found during rehearsal. We also see that they're watching the audience: is it "getting" it or no? Such is the obvious *process* which stems from their souls.

But here comes an actor on tour in one of his crowning roles.

An emotional or affective actor, like Fyodor Gorev [1950–1910].

I can see him in the *Old Landlord* (a 1873 drama by Alexander Pal'm [1822–1885]) as if he were right in front of me. It was in a provincial town. He was performing in the company of depictors.

He came onstage, and it was as if someone brought a candle into a dark room. The *truth* came out onstage. The "old landlord" came out onstage. A soft, kind-hearted, well-mannered, sensitive man . . . He's not trying to "depict" anything, to "play" anything, to "show" us, he's not even interested in the impression that we get out of it, his *process* of life is completely different – and we see it, this process, firsthand.

Our first impression is very strange . . . and possibly not even pleasant – we've grown so used to the falsities of the other actors that our souls cannot receive anything at first . . . And so you are somewhat uncomfortable for the first moments . . . Of course, soon, you adjust to it – the truth takes hold of us and enthralls us.

But here we see that our depictors, who felt at such ease with each other onstage, are also beginning to feel a bit, and maybe even significantly, uncomfortable. Judge for yourself: they delivered their lines into the air, received the same in response – everything was going smoothly, but here comes this man, this real, living, simple man, "the old landlord," and he asks them simply, amicably . . . looks into their eyes . . . and not with the usual glazed, unseeing eyes, but looks right into their souls . . . What can you do? And what is this "acting?" They aren't used to this, nobody taught them.

But there's nothing to be done about him! He won't be derailed now! Unwillingly, they start meeting his gaze, looking at him with similar eyes . . . His questions start tripping them up . . . They don't sound like those asked by an actor onstage, but unpretentious, like in real life . . . What should they answer him? All their lines have already flown out the window. It's a scandal! . . . But there's the prompter, feeding them the lines, and they're so appropriate and necessary – it's as if they fly off the tongue themselves . . . The actors pick up on this accidental truth, don't let it go cold . . . Something has changed in them, it's become easier, simpler, and at the same time, fuller, more comprehensible, and the scene starts cooking now that the actors are alive.

And this was all easily discernible from the audience. And the audience was happy for the actors. Today, instead of their usual process, the process of primitive depiction, they touched upon . . . or maybe we'll even risk saying it like this: they were drawn into the process of living onstage. The life of a character living in the circumstances of the play.

In such a manner, there is an *involuntary process* and the *external manifestations of this process*, or, as we like to say for time's sake: "*results*" (of this process).

"Results" can be different: from the most primitive "real life" forgeries to the finest ones.

The only things a wooden doll can do is bend, wave its arms, cross its legs, lie down, turn its head . . . A primitive actor can do more: he can depict on his face "the life of emotions" – honor, joy, sorrow, and whatever else he desires. No worries that it's all rough, harsh, schematic, and unconvincing – it's still better than the wooden marionette.

Finally, a more skilled actor can *depict the "process"* of life: he hears rustling . . . he grows wary . . . turns his head . . . searches . . . sees that someone is lying under a bush . . . he tries to make out who it is . . . he recognizes them . . . smiles . . . comes closer . . . etc. As if everything is real, everything is in order – that's exactly how it is in real life. But this isn't the *process*, this is only the execution of painstakingly chosen "*results*" of the process. Only a subtler lie – and nothing more. *Only the dead "verisimilitude."*

In the acting of an IMITATOR and a RATIONALIST, you won't see any *process* onstage – you'll only catch the *result*. Process isn't in their power.

Process is the privilege of the other two types of actors: the EMOTIONAL and the AFFECTIVE.

With regards to the question of process and result, it's worth saying a few words about form.

Usually, you hear and read about how actors should be divided into two categories: those who move from form to content, and those who go from content to form. And it's assumed that the result will be the same for both of them: form will become infused with content or content will express itself in form.

Actors really can be divided into two categories (it's not for nothing that they war amongst themselves), their very nature divides them, but not because ones are followers of form, while others are devotees of content; it is because ones are capable of *giving themselves over to the process onstage*, while others can only *depict the result*.

As for the words "form" and "content," they got into the mix here only because of a misunderstanding. In a real (not a false) work of art, form cannot be separated from content, nor content from form: anything that has authentic content has a corresponding form, and that which has an *artistic form* has appropriate content.

The actor that *wholly and entirely* gives himself over to the process will inevitably uncover an expressive form.

Here are two accounts of Mochalov's performance of the same scene from Nikolai Polevoy's tragedy *Ugolino* [1838]. (Mochalov played the role of Nino):

When they kill Veronica . . . offstage, and Nino is coming down the hill, singing and almost jumping in joy . . . he calls for his wife . . . looks for her . . . saying, "I know, she's a trickster, she's probably hiding . . ." and walking into the house, he sees her, killed . . . Oh, then . . . you can't even express in words what happened to him! . . .

. . . Sometimes, he would run joyfully into the house; then he would scream so frightfully, and, having walked outside, direct his gaze to the open door. Quietly . . . quietly backing away, he would whisper with his melodic voice: she died . . . she died . . . He would repeat this word, crossing the whole stage, as if wanting to convince himself; finally, he would stop and yell out, "Murdered!," his face covered with *true tears*. A long silence would follow – because the audience would be crying with him, and no one would applaud.

And sometimes, he would dash across the whole stage, and stop right in front of the audience . . . Looking at them with his dulled eyes, he would ask: she died? . . . she died? . . . and then, as if answering himself, he would say: "Murdered!" and fall into a rage and despair! [Orlova–Savina 1994: 143]

. . .Having entered the house and seen his murdered family, Nino returned to the stage, mad; in one performance, Mochalov did this: with a deranged smile, he ran out of the house, crashed to the ground, and scrambled across the stage on all fours, while the audience went numb from horror . . . [Sadovsky 1889: 45]

How Depictors Are Made (A Necessary Elaboration)

And so we have two movements in theatre - experience or depict, as if you are experiencing. Theoretically this is so.

But in practice, we get a fairly unexpected picture: actors, who, based on their capabilities and their dispositions and their convictions, should be adherers of the principle of experiencing, often turn out to be the most inveterate imitators, and if you look at it under a microscope, the army of actors turns out to be 95–98% full of imitators of different sorts.

How did this happen? This deserves a closer look.

One of the most common objections against experiencing is that an actor, when becoming totally immersed, forgets himself to such an extent that his own temperament gets the better of him. He becomes semi-deranged. In such a state, he might very well do something on stage that he himself won't be proud of afterwards.

Oh, if only it were like that! If it were true, it wouldn't bother anyone. After enough repetitions, the actors would inevitably become *accustomed* to this new condition and *orient themselves in it*. What's more: they would eventually **learn to control it**, and that would be just perfect.

The *real* problem is different. The problem is that nobody has this heat. Everyone is too cold. This very coldness, as well as the **lack of approaches to one's own creative instrument (the inability to tune it correctly)**, forces actors not to rely on experiencing emotions and accidental successes during rehearsal, forces them to choose the easier path of depiction. [It's worth discussing the following somewhat delicate position. An actor who is inclined to succumb to the abandon just described should not fancy that he is in possession of some unbridled temperament and an ardent imagination. Rather, he should think that his nervous system is in quite a pitiable condition and that he should tell these symptoms to a pathologist or a psychiatrist. This "creative" phenomenon has more to do with their competence, not at all with the realm of the actor's creative inspiration. Creative state, let alone inspiration, is primarily the harmonious apex of the actor's entire physical and psychological powers. It is the highest stage of his health and might. As for derangement, disorientation and complete abandon – these are the signs of pathology. – *Author's Note*]

Here's another obstacle. As it seems to him, the actor "experiences emotions" onstage, he is moved . . . But the audience isn't satisfied, it says: it's a weak performance, uninteresting. The actor's first thought: they don't get it, they're dumb . . . I was immersed, I really felt those emotions, that's a fact: even my heart was beating quickly. It must be that the audience is bad. After a while, he hears the same response to his acting from people that he usually listens to . . . Here, he begins to have serious doubts: "maybe it's true that when you feel emotions on stage, it's not as lucid as I thought up to this point . . . maybe 'experiencing emotions' really isn't the best way to affect the public? . . ." At this thought, many actors crack and become out-and-out depictors.

But in the meantime, the reason for the actor's failure here is completely different: the thing is, the actor is simply *inhibited*.

For a person with vivid emotions, every feeling instantly gives birth to a movement (a reminder: the word "emotion" comes from the Latin word *moveo*, which means "I move"), and so, every feeling inevitably results in external actions or apparent changes in facial expression. An emotional actor is very spontaneous and reactive. We decidedly *see everything that happens inside him* – he's somewhat *transparent*. For the stage, such "transparency" is good. But is it good or convenient for *life*? . . . Is it really a good idea for everyone around me to see exactly what I'm thinking and feeling? . . . And in this manner, the person develops a beneficial braking system. This development begins since childhood . . . After all, you can't do everything that you want. Usually, you want something, but can't have it. And so, the braking system is developed . . . When all is said and done, even though I'm emotional, not a single movement, not a single feeling will arise, not one thought will leave me spontaneously or freely – everything will be cold, curbed by the control of my "upbringing."

As such, I'm well-defended against any of my childish hi-jinks and am quite ready for everyday customs. But, having won one battle, I lose another: for the stage, I become completely *inexpressive* – too careful, reserved, and, as they say, even cold! And meanwhile . . . onstage or in classes, I often hear: "too pale," "I don't get it," "not theatrical . . ."

It turns out that even though I'm emotional, I'm very "closed," "tense," "inhibited!" The play's circumstances move me, but apparently, first of all, without *even suspecting this*, I *don't admit them to me*, and the ones that do reach me do so with a reduced effect, and second of all, *I inhibit the expression of my feelings*. They remain hidden, unseen, and, of course, I can't satisfy the audience.

What to do? How can I fix this?

Some, who are more talented and stalwart, are saved by their decisiveness, determination, and dedication to their ideal. After many years of hard labor, they developed some techniques that helped them enter into the truthful creative state. That state allowed them to perceive circumstances as authentic and true. Repeating it often, they would get used to this condition of authenticity, and it would become second nature to them. Many great actors did it this way, without a teacher − or rather, practically all. Garrick, Aldridge, Shchepkin, Prov Sadovsky [1818–1872], Yermolova and Duse.

It's a difficult job, truly heroic, without exaggerations. Not just anyone can do this. And so, despite all their talents, one after another, the actors slip and find themselves on the easy little road to depictionism.

And it'll continue like this until the time when the scientific thought of a physiologist or a psychologist sheds light upon this problem, and the art of the stage moves beyond mere craft. In short, things won't change until there is a *true, indisputable school of theatre*.

★★★

How will an *inhibited emotional* actor behave in the birch grove? Just like any other spontaneous person, on a hot summer day, in full view of the river, he too will probably want to take a swim. Another would simply throw off his clothes and, without much thought, throw himself into the water. This one functions differently: every thought, every passion that arises doesn't result in a movement or an action, but in a halt: *stop!* You want to swim! You can already feel the pleasant coolness of the water, your hands are already reaching for your belt and your buttons . . . Stop! Should you really do this? You want to climb up the old, bent birch tree over the water . . . Stop! Should I or shouldn't I? And this happens everywhere with everything: the first thing that rears its head at any thought or desire: stop! The first thing that happens immediately turns the brakes on.

Doesn't he remind us of our old friend − the prudent rationalist with the thermos slung over his shoulder? These two boots seem to make a pair. In some respects, that's exactly how it is.

But there *is* a difference between them, and it's a very big one. We are interested primarily by the difference in their prospects as actors (and it's very big). That's exactly what we'll discuss here.

The rationalist, when it comes down to it, has a smooth temper − without any leaps or surprises. He too doesn't spend a single minute without his brakes on, and doesn't take a single step without thinking about it − should he, can he? − but since he is not burdened with emotionality (he does have it, but in such a small amount that it can be ignored), he doesn't have to expend too much effort in curbing it (he's innately cold and dullish).

As for the emotional actor, his emotionality isn't destroyed completely, and his imagination and ability to give himself over aren't dead either. This is why he's capable of surprises.

In an actor's work, this manifests itself like this: everything is uninteresting, it's at one-tenth strength, it's too small, shallow − verisimilar, rather than authentic . . . Suddenly, during a random rehearsal or some noncritical show − it's so good, everything comes so easily and freely that you can't believe it − anyone would wish to act like that. You look at it and think: no, think what you will, but that's a gifted person! But why does this gift hide, when he needs it the most?

But regardless of how great the difference is between the rationalist and the inhibited emotional actor, regardless of how often his watchful guards—his brakes—let him out, neither is very suitable for the *art of experiencing* onstage. Not just to their depths, but they are unable to feel anything on an external level either.

At home, in solitude, the unfortunate "emotional" actor might sometimes be reciting some poetry, or his favorite role, and then might get so emotional − a rare touring star could compare with him. It seems like it's all there: the emotionality, the freedom, the imagination, the talent altogether – it's almost there! But when he needs it – it's gone. What remains is coldness, emptiness, and restraint . . .

Is there some way to get out of this mess? Is there a way to get around the malicious brakes?

But, of course, there is a way out: re-training. Or rather – continuing with training, and leading it to *completion*.

The brakes that are acquired because of the demands of life, they can stay – they're necessary, and the energy expended on acquiring them weren't a waste. It's a capital and useful gain. But now it's necessary to build something above this permanent building – a mezzanine, if you will.

This superstructure amounts to the newly created *conditioned reflex*. The latter manifests itself in the following way: when one sets about engaging in an actor's creative work, to say nothing of when one gets onstage – one must throw off the shackles of the brakes, throw away the everyday "prudence," and not get in the way of imagination and involuntary reflexes. In an actor's work, allowing yourself to do so isn't just permissible – it is essential. This is the whole point of our work, and our only salvation.

Otherwise, you'll pop out of the actor's creative atmosphere like a cork out of water. [It's necessary to say that this is an interesting phenomenon: a person who's gone through such a school (it'll be described in the next book), noticeably changes for life as well. Close ones and family members typically say: he's become slightly different, simpler, more spontaneous, more responsive and sensitive. In this way, new habits seep down into the "permanent building." Without ruining it, they expand and enrich it. – *Author's Note*]

Aside from restricting orders, orders that limit – there are opposite orders as well, orders to do something. You don't want to get up, you didn't sleep much, who cares! it's time! get up, don't think about it, that's it! And you get up. Or you're tired, you can't keep walking, you'd rather sit . . . but you HAVE to! And so you go on, stumbling, but you go on.

And so, there are two kinds of orders (imperatives), one which stops, forbids: *you can't! stop!* One which propels: *you have to! do it!*

The described rationalist and inhibited emotional actor live without really giving in to their innate desires or needs as much as they listen to the orders: YOU CAN'T and YOU MUST. These two orders replace everything: desire, needs, independence, freedom . . . Such rationality is highly undesirable for an actor's work. Then again, a person who controls himself so well should hardly bat an eye at such trifles: can't I overcome this rationality and inhibition within myself (if I want this!)? So what if it seems difficult or if I "can't do this" – I MUST, therefore it will be done.

However, it turns out to be much more difficult than that. To order himself *not to do* what he wants, like not going for a swim despite wanting to, or even the opposite: to *force himself* to swim despite it being cold and not wanting to, he can do that. In a word, to force himself to *do* some action – that's possible. But to force himself to fill up with one emotion or another – that's not an action! In the meantime, the author has clearly written – "sadly," or "in despair," or "passionately," "through tears," "while laughing." The author had an easy time writing it, but to actually do it . . . It's possible to evoke in yourself some ambiguous feeling, quite distantly reminiscent of one emotion or another. But is it really love or hatred? If bad theatres are satisfied with this, then it only means that to limit yourself in such a manner is the same as calling yourself a lousy actor . . . good actors don't "almost" experience things, they feel them to the core . . .

So how does one evoke the necessary feelings?

In life, there's no need to worry about this. In life, feelings arise on their own. They take over a person . . . And they leave the same way they come. There's no need to worry about either process. Here, onstage, it's different. You try, try, order yourself, try – but nothing works . . .

A persistent person will look for a way out: how *can* I find this elusive feeling? how can I rouse my dormant *creative* soul?

Those Who Depict and Those Who Live

Let's imagine the following situation: I want to tell you something. In order to do it in as clear and vivid a manner possible, I accompany my words with the "impersonation of characters." Unconsciously, I fill in the gaps left by my words — with movements, facial expressions . . . If need be, I imitate the voice, intonation and gestures of those involved in the fascinating scene I observed.

What is this? Doesn't it remind us of theatre? I'm not *just* telling a story — I'm "acting out" the whole scene in front of my audience.

"Acting out" consists of two processes (and both processes flow through me simultaneously — the first: I remember how things happened and recount it, and the second: I observe the audience, the person that I'm telling this to: does he see what I want him to see? Does he understand exactly what happened? Does he get it?

That very same urge — the desire to tell the audience some entertaining or didactic story — inspires the actor to do his work. In order for the story to be more clear and interesting, the actor doesn't do it alone, but gets into a group with others, and each of them "acts it out in character."

It would seem like that's all.

But no. Theatre itself, the conditions that come with an actor acting out some role or other in front of an audience, carry with them the buds of a completely new and fundamentally opposite process. It all began with the desire to "show," "depict," but all of a sudden, the role carried them away. They got so carried away that they forgot about the audience (they stopped keeping track of whether "they get it or not"), forgot that they have to "depict," and simply *felt like they were their character.* Perhaps this abandon lasted for only a quarter of a minute, but it took place . . . As it turned out, that part of the show, done with such feeling, left the biggest impression on the audience. There you have the beginning of another theatrical principle and another goal for the stage actor. And it's accompanied, of course, by a different kind of the actor's creative "*technique.*"

And so, the paths were set to diverge.

Actors who were more likely to get carried away and become immersed in a role to the point of partial or complete abandon naturally took this second path. Actors for whom such immersion isn't characteristic to such a great extent were left on the first step of depictor-imitators. They didn't become defenders of feeling, but of the verisimilar depiction of feelings (results).

But, of course, both groups, on their separate paths, set about to perfecting their respective crafts and techniques. This involves a massive amount of work on the part of theatre designers. This involves the incredibly skillful imitation of sounds — the wind, rain, thunder, trains, gun-shots, etc. This likewise involves crafty lighting, which, at will, creates onstage: day, evening, night, and setting and rising sun, fire, lightning flashes, cannonades, etc. It also makes sense to add to this list the art of makeup and costume design, which makes people thin, fat, hunch-backed, old, young, beautiful, horrendous, etc., etc. And, finally, this list also needs to include the gradually perfected art of the actor-depictor — to be able to adeptly copy life.

Although our sympathies lie wholly with those who "live on stage," although we see theater's bright future only with them, we have to give the depictors their due. After all, the "art of experiencing" is only being born, while imitation has many centuries behind it. The majority of actors in the whole world, with very rare exceptions, belonged and currently belong to this type – the depictor-imitator. One should not be fooled by the fact that some of them sometimes give in to immersion on stage and forget themselves – abandon that lasts for a second means very little. These are sparks, accidental flashes and nothing more. They bear witness only to the fact that, *given a proper school*, this actor *might* develop a proper emotionality.

Even the theaters that were the first to adopt the mindset of battling "presentation" (a.k.a. imitation), without even noticing it, they plunged right into the very same presentation, and have since been occupying themselves with nothing if not imitation. Let them consider this thoughtfully and seriously. They will see that this is so without too many difficulties. They can, of course, fool themselves . . . but, really, is it worth it?

Experience has shown, however, that the audience always gives the palm of victory to the actor who is *experiencing* onstage. The great masters of this kind of acting, like Garrick, Aldridge, Duse, and others, never have any "catastrophes" – while experiencing intense emotions, they can still govern their feelings.

And as soon the school of the *emotional and affective actors* crystallizes, so will the glory of the imitator's craft begin to fade.

Distinct Qualities of the Four Actor Types

We have identified four clearly distinct creative actor types. It seems that they have nothing in common, that they should be unable even to understand one another . . . They war, despise each other . . . But the whole time, like a team of four horses, hitched to the carriage that is theatre, unanimously or otherwise, they keep on galloping. Quite often in their zeal, they flip it into a ravine or force it into a boggy quagmire for a long time . . . In general, though, despite the zigzags, despite the delays, despite the occasional double backing, despite the breakdowns – they keep going and they keep theatre going.

We spoke about how they are categorized by their attitude towards the principle of "experiencing," and that of "depiction" onstage, but it's necessary to discuss their unique qualities, regardless of such a categorization.

The Imitator

When you meet a talented imitator, he will undoubtedly prove to be an instant source of charm and interest for you. He has one incredibly useful weakness: he loves to tell a story. Loves it so much that he can't keep it inside. And he acts it all out. And he'll doubtlessly tell you something on the spot. He might tell you a little trifle: how five minutes ago, he was walking down the street and saw a respectable lady with a dog . . . What were the comical situations that followed, and how embarrassed and upset the respectable lady was . . . It's a trifle, but he'll tell it so well that it's as if you're seeing it for yourself, maybe even better than if you had seen it with your own eyes. He'll relay everything so livelily, clearly, colorfully . . . you see the lady, and the interested passers-by, and the ill-fated little dog, and the scary, ill-mannered hound . . . and all the details that he describes with his sharp tongue. Details that you would have probably missed.

You look at this person and are amazed: so talented, so marvelous, he's so observant and subtle. What biting humor! He's so clever. Now this is a real actor! This is what art should be: festive, dazzling, sparkling, like champagne. When you see such an actor-imitator's rehearsal, especially if he's also the director – then you understand what hefty, in-your-face "theatricality" truly means. He's a master of form. He is out of his element when digging around in psychology – instead he creates such a keen form that it acts by itself. It's so rich, so sharp, so daring. Form is precisely what he puts all of his fire and creativity into.

His forms are special: condensed, caustic, with salt, with pepper, with mustard – it sears you to your soul. Let's say the actor is playing an adulatory and subservient man – the director will, no doubt, take this subservience and drive it to its extreme: it won't be a man walking across the stage, but *subservience* itself: all of his movements, postures, gestures are such that it seems like he'll explode from his subservience, fly apart – legs in one direction, arms in another: that's how badly he wants to serve everyone. The director will make his makeup such that his face will be partitioned, sectional: everything is sharp, everything is directional – sharp eyes, sharp nose, sharp lips – it's not even a person, but a thousand bolts of lightning: he wants to please everyone, serve everyone, manage to be everywhere . . .

Oh, and how he'll manage the simplest of scenes, one that doesn't seem promising at all!

An old clerk, the head of the office, is summoned to his boss. So what? You'd think it was the simplest of scenes: he gets up and goes. But no! This is too primitive and says nothing.

This clerk clambered out of his lowly roots via subservience and bootlicking. Now he's important and unapproachable, especially with those that need his help. Now we bear witness to a scene in the office, where this throned nobody has reached the height of importance and apery before his employees. But here he receives a summons to his own chief's office. His importance instantly crosses all human boundaries: this isn't a clerk any more – it's Jupiter himself. He preens and steps out . . . Here, the director does something really genius: using nothing but external strokes, he uses this walk to the boss's office to depict this "Jupiter's" insignificance and the primitivity of how he attained his status.

While he's walking to the boss' door, he undergoes a complete transformation: the first steps are taken by a great "Jupiter," but with each step, his "divinity" gradually slides off, the clerk becomes simpler, more modest . . . taking a look at the boss' door, he shrinks and, little by little, begins to bend from deference, his steps become soft, delicate – he is before a sacred place . . . and, finally, it's not a man that walks through the door, but rather an slimy worm that crawls through.

Is it good? of course it's good, it's more than that – it's excellent.

It's strange, though, why such a great and interesting artist should be called an *"imitator."* Imitation is perfect reproduction. What reproduction is there? On the contrary, here, the most typical features are taken, driven to the limits, to the height of expressivity . . . This is a pure act of artistic creativity.

But are we saying that the imitator can't be an artist in his own right? It's just that his mode of art is *external manifestations*, an expressive form. The word itself can confuse: *imitator* . . . Yes, the word isn't very pretty. But there's nothing to be confused by. – How do we interpret life? And how, by what means, do we *understand it!* One of the most frequent means by which we understand life is *mimesis*.

Say a pedestrian is crossing the street. A car zooms around the corner. The pedestrian doesn't see it, he's busy reading the sign on the store on the opposite side of the street. The car honks . . . The pedestrian doesn't hear it. The car tries to brake, but skids across the snow . . . knocks the pedestrian over. – Don't you feel like the car didn't hit just him, but you as well? As if *your* heart joined in with his and also went still, and you shrunk into yourself . . . on the ground . . . under the car? . . .

This might last for just a second, and then you'll either scream in horror and nearly lose consciousness, or you'll run to save the ill-fated pedestrian, or you'll observe what happens next with greedy curiosity, or, so that your psyche isn't overloaded, you'll turn away, try not to pay any attention and walk by the scene . . . In a word, the very next second, you'll behave in a manner that's characteristic to you. But the *first second* will be the same for most: you're watching, unwillingly empathizing, putting yourself in the pedestrian's place, and by these means, *by means of mimesis* (a.k.a. *imitation*), you understand what happened.

Once time has passed and the impressions have cooled, an emotional actor will tell you *what exactly* happened at the moment of the accident, and then how it all progressed: they got the injured out from under the car, took him away in an ambulance, he has a family, etc. He'll tell all this with complete sympathy and an understanding of the weight of what just happened.

At the thought of what happened, an affective actor will be shocked by some horrible detail: either the soul-rending scream, or the crack of bones (neither of which might never have actually happened, but . . . that's how he remembers it).

As for the one that we call the imitator, he won't turn our attention to *what exactly* happened while recounting it, but *how it all happened*. As if the most important thing wasn't the heart of the matter, but the external form. And he'll undoubtedly show you who was standing where, and how some person waved his arms, and exactly how (funnily or horribly) the injured man got mucked up . . . It's all − how, how, how, and how! Judging only by these *hows*, you're required to deduce what they thought and what they felt. First and foremost, *he is an observer*. Of all things, his perception picks up on the *external manifestation − on form*.

The Emotional Actor

A good emotional or affective actor achieves the point when the audience, as they look at the stage, see not the actor, but life itself − authentic life and real, authentic people.

Probably, some readers will think: "Life? . . . then this is a formless, amorphous show, as formless as self-flowing life itself . . . How can an audience derive any pleasure from a show like this? What's the point of everything being 'alive'? A pile of plaster arms, legs, noses, chins, be they done very well, still do not add up to a statue. So does a collection of unconnected scenes, be they ultra-alive, fail to become a show − for now, it's just a tangled mess."

One must remember that life in a show follows the plan created by the author-playwright. Therefore, if an actor has read the play carefully, there cannot be a mess. On top of that, if you watched, listened, and understood everything, then the form was convincing enough as well.

What it's like and how it is achieved are easily enough understood after reading a review like this:

> Moliere's Argan was a living character − as profound as life itself. The actor completely immersed himself in the imagined character's life and drew the audience in with him, into all of its chaos, and even its complexity. He brought the audience closer to the worries and concerns of this man, who is funny, but often deserving of pity, as foolish as he is good-natured, as capricious as he is kind. From top to bottom, Stanislavsky held the audience captive with his charm. And by immersing himself into his character's soul, he found Moliere's style, along with everything necessary for a truly artistic performance. [Demidov retells a review by Natan Efros (2007: 484–485).]

If we have seen enough shows and actors − then how do we look at the stage? We see both, the good and the bad. We derive pleasure from the art of the actor itself. We say: he (the actor) played that so well! He said those words so well! And we'll immediately follow up with displeasure: but *this* was weak, bad, talentless.

But when the stage plays host to real, authentic *truth* − then regardless of how big of an expert we consider ourselves and despite all our attempts to retain a critical gaze − one fine moment, the *truth* knocks us off this position, and we'll begin to regard the actor not as a "master" or an "artist," but as a real person. Which is to say that we'll regard him as we would do it in ordinary, real life. Do we look for showiness, form, vividness in life? No. We look at *life itself*, we look at different events, we look at *what happens*. That's exactly how we watch a show when good emotional or affective actors take the stage in their finest roles.

Is the form sharp enough? Vivid enough? Could it be sharper and more vivid? I don't know, maybe. That's not what interests me. I've seen real people . . . I've lived with them, suffered with them, celebrated with them . . . To discuss the acting of this actor or that one, discuss the form, the structure of the show or play not only doesn't interest me, it's even unpleasant: it kills all impressions. Those weren't actors – those people were close, dear to me . . . I want to see them again tomorrow: that's how familiar and human they are to my heart.

The Affective Actor

The MAT had an actor – Leonidov. A good actor: he played very realistically, honestly. Didn't really stick out from the leading actors of his theatre.

That's how he was. Then, all of a sudden – he gets the role of Mitya Karamazov.

That's when we truly saw him for the first time. Could it be the first time since Mochalov that our Moscow stage has heard such authentic, heroic, tragic male passions, without a hint of false pathos or straining?!

Is that even an actor? Could it be a never-before-seen creature in the theatre? The "Mokroye village" act was over – the hour and a half flew by so quickly that nobody even noticed. Aside from the awe that everyone experienced, we all had a question: what was that? An actor? Acting? Theatre?

The curtains have fallen, you're sitting there, at a loss for words, and you can't, you just *can't* wrap your mind around it: how did that happen? What is there in common between the stage and – this?

There is a unique phenomenon: a detonation velocity.

The powder depot is a dangerous place, surrounded by incredibly tall stone walls, armed guards on all sides so that nobody could even come close. They guard it so well that you can be at ease: there's no danger. And the depots are located significantly far from each other – also for safety purposes. And then, for a trivial mistake, a spark gets into one of them and . . . the depot lights up the sky.

What about the others? They explode too. One after another – it's over!! The tremors are so great that they sweep aside all obstacles, and boom – up into the air!

Same thing here. Each one of us has erected enormous walls about himself. There are guards [our braking system] that don't just protect our sanctuaries from people – they won't even let anyone approach the outer gate. Everything is quiet, calm, and dead . . . And then suddenly, inside each of us, a colossal, unprecedented detonation takes place as a result of sympathetic shock . . . Everything flares up, and just like that – no walls, no roofs, no guards!

The "Mokroye" act caused a detonation exactly like that. A benevolent catastrophe I was never ready for, and couldn't foresee or predict . . . You sat there, indifferent, protected from life's wounds by armor forged of restraint, and now . . . you're sputtering from the aftershocks, scorched by your own flames, which you never even suspected in yourself. Such is the strength of an artist of great, authentic inspiration. What could compare to it?

You can't remain seated during the intermission of such a "cataclysmic" performance: you walk down the hallways, the atrium, up and down the stairs, the whole time looking into other people's eyes, while the others, equally excited, are looking for yours . . . People wonder out loud: how could that be? . . . Did that really happen? And each person carries with him the remains of the healthful explosion, everybody's eyes are on fire: me too, me too! I have the powder too! And everybody is happy, everyone is eternally thankful to the great artist.

The thing is, it's true that everybody has powder – it's just that one has half a pound of it, while another has a whole barrel – tons. When those tons explode, that's when a new artist is born.

Only after a shock like that does it become clear why great artists always appear in groups: if Pushkin hadn't "exploded," there wouldn't have been a Gogol or a Mikhail Lermontov [1814–1841]. In painting – a glorious group: Leonardo, Michelangelo, and Raphael with their disciples. Mochalov exploded a whole wave of talent in his wake. That wave rolled over all of Russia. (Ivanov-Kozelsky, Strepetova, Yermolova, Komissarzhevskaya, Mamont Dalsky [1865–1918], and others).

But what about Leonidov? Who lit *him* up?

Who lit him up? The director, evidently. At least, if the director is a true artist in his field, then who else could the "firebug" be but him? Although, maybe the actor detonated on his own, having felt the echo of the explosion in Dostoevsky's soul, and the director was tactful and smart enough not to get in his way.

"It's interesting to recall," Leonidov [1960: 217] wrote, afterwards, "that the 'Mokroye' scene had only seven rehearsals. Vladimir Nemirovich-Danchenko said that there's no need to grate everyone's nerves any longer."

But explosions, flights . . . does it even make sense to talk about them? That's all just inspiration! Doesn't it come and go as it pleases?

Yes, it's inspiration. Yes, it comes and goes. But all the same: it happens to one, but another never experiences it. Some experience it *often* and *for a long time*, but others . . . only in their dreams. Some have *grown into it*, while others don't even suspect that it can visit us like a

Figure 14 Leonid Leonidov as Mitya Karamazov in the "Mokroye" scene; Moscow Art Theatre's production of *The Brothers Karamazov*, 1911; Vladimir Nemirovich-Danchenko, dir. Courtesy of Andrei Malaev-Babel.

frequent and familiar guest. They're rational skeptics who have become convinced in their years of experience that it's unhealthy even to think about it. When does it happen? Unless it's during some natural cataclysms: earthquakes, maybe a solar eclipse?

Fortunately, that's not exactly the case. Apparently, for an affective actor, it's not the case at all: it's inherent to him, intrinsic to his artistic nature.

There are opinions about the greatest of affective actors—Mochalov—that say that, usually, his acting was inconsistent: when he's seized by inspiration, his acting is godly, but the rest of the time, it's just fruitless attempts to ignite his own spirit. This gives rise to the conclusion that this sort of acting, affective acting that's based on inspiration, is not subject to someone's will: inspiration and affect do not heed our orders.

It's true that Mochalov was not always in control of himself, it's true that he did not develop his subconscious methods into a full-fledged *technique*. But should we not be inspired be the fact that, according to Belinsky [1953: 391], "he was often capable of making the audience irresistibly captivated by his passionate, simple, and highly natural acting, and by the painfully-sweet impressions it produced on them *during a whole role*."

Doesn't this fact cast some light onto our somber and hopeless darkness? And anyway, this "somber and hopeless darkness" isn't all that scary, all things considered . . .

Can there exist a specific *technique* (I assume a psychological technique)? Is it possible to find a way to these depots?

As it turns out – it *is* possible. Experience has shown that even a rationalist school, which is so foreign to an affective school, has a lot in its arsenal that equips it to clear the path for these explosions and flights. If we take a good look at the heart or, we'll take the liberty to use this term, at the *mechanics* of affective art, then the *paths to inspiration* open up on their own. Moreover, it becomes obvious that the *means* of this hitherto unexplored technique are simply begging to be used.

"Technique! . . ." *the technique of affect . . .* to the enlightened listener, that sounds either ignorant or, at best, impudent. What *technique* can there be?! This is how it was and how it will be as long as **the school of affective creativity** does not have **firmly established principles**.

The affective actor's art is saturated and oversaturated with feeling. It's the lament of a string at its tautest. Because of this, it is uneven, and does not neatly fit into any designed form. It consists of rises and falls, it is fire and ice. These people are not like this only in their art – in life, affective actors are also people of exceedingly unstable psychological conditions: one day, they firmly believe in themselves, in their talent, their future; the next – utter disappointment, loss of faith, despair . . . Everything is deep and grand with these people: these periods of depression last for whole days, weeks, maybe even months. Think about Duse, who was in the prime of her artistic life when she suddenly abandoned the stage for 12 years.

And anyway, despite their massive, sometimes elemental, talent, actors of this type often leave the stage for a year or two or even more. And the bigger and deeper their personalities were, the more inevitable this was. They left the stage because the stage was never their *goal*. It was only a *means*.

Their goal was completely different. They looked BEYOND the boundaries of the mundane. They looked for the meaning of life, they tugged at the strings of existence, they were tortured by the answerless questions of humanity. Not even suspecting it, and possibly not even wanting it, they were philosophers, thinkers, and moralists. Without suspecting it, they were the very prophets, with "flaming coal" in their breasts, with a prophetic gaze, with ears that were able to pick up on the secrets of nature and life, and with the Word, capable of burning the hearts of men. [Demidov is paraphrasing Alexander Pushkin's (1936 v. 2: 16) 1826 poem *The Prophet*.]

If they got even a hint that another path, a truer path was coming up, they got on it without any reservations, leaving the stage behind. True, they returned to it as soon as they understood that elsewhere they were not as well-equipped as they were for the stage, and that their life's work was there. They came back, but not because they "couldn't live without theatre." The stage, with its lights, set decorations, and hustle never attracted them *for its own sake*. They are not *theatre artists* in the technical meaning of that word. For a theatre artist, the theatre is everything. He cannot exist without theatre – it's his natural environment.

"Without theatre" . . . but what is theatre? Is it really only the magical moment when an actor – heart to heart – stands before an audience and burns with a flame, igniting the entire house?

No. Theatre is not just that. What's more: theatre has so much more that is in opposition to the "magical moment" that the "magic" either wanes or is destroyed, or maybe never appears at all.

Theatre is a big, complex, and capricious organism. It consists of tens, and sometimes even hundreds of people that are painfully sensitive, easily wounded, vain, and that involuntarily compete with each other all the time . . . Because what each actor "creates"—*impressions* – is so fickle and elusive that it causes the actor to always be on guard, always concerned and worried. Failures first cause fear on one's own behalf, then anger and jealousy with regards to others, and then revenge, intrigues, and unscrupulousness . . . What then becomes of the place where the actor-creator melds with the audience by means of artistic experiencing – with the place that, as it seems, is supposed to be pristine and taintless? It turns into a place for squabbles, into haggling, a skirmish of intrigues, and a breeding ground of despicable, low, angry betrayal.

A theatre like that cannot be resonant with an affective actor's soul. He can easily do without a theatre like that. He *can't* do without something else: he can't do without lofty thoughts, without the burning passion for the sake of a moral or social ideal, without enlightening, prophesying, without showing others the way like a bright torch. That's what these people *cannot live without*.

For now, the affective actor is a roaming wanderer, having descended here from some unknown heights. He showed up like the dearest of guests, sang his inimitable song, raised the theatre to the skies, and . . . flew away.

As comfortable as a "theatre person," or someone that "can't live without theatre," feels in a theatre, so does an affective actor feel oppressed and helpless among the theatrical squabbles, among the backstage intrigues. After all, the affective actor is a person who is so deeply turned inward, a person who is ill-suited to so-called practical life in general, and who isn't suited at all to theatre life. In the majority of cases, he is ostracized, undercut, and ousted. Alas!

One day, theatre will become different – the future of theatre is immense. This means that the atmosphere of a theatre's backstage also cannot remain unchanged. It will become the realm of the affective actor. Let's help this cleansing of theatre: let's think, let's dream, let's speak everywhere in all places about a different, new theatre, which is worthy of our future. Those who are repulsed by the atmosphere created in other theatres by inborn dilettantes or careerists will inevitably be drawn to one another. They'll unite, and what's better – they will be victorious.

"A born artist," "an artist by nature" values *form* very highly. For him, makeup, costumes, *mise-en-scene*, and *form* in general hold great significance. And this is natural, this is natural for theatre.

For an affective actor, form has no meaning in and of itself. He doesn't really worry about makeup or costumes. The most immaculate makeup can get in his way, as can the best and most expressive *mise-en-scene* that the director thought up for him. Owing to the fact that he feels the very depths, the very heart of a role, he will, naturally, involuntarily, not even suspecting it, undergo appropriate external changes, perhaps even to a point beyond recognition. However, these changes will only be the natural results of *internal* changes.

"In front of my eyes appears Mochalov dressed in some kind of ugly, faded, skin-colored costume . . . – remember it? – and set pieces that might have indicated Paris, Florence, even

Peking, as well as London; . . . Out of all of this emerges the ominous figure of a limping demon (Richard III. – *N.D.*), with spasmodic movements, with baleful eyes . . . The faded, skin-colored costume disappears; the short figure grows into the titanic image of some kind of serpent, a massive constrictor. A serpent, specifically: like a tempting snake, he stood next to Lady Anne; he magnetized her with his blinding phosphoric gaze, and the melodic tone of his voice . . ." (Apollon Grigoriev [1985: 147], *Memoirs*).

By the way: how clearly do you "see" all of Dostoevsky's characters? Do you know what they were wearing? Their facial features or hairstyles? You see their souls, their thoughts, their actions, and their internal lives. Everything else is drawn up according to each reader's own imagination. Dostoevsky is a pure affective writer. His artistic sight was constantly pointed "within" – not "without."

The affective actor has an equally careless attitude towards form in everyday life as well. A pure "artist" always tries to dress well; he pays attention to how he looks. He teaches his students that an actor is a priest of beauty and, as such, doesn't have the right to let himself go, to not look after himself; not just onstage – in life, he must train the *artistry* in himself in all respects. This is wonderful, respectable, couldn't be any better, but . . . It wasn't for nothing that Michelangelo, a man who understood and loved beauty like none of his contemporaries (and perhaps not only his contemporaries), dressed in god knows what, sometimes slept in his clothes. According to the stories, when working on the Sistine Chapel ceiling, he went whole months without taking off his boots, because he "didn't have time . . ." Of course, we won't be doing that today – at least for the sake of hygiene, but Yermolova, who never had any ostentatious "artistry," who dressed in simple clothing, had a simple hairdo, and looked like a modest schoolteacher – I don't think we'll condemn her.

The Rationalist

Is it possible to speak of the rationalist's creative attributes? The creative process and cold reason are such irreconcilable things . . . Yet it *is* possible to speak about it. Let's, at least, remember the shows of the Meiningen Company.

Organization, forethought, calculation . . . in a worst-case scenario, it could be a fair replacement for talent. And if combined with other abilities, it can be used to construct very interesting things. Sure, they'll be a little bit frigid, but this would be compensated with so much thought, taste, logical sequencing and verisimilar feeling. On top of that, the play would be analyzed with such a high degree of psychological realism, any scene and any character, that people will start thinking: maybe this isn't worse, but *better* than dazzlingly talented, but unorganized performances? And only after you've gone to enough of these cerebral shows and seen enough of these "reserved," "modest," well-mannered actors (who are in reality cold and dull, i.e. not actors at all), you'll feel a longing for authentic emotionality and affectivity.

As for the rationalist's potential for the art of experiencing, well, if the school is true enough; if the teacher is experienced, artful, and stubborn – it's possible to teach anyone to act. But, of course, within the limits of his abilities. To calmly walk across the stage, say peaceful things, live within the boundaries of calm and mundane life – you can teach anyone to do that. And, if he's not given roles beyond his strength, but is instead limited to playing a restrained *raisonneur*, then everything in that respect can also be satisfactory, even with strict expectations. (Pavis [1998: 300], in his *Dictionary of Theatre* defines *raisonneur* as "character representing the proper line of reasoning or morality, whose commentary is supposed to give an "objective," or "authorial" view of the situation.)

The rationalist has one more attribute, and you can't put a price on it! He's a businessperson. And theatre is a business. A huge, difficult business, combining finance with the creative and everyday sides of things. To manage at this business, you need brains, willpower, tact, and, of course, a certain giftedness. And so, *rationalists*, they're the ones that most often stand at the head of a theatre. Sometimes, they don't even have enough acting or directing or pedagogical abilities, and nevertheless, despite everything, these stoic, reliable people with good heads on their shoulders become managers, directors. They attract gifted actors, "big-name" actors. They never give up, regardless of whatever hardships and misfortunes they encounter, they are always able to find a way out of the most hopeless situations. In the end, their theatre achieves good standing and attracts an audience. If such a rationalist were to possess, in addition to all of his positive attributes, qualities like principality, consistency, and incorruptibility of thought, and a strict sense of duty to humanity – then, of course, his primary concerns wouldn't be his own comfort and gains; he would only be satisfied with dignified goals and serious undertakings. And once he steps onto this road, he will see it through to the end.

If, by some special or important circumstances, a person of such intellect, character, and will decides to go on the stage, then, having finally found the right paths, the true school, after an enormous effort, he is, after all, able to train specific attributes in himself – they lay dormant in his deepest depths. In this case, it is necessary to call what this powerful and fearless person has done a miracle, a miraculous second birth. But after his second birth (or rebirth), he, naturally, no longer belongs to the *rationalist* creative type.

This is a special case, a case of training, retraining, and the perfection of one's abilities, and that deserves its own discussion in its own time.

"Ailments" and Weaknesses (Shortcomings) of the Four Actor Types

The Imitator

1   Regardless of how talented an imitator might be, regardless of how theatrical, sharp, and expressive his external form is – his art, excepting certain very rare cases, *always lacks harmony*, and, every now and then, a moment of brilliance is followed by a blot. Nothing can be done about this, such is his essence. Harmony and general unity are not in his nature. For this reason, his creations (be they an actor's role or a director's show) never achieve the status of art. He only has occasional flares . . .

2   By the very nature of his giftedness, he is a *caricaturist*. Sharpness and vividness of form lead him to *grotesque*. Exaggerate any distinct characteristic or gesture, or someone's external shortcoming – and there you have a caricature. But try to exaggerate a *positive* characteristic . . . Intensify it so that you're able to enthrall and captivate with it . . . If you're not a "Mochalov," you'll pop from the strain, like the frog in Aesop's fable, and you'll make everyone laugh . . . Heroism, just like poeticism, cannot be depicted with vivid form alone. They need to be "internalized."

3   He is quite capable of "internalizing," his form is not empty. But here's his weakness: he can only flesh out the form *for a short while*. It pops into his imagination . . . he plays it, soaring on the wings of a momentary impulse, and then . . . it ends. The charge is gone. He tries to repeat it – there's no charge, only the memory of the external form . . . This actor is only capable of quick sketches.

4   His ability to take hold of a single feature and blow it up to extraordinary proportions, results in one more shortcoming, which very few imitators are able to avoid: *bending too far*. In search of vividness and sharpness, he bends the stick too far and . . . breaks it. The imitator has broken many roles, many plays, and many actors . . .

5   The imitator's natural element is that of the storyteller. He always needs the prototype of his story to stand before him (in his imagination). He *himself* doesn't live, but *imitates* it.

6   Most of the imitator's work on his role involves a search for a vivid, eloquent form. One needs a significant amount of talent, and has to do a significant amount of work, to find such a form. Once you've found it, you can rest calm: play the form well and that's it. Except, here's the drawback: regardless of how well the role is done, if another actor of even middling ability takes it up, he can *copy* it so well that the creator (the actor or director – it doesn't matter) will be *robbed*. A role or show that is built on external devices is not so difficult to reconstruct – when there's a will there's a way. An affective actor cannot be robbed no matter how hard you try. In order to do that, you have to steal his talent, his skills . . . Moreover, if you manage to steal his *ability to live onstage*, you still won't be playing exactly like him – you'll play it differently. Worse, better, less, deeper, but differently – as is characteristic of you, and of your actor's individuality.

The Emotional Actor

As we already said, the emotional actor's greatest performances and roles are *artistic* reproductions of life. But these are the best cases. His immersion has to release him for just a bit; his living in the given circumstances become just a little bit *underfulfilled* – instantly, what he's doing isn't the "truth," it's "verisimilitude."

"Verisimilitude" cannot affect the audience so enthrallingly as the "truth," and the audience stops believing. And seeing as the form here is, for the most part, quite meager, and *doesn't act on its own*, the audience grows bored. Everyone acts as they are supposed to in this theatre – realistically and seemingly authentically; I appreciate and respect this, but . . . I'm somewhat bored. Why the boredom? Because they're acting, let's be perfectly frank about this now, they're acting *badly*. This *isn't the truth, but the appearance of truth – it's acting à la truth.*

Yet, actors who have been trained "in restraint" do not allow themselves rough and vulgar "play-acting," nor do they resort to cheap theatrical tricks. And so you are fooled, you think: they're acting well – the play must just be boring, or the role isn't good . . .

This kind of acting does not deserve any appreciation or respect. It's stale bread, champagne without bubbles, a sword that has feathers for the blade instead of steel.

The second "ailment" of the emotional actor: some of them play the same thing everywhere and in everything – it's always themselves, or rather, the same thing they play in real life. The costumes change, the makeup changes, but inside – it's all the same. It's all the same "natural" way of speaking, the same little mannerisms . . .

The reason is that not all given circumstances are taken into account, and the actor – though he may be a very pleasant person – is still a simple layman, not capable of lofty flights of fantasy. And so he sees everything through the lens of his personal, layman's soul. When challenged with Shakespearian characters, however, the emotional actor proves to be utterly helpless. His acting seems true, his characters – breathing living beings . . . but it's all so small and pedestrian. All of his thoughts, all of his passions are of such dwarflike proportions that it makes you mad.

The Affective Actor

He doesn't know soft, obedient emotions. As soon as his inner life is struck – there's an explosion. The "internal life" of the affective actor is *Something*, which is stronger than him, and which he cannot control.

It would be easy to deal with a modest, convenient emotion – it's something like a house pet, which obediently listens to its master and fits into the frame of our everyday life; – Affect reminds us of some horrifying beast – once it's gotten loose – there is no telling what it might do!

We've already spoken about the miraculous, inspired explosions – here, we must speak about the failed ones. What *is* an affective actor's "explosion," after all?" His soul has particularly vulnerable spots. (Sometimes they are caused by one catastrophic blow – once and for all; sometimes – by thousands of little needling scratches.) These spots are unbearably painful. All it takes is for any one of them to be lightly grazed, and there's an explosion. Duse had an example of such a spot – scorned, trampled love. As soon as that spot was grazed, Duse wasn't herself: from the bottom of her soul, fountains of such powerful passions started erupting that the actress and the role broke their banks and flooded everything.

Duse, Yermolova, Aldridge were able to harmonize their eruptions just in time to direct them where they were needed. But we know of tragedians who, for one reason or another, were unable to do so, and did not know how to control their temperament. It so happened that they were often "carried away" during the most unexpected and unimportant moments in the performance. An affective actor like that would waste all of the day's charge on such an insignificant spot in the first act, and he won't have anything left for the big, climactic scenes. Or else, in a comedy, the actor would inopportunely tear himself to shreds in some sensitive scene, and the whole play would become completely disfigured.

Much bigger problems are so-called "internal explosions" – explosions, which do not find an outlet. For example, an affective actor's sensitive spot is hit – and his insides start boiling in response! And it'll stay inside like that . . . he'll start shaking, he'll pale like a tapestry, his breath catches, he can't get out a single word (or he says not what he wants to), his face starts twitching all over . . . Minutes of this internal fire can cost several years of life . . . If this happens to an actor in the middle of a show, he will inevitably crash and burn. Earlier, during rehearsals, or maybe even during other shows, the scene was fine, but today – the actor's closed up – nothing springs to the surface: everything burns up inside! Such internal explosion is always followed by fatigue, weariness, hopelessness, and despair.

Thus, the chief difference between the affective actor and the others is *explosivity*. But, as strange as it may seem, aside from explosivity and extraordinary sensitivity (vulnerability), he also has the exact opposite qualities: *icy coldness, deathly insensitivity, and even bluntness*. He depends entirely on his internal world: today, he's open like a flower greeting the sun, and everything hits him right in the heart – as they say, he's ready to give his last shirt to somebody he just met, if they need it. But tomorrow, the flower closes up, and nothing can reach his heart, and even in the heart of a fight, he is still cold and absent. It's very strange. But that's how it is.

However, this is very easily explained. Exploding for any reason, great or small . . . Can even the healthiest and most stalwart of psyches sustain that? And so, the psyche begins to defend itself from worries that are too dangerous: it takes cover under a glass dome. Although the person sees everything, he doesn't hear or feel it. It doesn't *affect him, it glides past him* and fails to deliver a single wound. You can imagine the hopeless state of the actor when this dome drops around him during an actual show! You couldn't come up with anything worse!

And in order to get out of this oppressive situation (since there's no school of his own yet), the affective actor attempts to reach the heights on which he soared the last show in a single swoop, and he overexerts himself – he enters a state of extreme physical strain, almost convulsions. Instead of the heightened creativity (which is simply the harmonious function of all psychological aspects reaching the heights of strength and clarity), instead of this heightened creativity, the actor enters a state of meaningless agitation: he yells, screams, waves his arms, smacks his chest – he's become inebriated with his own convulsions.

The most pitiful of all falls.

★★★

The affective actor can sweep you into a delightful moment not just during his creative minutes onstage, but in life as well. He'll sweep up your thoughts and feelings and send them to hitherto unreachable heights, opening up whole new worlds in front of your eyes . . . But he can also easily make you boundlessly miserable . . . An exceptionally heightened sensitivity can make him exorbitantly expansive, happy, and joyful without any reservations, but it can also throw him into the depths of sorrow and despair! Sometimes, when this happens, no amount of caressing or convincing can bring him out of this state: it only exacerbates it.

The amount of pain and disappointment that his "dullness" and "coldness" can bring to those surrounding him also isn't insignificant. This is the flip side of the coin that also holds his sensitivity, kind-heartedness, and vulnerability, and these two sides of the affective actor are *inseparable*. So, when you most need his humaneness and attention, he'll suddenly close up, lock himself in himself – and you're just a foreign and endlessly strange person, far stranger than any pedestrian out the window . . . You might be thinking that he's simply an *egotist*, a person who is so preoccupied with his own precious self that he isn't capable of speaking or thinking about anything or anyone else? You're wrong! Typically, he worries about himself least of all. The most delicate of souls, like Dante, Michelangelo, and Beethoven seemed so cold, closed off, and cantankerous to their contemporaries.

★★★

In conclusion, it's necessary to say that the described ailments, or to be more exact, the mistakes in the art of these three types, most commonly occur because they do not yet have a finished and flawless school. The affective type doesn't have *any* school yet . . . at all! When there is a school, there won't be these mistakes.

Another reason for these mistakes is that people who strive to become actors aren't always suited to the job. In this case, regardless of the school, there won't be a road forward without a few dips . . .

★★★

The affective actor's instability, the expansiveness and quicksilver irritability of the emotional actor may be misunderstood.

Many sensitive and neurotic, or maybe even simply spoiled, people, who are incapable of dealing with their capriciousness, will read this text and, in their simplicity, decide that they've been marked by the stamp of genius. This would be a blatant and egregious mistake.

Of course, genius and talent might have certain flaws in their nervous system, but they are not what make them so creatively gifted. On the contrary – these people are creative *despite* these shortcomings and even *in defiance of* them. As soon as they touch art, no matter how poorly they were feeling just a moment ago, they instantly become healthy, strong, calm, and harmonically balanced. This happens as if they come into their natural element from a foreign one.

If someone is psychopathic or neurotic, it's necessary, first of all, to see where these qualities are directed. *Towards art* or *away from art!* For Duse – it was away from art: at the thought of the stage, any hint of being neurotic or weak disappears. But for the delicate, nervous people – their psychopathy is directed towards art: as soon as they start rehearsing – immediately, they begin complaining and having fits . . .

The Rationalist

What can we say about his "ailments?" He's made up entirely of "ailments." What can someone who is incapable of giving himself over to emotion do in art? He's rational, cold, constantly observing himself. Essentially, he has no place in art. But since he's gotten here for one reason or another, he has only one choice: to try to fool the audience by any means possible. This is what he dedicates all of his strength to: he deftly distracts the audience with showiness, and a complex staging, while simultaneously affecting them with music, sound, and light effects . . .

As for the *art of acting* itself – a pure rationalist doesn't even worry about it. He replaces it with sound, clear delivery of the playwright's words (let the *playwright* act) and precise, smooth execution of the *mise-en-scenes*. To this end, he develops a flawless diction, a clear voice; the way that he says each line is immaculately "logical"; he pays an enormous amount of attention to his physicality and the expressivity of his poses and gestures . . . In a word, he unleashes every effort to make a deft imitation of art. [Flawless diction, a clear voice, logic, pronunciation, etc. are necessary for actors of all types, but all of this typically plays only a functional role. For example, it's vital to have a strong, developed voice and good diction, otherwise, regardless of how well you act, nobody can hear you. But here, the rationalist *limits* himself with all of these mechanical achievements. – *Author's Note*]

Imitation, falsification – is not the worse thing on earth. Tolstoy [1984: 92] wrote in his notebook: "Art does not tolerate mediocrity, but it tolerates self-consciousness even less." And a true rationalist is made up wholly of "self-consciousness."

Complex Types

Most likely, every reader, especially the actors, almost from the book's very beginning—from the "birch grove"—started trying on each of the types: what about me? what type do I belong to? Probably, one of the types seemed the closest to his heart. However (and this is also highly probable), he found that he had some qualities belonging to other types. It's true that these types very rarely come in their pure forms. There is no such thing as a straight line or a perfect circle in nature, and yet we still use these abstractions to our great advantage. And so we'll use *this* abstraction as well. Let's only note that, if it's only to a small extent, every person has the qualities of all the types within him. So we're practically always dealing with a *complex type*.

How do these complex types form? We've already spoken of this. In the embryonic stage, we all have all attributes. But they do not develop uniformly. This depends on thousands of reasons, from innate and genetic ones to random external ones. One single attribute begins to get ahead of the others and develops more quickly – to the others' detriment. But the others, though they've slowed in their development, haven't stopped entirely. And as a result, we get a complex organism with one of the main attributes as the dominant one.

Of course, it's possible to imagine that all attributes do develop uniformly. Then we get a complex and quite harmonious person. In reality, this happens as infrequently as you encounter perfect human beauty – without any deviations in one direction or the other. But, it probably does exist.

It's equally difficult to imagine that, in a single individual, all three emotional qualities develop uniformly and harmoniously: imitation, emotiveness, and affectivity. Something will inevitably be dominant and something will lag behind.

We've already given examples of how an early development of reason slows the growth of emotional attributes; we've even spoken of how it can stop it altogether. But a more hopeful case is also possible: the development of reason, and the ability to judge, can go hand-in-hand with the development of emotional attributes. Then we get a fortunate combination that we can only fantasize about: cold reason and conscious effort are not at war with ardent emotion; they don't suppress it, but instead direct it, support it, and *serve* it.

Same goes for emotions – as it turns out, they can not only muddle one's thoughts, but can enlighten as well. Under their effect, human thought can become sharper, more flexible, and stronger. The fortunate combination of affective attributes with rationalist attributes has given the world actors like Salvini, Rossi and Illarion Pevtsov [1879–1934].

It turns out, even Aldridge's fiery personality was surprisingly well-tempered by great self-possession and keen reason:

This was a great actor, that is, an actor whose analytical (preparatory) work brilliantly synthesized with the other kind – with the authentic creative work that took place before the eyes of the audience . . . . Desdemona was played by a local, fairly talentless, actress, who was under the wing of the mayor. In the scene where a volcano of jealousy is boiling in Othello's chest, she must have wanted to act as well, and so she began straightening her wrinkled dress with remarkable calmness and apathy. Aldridge was offended by her indifference, so he ran up to

Figure 15   Ira Aldridge, as painted by John Simpson in 1827. Courtesy of Andrei Malaev-Babel.

her and intentionally grabbed her arm so painfully that Desdemona's face immediately reflected a deep internal fear and physical pain. Suddenly cutting off his speech, the tragedian, smiling, looked into the actress's face and added tenderly: "Very good! Thank you very much," and then continued the interrupted scene . . . [Davydov 1962: 40–41]

As for the combination of emotionality and rationalism – it's given us Shchepkin, Stanislavsky, and a great amount of excellent actors.

The combination of imitation with rationalism, self-possession, and a portion of emotionality, has given us an enormous amount of actors with external expressivity.

There is a countless multitude of the combinations and proportions in which 2–3 or even all 4 types have blended. But let's again note that every blend always has a clear *dominance* of attributes of one of the four types (the other types' attributes being more or less auxiliary). This is why it's always useful to know the differences between the signs and characteristics of the basic types. What's more: for a director, it's essential. A lack of knowledge can lead to enormous, irreparable mistakes.

★★★

In the history of theatre, it seems that there is only one exception – Garrick. He was an amazing, inimitable, harmonious combination of all four types. An excellent imitator and mime, he frightened people by instantly transforming from one person into another without any makeup. He drove Parisians mad during his tour across Europe with his mimed depictions of everyday life . . . And right next to that is the role with which he started his artistic journey, which took London by storm and turned the old tradition of false "theatricality" on its head. This role was Richard III. Judging by accounts, it was a deep and intense "experiencing," and a temperament, which would be more typical of an affective actor.

And finally, over the course of 30 years, he becomes an entrepreneur, a director, manager and artistic director of the Drury Lane Theatre. His biographer Arthur Murphy [1801: 381] says: "There existed in England a *fourth estate*: King, Lords, and Commons, and *Drury-Lane play-house*." That may be an exaggeration, but a theatre which hasn't gotten a single shilling of support from the government must be very impressive indeed to merit such a quote.

There you have it – a perfect blend, in every meaning of those words, of a harmonious artist.

It's good when everybody does what's characteristic of them: Leonardo and Goethe combined scientist, philosopher-researcher, inventor, poet, and painter all in one, while Raphael only painted. It's a shame and a mistake when a person goes against his inclinations or strength – very little good typically comes of this. Instead, it's important to focus on the attributes which you have in hand, and drive them to perfection.

Unfortunately, we focus very little on utilizing our main abilities. We spend more time chasing after the ones to which we're drawn in others. The imitator and the emotional actor probably want to be affective, while the affective yearns to be an imitator, or a pragmatic reasoner . . . The comic wants to play a tragedy, and the character actress believes herself to be an ingénue or a leading lady. As a result, everyone suffers and grumbles . . .

Rarely is someone so fortunate to receive an unexpected role and thus find one's true calling. Most of the time, fate is not so magnanimous. But, truth be told, it's not always just fate . . . It could happen that you get a role (the one you've always dreamed of), but when you play it, you crash and burn! . . . Either your soul hasn't matured enough to play this role, or you don't have the skill (and nobody is there to teach you!) – but either way, the bruise stays with you forever . . . And so these actors who have yet to find themselves and unlock their talents are wandering about the stage – veritably misfortunate people. They can feel the strength

Figure 16   David Garrick as Shakespeare's Richard III; a detail from William Hogarth's 1745 painting. Courtesy of Andrei Malaev-Babel.

inside themselves, but this strength can't break through – it stays inside, only causing pain and restlessness.

Others, though their talents are yet to be unlocked, aren't concerned about it at all. They don't even suspect how massive their untapped strength may be. Some 5–10 percent of the total talent they end up using turns out to be enough for them (in combination with a good body and a pleasant voice) to assume their spot in theatre. This satisfies them and quite fulfills their needs, because really: why try so hard? – I've "achieved" something, I'm "renowned" – everything is fine. And if I've even succeeded at attaching myself, like a snail, to some enormous ship of a theatre – I swim with it across all the seas and oceans, and I'm happy: what could be better?!

The "Types" in Directing

The most important thing for a beginning actor is to come upon a director or teacher who'll be so keen, that he'll lead his pupil over the path that is right for ***him***. Having gotten on ***its own (suitable)*** tracks, talent starts rolling forward quickly and freely.

Today, the director means a lot, if not everything. He won't draw the line at simply establishing the *mise-en-scenes* – whether he wants to or not, he starts poking his nose into the acting as well. It's here that he can either save the actor from dangerous strains, or do a fair bit of harm.

If he's predominantly an imitator, a director without the necessary tact will probably be unable to restrain himself from constantly pulling you towards imitating. He'll make faces himself, search for all the possible "types," "characterizations," and forms – and he'll be coaching you this way in the roughest possible manner. And if you're more of an affective type, then, of course, he won't get anything out of you, he'll label you – "ungifted" and take away your role. And if he doesn't take it away, you yourself won't be pleased at all – he'll torture you so much with his mimicry that you'll lose any respect you may have had for yourself. And you'll still act poorly – it would've been better had he simply taken your role away.

Or, imagine this – an affective director: he feels everything with his "gut;" every trifle will cause a storm to rise up inside him. He doesn't like to explain anything, and, truth be told, doesn't know how: after all, there *is* no affective school of art yet. He would have to come up with everything on the spot. But not everybody has that skill, and it might just happen that he doesn't even have a hint of pedagogical talent. And so, without any artifice, he simply demonstrates *"how it's done."* He'll walk across the stage as a tiger, for example . . . he'll flash his gaze so that your knees will start shaking! . . . He'll say a line from the very depths of his soul – learn from him, take it all in while you can! . . .

But you, let's say you're predominantly a rationalist, you need to break everything down and reengineer it, think it all over, understand what you "want" where, what you're "doing" where . . . and what to think in each spot . . . To simply light up on the spot – that's not your style. And here's another misunderstanding: he'll be confident that you have no temperament, and that you're good for nothing, in general, while you'll quite reasonably reach the conclusion that *this* is no way to direct . . .

A director must be very perceptive with regard to the actor. Only then will he find his way to the actor's intuition, which is so crucial. Drilling is a last resort. It's permissible only if an actor is utterly unprepared and inexperienced, and even then only if it's a hurried production. Typically, though, this rather widespread method points to a director's helplessness. The most important thing in the world is awakening an actor's own individuality – any difficulties will be compensated ten times over.

Lately, a new kind of director model has become fashionable – the director-producer. This director approaches a production with a plan worked out to the tiniest details. He typically spend his first meetings with a collective captivatingly explaining how interesting and spectacular the show will be. The actors' heads will spin from the vividness of the images, from the showiness of the scenes, from the depth of the psychology . . . And they gladly applaud the director. During rehearsals, though, this ardor quickly wanes: for many of them, what sounded great during the telling of it all turns out to be unsuitable, foreign . . . They want something else . . . something closer to home . . . But there is not and cannot be anything else: the plan is set, confirmed, and approved. (By themselves, no less! each one of them applauded . . .) They'll worry about it for awhile, and then, out of the simplicity of their hearts, they'll decide that he's a wonderful director, he's just not very good at working with actors. Which is the same thing as saying, "He's a wonderful painter, only he doesn't know how to put a single stroke of paint onto the canvas."

An actor, a living, creative actor – that's a director's paint, and not knowing how to use it means to lack directorial skills. This sort of "producer" is not a director: he ruins and breaks the most important component: the actors. He may be very useful in theatre, but only as a consultant to another director, as an advisor, giving ideas, as a fantasizer – but he cannot be allowed anywhere near the "canvas" of the stage.

It would be misguided to make the conclusion that the author believes it to be harmful to have a preliminary plan. A plan is vital. But what kind? An exact, detailed description of every external form of the show? In that case, that's not a plan, it's a finished work, already performed by some abstracted, imaginary actors, and all that's left for me as the performer is to recreate it to the best of my ability, to copy it . . .

But regardless of how detailed the plan is with regard to a show's external features (exact or approximate), an actor *must* be caught up in a *play's internal content*, he needs to get its main idea, needs to become excited about his role, find the echoes of the role in himself . . . This is what the actor needs help with. His creative thirst needs to be stoked. Afterwards, he needs help educing what begins to take shape, what grows in him. Without losing sight of the play and the plan, it's necessary to dedicate the most attention to them, the performers. Because, ultimately, they're the ones who are going to be onstage living the lives of the characters, not me, the director.

Of course, the ideal case is when a director belongs to all four types, but . . . that never happens. Therefore, it's better not to force the actor to dance to your own tune, but *listen to what is happening in the actor, and retune yourself to harmonize with him.* Only then will you be of any use to him.

Great directors subconsciously do just that. They might start by searching for the right "tasks," suggesting them to the actor. Then suddenly they themselves will start acting – "demonstrating." The actor picks it up, and everything rolls on at full speed. In other cases, if the demonstrations aren't enough for the actor, they'll sit him down, calm him, start speaking with him about this, that, and the other thing. Gradually, having awoken the actor's sound creative state, they'll start questioning the actor about the play's "circumstances." Once the circumstances begin to work on the actor, they will ask him to move onto the role's lines. Or else, if the actor is cold or absent-minded, they'll *get* to him on a personal level, provoke his emotions, and then, while he's still experiencing these feelings, they'll immediately make him rehearse.

These aren't the only methods – directors come up with hundreds of others on the spot. That's how true mastery manifests itself: by finding a way into the soul of an actor – a living human.

"Types" Of Theatres

When a very strong director stands at the helm of a theatre and most everything passes through his hands, then, of course, everything will bear his mark. Can we say that, in this case, the theatre is of a certain type? If the director has picked out actors of a suitable type and has managed to impassion them with his methods, then why not? And the question is: *should* a theatre belong to one type or another according to the methods practiced within its bounds? In some very rare cases, it probably should. In the rest – definitely not.

In reality, there aren't really theatres that limit their repertoire with a single type of dramaturgy, or a single playwright. Everything goes: from tragedy to vaudeville (this is equally applicable to drama, opera, and ballet theatres). Most importantly: one shouldn't create templates or rules that say that tragedies can only be put on by affective techniques and affective actors, dramas – only by emotional ones, and comedies, vaudevilles, and parodies – only by imitators . . . Tragedies aren't tragic throughout, and not everything in them requires an affective grip; dramas, on the other hand, might have some parts that are highly tragic and call for a dizzying flight of emotions, while comedies might possess utterly irresistible affectivity. Affectivity doesn't necessarily imply tragedy: recall the walk through the birch grove.

Keeping this in mind, is there even a single play that requires the participation of only a single type? Doubtful.

Let's take *Hamlet*. Only two to three of the main roles are affective. The others are by their very essences closer to the actors of two other types.

Unfortunately, affective actors and directors are in such a stranglehold nowadays that even an affective and tempestuous play like *Hamlet*, which demands to be played from the depths of one's soul, is mostly staged in a very smooth, diluted, and ornately combed-over manner, like an old lady's poodle. Or it is crudely "defamiliarized," so as to surprise the audience.

When a director or an actor doesn't have the necessary strength to soar on the heights of tragedy, they lower the play, bring it closer to their own capabilities. Even if they have to completely put it on its head, that doesn't weigh on their conscience in the least. As soon as this tragedy falls into the hands of a director without any hint of affectivity, the first thing that happens is a new *interpretation*: "Hamlet has no willpower, Hamlet is inactive and indecisive . . . Hamlet isn't a hero at all, he's just neurotic . . ." A "brave" interpreter doesn't understand that Hamlet is "inactive" only from his point of view, from the standpoint of a person who has a very narrow and straightforward understanding of action. He doesn't understand that action can be much more intense and precious.

> The time is out of joint: O cursed spite,
> That ever I was born to set it right!

Here is the most important and torturous of Hamlet's questions: How? How to "set the time right"? . . . Vengeance? . . . Murder? . . . and . . . that's it? It would be so simple. All you need for this eventuality is a single hot-headed youth, like Laertes.

Hamlet himself truly believes that it's all about this murder. But in the meantime, some instinct stays his hand from the hasty and premature action. He incessantly accuses himself for his own willlessness, for slowness of action, for weakness, and . . . for some reason, he keeps delaying, putting it off, waiting for something . . . All the while, he keeps riling the castle's atmosphere with his "madness," the mysterious incoherence of his words, and scores of seemingly pointless actions. This, at first, gives the king pause, then causes him to worry, and finally panic. Entangled in malefactions, he entangles others. Finally, when everything ripens, at the right moment, the sole correct moment (before the invasion of Fortinbras's conquering forces) – the whole nest of villains is uprooted, along with those who were entangled in it. And look: what a strange heap of corpses: Hamlet's father, Polonius, Ophelia, Rosencrantz, Guildenstern, Gertrude, Laertes, the King, and finally, Hamlet himself – nine!

"Hamlet is a cold reasoner, unable to feel or act, he can only deliberate." This is said by those who want to adjust the role to suit their own feeble forces.

But what about the decisive pursuit of the ghost in the darkness of night?

> Still am I call'd. Unhand me, gentlemen.
> By heaven, I'll make a ghost of him that lets me!
> I say, away! Go on; I'll follow thee.

And what about the snap decision to play the comedy of a madman, and the brilliant execution of this plan? What about the murder of Polonius? What about the brazen theft of the king's order? And its substitution? And being first to step foot onto the pirates' ship?

Of course, it's difficult for an actor to throw himself down into Ophelia's grave and flare up so much that, from the depths of his soul, the following words fly out, full of such grief and such despair:

> I loved Ophelia: forty thousand brothers
> Could not, with all their quantity of love,
> Make up my sum.

Of course it's difficult! Let's be quite frank: for a non-affective actor, it's impossible. And thus is born a "brilliant" way out: "Hamlet doesn't love Ophelia at all. All the words on her grave are apery and show for the onlookers." It's simple, new, and "original" . . . and everything else has a similar fate.

Ophelia has a particularly poor fortune: some directors make her a prostitute, for some reason, while others make her a naïve, limited, pretty, foolish girl. And they all insist that this is an immeasurably deep insight on their behalf.

But what is there to do about her monologue (after the scene with Hamlet's "madness")?

> O, what a noble mind is here o'erthrown!
> The courtier's, soldier's, scholar's, eye, tongue, sword;
> The expectancy and rose of the fair state,
> The glass of fashion and the mould of form,
> The observed of all observers, quite, quite down!
> And I, of ladies most deject and wretched,
> That suck'd the honey of his music vows,
> Now see that noble and most sovereign reason,
> Like sweet bells jangled, out of tune and harsh;
> That unmatch'd form and feature of blown youth
> Blasted with ecstasy: O, woe is me,
> To have seen what I have seen, see what I see!

Obviously, this monologue needs to be crossed out. It speaks not of her foolishness and frivolity, but of a great mind, of crystal purity, and depth of feeling.

The most important thing to see in Ophelia is a creature that is tied together with Hamlet with significantly tighter threads of feeling and closeness than it seems to her (or him).

And, finally, the father's ghost. Typically, an actor with an immense, booming basso performs this role. But something completely different is needed here: what's necessary is a person who is able to imagine that he is walking feeling, unexhausted passions and is, in his entirety, nothing but the affect of unbearable suffering.

> But that I am forbid
> To tell the secrets of my prison-house,
> I could a tale unfold whose *lightest word*
> Would harrow up thy soul . . .

And so, when the appropriately strong affective actors have been cast in these three roles, then one can start thinking about Horatio, Gertrude, and Laertes. These are people that do have passions, but not of the same level, the same depth or breadth. Emotional actors can handle them.

The third group of roles: court gossips and fools, common malefactors, who can, without even knowing it, cause time to be "out of joint": the King, Polonius, Rosencrantz, Guildenstern, and many others can be handled by actors with "a bit of cold," a mixture of rationality and imitating. There's no need to fear a "mixture of styles." Such is life: it's full of people of different types who are unable to understand each other.

If this is how the show is structured, staged, directed, and, finally, acted – I dare to think that it'll be a Shakespearean *Hamlet*. Of course, if actors who have a bit of affectivity in their blood play Horatio, Gertrude, the King, Polonius, and the others – the show only gains in strength. But it will completely crash and burn if the tragedy's main roles are played by *non-affective actors*.

How do you think things were in Maly Theatre's golden days? The director would come in at the agreed time, pick up a bell that was situated on the director's table, ring it, and announce: "Rehearsal is starting."

And so, Yermolova, Glikeria Fedotova, [1846–1925] Ivan Samarin [1817–1885], Konstantin Rybakov [1856–1916], Prov Sadovsky and his son Mikhail [1847–1910], and others would begin to rehearse. They agreed, negotiated, helped each other, and then, when the clock showed the appropriate time, the "director's" bell rang once more, and he grandly announced: "Rehearsal is over!" No harm came from this.

No harm came from it because apparently the actors weren't just strong, but of the same aspiration – to the "experiencing" – and they were all affective or emotional. It was easy for them to agree, and out of the similarity of desires and commonality of talent, an affective-emotional theatre rose up on its own, with all of the qualities that are intrinsic to it.

Out of this friendly, communal work a sort of "school" would also rise up. It did not concern itself with theorizing or with psychological and psychophysical discoveries, but simply with striving for the truth, for authenticity. It also taught each of the actors to *practice* "infecting" their partners with the same truth in which they lived onstage.

That was the whole "school," but this "school" worked miracles. In those "theatrically unenlightened times" (as some people think today), the Maly was an exceptional and mighty theatre. It was, without exaggerations, the brightly blazing torch of genius. Truly a Second University!

If only it could be repeated! What's more, if only it were possible to carefully and wisely add to it the best and the *truest* from the directorial and pedagogical school that have risen up in recent times! It would have no equals not only in our own time, but for the following hundred years . . .

Rationality and Imperativity in the Actor's Technique

Many memoirs are coming out today. They speak of the entertaining moments of the actors' lives, of how an actor played this role or that one . . . As for how he worked, what he searched for, and how he trained himself – not a single word, not a single implication, as if these things didn't exist. Nothing is said about the process, the technique of transformation, the methods used to prepare for a performance, or the techniques utilized while onstage (an implied technique, of course, is one that isn't external, but internal – psychological). Either it was too difficult to describe these methods, or else these major actors considered them self-evident and not in need of additional explanations; regardless, it's as if everyone made a pact not to discuss them.

Finally, one person undertook something that everybody else avoided in the past – to reveal the psychological "mechanics" of an actor's creative process. An excellent actor in his own right, he set the objective before himself to find the paths and rules of an actor's creative work, systematize everything, and finally, create practical guidelines for navigating the winding paths of creative work onstage. This man is Konstantin Stanislavsky. And this heroic labor is what was called the "Stanislavsky System" – the endpoint of his 40 years of work.

But (one would have to confess this eventually), in the end, the result turned out to be strange and unexpected.

Alongside advice and demands that could be expected from an actor or a teacher who has "experiencing" as his primary goal onstage – alongside "I am," "communication," "what if," "life within given circumstances" – the "system" also proposes such rationalistic approaches that it's as if it wasn't created by an emotional type, but by a rationalist much like the one that visited the birch grove with the thermos slung over his shoulder.

How did it happen that an emotional actor created such a contradictory "system"? By some cruel irony of fate, he always used to put this word in quotes: "system." How did it happen that alongside the demands of a true, strict artist of the stage, about three quarters of it is rationalism, analysis, and imperativity – all that is foreign to his own artistic nature? And is this "system" really that "universal key" that he used to open up himself and others for the sake of art? And does it really serve as an expression of his creative genius? . . .

That will be discussed later in a special chapter. For now, recall the main points of the "system," and you won't have any doubts that rationality, cold analysis, and imperativity are standing at its helm.

Here are these points:

1   Every moment of his life, a person *wants* something. This is unavoidable. You have to *want* what your character wants right now – then you'll live on stage correctly.
2   When somebody starts wanting something, he begins to *fulfill actions*. If he is wanting correctly, he'll act correctly. And when you're onstage, you have to act all the time – the word "actor" comes from the word "action." Actions can be physical or psychological (without physical movements on the stage.)
3   An actor shouldn't take on a role all at once. He should divide it into bits: big bits first, then dividing them into smaller ones. Every bit needs its own *task*, e.g. what do I want in this bit? And the whole role needs to be broken into tasks, small and big ones, ultimately (it's not immediately evident) finding the most important task: the *supertask*. It will serve as the magnetic pole attracting the compass needles of all other tasks. In this manner, the actor gradually creates a *volitional score*, and just like a conductor leads an orchestra by a musical score, so does the actor lead his role by a *volitional* one.
4   In no case should you worry if the emotions would arise. This will inevitably lead to a false state of being. Onstage, it's necessary to *truthfully want* and *truthfully act*, taking into account the circumstances that have been proposed by the playwright ("given circumstances") – then the necessary feelings and emotions will involuntarily rise up. If these desires aren't active enough, and the emotions aren't the necessary ones, that means that I'm not fulfilling the right task. I have to more accurately find what I want here, what my task is, and fulfill that one. Rehearsals are typically spent in this sort of search.

These positions make it evident the importance that is accorded **to reasoning, analysis, and imperativity**. (In his last years of life, Stanislavsky spoke less about "tasks" and more about "physical actions." Although this isn't a direct departure from rational or imperative principles, it's still a step into another sphere – an "emotional" one.)

The majority of people are convinced that the Moscow Art Theatre's creative work is built entirely on these principles. But does the theatre owe its success only to them? Definitely not. Other methods and principles managed to contraband their way into the Art Theatre as well. Not only those directors opposed to the "system" used them, but more than anyone else – Stanislavsky himself. People employed these principles without even suspecting it . . . People used them and immediately justified their success by the faithful execution of the "system's" tenets.

We'll look more closely at these methods and at their contradictory union with the "system" later.

Will and Imperativity

The rationalist-imperative "system" of an actor's internal technique insists that *volition*, or will, is at the heart of the actor's score. Let's see if this is true.

According to the latest psychological definitions, will is a complex act, and it involves an organism's whole multifaceted life. Will is an organism's expedient striving. It's conscious, but can be unconscious to an even greater extent – it's a sort of resultant force of all needs, impressions, and desires. It can include a conscious command, an imperative: I want this! But it doesn't have to be involved. A person can strive for something with his whole being, and even succeed at it, but he can do so *without any commands* – he does so because his whole being (his *will*) is directed at this.

Thus, a command, the imperative does not make up all of one's will, but is *only a small part of it*, and not even a required one. To tell yourself, "I want this," does not mean to employ all of your willpower. The imperative is not only not willpower's heart, but it isn't even its beginning. In all likelihood, it is its end, the final push. The pull of the trigger. Bam! – a light touch, the hammer hits the cartridge, and the bullet flies off.

When the objective is clear, when the path is understood, when all circumstances are given and evident, then the lightest of touches is all that is necessary: it's time! act! – and the person's willpower discharges. The imperative is the last push, the pull of the trigger.

It is common to think that willpower is everything: all you have to do is want something to happen, and it'll happen. Tell yourself, "I want to fly, like a bird" (as we often do in dreams), yet it's not enough – you won't magically grow wings.

If I want to shoot without a rifle, if I want to use the first stick that I see, then although it has a small knot that looks like a rifle's hammer, although I pull on it again and again, there won't be a shot. "Open fire!" "Shoot!" This is the final act, the last step in a very complex volitional process, and to interpret the last step as *the whole process* is very careless.

In the meantime, if we tell an actor who is playing the ghost of Hamlet's father: here, in this bit, you want to push your son on the path of vengeance. Want this! Push Hamlet, inspire him to do so! – If that's how we say it, then it won't be enough, and . . . the stick won't fire.

For a very, very talented actor, especially if he's currently in an inspired creative state, and is immersed in the tragic character of the suffering ghost – then maybe these words will be enough for him. But only because he himself is an excellent rifle, loaded and cocked. All you have to do is aim and barely pull on the trigger . . .

But if an actor's soul is inert for some reason, if his soul has no powder, and its bolt assembly is rusty or lost some necessary parts . . . Then command him to "want" all you want – it's no good. Besides, it's necessary to note that a human is a much more complex machine than a rifle.

Anybody who'd trained in sensible internal technique (even just a bit) laughs at the naïve role development that's based "on feelings" – this is played "irritatedly," this is "happily," this – "in shock," this – "in love." They are quite justified in their laughter. Any emotion is a distant and complex response to a thousand impressions, and you can't just grab it out of the air. The only thing you'll grab is a pathetic semblance of emotion – a result with all its qualities, rather than a process. But it's the same with "desires." Telling yourself: "you have to want this thing!" isn't much better than demanding yourself to suddenly feel joy or despair or ecstasy.

So, in the end, what happens? Does breaking a role into tasks really create a *volitional score*? Of course not. It's an imperative score. A *commanding* score. And, finally, a forcible score. This is why, at the end of his days, while searching for the true path, the "system's" own author completely turned away from *psychological* tasks (which is what most directors continue to employ) in favor of *physical* tasks, and ultimately *physical actions*.

In this way, he departed more and more from the shackles of imperativity. And approached *nature*.

What was his main goal? – that's where we should turn our attention. His goal was the following: he always wanted to see only one thing onstage – genuine sincerity and boundless truth, i.e. *life* onstage or, to put it another way, *process*, not *results*. And it's so strange! This is what is almost always missed – probably because this achievement is considered to be easy, simple, and self-evident: "of course, authenticity! of course, sincerity! What else can it be? I always strive for this!"

I'll say the following, leaning on the bitter experience of a teacher and a director: whoever says this and thinks that to himself, typically has no idea, can't even imagine, what "truth" Stanislavsky is talking about. It isn't "self-evident" at all, you have to search for it, search some more, and keep on searching! If, for some reason, an actor falls into this state of utter truth while onstage, instead of giving himself over to it, he gets scared, he trips up, he says, "I've lost it . . ." That's how foreign, strange, and even scary this feeling is for him.

There is a myth that Stanislavsky changed all the time. People who worked with him (or came in contact with him) for a year or two would disdainfully say to those who worked with him before, some 10–15 years earlier: "Oh, you've really fallen behind! Stanislavsky's let go of that long ago! It's been forgotten and abandoned! Here's what he's doing now!" Those who said this knew Stanislavsky very shallowly.

I worked with him side-by-side for some 30 years (mostly on theory and the practical techniques of an actor's creative state onstage), lived directly next to him for a long time, and I can bear witness: in his essence, Stanislavsky *never changed*. He always strived for one thing (*for one thing only!*): he tried to find a way to *truly live onstage – as the world's greatest actors did in their finest moments*.

This alone is what united two of the greatest theatre artists of our time: him and Vladimir Nemirovich-Danchenko. This is the one thing that *never changed for them*. Whoever missed this missed the most important thing. They do not know either Stanislavsky or Nemirovich-Danchenko.

Stanislavsky changed the *methods* that he employed while trying to reach the *main goal*, but the *goal* itself was always unchanged. This is why he changed method after method – because the designated goal was too difficult to achieve, and the given method didn't give the necessary results. So he looked for a new one. New approaches, new methods, from this direction and that, trying to *get at* the main goal from every direction possible.

Stanislavsky's attitude towards his "system's" methods was very clear in these cases: sometimes, he'd stubbornly make an actor employ a single method of the "system," but as soon as the actor (either because of the method or another reason) became truly immersed, he would yell: "Now forget all the 'systems,' and keep it up – keep doing what you're doing!" Then he'd sit back and take pleasure in it.

Book Three

The Art of Living Onstage

From a Theatre Teacher's Laboratory

Translated by Andrei Malaev-Babel and Alexander Rojavin

Preliminary Notes (From the Author)

Creativity . . . Perhaps, no other area tempts one so strongly to stray upon the path of esoteric reasoning and philosophizing. On the other hand, no other area requires as much practicality and concreteness from those attempting its study.

The creativity of the actor is no exception. This is why the author took all possible precautions against the natural tendency of getting carried away with theorizing; instead he kept returning to the austere language of facts. A fact always strikes one as being too primitive and unworthy of thorough contemplation. In the end, however, the fact alone has decisive power.

Theoretical discussions, however, deserve special mention.

This is not a theoretical, but a *technical* book. Its goal is to describe a **method** that allows an actor to enter a state of creativity, and to master it. In this book, the method is explained as it developed throughout many years of practice, and as it has been taught by the author and his followers – to theatre students *throughout the first months of training*.

During these early stages, abstract reasoning should not amount, in the eyes of the students, to a finished theoretical construction. On the contrary, the single goal behind theory, at this point, is to lead a student toward a proper emotional state. This is why, firstly, each of these discussions (or rather, pieces of advice) has to strictly apply to those concrete cases described before the discussion. Secondly, these discussions take into consideration the age and experience of the student; therefore, theoretical discussions in the first period of training must be kept extremely simple.

On the other hand, I must console the more impatient readers. Later in the book, they will find entire chapters dedicated to freedom, involuntariness, and other, equally important, subjects. It is important to note, however, that one cannot fully comprehend these sections ahead before this material has been sufficiently absorbed – through practice. Even the final sections of this book do not provide exhaustive and concrete explanations. An attempt at greater precision and completeness has to be delayed until subsequent volumes of this collection.

If one reads this book in a practical fashion, striving to obtain the experience and knowledge essential to the theatrical practitioner and teacher – this deeper theory will become apparent without explanations. The most important aspect of the book is the method, explained in the language of sequential facts. Everyone, who wants to permeate the essence of the book, and those innovations it contains, must comprehend this method *in its practical power and succession*. In this case, some accurate theoretical deductions will inevitably be made.

The author is far from asserting that everything told here would remain unchangeable *forever and for all future times*. There will be new knowledge and, in its light, our present knowledge perhaps will seem ignorant.

At such a time, some beliefs that we consider unshakable today, will no longer be relevant.

Part I

The Significance Of The Actor's Creative Experiencing

Paths Leading Toward It

1
Initial Steps Toward Mastering the Art of the Actor's Experiencing

First Attempts to Create the Science of Actors' Art

When one observes great actors at work, their acting seems utterly simple and uncomplicated. One feels that he or she could get up, walk onstage – and act just like these actors – as effortlessly. Even their flights of inspiration and their power seem easily obtainable.

Why so? What causes such blunt self-delusion?

The reason is quite simple. While being among the audience, one involuntarily gives in to the impressions that come from the stage – one becomes subjected to the actor's power and begins to "share their feelings." A masterful artist takes me into his powerful hand and carries me along . . . But as soon as he lets go – I fall down from the clouds.

Let anyone who felt such a high, caused by an inspiring artist's acting, try to recreate it, on their own – they will learn that it is impossible. Many actors experience this phenomenon. Name an actor who, at the start of their journey, did not expect a sudden descent of inspiration. Nothing came of it, however. The majority fails again and again. Gradually, they abandon their expectations, and resort to mastering the simplest devices of their craft.

No one escaped such attempts to catch the heavenly fire with their bare hands.

Stanislavsky was no exception. He too, like the majority, soon learned that this is no path toward the lofty art. However, he did not give up or capitulate, like the majority, and began to seek for himself, and for others, some more practical and realistic ways.

On this path, he often got carried away; his methods were not free from mistakes that he himself soon renounced . . . Mistakes, deviations from the path, or imperfections are not essential, however. Every invention, at an early stage, is full of mistakes and incompletions. Take the first airplanes, for example. Their constructions had nothing but mistakes in them. The very thought, however, to move from air balloons to machines that are heavier than air, and to seek the solution to the question of aeronautics in this direction, was a genius foresight. This foresight, in our time, resulted in our super-powerful airplanes. Imagine what we could expect in the future!

Stanislavsky's thoughts and strivings were an equally genius foresight. He saw the future of the actors' art in the scientific development of their creative technique, or, as he called it, *psycho-technique*. The honor of originating this path belongs to Stanislavsky, this new science of the actors' creativity that ushered in a new epoch in theatre art. Moreover, Stanislavsky lay the foundation of the science and sketched its basic future plan. As for us, we must, as far as possible, continue this work.

It is not Stanislavsky's fault if some of what he suggested is misunderstood or sometimes distorted, according to the *abilities of the interpreter*.

Stanislavsky wanted to create (and he achieved his goal), a harmonious artistic production. This fact has been accepted in Russia, and in the world.

Stanislavsky wanted to create, and he has done so, a theatre – the best theatre in its time.

However, Stanislavsky himself looked at the accomplishments that satisfied others, and seemed a miracle of perfection, as at a mere threshold to theatre, and to the art of the actor. To begin with, Stanislavsky believed that this latter area was the weakest – despite his tremendous attention toward the work of the actor. The reasons behind the lack of achievement lie, according to Stanislavsky, in the theatrical working practices, but also in the actors. When it comes to working practices, he considered haste as the main shortcoming. As for the actors he had at his disposal [at the Moscow Art Theatre], he considered them established in their habitual ways and unwilling to move beyond those.

This is why, in order to continue his experiments, he had to create a "studio," i.e. a young theatre, where actors could practically study the discoveries he made in the area of the actor's mastery. The [First] studio [of MAT], however, also carried the atmosphere of theatre. Although less harmful, it nevertheless interfered with Stanislavsky's ability to investigate, in full, the effectiveness of his methods. Things like professionalism and haste once again came into the mix. Stanislavsky was forced to give the studio the freedom to develop in its own professional way (thus several theatre-studios were formed). At that point, Stanislavsky decided to create a theatre *school* by recruiting a new and completely fresh group of actors, and separating them from the theatre – or at the very least, freeing them from any obligation to develop a repertoire. By doing so, Stanislavsky hoped to obtain the "system's" unpolluted results.

In the early 1920s the Moscow Art Theatre, almost in its entirety, embarked upon a trip to America and I, the author of this book, as a specialist in the system, was entrusted to head this school and to teach the system. Everything in this school was established, based on a predetermined plan. Every "element" constituting, as we thought, the creative state, was trained separately – both theoretically and practically. The course as a whole was allowed as much time as seemed necessary.

Two years went by, however, without bringing the expected success. Young people, admitted to the school based on rather selective auditions, did not impress with their abilities or talent upon completing the required course . . . This somewhat disappointed the founders of the school. The students, however, noticeably improved in terms of their culture, their understanding of theatre, and an elevation of their ideals. In the end, it was concluded that the school gave even more than was expected from it.

The teacher himself, however, could not console himself with this flattering conclusion. He kept asking himself: what happened? Why did the spark that so noticeably gleamed in these young people during their auditions fail to flare up?

No thought of the "flop" of the system even came to mind. Therefore, the teaching technique is to blame? So, why would a more detailed study of every element, and its more systematic application, did not achieve a more effective result?

Two Paths Toward Experiencing, Indicated by Stanislavsky

At the basis of the art of experiencing there lies a ***process*** that causes an actor to transform into character and to live the character's life, to assume their personality, passions, and ideals.

Stanislavsky firmly outlined two paths that lead an actor toward this specific state of creative experiencing. The first path consisted of bringing the actor to a sound understanding of the role and the play; its whole and its every separate part, and, by doing so, bringing the role close to the actor and the actor to the role.

Another path, outlined by Stanislavsky, consists of learning the laws of the creative process and *applying the methods of a psycho-technique*. In practice, these two devices are typically applied simultaneously and complement each other.

As for the most talented actors, their process of creative experiencing emerges on its own (as an exception), as soon as they understand a role, feel it, and begin to burn with desire to act it.

Gifted actors, or even modestly-gifted ones, in their most successful moments ("at their best") enter the process of experiencing. This process is often triggered by the mere thought of the role and its circumstances. These cases, however, when they occur, do not guarantee the firmness of the experiencing; nor do they prevent its tendency to disappear at the first unfavorable condition.

Stanislavsky understood that this process is quite concrete and objective, and that it consists of a series of "elements", such as "attention," "communication," "imagination," "muscular freedom," "circle" – and others, indicated by him. When an actor, during rehearsal, was not conducive to creativity, it was sufficient to restore in him or her one of the given elements in order to cause the actor to enter a state conducive to entering the creative zone.

This solution, however, only worked today. Tomorrow, the work had to be started anew. It seemed that these elements, if developed in advance, would take no rehearsal time to develop. It was with this goal in mind that this work was outsourced to theatre school. Naturally, Stanislavsky himself never had a chance to engage in this kind of actor training – he was busy with artistic directorial work. While there were no actors with such a school, he personally worked on this in rehearsals.

This division into *two* equally important parts of the creative act – work *on the role* and work *on psycho-technique* – can be found throughout the entire book *An Actor's Work*. Nevertheless, Stanislavsky never made a clear and definite differentiation, nor did he formulate this division clearly in the book. Those who have read Stanislavsky's book or worked with him either did not notice this differentiation or perhaps noticed it, but did not consider its important meaning.

The majority of directors using the Stanislavsky "system," chiefly see in it only one of the paths toward creativity: play analysis, bringing near to oneself the circumstances of the role, the play's supertask, the through-action, the idea . . . while completely ignoring the development of the very process of creative experiencing. They do so, assuming that it is always at our disposal, as long as the actor understands the role and its meaning in the play.

Stanislavsky, as mentioned earlier, thought and acted differently.

2

New Paths

Departing from the Principle Of "Elements"

A school deals with the task of cultivating actors and developing their creative qualities. A school, therefore, does not concern itself expressly with the task of creating works of art – performances. This task plays a secondary role. This is why a school allows an opportunity to separate out this 2nd path – *"psycho-technique"* – in its pure form.

The first attempt to create a school, as it was described earlier, did not yield positive results. Things changed, however, going forward.

While teaching the "system," I continued to train students in its "elements," by offering them appropriate exercises. At that point, my attention was drawn to peculiar short etudes. They first flashed by as early as 1921, as a kind of a creative pedagogical find. At that time, busy with the "elements," I did not understand their value, but later I started applying them more and more, with greater and greater courage. These etudes, in turn, moved me toward a specific, peculiar way of conducting them.

As it turned out, the etudes, in their new modification, did not lose their simplicity and, most importantly, they contained all of the conditions that evoke a *sound creative state*. Gradually it became clear that these "etudes" allow us to see the very ***process of creative experiencing*** – in a form that is purer and easier to observe. Needless to say, all of my attention now switched to observing this process – tracing its origination, its flow, as well as the reasons behind its fluctuation and shutdown.

The former goal of developing "elements" yielded to a more practical task: working on the very process of the creative state.

While studying these newly developed etudes, and thanks to them, I managed to trace the following:

1   Chief conditions essential for the origination of the creative process of experiencing;
2   Conditions essential to its sound flow;
3   Mistakes that can occur during this process;
4   Ways to correct these mistakes.

These etudes paved the way for originating the process of creative experiencing in each of the 20–30 students in a class. Provided the discovered conditions are met (rather uncomplicated conditions, I might add), this process originates *without fail*.

Etudes are common in school work. We used to conduct etudes "in attention," "in fantasy," "in communication" etc. In general, these were etudes dedicated to "elements." Etudes introduced in this book, however, might be called etudes in *creative experiencing*. Through their use, the process of creative experiencing originates as a normal working state of creativity, and it proves to be entirely at our disposal.

3

On Freedom and Involuntariness in the Process of Creative Experiencing

On the Process of Creative Experiencing

What does it mean to "experience" onstage? Does it mean living just as we live in our daily lives and taking everything as real?

Everything onstage is a contradictory mix of things imaginary and real. To take all imaginary things as real equals hallucination.

What constitutes the process of our life? According to Sechenov [1965: 88–89]: "The initial cause of any action always lies in external sensory stimulation, because without this, thought is inconceivable." Therefore, the process of our life, from a materialistic standpoint, consists of a reciprocal response to a stimulation coming from without.

Imagine yourself, in mid-winter, sitting in a warm room, busy – reading or writing. Suddenly, the room grows cold . . . You shrink, shiver; you want to put on something warmer, you look around. As it turns out, someone opened the window. Quickly, you shut it down . . .

Here is a different scenario. You sit in the same room, also in winter, busy with your task. Someone walks in – perhaps your brother – and goes straight to the window. Apparently, he is about to open it. This same fresh-air-enthusiast was probably responsible for opening the window the last time. His preparation toward opening serves as a sufficient *signal* for you that the window will soon be open and that the same unpleasant "ventilation" will take place, as before. Although it has yet to become cold, you already find yourself under the impression that it is, and you become irritated.

And, finally, imagine a third scenario where your brother, this fresh-air-fanatic, having done absolutely nothing as of yet, would simply say: "It's so stuffy! Time to open the window." Although he has done nothing yet, these words alone serve as a *signal* of what must come next. Thus, in the first case, your organism reflexively responds to real cold. This is the ***first-signal system***, according to Pavlov's terminology, where the very fact serves as a signal for the reaction. In 2nd and 3rd cases, the fact itself is absent; it only exists in the imagination. This is the ***second-signal-system***; it equally evokes a human reflex, just as real facts do.

It is clear why a real fact would evoke a reflexive response. How is it possible, however, that a similar response is evoked in the absence of a real fact, just from its mention? The answer is quite simple: the fact is equally present in both of these cases. In the first case, however, it is an actual, present-time fact. In the second case, the fact existed in the past and, for the time-being, it lives in the *depths of our memory*. A mere word or thought about this fact (or something similar) evokes it again, along with all the accompanying sensations, physiological, and psychological. Here is another simple yet convincing example that speaks of the second-signal-system and its effectiveness. Imagine, or merely consider a slice of fresh lemon in your mouth . . . That very second, you will experience a seemingly real sensation, a *reflection* really, of irritation caused by the sharp-tasting acid; your mouth will fill with saliva. This won't last long, but it will happen. Now you have a choice: to either give in to the continuation and growth of this involuntary reaction, or to stop yourself by thinking: "What nonsense! In actuality, there is no lemon. I only *thought* of it . . ." At that point, the incipient process will be prohibited, and nothing will come out of it. This is how we act in similar cases – we inhibit our involuntary reaction. Truly, it would be quite dangerous and irrational to give way to all our reactions that are connected with word and thought.

This is how it happens in life. We are used to restraining ourselves – inhibiting all the manifestations that are connected with our spontaneous sensitivity. The work of the actor, however, almost exclusively consists of reactions to imaginary facts or **imaginary** circumstances. The law of the second-signal-system – an **indispensible reflexive response to word and thought** – is at the foundation of the actors' creative act. This is why actors, first and foremost, must **develop and cultivate their own ability to freely give in to reflexive reactions resulting from their perception of the imaginary**.

Physiologist Pavlov [1949: 338] says: "Life definitely reveals two categories of people: artists and thinkers. Between them is a marked difference." . . . An "artist's" cognition is predominantly "imaginatively emotional"; an artist is capable of "imagining objects and phenomena vividly, often to a hallucinatory degree." As for the "thinker," their cognition is predominantly "abstractly verbal."

People, who possess exclusively "imaginatively emotional thinking" don't exist; just as those with exclusively "abstractly verbal thinking." Every person inevitably combines both, with the exception that in one person an "artist" would prevail over a "thinker," while the other would be predominantly a "thinker," and not enough of an "artist."

Actors must give in to imaginary circumstances; they must believe in them and live with them, as if they were real. Needless to say, only those people with "imaginatively emotional thinking" are suited to that, while those predisposed to "abstractly verbal thinking" are completely unfit for the job.

Mochalov in his *Discussion* of the actor's art says: "Depth of soul and fiery imagination – those are the faculties constituting the chief part of talent." Fiery, vivid, and strong imagination is not inherent to everyone, but only to rare talent. As for the middle-of-the-way imagination, however, no one is deprived of it.

As stated previously, every person's organism reacts to thought and word. While this reaction originates in everyone, the real question at hand is whether one would extinguish this involuntary, organic reaction, or give in to it. In the latter case, the reaction would spread and might end up taking hold of a person entirely, until it could justly be called "fiery."

Great power can be found in such stimulation of free reaction or, to be more precise, in such surrender to a reaction. This is the key to one of the paramount qualities that distinguishes an actor. **To have courage to give in to a reaction fully, entirely is to solve numerous questions of the actors' creative process.**

Let us trace the path of this power, as it manifests itself in an actor's creative act, while also tracing the kind of things that help and interfere with this power.

I   I have a thought: in a moment, I will enter the stage; the audience will watch me, and I will turn into a character (perhaps, Liubim Tortsov from Ostrovsky's *Poverty is No Vice*). I will live with the same feelings, thoughts, and circumstances as the character I took upon myself. This thought alone has already *shifted me away* from my everyday, mundane experience of myself. To be precise, I no longer feel myself a mere everyday self, but an actor at work – a man who lives with the imaginary circumstances. Personally, I would not bare my soul in front of a crowd of people. In this instance, however, it won't be me, but Liubim Tortsov, whom I play. Isn't it so? This is why I don't need to restrain and stop all my impulses and manifestations, as they burst out of me, Tortsov. Let him, Liubim Tortsov, live and manifest himself through me . . . If one is bold enough to give in to this shift completely, to the end, it already makes an actor open toward creativity.

II   "It's cold!" . . . Not generally cold, but I, personally, am cold. Since I am Liubim Tortsov – this means that I am cold.

Having felt the cold, I don't fight it, but give in to this sensation. In the meantime, I add: "It's so cold that, unless something is done, I will freeze. . ." Having felt the temperature of minus 30–40 degrees, and having added to it: "I am poorly dressed" – I feel the cold penetrating me down to the bones . . . I shrink, I shiver . . . On top of it all, some new thoughts: "Brother turned me out . . . no one would let me inside . . ." Why won't they? – "Because I am a drunkard . . . a beggar . . . a sponger . . ."

III   As I add the new circumstances, one by one, I feel myself mysteriously change. Although I remain myself, I become somewhat different, not my usual self. Let's take an utterly different point of view on myself, on my surroundings – the point of view of a starving, degraded, homeless, hopeless drunkard . . .

"Mitya! Please take in the merchant's brother, Liubim Tortsov . . . . My brother turned me out! And in the street, in a coat like this – one has to dance about a bit! The frost – at Christmas time – brrr! – My hands are frozen, and my feet nipped." [Ostrovsky 1917: 86]

In the meantime, the imagined circumstances that accompany me, Liubim Tortsov, as well as my new state – all these factors permeate each other, creatively merge; I begin to rely on the process, give in to it, and this results in a phenomenon of creative transformation, and in me living with the creative circumstances of the character.

IV   The most interesting thing, however, is this. While I change, I simultaneously *mark these changes that occur in me*. Although I transformed in a character from the play – a character that lives his own life, foreign to me – my own, personal "self" did not disappear. It observes with curiosity, at times with astonishment, this new, unfamiliar fellow . . . Moreover, while watching, as an artist, I am satisfied with some things, while others don't meet my approval. Most importantly, I guide the actions of this newly developed person. At times, I encourage: "That's right, that's right . . . bolder, bolder . . . even bolder . . ." At times, I restrain: "Take care . . . take your time . . . take your time . . ." In short, there comes, in its fullness, the process of doubling, discussed by all significant actors of all times and countries.

At first glance, this creative process is full of contradictions. Here are some of them.

On one hand, an actor feels himself onstage and sees a large body of audience watching him. On the other hand, the play prompts him to experience himself as part of those conditions given by the author, i.e. alone with the partner, if not completely alone.

On one hand, the actor's personal "self," with all its special qualities, remains intact. On the other – he must transform into a character, often completely foreign and alien to the actor.

On one hand – the actual, matter of fact life of the actor; on the other – he must live the imaginary life of the play.

On one hand – the actor's personal point of view on the circumstances, characters of the play, including his own character he must play; on the other – this character's own point of view on all of it, etc.

In short, we are dealing with utterly irreconcilable contradictions that should, in theory, confound anyone who enters the stage. In the meantime, these very contradictions contain the powers that create "life onstage." One should not fear these contradictions. On the contrary, one must **exploit** them. These contradictions, or rather their dialectical struggle, create **truth onstage and artistic transformation** (instead of a complete, selfless merger between an actor's persona and that of the character).

This creative state of an actor, in its paradoxical nature, can be compared with the equilibrium of a spinning top. It's only due to the movement that the top can preserve its balance, and it falls as soon as this movement ends.

On Freedom and Spontaneity

Freedom and spontaneity in rehearsals used to come only at the completion of a given work.

Acquaintance with the play, and its analysis, persistent and careful work on a scene, plenty of repetition and corrections – these were the prerequisites to achieving from an actor a feeling of truthfulness and confidence in a given scene. When an actor grew accustomed to a scene, he could finally act it freely. Without violating these essential aspects established for the scene, he could nevertheless vary its nuances, according to his immediate state and based on the peculiarities his scene partner would have on a given day.

This freedom, however, did not appear without fail, but only in the case that a skilled director guided the work. In this case, this method could be used to enliven an entire role, not just one scene, having worked through it consecutively, bit by bit.

The problem is, the creative freedom – even if it did visit the actor in some scenes of the role – was not won firmly or once and for all. No sooner than an actor approached a new role, this freedom disappeared. An actor had to start from the scratch, seeking the truth in every scene and fulfilling the same amount of work of the same kind, as he did in the first play.

As a result of lengthy, painstaking (and necessarily sound!) work, an actor might again discover creative life and freedom for this new role.

Needless to say, the difficulty and inconvenience of having to *start from scratch every time* complicated the work. One would think that the sound state of creative truth, having been achieved in one case, would inevitably apply to everything else. After all, a human who learned how to walk on the house floor will now walk on the street and in the forest.

As it turned out, however, an actor had yet to learn *how to walk*.

As long as he existed in the given role, he was constantly supported and prevented from "falling" by one thing or another (such as "task," "object of attention," "action," "tempo-rhythms," etc.) As a result, the actor "moved" along the role with seeming ease. This freedom, however, was not the real creative freedom that could amount to one of the actor's chief and constant *qualities*. It was a deceiving freedom, akin to that of a locomotive running upon rails. A locomotive can run faster or slower; it can go forward and backward; yet it can only run upon a given set of rails, and it cannot go to the side.

One more thing pointed toward the fact that the actor had yet to learn how to "walk" (although he never strived for it either). This comparative truth and equally comparative freedom and spontaneity evaporated from a performance with repetition . . . Close inspection would reveal that only the external form remained. This form, fulfilled with habitual deftness (blockings, external actions, gestures, movements, intonations) was deprived of content, of inner life. This led to a misconception: as long as the discovered form was interesting, expressive, "logically coherent," it must be repeated in the appropriate rhythm and tempo. It will make its impression and *seem* as a manifestation of life. So, why bother with actual life onstage? This is the downhill path of an actor who capitulates to his own laziness, his tendency toward presentation, if not to mere craft.

Did Stanislavsky consider the actor's freedom? His entire directorial path was a journey from initial "despotism" toward freedom. Despite his directorial "despotism," he and his accomplice and closest associate Sulerzhitsky, would drop a word or two, somewhat by chance, about freedom, or would personally demonstrate such captivating spontaneity and independence from their own prescriptions, whatever they were, to make those present think one thing: how fine, how brilliant! Go ahead, try repeating it! This stunning, blinding beam of light was not an exclusive attribute to the later years; it also appeared at the time when there was no talk of any "system." The freedom and spontaneity of life onstage was at the base of Stanislavsky's talent, but also of Sulerzhitsky's. These words and deeds, however, did not turn into the seeds of "life onstage." Instead, they remain undervalued to this day. This became especially true following the emergence of the "system," when its "elements" were considered as the roots of a creative state.

At times, having conquered the actor's "inhibition," "tension," and falsehood through the use of many different means that fit the moment, Stanislavsky would situate an actor in a sound state. In these moments, he would say: "And now – complete freedom! Do what you want and how you want! May nothing bind you." In such cases, actors would rise to the highest manifestations of their talent.

To recreate this effect, however, lengthy and careful work was needed yet again to rid the actors of all those things that prevented them from being free and creative.

In a given scene, freedom seemed to come on its on, as a *sum effect* of correctly fulfilled work. Two questions arise. What is to be done, firstly, when this freedom is only suited for this given scene? Secondly, what is to be done about freedom being so unstable and easily lost?

In the end, pedagogical experience and practice supplied the answer. They showed that instead of waiting for freedom to grace us with its presence – at the end of lengthy and highly-qualified directorial work, *it must be cultivated as one of the chief creative qualities from the get-go*, beginning with the first lesson. Apparently, it can be cultivated so strongly that the actors' presence onstage, as well as their very entrance – the crossing of the stage threshold – would already serve as stimuli for freedom.

These observations revealed that freedom, spontaneity, and the creative state are inevitably tied together, and that they inevitably coexist; that *this freedom is always present* already in a simple, even simplest creative event; moreover, that freedom is *the very essence of creativity*, and an *integral part*.

Furthermore, the foundation being built out of this freedom – so firmly as to become the actors' second nature, their only way to exist onstage – such a foundation allows us to later affix to it the analysis and rationality of a commonly accepted approach to a role. Moreover, even in those cases when a certain measure of the imperative (command and order) is affixed – even then it does not extinguish the most important aspects of an actor's creative process – its freedom and spontaneity. In many cases, this will even prove to be fruitful and necessary.

If, however, at the start of actor training, one is to stress the development of rationality, of the imperative, and of the habit to analyze – these qualities will then form the foundation. Such qualities being the direct opposites of any freedom and spontaneity, may not completely extinguish the natural acting talent in a student; they will, however, produce the kind of stifling effect that will make it unrecognizable.

The New Approach to Creative Freedom and How It Emerged

Thus, the author began by teaching the "system" – "element" after "element." Due to his particular personality, however, and his pedagogical breed, he began to observe his students closely – not only with regard to the presence of a task, or attention, or object, or some other "element." While empathizing with the actors – living their lives – the teacher began to feel other mistakes that seemed less important but, nevertheless, interfered with the actors' life. At times, actors would push themselves – they would begin to rush; at times they would be afraid to give freedom to their feelings, or actions, and hold them back instead; at times they would make too much of an effort and thus creatively contract.

During an etude, the teacher would correct an actor's state by simply saying: "take your time," "yes, yes – this is correct!" (i.e. don't work too hard, don't push yourself, don't demand anything of yourself – everything you need is already there; everything is correct). This was just one of the devices aimed at enlivening the actor – this device belonged exclusively to the teaching practice. The time would soon come, however, when this tactic, rectified in school exercises, caused changes in my directing.

An actor, as before, would be given a *task*: what he must presently "do," and what he must "want." [In Ibsen's *A Doll's House*,] Krogstad comes to Nora in order to enlist her support in keeping his job at the bank (avoiding being fired). This is what he *wants*, and such is his *task*.

In order to successfully fulfill this main task, he also performs some others: to find out what is going on with Nora and, afterwards, to ask her to interfere on his behalf. Having met with indifference, he alternates between trying to move Nora and giving her an ultimatum. "Tasks" are clear to the actor, and so are his "actions." He *acts* and he *wants*. In the meantime, it is obvious that he is somewhat bound, constrained. Look, his interlocutress just upset him . . . he wants to get up from his place, but this is not included in his "task," so he forcibly remains seated. . .

The teacher, wishing to rid him of harmful constraints and, by doing so, clear the way for his main task, says: you wanted to get up, didn't you? – then why did you not do it? Why did you fight yourself? You must defeat Nora, and instead you are fighting yourself. Why couldn't you continue talking to her standing up? If this is what you felt like doing – don't interfere with yourself, do what you want.

- I don't want to draw away from my main task.
- Here, while we have been talking, you brushed a fly off your cheek several times. Apparently, this did not distract you from talking to me, and it did not disrupt your main task. Both of your needs were satisfied, without disrupting one another – the issue was solved, and you got rid of the fly.

Bit by bit, the actor begins to allow himself greater freedom . . . At some point Krogstad, while speaking of his downfall, of his disastrous situation, of his motherless children, picks up from the table an album with the sites of Italy . . . He picks it up without even noticing . . . Automatically he turns the pages, not seeing the marvels Christine and Nora just admired . . . And yet, this does not distract the audience one bit; on the contrary, his pointless, nervous movements inform them of his uneasiness, and of the high price he is paying for these forced confessions . . . The actor's creative process has begun; its first signs are apparent. We understand that these are not the signs of an actor's personal agitation, but are those of Krogstad's. Dare to stop him, and you would stop the entire process of carrying the circumstances of the role over to the actor. Give it way – and the actor will become Krogstad more and more and begin to live his life.

The actor, encouraged by his success, is less and less prone to forbidding himself to engage with what he "feels like" doing . . . Apparently, there is nothing bad or dangerous about it. When it comes to "I want" and "I feel like" – aren't they both manifestations of a singular life in a human being? At the very least, they get along together quite well. "I feel like" – is even somewhat more intimate; it tends to grip my entire psyche and, perhaps, my entire self. As for the word "want," upon close observation, it is not as all-powerful as they used to assume. Suppose, I said this word to myself – I did, but no desire seems to have appeared – I simply *don't feel like it*. At this point in the work, a more careful and serious attitude toward this seemingly insignificant "*I feel like*" emerged. Step by step, I started cultivating it in my students, as well as in the professional actors I worked with.

The work of cultivating actors conducted in the course of many years eventually led the author to directives and methods that were quite different from those he previously practiced. Today, some 30-something years following the inception of my initial thoughts, two things became obvious. In the first place, the new did not pop up suddenly, but rather burst in bit by bit, over the period of several years. Secondly, this new was born in the depths of the "Stanislavsky system" as a natural and inevitable consequence of my ongoing pedagogical search and observation.

Is it Feasible to Reconcile the Principle of Creative Freedom with That of the Imperative?

Those who carefully followed the entire flow of these new thoughts, starting with their inception, and down to their present condition, firmly grasped that these discoveries, and these new ways, cannot be seen as further developments and expansions of one of the **methods** belonging to some existing schools of acting.

This is a totally unique approach to cultivating actors, *fundamentally different* from other approaches. Having just emerged, this trend of theatre pedagogy that stands up for freedom and spontaneity in the actors' creative process started developing rapidly. In its development, it took the form of an opposition, if not to say protest against the former principles of teaching and cultivating actors – principles that often bound young people creatively, made them rational, and turned many into truth-like presenters onstage, rather than artist-creators.

As one moves from the first steps of actor training in school toward directing or staging a performance, one can not do without analysis of the play and the role, without prompting some "tasks," "actions," and blocking to the actor. At the same time, having discovered the true worth of creative freedom and having mastered its principles, it was impossible to reject them. I had no choice but to merge them, while keeping the *principle of the actor's creative process at the heart* of this merger. Both sides won from this synergy. The side of freedom in the creative process was enriched with artistic integrity, ideological directedness, and intelligent coherence, essential to a production. As for the analytical treatment of the performance and its every role, it became alive, inspired by actors' creativity and action. This new type of production no longer grew stale; it did not mechanize, nor did it fall apart with time. On the contrary, it began to grow, time after time it grew deeper and richer in content, and it excited the actors more and more.

It is not too late to engage in the cultivation of actors' freedom even at the stage of working on a role as a director. It is much more important, however, to *begin cultivating freedom while still in school*. Practice teaches us that this must be done at the students' very first steps, before they are corrupted by bad habits. Fighting such habits is never easy. From the very first meeting, the teacher takes to task developing the required QUALITIES in a student-actor: he starts with the sense of self (I am), with freedom in the creative process, with the "truth," and with that very state when "inside, beyond the actor's will, the organic nature with its subconscious joins the work" [Stanislavsky 1954: 356]. This is especially important for beginning students. They are like a virginally white sheet of paper: the first words written permeate it so deeply they cannot be erased; whatever else you might draw on it, the initial pattern will still shine through.

This book describes my attempts to embark upon this path of work with the students.

On Some Peculiarities of the Methods Used Here

Experience has shown that preliminary theoretical discussions introduced at the start of training create serious obstacles in the way of a practical mastery of the technique by the young actors. Such discussions scare students, put them on guard, and kill the spontaneity essential to an actor's creative process. Only the most essential explanations and remarks are needed, primitive enough to suit the first lessons, and adjusted toward the students' age – their lack of experience and knowledge. In such form, they are fairly harmless.

Training and cultivation during the initial steps consists of *leading the students toward creative freedom and spontaneity*. Creative freedom, spontaneity, and 3–4 other qualities that need to be developed make up the hidden *essence of an actor's creative state and are its chief motivating factors*. Is it necessary then, from the get-go to, plunge the student into the depths by analyzing these wisdoms? Students need to master the creative process, rather than philosophize about the subject. Would you, while teaching a child to walk, care to go into the laws of gravity?

A student can only accept and comprehend what becomes clear through *practice*. He can't even know what you are talking about, having not experienced it in deed. Thus, the job of the teacher is to give a short guiding message – and immediately move to practice. In the course of this practice, some things might require clarification, at which point, and only as it becomes necessary, a few more essential words – as far from a lengthy and complex theorization as possible. These words should merely provide explanations of the case at hand (the fulfilled exercise), to aid the given problem. A few words, capable of strengthening sound behavior in the students, of encouraging them, or carefully delivering them from an unsound, false state. This is the most fitting "theory" for the students' "age." It will strengthen everything that the students do right, and it will keep them from mistakes. In addition to that, it will clarify what's happening. With such answers and explanations, a teacher often has to resort to significant oversimplifications of our work. This is a temporary measure, however, aimed at redirecting the student away from rationally digging into their own state and its cooling effect.

As the students gain, step-by-step, practical mastery over the required state, as well as ways to approach it, they develop a need for more nuanced and precise knowledge of their work. They will no longer be satisfied with the old definitions – different explanations are needed, more complex, and closer to the theoretical essence of the process. At this point, while already at this new step of development, students will easily digest them. They won't interfere; on the contrary, they will arm the students with knowledge they most need. This is how practice and theory become one, while supporting and developing each other.

Part II

The Path of Spontaneous Reaction

4

Mistakes of the Past and Glimpses of the New

The year was 1921. The course of "actor's psychological technique" was huge: along with my assistant, I could hardly fit it into two years. We familiarized the students with all the "elements" that constituted, according to our deep conviction, an actor's sound creative state. We trained in our students each of the elements separately . . . As for the results we counted on, they were missing: the students' heads were full of fascinating information; they clearly distinguish the shortcomings and merits of someone else's acting. Personally, however, they, could, alas, do very little . . . This is considering that there were no ungifted people among them.

Perhaps you might think that there was too much theory and not enough practice? No. There was plenty of practice. The mistake was hidden elsewhere: by rationally dividing into elements the indivisible creative process, we murdered the main thing: spontaneity and the involuntary nature of life onstage, i.e. we murdered the creative process itself. Our poor student repeated the sad story that happened with one hapless centipede in a well-known tale.

There once lived a centipede. All of its 40 legs carried her everywhere with such speed that no one could neither catch up with her, nor escape from her. How many people envied her! But the scorpion envied her most of all. And so he came up with a devilish thought. One day, he came to his friend, the centipede, and started gashing:

- Oh, what a runner you are! Ah, what lightning speed! Tell me, I pray, how you do it? This must be awfully hard, I would think!
- What's hard about it? So, I run – no big deal.
- What do you mean: no big deal . . . My heart stops when I just think of it: you have *40* legs – how do you manage them? Above all: they all work together at the same time, and each does its own job.
- I swear, it's very simple: I just lift up the first leg, and all the rest simply follow.
- What a liar! Look: your first leg is lifted all the way, while your sixth leg is merely bent; the 32nd leg is only thinking of bending . . . look, look!
- Goodness me! – the centipede got a fright, "it is true: each leg is on its own. How is it possible?"

She started watching herself: "let's see, what's my 37th leg doing, while my 13th . . . in the meantime, my seventh . . ." She wanted to give it up – impossible! – thoughts kept crawling back in: "what is this leg doing while . . ." She stopped running, she could hardly even walk . . .

This was true of our students: what is my "task?" Let us say: to apologize. What do I need to do to succeed? Above all, I need to "concentrate" on my partner. OK, I will concentrate. In order to truly concentrate, however, I must "enter the circle." I entered the circle – my task went away. I rediscovered the task – tension crept in, out of nowhere. As soon as I released my muscles – I lost "communication." Etc., etc., etc. . . . This makes me laugh now. At the time, however, it was a disaster.

An accident, quite insignificant, came to the rescue. I visited the provinces and accidently found myself in a theatre. In the third act, when the leading man and his leading lady reached their climactic scene – a cat walked onto the stage. How did she get there? Who knows? I suppose, it was an oversight. The cat entered quietly, calmly, lazily . . . She sat down in the middle of the stage and wrapped her tail around . . . It looked at the audience . . . and found nothing exciting there: ordinary people . . . sitting there . . . gaping . . . The cat yawned . . . it looked around. Behind her stood a table, covered with cloth, some paintbrushes stood on it. The cat found them attractive. She jumped up, touched the paintbrush with her nose a few times, rubbed her face against it, touched it with her paw, played with it, then got bored . . . A few times she wagged the tip of her tale in displeasure, and, without any hurry, walking into the opposite wing, quite disappointed.

Needless to say, I completely missed everything said by the "leads" – the cat upstaged them.

The same is true of little children: someone brings in a little guy – you can't take your eye off of him. What is the trick? What are they doing so that they upstage everyone? Nothing, of course. Yet they do upstage. Do they *really do* anything at all? Perhaps, something in them **acts on its own**?

Let's take that cat, for example. She was promenading backstage – she got bored, got tired of strolling. Over there, on the stage, someone's making noise, stamping their feet . . . and, quite of its own accord, **something in her walked** to the stage, **something sat down on its own** . . . Her head turned on its own to look around the room . . . something exciting – over there . . . and her legs, on their own, carried her toward the brush . . . the cat does nothing she does not feel like doing. Moreover: *she does not act* at all – **something in her acts on its own**. Could this be the secret? Actors are usually "active:" they *do* things. When it comes to the cat, however, things are **done** in her; they are done *on their own*.

If one strives to achieve *life* onstage, one probably must get involved very little. One must learn, I suppose, *not to get involved at all*. One must achieve through training the kind of state where things are **done on their own**. In our mundane, **everyday life**, things probably happen this way. Our behavior is a natural reaction to the impact, both external and internal. Then, all of the actors' behavior onstage must be a natural creative reaction to their perception of the play as a whole, and each of their partners. This is no big discovery.

A few days later, I was overcome with doubts. Is it truly so? Perhaps this cat simply distracted me, as an accident that had nothing to do with what went on? . . . I even made up my mind to reject the "feline technique" when I remembered one story . . .

It happened long ago – also in the provinces. Mamont Dalsky, a well-know provincial actor at the time, performed the role of Corrado in a touring show of *La Morte Civile* by Giacometti. He performed it splendidly; one would say, he did not perform Corrado, but rather that he **was** Corrado.

For greater clarity, I should, perhaps, sketch the plot of this long-forgotten play. A girl marries a young painter, Corrado, in secret from her father. The girl's brother decides to rescue his "dissolute" sister and return her to their father. Corrado, in a clash, kills the brother. The killer is caught and sentenced to penal servitude for life. The shamed girl falls into hard days of hunger, cold, and poverty. She would perish if not for a tenderhearted man, who takes her in – sick, abandoned, on the brink of death, with a newly born little girl. To avoid gossip, the two move to a different town. The hard times pass, and good fortune follows. The child grows and becomes attached to her new father; the mother mentally buries her husband; when out of the blue – 14 years later – he walks in. This unsociable, embittered escaped convict demands that she follow him: they will escape to the mountains, where they will take cover from the police. She agrees: she must save her daughter from a new catastrophe. She will leave with him, but the daughter will be left in safe and loving hands . . . The convict's face begins to grow serene with joy. His eyes soften and become human, as if he is returning to life. At this point in the performance . . . a cat walks onto the stage . . . I remember that something pricked me as if I witnessed a crude and dumb practical joke. Corrado keeps looking at his wife, keeps looking around, as if he just came to from a long, grievous dream and did not quite believe in his own awakening . . . His soul warms up and thaws; his dim, gloomy eyes cleanse and grow radiant. He slowly looks around the entire room . . . he sees the cat and reaches for her, as if she were an old friend. The cat approaches. He pats her, and his eyes fill with tears – he feels himself at home. Tenderly, he picks up the cat and starts petting her, while shyly telling his wife of his gratitude and love.

He asks her to tell him everything, and the wife frankly tells him about her bitter wonderings, of growing to consider her sentenced-for-life husband as deceased, of the noble man and his deed – the man, who saved her life and the life of her daughter. She speaks of the daughter's love for that man.

"Could it be that you also grew to love him in all this time?"

Without noticing it himself, he puts the cat down on a chair next to him, thinking of something else . . . Gradually, bit-by-bit, he begins to understand that he brings with him misfortune and nothing else . . . Why ruin his wife's happiness? Why leave the daughter motherless? Why separate two noble people, who grew to love each other? . . . In his soul, he reaches a turnabout: he must leave . . . Leave this life for good . . .

Where did the cat go?

I don't remember. I was no longer following such trifles.

When a great "truth" graced the stage, and the cat walked in with its small "truth" – she turned out to be powerless. Next to the great "truth," hers was like a candle in the sun.

What did the actor do in order to achieve this *great truth*? And did he do anything at all?

He *did nothing*. Everything was *done on its own*. I saw at the start, when his wife recoiled upon recognizing him – blood rushed to his face, and he could hardly get hold of himself. I saw his face beaming with joy, and tears start in his eyes when his wife agreed to flee with him. I saw him grow pale, as soon as he understood the real state of things . . . I saw him get up involuntarily, walk, sit down again – not thinking of it, and probably not even suspecting: his hands bent on their own, took, let go, drew in, pushed away . . .

Doubts might arise: did the actor upstage the cat by making her play along? He took her in his hands, he petted her, etc. And what if he paid no attention to her, like those two provincial "leads," – in such case, perhaps, would the cat "upstage" him? Not so. Things went differently as soon as the cat appeared. In the first case, the cat attracted my interest the moment she entered the stage. Something more engaging emerged than what was there till this point. In the second case, the cat angered me right away: what are they thinking! A certain actor's sense of smell told the gifted, experienced actor that the audience listens to him, follows him, afraid to make a sound, or a glance. When the cat came in, he immediately sensed that it might anger, distract . . . For a second, he *partially* came out of the role and took the cat in his hands (for our sake, not just for his own), as if saying: "Don't be concerned; she does not bother me. You see, I am holding her . . . she even helps me. . ." Thus he put us at ease. Moreover, the actor felt himself differently than the other "leads." They only "portrayed" their "feelings and passions for the audience," while he felt himself inside the room, in the house where his wife lived . . . Here are the table, chairs, walls, windows, doors . . . A cat walks in . . . and why not? This is his wife's cat, and his daughter's . . . Affectionate cat . . . you feel like picking up and petting . . . And so he does.

This recollection dispelled my doubts: the truth of life onstage can only be achieved when one learns to be completely **natural**, i.e. freely **gives in** to the kind of state where something in you acts and speaks by itself.

The reader has probably developed some doubts and objections by this point. The first doubt: "acts by itself" . . . And what if it doesn't? And how could it, really? Freedom, naturalness, involuntariness – all these things will cause me to act based on what I, the actor Ivan Ivanov, personally need at the moment – rather than what the author and the character need. Let's use your example with the cat: she did have the utmost freedom and complete involuntariness; however, they went beside the play – perhaps even against its flow. This is objection number one.

And the second objection is even more significant and fundamental. Doing everything involuntarily . . . i.e. without the participation of one's consciousness and willpower per se . . . The actor, however, consciously arrived at the theatre; he put on his makeup and costume and, finally, he entered the stage – all consciously, and not because "it entered on its own."

Yes, this is definitely true: all of it happened consciously. I do not claim that good actors, as they create onstage, do so without any input from their consciousness. I do insist, however, that good actors are marked by *a correct distribution between the work of their consciousness and their automatic creative involuntariness, with all their quantities and qualities.*

These thoughts of the concurrent harmonious work of consciousness and automatic involuntariness came much later and were clarified later yet. We will have to return to them in this book. As for the time period in question, it brought clarity as to the power and irresistibility of the non-rational, involuntarily, *reflexive* behavior onstage. At that time, I felt that it solved all issues, and that it alone must be cultivated, while deliberativeness and self-observation must be scratched once and for all.

Was it an overzealous mistake and blindness? Theoretically, it was, but not *in practice*. Practice revealed that it takes telling an actor: "completely reject *all* rationality" – to entice them to give miniscule, merely perceptible freedom to their spontaneous creative manifestations. Otherwise, they almost entirely *prohibit* them. This became evident with practice. It is in this very light that one should perceive the aggressive "persecution" of rationality and praise of involuntariness that are to be found here.

Moreover, this directive has proven itself equally correct and effective in areas, such as one's approach to a role and a character, as well as in the area of directorial work, let alone actor training.

If one were to look closely at the psychological process that distinguishes significant actors in moments when they are at their best and act well, one would see that this very process, or something similar, takes place inside their creative instrument – they are free and involuntary.

5

Freedom and Involuntariness

About 30 years ago, at the first meeting with the new crop of students, we got acquainted, congratulated the young people on being admitted, told them all kinds of nice words about their giftedness (after all, we accepted 10 out of a 1,000!). After that, without further ado, we declared quite categorically: "Nevertheless . . . dear young men and young ladies, do bear in mind that you are essentially ignorant. You are just raw material, and we, great masters of our craft, will strive to transform you into brilliant talents." We were not as blunt, of course, but . . . this was the meaning of our speeches.

These speeches were immediately furnished with proof: please enter the stage and walk about. Who walks this way? Just walk about, take a stroll, as if you are strolling alone in a garden, or forest. That's not it: you are not strolling, you are marching convulsively, while trying with all your might do deceive us that you are comfortable, at ease, that you are resting . . . Please take a seat . . . now turn around . . . smile . . . Everything proved to be wrong: they could not look, or listen, or walk, and as for speaking – you just wish they would not open their mouth.

We were quite ingenious and persistent in this work: in a month or two, the young people had no doubts left: they can do nothing, and they have no skill. Whatever gift they revealed at the auditions was just raw material, and what they considered skill was total dilettantism and amateurism. "We know nothing, and we ought to be taught everything from scratch."

And so we did . . . the very same way the scorpion taught the hapless centipede.

Time passed, and I came to begin quite differently. The only thing left from our former devices were the words: "Hello, I congratulate you on your acceptance and wish you all kind of success!"

After that, everything went backwards: "There is not much I can teach you, really, as you know everything and can do everything."

- What do you mean? We came here to learn. We know nothing.
- Do you not know how to walk around the room, or look out the window? Do you not know how to talk to each other? sit, lay, eat, drink? Do you not know how to watch and listen? Pardon me, how old are you?
- 20.

- You see, for the last 18 years, at the very least, you've been doing nothing but walking, sitting, listening, talking, thinking daily, – in short, *living*. When you sleep, your life also does not stop. This means that 24 hours a day every day, you've been training and practicing. What can I possibly teach you? Moreover, life taught you the kinds of intricacies I could never manage to teach you. For example, if I was now insincere, wouldn't you immediately notice and think to yourself: oh no, come on, man, you are being coy! You are so good at watching and listening, I doubt I could trick you. Tell me frankly, not fearing to upset me, do you not see that I am completely sincere with you?
- We do . . . But what do you mean we have nothing to learn?
- Nothing! There is only one thing I can help you with: actors, from the start, can be disturbed by the audience – it distracts them, agitates them . . . I can help you with one thing: *get used to doing in front of the audience* what you already do so well without the audience – *living*.

  Without further ado, let's get to work on this. Let's sit in a circle so that we can all see each other well. Let's start with what you are all so good at: let's converse with each other. Something quite uncomplicated. One, two lines – a question; one, two lines – an answer.

  Who should we start with? Let's start with you. You will ask the girl next to you: "How do you like this weather?" and she will reply: "The weather is great". . .

Many students admitted to the school were informed people, more or less. Usually, I immediately received a question: And what is my "task?" What are my "given circumstances?"

- Don't think as of yet of any "task," "given circumstances," or anything else. I give you the lines . . . nothing else. Let these lines come out on their own, as they want to be said. It's OK. Do repeat what you are going to ask her.
- How she likes this weather.
- And what will you reply to that?
- The weather is great.
- Very well. Do begin.

What happens at this point is usually quite predictable: people do the opposite of what they really want to do and how they want to do it. They get agitated; begin to rush and say their lines "just to say them" or quite artificially, trying to "present" something, to "portray". . .

  Without going into analysis or criticism, I would say:

- Wait a second, you are rushing – you did not want to speak yet; the words had yet to ripen in you; there was no *desire* to say them, yet you made yourself say them all the same.
- True, I spoke these words a bit . . . for no reason.

As for his partner—the girl, who responded to his empty, forced words with a similarly forced and artificial reply—I would ask her:

- Did you understand what he was asking you?
- Yes, how I like this weather.
- No, the *words* he said were about weather, but he had no thoughts about the weather – he hardly took any time to understand what was going on, and just forced out the assigned words. We all saw and heard it, and he admitted as much.

You also rushed: you had no time to understand anything; nothing reached you yet – all the same, you replied. Let's do it again. But no rushing, and don't speak until you really want to.

Usually things would be sorted out quickly – the students stop rushing. However, forcing and intellectual strain remain. They continue to invest their words with things they do not feel or think. While striving to lead a student onto a clear path, I might say:

- Here, you looked out the window, addressed your neighbor and asked her how she likes this weather, and she replied: "The weather is great." Perhaps you wanted to take her out for a walk in this great weather?
- Yes, I wanted to invite her to take a walk.
- But it's raining. It's October, autumn, mire, cold – you looked out the window and didn't see it?
- No, I saw, but my partner has the lines: "The weather is great," so I tried to imagine it's summer, and the weather is good.
- Is this what I asked of you? I gave you the **words**. And I asked only one thing of you: do not interfere – live as you feel like living. Did I say: force yourself? Remember what you did? You looked out the window – cold autumn rain drizzling . . . leaden, smoky clouds; a naked, wet tree swinging in the wind . . . Bleak, nasty feeling . . . Don't interfere with yourself: just as you feel: shivering from cold, with this very disapproving grimace you now have on your face, ask: "How do you like this weather?"
- And how should I reply? – the girl is perplexed. – The weather is nasty, and I should say that it's great?
- But why? No one forces you to say that the weather is great. You were only assigned the *words*, as for how they want to be spoken – this is none of my, and even none of your, business – they will come on their own, as they wish. Go ahead, tell us what you saw! Did I, your partner, look out the window?
- You did.
- I asked you how you liked this weather. What did you hear in my question? "Look at the nastiness outside of the window" – that's what you heard. Do you agree with me that it's nasty?
- I do.
- Then just say so.
- In that case, I want to say it with annoyance, with disappointment: it's so great it couldn't be any worse.
- So do it.
- But I thought I was supposed to speak of great weather; I thought I was not allowed to mention bad one. . .
- Not allowed? You are not allowed to *interfere with yourself and force yourself to do and say what you don't want to. Everything else is allowed.* All of a sudden, your head turns toward the window – let it turn . . . This rotten autumnal sight makes you feel bleak and hopeless – let it be so, don't interfere . . . Your head turns away from the window – you don't want to look. . .

Most importantly, don't interfere with yourself, don't try to invent anything: everything must happen beyond you. Be as simple and spontaneous as a child.

- I have a question! – says one of the students.
- Go ahead.

- How can this be? When onstage, I am always given something quite definite. If you get used to "giving in" to your "urges," you will end up mixing up all the blocking and confusing your partners.

It is clear – this man has performed a lot, and he is the kind of person who needs to decide and come up with everything in advance, so that he could just "execute" it onstage.

- We must learn how to *live* onstage – I would reply, – so let's work on this now. Later, when we've learned how to do this, we will be learning how to guide this life. If we start *guiding* now, nothing will come of it: we've got nothing to guide as of yet – there is no life yet. If you start restricting yourselves from the first steps – you will never find out what living onstage means. On the contrary, you will develop a habit: at the first signs of life, just as the bud begins to open, you will say: this is incorrect! how dare you! wrong way! – and begin, according to your comprehension, to tear apart its tender core. . .
  Where will this habit lead you? It will lead you to the death of creativity. Corpses walk upon the stage – they think they are busy with art. A cat comes on and "upstages" them. Restrictions are needed, only not now. Don't even think of them at this point. Now – complete freedom: give way to everything that originates in you creatively. Only, as much as possible, don't break windows and furniture and don't tear your clothes to bits, and those of you partners. . .

They would laugh, liven up, and become a bit braver.

For several months, I forbid myself to speak of any restrictions. Instead, I demand only one thing: complete and unconditional freedom. Let's, however, be honest. Look, from the very first steps, I gave them a restriction, and what restriction! I *gave them some very definite words*!

Later, with time, I would throw in some new circumstances. Once again, I will do it so that they don't seem restrictive. On the contrary, they will *instigate greater freedom* by enticing and igniting the actors' fantasy. We will discuss this device later.

I am not a proponent of pedagogical methods like improvisations on a given theme with free words. These improvisations usually turn into empty babbling – people are scared of one thing only: God forbid, they might grow silent – so, they put all their effort into talking some nonsense non-stop.

Such improvisations are hard for actors; they consider them a burden. As they go to do them, they think of it as punishment. How could it be otherwise? Such improvisations are alien to the very nature of theatre.

Does an actor need to have the skill of composing lines or even entire plays? Is it not the other way around? The words are given, and changing them is not recommended. Verbal improvisation in theatre bears the rather indecorous name of "ad-libbing."

True, these verbal improvisations sometimes give birth to amusing things – complete little plays . . . Where does this point? This points at some *dramaturgical giftedness* on the part of the actors. There is nothing wrong with actors who are also playwrights. Yet, first and foremost, they must be *actors* – people capable of investing the alien characters they receive from the author with life and meaning.

In order to do so, they must yield their thoughts and feelings, their entire self, in fact, to someone else's words and to some foreign character. This is intrinsic to an actor's nature; without this actors cannot create. Moreover, living creatively in someone else's character is not merely the attribute of an actor – it is a necessity of certain true talent.

This quality must be encouraged without fail and developed from the very start.

How does it happen, in our etudes that the alien words do not interfere; on the contrary, they help, and they fit like a glove?

It happens like this: scene partners, the surrounding environment, my personal state and my fantasy, ignited by given words — all these factors merge together and shape my creative life. Imperceptibly, *mandatory words guide* this life.

In my lessons, I do use improvisations that are absolutely free, although I use them in small doses and with a certain goal.

Students, who ask their partner a question know perfectly well what words they will use to ask it. These words are never unexpected. Those who respond also know and anticipate them. This is a prohibiting fact, as it goes contrary to life. In life, we never know what we might be asked. This is why I need my students to *practically recall how it happens in life*. For that purpose, I offer them the following exercise: please, ask your neighbor some question, and you, neighbor, reply what you want. Let's agree, however — no empty chatter. One, at the most two phrases for the question and, similarly — two, three, four words for the answer.

This exercise is especially instructive for the people that are asked a question. They don't know what question to expect and, therefore, each question comes to them as a *surprise* and catches them off guard. This suddenness and unpreparedness constitutes one of the chief distinctions between life and the kind of predetermination we always have onstage.

To ensure the process of *living* onstage, we must ensure that the actor does not know and is not prepared for the question or for the answer. The exercise with "free text" makes this practically evident. This is why I offer it to the students.

A young fellow sits in his chair; he knows he is about to be asked something, but he does not know exactly what. He is, apparently, from the provinces; I remember, he came to the audition in some embroidered, eye-popping, collarless shirt, his hair long and shaggy. In the three days he spent in the capitol, he managed to change his haircut; he found a shirt with a collar, a tie, and he got hold of a suit. His good taste, however, is still in its very inception . . . One thing is clear: he is doing his best to enter the "civilized world" as soon as he can, and he is scared of making mistakes.

A young girl, his partner, glances at him, laughter in her eyes. She turns away and breathes out:

- Why are you wearing such a . . . green tie?

He blushes, grabs his tie, quickly looks the room over and prattles in response, scared:

- What's wrong? Is it so bad?
- You see, — I would say, — how it pricked you. This is what it means — to be unprepared!
- Yes, I could not expect she would ask about the tie.
- Did it embarrass you?
- Yes. . .
- Then mark what it feels like, when you do not anticipate the words. In life it is always so. A live scene is only possible when it is equally unexpected for both partners.
- How do we achieve it, though?
- Everything in due time. . .

Many of my readers will wonder: why do the students say the very words they are assigned? Since they are infinitely "giving in" to boundless freedom and involuntariness, propelled by some unexpected feelings and actions, then the words should also come by surprise. Nevertheless, they still only say the assigned text. Could this be a matter of constant self-observation? If this is so – what kind of involuntariness is it really?

This suspicion is fully legitimate. My assistants and I spent a long time in the beginning, distrusting ourselves and our actors, not understanding what's going on: an actor would repeat the lines once or twice and, going forward, these very words would jump out of their mouths *without fail, for no apparent reason.* Several years passed before we understood the real reason behind this phenomenon. A special chapter in the third part of the book is dedicated to it.

6

Actors' Fantasy

All these beginning etudes are built so that their text would provoke the young actors' fantasies; so that, whether they want it or not, they are affected involuntarily by the words. Here is an example: "We need to have a serious talk." – "I was expecting this for awhile."

I would ask an actress:

- Tell us, why did you address him so embarrassedly, but also so seriously and business-like? How did this happen? Who is he? Who did your partner become for you?
- It all happened on its own. I wasn't thinking anything . . . just looked at him . . . he sat so importantly . . . I thought he was a big boss . . . I even felt a bit shy . . . It looked like my little brother got into trouble at school, again, and I have to rescue him . . . At that point, he looked at me, saw my embarrassment, but that made him puff up even more. So, my lines just burst out: "We need to have a serious talk."

Then I would ask him, her partner:

- What about you? She says: important, a big boss . . . Why did you have this air of importance about you? How did it happen?
- Did I really? I did not want to be important . . . You said – don't get involved, let everything come on its own . . . Well, this morning they made me angry at home, even hurt my feelings . . . for some reason, all this came up . . . that's all.
- You remembered your offenders and wanted to give them a piece of your mind?
- Yes . . . I wish I had . . .
- Then you didn't see your partner?
- I didn't at first, but then my head turned to the right, on its own, and I saw. . .
- Saw whom?
- She was embarrassed, confused . . . I imagined that she had something to do with my trouble, directly or indirectly . . . She must have felt guilty – conscience stricken. Look at her, – I thought, – she did something stupid and is now apologizing . . . Here, she told me she needed to have a serious talk. There, – a thought popped in – finally you feel

yourself in the wrong! I will teach you a lesson. I will give you a piece of my mind! At this point I said, as calmly as I possibly could: "I was expecting this for awhile."

- There you go, – I would say, – you asked me to give you "circumstances," a "task" – see how the circumstances swept you over, on their own – good luck keeping up! The task also appeared . . . just as everything else you were concerned about . . . .

Influenced by the teacher's comments, by the partners' lines and behavior, actors enter a *different state; desires and thoughts arise, gestures burst out, words are spoken on their own* – in short, **they live, as they feel like living.** Just go ahead and *give in* to your internal and external impulses – to all this *life of the imagination and fantasy.*

The state of *"living, as one feels like living"* equals actors' creative fantasy.

Students (as well as experienced actors) must be trained *not to get involved* in their own manifestations. By doing so, they would develop and cultivate a specific type of fantasy, intrinsic to them as actors. *This particular fantasy instigates action and creates* **life onstage.**

- Now switch the lines around. What will you tell her?
- I will say: "We need to have a serious talk."
- And you?
- "I was expecting this for awhile."
- Go ahead. But take your time.

He looked at her, gave a faint smile; his hand was on the point of moving . . . but he suddenly stopped it, grew serious and earnestly asked her about some business. She replied. It looked truthful . . . but it wasn't truth.

- Remember, at the very start, – I would tell him, – you looked at her and smiled? Did you like her?

He is blushing.

- Did I smile? I don't remember. I did smile, didn't I? . . .
- And you wanted to put your hand on the back of her chair.
- No.
- How come? You hand began to move on its own. But you held it – you didn't let it. Like this (I would show him). Try to remember.
- That's right, now I remember.
- You see. Life began; it was an interesting life, but you cut it short, all of a sudden. Instead, you *forced* yourself to live with something that did not interest you whatsoever. Needless to say, it did not interest us either. It wasn't truth, but something truth-like instead. Go on, take a chance: give yourself full freedom. Don't be embarrassed. This is just an exercise. An etude. Search for the technique of "free life onstage." Go ahead! Risk it! What will come will come!

The young man, full of resolve, sets about his work, but suddenly he stops, puzzled.

- What's wrong?
- I want to get up . . . I thought, someone's behind that door, and I must ask her in secret. . .

- They why didn't you get up, walk up to the door, and look? If this is what you want, then go ahead; don't interfere! One more time! Just don't try to repeat what came before. Most likely, something different will emerge, something new; don't get in your way.

This is how, step by step, I lead people onto the path of freedom and spontaneity. I catch their every breath, every miniscule movement, every quiver of an eyebrow, each change in the life of the eyes. Just as soon as I feel that my actors might apply the break, disallow something, – I help them with a gentle tap on the back: "Give in! Bravely give in!" – and they take risks, they dare.

They take risks once, twice – in a week or so, you can't recognize them: such boldness, such involuntariness, such unpredictable flights of fantasy . . . Even the actors are surprised: where is all this coming from? They don't prepare; they don't plot it out in advance. Suddenly, the surrounding environment is transformed through the prism of fantasy; imaginary facts are felt tangibly, as existing facts. Beyond their own will, they begin to react to all this – and life begins.

This is what *actors' fantasy* is. It is this fantasy that must be encouraged and developed.

When students sit and *contrive* interesting etudes; when actors lean over backwards trying to invent the more exciting "treatment" for a scene, it may not be as bad; except those are the beginnings of the kind of fantasy suitable for stage directors, and the end of the certain fantasy intrinsic to an actors. This very fantasy, which needs to be stimulated and developed, is murdered instead. Gradually, it begins to die down, and soon, it will be forever gone.

7

Students' First Steps "Onstage"

We began our exercises while sitting in a circle. This way everyone could see each other well.

Meantime, during the second lesson, one of the students would definitely "want to get up." I would catch this, bring it to everyone's attention, and emphasize: you didn't want to sit, did you? If you wanted to get up, why are you sitting?

- Yes, I wanted to get up. But you sat us all down, and I understood it in such way that we are not allowed to get up.
- Not allowed? There is only one thing you are not allowed: interfering with yourself and doing what you don't feel like doing. Since you want to get up, to walk, to do something – how dare you interfere?

By saying this, I make an inconspicuous, barely perceptible transition toward movement. During this same class, or the next one, I make an equally inconspicuous transition toward *mise en scene*. I give the students a text like this:

- I have something to tell you.
- All right. Would you please make sure no one's listening? I think someone is standing behind this door.
- (Goes, opens the door, checks and comes back.) Nobody's there.
- Say it . . .

During the third or fourth class, I take one step further: I put two chairs and a table in one part of the room, move the students to the other part and sit among them. What we've got is an "audience" and a "stage." I would call students onto the stage and give them some uncomplicated lines, such as:

He and She. Sitting silently.

He.   Well, I must go.

She.   Stay a little longer.

They keep sitting.

He.   I must really go now.

She.   Come see me again when you can.

He.   Thank you. Good buy.

She.   Good buy.

He leaves, and she remains.

By the way, leaving the stage is easy, but coming onto the stage is not. This is why I postpone entrances as much as I can.

In some cases, I have to move a student onto "the stage" ahead of time, whether I want it on not. This happens when I come across a very communicable, outgoing guy. You give him and his partner an exercise, but he "pulls in" everyone in the room, not just his partner. He trades glances with them, makes exchanges with his eyes and face. . .

I would tell him: "You are alone with your partner, no one is around." This tears him apart from the audience for exactly one minute, after which he goes back to his old tricks.

What is there to do? Forbid him to look at those around him? Forbid him to feel them? This would mean scaring him off: first, I was told that everything is allowed, let *it* do what *it* wants – and now, suddenly a prohibition . . . The student would get confused, alarmed, contracted.

In such cases, I choose a different path – one prompted by the actor himself.
"Evidently, the close proximity of your colleagues distracts you. This is easily fixed: take your chairs and move, along with your partner, to that corner over there. We will also move away. No one will distract you, and you will feel easier."

Done. And indeed, things went much better for the communicable guy as soon as he moved away from us.

At the same time, we managed, quite easily, this serious transition "to the stage," away from the partners, "before the audience."

Practice tells us that, having been moved "to the stage," students should not be kept there forever. It is essential to sit them back in the circle and do the circle exercises again. Here, in close proximity, even the smallest mistakes are easily noticeable, while there, "on the stage," many of them slip unnoticed. They slip by once, twice – the student gets used to mistakes.

A few words about entering "the stage."

This is a very critical moment. You open the door and, immediately, before you even cross the threshold, you see 10–20 people looking straight at you . . . You get muddled, mixed up feeling inside . . . You have only to yield to this feeling for one moment – nerves will kick in, you will start rushing . . . before you know it, you will panic. . .

What's there to do?

The answer is quite simple: **take your time**. Do approximately the same thing you do when walking out of a dark basement into the bright, blinding daylight: give your eyes some time to adjust – look about, adopt. . .

Every new, strong impression causes momentary confusion, disorientation – this is the nature of things. Some people, when they hear someone shout: "Fire!" yield to their confusion and panic; others take a few seconds to adjust and, having received a psychological boost from a strong impression, perform miracles of bravery and self-control.

8

Some Thoughts on Pedagogy

Tactics

One of the actor's chief weaknesses is his lack of self-trust. He dismisses his small, mundane, everyday manifestations as unworthy and unsuitable. After all, he thinks, the stage is the stage. Hundreds, even thousands of eyes are looking at me – how could I possibly keep their interest if what I do before them is not done well and is inarticulate. Moreover, how could I keep their attention if I were to *do nothing*? So, the actor bends over backwards, works hard, spurs himself, and rushes. As he starts rushing, he simply "jumps over" his truth, over his life – and lands in a pile of lies and play-acting.

To aid this problem we must use all means necessary to develop the students' *faith in their own gift*. Their giftedness, I would assume, is beyond any doubts – otherwise they wouldn't be here. To achieve this goal, I use every opportunity to say how simple this is; how well they succeed, when they trust their talent.

- Here you felt like looking around, and so you did. Excellent. You looked at him – his face amused you, you smiled . . . and then, why did you get scared, why did you make a serious face?
- It felt improper, laughing in his face.
- Too bad. Why restrain yourself? You felt like laughing – you should have laughed. Improper, unbecoming? Leave these things for life. Here, onstage, be closer to nature – in fact, *be nature itself*. This is not as hard, really – as you see, it's begging to be released, on its own – just don't interfere, don't prohibit it.

How shall we deal, however, with a student's obvious weaknesses?

For the most part, avoid any word, any gesture that could betray that you see them. Wisdom and power for a teacher and director, as I see it, does not only rest on them being able to give good speeches and notes, but also on their skill to keep quiet at the right moment and pretend that everything is going well.

For example, at the start of the first lesson, a student resorts to crude, shameless "playacting," or "presentation," yet I pretend that it never happened, and say: you *rushed* –you did not feel like saying anything yet, but you forced yourself. Take your time: everything will come in good time . . . If, however, from the get go, I begin to pull him up and drum into his head that he acted falsely – I will ruin everything.

So, I pretend that I noticed nothing. There was no playacting, and no bad theatrics – he simply rushed it.

After all, is this inaccurate? Rushing was, indeed, the main cause. Had he given himself enough time, life would have begun . . . Yet he rushed, felt himself uncomfortable and uneasy, as a result . . . and "covered it up" by making himself do something, by resorting to depicting, playacting . . .

Is it accurate, though? "Do what you want," "act as it acts" – perhaps this is good for initial pedagogical steps? But what about directing? Might there be some excessive enthusiasm here? If things develop this way, you will end up dragging all the nasty mundane habits onto the stage.

This can't altogether be avoided. Such incidents are possible. Nevertheless, don't ever forbid anything from the actors. They lived; they felt good, and suddenly you say: not allowed, throw it out, it won't do! This would confuse them, and good luck restoring their spontaneity!

There is a special method for "removing" something from an actor's work. In *The Legend of Thyl Ulenspiegel* [by Charles de Coster], there is a chapter that tells the story of how fools built a house. The house turns out very uncomfortable to their complete surprise, because they haven't thought of building windows and doors. They dig an underground passage to access the house. Inside the house, however, it is pitch dark. Ulenspiegel catches them at a peculiar job: they are carrying something out of the house by sacks. As it turned out, they decided to take all the darkness out of the house: they would fill a sack with it, tie up the sack, so that darkness does not escape, carry if far off from the house and shake it out on the ground.

They worked on this all day long, but for some reason, they didn't get anywhere. Ulenspiegel came to their rescue: he brought in a candle, and the darkness dissipated on its own.

The same is true of an actor: removing darkness (you can't do this, you can't do that) will amount to nothing – a new darkness will come in the place of old one, even more impenetrable.

One must bring in a candle.

It is anti-pedagogical, pulling up actors, forbidding them all kinds of inappropriate poses and movements. It accomplishes nothing.

Remind the actors instead what and who surrounds them in a given scene; how this surrounding obligates them to behave, etc. These *circumstances*, on their own, would "draw" the actors toward the appropriate behavior. From this point on, an actor just needs to get used to the new in order for it to take root. That is all.

In short, the actors are given full freedom of actions in those circumstances offered by the author (in our case – by the teacher); however, *they are not given freedom to restructure these very circumstances, according to their taste.*

There is nothing unnatural in it. On the contrary, it's quite familiar – just as it happens in life. In life, circumstances are always given. If it is daytime, and the sun is beating down, a normal person won't behave as they would on a frosty winter night.

Therefore, in addition to pedagogical and directorial technique, there also exist pedagogical and directorial *tactics.*

As is often the case, a director deprived of any knowledge or technique, but rewarded with the gift of tactical instinct, produces a near miraculous effect an actor, instinctually. The opposite is also true: directors armed with knowledge of the directing technique "dislocate" and "murder" an actor simply because they don't even suspect of the existence of such silly thing as "tactics."

Tactics are the heart of pedagogy. The future of the school of theatre lies in complete and harmonious combination of the technique (meaning psychological, or "psychic" technique, as you would say it in Russian) and tactics ["Psychic technique" is *psikhicheskaya*, or *dushevnaya tekhnika*, in Russian. The Russian poetic symbol for the human soul (*dusha*) is the Greek mythical heroine Psyche. –*Author's Note*]. Timely support, timely indication of a spark of truth that flickers in an actor . . . This is just a flicker of truth, and it dies almost before it is born. Yet, the soul of the embarrassed actor must be pointed toward it. His soul must be moved to recall it and sense it. His soul must be moved to light up inwardly from the very memory – "it" was just there, just flashed by . . . Even if it vanished; even if I failed to grab onto it in time, it's all right, it will come in due time . . . It was there once, this means it is there, and it will come back. . .

Timely praise, timely help, timely abandonment to the whims of fate, timely correction. It's not as simple as it seems. There is much work to be done yet to develop this section of pedagogy.

As for those teachers deprived of the tactical scent – it would do them good to consider the incredible restraint, patience, and tactical sense of a mother. The cause of these qualities is simple: *love*. Love gives them sensitivity; it gives them patience, wisdom, and the power of authority.

You must *fall in love* with the actors. Not in theory, but for real. To fall in love with them and fight – fight them for their talent, their artistic conscience, and their human grasp.

Patience and Responsibility

Every once in a while, you get a difficult student. In the absence of sufficient experience, you are sure to make mistakes. At first glance, this student does everything you ask of him; tries to do his best. Seemingly, he "gives in" more boldly than everyone else, but . . . he is **dodging**. He does not want to dodge, and yet he is dodging: "giving in" exclusively to the peripheral, while artfully traveling over everything internal, deeply psychological. You think you've "unlocked" him, while in reality he has receded even deeper into his shell.

Don't even think of getting into an argument with him about this! Even if you win the argument, it will do little good. Keep silent and watch. Take your time. He cannot but get caught. One day he will be visited by a strong, definitive emotion: anger, indignation, or, the opposite – joy, affection; he will get emotional . . . and then, he will dodge to the side: he will jump into his *would-be freedom* and begin to yell, stamp his feet, or hug someone, grabbing his partner's hands. This is the time when you can't let him escape. Use this chance!

However, don't scare him off – be a tactician! Did he progress in comparison with his first days of training? Yes, he did. Did he loosen up, at least a bit? Yes again. So, tell him just that: "You've gone through the first and the most difficult stage. You've gained courage; you've lost your inhibitions. Now let's move onto the next, equally important stage. Now it's easy. Let's recall how things went."

Evidently, the text and impression you received from your partner nudged you to turn this etude into a farewell of two people, who are intimately close. (The participants have long outgrown their youthful years.)

The two of you sat at the table . . . She got up and said: "Well, I must go." Trying to compose yourself, you asked: "So, we won't see each other again?" She looked away and whispered: "We won't. . ." You looked: she bowed down her head; her shoulders drooped . . . Don't you remember how, at that moment, your hands sank down heavily? . . . Several years of your life – the best and happiest years! Nothing to be done! . . . It was meant to be! You stood long, your your eyes looking BEYOND this day and hour . . . At that moment, you understood it all: mistakes, and how inevitable and irrecoverable it was . . . Then you looked back at her . . . These were totally different eyes. I could see your whole soul through these eyes – all of your humanity, all the tenderness you are capable of. You started to move toward her . . . passionate words about to burst from the bottom of your heart.

But you did not say them . . . you didn't dare. When feelings overcame you, you got scared, silly man! Scared of what? Talent! That's right! Talent was asking to be released; it was ready to burst through your shell, but you screamed bloody murder! In panic, out of fright, empty inside, and only peripherally agitated, you rushed toward her, turned her around, grabbed her into your clutches . . . she felt awkward, we felt awkward . . .

Up till now, this kind of courage was an achievement, but now it's not enough: *something else has ripened.* Give it way. Your depth, your concealed feelings – give in to this first impulse whole-heartedly, without a backwards glance!"

You caught the actor at the time when he reached his true creative height. You let him *sense* his talent and its perspectives. You also caught him at falling down from this height, fearful of his own strength.

Now you've gained power over him. Now he knows why you will shout: "Green-light!" when he hesitates in fear. Now he knows that you are not fighting with him, but with his coward – the coward sitting in him and constantly stifling his own gift.

Don't think, however, that you've done it all. The work is only now beginning – the most delicate, difficult, and critical work. Left to his own devices, the student won't be able to navigate this dangerous path of his *absolute revelation. You must do that for him.*

Now, your every negligence equals retreat; your every mistake is a wound; every hesitation and doubt – a fatal push off the edge. This is why you should now be especially demanding of yourself with regards to this student. Don't take your eyes off of him, so that at any second you could come to the rescue!

Look how many damaged and wasted actors walk the earth . . . How many painters and musicians walk around with their brains polluted with rubbish and their souls demagnetized! How many handicapped singers, who lost their beautiful, rare voices because of some ignorant "maestros."

Who will answer for that, and when?

9
Weakness of the Actors' Creative Ties

Switching Off

Numerous are the mistakes that trip up young actors. Unless you know them and know how to correct them, they will strengthen and expand to destroy the very possibility of the creative state.

It is better to start with explicit mistakes, those glaring right at you.

She is asking him:

- Are you going to the theatre tonight?
- Yes, I am.
- And what if I ask you to stay?
- I will stay.

Everything seems correct; it looks like they were on the same page: with childish playfulness and slyness, she asked him to stay, her tone and eyes promising that they will be better entertained and amused here than he would be at his theatre. He glanced at her and suddenly smiled; he felt he could not refuse her and, without thinking twice, decided to stay. In short, everything seemed correct, except that, having replied: "I will stay," he immediately *turned toward me* and looked at me expectantly, as if to say: voilà! It seemed to have turned out well this time – can I have my praise now?

- Pray tell, what do you need me for? – I would ask him.
- That's it. I said all the lines.
- What do you mean, that's it? As far as I understood, it is only just beginning. You agreed to stay, said no to the theatre; evidently, this is going to be more exciting . . . Now, when things are just starting to get interesting, you abandon her and turn toward me.
- I am out of lines.
- Why do you need the lines? It's a good thing there are no lines. Based on what just passed between you, you would hardly be able to speak right away; look, she is embarrassed, and

183

you are in a similar place. I doubt you would immediately find a subject for conversation. Don't you think you would say more to each other with this silence, this pause, than if you began to chatter right off the bat?

Obviously, all these notes are nothing but pedagogical diplomacy. He did not abandon anyone, nor did he break anything off – it broke off on its own. It broke because there were no strong ties. If the ties were there – they would not be so easy to break.

I use this case, in order to reiterate: don't interfere – believe yourself; don't dare tampering with your life, once it's begun. Suppose I say: "That's enough, thank you," and you can't separate from each other. Suppose I begin to yell: "I said, that's enough!" and you, having left our "stage," sit down in your places, still unable to empty your minds of each other, exchanging glances again and again. Then I would say: this is life, this is a sound creative state, and your "technique" is sound.

- Technique? – someone would exclaim. – To have technique probably means to be able to get into character at the right time, but also to be able to come out?
- You will never have to worry about learning to "come out," – I would tell them. – Just look around: everything is conducive to this. The house full of audience members pulls you in; faces, poking out from the wings distract and interfere . . . and what about the footlights? and the spot lights? and the front lights that strike your eyes? and what about a partner's bad acting? and makeup that might look good from a distance, but always looks crude and rough up close? and the set? . . . All this rises in arms against the actor, screaming: this is theatre, this is false and fake!
   Is there anything at all that wouldn't distract and break your concentration? You hang on by the single thread of your fantasy. The moment it breaks – down you fall!
   Never mind if, having finished your role, you can't cool off for a while. All it means is you've given a part of your soul to the role; that you are no craftsman, but an artist; that you have lived, instead of pretending.
   Yermolova, having finished her role, took a long time coming to. She answered back, when addressed, asked questions and did things; yet her soul seemed absent. In her soul, she was still onstage as Joan of Arc, Mary Stuart, or Sappho [title character from an 1818 tragedy by an Austrian writer Franz Grillparzer (1791–1872)].

I would tell them how unpleasant it was visiting Stanislavsky in his dressing room on those nights when he played Famusov [from Aleksander Griboyedov's 1823 comedy *Woe From Wit*] – he was picking on everyone, nothing could please him, he would constantly sermonize . . . But then, you couldn't imagine a more friendly, kindhearted, and good-natured man in the world, than he was those nights when he played Stockmann [from Ibsen's 1882 play *An Enemy of the People*]. Having figured this out, crafty people, on those days, slipped in the most delicate papers for him to sign . . . This became evident soon, and a memo was issued forbidding anyone to approach him for business on the days he played Dr. Stockmann.

Sensing the Imaginary

He sits at the table.

She (enters). Hello.
He. Hello.

She.	Would you please tell me, does Skvortsov work here, an engineer?
He.	He does . . . Except, he is off today. Come back tomorrow.
She.	Thank you. (Exits.)

He sits down at the table and begins to scribble something. No pen in his hand, and no paper – just a bare table surface. Yet he pretends that he is very busy, and writing – none of it convincing at all.

When the etude is over, I would ask him:

- What were you scrawling?
- What do you mean – scrawling? I was writing. I felt myself at the drafting desk, and I felt quite busy.
- Busy with what?
- Writing something, considering things . . .
- What specifically were you writing, and what were you considering?
- I don't know. Something serious and critical.
- What specifically?
- I can't say specifically. I was writing without paper or pen – using imaginary objects!
- That's the thing. You've got a real table, correct? A real partner, right? Why in the world did you need imaginary objects on top of it? You say, I felt myself working at the drafting desk . . . Suppose so. Yet, in actuality, you've got nothing but an empty table. So, you decided to act that you are writing? In other words, you've done the opposite of the first impression you received from the empty table. You killed your real life, and decided to cook up an artificial life instead. You went against our guiding principles?

Let me tell you this: imaginary objects are used in acting, and we will use them too . . . Acting with imaginary objects, however, is not an easy thing, and it requires special training. Secondly, imaginary object exercises pursue a special goal. As for now, there is no need to invent anything. Rather, take your environment as it is, and proceed from it. The table is here – it's a fact. Is there anything on the table? No. Let it be so. Why can't it be bare? Perhaps, you finished all of your business and put your papers away. Perhaps, you are ready to go home and are only waiting for someone to pick you up. Perhaps, you may not be working here at all, but merely came to see a friend?. . .

Gradually, students are taught to treat everything around them *as real*, as truly existing. Since our main goal is to cultivate in them a bulletproof *faith in imaginary circumstances, as if they were real*, at the students' first steps I am a sworn enemy to all these imaginary watches, coats, shoes, written notes, glasses of water – etc. All these things belong to a different chapter of work: a chapter dedicated to the development of "imaginary sensations." As for our particular stage of work, the untimely addition of this different chapter could only cause a new trouble.

"Just a second," some would say, "from the first steps, you are killing all fantasy? A man sits at the table and sees himself in a large room; dozens of desks around him; everyone is drafting, scores of people – what's wrong with that? Why don't you encourage this? Even worse so, you say – this is harmful. Instead of their bold, far-reaching fantasy, you offer the student the meager concrete environment of the classroom?"

That's right; I don't encourage it, and I do call it harmful. And here is why. Taught by experience, I say – they won't manage. They won't manage anyway. All kinds of things might *flash* in the imagination. The real question is: can the students give in to their fantasy as to a concrete physical reality? Can they live and act in it as they would in real, concrete conditions? Fantasy might flicker for a moment and dissipate. As for the real environment – it remains; they keep seeing it, and it keeps acting on them.

In due time, I will give way to fantasy (and what fantasy!); by that time, actors will approach it *prepared*; everything that flickers in their imagination will transform into something *real, concrete, physically tangible*. As for now – it's reckless audacity and nothing more.

When cultivating fearlessness and skill in a tightrope walker, would you immediately make them practice under the big top? It might happen, perchance, that a gifted, courageous young man, a future acrobat, might accidentally run the full length of the rope on his first try. Is this, however, a sensible training method? The next time, the tiniest waver could cause him to break his neck.

Actors don't break their necks, yet they get into other trouble. Although it is lesser trouble, it is also extremely difficult to fix. Here is how it occurs. "Does Skvortsov, an engineer, work here? – let us suppose, these words suddenly caused me to imagine, even caused me to sense myself sitting in a large room; twenty drafting desks around me; each desk houses an engineer like myself. Everyone is bent over their huge design drawings, busy with calculations . . . I also bend over my design; although I have to draft, and my table is empty, that's all right, I try to make sure it is not empty, and I am also busy. . .. also drafting, calculating . . . I frown, preoccupation written on my face . . . To tell you the truth, the sensation I had at the first moment (when I fancied, sensed, imagined myself in a huge design workshop) has long dissipated. I tried to hold on to the sensation; I thought I was keeping it; yet I only managed to keep the *external manifestations* caused by that state. I bend over an empty table; I shuffle the supposed drafts, my movements quite uncoordinated; I frown – in short, I strive to *depict* the inner state I experienced one to two seconds ago.

When striving to forcefully keep this fleeting state, actors believe that they "experience." Having done this kind of thing once, twice, three times, and then again and again, they become firmly established in this "technique" – they solidify their mistake and get derailed from the creative process. Good-bye, artistic truth, good-bye life onstage. . .

Developing the Skill to "Tangibly Perceive" the Imaginary

Exercises with non-existing objects are aimed at developing tangible perception, so to speak. You hold a nonexistent glass in your hand; you sense its coolness, hardness, the roundness of the glass; coolness evokes a pleasant feeling if you are hot, and unpleasant if you are cold . . . "Tangible perception of the imaginary" has begun. Simultaneously, a reaction begins: you feel like bringing the glass to your mouth, or, on the contrary, putting it on the table. . .

In our work, the work of the actor, you would agree, 90 percent of all things are imaginary! Turning everything imaginary into the *physiologically tangible* is an essential tasks.

"Mitya, please take in the merchant's brother, Liubim Tortsov . . . My brother turned me out! And in the street, in a coat like this—one has to dance about a bit! The frost – at Christmas time – brrr! – My hands are frozen, and my feet nipped. . ."

"Warm yourself up, Liubim."

"You will not drive me away, Mitya? If you do, I'll freeze in the yard – I'll freeze like a dog . . ." ([Ostrovsky [1917:86] *Poverty Is No Vice*)

The main psychological key to the character of Liubim is in this *physiological state* of a shivering, half-frozen man. As soon as you sense it, other things will join in: his humility and estrangement from everyone, the feeling of being unneeded . . . Just catch this thread of the physical (physiological, to be precise) truth, and the emotional truth will follow it.

Work with imaginary objects is the first step toward developing this precious quality in an actor: *imaginary sensation*. What will result if you develop this quality in yourself? Everything you think of and imagine, i.e. all of the "given," "supposed" circumstances and facts would become *alive and tangible*, rather than theoretical and abstract. You won't be able to help but become emotionally involved, because of this experience. If this is the case – you've become a passionate and responsive actor. The kind of actor, who is organically captivated by the events of the play. You can't find an actor like that for love or money!

This chapter of our school is too important to practice it in passing. It requires much time, and one must train in it until it endows an actor with its miraculous power.

Our current exercises have a different aim: to teach people how to truly live among the stage conventions.

Everything is conventional onstage; everything is unreal. Only I, the actor, am real (unless I ruined myself, spoiled my sense of truth!), and my scene partners, and the environment: the table, the chairs, the floor, the glasses, a pitcher. . .

One must hold on to these authentic, unconventional things. They are factual, they are real. They must be approached as a fact: just as they are.

The first flicker of a thought: this is a design workshop ("Does Skvortsov work here, an engineer?"). Yes, here is a table, a chair, a picture on the wall . . . some landscape . . . Momentarily, another thought comes: this must be a railroad construction office; the landscape depicts the place where they will lay down a railway . . . You are inquiring about Skvortsov, an engineer? Yes, he works here, but today is his day off; come back tomorrow, you'll find him here.

Generally speaking – I recommend fewer talks about psychology and fantasy, and more practice in *sensing concrete facts*. As for psychology and fantasy – they are organically connected with the facts and flow out of one another, just as consequences flow out of a cause. Therefore, psychology and fantasy will join in on their own.

What I call "physiological sensation" is, of course, no hallucination. It is also an imagined sensation, a product of the actor's creative fantasy. Although, acting classroom is no place to expound this – it will only result in confusion. Instead, you just ask: "Do you sense it?" – and an actor receives an imaginary feeling. This is plenty. As it happens again and again, a new ability is developed to easily evoke imaginary sensations.

Seeing and Hearing the Partner

Two men.

- Say, do you know Streltsov?
- Pavel Ivanovich? Yes, I do.
- Isn't he a nice man?
- Yes. A very nice man.

They repeated the lines so as to better remember them, and began the scene. One of them got up, lazily looked around, and walked toward the window. The other lounged in his chair, looked in front of himself, smiled, as if remembering something pleasant; then he turned his head toward that man standing by the window and asked in a friendly manner: "Say, do you know Streltsov?"

The other man became guarded, as if he heard something dangerous, unpleasant . . . He turned around, and saw his partner in the most serene state. "Pavel Ivanovich?" The first man repeated as complacently as before. "That's right, Pavel Ivanovich." The other man smiled an ambiguous smile: "Yes, I do."

The first man was surprised – apparently, he did not expect such an attitude toward Streltsov, yet he immediately brushed off his confusion and, as if nothing happened, entirely under the spell of his new acquaintance, Streltsov, and his charm, continued: "Isn't he a nice man?"

The man standing by the window looked his partner in the face for a while, searchingly. Then he understood something, turned away and pronounced with sudden indifference: "Yes." He paused.

His next reaction burst out of him, and it was even more sudden. He said "hmm," jerked his head, smiled an evil smile, restlessly paced the room, and said slightly mockingly, while looking his partner straight in the eyes: "A very nice man!" As if he wanted to say: he will give you a hell of a lot of trouble, that Streltsov.

Once again, the first man hesitated for an instant – he sensed something strange and unpleasant . . . Yet he crushed this feeling at once and settled into his serene state. . .

- Well. Now please tell me what you asked him about?
- About Streltsov: whether he knows him.
- Does he?
- He does.
- Does he like that Streltsov?
- Yes, he does.
- Now you tell me – did he ask you of someone you knew?
- Yes, I knew him.
- And you indeed like him?
- No. The partner misread me. Streltsov just pretends to be nice. In reality, he does awful things to people. He did something to me – I am still recovering.
- And now I want to ask you all, – I would address the students, – how do you feel about this guy, Streltsov?

Students start drowning each other out: "Obviously a bastard! That Streltsov played a dirty trick on him!. . ."

- Well, well, well! Did you hear that? It looks like everyone was clear on what your partner told you about Streltsov except for you. How could this happen?
- I have no idea . . . I thought I got it right . . . He was supposed to say Streltsov is a nice guy. In my opinion, that's what he said.
- Oh, this is in your *opinion*? You did not listen carefully to his intonation; you did not take a good look at his eyes, his face; you did not try to grasp what your partner was actually saying and pre-decided what he is *supposed* to say. Did we pre-agree on **how** to speak the lines and **how** to understand the text? Your partner said what he thought and felt. Why didn't you understand him? You saw and heard as well as we did.

  Don't you recall the weird, ambiguous smile he gave as soon as you first spoke about Streltsov? Didn't you see it? You even got mixed up for a moment . . . Don't you recall this; don't you recall that and the other? (Gradually, I move him through the entire etude.)

  How would it go if you did not interfere with yourself and trusted your own nature, your own actor's talent? Let's recall: having repeated the assigned lines and having (as we usually do) freed yourself from the lines for a second, you "give in" to the first impulse. Now you tell the rest. . .

- I was comfortably sitting in a chair . . . I felt like making myself even more comfortable – and so I did. I felt calm and cozy inside, and inwardly said to myself: this is good. All of a sudden, a single word popped up: Streltsov. What about Streltsov, why Streltsov – I did not know as of yet, but I did feel something pleasant.

  I had the image of having been talking to some very interesting person yesterday, some tall blond guy. I also had the urge to share this with someone. I turned and said: "Say, do you know Streltsov?"
- What did you think just before asking him – does he know him or not?
- I thought that he probably does know him.
- Then you just wanted to tell him about this new acquaintance you made?
- That's right.
- It turned out he knows Streltsov. Didn't he ask: "Pavel Ivanovich"?
- Yes.
- Did he know him closely – what did you gather?
- I suppose . . . he knows him.
- How well? Are they friends?
- Now that you reminded me of my hesitation and of his strange smile, I recall this fleeting impression . . . that he lacks enthusiasm for Streltsov.
- But you did not yield to it; you brushed it off, tried to deceive yourself that it did not happen . . . We know all that. We saw it . . . Instead, let's follow the path of your nature.

  So, he lacks enthusiasm. But I liked my new acquaintance; he captivated me . . . I thought: what an open-hearted man. Where is this smirk, this innuendo coming from? What's the matter? Perhaps, I misunderstood his reaction, or it just appeared this way . . . So, I double-checked: "Isn't he a nice man?" (Perhaps I made a mistake, and you know something of him I don't know?)

  Your partner would see that his smile did not go unnoticed, and that you started guessing something about your new buddy. Having noticed concern in your eyes, he would guess that you've genially trusted Streltsov and hastily connected yourself with him. "Yes, my good friend – this I know from experience – such a good, naïve soul, he just wormed himself into your confidence. Run away from him as fast as you can: "A very nice man!. . ."

  Isn't this a more engaging treatment of this etude? Moreover, it was inherent *in you and your partner*. I did not add anything from myself; I only showed the way you would have inevitably taken, if you stopped interfering.

  Nature is always engaging, so just rely on it. Rely on talent – it is more engaging, and it is smarter then your intellectual reasoning.
- True, why did I brush all this off? It was definitely there. Why did I get scared of these things, and decided these were irrelevant thoughts – a product of my distraction, of a lack of concentration. . .
- You see how you distrust yourself. Your actor's talent was already pulling you somewhere, but you dug your heels in . . . it pulled you again, and you became even more obstinate.

  Trust yourself, don't get involved, give it a try – I swear, nothing bad will happen. It will feel a little weird at first . . . just at the very start. This is because you found yourself in a new element. Don't mind it – you will get used to it.

  Don't be embarrassed! Do you think that you are the only one with this mistake? You have it in such a small measure, it's not even worth talking about. Think of those who have acted a lot and acted incorrectly – this mistake took such root in them; getting rid of it is difficult and sometimes impossible. For many actors, self-constraint has become *habitual and natural.* They either "compel" themselves to submit to the director's will or to the traditions of their craft, or else they keep repeating their own successful finds from yesterday . . . Each manifestation of life and spontaneity they now see as a disastrous "lack of concentration." As soon as these actors truly see something onstage in a human way, as they usually do in life (i.e. when they get on the right path) – they think they've "*lost it*" and must immediately pull themselves together. . .

To be honest, we see this in the majority of theatres. Everything has been *learned in advance.* Every actor knows exactly how his partners will say their lines. This line comes with this intonation, that line is accompanied by such and such gesture, and followed by such and such pause . . . In the event that a partner, for some reason, says the lines *differently* today, it's better not to notice (he must have made a mistake) and to reply as before: respond with deeply ingrained intonations and memorized "acting" to similarly memorized, learned-by-rote lines.

Never mind that the entire audience saw, heard, and understood what happened; the actor decidedly makes himself deaf and dumb. As a result, out of the thousand people who sit in the theatre and follow the scene, only one did not understand these lines – the very person to whom they were addressed. The entire audience has only one interest in mind: how will he react to *these lines*? What will become of him when he hears *this*? How will he respond to *these lines*? As for the actor . . . he saw nothing, understood nothing, and he responds with something he memorized on his own.

10

On the Beginning

Mistakes of the "Beginning"

- Yesterday I saw you at the Tverskoy Boulevard with some girl. Is she a relative?
- No, not a relative; she is my fiancée.

They repeat their lines, so as to better remember them. A student is "yet to enter the etude," has "yet to begin," so he sits calmly, he is his usual self. Besides, he is occupied with repeating his lines. All this is usual . . . But now something *unusual* is about to start – a **creative act**. I don't yet know what is going to happen to me. I have no idea what I am about to *create*, but you would agree – a creative act is *no joke*!

The person immediately restructures – he mobilizes, pulls himself together, and concentrates. In the event that he was sitting naturally, he would sit straight; in the event he was sluggish, he would rouse himself, etc. This is how he "distorts" himself, becomes unnatural, all wound up.

Overexcitement, excess tension can be almost imperceptible – the more dangerous they are. The mistake is unnoticeable, but it exists, and it is doing its work. Everything that follows will be incorrect. *It cannot be correct* – incorrectness is at its very essence.

This moment of transition from one's mundane state to the state of creativity is quite delicate and critical. It can be compared with a train switching to a different track. It's a railway switch situation! Which train engineer would accelerate at a railway switch? On the contrary, you must slow down! You must pass the switch at a slow speed, running as steadily and softly as possible . . .

"Experienced" actors have the greatest trouble switching from a regular, mundane state to a state of creativity. They would repeat the assigned text, get up, and walk to the "stage." They've decided they are "yet to begin," they are so genuine, attractive, and touching! You can't help but think: that's how you do it! well done! But as soon as they've reached the stage . . . it is now time to "begin." So, they pull themselves together, make an effort and . . . "give in" to the unnatural state. In their mind, this is the start of the the creative act. In reality, however, this is the start of their habitual false and pretentious state. For years, it has been standing between them and the *art of living onstage*.

In addition to this transition to the **creative act**, there exists yet another transition – before the "creative act." I calmly sit in class, I follow everything, I am engaged . . . "It's your turn," the teacher tells me. Even if I were expecting it, all the same, his words would nudge me and whip me . . . I would contract, pull myself together . . . and – the first distortion has been done.

The opposite is needed: a teacher must conduct things so that his students are not afraid to go onto the stage, but enjoy it, *want* to do it. As a student, I must be impatient – when will my turn finally come? I listen, I watch the other students working, and yet I wish it were me. "Now – your turn." At last! These words bring me pleasure.

"What kind of text shall I give you?" the teacher says and, for a moment, he is deep in contemplation.

"Any one you want," I think. I wait, looking calmly in front of myself . . . a sunlight spot is dancing on the wall, changing the color of the wall beneath it. "Look what the light can do," I am thinking, "it can even transfigure this dull, boring wall . . ."

"Here is the text for you: 'Yesterday I saw you at the Tverskoy Boulevard,'" etc.

I repeat the text, so as to better memorize it. I try to perceive it as indifferently as possible; try not to "act" it ahead of time. Done. I think I got it. Now I turn myself off for a second; empty myself, as if breaking away from all my impressions and . . . open myself anew to perceive them – it's like waking up. The first thing that pops up . . . ah! the familiar sunlight spot. Why is it dancing like this? It must be a reflection of a pothole in the yard . . . At the same time, I detect a parallel flow of a different life: I am filled with some inner unrest – there is something I need from my partner . . . as if I ought to tell him something, but what?.. The sunlight spot is dancing again . . . Which window is it coming from? Ah, here! It looks like it's pleasant outside; the sun has lit up this yellowed autumn tree . . . A sudden image pops up: a boulevard, a bench, a young couple on it . . . I turn to my partner – he is busy studying his shoes. Just look at this prude! "Yesterday I saw you at the Tverskoy Boulevard . . . with some girl." He looks a bit embarrassed. "Is she a relative?"

Clearly, I hit the spot; I couldn't foresee such an effect – the guy turned pale, but then he threw a wrathful glance at me, as if saying: how vulgar . . . "No, not a relative; she is my fiancée!"

Dammit, this turned out awkward . . . I offended the guy . . .

Among others, I shared this chapter with one of our respected directors and actors. To my great embarrassment, he completely misunderstood it. "Why do you *interpret* this etude so? Why am I vulgar, not him? On the contrary, if I were him, I would reply with pride and joy: not a relative; she is my fiancée. What am I to be ashamed of? You are not analyzing it correctly. It turns out that the guy that hid from everyone at the boulevard is a vulgar man."

Did I really *interpret* anything? Generally speaking, are we striving for an engaging *interpretation* in any of these etudes?

I need to teach my students how not to get involved in the actual flow of their **life** onstage. This is the first step.

All these examples are taken from actual practice. They are not thought out; they are aimed at *precisely* conveying the process of the school lessons.

No one worries about some *engaging* interpretation. No one can ever predict the direction of the etude. It will go the way it goes. . .

Later on, these etudes will include precise circumstances and later yet – we will repeat the same etude several times, making sure that the circumstances remain the same. As for now – let it be as it turns out, "as it goes." At this point, an etude that goes in an old direction or has the same circumstances or mood upon repetition is considered a flop and is rejected. It is a pure sign that actors did not live. Has it ever happened in our lives that we said, did, or felt the same thing twice in a row, back to back?

This is why a student, guided by his sound instinct, does the etude differently in repetition. True, in the beginning, this difference is quite primitive: a serious etude would be followed by one that is cheeky and lighthearted, or vice versa. During the initial stages, there is no need to be afraid of this primitivism.

At the time when students become so accustomed to living onstage *they can't help but live*, then we can think of engaging interpretation.

However, based on my experience, I must say this: an etude is always engaging that features an actor's sound creative state; lack of interference with their own nature; courageous "giving in" to everything that comes out of them. In short – **sound stage behavior** (or, to put it simply, sound **technique**) guarantees an engaging etude.

I need to explain why the "Tverskoy Boulevard" etude went the way it did. At the heart of the matter was specific human material. The student who asked the question was a nice, simple guy, who did not ponder his words; an open and direct man. The other student – the "groom, who sat at the boulevard with his fiancé" – was outwardly very composed and a seemingly cold person. On the inside, however, he felt everything strongly, deeply. Always withdrawn, mysterious at the first glance and "complex," such a man reveals his qualities slowly – over months, if not years.

One well-known psychologist defined this type of person approximately like this: they resemble roman villas – unpromising, gloomy, and meager on the outside – on the inside they are furnished with fairytale richness. Death and stillness on the outside – rich and complex life inside.

Now imagine that this kind of a man had to sit on the Tverskoy Boulevard with his fiancée. First and foremost, who is his fiancée to him? His secret, his "sanctum." Not only does he not want to speak of his fiancée – he is upset when a mere stranger pesters him with his questions, praises, congratulations . . . Not to mention this windbag . . . How could it turn out differently! . . .

By the way, these etudes allow me, in a matter of two weeks, to almost unmistakably guess every student's psychological type, and also their specific character, tastes, and dreams, if not secrets. Why? How? This is simple: they betray all this . . . even things they do not suspect.

On Repetition

We just said how it was impossible to repeat an etude exactly, and that living identically several times in a row is against all natural laws.

This raises a question: what are we to do about repetitions of the same scene in rehearsals? Rehearsals require repetition all the time.

Moreover, only through repetition does an actor begin to discover and digest a scene.

Finally, performance itself is nothing if not a repetition of what was found in rehearsals.

In this book, you will find the initial approach and methods to truthful, artistic **repetition** in rehearsals and performances, without sliding backwards from art into craft. As for the repetition at large, this is not a simple matter, and it cannot be discussed seriously until much later.

At this point, I can only express some preliminary thoughts on regular rehearsals.

Different kinds of repetition are used, depending on why a scene is repeated and how.

Let's discuss two of the most frequent types of repetition.

The first type. Let us suppose, an actor does something contrary to the idea of the play, or else his acting is weak – for example, it is too schematic, or sketchy, and lacks inner fulfillment. In such a case, a director would try to remedy the situation by delivering notes, and then suggesting that an actor repeat the scene with these necessary changes.

The second type of repetition – the desire to solidify. The scene went well, and it was powerful; so as not to lose these results, the director makes an actor repeat it again. The director thinks that, by repeating the scene, they will "fixate" it. The actor would "learn" the scene, like a musician learns a difficult passage.

And if a scene is repeated not once, but several times – then the director can rest easy: the scene is "done," and it won't ever flop.

In the first case, you can't really call it a repetition. It is a search for the correct interpretation of the scene. With each of such "repetitions," the scene is played differently.

In the second case, when repetition is aimed at "learning," "fixating," what was successful in the scene, we are dealing with naïve self-deception.

From the standpoint of theatrical craft, this method is practical and sound: after such "drill," the actor will always be able to conduct the scene in the same way, boldly and confidently.

This forced repetition, however, is not able to "cement" psychological life. It cannot solidify organically developed emotion; nor the thoughts evoked by the circumstances of the scene. It can only "fixate" outer manifestations: movements, intonations, rhythm, tempo, and some specific actors' theatrical "agitation," meant to portray the genuine feeling.

At a first, superficial glance, the actors perform exactly as before, but this is a gross misconception. The actors only repeat the external aspect of their work. Inwardly, they are cold to the scene – they are primitive craftsmen.

The actor's very human nature protests against such mechanical repetitions. It is well known that actors **cannot stand** repeating a scene if they just played it well and with inner fulfillment. They don't feel like it! If, however, they have to repeat, they will always give a weaker performance, deprived of soul.

So, why is it that they don't feel like repeating?

We find a clear answer to that in Ivan Pavlov's teaching. Each activity causes excitation of a certain part of the brain. As soon as the activity ends, however (especially when it was intense), that part of the brain undergoes a process of *inhibition*. This is why one does not want to, or rather can not experience identical thoughts, feelings, or live identically two times in a row, let along several times.

Every "repetition," therefore, would either be a mechanically "truth-like" external portrayal of the previously experiences scene; or, in the event that it happens with various unexpected, new nuances, it practically stops being a repetition, and becomes *life*, a "first-time" experience.

An actor, of course, can resort – and multiple times – to the repetition of the pre-discovered. If it is mere repetition, however, then one cannot speak of creativity – this is merely the craft of truth-like depiction.

Sound Technique of the Beginning

- I was mending your jacket and found this note in your pocket.
- You read it?
- I read it.
- This is just as well.

When you now skim this text, you already imagine something – perhaps, brother and sister . . . difficult, dissimilar personalities . . . misunderstandings, resentment . . . If it's not this, then it's something else; some scenario comes to mind, at any rate. The same is true of an actor who is assigned the lines. I almost never succeed at assigning the text *completely indifferently*, and my personal attitude always slips in. Therefore, the actors receive images that move them approximately in the direction in which I unintentionally propelled their fantasy.

This propelling can be intentional. By partially "acting out" the etude's text, a teacher can prompt a certain interpretation to the actor. It's better to refrain from such prompting, at this stage. On the contrary, one must try to offer the text as coldly, indifferently as possible, without imposing one's own interpretation.

No matter how you "read" the lines, an actor still receives one image or another – everyone gets their own image, and, it might change for an actor, based on their current mood, psycho-physical state and many other incoming circumstances and conditions.

Let's take the first impression that appears when reading the text above. For the most part, an actor imagines his wife or mother or sister finding a note in his pocket. The note is of the kind that exasperates their animosity and dissatisfaction with each other. The actor stops looking at his female partner as an actress and instead perceives her as his wife (let's take this variant). As he looks at her, he imagines that she is as, as usual, dull and unpleasant . . . When she says reproachfully, referring to the note, "I read it," his "It's just as well" bursts out on its own – it's better to sort things out as soon as possible, to stop hiding, to do away with lies and innuendo . . .

Was this etude done correctly? Yes, it was. This is how the actors imagined the state of things when they heard the lines and, most importantly, this was the actors' actual *inclination*. There is nothing to correct here – there were no mistakes. There could have been some mistakes in the acting technique – let us suppose there were none.

Things could have gone not as smoothly, however. Let's imagine a similar beginning: as soon as I, the actor, hear the text, I immediately imagine an unhappy, failed marriage. I imagine that the note that was found in my pocket speaks of some marital disaffection . . . This is how the etude has shaped, this is how the play has "written itself."

We begin. Suddenly, at a first glance at my partner (up till this point, I was not paying attention to the person I was paired with), I see the most charming creature before me . . . it would be bliss to have such a wife . . . Yet . . . the etude has been "decided," so I force myself: I strive to destroy the spontaneous and live impulses that *actually* appeared; I kill my real life and strive to follow the "outlined plan." I make myself feel something else, think something else: "failed marriage, a difficult, unpleasant person – my wife . . ." etc.

The outcome is rather vague, "betwixt and between." Let's even suppose that it was either "betwixt" or "between." Even so, can it be compared with what was coming to me on its own, at my first glance at my charming partner? That impression completely took hold of me, while the other took hold of me with only fifty percent power. In art, the only thing that's genuine is the one that happens in full. One fourth, or one half, or even nine tenth of a truth is still a fake, and a falsity. [Some of the actors reading this passage will probably think: you say don't kill your own life; do not force yourself to feel something completely different . . . Yet in actuality, in practice, you have to do it all the time: suppose, I am just not attracted to my partner, but I have to turn her into a queen of my heart. What are you teaching? Something completely inapplicable to what the actors will encounter later in practice.

There is plenty to say on the subject. First and foremost, if a beautiful Juliet, Ophelia, or Portia are played by an ugly actress, devoid of charm, we are probably dealing with a very bad theatre. If such a case really presents itself in practice, a partner of this kind should be considered as a huge hurdle, as a ravine across the road, which the actor must be able to jump over. This should not be discussed at school and, in any case, not in the first lessons.

Let me better ask the doubting actor: how often has he met a young, beautiful, charming actress (such actresses are also plenty) that arouses genuine true passion in her stage partner? I confess that I have almost never met such a person. The actor magnificently recited the words of love – but did not burn with love . . . The actor "depicted" love and passion, but did not feel either one or the other . . . –*Author's Note*]

The student, from the first steps, must develop a taste for things genuine and real. From the first steps, he must become accustomed to *living in full*, not partially.

Experience teaches us that it is, after all, not so difficult. To do this, first you just have to *get him away from fighting with his own self*.

This is how it's done: you've listened to the text, trying to remember it . . . If some image appeared, so be it. The etude might go this way or another – how could I tell.

Now let's repeat the text aloud. We won't act it out, but just repeat – for *myself*, and not for the partner. Simply to check if I remember it or not.

So we repeat the text. I remember it. And now – for a moment I toss everything out of my head, out of my heart, as far away as possible . . . As if, for an instant, I've shut off, withdrew from life, and then . . . I open myself to experiences and impressions.

My partner immediately catches my eye – she is very pretty, petite and playful – almost a child . . . She looks at me with cunning little eyes, and right away, in one imperceptible moment, I imagine that this is my younger sister, my dear and faithful friend.

Her little eyes become even craftier, "I was mending your jacket . . ." For some reason I imagined that it was my gray jacket I tore yesterday at tennis (although there was really no tennis practice yesterday, and I have long since abandoned all my athletic pursuits; but then for some reason I felt myself a young man and . . . the etude took this direction).

"I was mending your jacket and found this note in your pocket." (I know the contents of the note - the teacher wrote it and gave it to me to read and only then handed it to my partner). She laughs; she is triumphant; she caught me, she knows my innocent, yet precious secret.

"You read it?" (You minx, you naughty girl . . .)

"I read it." (Now you won't deny it; now I got you!)

Well, there is no point in hiding it any longer. At least now I can count on your help – this is your kind of adventure . . .

Although I was sure that no one knows my secret, but . . . this cheat already spied on me and now caught me in the act . . . "This is just as well!"

What had happened to the scenario that popped into my head at the very first moment, when I was just assigned the text of the etude? Where did this failed marriage go? and the bitterness? and the exhaustion from living with a wrong, tedious person? All that vanished. It vanished on its own. I did not have to fight it. Regardless of what I initially imagined – in just a minute, there came something totally different and new. I gave in to this new impression, and it overtook me.

So, here is this method, in general terms, speaking *primitively*:

FIRST stage: calm repetition of the text (without "acting," just to remember).

SECOND stage: "putting the text out of your head" – so as to forget everything, as far as possible, for one-two-three seconds, to silence your imagination, to become "empty," to turn into a virginally white sheet of paper on which nothing is written.

THIRD stage: I quit interfering with myself – I no longer arrange for any "emptiness." In this instance, my life begins or, rather, *returns* to me. When I interfered with myself, it was as if it were not there: I did not see or hear; there were no thoughts – it was a second of "confusion." And now everything goes back to normal: thoughts come; I start to see objects; things I perceive evoke certain attitudes (as the aforementioned sunlight spot on the wall, and now this young actress). I begin to hear the noise of the street, the music next-door, the movement of the neighboring actor's chair. I feel the cold or the heat; I experience my posture as being comfortable or uncomfortable. None of it should be fought. There should be no interference:

thoughts flow, feelings change from one to another – this is what life happens to be at the moment. Nothing more and nothing less. To this, and this alone, I must surrender. "*Let* all of this *live on its own.*" I have nothing to do with it.

And here comes

THE FOURTH stage. Apparently, the words of the etude you just repeated are not lost – they were just waiting for their time, and are starting to *break out*.

Their first appearance is vague and indistinct; they don't sit on the tip of your tongue; they do not even occupy your thoughts. Yet for some reason, your imagination arranges out of your surroundings—people and objects—a very particular set of circumstances. These circumstances will, in a minute or earlier, make all these words quite handy.

In short, the repeated text *organizes the entire etude on its own, bypassing any conscious, rational fabrication.* Apparently, the text has not been forgotten, and it is doing its job.

And here comes the

FIFTH stage: one must have the *courage to give in to all this*. To give in entirely, without looking back.

Ah, that looking back! It plays the same kind of trick on an actor as it once did with the wife of the biblical Lot. As soon as you look back, you will turn into a pillar of salt. When on stage, act as you feel like acting, live as you feel like living, and do not look back! As soon as you look back – creative life ceases.

Students, for the most part, are not in the least concerned with how and why things work on their own, and why they go well. For them, practice is more convincing than any theoretical reasoning.

The readers, however, can only theoretically perceive these writings. In that regard, the statement that the *assigned text organizes the entire etude on its own* strikes them as being obscure and doubtful. How come the assigned words, on their own, organize an entire etude? How could they do it on their own?!

It's very simple. Haven't all of you experienced the following: you are asleep and dream of being somewhere in the province. It's summer, the window is open, some shrubs and trees outside of the window . . . Suddenly your hear drumming and a song – along the street, past your windows, in perfect formation, with the song and drum, soldiers come marching by . . . You wake up and discover that it's your alarm clock rattling.

During this short rattling – not just a single image, but an entire complex segment of complex life passed before you. You did not invent it, did not fantasize what could sound like alarm clock rattling, and what kind of images it could evoke. It came without you inventing anything, in an instant: voila!

Do we really need to mention that the rattle of an alarm clock does not organize images and thoughts in people, but that people organize them, influenced by the rattling sound? I also doubt it is worth saying that the words of an etude, entire combinations of phrases, as well as the impressions from the partner – all this is much richer and more complex than this monotonous and familiar alarm rattle. Finally, I can't imagine we need to be reminded that words, according to the physiologist Ivan Pavlov, are a "second-signal-system," and are no less significant than real sensations.

What is interesting and new here is this: in a dream, when the cortex is inhibited, as are all the activities of consciousness – even the smallest external impression can move us to create not just images, but entire segments of life, in which we supposedly participate. When we are not asleep, however, and the work of our consciousness is in full swing – it *overshadows* everything that happens below the threshold of our consciousness. We do not perceive what happens in those layers and think that it does not exist. Yet it does exist – our etudes, among other things, make it obvious.

Now the readers will, perhaps, understand how an etude can be organized by its own text, with no prior composing and devising. Moreover, they will understand that the described etudes and this approach do not remove or isolate the students from the processes that connected with imagination and creativity. On the contrary, they cultivate and master the most organic and subtle kinds of imagination and creativity.

In These Etudes, Everything Appears On Its Own – Creatively

It would seem people are so diverse! Each has his own unique qualities, differences, mistakes . . . Yet in practice, take any group of students – the major mistakes—the major types of mistakes—are the same.

There has never been, for example, a group without a person, who would never start an etude without thinking everything out in advance.

I see all his tricks, but I keep silent, waiting for him to get bored.

At first he feels himself a hero: his etudes are amusing and engaging . . . Though some of the students grumble under their breaths that, well, it's all "invented" and predetermined, I act as if I do not hear them. Finally comes the turning point: he himself becomes bored with his "creativity" and eventually starts to share his doubts.

- You keep saying, "it appears right away," "it happens on its own," "it can not help but come," yet I must confess – nothing comes to me. I repeat the text, toss it out of my head, I do the "emptiness" thing, and then . . . nothing. Nothing comes, nothing appears . . . And I'll tell you honestly, not to find myself in an awkward situation, I always take precautions and think it all over in advance . . .
- What bothers you then? Aren't you very good at it sometimes?
- But the others don't come up with anything in advance, and for them it does "appear!" So, it's me . . . And why are you saying nothing? After all, you see, but you don't speak up . . .

If he is so worried – things are looking up. Clearly, the man has felt some flaw of his and has decided to get rid of it. This means he will now listen with his mind and heart, not just with his ears. Now, in a mere ten minutes you will be able to direct him onto the right path.

- It does not come to you – I would tell him – because you expect something supernatural. Don't demand anything at all . . .

Recently, I came across just such a case.

I was speaking with a very capable woman, spoiled by bad school, and also too lazy to be able to think everything through to the end. This was despite the fact that she had spent several years working as a director and teacher. She ambushed me as I was leaving class and asked for permission to walk with me. What she said to me concerned the very topic of this chapter. And I told her the same thing I said to the student. We walked along the boulevard, and I suggested: Well, let's see how it happens in our everyday life. Let's sit down on this bench . . . We sat. Opposite us, an elderly bearded man concentrated on reading a newspaper.

As soon as we sat down – he folded the paper, stood up, and began to walk. My companion noticed a parcel he left on the bench and shouted: "Sir! Sir! You forgot something!" He did not hear her. She took off, having grabbed the parcel, caught up with the man and gave it to him.

When she came back, she said:

- What an odd man! Can you imagine, he was upset: he said "thank you," as if I just stepped on his foot.
- Say, have you been contemplating your every action? – I ask her.
- Contemplating what? what action? – she can't understand.
- I mean, when you called to him, took the parcel and ran to take it to him.
- How could I contemplate it? When? I look: the bundle is on the bench . . . I yell – he does not hear, and I run.
- So you ran without thinking?
- I thought nothing – I had no time!
- So, everything happened by itself?
- Well, yes.
- And why did you tell me he thanked you so badly?
- Why? I don't know . . . He surprised me so: he was either angry with himself, or with me.
- Once again, the words jumped out of you on their own? He was so queer you could not help but say, "What an odd man?"
- Of course. He is awfully funny. He had something heavy and soft in his bundle - probably chicken.
- And why is this your business? Curiosity killed the cat!
- No, I'm not curious – my fingers could not help but feel it.
- Could not help but feel it? Did they act, once again, on their own? What have you got going on here, what is this anarchy – everything is done on its own? Why have you "let yourself go" so?

She, of course, realizes that everything I say is related to the main topic of our conversation, and that everything she has done and said is the most direct and convincing answer to all her questions and doubts.

- It really is so! – She smiles.
- You see. In life, as it turns out, this occurs at each step, and you take it for granted, you pay it no attention – that's how natural it is! When I ask you to do this in class, however, you get scared; you imagine that I demand something incredible.
- Yes . . . it's true - she agrees.
  (But suddenly her face lights up – she is delighted. What is it? Just listen to what she says.) Yes, but this is *in life*! Life is one thing, and art – another. In art, on the stage, everything is pre-determined and pre-decided. That's why in art things don't work like that, for no reason at all. (All this is pronounced with such joy and satisfaction as if a person has made the happiest discovery of her life!)
- Why don't we try it out practically to see if it's really true? - I propose to her. – Let's take the following text: I will ask you: - "What did you do yesterday?" You shall say, "Why?" – "What did you do with my papers?" – "Why?" – "They are gone!.."
  Let's start, as usual, by repeating the text – let's see if we remember it correctly.

So we did.

To tell you the truth, her spiel did not entirely "fall on deaf ears" – it got marked somewhere inside of me.

What could it trigger in me? Only annoyance. How many speeches like that I have heard in my time! . . . They are shallow, superficial, irresponsible . . . They are filled with so much stagnant confidence, and they do so much harm to art.

Of course, this annoyance did not remain my own personal annoyance as a teacher at a lazy, complacent student – the text we just repeated redirected my annoyance . . . I "gave in" to it . . .

Suspecting nothing, my partner turned to me and suddenly got burned by my fiery eyes and recoiled, her face distorted . . . Not giving her time to recover, I squeezed her hand:

- What did you do yesterday? . . .
- Why? – she blurted out.
- What did you do with my papers?
- Papers? – she whispers, frightened by my threatening manner and by her own uncertain suspicions.

Genuine fright combined in her with those creatively emerged "papers" . . . Suddenly I see that a comforting inkling is about to sneak into her head: "Oh, it's just an etude!.." All her horror is about to vanish – she will calm down and become, as always, her "ordinary outside observer." To break off her "awakening," once again I squeeze her hand hard and, with even greater indignation, whisper to her:

- Are you going to tell me what you did yesterday?

Apparently, pain kicked the comforting thoughts out of her head, and my double attack brought back her fear, and the thoughts about ill-fated papers . . .

- Why? – she babbles faintly.
- They're gone! . . .

She understands something, remembers something . . . she jumps up and is about to take off . . .

- Wait, where are you going? – I stop her in a reassuring and friendly manner. – Please have a seat!
- You can be so scary! . . . Oh my!
- What did you imagine? What kind of papers? Who am I to you? . . . Well?. . .
- I do not know . . . I only just understood that some important documents are missing and that it's all my fault . . .
- What kind of documents?
- I have no idea . . . I just now realized that something irreparable may have happened . . . and that it's all because of me.
- When did this happen?
- Yesterday . . .
- Why did I get so angry, so furious? Or am I always like this?
- No, it's because of the papers . . . Your very life, I think, might depend on these papers! . . .
- Why did you jump up? To get away from me?
- No, to get the papers . . .
- You see how this captivated you. A real tragedy: the mysterious disappearance of the papers. And you say, "it does not appear."
- Yes . . . it did appear . . . Except, this must be because of your "toughness" – it got me going. With another partner, it still won't work.
- Oh, yes it will! However, why wait for other partners; let's do another etude together. Let's concoct some new text. One condition: don't invent anything in advance. Be a hero - take a chance. As soon as you repeat the text – try to toss everything out of your

head, and don't worry about anything, do not think. If nothing comes out of it - no big deal.

Let's do this. You will ask me: "You are not bored with me, are you?" – And I'll tell you: "Why bored? On the contrary, I am afraid to bore you."

Having repeated these words, she truly turned herself off for a second, and then suddenly smiled at her own thoughts . . . In the next moment, she had suppressed her thoughts and began waiting. Something must come, after all.

- Nothing good will come, do not wait. It already came to you, but you did not give in, you rejected it. What were you smiling about at the beginning?
- These were extraneous thoughts.
- Nevertheless?
- It occurred to me: here, I cornered the man in the street and forced him to work with me . . .
- And?
- As I said, extraneous thoughts . . .
- Why extraneous? Perhaps, they are quite fitting. Let them develop, give it a try: cornered the man in the street, forced to work, well, then - go ahead.
- Forced him to work with me. I doubt he is particularly excited . . . – Suddenly she got embarrassed. – You know, I do have this line on the tip of my tongue: "You are not bored with me, are you?"
- Then say it, if it's on the tip of your tongue.
- You are not bored with me, are you? – she breathed out bitterly, annoyed with herself, violently squeezing her handkerchief, and hiding her eyes.
- You see, it worked.
- Yeah, it seemed to have worked . . .
- If you assigned the text correctly – no "extraneous thoughts" can appear. Any first thought, or action, or feeling – give it way. Know that it is not extraneous – it is exactly what you need . . . Well! while it's still hot – let's go again! The same text. Let's repeat it!

So we did.

Somehow she hung her head, her face became sad, her hand drawing something on the ground with the tip of her umbrella. Then, all of a sudden, she became worried and agitated:

- Nothing at all comes. Not a single thought. Then I at least had some extraneous, unnecessary thoughts, and now nothing: just empty.
- What do you mean "nothing"? And what about your hand? What was it doing?
- Nothing.
- How come? It drew something on the ground – you see these hieroglyphs?
- So what! The hand was drawing something, but the head was empty.
- Don't you rush nature – don't interfere in its affairs. Let's give way to what you had. You were drawing something on the ground . . . Well, go ahead, keep drawing as before. (She began to draw.) Remember, all of a sudden you felt sad . . .
- Yes.
- You are sad, no thoughts appear, and only your hand keeps drawing some lines on the ground. You don't even see them . . . Go on drawing, just go on. This is what you must need: sadness, silence, drawing.

Suddenly, she said with great pain and grief:

- You know what I just thought? I've worked in the theatre for so many years, and have done nothing worthwhile . . . Nothing to give me joy . . .
- You see, this is the reason for your sadness. This is not a trifling question for you. May be a life-defining question. This kind of question would make anyone grow silent and thoughtful. The work that is happening in you is serious and titanic – give it time to run its course deep within. In due time, the thoughts will come and words will flow – just take your time and do not interfere – believe yourself.

  What are you expecting? Hallucinations? They won't come – thank God, you are not insane.

  Or may be you are expecting, all of a sudden, the kind of strong urge that one can't fight? The kind of urge that would pick you up and carry you like a feather? Don't worry – nothing of that magnitude will come right away, and nothing will carry you.

  Your main mistake is that you are waiting for *something special*. What comes instead is more usual, mundane, immediate: vague impulses, unconscious, almost imperceptible urges, indistinct thoughts, or fragments of thoughts, out of the blue, mechanical and small automatic movements, like scratching the ground with your umbrella – that's all.

  Be aware that this is creativity. Its origins are in subtle and almost imperceptible sprouts. But give them freedom, give in to them. Don't complicate things. Believe in nature. Nothing is more necessary as of yet. And do not say that "it does not appear" – it always does. It either flashes by too quickly – and you miss it, or it appears as something vague and obscure – and your inexperienced self decides that it was "for nothing" and discards it. Nature always comes to us on its own and, one might say, imposes itself on us, while we are always fending it off and trying to concoct something nature-like using our own means.

11
On the Theatrical and Non-Theatrical

Interesting and Boring Etudes

Students often come up with very engaging etudes. The texts can even be "bland," but when they start acting them out – these etudes turn into entire dramas or comedies. It is so exciting; everyone likes it so much (it's real theatre!) that the students unwittingly begin to think: it's only good when it turns into an interesting little play.

If an etude, however, turns out less interesting and does not amaze, the student thinks that he has failed. He loses his taste for "technique," and begins, in advance, inventing effects that would embellish the etude and captivate his viewers.

I would tell the students:

- We don't need it to be amusing, but *true*. When it's correct in terms of the inner technique, it is always engaging, because it is so true to life. If it turns dull and pale, this means some mistakes were committed in the technical approach.

Having said that, I would give them an etude. Quite purposefully, I would offer the kind of text that does not inform the actors of any dramatic collisions.

Moreover, my statement that there is no need to chase after amusement would also have an effect. In this unconscious pursuit of simplicity, the etude comes out a bit boring, but without any glaring mistakes.

One of the students, the most overly-emotional, would explode:

- This is, of course, "truer," but . . . boring, not artistic. On stage we need truth, but not simple, mundane truth. We need artistic, theatrical truth.

Everyone becomes all ears, waiting: how will the teacher respond to this challenge. But the teacher agrees, in a calm and friendly manner:

- Yes, of course, you're right – you need artistic, theatrical truth . . . But more about that later. At first, we will work on everyday truth. When we master it, then we will move to artistic truth.

Everyone's face falls from disappointment: the conflict was avoided, and working on some uninteresting "truth" is no fun.

- Let's continue our work gradually. Let's take the same modest text – we are yet to get tired of it. Let's not aim at making it into a drama, or a tragedy, or a farce. What happens – happens. Our goal is to develop certain qualities, without which creativity is not feasible. We will only worry about the correctness of the creative process. In short, we *will work* – search, discover, solidify our finds – thankfully no one presses us (no management urges us to open a performance as it happens in theatres). Let us use the advantages students have, and, having understood the full value of a leisurely, systematic creative work on self, let's not drag ourselves ahead of time toward "artistry," "theatricality," etc. We don't have to amaze or captivate anybody. Let's do our modest job at hand.

  To sum up – our old, unpromising text and calm, proper technique.

Although my words disappointed the students, they also absolved them from having to play something interesting; as soon as this sense of obligation disappeared, people immediately calmed down, felt free, and found a normal creative state.

- Have you been to the Tretyakov Gallery?
- No, I have not. I am going tomorrow.
- What time tomorrow?
- At noon. Why do you ask?
- Nothing. I just asked.

Without any concern for success of the etude, they repeated the lines, "forgot" them for a second, and then "gave in" to the will of the accidents and their own overt and covert motives.

He sat in a contemplative state, his gaze wandering lazily across the floor. She glanced at him with good-natured smile. Then she became occupied with her own thoughts, went to the window and started looking at the spring sky with running clouds, at the bare poplars, at the remnants of snow on the roofs . . . And then, somehow, quite unexpectedly, she asked him: "Have you been to the Tretyakov Gallery?"

The question caught him off guard. He apparently did not immediately realize who was asking him, and, without thinking twice, just to get rid of the question, he replied: "No, I have not" (based on his tone, he was about to add: and I am not going to). Having looked at the partner, however, he felt that he said something wrong . . . So, he recovered: "I'm going tomorrow."

It was clear that, up until this moment, he had no plans of going there. He simply felt awkward admitting to her that he had not been there . . .

She did not listen very closely; she kept looking out the window at the sky, and the tree-tops . . . Somewhat mechanically, without giving any special significance to her own words, she asked: "What time tomorrow?"

He was quite taken aback. Realizing that she, probably, did not notice his confusion, he quickly recovered and decided (it was clear that he only decided it just now, at this second): "At noon." And then a question flashed in his mind: "Why is she asking? Does she also want to go?" It was something new for him . . . quite unexpected . . .

- Why do you ask? – he inquired, as if he wanted to know: you're not kidding, are you? Do you really want to go with me? It would be nice . . .

She heard something unusual in his words, and it drove away her dreamy state. Waking up (but not turning away from the window), she, probably, tried to remember the whole conversation . . . She realized that her absent-mindedness caused her to say something wrong, or at least lead him to a totally inappropriate suspicions. As if nothing had happened, she said: "Nothing." She assumed an independent, aloof look and, slowly and carefully (so as not to lose her aloofness) turned to him . . . But he looked at her so fondly, so friendly, so gratefully, that her aloofness dissipated, and she could not help but smile (albeit with restraint) . . . She looked at him for some time, noticing in him something new and not unpleasant – quite the contrary . . . She turned away . . . then looking back at him and, as if to say: well, why are you looking at me? – she added, "I just asked."

Not to embarrass her more, he diverted his eyes to the side – they fell on the piano, but he did not see it. One could read in his face: she is so nice.

She looked again at the window, looked at him, at the piano, and, soothed, quietly left the room without looking back.

He stared for a long time at the closed door. His eyes were puzzled: why did she leave? Have I offended her?

Careful not to disturb his reflections, I ask him:

- Will she go with you tomorrow, or will you have to go alone?
- I do not know . . . It would be nice though. It would be nice to go with her. But I don't know if she would go . . . I must have said something wrong. She got offended and left . . .
- Do you single her out among your colleagues?
- No, why? She's just smart, serious; you can have a good talk with her, about art; she reads a lot . . .
- Why did you upset her? . . .
- Yeah, you know, it got awkward! I am not very clever with women . . . and it shows . . .
- Oh, you philosopher! – someone from the female half of the class could not resist the urge. – You got it all wrong! Do you really think she got offended?
- Then why did she leave?
- She left . . . because she understood.
- What did she understand? About the trip tomorrow?
- Not about the trip – about you.
- What do I have to do with it?
- Well, well! He really got it! – the young people laugh.

Hearing that we are having a lively conversation, his partner comes back.

- Go ahead, tell us how it went for you, from start to finish. How did he strike you; why did you start talking to him about the Tretyakov Gallery; why did you leave? . . .
- How did he strike me? . . . just Vasya Prygunov. Only, he's kind of strange today . . . I saw in the window – spring, snow melting . . . the wind stirring in the tree, as if it is waking it up . . . and I remembered – *The Rooks Have Arrived* [iconic Russian painting by Aleksey Savrasov (1830–1897)]. I asked – if he has been to the Tretyakov Gallery; wanted to know if he saw this picture . . . It turns out he is going tomorrow. I also wanted to go. But then something stopped me. What if he decided I'm going because of him. And, truth be told, I spoke with him so stupidly that he really could have decided that . . . And I don't really

know this Vasya. He is kind of quiet, always alone, reading his books . . . What kind of ideas can get he into his head? . . .

- Well?
- Well, I dared and looked at him . . . and he (I certainly did not expect that) looked at me . . . exactly like my younger brother – he is also a serious guy . . . And it turns out, he is not such a weirdo as he seems, this Vasya . . . he is . . . how should I put it . . . gentle, or something.
- Will the two of you go tomorrow to see *The Rooks*?
- Sure, we'll go.
- And he was afraid he offended you.
- How? What a funny guy.
- If so, then why did you walk away from me? – Vasya asked. – I don't understand – why did she leave?
- Look at him! – someone from the female half could not keep silent again. – She just told you – you are gentle.
- Who is gentle?
- You . . . You had tenderness in your eyes.
- Tenderness toward whom? Her?
- Who else then?
- That's not true.
- Not true? – we all saw it . . .
- Well, my friends, did the play come out well? Were you bored during these long pauses? Were you not interested?

   Here is your theatricality, and your artistry. Never mind that the "play" was well known – and its text probably tired you today – yet you watched it with enthusiasm.

   There is no need to chase after "theatricality." Where there is real truth, and full faith in all circumstances, as if they really exist, where there is freedom and ease – there is theatricality and engagement.

   Let's go back for a moment to the start of the lesson: why were we so bored with the same exact text? Because people made mistakes in technique; they used self-restraint – they would not give in. Why didn't they give in? Because they wanted to be as "simple" and "truthful" as possible. I told them not to worry about making etudes engaging, and, naturally, they have tilted in the opposite direction – they've begun to limit themselves, and chase after "simplicity" and "undershooting."

More on Non-Theatricality

On Long Pauses and Dragging

During the first lessons, students' excitement and lack of understanding of what is asked of them causes them to rush, "blab," and "press through" the words.

The teacher, while fighting these tendencies, keeps repeating at every step: "Take your time, don't be afraid of pauses"; "if you do not feel like speaking yet – keep silent"; "don't compel yourself – act or speak only when you feel like it, when it is happening on its own."

Under the influence of these tips, and encouraged by their first modest successes, students are no longer afraid to be silent on stage.

But time reveals a new problem: etudes became unbearably long – students endlessly sit in silence, then finally oblige us and utter a word.

This tedious slowness becomes nauseatingly boring. Yet – you suffer and even purposely hold them, torment them until they reach their fill. At last someone yells, "This is awful! Deathly boring! We would lose all our audience!"

- Why, do you think?
- Very simple: you cannot wait until you "feel like it." What if it takes an hour for me to feel like it – should I still wait?
- Then, sometimes you have to do what you want, and sometimes not?
- Yes, it means sometimes you've got to intervene, to force yourself, instead of waiting when something happens on its own.
- Why don't we examine it practically. Let's recall how things went.

Two men are on the stage. The text is as follows:

- Is it eight yet?
- I think it's after eight.
- I have to go.
- Will you be back soon?
- Don't wait for me. I won't be back until after one.
- Another meeting?
- Another meeting . . .

- Tell me why it took you so long to start the text?
- I did not feel like speaking just yet.
- Then tell us in detail how it happened. You repeated the text. Then?
- Then I tried to forget it, and then . . . freely gave in . . . to yawning and sleepiness (I slept poorly last night), I felt it was evening - eight pm . . .
- The text was already on the tip of your tongue, but you delayed it . . .
- Not that I delayed it; it was, perhaps, out of place – it wasn't time yet.
- Then it was running through your head, was on the tip of your tongue, but you thought it was out of place, so you did not give it way?
- Yes, I think it was early.
- Well, there is your problem – we've got to the truth: it means the text wanted to be said, but you did not "give in" to it, because you decided that it must come to you differently. So, what is going on? The unbearable pause did not happen because you *did not feel like* saying the lines. It happened because you missed out on your urge to say them.
  You know what this feels like? You need to leave with an express train. You are on the platform. The train flies in – it only stops for a minute. You hesitate, for no apparent reason. The train takes off, and now it's too late. You have to wait for the next train. And so you wait. You now have to go with the postal train, which is far worse. In an hour, the postal train slowly approaches. And here, too, you begin to choose which car is better or emptier. In the meantime that train also leaves. Again, you are stuck. What is left is some freight train – just wait for it an hour or two and board it – but don't gape. One way or another, sooner or later, it will drag you there.
  It is the same with the long pauses. They do not occur because you "do not want anything," or "nothing comes," but always because you miss the moment – the express train leaves, and you have to wait for the next one.
  Do trust yourself more. Moreover, do know that the first urge is always the best and most convenient. Why? Simply because it is *your* reaction, it is *organic* for you.

The humorous term "missed the train" usually comes into use, and a student who drags an etude, when asked: How did you feel? What do you say? – usually replies, without thinking twice: here "I missed the train," there I "let it go by," please let me repeat the etude. [On the "train," also see Book Five, page 685.]

"Muffler" (Muting)

In a month or two, the very essence of the technique – freedom, ease, and yielding to impulse – is more or less digested, and the students begin to live in the etudes somewhat successfully. At that time, however, a new worry creeps into the teacher's soul. Things seem to be going well, but . . . why do they speak so softly?!

Up until this point, this was of no concern – as long as they were mastering freedom. The volume is loud enough for the room, but it would never do for the stage – they are just whispering something under their breaths!. . .

You want to shout: "Louder! I can't hear you." But this would violate the basic principle – they do what they *feel like* doing. This would even be justified: they are having intimate experiences – why shout? They can hear each other, what more do they need? This is precisely what happens in life.

Moreover: they can perfectly see some strangers sitting near and looking intently at them. How can one live freely and with ease, under such conditions? And, on top of that, they are supposed to speak so that everyone could hear?

But then, why do we have theatres?

In some theatres, actors resolve this question quite simply: they set aside their own psychological state, set aside the partner, and simply shout their words at a level that could be heard in the back rows. Their partners feel uncomfortable – they sense that the words are not addressed to them, but to the audience. But what is there to do? . . . The audience sits there; they paid for their ticket – they must hear and see everything. How could it be otherwise? This is too crucial of a moment to be thinking of their partners' convenience. They will wiggle out of the situation somehow.

Of course, it is not art as we understand it.

But what is there to do? How can I make myself speak loudly about my intimate secrets, before a huge crowd of people?

After all, every actor, no matter how young, knows that the audience has come to see and hear it all . . . And they, the actors, have come onstage to be seen and heard.

Let us not go so far as to tackle the issue of the relation, and the interaction between the actor and audience. Not just yet. This is one of the basic, fundamental issues in the creative work of the actor. Only the right solution of this issue can reveal the main springs of the creative process onstage. Let's confine ourselves to a few practical methods, liberating students from "muting" the lines.

The first thing that can interfere with the actors speaking loudly enough is their habit of speaking quietly in life.

After all, people in everyday life speak quite differently: some yell, quite unnecessarily, as if people around them were deaf; others mutter under their breath. Sometimes this is a familial issue: you come into someone's home – everybody shouts, interrupting each other. You sit completely confused and leave with a headache . . . You come to another home – it's quite the opposite – it's silent: everybody speaks softly, almost in a whisper.

Actors who come from such families of "whisperers," needless to say, begin whispering in etudes. It would be bad enough if these actors were the only "whisperers." But no, they move their partners to do the same by the power of their example. Before you know it, they infect the others. You end up with an entire classroom of whisperers!

First of all, you can advise these whisperers to radically change their habits and get used to *speaking loudly in everyday life* . . . This is not so difficult to learn.

Practice reveals that this is often enough, and the "whispering" painlessly disappears.

More often the opposite is true: people speak loudly enough in life, yet they begin to whisper as soon as they hit an etude.

For the most part, this results from some absurd self-deception. This phenomenon was discussed before, and it will be spoken of again. In life, a man lives, moves, speaks, listens, looks freely and easily, without any special effort – what is there to try to take care of? everything happens by itself! As for the *stage* (!), it calls me to "demonstrate" something else – something special. This begets diligence: a person begins to listen diligently, to see, feel and even truthfully live – everything with diligence.

Needless to say, this instantly breaks out of the natural, normal state.

Heaven help them if the text or their partners give the actors an inkling of something heartfelt, serious, and deeply emotional. Actors feel responsible to conjure special "feelings," and sink to special depths of "experiencing." They contract, become highly strained, and . . . start whispering.

As you see, in such cases, "muting" comes as a result of a sad and ridiculous delusion. Actors sincerely think they are deeply involved and that they are *experiencing*, while in fact they are just very tense and inhibited.

This tension is not immediately visible to the untrained eye – the actor is seemingly free, yet tension exists, and it chiefly affects the laryngeal and respiratory muscles. Moreover, it is so strong that dealing with it is not so easy.

Each of us has probably observed in school how the most loud screamers, the ones who make such an incredible hubbub during recess, turn into modest, barely audible whisperers when they approach the teacher's desk, "secretly" sharing with the teacher the scraps of their imperfect knowledge.

A whispering actor is no better than them. He too did not learn his lesson – the basics of an actor's sound creative state.

Blame the teacher. He allowed the habit of "muting" to strengthen. Fighting it at this point is, of course, a lot harder.

What mistake did the teacher make? What did he miss? He missed the right moment, missed an opportunity. This moment and this opportunity are to be watched for, from the second or third lesson. Actors, even when they are students, still possess a special instinct that compels them to speak loudly enough, so that the audience could hear them. And as soon as you, the teacher, notice that a student just barely reined himself in and said a line more quietly than it was coming – catch that immediately! Use this chance, otherwise the right moment will be lost, and the disease will take root.

"You said it quietly . . . But you wanted to say it louder, why did you hold it back? Green-light it; green-light it as freely as possible!" – this, or something like this, must be said to the student. Saying it once or twice is not enough. As a teacher, you need to watch him closely and persistently in order to eradicate this "muting," as it originates mostly from an unsound creative state.

There is another method that often helps. When students repeat the text to remember it, a teacher must ask them to *speak loudly enough.*

And sufficient volume in repetition, for the most part, finds its way to speech in the etudes.

Explaining this phenomenon is not so easy, and it can be partially found in the chapter on *Assignment.* For now, however, we will leave it at practical advice.

12
On the Text

Frivolous Treatment of the Text

During the first lesson, before the teacher and the students have come to an agreement, students do not yet understand freedom as they should, and, above all, it affects the text.

They understand lines as being *approximate*. Therefore, without hesitation, they change the lines; alter them – as they choose.

Without delving into this phenomenon yet, I would stop them with some simple joke, such as, "Listen!.. I'm offended! What is going on!? A brilliant playwright like me—practically 'Shakespeare' – has given you brilliant words, and what do you do? In front of the author, you ruthlessly rework and shred to pieces the product of his inspiration!". . .

This joke won't intimidate anybody, but it will still do the job: everyone will realize that they should not treat the text with carelessness, and that they need to be more exact when learning the lines. In the future, if a lack of respect toward the words persists, I would draw special attention to the need to say the exact lines. "You will have to act in classical plays," I would tell them, "and in those plays, written in verse, you will not have the opportunity to mess around with the text. If you get used to being careless with the text, this habit will be hard to break. This is why at this early time, starting with the first steps, let us get used to the fact that the *words are given* and . . . that's the end of it. You can play them in a thousand different ways, but the words per se are inviolable. This habit is very beneficial. And even if you now feel that the construction of the text is not very convenient – it should not stop you. You will be thankful later, when no turn of speech will feel uncomfortable."

At the outset, and also because of the lack of agreement with the students, other confusion can occur with regards to the words. The students say all their lines to each other – and since they still lack the basics of the creative state – they are uncomfortable with long silences, when in front of the audience. They feel rotten, and they seek rescue in speaking. Although the text the teacher gave them has been used up, they continue to chat . . . just to avoid the silence.

I would stop them again with a joke: "Wait a second, I would say, the author wrote a 'finished play,' and he invested so much of his soul in the last act, yet you went ahead and added two more acts. Spare the author – he is sitting right here!"

They would laugh . . . and again realize that no verbal improvisations are needed.

Later, this ban on superfluous words can sometimes bind the students – an etude would gather such force that it would spread beyond the boundaries of the given words; one or two new lines are ready to roll off the tongue. Without them the etude would have no end. But the actors, remembering that "ad-libbing" is not encouraged, restrain and silence themselves. This restraining is so harmful that it must be avoided at all coasts. So, I would say to the students: "Next time, if you feel the need to say something else, please, do not hold back. At this point, what is most important to us? It is important to learn giving in to **complete freedom**. So let us do just that. And if some words are bursting out – let them, give them way, do not extinguish them. Just don't turn the etude into pointless blather; do not speak unnecessarily."

"As for a couple of words, two of three phrases – don't you dare hold them back. Since they are asking to be said – they're not yours."

"Remember the most important thing – freedom and ease."

Incorrect Attitudes toward Words

a)   Overestimation of the words, and its types

If the students, in the beginning, treat the words rather casually, mangling them in their own way, the actors make the opposite mistake.

This is not surprising – everything is nudging the actor toward this special attitude.

You can stage a play in many different ways; you can interpret it from different perspectives, using different treatments for certain scenes, or characters; you can change a *mise en scene* – but changing the *words*, altering them to your taste and understanding, is considered unacceptable. The most that is allowed with the words are certain cuts and, perhaps, rearrangement.

This is why actors acquire a special attitude to the *text of the role*. To begin with, the value of the role is determined by the number of lines in it: plenty of lines – this is an important role; fewer lines – a minor role (even if an actor does not leave the stage for the duration of a performance).

See how the roles are copied – you will find the character's words, and the scraps of someone else's lines – "cues" given by some unknown partners. These scraps don't give you a single clue as to what you are told or asked; what you are responding to.

And so, gradually, step by step, a belief is developed that a role is just words.

This leads to a whole slew of various misconceptions.

One of them: since everything rests on words, consequently, we must somehow *try* to give them some special treatment. And so the actors try. They endow the words with some special "content," some special meaning. They try to highlight those words they consider important. These unnatural efforts make them false and cause them to act badly. How could it be otherwise: in life we **do not try**, not a single bit, to speak our words; we do not even notice how they come out.

They don't act poorly because they are weak actors. Look: as soon as they've dragged their poor selves to the end of their "scene with lines," and got the text out of the way, they move to the side and sit on the sidelines, silently present in the scenes that take place between the others.

Since a heavy burden (the words) has been lifted off of their shoulders, they sit calmly, naturally . . . listening and looking, following what is going on, and they turn . . . into good actors. You cannot help but watch them with pleasure as they **upstage** their partners, without knowing it (like the cat we praised so much at the start of the book).

However, at the end of act, the lines resume, and (enough relaxing and doing nothing!) they begin to toil again, like conscientious workers, trying to squeeze the words out, and it becomes revolting.

Alas, such cases do not instruct anyone, and their attitude toward words remains the same.

Even students, people inexperienced in the theatrical business, having gotten to the end of their lines, consider the etude over and come out of it. This tendency has been described in the sub-chapter under this very title: "Switching Off."

It told the story of a student who, having said all his lines, immediately severed his ties with the partner and turned to the teacher, looking at him questioningly: What do you think? Not bad, eh?

To evoke in the students the right attitude toward the words, you should not philosophize and expound the subject. Instead, you should put them in the kind of situation that would *send them to the right path.*

Two students are called to the stage – he and she. It so happened that they were brother and sister. This could not but influence the course of the entire etude.

He. Are you mad at me?
She. I am.
He. Why?
She. You know perfectly well why.
He. This is exhausting.

Since they were not yet free from the actors' disease – considering words the main part of the etude – they unconsciously and imperceptibly sketched its content, while repeating the lines. The text itself seemingly indicated mutual irritation. How else would you explain words like "mad" and "exhausting"? Yielding to this, both of the partners – as soon as they finished repeating the text – felt some mutual dissatisfaction. She turned away from him and nervously twitched her shoulders . . .

"Are you mad at me?" he asked. One could hear neglect and contempt in his word. It was as if he said: "Just look how she puts on airs!"

She did not catch these subtleties in his voice, but only felt his hostility, and she reacted to it with an even greater irritation.

"I am!" she threw this at him over her shoulder and turned away even more sharply, as if to say: "I don't even want to talk to you!"

This hurt him, his lips instantly curled (Big deal! She does not want to talk!..), and some force turned him away from her as well. A second later he abruptly turned back to her and even slightly opened his mouth to say something, but, apparently, looked back at himself, and at his technique – he decided that he was rushing . . . So, he detained his urge and started waiting for another – a sound, unhurried impulse . . . Of course, he cooled himself off quite a bit, and broke the flow of his life, but he was saved by inertia: the irritation in him was still in effect, it is not as easily stopped – this is what saved the situation. Somewhat chilled, but still alienated and hostile toward her, he sat for awhile, looked around, and straightened his collar. . .

"Why?" – these words squeezed out of him reluctantly – they must have been on the tip of his tongue for awhile, but he kept them there, delaying them, thinking he does not need them yet. (In short, he missed the first train (the express) and did not want to go with the cargo train. . .) Finally, he squeezed them out of himself: "Why?"

She was not looking at him, and did not see his transformation. She only heard his reluctant "Why?" and exploded: "You know perfectly well why." She blurted these words out in a strange, squeaky voice that was not her own . . . Insulted, offended to the last degree, she could no longer contain her feelings. Tears of resentment and anger appeared in her eyes.

He (somewhat cooled off, due to his mistake), having received such an unexpected jolt, took a second to recover . . . Then he, apparently, remembered that she had annoyed him, tried to search for some rage – to counter her, but his anger has long subsided . . . The lines "this is exhausting" had come to his memory, and were ready to fly off his tongue, but he was still afraid of "rushing." So, he waited for a second, and then a third urge, and only then spoke.

Not giving him any time to recover, quietly and calmly I would prompt: ". . .continue . . . continue . . . let it keep going . . ."

The etude is not yet resolved, the scene is not over, and the student knows that . . . This is why my suggestion does not disturb him. Besides, the text is all over – this burden has fallen from his shoulders, and he now feels a lot easier . . . Now the burdensome words won't be creeping into his head, demanding to be spoken . . . now life flows as usual . . . everything is normal, and, therefore, his creative nature comes in its own rights.

He looked at her . . . not as an actor who will have to say certain words, but simply as a human being . . . He looked at her as a brother, and he felt sorry for her . . . For a moment he hesitated, then got up and went to her. She heard his footsteps, quiet and cautious . . . She felt the touch of his hand . . . she shivered, and at once became softer . . . Lowering her head, she turned to him and leaned against his shoulder . . . Quietly, barely audible, so as not to scare away what they've got, I would whisper: "Correct . . . this is correct . . . If you feel like saying something to each other – go ahead, say it."

Obviously, I guessed the right moment, and my words were timely, because they were immediately followed by her whisper: "Forgive me – I am such a difficult person . . . but it's hard . . . so hard."

He choked up . . . wanted to say something, but could not . . . Having cleared his throat, he uttered: ". . . I know . . . I can see it . . . I'm . . . It's me . . . I've hardened . . . got stuck in a rat race . . ."

"No! No!. . . Don't say that. Don't . . . " And he grew silent.

They stood there, leaning against each other, reconciled, quiet, exhausted from their stupid quarrel. We looked and . . . admired them and felt good . . . a sweet longing seized our hearts. . . a longing for friendship . . . for beauty . . . for a kindred human soul . . .

- Tell me, was there a difference between your state in the first part of the etude, when you had the words, and in the second when the words all ran out?
- Huge! Words get in the way . . . get stuck in the head . . . distract.
- And when the words run out?
- A weight off my shoulders! My path was cleared. This is when I saw her for the first time. Up until then, I kept talking to some phantom . . .
- I don't understand – why do you nurse these words so . . .

It is essential, at all costs, to distract them from caring about the words. Therefore, I do what I can to even exaggerate negligence toward the words.

- In life, you do not even know in advance what you are about to say and how. The words come out on their own, and they do not require your special effort. After all, at the end both of you also spoke. However, the words did not bother you.
- This is because at the end we did not know we were going to say them – we didn't even know there will be any words . . .
- Then why did you say them?
- They kind of came on their own . . .
- Here, here. This is how it happens in life. They come on their own; moreover, we do not know in advance if there will be any words . . . Let's strive for the same in our etudes.

- Easier said than done! – We know them beforehand, and that's that.
- Then forget them.
- How can you forget? . . .
- Put them out of your head, and be done with them. Out of your mind, out of your heart. I remember in some Ostrovsky play, a girl says, "Why don't I put that love out of my heart? . . . Out I put it, and forgot to think about it." Haven't you ever "put out of your head" a tedious, pesky thought? – I don't want to think about it- out! . . . Case closed.
- ???
- What is there to talk about – let's actually try it. Do this: speak your text smartly and intelligibly, listen to your partner's text and . . . put it all out of your head. It's gone! Vanished. And now . . . don't interfere: do what you feel like doing, feel what you feel like feeling, think as you will, say what you will . . . and only that. Take a risk. Try it.

They would give it a try, they would risk it . . . and, evidently, everything would work: the words would jump off the tongue on their own just when they are supposed to, and things would go as well as they could.

Why does this happen and how? We will encounter this phenomenon again in the future, and we will explain it. It will appear in this book more than once; specifically in its third part, in the chapter titled "Assignment."

The experience of this etude shows that delays and unnecessary pauses, and dragging, are mainly committed by actors **prior to speaking their lines**.

Rather than practicing freedom in saying the lines **how and when they want to be said** – people hesitantly stop and miss the moment, as well as their own desire to speak.

Why do they do that? All because they overestimate the importance of *saying the words* – just saying them, as it happens in life, seems strange and out of place . . . Surely, something special is required here – something "stage-worthy," "theatrical," and "expressive". . .

b)   Underestimating the words

Going forward, this overestimation of lines leads the actor to the opposite phenomenon – to underestimating the lines.

This inevitably occurs, and here's how: words are "special," a titanic work was invested in them, with all these "upward" and "downward" inflections, all these "intonations," and so on. They have become "a work of art." To make this artistry even more solid, the lines have been endlessly repeated. They've been drilled into this "artistic" form. Once they were drilled in, they became mechanized. And once mechanized, their original content vanished; they lost their lives, and turned into little corpses.

These little corpses pop out of the actors, colored in different ways with various vocal tricks. Still they are dead, empty, and unnecessary, both to the actor and to the audience.

The actors "pronounce" them, while easily thinking their extraneous thoughts.

How do the actors treat their lines now? Clearly, without any respect and awe. These are now just stiff forms of speech that used to be alive. And this is underestimation if ever there existed such.

This underestimation leads to another extremely curious misconception.

Surprising as it may be, the origin of this different kind of underestimation is also very simple and logical – the actors ceased to appreciate their lines, as these lines have become mechanical.

Instead, they now begin to appreciate *a certain actorly excitement*. The actors are now concerned whether they are emotional enough when speaking particular words. This preoccupation takes up all of their attention. With bare hands, they are fishing for emotions, for what they consider to be an "emotion." They try to be "full of emotions," try to become emotionally immersed. No, they've got no time for nonsense – at least, not for trifles such as thoughts or words – as long as they are filled with "*emotions.*"

Taken up by their own agitation, they ecstatically spew ten words per second . . . firing them like a machine gun . . . Their speech turns into continuous rattling, and inarticulate sounds . . . But what does it matter – they've got temperament, inspiration, power! . .

No one understands what they are saying (least of all they themselves), but that is not important at all – they've got this hightened "dramatic" tension in their acting . . .

Stanislavsky, in such cases, used a rather unaesthetic, yet convincing comparison. He used to say: "The actor threw up the lines."

We have far from exhausted all the mistakes and misconceptions connected with the text.

These are just some of the most common mistakes and misunderstandings.

13

Incoherence

The etude is over, and it went strangely . . .

- Tell me, who is she to you?
- My wife, obviously. Although she is kind of strange today . . .
- And whom did he strike you as being? Truly your husband?
- No. Absolutely not. – My brother.
- How so? . . . We've got a problem: husband . . . brother . . . wife . . . sister . . . . Do me a favor, tell us how it went from the beginning. You repeated the text . . . and then what?

It turns out that each of the partners started off of "themselves," from their respective inner state. Seemingly everything was done correctly, yet the etude turned into nonsense. Whose fault is this?

My fault, the teacher's. Students have nothing to do with it. I did not warn them that if they both draw exclusively *from themselves*, things could easily become incoherent. Until now this did not happen only because one of the participants unconsciously *used their partner as a point of departure*: they would look at their partner and immediately feel how the partner relates to them.

Similarly, in our etude, for everything to fall into place, it would have taken one of the partners to feel, understand, and guess another, or to start "from the partner."

It hardly matters who starts from whom, they just need to pre-agree.

- How do I *take it off of him*? What does it mean?
- You have already done it many times . . . Haven't you had plenty of etudes when you guessed each other and achieved a complete merger? Let's recall this . . .

Here begins our common, collective research of how this was previously done.

One student would say he's done nothing special: "Just looked at the partner; nothing else was necessary . . ."

Another says: "I do not look – I just listen to them when they repeat the text . . ."

I would ask them questions, leading them to discover the subtleties in their process they have not noticed. Eventually, I help them get to the bottom of the matter.

Why not just tell all this to the students right away? Why waste time?

First, any technique takes deeper root and "hooks" the students more strongly if they discover it on their own. Second, I must encourage observation and practically convince them that a bright mind and good will are an artist's best assets. This is especially true of our under-explored field of inner technique.

Let's, however, return to incoherence.

Many methods exist that can prevent (incoherence) in our etudes. Let's consider one of them.

As they repeat the lines, a student who is supposed to take his cue off of his partner *listens to the partner's lines with special attention*. There is no need to "ponder" the lines or to "feel them deeply" – it's enough to just *hear them well*. This alone establishes the connection and a certain dependency on the partner. This usually leads to a student feeling the need to look at his partner, at the start of the etude. Having looked, he receives an impression from the partner. Whatever he catches at this first look, penetrates him, and seizes him.

The rest of it we know well – do not interfere with your own life; give in to total freedom. Once received, an impression will inevitably lead to a reaction.

It often happens that an etude that starts with incoherence suddenly adjusts on its own. It aligns, and safely comes to an end.

Why does this happen?

What happens is that one of the participants, having felt that something is off, lets go of their path for a few seconds and begins to carefully study the partner. He looks at the partner differently from how he observed him so far, more keenly – after all, he's interested in finding out why the etude is not working, what's gone wrong.

Having stepped off their path, an actor becomes more passive and, therefore, more disposed to perception. And there is plenty to perceive: his partner keeps following his own path strictly and firmly. This spontaneous way of perceiving the partner causes an immediate and unconscious restructuring . . .

Perhaps the reader has already noticed and has even begun to get annoyed by the fact that all these etudes are kind of similar. Could you think of something else?

True, this is how things go. But it happens on it own. The actors are offered no circumstances, and nothing is pre-conditioned – it goes as it goes. A man and a woman, having met in an etude, develop some specific interest for each other, whether they want it or not . . .

Initially, I do not fight this – let it be so. After all, our main purpose is to learn how to live onstage – to yield to our spontaneous urges, manifestation, thoughts and feelings. If this specific interest gives everyone a certain extra charge – so much the better.

But then, I confess – this "specificity" gets old; so I would create a text that would inevitably steer the actor toward something else. This helps to solve the problem.

Generally speaking, it does not matter what they play in the beginning, as long as they learn to fully give in to their inner urges spontaneously and creatively.

Later, by adding the circumstances, it's easy to guide the actor anywhere, and any way you like. All in good time. After all, these are only the first stirrings of creative truth, the first leaves, the first sprouts – let them develop first. The time will come for you to begin to cultivate them, and direct their growth.

Here, in this nervous atmosphere – in the eyes of the entire class (i.e. the "audience"), out of fear of failure – primitive and selfish impulses arise the easier. There is nothing wrong with that. Let's give the actors a chance to calm down and to become established on their path to a sound creative state.

14

What Do We Gain from these Etudes?

Now that the reader is generally acquainted with our etudes, we can discuss their significance in greater detail.

Which "Elements," Essential for the Creative State Onstage, Are Developed by These Etudes

In 1932, I had to teach a "refresher course" for community theatre directors.

Stanislavsky's book had not yet been published, and his "system" was known only by hearsay. Speaking about an actor's proper behavior onstage and the "elements" identified in the "system," I illustrated many things with scenes, and many others with the etudes described herein. Actors in these etudes were participants in the same courses. They soon got used to the etudes – they lost all their initial tension.

At one of the last meetings, summarizing the results of all the classes, I asked the question:

"What do you think these exercises develop in an actor first and foremost?"

Immediately, one of those present said:

"Attention, of course. Whoever is participating in an etude is attentive toward his partner and toward everything that concerns him in the etude. This is genuine, substantive attention."

"No," said another, "these etudes are more about communication. When an etude is successful, the actors feel each other. The very construction of an etude lead to the fact that they can not *but* communicate."

"It's true," chimed in a third, "but the most important thing here is that an actor is fully directed by a 'task.' Without a task, you can not communicate and be attentive."

"Right, right!" a few other people picked up the idea, "If there is no 'task' onstage, then it's not an actor that we see, but an empty gun. The most important thing is a 'task.'"

So as not to cool common interest in the issue, you agree with everything, you support everyone's opinion . . . Someone says that it seems to him that the most remarkable effect of these etudes is that, in them, an actor holds on to an "object" very firmly, that he is so taken up by the object that nothing else exists for him, and that he gives over wholly to the life of the etude.

Someone was most attracted by the various interesting "adaptations" . . . Someone noted the distinctiveness of the "bits."

Two others made note of the astounding "muscular release" and insisted that's what grants them a proper creative state.

One young man with a vivid imagination was struck by the phenomenon that, the "system," is called "emitting" and "receiving rays." He said: "Sometimes, it's like you see currents emanating from actor to actor, it's like you notice the finest threads that are binding them – when they are speaking with each other, or when they are silent, or even when they're turned away from each other."

One was struck by the "public solitude." "It was as if they didn't even see us, even though there are sixty of us here. How did they do that? . . ."

So one by one, all the different "elements" of the "system" were named, and all I had to do was to sum things up:

"As you can see, in our etudes – if they are done correctly – all the "elements" are present. And they all exist in harmony with each other. That's why you had difficulty determining what was the main thing.

On Creative Transformations in an Etude

Many aspects of these etudes seemingly coincide with the usual exercises practiced in theatre schools [These are aspects such as the presence of spectators, the partner, or work with the given text (also practiced in other schools in scene study classes). –*Author's Note*]. But the main difference lies in the special method of application used by the teacher; in the "assignment" of the text; free and spontaneous reaction; and finally, in the specific paths to creative experiencing and transformation.

How do we realize transformation in our etudes?

a)   Redirection onto my own self.

After being assigned a text, and having "put it out of his head," an actor "green-lights" his spontaneous reaction – something in him that acts, thinks, and feels on its own.

IN HIM!

After all, he is still himself. There has been no requirement to be any particular "character." When the etude is over, the teacher asks him: what did you want? . . . What did you notice in your partner? . . . Who is he to you? . . . Why did you restrain yourself if you felt differently? etc.

All questions suggest that my "I" – the seeing, feeling, thinking "I" of the actor – is always present and always participates in the creative process. Moreover, it is the main participant in the process.

b)   A shift toward transformation.

The process of artistic transformation takes place simultaneously.

The class environment, the teacher, the classmates, and the partner – all of this makes the actor prepare for the fact that he is entering a creative path. All of this has already "shifted" him off the fact that he is merely his own, personal self. He is already an actor.

Repeating the text and listening to the partner's text "shifts" him even further.

The actor does not interfere with this shift, as he does not interfere with anything that happens in him – his thoughts, his feelings, and his action.

And now, the text, the partner, his own state, and all the rest, evoke in the actor some first hints of new imaginary circumstances. Then the circumstances of his new life, created in his imagination, solidify.

Alongside the circumstances and immediately following them, an actor receives a new *sense of self*: he feels himself being somebody else – the circumstances, and new imaginary life have "remade" him. [This new sense of self in the Stanislavsky's terminology is called "*I am*" (I am such and such character). –*Author's Note*]

And now, giving free rein to all his movements, sensations, emotions (he restrains nothing and "gives in" to everything freely), the actor perceives them as the manifestations of *his new "self."* These manifestations, therefore, confirm and prove to him the emergence of this new life – it becomes a fact.

Encouraged by this, the actor gives in more boldly, and so the process of transformation takes place.

c)   Unity of the actor's personal "self" and of the emerging "character"

While experiencing himself as somebody else, he never loses his personal "I."

This total unity of the actor's persona and of the character is a prerequisite to creative life onstage.

On the Creative Change of the Actor's Persona in an Etude

The text is given. Purposely, it is very unpromising and simple. Some conversation "about the weather."

- God-awful weather.
- Yes. It keeps pouring.
- We're stuck here . . .

My partner – a gangly guy, gloomy at first sight, but probably very nice. He is wearing a sweatshirt and boots. We are repeating the lines . . .

But even before I am assigned these lines, something else has already been added to my usual state. What is it exactly?

First of all, it is the sense that I am not just me – Petrov, but that I am also an actor who will now *play* some scene; the fellow with whom I will act is not just my fellow-actor – he's my *partner* in this etude.

I don't keep anything like this in mind, but it is there, and it is working in me; despite my own will, I already exist on a different plane – I have been moved off of my usual, mundane one.

And now, being in this new state, inwardly tuned to creativity, I perceive the proposed text; then, as I am supposed to, I "switch off" for two or three seconds, and finally freely "green-light."

The first thing that catches my eye is my partner's bored and gloomy face. He is upset by something, and he leers at the window . . . I also look there. A piece of gray sky . . . the autumn rain. I too feel dreary . . . He goes to the window, shakes his head and, hopelessly waving his hand, turns away and sits down. I begin to feel even more tedious. And it seems that this damned rain has been pouring for a long, long time – for ten days or so . . . And we are stuck here . . . We feel restless. The road has been washed away, you can't get through . . . And somewhere, hundreds of miles from here, somebody is waiting for us.

All of this is happening somewhere far from here, in the taiga, in Siberia . . .

Let's not bother going any further, and focus instead on the very beginning.

Notice how, in a few moments, a slice of near-real life emerged.

What remains now for me to do is to give in, to rely on what has risen in me, and to "green-light" it: let this complete, independent life grow out of my thoughts, feelings, and urges.

This life consists of a merger between my actual personal sensations and new content – a product of my creative imagination. While looking out the window at the autumn rain, I instantly feel "blue" – this is my personal. But next to this – an imaginary "taiga." I was under the impression that we were transporting some cargo – some mechanical parts. Personally, I have never had to do something like this. My partner is also an actor – not a driver or a mechanic. In general, the psychological space I am in, and all of my inner state, is quite foreign to me and unexpected.

Of course, I myself did not vanish, I stayed here: I still have my arms and legs, my eyes and my ears, and my heart. Yet I am somewhat . . . different. Some of my qualities, usually hidden from the others, here enlarge to such an extent that they become my leading qualities, and overshadow everything else. As a result, a seemingly different person emerges. This is as if some imaginary "I" has been added to my own "I." It is as if some imaginary Stepanov has been grafted to me, Petrov. He has been grafted to me, like gardeners graft a small twig of one tree to another. This twig strikes root, and the tree – in addition to its own qualities – receives all the qualities of the tree that supplied the twig.

The same thing happens here: we have the personality of the actor, Petrov, and a fragment of some other foreign person flickering in his imagination – some Stepanov. This fragment of an imaginary, foreign person creatively enters Petrov's persona. It alters it in its own way, and this merger with some imagined persona forms an embryo of some new man: Petrov-Stepanov (or Stepanov-Petrov – whichever qualities prevail). What is left now is just to ensure that this new person is given creative freedom. [Of course, if no merger happened and he, Petrov, remained intact, then there is nothing to be said: no new personality of "Stepanov – Petrov" exists. In such a case, Petrov would have nothing better to do but *portray* some "Stepanov," to imitate him.]

Some doubts may arise: things that instantly flash in your imagination are inexact and unclear . . . Which taiga, in what region? Who are you? What are you doing there? What do you do for a living? Do you have a family or are you perhaps single? None of it is in you and, therefore, this is not a life - in life you know perfectly well who you are what you do.

These are superficial, groundless considerations.

In life, do we always know everything about ourselves? Here, for example, I am writing – not thinking about my past or my present or my future – just as I am not thinking of who I am, where I am, whether I am married or single, healthy or sick. I only think of what I write, and everything else – *it exists somewhere* . . . If you ask me, I will answer, but it is of no use to me now, and, therefore, at the moment it has no place in my mind.

The same is true of our etude. Without any effort on my part, in one second, I, Petrov, was visited not just by a mere thought, but by an entire state of being: atrocious weather . . . we are stuck . . . and we must hurry . . . we have been hanging around here for no good reason . . . taiga, impassable mud, and floods . . .

At the same time, I feel completely calm – I have absolutely no worries about who I am, where I am, and so on.

This calm, this feeling of confidence is a fact of great importance. It alone is enough to dispel all doubts.

Why am I calm? Obviously, I feel quite normal; that is, I know who I am, where, and why.

If all these thoughts you require of me are not currently in my mind, it does not mean that they are not present *beyond the threshold* of my consciousness. Go ahead, start questioning me, carefully and skillfully, (as I interviewed my students in those previously described cases), and you will see that I know everything about myself: who I am, what is going on, and what's what. [Naturally, actors' calm and confidence onstage do not always indicate a sound creative state. Actors' calm may have nothing to do with creative calm. This can be the poise of an experienced, skillful craftsman.

Such a type does not even think about "life onstage"; they are only worried about the utmost skillful and showy *portrayal of the semblance of life*. Neither do they worry about creative transformation into character. They are not interested in becoming a character, but only in how to portray, or "present" it.

In order to skillfully depict, to deftly fake life—they know this from experience—they should first of all remain uninvolved; to not forget themselves, even for a second, and stay cold, calculating, and sober-minded. – *Author's Note.*]

Therefore, the absence of distinct, conscious thoughts of who I am and why, coupled with the sense of calm and normalcy of life in an etude, is a sure indication that my creative state is sound: it is the exact same state we experience in life.

Next question: where did the embryo of this life come from? Perhaps, it came from my gloomy, gangly partner. Maybe, it came from the cold Moscow autumn? Or maybe this taiga and the floods, the car stuck in the mud, and the long-expected cargo came from a book I recently read – so much construction is going on, and machinery is needed everywhere . . .

Yes, everything likely came from all these sources. No matter how many things you list, the picture will still be incomplete. Every moment of our lives is a result and a consequence of thousands of reasons that cannot be precisely determined. Let us not split hairs and philosophize, but rather practice trusting the forces of our creative nature.

Etudes and the Actor's Creative Process

These etudes are the most accessible and direct way to explore an actor's creative process.

A mere observation of their flow enables us to establish:

1   Conditions for the creative process.
2   Conditions for its sound flow.
3   Its errors.
4   The scheme of the creative process: assignment – free reaction – perception – another involuntary reaction . . .
5   These etudes alone made it clear that the creative process must not be **compiled** like a mosaic, by laying its fragments (the "elements") together. Rather, one should **not interfere** with the creative process that **already exists**. The fact is, as soon as an actor steps out to do an etude, and the assignment has been given – creativity **has already begun**.
6   When observing etudes, we notice that every attempt to break down the creative process into its constituent parts (as we used to do) leads to its destruction. Therefore, it is not just undesirable to do so, but it is **impermissible**.
7   We used to *make additions* to what we saw in an actor. We added what we deemed missing: attention, a circle, an object, a task, and so on and so forth.
    Our practice has taught us that, instead of adding what is not there, we must remove what interferes: excessive effort, haste, the "braking system" – "It's correct . . . correct!", "Give it a green light," "Take your time," etc.
    In short, we must proceed from the sound impulses that exist in a student; we must affirm them, rather than demand the non-existent, and thus extinguish the student's creativity.

Part III
Some Basic Principles and Techniques

15

The Threshold of Creative Experiencing

If you stick your hand out of a moving train, you will feel the force of the air. As the train approaches the station, gradually coming to a halt, the air ceases to press on your hand. The train is at a stop, and you lean out of the car window, smelling, in turns, the aroma of wild flowers, the stench of overheated steam, and of the locomotive soot. The air moves and brings you one smell or another. You cannot feel the pressure of *this* air on your hand; it exists below the threshold of your perception.

The train moves off quietly, but your hand still does not feel the movement; there is no sensation; the air seems to be standing still. The train picks up speed, and, finally, there is sensation: the wind begins to quietly strike your hand.

For each of our senses there exists a certain ***threshold***. If the irritation is too weak, we do not feel it; but as soon as the power of irritation increases enough, we begin to feel it.

The boundary between "I feel" and "I do not feel" in psychology is called a "threshold."

In our field, the field of acting, there is also a threshold.

Imagine one of the first lessons of the "psychological technique." The group is mixed: inexperienced novices are intermingled with seasoned actors. I call on one of the "seasoned" ones, who had recently entered the group, and I couple him with a very young girl. I offer them a simple text:

She.   Where are you going now?
He.   Home.

That's all.

He (a "veteran actor") repeats the text with a condescending smile – you have to obey, do all sorts of nonsense with boys and girls. Boring, stupid, but nothing can be done – orders are orders . . .

The most important thing for him is to show everyone around that this occupation is beneath his dignity. This is also necessary because somewhere deep down, he is not very sure of himself. So, if something does not work – he has got an excuse: "I wasn't really trying. In my opinion, it's not necessary. One needs to *act* well. What do these childish exercises have to do with it?! . . ."

Like it or not – he has to begin.

The girl looks at him. He sits with the air of dignity, performing the role of an offended man. Naively, she fills with respect for him and, after some hesitation, like a modest first grader, reverently asks: "Where are you going now?"

He hears her, of course, but vaguely – he is too busy with himself – how to best depict that he is natural, free, and captivating in his simplicity . . . He hears her words, but for some reason, *pretends* not to hear them (probably because he thinks it more "interesting"). Then, as if suddenly coming to, he mutters something like, "I'm sorry, I did not hear you . . . did you just ask where I was going now?" I did not give him these words, but so be it! Why should I not indulge him? After all, he feels himself rather rotten. Let him do whatever he knows to save himself. It's even amusing and instructive for the young people.

"Where?" He fakes thoughtfulness, while mulling this over (simultaneously peeping at us, out of the corner of his eyes – to check on our impression). Then, suddenly, his face swiftly assumes the expression of extreme business. Paying the least attention to his partner, he says "Home" with an air of importance, and mostly for our sake. He says it as if he has to attend to some state affairs at home.

After a pause that is meant to ensure that his masterful acting has "landed" with the audience, he looks us over forwardly, even triumphantly, as if saying: "See how it's done?!"

"All right, this is good . . ." I would say without much enthusiasm, "Let's do this . . . Without any discussion or critique, repeat it again. If things go like before – so be it; if something pulls you in a different direction – give it way, don't constrain yourself."

Wasting no time, he performs something else – equally ridiculous. Unsuspecting the true state of things, he gets a taste for it. When I tell him: "Come on, let's do it again," – he willingly goes to work: a hundred times, if you want! he is no stranger to creative work.

The students begin to understand the meaning of what is happening – they eye one another, restraining their smiles . . . The girl, our debutant's partner, is at first embarrassed, but then she begins to suspect that he just does not see or hear her, forcing himself to do something unnatural, and playacting with all his might. She sees that everyone else is also amused at his tricks, overconfidence, and complacency . . . She is also amused, but then she looks at him, and feels uncomfortable . . . she feels very sorry for him, and she is determined . . . to save him.

When I suggest to do the etude for a fourth time, she stares long and hard at her partner – she keeps trying to find a way to him, to "break" his shell. Finally, she moves closer to him and touches his hand . . . He looks at her in surprise; she survives this look and asks him cordially, friendly and simply: "Where are you going now?"

He keeps looking at her, and it is clear that he only just now sees her plainly. Before, he spoke to her as if to a fake doll; now her glance, her eyes, her appeal touched him to the quick. He cannot remain indifferent and apathetic. Reciprocal trust and tenderness flash in his face. "Home" – the word bursts from him, in the sense that "I'm free; I'm going home, but if you need me – please, I can stay, or I can go with you . . ." Somewhat embarrassed by his sudden fervor and his oblivion to everything but her . . . she stands up. He stands up with her . . . and they both go to the door.

Now it's really good! It works! – I would tell them and, without further discussion, invite them to take their seats.

I would call up another couple and give them a text, while continuing to watch my previous duo out of the corner of my eyes. They have yet to cool off; he keeps throwing glances at her, she – at him. As if some thread now ties them.

Aha! You're still going? Still unable to break apart?

They are both embarrassed.

This is as it should be: life began, real creative life. You *crossed the threshold*. Before this threshold, there was no life; it was all fake and false. And when you crossed the threshold, it all appeared – truth and life.

The second pair would finish their etude, return to their place, but the first continues "finishing up living" what just happened to them; both self-absorbed, they keep stealing looks at each other.

They do not realize that I have been watching them. Both get embarrassed and blush again, when I suddenly turn to them:

- I see your etude is still going? Don't be embarrassed, but celebrate! You just experienced what it means to truly *live onstage*. If this connection were to break at the end of an etude, this would mean that there was nothing to begin with. And if the connection exists, it cannot break, even if you wanted it to.

  Now tell us, Lyubochka, how did it all happen for you? From the beginning.
- From the beginning? . . . It began, perhaps, with Vasily Petrovich, in those first etudes, doing . . . not quite what we were doing here . . . I felt a bit tickled, and the guys were smiling . . . Then I felt uncomfortable: why laugh, when a person does not yet know what is needed . . . You told us to do the etude again – it was our fourth try. I repeated the text . . .
- Did you *want* to do the etude again?
- Yes. I felt we can do something real. . . perhaps, it's not working because. . . because I get in Vasily Petrovich's way . . . Well . . . we repeated the words. I put them out of my head, looked at him . . . he looked like a superficial person . . . sitting there, rocking his leg, adjusting his tie . . . "No, this is not the real him; he is better" – I thought . . . And suddenly I saw him as my cousin . . . he recently came to town . . . does not even know that we are related . . .

  I felt a bit awkward: he is my cousin, and I have not told him who I am in all this time . . . I just keep spying on him . . . Folks at home have been telling me all along: "Why don't you invite him over? Where is he staying, and does he have everything he needs?" I felt even more embarrassed, so I decided to tell him right away . . . I took his hand . . . he was surprised . . .
- Well, what can you tell us about yourself, Vasily Petrovich? What was going on with you before she took you by the hand, and what happened after?
- At first, I was playing an etude where I was a design engineer. I was vacationing on a cruise boat.
- Did you come up with it in advance?
- Yes. This is the task I set for myself. I am on a boat deck. The shoreline is moving . . . Other steamers are sailing by . . . Everything was good. Suddenly she puts her hand on mine. I must admit, I was taken aback. We hardly know each other . . . I look at her: what are you doing, my dear girl? And she looks at me as if nothing had happened. Either she knows something about me, or she wants to have a talk. "Where are you going now?" – she asks . . .
- Maybe she was joking with you?
- No, she was serious.

- So you believed her?
- Sure! She is such a nice, simple, sweet girl.
- Why did she ask you then?
- Apparently, she wanted to walk with me and tell me something, or ask me something.
- And you?
- And I'm free; I am going home after class . . . Why not take a walk with her?
- And what happened with the boat?
- What's that?
- You were sailing on a steamer.
- Ah, the steamer! Well, it was . . . it was nothing. I was acting.
- And here?
- Here . . . no, it's not acting, it's something else . . .
- Closer to life?
- Yes. Perhaps, it was life itself.
- This affected you personally?
- Yes, that's it – *me personally.*
- And before, it was something foreign, and personally did not concern you?
- Exactly. And now – as in life, it affected me personally. The real me.
- Well then, if the whole scene took place between you personally, that is, between Vasily Petrovich and Lyubochka – this means you will leave the class together? Will she go with you?
- Will she? I don't know. After all, it was an etude . . . an exercise . . .
- What do you mean an etude? After all, you just said that it was life. Real life. And if it happened in life – how could it go any other way? You met; she wants to go with you, to tell you something. You liked her, you are free – of course, you will go.
- Yes . . . but it wasn't life . . . And, at the same time, it was . . .
- Now that's interesting. I think you've quite confused us: first you say it's life, then you say it's not life. All right, let's check something. First of all, look at her. Is it her, or not? Is this the girl you talked to and wanted to go with?

He looks at her intently and says:

- You know what? That's not her! (General laughter.) Yes, yes! Don't laugh – it's not her! Here I look at her, and she feels kind of alien to me, a stranger . . . This is a young actress . . . a talented actress, even . . . and the other one . . . she was not an actress . . . she was an ordinary girl, and her eyes were the eyes of a child . . .
- Well, let us suppose you are right, and this is not her – things happen. But what about you? I hope you remained yourself? Or did you also get replaced?
- It seems not.
- Who are you now? An actor?
- An actor.
- And did she want to walk with you – the actor Vasily Petrovich?..
- Wait, wait! Hold on! This is very interesting! Let me tell you . . . When she took me by the hand, I was just surprised . . . But when she looked at me with her baby blue eyes, and then asked: "Where are you going now?" – something in me shifted . . . She is a sweet, simple girl, some tenth grader, and I felt that I was also some modest working guy . . .
- An ordinary mortal . . . – one of the students can't resist.

He does not notice the sarcasm and passionately continues his story:

- Yes, ordinary . . . very ordinary . . . some accountant or technician . . . I felt so relaxed and easy . . . And her eyes were looking at me so honestly . . .
- Well, and what about us?
- What about you?
- How did we perceive it all?
- I didn't know . . . I did not see you.
- You only saw her – the girl, the tenth-grader?
- Yes.
- And got quite emotional?
- Imagine so!
- Who got emotional? You – Vasily Petrovich?
- Yes, me, Vasily Petrovich . . . just somewhat different . . . accountant, technician . . . younger, and single (I am married in real life). This is miraculous!
- Well, now everything is in order. You actually felt the most important thing: what it means to exist up until the threshold, and how it feels *to cross the threshold.*
- What "threshold"?
- The most important threshold of all, as far as we are concerned: the threshold of creativity. When, for some reason, you become emotional and take to heart the words and facts that, strictly speaking, have nothing to do with you. When you begin to personally live some imaginary life – to live and act in it . . . All this is called stepping over the threshold.

  At the same time, you change. Suddenly, you depart your own persona and your actual surroundings. Your imagination takes hold of you. You are alive – not dead, or asleep – yet you are no longer your ordinary self. You are someone else – an accountant, a technician, Liubim Tortsov, Hamlet, Othello . . .

  Let's not dwell on this, as interesting as it may be – your whole future life onstage will consist of concerns about this creative state, about acting, while being "beyond the threshold."

Practice has taught me that work with students should also begin with establishing *a sound creative process.* More precisely – with cultivating the creative process of experiencing. To do so, one must primarily remove all interfering factors.

A creative state should be thoroughly sought from the outset, without putting it off to a future time. Otherwise, the most insignificant error made at the beginning will escalate with each step. The initial intentions to correct it "someday," "in the future" are never realized.

Imagine a circle. Somewhere deep within, it must have a center. Although it is unmarked, it serves as the foundation of the circle. If you find yourself on the "periphery" of a circle while you ought to get exactly to its center, then from the very beginning, you should take the right direction.

If you make a mistake in the very beginning and deviate from the exact path even a little, you're inevitably going to miss the center. *Seemingly, you would be moving towards the center.* Every minute and every hour of your journey, you would be expecting to reach it. In fact, you won't even notice how you moved **past the center.** Your might miss it by just a little, and yet . . . from that point on you would continue getting further and further away from it, until you come back to the "periphery." Except, instead of returning to your old spot, you are now at the *point opposite* to where your initial hopes and plans have resided.

The same is true of the student-actors. If you do not immediately give them an absolutely accurate direction (this is what it feels like "before the threshold", and this is how it feels when you cross "beyond" it), all future work will take them past the goal worthy of a true artist, and of genuine art.

16

Solidifying an Actor in the Creative State ("Support")

The Technique of "Support"

In my early practice, I would assign an etude; students would act it out, and, when it was finished, I would give my notes. Or else, seeing some mistake, I would stop a student, give notes, and make them either repeat the etude, or continue it from the same place.

Soon, however, I arrived at a new way of affecting the flow of an etude.

A young man is no longer trying, as he was in the beginning, to spit out his text as quickly as he can; slowly, he looks around, and glances at his partner . . . She feels extremely unfree: afraid to move or turn her head . . . He keeps studying her. Then something begins to bother him – a thought must have flashed in his head: "They are looking at me! I forgot that I am 'acting' . . . " His own silence strikes him as being excessively long – he is about to become nervous and spoil everything by pushing himself . . . Unable to restrain myself, I whisper: "Take your time; everything is right, take your time, do not be afraid of pauses . . . everything is right."

At first I would get scared of my own impulsivity and think: I distracted him. But it turns out to be a false alarm – my intervention does not spoil things. Apparently, my words hit him just in the right spot and are quite timely. He takes courage, feels himself on solid ground, and safely gets to the end of the etude without missing a beat.

Here is another case. When you see an actor (or a student) truly getting carried away by a scene and growing quite emotional, you become especially sensitive while following him. You begin to live in unison with him, so to speak. The scene develops; the excitement increases and suddenly, when it comes to a high degree of tension, some inkling suddenly prompts you: he is about to get scared of his own emotion, not being able to withstand it . . . he will slam his foot on the brakes . . . he is already doing it. Suddenly, these words burst out of you: "Green-light it boldly! . . . Everything is right! . . . Bolder!"

It turns out, that this too does not interfere . . . On the contrary, it helps him – the actor suddenly reveals his depths; his classmates are all amazed, and so is he.

Not wasting a moment, I would tell him, "You see – it turns out, you can do anything. You can, and it's not hard at all." At that moment, he also feels that it actually is easy to handle. He would believe in himself, in his own capacities. Having led him a few times by the hand, you establish him so firmly on the path – nothing will ever lead him astray.

Had I not supported him in time, he would have, perhaps preserved his "modesty" for another year, not even suspecting his own powers – and neither would we.

This became a habit – during the first etudes, time to time, I would do my prompting – "supporting" them – sometimes in a whisper, sometimes loudly. I would do so, as if leading them along a tightrope. So I would stand by, afraid to take my eyes off of them: the second they tilt – I would be right there.

They *don't even notice* my "support" – it's so timely, so empowering and affirmative.

This skill is not acquired overnight, of course, but gradually developed. As I closely follow the student's every movement, I begin to *live in unison* with him, feel what he feels, and even guess his thoughts, based on some barely-perceptible movements . . . When your connection with the student is that strong, no support will miss the target – it will always hit the right spot.

*Without being tuned in perfect unison with the student (being tuned to the very same note, the very same rhythm), whatever you say – however intelligent it may be – would **upset** the student's creative state. Instead of helping – you would just make a mess of things.*

It is more than sensitivity. At the end of a class, I would recall myself using, quite unconsciously, a variety of different "support" tactics: sometimes I would speak in a barely audible low whisper, then loudly, like the crack of a whip: "Correct! This is correct! . . . " When I feel that a student has got no strength to do a difficult, dangerous jump, I would shout – and the strength is found . . .

At times, I would deliver these prompts from my seat; then some force would carry me onto the stage, and I would walk in the actor's footsteps . . . guarding him, supporting, encouraging . . . Sometimes I would speak in such a quiet whisper that no one but the actor and I can hear it . . . In short, it is different every time. One condition never goes away, though: you must become one single being with the student – then you will never make a mistake.

A serious concern may arise: what if the students grow accustomed to constant assistance from the teacher, who keeps leading them "by the hand," as if they were children? Would this not deprive them of creative independence and individuality?

On the contrary – as a teacher, I do not prompt my students **what** to do, or **how**, but rather reaffirm their faith in their own creativity ("right, right . . . ", "that's correct . . . ") and anticipate their errors and haste (Take your time!").

In order not to spoil students with nonstop support and train them to work without any supervision, I would gradually, little by little, let them travel alone. Soon I would narrow my support down to sending encouraging words their way in the most dangerous moments – or else pulling the reins when they dart downhill . . . to keep them from falling, from breaking their necks, so as not to have to "treat" them afterwards for two or even three months.

In time, support will not be needed at all.

The Role of "Support" in Cultivating Involuntariness and Freedom Onstage

"Support" plays a tremendous role in the work of actor-cultivation. It accelerates it many times. With the help of this technique, already at the end of the first lesson, the students receive personal *practical experience* of what it means to not interfere with their own selves and to live onstage. Moreover, they experience how easy, uncomplicated and pleasurable it is . . . They already feel that, if things continue going this way, very difficult tasks will get accomplished on their own . . . Their job is to solidify this technique. Their job is to train . . .

Moreover, "support" enables us to bring to a sound state even those people, who are hopelessly distant from it – spoiled actors, only accustomed to stereotyped patterns, whose false state has become their norm; singers, deprived of acting talent; circus athletes and, finally, amateur actors.

None of these difficult cases would escape an experienced teacher. Whether they want it or not, they would arrive, in a matter of minutes, at the amazing state of the free creative experiencing.

My class consists of several dozen of community theatre directors. They are taking a "refresher course." The classroom population is quite diverse. There are young professional actors, waiting to be challenged. I know from experience that they are hungry for new ideas. I can see young women involved with children's theatres, and old actresses who left the stage under some kind of pressure. Old experienced provincial actors, who moved to this obscure, yet more peaceful path. Provincial "leads" who got unlucky, temporarily drawn to the amateur shore – they are ready to sail away at the first opportunity, to once more dash through the waves of the fickle theatrical sea. There are, of course, two or three true enthusiasts here, versed in the matters of acting techniques.

For the first experiment, it would be easier to invite someone who understands the heart of the matter and won't "fail." But wouldn't it be more persuasive to walk straight into the lion's mouth? So, I would choose someone who is a definite failure.

An old man I call to the stage is embarrassed and keeps making excuses – he did not expect that he would have to "act," especially before such a difficult audience as his colleague directors.

He was once a provincial actor . . . probably not a bright talent, he succeeded because of his experience . . . the years have flown by and carried away his vigor . . . he moved to Moscow and took up two theatre clubs at a factory. Simply and unpretentiously, he puts on performances with the theatre circle members.

As a token of recognition, he was invited as a veteran theatre worker to attend the "refresher courses." Why not go? It is, of course, too late to learn anything, let alone relearn . . . still, it is interesting to listen . . . In his day, they used to act the good old way, simply and unpretentiously, and now there is "system," and all that . . .

He listened to all of the "experts" – it sounded interesting. Only it's hard. Apparently, you need to develop attention, seek out the "logic" of feelings and actions, enter the "circle," know your "task," find your "adaptations"; sense the "public solitude," "relax your muscles," take care of "the verisimilitude of feelings in the given circumstances," of the "I am," and finally, to pierce all of your "tasks" with "through-action" . . .

Of course, it's all true. There can be no doubt. This is how it is, according to the latest theatrical science. Except, he must have grown too old for this: it's hard . . . things just don't fit into his head . . .

And this is the old man the teacher "drags" to do an etude.

- Please, please . . . don't be shy . . . Well, what shall we do?.. Do you see this miniature palm on the window-sill, in this dried-up flowerpot? Walk up to it, look at it and say: "Well." That's the whole exercise. Understood? – Understood . . . – If, at the end, you feel like doing something else, please go ahead. Don't hold anything back; give yourself full permission. So, what will you do?
- Walk to the window, look at the palm and say, "Well" . . .
- Very good. Take your time. Begin when you feel like it.
- Easy to say, "when you feel like it!" – thinks the unfortunate old man. – What if I don't feel like it at all? Why did I agree to this?! . . .

- That's right, right. This is correct. – says the teacher suddenly, sounding completely convinced.
- Correct? . . . – the old man is taken aback . . . – What about it is correct?

But there is no time to think; since he's saying "correct," that must mean I haven't failed yet; that I'm still keeping afloat. This means I must use it, hold on to it, and keep doing what I'm doing . . . But what *am* I doing?

After two or three seconds he would have floundered, gotten confused, and finally lost it. The teacher, knowing this, calmly and quietly whispered: "Right, right. You are dissatisfied with something, so be it; keep it this way, don't fight it, continue."

"I am dissatisfied, am I?" the old man is guessing. "Yes, yes, of course, I'm upset: why did I agree to come out? . . ."

"That's correct, correct!" the teacher does not give him a chance to recover. This "correct" seems to have propelled the old man forward . . . and he rushes headlong into his "dissatisfaction."

"Why *did* I come out?!" he thinks, "just look at them, they are all pleased, happy, smiling . . ." He looks angrily at the audience.

"Correct . . . correct . . . that's it . . . well done!" continues the teacher.

"'Correct . . .' I know myself it's 'correct,'" a thought flashes in the old man's mind.

Well, what about it: is it correct or is it incorrect, after all? Yes, in this case it is *correct*, without a doubt. His own mundane, living feeling strangely united with the consciousness, or rather, sensation of being a performing actor. These two feelings connected and, instead of colliding, reinforced each other. He looked with displeasure at his colleagues in the audience . . . then turned away and looked around the room. The room also felt unpleasant . . . he looked out the window . . . saw something interesting . . .

"That's right, that's right," the teacher tosses in. "Correct." And . . . the window pulled him. If the teacher kept silent – perhaps he would have restrained himself, and not gone to the window. The teacher's words erased all his doubts and even slightly nudged him and helped – his legs carried him to the window. Having dared to walk across the stage, he felt even better. And then there came the teacher's voice:

"Well done! Well done! . . . Good for you!"

The old man was delighted; his success began to agitate him. "Take your time, take your time," the teacher kept whispering calmly and evenly, "yes, yes, that's it, take your time." He felt calm and confident . . . His discontent came back – the same mood he "gave in" to in the beginning. From the window he saw people walking down the street . . . some couple . . . on the opposite side of the street, children poured out of the school . . . – they were running and jumping around – it must be a recess. They will catch the cold – it's chilly and damp, and they are dressed so lightly . . . Nothing interesting was on the street . . . A mere disappointment. What's that? Just look at this flower!

The teacher immediately catches a barely noticeable, involuntary movement of his hand toward the pot with the plant: "Yes, yes, do it! You can do anything you want!" Encouraged by this nudge, his hand continues to move more boldly . . . the other hand follows suit . . . "That's right, that's right, well done . . . " His hands take the pot and lift it up . . . All these movements are completely involuntary. Previously, such "anarchy" would have disturbed the old man; it would have seemed harmful and unrelated to business. He would have been scared by it (this is outside of "the task!"); he would have tried to suppress it. Now he hears the encouragement and gives free rein to his own movements. *His involuntary life awakens, along with a different attitude towards it: apparently this is what's needed! It has saving power.* For some reason, he carries the pot to the table. Another second – he would have gotten scared of his own boldness, and it would have spoiled everything.

"Good . . . Good . . . Correct!.. Take your time . . ." This whisper reinforces the old man in his state. He calmly puts the palm on the table. Picking the completely dry soil with his fingers (he must be a lover of flowers!), he shakes his head disapprovingly and lets out a sad sigh: "We-e-ell!"

"That's all," interrupts the teacher. "See how easy and simple it is. You didn't have to invent anything; didn't have to work hard. It all worked out beautifully on its own."

The old man is happy; the old man feels himself a hero. He got so excited he is not going back to his place without telling us how it all happened . . . And we hear from him approximately what was just described.

On the Subtleness of this Technique

The reader may still be perplexed: Wouldn't the words of the director, said at the most emotional moment, interfere with the actor's creative process?

It all depends on how you say them.

If the director has such a fine sense for the actors that he almost **merges with them**, then he won't make a single mistake. Instinctually, he will deliver his prompts so carefully and in such a timely manner that the actors will accept his voice as their own. Alternatively, the actors would sense that someone else, so friendly and indispensible, has joined in their work and won't abandon them at a difficult moment. They cannot help but obey such a voice.

Most importantly, the director should bear in mind that, during etudes, the students (and actors during rehearsal) *live in a particularly sensitive and receptive space*; every word, every breath coming from the outside hits them in the very center of their psychological life.

Many directors, seeing the effectiveness of this device ("support") will, most likely, begin to use it. If some of them do not receive the expected result – the main mistake will likely lie in them missing the very essence of the device and not realizing that its power lies in its subtlety – *in extreme sensitivity toward the actors; toward the flow of their life onstage.* These directors will begin to boldly give their orders to the actors, regardless of their current thoughts, emotions and their life at large . . .

The other error – instead of two-three essential words, they would start lecturing the actor, delivering entire speeches.

Both of these mistakes, instead of supporting the actor, and establishing him on the right path – they, would violate the actors' complex, intense, and simultaneously delicate process. Such insensitive intervention causes the actors to fall off the clouds of their imagination to the hard ground.

17

The Role of Automatic Movements in Cultivating Freedom and Spontaneity

Simplicity and Naturalness

Many actors believe that one should be natural onstage, "as in life." So, they try to find simplicity and naturalness, this "truth of life," as if it were some kind of a separate thing.

Truth be told, it does not exist. What is simplicity and naturalness, and when does it come? It comes when *life flows spontaneously*. You breathe and do not think about it. You breathe habitually, as it is natural for you. Try keeping an eye on your breath; try catching this simplicity and naturalness – in three or four seconds you will feel that your breathing has been disrupted. You breath is no longer normal or natural, but strained and deliberate.

Only organic and natural things are free and spontaneous.

What is freedom and spontaneity onstage?

It is very difficult, almost impossible to explain to a person what spontaneity and freedom really are. This is not at all surprising. Such things can only be understood in practice. If you describe to a person how a certain fruit tastes, no matter how vividly, this person's idea of the fruit will be distorted until they actually try it.

Imagine a student approaching you after class, smiling shyly and continually adjusting his glasses, for no particular reason: "I am sorry, I don't think I quite understand . . . I don't doubt that one has to be free and involuntary . . . but you're saying that everything should be happening 'on its own' – I don't understand that. Let us suppose that I go somewhere – I do so because I know where I am going. If I didn't know that, I wouldn't go; nothing in me is going to 'go on its own.'"

- Tell me, why have you now, while talking to me, adjusted your glasses five times?
- I did? My glasses?
- Well, yes. I counted – you have adjusted them five times. Did they bother you?
- No, they didn't . . . I don't know why, I didn't notice.
- And now you fixed your hair. Why?
- I don't know why . . . For no reason . . .
- You see. Then, you are not aware of everything you do, and things take care of themselves, as if beyond you.

- Um . . . Yes.
- Here, you took out your handkerchief, wiped your hands and hid it in your pocket again . . .
- Yes, yes – he is embarrassed (this is because everything he has done with his handkerchief was also done involuntarily) – My hands must have been sweating . . . so I wiped them.
- "Must have been!" So you do not know, you're just taking a guess: I don't know why, my hands *must have been* sweaty . . . These are *involuntary movements, involuntary thoughts* (I do not know why I thought that – the thought must have come on its own), *our life is full of involuntary feelings.*

  It is true, many things we do are predetermined. Here, let's come to the window. Can we? Yes, we can. Come on. And so we did. We decided to do it, and we've done it. By all indications, this action was arbitrary . . . as for why you've grabbed the window handle, I do not know.
- It happened by itself. (He is again embarrassed that I caught him in an involuntary movement, and he smiles.)
- You just smiled – that too happened "by itself," didn't it? (I would keep torturing him, not giving him a second of rest, until he began to feel what a great number of things in him happen involuntarily.) Then I would say: I demand nothing special – just give free rein to all of your small involuntary movements, as well as thoughts and feelings . . . let your fingers drum on the table if "they feel like it;" let your eyes look out the window if they saw something interesting there, and don't worry about anything else.

  Let's be humble – let's content ourselves to the most primitive – the physical, if you will – freedom and spontaneity: let's give freedom to our smallest automatic movements and actions.

  How can we dream, from the first steps onstage, of heightened creative freedom? We have yet to be able to give in, immediately and completely, to our usual everyday feelings and desires. Or else, we will keep straining them through a sieve and holding on to all those manifestations we deem "inappropriate" or "immoderate."

  We are so used to holding back our every urge, we must recapture "freedom" and "involuntariness" – cultivate them step by step.

  We should start with the smallest things. No need to look for them on the side – they are always with us. I am referring to those involuntary automatic movements which we do constantly without suspecting it.

What are these unconscious automatic movements? Imagine a man sitting, listening to his companion and constantly fidgeting in his chair. What's the matter? Why is he doing this? The answer is very simple: he is tired of talking; besides, he had long wanted to leave, but it would be rude to do so. He forces himself to sit, but all these movements break out beyond his will; these movements are nothing else but *the beginning of getting up and leaving.*

Or imagine an unpleasant man entering . . . I have to make an effort to turn to him, approach him and say hello. This is because, apparently, I involuntarily turned away from him in the first moment and wanted to leave.

A pleasant and dear man comes in . . . I have to refrain myself – otherwise, my legs would carry me to meet him too quickly; my hand would seize his too hastily and too hard, and too much joy would glint in my eyes.

Imagine a boring interlocutor you have nothing to discuss with; everything you could say to each other had already been said . . . engaging with some business in his presence is improper, and your energy finds its way out: you are drumming the table with your fingers. You hum. Thoughtfully, you utter from time to time: "Yes-s-s . . . "

A man is tired, and his hand involuntarily reaches for his forehead; he is rubbing his temples . . . he has probably got a headache. Try refraining from these movements, however meaningless, purposeless, and motiveless they may seem. When holding back these movements, you hold back your inner life that spawned them. When green-lighting them, you give freedom to your inner life with its unconscious manifestations. This is the essence of our method.

Many of those working in theatre consider these small movements harmful for the actor. "If you give in to small movements, you will only create hustle and bustle" – they say – "an actor keeps shifting from one foot to the other; constantly moving his arms; he keeps shrugging his shoulders and turning his head . . . We must, on the contrary, make him stop, cease this hustle; he would then be able to think clearly, and the audience would be able to see, hear and understand him."

This seems quite reasonable; yet, when we are alone in the room, we permit positively everything, and no hustle results from this. On the contrary, we feel complacent and freed.

And vice versa: every ban, every constraint creates anxiety.

Moreover, refer to life and observe: how long you can sit *perfectly still*? Not even one minute.

If you decide to make yourself sit still for a whole minute, you would do it, but how? You would need to deliberately bind yourself, refraining from subtle movements. These movements accompany our every moment: some thoughts of ours cause us to hold our breath; our eyes shift; we move our head. Our feet or hands change their position – the inconvenience causing it is quite unconscious, yet it exists. And so on, and so forth.

What do most actors do, as they start rehearsing? *To begin with, they bind themselves,* removing all their involuntary automatic movements (some of them call it "getting ready", "concentrating," "mobilizing," etc.). Up to this point, there was "life," "mundane life" – that was just trifles; *now* I am about to start working, making art – this is serious. Therefore, away with everything mundane.

They throw away everything "mundane," and with it they throw away everything "alive," i.e., all of those manifestations that feel normal and natural to them . . . They are left with dry reasoning and a cold-minded willingness to "perform on command." This is the end of everything.

It turns out that encouraging actors' own involuntary automatic movements is one of the most effective and speedy means by which we can regain the lost natural involuntariness, freedom and ease. This is not in the least surprising. As mentioned earlier, the actors primarily start by depriving themselves of their "mundane freedom": they forbid their own involuntary habitual movements, considering them extrinsic and distracting. What do they achieve by this?

After all, these involuntary movements were free manifestations of their inner life. This life flowed as continuously as breathing, yet the actors went and forcibly stopped everything that revealed this life.

The consequences are comparable with plugging one's nose and mouth, i.e., suspending one's automatic and involuntary breathing . . . Such an unnatural condition cannot result in anything good.

How would one go about destroying this condition?

First of all – unplug your nose and mouth . . .

In practice, this is very simple. "You are not quite comfortable in your seat. Sit any way you want" – an actor sits more comfortably. In the meantime, the director starts talking with other actors. This is done to give the actor time to calm down. When the actor sees that the director is distracted, he ceases to feel the responsibility of the moment, and starts to behave "mundanely." He leans with one hand on the table, and rests his head on his hand. With his other hand, he rolls a pencil he found on the table. – Let's begin.

The actor straightens up and leaves the pencil alone.

– No, no, why? Sit as you were sitting . . . You were comfortable, weren't you? Keep sitting this way. And . . . keep rolling the pencil as you did before . . . The actor looks questioningly: perhaps the director is laughing at him?

– No, no, I am serious. Why wouldn't Mitya sit leaning on his desk and roll the pencil out of boredom? After all, he is by himself – no one else is in the booking-office. (We are rehearsing Mitya's first monologue from Ostrovsky's *Poverty is No Vice*.) Sit the way you want (no doubt, Mitya sat quite comfortably) and roll the pencil . . .

The actor finds this amusing – rehearsing not "seriously," but by some new, funny method . . . He leans down as before . . . After five-six seconds, however, he becomes worried: time to "deliver" the lines!

In order to prevent this misfortune, the director says in a calm voice: "You can wait with the lines: after all, he wasn't talking all the time; he must have been silent a lot, left alone in the office, on a holiday . . . "

The actor calms down . . . and goes on with his business. The director notices that the actor is growing tired of rolling the pencil. Catching the involuntary movement of the actor's head, the director helps out: when you get tired of the pencil, leave it be. After all, you are alone, no one is there, you needn't be concerned with anybody.

The actor looks around. – "That's right, that's right," – calmly and quietly, the director encourages him. The actor sighs . . . "Correct, correct," – joins in the director in a barely audible voice. Noticing an actor's subtle movement, he says: "If you want to get up, do get up, don't keep sitting . . . you are by yourself . . . everything is permitted . . . everything . . . " The actor goes to the window and begins to draw with his finger on the misted-over glass . . . "Good, good, that's right"– the director reinforces him quietly, but firmly and authoritatively . . .

Encouraged by this stimulation, almost a command, the actor completely gives in to his involuntary urges . . .

It does not take 10–15 seconds, and the director notices the all-growing anxiety . . . "When you feel like saying the lines, do not interfere – green-light them." The actor, it seems, was just waiting for this permission. "Oh Lord, what misery!" – he says, abruptly turning away from the window. He waves his hand in some unknown direction, as if pushing away something unpleasant and heavy . . . "Right, right – the director does not give him time to recover – go on."

The actor is carried away. A glance out of the window . . . and the director, guessing the moment, urges the actor: "Yes, yes, correct."

– "Everybody in the streets is having a holiday, and everybody in the houses too!" – the actor has become bitter; he feels hurt, humiliated . . . The emotion keeps growing . . . He is not used to giving in to such emotions – live, involuntarily flowing from some unknown source, and gripping. Another second, and he would slip, unnerved by the novelty of the sensations . . . Anticipating this, the director speaks quietly, in a barely audible voice: "Correct, correct . . . well done, right . . . take your time . . . everything is correct . . . " The actor feels affirmed in his psychological state . . . He looks around and says with sadness and longing: "And you have to sit between four walls!" Having groped his way to the chair, he sits down and bows his head.

By these means – by constantly encouraging, anticipating mistakes and urging – the director, from the first rehearsal, guides an actor through his entire monologue. In some half an hour, the director gives him the delightful experience of *living onstage*.

When the actor tries to repeat this on his own, he isn't able to do it. This does not matter: the first step has been made, and the actor is now interested. With time, he will master this technique.

In addition to the state of freedom and spontaneity onstage, this method leads the actor to what he needs most of all: creative transformation.

If he has no experience with this, the new sensation may even perplex him.

- It's a good thing, no doubt – I did live – he would say – but it wasn't Mitya living, but me. *I* felt like rolling the pencil on the table, *I* was sad, *I* was envious that I cannot go anywhere – no decent clothes, nor shoes, and wearing the old stuff is embarrassing. *I* was the dependent poor steward to the rich merchant Tortsov. *I* had an old mother living somewhere in the city . . .
- Well, tell me – the director would ask, as if out of curiosity – what kind of a feeling did you get about your mother, what is she like?
- She is a little old lady . . . she loves me . . . wears a dark dress, short jacket . . . and she likes to sigh, "Lord, have mercy on us sinners."
- Does she spend all day reading? . . .
- She's got no time to read! She is always busy, running around . . . She only reads on Sundays . . . her hymnal . . . and "Lives of the Saints" . . .
- Where does she live? In the center of the city?
- No, no. On the edge . . . and not in the city, in the village.
- She's got a big house?
- How could she? A small shack . . . shabby, with a straw roof. To enter it – you have to bend down your head. Tiny windows, all chipped, pasted over with paper . . . cracks in the floor . . . draft coming through the cracks.
- Now tell me: are you telling me about your mother, or Mitya's? Do you personally have a mother like this?
- Me? My mom?
- Yes, you personally?
- No, my mom is a teacher . . . She is tall . . . Wears a pince-nez . . .
- How could it be? Apparently you turned into Mitya without even noticing. Look: you are telling me about this little old lady, as if she was your mother. Remember, you said: it wasn't Mitya, but me. Well, perhaps it was you, but it must have been some other, changed you – with a different mother, a different life . . .
- How could that be? (He is somewhat puzzled.) Don't be taken aback: this is normal. You should be glad it happened this way. You didn't even notice how you "slipped into Mitya" and felt like a different man. Do you realize that your external appearance, during the monologue, was also different – unlike your everyday self, you were less sophisticated, humbled, in short . . . almost Mitya. Here you have the beginnings of the character. You did not concern yourself with character, and yet it started to form – whether you expected it or not.
- You are probably right . . . the character appeared . . . But it isn't the right character. Why is he "humbled?" Mitya, in my opinion, must be heroic, "Oh, just give us a chance! I want some joy in life!"
- Well, this is just an outburst of an overly-emotional young man, who constantly had to constrict himself and restrain his feelings . . . Naturally, he would want to spread his wings, at least once. Other than that, just look at him with his constant "Yes, sir," "No, sir."

However, this is not the time to argue about who Mitya *actually is*. No matter how we *define* him now, it is irrelevant, if we want to make the role organic. If we want Mitya to come from your heart and from your individual "I," your Mitya will come out . . . as he comes out. [The reader should not be perplexed by the director's prediction: "Your Mitya will come out . . . as he comes out". This is said so as to keep the actor from the pursuit of character he is yet to develop. While perusing this kind of a phantom, hastily fabricated in the actor's head, he can only run away from his true "Self." – *Author's Note*]

We don't yet know what kind of Mitya will grow out of you. It depends on the thousands of reasons we are not able to take into account. And we do not really need to take them into account. These reasons include your complex personal "self" with its heredity, upbringing, joys, sorrows, doubts; your conscious and unconscious hopes, dreams and fears.

Everything in you that is near and dear to Ostrovsky's Mitya will respond to the character. What does not exist in you (at least marginally) will not be found in your Mitya, no matter how hard you try, and how you "define" the character. True, sometimes, we may need to "extract" from you those qualities that are well-developed in your character, but poorly developed in you. We will speak of that later, when there is a need. As for now, your present qualities are quite enough.

With some patience, even such a simple device as attention to the most primitive manifestations of life – small automatic movements – is able to clear the actor's way to the most important and difficult things, such as naturalness, simplicity, and to what is called truth. This subtle, yet simple technique is well illustrated by an Indian tale – an allegory.

A minister angered his master-rajah, who ordered him to be shut up in the "Sky Tower."

This tower was a very high stone pillar, inside which there was a spiral staircase leading all the way to its top. At the top was an open platform. A prisoner was scorched by the sun, lashed by the rain and torn by the wind – there was nowhere to hide. He was not given any food or drink, and when he grew weak, black kites swooped down upon him, tearing him to shreds. The ravens finished the job . . . When a few days later people came up the stairs, there lay only clean bones.

They dropped the bones over the railing to the dogs . . . It was in this tower with such a poetic name that they locked the unfortunate minister. They locked him in and left him there. Guards were not required. The strong locks were unbreakable, and no ladder was tall enough to get to the top. The prisoner sat under the scorching sun, and the kites circled up high, anticipating an easy pickings . . .

When the night arrived, the minister's wife came to the tower. She began to cry, complaining about her fate, cursing the unjust Raja, and assuring her husband of her love and eternal loyalty . . .

The night was calm, the wind did not ruffle the tree leaves, and her every word reached the poor prisoner's ears . . .

"Listen to me," said the husband from the top, "dry your tears, go home, catch a black beetle, find a ball of silk thread, a ball of fine twisted silk thread, and a ball of thick yarn. Grab a spoon of honey, and bring it all here."

Without saying another word, she quickly went and brought everything her husband told her to bring.

"Now, tie the end of the silk thread to the rear foot of the beetle, smear his mustache with honey . . . put him head up . . . and release him."

241

The beetle, smelling honey ahead of him, kept crawling up. The silk thread did not burden him — it is not much thicker than the webs of a forest spider. Up, up, up crawled the beetle . . . and he ended up in the hands of the minister.

Along with the beetle, the end of a thin, barely perceptible silk thread also ended up in the minister's hands . . .

The night was calm, and the wind did not blow away the thin silk thread, nor did it tear it. "Now tie the thinnest twisted thread to the end of the silk thread."

Carefully winding the silk thread around his finger, the minister soon got hold of the end of the twisted thread. The wife understood everything. Without waiting for new orders, she tied the end of thick thread to the end of twisted silk thread . . .

"Go get the twine," ordered the husband.

The wife ran, brought the twine and tied it to the end of thick thread. Soon the end of the twine was in the hands of the prisoner.

"Pull again!" shouted the wife from the foot of the tower. The minister pulled the twine, and soon in his hands was the end of the rope brought by the quick-witted woman. Minister firmly tied up the end of the rope, went down it, and was gone.

We're doing something similar. We don't indulge a vain hope of immediately achieving heightened emotions and passions . . . They are thick ropes that are unreachable at first. In the beginning, we're satisfied with the most insignificant of things — the small automatic movements.

They are the silk thread that will eventually, given patience, lead us to the thick rope.

Freedom of Automatic Movements Will not Lead to Anarchy

"I beg your pardon," some people might say, "what are you preaching – the freedom of involuntary, automatic movements? What do you suggest? Down with intelligence, consciousness, and harmony, and long live primitiveness and anarchy?"

But what is our every movement, large or small, unconscious or deliberate? It is a *reaction of our body*. A response to some impact from the outside, or from the inside.

Take a very simple case: a fly lands down on my cheek while I am writing . . . My hand does an unconscious movement and brushes off the fly. I do it unconsciously, while continuing to write.

The fly irritated my skin, and my body responded: my hand brushed the fly off. Did this semi-automatic movement distract me from my activity? Practically not. I kept sitting calmly and working – before and after the movement. If, however, I would refrain from brushing of the fly, then I could hardly sit still and write.

Let's take some physical object – for example, a button. Imagine that your hand, for some unknown reason, moves up to take hold of the button of your jacket. Why is it doing this? Perhaps this is your habit, perhaps for some other reason. In short, you would feel more comfortable if you were holding the button. Your hand already made a slight movement – it moved up toward the button.

At that moment, you say to yourself: this is not appropriate; this is awkward. Your hand obediently moves down, yet this results in the feeling of dissatisfaction. There is an inner need to raise the hand and hold on to the button, yet the need has been stopped.

Frustration creates anxiety – this anxiety is very small, barely noticeable, and yet it is quite real and concrete. Soon this anxiety urges you to make a similarly small movement, but you hold yourself back again. The first feeling of discontent is followed by a second, and then a third, and a fourth . . . Soon your anxiety accelerates to the degree that it practically takes hold of your entire being.

Thus, constraint leads an actor to anxiety, and to a state of tension and inhibition. When repeated often, such constraint causes a state of *habitual* tension and inhibition.

The opposite is also true: if you give full freedom to your small automatic movements . . . there will be less and less of them.

The reason is the same: every external manifestation, and therefore every movement, is nothing other than the reaction of our body.

Let's go back to the old case with the fly. There is a fly on my cheek . . . my hand brushes it off . . . the fly is gone – things are back to normal, and there is no reason for further movement and bustle.

Or let us take the case with the button again: my hand reaches for the button . . . it takes hold of the button . . . my fingers play with the button. Why are they doing it? Perhaps it is an expression of some inner unrest. Does it really matter? Let them play with the button. If the inner unrest does not spread beyond the hand touching the button, and is satisfied by this movement, what harm does it do? This is nothing to worry about. Wouldn't it be worse if, by delaying the movement, we would detain this anxiety in our soul? It would keep rising and distracting us from our main task.

It is better to let the hand continue with its harmless business. In the meantime, there comes a partner's line, or some event takes place onstage, or my own thoughts arise, evoked by the action. Before long, I get interested; the situation pulls me in . . . And the small movements stop on their own: they die out. The former anxiety is replaced in my psyche by some new, more powerful experience – true to the course of the play.

Some actors are prone to constantly running around the stage, waving their arms and generally bustling. At first sight, we would say: here it is – there's your freedom of automatic movements. See what it leads to!

But this is absolutely not true. The reason for such an abundance of unnecessary, extraneous movements and actions is not freedom, but *on the contrary*: the prohibition of freedom.

In this case, it all begins with these actors' inhibition of their first spontaneous movements. They don't allow them to fully develop, and they remain inside, unresolved.

The first prohibition is followed by a second, and then a third. This results in a blockage that causes a restless, nervous state of tension. Such tension is only looking for a chance to be discharged. And it does discharge itself at the first opportunity.

How does it discharge itself, though? Completely and in full? No, full and complete discharge is *no longer possible*. This *inappropriate inhibition took such a deep root, nothing is done in full anymore; everything exists in this inhibited state.* All this running around and bustling – these are all scraps, started and unfinished actions. The more of them, the scrappier they are. They pile up on each other, urge each other out, collide with each other . . . In the end, we have confusion, a crush, a broken-loose pack of animals, a runaway car . . .

Is this really freedom? This is only a state of nervous panic – one of the varieties of inhibition and tension.

18

Don't Interfere with Living

When you watch good theatre, you can't help but think: "This is so easy – I could walk on that stage and act just like this. After all, they are not doing anything special – walking, sitting, talking to each other as they please, feeling quite "at home." How could this be difficult?

But as soon as you take a single step onstage, something in you gets distorted – you begin to observe yourself, making too much effort . . . something completely unexpected and quite unpleasant happens in you . . . In the end, having fought with yourself in vain, you conclude: "This turns out to be a hell of a tricky business!"

So, how do we calm the actors and distract them away from self-watching and from the audience?

There is no need to distract the actor, or attract him to something else. He must allow the flow of life, which is already flowing (as described in the beginning exercises), to keep going.

These exercises will cause you to live, feel, think, and act on stage freely, naturally, fully yielding to the imaginary life, just as all significant actors-creators.

It does not come as a surprise that highly artistic, genuine acting makes you feel that you could step onstage and act as well. After all, such acting is grounded in freedom and ease. Actors do not force anything at all; they don't coerce their nature, and their life flows freely and spontaneously – on its own.

As a teacher, I have been searching for this "technique" from the first steps, and so were my students. All the previously described exercises have been directed specifically toward this goal.

Soon, a student becomes so sensitive and responsive, that a single mention of "cold," for example, would immediately cause them to "live" accordingly.

As soon as they hear the word "cold" – they can't restrain the respective movements: they shiver, wrap themselves in blankets, tuck their legs under. Simultaneously, they receive the feeling that they are truly and irrevocably cold.

All that remains is not *to interfere*, to "give in" to all these small and seemingly insignificant movements – *not to interfere with living*.

It is, no more, no less, the awakening of the *actor's creative nature*. The whirling top begins to spin; do not stop it, otherwise it will fall, and everything will be over.

The day will come when the students master the art of *living onstage creatively – freely and spontaneously – in front of any audience*. Moreover, they will arrive at the point when they are unable to live any other way. At such a time, it would be quite easy to *lead them to any role by carefully tossing at them certain thoughts on the play's circumstances*.

Having practically worked on this freedom, involuntariness and, to put it simply, "life" onstage, it is not easy to see theatre. Having experienced firsthand its power, and how easily it solves the most difficult hitherto unresolved issues, you want to scream, to yell in a loud voice to the actors onstage: "Stop interfering with your own creative life! What are you doing to yourself?! Why do you disfigure your own art?!"

Here I see an actor who does not want to sit still; the scene has excited him, and he even tried several times to jump up. Nevertheless, he does not listen to his own nature and continues forcing himself to sit – such is the blocking!

Or else I see an actress who does not want to answer her partner's lines right away. Her response is not ready – yet she forcefully pushes out the words, out of fear she might slow down the *pace* of the scene!

The partner says or does something unexpected; the actor has yet to realize what it was, yet he is quick to "indicate" it on its face – to "mimic" some pre-ordained feeling (joy, fear, resentment).

Here, the actor is about to be consumed by an emotion. If he were to give in to it, it would permeate him entirely. Instead, he forcibly cuts the emotion off. Why does he do so? Why does he kill his own creative life? Apparently, according to his preliminary plans established in rehearsals, it was time to move onto the next "bit." Not for one minute, not even for a single second do these actors leave themselves alone. They keep altering their life by force and dragging themselves where they presently don't feel like going. They keep whipping and inhibiting themselves . . .

Do you, as an actor, truly enjoy this coercive treatment of your own inner artist, and this kind of inner state onstage? Are you yourself – if you are a creative person, and not a craftsman or a charlatan – not ashamed and devastated to do this?

All right! Let's suppose you are a craftsman. So do you think the audience cannot see your gross forgery and lies?

They are perfectly visible. An elevated stage, theatrical lighting – these are like a magnifying glass.

You think it is sufficient to show us your teeth and have us believe that you are having a good time and smiling? You are much mistaken! We see the whole **process** that takes place in you. We cannot help but see it.

If you are applauded, if the audience cries, it still does not mean that you played well. It only means that the audience filled in all of your gaps – they completed your acting on your behalf, while you have nothing to do with it.

How does the behavior of a significant genuine actor differ from that of an actor-forger?

First of all, it is marked by honesty and freedom.

Truth and freedom immediately follow in each other's footsteps; they are completely interdependent: a moment of truth, when not allowed to freely manifest, is swiftly extinguished.

What is stage freedom, as we, actors, understand it?

It is the freedom of manifestations; the freedom of reactions – responses to the impact of life. [Our small automatic movements, as well as all of our actions, thoughts and feelings, can be considered as manifestations. – *Author's Note*]

This does not mean, of course, that a "free" actor is different from his non-free colleague in that he does absolutely everything he pleases – breaks furniture; tears his costume apart; plays Othello instead of Hamlet . . .

245

He is free to go where he is carried by the artistic image of the role, and by the circumstances of the play.

And nowhere else.

Providing the character is understood correctly, and the circumstances of the play are truly and fully perceived, an actor can do nothing wrong.

If the actor, nevertheless, does something contrary to the play, this only means that he misunderstood the character he plays, or incorrectly sees the circumstances surrounding him in the play. In this case, give him the right hint, help him.

There was a famous Russian director, teacher, and theorist, who spoke and wrote approximately thus. "Orient yourself; enter the circumstances of the play and, when your 'engine' gains some momentum, in the heightened emotional moments, don't restrain yourself – allow yourself full freedom – do not interfere with *self-revelation*."

This seems sensible. But why call just this self-revelation and this alone? Absolutely everything is self-revelation. Even such a thing as inhibition is nothing short of self-revelation. The concept that treats self-revelation as something special is utterly erroneous. One error leads to thousands of others.

Almost all directors and teachers claim that they never interfere with the actors and, of course, do not harm them – they just help them by always meeting "the actor's nature" halfway. In actuality, however, the vast majority of directors do quite the opposite.

Let's set aside those directors prone to "breaking the actors in," to "whipping them into shape," and requiring mere imitation. Let us take those directors who really want to help the actor. Even they, while searching for truth, force their actors' genuine nature. Or else, they chase the truth, as a hunter chases a rabbit, and they end up driving it to exhaustion, hunting it down.

Why "search" for truth and, what is more, create it? It is always with us. We sit – this is our truth and our nature. We breathe – this too is our nature and truth. Thoughts run through my head; I experience pleasant or unpleasant sensations – this *is* my truth and my nature, and *I don't have* any other at the moment.

If I now start creating for myself some "new" truth (which is commonly done), I would look quite ridiculous: I am chasing after the truth, while it follows at my heels – naturally, we never meet.

What is the solution? Not to interfere with the truth I now have in me – not to interfere with living. What if this truth does not match what the play requires at the moment? Speaking from experience, this does not matter.

I recall one very illustrative case. One of the studios of the Moscow Art Theatre had been performing W. Somerset Maugham's play *The Land of Promise*. They had already done about 200 performances. None of the actors were especially proud of their work. The performance was well coordinated, "well-made," quite measured and rather stale. With time, it had mechanized and bored the actors. Yet, the show must go on. And so it did. Actors braced themselves and performed, i.e. they fulfilled the external pattern of their roles, and even tried their best to "justify" it inwardly. They excited themselves somehow, to give the appearance of passionate acting.

That night, too, they had to play this odious show. In the meantime, rehearsals for a new production left all the actors exhausted. Afternoon rehearsals were followed by evening performances of *The Land of Promise*. In the last two days, they were also holding late night tech rehearsals. The actors asked to cancel today's performance – they were so worn out. But the management said it was impossible.

"Well, so be it," thought the actors, "just don't expect too much from tonight's performance."

They put on make-up and costumes . . . Then one of the actors said: "I cannot act – I am so fatigued – I'll just say my lines." All the other actors echoed him. They decided: "Let's all calmly say our lines – and that's all. This will teach the management to pay attention to the actors' condition."

Before the start of the show (still behind the curtain), the actors entered the stage as they were, without forcing anything onto themselves – tired, lethargic, distracted, sometimes irritated. They demanded nothing of themselves, and they remained shamelessly careless and calm. After all, they are not acting tonight – just saying their lines . . .

The performance begun. The opening lines did produce an odd impression. They sounded truthful and natural, yet they were completely unmatched with the style of the play or the characters: an actor would come out and say the lines from his personal point of view. An actress (some Maria or Claudia) would take the words personally and, without bothering to think about her character, she would just respond to the lines *as her real self.*

Since all the actors were completely truthful and did not hold themselves to any unnatural manifestations, their personal "I" gradually became pulled into the circumstances of the play. They got carried away with this new and hitherto unfelt creative state, and the performance was acted brilliantly, as it never was before or after.

Here is one of the most telling examples showing that the search for truth is useless, as it's looking for you. Just learn to not interfere with it and not to drive it away. [The Russian actor Pevtsov [1935:41] refers to such cases: "It often happens that at some three hundredths performance, or at some matinee, I act better than at the opening night. Often at some "unimportant" performance I act particularly well. Sometimes you come to the theatre in the morning, having spent a restless night. You shiver, and you don't feel well. Suddenly, having started some monologue *sotto voce*, you feel the kind of excitement and inner strength you don't experience when you most need them, in the crucial moments. – *Author's Note*]

From time to time, actors complain: "I can not rehearse, I cannot do the scene – I don't feel well."

In such cases, the director usually makes one of the most heinous mistakes by saying: "You must overcome yourself, you must make yourself do it! An actor must be able to control himself!"

As if to control one's self means to overcome one's nature. However, the director did not misspeak – he truly thinks so: an actor must be able to overcome his or her own self.

Why does he think so? Firstly, because he does not know any other ways; secondly, because to say "overcome yourself" is much easier than digging deeper, helping the actor find a genuine creative state; and, thirdly, because the director does not require much of the actor. He is easily satisfied with the distant resemblance of the "truth" – why look for some kind of "authenticity" and "perfection?"

In just a few years of work, he forgot what he used to remember about genuine artistic truth.

Is it possible to instantly alter yourself? Can I overcome my actual nature without running the risk of spraining my artistic soul?

Imagine that you and I, we are sitting in this very room. An hour from now, you are flying out of Moscow to Crimea, or even taking a plane overseas. Would you instantly make a five-kilometer step to the airplane? I don't think so. You would get up from this chair, in which you have been sitting, take a few steps, say goodbye to your friends, make another few steps across the room, cross the threshold, go down the stairs, walk out (as always – without any unnatural jumps and "flights"). You would get in a car; it would drive you to the airport; there you would again walk to the plane. Only at that point will the plane lift you into the air and carry you to your new destination.

We should be equally firm in our logical sequencing and equally gradual – providing we want to join the flight of our creative imagination without any dislocation and self-inflicted injuries.

I am referring to the creative imagination of the actor. After all, it is very different from other types of fantasy – those belonging to different art forms. It involves the *actor's entire being*, with all of its physical and psychological apparatus. Actors cannot escape their physical apparatus.

The neglect of these normal intermediate steps leads to dislocation and hollowness – an actor cannot *step into a role at once, in a single swoop.*

Let us return to the case when actors try to excuse themselves from working, because they don't feel well (physically or psychologically).

Instead of suggesting that the actors *overcome* their state, the director should offer them to utilize their current state as they experience it at the moment. "You don't feel well? You are tired? Upset? Let's bring this to the scene.

After all, the character you are playing is not an inanimate doll. Why can't he be upset, tired, or sick?"

The actor begins the scene precisely in the state he actually is in, including the state of his health. *Since this constitutes his doubtless, unadulterated, organic truth,* his lines (be they even foreign or unnecessary) adapt to his experience, merge with the general state of the actor, and become alive and fitting. Since the lines do belong to the character (and the actor somewhere deep down knows it), saying these lines as his own, causes the actor to *graft* his character's personality to that of his own. This includes the character's circumstances and life.

This grafting continues to do the trick, strengthening with every moment. With each word said by the actor or heard from his partner, his new identity further solidifies – this is the persona he should play today. Most importantly, this new solidifying persona, at the same time, merges with the personality of the actor. He feels that he is the character, and the character is he.

It happens quickly and easily simply because there is no "dislocation" in the beginning, and the actor does not immediately step over all the obstacles onto the airplane, but gets up and goes "upon the floor" of the *room where he actually is.* The laws of nature were not violated, and the transition is natural, without disruption.

Never mind that the actor is initially weak, sick or distracted – in two, maximum three minutes, the actor will perceive the text of his role, and its circumstances, as his personal, living truth. As such, they will pull him into the state of health and the mood that he is supposed to have in the scene.

Such is the case with the actor.

The same is true of a student. Let him start an etude without overcoming or altering his genuine self – in his current state. Soon, the text of the etude, or the partner's behavior, will alter him (if need be), and everything will be as it should.

A student says: "I don't feel well." – "Not a problem! Please carry on without altering how you feel. Let the etude develop as it does."

A student says: "I am empty; my attention is scattered . . . I cannot concentrate." – "That's great! Start just like that. What are you afraid of? We often feel 'empty.' Sometimes you see someone sitting silently, 'lost in thought.' Judging from their appearance, their brain is occupied with serious thoughts. Yet, ask them a casual question – what are you thinking? Apparently, they cannot tell. It turns out they were 'empty.' Something has been roaming in my head, as for what it was – tough to say."

"Therefore, do not discard this state. You are presently empty. Well then, this is your start. We will accept this emptiness, since it is your truth."

This is how we treat the beginning moments: whatever the condition, or mood may be – we will start with it.

In the meantime, a student might "feel bad" somewhere halfway through an etude, rather than from its start. What is to be done then? Once again – "don't interfere with living."

Two men have been invited to do an etude. A middle-aged man of 40 and a young man. The text is as follows:

Young man. – Are you leaving?

Middle-aged man. – I am.

Young man. – Will you be back soon?

Middle-aged man. – Don't wait for me; I won't be back until after midnight.

Young man. – Where are you going? Another meeting?

Middle-aged man. – Yes, a meeting.

The circumstances are not given. Let them arise in the course of the etude – whatever they may be.

The etude ends, and the middle-aged man immediately starts complaining: it did not work for him. He felt awful.

- What do you mean?
- Just awful, and that's it! I felt fake and pretentious . . . not my genuine self. For some stupid reason, I kept trying too hard . . . tried to perform something, and nothing worked . . .
- And what about this young man, who did you take him for?
- I thought he was my son.
- And, do you have a good relationship with him?
- The relationship is fine . . . only he's somewhat restless today . . . He doesn't look me in the eyes . . .
- This is only today?
- No, I feel that he's changed in general these past several days: he's concealing something . . . hiding from me . . .
- Are you definitely going to a meeting?
- No, I want to catch him. Let him think that I won't be back for a long time. He's up to something.
- So, that means you were telling a lie, you were lying to him.
- Yes, I was lying. For his own foolish sake. I can't stand lying, but I had to here . . .
- So, you're saying that you don't like to lie (and you're probably rather bad at it) – it was probably difficult for you to tell him a lie?
- Yes, it's a horrible state. You start to feel like you're some kind of a thief or a criminal . . . And I have to act like I don't suspect anything.
- A horrible state?
- Awful.

- So if you're a truthful person, but you have to lie, it's natural that you didn't feel right: that's how it should be. I don't understand – why did you question your unpleasant emotional state? It's the most suitable here. If you had felt well, and calm, that wouldn't have been right.
- Hm, true, I should have probably been feeling false and rotten . . .
- Which you were and which you should have, it's just that you didn't give in to it courageously. On the contrary, as soon as you suspected that you were insincere, you became scared and thought that you as an actor were lying (although you were lying as a father). You got this into your head, and you began to fight this "falseness." You shouldn't have done that – you should have green-lit such falseness.

  Let's repeat this etude. Let's take the same circumstances. Your son has been unimpeachably honest and sincere, you have a wonderful relationship with him, but this relationship has, for some reason, soured recently. He's started avoiding you . . . You overheard fragments from suspicious conversations over the phone . . . Something about parties . . . He is unresponsive to all of your questions, or answers evasively . . .

  As for you, – I address the youth, – Have you truly taken up with the wrong guys?
- You see, I was a good student, a good son . . . And suddenly, something changed. All things considered, it's not too bad. Why sit home all day and waste away over your homework?
- Don't you feel sorry for your father? After all, he suspects something . . . He suffers for it.
- He does . . . And I do feel sorry for him. But so what! You get one chance to be young!
- And you've slackened on your studies . . . You're now lagging behind everyone else . . .
- I am . . . I'll catch up!
- Alright. Let's do it like this. Only I'll add a little more. No matter how exciting all these parties seemed to you at first – admit it, there's something wearisome in them. Your new friends, once you got a chance to get to know them better, they don't seem as joyful or sharp-witted . . . their arsenal of jokes has long ago been exhausted and is now on a loop . . . you also have your doubts about their intelligence . . .

  And in general, you're growing weary of all these parties and get-togethers . . .

  Tonight, it's your turn to host the party – everybody is going to gather in your apartment today. As soon as your father leaves, you have to call your friends over the phone, and the party will flood in.

  Now then – proceed.

The young man grows pensive and somber. He steals a few glances at his "father" . . . The "father" is standing at the window, looking out . . . shaking his head. He sighs, and finally, turning away from the window, he makes as if to leave . . . "You're leaving?" The words seem to burst from the "son" on their own.

The father stops. Apparently, the query's suddenness has concerned him – he heard both joy and confusion in the tone . . . apparently, my "son" desperately needs me to leave . . . Alright, let's see where this goes.

- I'm leaving, – he says, avoiding his "son's" eyes.
- Will you be back soon? – the "son" asks in a voice that isn't his own, as if someone else has squeezed this question from him. He himself is frightened of his own words, of his bravery, of this strange voice. To restore his own voice, he coughs a few times, as if his criminal question got stuck in his throat . . .

The "father" notes his "son's" strange behavior, but pretends like he didn't notice anything.

- Don't . . . don't wait for me . . . – he opens his suitcase, which was lying on the table, takes out some papers, looks them over, shakes his head significantly while examining a few of them, and, putting them in a different order, carefully places them back in the suitcase. "I'll be back in an hour," he says and makes for the door.
- Where are you going? Another meeting?
- Yes, a meeting, — the "father" responds almost mechanically. It seems like he's only thinking about his papers and his big, important meeting, and that he has no time for his son.

The "son" observes him, and when he closes the door, he sighs in relief.

- Well – how'd it go?
- Ugh! I felt so awful . . . and it was so good! I didn't even know what to do with myself! I don't dare look in his eyes – I pity him, and I'm angry at him, as I go on lying.
- In a word, you green-lit your awful emotional state?
- Yes, I took a risk – come what may.
- And what happened?
- Something very strange happened. As soon as I saw that he was happy I was leaving, I understood that he really was planning something. Now, all I had to do was not scare him off, not give myself away. I do some completely unnecessary things . . . I open my suitcase, dig around in my papers, pretend that I'm busy, that I'm entirely in my work. He asks me, and I pretend like I don't hear him, like my mind is elsewhere . . .
- And so? Was it difficult, uncomfortable?
- No, on the contrary, I was doing it, and I felt like it was all very appropriate . . .
- So what's giving you pause? I can see that something is still bothering you.
- Yes. What gives me pause is that I was observing myself . . . This self-observation was telling me that something wasn't quite sound.
- That's nothing! You were observing yourself, because it was an entirely new phenomenon for you. Once you get used to it and begin to treat involuntary and alien life as ordinary, you'll stop observing. And even if you do observe yourself, you'll do it in amounts that won't bother you.

To conclude this chapter, I would like to repeat what I already said in the beginning.

One of the main reasons, perhaps the most important reason why an unnatural state might prevail in an actor onstage, is an actor's tendency to *interfere with their own life*.

Their whole being, their entire nature acts, feels, thinks – in short, lives in a non-arbitrary way, but rather in obedience to the creative process (after all, the actors carry deep within their character, and the circumstances of their lives). As for cases of incorrect behavior onstage, actors also live during them, yet they simultaneously interfere with their living: they constantly brake, spur, alter their inner state by force, etc. They hinder their life so much that even big talents cannot rely on a sound creative state onstage.

As we could see, aiding with this is not that hard – as long as you move in harmony with nature, and not against its flow.

As for actors, who are not willing to systematically go through the school of freedom and involuntariness, I won't grow tired trying to convince them: at least do not spoil yourself beyond hope! Do not interfere; do not deprive yourself of life onstage. Rely, at least sometimes, on your creative nature.

Not only in our art (where everything rests on the truth of our organic life with all of its manifestations), but also in other art forms, creative laws are the same. Just take a look at the following thought by Tolstoy:

"Don't try to be original; don't impose your own will on the events of the story, but rather follow them wherever they lead you. Life is wherever it leads you.

Life is not defined by symmetry, but rather by the *apparent randomness* of its events – such are its chief indicators." [The editors could not identify the source of Tolstoy's quote.]

19

Carelessness

Among actors, we find plenty of those who decide everything in advance. During their performances, they control every move, every word, and every breath, to make sure that everything is done as has been "decided." *Living onstage* is outside of their realm of possibilities.

When you tell such actors to not interfere with living, they simply don't understand you. The time they've spent onstage has never included "freedom" and "life."

Here, as in other cases of actor's inhibition and lack of freedom, you can lead the way to freedom through "small automatic movements." In addition to this, there are other techniques, which are also quite effective. The time has come to describe some of them.

Carelessness, as a Path to Creative Freedom

This technique originated from practice, just like all the other techniques.

Some actors or beginning students *try so hard* to fulfill every task (with the best of intentions), their efforts consume the most important thing: freedom and involuntariness.

You keep struggling with such actors, striving to bring them to freedom by all possible means . . . Nothing comes out of it.

You would tell them: "Freer, lighter, easier . . ." With all their heart, they try to meet you halfway, working their hardest to find ease – to no progress!

Finally, some sixth sense of yours prompts you as to what the matter is, and you suddenly say: "Oh, just quit your 'diligence!' It gets in your way, and it hinders your work. Try to act sloppily – as carelessly as you can! Don't pay any attention to anything and, most importantly, care less about us."

"Why do you look at me in disbelief? I'm telling the truth. As for caring less about us, the audience, perhaps you already have some experience in this regard? I'm certain that you had some performances in front of some undemanding audience and acted with freedom and ease that bordered on true inspiration. But here you keep trying so hard, wanting to make it better, that you destroy all the freedom of your creative process. You're probably thinking: I can be irresponsible there, but here I can't."

"And why not? Give it a go! Act as you used to act! Go ahead, recall what happened back then? . . . There was a lack of responsibility, you did not demand anything of yourself, and acted as you felt like acting. So let's now do the same thing."

The actor gets rid of excessive effort, and begins to come to life. As he gets carried away, you keep telling him, "Could you be even more careless? . . . That's it! Good for you! Even less diligence! . . . " Finally, after my fifth or seventh comment, the actor completely lets go of his effort.

Having let go, he becomes truly immersed in the circumstances of the play and "hits freedom," as he did back then, with his undemanding audience.

The reader is probably unpleasantly surprised by my call to irresponsibility, to negligence and a lack of consideration for the audience . . .

I am far from trying to cultivate such qualities in an actor. This is only a temporary measure.

The whole point is to unsettle the student's unwavering and persistent diligence.

Based on experience, some cases can not be solved by conventional means and require desperate measures.

Harmful Forms of Carelessness

Quite often, this technique of *"carelessness"* yields amazing results. However, it is not always suitable. There are young people who possess such self-confidence that they do everything more than carelessly and not very well, at that. You've got to keep an eye out for such cases.

Here is one such example.

A young man is not without talent, but very self-confident, and "knows his own worth . . . " This "freedom," and the tactic of encouragement, it seems could not be more to his taste. He picks it up quite easily and quickly – no need to do anything; let things happen on their own! He does not require anything of himself, and does not coerce himself at all . . . An inexperienced teacher looks at him and rejoices – what a free and involuntary man!

Little by little, the teacher begins, however, to feel somewhat awkward – something is *not quite right*.

Not right indeed! That is not freedom, not involuntariness; this is just outrageous, cynical negligence.

He does not properly see his partners; hardly listens to what they say. He is completely occupied by his own persona. If, on top of that, he is also a bit thoughtless and shallow, our deceived teacher, constantly treated to this *would-be* freedom, will soon get a sour taste in his mouth.

Through the use of this technique, even the most inhibited, "most diligent" actor can sink down into "negligence." This is nothing to be afraid of, as this condition is easy to fix. In the meantime, this period of "negligence" usually brings a lot – people practically discover that freedom is not such a difficult thing.

This kind of freedom is incomplete. It is peripheral – the actor's head and heart remain quite empty. Even so, in comparison with an actor's state of utter inhibition, which is what we had at the start, this is freedom, isn't it? For the moment, it will suffice. As long as the actor sets foot on a new path, he can be further grounded in it later.

Going forward, a teacher can make two kinds of mistakes. The first is to remain satisfied with this kind of freedom. This usually happens when an actor possesses so-called "stage presence." No matter what such an actor does onstage, as soon as he comes in, the audience begins to enjoy his presence; they want to watch him.

In this case, it is easy to overlook the superficiality and shallowness of an actor. [By the way, "stage presence," as well as other fortunate inborn qualities, have caused art a lot of harm. An actor might have a pleasing appearance, beautiful voice, or pleasant demeanor. When such an actor comes onto the stage, he is a delight to watch; you enjoy listening to his voice . . . If you look closely and discard the impression produced by these natural qualities, you might notice that the actor has nothing inside. In fact, there is no actor there at all. There is just a very sweet, beautiful, captivating young man (or woman) with a sufficient dose of self-confidence. But the audience admires him, loves him and spoils him, and sometimes even creates the illusion that he is a major actor. – *Author's Note*]

The second error occurs when the teacher (or the director), seeing that "carelessness" had overstepped all limits and not knowing how to manage it, *gets it into his head that freedom onstage must be* **relative** *– full freedom, apparently, can cause trouble.*

Such a teacher would then begin to limit the actor, tightening the reins . . . in short, all of his previous achievements would be destroyed.

The point, however, is quite different: carelessness entices the actors to "green-light" their most **superficial** impulses. This peripheral, superficial freedom must be *supplemented* with deeper freedom – the *freedom of the soul.*

- Zina, you are still up . . .
- I've been waiting for you. Didn't you ask me to help you with your presentation?
- They kept me late.
- You have a presentation tomorrow. Did you forget?
- How could I forget? I just couldn't leave any earlier. I am telling you, they kept me late – it was very serious business.
- Why didn't you call? I would have left – I've got my own things to take care of.
- You are right. I am so sorry. I wasn't thinking.

The content of the text, it would seem, points to a serious exchange between the partners. The actress is sensitive and not at all thoughtless. However, she flies into the room and chirps out all of her words, like a carefree bird.

Her partner ("Zina"), is surprised, hurt and finally annoyed by her carelessness, and inconsiderate attitude. Especially since, based on her mood, it is unlikely that she was detained by anything serious.

The etude is over, and the student feels victorious.

- Not bad . . . – I tell her – only why are you "green-lighting" so incompletely?

She is dumbfounded – she thought herself to be so free, so involuntary, as she never was before. And, suddenly, the teacher says: "You're green-lighting so incompletely."

- What else can you call it? Of course you're not green-lighting! Let's recall how things went. Knowing your tendency to be too dutiful, diligent, and to restrict your free creative manifestations, you wanted to test this device. The very word "carelessness" apparently made you think that the entire text should be nothing but empty chatter. It was with this understanding that you repeated the words and walked out of the classroom. This is how you started the etude – hardly seeing "Zina," and not noticing her discontent and irritation. Or, perhaps you did notice them?
- At the start, I truly did not notice them. When she reminded me about the presentation and that she was waiting for me, something in me shuddered . . .
- Why?
- How could it not? Tomorrow's presentation is no joke.

- Now you're saying it's no joke – what about back then?
- I was afraid it would knock me out of my new freedom and ease, so I . . .
- So you brushed it aside, as if nothing had affected you, and nothing made you anxious. What do you think this is called – green-lighting or not green-lighting?
- Yes, apparently, here I stopped myself, I didn't green-light.
- And by doing so, you trampled upon all of your living, unexpected manifestations!

An actor may be sure that he is extremely free, and fully gives in to his creative life. In reality, however, he inhibits all that is most important.

To set the actor right, you should catch him and practically explain to him that the freedom obtained through carelessness is still quite limited. Although it is an achievement, it is now time to move further. **External** freedom and involuntariness must be now supplemented with their **internal** counterparts. An actor must release his inner world, and not interfere with its manifestations.

20

Take Your Time!

Nervousness, anxiety and haste are the actor's most common enemies. The very atmosphere of the stage includes numerous sources of nervous excitement: the limelight, spotlights, hundreds of watching strangers, stage partners peeping from backstage – all of this lashes the actor's psyche, like a whip.

This is why the teacher's first and most frequent request is "don't rush" and "take your time."

Seemingly, it would be better to say, "calm down," or "don't be nervous." However, advice to "calm down" is, at the very least, naive. It is simply impossible to fulfill. Is it in my power to just go ahead and settle my nerves? On the contrary, this kind of advice will make me even more nervous.

"To take one's time" is quite a different matter – it means to suspend what I have been doing, to slow it down. This is not difficult. Having suspended my actions, I dissolve my excessive nervousness. As a result, I begin to better see and hear everything around and, in general, better navigate my way onstage . . . In the meantime, the director tells me: "Correct, this is correct . . . take your time . . . that's right . . . " I suspend my actions even more . . . In the end, all excessive haste has been cut down to size, along with anxiety and nervousness.

Therefore, more often than not, it is necessary to tell the student (or actor): "take your time," "no rushing," "don't be afraid of pauses," "don't be afraid of dragging it out," "continue this way – good, good."

These simple tips quickly restore any lost calm.

This technique of "taking your time" has been frequently used in our classes. The reader will keep encountering it in the future. Therefore, this chapter will only describe a few aspects of this technique.

These simple words become even more powerful when used as a preventive (or preemptive) measure, rather than a corrective one. In such cases, the effect of this technique is short of miraculous – cold, inhibited actors show unprecedented freedom and power; coarse and primitive actors become more subtle and sensitive.

Let us take, for example, the so-called "emotional availability." The actors commonly apply this term to the richness of their experiencing, and to the unrestrained expression of their feelings.

To put it simply, actors commonly understand emotional availability as passion, fervor, impulsiveness.

Many actors, especially those of the rational type, are deprived of this quality – their habit to rationalize everything and to watch over every step they make onstage detains all their immediate reactions. As a result, they come across as cold and insensitive, although in actuality they have not lost their sensitivity and impressionability.

If this kind of actor, while in a sound creative state, is suddenly called a "scoundrel" during the play, his heart would sink, and his feelings would mix up, as with every normal person. He would feel completely dismayed and be paralyzed with confusion . . .

This scares the actor; he thinks that he has "broken out of" a sound state, out of the role. Hurrying to fix this, he forces his nature, takes his feelings under control, and does what he considers befitting the occasion – on his face, he shows fear, resentment, anger, and begins to speak the character's lines . . .

He does not feel like depicting anything on his face; neither does he feel like saying the words, but what is there to do? His state of unease and confusion is so great that he has to mobilize all his self-control in order to "save" himself.

He should have done just the opposite: he should have *waited*.

Why be afraid of confusion, emptiness, and awkwardness? Are these not normal manifestations of the human psyche?

Let's look at real life. As a decent man, if you suddenly heard "You scoundrel!" thrown in your face, would you not feel mixed up and lost? Would you not, at least for 10 seconds or so, feel totally confused? It could not be otherwise.

Those seconds, or even those tenths of a second, are crucial. If you have the courage to withstand them, the complex inner process of digestion would run its course. Your words (or actions) in response would then pop up on their own, with all their rich, unexpectedly deep content, all their significance and emotional power.

This "emptiness" and "confusion" strike the actor as being incredibly long and tedious . . . An actor feels that he has been "dragging" the scene and boring the audience. In the meantime, this is mere self-deception. In actuality, the feeling of tedium and slowness is caused exclusively by the actor having *looked back* at himself. This means – coming out of the role and ceasing to "live." Having come out of a role, the actor feels fake. No wonder he experiences a few seconds as hours.

Anticipating these moments in rehearsals, I would come closer to the actor, standing almost behind his back. As soon as his partner's unexpected words hit him, and he feels thrown into confusion, emptiness, and helplessness (a state of near panic) – at this very moment I would tell him in a calm, quiet whisper: "Take your time! Everything is correct."

At times, I would see that the atmosphere has become so tense, the string is wound so tight, that one more second, and it will burst . . . Here again I would speak behind his back – even calmer and more firmly, "Take your time! Good . . . good . . . this is right! Take your time." And the actor performs a miracle. He comes through. Easily, without any effort.

The expression "take your time" can also interfere, when used incorrectly.

For example, an actor might get nervous and push himself when overwhelmed by a strong emotion . . . In order to avoid this, a director would say, "Take your time." An actor, taking this for a reprimand, would inhibit his entire inner life. This causes a scene to fall through.

Who is to blame? The director, of course. Before advising the actor to not interfere with his own inner life, the director must make it clear to him that *everything is going right*. Just do not interfere with yourself, take your time (the actor has apparently already started to rush and to force his own life).

This is why, in practice, I would usually say "Correct, this is correct . . . just like that . . . only take your time . . . it's all good."

The words "take your time" must *establish* the actor on the path of his sound inner process and merely *prevent him from mistakes*, without destroying proper life onstage.

21

Play-Acting

Underacting

When an actor lives soundly in an etude (or a scene), and nothing is impeding his creativity – be it self-interference or some external factors – his emotional life can reach an extraordinary force and richness. In such cases, the actor himself might become scared of having deviated too far from his own persona, and having reached too deep a level of transformation.

In rare cases, the intensification of the actor's creative process does reach its natural resolution and peaks. This happens in instances when an actor stops nothing in his intensifying internal life and refuses to turn away from this seemingly risky path. Very few actors can manage that.

It must be said, however, that with the help of a skillful director or teacher, even an average or inexperienced actor can achieve this.

More often in practice we encounter the following two ways out of this predicament:

1   An actor feels that the process is so strong and is developing so rapidly that it could, very quickly, uncontrollably drag him somewhere, like a heavy cart rolling down a mountain slope. In this moment, a fearful actor indiscriminately suspends and inhibits all of his ongoing inner processes. The creative process overall loses all of its strength, swiftness, and depth. The actor arrives at the finish line cold and practically empty.

2   An actor, scared of the depth and authenticity of his own process, *does not inhibit it completely*, but in part – he inhibits all of his deep inner life . . . At the same time, he knows that, according to the play, he is supposed to act an emotionally intense scene (it has already begun and should be developing further). However, all that survived from his genuine creative state is sheer nervous agitation – it has had no time to subside. So the actor, having inhibited his rich creative life, gives in to this external agitation instead. Having taken such a path, the actor may burst into yelling, convulsive clenching of fists, even into a nervous frenzy and hysteria. Since he is a little "out of it," subjectively, he imagines that he has reached his creative high and has obtained "inspiration."

When observing such cases, one always assumes that the actor is **overacting**, giving out more than what he has inside. In actuality, the actor inhibits his creative life, and, therefore, *underacts*. Simultaneously, while still trying to do something more or less suitable for the occasion, he gives way to his own nervous agitation, mistaking it for creative expression.

Play-acting – this fierce enemy of creativity onstage – is thus revealed to us in a quite unexpected light.

Play-acting, or rather *underacting,* is met not only in students. It is often met in good actors, familiar with an organic creative state onstage. In such actors, it comes without hysteria, without the nervous frenzy. As they say in such cases: "Today in this moment or other, the actor was fake."

Overacting

Does this mean that "play-acting" and "overacting" appear exclusively as consequences of "underacting" and don't occur without it? I repeat: not in gifted and especially well-cultivated actors. In such actors, we only meet "underacting," as described above.

Neither do "play-acting" and "overacting" occur in students trained in this system. Why don't they occur? They are simply unnecessary. After all, no one forces the student to achieve "passionate" experiencing: whatever you feel may exist. A student gets used to this. In the future, emotional strength and passion are achieved by completely different means.

As for insufficiently talented actors and those with incorrect training – they are, of course, prone to "play-acting."

After all, they have not been trained to "live" onstage; they have not experienced creative freedom and involuntariness. They know nothing of this; in the meantime, the author has written that a particular scene calls for tears or excitement . . . It was easy for the author to write it, but how do I do this in practice? In the meantime, the director demands: "Come on, come on!" It figures, one way or another, that I must generate excitement. I must do it for no apparent reason – "out of the blue."

When the actor is empty inside, but nevertheless "must!" – an actor begins to "fake," to "depict" the illusion of experiencing.

This is, in fact, what we call "play-acting."

In practice, we meet with different kinds of "fakeness." Starting with the utterly coarse and primitive play-acting, and finishing with such subtle and skillful play-acting that an inexperienced eye could be easily deceived and take it for truth, for a natural reaction.

There are entire schools dedicated exclusively to teaching their students some external ways to skillfully depict feelings, passions and even . . . truth itself. That's right! – "to present truth!"

Play-acting has even become a feature of actors' everyday lives. Actors can be distinguished from all the rest by this blatant and glaring fakeness – affectation, deliberateness . . .

Common methods of fighting play-acting are, alas, very primitive. Although they reach their goal of eliminating play-acting, they cause an equally serious disease in students – "closedness" and a lack of faith in their creative powers.

A war with play-acting is usually fought by direct prohibition: don't do it! An actor makes a fake move – Stop! I don't believe it! It was fake!!! An actor just starts faking: Stop! This is untruthful! . . . An actor is just about to start faking – I don't believe it! Play-acting! Cliché acting!!

This strike, to give it full justice, swiftly reaches its target. It uproots play-acting, but along with the bad habits, it also roots out precious commodities, such as faith in yourself, initiative, and the need to create freely.

If an actor is not scared off by such a brutal operation and does not run away from the theatre to save the remnants of his talent, then he undergoes further treatment.

An actor now knows what *not to* do. As for what *to* do, he does not know yet. This is precisely what they are about to teach him. The training begins with simple "physical actions" and "tasks," such as cleaning a room, rehanging a painting, pouring a glass of water, and so on. At the slightest attempt to "fake" something (an old habit), the actor is stopped – don't! do strictly what you were asked. Thus, gradually, an actor learns to avoid play-acting.

Naturally, such a tactic does not go without extremes. There is no play-acting in sight; on the contrary, an actor does something live, something that sprung from spontaneous feelings. Nevertheless, the overly-suspicious eye of the educator already sees this as a manifestation of untruth, and shouts: "I don't believe you! This was fake! Cliché acting!!"

This kind of vigilance and diligence leads to the following results. They are intending to restore a precious painting. A bad artist painted over it, so, layer by layer, they remove his daub (i.e. those clichés acquired in bad theatres). They keep scraping, and suddenly, to their own surprise, they see that they've scraped down to the very canvas . . . They see that nothing is left – no precious painting, but just a bare canvas, perhaps even rotten . . .

The unfortunate restorer sadly sighs and says: we were so wrong! At the auditions, we thought this was a talent, but he turned out to be an empty shell, a complete nonentity!

Less zealous teachers, acting according to the same method, do not "scrape down to canvas." For the most part, however, they extinguish the actor's fire, down to the last spark of creativity.

Having sown and grown the fear of every bold creative manifestation, willingly or unwillingly they sow in the student's soul the malignant idea that artistic truth onstage is just something small and truncated – with no arms, legs, and, most likely . . . without a head . . .

It is laughable seeing these sterilized actors. Supposed to be protected forever from any play-acting, they do nothing else onstage, but fake – "present" or forge life . . .

Strange, isn't it? If you think about it properly, however, – how could it be otherwise?

Just look: all life in such an actor has been destroyed; he perceives every free expression as a falsehood, as play-acting; he is accustomed to the idea that only the most unpretentious physical actions can be called "truthful." In the meantime, he must act something! Somehow he must carry the scene! What is there to do?

First, he breaks his scene into tiny scrupulous physical tasks. He executes them diligently, one after the other. His acting is pale, weak – "verisimilar," but not truthful. He feels it, and slowly, carefully, modestly, oh so delicately! he attempts to "touch up" his acting by throwing in some play-acting. At least, it is a bit livelier this way. It goes from bad to worse, and before you know it, it turns into one big case of play-acting! Only this kind of faking is not as crude and harsh as that of the vulgar provincial actors. Our actor fakes "à la truth," "nobly," "tastefully" and "with restraint." The essence, however, is still the same – play-acting and falseness.

Here is how the slightest violation of the creative nature and its laws ironically avenges itself.

A completely different way of fighting cliché and play-acting must be found. Strange as it may seem, its secret lies in allowing greater freedom. Total freedom, in fact. [In addition to this discussion, also look further, in the special sub-chapter – "Green-lighting Cliché Acting" [pp. 285–286]. – *Author's Note*]

Of course, even the device of "green-lighting" can lead to an extreme. An overzealous and therefore insensitive teacher can cause a lot of mischief. Day after day, he causes a student to green-light things beyond his strength. In addition to that, he has planted in a student contempt for everything that is ordinary, not "grand," not "tragic," not "talented." Before you know it, this teacher injures a student.

It is essential to resort to all possible tricks to keep a student from frequent encounters with the insurmountable and to only give him tasks that he can manage. A teacher's talent manifests, first and foremost, in this ability to adapt to the student's forces, and to his every immediate moment.

Legitimate Play-Acting

In our school, however, we also find another type of play-acting . . . It deserves to be seriously discussed.

A simple, good-natured young man, somewhat shy, is called to do an etude. He is partnered with a saucy, sociable girl.

She — (alone at her place. A knock at the door)
She. Come in.
He. Could you tell me if this is Parfilyeva's place?
She. Yes.
He. Are you Ms. Parfilyeva?
She. Yes, I am.
He. I am Porznev. My sister, Tanya, asked me tell you not to wait for her – she cannot come – she is sick.
She. What's wrong with Tanya?
He. I am not sure. She has a cough and a high fever.
She. Can I come visit her?
He. Sure. She would like that.
She. I will be there in two hours or so.
He. OK. I will tell her. Good-bye.
She. Good-bye.
He. — (leaves).

The young man behaved very formally. He carried the whole conversation with an air of correctness and restraint, perhaps even dryly. He hardly looked at "Vera" and, having completed his errand, left without delay.

As soon as he was gone, I asked his partner: Well, how did you like him?

- You know . . . I liked him a lot . . . Except, he didn't look at me even once? . . . As if I wasn't there . . . Still a very nice young man, straightforward, bold – as a real man should be. And so mysterious . . .

A young man returns.

- What do you have to say about yourself?
- What do I have to say? . . . I put on some pompous, impregnable mask . . . Like a count or something!
- So why are you unhappy with yourself?
- What's there to be happy about? It's pure play-acting.
- But she liked you. She did not notice anything false. She says you were genuine.
- Who's genuine? Me? Well, I don't know . . . Maybe she's a bit short-sighted . . . How genuine could I be when it was all feigned.
- Oh, I get it! – the girl begins to guess – This is because you did not behave with me as your equal, and kept me at a distance? What's wrong with that? After all, we don't

know each other . . . you came to me for the first time . . . naturally, you behaved strictly officially . . . What's wrong with that. Why is this faking?

- Why? You're a friend of my sister.
- So what? You meet you sister's friend for the first time – and you are supposed to smile? On the contrary, I really liked it that you were so independent and earnest . . . and held yourself with such dignity . . .
- To hell with my "dignity!" I just put on some stupid importance, and that's it.
- You put on nothing. Just a well-brought-up young man came to visit for the first time . . .

I would let them argue some more and, when things get completely confused, I intervene.

- We-e-ell! This is curious! He argues that it was all feigned, and she says that that's is how it should have been. He is convinced that he was false, and she goes out of her way to convince him that he was truthful. It's no accident – something curious must be going on . . .
  So you insist that you were deliberate and fake. She, however, did not notice it, and interpreted it quite convincingly, and to your advantage. Let's check on how it happens in life. Tell me, in life do you approach everyone equally? Are you genuine with everyone?
- What do you mean?
- For example, do you hold yourself in the exact same manner with your classmate and with your teacher? There must be some difference: with one you are more direct, with the other – restrained? With one you never hesitate, with the other – you control yourself and, out of respect, do not allow the same behavior as you do with your classmates?
- Certainly. However, this happens on its own.
- Similarly, you would speak differently to different people, correct? Let's say you have a negative attitude toward someone – someone not very bright and dishonest . . . and intrusive to boot. How would you behave with such a person? Would you be honest with him? Would you open up your soul?
- Of course not. I would probably try to behave with him so as to get rid of him as soon as possible.
- So, why did you do put on such an air with this "Vera"?
- I don't know . . . I felt that she was a bit frivolous . . . What if she decides I purposely came to her . . . under the pretext that my sister was ill . . . To make sure she does not get the wrong idea . . .
- . . . You put on, quite preemptively, a cloak of inaccessibility, all cold and businesslike?
- There you go. That's probably what happened.
- Then it was inevitable to play it *this way*?
- Yes, it happened on its own . . .
- Truly, in life we quite often resort to *"play-acting."*
  Take this: you've come home after some failure of yours, after some unpleasant event. No one is home, and you give in to your mood. But as soon as anyone comes in, even if it is a very close person – not wanting to show your real state, you pretend that nothing has happened. Would this be truth? Is it not a lie, falseness, play-acting? It definitely is. However, this is so common that we would never even think of calling it falseness and play-acting. Then why, I ask you, why is it so frustrating to see play-acting onstage?
  The answer is very simple: because in life we fake (or "present") *for our partner* – in order to influence him – this is not only full of deep meaning; this is a part of all our *social interactions*.

Onstage, however, actors resorts to play-acting *for the sake of the audience*. A partner is not important; they don't even see their partner – they play "to the audience" and for the audience.

This state of things is highly unnatural and, therefore, unpleasant and insulting to look at. You, for example, did resort to play-acting (you were right about it), yet you did it *for her*. You wanted to put her in her place, to protect yourself from unnecessary misunderstandings – so you played the unapproachable, self-important young man, who is not up for frivolous conversations. You did your job and left. It was your way of influencing her. It was *truth*. Your genuine truth. This is not false acting; this is none other than **transformation**.

After all, transformation is not such a rare phenomenon, both onstage and in life.

It (transformation) is not a sign of hypocrisy and duplicity, but rather our natural reaction to the changing circumstances of life. With one person we exhibit one kind of persona, with another – we are quite different: so different in fact, we don't recognize ourselves. In one set of circumstances – we are one person, and other circumstances awaken in us the kind of qualities and powers we have never suspected; they seemingly have nothing in common with us. As if, by some magic power, we have been switched. And what about costume! How drastically it affects our state and our identity! At times, such "transformation" is very jarring – it catches us by surprise; at other times it is subtle.

Thus, "transformation" is not only the prerogative of the actors, and of their art – it is one of the main qualities belonging to every person.

This, by the way, is one of the reasons why so many people are eager to act on the stage; why community theatre is so popular, and why some people, without special training, do such good job of acting on the amateur stage.

This disposition toward transformation is at every person's core. The main thing is not to distort it, not to turn it into "play-acting" and "presentation" and, in general, not to follow the principle of bare external form.

22
Perception

Perception: The Source of All Action

Our every manifestation, every thought, every feeling is nothing if not a reaction of our being to an external or internal impact.

Imagine that a person is sitting quietly and resting, even dozing off . . . his life seems to be on hold. Suddenly outside the window, on the street, there is noise, shouts, music – this produces a direct reaction: the person gets up, walks up to the window, and so on.

Hence, first there is an impact of sorts, and only then, in response to it – a reaction. "The initial cause of any action," says Sechenov [1947:157], "always lies in external sensory stimulation."

However, an impact alone is not enough – it has to be felt. If, for one reason or another, we do not feel this impact, there will be no reaction either. For example, in our sleep, we can be surrounded by all kinds of life; since we do not see it or hear, it therefore produces no reaction. Or else, when we are absorbed in something, we also do not see or hear what is happening around us.

A man's life is, therefore, a reaction. Those who perceive clearly react strongly. Those who perceive vaguely and weakly react accordingly. Neuropathology tells us that there is even a disease of the nervous system that manifests itself in reduced perception. People affected by this disease are distinguishable by a dull and sluggish reaction.

An actor onstage perceives two lives at once: the real (audience, stage, backstage) and that of the imagination – the author's and his own.

For a person deprived of certain actor's qualities, real life will, of course, overpower the imaginary. For a person, who possesses a talent for acting, real life (audience, stage, backstage) will only act as a stimulus to give in to imaginary life, meaning to those circumstances that govern their character's life.

Some theatre people like to say: you must *act correctly* onstage – this will cause you to *live* correctly.

Seems logical.

However, how does one go about acting correctly?

In life we act because there is something instigating our actions. All things considered, our action is our reaction to everything that happens within us and around us. If we do not perceive (for whatever reason) our surrounding, it is as good as nonexistent, leaving us with nothing to react to.

This will become clear from several practical examples. Thus, a different law of stage behavior will develop and formulate itself: action does not constitute the primary cause of our emotional state; rather *our perception should be considered the primary cause, both of our actions and of our emotional state.*

It is true that a skillful director can lead an actor to right actions onstage – in full accordance with the play. He will do so, however, *by directing the actor toward a right mode of perception.*

What does an actor need to perceive in order for his actions to be correct? Naturally, he must take in the *circumstances* under which these actions are committed.

Even the simple act of opening a door and walking through it onstage depends entirely on its *circumstances*. If it is a noisy train station, you would walk in without standing on ceremony. If this is the room of a seriously ill person, you would go in gently, so as not to make noise, not to bother the patient . . . If you want to ambush and capture a criminal, you would burst in at once, hold up-style. One can use numerous examples. It all depends on the circumstances. They will make you act correctly. As long as you perceive them. After all, this is how we act in life – according to circumstances.

Some directors would object: there is no need for action or perception . . . I would never say a word about the circumstances; I would just demonstrate – do it myself as it should be done and make the actor repeat.

- Well, demonstrate. Let's take the example of walking into a sick person's room.

If the director is capable, he would play the scene well, as a real actor. What would he make you see? You would see a man opening the door quietly and gently . . . making sure that it does not squeak. If it does squeak, he would instantly stop, frightened, and freeze . . . He would wait . . . and again begin to open the door . . . He would stick his head in . . . inspecting the room . . . and quietly tiptoe toward the bedside.

What did he demonstrate? Was it a mere action? First of all, he felt the presence of a very sick man, a loved one. This person is so close and dear that he fears causing him the slightest trouble – God forbid he might disturb him.

This is true of every demonstration: provided it is true and successful, it always elucidates the *circumstances*, first and foremost, making it clear to the actor what he must "live by" and what to perceive.

To play correctly, it is necessary to perceive correctly. We must perceive exactly what our character perceives in the play, and how they perceive it. This evokes the very reaction that occurs in the character.

Training Perception Onstage

Perception is at the basis of everything onstage. Errors in perception entail errors in everything else. Therefore, we must first attend to evoking correct perception in the actors (despite the unnatural conditions of "life onstage"). Then we must show the actors the ways toward this correct, live perception. And finally, we must help them habituate creative perception, make it their second nature.

In life, we always perceive. However, we do not think about it. Perception happens on its own. The process of perception onstage should be equally involuntary, and arising from the necessity to live in all those circumstances of the play.

To preserve it in all its natural purity, not clogged with self-observation and dry reasoning, above all I try not to say the word "perception." As if no such thing exists on earth.

Secondly, actors' problems do not come from their inability to perceive, or from their lack of perception skills – their perceiving apparatus is in good order; it does not need to be fixed. The actors' trouble is that they perceive the *wrong thing*.

They perceive the audience, the backstage, and so on, rather than what they need to perceive according to the play.

All the same, not a word, not a hint must be dropped to the actors about this trouble – no matter how alarming it may be. We must quietly *redirect them away* from it, and that's all.

Redirecting is done by means of the same simple words, as previously described: "Take your time . . . you still don't feel like it . . . you are yet to see, to hear . . . that's right . . . give it a green light . . . don't interfere . . . " Apparently, these means are enough to redirect the actors' perception away from the audience, and onto the partner – from the house to the stage.

During the first etudes, I try to strengthen the actors' faith in the correctness of their perception. To do so, I usually ask after the etude: how did she strike you?

When you look at your partner, you always receive an instant impression: your beloved, or a stranger . . . close, or alien . . . pleasant, or unpleasant . . . You can give in to this tiny spark, or you can miss it, and it will die out.

An actor holds his reaction, hesitates, and this results in an uncertain relationship. I would inquire: who did she seem to you in the beginning?

- I don't know . . . I didn't get it . . .
- Tell me all the same . . . . Maybe your mother?
- A mother!

If he protests so strongly (and how could he not – his partner is 17–18), this means that in the back of his mind, he did have some *definite* impression. He simply missed it, and it did not develop. So, I go on provoking:

- Maybe your grandma?

This even makes him mad: what insensitive, stupid people.

- Even better! How could she be my grandma!
- Well, maybe your sister?
- Yeah, this is closer . . . and even then, a younger sister.
- Still, she seems to be holding you under her thumb? – this is again a provocation. Against these, obviously wrong assumptions, a precise point of view, missed in the first moment, emerges and solidifies in the actor.
- She holds me under her thumb?! Her?! . . .
- There, you see. From the first moment, you apparently felt who she was, but for some reason did not give in to the correct impulse.

He is taken aback a bit, and pleasantly surprised.

- It seems so.
- It is so. Let this be a lesson to you. Everything inside you was instantly ready, and you did not believe yourself. You yielded to doubt, and did not give in to your own impressions and urges. And they went away.

  Do believe yourself. Surrender control and give in without looking back.

Thus, time after time, you sow and cultivate the actor's faith in a "mere flash," in "just a fancy." What kind of faith is it, to be precise? – Faith in perception. Something "flashed by," I "fancied" something . . . – this surely means that I have already *perceived*.

Here is another example. An etude goes well: everything is clear, correct and true; still I ask:

- What did she want from you and how did she strike you? Why did she smile so slyly?..
- No! – he would reply, – she was just shy. She was embarrassed.

And so, by asking these questions, you direct the student toward involuntarily seeing and hearing the partner better, and generally getting a deeper sense of the partner, and of the circumstances. With time, this process grows to be freer and more nuanced.

Now we only need to have patience to finish what we started: by thorough exercises to habituate this correct creative state in the students – so that the moment they cross the threshold of the stage, it inevitably evokes the needed condition.

Perception Occurs Involuntarily, by Itself

At times, an actor gets so carried away in the course of an etude, he misses the partner's lines and responds to them at random. I would use this pretext and ask:

- What did she really tell you when she said these words?
- I don't know, really . . . I missed it – he would frankly admit. (Or else, he would say something incorrect – after all, he did not really hear her.)
- No need to be embarrassed. Did you really make a mistake? You were busy with some – thing else. You could not hear her.

  If you forced yourself to listen, you would do something you did not want to do. This truly would have been a mistake. In life, when we are passionate about something, do we not often miss what we are told; do someone else's words not fall on our deaf ears? This is normal. This is life.

Sometimes it is regrettable that he missed something significant coming from his partner, and thus shortchanged the etude a bit. Nevertheless, it is best to make this temporary sacrifice – so far as the student is learning to live freely and naturally onstage. [A careful attitude toward the partner's lines is developed later, by adding and clarifying the circumstances (as indicated in Part Four of this book). – *Author's Note*]

I also say all this so that the student *does not make a fetish and a cult out of "hearing" and "seeing,"* but rather treats them with ease and simplicity, as in real life.

After all, hearing and seeing do not require any particular, special effort in life.

Even when we watch something keenly, it happens on its own, without any effort on our side. It happens when we find something *particularly interesting*.

Just a second – someone would tell me – you're contradicting yourself. Earlier you said that perception is the cause, and that it all starts with perception, and now you claim that perception does not require special attention, and that it occurs on its own!

Precisely, it occurs on its own. Our senses are in perfect order: as long as there is something to see, hear, smell or touch – we certainly would see, hear, and so on. That is: perception would take care of itself. Life itself begins with that. Anyone who has been in a dead faint probably remembers how they regained their consciousness. First total darkness – without time, space or thought . . . Then a noise . . . then some other random sounds: a clock ticking or the sounds of the wind . . . I open my eyes – light . . . objects . . . people . . . and my mind begins to work.

Therefore, the only thing we ever need to worry about, when in our normal state, is *not interfering with perception*.

In other words, the secret of perception is unlocked with the same two golden keys familiar to us from the very first pages of this book: freedom and involuntariness. They are everything.

Students brought up in the school of "involuntariness and freedom" cannot help but "live," when coming onstage, to see and to hear all around, and to be in the character's circumstances.

They need not worry about their "creative state" and "the truth" – everything they do is always truthful, as they are the truth.

The only thing they ever care about is how to not miss some important facts of the play – otherwise a scene would not develop as it should. It is enough, however, to take into account the lost circumstances, and things are set right.

"To Give" and "To Take"

Those recounting the art of great actors often use expressions such as "he emphasized," "he singled out," "he imbued it with," "he gave it particular tone or meaning."

> "'My dear bedraggled little dove! . . .' [Pushkin 1962: 152] – Yermolova *imbued* these words with deep affection, characteristic of her talent."

> "'A maiden pure and chaste achieves whate'er on earth is glorious, if she to earthly love ne'er yields her heart' [Schiller 1883: 340, *The Maid of Orleans*] – she gave these words a low-pitched tone . . ."

> "' . . . To blot thee out from the fair light of day/An irresistible desire impels me' [Schiller 1883: 361, *The Maid of Orleans*]. The word 'blot' she invested with immense anger . . ." [Shchepkina-Kupernik 1940: 58,61]

It is impossible to express the measure of harm brought on by these and similar expressions utilized by our critics and theatre "experts."

A gullible actor would read about this method of acting and begin following the example of the great actors by investing one line with "anger," another with "deep affection," and trying to "express" passionate love. He would "give" the low-pitched tones to these words or some others . . .

In the meantime, this actor has nothing to "invest" or "express:" nothing has ripened for it in his soul . . . And so the actor squeezes out the kind of artificial agitation he mistakes for emotions, and he crams it into some lines – alien to his heart and to his mind.

It is somewhat excusable when critics and biographers, who have never acted on the stage, toss around these harmful words, however frivolously and irresponsibly. In the meantime, people who have spent their entire lives onstage or near it make the same kinds of mistakes. Moreover, these *suspiciously inaccurate expressions* can be found in works by such authors, that you can't even believe it yourself: he's *also* saying that an actor should "try to express" or "invest" or "give it a quality" or "deliver to the audience" or "emphasize," or "stress"! . . . These authors, you would think, surely know well that the actual state of things is quite different – quite the opposite, in fact. An actor – if we are talking about the actor, who creatively experiences his role onstage – *does not invest* his words with anything. On the contrary, he gives freedom to all these circumstances and all these facts that occur onstage *to act upon him*. These facts (as well as the words and the behavior of his partners) put him in such a mood and ignite him so much that his own words fly off his lips on their own, saturated with anger or joy, depending on the circumstances.

This is so obvious to all those present that the same biographers, on the very same page, would unknowingly contradict themselves, while describing superb artistic truth. This truth is priceless and unites the great actors, who all create according to its laws.

Browse through a few more pages of the very same book, *On Yermolova*, and you will see this:

"When Yermolova acted on the concert stage, it seemed that she was not so much reciting, but rather sharing her innermost, precious thoughts."

"The figure of Yermolova, thoughtfully bowing her head, eyes contemplating something intimate, engrossed the audience's attention from the moment the curtain was raised . . . Only the entrance of Bertrand (scene 3) with his helmet, and his story of the gypsy who gave it to him *suddenly made Joan raise her head and, without looking at him, listen to his story*."

"She powerfully took the helmet, slowly raised it above her head and put it on over her loose curls. *This touch transfigured her face . . .* "

"When she looked upon her familiar places, *a gentle expression lit up* Yermolova's face."

"When Roman, in his turn, said to her painfully that he had not asked how *she* lived in his absence, a *triumphant cry escaped from her*: "Roman, oh, Roman, forget to think of it!" [Shchepkina-Kupernik 1940: 76, 77, 84, 118] [Roman is a character from Alexander Ostrovsky's 1865 play *The Province Governor*, where Yermolova played the role of his wife, Olyona.]

These descriptions, as you can see, don't carry a hint of Yermolova "imbuing" her words with anything or "giving" them any tones. Here, everything is described simply, as it really was.

How deeply have these malicious words penetrated our daily theatrical practices!

Fellow actors tell you: you "give" this, but instead you must be "giving" that . . . Or else they say: you've not "conveyed" it well – it "did not reach" the audience . . .

The director says: here, I want you to "give me" passion. More passion! Here, "give" me anger! . . I want you to "put" contempt into this word . . . or jealousy . . . or despair . . . I want you to "land" this line with the audience . . . to "stress" this word . . .

A less eager director advises: don't play the feeling, just "give me the thought" . . . "highlight the key word in the sentence . . . "

The audience screams: louder!!! This also means "give it to me"! . .

Finally, critics and biographers write about genius actors that they also "invested" and "gave" – and the circle is complete.

No wonder that this mistake, one of the worst, enters our flesh and blood.

Perhaps, one cannot find a more common error than this among the actors (especially storytellers).

An actress rehearses a scene between Katerina and Varvara from the first act of Ostrovsky's *The Storm* [Scene 7]. In this scene, Katerina tells Varvara the story of her childhood.

- Tell me, why do you press Varvara so hard?
- I want to get her attention, I want to interest her, I want to inspire her with my story – how "I lived without a care in my heart, as free as a bird. Mother adored me, dressed me up like a doll . . . [Ostrovsky 1899: 27]"
- You want to interest her . . . And why should you?
- This is my task.
- How did this "task" come about? Maybe you, Katerina, now live such a good life, that it prompted you to remember the time of your happy childhood?

- Oh, no! Quite the contrary. My life is so bad, so hard now . . . because of my mother-in-law, and my husband . . . who's like a stranger. I never imagined it would be so hard.
- So, only now you've grown to appreciate your life before marriage? . . . You want to bring back these old days, so serene and happy?
- Yes, when you tell someone – it's as if you live that old life again . . .
- Suppose, you were now living a happy life – would you speak of your past with such passion, with such enthusiasm?
- Of course not. When life is good, you don't think about the past.
- Then it's not so much that you want to convince or interest Varvara, as to recall it for your own sake . . .
- Yes.
- To escape your present life, at least in your thoughts?
- Yes.
- You see how different this is from what you told me earlier?
  Let's examine, practically, how it happens in life. Tell me about your room. Tell it to me, so that I understand it well. Let's start with the front door. You open it . . . you come in . . . what comes next?
- Next is the corridor. It's always dark . . . here, to the right, is the switch.
- You flick it on . . .
- Yes, I turn on the light . . . A coat rack is on the left – I take off my coat . . . I hang it . . . I turn off the light and walk down the corridor . . . The second door on the left is mine . . . I open it . . . My room is spacious and bright . . . two windows . . .
- Large windows?
- Yes. And now that it is spring, there is plenty of sun . . .
- Say, do you "give" me something, or do you "take"?
- What do you mean "give" or "take"?
- Just so – don't you *perceive* your room . . . large windows . . . sunshine? . . . Then you must be "taking" these familiar impressions?
- Yes . . . I perceive . . . I take . . .
- And you weren't trying to "give" them to me?..
- No, I was not . . .
- This is how it always happens in life: we "give" nothing. We only "perceive." The *giving* happens on its own – it is an involuntary reaction. Just don't interfere, "give over" to it. While it's still fresh, let's go back to Katerina. Tell me your story from this point on: "Do you know how I passed my days as a girl . . . [Ostrovsky 1899: 27]"
- Do you know how I passed my days as a girl?
- Tell me how.

There are no such words in the play, but I need the actress to feel that her story interests me vividly. I need her to tell me her story in earnest. This is why I take her, so to speak, into the orbit of my influence. Eagerly, and with great sympathy, I follow her story, echo her words, ask again, and want to know the details . . . The actress has no other choice, but to surrender to the events of her sweet past.

- I'll tell you. I used to get up early.
- How early? Was it still dark? – I keep asking her, but not as a director, but as her partner, Varvara, who wants to know it all. At first, she looks at me, puzzled: how should she reply?

There are no lines for it in the text. I would reassure her: don't be concerned that the text says nothing about it – let's converse using *approximately* the lines given in the text. If they are not enough, we will add our own.

Consider what we are looking for, you and I. You are looking to tell me, and I am trying to find out from you how you used to live . . . So, go on. How early did you get up?

- Quite early . . . the sun was still low . . . In the summer, I'd go to the spring to bathe . . .
- Was the spring cold?
- It was . . . I would walk barefoot . . . the dew on the grass is icy cold, and it bites my feet . . . The air is fresh, life is merry . . .
- Where is that spring? On the hill?
- No, down in the gully. It's so clear . . . It bursts from the ground . . . stirs up the sand . . . the sand is clouding the water on the bottom . . .
- Is it a quiet place?
- Yes, no people in sight, only the birds are chirping. And the air is so clean, so fragrant . . . you want to drink it in . . .
- Do you perceive all these impressions, or do you "give" them to me?

For a moment she is confused, but then realizes that it is no longer Varvara talking to her, but her director. She would look back and, surprised, she would notice:

- Yes . . . I perceive, and I "give" nothing . . .
- Well, keep going, keep going . . . Why do you go to the spring?
- To bathe and to bring back water with me and water all the flowers in the house, every one of them.
- What kind of flowers? Tell me.
- All kinds: big and small . . .
- Do tell me what kinds. – I keep asking, because I see that no flowers appear for her – she is just saying empty words about some generic flowers.
- Geranium, a fig . . . I don't know what else . . .
- It's true, you don't know, and you've got nothing to perceive. You are saying "every one of them," and I do not believe it. I see that you don't have them in front of your eyes. Remember how at flower shops they've got flowers everywhere – on the floor, on some benches and tables, on the windows, and on special step-ladders. Some flowers are familiar, and others you don't know. Some are blooming, others are budding, and some look like simple greenery. This is what you used to have at home – you are such a lover of flowers. Can you imagine it?
- Yes, I can . . . I've been in flower shops, I know.
- Well, you bring back water, and what next?
- I'll bring back water, and water all the flowers in the house, every one of them.
- Now you feel the difference, how easy it is to speak, when you've got something to speak about - when you perceive? And how difficult it is, how empty the words are, when you perceive nothing? Then you have to search for the *intonation* that would make these words come out more alive. They don't say themselves, because no facts stand behind them, so you have to color them, to put them to music – to come up with upward and downward inflections.

When this idea of putting forward *perception over task and action* falls on the heads of some inveterate followers of the rationalistic and imperative school, they raise quite a scandal. Such a person might attack . . . as if about to hit you.

- "In theory," "according to science," it may be true, – he yells – but in practice – just the opposite. Look, I urge you – I act on you, I send, I **give**!
- You send nothing, – I tell him – on the contrary, you restrain yourself with all your might. You received such a charge from me, you are bursting with words meant to destroy me, bursting with threats . . . and if you were not so well-mannered, you would have told me the kind of things that would knock me off my feet.
- !!!
- Yes, you do *need*, or rather *you have the need* to affect me, but this is only because you see – instead of your student and admirer, slavishly catching your every word, you are faced with a dangerous man, "sabotaging the very foundations." You "perceive" it perfectly well and you experience an inner storm that is hard to contain, despite all your restraint.

Whatever the end of our conversation may be, in his soul, he will leave with one thought – *this fellow is unpleasant and harmful*. The actor "perceived" this once and for all, and, against his own will, his excited mind will be swarming with all kinds of measures aimed at crushing the "enemy."

And all this, not because he consciously "wanted" or "needed" it, but quite involuntarily: because he sensed danger.

Suppose he saw this new idea for what it is, namely, for something new and important to be added to what he already knew; something that would make him even stronger if he were to master it. In such a case, he would have grabbed for it and would not have left me alone until he squeezed it all out of me.

However, the *seekers* are very rare, and the majority ends their quest at the first sign of success. Everything new – even if it is the truest truth – simply annoys them: I should re-learn and why? Just as I got my success, have been "recognized," have "achieved," and have my peace of mind . . . there comes something unknown . . .

And the most annoying thing is: what if this happens to be the truth?! Then I am facing the most dangerous competition!!!

Perception Under the Guise of "Point of View"

They say that in order to create a role, it's most important "to find the character's point of view," find how this given character relates to the other characters in the play, to all kinds of things, circumstances, and facts. These "points of view" constitute the personality, the inner content and, in general, the entire "I am" of the character.

Is this true? – If we have the point of view, we have discovered almost everything. This is true.

However, what is a **point of view**? Is this something volatile that appears by our choice and order? Think of the many examples from our lives when things that we perceive *slip right by our consciousness*! We perceive something, but we don't necessarily cognize it! . . . After a business discussion, you are supposed to feel calm – your partners promised to do everything that was discussed. But for some reason, you're upset. Why is this? You might not even recognize it, but the problem is that you caught on to *something* that leads you to conclude that all these promises are mere "diplomacy," and they will never come to fruition. If someone were to ask you: "What exactly did you catch on to?" – you wouldn't be able to tell them.

Perception through cognition is *incomplete*; it doesn't include the whole sum of occurring phenomena, as we organically perceive it. It doesn't involve the world of our feelings, and subtle and subconscious spiritual movements. It doesn't grant us the sincere excitement and passion that are so precious in the art of the actor.

A point of view is our reaction that appears quite spontaneously as a result of all sorts of impressions (conscious and unconscious, correct or incorrect) that we receive from people, objects, or facts.

Your mother, father, brother, wife – just think how many diverse impressions you receive from them over the course of your life. As a result, you have formed a *point of view* for each of them.

Take any point of view, no matter how quickly or slowly it has been formed, it has *formed on its own*. It has been forming as a sum effect of *what exactly you have been perceiving* from a given object, person, or fact.

Let's say you are playing Plyushkin. [The Russian "equivalent" of Moliere's Harpagon (*The Miser*), Plyushkin is a character from Nikolai Gogol's novel *Dead Souls*. Thanks to Gogol, the name "Plyuhskin" has become a Russian common noun for "miser."] He is a miser, a skinflint, a cheapskate. What is his point of view on all those around him? – Enemies all around . . . everyone wants to steal from him, to deceive him, to cheat him. But how can you assume such a point of view on people, for no apparent reason?

Yet a talented actor somehow does it. Take a look at him, and you will marvel at how his entire being has changed: not only his face and his manners, but apparently his thought process and his entire point of view on his surroundings . . . He looks at you with suspicion and hostility . . . his eyes keep feeling you cautiously: do you want to steal something from him?

How does he achieve this?

If you are a good observer, you will see that his secret is, in fact, simple: in everyone around him he sees only thieves, swindlers, robbers, idlers, and parasites, who are only looking for something to steal. They seek out gazers and gullible fools, who are easily bamboozled . . . Take his servants for example. Why do they look at him with such honest and innocent eyes? They are doing it on purpose, so as to lull his vigilance . . . Try trusting them to fetch a thing from the cellar – they will swipe something or gobble something up. Especially since they are all hungry. How could they not be – they are lazy-bones, and gluttons to boot . . . Everyone is, in fact, a thief, a rogue, and a loafer through and through – they will rob you in no time!

No wonder he is on constant alert: his eyes, thought, movement, actions . . . In everything around he sees something hostile, suspicious, and dangerous. In other words, his point of view is the one of a miser, a skinflint – the one of a Plyushkin.

What is the origin of this? Does it really start with a point of view? To begin with, the actor sees (that is *perceives!*) everybody around as rogues and thieves, and only this produces a **point of view** as a consequence. This point of view being: everyone is a dangerous person; I should keep away from them, be on constant alert, and trust no one.

There is another misunderstanding around the word: attitude.

One of our prominent theatrical figures, [Yevgeny Vakhtangov] who in his time did a lot for theatre art, said something like this: "I cannot believe that this ashtray is a frog. Seeing, in a hallucinatory way, the ashtray as a frog is pathology. *As for having a point a view with regards to the ashtray as to a frog – that, I can do.*"

Truth be told, this helped the actor in practice: he **ceased trying to force himself to believe in the impossible** – that this ashtray is no ashtray, but a real frog.

"Then I don't have to believe?" he thought with relief. "It is enough to just have 'a point of view,' which probably means to just handle it *as if it were a frog* . . . This is certainly much easier, this I can manage."

From this point on, a mere glance at the dark glass ashtray awakened in his imagination the memory of the cold slippery body of a frog . . . The "point of view" was good to go.

If, in addition to this, he would touch the ashtray and instinctively receive a cold, weighty, and smooth sensation, his "point of view" would strengthen, and the ashtray would practically become a frog.

This teacher's disciples and followers picked up the definition of "point of view" he casually tossed in the heat of the moment, in class, and they made it into a psychological law of theatre: "it is impossible to believe, but it is possible to evoke a point of view."

Is this truly so? What is the real meaning of this method? Does it prove that a "point of view" is the origin of it all, while everything else is a mere consequence?

This method consists of several parts. First of all, it *redirects* an actor away from the unnatural and literal demand to "believe," "feel," and "want" for no apparent reason. This redirection is quite legitimate and rather witty.

Secondly, the actor, having heard the word "frog," immediately receives the image of a frog in his imagination.

Thirdly, the imaginative perception of the frog is supplemented with the perception of an actual ashtray he sees before him.

Fourthly, the ashtray and the frog merge in his imagination for a second or two; provided that the actor touches the ashtray, he even receives a physical sensation, as if from a frog.

Fifthly, this complex sensation is instantaneously followed by a reflexive response via action (withdrawing one's hands, tossing away "the frog," or something else).

This is how this "point of view with regards to an ashtray, as to a frog" comes about.

As you can see, a "point of view" is not the origin, but a *result* of a rather complex interacting processes – both mundanely physiological and creative. Among them, perception, once again, plays the leading role.

However . . . those who use this definition of point of view probably do not really want to think things over, let alone think them through to the end, all by themselves. Especially since the man from whom they first heard these words seems to be such an inerrant authority . . .

Is this method wrong or even harmful?

Not at all; it is correct and witty, and it can be used. As long as one is cautious when explaining it theoretically.

It is imperative, for example, to know that this method is nothing if not an *evocation of* **creative perception** *in the student or actor*, only cleverly disguised; creative perception being, in actuality, the origin of it all.

Mistakes of Perception

At times the actor perceives nothing of what is happening onstage. He does not see his partner, is not listening to his words. He has grown quite tired of them; they no longer carry anything – why bother listening? He monitors only the timely delivery of his own lines and the established blocking.

These cases are frequent; more frequent then we think. They have nothing to do with the art, so they are not worth discussing. These are not mistakes of perception, but rather the lack of any attempt to perceive. This is primitive craft.

Let us talk about mistakes.

An actor is in a sound state: he *sees and hears* onstage; he does not stop his reactions. Still, something is missing.

The director usually advises him to carry on, but . . . to give it a bit more power and passion. To put it simply, he is advising him to "step on it" and "to push." Or else, the director says something like this: you live truthfully, but now what you feel needs to "reach the audience." The meaning is the same – "step on it!"

The result of all these tips are always the same: they extinguish truth and instigate falsity.

In the meantime, the problem is very simple. If an actor lives truthfully onstage, yet his acting is rather dull, it only means that he is living in some circumstances *rather than his characters'* (as they are given by author). That is: he does perceive, but *not what he should.*

Take for example the recently discussed Katerina's story from *The Storm*. The actress might see "the spring" and "the flowers" . . . they might affect and excite her . . . Yet, something is not right . . . Why would a grown woman be so ecstatic about getting up early, going to get water at the spring, and then watering all her flowers! What is particularly exciting? No wonder it turns out a bit boring.

The mistake lies in the fact that it is a story about the days of her youth, almost her childhood. "Do you know how I passed my days as a maiden?" What does this mean: "as a maiden?" Fourteen, fifteen, sixteen years old. In those days, they used to marry off a girl early in life. An unmarried woman of 18–19 was considered an old maid. As for Katerina, she was probably married off at 16. Considering the life she led, her 15–16 equals the life experience of a contemporary 11-year-old. So, she took life as a girl: flowers, church, pilgrims' stories, religious songs, and embroidery . . . She probably did not even have any dolls. The psychology of a child, a child's world, and a child's freedom. This freedom is most important! (Otherwise, she would not have said, referring to her present life: "Here one feels somehow in a cage.")

And now Katerina recalls how she, as this girl-child, rises very early . . . runs barefoot on the dewy grass, runs down to the gully, bathes, splashing in the water like a duckling . . . She draws water, lifting the heavy buckets like feathers. She is bursting with strength and joy – carrying a heavy yoke uphill feels easy. She has the strength of a grown-up woman and the soul of a child. She brings the water home. Watering the flowers! My flowers! ("Every one of them.") Today children have everything: paintings and books, radio, theatres and film. Back then, especially in these remote provinces – they had nothing. Flowers were everything for them. They had to satisfy all their aesthetic and scientific needs – they are all her children, planted by her own hands, grown through her care. She knows the life of each flower, watching as their leaves unfold, as they open their buds. It's all so mysterious, exciting and marvelous . . .

The actress realized what is at the source of Katerina's life, as Ostrovsky wrote her. She unconsciously reached over to her own childhood . . . began to see and perceive things differently – the very images that used to bore her, captivated her imagination. As for us, the audience – inspired by her feelings, we remembered our own childhood joys . . . All boredom vanished at the sight of this carefree, happy childhood.

This example shows how difficult it is to *properly understand* all the "given circumstances" and *to live*, drawing from the kind of sources that fuel the character's life. Actors often assume their given circumstances *incorrectly, approximately* (I am referring to good actors, who live onstage). This makes their acting and their lines unconvincing.

Speaking from experience – good actors and a good author producing a boring impression points to the fact that the scene has been interpreted *incorrectly*. It means that something elusive, yet important, has not been clarified.

Here a different kind of mistake. It is not caused by the fact that the actor perceives incorrect things, but rather that he perceives incorrectly. His perception is not of a kind we have in life, when something *interests* us and concerns us directly. When observing such an actor, it is easy to notice that everything he now tries to see does not touch him. He sees it, even marks it in his mind, but what he sees leaves him completely cold. *Personally*, he is not concerned with any of it, and he looks at it as if from the outside. He just notes everything coldly – as if cataloguing it.

In the meantime, we need to *see* onstage in such a way so as to trigger a reaction. He does not see like that.

It is almost impossible to explain exactly how one should see. You must be able to show it in practice.

To follow is a simple practical method developed exactly with such an issue in mind.

We have before us an actor who thinks that he *understands everything and sees it all*.

- You believe that you see? Let's check it out. Here, for example, is a nail, or rather just the tip of the nail (I point out a nail hammered into the floor. In general, you should take some small object). Tell us what you see.
- I see the head of a nail half-centimeter in diameter; it is ribbed, slightly crooked, edges notched by a hammer. The nail has not been driven in all the way – its head is spaced a whole centimeter above the floor . . .
- Very well then . . . do you like this nail or not?
- What do you mean "like it or not?" It's a nail. What is there to like or dislike?
- Yes, but the sun is also always the sun, and the rain is the rain. And yet, if I ask you: are you enjoying the rain today or not, it won't be hard for you to answer.
- Oh, in that sense! How shall I put it – do I like it or not . . . The nail is all right . . . it is new, not dirty or rusty, it even sparkles in the shade dark. Only, you know, this is a treacherous nail: if you catch on it, it will take your sole off just like that. Yes, as far as my sole is concerned, I do not like it. As soon as the rehearsal is over, I'll personally pull it out, or hammer it all the way – that's for sure.
- Now you do see. You see as a normal living person, not as mechanical cataloguer. The kind of seeing you had before left you cold, and although you were seeing dozens of details, they did not bring the object any closer to you, but rather moved it further away. As for this other way of seeing – normal, without unnecessary complications, and so familiar to you from your mundane everyday habits – it just revealed in a nail what it really means to you.

Now you will approach your partner and the circumstances with this way of seeing. Not objectively, but *subjectively*. Objectivity onstage is unnecessary; moreover, it is harmful. We must perceive everything purely subjectively: *what is it for me? and how does it strike me – the character?*

23

Free Reaction ("Green-Lighting")

Free Reaction ("Green-Lighting") as the Basis of the Actor's Stage Behavior

The very word—"green-lighting"—sounds primitive and completely unscientific. For the sake of accuracy, it should be replaced with "free reaction" or something like that . . .

However, in practice, any such expression as "free reaction" only scares off the actor. In practice, you may only resort to simple everyday words – they do not interfere with the actor's process and produce the right effect. Usually I say: "Give it a green light," and it does the job. Try saying: "react more freely" (or something like that) – it would spoil everything. It would spoil it because, as a complex abstract expression, it would force the actor to think it over, at least for a second – this takes him out of the sound creative state.

This is why I do not deviate from what life and practice have taught me, and do not give up our "working" vocabulary: "green-lighting," "green-light," "you did not green-light."

A chief and basic task of a theatre school should consist of identifying and developing an individual student's natural talent. To do this, you need to *go along with his talent – not against it.*

The path of imposing anything onto the student would be the way "*against*" his talent. The path of freedom and involuntariness would be the one of affirming and further developing his natural gift as an actor.

This leads one to the following principle: to allow your own creativity; to free yourself in it, to be involuntary – such is the foundation of our theatre school.

The more you work on cultivating actors, the more insistently the question arises: could it be that one single mistake exists in the technique of the actors' creative process – "the lack of green-lighting?"

"Pushing," "rushing" – they also result from "a lack of green-lighting." A line is yet to ripen in the actor's soul; he should have kept silent – yet he does not green-light this need for silence. The fear of a pause causes nervousness and . . . he "pushes" himself. Thus, there is likely one cause of most ills: "a lack of green-lighting." All these recommendations to "not rush," to "not push" are all bits of advice that tell one not to interfere with one's creative freedom and ease, i.e. with "green-lighting."

Not just these two recommendations, but all of the advice and methods described herein, can be reduced mainly to developing the habit to freely "green-light" this involuntary, organic life onstage.

Laxity Is Neither Creative "Green-Lighting" nor Creative Freedom

There was a young, very cultured woman among my students, an artist by training. She frequented theatres and had already formed her own opinion of the actor's art. Undoubtedly gifted, she nevertheless remained very restrained in her work. I told her about the freedom of Mochalov and Yermolova . . . To my surprise, this actress (despite all her talent and love for art) remained completely indifferent to all of these stories. It was easy to read distrust and even prejudice in her eyes . . .

I tried to overcome this attitude and seemingly succeeded at this. But then, all of a sudden, she became quite upset and said:

- If this is the case, I'll probably never be an actress . . .
- And why do you think so?
- Because I could never be as open and involuntary . . . Not long ago, I was visiting the X family, and there are three sisters, all actresses. They must have wanted to make my day, so they decided to show me their skills – they played "etudes" . . . They were so spontaneous, so bold, so explicit . . . I never thought one could throw off reserve like that . . . I was astonished . . . and at the same time . . . embarrassed for them . . . I think I would never dare to be so free, as you call it.
- And what was it like – their freedom?
- What was it like . . . When it comes to these girls, you can truly say, without exaggeration, that they gave themselves free rein . . . They were talking about all kinds of subjects, did not mind their language . . . They were not afraid to be frivolous, obscene, nasty, ill-mannered . . .

Even now, at the mere thought of these "etudes," she apparently felt uneasy – her mind kept recreating details, and they made her feel sick . . . Finally, she said:

- No! I still think that freedom and involuntariness are not such a necessary thing for an actor . . . At times they can be unbearable . . . Here, take our L. and B., for example. They are also quite free and open on the stage, but I can't look at them. Everything they do is so vulgar and tasteless . . .

The resolution of these misunderstandings is very simple: creativity does not only *require* sincerity and authenticity – it *instigates* them. When being in the throes of the creative process, one cannot help but be sincere.

Naturally, "green-lighting" is a double-edged sword – you might green-light, and reveal quite the opposite from what you want to show. Vulgar people, in this case, would hardly be able to hide their vulgarity; limited or narrow-minded people would reveal their limitations; depraved people would show their perversion. The opposite is also true: smart, determined and pure people would reveal their complex psychological constitution, all their strength and beauty.

As the saying goes, "welcome to our potluck."

The question arises: what if vulgarity keeps coming out of me – does it mean that I can play nothing except vulgarity onstage?

It is true that each of us has some negative qualities, but the opposite is also true.

When an actor is prone to his "base" manifestations and cannot redirect himself, it is the job of the director and teacher to guide him towards things greater and more dignified. If the director does not know how to do this, clearly he does not know how to manage the most important part of an artist's job. A true artist cannot help but feel beauty and strive for it.

To Stay the Course or to Give in to It?

Two-three chairs joined together represent a bench – in some garden, or in some exhibit or museum.

She (sits).
He (comes in).   – Have we met before?
She.   – Maybe we have.
He.   – Have you been to Yalta?
She.   – I have not.
He.   – And how about in '48?
She.   – Not in '48 either.
He.   – I guess I was wrong . . .
She.   – It happens. (Leaves.)
He (alone).   – It was her!

She sat, apparently waiting for someone. Her partner came in, absently looking around. He gave her a quick look, and slowly walked past . . . Then he stopped . . . He clearly wanted to sit down, but the bench was occupied. She understood this and moved to the edge. He settled on the other edge.

She had been expecting someone else, and was annoyed by his company. Having looked at him with displeasure, she was suddenly startled – she paused and froze . . . She started remembering something . . . she stole a quick look at him . . . glanced again and, having remembered something – smiled. Then she hid her smile and began to wait for what would happen next.

He felt her attention and, once again, gave her a quick look, thinking to himself: "What's the matter? She must need something from me." In the meantime, he himself became interested in her, for no apparent reason . . . He looked at her again . . .

She was turned away from him. He kept waiting – she would not turn back . . . Then he carefully looked into her face. She closed it with her handkerchief, as if attempting to wipe her temple. A modest, well-behaved young man, he stood up, walked around, as if studying things around. Although she tried to close off from him, he still caught in her something familiar. Apparently, he had yet to remember who she was . . . Hesitantly, not wanting to be intrusive, he said, almost to himself: "Have we met before?"

Suppressing a smile, she looked him straight in the eyes, like a close acquaintance: "Maybe we have."

Her direct gaze made him feel embarrassed, confused. He hesitated for a few seconds. Then suddenly, some insolent demon possessed him. He sensed himself an outgoing, frivolous man, and asked her, as if hinting at some jolly adventure: "Have you been to Yalta?"

She was taken aback – where did he disappear, that humble, quiet man, a touch absent-minded? There was suddenly some fop standing before her . . . Very strange . . . She stole a glance at him – no, she wasn't wrong – it was a different man. Unless something happened to him in these two or three years she has not seen him. Just in case, she made a stern face and dryly replied: "I have not."

He was not letting go. He came from behind and, leaning over her shoulder, whispered a reminder: "And how about in '48?"

She blushed, offended, pulled away from him and abruptly snapped: "Not in '48 either!"

This knocked him out at once . . . He looked at her closer . . . His "swagger" and frivolity evaporated, and he came back . . . to where he started – a modest, absentminded, well-behaved youth. – "I guess I was wrong" . . . It sounded like an apology: "I'm sorry . . . I was wrong . . . "

That surprised her even more – an awfully strange young man! I better go . . . She muttered, as she went away: "It happens."

He remained, stunned . . . Silently, for a long while, he followed her with his eyes. Kept looking at the place where she had just sat . . . He got up, still trying to figure out how it all happened, and what actually happened . . . Again, he looked in the direction where she went, sighed, and said sadly: "It was her . . . " He shook his head in disapproval, and dragged his feet in the other direction.

- Well, what sort of disaster just befell you?
- "Disaster" indeed, – he said, still in a state of bewilderment and sadness – I started as one person; then I was drawn to somebody else – someone not very pleasant . . . how should I put it? – some frivolous fellow, or something like that . . . I "green-lit" this guy, but I could not sustain the act, and things went south.
- Can anyone tell me what mistake he made?
- He couldn't stay the course he shaped at the top of the etude.
- And what course did he shape at the top?
- At the start, he green-lit this ordinary, modest young man in him – so, he shouldn't have strayed from this course.
- He should've stayed it?
- "Stayed it" – precisely.
- "To stay the course . . . " This must be it . . . You seem to have a point . . . Let's, however, take a closer look . . . . Tell us, in the right order, how things went. You came in . . .
- I came in . . . The place felt like a museum . . . Or a memorial apartment that used to belong to some writer or composer . . . It did not feel like a comfortable place – perhaps they couldn't preserve all of the furniture – it felt empty.
- Aha. What then? . . .
- Then . . . At first I did not notice her: some girl's there – no big deal . . . Then I felt I had seen her before . . . And she herself keeps examining me . . . I don't know who she is, but I know I've met her somewhere . . . I asked her gently . . . And she suddenly looked at me so directly, so freely! "Maybe we have met," she says. Out of surprise, something inside me got unhinged . . . And she keeps looking . . . To show her that I'm not embarrassed – I keep looking at her . . . At that moment, some kind of insolence rose up inside me . . . That insolence made me feel myself a daredevil, who couldn't care less! That's how it went . . .
- So, all that trouble began with you getting embarrassed, confused, lost?
- Yes.
- And, in order to avoid this painful and stupid state, you grasped at the first thing that turned up?
- Yes.
- And that first thing was her face, and his eyes . . . looking at you slyly?
- Yes . . . and I felt myself being somebody else . . . somebody at the boulevard.

- A new etude, you mean?
- Yes, probably a new etude.

The proponent of "staying the course" cannot restrain himself:

- What did I say?! He should have stayed the course!
- Wait, wait: it's too early to draw conclusions . . . You feel embarrassed, confused, lost . . . And what were you so afraid of? Do we not often feel lost and confused in life? What is so special? It's quite a common occurrence. When this happens – what do we do in real life? We try to understand, to figure things out . . . before we know it, something always emerges.
Let's approximate what would have happened, if you did not get scared of your confusion? . . . You got confused . . . I don't understand . . . I look at her . . . can't see anything clearly . . . So be it; this happens often. And she keeps looking at me and smiling . . . My stupefied face makes her laugh . . .
- I got it! I got it! Something flickers in me – memories, or something like that . . . Who knows what it is . . . And it does not matter a bit that I cannot remember her! It happens all the time – you recognize a person, but who it is, and where you've seen them or when – this does not immediately come to mind!..
- Exactly . . . Then everything is all right – you don't need to "restructure"?
- No, no! Now everything is going as it was.
- That's staying the course for you! – the advocate of "sustaining" does not let go.

It is true that we do "stay the course," – at least this is how it seems. But this course is formed on its own, and we do not stay it. On the contrary, *it stays us*. That's right! We have before us a living example. This ardent supporter of "staying the course." Could he control himself? Apparently not. Some force kept nudging him to chime in, and it urged him to speak – from impatience, he stirred in his chair, as if it were a frying pan . . . What happened to him? Was he staying his course? Of course not – he was sustaining nothing. His firm belief was acting beyond his will and giving him no peace.

After this incident, he is likely to reconsider this belief of his. He will understand that in such cases, the "disaster" does not occur because of the actor *not staying* with the first thing that appeared in him. It occurs because he did not fully give in to this first thing. As he is not completely immersed in it, naturally, a more or less powerful bump can mislead him.

Wait until this ability to fully give in to his creative life is firmly embedded in him, and turns into a habit – a tangible quality. It will replace his present belief in the need to "shape" and "stay" the course..

"Green-Lighting" in the "Beginning" ("The Lad with a Cane")

He is no longer a young man. But since he is puny and short, he is still considered a "young man" at his theatre. His specialty is the crowd. He is a crowd scene actor. His favorite role – a cheerful, sassy lad with a cane. For many years, he has been acting this role in different plays, changing costumes and names. He plays it boldly, confidently and "reliably."

Many years of work without cleaning and maintenance, resulted in the build-up of bad habits. Imperceptibly, these habits turned art into mechanized craft . . .

On top of it all, based on his psychological qualities, this actor belongs to the category of those rationalists, who have a tendency to think everything over, to comprehend it all, and to control the executing of the plan.

As soon as I started speaking about freedom and involuntariness, he met my words with hostility. The unnatural habits were so deeply ingrained in his flesh and blood that anything natural strikes him as ignorance and heresy.

As one would expect, the mistakes began with the "beginning." Boy, did he "begin!"

Here he enters the stage to do an etude – pleasant, polite, business-like – just as people perceive him in everyday life. Having reached the stage, however, he changes dramatically: he throws out his freedom and truth as unnecessary and harmful, "concentrates," "takes" his pre-invented "task" and begins to bend over backwards, according to all the rules of his craft.

With some difficulty, I managed to convince him to try to not "begin," but give in to what comes out of him on its own, without preparation and adjustment. He took a chance . . . he tried . . . and . . . began to play his "sassy lad with a cane" . . .

- Why? Why did you do this? Didn't you feel something else entirely? When you started the etude for the second time, you felt bored, tired . . . You looked at her with indifference. Maybe because you have been seeing her every day for several years, and have gotten accustomed to her, or for some other reason – you felt even more bored. This is how it went. Yet, you suddenly broke all this life inside of you and "cheered up." Why?
- Why would I bring onto the stage my personal, mundane life! Who needs it! And besides, what was going on inside me was too simple. I'm tired, I'm bored, I do not want to do anything . . . Yes, it is truth, but is it art? This truth is completely uninteresting and vulgar. Who needs this kind of truth?

Notice: "Too simple" – obviously, simplicity is beneath him, and he chose something more "engaging" and worthy of him, because of its complexity.

And besides, the man is so used to forcing his own nature, simplicity and ease even seem *incorrect*! Not worthy of art!

His colleagues lost their patience, teamed up, and, after much wrangling, persuaded him to give this new way a thorough try. "Let it be wrong – all the same, give it a try. If only out of curiosity . . . So, we will have a tedious time – what of it? Just green-light it, give it a try. Take a chance.

They persuaded him. He agreed.

What followed was a true catastrophe.

The text itself was very peaceful:

He.   – Are you going out today?
She.   – No, I'm not. I am staying home.
He.   – Very good.
She.   – Why do you ask?
He.   – Nothing . . . I don't get to see you often.
She.   – I've been busy.

Since the actor had just endured an argument and did not come out a winner, naturally, he continued to carry some muffled irritation inside. The etude kept developing under the influence of this irritation.

As soon as he and his partner repeated the text, he turned beet red . . . for two-three seconds he restrained himself, and then – switched off his usual internal fuse box: "All right! You want me to green-light it?! You asked for it!"

He cast a heavy, hateful glance at her.

- Are you going out today?

She did not see his face, but the sound of his voice lashed her, like a whip. She turned around and shrugged: someone else stood before her – a strange man, unpleasant and scary . . .

- No, I'm not. I am staying home. (Why do you ask? What is the matter with you?).

He spilled his muffled irritation all over her . . . Apparently, she struck him as a woman, over whom he had some unlimited power. And, from the bottom of his soul, there rose such rage, such gloom!

- Ve-e-ery good! (It's a good thing you are staying home). Ve-e-ery good!!! . . .
- Why do you ask?

She froze in fear. As for us – astonished, we watched such horror crawl from the depths of this polite, reserved man (although, truth be told, not everyone's favorite)! . . . Wait a second! This is what you are like! Inside your soul, it's not all politeness and pleasantness . . . and to such a degree that it's horrifying to look at . . .

He glanced in our direction, and . . . came to.

Realizing that he just accidentally opened up his heart of hearts – he caught himself and rushed to play his salvational "lad with a cane" – he laughed, turned around on one leg, and successfully gabbled out the rest of his text.

When asked what just happened, he said, as one would expect, something like this: "I wanted to play a joke on her, to scare her a little . . . "

It was clear, however, that he was not joking, but that he just experienced the worst thing that could happen to a false and private person – he suddenly opened up, beyond his own will. Always so decent, well-mannered, and courteous, he suddenly showed us his true nature, his blood, his primitive instincts. A true catastrophe!

Proper "beginning" and "green-lighting" broke through all the barriers.

Now, just do not back away, just continue this work. Above all, reassure and convince him that there is no need to worry about all these horrors that crawl out of us, on their own volition. They lurk, unknown to us, at the bottom of our soul . . . Without these "horrors," we could not play Iago, Macbeth, or Richard, or Shylock – they would be flat without them. Reassure him that there are not only dark and negative qualities lurking in his heart (and who doesn't carry this darkness inside them?). Just look closely, and you will most likely discover beauty . . . Except, he keeps hiding it – in his shyness. (Yes, imagine, this arrogant, selfish, embittered egotist is essentially a timid man – this is why he is secretive and artful – and not an artist.) In his shyness, he hides all that is truly valuable, and brings to light only his politeness, balance, courtesy, and other husk. They come in handy in everyday life, but for creativity – it is empty husk.

"Green-Lighting" Cliché Acting

There are many of those, who will begin to doubt: is "green-lighting" such a panacea for all ills? And what if an actor has bad habits? What if stereotypical patterns or cliché acting became his second nature? Is it wise to simply leave him alone – let him "green-light" all that? He will be "green-lighting" . . . and what would become of it? He will drown you in clichés.

A class of internal technique is in progress. An old, "experienced" actor was merciless, as he treated us to a whole slew of clichés: he imitated all kinds of feelings; he kept one eye on the audience – checking whether his masterful acting reaches the target; he held effective pauses . . . in short, he was doing everything one might expect from a patented craftsman, with questionable taste to boot.

Everyone is expecting me give him a good dressing down . . . Instead, I begin to praise the actor. I praise him for his wonderful "green-lighting," for playing so brilliantly the role of a poseur, who is all airs and graces. At such and such moment, he perfectly did this, and in this other place, he brilliantly acted that . . . and then he also wanted to do such and such a thing. What a pity that he did not allow himself to do it – it would have been exceptional!

At the moment, I am not concerned whether my students understand all of my diplomacy. What is important for me is he, the actor. There is a battle going on. I attempt to break through his habits of a craftsman – to artistic truth.

Over the course of many years, he got used to play-acting and falsehood; he can no longer do without them onstage – they have become second nature to him. He just gave it full freedom: for that freedom I praised him.

Only up till this point, he did not suspect that those watching him from the outside could clearly see falsehood. He was used to thinking that his acting gives the impression of "truth," but apparently . . .

He is experiencing some inner shift. He looks back at his inner experience, and sees a large measure of artificiality, which used to save him until now . . .

For several seconds, he does not know what he should do. On the one hand, he is being exposed in the most insulting manner, and on the other – praised! He is confused, unsettled, but he sees that he is being treated with kindness, friendliness even, and taken quite seriously . . .

So, I keep praising him more and more, and then immediately suggest: let's now take a different character – a man who never lies and does not even know how to lie. Give in to it as whole-heartedly as you gave in to that poseur . . .

Of course, it would be natural to expect failure – after all, he is so accustomed to falseness onstage, so hopelessly cluttered with clichés . . . And yet – imagine that! – perhaps because his trick has been exposed, or because I praised him so convincingly and persistently – his soul has opened and he . . . took a chance! And as long as he takes a chance, he will do it. Just do not give him anything difficult, to begin with. If, on top of it, you help him with your "support" – he will do it!

Having done it, having tasted the truth – he will want it again and again.

The Nature of Consciousness during Creative Work ("Doubling")

"Give yourself freedom," "don't interfere with yourself . . . " – these tips may not help. What do you mean? How would I give freedom to my own self? This is some kind of an oxymoron. I can give freedom to someone else. But how would I give freedom to *myself*?

Many actors, who grew accustomed to self-observation, are thrown into confusion by this advice to "give freedom to yourself."

In such cases, I use the following device. I say: "That's all right, don't give freedom to yourself – give it to your hands – let them do what they want . . . Give freedom to your body – let it live and act independently, as it wants . . . Give freedom to your thoughts – let them live: appear and disappear, merge with one another . . ."

"In general, outsource your life and actions to some kind of 'it.' Do not interfere personally. You could not care less. Let it be. You are passive. You've got nothing to do with it."

"After all, many processes take place in you on their own, without your control and intervention. For example: digestion – you ate your lunch and forgot about it; everything else is done without you – digestion, assimilation – you do not interfere. Your job is to eat, and then 'let it be,' as it should. The same happens with breathing, with blood circulation. Something in you keeps breathing . . . blood circulates as it knows how . . . The same is true of sleep – you lie down, wrap yourself in a blanket, and let sleep come on its own. You've got nothing to do with it."

"This state – 'let it be' – is not alien to you; on the contrary, it is very familiar. So, let us try it here, in our work."

"To make things clearer and more distinct, let's skip a partner-etude; let's put together some sort of a monologue. With one person onstage, it will be easier to follow this device."

"Weren't you quite puzzled by the issue of giving freedom to yourself? So, let's start with you. Please come 'onstage.'"

A modest, reserved girl, very strong-willed, from an educated family (a daughter of a university professor) steps out willingly – you can see that she really wants to understand and master this "freedom."

Her intellectual tendencies, and her self-control, so precious in life – here, in the arts, have not only interfered, but simply barred her path, not allowing to take a single step forward. Not for a moment is she able to forget herself and stop watching her own life. She has got not a trace of living, let alone freedom.

She is smart and understands it well. Especially since she has seen this freedom (alien to her, and, therefore, fascinating) in the other, more spontaneous students.

"Here hangs our all too familiar classroom clock. Let's construct your monologue around it. How about this: 'It's almost two, and he is not back yet. What's wrong? . . . He was supposed to be back at twelve . . . Did something happen? I can't wait any longer – I must hurry . . .' Runs out."

"All the rules we have followed so far in our etudes remain the same. Don't change a single thing; just aim to give freedom to your hands, feet, and body . . . to your feelings . . . and thoughts . . . Let's see what comes out of it . . . Let them proceed at their own risk – "let it be!" You've got nothing to do with it! Absolve yourself of any responsibility – take this load off yourself – let them manifest themselves as they want! Be what may!"

The actress, weary of fighting self-observation, sensed that I offered her some *new way to bypass* her constant self-awareness.

Having repeated the text, as usual, she "put it out of her head." It was evident, that she also made an effort to toss aside her observing self.

"That's right, that's right . . . this is correct, correct, "let it be" – don't get involved. Just so, just so . . ." All these encouraging comments are made so as not to scare off the actor's new experience, to reinforce it.

Be it because she truly threw off the yoke of self-control, or for some other reason, but she quickly fell into a state of pleasurable rest – she stretched, made herself comfortable in her chair, closed her eyes and leaned back, smiling blissfully and settling her head – as if about to take a nap.

"Correct, correct . . . 'let it' live as it feels like living . . ."

She allowed herself to slip even deeper into this state of self-forgetfulness and irresponsibility.

"Correct, correct," I whisper to her, calming her as much as possible, and strengthening what is happening in her now. She is yielding to it and is on the verge of completely losing herself . . .

Suddenly she abruptly opens her eyes, as if someone pushed or pricked her, and looks around nervously – apparently, she still does not understand what is going on . . .

"That's it, that's it . . . this is correct. 'Let it be' . . . this is none of your business . . . do not interfere . . ."

She looks around, searching for something . . . accidentally, she glances at the clock: "Ah!" she cries out. She is recalling something, trying to gather her thoughts . . . ("Let it be" . . . Correct, correct . . . just let it . . .). Still oblivious, trying to comprehend and remember something, she looks at the clock and mechanically says: "Two o'clock . . . almost two o'clock . . . " She still does not understand why she is so worried that the clock shows ten to two . . . (Just let it be . . . don't get involved . . . none of your business . . .). She completely gives in to what is seething inside her—anxiety and bewilderment—and suddenly remembers: "It's almost two, and he is not back yet. He was supposed to be back at twelve . . ." (That's it, that's it!.. Just let it be, don't interfere . . . Let it proceed!)

She jumps up and runs to the window . . . to the door . . . she opens the door and shuts it again . . . once more, she looks at the clock . . .

"What's wrong?.. Did something happen?" – she is in a hurry to figure it out, to compare the time and the facts: where is he? Why is he late? What could have held him up?..

She forces herself to sit back in her chair . . . but her anxiety keeps growing. (Good, good. "Let it be," let it move – full speed ahead . . .) Suddenly, she abruptly jumps up. Having tossed, on the go "I must hurry . . . I can't wait any longer!" – she shot out the door.

A minute later she returns to the classroom. Her face and her entire self beam with joyful amazement. Apparently, she had just experienced something so new and pleasant – she still cannot go back to her balanced self.

- Well, now? What do you say?
- That's interesting! You see: it as if it was me and not me!
- Tell it to us, step by step.
- Step by step? . . . I don't remember . . . and I would hate having to come out of this new state.
- Aha! Well, then don't. Just go back to your seat and enjoy it quietly. We'll talk later.

One of the students who has the tendency to examine everything in detail, to understand and systematize it all—one of the future teachers and "theorists"—asks:

- First, you told her to carry on as usual, but "aim to give freedom to her hands, feet, and body – to let them act independently, at their own risk" . . . I think we already used this device. We called it "freedom of small automatic movements." There, too, we gave freedom to our hands, feet . . . I would like to clarify, because I can see – the results are somewhat different, more profound, more enthralling for the actor.
- You're right. In its initial stage, this device almost entirely equals "freedom of small automatic movements," but then we introduced something else. Remember, I added: "Give freedom to your feelings, thoughts . . . let them live – appear and disappear, merge with one another." In short, give freedom to your *life*. This point of transition is most important – the transition from the freedom of small automatic movements (physical freedom, so to speak) to *psychological* freedom.
  And then we said that, in addition to letting our hands and feet do what they want, we also let some kind of an *"it"* live, move, feel, think, and want. What is this *"it?"* Liza here

said something strange: she felt as if she − was not she, but someone else. Well, Liza, share it with us; please tell us what happened inside you? You've now had time to sit it out, to "recover" from your new sensation.

- What happened? . . . It started before the etude . . . I was affected by what you said about giving freedom to feelings and thoughts − not interfering in their lives . . . Suddenly, for one second, I felt that it was possible, that I actually can completely give in to my thoughts and feelings − while simultaneously watching myself from the outside. As if "it" was actually feeling and thinking in me, and I was watching it . . . as some foreign thing . . . I tried not to lose this sensation . . . I repeated the words, and plunged into it! And here you encouraged me more: "Correct, correct . . . let it be . . . you've got nothing to do with it" − and I lost all caution . . . I felt so good and easy, as if someone lifted a five-pound weight off of me. I felt like stretching and sighing . . . The chair was near, and I dropped into it. It was so nice to feel freedom and peace . . . Everything in me felt so clear, unclouded, and I looked at it as if from the outside, and did get in the way. You repeated: "Correct, correct . . . let 'it' live as it feels like living . . . " I gave in even more to this new sensation, forgot everything else . . . And suddenly something jolted me so! I initially got scared, but you said: "That's right, that's right, good, just let 'it' be . . ." Well, I think, be what may! Somehow, I gave it a green light: I let "it" be worried and terrified, as if it was none of my business! . . . My fear and anticipation of something kept growing, and when I saw that the clock was showing two, I got completely confused . . . And again, you said: "That's correct . . . let 'it' be . . . leave it alone, it's none of your business . . . " Then I got carried away!.. I imagined that my little brother was supposed to come to me for a lesson. I've been waiting for him, and he is not showing up . . . Two hours have passed . . . he is a mischief-maker . . . what if he got hit by a tram or something . . . I think, you shouted again: "Correct, correct . . . just so . . . let it . . . " You probably did not have to: that "it" has become stronger than me. I am running around the room, dashing to the window, and then to the door − I am beyond myself, out of fear for him. In the meantime, I am stealthily watching − watching, but not interfering . . . and just rejoicing. I hear you too, giving me extra courage: "That's it, that's it . . . let it be! Don't interfere . . . " Something keeps swirling and tossing me around the room . . . And I am not scared a bit . . . I feel that I can suspend it at any moment . . . Except, I don't feel like suspending. I want it to last; I want more, more, and more! Because I can see − this is truth!
- Who is it bossing around inside you?
- I have no idea . . . Perhaps it is her − that girl who is afraid that her little brother got hit by a tram . . .
- Do you personally have a little brother?
- I don't. I am the only child. It's just Dad, Mom, and me.
- And here you thought that you had a brother?
- Yes . . . shaggy hair . . . a trouble maker . . .
- And you thought he got into some accident?
- Yes . . . my heart sank . . . I was so flustered . . .
- And you're watching all that?
- Yes . . . somehow I still managed to look at it from the outside . . . and then I saw that even though it was "I," at the same time, it was not me . . .
- How come? Was it some kind of dual state of being?
- Yeah, yeah. Precisely: dual.
- And . . . it's OK? It does not break you out of it? Does not get in the way?

- It does not bother me – on the contrary.
- A dual state of being . . .
- That's it – a dual state of being! A perfect way to describe it!
- Well, let's not dwell too long on this phenomenon. Just note that it is present in any creative process, especially in that of an actor. This phenomenon is the first indicator of the presence of a *sound creative state*. You are happy, you are triumphant. You're right – you have every reason to be happy: now you've experienced, in practice, the creative doubling of an actor.

The Significance of the First Reaction

The ability to follow the first impulse *without delay* is so important for actors that every one of them—regardless of their persuasion—consciously or subconsciously prizes this particular gift.

Let us take a closer look at it. Any impression we receive evokes in us a certain response – a reaction. In a spontaneous person, this reaction is immediately visible – it meets no obstacles on its way. If someone unpleasant walks into a room, at that very moment his face would pout – without even noticing it, he would turn away. That would be his first reaction.

The next moment would bring a delay of this first reaction – its inhibition. With it would come the *orientation* in the surroundings: the person understands that such a direct expression of his attitude is awkward and indecent – finally, it is insulting for the newcomer.

This brings about the third moment: a reaction in view of the surroundings – this reaction can be called *secondary*. Now the person may, on the contrary, make a friendly face and even offer his hand to the newcomer.

The conduct of a well-behaved adult would be closer to this second reaction; the one of a child, or spontaneous person – closer to the first.

These are our mundane reactions.

The actor's creative reaction cannot be like either of those. It is much more complicated.

Actors must transform into a character with his or her nature, beliefs, feelings and tastes. In addition to that, actors have to live with all the circumstances of the play.

At the same time, they are surrounded by artificiality, convention and falseness of the stage, and by the watching audience . . . If actors begin to naturally orient in all that – how could they transform and live the life of their fictional role?

In the meantime, the natural orientation cannot disappear: actors cannot forget that they are actors, performing onstage.

However, despite these indications of the natural orientation, actors also know that, if they are to strive for true art, they must perceive all the circumstances of the play as their own.

And so, while orienting correctly, as people (this is a stage, and everything about it is false), they should at the same time be oriented as characters – that is, perceive all the imaginary circumstances as quite real and personal. And react to them accordingly.

But how is this done?

The First Reaction as a Source of Imagination and Faith

In the words of Stanislavsky, you must *believe* in the given circumstances, as if they really do exist – make them your *truth* (his constant wording: "The truth for me is what I sincerely believe at this moment").

How can I believe this? How do I make it my truth?

A gifted actor does it quite simply: a single thought – and it's done. A mere idea that it is cold – and the actor experiences all of the effects of the cold; it happens right away, like the first reaction. Similarly, a mere thought about all other circumstances of the play, about his character's nature and qualities – and he is in the power of these circumstances, while his whole being is that of the character.

In a less talented actor, a reaction to a thought is not as visceral and quick. Although it exists, its lifespan is short – it is overpowered by sober reality: "it is only my fancy – in fact, there is no cold, and no such circumstances – they are fictional." And the short-term experience, which was sparked by benevolent creative imagination, disappears.

Thus, both actors have a reaction. With one, it's stronger; with the other – weaker.

What does the gifted actor do? Maybe he is completely deprived of normal orientation, which is why he is able to freely give in to imaginary impressions and to his reaction?

Like any normal person, he is fully oriented in actual reality. However, he is an actor. As this fact is of paramount importance to him at the moment (for such is his nature), he does not allow the normal, mundane orientation to seize him. Otherwise—he knows this well—it might destroy him . . . The most important thing for him now is creativity – the character and his life. The real situation, from his standpoint as the actor-creator, no longer distracts him from his creative process; on the contrary, it brings this process into greater focus. He courageously frees his reaction, while "green-lighting" the life urged by his creative imagination.

Let us remember our walks through the forest at night, as a child, when the slightest rustle, the crackling of broken branches, a bat darting past our faces – all this immediately strikes us as so horrific and dangerous that it takes all our will-power to control fear . . . Our heart is pounding; we are ready to fight, or to flee, or to fall to the ground in horror . . .

In the meantime, all this is merely the result of our imagination.

Why is our imagination captured so completely? The darkness, fear of the unknown, and the mysterious nightlife make our every impression so significant and vivid, it fills our entire consciousness. Under the influence of such impressions, our imagination creates its events and facts – fantastic, yet real.

Simultaneously, our entire being reacts to the picture created by our imagination.

All together – this is our *first reaction* that precedes any kind of orientation.

Of course, the orientation begins immediately. However, it differs from what it would have been in daylight, when reality can contrast the imagination.

In the dark, we cannot see this reality; this inevitably limits us to what we imagine. Therefore, our orientation is also restricted to *what arises in our imagination at the first reaction*. More specifically: these fears and dangers do not dissipate. They remain, and we orient *in them*, in those pictures drawn by our imagination.

Nighttime in the forest, full of all sorts of surprises, brings the young traveler into a state of extreme sensitivity and receptivity. In such a state, every new experience captures a child's entire being. What occurs is some kind of a *shift* from the usual mundane reality to a semi-imaginary life.

Similarly, entering the atmosphere of creative life onstage immediately shifts a gifted actor from his usual, mundane state into creative state, where the imagination plays the main, the crucial role.

Alas, the stage does not always produce this effect on the actors. And not all actors, having entered the stage, experience this immediate *shift from the real life – to the imaginary*.

In this case, Stanislavsky offers a device he called "*what if.*" When an actor cannot make a switch from real to the imaginary and *believe* in the circumstances, given by the author,

Stanislavsky suggests the following thing. Don't worry about believing, he says, just ask yourself: what would happen *if* I really was such and such character, put in such and such circumstances? The *shift* occurs instantly – the actor feels his new "I" and the circumstances. But it lasts only a few seconds – not supported by anything, this sensation leaves as quickly as it comes.

What was it?

It was a flash of imagination; under its influence, for a second, all the circumstances came so *close* to me that they became tangible. My entire being felt them – the ***first reaction*** occurred.

This is our common reaction to a word or an idea, and it is inherent in absolutely everyone (not just actors). In Pavlov's terminology, it is a reaction to the "second-signal-system." As soon as we hear a word or think about some more or less acute sensation (the taste of lemon, the touch of something soft, cold, or slimy), this immediately stimulates our physiological response.

This is a normal reaction that does not require any specific abilities. This is confirmed by the fact that this device – "what if" – is offered at moments when the actor cannot enter the space of creative imagination or "believe in the circumstances," i.e. when he is not disposed to creativity.

The "what if" affects every human being with one important stipulation. An exceptionally gifted actor's reaction can seize his whole being and last a very long time; an average person's reaction, being weaker and not supported by an actual fact (after all, this reaction belongs purely to the imagination), soon fades and dies away.

On the Development of Imagination

Is it possible, however, to develop this ability, as we develop other necessary skills?

No doubt about it – *the ability to give in to the first reaction with its inherent imagination, sensations and manifestations, can be cultivated and developed.*

Mochalov [2000: 373] in his unfinished manuscript on the art of the actor writes: "Depth of soul and fiery imagination are two abilities that make up the major part of the actor's talent."

Theatre schools often use the following method in order to develop imagination. They give you a topic. (For example, you are a skydiver. You just made your first jump. Tell us – how did it go?) A student or several of them sit in chairs and fantasize on this topic. Sometimes this leads to quite coherent and even fascinating descriptions or stories.

But this is no way to develop the actor's imagination – rather the one of a storyteller, or, perhaps, that of a director, or someone like that. One's ability to make up stories or to communicate them in verbal, literary form falls short of the actor's imagination. The latter consists of organic perception of the imaginary world of the play, and in reacting to it with one's entire being – within the frame of the given role.

Improvisation on a given theme is yet another method they practice. This type of improvisation is closer to the realm of acting, as it is not descriptive or narrative – an actor lives and acts in it, while engaging in dialogues as far as necessary. Stanislavsky describes such improvisations in his book *An Actor's Work* in the chapter titled "Imagination."

The introduction of such kinds of improvisations in schools, especially when working with trained actors, often meets discontent. To submit to it, actors must first overcome some resistance, and coerce themselves – while the teacher convinces them that such improvisations are "very useful" and "necessary."

It is not that difficult to explain their resistance. These improvisations are not inherent to the art of acting. Actors are always given their lines, while here they are invited to partake in another art form. Not all actors are disposed to this art – the art of the writer, playwright, or the ancient actors of the Italian *commedia dell'arte*, who had to improvise their lines right there, onstage. The job of the *commedia* actors was made easier by the fact that they always played the same, familiar character. In these other improvisations, however, it was necessary, without preparation, to improvise the character, the entire situation, the actions, and the words.

All this is so difficult and, most importantly, foreign to the art of the actor, that they have to use all their will to carry on the forced role of the improviser. No wonder that, having dragged themselves, against their will, to the end of this alien affair, they sigh with relief.

On Faith and Naiveté

Stanislavsky, when speaking on the importance of "faith" in the actor's creative process, almost always added, "and naiveté." For him, "faith" and "naiveté" have always been linked together.

While often talking of the necessity of faith, he said very little about naiveté. He cited the example of children's play, and encouraged actors to follow their naivety and trustfulness. But what is naiveté, and how does one gain it, or at least come close to achieving it? What is clear is that the need for naiveté in our art is as great as the need for faith.

Let us see what distinguishes the adult from the child when it comes to naiveté. First of all, children believe everything and don't criticize – they accept the first thing they hear or see. Adults do not content themselves with this – they juxtapose everything they perceive with other known facts.

Therefore, a child's naiveté and trustfulness is, perhaps, nothing more than a tendency to give in to the first reaction.

A state of "faith," i.e. giving in to the imaginary, is one of the actor's chief qualities. To cultivate and develop it must be one of the chief tasks of our theatre pedagogy.

Like any quality—be it an athlete's muscular strength, the precision of movements essential for a musician and a skilled worker, or the actor's psychological technique – it should be developed gradually. It should start with small and feasible tasks, their difficulty increasing step by step, carefully and slowly.

A tightrope walker would, once again, make a good example. At first, he could hardly manage to stand on the wire for a single moment before he lost his balance. But gradually, balance is mastered; in the end, it becomes so familiar and easy that it requires no conscious effort.

The actor should be put in a similar situation. We must consistently, patiently, and persistently exercise and develop his ability to believe and give in to imaginary circumstances, however insignificant this ability may be at the start.

The beginning of faith is naiveté, while the basis of naiveté is the first reaction – that very first reaction, which appears immediately when we receive an impression. There, in the first reaction, lies the *source of creative imagination and faith*. Therefore, we should hold on to the first reaction, as to a real, concrete possibility to develop imagination, and with it, the creative naiveté and faith in all circumstances of a play and a role.

To give in to the first reaction means to cultivate a specific actor's imagination and the needed naive faith in the circumstances.

As for strengthening imagination and faith, it's necessary to green-light them, and the evoked reactions. This we already know.

In addition – and this is also very important – this art of giving in to the primary reaction hides the secret of *expressivity*. Actors whose every thought and feeling can be read in their faces do not inhibit their primary, involuntary reactions. Such actors don't have to worry whether what they experience will "reach the audience" or not. They are so open, so transparent that their inner life is visible in their face and body, in every word and movement.

Practical Methods of Developing Free Reaction

Just as in other fields, we also need to begin by identifying the correct and necessary reflexes of our creative process, and then develop those. In doing so, we might discover that many of the reflexes formed by everyday life that are quite suitable in mundane situations have to be restructured and retrained for the stage. As an example, most beginning actors are disturbed and distracted by the presence of an audience. We need to make sure that the audience, on the contrary, inspires their creative state and focuses them on the circumstances of the play and the role. This reflex, necessary for the actor, does not appear immediately and grows with practice.

Another example: giving in to the first reaction is completely unnatural for us in life – in creative work, however, it is essential, and this habit must also be developed.

A true school of acting consists of the skillful cultivation of creative reflexes; it restructures existing reflexes and develops new one, which are specific for the stage.

The experience of working in theatre schools has taught me that the *development of creative freedom cannot be postponed until the time when students have learned the other aspects of acting*.

This is why we begin this work *from the first day of our classes*.

During the first lessons at school (or in the first rehearsals), I am completely satisfied when the students, having extinguished their first urge, "green-lit" the second or third. So be it. As long as they dared "green-light" something. As long as they have experienced in practice what "green-lighting" feels like.

When this experience strengthens, I lead the student to the *first impulse*, nearer to his true nature, to the first reaction.

And now I will describe one of the special exercises as we practice it in the classroom.

Before us is a class of students. You ask them to sit as calmly and freely as they can, anticipating nothing, and not preparing for anything at all. You tell them in advance that, at some point, you will say a word or two. As soon as they hear these words, they should feel free to do what they want, allowing movements and actions to come on their own.

Then, having chosen the right moment, you name something that would cause a sensation – for example, "wind, strong cold wind." The students immediately begin to shiver, to wrap themselves up, to make movements aimed at warming up; they go to pick up a scarf, or a wrap, to close the window, if it is open . . . And some, having immediately made a barely perceptible movement, won't "green-light" it further. The movement would stop; the life, having just begun, would die out . . . and the reaction would end there.

I do not recommend saying words aimed at a very strong reaction. Externally, they do produce a great effect, but starting with them is harmful. Going forward, I also would not recommend using them excessively. For example, you can say "fire!" Everyone would jump up, scream, make a lot of noise and run around . . . But this would contradict our goal – to develop and refine the students' sensitivity and reaction, so that they could receive a distinct, real, and sufficiently strong physiological *sensation* from seemingly insignificant words.

You can vary this exercise as much as necessary. Instead of saying one-two words, you can speak an entire phrase. You can speak with a different feeling. You can not speak at all, but instead show some object or picture; you can turn on or switch off the light, make sound by dropping an object, tapping it, breaking a stick or tearing paper, and so on. Endless possibilities.

Some students may deceive you unwittingly – so be ready for it. As soon as you say, "cold wind," a student like this would leap up to his feet, begin to warm up, move, hide from the wind . . . From lack of experience, you would think, "What an excellent, quick reaction; such easy, dynamic nature; such brilliant imagination!" – while in actuality, this may not be a reaction coming from genuine sensations, but rather from typical pushing. Not life, but an intellectual idea. He said "cold wind" – this means I must bundle up, warm myself, hide from the wind, etc. The better he does it, the more enthusiasm he exhibits – the more likely he is to deceive you and himself. And, therefore, the more hopelessly he would *pollute* the most important – the *first moment* of his imagination, of his spontaneous physiological sensations and his surrender to them.

Perhaps, having realized how important it is to cultivate free reaction, the actors would acquire a taste for these exercises and want to practice independently, at home. [Prior to starting these exercises, students should review the first chapter, this chapter, and chapters titled "On the Beginning" (Part Two, Chapter 10) and "The Role of Automatic Movements . . . " (Part Three, Chapter 17), "Don't Interfere with Living" (Part Three, Chapter 18), "Carelessness" (Part Three, Chapter 19) and "Perception" (Part Three, Chapter 22). Having done this, they should gently get down to work. These first reaction exercises can be practiced both at home, individually, and in rehearsals. – *Author's Note*] What follows is a brief description of the technique behind these exercises. There is no need to brace yourself, or spur yourself on; on the contrary: loosen all those strings we keep wound up tight in everyday life – *let yourself go*. We always live with unnoticed, unconscious muscular contractions, with tension and stiffness – all this should be removed. After that, do not interfere with anything: you feel like sitting down – go ahead; you are in the mood to move – be my guest . . . Give way to everything. Do not interfere with your nature: you are feeling bored – so be it; annoyed – give freedom to that too.

At the same time, *do not push* – just *don't abstract* anything! Don't abstract your life and manifestations, as they occur **in your whole being**. Give in to them.

Here are some techniques that help to carry out this training.

Make several lists. Each list should contain over 50 various topics. One list may feature general topics, assigning certain sensations: hot . . . cold . . . lying in a warm bath . . . I sit on a wet surface, and so on. Another list would consist of topics featuring more complex circumstances: someone just knocked on my window . . . inside a ship's cabin . . . in a one-man cell . . . I am expecting a phone call . . . I am expecting the arrival of a loved one . . . and so on. Let me stipulate once more: in no way should you be choosing powerful and provocative topics. Otherwise, the results would be as with the topic of "fire."

Write down these topics one under the other to form a tall column. The exercise technique is as following: pick up a sheet with a column of topics, and – to receive an unexpected impression – put your finger on the sheet at random, without looking. Then see what you've got. Suppose your finger landed on "mosquito bites" – immediately, without a moment's thought, yield to involuntary sensations, movements, thought – to everything that comes to you as a reaction to these two words.

Don't rush to move to the next topic until you've exhausted the previous one. Rest for a few minutes, and then take up another theme.

No need to exercise many topics – otherwise you would get accustomed to reacting approximately, anyhow. This won't be truth, but rather skimming on the surface of truth – one of the worst evils for an actor . . .

Here is another variety of exercises at home, without a partner. Calmly sit down, (lay down or stay standing), and then let every miniscule, almost imperceptible impulse and small movement develop freely.

And don't *choose* the impulses: "this one is a go, I like it; this one is not worth following." On the contrary, yield to whatever comes first; let them flow on their own, as if without any participation on your part. Just let them change one another. As these impulses develop, they will probably engage your whole being, with your entire intellectual and emotional apparatus – do not interfere with this either.

Please take a note: do not do these exercises for an extended period of time; be sure to take breaks, and rest between exercises.

These exercises train the actor to inhibit himself less and less in his creative work – to give in to his creative impulses more, and with greater ease.

But how could this happen? After all, these exercises are not done using creative material; the actors don't "green-light" their impulses in a play, but rather in an etude. One-on-one with himself, the actor does "what he wants to" or gives in to his reaction that occurs under the influence of some words or thoughts. In other words, he obeys impressions transmitted through the second-signal-system. All this does not seem to have any connection to the process of creativity.

This is how it is on the surface. In actuality, however, the process at the heart of these exercises is fundamentally different from ordinary, mundane life – which is what makes it creative.

Many hours a day we allow ourselves to "do what we want" unrestrictedly – be it when we are alone, or in the company of our loved ones. We do this without noticing. Before the start of these exercises, however, we subconsciously say to ourselves: "My life is about to flow on its own, and I won't interfere." By doing so, we create a **shift**. From our usual, mundane state we transit to another in which a person not only gives himself freedom, but on top of it, his consciousness doubles. He lives, acts, and at the same time something in him oversees these actions, thoughts, and feelings. He monitors them and, to some extent, can even influence their course. In other words, under the guise of exercising his freedom to "do what you want," he trains in the essence of our creative process – in the **creative duality of consciousness**.

The same thing happens when you exercise with a list of different topics. After all, prior to all these exercises, an actor always has a certain preliminary task: "Now I shall practice giving in to the first reaction." Therefore, the transition into the state of doubling has already been made; what is left now is to stay in it further.

A Few Additional Thoughts on the Importance of Free Reaction

This "freedom of reaction" ("green-lighting"), might seem, at a first glance, a mere pedagogic device. This is not true.

At the heart of it all is **the very beginning**. Creativity enters our theatre work more often than we think. However, it is merely perceptible at its inception: "I just happened to think this," "I just did it for some reason" . . .

These subtle manifestations – be they movements, feelings, or thoughts, or some vague general sensations – they are not random. They are the *result of an assignment*, the result of impressions from the play, the result of thoughts about the given circumstances. They carry the most value. Let them develop, and they will grow to their full size. But we consider them trifles – something interfering, distracting us from our direct cause.

Such an attitude *towards this crucial moment*, skipping, oversight, and a complete disregard for it – this is what has so far been inhibiting the development of the actor's creative technique.

The most talented actors, at their own initiative, intuitively do not quench this moment and let it develop. As for those teachers and directors who need to "stage a production," rather than nurture the actor's creative process – they do their best to get around this *moment of uncertainty and ambiguity* and quickly hurry to intercept it with precise and specific "actions" and "tasks." In short, they go for intentional "activity," instead of these bursts of spontaneous manifestations that come out of the artists' soul.

Some may say, you never know what you might "want," and what might "come"- what if this is all wrong?

This is not a difficult question, and it has been already answered in part: haven't you forgotten the preliminary "assigning," familiarity with the text of the play, and the "given circumstances?" Put together, they direct what "comes," what you "feel like doing," and what is "done on its own."

If, in spite of "assigning" and acquaintance with the text, the actor does something wrong, it is not hard to fix. Reminding the actors of the circumstances they overlooked appears to be enough. It is important, however, that the actors, while perceiving these new circumstances, immediately "green-light" their first reaction – the one instigated by the first impulse. At such a point, these new circumstances would merge with what was there before, without violating the creative process.

At times, a free reaction ("green-lighting") bursts through on its own. It does not happen at the start of the run, bur after the play has been performed over thirty times or so. With time, the actors cease to strictly execute their assigned actions and tasks, and gradually give in to spontaneous impulses.

Finally, freedom and ease *come with experience*. The main difference between experienced actors and beginners is that beginners are bound, tense, they've got hundreds of "musts," while the experienced actors feel at home onstage. Their 20 years in the theatre made them that free. As was mentioned in the first chapter, why wait 20 years when this can be accomplished much earlier? Rather than finishing with it, we must make it our *starting point*!

24
Braking

Braking – in Life and in the Creative Process

Much has been said of the actor's tendency to "not green-light," to "inhibit." The words "braking system" have been used.

To gain a tangible understand of the human "braking system," we must trace it down to its roots – how it was formed and why.

It all begins almost from the first days of our life.

A baby reaches for anything he sees – especially colorful and bright things. If you don't keep an eye on him, he could grab a burning candle, a sharp object . . .

He would grab it once, twice; in the end, he would learn from bitter experience to stop in time. The urge would still be there from the start, but the next moment would see *something stopping him*, slowing down his movement. His hands, instead of reaching for the tempting object, would resist the urge.

Later, due to the same painful experience, he will stop putting any random thing in his mouth. And over time, he would learn to watch his every word, every movement, and even every thought.

Thus a person, little by little, develops a reflexive braking system. He inhibits and checks everything, in case it might be harmful. Similarly, he inhibits his perception, as well as his reaction.

No matter how delighted he may be – he won't rush to you with open arms. If his hands, without asking permission, begin to move toward you, at the same moment some inner mechanism would pull them back down. The impulse has been neutralized, and restricted to a calm welcoming smile.

And good thing, too! Is it really possible to be so excitable, spontaneous and openhearted?

Composure, self-control, restraint – these are universally recognized virtues, indispensable in our everyday life. It is impossible to conceive a man completely devoid of this ability of self-restraint, always acting and speaking on the first impulse, without thinking. We would not hesitate to say that this man is abnormal, unfit for life.

In short, the braking system is not only useful and necessary for our lives – it is essential. But, of course, like with all things, one should seek moderation.

And yet, this very braking system – so necessary in our everyday life – turns into a serious obstacle as soon as we go onstage.

Among actors, there are plenty of people who are inhibited in their art. Some inhibitions result from their psychological makeup; others are developed by a wrong school.

People say about such actors: he is "tense," "stiff," or he is "not in touch with his emotions," or "cold." And sometimes they simply say: "he is no actor." Actors, who are deprived of spontaneity, "flammability," and quick responsiveness, are truly inadequate – a bit like a runner with aching and weak legs. These actors originated the "theory" that it is not enough to feel onstage – you must also be able to demonstrate your feeling to the audience. For this purpose you must be able to "land" your feelings – otherwise the audience will never "get it."

In order to destroy this common misconception, in practice, by a living example, you must expose the hidden mechanism of this phenomenon. So, I would call one of the most reserved and "closed off" students "onstage," and offer her a rather intense etude. For convenience, to avoid incoherence, I would also offer concrete circumstances.

- Yesterday you were at a dress rehearsal. I seem to remember you both liked the role of Iago . . .
- Oh, no, – interrupts the girl – he liked it, and I find Iago disgusting . . . I cannot accept him. Othello – that's a man! That's the kind of role I would love to play!
- All right. Let's take something similar. Here is an etude for you . . . The theme is not current, but yesterday's Othello already transported your imagination away from the present day. You won't have a problem connecting with the old times, when the powerful and rich could get away with torturing the unfortunates – destroying them, slandering them, shutting them up in prison . . .
  Some time ago, he (I pointing to her partner) brought you and your entire family to utter poverty and humiliation. (No wonder he was so taken with Iago.)
  Fortunately, things have changed, and he himself has fallen on hard times. Now that you have forgotten all about him, and do not expect to see him ever again, he has found you and pays you a visit, like a good old neighbor.
  The text is such and such.

Let us suppose that the etude comes to a safe end, and no glaring mistakes have been made. Nevertheless, it does not reach the "high pitch," as expected.

- Well, how did you feel?
- I felt good . . . At the start, I was lost in thought and got really scared when he came in . . . I did not expect him. So, I got scared . . . and then annoyed and angry . . . And he, with his sentimental, disgusting smile, comes to me with his greetings . . . And this is after all he had done to us! My heart was pounding . . .
- And when he said that he keeps no record of wrongs and bears no grudge against you? . . .
- Ooh! How do I describe it?! – she interrupts me. – I could not catch my breath. I felt indignation, resentment . . . I did not know what to say, what to do . . .
- Really? Why the outrage? . . . I thought he came to make peace, he was quite sincere and . . .
- Peace? . . . Are you kidding me??! How about kicking him downstairs?! I can't stand the sight of him!

Two minutes ago this actress, although somewhat agitated, acted her etude with modesty and restraint. Now she is excited, flushed; she is gesturing, and can't keep still in her chair; she can't let go; she is spitting harsh words.

- You see – I turn to the students – she got quite worked up. And, of course, she is telling the truth: she did feel all that. But how did it happen that we did not see it? It was clear that she was uncomfortable and upset. But who could have thought she lost her temper to that extent . . . Maybe, in fact, it's not enough to feel – you must also know how to *demonstrate* your feeling?

  Not at all. We did not see her true feelings only because she would not green-light them and kept it all inside. Now she is "green-lighting," so we can see them, though she is not trying to "demonstrate" her feelings to us. If she did not control herself, what an exciting and powerful etude it would have been!

  Instead of being concerned with *landing* our feelings, we should only worry about *"green-lighting" these feelings – but fully, to the end.*

- I do not quite understand – interrupts one of the students, – I think she had no certain feelings as of yet. His arrival was so unexpected, in the first minute she couldn't put two and two together. What is there to "green-light?" Just some confusion inside.

- That's right – confusion inside, and no definite feeling as of yet . . . Since you've noticed such intricate details, perhaps you can try to figure out what she should have done, and what would come out of it?

First he feels embarrassed, but soon sees that I am not trying to catch him, but just want them to learn how to find their own way out of difficult situations. By this time, they have had enough experience with the technique.

After some hesitation, he does give a correct analysis of this case. Here is the essence of his discovery: as soon as the partner entered, the actress instantly recognized him and immediately began to relate to him as to her enemy. In the meantime, the suddenness of his visit made her feel all confused. She was seized by a moment of panic: what am I to do?

This confusion and panic point to some strong feeling (a great catch for the actor), and you just need to give it way and not interfere. For this, first of all, one needs to "take time" while in a state of inner turmoil. It would subside after a few seconds, and in its place a feeling of burning animosity would form – the initial natural reaction of the actress. After the feeling defines itself, she simply has to green-light it.

From lack of experience – she did not recognize the true value of this panic as one of the first stages of a strong creative emotion. Instead of using it – reflexively, hastily she gave way to the first available defence mechanism. For her, this was her habitual way of inhibiting everything inside. And that's what she did. Hence her coldness and haughtiness in dealing with her visitor.

Having found out, by common efforts, which mistakes the actress had made and how she should have behaved – let us return to where we left off.

So, I repeat: instead of thinking about "landing" our feelings by means of seeking their expressive outer manifestations, we should worry about *"green-lighting" these feelings in full, completely*.

Every feeling, especially a strong one, is always connected with its manifestations. An involuntary movement of a hand, a smile of joy or a hostile frown, eyes beaming with wrath – immediately reveal our feelings, thoughts, and attitudes.

And so, to stop our manifestations from betraying us, we inhibit them. As for the feelings – we cannot extinguish them, just as we cannot immediately put out the fiery glimpse in our eyes. As for stopping crude movements – that we can easily do. This is where we begin.

And once we stop some of the manifestations of feelings, in doing so, we change the feeling itself – it's no longer the same.

When people with such habits get onstage, they begin to behave according to their life habits (staying within the "permissible" and "modest" bounds). Their feelings, having been deadened from the start, naturally "do not reach" us.

In the meantime, *landing* the feeling is a sure way to kill it, and it cannot be actors' concern. Instead, actors should take care of being infinitely free in their creative process of "green-lighting" all emerging thoughts, sensations, desires, and actions. These will then grow to the extent where one cannot help but see them. Otherwise, they die out from the start.

Convulsion and Spasms as a Consequence of Inhibition

There are many actors, who can satisfactorily cope with all sorts of "calm" roles – those not requiring great emotional power. But as soon as they take on a role that requires great depth, spontaneity, and passion, they immediately discover their powerlessness and superficiality.

Their psychological apparatus appears to be made out of poor and brittle material. It cannot withstand more or less significant stress – it bends, creases, or tears under pressure . . . This impression is often true.

In other cases, this does not result from the actors' lack of power, but rather from their overdeveloped "brakes." As soon as the pressure increases, the breaking system kicks in. The circumstances of the role do not reach the actor; and neither does his own excitement (even if it awakens). It does not find an exit and stays inside the actor; invisible to anyone, it dies out, like fire deprived of air.

In all such cases, actors are faced with a choice. The most intelligent and honest of them do not take up such backbreaking roles.

Others – those, who are given no choice or do not care – are forced to cleverly deceive the audience with stage "tricks," or to explicitly evoke neuroticism and engage in hysterics . . .

I feel so sorry for these actors. They use a mere tenth part of their potential, hidden powers.

Yet, it is truly heartbreaking to see an actor who has power and depth, and the ability to easily ignite his passions, to still be controlled by these brakes.

A few days ago (quite apropos) I saw one actress . . . Based on her inborn talent, she apparently belongs to the type of impulsive, emotional actors, capable of deep feelings and psychological "explosions." Yet, she went through the rational, analytical and "imperative" school, unsuitable for her talent. On one side, her natural talent remained undeveloped; on the other, the school she trained in could not take root in the foreign soil of her soul.

And now this actress is constantly struggling with herself. Flashes of passion keep bursting from her inner depths; yet . . . they have to be subjected to precise inner and outer patterns – such is the requirement of her school . . . Never mind that her inner content today is much greater than before, and it no longer fits in the established pattern – to break the pattern is unthinkable. Like it or not, you have to adjust to it.

How can she do this? To begin with, she must probably cut herself down, refrain from new and bold manifestations – to inhibit them all . . . Before you know it, her inner flashes have been inhibited, one by one. Yet, they are not extinguished; they remain inside – unused, unrealized . . . They accumulate, pile on top of each other . . . this cluster wants to break out . . .

The actress is bursting from inside . . . Were she able to set in motion this tremendous emotional charge, we would see explosions worthy of great actors, of Strepetova and Yermolova. But she has been taught very differently. This precious stream, finding no way out, completely choked her – she shrank into herself from tension, her voice became hoarse, not so much from yelling as from the spasm of her throat muscles . . .

Watching her makes your head ache. As an audience member subconsciously imitates the actor, you also begin to strain, choke and fight with your own self.

Who taught her these terrible, ugly expressions? No one. This happens on its own.

She needs a completely different school, one that would grant her total freedom – freedom of both perception and expression.

Some Types of Inhibition

Withdrawal into coldness and insensitivity

There are other cases. The actor rehearses truthfully and well; the scene is developing, becoming more and more intense – it is approaching the most crucial moment. As a director, you expect two possible things: the actor will either get scared, contract, and lapse into yelling, tension, and "clutching of fists," or else he will safely pass this treacherous point . . . Suddenly something quite unexpected occurs: an actor grows cold, becomes empty, dull, and indifferent – he drops out of the creative state. Tell him what you will – nothing works.

Sometimes, he tries to rouse himself, but . . . to no avail. As if a deep river was running, but suddenly – the water is gone. Gone without a single trace. It must have disappeared through sinkholes, continuing underground, as is the case with some rivers.

What has happened? Foreseeing a dangerous place, the actor unintentionally applied the brakes. The trapdoor has closed, and not a single drop leaks in or out.

The director struggles with such an actor for a while and, not having experience in these matters, decides: this is an untalented, insensitive man. Why did he ever bother to become an actor!

But this is not the point. Apparently, the actor, fearing his unprecedented and seemingly risky feeling, abruptly "slammed his foot on the brakes."

He started with something small and mundane; it grew as the scene progressed. The actor became excited, as something grand and wild emerged from the depths of his soul. So grand and wild, in fact, that it feels scary . . . Out of this fear arose anxiety and haste . . . This grand and fearsome thing is no longer just approaching – it is springing at him, like a hurricane. He is horrified; another second, and he won't be able to withstand it – he will fail . . . Suddenly, beyond his will, something inside him clicks, like a protective device. At this moment, he becomes someone else (as if someone replaced the man) – calm and indifferent. For an actor, this equals creative death.

To teach him how to skillfully avoid such a dangerous spot, we use the saving measures already known to us, such as "support" and "take your time."

It's coming nearer! . . . it's dashing at me . . . it's huge!! I am awe-struck! . . . We must seize the moment when the actor feels awe-struck – it is the turning point. If the actor cannot withstand it – this either leads to terror and panic or to brakes and coldness. At that point, all is lost. An actor who withstands this moment, braces himself and mobilizes. Out of nowhere, come unprecedented power, composure, and calm. In such a state, he can perform heroic feats, miracles – he can succeed beyond his wildest dreams.

Seize this moment. Be prepared – listen to the actor, penetrated his inmost soul. When you feel that he is on the verge of hesitating, calmly and firmly (though, perhaps softly, barely audibly – depending on the situation) reinforce him: "That's it, that's it . . . correct, absolutely correct . . . " He will grow stronger. So will his emotion and excitement! . . . Once again, you say: "Very good! . . . excellent! . . . well done, this is good – take your time!.. Just let it happen – don't interfere! . . . "

Sensing the subtlest shifts and fluctuations in the soul of the actor, monitoring every dangerous moment, support and guide his apparatus – powerful, as never before, but also sensitive and also as obedient as ever. With some practice, you shall see that mastering this skill of a facilitator is a worthwhile endeavor.

Hidden Forms of Inhibition

This form of inhibition is rather crude – even an inexperienced eye can see that the student is "not green-lighting." Yet, there are other forms of inhibition that are easy to miss or mistake for something completely different.

Let us discuss these cases.

"Good Manners"

Using the methods described, a student (or actor) quickly gets rid of the brakes and of the unnecessary effort.

Here is an actress, formerly timid, unsure of herself. Look how easy and free she feels! The etude has ended, and . . . you have no notes for her – it was good; it was true.

Satisfied, she goes back to her seat and begins to watch the next couple.

But what is wrong with her? She is flushed, agitated, frantically squeezing her handkerchief. She is on the verge of tears . . . What is the matter?

The answer is quite simple: she did not "*green-light*" her life in the etude. It is obvious that she had much, much more inside! But she did not give it free rein – it stayed inside and is now bursting to come out.

This means that her freedom was quite deceptive.

Try talking to her during a break – you will learn a lot of interesting things.

- At first, when the etude just ended, I felt that things went well. But soon I became restless . . . my restlessness kept growing . . . I saw that I was not quite doing what I was supposed to.
- What do you mean?
- When he asked, "So you're that very Lyolia?.. And we used to be friends, when we were six-seven years old?" – he looked at me with such openness and kindness . . . I felt all cozy and warm from that look . . . I remembered my late mother . . . our little house with windows looking onto the Volga . . . my childhood . . . He became so close . . . I don't really have any close friends, just acquaintances . . . and suddenly . . . Somewhere deep inside I felt such comfort and joy! . .

  Why didn't I go straight to him with this joyful excitement, take him by the hand, or something like that?.. Instead, I turned away and walked to the window . . .

Listening to her story, you will realize that two people kept living in her all this time. One – tender, simple, open, weary of loneliness, and longing for sympathy; the other – discreet, "good mannered," and mistrustful. Her genuine, sincere self she hid inside and gave way to her other self – reserved and pleasantly proper. The etude turned out quite well, without a single mistake. Yet, what was most intimate in her was held back and suppressed.

She feels frustrated and anxious . . . This is a good thing . . . However, do not frighten her, do not tell her that she made a mistake. She truly did not make one – she did "green-light" her freedom, just not enough . . . She allowed as much freedom as one does in everyday life – within the boundaries of modesty and restraint. Tell her instead that the etude was done correctly (it truly was); however, since something more powerful and bold is rising from her depths, it is time to give way to these new, unfamiliar urges – they are more important and exciting. Next time, just be bold, take a chance.

For your part, you now need to keep a keen eye on her. As soon as she begins to waver in an etude (or a scene) – look out! Help her without delay!

The Mask of Sincerity

This following kind of actor is highly deceptive. (In this particular case, his human qualities usually coincide with the quality of acting.) The first things that strike you in this person are his extraordinary sincerity and simplicity. His eyes look at you with such openness and directness that you feel that you can see his very soul through these serene and clear eyes. He carries himself so directly, with such empathy and child-like simplicity.

However, upon closer acquaintance, you realize that these are just appearances – he is actually very cold, callous, and self-contained.

He is no different onstage: at first, he impresses you with honesty and directness. Upon a closer look, as you penetrate his essence, you discover nothing of this kind, and you feel that his directness and sincerity are mere pretense.

He is so inhibited and so closed – he does not permit any impressions *inside*, let alone green-lighting involuntary manifestations or reactions. He looks at you with his open, trusting eyes . . . Yet, don't let him deceive you into thinking that everything you say and what he sees enters his soul – it does not.

In the end, you find his affected sincerity to be unbearable, if not disgusting.

This actor won't blush or grow pale at the end of an etude, "finishing the scene," while back in his seat – he has nothing to finish: he never had anything and never will, except for appearances.

★★★

Is it possible to fight one's brakes?

What if there is no keeping them in check – these precious helpers and guardians of ours? What if, while wanting to do us good (to protect us from all our rash impulses), they totally deprive us of all spontaneity and freedom? In this case, our situation in art is pretty sad.

You can fight them. You can, and you should. This entire book speaks of this, starting with the first lesson.

Inhibition, as Part of the Creative Process

Since inhibition is so bad for the creative process, you might think that true creativity has nothing to do with it at all. On the contrary: not only is it included in a creative act – it **takes place all the time**.

However, it is quite different in its essence.

First of all, the actor knows that his experience onstage, his "life" there, is play, art, and not a reality. This awareness, on one hand, instigates greater freedom (fear of repercussions is not as severe onstage, as in life), and, on the other, decisively inhibits a lot of things.

To begin with – over one hundred people are watching him. Here it is – the true reality. And, it is surely the most important part. Theatre without an audience, without a single viewer, loses all its meaning.

This impression, however, must be **inhibited** a bit, so as to give priority to what is onstage – to this environment, spiced up with my imagination: the circumstances given by the author, my partners, and my own character.

Secondly, there is another undeniable fact that I also cannot freely allow – the fact that I entered the stage as an actor.

However (let's not forget transformation!), it's not exactly me, but the character in the play. To put it differently – it is me, but in such unusual circumstances, with such uncharacteristic qualities and manifestations, that it does not really look like me. My personal "I" with all my likes and dislikes, habits and characteristic features, is also inhibited. Other qualities come to the forefront – if not completely alien, then so expanded and exaggerated, that I become completely unrecognizable (from thriftiness – to avarice, and then – to Plyushkin-the-miser).

Because of this phenomenon, many of my usual brakes become removed; at the same time, new brakes appear in those areas where I usually give myself complete freedom.

When playing Nozdryov [Another iconic Russian character from Gogol's *Dead Souls*, Nozdryov is a common name for a rowdy fellow – a boor, troublemaker and a brawler] or anyone else, I perceive everything and react to it differently from my usual self. My feelings, thoughts and actions are now based on my notion of these characters, on my "images" of these characters . . . For example, when playing Nozdryov, I give myself the kind of freedom I would inhibit in my personal life, and vice versa – I hold a lot of my own impulses, because for Nozdryov (whom I now play) they are alien and atypical.

Thus, the brakes, although they are active at all times, do not belong to me personally, but seemingly to Nozdryov.

Finally (thirdly), I cannot get carried away to the point of complete oblivion – at least, not in all moments of my life onstage. There are plays where a character, in a fit of anger, despair, or revenge – kills, poisons, strangles, or throws off a height his enemy or himself. Can you practice full, unrestricted freedom at such moments?

There is a limit to everything.

Hence, inhibition is not only possible during creative work – *it features in the very process of creativity* as an integral part of actors' creative experience.

Given all this, we still must be concerned with greater freedom of our creative expression, as opposed to inhibition. Then our perception, as well as our reactions and our inhibitions, will be fully consistent with the notion of the character we embody.

25

Stepping on It

We have gotten acquainted, more or less, with the error of *inhibition*. There is another mistake, diametrically opposed to it, which consists of *stepping on it*. Actors, feeling an urge of some kind, are afraid to miss the moment. So, they *step on it*, urging themselves to move ahead of the next moment, before it ever arrived.

We know this error well, and we even know how to fight it: "Take your time."

This is stepping on it *"time-wise"*: you feel that things are moving too slowly, so you step on it: let's move on!

You don't feel like speaking just yet, but you squeeze out the lines all the same; you don't feel like moving, yet you force yourself to get up and walk . . . You saw or heard something new and unusual . . . so new, in fact, you are still trying to fathom what is going on . . . In the meantime, your inner voice tells you: "There is no time for that! Move it, move it!" And you force out *surprise*. You are yet to become surprised – you are yet to even understand what is before you. But the actor onstage feels that things are taking too long: let's skip straight to surprise!

And so, skipping all the usual stages of the normal reaction, the actor hits the highlights, breaking all the natural laws.

Besides stepping on it time-wise, there is also stepping on it *"strength-wise."*

The actor feels that everything he experiences, says or does is too subtle and weak – it should be stronger. And so he steps on it, nudging himself: intensity, power!

This turns into "pushing," as theatre people refer to it. We can "step on" walking, and go faster than before; we can "step on it" and hit the table top with our fist stronger than we have hit so far. However, could we use such primitive means to force ourselves to feel stronger?

Reasons Behind "Stepping on It"

It all seems so obvious, so undeniable . . . Meanwhile, actors, in their vast majority, either do not know any of this or do not want to know. With a clear conscience, they step on it, spur themselves, push . . .

What is this? Thoughtlessness? Primitiveness?

There is a measure of that, of course, and not a small measure. And yet, there are also justifications.

The fact that – as has been said before – the stage, the limelight, the music, a crowd of people in the audience, the excitement backstage – all this whips up the nervous system, causing its increased excitation and hypersensitivity. The balance is destroyed.

Add to this the involuntary thoughts of a man facing an audience (he might not notice these thoughts, yet they exist): "I've come to the stage, so I must be **doing** something. People have gathered; they are watching, waiting for me to do something exceptional and engaging . . . "

Anxiety and effort come involuntarily. An actor tries to sit better, to speak livelier, to gesture more expressively, to feel stronger; or, on the contrary, he tries hard to be more "natural" onstage – "simpler" or "more truthful" . . .

In the meantime, there are also those actors who undergo a different process when going onstage. Having done their fair share of worrying backstage, they make a great effort and enter. As they cross the stage threshold – all of a sudden they strangely calm down. They look at everything around them with new eyes; they are seized by feelings of faith and truth . . . At the same time, they feel elated and joyful . . .

This is a manifestation of true talent, a sign that for these people the stage is their element, and the presence of the audience does not throw them off; on the contrary, it mobilizes all their creative powers.

A moment comes, however, and something knocks the actors out of this marvelous state.

At such a point, all-too-familiar feelings of unease and anxiety attack them. With it, come things such as "demanding from themselves," "trying too hard," with all their consequences . . .

There is no actor who is not familiar with this painful experience . . .

Beauty and Credibility of Truth

To find a natural experience in the conditions of the stage, the actor must, first and foremost, discard all involuntary effort.

It must be well understood that **nothing should be added** – what is taking place in you is quite enough. Whatever you feel, it is all visible – this includes your embarrassment before the audience, your inhibited state, your efforts to conceal and alter your true feelings, and your desire to convey something else to the audience – in short, all the negative and artificial things you are hoping to hide. The opposite is also true: if you are spontaneous and free, this is also visible . . . The truth is visible.

This is why the only thing one must worry about is the truth of living (in accordance with the circumstances of the play) and freely giving in to his own manifestations.

Life can slip in some striking cases, as if saying – look, here you have, side by side, truth and falsehood, beauty and ugliness, spontaneous life and the most vile pushing. Astonishingly, you see all that in the same person.

A new leading lady has been admitted to the troupe. Today, in the presence of all the actors, she joins the rehearsals of a new play, in which she plays a village seductress, *la belle Italienne*.

The rehearsal takes place in a large hall. The actors are solemnly sitting along the walls; she is among them. Opening scenes are rehearsed first. She sits there waiting, excited . . . Today is the day. If she is lucky, this will secure her position at the capital-city company. If she is unlucky – things could turn out differently . . . Her eyes are lit with excitement, and she is what they call "chomping at the bit" with impatience.

Her turn. Slightly pale, she gets up . . . We can see everything inside her mobilize and gather in one lump: it's now or never!

She looks everyone over, throws a shawl from one shoulder – over to the other, carelessly tosses her purse on the chair . . . Then she turns to her partner . . . She stares straight at his face for so long that he gets embarrassed, and then she goes straight to him across the room.

She walks calmly, slowly, stepping like a strong beautiful beast, playing with the edge of her shawl . . . Everyone freezes: it is brilliant! It surpasses all expectations. If that's just the beginning, can you imagine how she will spread her wings next! Everyone sits spellbound and conquered . . . What strength and ease! . . . What a genuine, lively, attractive . . . and dangerous woman! She comes up to her partner – now we are up for something awesome . . .

Suddenly she turns to the director and asks him with an inconspicuous smile on her lips:

- Can I begin?
- Yes, yes! Absolutely! I thought that you have already started . . .
- No, I have not started just yet.

She makes some kind of an effort, forcing an unnaturally upright posture, raising her head "heroically" . . . She begins . . . and drowns us all in a stream of theatrical clichés . . .

Actors often cannot imagine how beautiful they are onstage – how convincing and artistically captivating – when they do not add anything, do not impose anything on themselves, but live – simply live as they feel like living.

Nor can they imagine how far they are from their goal when they are stepping on it, forcing, interfering, and ordering themselves . . . Then they are pitiful, helpless, and not at all convincing or attractive to the viewer.

But they are not aware of this. On the contrary, they are quite sure that, when they try hard, they are irresistible.

On Retraining

Is this a spoiled actress? – Very much so. – Is she fit for serious work in her current condition? – No. Does she exhibit some signs of talent? – Definitely. Moreover, she exhibits the signs of great talent. Can this ridiculous husk be removed from her? – Of course. A large part of her talent is still intact; it did not have time to perish; as for the inner fire – she has enough for two.

What became of her in the end?

Nothing much. An ordinary actress. – How so? – They began removing the "husk." Husk removed, they not only forgot to awaken new freedom and spontaneity in her; they dampened what she already had. In the end, she turned out like in the Russian saying "a pie without a filling."

As for the "husk," they should not have bothered with it at all. Instead, they should have encouraged her *genuine nature*; the husk would have fallen off on its own with nothing to hold on to.

In this case, the actress was unlucky – she fell into the wrong hands.

But is it possible at all to "*retrain*" an actor?

Why would it be impossible? For some, it is even very easy. No matter how hard someone tries to break them, artistic truth is still in their veins. As soon as they sense the right path, they rush straight to it, driven by their instinct.

Besides, they have suffered so and grown so tired of an alien atmosphere – they rush to a new path with redoubled force, at a mere sign of deliverance.

Things may be different when it comes to people who are not gifted, but just have some abilities. They find it difficult. Firstly, they are more easily satisfied with what they can already do. They could care less if their art is far from perfection – this is because they have no craving for *genuine* art. True talent cannot live without it, but simple "ability" can. Talent does not tolerate compromise, but "ability" and mediocrity is all compromise.

And so, at the sight of some sort of semblance of success, not suffering too much because of a lack of perfection, they do not see the need to search and to change . . .

Why bother? Things are good as they are. And if they are also a bit cold and restrained, then . . . why should they upset themselves? Why? Especially if people around keep praising them, while their own artistic instinct is silent.

The Threshold of Calm

To free an actor from the harms of effort and pressure, practical experience prompted us to develop a new device. The director tells the actor "You try too hard. Why? Here, you sit and listen to me – and you're not trying. Then why, when starting to talk with your partner, you keep demanding something from yourself? Let's start again, only lose this effort – at least some of it . . . That's it, that's it . . . Release some more . . . More . . . Now, don't try at all. Absolutely no trying . . . Now even less . . . "

And so, with patience and tact, bit by bit, you "remove" from the actor all that is unnecessary; he stops requiring anything of himself, ceases to "try hard" and becomes calm, free and involuntary.

No matter how skillfully you "remove" this excess effort, the actor will probably still complain to you, saying: "When you watch me and guide me, it turns out right, but when I'm on my own – in performance or rehearsal – I again begin to 'demand' things from myself and 'step on it' . . ."

If you – the director – once more begin to speak about the need to release, get rid of the effort and so on, you will achieve nothing. He himself knows it; he just cannot implement it.

In such cases, the following practical advice has proven to be effective: "All right, since you can't help but 'demand' things of yourself – keep 'demanding' . . . However, instead of demanding that you step on it, demand that you 'let go' – set yourself free and completely give in to the imaginary circumstances."

This *change of direction*, for the most part, puts things in order.

A smart actor soon becomes convinced that "demanding things from yourself" and "exerting too much effort" is harmful. He asks for help and takes his own actions. He rids himself of these bad habits and soon achieves a more or less sound emotional state.

And then there are actors who are not only smart, but also rigorous and strict. They don't settle for partial achievements – they want perfection. These artists soon begin to feel that the state they have considered sound is far from being such. The harmful "effort" is still present in it – at least in some small, microscopic measure . . . It is present, and it does its distractive task. It is like an invisible, imperceptible gas – it does not seem to exist, and yet it carries poison and death . . .

Everyone – along with the director, perhaps – thinks that they have achieved truth, and that everything is in tip-top shape . . . However, a strict artist knows for sure that *this is not it*; his delicate scent detects falseness where everyone else cannot feel it.

He tries to fight it, but the old methods that used to help with crude mistakes prove to be useless.

He looks at his comrades . . . he listens to them philosophizing on the harm of "effort" and "stepping it up." They speak, as if they have perfectly mastered this art, but in reality they also rely on "effort" and "stepping on it," adding something to their acting – something invisible to them, and yet completely unnecessary . . . Most importantly, they don't even suspect it.

Well, perhaps this is inescapable? You can remove crude effort, as for this subtle, barely perceptible trying – perhaps it has to remain?

But his inner artist gives him no rest . . . What if it is possible after all?

Having shut himself up in his room, he continues his attempts – gently and patiently, day after day, month after month – until perseverance and instinct triumph over his inert and stagnant soul.

Having come out in front of an audience, he loses it again! Once again, he begins to "demand from himself" and "spur" his inner artist . . . But now it does not frighten him at all.

Once he held his creative dreams in his hands, he knows that reclaiming them is only a matter of steadfastness and perseverance.

> I became convinced that the secret lies in a state of calm – the kind of creative experience that causes me to forget all the worries around me and lose interest in anything other than the life of my character.
>
> When I speak of creative calm, I do not mean indifference. Creative calm is a state in which thoughts are not distracted by outside influences . . . . We must be able to preserve the greatest possible degree of creative calm, which is present when you are at home, alone, and your creative experience has been born . . . .
>
> You must achieve four times as much at home. This is because the outside influences present onstage will take away from you part of the inspiration you have achieved, and they will leave you only a quarter of the creative calm!!.
>
> *(Pevtsov [1978: 31–32])*

In other words, a true creative state can be achieved (and not without difficulty) when working at home – in private, when you are calm, not in a rush, and without excessive "effort." In such a state, you can believe that the circumstances of the play are your personal circumstances, while you *are* the character – his concerns are yours, and vice versa . . . Under these conditions, you can even achieve inspired acting.

But what you have found is very fragile. At home, nothing interferes with your creative experience, and no one demands anything from you. This is not the case when it comes to a dress rehearsal or a performance in front of an audience. There, surrounded by new impressions and numerous distractions, you grow wary and start applying "effort." At this point, everything you have achieved yesterday, at home, comes to nothing.

To arrive at the desired result onstage, you must achieve four times as much in the comfort of your study – this is because three-quarters of it will evaporate from the "outside influences."

Thus, it is necessary not only to reach the threshold of calm (as you have done until now), but to go **beyond this threshold**.

We must achieve so much that this quantity transforms into new *quality*. And not an ounce less.

This new quality lies in the fact that this state of special calm – complete and truly creative calm – causes you to tangibly become a *character*.

At this time, although you can see the audience, it no longer distracts. On the contrary, it further strengthens your calm and concentration; instead of interfering with your creativity, the audience supplements your creative high with its own – it *creates* with you.

Some of the "Legalized" Forms of Stepping on It: Tempo ("Rhythm")

The kind of "stepping on it" caused by specific stage conditions is natural, though still unwanted. In addition to it, we encounter "stepping on it" of a different kind, adopted and "legalized" in many theatre schools – these are even more harmful.

Nobody speaks so much of rhythm as some of our directors. Meanwhile, their "rhythm" has nothing to do with Stanislavsky's idea of rhythm. When he used this word, he meant internal, psychological rhythm – the rhythm of thought and blood. As for these directors, they only have the notion of external or outer rhythm. In addition to this, their "rhythm" implies something quite different from what it actually is. For them, rhythm equals quickness. Speed up the "rhythm" . . . slow down the "rhythm" . . . this exhausts the wisdom of their teachings on rhythm.

Anyone remotely familiar with music knows that this is not rhythm, but tempo. The phenomenon of rhythm is much more complex.

I had to attend a rehearsal in one of our prominent theatres, where the director (one of the devotees of "rhythm") was doing his usual thing.

"Rhythm, rhythm!" – he constantly yelled at the actors onstage – "Pulse!" – he urged them on. The actors tried with all their heart and soul; they spared no effort spurring themselves. Everything went smoothly.

But here comes a well-known veteran actor, well liked and respected. He is free and calm. He is in his usual state of creative living, developed through decades of experience. Watching him gives you such a pleasant and easy feeling – your soul begins to rest from constant playacting and pushing. You even breathe a sigh of relief – finally a living soul!

But, it did not last long. The director interrupted him, impatiently and angrily: "Pulse!!! . . . Don't slow down the 'rhythm!'"

The actor, lost and confused, broke out of his sound creative state, and, having stepped on it . . . got into the general stream of "good rhythm." Against all natural laws, the play kept flying through trenches and ditches, giving no time to the audience or the actors to catch their breath.

Sure, it happens that a heated scene must go at a fast pace. However, just spurring the actors on: faster! faster! – does not solve the problem. They would move faster, speak faster, tensely clench their fists – but they don't feel or think any more quickly. On the contrary, they cease to feel and think as a character, concerned with one thing alone – faster, faster . . . rhythm . . . rhythm . . .

An actor is not a phonograph record you can play slower or faster, as you wish.

Even a phonograph record would not satisfy you unless you found the exact speed at which it was recorded; any acceleration or deceleration would sound artificial and false. And what about a living person!

A director enamored with "rhythm" usually claims that by repeating a scene 20 times in a row at this accelerated pace, the actor gets used to it and comes to life. Even the actor notices that, indeed, each new repetition makes things easier.

Of course, it does, but why? Because everything becomes *mechanized*. The psychological life of the character comes to a halt. It becomes substituted with clever and quick delivery of the text, external mimicry, and the *depiction* of life, crude and peripheral.

Acceleration of pace is not achieved by a whip or by shouting at the actor, but by taking an example from life – that is, through circumstances. If you, while reading this book, suddenly remember that your train takes off in an hour or two, and you have yet to get packed, you will alter your state at once, without even thinking about it. The new circumstance will do the job – you will drop the book and quickly begin to pack your belongings.

The same is true of the actor. If you need to speed up the pace of a scene, remind the actor of the circumstances that will excite and ignite his cold soul . . .

If he needs to enter the stage in a state of *excitement*, he should, prior to his entrance, act out backstage the things that brought him there. Without this, there would be mere pushing.

As for the director, he should keep one thing in mind – do not ask the actor to "step on it!!" Everything onstage is urging the actor to do so *without* your help.

The Connection and Interplay between Inhibition and Stepping on It

These two processes – inhibition and "stepping on it" – are deeply interconnected onstage. One begets another. For example, an actor about to go onstage can be very simple, natural, and free. But there comes the time to cross the threshold, and he feels that everything he had before is no good – something completely different is needed . . . Naturally, he *inhibits* everything natural – he must "act" what the author wrote, what the director required, and what the audience wants. To do this, you need to evoke a special state of "attention," "activity," and all that – the working state of an actor. This state, as he has been taught, consists entirely of demands and orders – he must have a "need," he must "concentrate" on something, and so on . . . Or even worse: he must "depict" something. And to "convey" it to the audience, he must "deliver," underline, highlight, demonstrate . . . And then, it must be loud, clear, and expressive . . . One "must" on top of another . . . In short – typical "stepping on it."

In this case, pushing follows inhibition, and in some other – vice versa.

This intertwining of the two processes is never-ending. It does not only take place when an actor goes onstage; it occurs at the slightest provocation, during the actual course of action. It "attacks" all actors, even those who are aware of this danger and seemingly well protected from it.

Sometimes it ambushes the actors, "attacking them from behind." Here is a curios case of failure. A scene is going very well – so well, in fact, that the actor cannot help but look back at himself: this is really working! This causes distraction – something inside the actor stops, inhibited . . . He feels that the scene has weakened; another moment, and he'll be lost . . . To help the matter, he must "stir it up," "spur it," or "step on it" . . .

Having gone off the rails – it takes time to get back.

26
Physiology

The Power and Importance of Physiological Processes in Creativity

Dinnertime has come, yet I am not hungry; even thinking about food is unpleasant. Nevertheless, I sit down and force myself to swallow one, two, three spoonfuls of soup. I seem to like it – the fourth and fifth spoons go down not without pleasure. Before I know it, my appetite has come.

What is the matter? The fact is, a new phenomenon takes over – *physiology*.

This phenomenon is powerful – much stronger than human will. I engaged it by forcing myself to swallow the first few spoonfuls of soup. Put a candy into your mouth and try to stop salivation. Your mouth won't dry off – it is impossible. In response to the candy, all of your glands begin to work. Your tongue, without your will, begins to rotate the delicious sweet. At the right moment, the tongue moves the candy down to the tongue's root. Down there, the act of swallowing occurs – also involuntarily, followed by all the other processes connected with the delivering of the candy into your stomach.

You don't have to make a special effort – just "taste it," come into contact with the object (put a spoonful of soup, or a candy into your mouth) – physiological perception and reaction start on their own.

You can even "come into contact" inertly, reluctantly. This is almost the same as bringing a match to dry hay; you can do it absentmindedly and aimlessly, or you can do it with vigor – the straw will burst into flames all the same.

Just consider this power - like it or not, it forcibly takes control of your whole being! Is it possible to make use of this irresistible force in our art?

Intuitively, instinctively, this force has been used in theatre for a long time. When you drink, eat, or smoke in a scene, acting seems to get easier. Why is this the case?

Many years ago, I understood the value of "physiology." This happened while working on a stage adaptation of Gogol's *Evenings on a Farm near Dikanka*. "Have you, gentlemen, ever tasted pear kvass flavored with sloe [blackthorn berry] or raisin and plum vodka? The delight in your mouth is too good for words! Really, when one comes to think of it, what can't these women do!" [Gogol 1926: 18]

313

The actor who played the narrator (beekeeper Rudy Panko) did not know what to do with his role. Try as he might, it was just boring. I even had the thought of striking the role from the play.

Then I added an extra scene - he is given a pitcher of "pear kvass," and a mug. He makes himself comfortable in his chair, pours the kvass, tastes it, relishing every drop . . .

It's a hot day – he is thirsty; the kvass is cold . . . and besides, the "delight in your mouth is too good for words!" A sweet smile spreads across his face. He wants to share his pleasant sensations, but cannot bring himself to open his mouth – the taste is so nice and sweet. He just growls approvingly, suggestively raises his brows, shakes his head, points to the mug with his spare hand, and taps it with his finger. Finally having had his fill, still overwhelmed with the taste of this heavenly drink, he speaks to us, as if we were his most intimate friends: "Have you, gentlemen, ever tasted pear kvass flavored with sloe? . . . " He takes another sip. Further inspired by this nectar, he silently marvels: how can such a bliss be obtainable on earth? Overcome with delight, he suddenly recalls something else entirely out of this word: "Or have you ever tasted raisin and plum vodka?" He sees that we have never tried such things, and don't even suspect that they exist. He wants to make our day, and to sweeten our meager existence – life without kvass and plum vodka. He wants to at least describe them to us. He wants us, at least in our imagination, to experience these delightful sensations. An ecstatic smile spreads over his face, his words trickling off his tongue like syrup: "The delight in your mouth is too good for words!"

He takes yet another sip of kvass; he growls some more, and says grievingly, almost with reproach: "Really, when one comes to think of it, what can't these women do!" As if saying: these temptresses, these breeders of sin!

The pear kvass seized his entire self – nothing else exists for him at the moment. Nothing on earth, except for this indescribable sweetness – and us, with whom he wants to share it, so as to relieve the abundance of his heart.

Imperceptibly, he moved onto other things – he began to tell us about honey, "clear as a tear," and about the pies so delicious "the butter fairly melts on your lips when you begin to eat them." [Gogol 1926: 18]

In speaking about these new things, he preserved the same force of physiological perception, as if his entire actor's instrument was so well **tuned** – there was nothing else to do but stay out of its way. Without losing this state, the actor and I "skimmed through" his entire role. In a mere hour, the character was born – the bee-keeper turned out lively, comical and charming. The puzzling lock opened on its own – as soon as we inserted the right key . . .

Needless to say, I did not give the actor any real pear kvass – I merely poured some cold water into his mug. The taste of liquid and the swallowing of this liquid, multiplied by the actor's imagination – those were the devices responsible for the power of sensation, and for the **physiological** concreteness.

If, however, I were to give real pear kvass to the actor, things would not have gone as smoothly. The kvass could have distracted him, possibly causing him to break out of his entire imaginary circumstances. [For more on this, see "On Real and Imaginary Objects," p. 524]

The important thing is to evoke the physiology, while making sure that whatever goes into an actor's mouth does not take up all of his concentration.

Giving the actors something to drink, or to eat, or supplying them with an enticing action – this is nothing other than offering them a new **given circumstance**. This circumstance begins to affect the actor in a physiological way.

A gulp of water is perceived without fail. It evokes a reaction – whether an actor wants it or not. If this water has got anything to do with the action of the play, or with its text – it becomes a safe bridge connecting the **real life with that of the imagination**.

This suggested circumstance does not require any perceptive effort on behalf of an actor. *It seizes you on its own. It is real, not imaginary.*

Once it has seized you, it will let you into a scene as a whole, with all of its imaginary circumstances.

This is exactly what we need – to evoke in an actor a complete, tangible merger with his environment, as the author describes it.

Completely merging with everything you think and speak of . . . being captured, and carried away by these things. Finally, *living* by them . . . This is nothing short of a different way of existing onstage, a new way of acting, and a new "technique." This art cannot be mastered after one or two repetitions. After all, it contradicts all our mundane habits.

A new habit ought to be implanted, while an actor's entire instrument must be restructured. A new school is needed, and a special new culture of an actor's creative state.

Physiology of Movements

When going back to Rudy Panko, and to his drinking of kvass, we will notice something besides the sense of taste. Plenty of physical actions were associated with the act of drinking. He brought the mug to his mouth, and his lips touched the edge of the mug. He sipped in the liquid, and he made peculiar movements with his tongue to push the liquid deeper into his throat. He swallowed the liquid, etc.

These actions and movements were also perceived by the actor, and they also evoked his imagination.

Actions are widely used in theatre. In the most cases – *they* serve as physiological stimulants of the actor's creative process.

To achieve physiological concreteness, however, it is not enough to just be doing something. One must *busy* himself with the action at hand in the same way in which the bee-keeper busied himself with his pear kvass. Only this will lead to a merger, and to the crossing of a threshold between the usual abstract point of view on an object or action – and the "physiological" sensation of the above.

Just as one can "savor" the taste of plum vodka, one can also "savor" sweeping the floor, sewing, and any other action.

One can eat, drink, or do something without "savoring" it, mechanically.

Similarly, one can speak without "savoring," without sensing or experiencing what he says.

One can speak of anything abstractly, as if it does not concern him at the moment. And then, one can speak in such a way that he experiences and senses it – tangibly and physiologically concretely.

"Physical Busyness" and its Impact

Actors are often given some physical business that does not require much concentration. Directors resort to it in order to calm down their actors, and to distract their attention away from the audience. This business can include needlework, tidying a room, straightening one's clothes, brushing hair, drinking tea, smoking, etc.

It would be a mistake to think that this is done with the goal of evoking the very "physiological perception" just described. Instead, we are dealing with a different phenomenon. This phenomenon, while less significant as far as an actor's creativity is concerned, it is yet worthy of a discussion.

Actors, while in front of the audience, are always somewhat unfree and agitated. The theatrical environment makes them nervous. Once you give them some simple business, however, it begins to distract them from the source of their agitation. (Providing that this business fits the given circumstances.) Actors begin to feel freer, they begin to truly see around them, hear, and even think.

In short, "physical busyness" often helps the actor.

At the same time, it can interfere. Imagine, for example, that what happens onstage is so important that it must *captivate an actor's entire self*. In such a case, being distracted by "physical busyness" diminishes an actor's power. Thus, overusing this device can lead to halfhearted, peripheral perception and, therefore, to a similarly weak reaction.

How often do we see actors onstage excel at eating, drinking and brushing hair – while the subject of a play remains somewhat obscure.

On "Physical Actions," According to Stanislavsky

(One of the Ways toward Tangible Perception of the Surrounding Circumstances, and the Character)

In his later years, Stanislavsky spoke much about "physical actions." Death stilled his attempts to perfect this method, which differed greatly from the physical actions as just described. It aimed at immersing an actor into the circumstances of the play and the role.

Let us suppose that an actor feels helpless – he does not know "what to live by," and "what to play" in a given scene. In order to point the actor onto the right path, a director [Stanislavsky] would suggest: "You've come a long way; you are tired, and out of breath – so go ahead and wash yourself. Here is a washbasin, water, soap . . . (For the most part, the water and the soap are imaginary. This serves a special purpose, as described in Stanislavsky's *An Actor's Work*, part one.)

So, the actor sets himself to work. In the meantime, the director keeps interrupting him, while offering his corrections.

- Wait a second, you are washing as you are used to doing it, yet the play takes place in the south. It is summer, and you just drove 120 miles in a hot car. You are covered with dust – you are dying to take a bath, to refresh yourself . . .
  Now, this is different. However, you keep washing as if at some place where you can't make yourself at home. In the meantime, you've come to your best friend's – his house is your house.
- If this is so, I want to take off my shirt and wash myself down to my waist.
- Be my guest.

The actor does so.

- Excellent. Except, your pants will get all wet, if you wash like that – how about tying a towel around your waist? By the way, you keep washing with warm water, which contradicts the play. He brought you the water from a spring. It is cold. The air is hot, and the water's stinging cold.
  Now go ahead and wipe yourself with a towel. And now you can put your shirt back on. Don't you feel refreshed? You must be less tired. The bumpy road, the scorching sun, and the wind – aren't you beginning to put it all behind you?

Thus, by fulfilling the physical actions with greater precision, the actor's perception of the scene's circumstances grows more *tangible*.

Having sensed himself in the plays' circumstances, the actor begins to feel himself as a character. Stanislavsky called it the "I am," meaning "I am character."

Stanislavsky had grown to appreciate this device – physical actions under the conditions of the play's circumstances. He began to resort to it more and more often – especially since the actors kept losing the "I am," the circumstances and the truth at large – as soon as they ran out of physical actions. This inspired a thought. Would it be possible to construct an entire role in such a way that physical actions would follow one another, like links in a chain? If one could avoid any breaks in a chain, wouldn't an actor always be supported by some external device, and never slip off the tight rope and fall?

In some cases, the regular physical actions were not applicable. For example, during some serious, weighty conversation we would not be able to carry on – if occupied by some business. So, what is there to do in those cases when physical actions would just get in the way and, therefore, not be appropriate?

While observing yourself, it's not difficult to notice that the life of our imagination is uninterrupted. Our thoughts keep flowing at any moment. Moreover, we constantly perform some imaginary movements and actions – at times, we follow our thought down a street, at other times we ride with it in a car, climb up the stairs, eat, etc.

And so, Stanislavsky referred to all these involuntary movements and actions (often imperceptible) as "physical actions."

Needless to say, he was perfectly aware that these were not true "physical actions." He continued to use this term out of habit (as he himself put it), and because he was yet to find a better one.

Strictly speaking, he used to say, this new type of "physical action" is not an action in a literal sense. Rather, it is a physical *impulse*. (See Prokofiev 1948.) So, he insisted that – action or no action – an actor should always at least have an *impulse* like that.

This caused him to decide that an entire role could be broken into "physical actions." In part, it would be actions in the literal meaning of this word; in part – "would be-physical actions," or *impulses* for physical activity.

Later yet, while seeking a wider use for his device of "physical actions," Stanislavsky began to look for the characteristics of "actions" in the human speech. Thus, he began to speak of "verbal actions."

It would have been difficult to predict the final conclusions of his research and experiments of the later years, if he were to have continued them.

Meanwhile, the first steps in this direction greatly encouraged Stanislavsky. At one time, Stanislavsky [as quoted in Sibiryakov 1974: 12] even addressed his students by saying, "Instead of learning how to act, learn how to correctly fulfill actions onstage, and you will become accomplished actors."

Nevertheless, one should not understand this literally and, therefore, narrowly.

It is sufficient to recall that Stanislavsky, in order to achieve the *correct actions* from an actor, continuously supplemented them with such circumstances that evoked the actors' sound creative state, and caused these correct actions. In other words, the *correctness* of actions depends entirely on the perception of the given circumstances.

★★★

It would be advisable to supplement this device with "green-lighting," as described in this book, not to mention an actor's general skill of practicing creative freedom onstage.

Once an actor, by the use of "physical action," achieves the correct "I am" – it is enough to green-light this newly born creative life, and this "I am," as it was described earlier. By doing so, an actor would solidify in himself the feeling of the character in the circumstances.

A state received from the correctly fulfilled "physical action," would serve as a tuning fork, striking the right note in regard to an entire role, and to an actor's creative state in this role.

In such a case, it would no longer be necessary to endlessly proceed from one action to the next, and then to the next, and to the next, etc. One, two, or three actions would suffice even for a sizable role. Not to mention that not every play permits an actor to continuously resort to physical actions.

Every Action Is Simultaneously a Perception

The chapter on perception spoke of the fact that any perception is already an action. Moreover, every action is simultaneously a perception.

Action, especially "physical action" can only entice us as it triggers **perception**, be it even in a masked form.

Here is an example. Let us say, my director tells me, "In this scene, I want you to brush your hair." I, the actor, begin to do so, without any interest or desire. I move the brush through my hair . . . The brush gets stuck: there is a tangle in my hair, and it resists the brush – I can sense this with my hand, and with my scalp. Reflexively, my hand stops, and it now proceeds more carefully, while trying to brush through this tangle.

In several movements, I manage to do so.

Having managed one spot, I move to the next. There, I am stopped by a similar obstacle, causing me to seek ways to overcome it. One by one, these obstacles, along with my struggle, pull me in. This occupation, originally suggested by my director, seizes me – I am no longer disinterested, while brushing my hair.

Yet why do I do this? If my occupation is aimless, it will soon bore me. The good news is that I have already been woken from my inertia, and I am now ready to even perceive things outside of my physical activity. At this point, my director (or else my own mind) toss my motivation at me: **why** I brush my hair. Perhaps, I must go out, according to the play, and so I am brushing my hair, I am getting dressed, etc. This motivation gives my actions a purpose, and a sense of direction.

I must go out. This becomes even more tangible, while I am getting dressed and brush my hair . . . And so, the circumstances of the play become, one by one, **my own, my personal business**. I now begin to perceive where I am going, and why, as if it concerned me directly.

In short, by starting with an action, I awakened my perception. Perception provoked the next action. Action lead to further perceptions, and so I arrive at the place where my character's circumstances become my own. I perceive them, and I react to them, as if they were my personal business.

What is left is **giving a green-light** to this new state of self, and to the perception of all the circumstances.

Any physical action given to an actor is significant to him only as it has a tendency to be **sensed**, i.e. to be perceived physiologically, not as an abstract thought.

This sensation evokes a reaction, without fail. This reaction is also sensed, in its own turn. What follows is a reaction to an entire spectrum of things. To put it simply, the "physical action" is not a self-sufficient principle of creativity, but merely one of the ways to evoke perception, and to originate the combined work of perception and reaction, as they evoke each other. This, in turn, evokes the creative life.

Those who mistake action, and especially "physical action" for the alpha and omega of an actor's art – they have failed to carefully analyze the process of creative experiencing. Although, in practice they may be well familiar with it.

On the Unity of Perception and Reaction

When approaching the creative process like this, it does not matter where to begin – with action or with perception. The result will be the same. As long as one does not draw the wrong conclusions that actions, and *activity* at large, dominate the art of the actor.

For the most part, an actor understands the demand for activity as the demand for pushing, spurring, and greater tension. In pursuit of activity, an actor restricts his work to crudely and linearly performing his "tasks" and "actions," while completely forgetting what is most important – the live perception, along with the live reaction. In the meantime, *perception and reaction constitute a complete harmonious whole*. One begets the other, without fail, as long as this harmony and this unity remain undisrupted.

Stanislavsky [1954: 6] always claimed that "one of the main objectives pursued by the "system" is the natural stimulation of the creative organic nature with its subconscious." The subconscious, in his understanding, equated with the organic, involuntary life.

This is what he did. He would give a task, or an action, and then would immediately prompt circumstances to an actor – as described above, when discussing "physical actions." Thus, while beginning with formal activity, he at once brought an actor into perception. The circumstances would then begin to act upon an actor, who went to ignore them up until this point. Under their influence, he could not but behave as they demanded – that triggered correct behavior.

However, an actor trained to be "active," to "fulfill actions," and have "tasks" – such an actor will soon slide downhill – off of the perception of circumstances, toward his habitual way of behaving onstage. His perceptive mechanisms (those responsible for the sound creative state) are inhibited. With them, his entire natural creative life comes to a halt. His manifestations then begin to result merely from the fact that *this is how it must be, this is what's been decided, this is what's been preplanned*.

On the Mistake of Treating Action as a Dominant of an Actor's Creative Process

Theatre people today seem to be fond of the following trivial formula: "A sculptor implements his idea in stone, an artist – in paint, musician – in sounds, and an actor – in actions. There are no other ways of implementing ideas in theatre, except actions."

It is true that a sculptor implements his idea in stone, an artist – in paint, i.e. in dead matter.

As for the actor, his material is alive, and he has to implement his ideas by the means of his entire *living* organism.

Why, mind you, restrict an actor by stating that he only has this one means available to him – action, and nothing else. There is more to it – an actor has at his disposal *his entire instrument with its ability to live and create*. It certainly includes action. Although, first and foremost it includes the actor's *being* (what he is like, and who he is), then his *perception* (what he perceives and how), followed by his *reaction* (how does his entire organism respond, as a whole, to an external impression).

This explains the term that defines our art: "experiencing," as well as its main prerequisite: "truth."

The proponents of action appeal to the fact that the very word "actor" is derived from *action*, and that a play is broken into "acts," and that even characters in a play are called "actors."

This proves nothing. Do we not say plenty of things without any consideration for the reality of the matter? For example, we say: "sunrise," while in actuality the sun does not rise above the horizon; on the contrary, we, the earth, keep turning one of our sides toward the sun.

27
Assignment

Assignment and its technique have been described in the previous chapters, directly or indirectly. Remember, we were surprised and baffled why the actors, having repeated a suggested text and having then "put it out of their heads," would begin the etude, and, without any hesitation or confusion, the words would fly of the tongue – the exact words and in the exact order they were assigned.

Not knowing how to explain this, we still continued our experiments and gradually, time after time, became convinced that this repetition of the text is not mere repetition just for the sake of "memorization," but is *a crucial device*.

I understood that this device is, perhaps, absolutely essential for the creative process. At any rate, an actor always uses this device in one form or another. The only question is: would it be used correctly or incorrectly; with the benefit or detriment to one's creativity and, finally, consciously or completely involuntarily, unnoticed by the actors.

I have managed to observe certain steps (or stages) of assigning. Finally, I was able to trace its correct or incorrect flow.

In life, we quite frequently use the device of "assigning" or "placing an order." For example, having woken up in the morning, before leaving the house, we mentally review all we have to do: go there; call such and such; don't forget something at work; get somewhere by a certain hour, etc. Calmly we leave the house, and our businesses come to mind, in the right order, one after the other. Whatever we "assigned" is now being executed. There's nothing unusual in that.

Creative "assignment," however, is much more complex.

Firstly, an actor (in this case, a student) knows that what is about to come is not "life," but "art," a theatrical "performance" – this is the first assignment. The second assignment – what's coming is creativity, i.e. the creation of something new. Third – it must be a work of art that is artistic truth onstage. Special assignments of this kind do not exist, but they are implied – the entire environment speaks of them.

Only now, in fourth place, do we find the process of special "assignment", the text of the etude is assigned. Sometimes it assigns who my partner and I are, as well as our circumstances.

Everything else – our inner content and our behavior during the etudes – is our creativity.

This complex "assignment" begets a thought. Having engaged with the inner content of the actor, this thought creates an embryo of the work of art – the embryo of the actors' future creative manifestations.

Manifestations of the Artistic Embryo of a Role

Like any inception in the organic world, this also originates from the collision and merger of two related, necessarily complementary, and, at the same time, diametrically opposed forces.

In our case, there are two such moments.

The first moment. The "I am" of the actor – the entire content of his or her personality, with its clear and hidden abilities and properties; its life experience; its centuries-old experience; its current condition, at this given moment – all these factors collide with the fact of having to perform in front of the audience.

This collision causes a person to undergo a certain inner shift: a regular human becomes an actor-human. This actor is now ready for creativity (in fact, he is already in the realm of creativity). The only thing that is missing – what is he going to play?

And the second moment: the actor is offered the text of the etude, a partner and, sometimes, given circumstances. The interaction between this material and the personality of the actor begets the embryo of the role.

No need imagining it as a specific, distinct "character." Not at all. What appears in the actor, at this point, are just sensations, urges, thoughts, and movements. What this means, however, is that the life of the role has begun.

It is also incorrect to think that such unformed "embryo" is only characteristic for the art of acting, while in other arts it always appears as a clear image, or it can be labeled with certain words – like a title of the work, or a clearly formulated theme. The creative embryo in other arts is also just a nudge, a beginning thought, a point of departure, and a vague foreboding of the future creation.

> "I know not yet what I shall sing,
> I only know the song ripens."
> *Afanasy Fet [1949: 108]*

> "And thoughts stir bravely in my head, and rhymes,
> Run forth to meet them on light feet, and fingers
> Reach for the pen, and the good quill betimes
> Asks for the foolscap. Wait: the verses follow."
> *Pushkin [1936: 81]*

> "Oh, many, many days have fled
> Since young Tatyana with her lover,
> As in a misty dream at night,
> First floated dimly into sight –
> And I as yet could not uncover
> Or through the magic crystal see
> My novel's shape or what would be."
> *Pushkin [2009: 211]*

But the appearance of the embryo does not end the work. Now we have to be able to seize the moment and create favorable conditions for the development of everything that has been born in an actor.

Let's start with the fact that a momentary delay would cause the irreversible death of the "embryo." Death is common in nature – it is not afraid of death: not every bird egg will become a bird; not every fish-egg – a fish; and a plant won't grow from every seed.

No such person exists that has not been visited by promising thoughts, or did not make ingenious and courageous plans. But not all of these thoughts, plans, or aspirations are realized.

A glimpse of thoughts, vague desires . . . these manifestations often make us believe that *they are not yet real*. A man is waiting for something finished and well defined: it will come any moment now . . .

Yet it does not happen like this in nature: everything organic must first pass through the stage of a nondescript embryo.

And we often do not even notice them, these precious germs, or else we consider them trifles, saying to ourselves: these are idle dreams, pathetic fragments of thoughts, and silly glimpses of the soul's unrest.

The ability to sense the artistic embryo of the role and to give in to it boldly is the main quality of the **actor–creator**.

Our unpretentious exercises, among all other required qualities, develop this precious skill in an actor.

How do you determine the appearance of these germs of creativity? And how do you help them develop?

A previously described method comes to the rescue – the so-called *emptiness*, when an actor, having repeated the text, tries to "put it out of his head," and for a moment "stays empty of feeling, thoughts, desires."

This "emptiness" is needed in order to clearly distinguish the moment when the "embryo" appears: *everything that comes on the heels of this emptiness is to be treated as the sprouts of creativity*.

I repeat again and again: this is not about formation, in the mind of the actor, of some character they are supposed to implement. *An actor's artistic embryo is* **a new sense of self**, the beginning of creative transformation, an anticipation of the new "I."

But do not think, however, that this new "I" will overcome your entire being. It does not yet exist in its established form. What exists is only its premonition, its timid germs.

Now for the main concern: how to help it grow and become realized?

Practically this is solved like this: just give way to all these germs – nothing else is required. Some thoughts occur? Let them flow. Some feelings, sensations rise up? Do not interrupt them. Don't inhibit your unconscious needs and desires – give complete freedom to various small automatic movements as they burst out. Completely give in to the will of anything that exists in you and asks to be freed.

Give in to all these impulses with utter trust, without hesitation or doubt. This is one of the greatest secrets of our "technique."

Give these living germs a chance to live. What comes will be very different from what you pictured – especially at first. Do not be discouraged by this fact – this is as it should be. A month-old infant looks nothing like a young man of 20. How could it be otherwise? If they looked alike, you would be the first to call him a non-viable freak!

School practice often yields something "less than thrilling" – something far more engaging, smart, and beautiful than what we could have invented. We should not worry about this. After all, what is the task at hand? We want the actor to *learn the process of creative inception and how to give in to it*. Whether it will be exciting or not from a theatrical standpoint is of no importance.

The "technique" described may strike one as repetition: we've already discussed it a lot. Yes, but these significant words—artistic embryo—had yet to be said.

Now that they have been said, the creative process becomes more understandable.

Gabbling the Lines

In describing the first lessons we mentioned, in passing, those cases when students would gabble all of their lines all too quickly. An etude would be over, yet we, the audience, would have no idea what just took place.

This incident occurs in almost all beginning lessons. It is not even a mistake – simply a misunderstanding: students have yet to understand what is required of them. They heard that you asked them to do everything so that all the acting and speaking "happens on its own," without holding it back, or "stepping on it." They had no time to think this through, so their understanding is extremely primitive.

However, this misunderstanding affords you an opportunity to suggest one very important detail in the technique of "assigning" the lines, as well as in the technique of "beginning."

- Great weather. It's nice for a change. I wouldn't mind playing some volleyball!
- Let's go then. The guys are already playing.
- Really? Let's go.

They repeat the text. As soon as they repeat it, the girl instantly gabbled out all of her lines: "Nice weather . . . " etc. Her partner catches her hastiness, and the whole scene goes by in a flash.

When they finish, I tell them: "Let's skip the discussion, and just do the etude again. One tip: having repeated the lines once more, put everything out of your heads, forget the lines, as if you have been 'assigned' none."

She repeats the lines and fulfills my instruction: tries to *forget* and put the text out of her head. She succeeds at that – clearly, in the next few seconds, she does not think, but lives with some unconscious and, perhaps, very primitive sensations. One can see that she is a bit uncomfortable; this is residual dissatisfaction from the unsuccessful etude . . .

"You are uncomfortable, for some reason, and restless," I whisper her, "so be it; just 'greenlight' it: let it feel uncomfortable – it's meant to be so."

She establishes herself in this state, and looks around – prompted by her unrest . . . Her gaze falls on the window. She is quite surprised: the sun outside is shining so brightly.

"Great weather!" – the line comes out like this: "Who could of thought the weather was so great! And we've been sitting here sulking." – "It's nice for a change. I wouldn't mind playing some volleyball!"

Her partner clearly does not care whether the sun is shining now or not – he just loves playing volleyball. He has been listening closely, for a while, to some sounds coming from the yard. As soon as he hears: "I wouldn't mind playing some volleyball!" he immediately chimes in: "Let's go then. The guys are already playing." "Really?" she exclaims with joy. He nods toward the yard where one can hear sounds similar to the striking of a ball . . . "Let's go!" she says hurriedly. And they rush out of the classroom.

- What was the difference between the first time and the second? – I ask her.
- The first time I rushed, but not the second.
- Is that so? Remember: the first time you repeated the text to better memorize it, but then you did not try to forget it; you did not "put it out of your head," and the text . . .

- Yes, yes! the text immediately jumped onto the tip of my tongue.
- And what did you do?
- I think I did the right thing: I did not resist: I felt like speaking it, and so I did.
- Quite right. So, you can't blame haste (although you did spit out all of your words with supernatural speed). Your mistake was not bothering to *forget the text*, not casting *it away*. No wonder it immediately spouted out of you. It had no choice.

Skipping and Mangling the Lines

A pert, somewhat light-minded girl steps out to do an etude. Her partner and she are given the following text:

He.	(sits, looking through a book, turning the pages).
She (approaches).	Excuse me, did you find that book here, on the bench?
He.	Yes.
She.	That is my book. I left it here . . . by accident.
He.	Well, if it's yours, please take it.
She.	Thank you. I was afraid I lost it for good. Sorry. (*Exits*)

Having gathered from the proposed text that the etude deals with a book forgotten on a bench and with a search for this book, she repeated the lines – correctly, but somewhat carelessly – and walked out of the classroom to return in half a minute. This gave her partner enough time to see the forgotten book, pick it up, reluctantly, and turn the first few pages.

She quickly entered, looked at the bench, at him, at the book . . . Then she sat next to him and started the conversation.

- Tell me, where did you pick up that book? Here, on the bench?

He looked at her, understood that she was looking for this book, that the book was hers, and replied:

- Yes – and curiously waited for what she was going to say next.
- You see, that is my book, I lost it . . . left it . . . forgot it here . . .
- Well, if it's yours, please take it.

She was delighted, grabbed the book, opened it to a random page . . .

- That's good. And I thought I lost it. Sorry! – she shut the book, nodded, and ran away.

Everything was good except for one thing: the text was mangled, all the words were mixed up – she performed a "loose translation" of the etude.

This was to be expected. When she was repeating her text, it was already clear that the *words were not important* to her (though she repeated them correctly at the time). She only valued the general line and the fact that a book was lost.

Naturally, this is what she *assigned*. And she also assigned some negligence with regards to the text – the words are not important, but just the gist of them. This tendency immediately became evident in practice.

Similarly, I can always predict in advance which words an actor will stumble over, which lines will be mispronounced, and which forgotten. To do this, one just needs to closely watch the actors as they repeat their text: a line missed or said wrongly in repetition – this very line will be skipped and mispronounced during an actual etude. Any hesitation before a certain word in repeating – this will also translate into the etude. In short, the way I repeat my lines; the way I "deposit them" – the same way they'll emerge later.

When, prior to an etude, you repeat the lines, you must also say your stage directions: I leave, I sit down, I take a book, and so on. Otherwise, the words will get spoken on their own, yet the actor won't feel like leaving or doing something else specified in an etude.

I would ask students: why didn't you leave, or why didn't you do this or that? The answer is always the same: "I did not feel like it." And they are right. They were correct to completely "green-light" their desires and urges. There was no error there. The error was elsewhere – in the assigning. As it always turns out, assignment is to blame – students forget to say: "I leave," or "I do" this or that.

An actor who clearly tells himself a stage direction – for example "I go to the window" – that actor will not notice how he finds himself by the window. Some force will inevitably lead him there.

There is nothing miraculous and supernatural here. This phenomenon is rather common-place. Going to bed in the evening, fearing to oversleep, we say to ourselves: "Tomorrow I need to wake up at seven o'clock." In the morning we wake up from some jerk or from some thought. We look at the clock . . . and the arrow points to seven.

The same thing happens with the assignment we practice in theatre, in our classes.

Assigning the "Ending": "Full Stop"

During initial lessons, students usually think acting is saying lines. As soon as they get through the words, they either end an etude, or they begin to "improvise" and talk a lot of nonsense just out of fear of silence. So that it doesn't become habit, you have to delicately temper the students' zeal and lead him away from such unnecessary additions.

"Improvisatory" chatter stops, but they begin to forcibly restrain themselves even when they do have the need to say something. The words are on the tip of their tongue, but, seeing as they're not in the text, students inhibit them and fail to green-light them. This is no good. Encouraging such restraint means killing what is most important – involuntariness, freedom, spontaneity, i.e. the basis of creativity of an actor.

This is why in such cases, you say: "No, it's best to say the words. If they are begging to be said, if they are the result of your *life* onstage, that means that they truly were necessary – by no means should you hold yourselves back. Remember the rule: only one thing is forbidden – you're not allowed to interfere with your own life." This is what you do, saving what is most important – freedom. And you temporarily allow the addition of extraneous words that come from the actors themselves.

But soon, you arrive at the real reason, explaining why the actors do not want to stop once they say all their lines and instead feel the need to keep adding more words. The issue is once again in ***assignment***.

Here's a text:

- You've paid off your debt to Victor?
- No, I forgot.
- That's not good. I heard he asked to borrow 10 rubles from Sergei.
- Damn! . . . How could I? . . . That's not good . . .

If we allow that this is the *beginning* of a conversation, then we allow the thought that *there should be a continuation*, i.e. we **assign** ourselves a continuation. And since this is the case, we will inevitably want to keep talking.

Is this bad? No, it's not bad. But we're training our students not for free improvisations, but for theatre in which we act out the works of drama with very precise text. We have to teach them to view a given text as having everything – a beginning and an end. Repeating a text before an etude, students should automatically assign the following thought: "These are the words I have to say, and here is their end." **Full stop.** Then, they won't feel any need to keep talking. In the given example, having said "Damn! . . . How could I? . . . That's not good . . . " the student can pick up a phone in order to talk to "Victor," or maybe he'll go to him personally. Whatever he does, his conversation with his scene partner is *over*. The same will happen for his scene partner. Her words have done their job – she sees this by the actor's face and behavior, and she is satisfied. She feels no need to continue the conversation.

"Refrain from Acting" while Assigning the Text

- Why aren't you talking to me?
- Oh! You know exactly why.
- Enough is enough. It's interfering with our work.
- And whose fault is it?

The young man, while repeating his text ("Oh! You know exactly why") was already acting – he was giving his partner a contemptuous, hurt look, irritatedly moving his foot, and so on.

While assigning the words, he already assigned not only the mood, but the whole situation. He has already made a "rough sketch" of the etude, and now has only to play its "final draft." [Can this be done? Yes, but it won't be an etude "without circumstances." – *Author's Note*] Moreover, he invested this "draft" with so much feeling, the etude has been practically played, and the actor now has nothing left in him for "the clean copy."

Actors will easily understand this – they have probably experienced similar cases in their work.

All of them must have, at some point, rehearsed, or acted a scene shortly prior to their entrance. They did so, wanting to tune up their instrument, or simply to test their strength before going onstage. But, strange to say, the better they managed to play their scene offstage, the more it carried them away and excited them – the weaker it went later onstage . . .

Having acted it out (moreover, having acted it well), it's as if they emptied themselves out – all they had left now was to try repeating what they had just done offstage . . . A living thing defies repetition – it passed, and is no longer there . . . One can only repeat the external manifestations (movements, facial expressions), and even then only approximately. As for the feelings . . . Using a willful effort, one can only evoke some abstract excitement – that is all.

And an even stranger thing – those scenes they did not touch went easily and even with inspiration.

On a small scale, this can be observed in our classwork, when, in assigning the text, an actor already plays an imaginary scene.

To assign a text does not mean to play it. On the contrary, to assign is to load it in. When loading – be it a photographic camera or a rifle – you will not be trying to take a picture or to make a shot at the same time for the sake of testing it or "rehearsing the shot."

The same is true in our case. Once a shot has been made—timely or untimely—it has been made.

This is the explanation I usually resorted to in such a case.

A Pavlov-school physiologist would probably put it differently. Why, he would say, implicate various household analogies, when the fact is so simple – while you played your etude, you excited a certain area of the cerebral cortex, and the more your etude captivates you, the greater the excitation. At the end of this etude, the excited area becomes inhibited, as a rule. And the greater the excitation (the stronger the etude went) – the stronger the inhibition that follows this excitation. Thus, it is understandable that having played through an etude once (not just sketched it, but playing it well), you cannot play it as well and as strongly the second time – the required area of the brain is ***inhibited***.

Part IV

Guiding Freedom and Involuntariness

28

Circumstances

Acting with Predetermined Circumstances Is Easier

"Don't interfere with living," "let it be," "pre-decide nothing; prescribe nothing, and do whatever you feel" . . . and so on.

Could these techniques, well suited for developing freedom and involuntariness, lead to unfortunate consequences? Could it be possible that an actor accustomed to such absolute freedom would not be able to play a single role?

After all, theatre requires the opposite – it predetermines everything that is important, while our student of freedom is unaccustomed to it.

Sooner or later, this sort of question will inevitably come from the students.

I do not argue. I simply suggest: let's check it out.

You have come up with this disturbing idea – so, you give it a try.

Let's keep our technique: as always, "avoid any acting" while going over your lines; as always, "toss everything out of your head" for a few seconds and go with the first thing that pops up.

Prior to repeating the text, I will give you some *circumstances*. How about this: you are a young construction engineer. Very fond of your work. You have got your own inventions. You've recently married . . . this lovely young girl. You have a wonderful relationship, and you seize every opportunity to be alone. She is a violinist; this year she graduates from the Conservatory; professors are predicting an excellent future for her . . .

Yesterday you received a note from a friend, a fellow engineer . . . I'll now write it for you. Read it silently and then give it back to me.

Apparently, it mentions a long-term assignment – they seem to want you to work in Siberia for a year. This assignment is of great interest to you. They are entrusting you with a huge, important project. Accomplished, experienced engineers could only dream of such work – let along a young engineer like you. This is great news, but this also means separation from your wife . . . for a long time . . . for a whole year! After all, you can't expect her to leave the Conservatory because of your trip!

Just in case, you did not say anything to her. This may be just speculations and they'll send someone else in the end – so why worry your wife?

This morning at work, however, it got confirmed: you are the one to go. How do you bring it up with her? How do you broach the subject? After all, a year is no joke!

You've come back from work, washed and changed, walked into your living room, and you still don't know how to start the conversation.

As for you – I address his partner – let me add one more thing to what I have already said. You are a violinist, about to graduate from the Conservatory; the beginning of your concert career has been very successful. You married your husband for love, and so did he. Lately, you have not been seeing each other a lot – both of you have been busy. You can't wait until the summer, when you are going to travel to the Caucasus with him. An hour and a half ago, you were sewing a button to his jacket when a note fell out of his pocket. Here it is – please take it. You will read it later.

Now let's repeat the text and start with whatever comes – without inventing anything in advance, or predetermining how it might go.

They repeated the text:

- I was mending your jacket and found this note in your pocket.
- Have you read it?
- I have.
- This is just as well.

After repeating the text, the young man quickly left the room. The girl remained. She looked at the piece of paper in her hand, unfolded it, began to read, and her eyes grew serious at once. The note said: "Dear friend, it seems you've got to quickly pack and leave. The matter seems to have been decided. Yours, Peter." At first, she did not seem to understand the content of the note or did not attach too much importance to what she had read. Then she began to worry . . . reread the note again, and then again . . . Got scared . . . At this moment, she heard his footsteps outside the door and quickly put the note on the table.

The young man opened the door. Trying to seem more relaxed than he actually was, he went to the girl and gently took her hand . . . After that, he wanted to withdraw and sit on the sofa . . . She kept his hand in hers . . . Then she looked narrowly at him, staring straight into his face with her earnest, searching eyes . . . She was silent as she kept peering at him. Finally, she took hold of herself and uttered, almost calmly: "I was mending your jacket, and found this note in your pocket." The young man saw the note on the table. He recognized it, became agitated, and flushed. "Have you read it?" She was touched by his emotion. "Yes, I have," she said sadly.

He saw that she looked at him lovingly and with great tenderness, and he brightened up: "This is just as well!" He picked up the note, glanced through it, and switched his glance to his wife. She was waiting.

I needed nothing more, so I stopped the etude.

- Well, how do you feel?

Both of them spoke at once, hastily and joyfully interrupting each other:

- Very good! You know . . . – very good! And oddly, it's much easier to act this way than without the circumstances. We felt like we did not have to do anything – things were already there, taking care of themselves.

- Precisely – I tell them – that's how it is: acting "with circumstances" is as easy as swimming with a float. The float (the circumstances) holds you and does not let you sink. You see, and you were afraid that you won't manage the circumstances!
- How is this possible? And why?
- It's quite simple. When you start with "no circumstances," the circumstances appear anyway: when you look at your partner, you feel that she is your wife, or sister, or friend – is this not a circumstance? When looking at the room, at the walls, at the ceiling – you feel that you are at home, or at work, or at some public institution – are these not circumstances?

  They are created on their own, at the slightest clue. Now you are so trained that the tiniest impulse restructures your entire inner life and creates in your imagination all the major and minor circumstances.

  Ordinarily, I don't offer you a path – you find it on your own. And now, when I offer you basic circumstances – strictly speaking, I put you on a path. Now you don't have to look for it – you've got the path to travel on. Now everything is clear – you won't misroute, so you don't have to worry about a thing.

  You can no longer help but perceive things as a living, breathing person; so everything around you, including you partner, gives impetus for *further* development and enlivening of the circumstances you were given.

  Usually, when you do an etude with "no circumstances," your creative imagination gives birth to all the circumstances, major and minor. Now, when major circumstances are given to you, naturally, it is easier to create the minor ones. They grow on their own, like leaves on a living tree.

  Now tell us why you met him so severely, and then relented, and even smiled?
- When I found the note, I was upset – why did he say nothing to me? What is this hasty departure? Where is he going? If this is a business trip, why make a secret out of it? And then, when I saw his embarrassment and looked into his eyes, I realized that he kept silent because he did not want to scare me. He himself was upset because of it, and even suffered. I understood everything at once and was glad – for him and for us both . . . He felt so dear, so close.
- And you?
- Me? I've come to the point when I needed to tell her everything, but I could not start right away – I needed some kind of a pretext . . . A difficult conversation.
- What were you afraid of?
- What do you mean?! She knows everything, she is worried, offended that I hid it from her . . . I should not have waited; I should have told it to her yesterday, but I was a coward! The moment I received this note, I felt this trip was inevitable! And I felt that they will send me, not someone else! So, why hide it from her, why drag it all out! . . .
- And then, when she smiled at you . . .
- Then all my fears and embarrassment . . . just vanished!

What is this about? Preplanning the course of an etude constrains and binds the actor. Not so with "circumstances." Preplanned "circumstances" make it easier to act. Yet, these "circumstances" are also predetermined!

The issue here is very simple. Our feelings, our thoughts, and our actions are caused by what happens to us.

This is why, by suggesting the circumstances, I only do what life does – I supply material or an impulse – this causes a reaction and starts up life.

Suggesting or even prescribing feelings or actions, on the contrary – equals prescribing a result, or prescribing consequence without any cause. This never happens to us in life – it is unnatural.

That is all.

But I don't say this to the students. All they need at this point is reassurance that "circumstances" will not hurt when they encounter them.

The exercise described above convinces them beyond any doubt.

What I do tell the students is this: Since in the future you will have to deal a lot with circumstances, let's use this time to work "without circumstances." The more you work "without circumstances," the more you will perfect your ability to "take" the circumstances.

The Technique of Transitioning to Etudes with Predetermined Circumstances

The reader may have already noticed that our earlier etudes were also not without circumstances; as a matter of fact, the circumstances were offered to the students from day one. To begin with, they were recommended not to invent anything, but to take this actual room, this interior, this view from the window, and this weather outside.

Similarly, in the chapter titled "Incoherence," the students were advised to look at their partner before starting an etude. If a partner turned out to be serious, focused, and, accidentally, wearing glasses, the student could imagine that this was a young scientist. Is this not a circumstance? Although it was not given beforehand, it still appeared in the first moment – therefore, prior to the start of the etude.

At that time, however, there was no reason to raise these questions – what are circumstances and what purpose do they serve? Students were coping with the circumstances – and that was enough. Why frighten them with a new word. This special chapter, on the contrary, demands that we speak of them.

In classroom practice, the transition "to circumstances" is inconspicuous – as if by chance.

When some pair finishes their etude, you ask them who they thought the other was and what the circumstances were. They say something like this: brother and sister . . . She is unhappy with his irresponsible behavior. As the elder sister, she wants to bring him to his senses . . .

The text, as well as their age difference, prompts these circumstances.

You begin to clarify and specify the nature of his irresponsible behavior.

- Instead of preparing for his exams, he's become keen on sports . . . all he does at home is sleep.
- Perhaps he has got some other interests?
- Oh, no! He speaks of nothing else other than his rowing. He just took it up, and he is going to be a champion! He will fail his exams, for sure . . .
- And you – I would address her partner – what do you have to say about it?
- What do I have to say . . . well, in some way, she is right. Exams are awfully close, it is true. It would not be a bad idea to cut down on practice. But it's so exciting! Plus, I get to spend time on the water! . . . The air is out of this world! I'll catch up to my studies at night. My grades from last year were not that bad.
- Here's what we will do: let's repeat this etude. We will repeat it just as it went – you, once again, are the older sister, entrusted to watch after her younger brother. And you are this very brother whose freedom has been so restricted. Let's recall the text . . . and go.

The etude usually goes with greater clarity; it captures the actors more than it did before. Talking through their own story excites them; it makes *more tangible* both their relationships and their vital interests . . . Their circumstances become *more concrete*, and the tracks they followed before, so cautiously, have already been trodden. Subsequently, everything goes like clockwork.

As a result, this novelty – a shift to precise circumstances, offered by the teacher – instead of being difficult, becomes a transition to easier things.

Actors do not even notice how they make one of the most important steps: the move toward working on a play – a translation from their personal experiences to the circumstances and role. [Some actors, having been asked, after the end of an etude, who are you? and so on, give glib answers and speak extraordinary smoothly. It means – they are lying. Consider yourself warned. They want to impress, to amaze, and to deceive the teacher. Most importantly, they do not understand the fact of the matter: how could one possibly speak of exact circumstances or precise facts at that point? So far as the circumstances are not given, but formed on the spot (in one or two seconds), they cannot possibly be distinct and specific from the get-go. – *Author's Note*]

A Change in Circumstances Changes an Etude

To clarify this etude, I must explain that it was done in the midst of World War II, in 1943, when many Russians were evacuated to the far north.

The text was offered without specific circumstances.

HE.	(sitting at the table).
SHE. (enters).	Excuse me, does Peter V. Stepanov work here?
HE.	He does. Down the corridor – second door on the left. You'll find him there.
SHE.	Thank you. (Exits. Comes back after a while.) He's not there.
HE.	Well, he must be off today. Come back tomorrow.
SHE.	Thank you. (Exits. Returns after a while.) Excuse me . . . Has he been working here long?
HE.	I think so. Just come tomorrow – you will find out.
SHE.	Thank you. (Exits. Comes back again.) I'm sorry . . . Do you happen to know if he is married?
HE.	Come back tomorrow, would you . . . He will answer all of your questions.

Enter an actress. She is not beautiful, with peculiar features, extremely thin and tall. She is wearing a shabby coat and sewn-up felt boots; her head is covered with a shawl . . . He clearly dislikes her from the start. Moving forward, her entire behavior convinces him that she does not deserve his respect.

Annoyed, even resentful, he sends her on her way . . . What an importunate creature, he thinks, walking about, panhandling . . . You can see right away, she has come to scrounge. And what was it about him being married? Is she hoping to seduce him with her charms? . . .

After the end of the etude, I ask, as always: Well, tell us what came to you – who is this Stepanov and what do you need with him.

It turns out her husband was recently killed in the war. She was left alone with the children. A bomb has destroyed the house where they used to live. She was evacuated to this city. Somehow, she settled her life here. It's very hard. Her husband had a friend – Peter V. Stepanov. (The husband always called him Petya.) His closest friend. At the start of the war,

Petya was wounded, and they lost touch. Accidently, she learned that a fellow by the name of Peter V. Stepanov works at this place – what if it's him?

While telling her story, she remains quite demure and brief . . . When she spoke of her husband, and the children, something warm and gentle flickered across her face . . . This too she immediately hid . . .

- Why did you want to know if he was married?
- The Stepanov I look for was married – my husband used to have a photo of him with his wife.

I suggest repeating the etude with those same circumstances.

They repeat it. The entire etude is completely different, from start to finish. The words are the same, but their content has changed dramatically.

The greatest change was with him. His contempt and disdain for her has vanished without a single trace. On the contrary, as soon as she spoke, he started treating her with great care and sympathy.

He was not alone – her life in the etude was also drastically different. She behaved with great dignity and strength of mind. She was sorrowful and moving . . . The former insecurity, which used to make her pathetic, was gone . . .

What was the matter? What were the reasons behind this change? After all, their circumstances did not change.

Her story about her husband, the children, and the difficulties of her life touched him. Her careless costume and her excessive perseverance impressed him differently this time . . . Her appearance also no longer seemed ridiculous and absurd – on the contrary, it spoke of her grief, distress, and dismay . . . Besides, she herself had become a different person . . . He wanted to help her, ask her questions, and do what he could for her.

What caused all these changes in her? Once again, the questions I asked her between the etudes. And, most of all, speaking through her own story. Having put her vague worries into words, she made her tough situation concrete for herself. She clarified the facts of her life, including the loss of her husband, her orphaned children, her distress, and the hopelessness of her situation . . . Although all this was present during the first rendering of the etude, it was not as definite, not as precise and specific. Now it came to life and started existing for her in all its concreteness – *as a fact of her life*. This caused the actress to walk upon her old path with greater faith and certainty.

The circumstances, as you see, did not change – they got clarified. *Their nuances* became different. Notice how this led to a complete turnaround in the interpretation of this etude. This shows the importance of *accuracy, correctness, and concreteness of circumstances* when working on a play. The slightest deviation in nuances, and everything goes topsy-turvy.

Needless to say, this effect is only observed when the actors are *living* onstage – when they hear and see the partner, as we hear and see each other in life. Although in the majority of cases, actors do look and see, they do so not as in life. They see the very surface, without looking too deeply.

They do not see the essential and do not notice what their partner thinks and feels. They see what they are "supposed" to see. Even then, they mostly think that they see it.

Circumstances Change with Repetition

- Sergei, is that you?
- Hello, Vera.

- When did you get back? I'm so glad to see you! Have a seat.
- Thank you. Is Dmitry home?
- Dmitry does not live here anymore. He moved out.
- Moved out?
- Yes, recently . . .
- I see.
- Yes . . . Well, tell me about yourself – how have you been?
- Alright . . . Thank you . . . Working . . . Where did Dmitry move?
- Not far from here. 12 Maple Street, apartment 7. I think it's 7.
- I see . . . Well, I better be going, Vera. I have to see him . . . Right now . . . It's important . . . I am sorry . . .
- Of course, if it's important . . . 12 Maple Street, apartment 7.
- Thank you. Goodbye.
- (alone) 12 Maple Street, apartment 7 . . .

The circumstances have been given: Vera is a bride whose fiancé left her unexpectedly and for no apparent reason. He just moved out for good, having left her a letter. Sergei is his friend.

At the beginning of the etude, "Vera" was sitting in her chair, looking fatigued, her fingers absently playing with the tablecloths' fringe. Then she stood up, walked to the window and leaned her hand on the windowsill. She looked at the street with an aimless, mechanical expression, not really seeing it.

Someone knocked at the door. She did not hear it. They knocked again. She came to – "Come in." He came in.

She must have expected someone else – less familiar and not as important . . . His arrival brought her surprise and great joy. Her face instantly brightened, her eyes started shining, her cheeks blushed.

- Sergei, it's you!!
- Hello, Vera.

She could still hardly believe his arrival.

- When did you get back? I'm so glad to see you!

She put his briefcase on the table, took his hand, and led him to the armchair. Excitedly, she was seating her dear guest:

- Have a seat.
- Is Dmitri home?

These words struck her like a whip – everything turned upside down inside her; the blush went out of her cheeks; her hands froze in place when she heard these awful words.

Finally, feeling the awkwardness of her silence and seeing his searching, anxious eyes, she made an effort and said, in a muffled voice:

- Dmitry does not live here anymore.
- He doesn't? – the guest asked, not believing her.

She lowered her head.

- He moved out.

Having understood everything from her crushed look, the guest asked again, in shock:

- Moved out?!. (Really???)
- Yes . . . – She too did not seem to understand how this could happen . . . this terrible, catastrophic event . . . – Recently. – She still saw him; her entire being was full of him, everything in this place was connected with him . . .
- I see! – these words escaped from him beyond his will. They were filled with perplexity, resentment, fear, and shame – what had he done!

Suddenly she caught herself – realized that she might bore him with her grief and complaints.

- Well, tell me about yourself – she said hurriedly, and fussily. – Tell me about yourself – how have you been? (Let's not speak about us. What is there to say? Most importantly, how are you doing? Well?)
- All right . . . Thank you . . . Working . . . – He answered mechanically, thinking about something else. He was shaken by the news. – And where . . . where did Dmitry move? – It seemed like he wanted to intervene, to untangle this stupid mess . . .

Busy with her own thoughts, she could not see his emotions – she only heard the words, "Where did he move?"

- Not far from here . . . 12 Maple Street, apartment . . . 7 (I may be wrong). I think it's 7.
- I see . . . Well, I better be going, Vera.

She woke up . . . through some fog, she began to realize that her guest was suddenly in a hurry to leave . . . She looked at him questioningly: Why?

- I have to see him . . . Right now . . .
- Right now?
- It's important . . . I am sorry . . .
- Well, if it's important . . . – To help him remember, and to ease his search, she added: "12 Maple Street, apartment 7".
- Thank you. Goodbye. – Frustrated, confused, he shook her hand, and left quickly. The meeting broke off awkwardly. And it was clear that he was about to give his friend Dmitry a piece of his mind . . .

She did not notice his emotions. For her, things were over. She looked like a shattered, fragile boat, tossed onto coastal sand by a storm – dimmed eyes, arms hanging, lips automatically whispering: "12 Maple Street, apartment 7" . . .

No, reader, this is no fantasy, and no fiction – this is a school exercise.

Plenty of those, even more poetic and exciting, happen in our modest classes!

The etude is over. Everyone is silent. Some are ashamed of their emotions, of their "weakness" – they are trying to hide their eyes, wet with tears, and a smile of joy, illuminating their faces . . . Beauty just walked by them with its light step – the beauty of our theatre. Talent, if not interfered with, or clogged, shines and sweetly grips your heart with its first steps . . .

I speak a few words of encouragement, and wait for the actors and the audience to cool down a bit. Then I suggest: let's repeat the etude. We won't change anything, and we'll take the same circumstances. Forget that this etude has just happened. Do it as if it's the first time. After all, we always have to act as if "for the first time." No matter how many prior rehearsals have been conducted, Chatsky, having spent three years abroad, still comes back to Moscow for the first time . . . while Hamlet hears about his father's ghost for the first time, and so on.

Here are your circumstances again: you are alone. Your beloved, your fiancé has left you. He used to live with you at your parents' apartment, and now he moved out and rented a place of his own . . . How did this happen? And why? Maybe it was a misunderstanding; perhaps his difficult nature was to blame . . . This is up to you, choose any reason . . . Perhaps you yourself made some mistakes of your own . . .

In the meantime, you are coming off the train and are headed straight to your friend Dmitri. He is so lucky with his wonderful bride . . .

Let's repeat the text and begin.

Just like the first time, "Vera" was sitting in her chair, pale and subdued, her vacant eyes wandering over the walls, the ceiling, her own hands . . . Yet, there was something new in her – it will reveal itself later – the actress was not the one to lose what was living in her from the start. No, she would let it develop and fully give in to it.

Once again, she did not respond to the first knock, although not because she did not hear it. Although she heard the knocking, she could not tear herself away from her thoughts, intimate and entangled.

At the second knock, she replied softly: "Come in."

The door opened quietly and cautiously – the person must not have been certain if he was given permission to enter.

She did not turn to see who came in: she was not expecting anyone she needed or loved. He had to cough to make her turn at him. Delighted, she quickly approached him: "Sergei, it's you!" She grabbed his hand, as if she had wanted to see him for a long time – and now he was here.

- Hello, Vera! – The visitor's words also revealed something new – they had more warmth than before and more friendly intimacy.
- When did you get in? I'm so glad to see you! – As before, she was pulling him to the armchair and sitting him down . . .
- Thank you, thank you – the guest was thanking her as a good old friend who used to frequent this house and often sat in this comfortable armchair.
- Is Dmitri home?

This was a blow to her, as before, but a different kind of blow. Last time, these words lashed her so suddenly that everything inside her got mixed up. It took her awhile to overcome this state . . . Back then, her fiancé's departure was still very fresh – as if it had just happened, leaving her with nothing but bewilderment, confusion and fear . . . Now – quite the opposite: she had no confusion – a *fait accompli* – he is gone. She felt bitter and hurt . . . Yet, it felt as if it has been a long time since this happened . . . She said "just recently." "Recently," in the usual sense, means a few days, or a week . . . In a different sense, however, it may mean an eternity – this is how much she had suffered during this time, and what kind of thoughts she had thought. A different woman was standing before us – matured, thoughtful, and strong-willed. Woe did not crush her; on the contrary, it had enriched and deepened her soul. Her youthful carelessness was completely gone, true, but there was a time and limit set for it anyway . . .

We looked at her head, slightly bent to one side, at her slower movements; we found ourselves immersed in her serious, thoughtful, and somewhat weary eyes. With this, the power of the other beauty stirred and captured us. Previously, we saw a human being defeated by suffering – but now, we saw her rise above her suffering. Captivated by the actress, we experienced this victory with her.

The etude ended. There were no emotions like those awakened by the first etude. No tears came to the viewers' eyes . . .

Instead, there was something quite different – all of those watching, sat serious, immersed in themselves.

Having looked into the eyes of this new woman and having heard the new music in her voice, the viewers had measured in their own heart the kind of journey she had made. Once more, they felt the amazing power of art . . . Which etude was better or stronger – the first or the second? It was impossible to choose.

However, as researchers of the "technique," we cannot stop here. We need to know how it happened that the actress, wanting to repeat the same thing, ended up playing something completely new and unexpected.

Could it be that this fact discloses an important law?

Let us look closer to what occurred.

Before the first etude, I told the actress that her beloved, her fiancé, recently left her and moved to another apartment . . . Clearly, this caught the actress by surprise. She had no time to get used to this new situation, far less to grasp everything that happened.

At that confusing moment, here comes her old friend. Naturally, his sudden arrival makes the abandoned woman happy – she is eager to talk with a dear friend who is almost part of the family . . . All of a sudden comes the most terrible question: "Is Dmitry home?"

It is a frightening question – she herself has not yet decided how to answer it: "is he or isn't he?" What if he just went out for a while? Suddenly, reality demands an answer: is he home or not? Yes or no? It knocks her off her feet.

The etude is over . . . She has lived a part of her life . . . She has closed one of its chapters. But a memory of what happened remained in her soul: a friend came by; he inquired about the closest person I have in life, and I had to say that he left me . . . Now it's clear – I know it, and so does everyone else.

The second etude begins . . . Once again, my old friend arrives . . . once again I am happy to see him in my loneliness, and once more he asks me "Is Dmitry home?" One more time, I have to say that he left me and does not live here anymore . . . But . . . this is not the first time . . . I already told someone that he does not live here, that he has left . . . and that his new address is 12 Maple Street, apartment 7 . . . I am about to say it now, but this is no longer a new thing to do . . . This is something from my past . . .

In short, it happens just like in life: the first time I am asked about something intimate, the question catches me off-guard; the second or third time I am asked the same question – it affects me quite differently . . .

If the actor is *living* onstage, the second etude cannot become a *repeat of the first*. Moreover, his very inability to repeat the etude exactly indicates that the actor is *living*.

However, as we move to scene study or begin to work on a play, this cannot help but bother us.

How could it not? Just imagine that nothing of what was found in rehearsals, however valuable, could be repeated tomorrow – it vanishes along with yesterday, and each subsequent rehearsal (and, obviously, every new performance) becomes something completely new . . .

Yet, in a play everything is firmly set. If our etude was a segment of a play, it would firmly establish that this is the *first* visit from the friend, and the *first* question "Is he home?"

Doesn't this mean that this school is not suited for regular theatre? Perhaps, it is only suitable for some special, improvisational theatre, where the actor is simultaneously the creator of the play? A play like that would only be valuable as it is created here and now, right in front of the audience . . .

The students are rarely fazed by these fundamental theoretical questions – except for those students who had already experienced the iron hands of some form-driven director. Such directors, of course, have no idea about an actor's creativity and do not suspect that it chiefly takes place onstage, before the audience. Neither do they suspect that rehearsals are mere preparation *for the creative act during performances*.

Trained by such directors and having never seen a single creative spark, these actors naturally begin to worry about the execution of exact form. However, these fears soon go away. They quickly find other sources of their art other than those connected with endless self-duplication (or duplication of the director). They realize that non-stop repetition of the exact same pattern inevitably leads to deadening and mechanization. This helps them put their worries to rest, especially as they become practically convinced that there are means to repeat the essence of a play or a scene.

29

Forgetting

The Importance of Forgetting

So how do you make sure that more-or-less exact repetition does not violate the natural laws of an actor's life onstage?

In the case described, the etude completely changed from **repetition**. When performing it for the second time, the actress, naturally, could not feel quite as she did the first time – she was under the impression of the meeting she just experienced in the first etude.

Therefore, would being able to *forget* the first time as if it never happened cause the second meeting to go as the first?

Certainly. After all, the actress would be put in the conditions of the *first time*.

The only question is: how does one learn to forget? The issue of "*forgetting*" is an essential one for the actor. Many significant actors, when asked what they consider the most difficult part of their art, reply: "Forgetting the play."

In fact, how could Othello be serenely happy in the first act if he knows (that is, remembers) what life has in store for him?

We practice this "art of forgetting" all the time, beginning with the very first steps.

However, the techniques we offer at the start are very primitive – we simply say: Now forget what you just did, put it out of your head (as best you can), and begin again as if it were an entirely new etude. The students manage, each in their own way.

But one such primitive method is not enough.

The Creation of the Past Circumstances

Let us take the same etude. Its participants, having experienced their first meeting, cannot forget it. The impression is stored in their psyche as an actual event, as a *fait accompli*. Let us suppose, however, that we need to create an etude (or a scene) with the exact circumstances from its first version.

We could do this at any point, no matter how many times the etude has been performed. To do so, we should bring into special focus the kind of circumstances that would make this a **first** and unprecedented event.

You say to the actress:

- Let's repeat this etude one more time. Just let us play it completely anew, trying not to repeat what happened before. However, if some things return on their own – don't interfere – let them happen as they will.

  To help you let go of what you've experienced, let's imagine with greater concreteness the circumstances that initiate the etude. You are young, you know very little about life and people (the actress is actually 30, however, by some creative whim, she played a 20 or 22-year old).

  You recently graduated from a theatre school; you like music, poetry, and nature . . . Last summer you visited Crimea with your family. There, at a resort, you met a young man. You met him by chance: your restaurant tables were next to one another . . . This young man is not a writer, nor is he an artist . . .
- A scientist – she interrupts me.
- Let it be so. He had proved to be an interesting person to talk to – well-travelled and smart, he captivates you when he speaks about his profession . . . What field is he in?
- Physics.
- When talking about new discoveries and the brilliant prospects his science has to offer, he becomes so excited . . .
- And I begin to appreciate his science too.
- Southern Crimea, a carefree vacation, walks on the beach, excursions to mount Ai Petri and Gursuf . . . Life seemed like such bliss . . . You soon became great friends. Your parents also grew fond of the young man and did not interfere with your mutual sympathy. And when you came back . . .
- To Kazan.
- Why Kazan?
- He was from Kazan – just like myself.
- And when you returned to Kazan, your parents invited him to move to your apartment. His own living arrangements were quite poor.

  Although urban life did not allow you the same kind of freedom you enjoyed in Crimea, and each of you had been busy with work (you – at your theatre, he – at his lab) – your friendship grew even stronger. He used to say that you being in his life did not interfere with his work, but made it even easier and more joyful. You had even begun talking about marriage.

  However, recently, he started spending less time at home and more at his laboratory. You saw each other less often. He talked about some new discovery of national importance and of the need to conduct extensive experiments. He mentioned a lengthy business trip. What kind of discoveries or experiments, he did not tell you, but with bitterness and fear, you began to notice how the importance of his work has grown for him and has completely replaced his personal life. It ceased to exist for him – he was concentrating entirely on work. Sometimes—you now recall—he spoke of the need to go away . . . for a long time . . . Jokingly, he asked: "You won't cry much if I leave and don't come back?" Remember?
- Yes! I did not understand how serious it was . . . that circumstances might force him to do so . . .
- He was still gentle with you, attentive and sensitive . . . Although, at times, he would lock himself in his room. When you knocked, he would answer that he was very busy . . . Then he would suddenly disappear for a week . . . Where to – you never knew. "On business," he would reply briefly.

Ten days ago, he took his belongings and left again . . . And the next the morning, you received a letter in which he asked your forgiveness – he had left you for good. Your marriage, he wrote, would have been a mistake; you do not fit together, you are strangers . . . He wrote that he does not deserve you. With time, your pain will subside, and you will find another man, more worthy of you. He asked you to forgive him, again and again . . . Only his own thoughtlessness and selfishness are to blame. He cannot continue deceiving you and asks you not to seek a meeting with him.

This is it. You are alone. Your father is on business trip in Siberia. Mother went to visit him. You probably went to see Dmitry . . . Since you know his address . . . .

- Of course I did. I don't believe what he wrote – he invented it all. Something else must be going on. He is trying to humiliate, to denigrate himself in my eyes so that I become disillusioned with him. He wants to ease my pain. But I see through it, I know that it is not true. There is some force at work that divides us. I may truly be in the way . . . Not the right match for him . . . And he, out of pity for me, wants to portray himself as a careless, petty egotist . . . I still can't understand a thing . . . I'm filled with confusion.
- You said – you went to talk to him. How did it go?
- I did not get to see him . . . I was told that he was not home . . . Only it wasn't true . . . He must not have wanted to see me. I walked around his house for a long time . . . In the evening, I came again, but he really was not home. I saw his things in the apartment . . . wrote him a letter . . .
- Maybe there's another woman involved?
- No, no! No!! – she protested hotly, – This is impossible! . . – She grew silent . . . lost in her thoughts . . .
- I see . . . So, now you're alone . . . Wandering around your deserted apartment, from room to room, from corner to corner . . . You've been doing this for a while.
- For a while, – she repeated mechanically, – for a while . . . In my mind, it's been a year . . . or two . . . my whole life . . .
- That's how you start. Or rather continue, without interrupting your inner life.

These specific circumstances made her past more tangible. They captivated the actress, thus freeing her from the influence of the previous etude.

It was replaced with her *actual past life*. "This is true, this is real, this is what's happened," the actress now thinks.

The more we would repeat this etude, the more *facts and circumstances of the past* would emerge for the actors.

We know this from our everyday experience – as soon as we touch upon some part of our past, memories just spring on us – all sorts of facts and details appear. You thought you had forgotten them all, but they are alive. In our case, too, imagination prompts thousands of tiny details for the actress.

For the most part, actors (especially students) become so engaged, they continue, along with their partners, to *gather and develop* material for their etudes. They do so both inside and outside the classroom.

The past of their role in the etude, and thereby the role itself, is revealed to them step by step. It captures them, it draws them in. They become interested and amused by this new, unfamiliar experience when the role merges with the actor so and leaves him perplexed – where is the role and where is he? As if he was no longer just himself, but the role . . . And the role stopped being something extraneous and became him.

The same thing happens with the circumstances: he feels that all these stray circumstances and facts happen to him personally, not to anyone else.

Thus begins his acquaintance with one of the most important stages of an actor's work – artistic transformation.

Here is one important stipulation.

In our case, the teacher-director personally explained all the preliminary circumstances of "Vera's" life. This method may not always reach the desired goal. For the most part, the director, while fantasizing and talking, gets carried away, becomes excited, while the actor listens to him calmly – as if it were an amusing story that has absolutely nothing to do with him. He listens and remains unaffected.

In this case, however, the actress was such that she drank in all of the director's words. Moreover, she prompted new facts of her life, fueling the director's story. Such cases are rare. The usual tactic is this: the director begins the story in order to bring the actor to the point when he becomes somewhat engaged by it. At this point, the director must *switch to interviewing* the actor so as to immerse him in the character's circumstances: where did you meet? how? and when? what was your first impression of him? what happened next? and so on.

Thus, by using questions, the director should involve and engage the actor in this imaginary life.

30

Concreteness as a Path to Authentic Perception

On the Concreteness of Objects and Facts

In our etudes, there are, of course, no sets, costumes, or makeup. Seemingly, they are relying exclusively on the imagination of the participants. In the meantime, there is more authenticity here than there is on stage.

Here, walls are walls; the floor is the floor; windows are windows; a cabinet is a cabinet. And my partner is exactly as I'm used to seeing people in life – no makeup, or wig; just an ordinary person without any forgery.

And so, I perceive him simply as he is; I see what mood he is in, and what occupies him; I see how he relates to me – I can't help but see it: it happens on its own accord, through our everyday habit. By his facial expression; the tone of his voice; the involuntary movement of his hands, fingers, head, and so on – I guess at his thoughts and feelings . . .

And in this way, I immediately fall onto *the correct path to actual perception of my concrete partner*, with all of the subtleties of this process and with all of its truth.

This genuine, live perception is the basis from which the life of the actor onstage flows, and upon which it feeds.

It is the stream of that truth through which, in falling into it, the actor becomes faultlessly truthful.

Now, all of his strength should be directed only toward the preservation of this correct perception, and its development.

In order to nurture this authenticity and concreteness of perception, you must constantly remind the actor that he doesn't need to invent anything, but rather that he needs to take the situation, the partner, and all of the other things only as they are in real life. He needs to take precisely that very room and not any different one; the one with this stove, with this cupboard, with these cracks on the ceiling. That window. Through it, you can see a yard with benches and trees. Two or three of the trees have withered – accept what is before you in real life.

If you allow an actor (especially in the early stages) to imagine or picture something for himself in place of this room, then he isn't going to be able to do this; and even if he is able to, then he can only do it for a short while. In a few seconds, the vision dissipates, and he (assuming that, since he's already taken up this matter, he must stick with it) will go out of his way to convince himself that he still sees that fleeting image.

In this way, he loses his balance and is displaced from the correct emotional state; if he continues like that, he will assert himself in this falsehood.

In order for the student-actor to not only understand in his mind that he must perceive things that aren't imagined but are true, but also *to become accustomed to this in practice*, you must patiently point him to it every step of the way.

This authentic perception has already been discussed in part in one of the first chapters of the book (*Weakness of the Actor's Creative Ties*); an example was given of how a student tried to see "good weather" through the window, while at the same time, dreadful autumn rain fell outside, and how the teacher, using this mistake, clarified for him the essence of the matter in practice and showed him the correct path.

In order to train someone to perceive the truth and reality, it is necessary to not miss any occasion to suggest a text that would point to what is there in actuality. If it is evening and through the window the setting sun can be seen, you must use this opportunity to give a text featuring that setting sun. Everything, beginning with the most minor details, just so long as it had some bearing on us personally (rain, the moon, thunder, a sunny day, an evening sunset, frost, the details of the actor's appearance or costume, his physical state, the performance that everyone attended yesterday), and ending with significant personal and social events – everything should be put into use.

And you shall see that *this one genuine existing* phenomenon, or event, or object *will revive and make true everything else in the etude*.

A storm has just passed; the first spring storm. The sky is beginning to clear, and the bright sun struggles through the gaps between the evaporating patches of cloud.

It's stuffy in the room; you want to open a window. It's likely that out there the after storm fragrance of the resinous poplar standing near the window can already be sensed, and that the birds are chattering cheerfully . . .

Two young people are called up; they are given the following text:

First: The storm is over . . . it's clearing up . . .
Second: It'd be nice to open the window . . .
First: Let's open it. (They open it.)
Second: Ah, what air.
First: Yes, I feel easier now; I had this heavy feeling all day.
Second: My injured shoulder has been aching since last night . . . And what's more I received an unpleasant telegram . . . It turns out that my mother was very ill – she's getting better now.
First: Anna? What's the matter with her?
Second: I don't know. I only found out through this telegram. "The danger has passed." But what the danger was, I can't even imagine. I sent an inquiry.
First: It's all right, things will get better. All things will pass. Just like this storm.
Second: I hope so.

During the class, the downpour, the claps of thunder, the sparks of lightning, of course, distracted everyone from the task – even more so for it being the first rain of the season. And now, after the text has been repeated and the students have begun the etude, their impressions from the storm are still with them. The text doesn't contradict these impressions – therefore both of them, giving into their natural inner urge, approached the window and began to look out of it with curiosity. For whatever reason, one of them looked down, at the earth and the puddles; the other – more so at the sky, at the clouds, and at the bright young green of the poplar . . .

Both of them were so immersed that, by all appearances, they even forgot that they were in class, and that they were acting at that moment. Truly, how could you remain indifferent to this sight of awakening nature, especially after our hard, gloomy northern winter! Your entire body longs to be free, to live and enjoy the sun! And they are young, full of strength, hopes and dreams; they are probably overflowing with power, trembling from a surge of energy . . .

How interesting it was to witness this eloquent silence. How much could be seen in it. How readable were their thoughts; how clear were the differences in their characters. One is some kind of abstract dreamer, "a poet" – he rapturously looks at the sky . . . the other is a realist, a practical man, and for that reason his thirsty gaze is glued down to the earth . . . What awesome puddles! Oh, these lucky kids who splash through them, spraying each other and squealing with delight!

Suddenly the other, the one who looked at the sky, doesn't so much say or sigh: "The storm is over . . . " He's still looking up, following the racing of the clouds . . .

The second also glances up. With his practical eye, he immediately appraises the situation, and comes to the conclusion: "Yes. It'd be nice to open the window."

The first happily jumps on this idea. "Let's open it!" and leaps up onto the windowsill, unlocking the upper shutter with a stroke. The second unlocks the lower, and both halves of the large window burst open.

They both shiver from the crisp, fresh air. The first stays above and, leaning out the window, breathes greedily, raising his head up, as if he is breathing the sky and the clouds, and not "our" air that is left down below for our share. The second takes a few deep breaths with pleasure, smiling and booming contentedly: "What air!"

The first one doesn't have time for this – he needs to gather as much of the air that is reserved for him up high. He just nods his head and hastily throws out a "Yes, yes! . . . "

Having inhaled plenty, he finally brings his head back into the room with us, and he says to the one below him: "Yes, I feel easier now; I had this heavy feeling all day . . . "

This is very curious and very instructive. It would seem that the surrounding reality should have upset the *imagined* life suggested by the etude – the kind of life where everything is non-existent and fictional. It would seem that the real sun and the authenticity of the surroundings should have been "sobering," and that it should have returned them to reality. Meanwhile, the opposite phenomenon is occurring: the reality of the setting, the concreteness of the facts is carried over to the imagined.

How is this so?

The Fishing Rod

An interesting phenomenon occurs: the actor gets hooked on the fishing rod of truth. The bait is concrete reality. Concrete reality arouses my personal emotions. And as soon as my emotions have spoken up, they push back my reason. Instead of correctly and objectively seeing my surroundings, I begin to see them through the prism of fantasy, evoked by my emotions.

Just allow yourself to get caught on this wondrous fishing rod – it will pull you, the actor, exactly where you need to go. It will do so on its own accord, without any participation from your side.

When repeated frequently, this process of crossing *over the threshold* becomes progressively easier. After some time, a habit is fostered – as soon as you have crossed the threshold of the stage, you begin to relate to your surroundings, and to all circumstances of the play, as if to something actually existing and concrete. That is to say that the imaginary circumstances become as concrete as that storm, as that window, as that air after the storm . . .

This quality (and it is nothing other than a new quality) is fostered fairly easily and quickly. It leads, in turn, to an interesting phenomenon – paradoxical, at first glance. The actor is accustomed to perceiving only what he actually sees. At the moment, he sees a room, a window, a door, a floor, a ceiling . . . In spite of this, the teacher gives him the following etude: You're standing in some corner with heavy pedestrian traffic. You're selling matches. To every passerby you say: "Citizen! Buy these matches." The rest of the text points out to an unexpected meeting of old acquaintances. What kind of meeting it will become—dramatic or comedic—that will depend on the actors' personae and inclinations, on their present moods, on the nature of their interaction . . .

It would seem that the actor who is used to perceiving the settings as they are in real life, in accordance with reality, should become confused that there is a room here, and neither a street nor a street corner . . . However the etude comes together very cleanly, strongly and without any hesitations.

The teacher asks the actor:

- And where was that?
- I don't know, he answers. Somewhere on a corner, where many people are passing.
- Does this mean on the street?
- It seems so . . .
- Didn't you see the windows? The floor, the ceiling?
- I saw it . . . the floor, the ceiling, the stove.
- So how could this be a street?
- Well, it probably wasn't a street, but rather . . . some shopping arcade, or market stalls . . . It didn't really make a difference to me – for me it was all "street" . . . foreign, hostile . . . Although I did see the windows. Now I remember – I even looked out the window . . . children were playing in the yard . . . and I even thought about it: they're playing, they're having fun . . . And my little brother is in the hospital . . .
- Then it was a shopping arcade?
- Yes, only it's not in Moscow but in some small town abroad somewhere.
- In France? In Italy?
- No. In Sweden.
- Why?
- I don't know. Anywhere but in the south. Just look at the sky – what a dreary day . . . Trees like you find in the north . . . double window panes . . .
- Maybe it's Russia?
- No. You won't find inside patios like this at a Russian market, especially not in a small town.

This is how the actor's free imagination, without any particular command on his behalf, instantly transforms his surroundings into a different reality, harmonious with his current inner state.

Most importantly, the genuineness of the reality and the serious attitude toward it create such a psychological setting that everything connected with it is accepted as authentic and actually existing – even though it isn't there at all, but has only been described in words and flashed through your mind.

Windows, doors, the stove, the arcade, matches in his hands – these are all facts, they are all real . . . "Citizen! Buy these matches!" – this means that I am selling, and this is just as sure and real. I'm selling something, and it means that I have to . . . It means that I can't help but be out there selling . . . and reasons compelling me to become a salesman appear instantly in my imagination.

Here is a different situation, the complete opposite of this one – that which is practiced more often than any other in theatres. Actors are not only not trained to adjust their creative state in genuine settings through the use of genuine facts and events – on the contrary, they are trained to believe that everything around them is fake and false. We are rehearsing in a room, but this isn't a room, but a forest, a palace, or something else . . . You have a stick in your hands, but it isn't a stick – it is a weapon, and so on.

Following this, everything else is perceived as completely approximate, and as if it is false: people, words, thoughts, feelings . . .

Stanislavsky, who had an implacable attitude toward falseness onstage, always strongly exposed even the smallest hint of it in an actor. But, like a genuine artist, he demanded it of himself even more strictly and mercilessly.

He used to tell the following story that happened to him personally. In the Art Theatre, Turgenev's play *A Month in the Country* was being put on. Stanislavsky played Rakitin. As they always did in this theatre, the actors and their director together strove for achieving truth, and they achieved a lot. The play was widely recognized as a great success.

Over the summer, a group of actors went to vacation at the estate of one of the theatre's friends. And there, when taking a stroll with their hospitable host in the wonderful old park, they suddenly came upon a gazebo in an alley that looked exactly like the one that they had had in the theatre during this play. Centuries-old trees . . . the scent of the forest, the flowers . . . the bright sky . . . the birds' song . . . And they suddenly wanted to perform a scene from the play that perfectly matched this genuine setting.

"The audience members" settled into their places, some here and some there; and the actors sat on the bench just as they always had in their own theatre.

They began the scene . . . and after a few lines they ended it. They ended it because they were embarrassed by their falseness, their fake theatrical verisimilitude.

And no matter how many times they started again, they couldn't do anything with it – everything turned out completely false. And it turned out that it was impossible for them to handle this, to step over into the realm of authentic truth. This is how Stanislavsky told it.

His explanation for it was that the authenticity of the surroundings pushed him (as a sensitive artist) to a similar authenticity of feelings and of all of his life. It demanded the kind of authenticity that, until that point, his artistic life had not reached in this play. In the theatre, its habitual convention of the set pieces, and of the environment in general, did not reveal this gap, and it left the actors in a pleasant delusion with regards to the perfection of their performance.

Concreteness: The Path to the Personal

The atmosphere of the park, of course, has a very strong effect on you – here, all of the senses are immediately attacked: sight, hearing, smell, touch . . . We cannot get this kind of strong impact in our school classes, or during rehearsals in a theatre.

Therefore, it is all the more important to select and use such objects that not only speak to the actor's eye, but also to his other senses. One impression will be formed from a simple handkerchief found in a pocket or on a desk; another – from the discovery of a lacy, perfumed woman's kerchief . . . In general, objects make moods and feelings more concrete: a favorite toy of a dead child will say much more than a mere recollection of him.

However, an especially strong and decisive impact occurs when things become personal for the actor, either directly or indirectly.

I'll quote an example from practice. Once, when searching for new material with which to verify all of these methods, I struck upon a group that was made up not only of actors, but also of singers, musicians, dancers, and one juggler.

The leader of this group was a person who correctly understood the stage. He voiced the idea that it would be useful for everyone – not just the actors – to become acquainted with the basic principles of the proper creative state onstage.

Not all of the participants approved of this project. And, since I wasn't about to do without any speaking, a few of them protested: why do we have to speak if we're never going to have to open our mouths onstage?

However, in spite of their misgivings, they took part in the lesson. They came and sat somewhat aloofly, showing their disinterest and unwillingness to participate in such a strange and unnecessary task.

The juggler carried himself with a particular air of independence.

He was a very tall, thin person – like a stick, this awkward fellow. He was at that age when his arms, legs, and neck rushed to grow – they outpaced everything else and seemed to belong to someone else. He gave off the impression of an awfully clumsy fellow; sort of like a cheerful sweeping windmill, bursting into the room, visiting people.

By all accounts, he was enthusiastic about juggling to the point of forgetting himself: even before our exercises began, I could see how he didn't stop for a minute tossing, catching, balancing, and in general "working" with different things that fell into his hands: cigarettes, matches, someone's hat, a shoe, a watch, a book, a flower pot, a chair, a walking stick, a pitcher, a woman's powder-case, a bunch of keys – all of these things flashed through the air, making their owners concerned for the safety of their possessions . . .

And why, in fact, would he need any kind of "actor's creative state"?! He only needs to "work" well, without accidents; nothing else matters.

Having gotten the actors interested in the obviously tempting results that came about with these new methods, I began, bit by bit, to engage the non-actors.

It finally came down to the juggler. At first I gave him an easy, neutral text. No big deal – he more or less handled it . . . it was obvious that he wasn't a person devoid of actor's instinct and, what's more, he was extremely vain, and had a high opinion of himself, characteristic of youth. I gave him an exercise that was a bit more complex. Imagining that he understood and had mastered everything after the first exercise, he became careless and, of course, it got worse . . . and he sensed it. Wounded, he barely hobbled along to the end of the etude, and without even waiting for the teacher's comments, he stood up and went to his seat.

- Whatever are you doing?
- What's wrong? I said everything, I did everything . . . what else is there!

"Oh, so that's how you are!" I thought to myself, "You want to show your total disinterest and even disdain, and you do it in such a primitive and unceremonious way . . . And all the while, you're just covering up your own limitations and helplessness! Well, hold on! Now you'll learn a little something!"

- No, it's not enough. Let's try something else, something more interesting . . . I'll give you a different partner . . . who should it be? How about you? . . . Please!

The new partner is chosen not without intention. Even before the beginning of the lesson it was obvious that he liked her. More so than with anyone else, he performed his jugglery in front of her as a way of flirting: he would either take away her purse and toss it in the air along with his own cap or pitcher, or he would scare the girl, acting as if he was going to drop something on her . . . In general he showed great preference toward her.

At the beginning, she acted like she liked it. She smiled and laughed . . . When she felt that something was going to fall on her, she would yelp softly from surprise. As time went on, however, she seemed to have grown tired of such attention: she started getting annoyed, and began to grimace . . . The juggler, in his rapture, wasn't in the least concerned, and he continued his actions.

Seeing before him this attractive woman (on top of everything else, she was a ballerina), he was almost noticeably confused and . . . he couldn't refuse.

- Imagine that you are husband and wife. You've been married for two years already. (He smiled smugly.) Let's call you Verochka, and you – Seryozha. You live here, in this room. Unfortunately, you don't really live in harmony . . . Perhaps it's that you rushed into marriage . . . you aren't really made for one another, you're too different: you only think about your work, and she isn't interested in it. She thought it interesting at first, but then she simply grew tired of it. She has her own work, her own interests, her own hobbies, and her own friends . . . Perhaps at some point, you'll patch up your family life, but for now . . . there is only grief, disappointment. In moments of anger she doesn't shy away from calling you boring and boorish. In annoyance, hurtful words always burst from her tongue. At first, it was rare, but then it began to happen more and more often . . . Finally, you see – she is completely shunning you: she always has things to do at her girlfriends' or her friends' who are closer to her – to her, they seem smarter and more interesting . . . You put up with it, watching, holding back (after all, maybe later your life together will get better). But today, after an ugly scene and quarrel, a letter of some kind was delivered to her . . . She read it, tuned her mocking, derisive eyes to you, quickly dressed, and left, slamming the door behind her.

This is the interesting little note that you received (I hand her the note, which I've just written here, on the spot). Read it and give it back to me. (She reads it, starting from surprise, looks toward her admirer with childish, impish malice, and then returns the note.) Having received this pleasant letter, you naturally don't waste precious time, and you leave.

Everything turned out quite well where you went. There's just one little unpleasantness: it would seem that somewhere, you dropped your little note. Maybe on the street, maybe in another place . . . ultimately, these are just minor details . . .

Now, this is what happens after she leaves. You're left alone in the room. Then, she returns.

Don't rush, let her stay in the room, watch her closely, and later, when you want to, just ask: "Nice weather?"

She answers: "Yes."

You ask her something else: "Did you take a walk?"

She says: "No, I was at rehearsal."

And that's all. If, after this exchange, either of you wishes to say or ask or do something else, don't be shy.

Let's repeat the text. What are you asking? And what are you answering? . . . Right. Now you will walk out the door; let him stay there by himself. And don't rush to come back.

As soon as she closes the door behind her, I say to him: "And when she, this Verochka of yours, left, you noticed that in her rush she dropped a scrap of paper – it's lying right there, this scrap. Please, take a look. This is a secret note; you're going to read it now, and everything will become clear to you."

Daunted by my hints, stung by her triumphant exit and sneering glance, spurred by general interest, he picks up the note that I've dropped on the floor (as if his light-minded wife has lost it). He unfolds it, and reads it.

This is what the note says: "Verochka! I am entertaining some people who could do us a favor. Ditch your beanpole, your giraffe, and come over as soon as you can. Something good might come out of this for you and I. Your Lily. Come quick!" He grows pale, looking at me with hostility – after all, I'm the one who wrote the note. If I hesitate even for a moment – there will be a scandal – how dare I offend him! To call him funny names . . . to snoop into his private feelings!! . . .

"That's it, that's it! Good! Excellent job!" I say assuredly, looking him straight in the eye. "Be angry, be outraged, don't hold back!"

But I am not at ease either – I live together with him, I'm no less excited than he is. I'm no longer the teacher - I am his double! He senses this – his anger has just been deprived of a target . . .

"That's right, that's right!" I kindle him, "How fortunate that no one else knows the contents of this note . . . just you alone . . . But what kind of dirty tricks are being played under your nose, undermining your relationship, your married life!"

At this moment, the door opens and "Verochka" walks in. Glancing at him, she turns away in order to hide her smile.

He pales . . . he is at a loss . . . he is about to fly off the handle, to lose it, to run away, to curse all these insulting and useless "exercises" . . .

"Yes, yes . . . that's right! . . . take your time . . . watch her closely . . . " I redirect his attention onto her. "She seems to be very cheerful . . . it must be that she had a pleasant walk . . . the weather must be nice . . . "

I say it all quietly . . . with long intervals . . . during a huge, tortuous, awkward pause, when neither one, nor the other partner knows what to do . . . All the while, their emotions torment them . . . they feel that they must be doing something . . . In the meantime, from the outside, they hear that all of this is correct . . .

"When you feel like saying something, or asking – go ahead, don't be shy."

Turning away from her and pulling himself together, he utters under his breath something that has come to his memory: "Nice weather?"

She senses that something is amiss with him; she has never seen him this way, and she responds with what sounds like a question:

"Yes . . . " (as if asking: "and what about it?")

"That's it, that's it," I encourage him. And he, sensing that she is afraid, rallies and, already without any prompting from my end, questions her further:

"Did you take a walk?"

"No," she answers and then – noticing that he is concealing something, and carefully watching her – she tries to avoid explanations. So, she snaps at him: "I was at rehearsal." ("and leave me in peace.")

He begins to boil.

"That's right!" I say to him.

He pulls the note out from behind his back, where he had been hiding it until now. Waiving it in the air, thrusting it into her hands, he keeps asking: "At this? . . . at this? . . . at this rehearsal?"

She is taken aback and, recognizing the note, she becomes scared . . .

"Why are you laughing?!" He screams at her (although she wasn't even thinking of laughing.)

"I'm not laughing," she babbles, and storms out of the room. He follows her . . .

"That's all! Good! Excellent job! Where are you going?! That's enough! Stop! Come back!"

He comes to a halt, turning around . . . and he's still excited and full of passion! . . .

"Look at you! You're wonderful! And you didn't want to exercise."

He clearly doesn't understand anything – everything is mixed up: his own anger, the humiliation, the lie, the mockery . . . and here he is being praised, looked at with admiring eyes . . . And all of his colleagues are whispering: "Look at him! Was this our Fyodor?!"

This is how the dam broke.

Later, this young man would not leave me alone: dogging my footsteps. Juggling became less interesting to him than it had been before. It was sidelined. Unfortunately, I lost touch with him – the group left for a tour, and then the war began.

This Fyodor, obviously, was not devoid of acting talent. With tenacity and love for work, he could have achieved good results – and it seemed that he did possess tenacity.

This was not the first time that the awakening of an actor began with such a provocatively designed etude.

This isn't only true for gifted people – a well-aimed note can even knock an ungifted person completely off-balance, and immediately ignite him. Just don't lose it – seize the moment!

What happened in this case?

The actor prepared to perform. All of a sudden, a wound to his pride was inflicted – it affected him personally. In response, his emotions arose and seized him – they weren't fictional – they were real. He was genuinely hurt and offended . . . He was indignant, he won't forgive this, he'll show you who he is, he'll repay this right now!

All of this is him, him, and him! Having established his own "I," he stands firmly upon it. And beyond that, he is already boiling with the living feelings of hatred and living demand – to repay an insult. To hell with any "acting!" All of a sudden, he hears that this is what's called truth, that this is what is needed. Just a second ago, he experienced an insult. He felt it with all of his being, and it had nothing in common with acting or with art, and then suddenly – it's art! This, his personal irritation, this, his emotion, is **creative**! . . . "Just don't do anything differently, don't restructure! Everything is right!"

This turn of events knocks him out of his usual state of self-awareness – it turns out that his identity is being taken for a completely different identity, and here they are slipping him imagined facts and circumstances that suit his real mood.

At the start, having been struck with surprise, he accepts it all with hesitation . . . he is encouraged in this . . . this causes an imperceptible "shift" – his **transformation**.

He had just established himself, and established himself completely, dropping the conventionality and falseness of acting under the influence of genuine anger – and then there are these circumstances that, without destroying his "I," transform him into a different person.

And now, as someone else, he is already giving in to what the circumstances are pushing him toward.

Therefore, the phenomenon of transformation *above all requires for the actor to be himself.*

In this case, it was necessary to affect the actor personally. But this does not necessarily have to be done by means of agitating emotions such as anger, rage, or offense. It is important to arouse strong emotions that will touch the actor personally – that is all. These emotions could also be happiness or satisfaction.

There exists an opinion that transformation can be achieved by two paths: internal or external.

If we look at them closely, however, we'll see that each of these methods is based on the phenomenon which was evident in this etude: from the very beginning, the actor establishes his "I," his identity.

When the actor is able to catch the characterization while proceeding from the external, this is done in the same way. It is just that it happens unnoticed: the moment of the identity's establishment is overlooked.

In searching for a character, the actor changes outwardly. Suppose, for example, that he hunches over, he peers out from under a furrowed brow, half-closing one eye, wrinkling up his face . . . Yet all the same, he remains ***himself***. But his self-perception is changed by these alterations in his face and figure, by his new temper or the rhythm of his motions – these purely external changes lead to an immediate and reflexive change of his inner state. Although he remains himself, he still feels different, like a different person.

This sensation of his new being only lasts for a few seconds. It is merely an instantaneous ***first reaction***. One must give in to it. A person who knows how to do this is on the path to mastering the character.

The case with the juggler is not described here in order to tempt the inexperienced teacher into testing his own strength against such a potent method. A teacher might easily lose his footing, if he doesn't have enough experience under his belt, or if he overestimates his own strength. As a result, he would ruin his relationship with his students and lose their faith and their love.

Let him write notes, but . . . carefully – for now, not touching the personality of the actor.

Let this case serve solely as a convincing illustration of the *strength of concrete things and facts for the actor.* This is the force before which all obstacles fall; the force that allows us to go beyond the highest "thresholds."

Of course, one could surround oneself with very real things, drink real tea or wine, smell real roses – and yet nothing good would come out of it.

It is necessary to develop in oneself a particular inclination and ability to ***grasp*** everything that is real and concrete. One must grasp it and give in to it – along with all of the sensations and reactions that arise from it.

31

The Ambiguity of the Given Circumstances as a Motivating, Driving Force in the Actor's Art

Is it worth occupying yourself with "sketches" or "drafts" when these things are not going to be needed onstage?

It's customary to think that what is needed onstage are finished, elaborated canvases. Therefore, it is necessary to learn how to create them. That is the first question.

And then, there is another: our exercises and, in part, our etudes "without given circumstances" – do they not train the actor to become accustomed to imprecise, unspecific, approximate given circumstances?

All of these barely outlined circumstances and relationships these "Skvortsovs," these "Zinas" and so on – are they not merely a shadow, only the first vague inkling, first unclear sensation . . . what good is it if the actor is trained to be satisfied with the imprecise, the unspecific, the undetermined?

After all, Shchepkin, Yermolova, and Stanislavsky all spoke about realness and tangibility . . . This is exactly what our most advanced theatres strive to do – there, dozens and hundreds of rehearsals are spent helping the actor get the perfect feel of the role and of its every scene . . .

And thus, there are two questions: one – is it worth doing sketches and drafts? And the other – is it harmful?

The answer would seem clear: it is not worth it, and it is harmful.

"I Know" and "I Don't Know"

At any given moment in our lives, we are simultaneously experiencing two diametrically opposed states. One: we definitely know a little something about ourselves, about our surroundings, about people and given circumstances. We know and we can anticipate the future. The other: we don't know anything about ourselves at all: nothing about our surroundings, or about people, or the given circumstances, and we can't anticipate anything.

For example, this morning I set out, as always, for rehearsal, but as soon as I walked out of the gate, I was nearly knocked over by a piercing northern wind to which I am completely unaccustomed. Well there you have it! From the window, it seemed calm to me, and I hadn't dressed warm enough . . . While walking to the theatre, I became completely chilled. At the theatre, it turned out that the lead actor had fallen ill and instead of the planned scene, we had to scrape up something completely different. See how many surprises there are in such a short period of time, and in the most simple, habitual, everyday conditions!

And so, it is from these two contractions – "I know" and "I don't know" – that our lives are composed. (Some things we know, but many other remain unknown to us.) Throughout our lives, we constantly encounter new circumstances and "surprises." We are constantly investigating them, and getting our bearings – we clarify the circumstances, and we adapt to them. The uncertainty of future moments is natural for us, and a completely normal phenomenon.

And how is it in a play? There, we know everything. We know not only the past and the present, but even the future.

This condition is completely unnatural for us.

And how is it in an etude "without given circumstances"?

There, on the contrary, we know nothing: neither who we are, who our partner is, nor the circumstances of our lives, nor our relationships . . . we know only words – a few phrases whose meaning could be interpreted in thousands of ways . . .

This condition is also unnatural.

Nevertheless, in each of these cases, the actor finds the path to creativity.

Let us see how he does it.

We'll begin with etudes. The actor doesn't know anything. He knows only the text, and he even needs to "forget" it, to toss it out of his consciousness. For a second, he "empties" himself, trying to exist without thoughts, without feelings, without desires. But it is difficult to stay in such a condition for long. And as soon as the actor has "green-lit" himself to freedom, then his first impressions strive to fill that void: the window, the floor, the walls, the ceiling, the pictures, the partner . . .

But this isn't enough for creativity: it is all still "emptiness." What is all of this to me – the windows, the floor? Well, I see them, and so what? . . .

And then suddenly – with one glance at my partner, under the impression from her – in one imperceptibly short moment, this emptiness became creatively filled. I get an inkling that my partner is a strict sister with whom I am at odds, that our conversation is about money, and that we share this room . . . And thus the emptiness is gone. However, this emptiness got filled just as it does in life – I know some things (my sister, her strict principles, this unpleasant conversation about money), and there are other things I don't know. Moreover, this unknown part turns out to be the most interesting – will she give me the money or won't she? Will I be able to convince her or not?

One part of the emptiness got filled by "knowing," while its other part – by "not knowing."

It would now be worth considering how the actor's creative nature behaves when it encounters a different kind of unnaturalness – a play, where everything is known in advance.

This will be discussed in more detail in the section on "scene study," but for now it is worth focusing on the fact that knowledge of the play, after all, does not come to the actor straight away [Demidov must be referring to his fourth, unfinished book, *The Artist's Creative Process Onstage*. Although a section on scene study remained unfinished, the book contains much precious material that has to do with creating a character]. In the beginning, when he comes to the first read-through (this is only if he doesn't know his role well before this), then he only envisages his role in general terms: for him, many things are still unknown: his partner is an unknown; he doesn't know how they will approach their scenes; much of the text is still unknown.

This is the root of the actor's direct, immediate interest in his partner, and likewise in all of the words: not only those of his own partner, but of the other characters as well. This interest does not allow him to observe himself, and so he reacts to everything like he would in life; he utters his words without any particular preliminary forethought or preparation – it is all spontaneous. In short, what happens during the first rehearsal is almost exactly the same thing that happens in our etudes. In the etudes too, the only things that are known are general terms, and the rest depends on the environment, and on the partners and their behavior.

The First Reading

Let us take a look at this "first read-through" that is practiced in many theatres. Its goal is to get the actor acquainted in general terms with both the text of the entire play, and with his role. In order to accomplish this, all of the participants come together and read their roles, as if aiming for them. Whether they want it or not, they are trying their hand at their roles, however cautiously.

Perhaps you have come across this curious phenomenon – in a first read-through, the actor, even though he still doesn't know the text or the point of the play, sometimes reads his role so well that you think: "If only he would perform it this way!"

But imagine his embarrassment – he rehearses tomorrow, and the day after tomorrow . . . No one is interfering with him, and he rehearses as he pleases. One would have thought he would be discovering his role step-by-step, and becoming better acquainted with the given circumstances . . . In the meantime, his acting becomes worse and worse; it is growing emptier with every step . . . When he read it the first time, everything was as it should be: the circumstances, the facts, the relationship with his partner. But as he began to "work" further, the facts disappeared, the partner stopped being a living, moving person with whom life had thrown him together . . . In the beginning, when he didn't know the point of the play, he correctly interpreted the facts and his relationships. Later, when he began to become more familiar with the play and to determine its circumstances, then all these things – the circumstances, the facts, and the partners – receded and became less and less tangible. Isn't it strange?

Perhaps this stemmed from the fact that all further work on the role was carried out incorrectly . . . Perhaps. But the fact that the *first reading* was so encouraging cannot be overlooked. It would seem that in this, the *first reading*, there were some conditions that made it possible to subtly and deeply penetrate into the life of the role. Let's allow that this rough sketch of the role is far from being its completed version – nevertheless, there is still much in it that is *living*. Much in it is sincere, without falseness, without the actorly "delivery." The "rough sketch" turns out to be the that of the artist, and the finished play – the dull falseness of a craftsman.

Yesterday, at the first rehearsal, the role worked out well for the actor. He felt this, but he didn't try to truly understand the lesson that nature had just taught him – why did it work out well for him yesterday? What did he do in order for this to happen? Such questions do not even occur to him. It worked out well . . . probably because he is really talented, and the role really suits him . . .

Today, at the second rehearsal, he steps up to the task with more confidence: he knows everything; there's nothing more to learn and likewise nothing else to orientate himself to – everything is familiar . . . the role is understood, and many scenes have already been "discovered." The only thing left is to *repeat* and "fixate" them (in theatre jargon).

But here is the trouble: repeating them *does not work!* If something does work, then it is only the external manifestations of yesterday's creativity – intonation, a gesture – but it isn't the essence of the matter, nor is it a free, creative state.

Now, if he is left to engage in these fruitless searches of yesterday, then everything will become worse and worse with each rehearsal.

The Principle of the First Time

These days, many directors opt out of doing a first read-through. Some begin work by analyzing the roles; others require that the actor not know anything about the play or the role before the first rehearsal. Rather, they begin to go through the role with the actor by "physical actions" – from one "action" to another . . .

As for the "first read-through," as described above, – I have yet to see these first steps of the actor's creativity used sufficiently. And what is more – there are not any acting schools that would take up this basic principle of the "first time," meaning that they would try to set up matters so that when the actor studies the play and delves deeper into it, he continues to read it *for the first time* – not only today, but again tomorrow. And the day after tomorrow . . . and every day. So that on opening night, he played it as if it were *for the first time.* It is just that somehow, he knows all the words, he carries out the main, basic *mise en scenes* precisely . . . Why? It is not important . . . but he is acting . . . *for the first time.*

But what makes it possible to achieve so much from the first reading? Why does the actor have such a free and a largely creative state of being? Why does the process of creative transformation happen on its own, without any searching?

There was much that he *didn't know* about the play, the role, and the characters, and yet he wittingly-unwittingly took up the navigation of all of these things that were new to him; he had a real interest, a genuinely live attitude toward all of it.

But he doesn't suspect that this was the main stimulus of his creative state.

All this is easily confirmed by the following observation. Actors rehearsed a scene many times; they even performed it before an audience. They know all of the given circumstances, and everything about the play is clear. Perhaps from some irregularities in their work, it begins to feel manufactured, and mechanized – the actors are false, and they know they're false, but they can't do anything about it. You give them a few etudes to cleanse their clogged apparatuses – the first texts that come to mind. These etudes should be very simple, and, preferably, they should not in the least resemble the scene. They do these etudes, they adjust to "creative truth," with correct perception and reaction, and then you tell them: "Play your scene, take your time, don't demand anything of yourself – however things go will be fine." They begin carefully, on their tip-toes, until they become so warmed up that it would be impossible to require better of them. What a shame that this is a rehearsal and not performance night!

It is obvious that these exercises, these simple etudes contain some truth that you will not reach by any other path.

And so, *it is not just from the accurate knowledge of facts and getting used to the given circumstances of a play that this fount of truth flows, this spring of "the water of life." It turns out that this lack of clarity and definition, this obscurity – also exudes the living water of truth and creativity.*

The actor must know certain facts and circumstances. But apparently, along with this, the lack of clarity and definition of the circumstances, and the need to figure them out, are no less important conditions.

In these conditions, a creative fantasy can seize a middling actor almost as well a great one.

And, if the actor is lucky enough to be carried away by the force of this obscurity, then it is important to put all of one's efforts into helping him know how to remain in this state. Never mind that it happened just at the first rehearsal, and by accident.

Now it can be understood why many great actors consider that the most important, the most difficult, and the most necessary thing is to *forget* the play.

And here is yet another illustration for our conversation on the awakening force of unknown.

In the past, in the provinces (I'm referring to the second half of the 19th century) plays were put on after the third, the sixth rehearsal. Nevertheless, gifted actors sometimes gave performances that were quite successful in terms of their creative state, especially when the role was close to them.

The reason behind their success is similar to that behind the favorably formed circumstances of the first reading. The actor is acquainted with the play and the role only in general terms – his partners and even he himself avoided acting their roles at rehearsals. Instead, they just carefully said their lines, as if merely trying on their roles. The actor still hasn't seen his partners or himself in makeup and costume. It is only in front of the audience, on opening night, that he receives – for the first time – complete, concrete, and real impressions from his partners and his surroundings . . . [By the way, pay attention to this: the careful saying of a role's lines – not for a partner, but for yourself – this "trying on" of what will later be done in an actual show is very reminiscent of our "assignment" of a text before an etude. It was indeed our "assignment" – and that explains its significance and its power. – *Author's Note*]

Consider the necessity of quickly dealing with all of these new and unexpected things, laid out before the actor for the first time. Consider the responsibility that comes with being in this position in a play that is already going on. All of this mobilizes the actor's inner strength; it makes his perception particularly keen; it makes him particularly sharp-sighted and responsive onstage.

It is true that accidents can occur during these risky "travels" across the sea of the play's surprises. What's more is that these performances were often full of clichés, ridiculous and pitiful to the extreme. At the same time, all of these clichés were intermingled with such fresh and genuine moments – much can be forgiven for such spontaneity and passion. (I repeat – I am talking about gifted actors.)

I often met provincial audiences who went to the theatre in the Capital, hoping to see some kind of miracle among miracles, yet they sometimes returned from there surprised, bewildered, and even embarrassed. This is because . . . it's awkward and embarrassing to admit: they didn't like it . . . The setting, the consistency, the resplendence – this was all worthy of praise, but the actors . . . they were lacking something.

What did this audience member want and what did he miss? He missed this freshness, this creative flight that often occurred and seized him there, at home, in the provinces.

When he went to the theatre in the capital, he expected that there would be more than these creative flashes. He hoped to be dazzled by an uninterrupted creative burning, and he thought that the air of the play wouldn't be ordinary air, but that it would be full of life-giving ozone . . .

And suddenly – none of that was there! . . .

It is true that when he attended some of the best performances at the Art Theatre or, even more so, when they saw Yermolova perform at the Maly – he was not only satisfied, but he took out of it everything that he had dreamed of, and many times over. And he saw there how his demands of the theatre were just, and that he was not imagining anything fantastical or excessive.

A natural question arises: would it not be better to learn to perform such a play in one rehearsal? Or even without any rehearsals at all?

Of course not. In theatre, the complete play is necessary – not separate, short-lived, random creative flashes of two or three actors. The question is, rather: how to continue working on a role past the first rehearsal, so that it retains the freshness of that surprising "first time?"

Experience convinces us that this is possible.

Having reached an exercise with given circumstances, the actor, as well as the teacher, would likely feel that they are in a familiar atmosphere and, perhaps, they would not want to return to exercises "without given circumstances."

If so, they are making a huge mistake.

It is necessary to practice exercises with given circumstances (and not just approximate ones, but with exact ones – as an essential preparation for working on a play). But one must not be limited to this. Otherwise, the actor's "technique" *of living* onstage will vanish, along with all of its essential attributes, such as the spirit of improvisation and involuntariness. The actor would gradually *lose* the *living* character and its qualities, one after the other. Thus imperceptibly he would transform into a verisimilar "depictor of life."

This is why it is crucial to not let go of exercises "without given circumstances." It is through them, the actor will regenerate and cleanse himself of all the grime that has dangerously built up on him. From these exercises, he will draw the strength of freedom, involuntariness, and freshness without which there is no "art of living."

We'll now return to the two questions we asked at the start of the chapter. The first question: is it worth doing sketches and drafts when it is generally accepted that the only thing necessary for the stage is the finished and fully fleshed out paintings?

And the second: do these etudes, especially those "without given circumstances," not cultivate the habit of inexact, unspecific, and "approximate" given circumstances – a bad and harmful habit that breeds half-truth.

It hardly seems necessary to have to answer these questions now.

As for these simple etudes – they combine, in perfect proportions, the contradictions of the actor's creative nature. Although it may be more accurate to say that they feature its dialectical duality – the dialectical unity of real life and creative fantasy.

They contain everything: on the one hand, "I," my personality with all of its obvious and hidden qualities and inclinations, and on the other – "he," "the character," created by my acting fantasy . . . The real settings that surround me on the stage, and the imagined life; my real, concrete partner (my co-actor, whom I know), and the imagined character; the actual reality and fiction; complete solitude and publicness – the feeling of the audience; "I feel like" with its total freedom, and the assignment; "I know" and "I don't know" . . .

The actors who experienced first-hand the power of these etudes – they literally squeal if there haven't been any group etude exercises due to the haste of pre-opening night. They say that these etudes are vitamins, life-giving vitamins. The lack of them breeds all kinds of actor's ailments – every imaginable kind.

32

The Character

Can One Live Onstage Personally, "as Yourself"?

It has already been reiterated how the actor's personal, individual "I" strangely changes and becomes a complex "I" – providing that his creative state onstage is sound. In such a case, the actor preserves his own "I," while simultaneously acquiring someone else's – the "not I."

There are a few additional things worth mentioning here.

Theatre schools' curriculums prescribe that all of the first and second year exercises be performed exclusively "as yourself." It is only in the third year that they start upon the character, and allow the students to act not as themselves, but "as him" – the character.

This is done for the following reasons: to be in-character is difficult, it is even more difficult to act while in it. It takes time to master this skill. Meanwhile, acting "as yourself," as one's own "I" (being oneself) is easier.

This has long been accepted and almost legalized . . . It seems logical, true . . . Judge for yourselves – what kind of actor can perform Plyushkin, Khlestakov, or Shylock from the get go, bypassing serious preparation, and the gradual development of the role?

However, before we agree with this, let's examine a few facts.

A new actor enters a group. The group has already significantly advanced and, although he tries to master the skills and catch up as quickly as he can, there is much that he doesn't understand, much that he has not experienced for himself; and what he has experienced – he still hasn't come to understand it. Although, he honestly tries to overcome all the obstacles.

- Every one of them, – he complains, – they all say that they "sense themselves differently" and "feel as being somebody else" – one, that he is an engineer; another, a teacher . . . a father, husband, brother, son; serious, frivolous; hardheaded, a shrewd businessmen, an honest worker . . . And from the way that they do it, I can see that they aren't making it up . . . And I . . . I don't "imagine" myself as being anyone at all. I simply remain who I was . . . (He is discouraged and upset.) I suppose this means that I am not an actor: I do not have any talent for "transformation."
- Don't give up hope. To be yourself is no small thing in our line of work . . . However, let's make sure that you truly don't "sense yourself differently," and never "feel as being somebody else." We want to be positive that you are not missing anything in yourself.

We'll purposefully take something simple, something that won't require you to think about any "character" or "transformation." We'll take something that will allow you to speak and think completely "as yourself." And we won't go out "onto the stage," but instead you'll stay sitting in the chair, just as you are right now.

I'll give you and your neighbor some very uncomplicated text, something along the lines of what I gave you in our early lessons.

Let him ask you: "Do you want to say something to me?" And you answer: "Yes, I do." And that's all. Don't require anything of yourself, don't decide anything in advance – however it turns out will be fine. Repeat the text and begin.

When repeating the text, his neighbor, who is free from any tortuous doubts, begins to stare absent-mindedly off to the side, out the window . . . he glances briefly at our actor, who is sitting uneasily, preoccupied – it's obvious that he is still somewhat worried after our conversation.

And of everything that has caught the eye of the absent-minded young man (and he, sensing this absent-mindedness, has obviously green-lit it) – it was his partner's agitation that has attracted his attention the most. He began to examine the worried actor closely.

And that worried actor has remained as he was before. The assignment hasn't had any effect on him, or he executed it poorly, or he didn't give into his inner impulses. He would just sit there, occupied with his own thoughts. However, sensing the gaze of his neighbor, he turned toward him and looked at him questioningly: "What is your deal? What are you staring at?"

The other, not embarrassed in the least, continued to stare at him, and then asked, unexpectedly: "Do you want to say something to me?"

The first was taken aback. His face, his eyes, and his entire body seemed to have been saying: "*I* want to say something? Me? Where are you getting this from?" But he didn't say anything. He was silent, and then he suddenly turned to me:

- I can't say the words that I have to say. The words are "Yes, I do," but I don't want to say anything to him.
- It's alright, we won't get hung up on this minor mishap. Let's take the same text, only why don't you change roles: now you ask him, and he'll answer you.
  Repeat the text.
  Repeat it again.
  And repeat it a third time. Now you can begin.

What is the purpose of this? The actor was preoccupied with watching himself, and he could only think about how to not miss the moment when he loses his own "I." It was necessary to knock him out of this state of self-observation. And if it turned out that three repetitions of the text did not accomplish this goal, then it would have come down to asking him to repeat it a fourth time. In this case, three repetitions turn out to be enough. It was obvious that the text "permeated" the actor.

And indeed, as soon as the actor had come out of emptiness, then at that very moment he felt compelled to look at his partner (I "supported" him: "Correct, correct . . . just like that . . . ").

His partner turned out to be gloomy and anxious, listening and waiting for something unknown . . . The actor was infected by this; this uneasiness was passed on to him ("Yes, yes! Correct, correct . . . well done!"). Their eyes met, and the actor suddenly uttered: "Do you . . . have something to say to me?" The other, quickly glancing around, and whispered – secretly, as if was about something important, scary and urgent: "Yes . . . I do."

- There you go, that was good. Tell me, this time, there was probably no character either – just yourself?
- Yes, it was me.
- And him? Who was he?
- He was also himself. Just himself.
- And what *about* him? How does he feel?
- He's definitely afraid . . . he's scared.
- What is he afraid of?
- All this happened back then . . . during the war . . . there are planes flying overhead (and at that moment, planes really did drone overhead) . . . ours or the enemy's . . . it isn't clear . . .
- Were you scared?
- Of course I was scared. I still can't calm down.
- Have you always been so nervous and fearful?
- Me? No. For some reason I wasn't afraid of these raids. I'm a fatalist: what will be will be, and what won't be – won't.
- And here, now?
- Here, now, for some reason I became horribly uneasy: and he's nervous, and the house is somewhat gloomy . . . and the weather . . . from the window you can see the yard . . . like you find on the outskirts . . . and the planes . . . they're flying quite low . . .
- Yes, they wouldn't fly so freely over the city. And who is he – your neighbor? Why is he here?
- Some acquaintance . . . he lives next door . . .
- Does this mean that you don't live far from here?
- I suppose so.
- And why did you come here?
- To find out about something . . .
- About the evacuation?
- Yes, yes, perhaps about the evacuation . . . It's just that I don't want to be evacuated myself . . . this must mean that I'm here on someone else's behalf . . .
- For loved ones or for someone you know? Perhaps for children?
- Sure . . . for children . . . my brother's . . . or my sister's . . .
- And now tell me: where do you personally live?
- Not far from here, in a dormitory.
- Are you single or married?
- No, I'm not married – I'm single.
- And you don't have anyone in Moscow?
- I have a brother. He's a student.
- Is he married?
- No, he's also single.
- How can that be? There's something that I don't understand here – your brother doesn't have children, yet you're getting ready to evacuate these children; you live downtown, but you have a neighbor who lives on the outskirts of town. It's obvious that you aren't a timid person, and you're even a fatalist, yet you tremble from the drone of an airplane . . . Things just don't seem to add up here. Was this truly you?

- Me. Of course it was I! After all it was I who was seeing and hearing and imagining this the whole time, who was aware of all this . . .
- Yet if it was you, then, at the very least . . . there was something strange about you . . .
- What's strange about it? It's just that these given circumstances aren't my own.
- Yes, the given circumstances. But you must keep in mind that the given circumstances are not a minor thing. You're a bachelor; go ahead, imagine that you're a family man (with a wife and children, and with the in-laws) – you are no longer exactly as you are right now – you aren't yourself, rather it's you with something added and at the same time with something taken away.
- Yes but it's still just me.
- And if someone were to give you given circumstance after given circumstance – your profession would be different, your nationality would be different, your upbringing different, your ideals different, and your whole body different, your height different – perhaps there would be still much left of your current personal "I," but neither we nor you yourself would recognize you.
- If that were so, then of course . . . but all the same, no matter how much you spin me around, even if you were to stand me on my head or to turn me inside out, even if I were to change my habits and my tastes, or to change so much so as to be unrecognizable, I'd still remain myself.
- That's a good thing! Do you think that you need to disappear without a trace and to put someone else in your place? If such a tragedy were to befall you, then we would have to turn to a psychiatrist!

  Don't be afraid of *remaining yourself*. And what's more – *it is only in remaining yourself that you will be able to become someone else.*

But do not overload your inexperienced students unnecessarily; do not burden them with this dangerous analysis before the time is ripe. Refrain as much as possible from these superfluous premature conversations! It would be better to turn the student's attention to his successes: see, the second etude was already performed correctly; in any case, this time you followed the right path . . .

A Shift Toward Transformation

Now, let's take a closer look at what happened with the first and second etudes, as well as with the "I" and "not I." The first etude was such a failure that the actor couldn't even get out the words.

Why couldn't he say them? What is the reason?

Before the etude, he was advised not to worry about either the "character" or the "transformation" – he should have just stayed himself. He understood this in his own way: as soon as he repeated his lines, he immediately returned to the internal state he had just experienced – the same emotional state with the same thoughts and concerns. He sat there, preoccupied with his private matters.

When his partner, gazing at him strangely, unexpectedly asked: "Do you want to say something to me?" – how could he have understood it? Just an awkward, inopportune question, which is exactly how he interpreted it. And if he had the line: "What do you mean, my good man! I don't want anything, leave me be," then it would have been easy and simple for him. However, the words, "Yes, I do" were utterly out of place.

In general, if you remain yourself in an etude – so much so that all of the facts of your private life remain pertinent – then, naturally, all of your reactions (including your words) can only be a consequence of your own life. You will not be able to say words that do not agree with your immediate needs. And you cannot feel, think, or desire anything that doesn't correspond to your internal state.

You *can* force yourself to do something against your will, but that will be coercion, rather than a natural manifestation of your will.

Now, let's take the second etude.

It has already been said that the actor, who was too preoccupied with observing himself, had to be redirected from such a state. This is why he was advised to "assign" the text to himself a few times in a row.

As soon as it became clear that the text didn't slip by him, but *hit* its mark (you can discern this quite clearly with experience), the actor was told to "green-light" his freedom.

Seeing as the text was assigned well, it immediately started to "act" inside the actor, to direct him.

The words that the novice actor had to use to address his partner ("Do you want to say something to me?) required him to have beforehand seen something in the partner that would elicit such a question. That's how it happened. As soon as the actor assigned the text, his eyes turned to his neighbor on their own. Here, because of his habit of observing himself, he could have easily looked at himself, put his life on hold, and ruined everything. To prevent this, the teacher intervened with his "support," and cut off any doubts.

In this new state, the actor saw that his partner was worried about something, listening intently and waiting. Seeing as the actor perceived his partner's behavior without any doubts or criticism, he became infected with his partner's worry, and he clearly caught on – there is danger here! He grew scared himself, he shrank . . . he waited. Once again, he heard the teacher's affirming voice: "Yes, yes! Correct . . . well done!" – that means that the fear is appropriate; it's appropriate to prepare for something catastrophic; it means that I am justified to think and feeling as I do . . .

All of this (chiefly *his own physical and psychological reaction*) leads to the feeling of fear, to the sense that something is going to happen . . . Meanwhile, I hear the sound of approaching jets . . . they're here – over our heads! . . . The wind tears the last leaves off the bare poplar . . . The neighbor is looking at me intently and worriedly – he's about to say something important to me . . .

It's as if it's another life, other people. And I myself am different – someone from this new life . . .

This, in general terms, is that "shift" that happens in an actor's psyche.

It all begins with the perception of concrete realities. However, under the influence of the assignment, as well as a momentary lull in criticism and control, the "shift" occurs – real people and things are endowed with imaginary qualities and attributes; real life is mixed up with an imaginary one.

This "shift" is everything. The "shift" lasts for an instant – the actor takes everything in. Instantly, a reaction occurs (fear, worry, etc.). In a single moment, the imaginary becomes real, and it takes over the actor – he has "an inkling" of something, and he "imagines" something.

Now, all that's necessary is to not be afraid of this "shift," but to give in to it. The director's support helps an actor become grounded in this new state.

But, regardless of how distinctly I "sense" something, I, the actor, feel in my heart of hearts that it's *not real*: the war, the bombardment. I'm afraid . . . but in reality, all of this ***doesn't exist***. And so, without risking anything, I plunge into these imaginary worries and concerns all the more willingly.

I can completely forget myself and give in to this created, imaginary world for fleeting instants, or even tens of seconds. It, in turn, affects me in such a way that I become one of its characters more and more.

However, while in this new life, I retain my ability to observe myself.

At a cursory glance, this all seems like some sort of splitting of identity – one part lives one life, while the other observes and controls it. Or perhaps, it's a **doubling** of our being – we simultaneously live two lives: one – imaginary; the other – real and observing the former.

For the process of an actor's creative experiencing, such copresence and coexistence of two seemingly contradictory manifestations of his "I" – is absolutely *indispensable*. On the one hand – his ordinary, personal, mundane "I," and on the other – the "I" of his created personality with all its qualities, abilities, and life in general.

And now that we know that this dual life is necessary for the creative process, many questions are easily solved. Some of them, rather than being solved, never even arise. Beginning with: is it necessary to experience onstage or merely imitate life? . . .

Can You Play Yourself?

Now, armed with this new data, let's investigate whether it's possible to act out a role personally as yourself.

Two young ladies are called up for an etude, and are given the following text:

- Tell me, does Dad know about your problem with the broach?
- I think he does.
- And . . . ?
- I'm scared to even think about it . . . He avoids looking at me, he doesn't talk to me . . . And he walks around so depressed.
- What are we supposed to call each other? – one of the participants asks – It's kind of uncomfortable without a name.
- Whatever you want. Choose any name you like.
- Alright.

While repeating the text, they added names: Zina and Sonia.

They began the etude. But as soon as one of them said, "Tell me, does Dad know about your problem with the broach?" the other hesitated – some sort of internal battle went on in her, and finally, completely not wanting to, she forced herself to say, "I think he does."

At the second question ("And . . . ?"), Sonia could barely get the words out, and she immediately addressed the teacher:

- I'm in a horrible emotional state, I've never had one like this . . . and I can't get the words out . . . it's like they're foreign, unnecessary . . .

We searched for the reason – we couldn't find one. Everything seems to be in order.

- What's your real name? – the teacher finally asked.
- Sonia. That is my real name.
- Well, there you go, that's the problem. How did you ask her? – the teacher asks Zina. – As if she were Sonia Zvyagina? Or did she seem as someone else to you?
- Probably, as if she were Zvyagina. I always call her Sonia – and she was Sonia for me here too.

- And you asked her, Sonia Zvyagina, about the broach?
- Yes.
- And you, Sonia, you understood that she addressed you, personally you?
- Yes, that's how I understood it. Oh, I know, that's where the mix-up happened. She addressed me as Sonia, and was suddenly asking me about my problem with the broach . . . I don't have a broach, and I don't have a dad either . . .
- And if the text of the etude featured a different name, and she were to address you – let's say, as Vera or Katia? . . .
- Then, it would be easy, – she interrupted. – Then, there would be a broach and a dad. Otherwise, where would they come from?
- Hm, so it looks like the problem is in the name? In a single word: Sonia?
- It seems that way . . .
- But uncle Vanya's niece is also named Sonia – Sonia Voynitsky. Evidently, you won't be able to play her?
- Oh, no! No! That's my dream – Sonia! I feel her so well . . . I love her . . . I'll play her! . . . One day, I'll play her!
- Since you feel her so well, then you'll probably play her. But how will you deal with the name?

She became thoughtful and, evidently, started fitting herself to the character – could she become Sonia Voynitsky? . . .

- You know, for some reason, it's not getting in my way. I just tried one scene . . . with Astrov, and it was fine – very comfortable.
- So, it must be that the issue isn't in the name only . . .
- I'm probably the one who's at fault, – her partner butted in, – I looked at her and addressed her in such a way that she took everything personally, as if I were addressing her, Sonia Zvyagina. So I unsettled her.
- Yes . . . it looks like that's the truth. And what if you asked her not about a broach, but about something that actually happened to her?
- Why not! She was at a lecture yesterday, and it would be easy for her to answer about that. Right, Sonia?
- Sure.
- So, according to our observations, here's what we have: Sonia can play herself, Sonia Zvyagina, but only with the circumstances that she has in real life. As soon as they change just a little, she can no longer play herself. In order to live in the new circumstances, something in her has to shift.
  Let's see how this happens in our case – how to cause this shift in you. The broach, the father, who is saddened by the unfortunate events that have to do with the broach – what does this stir in your imagination?
- I think that I got it from my mother . . . that my mother died. My father loved her very much, and he liked it when I wore the broach. But I lost it . . . And so I'm worried and scared, I'm thinking: where could I have lost it?
- Is this you?
- Of course it's me.

But . . . if we dig a little deeper, it'll turn out that she is, in fact, she, but she's different – her father is alive, her mother died recently, while the actress herself didn't know her mother or her father from her birth, etc., along the same lines.

In a word, if we examine this sentence more closely: "be yourself, but in different circumstances" – we can see that this is merely a tactical pedagogical tool. On one hand, it displaces the obstructive self-consciousness, while on the other – it brings one closer to the fact. Somebody lost a broach – that doesn't concern me, it's distant from me, but: *I* lost a broach, *my* broach, a precious family relic – that'll worry me, even if I only think of it in my imagination.

And once it makes me emotional, I am already sucked into this new life – all I have to do is not interfere.

The *shift* has already been made: "I" am now "not I."

In general, since the actress has slipped out of her real life into an imaginary one, and knows how to keep afloat in this new life; since she's able to imagine herself (feel herself) in any circumstances and green-light any reactions that they evoke – why shouldn't she allow *any version of herself*? That is, why can't she act like she's no longer Sonia Zvyagina, but a girl that lost a precious broach, or Pushkin's Tatyana, or Sonia Voynitsky.

In order to understand what it means to act "as yourself," you have to understand first and foremost what the "I" is – my own, personal I.

This evidently consists of all my external and internal qualities, my past and present, my tastes, desires, opinions, ideals, character . . .

In a word, I am the whole complex world that I carry within me.

If there were a role that would entirely coincide with an actor's personality, as well as all of his life circumstances, then it would seem that there would be no need to alter oneself – an actor can play it straight.

But if the coincidence is even slightly incomplete, an actor immediately thinks: this fact isn't my own and cannot be my own – it's from another life, one that isn't my own.

An actor's reaction to this can only take one path: this fact is alien to me, it's not from my own life, but it exists, it's before me, it's a fact. That means I have to accept it. I can't reject it.

Everything that's my own, that's personal, takes backstage, and this fact seizes me. A "shift" happens: from my life to "someone else's"; from "I" to "not I."

I have a broach . . . I have a father . . . Some problem with my mother's broach . . . My father is upset . . . What is there to do? . . . What can be done? . . .

And in an instant, the stream of my life intermixes with that of another.

If it's a small stream, then it changes my own very slightly. If it's large, expansive and wild, like in tragic roles, then it drowns me, drives me to break my own banks, and my modest little river becomes completely lost in the new torrent; it changes its course, assuming one that hadn't existed before.

All of this makes it clear that a sound creative state onstage *inevitably leads to the formation of a character* – it appears as early as the first lesson.

As soon as an actor assigns another's words to himself, as soon as he begins an etude – this "shift" happens into the realm of imagination: the actor is no longer just himself – he is someone else too.

It is essentially impossible to obey the demand – "act as yourself." It is impossible to "act as yourself," to be only yourself onstage. An actor can **begin** by applying the circumstances to himself, while still remaining his own self. In such a case, the circumstances become intimately close to the actor, and therefore more tangible. They swoop the actor up and carry him away into the life of the role. Creativity commences – the actor steps into the realm of the imaginary.

But this is not the same as "acting as yourself" or "being yourself." It is *only one possible method of bringing the given circumstances closer to yourself*.

Being yourself and completely giving in to all of an etude's circumstances (or, even more so – those of a play or a character) and living in them – that already *is* **transformation**.

This departure from your own personality can be subtle and even barely noticeable – in this regard, an inexperienced actor (or teacher) might not even notice this "shift." But if the circumstances have enthralled an actor, then this "shift" indubitably exists. Such instances have already been described many times – instances when a teacher's questions helped an actor understand that he was himself in an etude, while simultaneously someone else.

Such a smooth subtle deviation from one's own identity is what brought about this mistake – people began nonchalantly discussing the possibility to "playing yourself" or even "being yourself" as an irrefutable fact.

The only thing worth pondering here is that in the first years of school practice, it is more advantageous for the majority of actors to pick roles *that are less removed from their habitual, everyday "character."* That is, characters that are closer to an actor's "I" and life circumstances. As for expressive characters that are far removed from an actor – they should be saved for later.

But it's also worth mentioning that not all actors feel themselves more freely when they are playing a character that is closer to them – there are many that, on the contrary, need to cover themselves up with a dissimilar mask.

They love putting on a mask so much that they do it at any chance they get. Between rehearsals, in the cafeteria, in friendly conversations, all they do is imitate each other or their buddies.

Some of them are so gifted in this regard that they manage to gather a crowd and put on a whole show, telling highly amusing stories and portraying all "characters." And this is done with such artistic subtlety that there can be no doubts – this is a talent before us.

But then such an actor goes to rehearsal, starts searching for "truth," for "himself," etc., and becomes mediocre, if not wholly talentless.

What's the matter here? Half an hour ago, he was talented and enraptured everyone with his creativity.

The problem is that he needs to stick to his own path – the path of sharp characterization and expressive characters.

Only by covering himself with a mask that doesn't resemble his own face, only by assuming characteristics that are not at all inherent to him can he find the path to himself, to his own creative "I."

Initially, his transformation into a character can be short-lived, but with a proper approach, it can be strengthened and become complete.

If this kind of actor, when playing etudes, is drawn to expressive characterizations while abandoning his own habitual persona, then do not interfere. This may be the only path that he is able to take to develop his specific kind of talent.

But you must carefully pay attention so that he doesn't become "derailed" and fall into the abyss of "depicting" – because of unnecessary rushing or effort.

33

Types of Characters

The Beloved Character

Circumstances alter us is absolutely *indispensable*. On the one hand – his ordinary, personal, mundane "I," and on the other – the "I" of his created personality with all its qualities, abilities, and life in general. Under their influence, we experience joy, grief, irritation, wrath, wistfulness . . . But we cannot always show the emotions we truly feel. And so, a person shuts off his true feelings, instead assuming a guise of calm when he is worried, a guise of cheerfulness when he is sad, a guise of sympathy when he is apathetic, a guise of joy when he is actually full of woe.

Some become so accustomed to it that they hide away nearly all of their true feelings and only show emotions that are not actually there. Very rarely do they allow themselves to be themselves – only when they are alone, or in a circle of close-knit friends, or when they are engaged in a favorite activity. At other times, they are constantly assuming some sort of guise: in the presence of some, they act like a simpleton; in the presence of others, they become strict and important; with yet others, they try to be serious and intelligent; with others still, they are exceptionally kind, sensitive, and attentive.

Naturally, they do have all these tens or hundreds or qualities – some are highly developed, others are less so. All they have to do is "evoke" these feelings as the situation calls for. But still, whenever they assume some sort of guise, these qualities are merely a veneer, a mask that is put on for convenience.

It is possible to see such veneers and masks in school during etudes. As soon as an actor assigns himself a text, he immediately puts on a mask of some kind: he either becomes modest, or concentrated, or serious, or tired; sad, disappointed, wistful, joyful, shallow, etc. – every actor has his own favorite guise or mask.

This guise becomes customary and comfortable with repetition, and with time, an actor becomes so comfortable in it that it is impossible to separate them; as soon as an actor enters an etude, he immediately assumes his beloved mask and becomes his convenient, well-tried and well-known character.

If an etude's content doesn't correspond to his beloved guise (let's suppose that it is a guise of apathy and disappointment), then he evokes a diametrically opposed mask – airiness, cheerfulness, etc. In turn, this new guise also becomes habitual, and then these two-three characters make up his entire arsenal.

He becomes so intimate with these habitual guises that he feels himself completely free when using them.

A Character Evoked by the Text

However, these characters that are very useful initially – they quickly turn into deadly enemies. They become so closely linked with actor that as soon as he enters an etude, they're already there! And they don't let any others join the party.

The actor becomes repetitive, playing the same thing everywhere. An inexperienced teacher can look at such an occurrence for some time and decide: "My dear, you're not so talented after all! . . . You keep playing the same thing . . . That's rather boring and hopeless." He might even say this to the student, which would be the height of pedagogical tactlessness. This will dismay the student, and frighten him – it's possible to ruin everything by doing this.

In general, knowing when to be silent is one of the most precious qualities of not only a teacher, but a director too, who needs to know how to simply sow the seeds – the seeds of the future character (which resemble the future character about as much as a small birch seed resembles the future alabaster beauty itself). If, however, he immediately paints a full-bodied picture of everything that an actor has to play, the actor will only be able to play it externally, but will be unable to live by it, authentically and truly. You have to carefully *cultivate* a given character's qualities in an actor – develop them, skillfully leading the actor to these qualities, without even mentioning them. More will come on this later.

And so, in order to lead an actor away from a beaten path, it is necessary to (without warning) give him a text that will, on its own, lead him away from his beloved and habitual mask.

If, for example, an actor plays an intelligent, distinctly proper youth in all of his etudes, you give him an etude like this, evoking the times of old:

- Tell me, are you from the tailor's?
- Yes, I am . . .
- Do you know Tasha there?
- Of course I do! She's a friend.
- Tell her Vanya says hi.
- Where do you work?
- At the market. I'm a butcher.

It's better to give a comedic text, half-mischievous, half-joking. Under the cover of comedy, the actor will more easily give in to a new character.

In these etudes, the text itself pushes the actor toward a character, and it evokes circumstances in the actor's mind that are alien to him.

It is similarly possible to help an actor to bring about a character by hinting to him the character's circumstances and facts.

But you should never speak of the character as if he were someone else: "he's a simple guy, works as a butcher, dresses meat, weighs it out, etc." The "he" is completely foreign to the actor. Having drawn a picture of him outside of himself, and having seen him from the outside, the only thing that an actor can do is try to depict him – imitate what he just saw in his imagination.

By suggesting this to an actor, you would be pushing him toward the path of the imitator. You would extinguish his ability to *live* onstage.

If you give hints about the circumstances and the character, you should never allow yourself to say the word "he/she." Only "you!" "You work as a butcher. (I can see this is hard to believe . . . Imagine that you were alive 50–60 years ago.) You're probably from a village, from some poor peasant family, no education at all. Hard times forced your father to cut you off from the family and send you to the city. The townspeople helped get you work at the butcher's. What can you do . . . It's not very pleasant, but you don't go hungry. With time, you've gotten used to it; you've learned the butcher's trade, and now man the shop . . . And now that you have enough experience, you left for the store at the market – this was three months ago . . .

As for Tasha – it must have been an incidental acquaintance. You met her on a holiday, while out on the town . . . "

Thus, giving the actor circumstance after circumstance without destroying his awareness of his own "I," you transform the actor's view of everything around him; he easily departs from his habitual character and becomes another. And he does so without losing himself.

With repetition, while working on a role, this shift can be taken very far, and even taken to the point that the actor's personality will be changed beyond recognition.

From experience, I can say that giving an actor his circumstances and facts should be done as distinctly and clearly as possible, without any grandiloquence, and without filling the actor's head with unnecessary details. At the same time, it has to be convincing and engrossing enough. Experience will teach the proper tact and measure.

The External and Internal Character

After working with such an expressively characteristic text, one actor would feel that he is Vanya the butcher, but without changing too much externally. He would not undergo any physical changes; he won't acquire anything physical from the old-time village boy. He would change, for the most part, internally – he would become more primitive. Another, however, might change more externally – he'd acquire a different bearing, manner of gesturing, manner of speech, etc.

Naturally, neither would be a finished character and only a sketch, but at the same time, it would be possible to make out in the sketch the principal difference in the creativity of these two actors.

You should not interfere with either – let each develop in his own way. If one demonstrated external expressivity – let that expressivity develop more; if the other more freely gave in to his internal, psychological life – let that quality develop all the more.

Either path of creativity will eventually lead to a finished work of art – each in its own right. However, a rich internal life can be enhanced with external expressivity, while expressive, external form can be infused with internal content.

How can this be done?

All you have to do is understand the internal creative mechanisms of each of these types of actors, at which point we'd have all we need to achieve this goal.

Let's begin with a case where we want to add external expressiveness when we already have great internal depth.

Where does this dearth of external manifestations come from? Most often, because the actor *does not "green-light" any external manifestations* – he halts them.

Let's take the last etude. The actor really felt that he was a butcher – a simple peasant youth, selling meat at a meat stall. However, he did not "green-light" the gestures and manner of speech that wanted to burst out of him. In doing so, he pared down the character and made it poorer.

How can we help him? First of all, we need to minutely observe him, and in the moments that some brave or extraordinary impulse is waiting to break out of the actor, we must support it: "Yes, yes . . . good, you're good! . . . Green-light it! Bolder! . . . "

Other than this, after an etude ends, you should sit down with the actor and recall how one impulse or another began to burst from him, and how it *was already emerging*, when he hit the brakes and stopped it.

As for the second instance, when an actor bravely green-lights external movements, but hits the brakes with regard to his internal life – this too can be fixed. A few previous exercises already featured similar situations. There, we recommended a method with which you can lead such an actor to the right path.

In short, it involves helping the actor note the moment when he becomes afraid of an emotion and stops it, while transferring all his energy elsewhere – to external manifestations.

Without taking away from his achievements, you have to show the actor that it's possible to make do *without shying away from a direct path*. The actor *was already on it*. He was, but . . . he grew afraid.

Depth and Shallowness

There is another scale with which to evaluate characters: one that ranges from shallow to deep. Two actors: give one any role, any etude, and it would always turn out powerful, deep, and significant. Give the other any serious subject, any dramatic role, and though he would play it properly, he won't really be very invested emotionally, nor would he enthrall the audience. And the character would always be insignificant, uninteresting, and pale.

Mochalov believed that aside from fiery imagination, a talented dramatic actor also needs "the depth of soul."

What is an actor's depth of soul? It is not enough, for such an actor, to possess wholeness, harmoniousness, and power; developed intellectual and moral qualities; acuity of understanding, and sensitivity toward everything around him. Aside from these human qualities, commonly associated with the term, such an actor should possess yet another kind of attribute. When in moments of creative flight, an actor is capable of an incredibly straining nervous activity, and he has his intellectual and moral forces vastly expand. In a word, "an actor's depth of soul" is a term that implies inspiration.

Every one of us has moments in life when we become shallow for one reason or another. Nothing really affects our inner depths; we think, feel, and grow excited, but not very deeply – not passionately, not with our whole hearts, but only shallowly, *peripherally*.

There are many actors whose performances are somewhere "on the periphery" of great, real thoughts and passions. These actors live onstage only shallowly or "barely." Or, maybe they don't have any depth at all – human or creative?

You observe such actors for a long time, and you still don't understand – what's the problem? It looks like everything's right: he perceives everything, and he "green-lights" various impulses freely . . . It's as if everything is the truth, but his acting brings neither satisfaction, nor joy.

Roles that require great depth are contraindicative to such actors. You can deftly structure such an actor's role so that it is logical and "verisimilar." In significant moments, you can mask his creative shallowness with various scenic effects. The audience might be tricked . . . But then we have to honestly call this a forgery.

If you feel depth, significance, and great spiritual content in an actor, but notice that it's inhibited in rehearsals or etudes, you cannot retreat. You have to get to work.

Usually, this is simply a matter of fear – *the fear of opening up*.

34

The Appearance, Strengthening, and Development of a Character

The Just-Born Character

"The butcher from the market" and other such exercises provide a sharp jolt for the imagination and direct it towards an unusual and uncharacteristic emotional state – towards an expressive character.

After being done a few times, these etudes allow students to break free from any creative standstill, but they do not rid them of their devotion to a beloved character that they've already formed. Given the first chance, they return to the beaten path.

And as long as an actor keeps using a single beloved character universally for any possible situation, he is still in the early stages of his development.

The first bit of harm – the actor's chief forces remain untapped, because the deep, fertile layers of his soul aren't touched.

The second – the habitual, beloved character doesn't give way to any others. It always beats them to the punch.

And, finally, this character isn't substantial enough, it's not deep enough. After all, it's artificial; it's just a grimace of the soul, a mask.

What can be done with this actor? The beloved character has done its job – it's time to move forward!

Two are called to participate in an etude.

One of them is a handsome, attractive young man whom everyone has already typecast as "romantic lead." And it's true, you want to see him playing if not Romeo (that would be too much to start with), then some other enthralling youth. And he himself wants to play such handsome, noble young men. In life too, he tries to avoid anything harsh or crude. And in an etude, before an audience, he, of course, wants to hold on to his beloved character of a proper, charismatic Adonis.

At times, either because of the text or his scene partner, he seems to be drawn towards mischief, expressivity, boldness – this is evident. It's also evident that he doesn't give in to these impulses and remains true to himself.

Nobody is too upset about this – everybody likes how he plays his etudes . . . The "romantic lead" type is becoming more and more ingrained in him.

For some time, this weakness is forgiven – after all, he's not green-lighting anything except for this "romantic lead" primarily because of cowardice: what if something ugly will come of it?! And this could stain his reputation as a charmer!

Finally, the moment comes, and you say to yourself: alright, enough is enough. Without giving a word's notice, you give him an appropriate text and begin.

And so, two people are called up. One is utterly unremarkable-looking, the other is our handsome devil.

The first is getting ready to leave. He gets dressed and carefully goes through his briefcase.

I.   Did you have anyone over?
II.   Nobody. Why?
I.   I had some money in here – 800 rubles – and it's gone.
II.   How can that be?
I.   I don't know, but it's gone.
II.   Maybe you lost it on your way, or someone stole it?
I.   No, when I got in, I checked to make sure it was there . . .

I carefully keep track of the text, making sure that not a single word is lost. I make them repeat the text two-three times, thoroughly empty, and . . . let them begin.

There can be no doubts: the "handsome one" took the money – a shameful act. Even if it's done as a joke, it's not very clever. At any rate, it's unbecoming.

And so they begin . . .

From the very first moment, the actor is seized by a complex flurry of emotions: fear, worry, the knowledge that there is no way out . . . It grows stronger when the partner starts digging around in his briefcase and is about to notice the theft . . . It's clear: he's panicked – he's the one who took the money, that's a fact . . . and he didn't steal them as a joke, that's clear too. He's getting ready for something . . . maybe even something scary . . .

And then, for some reason, all this worry and perturbation was gone – he's now entirely unconcerned about everything, including his frightened scene partner, who is feverishly rifling through his briefcase. He looks around and grows pensive about something.

The question, "Did you have anyone over?" catches him by surprise and seems to him so strange that it looks like he's thinking: "Who could have been here? Nobody's ever here!" and without understanding what his partner wants from him, he says: "Nobody. Why?"

When he finds out about the loss, he's only saddened by his friend's misfortune and that's it. He has no idea that he himself might have done the thing. Calm, clear eyes, a steady voice. He shows nothing but sympathy and a desire to help: "Maybe you lost them, or someone stole them in the street?"

It turns out that the money was in the briefcase just a few minutes ago, and here he . . . doesn't understand anything . . . He realizes for the first time that he is under suspicion. He doesn't believe it, he thinks that he's being joked with . . .

However, he sees by his partner's, his buddy's behavior that the suspicions are definitely there: there cannot be another culprit . . .

But he doesn't know anything, he's innocent!

And at this point, even the victim himself, having looked into those innocent eyes, started second-guessing himself and rifling about in his briefcase again, trying to remember – could it be that he himself took the money and forgot about it?

In short, it turned out to be fresh, interesting, and dramatic. Most importantly: his reputation didn't suffer – it was clear to everyone that there was a misunderstanding with the money, that our hero was the victim of an unfortunate misunderstanding . . .

Everybody liked the etude.

- So who stole your money?
- I don't know.
- Not him?
- Not him.
- Really, it wasn't you?
- No, of course not . . . I don't know a thing about it . . . I was hearing about the money for the first time.
- Alright, fine. But let's try to get to the truth here, let's specify a few things . . . Do you remember what your partner said in response to the question: "Maybe you lost them, or someone stole them in the street . . . ?"
- Yes, I do, he said: "No, when I came back, I checked to make sure they were here . . ."
- And do you remember your anxiety in the beginning of the etude? Why was it there?
- That's . . . I wasn't in the etude yet, perhaps that's why . . .
- But then you did 'enter' it – you calmed down, and everything went smoothly?
- It would appear so.
- Is that so? And not the other way around? Maybe you didn't "enter" the etude, but "exited" out of it?
- How is that – "exited?"
- Just like that. Recall your initial anxiety, when you repeated the text and "green-lit" yourself in the beginning of the etude . . . You became very, very worried . . . you even became scared of something . . . If you had 'green-lit' your worries, anxiety, and fear . . .
- Then it would have turned out that I was the thief! . . .
- So what? . . . Is that unpleasant? Uncomfortable? . . .
- Yes, of course, a bit . . .
- Exactly. And it's dangerous: how do you behave in this new, unprecedented situation? Maybe you'll even say something crude or tasteless? That's just right! . . . And so you shied away from utterly evident circumstances. And though everything afterwards was sound, we came away from it with an etude different from the one that was forming under the influence of the text.

Now you see that your *anxiety* was the etude that should have happened, but you "exited" out of that etude – you grew scared. What did you grow afraid of? Evidently the difficulties, the risk, the novelty . . . Yes, most importantly, you were afraid to appear crude, unpleasant . . .
- Probably. If I had "green-lit" that initial feeling, the initial worry and fear . . . I'm thinking about it right now . . . I think I would have become different.
- Unfamiliar?
- Yes.
- Not a "romantic lead?"
- Yes.
- A character actor?
- Exactly . . .

- What's wrong with that?! Be happy! Your palette is expanding, you're adding new colors, coming upon new strength and new resources. Your old resources aren't going anywhere – they'll stay with you, but you now have to acquire new ones.
- But how do you acquire them? – one of the more inattentive students that missed the essence of the lesson will ask.
- Very simply: *follow your first impulse*, answer the first call – that's it. It is the soundest one of all, and it is *always new*. If you hesitate for even a moment, if you leave the door open for one or two seconds, your favorite familiar character will immediately sneak in: it's waiting for this opening . . . And it won't leave any room for anyone else.

   The first call, the first impulse is most precious. Because this reaction is physiological and forms the foundation of our psychological life.
- What if these first impulses aren't interesting? What if they're insignificant and dull?
- If they're truly the first ones, do not hesitate – give in to them. Even if they're dull and uninteresting at first, who knows what may come of them. I repeat: if they're the **first** ones (if you didn't miss them and are mistaking the second or third ones for the first ones), they will inevitably lead to something unexpected and significant.

   You're asking why? Because they're the manifestations of the precious artistic **embryo**. Because only the first reaction is the reaction to given circumstances. The second reaction is to some other changed ones.

The Character Is "Being"

Let's look one more time over the whole process of getting ready for an etude and entering its flow. Let's look it over with a specific goal in mind – to note the moment when the character is conceived.

By analyzing this moment, we will probably find a solution to the question: how do you skip over to your beloved habitual character?

Here are the main parts of this process:

1   The teacher *assigns the words*. This doesn't slip by the students' consciousness or, concordantly, their reactions.
2   The partners *look at each other* for the first time, they get to know each other – who is the other one and what is he like? This is very significant.
3   The partners repeat the text, i.e. they *assign the text to themselves*.
4   The assignment is finished. *Full stop.*
5   *The words are "cast away."* The words are as good as "forgotten," and now they, along with the assignment as a whole, do everything on their own. These two-three seconds involve the collision between the text, my own personal life, and what impressions I get from my partner and my surroundings.
6   The actors *green-light* various impulses and manifestations. This is the *beginning*. The etude has *begun*.

Previously, we said that involuntary movements are manifested, and that there are involuntary impressions – the actors see each other, something else in the room, someone in the audience . . . Thoughts fly into their heads, they get various feelings . . . And we advised the students to freely "green-light" everything that pops up. As a result of all this, a character was born: the students became somebody else in addition to staying themselves.

Now it's time to say what it would have been too early to say previously – it would only have confused a new student. It's time to say that *not only movements, feelings, and thoughts arise involuntarily* – something else does too: a certain self-awareness; the sense of one's own *new being*.

And just as you can "green-light" your various movements, feelings, or thoughts, you can also "green-light" a whole new *being*.

Having felt that you are a village youth-turned-butcher, you could green-light this *being* and allow it to manifest itself in you, after which your whole being would submit to it: it'd change your perception, reactions, gestures, mannerisms and thoughts – everything would stem from this youth.

In a given situation, in a given etude, an actor's being is noticeably different from his everyday one. But in the majority of etudes, it is not so acute, and it might even seem like there *is* no special new being. But it is always there, because a dual state of being is non-negotiable. Without it, there can be no creativity on the part of the actor.

Up to this point, we have not spoken of it. Until now, we have simply said: "green-light" everything – movements, thoughts, feelings, but we never said anything of "green-lighting a new being." And we didn't have to up to this point: doesn't freely thinking, feeling, and acting already means *being*?

On the Technique of Giving in to Character

Without touching on how a character is born while working on a play, and how to look for it in that situation, we'll limit ourselves to only speaking about observations on the process of character creation in etudes.

It has already been said that a character always arises, that the assertion that you can act completely "as yourself," proceeding from your own persona, is based on a very surface-level observation.

We have seen multiple examples of how a character arises, of how it "permeates" an actor, unnoticeably taking over his whole being.

But here is an instance that requires special attention. A character that an actor has to play is so alien to his personality, to his own human "I," that it cannot stay rooted for long – special methods are needed in order to organically and naturally prolong this new, alien life.

I. *(Entering)* Forgive me, your excellency, I'm late.
II. This isn't the first time.
I. It won't happen again.
II. Let this be the last.

As soon as the actor "green-lights" his freedom, he thinks that he is some big boss – some kind of general of times gone by. He swells up, his head jerks up, his shoulders straighten out, the corners of his mouth turn downwards disdainfully, and he begins pacing about the room in irritation, waiting for the late subordinate.

It was very convincing. Along with the external changes, the actor changes inwardly as well: in his eyes, you could make out stubbornness, dullness, narrowness of vision. He looked down on everyone and tapped his fingers in such a way that it was evident that he was a paragon of hubris.

It was all alive and truthful. Looking at him, one would say: what a gifted, expressive, finished character actor!

But this didn't last long. The partner wasn't showing, and the creative explosion lasted only few seconds. Without any fuel, the irritation died down; the hubris and sense of personal significance, unsupported by any external stimulus, also disappeared . . . Everything became suspended in mid-air.

But once the actor has put this mask on, he has to keep going! He has to hang on to his fleeting hubris, disdain, etc. But how?

A feeling that isn't supported by anything evaporates without a trace, you can't hold on to it . . . What *can* you hold on to and retain? Only the pose, the posture, the mien . . . This is what the actor is forced to hold on to and retain – the external mask, the bare form: the thrown-back head, the raised shoulders, the disdainful grimace, the nervous pacing.

This kind of acting has its own name: people say that an actor is *playing character*. He's playing it, *imitating* it.

Naturally, this has nothing in common with that first creative moment of true transformation when the actor truly became the "excellency" for a few seconds.

In those moments, not only his body became the new person, but so did his psyche – his thoughts, feelings, impulses, and his whole internal life. Everything flowed from the character. There was total harmony: the internal state evoked the corresponding movements, gestures, poses, and facial expressions. These external manifestations, in their turn, supported and developed his internal state: the nervous pacing, the irritated movement of fingers, etc. added fuel to the fire of his internal fury and indignation.

What is the matter here? Why did the life of the first few seconds come to a stop?

The answer is the same – he didn't "green-light" it. He didn't "green-light" the internal life that sparked to life and took over him.

He should have given full freedom to the nervous pacing and the other physical manifestations of his emotions. It would most likely be followed by close listening: is he coming? . . . by looking at his watch: how late is he? . . . by involuntary impatient movements . . . In addition to that, he should have "green-lit" his emotions: when a person is displeased, everything irritates him and seems foreign or unpleasant. The weather, the walls, the objects, the people – everything is horrible, everything is annoying . . . He only sees that he is surrounded by badness and animosity. This would support his emotional and physical state – this way, the actor would become character.

Weak Currents

No matter how you look at it, the just-born character is associated with weak currents. Its manifestation may be delicate or rough, but its origins are nevertheless in weak currents.

With the rough manifestations, there is a jump over the gradual, the "logical" – the normal life. It is somewhat of a shock. However, a shock does not go outside the boundaries of the norm! Not everything should happen smoothly and slowly. Breakthroughs can also occur – the kicks.

The sharper and more expressive a character is, and the farther it is from an actor's nature – the more easily it slides off the actor. And, subsequently, the more skill you need to have in order to not scare it off, to hang on to it and let it sweep you up.

Here, just like onstage in general, the main enemies are either haste and pushing or braking. On the one hand, you must "green-light" yourself, but on the other, you cannot rush: the creative life will sweep you up on its own – just don't disrupt it or spur it on.

However, we have to admit that in the work of an actor, just like in etudes, the character is usually taken by assault, recklessly and forcefully. One mustn't rush, nor green-light this seizing of the character. Nothing fruitful ever comes from it: staying for a few seconds, the character disappears, leaving behind only one of its manifestations – a grimace (a facial one, a bodily one, or only a vocal one – this doesn't matter). The actor mistakes them for the character itself, and he begins to repeat them. This is called "playing character."

Instead, you have to *become* your character. Character is the new "I am."

In life, "I am" is formed over years, and hundreds of thousands of impressions.

On the Diffusive Transmitting of Character. A Faucet

How do you fill a glass to the rim? You do this with a gentle stream—the closer you get to the edge, the weaker it must be. This is the "diffusive" method of transmitting the character.

If you turn the faucet open abruptly, then the strong stream will splash out all of the water – you pull away from the faucet an almost empty glass. This is the same thing that happens when a character is taken by force, or when you give in to strong feelings without having the proper technique for it.

It's impossible to "take a character" – you can only *give in to it*. Give in to the sensation of a new *being* that arises on its own (in the beginning of an etude and in a sound approach to a role). You can do it in two ways. The first way is to simply give in, or rather, to slightly push yourself into this new, unexplored being – as it emerges in a form of a vague sensation . . . This is the pushing of yourself into something that is still unknown, just an anticipation. Having pushed yourself into this new being, and having had the courage to stay in it for a few moments, you begin to hastily orient yourself, and adjust to this new state.

Your actions intensify, and so do your other manifestations. This is because the push you gave yourself brings about a bit of a haste – this rush is probably unavoidable in the first moments. However, you need to be on the alert! In your hastiness, you might lose your balance, and then everything will be lost . . . you will begin to force yourself, and play character.

The second way is diametrically opposite. In the first, I threw, tossed or pushed myself into the just-born character. In the second, on the opposite—*I do not do anything*, and I act like this: The sensation of a new being arises, and I grow quiet, everything in me calms down and becomes primed to receive something . . . as for what – I don't know and don't want to know yet . . . I suspend everything . . . I am silent . . . *I take my time* . . .

And it enters me, flows into me . . . I soak it up, like a sponge . . . As if this happens in accordance with some inviolable laws of physics (like capillarity).

As for me? . . . I only open up even more widely and give in to it entirely. I give in to what's pouring into me – to this new being, this new life.

I let the character infiltrate all of the pores of my body and soul; I let it diffusely saturate my whole being. *I let the character carefully pour* through the narrow neck of the enormous vessel that is our multi-faceted "I".

And it's strange: in order to give yourself over, to enter a state of "passivity" – you need ten times more bravery than for the most desperate activity. You have to remain empty, knowing that something – you don't know what – will flow into you and fill you up entirely, displacing the rightful master . . . (This is the "diffusive" transmittance of the character.) Without experience, without many successful attempts, it is very frightening . . .

But it's frightening only in the beginning: with repetition, this becomes an ordinary event, not frightening in the least.

★★★

Just as they grow frightened of their own bravery and don't allow themselves to make any movement (even if it has already begun) – they similarly don't green-light character – a new being.

Under the influence of the text or the scene partner, an actor receives a new self-awareness: he makes a new gesture, his eyes change – something new flickers in them, an alien expression. A new person is before us. But . . . in two, three, four seconds, the actor grows afraid of his unusual new state . . . he halts all these new manifestations and . . . returns to his "beloved character."

Here is what needs to be done: first of all, explain to the actor that the first moment that drew him toward something new *was* the character's embryo. Of course, it was unusual for the actor – that's why it was uncomfortable. But it was alive and authentic – it came to life on its own, involuntarily, according to the laws of physiology and creativity – you have to believe in it and give over to it wholly.

Secondly, after this explanation, you have to carefully observe the actor when he just finished repeating a text. Everything happens in these brief seconds: either the actor allows the new character to live, or he extinguishes it. This is where you have to interfere: yes, yes! Good! Good! – he will stabilize and will keep risking. Then, you keep supporting him more and more.

Of course, the words aren't the only important things – your tone when you say them is also crucial. The words are simple, they're the same ones you use all the time. There's no need to keep repeating this – enough has already been said in the chapter on *Support*. It's only worth stressing that the effectiveness of support is chiefly determined by the degree of accuracy and acuity with which the director or teacher senses an actor's creative urges and hesitations.

For the most part, the teacher or director doesn't even suspect the sharpness and accuracy of his hits. He is so immersed in the actor that he has no time for observing himself.

How Repetition Affects a Character

We have already spoken of how an etude's "circumstances" change with repetition – how they become more specific and concrete, and become more tangible overall.

Now let's look at the effect that repetition has on a character: does it change it and how?

An elderly woman and a young girl are sitting in armchairs some distance away from each other.

- You're a teacher, right?
- Yes.
- And what do you teach?
- I teach mathematics.
- Never liked it: awfully boring.
- And what do you do?
- I'm an actress.
- Dramatic theatre?
- No, I do musicals.
- I see-e.
- What do you see-e?
- I see why you don't like mathematics . . . And it's not in the least boring.

After the actresses repeat the text and enter the etude, the one who has to play the "musical theatre actress" – the very modest-looking, but incredibly likeable, smart, lively, and gregarious

Sashen'ka N. – sits down comfortably in her armchair and begins examining the elderly actress (the "teacher"). She does it carefully at first, then quite unceremoniously and even superciliously.

The "teacher" is meditatively looking up at the ceiling as if she were admiring the open sky.

Sashen'ka also looks up and completely loses any respect she had for her neighbor: there is nothing above that is worth admiration or delight . . . Barely holding back laughter, she asks: "You're a teacher, right?"

Hearing the tone of the question, the other woman glances at Sashen'ka, sees that she is dealing with a fairly vapid girl, and, not offended in the least – responds: "Yes." After all, what point is there in being offended at such a doll?

Sashen'ka notices her calmness and attributes it to the other woman's obliviousness of being mocked. And now, without hiding her contempt (she won't get it anyway!), Sashen'ka asks: "And what do you teach?" (i.e. – and what can you possibly teach? You're so plain and simple and, above all, so dull!!).

The other grows interested – well, look at this little butterfly! – and, hiding a curious smile, responds serenely: "I teach mathematics."

Sashen'ka fails to notice the humorous attitude with which she is being treated. Without feeling embarrassed at all, she expresses her own disdain for this science.

The teacher now grows immensely giddy—apparently, she has a taste for observing amusing specimens—and as an experiment, trying to be as serious and delicate as possible, asks: "And what do you do?" (what do you deign to do?).

Inebriated with her superiority and not suspecting any tricks, Sashen'ka deigns to respond very briefly, but utterly destroying her opponent: "I'm an actress!"

The teacher assumes an expression of reverential astonishment. In order to egg the simpleton on further, and let her reveal her true nature, she shakes her head, makes a sound like "wow!" And altogether, this means: please! I'm so fortunate to meet a person like this! . . . And she carefully inquires: Dramatic theatre?

Sashen'ka blazes up – apparently, drama is something akin to mathematics. "I do musicals!" she says with an air of importance. Evidently, she wants to say: don't be so thick-skulled, my dear, and do not speak such obvious foolishness! If I were in drama, would I look so chic and refined?!!

The teacher has gotten everything that she needed and stops playing the role. Without hesitating, she immediately starts laughing in the little actress's face and says: "I see-e!" (i.e. of course, that's what I thought . . . you couldn't be anything else . . .).

Sashen'ka is startled by this. Though she wasn't expecting anything sensible from some blue-stocking, still . . . why did the teacher who was impressed with her so instantly lose any sign of respect and admiration? . . .

"What do you see-e?" she asks, somewhat losing courage . . . The poor girl is evidently not so spoiled by success . . . and thinks she has a greater effect on people than she actually does . . .

The "teacher" also didn't foresee such a turn of events coming. She begins to pity her. They look at each other for a long time. One is like a caught schoolgirl, the other is like her mother or older sister. And both are ready to ask the other for forgiveness: one – because she allowed herself to speak in an insulting manner to a serious and respectable person; the other – because she made a mistake, and didn't recognize the childish sense of importance and naïve haughtiness that was put on by a girl that maybe wasn't so foolish. And the words, "I see why you don't like mathematics" mean: "My dear, don't be afraid, I don't want to say anything bad about you . . . I just think that you've been running around with people who have littered your mind with trivial interests . . . "

- Tell me, where is this taking place?
- At a summer house of sorts . . . most likely, at a resort, – the "teacher" responds.

- Yes, yes, – Sashen'ka hurries to confirm, – a resort. You can relax, not worry about a thing, and enjoy the freedom!
- But apparently it's pretty boring?
- At first, it's boring, and that's fine, that's even a good thing. Later, though, once you get settled and get to know some people, things will be interesting.
- So you haven't been here long? You must have spent most of your summer at home, in Moscow?
- Yeah, not too long. But I'm not from Moscow.
- Ah! So you're a provincial diva?
- No . . . I'm not a diva yet . . . I'm very young . . . and my voice . . . isn't really proven yet . . . I'm still only in the chorus . . .
- But you're evidently going to be acting soon?
- Yes, they tell me I'm gifted.
- And do you want to?
- Of course! . . . It's pretty great when they bring you flowers . . . and applaud . . . And I think . . . I can act like they can . . .
- Besides, you're younger and better looking than the other divas who've faded with time?
- Yes, that too . . .
- Good looks are no trifle, when it comes to musicals . . .
- Naturally, looks are very important, – Sashen'ka announces proudly. Everyone smiles, because her looks aren't the most glamorous. But here, she thinks, for some reason, that she is irresistible: she is the future diva, a beauty that is held back by enviers, who keep her in the chorus, not letting her talents to develop . . .
- Evidently, people are telling you that you will have a glorious career?
- Yes . . . our director and others . . . lots of people . . . even Spiridonych, our old barber.

The "teacher" is also subjected to similar questions.

When it is repeated, the etude differs from the first one primarily by the fact that all circumstances, external and personal, are already established.

As the second etude begins, the "actress" needs a moment to grab a hand mirror and lipstick out of her purse; the "teacher," meanwhile, arms herself with book, begins to read it, but, seeing the sky, places it on her knees and, from time to time, breathes deeply the southern air, blissfully closing her eyes . . .

The second etude is followed by more questions. [I take this opportunity to once again show the reader the advantages of the questioning method over the method of telling. It's a great thing to point out to an actor the circumstances of his character's life that he has overlooked. But this doesn't always yield the desired results. Often, a director loses all his energy trying to inspire an actor, explaining to him all his role's circumstances. But an actor remains unperturbed and cold; he remains completely indifferent. For one reason or another, he's closed off, inhibited – it's like talking to a break wall. You have to change your tactics: don't tell him things – instead, point him in the right direction with questions: *make him himself start speaking*. Lead him into the life of the character and the play. You have to start with very simple questions, and then gradually reach more complex and immersive ones. – *Author's Note*] The third and fourth etudes are different only in that the most important things – the circumstances and the "I" – become more and more concrete. The "teacher" no longer feels herself a novice, but rather an experienced educator, a socially active person with definite ideals and life goals.

Sashen'ka becomes more and more a steadfast supporter of musical theatre. Her point of view with regard to her "career" becomes more concrete and definitive with every repetition . . . Her typically intelligent and thoughtful eyes turn simple and absent-minded, and her lips become capriciously coquettish.

If the repetition is done soundly, it determines and strengthens the most important things in a role: the chief circumstances and the "I" (or, as Stanislavsky called it, "I am" – i.e. I am a teacher or a musical theatre actress, or Hamlet, or Ophelia; in a word – I am the character).

As for the details – the book, looking at the clouds, the hand mirror, the lipstick – all this is unimportant, and can change. Moreover, it has to change – after all, the person is becoming more and more defined, and enters the life of the role more deeply.

Usually, directors chase after these details, which have absolutely no bearing on the role at large: books, mirrors, random expressive *mise-en-scenes*, and even intonations. And these are the things that they insist on during repetitions – without understanding that this paralyzes the creation and strengthening of the "I."

The growth of a role can be compared to the growth of a tree. The roots, the trunk, and the branches are the "I." The leaves are the manifestations – the flicker of life. Having appeared in the spring, they whither and fall every autumn. But the roots, the trunk, and the branches remain. They change too, but how? Not like the leaves – on the contrary: they keep growing, they multiply and strengthen. And eventually, they turn into a mighty giant.

By affixing all the tiniest movements and physical manifestations, an actor executes a murderous procedure with the trunk and roots of his role – he forcefully affixes and paints green the weakening, yellowing leaves, thereby murdering what is most important: the trunk, the roots, and the branches. The actor deftly repeats the same details with every performance – the "leaves" are in place, but there is no life – there is no "I," and there cannot be one. It hasn't been grown.

Practice shows that repetition is necessary most of all for the creation and strengthening of one's "I" – or, to explain with another more common, but less exact term – for the creation and strengthening of one's character. Each rehearsal strengthens and deepens the "I" of the character, and its basic circumstances, and it sheds its minor manifestations and "results."

If, however, you forcibly hold onto the "results," then the "I" will die – it will cease developing. Yet, life itself is development. It isn't just that the tree has to shed its leaves because it will die if it doesn't – if it is to live, it must strengthen its trunk and roots (or at the very least keep them unharmed).

Generally speaking, repetition is one of the most important conditions in the actor's work – many things, nearly everything, relies on the proper use of repetition.

For a film actor, the frightening question of repetition doesn't exist – he plays it once, they get it on film, and the job's done. If it's bad or something went wrong, then you just have to warm the actor up and get another take.

In theatre, however, things aren't the same (I am speaking of theatres that strive for the art of living onstage). Here, you have to live, experiencing the same things, for the duration of 10, 20, 100, and sometimes even 1,000 shows. And not just separate fragments, but the entirety of the role, from beginning to end . . .

And so, if repetitions in rehearsals and shows are all about strengthening the roots and the trunk, then the role grows, fortifies, and becomes richer; if, however, the actors are more concerned with the "leaves," then every subsequent performance grows weaker, and it becomes more mechanical. The words lose their weight, the characters – their substance, and the actors turn into dead, mechanical puppets. People say: the show has gotten stale. It cannot be any other way.

The necessity of repetition is what pushes an actor towards presentation most of all. Without a serious and proper school, it is impossible to repeat experiencing, but repeating form – all the external manifestations of experiencing – is not as hard. And this is the feasible job that most actors concern themselves with.

Part V
Conclusion

35

Practical Advice for Teachers

What to Begin With?

This book can be an aid for a teacher. However, it isn't an aid or a textbook in the traditional sense – it isn't broken up into lesson 1, lesson 2, etc.

Before beginning practical work in class, the teacher should first study this book in full.

After that, he has two different possible paths. The first – without rejecting his previous experience, he can carefully begin augmenting it in his everyday work with the new knowledge. And with practice, all the new will replace anything old that fails to give any positive results. The second path is more categorical and decisive: immediately switch over to the new method. In this case, here is what you should do: at first, take what was described in this book's first chapters, i.e. the exercises that you do while sitting in a circle: a short question and a short answer. But they have to be very simple in content, very straightforward. Mistakes will immediately be made (a lack of proper perception, rushing, braking, etc.) You have to pick out the more apparent and crude ones and fix only them, without going into nuances and details – otherwise, you will fill the students' heads with unnecessary things and will frighten them. They will be able to understand the nuances only once they have already dealt with their obvious, crude mistakes – this must not be forgotten.

Most importantly: it is necessary to *very carefully observe a student, coexperiencing everything with him and noting the slightest deviations from spontaneous organic life*. Such coexperiencing, such an emotional merger with a student would prompt the teacher as to what is happening to the student, how to help him, whether it's time to advance, and how to advance. Students are all different – you have to adapt to whoever is in front of you.

It's also vital not to rush with new exercises – return to the first, beginning steps often, as they are where you establish the right *direction*. And never allow any deviations from this course, or you won't even notice how you slip into verisimilitude. Our goal is absolute, creative, artistic truth.

The Centipede

The training methods recommended in this book arose in opposition to those that cultivated conscious self-observation and self-analysis, thereby creating the aforementioned "centipede."

However, with time, things have become more complicated in this new pedagogy as well. Now, next to the simple "take your time" and "don't stop yourself – green-light," we now have "freedom of small involuntary movements," the "just-born character," "perception," "depth," etc., etc . . . .

Here too, analysis has seemingly led to a kind of "centipede."

However, this is not the case.

What created the hopeless, catastrophic constraint of the "centipede?"

First and foremost, a multitude of simultaneous demands. You have to do one thing, and then immediately add another, and a third, and a tenth. And each of these "you have tos" requires a significant measure of deliberation, attention, and conscious strain on behalf of the students. Their whole creative apparatuses become overloaded, which means that there cannot be any free creative processes, to say nothing of their unity . . .

As for us – we're striving to give these processes free rein. We want to liberate these natural manifestations of life, *believing in their creative force*.

This means that we cannot overload a student with demands, or set him up for intellectual strain. On the contrary, we have to free him, unshackle him, and remove anything that might inhibit his creativity. The conditions of the stage inevitably result in an overload without our help (too much effort, stepping on it, etc.).

The theoretical knowledge of all terms and methods is necessary not for the *student*, but for the *teacher*. The student should first master the *practical side*.

And we teachers need, firstly, to learn *not to get in the students' way* when they are doing everything soundly; secondly, *to support and encourage* the students, so that they do not "lose their balance" in difficult moments; thirdly, *to assume the initiative* when a student doesn't have the strength to ascend to a new, higher step.

This is on the one hand. On the other, the teacher must learn to set a student on the right path if he gets derailed and cannot find his way back on his own. This is where you have to know how to approach him not just from one side, but from 20 or 30 different ones.

For a start, this book suggests a few ready, proven methods. The goal behind them is always the same – to achieve a process of creative experiencing, i.e. spontaneity, freedom, and artistic transformation. There are many reasons as to why this doesn't happen – depending on the given moment, every actor can encounter scores of obstacles. You have to be able to see them and dispose of them.

It's not enough for a teacher, at every setback, to simply repeat "green-light yourself!" This might not do any good (even if it's essentially right). A student isn't green-lighting, but why? What is the cause invisible to an inexperienced eye? And how can we remove it?

Without this knowledge, the teacher is no more than a student himself, one who has usurped power to which he has no right.

At first, a student actor might not even know the theoretical aspect of all of these techniques, but by utilizing them in practice in accordance with the teacher's advice, he will achieve good results.

And he will become acquainted with the theory only gradually, by practically applying it. And then, by deriving the theory from practice, it will not "overload" him, but will rather help him understand and cognize all of his new skills.

Attitude toward Mistakes

Do not dwell too long on mistakes. Do not pay them too much attention.

If a few mistakes pop up amidst what is mostly good and proper – let them be. Do not notice them! Only pay attention to what was good, what was correct – grab on to it. If the general direction is correct, then the mistakes will gradually fade away.

Behave as you do when you are learning to ice skate: you fall, you get up, dust yourself off – and onward! After all, you don't do the following: you fall down, get up, and start thinking: how did I fall? why did I fall? where did I make a mistake? You're not learning how to fall – you're learning how to skate!

Just as it is natural for a person to stand, walk, and simultaneously keep his balance, it is similarly natural for an actor to artistically create. You do not force yourself to think about the reasons behind your fall while skating – you simply get up without losing any time and keep going. The natural instinct of balance does everything for you and will teach you everything.

Similarly, an actor's natural instinct will lead him to the right path; just don't intimidate the actor with excessive theorizing and don't cause him to dwell on his mistakes; otherwise, these tendencies will develop, instead of the natural instinct. He will keep looking back, and he will grow more frightened, rather than acquire bravery and freedom. You can find another time for combating mistakes.

This is what's most productive for the actor. And the teacher should aid him in this – lead him away from unnecessary "oh mes and oh mys" with regards to his mistakes. The teacher has to teach him to slip by all the mistakes without getting hung up on them.

And the teacher himself should stay away from digging around in the students' mistakes and shortcomings – otherwise, you will get mired in them. On the contrary, you have to try to see: what is here that is good? And then you should grab on to it.

But, naturally, this does not mean that the teacher should pass by mistakes without noticing them. He has to know them and know them well! He needs to know the reason behind every mistake, how one mistake leads to another, how they combine to create a complex (a seemingly incomprehensible conglomerate), how to combat them, and where to begin.

For the most part, every student has his own particular qualities, his own weak spots, and his own chief mistakes (at least for this period in his life).

You have to note them and deftly pluck them out of the student like splinters, without scaring the student or overloading him with new concerns – he has enough of his own.

When a student is sufficiently readied and intellectually powerful, you can get him to join you in this work by showing him his main mistake, and teaching him how to battle it.

But this is only viable if there is no danger of overloading and frightening the student, and turning him into an ill-fated "centipede."

On Students' Deceptions

It has already been told in the chapter on the "beginning," and in a few others, what kinds of deceptions the students come up with in order to show themselves off to the class and the teacher.

For example, they predetermine how they will act through an etude. They do so out of fear that "nothing will happen 'on its own'" or that something will, but will be uninteresting. Or, when asked about what they "perceived" in an etude and what kind of circumstances they had, they spare no ingenuity and zeal making up whole stories on the spot, asserting that that is exactly what happened to them in the etude.

How should the teacher handle deception on the part of the students?

Sometimes, it must be exposed immediately, but for the most part, it is better to pretend that you don't notice anything. And this will lead to the student himself becoming bored with this farce. He would either fess up, or he would get so entangled in his own lies that his deceptions would become crude and obvious, and this would be the best lesson.

The advantage of this approach also lies in the fact that the student will stop fearing the teacher's eagle eye. Let him think that the teacher doesn't notice anything. Let him think that he is the smartest, most cunning, and most courageous student. The bravery and confidence will allow him to display more and more freedom – he will start having successes, and this will inspire him. That is what the teacher should grab hold of and encourage . . . With time, the deceptions will disappear on their own . . . And so will a need to address them.

Students utilize a vast array of tricks to impart a good impression on the teacher and their colleagues and to build themselves up in their eyes. This happens often with experienced actors, who have to go back to school.

Here is an example of one such trick: a student plays up his disappointment in himself: "No, this isn't it! This is weak!" Very rarely is this the self-torment of talent. For the most part, this is one of two things: either it is simple coquetry, or it is a lack of desire to overcome the difficulties. At the sight of hardships, he loses all faith: reassure me, instruct me, convince me, i.e. pick me up and carry me . . . and I will try to hang back as best I can.

There is another kind of deception – for the most part involuntary. A teacher must know of its existence.

The eyes! . . . Delighted eyes with which a student is gazing at the teacher or the rehearsal . . . He looks on and is delighted! He's found a spectacle to his liking!

An inexperienced teacher will see these "burning" eyes as a sign of enthusiasm, power, spiritual fire, creative delight! . . .

Time passes, and it turns out that these "delighted" ones are the ones who are lagging the most, and are the weakest and talentless members of the class.

When you have enough experience, you cannot look at these lovestruck, delighted eyes without irritation.

It's better to deal with cold ones – they'll grow warm with time. But anything not to have to deal with these eyes, glowing with the empty light of "adoration" . . .

But there are other eyes: thoughtful eyes! Seeing eyes, sensitive eyes, eyes that reflect the depth of one's perception, the strenuous work of the mind, the greedy determination to understand the *essence of things*.

You can forget all your fatigue, sickness, hardships, and everything for the sake of such eyes.

Everything that falls into such eyes will begin to grow. It will take root and will bear many fruit.

On Returning to the First Exercises

If done properly, our simplest exercises (short questions and answers) quickly lead to promising results: the actors pass over the "threshold" of the creative state.

As soon as this new state is felt, it is natural to immediately want to test it out on something more difficult. The text grows longer, the etude – more complex, everything is taken "onstage," and soon, the students' etudes begin to resemble complete little plays.

They involuntarily begin to compete with one another, and they chase what's "engaging." "My etudes must be at least as engaging as what everyone else is doing." And from day to day, the class's miniature plays become more and more theatrical.

Everything appears to be moving along well – success is inspiring everyone. But after a week, after a few classes, everyone grows bored with these etudes for some reason.

The cause is unclear. It would seem like everything is as sound as it was before . . . however, previously, everyone looked on with gripping interest at the simplest of exercises. Now, these complete "plays" cause everyone to yawn . . .

Maybe it's time to let go of these exercises and move on to scenes, or even whole plays?

No, to move on would mean to ruin everything. The problem lies elsewhere.

If the etudes are boring, the sole reason is that they are being done **improperly** – the actors in them are acting **poorly**.

How did this happen?

Quite simply. The chase for "intensity" distracted the students from what is most important: sound behavior onstage. It would seem that each etude is more interesting than the last, that all the performers are experiencing creative flights, but there are still mistakes. Small, insignificant ones. Concealed by the exciting plot, by the actors' excitement, and by the unpredictability of their fantasies – they slipped by unnoticed.

Today, they are few in number; tomorrow, there are more of them; the day after tomorrow, they have become legitimized. And it becomes habit to work with mistakes – actors stop striving for an absolutely sound technique, and instead they limit themselves to working with an *approximate* one. Most importantly, they want the etudes to be engaging, to "enthrall" the audience.

But the audience, at first enthralled by the manifestations of authentic truth, grows colder now that the truth is steadily waning, and eventually begins to become outright bored. All those present feel that the etudes have become uninteresting . . . the etudes are probably no longer necessary.

This is true: *such* etudes are not only unnecessary – they are harmful.

What can be done? Take everything back to the beginning?

Yes, to the beginning. The very beginning, with the first exercises while sitting in a circle (away from the "stage") with the few lines.

And the mistakes that managed to slip through at a distance "onstage" immediately become apparent here in a tight circle. There is nothing distracting, nothing theatrically interesting. The text is so simple that you cannot really make it too theatrical.

Only by returning to these beginning exercises can you see how the students (and the teacher) have gotten derailed with their engaging etude-plays.

They accorded the students great bravery. But they have done quite a bit of harm. They have sown carelessness with regards to what is most important: the nuanced, but inexorable laws of a sound creative process, which we began to learn in the very first lessons. The presence of an "audience," and the desire to make something exciting, caused the actors to involuntarily start spurring themselves forward . . . and the laws were broken.

If we do not stop now and take stock of the situation, then every subsequent step will bring us farther away from what flickered before us in our first moments of enlightenment. And both will be getting farther away: the actor and the teacher. Soon, we will step off the path of the creative process.

You must be constantly cleansing yourself from contamination and impurity. They are inevitable – not only for beginners, but for experienced actors that have mastered the proper technique too. Without upkeep and growth, this technique becomes shaky.

And you have to right and repair your weakening technique your whole life. You must sharpen your blade your whole life, as it becomes duller after every use. Or tune your violin, which goes out of tune after every performance . . .

Our little etudes in the circle are not just our first exercises – they are our scales.

And just as musicians and vocalists cannot disregard scales and elementary technical exercises (as soon as they do, their technique and tonal quality weaken), so will an actor lose everything if he does not keep warming himself up with these "scales," these first exercises that helped him understand the essence of things. With their help, he will again be able to properly "assign," "properly begin," "green-light," etc. – things that you cannot do in a scene study class, where the focus shifts away from an actor's process and instrument – onto the play.

Oversimplification

Regardless of how good a method or technique is, in order to successfully implement it, you have to have a *creative* attitude toward it, showing your own initiative in the right moments.

In the work of the actor, this is even more necessary: after all, we work with live "material," and you need to adapt to it in a very nuanced manner.

You must keep in mind: regardless of how well something might be progressing at first, there will come a time when a method that is giving you obvious results will, for some reason, stop being so effective . . . Everything will grow pale, nothing will be the truth, but something "approximate" . . . The actor and the director both wear themselves out; they keep using the same methods that, until recently, yielded great results, but nothing is working . . . Things become boring, tiring, and you want to abandon the whole endeavor . . .

This phenomenon is common and even inevitable. And its cause is *always the same: oversimplification*. Oversimplification with regards to one thing or another: the technique, the role, the play, or the partner.

How do we succumb to this oversimplification?

People succumb to it fooled by their first success. It seems like everything is fine. You have mastered the "secret" – you won't lose it, ever. There is no need to be as strict in your demands toward yourself.

It seems like you're doing everything as you have been. Everything is so clear – the method has been tested and mastered, the results are obvious. Now all that is left is to keep using it.

And so you start treating your work with greater and greater negligence, and . . . you lose unnoticeable, but essential details. And the more you use a device, the more you lose.

You should not be flustered or dismayed. You just have to know that repetition has led you to being *mechanical and negligent*. The technique has lost what it should not have lost: it has become oversimplified, overly primitive, if not null. That means that you have to restore it to its initial state.

An actor who has grown so "negligent" thinks that he is doing everything as he was at first, but if we take a closer look, we can see that he does everything *only approximately*: he "assigns" approximately, he "green-lights" approximately, he lives approximately, he's approximately free . . . He's not missing very much . . . But what he is missing is decisive: if it's not there, then everything stays *before the threshold*.

What is lacking?

These shortcomings are not new and are quite familiar to us: a student may have gone through the assignment stage a bit too formally; he didn't give in to his first impulse, maybe didn't even notice it; he "green-lit" it, but *not in full* . . . and there are more similarly tiny mistakes.

Now, having considered them closely, we can see how serious they are.

There is one more important moment that we need to note.

The academic year (or some other period of training) has passed successfully. Now there is a break. Then, the students gather again. What should be done with them? After all, they have already mastered everything they should have mastered. Do we keep going? If the teacher takes them further, he will ruin everything.

*It is crucial to restore an **absolutely sound** beginning technique.*

Sit in a circle again, do preliminary exercises again, carefully observe every single thought again, every single sigh. And only when you are confident that everything has been restored can you begin to progress further.

★★★

Although all of the etudes that have been described can be used in classwork, there are so few of them for prolonged training that you should by no means limit yourselves to them. Also, in order for the subject of an etude to have a greater effect on the student, the teacher should design the texts of a given day's etudes so that they would be full of content that it pertinent to that given day.

The Significance of these Principles and Techniques for Professional Creative Work Onstage

We have already stressed that the conditions in working on a show in a theatre are completely different from those in a school. Here, there is a *play* in which everything is assigned and established: the words, the thoughts, the feelings, the through-lines, the atmosphere, the characters. There is no room for improvisation or for "freedoms."

Yes, but in practice, in rehearsal with actors (regardless of their skill level), *you have to combat the very same difficulties and mistakes*. They rush, they don't perceive, they don't do what they "want to," they don't "green-light" themselves, they spur themselves on, they force various feelings onto themselves, etc. In a word – freshman mistakes!

Let's try to – thoughtfully, carefully, and tactfully – augment our everyday work with a fresh stream from our schoolwork with psycho-technique.

Wielding "school" methods, knowing typical mistakes and techniques of avoiding them from school, we can easily work through actors' mistakes.

As for the actors themselves – it is in their interest to master these preliminary aspects of schoolwork, because, having mastered them, they typically *do not need* corrections with regards to their ability to "live onstage." [They will only need to learn how to approach a role. – *Author's Note*]

These may be the very basics, the ABCs of the art of the actor. But let us not have a dismissive attitude toward them. We should not treat literacy as something very elementary and so easy, that it does not require too much effort to be learned. The literacy of an actor's psycho-technique involves **being able to see and hear onstage, think onstage, live onstage in-character and in a play's given circumstances**.

It is very difficult to meet all of these requirements, and not very many actors are capable of doing so. At any rate, without this actor's preliminary literacy, any further work is bound to have mistakes and distortions.

36

On the Way Forward

The Personal "I" in the Actor's Creativity

Let us return to the first chapters of this book – to the highest manifestations of an actor's creativity with which the genii of the stage so amazed and delighted us. After all, this is the creativity and art that we are thinking about as the future of our theatre. Only such art is capable of elevating theatre to the highest degrees of significance, power, and beauty.

However, natural talent is such a rare occurrence that it is impossible to build all our hopes around it alone. Usually, a troupe consists not of genii, but of simply gifted people.

We have to learn to develop these gifts to the highest possible levels.

We already know how to do quite a bit in this regard!

But it is so difficult to not be envious of circus artists – they develop their qualities and their art to such a high degree that their skills and power seem miraculous. They almost seem like unnatural phenomena. You look at it and think: no, in order to do that, you need supernatural abilities!

That's how it is. However, these abilities aren't inborn – they have to be cultivated and developed by means of enormous, stubborn, and systematic effort.

An actor's qualities and abilities can be cultivated and developed – we know this. This leaves one question unanswered: why does an actor's extensive work on himself not lead to the same wondrous results that a circus artist's do?

The reason (which we have already discussed) is that *an actor does not have indubitable and objective criteria with which to judge the soundness of his work*. There is nothing that can sensibly and without any doubts point to a lack of "equilibrium," to a **loss of artistic truth**. And so, an actor very easily "slides off" of truth and authenticity and falls into the realm of forgery and falsehood.

However, let us more closely investigate the lesson that we are taught by circus art. Aside from having exact criteria, the circus also involves determined training that does not allow for any concessions to be made.

What is this training?

Let's once again look at the tightrope-walker. How does he begin? After all, he doesn't begin by immediately forcing him to bravely walk across a tightrope. No, he cannot do this, nor does he want to. He only does what he can do without too much strain, or at least without any danger. Firstly, the tightrope is very low to the ground – just barely above it. Secondly, once he is on the tightrope, he spends a long time figuring out how to stand on it. And since he is not yet capable of standing, there is a rope that he can grab on to at the slightest loss of balance. He hangs on to it almost all of the time – he'll let go for a few seconds, then grab on again.

Gradually, he becomes able to feel his balance and instinctively maintain it, or restore it if it is disrupted. He practices like this until he is firmly rooted in his new state. He does not rush to advance further.

Then, he carefully begins to move across the tightrope, but still hanging on to the other rope for insurance.

As a result of such "school of hard knocks" that does not forgive even the slightest mistake, he develops the habit (or rather, reflex) to thwart *the slightest deviation from physical equilibrium – to immediately, instinctively restore his balance.*

More and more, this process becomes automatic and seems to happen independently of the artist. Aside from the fact that he senses any loss of balance, he now can somehow sense certain signs (which he could not sense earlier) that allow him to *predict* loss of balance and instantly, automatically, prevents it before it even happens.

The acrobat can walk or dance on a tightrope, even juggle on it (and the juggling demands a liberal share of his attention). At this point, balance and its conscious maintenance *moves beneath the threshold of consciousness* – it becomes its own mechanism, second-nature to the acrobat.

For a tightrope walker, balance is the most important thing in his work. But what is similarly most important for an actor, something without which he can neither experience, nor transform?

We have already spoken of this – this is *the constant presence of his personal "I" in all of a role's and play's circumstances, both external and internal.*

As soon as an actor's "I" ceases to participate in a role's life, the actor immediately slides off of artistic truth (like an acrobat falls off a tightrope).

The presence of an actor's personal "I," which happens to be the foundation of the actor's creativity, should not be disrupted as long as he is onstage. On the contrary, it should only grow stronger in order to become part of his creative nature, to become automatic.

In order to achieve this, it is important to remember what we saw during the acrobat's training: his main and, at first, only concern is balance! Balance at any cost!

With similar determination and perseverance, we have to train in ourselves what is most important for creativity onstage – fundamental, personal participation in all of a role's and play's circumstances.

The character is me, and I am the character.

If we do not firmly establish the *constant creative presence* of our personal "I," as part of our state, if we do not make it an **automatism**, then we will constantly be "derailed," and we will never achieve a state in which creative experiencing onstage will become second-nature to us. And without this, we shouldn't even think about mastering the art of the actor on a high level.

All the principles and techniques that have been described or mentioned in this book, like *perception, free reaction, physiology, physical actions, assignment, attention, etc.* – these are all **conductors** to a sound creative state.

As for our etudes, they are such that they automatically involve an actor's personal "I." It does not (and cannot) leave an actor for an instant. This is one of the main values of our etudes. They are part of the necessary "grammar" of the actor's art.

★★★

For a person that loves our art and wants to dedicate his life and his whole being to it, it will be a great consolation to find out that aside from this "grammar" – *the art of living onstage* – there already exists (at least in its initial stages) a higher "internal technique." It is possible to inculcate an actor with a whole array of qualities that he does not yet possess. Or if he does, then they only flicker to life in limited moments of inspired creativity.

What happens to him in these happy moments?

People who can split their attention have probably noticed on multiple occasions how, during moments of creativity, they are, on the one hand, carried along by a stream of creativity—they are immersed in a play's circumstances, they are experiencing properly—and, on the other hand, note that they are exhibiting some unusual behavior. It includes a certain way of breathing, certain state of muscular freedom, a certain way of perceiving their surroundings . . . In a word, in these moments, they instinctively perform a slew of physical and psychological movements and actions that are apparently closely related to their immediate heightened psychological state.

Naturally, a question arises: if this is all so closely related, then is it possible (even to a lesser degree) to evoke a heightened creative state by consciously performing all these movements and actions, physical or psychological?

By means of observation, experimentation, determined exercising, and prolonged training, we have managed to establish that creative power, passion, vividness of imagination, emotional subtlety, and even depth of soul – these are all achievable not only for great talents, but for the majority of people (that isn't entirely lacking theatrical ability). Most of them can acquire many of these rare qualities of an actor.

As tempting as it is to acquaint actors with this "heightened technique" on the very first steps of their training—why wait?—it is necessary to follow a *logical sequence* and use a *gradual approach*. A student that has not been properly prepared will not be able to understand any method, regardless of how well it is described. And an improperly understood method will bring only harm. [On Demidov's "heightened technique," see Books Four and Five.]

On the Necessity of Investigating the Process of Creativity

Any true knowledge is based not on assumptions, but on facts. If something unripe and mistaken makes way for something more accurate, this always occurs as the result of the revelation of some new, significant fact.

But it is not always easy to understand even a seemingly obvious fact. Humanity stared at the daily rising and setting of the sun for millennia, and only Copernicus figured out that things are not as they actually seem: the sun doesn't circle us – we circle it. But as soon as this fact became inviolable, we were forced to change not only the chief foundations of astronomy, but all of humanity's worldview. Such is the power of significant facts.

It is the same way in our young theatrical science – there are facts that are the key to many things, but there is much that we *wrongly* accept as fact.

Theoreticians and practitioners from other fields often deliberated on our subject without any concrete proof, or else they quoted the experience of actors that were *far from the true creative process*. There have been cases when a theoretician, who was greatly removed from the essence of the actor's creative process, used facts that were told to him by trustworthy actors *and perverted them so much that he caused much harm to the field*.

This is why, if we want to truly comprehend this process, we must concern ourselves with gathering the *fundamental facts* of our art, after which we have to test them to make sure that they truly are the unshakable foundation not only of the theatre arts, but of further scientific study.

They must be checked not only by us, but also by representatives of other sciences that are interested in higher nervous activity. True *scientific* research, armed with all the knowledge of contemporary science, will help us get on the right, direct, and quick path. And familiarity with these hitherto uninvestigated processes of creative transformation may also grant science much that is new and significant.

As for our case, we have discovered new facts gradually through our teaching and directing. Through observations, we have come to *facts of such great significance* that they led us to completely *new* conclusions.

Much of what has been found seems to the author to be true and in full accordance with science. However, this is no more than a stage – just the next stage. Further progress will find new facts, posit new hypotheses, and come up with new methodologies.

Additional Materials

Various Notes

On the Book 'The Art of Living Onstage'

This is only the freshman year – it's the basics. However, with these basics missing – there cannot be a second, third, and fourth year. Without these basics, there is no **art**. True, talent trumps the inaccurate "school." But the majority of actors perish, and the lucky few emerge "invalids."

On the Difference of the New School from Existing "Systems"

They are one-sided and cannot be useful for *everyone*. But this one is **universal**. It helps each person develop what is his own and personal.

It concerns itself with *cultivating and growing* **talent**.

Toward "Stepping on It" vs. "Let It"

Often, I say to a student in the middle of an etude: "Yes, good, green-light it even more! Just plunge into it! Bolder!"

Is this sound? Is this pedagogical? After all, this makes the student push and step on it.

Shouldn't I do the opposite? Instead of yelling at the student to give "even more," I should be telling him, "even less!" Instead of whipping him, I should remove everything that is extraneous? Remove the extraneous effort.

Maybe, I should yell to the student: *"Yes, yes!! Just let it! Don't interfere – **let it** do what it wants – **let it** knock itself out!!"*

This should come as a warning. If you say: "green-light! green-light!" – then what you get will be "come on, come on! Step it up!"

Meanwhile, what you should be doing is **clearing the path**. "Yes, yes . . . Let it be!.. Don't interfere, let it do what it wants!"[1]

On the Second Threshold

Anybody can get to the first threshold and *cross it*. An experienced teacher can teach a person who has absolutely no acting skills to do this.

As for the second threshold – aside from giftedness and immense commitment, it is also necessary to know several special **methods**. Without them, even if he is very gifted, a person will fail so severely that he won't even know how to hide his shame . . .

On Analysis and Synthesis

I'm not saying that analysis is never necessary. I'm saying something different. I'm speaking of synthesis, or rather methods that lead to the *ability to perceive everything through its prism*.

What Do our Etudes Give Us? (These Exercises Have Everything)

There is an element of *improvisation* in my "*intuitive*" system – this is one of its chief differences. It would not be a bad idea to reread Erberg's [1913] writings on actors and improvisers.

Only, improvisation does not follow the superficial path of facts, but rather a very delicate line of creativity and feeling out one's own truth, power, and temperament.

There is external improvisation, but what I'm proposing is *internal improvisation*. The text, as well as the actions and *mise en scenes* are given. Everything else is free, i.e. what is most needed in theatre.

In short: every other system leads to the result (which means coercion), while my school leads to the *process* (i.e. nature and life).

★★★

The etudes, large or small, have everything.

1   Assignment.
2   A period of "emptiness."
3   Stepping into a new life.

They feature one of the actor's main circumstances – the audience. What is it? In the actor's work, it is the *doubling of one's consciousness*. This doubling must be taught *from the very first steps*. This is *doubling in front of an audience*, this is doubling in class, or at home when there's no one there, yet an imaginary audience is still present. These etudes also feature the kind of constraint that does not hinder, but rather inspires and *pushes toward creativity*.

At first, the constraint is small – it's the words. The words, the partner, and the actor's own state give birth to imaginary circumstances. The actor surrenders to them. Beneath the mask of the imaginary circumstances, I say things that affect me personally. Beneath the mask, I break free from my brakes. The teacher's deft intervention aids all this.

Later, the constraints come from the author and the assignment, but by that point, the suggested constraints are instantaneously enveloped and pierced by fantasy and imagination, and they become galvanizing agents, rather than shackles.

The etudes have life with all of its unexpectedness. Along with all of its "I," "through-lines," "tasks," "objects," "internal and external lines," "communication," "attention," "logic of emotions," "appraisals," and, in general, every invented "element" that doesn't factually exist in life, but that bears witness to the resourcefulness of the imaginative pseudo-psychologist, and to the *powerlessness of the artist-teacher.*

All of our little exercises include ***everything*** that makes up the foundation of the actor's creative process onstage.

Everything, beginning with a transition from my private state of an observer into the state of a person, surrounded by the new, imaginary circumstances, and ending with such immersion in them that not a trace is left of my own private habits and mechanisms.

Everything is there, and it is already present during the very first lesson.

The Main Principle of the Method

You have to live onstage in the circumstances that have been given to you by the play. This means that you have to teach how to live, how to manifest everything that you can do in life.

Nature comes first. You have natural instincts – you have to develop them. How? With practice. A teacher can only encourage you and support you so that you "do not fall" (off the tight rope), and so that you know that you will be supported if necessary.

Walking onstage means "walking on a tightrope." A "task" is a means of running across the tightrope without seeing it. But isn't it better to see it, but know how not to fall?

Assignment: Suggestion

Let's allow that assignment is a wonderful and practical thing that *must* be used . . . But, if we take a closer look, we can see that there's a little bit too much of it.

First – an actor assigns the text.

Second – the teacher employs "support": "Yes, good, take your time," etc., not leaving the actor alone for a second . . .

And third – the etude ends, and the teacher gives his notes, advice . . .

There is perpetual suggestion. So what can there be of creativity? This is coercion, hypnosis.

There is no hypnosis here, but there really is suggestion at work. Relentless suggestion, even. Suggestion of three different kinds:

The first stage. The actor gives himself an *assignment* or, if you would like, a suggestion.

The second stage. As a result of this assignment-suggestion, he begins to display artistically-creative manifestations. He has neither the experience, nor the courage necessary to greenlight them, so the teacher takes the inexperienced actor "by the hand," as if he were a child, and leads him along step by step. This kind of a suggestion can be called *encouragement and standing by.*

The third stage. The etude is reviewed, conclusions are drawn, any growth in the actors in noted, and they are *encouraged to keep growing. This review is suggestion from the teacher's side, as well as from the student's.*

All three are suggestions, and all three are different; and all three are intended to develop one thing – *an independent technique of **creativity** at large.*

In order to achieve this last goal—independent creativity at large—the teacher sometimes lets go of the "student-child's" hand, and he takes a few steps on his own. His "hand" is let go more and more, for longer and longer, and after some time, "support" is rendered completely unnecessary.

In this way, this is a direct and undeviating path to *developing one's own power, one's will, and one's individuality.*

Fantasy and Imagination

Fantasy is not the same thing as imagination. Fantasy is imagination in action. I can imagine my room or my friend – that's imagination. But if his face or clothes begin to change, then that's fantasy; if the acquaintance begins to say or do something, and something that he hasn't done or said before (that is, not what my memory a.k.a. imagination tells me, but rather something new) – it is fantasy.

An actor's fantasy is very different from that of a painter or a writer. The actor fantasizes actively. He has the impulse to grimace, to go somewhere, to bend over, to speak in a completely unexpected voice – action is the manifestation of his fantasy.

The actor who can fantasize very easily in his imagination, outside of his own body, often lacks his main fantasy – the fantasy of action, bodily fantasy. This is the only fantasy that is specific to an actor. Such an actor may not be able to answer a question about how he sees a character that he is meant to play – he cannot imagine it outside of himself. But as soon as he begins rehearsing, trying it out on himself, it will turn out that his body, his face, his voice – they already know everything and will paint the entire living character.

On the Distance of the Imaginary

When you begin to remember something, the images are usually far away from you, at a great distance, and you are examining them.

In general, I habitually do not allow anything imaginary to approach me, and instead prefer, either out of a closed nature or out of fear, to observe it from the outside.

For example, I say, "I loved you . . . " and am observing myself and "her" and my love at a great distance, like an outside observer, who *is* saddened by these images, but is saddened at a distance, from the outside, like an onlooker.

Naturally, you can do this . . . you can, but you shouldn't.

It's better to train in yourself the habit to *see and sense* anything imaginary as if it were right next to you, rather than a distance away, and as if it were happening right now, rather than in some pluperfect times that were so long ago that you can barely remember them.

In order to better understand this, you have to sense that there is distance between you and the imaginary, and that it can be greater or smaller. Once you feel this, you can *decrease* the distance. You have to decrease it.

★★★

On how and what you should see. Do not see what is said with words – see what is behind them. Don't "breathe in" the *words*, but what is **behind** the words.

★★★

Imagination is a process. And this process can occur in different forms.

The imaginary can be close, far, living, dead, i.e. exciting or apathetic.

This is because the process of creation differs from that of perceiving what is created (imagined).

It was thought that two qualities were most important for a mage: imagination and equilibrium. This was for a good reason. I will not speak of equilibrium here, but keep with imagination.

You have to develop it. How can you develop it, and what kind of imagination should you develop?

For an actor, the imaginary should be living, tangible, physical, real, ultra-natural. I think that that's how it should be for a mage too.

With the help of *breathing*, we cultivate the ability to use our imagination in full, but our imagination can be exceedingly poor, indistinct, cloudy – this means that our reactions to it will be dull and passionless, heatless. This is why it is necessary to start going through these exercises. They have to consist of several principally different methods.

The first: physical communion and action with some very simple item – slowly pick it up, put it somewhere else – it can be a pencil, a handkerchief, a knife, etc., while sensing it rather tangibly. As they say (and I dislike this expression), "focus all your attention on it."

The second: recall and imagine this simple process, repeating it in your thoughts and with your senses. Do this one thing many times. In general, do not vary this exercise – variations will lead to weak, scattered attention.

The third: recall your "travels" along [illegible word].

The fourth: clearly imagine and maintain in your vision an object or a person. This last exercise is very difficult. Do not attempt it before you have mastered the first three. This requires no less than a few months.

Fantasy (see Affects, Admitting, In Statu Nascendi ["In the State of Being Born" (Latin)], Emotionally-Tactile (Imaginative) Reading)

Somebody says a word; you see an image – this is either concrete thinking or association, or the just-born image.

The just-born image is the fantasy's first stirring – it is often not obviously connected to the word.

It is necessary to develop the ability to evoke vivid just-born images, especially just-born images of movement and just-born images that are manifestations of a task (Actions?).

And develop the ability to green-light any just-born image-action.

A method of evoking just-born images: *reading a play very slowly* word by word, with long pauses almost after each word.

If your imagination is slumbering, you can wake it up by the power of your mind (in accordance with Stanislavsky). Fantasy is the life of the imaginary.

Additions to the Chapter on "Circumstances"

Why Are Circumstances Used Minimally and Improperly?

By the way, there is no great new discovery here: even Shchepkin said that you should "step into your character's shoes"; while working on a role, Yermolova used to put *herself* in the role's circumstances; Stanislavsky speaks of "given circumstances." This isn't new.

Yes, the concept of circumstances isn't new, but why is then that in practice, people spend some time discussing circumstances, as if they are an inevitable and unpleasant obligation, and then quickly begin searching for "tasks," "actions," and "justifications?" I.e. why do people spend some time discussing circumstances, but do not treat them as the foundation? Or rather, to be more specific, why do they not use them at all?

This is an interesting question! Think about it: all the great masters of the stage treat a role's life circumstances as the most important thing! . . . and nobody other than them uses this crucial tool!

There is much to think about here.

Circumstances and Facts in the Director's and Pedagogue's Work

Our attitudes, our thoughts, and our behavior in life are wholly dependent on two factors:

1   *Who we are* (peculiarities of our identity and our temperament, our upbringing, habits, our past, and, finally, our physical and psychological state).
2   *What facts we encounter.* There are facts to which we will all react identically. For example, if it is winter, and for some reason, we have to open the window, then everybody would either quickly leave the room, or they would shrink from cold and try to get warm. Such are all the facts that are roughly physical.

But such a reaction can only be evoked by a fact that isn't augmented by some additional psychological circumstance.

For example, we will all keep away from a fire, but if my children or my precious manuscripts are in the fire, I will, without thinking, launch myself into the flames!

Similarly, a fact that is insignificant on its own can evoke a stormy reaction. It was enough for Pushkin to see that a rabbit had run across the road, and he became scared (it's a bad sign!), refused to go to St. Petersburg, and turned back.

In this way, a fact is not important to us on its own – what is important is how we interpret it. After all, you and I will not jump into any old fire, and not all of us will interpret a rabbit crossing the road as a sign from beyond.

By helping an actor see certain circumstances and facts, we push him toward the internal state, thoughts, desires, and actions that we expect from him in accordance with the assigned etude. This is clear from the cases in the chapters on "circumstances." This is what should be done with an actor not only in etudes and scene study, but when working on a play too.

After all, this is how life treats us: it gives us circumstances and facts. And we either grab on to a fact that life has given us, or we try to wriggle out of a situation as best we can.

And a director is bound to know this not only theoretically—from books—but should be able to demonstrate this principle in his creative work with actors.

The first step toward this is the art of surrounding an actor with the circumstances and facts – as a result of which the actor will inevitably get the thoughts, feelings, actions, and words that have to be in the play . . .

This is a very delicate art – we have seen how abruptly life, our whole *existence*, changes, and how a given role's consciousness follows in kind, depending on changes in circumstances that, to an inexperienced eye, seem unnoticeable. The difficulty of this art lies, first of all, in the fact that you have to see whether the character's circumstances are causing the actor to live, feel, and think correspondingly, or whether he is living in the circumstances of his life as an actor, which has no connection to the character (i.e. he is observing the audience, he is keeping track of the execution of the stage's various formal demands, etc.).

Secondly, even if an actor is living in the character's circumstances, you have to be able to identify the facts that are causing the actor to behave not in the way that you were expecting.

Thirdly, you have to point him in the direction of the facts that *will* push the actor toward what needs to happen in the play. And not just any actor – *this* actor in particular. For another actor, you will have to find other facts – these might not have the proper effect on him.

Fourthly, you have to be able to point him toward a fact so that the fact has an effect on him.

In short, there will be many failures and disappointments before you master this delicate, but mighty method.

The word "method" isn't even really appropriate here. It should be called a "path." It is a *path*, a whole path.

And it is crucial for a director and a pedagogue to be able to master this path. Otherwise, you will never get to the roots of your art and will merely be skimming the surface.

Circumstances and Facts in the Actor's Work

If a director is so required to master the "path of circumstances," then the actor is even more so obliged.

You have to learn to treat them as reality, as facts that really occurred and affect you directly. Only then will your whole being provide a live reaction (psychological, as well as physiological).

It's not enough to discuss the circumstances and understand them intellectually. You have to sense them as real events and facts that did not happen to someone else, but to *you*.

The actor's mistake with regards to circumstances usually lies in him discussing the circumstances as if they are involving the "character," some kind of "him" or "her."

I repeat, and I will never grow tired of repeating this: you have to treat the circumstances as something that is happening *to you*, not to anybody else.

Then, you will sense the circumstances personally, and they will begin to affect you. Otherwise, they are nothing more than bits of fiction that do not involve you. Naturally, in this case, the circumstances will not affect you, and you will reach the conclusion that there is no need to waste time with them.

When you meet an actor who has acted quite a bit and has developed rather strong habits, you usually have to spend the most energy trying to get him to stop portraying some sort of "him" and instead have him personally step in and take the place of the character.

And when, after much effort, this finally happens, his eyes widen in surprise, and he, having experienced transforming into another person for the first time, finally understands the incredibly unique delight of an artist's creative transformation.

Given *our* methods of actor training, you don't have to worry about an actor taking a character's given circumstances as his own. That is *the only way* that an actor treats the circumstances. *He cannot treat them any other way.*

The actors are inculcated with this attitude toward circumstances from the very first lesson. From the very moment that student actor is asked to say to his neighbor: "It's stuffy in here. Maybe we should open the door? . ." or some sort of similarly simple phrase that more or less *corresponds with the real circumstances of the class* – from this very moment, he is under the influence of circumstances and facts.

He has been given permission to not force himself to do anything, to green-light complete freedom within himself: when he wants to say it, he'll say it . . . and he'll say it as it wants to be said . . . And he is constantly praised and encouraged, reminded to take his time, told that everything is good, that everything is alright . . .

He does not demand anything from himself. And in the meantime, he is distracted by the sight of the room, the room that he is seeing for the first time, and lots of people . . . Everyone is slightly excited . . . they are all sitting in a dignified manner . . . they are looking at him . . . he becomes a bit uncomfortable . . . "That's right . . . that's right . . . good job! . . . " – he hears the teacher's voice. "Everything is good . . . don't rush . . . " "Is it really good?.. Well, alright . . . it's kind of hot in here . . . " At that moment, his neighbor moves slightly . . . he looks at her involuntarily . . . "Ah, it's her. We took the train together yesterday . . . she's probably a pretty cool girl." "That's right, good, take your time! . . . " "Huh, even this is good? Great!"

At this point, the neighbor looks at him, blushes a bit, and turns away . . . why is that? . . . I wanted to ask her something, but she looked away, so she probably doesn't want to talk. Alright. I'll look away too. "Good job, good job! That's good!" Well then! still good. I'm not even doing anything . . . how is that? Well, since he's saying it's good – it must be fine. But still, why did she turn away? Maybe I should ask her something. Maybe she's hot too? "It's stuffy! Maybe we should open the door?"

And so, beginning with the first lesson, the student grows accustomed to not evoking any thoughts or feelings or desires deliberately – *they arise on their own in accordance with the circumstances, words, and partner's behavior.*

And this becomes second nature.

I am living. *I* am perceiving and reacting. Not some other imaginary person. Or rather, everything is happening on its own: my perceptions and reactions are working without my conscious interference.

It's true that "I" am not the same "I" that lives 24 hours of the day. At times, I think that I am a store clerk, or a jealous husband, or a bacchanalian and lazybones – the curse of the family, and everybody calls me Volodia. Sometimes, I feel that I am an old general – for some reason, I begin to cough, my legs barely move, and my back hurts . . . But it's still all "me." My qualities and tastes differ every time, and they are often outside of my usual repertoire. It's amazing, but . . . it's all me.

The Impelling Significance of Circumstances (Facts)

The director often despairs, because an actor *does not take hold of the circumstances*. The director describes this and that and everything to the actor, but he just looks back at him with cold eyes. "I understand," he says, but it's clear that the circumstances are not affecting him – he is simply checking them off intellectually. They do not affect him personally.

Why does the opposite happen in our etudes: everybody grabs on to the circumstances? They catch them while they're still hot?

Because our actors are assembled differently.

Actors not of our school usually treat a character's life circumstances as something foreign that does not involve them: "Sure, the circumstances . . . they're such and such . . . that's great, it's very interesting . . . yeah, I should probably know them, because I get a better sense of the scene. Without them, I probably wouldn't understand what exactly I'm supposed to act . . .

But . . . could we talk about something *more pertinent*? Could we talk about *how I'm supposed to act this scene*? Because I'm going to have to play it on a stage in front of an audience . . . Play it, not deliberate about various circumstances and facts! Especially those that don't affect the character now, but happen *in the past*! I'm sorry, but that's just fluff, and I don't need it *right now*. Give me something more realistic, more practical – show me "where to cross," give me the blocking, tell me what kind of intonation I should have here, what facial expression, what movement and gestures . . . " (this will be said by a professional craftsman). Or: "Tell me what my "task" is, or my physical action" (this will be said by a trainee of the emotionally willful school).

For us, it's the exact opposite. When we work on scenes or a play, everything progresses as it does in our work on etudes.

And it progresses like this: as soon as an actor "assigns" himself a text and "green-lights" himself, he immediately has an involuntary reaction to the circumstances that he perceives in a fleeting instant.

These circumstances are the actor's own physical state, the sight of the partner, his facial expression, his behavior, and his own surroundings . . . all of this leads the actor (along with the etude's text) to understand the circumstances in which he currently exists. From here, he senses who he is and what happened prior, i.e. what occurred before this etude.

And as long as the etude is going, the actor is only concerned with *figuring out the circumstances.*

If this seems doubtful to you, I will only point to the fact that the actor is put in a position that is close to lifelike.

And what do we do in life? Consciously or semi-consciously or even unconsciously, we are constantly trying to figure out the circumstances that we encounter.

We look at the clock to figure out whether we are about to be late. We look at the weather – how should we dress? We look in the mirror – is there something wrong with my face or my clothes? We look at an interlocutor's face to understand what he is saying, what he is thinking, and what he needs. What we notice, evokes our thoughts, feelings, desires, words, and actions. As for when we don't understand something, everything stops in us – we hit a "dead end" and remain in this state until we finally understand, at least approximately, what something means, i.e. what the circumstances are.

Our life process consists of us encountering new and old facts, thoughts, and sensations, and reacting to them. To some things, we react instinctively and subconsciously (reflexively or automatically). To some things, we react, understanding what is before us and what just happened. But both cases involve us encountering facts of life. And our reaction depends on how we understand or feel a given fact.

This is our whole life. This is natural and ordinary.

This is why our actor, who is always put into such natural conditions in our etudes, grabs onto his circumstances so greedily. He needs nothing more – only the circumstances. He does not worry about his own reaction – he knows that the reaction will come. It can't help but come. He just has to worry about not interfering – "green-lighting" it. For our actor, "circumstances" and "facts" are everything. Having developed this habit while working with etudes, he transfers it to scenes, and then to plays. He needs circumstances and facts there too – those that happened *before* the moment that he has to create onstage. But he is not remotely worried about *this* moment, and he is worried least of all about predetermining everything that will happen and how it will happen. It will happen . . . as it happens!

If he knows all the circumstances that occurred before today, if he knows who he is, if he knows everything that he has to about his partner, then he doesn't need anything more: the partner's lines, as well as his own, will lead him to the right path. If it happens to be the wrong path, then that means that the circumstances were wrong – if they are changed properly, then everything will be correct.

In order for Othello to not forgive Desdemona, all that is necessary is for him to improvise *in the proper circumstances*. He must not improvise **the circumstances themselves**.

You cannot forbid anything – you have to add circumstances.

Not: "No, don't pick your nose!" – Instead: "You're a prince!" – and the urge will go away on its own.

Crude Reactions

Short Circuiting

Actors who desire to master the new technique of spontaneity and freedom bravely green-light everything within them. In doing so, they find qualities in themselves that are crucial for creativity onstage.

But sometimes, though not often, there are embarrassing situations in class: an actor breaks the furniture, or rips his clothes, or starts hugging and kissing his partner, or, on the contrary, he starts roughly shoving him around, or hitting him . . . He is seemingly doing everything right: he had the impulse, it was in accordance with his nature, and he *green-lit* this free development. However, these "free developments" shock us for some reason – they seem inappropriate, "too free." What is the matter?

In order to explain this, we'll have to analyze some aspects of our internal life, even if we have to use the most popular analysis.

An infant's reactions are very primitive: if he doesn't like something, he will yell, cry, start kicking. If he does like something, then he'll jump from joy, wave his little arms, and, once again, yell something incomprehensible . . . This primitive life of desires, feelings, instincts, and motor reflexes is an effect of very primitive nervous activity.

The infant gradually becomes acquainted with the surrounding world, and with time, a properly raised person's brain gradually inhibits all his dark instincts, desires, and primitive reactions. Finally, they completely submit to its will.

However, the primitive animal, with its dark instincts and fierceness, continues to thrive. It is easy to see this. Get a person drunk – the mind's dominance will recede, and the person's reactions and actions will be exceedingly primitive.

Powerful emotions can similarly "inebriate" and put the mind's associative apparatus out of order, in which case a person behaves as if it is not him who is doing things, but somebody else – some part of him, and usually not the best part.

Later, when he "comes to," this behavior evokes surprise, embarrassment, incomprehension, and even horror. The mind is eclipsed (either by alcohol or by powerful emotions), and the primitiveness finds its way outside. It breaks free and does such things that the person himself doesn't quite understand afterwards: how could this have happened?!

The actor's situation onstage is far from ordinary. Beginning with the fact that the actor consciously becomes the center of a hundred strangers' attention. This exceptional situation evokes a certain state of excitement and even emotional "inebriation." Some find this beneficial, others – less so. When the effect is positive, the actor enters a state of *harmonious excitement* – a heightened creative state. When the effect is unfavorable, the person enters a state of disharmonious excitement: nervousness, worry, confusion. And in this case, he demonstrates not the maximum of his abilities, but the minimum.

If, on top of this, he does not know how to combat this state, *and* the content of the scene (or etude) evokes emotionality in him, then this foundation of nervous, uncreative excitement is augmented with his own conscious (or unconscious) demand: "this moment requires strong emotions!" And what are strong emotions? Not being always able to figure this out, he simply tries to *excite* himself, i.e. become more emotional. And so, these two different emotional excitements, both of which are being harmful, combine, intertwine, and give birth to a new excitement that is so great and enthralling that the actor cannot deal with it. This leads to emotional dislocation: he has lost control of the car – it's gone off the road and is now speeding across ditches, bushes, grooves, and hills . . . This is close to pathology: losing human rationality, the actor falls into a primitive state – the realm of the crude reactions of the infant and the animal. Once the actor, having forgotten everything in the world, in a state of extreme agitation, imagining that he is in an inspired state, zooms across the stage with clenched fists, froths at his mouth, and destroys everything around him – that's pathology at its finest, which, naturally, has nothing in common with creativity or art.

This is a cataclysm. A short circuit! Instead of going through the whole wire and lighting thousands of lamps, the current of life loses its way, slips by what is most important—the brain and its wondrous associative apparatus—and we see a spark, an explosion, and a self-destructive inferno.

Conditions Evocative of Crude and Other Primitive Reactions

When, for one reason or another, the cerebral cortex's associative activity (which connects and harmonizes everything) is impeded, there is disharmony. Parts of the psyche function in disunity, destroying each other with their contradictory behavior. The pedagogue needs to know the reason behind such occurrences, otherwise he might make quite a few ill-advised steps.

First of all, such an instance might simply be a *misunderstanding:* the actor did not understand what the director wanted from him. He thought that all of these exercises with green-lighting have nothing in common with theatre or the audience, and have only to do with training "freedom" in an actor – any kind of freedom, freedom at any cost. And the more expressive and courageous it is, the better it is.

Up to this point, his physical manifestations, his actions and behavior have been completely connected to his consciousness and reason. His consciousness and reason sometimes got in the way: they impeded and halted his involuntary reactions. So in order to work around these impediments, to keep reactions spontaneous and free, he is advised not to inhibit himself, but to wholly give in to these reactions. And he, while chasing after this new freedom, this liberation from his limiting braking system, pushes himself toward this new and unknown thing – toward the freedom of physical movement. Harmless at the start, it can grow and expand rather quickly. In some actors, this freedom of physical movement can cross a boundary that is set by aesthetics, and it even reaches the point of crude reactions.

But why is this? Why does this happen?

Because, while giving freedom to physical movement, the actor, mistakenly considering it to be the sole thing worthy of attention, does not give any freedom to his internal (psychological) life; he impedes it. Meanwhile, the unshackled and broken free primitiveness can only lead to crudeness and accidents.

As you see, this "freedom" is completely unsound – it is by no means the freedom that is needed for the actor's creativity. Besides, it is very unpleasant, both for the scene partner and the audience: it is not very pleasant to look at such uncontrolled behavior. As such, it is better to lead the actor away from such surprises beforehand. But I would like to give fair warning: this must be done very carefully and artfully, else you will scare the actor, and he will never allow himself any creative freedom at all. In short, you will not manage to achieve what is most important.

The most important thing that you should do in this case is let the actor know the following: *he should give complete freedom to his physical movements and everything primitive, but simultaneously **not stop his higher level cognitive functions and processes***. In short: *do not disrupt your normal, harmonious state.*

The reason behind such crude and primitive reactions might also be a student's nature.

In order to more clearly imagine this, it is worth recalling what we discussed in the chapter on "small automatic movements." It was said that any external manifestations, regardless of size, is an involuntary *reaction*, our response to some sort of impression that is coming from without or within. And if we impede these external manifestations (movements, actions, sounds), then the internal process that is associated with the external manifestation also stops (or, if it does not stop completely, it will change significantly). If, however, we give limitless freedom to all external manifestations, then in doing so, we give the corresponding internal processes the freedom to develop. If we practice this (seemingly external and peripheral) freedom well enough, then the processes in our center (i.e. in our psychological realm) will function unimpeded. This was all illustrated by the Indian tale about the minister that was locked in the tower, and how he managed to use a "spider web" to pull in an entire "rope."

In normal cases, this is exactly what happens to an actor – external freedom results in internal freedom. But sometimes, as a result of efforts to give in to external freedom, actors undergo such psychological dislocation – you just want to throw up your hands.

For the most part, at first, such a specimen of actor seems very spontaneous, sensitive, expressive, and skilled. Aside from this, he almost always astounds us with a unique, enthralling childlikeness and mobility of temperament.

And so, when giving an exercise, you expect that it will be executed lightly, freely, smoothly, and that, full of delightful freshness, it will be the highlight of today's lesson . . . Suddenly – blood is rushing to his face, or deathly paleness; a strange, unfamiliar, almost deranged gaze . . . awkward movements, pointless waving of the arms, and, finally . . . destroying anything he can get his hands on, rough treatment of his partner, or something else along these lines . . . What is the matter?

You have no doubts that the actor perfectly understood you: he knows full well what is required of him and what should come of it. But . . . his demands of himself, requiring that he be even **more** free, **more** spontaneous than he is in life – this demand (conscious or otherwise) hits the weakest point of his internal organization.

The problem is that, even without this extra freedom, he is predisposed to gaps in his organic processes, and primarily to gaps between higher-functioning processes and primitive desires. And here, he thought that such a gap is not only encouraged, but serves as the primary foundation for everything. This is why he gladly embraces it, and reaches the point of aggressive outbursts and excess.

When you carefully examine this seemingly easy surrender to impulses, this enthralling spontaneity and freedom, you will see to your great disappointment that it is nothing more than a weakly organized psyche, and an inability to live harmoniously. And the childlike spontaneity that was so endearing at first is merely immaturity, infantilism, and essentially psychological and physical inadequacy.

Naturally, there is no need to be hasty in one's diagnosis—it may be false—but it is vital to keep track of this person, and to attempt to avoid further misunderstandings. [This shortcoming, if it exists, sometimes smooths over with intense work. And the actor, though he failed to meet many of the expectations that were laid at his feet in the beginning, still becomes more or less suitable to playing more minor roles. – *Author's Note*]

And, finally, you often encounter the case when an actor that has chosen the path of "living onstage" is unpleasant, crude, and even repelling. The reason behind this may be an insufficiency of culture in his background, as well as a lack of moral and intellectual development. If this kind of actor will behave onstage "like he wants to," "according to his impulses," there will inevitably be narrow-mindedness, incivility, crudeness, and tastelessness in their purest forms.

People might disagree: "But how could then such and such actor, without any education or upbringing, play leading roles in Shakespeare's plays? And, as contemporaries tell us, how could he have been astoundingly good in those roles?"

Yes, great talents without enough commonly accepted culture and upbringing are capable of acting the roles of "princes," "kings," "philosophers," "great leaders," "poets," "Mephistopheleses," etc. – they can act them and not elicit condescending smiles. But how did they achieve this?

True, they did not do this by means of knowledge or erudition, or by polishing every physical pose, gesture, and facial expression. They achieved this by virtue of their depth of thought, the beauty of a gifted soul, and the limitless force of their passions. In a word, they achieved this by virtue of **talent**. And the audience, enthralled by their feelings, carried away into an abyss of thought and spiritual beauty, would overlook artificial, ostentatious aristocratism, which is seemingly so necessary for these roles. They forgot about it, because they had before them an authentic, inborn titan of thought and an aristocrat of the spirit.

But only rare individuals have the capacity to do this. Nobody who can sober-mindedly evaluate himself will list himself among such genii. We people of average giftedness have to expend great amounts of effort to achieve even a small fraction of what comes to a genius so easily and quickly.

But if we get even closer to the truth, we have to add that history shows that all people of natural gifts also had their fair share of failures when they were relying solely on their talent. What did they do in these situations? Did they wait until they were "stricken" by inspiration? No, they redoubled their efforts and began to work, study, and train even harder, attempting to acquire the knowledge and skills that they were lacking.

Psychological Stability and Spiritual Balance: A Necessary Quality for an Actor of the School of "Living Onstage"

Up to this point, the acting profession was considered very accessible . . . Although, this may carry into the future — as far as it concerns those theatres that are satisfied with the current state of acting technique.

If, however, we think about an actor who creates onstage before an audience, and strives for the *art of living onstage*, then not many people are suited for this profession.

First of all, only people with a mighty and harmonious psychological organization are suitable for it. True artistic creativity before an audience (i.e. the art of living onstage) requires a "doubled consciousness," "creative transformation," and everything that a weak psyche might not be able to bear. Its equilibrium may already be rather shaky, but with these requirements, it will promptly tumble down into an abyss.

Is there anything surprising about this? In order to be accepted into flight school, you have to pass through several selection committees that evaluate the fitness of young people's heart, lungs, and other organs, as well as their psyche. We therefore have no reason to believe that an unstable and unbalanced nervous system is suitable for flights into the "stratosphere of thought," as well as for performing aerobatic maneuvers up in those heights. Or, another example: can any average person easily fly beneath the big top from trapeze to trapeze?

The Harmonizing and Strengthening Power of the Audience

But regardless of how shaky or unstable an actor's psyche may be, or how low his level of culture, there is one aspect of theatre that can immediately, in a single swoop, bring harmony to a disharmonious psyche and replace seeming weakness with strength.

This aspect is the presence of an audience.

A youth might give off the impression of a weak and wan, or nervous and poorly-balanced person . . . But he goes out onstage, and you cannot recognize him. Where did his short stature go? Where is his weak, barely audible voice? His movements are full of grace and intention, his eyes are intelligent, his posture is noble and robust. Where does this strength come from? Why did everything become so strangely harmonious?

The cause is the group of people sitting in the audience. The knowledge of the fact that there is a mass of people that is waiting for you to act *for them* instantly *organizes* a torn psyche's disparate parts. You have to "live?" "Live as the character lives?" Why? So that 500–700–1,000 people – these specific people – saw and believed it. You know full well: if you do not live truly, then it will be a forgery, and no one will believe you.

In order to "live," you have to give yourself a "green-light" . . . but can you green-light yourself and everything else indiscriminately? Will that be necessary and interesting for the thousands of people that are staring at you and waiting for not just your random impulses, but for *appropriate* impulses that are coordinated with the play and are indubitably artistic? And a person **who is not lacking an actor's instinct**, who instinctively feels with his whole being the presence of the audience, his responsibility before the audience, and his **possible power over the audience** – such a person involuntarily mobilizes and begins to act unerringly as is necessary in this environment (the theatre) in this character (the role). Just like a duck that grew up alongside hens and turkeys on a poultry yard and has never been in a body of water – when it sees a river, it will make directly for the water in accordance with its instinct, and it will begin to swim and dive as if it has spent its whole life doing nothing else. It's the same for such an actor – in life, he may be timid, awkward, and unresourceful, but when he goes out onstage, he is a king! The strength comes on its own because of a proper relationship with the audience. And so does the trueness – artistic and creative responsibility points the actor in the direction of thoughts, desires, and movements that correspond to the needs of the play and the role.

In this way, the stage and the audience are the touchstone that can help certify whether a person has the instincts of an actor. If a person before an audience becomes more significant, calmer, more convincing, and more compelling, then he does. If, however, the audience causes an actor to lose everything and become ugly, pitiful, pale, or pathologically excited – then he has none of an actor's instincts. Or at the very least they are dormant and have to be awakened and developed.

There will be more on the wondrous and inevitable relationship between the audience and the actor later on.

On Work at Home

Simple assignments. It is not enough to do an exercise once. The first time will always be full of mistakes, restraint, and superfluity. When you repeat it again, everything calms down and becomes better. True, this also happens, because the circumstances become more concrete and tangible. This helps calm things down. But this second time will also be full of holes.

Do it a third time, and you'll see that you have gone even deeper. Or rather, to be more exact, the circumstances will enter you more deeply – they will immerse you even further, and you will feel what it means to *live* onstage.

The violinist that taught Volodia (my brother) allowed his student to tune his own violin only after five years of training. Before that point, though the student could almost tune his instrument exactly, it was still just slightly off. And then, playing on such a violin, he would have ruined his ear – he wouldn't be able to make out these slight deviations.

The tuning of the actor's instrument . . . It is such a responsibility! Only after I was submerged into the false quagmire of the Kamerny Theatre did I begin to study truth and learned to properly tune and calibrate myself, checking what was in order and what wasn't, where I am still "sitting," and where I am already "falling" (like Stesha Hertzog).

Such is the contradictory nature of life: on the one hand, you cannot learn on your own without a teacher. On the other, only I can know my own truth.

To some extent, bound by our braking systems, we can all be free and "do what we want" in life. But onstage, when thousands of eyes are looking at us, this becomes possible only after extensive practice and with great talent.

Exercises in school alone are not enough – you have to work at home too. Truth be told, homework is more important. Exercises in class are merely check-in sessions.

Together with a partner, or even better, on my own, when nobody's gaze is embarrassing me, when nobody is demanding anything of me, when nobody is waiting for me to finish the etude and give up the stage – I can endlessly repeat any exercise, I can stop where I want to, I can do the most boring, and / or riskiest things.

Students that can overcome their laziness and infuse their daily "ration" with even a few minutes of such exercises soon achieve, if not wonders, then at least results that nobody could have expected from them.

The first and most important rule that must be obeyed: the exercises have to be *extremely simple*. So simple that you could not make them simpler. The majority of failures and mistakes at home occur because of students trying to take on exercises that they are not yet equipped to handle. Meanwhile, when you are alone, when there is no audience, when you do not have to worry about entertaining anyone – this is the time when you should freely explore all the mechanisms of your psyche, investigating every cog and screw individually. It is unwise to ignore this opportunity and instead turn on the whole machine at full blast – you will not understand its secrets, and it'll just break instead!

Homework

1. Assigning short etudes.
2. Green-lighting the automaticity of movement.
3. Do a movement mechanically and green-light its further justification.
4. Create a list of circumstances and, choosing one at random, give in to the sensations that you get from the circumstance that you read (I'm caught in the rain; I'm sitting next to a burning fireplace; I'm sitting in a warm bath, etc.).
5. Green-light random movements, thoughts, and feelings (alternating between the three).
6. Tell yourself: "I am in front of an audience" (something like "public solitude").
7. *Restraint* exercises, i.e. follow your first impulse without becoming derailed, and without skipping to new impressions, as they turn up.
8. Exercises with imaginary objects and actions.
9. Monologues.

Some have no luck at home. They think that "doing the simplest things" means emasculating feelings. "Go up to a window and open it," and that's it. Meanwhile, they extinguish any feeling that arises. They think that will no longer be "simple enough." Naturally, this results in rubbish.

When a student does an exercise, he is observed by either a teacher or by his classmates. He knows this. But when he is alone, since there is no one there to observe him, *he begins to observe himself*. This is, of course, harmful. Especially if he is predisposed to doubling. Given circumstances help out in this situation.

It is also a good idea to assign a watcher: the wall (or the table) is looking at me . . . Put yourself in conditions similar to the classroom – at least there, you have an inevitable preliminary assignment: the teacher and my colleagues are watching me.

★★★

At home, you have to search for the greatest possible depth.

If a tightrope walker paid attention to the effect that he is having on the audience, he would immediately fall off.

An actor, however, is constantly observing the audience: are they getting it or not?

This disease begins with the very first lessons. The student acts, and the teacher watches, after which he gives his notes. And it turns out that the student is working for the teacher, trying to meet his expectations.

Even if this isn't the case, he will still constantly sense the teacher and be dependent on him. As a result of such work, the actor becomes entirely dependent on the audience. Stanislavsky or Nemirovich comes to a show, and the actor invariably becomes nervous and cannot cope with the stress. The actor must learn to *do his job* notwithstanding the audience. You have to learn to do this at home. You have to train to do this very, very well. So that, ultimately, the process itself can immerse you.

You have to develop every method to the greatest possible degree and firmly establish yourself there. Then you will never be unhinged by the teacher or the audience or by anybody that could be at a performance. You won't have the time to spare for such trifles.

Another equally important, if not more important, thing: you have to strive for *absolute* truth at home. Not approximate, but absolute.

The Dangers of Working at Home (and also, on "Scene Study")

An actor rehearses very well – confidently, freely, loudly. A day or two pass, and suddenly, something very strange happens to him: he starts whispering his lines, he is constrained, he goes through a scene so "timidly" that it's useless . . . It's apparent that something is weighing him down, that he's trying to tear through bonds of some kind that are preventing his development – but he cannot do it! What is wrong with him?

It turns out that he was "working" on his role at home . . .

But since he could not speak loudly at home (to say nothing of freely raising his voice), he observed himself so as not to yell or allow himself to do something inappropriate . . .

He was searching for "truth." But he found brakes instead. He found the truth, but it was the truth of an inhibited person. And he drilled it in (he "assigned" it to himself).

We needed five rehearsals to get rid of these brakes!

It is possible to rehearse quietly, but you should be aiming for volume, and for freedom. Sure, I cannot speak loudly right *now*, but this is a temporary condition – I am rehearsing with the view of the *future* in mind, when I will be able to speak as I want . . . as I want to speak at that moment.

On the Necessity of the Teacher's Training

From personal experience, as well as by observing other directors and teachers, I can say one well-tested truth: it is absolutely crucial for a teacher or director to be constantly training. If not in front of an audience, then he should at least act at home on his own. Only in such practice will you be able to find enough fuel to keep your quickly diminishing charge going. You have to keep yourself in the realm, the atmosphere, and the environment of the creativity that you are teaching – regardless of whether you are a director or a pedagogue.

Otherwise, you quickly lose your keen eye. Maybe because your eye and your actor's instincts disunite. You have to maintain their relationship.

On Evaluated Showings and Other Topics

During public showings, the instigative power of the stage significantly increases – it becomes five or even ten times as powerful. The actor's power grows, and he is able to demonstrate a lot more than usual. But his braking system might also be 5–10 times more powerful. And it is sometimes too powerful to handle!

There is one very frightful thing during showings: this actor and this actress were always exemplary during etudes – for example, they could play a very dramatic etude with exceptional strength. And so you call these most reliable and tested students onto the stage, and you give them a jaw-dropping etude. And you even hold them until the very end, like your trump card. But they're the ones that'll let you down. And not just let you down!!! They'll fail so spectacularly that you won't know what to do with yourself!!

Who is responsible here? Them? You. You alone and nobody else!

First of all, the showing is already enough of a whip – a "thrilling" topic is a second whip – and they involuntarily begin to *demand more of themselves*. They can also feel that you are saving them for the last, as your final, decisive blow, and they begin to demand even more of themselves. This is the third whip. The fact that you give them an old text that they managed to do *so* well at some point in the past is a fourth whip – they subconsciously want to do it *even better*. As a result of this overload, they are so bad onstage that you wish you could sink through the floor from shame.

In general, you have to do simple etudes for showings, or else you have to "prime" the students beforehand, or give a couple a very simple etude and then give them its "second act" (which is slightly more difficult), at which point they will be ready to handle it. But do not overdo it – do not lump too much hope onto their inexperienced and easily frightened "mastery!" Nothing good will come of it! And what's more is you'll wound them.

During "showings," extreme brakes come in two forms. One: a battle between a temperament that has been augmented ten times over and the brakes that have become ten times more powerful. And immense internal struggle . . . Five-minute-long pauses . . . people huff, puff, pale, shiver, "experience," but you can't understand anything that's happening – it's just pathology.

Another form: a person doesn't worry at all, he grows cold. Everything has been displaced into his subconscious. There is no visible struggle, but it's there. Extreme fatigue after the "showing" bears witness to this. After this, a person feels like a wet rag for about two days.

If a showing is difficult and comes with great responsibility for each student, it bears even more difficulty and responsibility for the evaluators! Their carelessness, inattentiveness, or lack of vigilance can lead to great mistakes and harm for the students.

Why don't people know how to watch public showings? Why do they want to turn a showing into an interesting performance? It's not because they do not understand anything and are unable to *see into it,* but because they do not come to exams, treating them as *the most difficult work that requires all of their efforts*. They treat it as time for relaxation, as a cabaret. The semester is over, and now it's time for exam week – hosting parties. Today, one teacher is hosting everybody, tomorrow – another is . . . Each one tries to give the guests something that is entertaining, original, tasty, and spicy enough. The more entertaining and interesting a showing is, the more it becomes like a merry cabaret – the more people find it successful. The teacher exerts himself, training the actors for the public showcase.

You have to check what every student has learned. You need the time and patience of people who will observe their public showings. There is no need to turn them into an exciting little cabaret – it confuses the students. It disorientates them.

Meanwhile, some of the students in today's cabaret got very unlucky roles – it's very difficult to judge their success . . . some are forced to do something that isn't their forte – oh well, such is the order around here . . .

It rarely happens that etude exercises turn into fully-fledged *stage etudes* that would be interesting for the average audience.

Usually, the first four or five are observed with interest (which means they make for good theatre), after which the rest all seem like unnecessary repetitions and become boring. This leads to the conclusion that they are uninteresting. And if this is a *critical* "showing," then many get the impression that it was a failure. Naturally, everybody forgets that the first four or five etudes were interesting and engrossing.

They similarly forget that the 16th, 17th, or 18th was also fairly extraordinary . . . This is written off to exceptional talent, and nobody thinks: "This is how it should be." And if there was no success, then people think that it was either because of the method's shortcomings or inadequate training. They don't realize that the actors were in front of an audience for the first time (*and* during an "exam") and were nervous – and that's why everything came crumbling down.

In general, this is the point of view of an everyman.

Imagine that there is a marksmanship competition. The first, second, and third marksmen all hit the target, and though they do not hit the bullseye, they hit one of the innermost rings. You are amazed: they shoot so well! But when the 103rd or 104th does the same thing, you begin to think that it isn't interesting at all! Look, someone's hit the bullseye – now that is interesting! Except, that was either an accident, or they probably used a different school.

And it's too difficult to consider that in their first lessons, nobody even hit the target itself – everyone missed it by a few yards. That's first of all, and second of all, the ones who do hit the bullseye – they have simply figured out the proper technique of shooting, while the others haven't "gotten there" yet.

And the fact that all 500 or more manage to hit *close to the bullseye* isn't boring – it's an amazingly enormous achievement.

What is improvisation in other schools' etudes? These are bad plays written by the students themselves. In other schools, the teacher never gives a text that is written *on the spot*. And since there are no such texts, then how can it be improvisation?

Seeing as everything in showings is always learned by rote, nobody ever believes that things can be happening **here and now**. When you try to convince them of this, they nod, "Yes, yes," but smile, as if to say, "Sure, we know all about these 'improvisations.'"

This is why it's a good idea to have the texts come from the *audience*. This can only be beneficial for the students.

The texts might be very awkward, and in that case, they should be adjusted a bit or lightly "spiced up."

In general, showing an unfinished painting, reading a newly-written novella, and especially having a public acting demonstration should only be done with great masters in the field. They know how to make out what is sound and fundamental amidst a heap of faults. Accidents will not deter them. Aside from this, they only need hints, the tiniest seeds, to predict what is going to come of all this.

At the same time, somebody who understands the work only at surface depth can make out only the faults. He does not see the *paths* that the artist's, writer's, or teacher's creativity is following. And certainly not **new paths** . . . And so, he begins to criticize: this isn't there, that's not good, this is terrible . . . The cherry tree is in full bloom, but has no berries! It's outrageous!

But if it's in bloom, then the berries will come. The berries do not come first – they appear only after the flowers.

The Necessity of an "Etude Technique" for the Actor's Stage Work

Working on scenes, or working on a role (which is essentially the same thing) is addressed in the next books in this collection. But so that the reader does not lose time or the knowledge that he has attained while reading the book *The Art of Living Onstage*, he should keep in mind that he can already use much of what he has learned for working on a role.

Firstly, using an effective method like "support."

Secondly, the essential principles of the art of living onstage — "green-lighting," "taking time," "assignment," and generally the "technique of freedom and involuntariness."

Thirdly, finally, he will find everything that has been said about circumstances and character useful.

The reader should not be deceived by the fact that etudes involved freedom and improvisation, while in a role, everything is already determined — the words, the thoughts, a scene's atmosphere, the major through-lines, the character and its physical appearance, etc. He should not decide that, in an etude, an actor can give in to his impulses, while here, on the contrary, he is bound.

Most importantly, the reader should not reach the hasty conclusion that etudes are one thing, while a role is another; that etudes are exercises for developing necessary qualities, while a role or a show is something more fundamental, and has no room for "freedoms." You can experiment with the "freedoms," but when push comes to shove, you have to abandon your entertaining and interesting amusements and do what is required for the stage — you have to search for a concrete, effective, expressive, and verisimilar form, and try to "justify" it (make it verisimilar, personalize it, etc.).

Without giving in to specifics (they're in the next book), it is worth saying that techniques that you use in etudes are the ones that you have to use while rehearsing for a show with experienced actors. They all "rush," "do not trust themselves," do not do what they want to, do not "green-light"; they "spur themselves," force various "emotions" onto themselves, etc. When actors act poorly (if they act poorly), they do so because they make the primitive mistakes that you try to weed out of first-year students.

All actors (beginning with the experienced ones), without exception, need the same advice: "take your time," "green-light," "do what you want to do," "do not interfere," etc.

When you encounter this in practice, you see how our theatre art completely lacks any efficient school. It does not exist, and nobody even suspects that it should. It is replaced by acting by numbers — one moment is played "as surprise," another "as horror," etc. Or, here you "have to want" one thing, here — another . . . here, you have to justify your pose, there — personalize some prescribed line-reading . . . Or, people try to pass off *distracting the actors* with "physical actions" as a technique.

It's amazing how the requirements of almost all theatre schools are so unnatural, and how there have been so few searches for proper paths that correspond to the laws of nature.

Can You and Should You Combine the "Stanislavsky System" with My Principles and Methods?

People who have previously studied the "system" and have gotten accustomed to it, upon superficial acquaintance with my methods, say, "We have to combine the two, and it will be great!"

Doesn't it seem like a sensible thing to do?

It's not at all sensible!

According to the "system," you do something, because somebody from the outside told you to do it. Meanwhile, the need to do something or other needs must *arise in you on its own.*

When compared to a genuine, live state of being, a state of being that involves "task" is a forced and false state, and is in no way creative. In life, we *never cognize* the fact that we are aiming for one "task" or another, that we want one thing or another.

One of the "insightful" reproaches that Stanislavsky got from stupid and ignorant intellectuals (one of the most hopeless kinds of idiots): "Seeing as you can use the system to teach a person to 'act naturally,' though in mundane circumstances, this eliminates the necessity and preciousness of *talent*. Before, you needed talents, but now . . . evidently, you can make do without them."

Such pitiful reasoning! Art does not consist of "acting naturally in mundane circumstances" – this is basic literacy, and that's it.

Nearly everyone is taught to draw in school – the art of painting does not suffer from it. This only results in the awakening of scores of extra talents.

Literacy remains literacy, and art stays art.

When using my methods you truly *can* teach anybody how to act. There will be "truth" and there will even be traces of art, seeing as every case will involve *creativity*. But this isn't art in the true meaning of the word. Everybody wrote essays in school, everyone writes letters. But that's not literature! In order to create literature, you require a *special talent*, just like you need a special talent in order to create great art of the actor.

A person who has grasped our technique well will not be a great artist yet – this is only the *basic grammar*.

The heightened technique is the affective technique.

Of course, I haven't said what is most important yet – the highest thing that every artist strives for in his dreams. But this comes later. First, we need to know our ABCs, our basic grammar. We have to learn to "keep our balance" – then we can speak of heightened technique – "the second threshold."

And a proper school or "system" can expedite the development of talent – it can uncover talent. An improper school kills talent. Which is what "Stanislavsky's system" always did when wielded by his bodyguards.

I am not a supporter of Stanislavsky's intellectually willful system, but the way that various ignoramuses implement it defies description. They seemingly say all the right things, but when they begin to *do* it, they deform an actor so much that he is not capable of thinking, feeling, or even breathing. And they support all their actions with references to Stanislavsky.

Regardless of how well you write something or of how clearly you explain something, there will inevitably (!) be people (and not just one, but thousands) that will keep doing what they were doing before reading my books, but supporting their actions with references to these books. And since they're directors and teacher, i.e. authorities in the field, there is no possibility of arguing with them. Regardless of how a book is written, it will still serve as proper direction for very few. For rare individuals, for seekers, for the very sensitive and subtle. The others will try these methods roughly and will, naturally, not achieve anything useful. And they'll say: "The method is bad, it doesn't lead to anything. ("Sour grapes.") If the author did use it well, then he simply influenced people with his hypnotic suggestions; he inspired others through the power of his personality and, in general, was under an illusion, kind of like Stanislavsky – he writes one thing, but, unnoticeably for himself, does something completely different. And yet he thinks that he is using newly discovered paths."

In a word, the same thing will happen that happened with [a Swiss psychiatrist Paul Charles] Dubois [1848–1918]. He achieved great results in employing his psychotherapy.

And Dubois's method consisted of *rationally persuading the patient*. In his opinion, a person's poor reasoning cause the majority of neuroses. He becomes hung up on topics of secondary importance and blows them up, while he *misses what is most important*. And Dubois, without making anything up, showed the patient what is most important, thereby bringing *balance* to his weakened and deranged mind – harmful ideas, fears, and expectations fell away, and the patient, under the influence of this directed train of thought, grew healthy.

And so, the majority of doctors that tried to implement this method of "reasonable persuasion" did not experience any success, and, naturally, everybody wrote their failures off as the method's inadequacies.

What is the reason? Only that successful implementation of this method requires **subtlety** and a good head on your shoulders. And it's a rare thing to see both together. Not just anybody can persuade somebody **reasonably**. Simply because not everyone has a lot of reason. Some have just barely more than the patient.

The same thing can happen with my book. People will begin to implement it and will immediately encounter their own . . . narrow-mindedness.

The Ideal

One sign of person beginning to follow a path that is foreign to him is that he very quickly surrenders his position and *lessens his ideal*.

Painters have painted hundreds of thousands of young women, but where are ones like Lisa Giaconda? Where are the portraits that resemble those of Rembrandt? Raphael lived, and he showed us the way. Why, then, do we not have another Sistine Madonna?

There are many people that spread their paints across a canvas, but there are rare individuals that reach the very limits of art. And it is a fraction of a fraction that demonstrate high artistic giftedness.

It's the same in other art forms. We had Mochalov . . . we had *bel canto* . . . we had the Art Theatre with Stanislavsky and Nemirovich at the helm . . . You'll say: it was always a genius, it was pure talent.

No. **The ideal. High standards.**

What should we strive for? There is no room for doubts. The choice is obvious – we have to strive for the highest possible manifestations of art and not the lowest. You can slide back down anytime.

Note

1 In the experience of the editors, a call for greater passivity takes care of Demidov's concerns. Once the students have been introduced to exercises in passivity, this term can be used as part of "support." While "supporting" the student, a teacher might say: "Be more passive! Even more! More passive yet!"

Book Four

The Artist's Creative Process Onstage

Translated by Andrei Malaev-Babel
and Sarah Lillibridge

Introduction

It is by logic that we prove,

but by intuition that we discover . . .

Henri Poincare

The work of a theatre artist (and that of the actor in particular) may be fascinating, but it is also difficult. Most importantly, we aren't always aware of the full depths of our ignorance, especially when it comes to the subtle, complicated, and timorous creative process. (Truth be told, specialists are equally ignorant in this regard.)

There is no other art that everyone discusses so resolutely and willingly, and with such careless ease. This is likely because the difficulties of acting technique are completely unseen: people walk, sit, speak, gesticulate, laugh, rejoice, mourn – what's so special about it, and what more is there to understand? Everyone pronounces such categorical judgments, as if he is the preeminent connoisseur or specialist in theatrical matters and particularly, more than anywhere else, in the creative work of the actor.

It would therefore be wise for theatre-lovers, and likewise people of theatre, to broaden and clarify what they already know about the main and fundamental questions of theatre.

It is, however, not easy putting this knowledge into words, and here is why. One need unites theatre workers – be it the director, the teacher, or the actor – with other professionals. It is the need for *the clarity of refined instincts* (or, to put it differently, the sophistication and precision of creative automatisms). It cannot be substituted by knowledge that has been passed on via words.

In order to make a complicated (and indescribable) process more comprehensible and tangible, it is necessary, firstly, to examine it from different sides. Secondly, it is necessary to extract individual laws from it, one by one, and to describe them as if they exist independently and separately (which in reality is not true, of course). These ideas and notions, by their very nature, nuzzle together, endlessly shaping and permeating one another. Yet we have to put them into a certain order, with each step in the sequence conclusively linked.

The matter becomes yet more complicated because "specialists" abuse conventional theatrical terminology so frequently that the genuine meaning of these terms has utterly eroded or changed almost beyond recognition (for the most part, it is completely distorted). Thus, it becomes necessary to renegotiate each of these terms.

★★★

Under what conditions does a new, more or less noteworthy hypothesis arise? It either arises when there has been unexpected enrichment of the given science with major new facts, or from obvious dissatisfaction with its current predominant doctrines.

Each of these factors played a role in our case. In addition to that, there were also unsatisfactory indicators from the *practical test* of the dominating theories.

I can say with certainty that the hypothesis before us is *new* and *reliable*. Proof of its newness lies in its persecution, and of its reliability – in its being put to the practical test.

My entire "system" consists of non-interference with the existing process, and in the ability to add fuel, and also to use that which already exists.

My job is to surround an actor with such materials so as to facilitate *self-combustion*. In short, I prefer not to lay claim to a God-like role, or even one of a Great Alchemist or Magus. Instead, I'll confine myself to the role of a **gardener** who knows the best conditions not only for the *germination of the seeds*, but for their further growth and development.

Take a look at my "green-lighting," "take your time," "support," "the freedom of small movements," "assignments," the particulars of "the beginning," "let it be," "letting go," "non-restructuring," and even at "breathing techniques" and "periphery and depth." There is nothing in them that resembles the "elements of the creative process" [of the Stanislavsky System].

In order to conquer and ultimately subjugate nature, we must try to discern all of its most subtle laws and learn how to use them. One cannot go against these laws; they must be utilized.

"Nature, to be commanded, must be obeyed." As paradoxical as it may sound, it is also true.

Our art still exists as if it were in the Stone Age; the actor's creative technique is still in its infantile stages.

The mastery of such an "invention" as "emotionally synthesizing thinking" is capable of transforming the art of the actor. Once mastered, it will expose the pitiful state of our present art. At such a time, it would be laughable to even refer to it as art. We won't believe that it was once called so. It would be like using a stone ax in our age.

Those who wish to move this art forward must think about inventing something new. About new discoveries.

There is another way: the ultimate improvement of the old. The fact is that by reaching and mastering the limits, *you go beyond them* – you take a step into a new area (see also Book Five, the chapter "Advice to Future Researchers of Creative Technique").

1
On the Difference of Acting Techniques

The theatre's influence on the audience is composed of many elements. It includes the actor, the author, the director, the artists, musicians, electricians; the actual theatre building – its intimacy, comfort, and splendor. The service staff, even the buffet, the cloakroom, the composition of the audience. Each of these, and many other elements I've neglected to mention, have their own place and play their own role.

But ultimately, the most important element is still the actor. No matter how bad the actual theatre is, even if there isn't a director – if Duse is playing the role, you forget everything.

If there is no actor, there is no power in the production, no heart, no life. But with him, everything else fades into the background.

All actors want to conquer their audience, but they go about it in different ways.

One school seeks to attract the audience's attention with the genuine truth of the actor's artistic transformation onstage. [Of course, we must not understand "life" and "experience" in the literal, narrow, everyday sense (for more on this, see Book Five). – *Author's Note*] This requires that the actor thinks, desires, feels—in a word – *lives* onstage as the character that he is playing. A different school considers a skillful lie, shuffling and falsification to be more reliable and effective. Its method is to divert the audience's attention, to throw sand in their eyes and to sneak in an imitation in place of the real thing – not even an imitation, but a placebo. If they have to, they'll even resort to hocus-pocus – rousing in the audience the impression of a psychological experience where there isn't one, and where one never existed.

It is impossible to compare these two approaches, just as it is impossible to compare an airplane and a sailboat. They each exist, doing their own thing – period.

There is a "reconciliatory" path: representational acting.

There are two components of such an actor's work. The first is creative: the actor creates his work using the path of intuition. This happens at home or in early rehearsals. The second component consists of the most exact and strict implementation of the discovered external form. The outer manifestations of feeling are repeated each time with complete accuracy, and without change. This consolidating of what was found happens in subsequent rehearsals, and during the performance, in front of the audience. Such an actor's technique is chiefly external. In order to manufacture the impression of truth, the actor should be an adroit master-imitator of the highest caliber. In order to be so, he needs to perfectly learn and develop his expressive apparatus – his face, voice and plasticity of movement – and to master them, just as a piano virtuoso wields his instrument.

This school happens to be most prevalent in France. Its best representatives are Mademoiselle Rachel [1821–1858], Sara Bernhardt [1844–1923] and Coquelin [1841–1909].

Some moments in such an actor's role are designed so well that they evoke his genuine emotions. They "bring the actor to life." The form is so perfect (or maybe he perceives it inwardly so well) that he becomes affected by it emotionally. Then suddenly – in one, two places of the role – he is living again through what he experienced when he first approached the role. But, having learned through bitter experience, he knows that it is impossible to count on this *accidental* emotional "immersion" in the role. If it happens, that's good, but if not – it isn't important; he is insured by his external technique. But in actuality, these are two *completely, essentially, and fundamentally different ways of acting.*

The normal experience of a genuinely creative actor (the one who is living his role) is a state of freeness, involuntariness, and naturalness. In short, it is the experience of continuous "life" onstage. Let us suppose that the actor, having experienced a creative state at home or in rehearsals, only brought the external results of his preliminary work (the external form) to the audience. Such a form would no longer have that same content as existed during its creation, while the actor does not have the same internal experience. His is now the experience of an implementing copyist, and not that of the creator. The audience, in such a case, would be presented with a *copy* of the artist's work – no matter how good said copy may be. If we do not learn how to create here and now, on the stage and in front of an audience, then we will be condemned to exhibiting mere *copies* of our works.

What sense does it make for an actor to restrict himself and be satisfied with the execution of lifeless copies?

When you read a play for the first time, your heart burns with the desire to rush onto the stage and act! Working at home alone and at rehearsals, you open up, get carried away and excited, and pour out your heart. Now, the time has come to fulfill all your aspirations. You are in front of a breathing crowd – it comes to life on its own, arouses and affixes its own excitement to that of the artist. How do you treat this most important, priestly aspect of communion? For some unknown reason, you turn it into a demonstration of agility, manual dexterity, and proficiency. Apparently, this sacred moment is completely deprived of creativity! Is it not upsetting, not vexing? And is it not incomprehensible to the outside observer? What was the point of such long and inspired preparation? What was it all for? For the act of transforming your own living being (pulsating and breathing, full of blood and excitement) into a cold mannequin – a corpse that has been drilled to appear as a living thing.

Who needs my body, my voice, my tears, if they are drained of life with all of its surprises, its flashes of inexplicable urges, its sparks of feeling, and its glimpses of *living* thoughts, no matter how miniscule and simple?

Ah! How many truths in the Persian adage: *a living dog is better than a dead lion.*

★★★

But why such a will-less capitulation? And what is with the satisfaction that comes from mixing unlinked things: genuine life and dead fabrication?

I have seen how, in anticipation of the object of her adoration, a petty bourgeoisie girl placed fake paper flowers in a vase. Then, probably wishing to create a poetic atmosphere of a fragrant flower garden, in her simplicity of heart, she sprayed them with eau-de-cologne – "Bouquet of My Grandmother" ("Persian Lilac").

Doesn't an actor do the same thing when externally mimicking his own elapsed, bygone feeling?

What is so surprising about this? We still haven't even begun to touch upon the creation of the true science of art. What do we know so far about the spiritual mechanics of the actor's creative process? Or what do we know about a different, contrary field: about the reflexes of the audience and how to govern those? So far, we are barely making do with the amateur craft.

At one point in each of our lives, we have all experienced an irresistible and sweet fluster from one spoken phrase, from one word, from one glance . . . This has happened both in life, and in the theatre.

This inexplicable heartiness, authenticity, and higher humanity stroked at our very heart! Without losing its melody or beauty, the sound carried in it such strength of will and feeling that it seemed magical.

Our grandfathers had certain phrases said by Mochalov resonating in their ears (probably, in their very souls) until the end of their lives.

The eldest among us cannot recall Duse's "Armando!!!" without a lump coming to our throats. [Armand Duval ("Armando," in Italian) is a lover to Marguerite Gautier, the title character of Alexandre Dumas, fils' 1848 popular play *La Dame aux camellias (The Lady of the Camellias*, also known as *Camille*). Marguerite was one of Duse's most important roles.] It seemed that all of her soul, all of her life went into that one word – the farewell, love, an undeserved insult, gratitude for all that came before . . . One word, just a few sounds . . . and an entire life. The life of such a woman as Duse – one of the most gifted, intelligent, enlightened, and most beautiful women of her century. Perhaps listing these qualities will in some way help you imagine the strength and emotional impact of that "Armando!"

And it was not without reason that Salvini, when asked what was required to play tragedy, answered "voce, voce, et voce!" (voice, voice, and voice!).

It is not known exactly how Mochalov worked on himself – this miracle-worker and wizard of the dramatic and tragic *bel canto*. Perhaps, a lot depended on his genius, on accidental insights. But the best of his followers, the glorious constellation of our tragedians, those actors of the "gut" (Ivanov-Kozelsky, Andreev-Burlak [1843–1888], Mamont Dusky), apparently had their own secrets. They passed them only to those select few whom they considered worthy and capable of keeping these secrets undistorted.

It is interesting that those secrets had *many things in common with the secrets of that very Italian bel canto* we have already discussed! Those same breathing exercises, that same blowing and whistling at the flames of a candle, and so on (this will be addressed in greater detail later). [See Book Five, Chapter 12.]

It is necessary to say that to look at the actors of the "gut" merely as dilettantes, waiting for sudden inspiration, or for the blessed (heaven knows why) descent of the Holy Spirit is a deep, fundamental mistake. Actors of the "gut" had **their own** school, or, at the very least, had *a path* toward that school.

The imitators ruined the reputation of this school. All of these "Oralovy" [Yellers] and "Rychalovy" [Bellowers] who, not having enough talent or skill, managed to absorb just one thing from their predecessors' heart-felt, superhuman power: one must act with the "gut," "as one pleases." Not knowing methods to achieve this, they barged straight ahead – they shouted, screamed, yelled, scampered about on the stage, trying with all their might to rouse their "guts." Of course, nothing fruitful came from this; it only cast shadows on the very word "gut," and quashed any desire to find the path to this most wonderful of the acting arts – our dramatic *bel canto*, the art of the "gut."

Figure 17   Eleonora Duse as Marguerite Gautier in Alexandre Dumas, fils' *La Dame aux camellias*, 1890s. Courtesy of Andrei Malaev-Babel.

(It is worth saying that the school of the "gut," and its methods, will hardly work miracles on everyone.

The fateful division into three types – imitator, emotionally willful, and affective – will reign here with all its might. These methods, so potent for the affective actor, might not produce their great, magical effects on the actors of the other two types; the very instrument and "mechanism" of their art is completely different. These methods might give them something, but they won't make a miracle. For them, the grapes might turn out to be too sour.)

In moments of inspiration, all of the actor's abilities converge, inevitably resulting in *synthesis*. Meanwhile, this synthesis is harmonious – without one thing dominating the rest. Predominance, in this case, amounts to a mistake. Maybe it should exist to a certain degree, but no more so than asymmetry can exist in a beautiful human face. Underneath this asymmetry, however, lie an indivisible person and the wholeness of his "I am." According to artists, symmetry in a living human face creates deadness. But the living asymmetry in a face is a permanent struggle, a permanent change: at times, one side dominates, then another . . . it is a *duet*, not a solo or a primitive tune.

Needless to say, I use the word "synthesis" not in its usual meaning. The so-called "Total Theatre" requires performers, who are able to act, sing, dance, perform acrobatic feats . . . perhaps it would be more accurate to call such an actor "a jack of all trades." Synthesis is something different – a fusion, and a transition to a new quality.

An actor who can do some singing, dancing, and walking on his hands without being able to do any of it perfectly – such an actor combines these arts only mechanically. This is not an organic synthesis, but a mechanically concocted mix. (If an actor must learn the basics of these disciplines, it is not so that he can demonstrate it onstage, but rather to keep his physical apparatus in shape.)

The higher the art, and the wider the circle of those abilities involved – the more complex it is. Yet the very highest of arts consists of harmonic creative fusion of all abilities at once. Only such an art may be considered genuinely synthesizing.

Perfection (Dramatic, Theatrical): The *Bel Canto* and Form

Perfection can come with bold external form, but then again – it may not.

Here is one example of perfection for you:

> The king rises, confused; Polonius shouts, "Lights, lights, lights!" The crowd hastily backs away from the stage, while Hamlet watches them go, mysterious look on his face; finally, the only ones left are Horatio and Hamlet, who is sitting on a bench. He looks like a man, whose feeling, suppressed and restraining with a colossal will-power, are ready to burst out in a terrible rage. Suddenly, in a single lion's jump, quick as lightning, Mochalov flies from the bench to the center of the stage. Stamping his feet and waving his arms, he fills the theatre with a resounding, hellish laugh . . . No! If, by some command, a thousand chests laughed in unison, melding into one, it would still feel like a feeble child's laughter in comparison with this furious, thunderous, paralyzing laugh. This is because such laughter doesn't require a strong chest and iron nerves, but a thunderous soul, trembling with bottomless passion . . . And what about the stamping of the feet, and the waving of the arms accompanying this laugh? Oh, it was the *dance macabre* of a desperate man, rejoicing in his own torments, and reveling in his own burning lacerations . . . [Belinsky 1953: 321–322]

One must not forget that all this burst forth from an actor who was overflowing with feelings and passion. Without such overflowing, the jumping about on the stage evokes only a feeling of awkwardness in public, and maybe even a shriek of laughter.

And here is a different example of perfection. Without any thunder and lightning, the acting of that same Mochalov on that same stage in a different performance:

> After the performance of the play, when the embarrassed king left the stage, followed by his court, Mochalov no longer jumped up from his bench. He remained sitting there, next to Ophelia's empty armchair. From the fifth row, we could see him as clearly as if he were just one step away. We could see that his face turned dark blue, like a sea before a storm. Letting his head fall, he shook it for a long time, with an expression of unbearable torment in his soul. From his chest rose a few muted howls, like the roar of a lion that has been caught in a snare – seeing the futility of its efforts to free itself, with a muted and silent roar of despair, he expresses involuntary submission to its miserable fate . . .
>
> The audience froze, and for a few moments nothing was heard in the vast amphitheatre except for fearful silence. It was suddenly torn asunder by cries and applause . . . [Belinsky 1953: 333]

431

How humble and subtle is this form in comparison with the "*dance macabre!*" No bold theatricality, no "thunder and lightning . . ." And at the same time, how perfect it is! Which of these two forms can be considered a dramatic *bel canto*? They both equally can. In both of them, the primary source of the actor's creativity resides in the very deepest subconscious – beyond the bounds of banal calculations or mere arithmetic.

When we speak of the dramatic *bel canto*, the meaning of this term is, of course, relative. One wants to find a word that could express this specific perfection – the one whose roots are found in the very technique of the actor's art.

For the actor or singer who has mastered the physical and psychological technique of *bel canto*, there is no need to search for form, to invent it, or to fix its intricate patterns (be it speech or plasticity of movement). I guarantee it. In doing so, he would just tie himself hand and foot. He would drag his arithmetic into the realm of higher mathematics and thus risk destroying everything. (What would he do with his fixed external pattern, as completely new things reveal themselves the next day?!)

It is important to know where to find the secret valve at the source of a fount and how to tap and open it. As for how it might decide to spurt today – this is impossible to guess in advance. In any case, it won't be like it was yesterday, or the day before – because it is the fount of life, of the very depths of our creativity. And there is no predicting it.

The *bel canto*! . . . A quality of sound . . . The essence of sound . . . A soul of sound . . .

The soul of sound! Or maybe – the sound of the soul. That soul itself must be singing or speaking. No more, no less. Just so. Just precisely so.

Authentic Experiencing

Usually, as soon as one begins to speak to a new group of theatre people about the possibility of "living onstage," one is showered with expressions of bewilderment, objections and protests – in short, by everything you can read in Diderot's renowned *Paradox of Acting*. It may be worded differently, but in essence it is the same.

There still has never been, and perhaps there never will be, a more dangerous book for the art of acting than Diderot's *Paradox* . . . Alas, this is what always happens when a layman begins to make himself a home in a field that is outside his area of expertise. And, the more talented the layman, the more destruction he causes.

People have already been learning by this book for a century and a half; they quote it like a serious classical treatise on the technique of acting, and it has confused so many people! How many living creative sprouts it has destroyed . . . There have been similar theories and hypotheses in science – fortunate to appear "at the right time," they proclaimed as truths. People take them as such and . . . fall into their clutches. Dozens or even hundreds of years must pass before someone finally grabs his head and shouts: what is this nonsense! Being led by a false hypothesis that sprung from a fake idea – with stubborn conviction we have been swimming toward the east, expecting to get to the north! Retreat! Retreat! It is hard to imagine how much we have lost on this way! . . .

How do we ensure that our discourses don't turn into pointless arguments with those who are blind from birth about what paper looks like? (You'd tell him that paper is white and lined with graphs, and they'd protest, claiming that it's smooth and thin, and that it rustles.) To avoid this confusion, it is necessary for both sides to *tangibly and practically comprehend* that every art deals with "life" that is creative (CREATIVE!), rather than real and mundane. There is an entire chapter dedicated to this [in Book Five]: "'Life' in Play and in Art." In moments of artistic creation, a person lives a fantastic, imaginary life. He lives and creates new circumstances for himself; lives and creates himself in the new circumstances. He lives in different kinds of environments – those of imagination, fantasy and daydreaming. Life in these environments is governed by different laws. This is why glue-on beards, conventional sets, etc. – rather than distancing the actor, bring him closer to this life.

The actor's creative act takes place in front of the audience. It will be explained later why the audience is essential for the actor, and what kind of harmonious interaction takes place between the audience, the actor, and his imagined fantastical world.

Having not experienced this practically, one cannot understand the most important thing – the nature of the actor's creativity. Discussing the creative act with those deprived of such personal experience equals a discussion of colors with those born blind. Such a person cannot say much even of Mona Lisa, or the Sistine Madonna, except that one is big, and another smaller, and both feel like a board with a rough surface . . .

For the fundamental questions of the actor's art, such as: *Life and Truth in Play, The Actor and the Audience, The Actor and the Author, The Actor and the Director*, and so on, I direct you to the corresponding chapters.

And yet I can't help but feel that I failed to write something essential. Well, at the very least: the actor lives the life of the character, yet in large spaces he would "live" differently: for *the larger number of viewers*. This means that his life is not restricted to his embodied role, but it *features the audience*. This is where the styles of acting come from, such as naturalism, realism, impressionism, symbolism. This is what inspires louder voice, clearer speech. The actor's life is "conciliar."

In a theatre built for five thousand viewers, some things are physically impossible to see. This, however, does not call for falsehood and over-exaggeration; instead, it calls for *impressionism* – a particular style of acting. And a talented actor with an instinct for a certain "publicness" would act quite differently in a big theatre than in a small chamber house. In the art of acting, loudness, richness of sound, boldness, and breadth all depend on the actor's correct perception of the audience. There are actors who, the bigger the audience, the better and more strongly they act; and there are others who do not possess this capacity for "expansion."

The Stage as a Magnifying Glass

And now on to the question of whether the audience ever notices all of these nuances of acting: do they "reach them" and is it necessary to over-exaggerate?

The actor's placement on the stage, well-lit and elevated above us, cannot help but draw our attention to him. We see him as if we are looking through a gigantic magnifying glass: nothing is hidden from us; every detail makes itself known.

The actor hesitates: we see how he stared at someone in the audience; we see that the actor doesn't know what to do with his hands – we see it all. The actor attempts to cover up his confusion by overprotecting – we understand. The actor feels charming, and puts the audience under his spell, using a certain arsenal: beautiful voice and fluid gestures, or perhaps a lovely "simplicity" of acting – "this must be the idol of the local public," we guess.

Everything is visible, through and through; such is the nature of the footlights that they make a regular person sharp-sighted, transforming him into an observer and audience member.

For some reason, actors think that their viewers perceive only what they want them to perceive. Why?! Far from it – the viewer perceives everything! The entirety of the actor's state of being.

That which *you are living by right now* is *experiencing*, and not some kind of *special* "exxxperrrriencing." If the actor chases after some kind of *special* experiencing, the viewer sees this chase – he cannot help but see it; such is the specificity of the "magnifying glass of the stage." The viewer may not always be capable of making clear sense of everything, or perhaps he may not be consciously aware of it, but he always feels it when "something isn't quite right."

In this sense, the history of film acting is quite informative. Those who have watched the earliest films remember perfectly well how the actors over-exaggerated, how they tried with all their might, mercilessly grinning, grimacing, and waving their arms – in pursuit of expressiveness. This was likely because the films were *silent* – so, the actors felt that they had to pitch in something that was *visible*.

In the end, it turned out to be a pitiful error; apparently, what was needed in film was *absolute truthfulness* and an economy of mimicry and gesture – in short, complete *authenticity*.

The same is true of the stage.

What can the audience see in an actor who is **creating** onstage?

They see involuntariness – clearly, inside the actor lives something stronger than him. Things are *happening in him*. He *lives*, or rather – something in him *comes to life*. His passivity is visible. It can be seen that he doesn't interfere, doesn't consciously "react" to his circumstances, but rather something *reacts* within him. In short, everything happens just as it happens for us in life. We are attracted by something – and we find ourselves lost in admiration; we encounter something unpleasant – unnoticed by us, we turn away and hasten our steps; we are tired – and our gait slows down, and so on.

What is visible in the actor who is consciously (rationally) imitating life, externally simulating it? In such an actor, on the contrary, we see voluntariness. Clearly, behind his each action and movement, there is a conscious directive. Clearly, nothing happens *in him*, but rather he *does it himself*. His willful intervention is visible, as is his duality (the actor and the character), and his *artificiality*.

This arbitrariness and artificiality might be carefully masked, but somehow it is felt. A dog, let alone a human being, can sense perfectly well whether you are afraid of him, whether you love him, whether you have forgiven him – so why think so poorly of us, people? We notice everything, feel everything, and understand everything.

Experiencing on Request

Is it possible to experience something when ordered to do so? Just go ahead – without any kind of preparation, for no reason at all, become inflamed with some kind of passion along the lines of love or hatred.

"And why not?" A person not without the actor's gift will say to you. "There you go – I'm already full of hate, I already want to say unpleasant things to someone, anyone. I want to hit someone . . ."

And it is true. Just look at him: in his eyes there is a flare of rage, his voice trembles with anger. You feel terrified – this isn't the actor's agitation that is spoken about in the "pseudo-experiencing" [see Book 1, "Truth"]; it is not nervousness or "generic" agitation.

Now, how did he do that?

A capable person can do this very easily and completely unconsciously. It is enough for him to think: "Hatred? . . . I hate . . ." and his quick fantasy draws a picture of someone . . . some kind of villain or scoundrel . . . "there he is, I feel him" . . . and when you face a scoundrel – rage, anger and fury completely possess you – just watch out so as not to do something stupid. Just be sure to encourage this feeling – to pour oil on that fire – and the deed is done. The psychological state has been evoked. The only thing left is to develop it, to strengthen it; to cultivate it and to take it in your hands – but again, not with bare hands, but with witty and psychological methods. Otherwise, this feeling is like a bird: you reach your hand out to it – flit! – and it is gone.

But for a capable actor, with his fervent and mobile fantasy, it isn't difficult for him to imagine that he is, for example, Hamlet. And if he has imagined and felt that he is Hamlet, everything else happens on its own. And what about a person with a less fervent fantasy? What is he to do? How would a person who is always watching and criticizing himself do this?

Instead of an answer, I will take your question one step further, and even add onto it – how would a person who is not fit to be an actor do this? This is a rather frequent case.

Among other things, negative criticism, self-watching, constant looking back at oneself, and many other basic sins, don't always come into the theatre with the actor. These diseases are often contracted in school or at the theatre itself. A faulty, bad school, a bad teacher, negative examples from colleagues, the unrestrained praise of "fans" – this is where this disease comes from. It eats up the very roots of talent. Such actors, with destroyed roots, are not as rare on the stage. True, the majority of them can be cured. But such treatment requires a shrewd expert.

There are some actors who acquire confidence only when the director has spoon fed them, drilled every moment of the role into them, dressed them up, swaddled them, and tucked them into bed . . . only then do they begin to feel themselves at home, and "create."

For some, such attentive care is paradise. For others, it is murder. Especially for actors of the affective type.

This doesn't depend only on the type of the actor's abilities, but also on the *school*. One school will unlock an actor's talent, his freedom, his creative intuition, and his ability to listen and submit to those. It teaches actors to go boldly beyond the borders of the commonplace; it teaches them the audacity of inspiration; it awakens a hero in them. It equips them with a special technique that makes them fearless – with the ability to listen to the prompts of their own intuition, to believe it and obey its most subtle hints.

Another school plants a lack of trust in one's own abilities; it dries up the spiritual sources of living waters; it clips the actor's wings; it knocks out of him any kind of courage, and substitutes the fire-breathing truth for the pitiful technique of "verisimilitude." It pulls out all of your teeth and inserts artificial ones. Sure, they make chewing difficult and they interfere with speaking. But for all that, they never hurt.

On the Virtuosity of Experiencing

Here is the constant, inevitable, and favorite argument of fans of representational acting, and "external technique": here some celebrity (for example, Chaliapin) in some highly dramatic scene, between his lines – that is, in the pauses – was telling his partner some jokes and stuff. In the meantime, the audience was crying and thinking that he is "experiencing." There it is, the power of mastery! This is what should guide one, what one should strive for!

I didn't see Chaliapin perform much, and when I did see him, I was out of luck. I must not have caught him during those kinds of performances "with jokes." He only truly touched me once as Boris, [the title role of tsar Boris Godunov in Modest Mussorgsky's opera, based on Alexander Pushkin's tragedy] but even that was not in the famous monologue (the pivotal moment of the role, its own version of "To be, or not to be"). I think that the performances that contributed to Chaliapin's fame were without these funny stories or dirty jokes.

Self-control is a good quality for an actor. Yet, maintaining control of one's temperament and fervor does not mandate frigidity.

As for the demonstration of the "technique" of using funny stories and dirty jokes onstage, it deserves as much regret as alcoholism in talented people – you want to forgive it, but you can't.

Not for nothing did Michelangelo [as quoted in Francisco d'Ollanda 1903: 320] say: ". . . it is not sufficient merely to be a great master in painting and very wise, but I think that it is necessary for the painter to be very good in his mode of life, or even, if such were possible, a saint, so that the Holy Spirit may inspire his intellect."

You don't have to believe in the Holy Spirit; armed with science, you can explain the influence of prayer however you like: as self-hypnosis, as an exercise in creative passivity, as a concentration of all psychological forces into one single power, and so on. One thing is undeniable and unavoidable. The actor's stage and the books, paintings, and sculptures invisibly radiate either intelligence or stupidity, greatness or baseness, spiritual richness or an artist's poverty.

All the great artists from any field were maximalists in their work, people of far-reaching demands: all or nothing. A tendency to compromise is a disappointing symptom. It is only by force that one can compel a significant creative individuality to settle for a compromise. The artist can accept it only with pain, by twisting his own arms and straining his heart. Maximalism and firmness of his own principles often make the life of such an artist completely intolerable, but . . . without maximalism or firm principles, an author, painter, musician or actor is **not an artist**. A master – maybe; an artisan – maybe; but not an artist.

A gift of virtuosity, like any dazzler, is very tempting and dangerous for its possessor. It is so tempting to resort to it more and more often . . . As a result, there is no time to *delve deep* into one's thoughts, feelings, or physiology. You are content with little. You are made a *slave* by your own virtuosity. But is it impossible to be a virtuoso *in depth*?

Virtuosity can come from somewhere else. Salvini, when strangling Desdemona, barely touches her throat with his soft fingers. The actor who does so can either turn himself off or be so in the element of "play" (that is, in the elements of fantasy and imagination) that to actually strangle the actress playing Desdemona would feel *false*. He cannot abide that falsehood; moreover, he is *not drawn* to this falsehood at all. So there is no point in turning yourself off. On the contrary, one should become engaged even stronger in *creativity* and in *play*.

Incidentally, why is it that only the ability to turn oneself off is considered virtuosity? Maybe, it is actually the opposite? Maybe Yermolova, who couldn't come back to herself after the performance, had it, and that is the most genuine virtuosity? And the other kind is just "foolhardiness" and cynicism? It's possible, of course. It's just that the word "virtuosity" is connected with "external technique" . . . And, when speaking of the higher art, can you really call it virtuosity?

The telling of a joke might be a deliberate *distraction of the consciousness* away from the basic *work of the subconscious*, which at this time is in full swing. This is when the joke is told **before coming out onto the stage**.

On "Convention"

It is extremely convenient to hide behind these words. "In the theatre everything is conventional, and nothing is real; because of this, life must not be real," – you are bound to hear such protests.

That everything in the theatre is conventional and just "as if" – it is, of course, so. But the genuine solution to the problem is more complicated than it seems to those confirmed craftsmen, who are *incapable* of *splitting (or doubling) and are deprived of imagination*. [On doubling, see Book Five.]

The Role of Physical Technique in the Art of Experiencing

One typical misunderstanding is when a creative element is confused with the physical technique, connected with the execution per se.

Voice placement and one's ability to direct the sound is a physical technique, even if creativity played a role in *acquiring* it. If the physical-technical methods in vocal training were always connected with such psychological conditions as openness, emotional release, the subtlety of psychological perception, then it would still be alright to talk about the "art of singing." In such a case, the sound – correctly and organically placed – on its own evokes the kind of state that is only one step away from the creative process. It also happens that the sound itself is what awakens the artistic chords in the soul. "Sound gives birth to tears."

Physical technique should not get in the way; it should be developed separately and in its own way. Physical technique is only the most basic part of an actor's work.

1   It might not get in the way (or it might get in the way, but there is no point in discussing that).
2   It might inspire (sound gives birth to tears), although in this case it would not be merely a physical, but also a psychological technique.

The Affective Actor (A Little Something on His Most Basic Distinguishing Qualities)

The First Distinction: Explosiveness

Every actor, no matter what type he belongs to, can "experience" onstage. The difference is only in the quantity and the quality.

Eleonora Duse never dropped out of her roles for one second: She walked onto the stage as Marguerite Gautier, lived her whole life there, and died the same Marguerite Gautier.

And here is an opposite example. A few days ago, I saw an actor who didn't give himself up to his role for one second. The whole time he "portrayed" and "represented," watched himself and led a triple life: one for himself, one for the audience, and the third for the director (who sat with a strict face in the house, monitoring whether the actor was doing everything just as he had been prescribed . . .)

And only once, when the choir began to sing from somewhere in the depths, the actor forgot to watch himself: he came alive and so spontaneously, so simply and genuinely spoke a few phrases about the quiet of the evening, the starry sky and the reeds . . . it must be that he himself loves music, loves nature, and the song touched him to the quick . . . within a minute he again glanced at himself and . . . continued his dead craft of "verisimilitude."

But I am grateful to him even for that one moment.

Here (in this comparison) the difference is *quantitative*. Yet there are instances when difference comes from the very *quality* of emotional immersion.

One actor experiences everything on the surface, and another in the very deepest, most deep-seated layers of his soul, as it was described in the book *Actor Types*.

What is the reason for this difference?

It would seem that the difference lies in the structure of one's creative apparatus.

In contrast to the other types, the affective actor has his own kind of psychological mechanism, so to speak. Thanks to this mechanism, much of what he sees, hears, and even what he thinks about, doesn't get trapped at the periphery, but immediately *sinks* into the *very depths of the bottomless whirlpool of his soul.* And from there, suddenly, with incomprehensible strength, a storm and a tornado unexpectedly break.

It is as if (as if!) unknown thousand-pound monsters lie at the bottom of these whirlpools, peacefully dozing. And an unsuspecting person, sitting on the shore, tosses small trinkets into the deep water – whatever he can lay his hands on . . . He comes across a piece of glass, and it flies into the water . . . It must have hit a monster smash right into the eye . . . A monster shoots up – who dared! It lashes its tail in pain and rage, brushing against its neighbors. The water is whirling everywhere; the whirlpool is seething, and from its depths the monsters throw onto the shore with their tails all kinds of wondrous miracles.

What kind of mysticism is this? What old thousand-pound monsters could live in the depths of our souls?

In fact, there is nothing special and nothing fantastical about it.

How many thousands of years has life existed on earth? For just as many thousands of years, life experience has been accumulating, and passing down through the generations (through the embryo cell). And, although you and I have lived on the earth for only a few dozen years, we use all this inestimable heritage of nature – it is ours. Abilities, instincts – everything is passed embryologically, through our DNA. They remain unchanged and transform, disappear and reappear . . .

These massive thousand-year-old sources that begat the monsters in the depths of our souls are not the only sources. All work that takes place beyond the threshold of our consciousness is another source and another nest for similar monsters.

Several chapters in the next book will be dedicated to this obscure topic, but for now it is important only to know that they exist, and that when you poke one of them in the eye, all this centuries-old force goes into motion. It does not spring from you, nor from your everyday "I," but from the depths of your primeval resources – completely outside of your control. Huge blocks of feelings and searing flames burst forth beyond any of your expectations.

When people want to bridle and manage the soul of such an actor, as if with an obedient horse, it always ends in a misunderstanding, a catastrophe, the end of all creativity. Who is right? The actor, of course. He becomes capricious, he doesn't listen . . . but, as a matter of fact, he cannot and must not listen. If he listens, his creativity would be instantly neutralized, and he would become like a flag on a windless day, hanging next to its pole like a useless and sad-looking rag . . . Can you force him to emit the same exact monsters from his depths every time, and ask them to play all the same tricks? Is that question even worth answering?

Of course, *armed with reliable psycho-techniques,* he can again call these monsters to action; he can even call up others . . . in short, this actor can also repeat some things, but not the details, of course. It is in his power to repeat only the main thing: the idea. The apex of the idea. The very essence, the very "I" of the role. In chasing after details, he loses the main thing, without a trace – because for him *it* is not *comprised of (not formed by)* the details, but (itself) *creates them* (it expresses itself through them).

The Second Distinction: The "Tangibility" of Perception

The second distinction of the "affective" actor is his extreme sensitivity – any impression wounds him; he has such sensitive thin "skin."

I'm not talking about neurotics, or others suffering from similar ailments – they also have sensitivity and vulnerability, but it goes hand in hand with their weak nervous system. Impressions don't nourish them or give them strength; they only temporarily excite them, as with a whip or alcohol, and then comes the response – an episode of fatigue and weakness.

For a healthy person it is the opposite: impressions play the role of magical vitamins and enzymes for him, boosting his spirits and giving him nourishment, strength, energy, and stamina.

Not only does the "affective" actor possess great sensitivity, but with him it is rather specific: he perceives everything *tangibly*. And this is the *second important distinction*.

Take a lit candle: I can tell you about its flame, how it is hot, how it would hurt if you were to stick your finger through it . . . but no matter how many fears I heaped onto you – I'm still not actually physiologically sensing the flame.

Well then, I'll try it for real, I'll stick my finger in it . . . and here only I can sense it, feel it – what a flame is and how it feels when it licks my finger!

There is a similar difference in the perception of life (real life or, as in art, imagined). On the one hand, you have a majority of people; on the other, you have the "affective" type. Most of us view the world around us *from the sidelines*, from afar, from a respectable distance, so as to not be wounded, to not burn ourselves, to not get dirty. For the affective, the opposite is true: they personally climb in the fire; they put their entire self into the flames. It burns them; they double up with pain in its heat; they cry out like a wounded beast – and that's all there is to it, end of story. Or else, having left their finger to burn and sizzle in the flames, they go on to tell how it feels. This, in essence, is what every "affective" tragic actor does.

> Wherein I spake of most disastrous chances,
> Of moving accidents by flood and field
> Of hair-breadth scapes I'th' imminent deadly breach,
> Of being taken by the insolent foe
> And sold to slavery. . .
> . . .This to hear
> Would Desdemona seriously incline.

So says Othello to the Senate about how and with what he won the love of his fiancée.

What do you usually see in the theatre? The actor recites this monologue beautifully, with some agitation, while all the things he is talking about stand far, far away from him and (just as in the example with the candle) they don't "burn" him. He does not feel them *tangibly*; he doesn't experience everything that he is saying **anew**, palpably and physically. You watch, you listen, and you don't really understand why the old Doge of Venice, this experienced and intelligent man, has softened and ceded so immediately:

> I think this tale would win my daughter too.

Shakespeare obviously didn't write for such an actor. What kind of actor did he write for? I came to understand this at one rehearsal.

A director who passed away 30 years ago [MAT's director Vakhtang Mchedelov (1884–1924)] explained and demonstrated to such a "lukewarm" actor how to act the monologue before the Senate. This director literally *burned* on every word. I can still hear and see how, when speaking "Of hair-breadth scapes I'th' imminent deadly breach," the director experienced his fall into the abyss so realistically, so palpably, so *tangibly in a physical sense*, that everyone around him experienced *the same thing*, and felt like they were flying, sliding into a chasm, grasping at a bush . . .

"Of being taken by the insolent foe . . ."

And we see him, wounded, *just now* regaining consciousness amongst wild, fearful, vile snouts . . .

"And sold to slavery . . ."

And we saw and heard how they were selling him, how he was escorted away, his hands tied . . . how he was carrying heavy rocks, how they beat him with a lash. "Saw" does not describe it; everyone experienced it first-hand. Each of his words burned with a fire, each of his silences made our hair stand on end.

If Othello addresses the Senate *that way*, then of course, even the worldly old man Duke would give in:

> I think this tale would win my daughter too.
> Good Brabantio,
> Take up this mangled matter at the best:
> Men do their broken weapons rather use
> Than their bare hands.

The Third Distinction: Grasp and Synthesis

The ability to "tangibly feel" is one of the most important, but it is still not the deciding factor. An infant or a savage can feel things tangibly. It is still a long way from here to the creation of a work of art.

Imagine to yourself that, in that same speech to the Senate, we *tangibly feel* that abyss, our fall into it, those wounds, the capture. We tangibly, vividly feel it, but we feel *only this one fact*, without any connections to our life as a whole: *I fall into the abyss*, and nothing else. Who am I? What am I? Why am I falling? Why was I telling this to Desdemona? Why am I telling this to the Senate right now? My story consists of disconnected fragments. It resembles separate dabs of paint for some kind of unknown painting; they don't fit together at all . . . these brushstrokes are vivid and passionate, but they are just that – separate brushstrokes.

Each of these separate facts and events are interesting in their own way, but they are only episodes from which life is composed. However, these are episodes from the life of Othello – that moor I am about to play. The life of Othello, into whom I should transform, must become mine, and my life should become his. In short, this is part of *my* life, because I am *Othello*. And the day of my meeting with Desdemona isn't just another day in my life, but the happiest, most delirious day:

> . . . I cannot speak enough of this content;
> It stops me here; it is too much of joy . . .
> As hell's from heaven! If it were now to die,
> 'Twere now to be most happy; for, I fear,
> My soul hath her content so absolute
> That not another comfort like to this . . .
> Succeeds in unknown fate . . .
> Excellent wretch! Perdition catch my soul,
> But I do love thee! and when I love thee not,
> Chaos is come again.

Each word blazes with such fire! Each glance and each breath are full of such energy! The rays of my entire life have now focused in one single spot! I embrace my life with one glance, one thought, one "*sensation*": my whole life led to this one thing – to that day of happiness with Desdemona.

This *moment of grasping* with one glance, one "sensation" also relates to the *fundamental* defining characteristics of the art of the "affective" actor. A role cannot interest him fragmentarily (in its separate parts). He is not concerned by how he might play its particular moments. He needs to grasp just one thing: the main point, the very heart of the role.

He may catch it immediately (after the first, second, or third reading of the play). Or else, he grasps it in his ongoing work, as he becomes absorbed in the play, reads himself into the words of his character, permeates his deeds deeper, and tries to pass it all through himself in his creative dreams.

The ability to catch *one – the whole*; the ability to discern one idea, one harmony, one soul in the thousands of varied and contrary things; and, finally, the ability to connect it all inside, and to become one with it – this ability is the *actor's synthesis*, the natural-born brother to "grasp."

Put together, synthesis and grasp represent the third distinction of the "affective" artist.

Not all "grasps" are created equal.

Take some people. The scope of their happiness, grief, and even entire life is restricted by their own *persona*: he is comfortable, he is fine, the sun shines on his roof, and he doesn't need anything beyond that. For him, everything is measured by the standard of his "I," of his mundane life. Naturally, we are not referring to this kind of "grasp."

2

Calling and Abilities

Talent is not just one quality (for example, emotionality). It is the combination of emotionality, enthusiasm, special mind, taste, commitment ("courage" according to Balzac), and lofty ideals.

Calling: Abilities and Choice of Profession

Yes, we often meet talent, but recognizing it isn't so simple. Oftentimes, its current manifestation doesn't remotely resemble its bright future. Similarly, a seed doesn't resemble the tree it will become, nor the rough diamond its polished self. This is so true that sometimes, when you first come across talent, you only see someone who appears to have an obvious lack of ability. [This seeming lack of ability comes from excessive demands on oneself. A person wants much, but, as of yet, he can do little. At the first failure, he contracts, closing himself off, and he loses all spontaneity and freedom. – *Author's Note*] Alongside it, though, you would see a kind of stubborn longing for his chosen art. You would notice complete fearlessness in the face of future difficulties, rare seriousness, and tenacity in everything that concerns art. From these signs you would surmise that something very precious hides in the depths of this person. It might not be such a bad thing after all that the talent has yet to surface – it has yet to ripen. It is imperative to help him now, at this time of hard underground work. The volcano hasn't erupted yet, but there is lava inside it – and it's boiling already.

How many of us can say that we are actually doing what we want to do more than anything in the world? Very few. For the most part, our occupations weigh down upon us like an affliction. Yet they should be our only joy and our life . . .

There are hundreds of questions we answer before we bind ourselves to our specialties . . . There is usually only one question we don't bother to raise: what is my calling? What can I do the *very best* way – better than others? What can I do that would combine all of my strongest abilities, without straining them? Alas, such a question is never raised – it is not a "serious" question or a "businesslike" one.

In the meantime, is it even possible to do the work *you are not fit for*, to create in it, or to be inspired by it?

I spent decades among actors – in drama, opera, operetta, and at theatre schools . . . It wouldn't be an exaggeration to say that 80 percent of them would be better off if they left. Although, about 20 percent of them had let the moment pass – they should have left earlier . . . There are so many untalented people! But that isn't even what I want to say here – only that theatre and art are completely foreign to them and don't interest them at all.

Just listen closely to their conversations at the cafeteria. What does this actor tell to his neighbors with such enthusiasm – he, who has driven his directors mad, as they try to get anything worthwhile out of him? Now he's come to life; he is transformed; he is burning with inner fire! . . . Apparently, he isn't speaking about his role or about theatre . . . Or about art.

You follow their deeds and their behavior in life. Some utterly undistinguished actress or actor suddenly disappears. What happened? Apparently, one of their colleagues has fallen ill, and the actor (or actress) spends days and nights at their bed-side. This selfless and talented tending does not go in vain – the colleague has been saved. I suspect some personal relationships between the two. Apparently, there is none. This is a case of an inner need, of calling, or talent.

Yet, how many talents in them go to waste – fine "businessmen," wonderful needlewomen and craftsmen, mothers, educators, accountants, waiters, tailors, and housewives . . . The theatre sucks them in, and all of these people get trapped in it. I could have cited many other professions, but why bother? Every theatre person can just look at his colleagues or perhaps at himself . . .

The opposite also occurs. An actor might get trapped at a theatre that is so insignificant and petty in comparison that all of his talents wither and fade. (Especially if he possesses a somewhat developed moral nature.) His theatre is an aggregation of hucksters, nonentities, dilettantes, and charlatans. The poor person is gasping for air, but he just can't bring himself to leave. He is so impractical and so unfit for life – he can't even make a move. Perhaps, in a stroke of luck, they would kick him out as useless; or perhaps, an accidental wind would carry him to some different, more fitting theatre . . . Just watch how this actor suddenly comes to life, and how he begins to improve with every new role . . .

Self-doubt; On Periods of Decline; On Huge Demands, and on Being Satisfied with Yourself (with Little)

Every person has periods of decline, of inertia and bad luck. During such periods, nothing turns out right; you can't get anywhere, and whatever you do – it's all poor and weak. You lose faith in yourself.

Unbalanced, sensitive, and easily wounded, people often fall into just such a pitiful state. A careless critical review or a look of indifference may be enough to send them into depression. It is also true that a fairly small success might lift their spirits and make them forget their hopeless thoughts. Once again, they are full of faith and power. This, of course, doesn't last long. Their entire lives consist of such endless fluctuations.

For our purposes, however, we are interested in genuine periods of creative stagnation, rather than neurotic fluctuations. We are interested in cases that are similar to Gogol's [1940: 173]: "Soon it will be a year since I have written a line . . . No matter how I force myself – nothing, and that's that!"

Such periods of artistic decline aren't trifles. They are complicated and tangled phenomena. We know too little about them to draw any kind of final conclusions. By all appearances, these [interchanges of] ascents and descents are subordinate to certain laws. We only know some of these laws.

Some of these known laws are prompted to us by the physiology. They connect periods of creative decline with physical exhaustions, the change of seasons, the movement of the moon, as well as solar activity. Most importantly, these fluctuations are connected with the critical cycles in the life of the body, such as changes in the endocrine system.

In addition to these genuinely disastrous periods, we encounter another that isn't genuine. False as it may be, it is quite dangerous. When misinterpreted, it can cause a lot of grief for the person affected and for those around him. It usually happens like this: an artist (be it an actor, an author, or someone else) is successfully carrying out his work, but suddenly hits a wall. No matter what he tries, nothing is working out – everything goes wrong. He seems to be fit for nothing. At times, this state is unbearably tortuous for an artist. However, with perseverance and tenacity, it always ends in a resolution of all the difficulties. It happens instantly, and without "prior warning," and it is followed by a new wave of inspiration. It is as if a dam that was blocking a river suddenly broke. It is such periods that inspired idioms, such as "throes of creation," or "difficult labor," etc. Such tortuous days resemble the crises during a serious illness – a beneficent battle of the body with the disease.

An experienced director knows the value of such low periods; he knows the meaning of such hard and hopeless rehearsals. The actor is losing it; he gives up the role; he's leaving the theatre! He's abandoning the art! But the director only laughs in his sleeve and further provokes the actor, making it seem that the situation is hopeless. Inexperienced directors would begin to console the actor, ruining the whole process.

Those completely devoid of any directorial sense, take the role away from the actor. By doing so, they scar him for life. In the meantime, this actor has been surmounting the most difficult mountain range of his artistic journey. If you give him a chance to cross to "the other side" – an artist will be born. Allow him to stay on this side, or let him slide downhill – he will remain forever crippled.

In such situations only one thing can save the actor: solid, unwavering faith – almost a physical sense of the presence of one's own talent. With it, no matter what people say – their words just bounce off of the actor.

I recall just such an instance. One of the most prominent figures in the theatre world at the time took a role away from a then-young actor. It was too much for the actor, who started an argument and said a few rude things to the director . . . The director grew angry and burst out: "I'll tell you openly, it's not just this role, but I think that, in general, you'll never make a good actor." The young man grew red with rage: "I will never make a good actor?! Is that what you think?!! Yet I feel him. He's sitting in me, and I will make him!"

And . . . he did.[1]

There is another phenomenon that may not be as dramatic, but all the same it can make life uncomfortable.

No true artist is ever entirely satisfied with his creation. Needless to say – the greater the artist, the grander and loftier his ideals. And, therefore, the harder they are to reach. Satisfaction is an unfortunate symptom. If you are sure that things are fine and well, and that you have reached the limit of achievements – it is a bad thing. "The painter who has no doubts will have small success," Leonardo da Vinci [as quoted in Merejkowski 1905: 78] told his students.

Many of the great writers mercilessly burned their own works.

Yermolova "was almost never satisfied with herself onstage. It was on rare nights that she felt how perfectly she played her role. On such nights, her admirers would exclaim, in exaltation: "Could you possibly be unsatisfied with yourself today?" To that, she would reply reluctantly: "No . . . I guess not . . . it wasn't so bad after all . . ." [Shchepkina-Kupernik 1983: 118].

It is always this way – and no other – when the ideal exceeds capabilities, skill, and technique. This happens on all those occasions when the material resists and doesn't yield to the dictates of thought and creative desire – even those of a genius.

As for the art of the actor – how could one ask much of it? The psycho-technique is still so unrefined. After all, it is so young in comparison with, say, music or painting.

And what about the pinnacle of our art – the technique of higher creativity or that of the affective type? It alone could satisfy those actors who are known to be demanding artists. However, "serious" people don't recommend going near this technique; they insist that inspiration is out of our reach. As for "not so serious" people, they all attempt to mount the inspiration, to take it by force. In doing so, they permanently scare everyone off from the technique of intuition – they "strut and bellow" as if "some of nature's journeymen had made men and not made them well" [Hamlet's "advice to the players"]. In short, they repeat those same mistakes that even in Shakespeare's day were considered ridiculous and ghastly.

And so, how can the actor-artist be satisfied with his own creation? How could they be content in the absence of the systematic technique of inspiration, or at least that of creative experiencing? This discontent, while burdensome, is nevertheless noble. After all, "being *satisfied* with yourself" is the surest recipe for the destruction of your individuality and talent.

Calling and Talent Are Not Always in Harmony with Specific Abilities

The greatest violinist the world has ever heard, Paganini, was known to perform miracles with his violin. His art bewitched and astounded his listeners. It also inspired rumors (as dark, as they were categorical) that, in exchange for his miraculous gift, he sold his soul to the devil. How should this man have played, if, out of all the musicians who have existed on the earth for all time, only he had inspired such a legend?!

From the fragmentary evidence that has reached us, it's obvious that he combined the genius of the musician and artist with physical genius (for the lack of a better word). His fingers were unbelievably long, and their natural agility and strength allowed him to easily do that which others would never be able to achieve – not with any kind of training. When need be, the power of his violin's sound was deafening!

The miracle of Paganini's art was created by this fortunate combination of artistic talent, musical genius, and physical abilities perfect for the violin. Similar combinations are more than rare . . . Most of the time, where there is talent, there are almost no fitting physical abilities, and where there are abilities – no talent.

Nevertheless, a genuine calling can do more than overcome these obstacles – it has been known to draw new strength in overcoming them! It can hone its talent and willpower on the grinding stone of these obstacles.

The greatest of orators, Demosthenes [382 BC–322 BC], was a tongue-tied, weak-chested, voiceless, and ridiculous looking man. He failed at his first public speeches and was ridiculed mercilessly. Yet, the awareness of his own talent and the sense of his own hidden powers forced him to *disregard* his clear lack of necessary oratory abilities. He locked himself up, shaving half his head so that he couldn't go out into the street. Having done that, he began to exercise his diction and speech. He put small stones into his mouth and tried – with a mouth full of stones – to speak articulately and clearly. He went to the ocean shore, and tried to cover the roaring of the waves with the strength of his voice . . .

Anyone who is not capable of undertaking such Herculean work doesn't have the right to speak about his own talent, genius, or calling. Where there is a calling, there is no place for doubt or laziness.

This is true of Demosthenes and everyone like him.

Taking into Account Your Abilities and "Gifts"

Talent and genius are rare phenomena. To put it plainly, not enough has been thought about fostering them. Students are usually heaped together randomly – be they capable, talented, or even genii. It's up to them to scramble out of this pile the best they can.

In the meantime, the very *nature of a genius is completely different* than that of the "capable."

All of this – calling, genius, talent – will be addressed in the coming pages. At the moment, it is appropriate to speak of the simpler things that are met at every step – "abilities" and "gifts."

I once had an acquaintance, Doctor K., the director of the Athletic Society. All applicants to the Society passed his inspection.

When a short-armed or short-legged youth would arrive and express his desire to box or wrestle, K. would say to him: "Of course, you can do these things, but I warn you that with your physique you won't achieve any exceptional results. All of your 'levers' are built in such a way that you should take up a completely different type of sport. It would be more beneficial for you to take up apparatus gymnastics or ground acrobatics."

If a tall, thin lad with shovel-like paws approached him, he wouldn't let them near weights or the apparatuses. "Nature itself," he would say, "made you a boxer (or a wrestler)" . . . In each individual case his diagnosis was completely accurate.

At first, he would make his decisions based on unsophisticated indicators, and later he would delve into the details. "Your hands (or legs) are built in such a way that you will have the most success with such-and-such movement. Work on it."

As a result of such sophisticated diagnoses, each of these young men was easily able to achieve *exceptional* results in his field.

Such a wise consideration of physique is a matter of utmost importance.

There are people (albeit not many) who are just *generally capable*. No matter what he picks up, everything bends to his will. If he ends up as an actor – it works out just fine . . . Although, a "*theatrical*" Doctor K., if he were around, would probably say to him: "Young man, I advise that you don't get too excited by your *first* successes. Your machine and all of its attributes are built in such a way that you will not achieve any outstanding successes or *exceptional* results in this field. It would be better for you to do *this* . . . you have exceptional *attributes* for it . . ."

Time and again, you meet capable actors . . . but life shows that nothing *special or outstanding* comes from them – no matter how much their directors and teachers try.

There is another mistake that happens in the theatre.

A person should be an actor – there is no doubt about it. In the meantime, he shies away from the kinds of roles he is *best equipped* to play. Women are particularly guilty of this. So often they want to play leading ladies, beautiful and young. Offering them a character part is a mortal offense. Yet, she has got so little potential (both external and internal) for her desired roles. This is how an actor can make herself unhappy for her entire life. She has the gift, yet it all comes to nothing at the end, except for big disappointment.

A Gift for Transformation

Can you imagine a musician with a bad ear? What's the use of a puny, weak guy dedicating himself to a career as an athlete, wrestler, or a weight-lifter? No matter what the field, it would be more beneficial to already have special qualities and abilities in stock.

So what are these special abilities that an actor should possess?

The emblem of the theatre is a mask. The actor's muse is Melpomene, the goddess of transformation. It just might be that a person who finds special joy in giving himself over to a different, imaginary character, without even suspecting it himself, is an actor – that is to say, a priest at the altar of Melpomene.

The level and depth of such an artistic transformation can vary widely, from a subtle hint to an almost-complete disappearance of the self that is scary to watch.

Leonid Leonidov tells of the scene in Mokroye [*Brothers Karamazov* at the Moscow Art Theatre, 1910, the role of Mitya Karamazov – *Ed.*]:

> Of what I did, said – I remember nothing. I, Leonidov, disappeared. There was a second life – not my life, but the life of a wretched man, about to endure his crucible. What was happening now, however trying, was just the overture. I came to myself when the arrested Mitya was escorted away, and the curtain closed. It's strange, but I didn't understand what was going on with me. I felt unusual ease; I could have played it again right then, even in a different, new way. It's just that tears were coming to my throat, and I wanted to cry. [Leonidov 1960: 125]

Actors who possess this ability – a pivotal ability really – tell us the following. In their best roles, as soon as they've put on their makeup and costume (or even actively thought about the role), they let this stranger inside. The stranger begins to live in their "shoes" and make himself at home, completely edging out their own persona. As for the actors – they only watch and witness. This person whom they've let inside is usually completely unlike them. Completely different are his nature, habits, worldview, manners, moral principles, and logic. He is so unlike the actor, in fact, that the latter finds his actions, thoughts, and desires surprising and even incomprehensible. Outside observers cannot make sense of this either: can it be that this wonderful person (the actor) is capable of even understanding a single one of these stupid and heinous motives – let alone acting or thinking as his "inhabitant?"

On the other hand, we see a contrary phenomenon – perhaps, even more surprising. He is a narrow-minded, dull-witted actor, from whom, in all the years you've known him, you haven't heard a significant profound word. Tonight, he puts on his make-up and costume (for example, those of Hamlet, or Faust, or Uriel Acosta [The title character of the 1847 drama by the German writer Karl Gutzkow, modeled after a true historical character, Uriel da Costa – a Portuguese Jew, a philosopher and an independent thinker]) and . . . and he transforms into a sage, a genius thinker, and a profound personality. Watching and listening to him, you feel like a pigmy and a pathetic fool. Of course, this isn't just because he speaks someone else's words (Shakespeare's, Goethe's, or Seneca's), but because of *the meaning* he puts into these words, of *how* these words *excite him*, and, consequently, us. Only now do you truly understand these words – having heard them from his mouth, saturated with his profound thoughts and illuminated by his passion. "Understand" is not the word – rather, you comprehend them with your entire being. As if a sage has arrived and rubbed it in for your simple self: this is what this means, and this, and this.

Alas, the opposite is also true: an intelligent actor starts playing Hamlet – and his Hamlet turns out to be a fool.

The most surprising of phenomena!

Transformation plays a pivotal role in other arts, but in acting it is *fundamental*.

Kinetic Responsiveness

I once knew a young actor [Mchedelov] who had an awkward, absurd way of speaking. If you were to write down what he said, you would end up with complete nonsense and gobbledygook: not one coherent sentence, not a single logical thought – just a mass of exclamations and completely inarticulate sounds.

And, imagine, this man was brilliant at directing and teaching.

He explained the most complicated things in his own almost-primitive ways. Yet, he did it so that everyone immediately understood it all. He would say some word, as if completely unfitting; his quick, agile fingers would draw something in the air; he would wink his sly eyes, suddenly spin around and . . . that's it! You looked at him and thought: this is what actors ought to be like! They shouldn't speak with words, but with their whole bodies, with their entire beings – words are just one of their means. And when he finally spoke a word, it would be with such subtle intonation – you wouldn't be able to describe it in 10 pages.

The actor expresses himself through actions, sounds, gestures, and facial expressions.

When young student-actresses asked Yermolova to help them, to tell them about a role, and to explain it, she was at a loss. She hesitated, and she could find no words other than general phrases, always ending with "I'd better show you – I'll act it." And she acted . . .

The better an actor is at describing his role, the weaker he plays it. That is quite common. Of course, it's not that actors have to be stupid, uncultured, or unable to say what they think. Of course not – just the opposite: the more sophisticated and refined the actor's inner world, the greater his ability to deeply penetrate life and perceive it in all its complexity. That is exactly why an actor is often at a loss for words: he feels things deeply, complexly, and subtly; and when he tries to describe it in words – they feel insignificant, primitive, and crude . . . Therefore, Yermolova's muteness is a sign of great, immeasurable inner content, while the eloquent, fluid speech of a windbag-actor – with very few exceptions – is a sign of his primitiveness.

This is yet another of the abilities that distinguishes the actor from the rest.

What is the best way to define it and how do we name it?

The actor's instrument is his own self – mobility and precision of the entire body, face and voice, and their obedience to the inner impulses of the artist-actor – that is what we need.

One should not understand this ability as excessive external mobility, as a splashy bustle, or as continuous fireworks. A barely noticeable change in the eyes is enough; a shadow flickering across the face is enough, or a blush coming over the cheeks: these will say so much that you won't be able to convey it with words or with sweeping gestures – not with anything . . .

What is this ability? Is this a gift of expressivity? Perhaps so.

All people possess it, to some degree. Although, it takes something irregular to destroy our poise and to force us to assume a not-too-ordinary pose. There are people whose every feeling, however subtle, is immediately expressed on their faces. They don't want to be so expressive; they want to be reserved, but everything is immediately visible with them. They just have that kind of locomotive system: whatever they feel or think is written on their faces. Or else it escapes through a telling gesture, exclamation or sigh . . . Before you know it, the enigma is revealed, the secret is out.

In other words, with these people, every thought and feeling immediately causes a muscular reaction. *If nothing is stopping them*, these muscular reactions are always expressed. Therefore, what makes an actor expressive is this *muscular responsiveness* – this ability to react with one's muscles *without delay*. In order to act well onstage, the actor requires the naivety, simplicity and spontaneity of a child, coupled with a sensitive, expressive and eloquent apparatus.

Desire to Be Featured

The actor's "inducibility" is his tendency to inflame when in front of the audience, and to draw strength from his spectators. This ability should be listed among the actor's fundamental instincts – his deepest organic impulses, connected with his calling. Meanwhile, this chapter discusses abilities, and abilities lie closer to the surface. This may be true. However, one cannot overestimate actors' qualities, such as their need for an audience, desire to act in front of the public and "to be featured." In conjunction with positive, useful excitability caused by the audience's presence, these qualities are essential. They are so essential, in fact, that one always wants to verify: does the actor possess them or not? When auditioning new actors, you always look to see how they react to the audience and how they change before it.

It is worth mentioning that this "ability" at times takes a polar opposite form. The actor gets so excited by the audience that his excitability turns into nervousness and spasms. These he cannot overcome and . . . he "flops." Nevertheless, experience teaches one how to deal with this pretty easily. Moreover, there have been cases when it took such a catastrophic failure to catch the scent of a great talent.

Emotionality

An artist perceives life with passion and fervor. He does it not so much with his reasoning mind as with his heart and emotions. This ability to feel deeply is fundamental for an actor. Let's call it *emotionality*. I saved it for last, because it is fundamental not only for the actor, but for any *artist*. Without it, there is no art. The greatest artists possessed it in great measure – perhaps, incomprehensibly to us.

Early morning, winter, frost, a blizzard . . . Hearing the jingle bells of an approaching sleigh, Pushkin jumps out on the porch of his country house barefoot, wearing only his nightshirt. Pushkin's dear friend, who has arrived in the sleigh, had to grab the poet by the hands, wrap him in his fur coat, and, as one would with a child, carry him into the house.

Pavel Mochalov gave all of his monthly wages, which he had just received, to a beggar who seemed horribly bitter and unhappy. He, Mochalov, heard from the neighboring room how one kind old woman grieved before his relatives that she had no money to buy back her only son from the soldiers. So, he brought her all the money he had, keeping just one ruble for himself.

Such examples are numerous.

Without this flammability, there can be no creativity in art. More than anyone, an actor should possess it. Moreover, his flammability should be especially quick. The performance begins on a given day, at a given hour, regardless of the actor's mood or readiness. In order to not be caught unprepared, the actor must start getting ready for the performance well ahead of its start. He must draw deeply into his shell (otherwise he might spill and squander what is meant for the performance). Or else, thanks to his quick flammability and responsiveness, he must know how to instantly immerse himself in the circumstances of the role – immediately before his entrance.

In short, this ability is one of the most essential.

While necessary for art, it is far from being convenient in life. Qualities such as ardor and passion, as well as emotiveness, rarely combine with genuine restraint. The same is true of nervous sensitivity (the latter obviously being much more common, like everything petty and average). Alas, without control, emotions always, in the end, bring about trouble.

Artists, consciously or unconsciously, treasure this ability to ignite and to give in to feelings. They value it in themselves and in each other – understandably so. Not only do they value it, they cultivate it. In doing so, they let themselves take the path of least resistance – from here come revelries, jolly, light-hearted diversion, ceaseless amorous pursuits, and everything that is called "bohemia."

This is characteristic of the *majority*. A great artist loves, works, and lives greatly. Dante and Beatrice, Petrarch and Laura, Balzac and Hańska, Leonardo da Vinci and Mona Lisa . . .

When asked why he wasn't married, Michelangelo [as quoted in Marden 1894: 107] categorically answered: "Art is a jealous lover. She requires the whole man."

In the end, the life of every great master and every immortal work of art is a feat of self-denial! The great master, philosopher, or poet seizes their passion with an iron hand and transforms it into a work of art.

Mediocrity

It is extremely important to distinguish mediocrity from a *closed nature*.

A closed, tense person often gives off the impression of someone who is obtuse and lethargic. But try stealing a glance at him as you tell something significant or exciting (for example, the story of Mochalov reciting Pushkin's *The Black Shawl*).[2] You will notice sparks in his eyes, and his face growing pale and thin . . . "Oh ho," you think to yourself, "this is who you are!" From this point on, it's only a matter of finding the right approach to this person.

Mediocrity is altogether a different matter. At the start, mediocre actors often give the impression of giftedness. A sweet girl or a pleasant, well-bred young man – they are very attentive and clever. The rest of the class is still afraid of something – they are either working too hard, or playacting, or else overthinking the technique. Not our sweet girl or the pleasant guy. They are quick to pick up the simple technique of "green-lighting your every wish." They march ahead, as if they were born for this art – correctly, easily, simply, naturally, and "truthfully" . . . Besides, he (or she) is such a pleasant, sweet youth . . . It must be that this one is the most capable!

As time has gone on, however, the others have gotten used to the new way of working. They have calmed down and begun to allow the kind of impulses that burst forth from their depths. In one student, the technique awakened his sense of humor; with someone else it inspired their sense of the dramatic; with a third actor – his lyricism. One became spontaneous and edgy (surprising everyone and even himself); another became mild and gentle (often completely in contrast to his or her outward appearance); someone else yet – tempestuous and explosive. They do lose control and make mistakes; however, you can see the glimpses of their unique individuality, of their creative "I."

In the meantime, our pleasant youth is still at the first stage of his or her development. Of course, in all this time they have become more confident. Perhaps, they have even become expressive and artistic. After all, they have now gotten so used to their habitual mask, and they now play so well together – they and their mask.

More time goes by. You begin to suspect, however vaguely, that this young person probably has got nothing inside – no creative excitement, no surprises, or bold imagination . . . This is just an average person – a well-bred nonentity, who brings his or her narrow-mindedness to the stage. Art, creativity, and daring quests are completely outside of his or her realm.

Can they act? Can they be an actor?

Whether they can or not – they won't ask our permission. They will become actors, and they will perform, charming the audience with their appearance, elegant manners, and with what they call "noble restraint in acting" . . . Just wait – they will be held up as examples for other actors!

No matter what kind of successes or accomplishments they achieve, they are *mediocrity* as far as theatre is concerned!

From the point of view of creativity and art, they are just *talentless people*.

Talentless people don't always produce the impressions of giftedness at the start. This only happens with actors who have good looks and a bit of intelligence. Without either of these qualities, you won't make a mistake.

Notes

1 One of Moscow Art Theatre's most celebrated actors Boris Livanov (1904–1972) –*Ed.*
2 While reciting Pushkin's poem, *The Black Shawl*, Mochalov had to hold a real black shawl in his hands, so that the "primitive sensation" would evoke a reaction in response – a flare of jealousy.

3

The Actor and Life

(Outline)

The Actor and the Theatre

The stage has its own specific temptations:

> It is a handful of people, united by the same interests;
> It is an escape from life into the realm of fantasy;
> There is mysteriousness in the atmosphere of the rehearsals, as well as performance;
> It feeds your vanity.

It absolves you from having to do any kind of special work on self – the kind a musician, artist, or writer has to do. We all know how to talk and walk – waving our arms also isn't exactly a tricky business. Neither do you have to devise anything. The author thought up the words for you, the director shows you what you need to do, someone dresses up you and puts on your makeup. People come to watch, the lights are shining, the music's playing – and all of it is for me . . .

The notion of escape deserves some elaboration.

A person escapes in the evenings to spend time with his close circle of friends – this is escape from the family, or from his own privacy. He doesn't live, but rather "plays at life" – this is a different kind of escape, one from life. He puts on all kinds of masks – this is the third type (escape from himself).

Yet, the escape of theatre amateurs and their enthusiasm has a share of parasitism in it. There is even a little something, God forgive me, of prostitution. What it is exactly, I don't know – but it is present. After all, it may not be completely stupid that in India an actor isn't seated at the same table with everyone else, and that in ancient Russia wondering comic minstrels (*skomorokhi*) and jesters were contemptible . . . There is a sort of slipperiness in the pursuits of this priest without altar, ordination, or grace . . . (However, does this slipperiness not exist in other arts?)

There is something else about actors that is close to parasitism – their wastefulness. Fast living, the squandering of life, drunkenness . . .

"Bohemia"

A rational, coldly calculating, and imperturbably calm person can't be a genuine creator in art. His "apparatus" isn't built for it. A creator, whoever he is (poet, actor, painter, or musician) perceives life ardently – not so much with his logical mind as with his heart. His passion and responsiveness are joined by his *vigilant and acute perception*, his *ability to feel complexly and subtly, and his profound thoughts*. This flammability and spontaneity of many gifted artists has deceived people in the past, and continues to do so.

If you talk with actors, you'll hear stories about celebrities' sprees and rowdiness . . . In the consciousness of some actors, it is obvious that talent and debauchery are inextricably linked. If a person is talented, then he must be a fast liver, a lecher, or a slacker. Or vice versa: if he isn't a fast liver or a lecher, then . . . he likely isn't talented.

This lifestyle has been "legalized." It even has a special and very euphonious name – "bohemia." However, what hides behind this alluring, poetic name? The most thoughtless debauchery of the weak-willed and, then, ultimately, parasitism.

Everyone knows this in the depths of their souls, yet the tradition has remained unshakable – talent is a law unto itself. The reasoning goes something like this: It is true that a talent is intemperate; in fact, it is unbridled. But why is it such? It is because of the irrepressible power that bursts from within it; and it is considered ignoble to restrain yourself when your soul is overflowing with "creative" fire! Let the masses restrain themselves – that is mediocrity!

This is how the "bohemians" glorify themselves – these self-proclaimed talents and genii who scorn the "masses" and "mediocrity."

However, aren't there just a few too many of them? You can count them in the dozens, hundreds, or even thousands – these secret and obvious bohemians. Is it really possible that we are dealing with an overproduction of talents and genii?

As you look about and examine their **deeds**, you see only the rare flash of giftedness against a backdrop of grayness, powerlessness, and clichés. These flashes just go to underscore that there *could be* talent here – a glimpse of it is seen, but . . .

Upon the final tabulation – it turns out that the talents are few and far between. As for genii, there are just none – you have to enlist those dearly departed . . .

It's true that this bohemian life sucked in, or even killed some major talents (especially here in Russia). One can only lament about this day and night . . .

Moreover, these talents themselves lamented about it, in moments of enlightenment. Here, for example, is a confession of Pushkin's [1888: 70–71]:

> When noisy day to mortals quiet grows . . .
> . . .
> Then for me are dragging in the silence
> Of wearying wakefulness the hours.
> In the sloth of night more scorching bum
> My heart's serpents' gnawing fangs;
> Boil my thoughts; my soul with grief oppressed
> Full of reveries sad is thronged.
> Before me memory in silence
> Its lengthy roll unfolds.
> And with disgust my life I reading
> Tremble I and curse it.
> Bitterly I moan, and bitterly my tears I shed,

But wash away the lines of grief I cannot.
In laziness, in senseless feasts
In the craziness of ruinous license.
In thralldom, poverty, and homeless deserts
My wasted years there I behold.
Of friends again I hear the treacherous greeting
Games amid of love and wine.

. . .

No joy for me . . .

Pushkin was not alone – other great servants of art made similar confessions.

A real person, a true creator of life never wastes anything. Scorched by one thought, he has been burning with it for years. Like a miser, he collects things everywhere – patient, relentless, and thrifty . . . The time comes, and the world receives a gift of inestimable value.

When I remember performances with Yermolova, or Leonidov, or Aleksander Moissi (in Tolstoy's play *The Living Corpse*), and a few others, I see what a significant and profound undertaking it was! Great is the feat of an actor, if he isn't a craftsman, but a genuine artist. Of course, such people are few. Almost everyone who has become a professional in art (especially actors) is not afraid of being wasteful; on the contrary, they do everything so as to maximize their wastefulness. And then the reckoning comes: the loss of time, strength, and health, and, in the long run, talent. In the end, they accuse circumstances, friends and, finally, fate. In the meantime, they've got nobody but themselves to blame.

A true artist has a need. This need is to fulfill his creative task – to contribute his share to the works of humanity at large, and to genuine life. With this his deeds, he contributes.

4

The Actor and the Author

Constraints of the Text: The Railroad Tracks

People speak of actors' creativity . . . Where does it lie, if their words are already predetermined? With the current "strict" directorial concept, everything is prescribed by a despotic director – makeup, costumes, the pattern of the role, as well as blockings and even intonations(!). It's all been fixed and approved. Any permissive interpretation means trouble for the actor.

So, where is the creativity? What is left to the actor?

There is a rail track laid through the forests, mountains, valleys, and steppes, spanning across rivers and gulfs. Trains dash along this line – freight trains, postal trains, express trains and courier trains.

If you put a steam engine straight onto the ground, it will imbed its sharp wheels into the earth, scattering dirt and sand everywhere; yet, the heavy monster won't crawl a single step. Pick it up and put it on the tracks – helpless on earth, it will fly with the speed of the wind . . . It will even pull tens of thousands of pounds behind it . . .

A good actor is a "steam engine" that shouldn't be put down on the earth. He isn't made for it.

A good author is a well-laid railroad track.

Perhaps now it's clear why the "constricting" circumstances – someone else's words, the author's text, the boundaries you can't escape – are the chief aid to the actor. It offloads the actor, freeing him from things that are outside of his nature. It provides conditions, and the very possibility for the actor's creative act. Light the fire, raise the steam, and we're off!

The Author Is the Inspirer: The Author Is the Awakener

Good authors don't just offload a burden. They inspire. They awaken the sleeping soul of the actor.

Have you ever happened to experience a strange transformation when standing on the peak of a mountain, or overlooking a river, or being in a meadow on a hot summer's day, or by the sea, or at some wondrous corner of the magical Caucasus Mountains?

The effect of nature's beauty and of its mysterious voice is so great that it leaves you in mute, overflowing rapture. The doors to the soul swing open of their own volition, and a stream of new, great force rushes in . . .

This is what a genius author "does" to the sensitive, subtle soul of the actor. Exhausted, lazy, and sleepy, it boils up at once – like water, when a drop of red-hot, sparkling metal has been poured into it. It begins to rage, to rebel, ready to move mountains. It wants to create, to take action, to burn!

Out of the multitudes of actors I saw, I remember one particularly well. A third-rate actor – undistinguished, plain-looking and inexpressive – Kostya M. didn't show much promise.

His attempts to take on more serious roles always ended in failure. He himself treated these attempts with humor: "I warned that I'd ruin the role, didn't I? Why'd they give it to me? The hat is not for a small head!"

We lost track of him for some time. Then, suddenly, a letter arrived from him asking permission to call on us for two or three days in order to "discuss a very serious matter." My father sensed [that there was] a real need, so he replied without delay. Kostya arrived.

When he and my father went into his study, we, children, kept speculating on the nature of Kostya's visit. In the end, we decided that he probably had had some misfortune, or else he was thinking about getting married . . .

It turned out that it was all much less intriguing than that, yet, at the same time, much more incomprehensible and mysterious.

About two months beforehand, Kostya had read Calderon's drama *Life Is a Dream*. He read it and, as he expressed it, he was stunned. What if, all of a sudden, it was true! A dream?! What then? And where is truth – in life or in our dreams of it. Perhaps truth is in what we imagine, in our "dream visions"? Then what is "acting"? Perhaps it's a dream? Or maybe reality?

We decided that the young lad was, perhaps, over-thinking things . . . In the meantime, my father, having sent Kostya off to bed after a sleepless night on the train, beamed at us with a happy, rapturous smile. With a cryptic significance, he whispered: "Well, my children, an actor has been born!"

Kostya lived with us for about a month. For several hours each day, passionate cries from the character of Calderon's play (prisoner Segismundo) were heard from my father's study . . .

Kostya went about happy and satisfied . . . At times, it seemed that he carried inside himself something invisible (to us) – he carried it and was afraid to break, spill, or damage it. Looking somewhere within himself, he would smile and beam. Then suddenly, embarrassed, would hide his face . . .

I saw him in that role . . .

One of our well-known actors was exempt from serving in the army, and a handwritten note on the order exempting him read: "You cannot shoe a draught horse with golden nails." Kostya was just such a golden nail. They shod the Japanese War with him and . . . a most remarkable actor was lost . . .

Would Kostya ever have woken up if Calderon did not come his way?

The author isn't the only factor that can wake up the artist inside an actor – an impression from watching a genius actor can also do it. Haven't more than a few people felt a "call to the stage" after a performance by a renowned touring actor?

Life, with all its catastrophes and trials, can also awaken the artist. John Milton [1608–1674], and our poet Ivan Kozlov [1779–1840] began to write only when they lost their sight . . . Love can do it too – if Dante hadn't met his Beatrice, we wouldn't have heard his name . . .

How does an author awaken the actor? What are the mechanics behind this phenomenon?

In my childhood, I had an acquaintance, a certain Fillip T. or, simply, Filya. He was about four years older than me, and he was self-taught on the violin. He was not too much of a violinist, but that's not the point here.

He once asked me: "Would you be afraid to go to the belfry at night?"

"By myself? I would be."

"No, with me."

"They won't let us, there's a watchman there."

"They'll let us, I know him."

"Let's go then, but why?"

"You'll see when we're there."

I didn't pester him, knowing that he won't tell. Filya was a tough cookie. Darkness fell as we went along.

"Why did you bring your violin?"

"That's none of your business."

We found our way to the top, bumping into the walls in the dark and, at one point, almost rolling all the way down . . . We made it there somehow, right to the bells. Filya said: "And now I'll do a magic trick." He sat underneath the bells on the floor, unwrapped his violin (it was wrapped in a cloth) and began to elicit lingering, plaintive notes from it. Not loudly, so that the watchman didn't hear from below.

I don't remember how long he had been delighting my ear, but suddenly, one of the bells began to hum in response to his note . . . I remember that I almost died from fright. And Filya nearly finished me off: "Ahh," he whispered, "it doesn't like it!" The musician kept sewing a single note – plaintive, annoying, and scary – and the belfry kept humming in reply. Having returned to myself a bit, I asked him, stammering, "What are you doing?" And Filya replied, as if nothing had happened: "I've touched its nerve!"

I soon learned that there was no miracle there; that Filya was absolutely not the magician he certainly wanted to seem, and that his violin wasn't at all magical. In fact, it was quite ordinary . . .

My father explained to me that this was "resonance phenomena," discovered by the physicist Hermann von Helmholtz [1821–1894]. He brought me to the piano and showed me how to make a sound from any string without touching it . . . you have to sing the note that the string is set for, and it will immediately make a sound in response.

What happened to Kostya M. when he read Calderon? Perhaps it was the sympathetic resonance phenomena? The "string" of his soul resonated after 30 years of silence. It was silent because life still hadn't touched it, and neither had a "sound" to which it could answer. Once that sound was heard, however, his "string" awoke and trembled with excitement.

Calderon is a powerful author. Yet, an insignificant author too can stir up an entire storm in the soul of a great artist – just as a feeble, cheap violin could make an entire belfry vibrate. Just so long as the author's "sound," however weak it may be, is in tune with the strings of the artist's soul.

Finally, this awakening of the *artist* can be instigated by a sensitive and competent director. As a matter of fact, it is the director's primary task. Moreover, it should be required of him.

The Ready-Made Mask

The phenomenon of resonance is far from being the only way that an author influences an actor. As I've said before, the "mask" plays a large role when it comes to art in general, and especially to the actor's art. Without the "mask," we aren't capable of green-lighting even our closest, most habitual and genuine feelings, let alone the unfamiliar ones. Having hidden behind "the mask," however, we are capable of saying everything about ourselves. Under the mask, we give up secrets that are known to absolutely no one, not even to ourselves.

The author presents us with a ready-made "mask." In addition to providing the "mask," the author puts the character in peculiar conditions. In these conditions, having become the character, you'll inevitably feel like behaving just as the character does in the play, and saying the very words that the author wrote.

Before I know it, it already isn't me, Kostya M., but captive Segismundo groaning in a dungeon, bound by heavy, tortuous chains . . . Not me, but Segismundo . . .

If, however, the appropriate strings aren't present in the actor's soul, then it's impossible to play the author's melody on them. The author's melody won't excite the actor, unless it speaks to him of things that are dear, close, and intimate.

Co-Creation

Even an inanimate, "lifeless" bell or a "dead" piano string responds to a kindred sound; they resonate. Yet, a man is a living being – complicated, albeit one that is uniform and whole. Relatively speaking – as one string of his soul begins to resonate, it evokes a response from *his entire being*. He begins to live entirely by this response. Having begun to live, he creates (especially when it comes to an artist-creator). Having begun to create, he originates something new. In other words, his "living instrument" begins to play on its own. The stronger the sound of the author's "strings" touches my soul – the richer, the more emotional and powerful my response; the sounding of my strings; my melody. Co-creation takes place. This mutual co-creation of the author and the actor gives birth to the role – the actor's artistic creation.

The Author's Fertilization of the Actor

The actor doesn't always echo the "sounds" or "melodies" of the author. It often happens that the author's words and images fall upon the soul of the actor like grain, like seeds, or like germs. They fertilize it, and then a third something comes into being. It grows, neither completely resembling the author's design nor the actor's individuality – even though it wouldn't be difficult to find traces of either.

This third something is a new, independent being; the child of two artists.

Different Approaches to Dramatic Works: The "Overcoming" and Murdering of the Author

This kind of approach to the author doesn't always happen in the theatre. Nowadays, hostile relations between the performer and the author are considered completely normal. In recent years a special term has come into usage: "overcoming." Nowadays, you won't score any popularity by solving the author's riddle, opening one's soul to him, and getting inspired by him (or filling his shoes). We must "overcome." Letting the author fertilize us and bearing some mysterious fruit by all known natural laws of art? What nonsense! We must "overcome."

It's true that the author is at times so bad that you have to mobilize your entire creative powers in order to "overcome" his mediocrity, dramaturgical ignorance, and lack of culture.

The problem is, we usually act the same way with the classics: instead of confessing that a play is difficult and not within the capacity of the director and actors, we say, for example, the following: "This play would bore the contemporary audiences as it is; it would not interest them; today's audiences need more dynamism and action." Thus, the "overcoming" begins. They delete three-quarters of the author's text, insert interludes and brighten it up with amusing extra scenes. The unrecognizably remade play, deprived of all its meaning and power, is then unloaded onto the audience in an "overcome" form.

In exchange for profound content, grand emotions, and the battle of the eternal passions, it has acquired external shine and amusingness . . . It is easy and fun to watch . . .

There is another form of "overcoming," which for some reason is exceedingly encouraged right now.

Great authors like Gogol, for example, rewrote their works many times. The first drafts were so weak and primitive that you couldn't even imagine that Gogol wrote it. Meanwhile, the matter is very simple: in order to not lose his thoughts, he quickly sketched what appeared to him. He wrote it down in a rather amorphous form. Later, step by step, draft by draft, his work changed and finally acquired the form and perfection we know today.

However, today it is considered a great merit to stage a play, based on its first transcription – that is to say the first sketches, discarded and thrown away by the poet as something useless.

If we were dealing with censorship cuts, that would have been a different matter. But no! For some strange reason, the directors are enamored with the authors' first attempts, when they are still groping in the dark.

For the most part, it is the director who operates on the author in such a way. At other times, it is the actor's "overcoming" that makes it uncomfortable to sit in the audience.

Who among us hasn't seen the titanic character of Hamlet "overcome" and dumbed down to a minor neurotic or a shallow philosopher with a handsome exterior and a pleasant voice? Who hasn't seen a crude animal in place of a noble Othello? Or an empty brawler? Rather than rising up to the role and overcoming *himself*, the actor, without a moment's hesitation, fits the role to his own height. He shortens its legs, chops off half its head – "Isn't it all the same? – it should have been fit to my measurements in the first place!"

"Overcoming" can also be of a positive kind. The actor and the director manage to create a living, convincing and telling character from an author's useless, false material. It is a service; it is a sacrifice; it is a feat.

If it becomes absolutely necessary to stage such an inadequate play, or to act such a role, then it's obvious that I *cannot help* but fix it; I can't allow ignorance; I can't keep tastelessness; I have got to beautify the dire poverty of the author's thoughts and fantasy.

How could it be otherwise? The entire life of a genuine artist is composed of such feats. This is not at all surprising.

Onstage, You Must Think

Thinking onstage is one of the most important skills. Of course, this isn't a discovery; it is just a method. If you "let go,"[1] that triggers your perception. Now that the actor is free to perceive, the flow of his thought begins. In the meantime, many actors inhibit a thought as soon as it appears. Point their attention to the thought – and they release these brakes.

It's interesting that, when learning a new language, the first sign of fluency is that the learner *begins to think in that language*. It's the same way for us: we have to learn how to think when in character (to think "in the language" of the character). This is similar to the manner of walking, shape of the body and other aspects of the external characterization – you have to practice thinking in character. Khlestakov [from Gogol's *Inspector General*] doesn't think like

Osip, his servant, or like the Mayor [Gogol's *Inspector General*], or like Podkolyosin [Gogol's *The Marriage*] – each of them thinks in his own inimitable way.

It's worth exterminating from the very depths of the actor the idea (and the feeling) that the role is *words*. In beginning to rehearse, what does the actor do? He's preparing to say the words. Or (which isn't much better), he is preparing to fulfill actions.

Above all, he needs to *be*.

There is no need to search for this. Don't you already exist? Sitting? Or walking? Well, just keep doing all this to your heart's content.

On the Past, Present and Future

The actor always tries to live by his character's feelings – to rejoice, to mourn, etc. Easier said than done. How is he to experience joy? In large part, the joy is evoked by the fact that, until now, things were bad; bad things being finally gone – this brings joy.

You always need to search for the *past*, yet the actor searches for the *present*.

Nora rejoices; she is happy – her husband became the head of the bank, and they will now have heaps of money . . . The actress "rejoices," and nothing comes out of it. How could it? There is no point thinking about joy, or about the new circumstances; you need to think about the horror of the previous years. As soon as you grasp that they are now in the past, your whole being will swell with joy.

Note

1 On the method of "letting go", see Chapter 12 of this book.

5

The Actor and the Director

The Director's Breathtaking Career

The director has assumed such power – he has the right to completely berate and offend the actors, and to order them around like pathetic creatures.

Vakhtangov's students, gushing with admiration, tell of how their teacher once threw a paperweight at the stage . . .

I've had the chance to hear actors tell with pride and rapture how their director hurled a pitcher at them! . . .

As for those who don't hurl anything, and don't scold them – they aren't worth much in their eyes.

The director has gradually become the master of the performance. And he can keep this title, as long as he is tactful enough, and knows how to spare the easily wounded pride of the most conceited of persons – the actor. After all, he doesn't get in the way of this prideful person collecting an abundant harvest of applause. (Although, this applause is now often addressed more toward him – the master, the advisor, visionary and teacher.) I repeat, if he is tactful and capable of keeping himself in the shadows, then there is no actor who wouldn't want his presence, need his advice and feel as safe with him as the bank of England.

Once this individual makes himself indispensable to the theatre, his influence becomes huge – especially if he is energetic, active, and authoritative.

Those actors who kept resisting him for a long time, would be finally forced to give up. Or else, they would be forced to leave this theatre, and search for another – where they could feel freer, at ease, and independent.

Such is the breathtaking career the director has accomplished in some 50 [now more than 100] years.

It is, however, too breathtaking to be long-lasting and deserved. Much of it is based on misunderstanding and even more [so] on usurpation.

It is time to clarify this statement, and to put two *equally valuable artists* – the actor and the director – in their rightful places.

The Necessary Quality of the Artist-Director

Who gave birth to theatre as a form of art? The actor. Whom does the audience see before them? The actor.

Yet, there is no getting around the fact: in most theatres this main person – the actor – is in the second, third, or fourth place.

In order for the actor and the director to take up their proper roles, there should most likely be a third person present: a wise psychologist, a connoisseur of the human heart, and of the inner creative mechanisms and laws. An artist unto himself, and should nevertheless be capable of understanding the other two, often hostile, sides.

In the absence of such a person, things usually happen this way: if the actor is strong, powerful, and active, the director becomes an almost-unneeded spectator. He sits gloomily, with pursed lips. Or else, if the director is domineering, judgmental, and vested with power – then the actor sighs a sad sigh and pulls the plug out of his creative outlet. Having extinguished the lamp of his intuition, he turns into a cog in a machine. He becomes a blind executor, dependent on every command of the often capricious and untamable director.

When the director is the *master* of the performance and the actor is *used* to obeying him, it destroys all initiative in the actor. It is one of the most dangerous influences that a director can have. The actor should be active, responsible, and independent. Without this, his creativity will never be roused.

The co-creation of the actor and the director, however, almost never happens.

Yes, it's difficult. Actors are many, and the director is one. However, if speaking about serious creative help and collaboration, you have to approach each actor on an individual and personal basis. Moreover, you have to approach them based on the laws of a totally different "school" – the one organically intrinsic to his "creative type."

As unpleasant as it may be to acknowledge, there still isn't a science on the creativity of the actor. In the meantime, only such kind of science could help every actor give free and talented performances at his maximum strength – regardless of his psychological (creative) constitution. So far, only the first timid steps have been taken toward this kind of science. So, long as the secrets (objective laws) of the creative artistic process remain unrevealed and **unknown** to the director (and so long as he does not ***practically master*** these laws and everything they imply), there can be no theatre that would approach a true artistic ideal.

The actor himself is an artist. The overconfidence of the director and his faith in his own unlimited strength and power (his ability to "mold" and "build") is nothing but self-deceit and narrow-mindedness. He needs to learn all the secrets of the multifaceted actor's creativity – although it's not likely to happen in the next hundred years. If so, with his way of forcing everyone into the same mold, he won't achieve anything worthwhile. Abusing the creative will of the actor and persecuting the actor's intuition (incomprehensible and unacceptable to him), won't get him very far. He shouldn't be kidding himself!

The only thing left for him to do is to pick the actors' material that is of his same type. Then, maybe, they'll be able to figure each other out somehow.

It's true that there is one miraculous force – love. Wherever it appears, you can expect all kinds of miraculous surprises. There have been cases when medical science capitulated, while a mother's love instinctively gave the sick child life and deliverance.

Can a highly artistic work come into the world without love or rapture? Aren't love and rapture inherent to any major creative flight?

The Co-Creation of Individualities

"Artists, like the Greek gods, are only revealed to one another" (Wilde [1909: 163]).

When Mussorgsky takes Pushkin's text of *Boris Godunov* and puts it to music, when Salvini takes Shakespeare's *Othello* and embodies him onstage, when Mochalov passionately electrifies the audience with his Hamlet, and when Yermolova radiates from the stage in Schiller's *Maid of Orleans*, then a genuinely miraculous unraveling of one artist by another occurs. Not just unraveling, but a merger, and a co-creation.

The author, actor, and director – are they not three artists? If even one of them isn't an artist, it's tragic.

If two of them *force* the third to become a non-artist and a cog, it couldn't be worse. Yet, this happens not so rarely.

We'll assume that, in each instance, the author, actor and director are all artists (otherwise they should take up something else that is more fitting for them). In such a case, wouldn't it be considered ideal (if not just natural and normal) for them to remain artists when working together, and even inspire and inflame each other? Who else could inspire them but their respective counterparts, who "like the Greek gods . . . are only revealed to one another"?

In practice, however, the author is usually either far away or, even worse, in a better place. The director often takes his place. Actors come to him with questions about the interpretation of the work, for explanations of obscure passages, and for the right to change the text . . .

Therefore, in practice it is usually just the director and the actor who collide with one another.

It's easier for two to make peace, of course.

Let's take a look, however, at how it happens in practice.

The main barrier that often crops up between two artists is their greatness, their independence and, what often happens here, their categorical dispositions.

The greater and more equal the artists, the harder it is for them to get along with each other. In a word, it is a classic illustration of the proverb: "Two dogs over one bone seldom agree." The most minor disagreement in taste, a small gap in worldviews, some difference in technique – and suddenly they can't stand each other. Moreover, each of them feels powerful enough so as not to need the other.

With the exception of a few singular instances, the matter ends in either a split or the tragic victory of one over the other. In the latter case, the defeated side puts down its weapons, extinguishes its creative fire, and turns into an obedient executor, deprived of creative flights and inspiration . . .

How then can these two equally matched personalities come to an agreement?

Just think what could be achieved if two outstanding artists like this managed to do so. The two of them wouldn't have just added up their strengths and capacities; they would have multiplied them. From five and five they wouldn't have gotten 10, but 25. Such a path, however rare, is possible – practice and life experience have shown that.

People are usually tied to each other by one common idea. A merger like that mostly occurs at a theatre's inception, when everyone is of one mind, and believes in their inspiring leader. As for the leader – at such a time he is yet to grow tired from having to overlook his young colleagues' shortcomings and lack of talent . . .

In the more established theatres, the fusion and co-creation of that kind is, alas, a rare phenomenon. To put it bluntly, it is almost a non-possibility.

Theatre, footlights, audience, and the press – with time, all of this truly spoils a man. Here, vanity is an unrestricted ruler, and noble ambition is a rare guest – empty worship kills everything else. Jealous plotting, intrigues, and the constant work of self-destruction rule those theatres that prefer petty vanity to a common guiding idea.

The question of co-creation in the theatre is painful and serious. The solution to this question chiefly hinges on two untapped cornerstones:

1   The science of the creative process onstage and the knowledge of this science.

I refer not so much to the physical techniques as to the psychological or, perhaps more than anything, to the internal technique of the performing artist. Besides, the laws that govern the artist of each type of performing art – be it drama, opera, musical theatre, or ballet – are everywhere, in essence, the same.

2   The ethics and philosophy of the artistic creativity that needs to be infused with tangible awareness of the grandeur, importance and power of art in general, and ours in particular.

Everyone thinks: "what **I** mean, what **I** am worth," and doesn't think about *art in general*, and what it means, stands for, and does; art at large, and his in particular.

It would seem that we are still far off from the tangible awareness of these things. We still don't have a real science of the creative process, nor a philosophy or ethics of this art. So far, there is only one salvation: the coming together of artists in the name of one idea, and the support of the unquenchable flame of this idea with all possible means.

A Few Words on Individuality and Mediocrity

We spoke about the *co-creation of several individualities*. It wouldn't hurt to clarify and to say a few more words on who is to be considered an individuality in art.

In life, an individuality is a well-known entity. It is a person who has his own "I," and his own opinion that was not hammered into his head. He has his own view on things, his own principles and, perhaps, even rules. He isn't a faceless mediocrity under the invisible spell of someone else's opinions, suggestions and traditions – with nothing of his very own.

An individuality in art is, in essence, the same, except that all of these qualities are manifested in art per se.

In life, an artist can be mediocre in many things. He can have a bland personality; yet, when the matter involves art, he is unrecognizable. He becomes firm and decisive. Contrary to how we see him in life, he is full of creative fantasies, unwavering in his views, unique and talented, unpredictable and convincing.

However, the opposite may also be true. A person who is unique in life often displays definite mediocrity in art.

From bitter experience we now know that such people destroy the theatre more than anyone else. It's understandable: strong, resourceful and energetic in life, they are a waste of space onstage. Coming to terms with this is extremely difficult; individuality, a strong person, can't do it at all. You would have thought – why not take a look at yourself, understand that this isn't your place, and look for a quick way out? Instead, he assigns the blame for his piteous state to the others and pulls the springs of his worldly cunning and intrigues, often eliminating and pushing out the most valuable people in that theatre, its foundation – either the colleague-director, or the colleague-actor, or even the very leader and inspirer of the theatre himself.

Of course, only individualities and people of talent have the full and inalienable right to be in art. The individuality radiates its unique light. Such a light just needs to be kindled into flame, strengthened, expanded, and kept safe from any passing wind.

A faceless, non-singular actor emits no light at all. He is capable only of carrying out what the director tells him to do. Having done everything that has been shown to him, he stands and waits: "And what next?"

Nevertheless, don't hold him in contempt. There are as many actors these days as there are grains of sand, but individualities are far and few between.

If an individuality can be compared with a lamp, emitting its own light, then we'll compare a faceless actor with another "illumination device," such as . . . don't be surprised . . . with a samovar. You can buff and polish this household appliance to such a degree that, if you put it under a strong light, it will shine so brightly that it hurts your eyes. Of course, the light isn't its own – it's someone else's – but what can we do? We must be thankful for small mercies. It means that it also has its own value.

I hasten to qualify my statement – with the smart approach, individuality oftentimes can awaken, and the actor from the polished samovar turns into something else. Restive and rarely blinking at first, flickering and almost fading, he nevertheless becomes a lantern. With skillful handling, this actor's light will grow stronger; it will kindle [into] a flame, and, finally, be established for many years.

Other things can also happen. Individual talent, ill-adapted for interacting with people, stumbles onto a director who is ignorant in essence (from the view of genuine directorial art) – rude, powerful and despotic . . . The lantern of this actor's talent at first begins to smoke and fume, and soon it fades, hopelessly and irrevocably . . .

Is his rehabilitation and rebirth possible? It is. It's just that here, with this director, it is unlikely.

An Individuality or an Impertinent Person?

There is one particular quality that could mislead us.

This actor amazes you with his bravery, persistence, decisiveness, and independence. Yet, everything he does has a hint of some rudeness and tastelessness . . . Before long, you feel shocked and want to pare down this bravery. Take away this daring, and you'll find that there is nothing behind it. It isn't bravery or daring, but just impertinence and impudence – hollowness hiding behind excessive forwardness. In our most gentle and delicate art, this quality, for the most part, points to a coarseness of soul and inability to figure out the springs of the creative mechanism.

On the other hand, it would do no harm to instill this quality in an unmistakable *ability* that is excessively timid . . . (I'm not talking about *talent* that of itself possesses all necessary qualities.) Timidity and complete lack of faith in one's powers has destroyed quite a few very sweet and pleasant abilities.

On the Director's Tyranny

Nothing good has ever come from director's tyranny: as the play leaves his hands and makes its way to the public, the balance shifts – when all's said and done, it's up to the actor (and not the director) to perform the play. If the actor isn't gifted, then he won't blossom in front of an audience; he will wilt away. If he is talented, the audience will inspire in him his own creativity, which, the more that the director tortured him, will take him that much further away from the director's pattern. In the end, it will sow in him an aversion to the established pattern, no matter how good it may be. If the director is inexperienced or jealous enough to demand at all costs that no deviations be made from his precious requirements, then a talented actor will get offended. (And rightly so – don't distort the *nature* of my creativity, don't turn me into a puppet.) He will withdraw, and do everything mechanically. Or in any case, he will act without flame or talent. In 10 performances he will have had absolutely enough and will be sick and tired of it all.

The director will rant and rave – "Mediocrities! I gave them *everything*, and they took nothing!"

In the meantime, the director's art cannot be compared to that of a painter or sculptor . . . His material fluctuates.

The director's art is more comparable to the art of a ceramic-potter who should know that his colors will surely change under fire and precisely how they will change.

I must admit that there exists one saving kind of tyranny – that of a very experienced, knowledgeable, and savvy director.

When a rescuer approaches a drowning person, he should be very harsh with him and even rude, if necessary; otherwise the other, panicking, would grab him and drown him. There is no need to be afraid of pushing him off, or even hitting him. Or else, having managed to grab him by the hair, dragging him in this humiliating way . . .

In the same vein, sometimes you can't do anything with a lazy or cowardly horse without using spurs and the riding crop. If you don't spur him right before the jump, then he may not jump far enough – break his own leg and cripple you.

I write this not without apprehension. It is so tempting for the director to dump the consequences of his own inaptitude onto the actor. Out of this temptation, he could rank all cases among those that require the crop, the spurs, and the rescuing of a drowning person. In the meantime, such cases are quite rare.

Here I'm addressing the actor, so that he truly understands the importance and point of the "crop." And so that he can name the reasons that lead to the crop being taken in hand, and why the director's rudeness and aggravation take place onstage. These reasons have the following names: laziness, apathy, inertness, sleepiness, irresponsibility, shortsightedness, a lack of understanding of the closest and most fundamental tasks and, probably, a wrongly chosen profession. When there is no commitment, how can there be a calling?

★★★

Sometimes an actor has certain select abilities, but lacks others. Or else, his physical qualities are not completely suitable [for acting]. Persistent and stubborn people overcome these shortcomings, while the majority give up.

If someone did give up, does it mean that he chose the wrong profession? Of course not. For example, a good lash from someone could have rescued the situation. It means that the matter requires the whip – from myself or from someone else – doesn't matter. The most important thing is to work. It's true that senseless work, or "monkey work," so to speak, won't do any good. The work should be conscious and systematic. With such work, things will soon click into place.

★★★

The director arrives, reads the play to the cast (or more likely performs "exactly how all of the parts should be played"), and then he begins to offer his "explication."

The actor listens humbly, taking his mental notes. He submits, and he tries to depict every-thing his "papa-director" (authoritative and faultless) has come up with.

If the actor, in the beginning, had imagined his character, his actions, or images of the scene outside of himself (as something that looms before him, asking to be recreated onstage) – then this creative process does not belong to the realm of the actor's creativity. It lies outside of the actor's nature.

For the actor, a completely different creative mechanism is intrinsic: the actor imagines actively. His imagination and fantasy work in a genuinely creative way (that is, with all of the surprises and trueness of intuition) *only in actions*. A true gift of an actor is never expressed in eloquent, interesting talks about the play, or profound philosophizing about the role. Moreover, the presence of such ability almost always reveals that we aren't dealing with an actor, but with a critic or, maybe, a man of letters. Even in such cases when an undeniable actor speaks too well, or too beautifully about some role – it can be surely said that he performs it badly, or based on the methods of cold representation (not as a creator, but as a mere imitator). Or else, he isn't performing it at all. If he is performing it, he won't wag his tongue about it. (Pardon my expression.) Why? What's with the sentimentality? There are two reasons: 1) Somehow he instinctively doesn't want to; it is unpleasant for him, and something holds him back; 2) From experience. It's happened a few times: you talk about the role, you let your tongue loose, and then you look – the role stopped working. You have troubles with it, and these troubles persist . . .

It isn't superstition or self-hypnosis – it is a psychological law. It is called the law of "catharsis." The actor-artist usually senses it himself, instinctively, and needs no warning. The director, on the other hand, doesn't know it and doesn't sense it at all. With his "explanations" and "descriptions," he destroys the actor's creativity at its very roots (at its buds).

But how then, they may ask, can you create? Without any plan? On serendipity – be what may?

A plan or, say, even an embryo of any work is one thing; a precise picture with practically all of the elaborated details is another.

The words of Pushkin [1979: 232] answer almost all of these questions in full:

a free romance's far horizon,
still dim, through crystal's magic glass,
before my gaze began to pass.

A broad outline of the plan, an initial idea, an approximate plan that can stay the same or can mutate into something unrecognizable – is it that same iron plan that the director feels it his duty to lay out at the very first rehearsal? For Pushkin, for example, it was a complete surprise that his heroine Tatyana [*Eugene Onegin*] married an old man.

The actor's creative nature keeps silent because it **has** something to keep silent about, and the director speaks . . . because **he has nothing to keep silent about**.

On the Preliminary Readings of the Play

Preliminary discussions are necessary for a few days – not of the play, but rather of some cru-cial things that find their reflection in the play. They are necessary so that the play becomes an *expression of all these accumulated ideas*.

"Falling in love" – under what conditions does this happen? Some preliminary state, a longing for love, loneliness, or a thirst for thrill and self-expression. The object of your love understands you without words; she is like your flesh and blood. The question is: what does all of it, or some of it, have in common with the play?

At the start, it is necessary to inspire in the actors the kind of thoughts and feelings that could find their expression and realization in the play.

What else is new in the *directing technique*?

To not explain the role to the actor, nor to interpret it. The actor will have his own interpretation – the one that comes out of him. When you notice that he doesn't see and doesn't understand, it is best to **ask questions**. Then his own sense of fantasy will begin to work.

Do directors think about the reason behind the following fact: the actor was doing more or less well, then they put their hand to it, and things started going badly – the role stopped coming together?

Or how about this: the director crafted the beginning of the role, and it is bad; the actor did the end on his own (because the director had had enough, and had given up on the actor) – and the end is good! How did that happen?

The director usually either doesn't think about this, or tries not to think. Yet, it is worth thinking about.

Fixating adaptations and intonations . . . acceleration of the rhythm . . . strengthening and heightening the tasks, or the stakes . . . all of these maleficent methods have been legitimated, and the director doesn't even suspect that they are the very evil. Poison. Death!

How Talent Overcomes the Incorrect School (the Unity of Opposites)

Everyone was taught the same way. Yet, the majority of them give a disingenuous performance, and a few – let's say, Boris Dobronravov [1896–1949] in *The Storm*, or Mikhail Tarkhanov [1877–1948] – perform creatively.

Both of them took something from "analysis," from "bits" and "tasks," but they work *as they think fit*. While everyone else got entrapped in mistakes.

6

The Actor and Form

To tell the truth, the actor's art begins only when the actor *upstages* the form – no matter how good it may be. That is, it begins when I, as an audience member, forget what the actor did or how he did it – I am entirely under the sway of the life of his spirit – everything else fades away.

"Tricks" (in the performance) should express the play's inner content. There are shows full of somersaults, falls, singing, dancing, and all for what? By God, it's impossible to understand. It isn't form, nor "theatricality." It is just trickery.

Proceeding from content to form – that is, from a live sensation to a reaction – is a proper path. Nevertheless, there undoubtedly exists a path from the external "dead" form to a live sensation.

The detail of a costume, the posture, grimace, gesture, or intonation . . . all of these can immediately give a living sensation of the character, of the experiencing and creative state. A fortunate, typical, or keen detail can release a lock, just like a tiny, but well-matched *little key*. Place it in a huge, disobedient lock . . . click . . . and the lock unclenches its jaws.

★★★

To start from the form is to grow a plant from a cutting. An entire tree would still grow this way, just as it would from a seed.

There are two kinds of form. One is subtle and profoundly human – this form (if it can be called form!) is spiritual, or internal. The other form is cruder. Flourishing, extreme and noisy, it speaks for itself. It is the bodily form. The first kind of form lives in the sound of voice, in its musicality and inner richness; it lives in the subtlest facial expressions (the shadows flickering across Duse's face). The second is found in the expressivity of the blocking, in makeup and costume.

The greater the actor's talent for the "first" form – the more the "second" gets in his way (if it is required of him). The less talented he is of it – the more necessary the "second" form becomes.

An actor of the "first" form functions best with minimal movements, makeup, and perhaps even a less elaborate costume. This kind of actor speaks for himself. An actor of the "second" form is practically silent on his own; effects and tricks speak for him. They are either of his own invention, or given to him by the director – it makes no difference. Here, onstage, his own creativity (the one that comes out of him per se) is kept to a rather low level of expectation.

We must give the "second" form its due, of course – it is needed and is especially valuable when the actor is ill or unenergetic – in a word – when the form performs for itself. However, it is necessary to emphasize that the path of the "second" form is very slippery. It disguisedly leads *to the destruction* of one of the most important things in an actor's art: *the actor's* **creativity**.

Roughly speaking, there are only two types of form, and they are *more or less antagonistic*. The harmonious combination of the two is something of a miracle. You can't find it, try as you might.

You Can Start with Form or with Content

Which appears first in the creative process: form or content? Is content followed by form, or is it the other way around – form comes first, and then the content is inserted into it? We'll suggest that it can work both ways. Although, this would only be true in relation to a certain phase of the creative work, but not to its very beginning. The first flicker of an idea is already the *meeting* of form and content. Everything after that is just the discovery (manifestation) of the *embryo*.[1]

The Wondrous Interplay of Form and Content

We can speak separately about the perfection of form and that of the content. The most important thing, however, lies elsewhere. It is found in the wondrous *interplay* of form and content that is past all understanding.

There lies a pile of gunpowder; a firebrand smolders right next to it. This can go on for a long time, and nothing will come of it . . . Yet, throw the firebrand into the powder! This is similar to what the artist does in the moment of creation: he fuses the powder of the content with the flame of the form.

In looking at the powder, you might think – what is so special about it? It is just some kind of dust. You would not think much of the firebrand either, would you? "It just reeks; hurry up and douse it, that's all." But the artist senses the hidden forces . . . he senses their affinity and he can't hold back from dropping one into the other! He's got an amazing nose for these hidden forces.

What is even more amazing is his ability to guess that these are related forces. And the most amazing thing of all is his other guesswork – how to connect them so that they come alive, and live in perpetuity.

These three abilities contain the mystery of the artist.

What is at the heart of this mystery? It has to do with the inception of the *embryo*.

External and Internal Form

When the performance doesn't leave enough of an impression, or when it seems boring, maybe it isn't because its form is weak, but just because the acting is bad?

When the acting is good, then even the plainest of "forms" is fun to watch and to hear. Elaborateness isn't really necessary here; on the contrary, in this case it is more likely to hinder and distract. In those performances where the acting is good, a different "form" comes into its own: not external, but internal; not physical, but psychological.

We can so clearly and distinctly imagine the life and characters described by Leo Tolstoy; they are so expressive and vivid, we can almost see them before us.

It's the opposite for Dostoevsky's characters – we don't know how they're dressed, and we can't claim that we see their appearance, or height. We each come up with our own images for the settings in which the action takes place . . . However, can we use that as grounds to say that form meant nothing to Dostoevsky?

The thing is that Dostoevsky assigns the chief value to the *internal, psychological form of his heroes*, while for Tolstoy the external, the *physical* is not at all unimportant.

And so, depending on where the center of gravity falls – on the internal or the external; on the psychological or the physical – two different kinds of productions come into the world. One is distinguished by vivid theatrical form. The other has a form that is modest, although it is imbued (and over-imbued) with the fervor of feeling and deepness of thought.

Which of these is better? Is that even a question?

I'm not talking about productions that are simply boring and bad, where both content and form are *fictitious*.

There is only one thing to remember. The artistic work that requires explanations (a commentary, or a special key to unlock its treasure), and doesn't affect or impress you on its own – simply *isn't artistic*.

Artistry is strong in that it affects you by the mere fact of appearing. Any analysis or critique only gets in the way: artistry makes my heartstrings resonate, sing and moan – so, leave me in peace and don't impose your understanding on me. Mine may be less profound than yours, but it is mine. Let yours excite you, and let me be excited by mine.

A profound, mighty author finds the path to my heart, to my inner sanctuary and depths; he excites me, and stirs my soul. If he doesn't do that, he wasn't strong or skillful enough in his work. This means that he needs some assistance – a critic. This critic can show and spoon-feed me those buried ideas – the ones that got cluttered by other things, perturbing and glaring.

If a thought doesn't affect you on its own, and it must be unearthed and pulled out by force – is it really there?

Every New Form Is New Content

Take any good classical play. If performed with competence and insight, it will be pleasant to hear and to watch.

If, however, some talented actors become enthusiastic about this play, then their creative fire will excite the audience and leave a profound impression upon them.

In a different case, certain aspects of the play may not satisfy the director – be it the author's remarks on the set, furniture and costumes, or the author's blockings. Having read the text of the play, the director might envision something completely different – more colorful and juicy, perhaps more expressive.

When the director sees a new form, prompted by his imagination – something interesting and unique – then is that not new content that he's seeing? In his dreams, the play's theme and plot – which is only *a certain part* of its content – might be one and the same. However, another "part" of the content – the play's rhythms, atmosphere and mood; its undertones, and often the very idea of the play – all this has been ignored by the director. In finding a new rhythm, atmosphere, undertones and details, he essentially creates a *different content*. This fact usually escapes those talking about *new form* – in actuality, they are referring to what is essentially *new content*. They are talking about a new play.

What Does It Mean to Find Form for a Good Play?

In Shakespeare's day, in place of a set, they brought out a pole with a banner, and placed it in the middle of the stage. On the banner were the words: "Garden," or "Palace," or "Seaside" – now you know where things take place, so imagine it as best you can. Back then, they saw the core of the matter in something else – in the human collisions; in the force of passion; in the inner content of the play, and in its poetic and philosophical substance (that is to say, in the "inner form"?).

How many "sorts" of *Hamlet*, for example, can you see these days?

A box setting; the traditional black tights and a rapier for a prince; a white shroud for his father's shadow and so on – in a word, everything is conventional, traditional, and "theatrical." Everything, except for the actors, who live behind those masquerade costumes; except for the excitement in their blood, the flight of their ideas, and their aroused passions.

Or else, take some gigantic golden screens that are so tall that they block out the sky. Everywhere you look, there is gold: the walls are gold, the people are imbued with gold, and the talk is about gold, prosperity and power. Hamlet alone, in his humble, austere, dark clothing, seems a stranger to the gold and the splendor.

This theatre is not concerned with the realities of life, nor with period features, but rather with a philosophical and symbolic interpretation of the tragedy.

A third *Hamlet*. A knight's castle with a drawbridge and cannons, with stairs and arrow-slits. People encased in armor – people with harsh knightly manners. Rapier and tights exchanged for a battle sword, warm fur clothing, and warrior's heavy boots. Such is Hamlet. A performance of the realities of life, of manners and customs, and social conflicts.

You can stage and perform this amazing play in thousands of other ways. Any of these discovered forms might seem appropriate and enthralling.

Has anyone ever found the most appropriate form? Is it even possible to find?

Imagine the massive, almost 6,000-meter-tall Mount Elbrus – in the morning it is one way, during the day another, in the evening a third, at night a fourth. In winter, in summer, under the sun, in stormy weather, from above, from below, from the side, on one side and on the other – it is always different, and always Elbrus.

The greater the dramatic work, the more it is like Elbrus. Any director and any performer who cherishes the illusion that his depiction of Elbrus is the smartest, the most profound and faithful is mistaken. Let's thank him for not slipping us himself(!) instead of Elbrus, but rather depicting for us *something* that is actually about Elbrus. Of course, he did not exhaust the subject, nor did he reveal some essential truth about it, for the times to come. What he saw today in Elbrus, what he conveyed to us – it is only a "form" that revealed one of the countless "contents" of that mountain. And that's all. To find a new staging for a good old play (to find a new form) is to reveal one of its countless contents – having forgotten about the others. That is all.

What Does It Mean to Find Form for a Bad Play?

It happens that a play sometimes represents only a scenario or synopsis. If you perform it that way, it will not amount to a play or performance. Everything in this play needs expansion and further elaboration; without this, it is only a sketch.

Perhaps, its inner structure is chaotic, or there are numerous contradictions. Whatever the cause may be, the play is far from being first-rate. In such a case, it is impossible to avoid intervention; it might even be necessary to remake it, as a good tailor remakes someone else's hackwork, cutting an elegant dress-coat out of a sack-like frock. As with any restructuring, the result will be a different play.

What does it mean to give convincing staging or interesting form to a bad play? It means to extract some aspects of its entangled, unclear content; to highlight and reveal these aspects, thus making them distinct – while, at the same time, crossing and dimming whatever confuses the content.

Seeking a new form for a good classical play is a different matter. It's likely that the form inherent in the play has not been discovered. They try to rehash it, and ruin a good play.

What Does It Mean When Form and Content Are Unequal?

When people say that they like the form but not the content (or vice versa), they obviously aren't talking of the wondrous *interplay* of content and form, which can create an artistic work all by itself. They are obviously talking about two different contents, or about two different embryos. This implies that there are two different creations someone has tried to fuse into one – to fuse wood and iron, which are non-fusible materials.

Moreover, one of these contents is obviously more ripe and mature, while the other is just beginning to take shape – it's still vague and unclear, and perhaps even a bit muddled. It therefore does not seem to be equally good and strong. A powerful artist picking it up, however, it will become strong and compelling.

Take Goethe's *Faust*. The content is excellent (at least for the next thousand years, after which, it's possible, that it will seem primitive), yet the form, truth be told, is boring.

Would this mean that there isn't a wondrous interplay between form and content? It would. Would it mean that *Faust* is not an artistic work? It would mean that it isn't artistic. It is a philosophical treatise put into a more or less belletristic form, and that's all there is to it. It has a few well-formed scenes, similar to Stanislavsky's *An Actor's Work*.

In contrast, take *War and Peace*, for example. Is it not full of grand philosophical thoughts? Then why is it not boring? The thoughts "enter you" in such a way that you don't even notice how they possess you, or how you change your view on life and death, and on good and evil.

The Minor Details of Form Are Stronger Than Major Things

A copy of a painting precisely conveys its form. Then why are copies always weaker than the original? Because, it would seem, it isn't possible to make a perfect, absolute copy.

There is no conscious way of conveying precisely the colors or draftsmanship (in other words, form). The nuances are too elusive and subtle; the lines are too gentle in their twists – to capture them isn't within human capacity.

This brings back that same old paradoxical thought: the power is only in the minor details. Things elusive affect us the most. Like the force of gravity – invisible and inaudible, it rotates the universe.

Unity of Form and Content: Content Is No Summary

A peaceful pedestrian is walking along the road. Suddenly, a car signals him from behind. The pedestrian jumps out of his skin with fright and recoils so far off to the side that he lands in a ditch. A different pedestrian would freeze up from the same fright – you can run him over all you want. A third would thrash around, running the risk of ending up under the wheels. And a fourth would simply flinch in surprise, and take two or three steps to the side.

These are different forms of manifesting fear, and different forms of reaction, evoked by that same frightening circumstance.

You could consider it like this: the *content* of each of these people was the same – it was fright. However, the form of its expression was different. Yet, it isn't exactly the case – the fright was far from being *the same*, and each of these pedestrians reacted depending on what he happened to be imagining at that moment.

Although we can speak about form and content separately, in actuality form cannot exist separately from content, and vice versa. So, what do we mean, when we speak of "inserting" that same content into different forms? Unknown to ourselves, we are talking not about the content, but about the **summary** of the content.

The word *summary* contains the solution to all debates on whether you can put the same content into several different forms. Of course it isn't possible to do so with the same exact content, but the same *summary* can be put into an endless number of forms.

A person walked along the road. A car signaled him from behind, scaring the man. This is not content, but rather a lifeless summary. What if the man went insane from suddenness and fear; what if he felt as if the ground opened up beneath him, and the sky fell down on him? Can this state be exhausted by the single word – scared? It requires an artistic description by a major literary master. Or else, you need to film this scene to accurately recreate all of his jumps, leaps, and grimaces. Only this kind of a form (precise, expressive and quite fitting for the occasion) could enable us to judge what that person experienced in this short moment. Otherwise, we would get the idea of fright, but some other fright, of a different quality and strength – in short, of different content.

Just as there can be a summary of content, a summary of form also exists.

A person fell into a ditch from fright – does that say everything?

A person laughed . . . and how did he laugh? What was in his eyes, and what could be heard in his voice? A person may laugh a million times in his life, and each new laugh will be different.

Types of Theatrical Form Today and in the Future

Productions often have only form, and absolutely no content. A theatre puts on a cheerful play – everyone is somersaulting, dancing, singing, and laughing, for no reason whatsoever. When the show is over, you are left with this feeling – "I just saw something amusing and cheerful (I think), but what? For the life of me, I don't know. I can't put it in my own words."

In theatre art, form – that is character, blocking or rhythm – only has the right to exist if it is filled with content [that is] relevant to the idea of the given scene. Only such a form is worth holding onto. If form is only form, interesting as it may be, it isn't artistic. It exists on its own.

From all of this we can gather that form should be **living**, capable of change, and with an inclination *to change*.

At the same time, in order to be *living*, form should be very precise. It sounds like a paradox, but it isn't. How precise are tree leaves, or those of a plant; or their flowers, stem and trunk – all of their contours, proportions, and patterns! . . . In a similar way, a genuinely living creation of an actor is so *expressive* (theatrically speaking) that it is *precise* in its form at every moment of its life.

A stillborn form – such is the symbol, and a driving force behind the art of several theatres (Tairov's Kamerny and others). A dead form – such is the symbol of the majority of our theatres. In the meantime, our theatre's best artists subscribe to the ideal of living form.

The life of the form is the ideal of future artists – a "living form" that changes depending on the circumstances. It is an ultra-modern and dialectical solution to the question.

Form in time.

This idea might be one of the most tempting for dialectical philosophy.

How Form and Freedom Combine

I am keen on freedom, and I zealously preach it. At the same time, I persecute firmly set "form." However, do I follow this in practice, in my productions? Indeed I don't.

It's true that I don't drill into my actors the miniscule details, but I still do find and preserve the most expressive blockings, or the most telling movements and actions supplementing the text.

Does it mean that I am not completely consistent?

One could say that, of course. The reasons here are simple and potent.

I persecute form, and I am the cursed enemy of form, as form is precisely what is destroying the art of the actor these days. They find it (or the director finds it), and they keep running with it – empty, deprived of content and senseless. And then they say: this is the actor's art at its best!

I too, however, find and secure it . . . This is because the actors are still no good. You can't allow them green-light complete freedom, as they are incapable of anything significant. They still can't act. So, having painfully run my head against their incompetent and ungifted selves, I resort to form. The actors might have involuntarily produced this form, or it might have been ascertained by my director's eye. At any rate, I am forced to piece it together, rehearsal after rehearsal.

The combination of these two paths could be seen in Aldridge: his enormous giftedness (the ability to ignite and give in to his emotions freely and to the end) and, on the other hand, the precise, expressive and pre-discovered form.

My method gives the actor giftedness, and it allows for the dialectic combination of freedom and form, fire and water – the steam and the boiler collecting it.

Note

1 For more on the *embryo*, see Chapter 8.

7

A Few Critical Thoughts on Some Methods and Terms of the Ruling Theatre Schools

The Object

We'll take "object," for example. Your partner is your object – that's a fact. But Ivan changes every second; first he is merry, then he is sad . . . he can't be stopped. As soon as you stop a motion, it ceases being life. Stopping the heart is death . . .

So it isn't Ivan that is your object, but the *changes* that constantly occur in him. You say to your student: "Ivan is your object." He stares at him. Yet, in the very next moment, the Ivan you've just pointed out to your student is gone! Ivan lives, while the student would unwillingly stop himself, forced to continue seeing the very Ivan you've shown to him. And so, that "old" Ivan becomes the "object" that now stands between the student and the living Ivan – the one who changes by the second. You've thrown the student for a loop; he is now trying with all his might to do things that never happen in life, and that never could.

In order to return him to normal, natural, living reactions, you use different methods, depending on the composition of the group. The general concept behind it is, nevertheless, the same: to immediately compare the artificial, affected state usually displayed by the student with the living – his completely natural and spontaneous state.

You do it like this, for example: You sit the student down across from you. "Try it with me. You say: you need an object? Well here, let me be your object. You know what it means to "take an object," right?"

- Of course I do. It means to concentrate and gather my attention on it.
- Wonderful! Concentrate, be attentive, and hold me as your object.

The actor begins to carefully examine me and "dig deeply" into me . . . I give him half a minute for this, and then disrupt this exercise in some way or another: I suddenly "realize" that I have an important meeting to attend that is about to start, if not already started. And here, I got so carried away with the exercise I completely forgot about it. I begin trying to figure out, hurriedly, what time it is? Am I late? What could the students do without me so that they aren't losing time while I am gone? And so on.

Another, even more primitive method – as soon as the actor has "taken me as his object," and immersed himself in the study of my serious face, I go ahead and misbehave: I give him a sneaky, sly wink. Flabbergasted, he stares at me questioningly . . . In my eyes he sees a cheerful, honest playfulness. He can't hold back, and he gives a snort of laughter. I also laugh and amiably ask: "What are you laughing at?" He can't stop, and through his laughter he blames me: "It was you . . . you started it . . ."

After we have both calmed down and come back to ourselves, preserving the cheerfulness, I would provoke the student: "I ruined your performance . . . All of your objects are scattered."

- Yes, I had just started concentrating and you . . . and then I lost it.
- Tell me then, you and I are having a conversation right now – am I your object or not?
- Right now? My object? No . . . Wait . . . now you are also my object.
- Come on, confess: which object is better, livelier, and truer?

At that point, all the students cry out in one voice: "This one, of course." When he looked at you before . . . he puffed up like a mouse in a granary.

- And now?
- Right now he's just talking with you.
- What's happening here? It turns out that before, in addition to me, there also was some kind of "object" that got in the way? When I broke his state of "concentration" with my prank, the "object" vanished, and only I remained. When this "third person" (probably unnecessary and even harmful, as you all could see) had disappeared, then we had a rather good laugh, and a decent conversation with each other.
  Let's abandon the "objects" for a time. Give it a try. No "objects": just you and I.

To make a long story short, it's beneficial to let the student experience two polar opposite states, one after the other – the artificial, devised, pseudo-creative state, and then the one that is genuinely living. Having experienced and compared them, he starts to come alive.

So, bit by bit, you remove a spoke someone had put in his wheel.

Concentration and Attention

We will talk in detail about "task" and "actions" all in good time. For now – "concentration." The way this method is presented to actors – I can't think of another that could do more harm. (And, apparently, presenting it in any other way is quite difficult.)

It's strange, isn't it? We're so used to thinking that concentration is everything . . . How can it be that advice to be attentive could hinder a proper creative state onstage?

In the meantime, take a look at how it happens in practice.

The actor is told: "Concentrate on your object." The actor forces himself to look and to listen; he stares, he keeps staring, and then he stares some more . . . In the meantime, as it has just been said, the actor has gotten firmly stuck in an unnatural and fairly useless state . . . while his "object" had time to change so many times.

Now we'll take a look at how the *process of attention originates* in life.

Your acquaintance and neighbor has never stood out in any way . . . he is a modest, quiet, and simple man. Suddenly, a full-page photo appears in today's issue of a specialized technical journal, captioned Vasily Grebeshkov. You flip through the pages, and it turns out that the entire issue is dedicated to a device that has revolutionized the technology of an entire field. You don't really understand how this device works, but it turns out that "Vasily," quite unexpectedly, is the inventor of the device!

How is it possible?

You continue to run into him in your ordinary meeting places – in the stairwell, at the bus stop, etc. Yet, now you feel different – he has become *interesting* to you, and you look at him in a totally differently light. He is still the same: that same shabby coat and that same modest (if not to say timid) gaze. His look does not fool you anymore. You know that it hides something impressive – deep inner content, great will, inquisitiveness and boldness of thought. Where are they hiding?

They are there, in that same shabby coat: he doesn't have the time to attend to such trifles. How he looks, what he wears – frankly speaking, it doesn't make any difference to him: just so long as it's comfortable and doesn't catch the eye. He has no time to think of all that . . . or go shopping . . .

His gaze is a bit absent-minded and timid. You used to think that it was a sign of a narrow mind, but now you see something different *behind* this absentmindedness. He is absent-minded because his thoughts are engaged in matters that are more important to him. He is timid because there are obviously two people within him. The first is the one who invents and researches – a bold and profound thinker. The second is unfit for mundane life and poorly oriented in it . . . And it's true. Look: in speaking with you he smiles his embarrassed smile; but when he has his nose in some book, his face is completely different – intelligent, willful, and calmly concentrated.

You begin to see him much better. Why? Because you have become interested. This is precisely how it happens in life: *attention emerges as a result of interest*.

You never force yourself to be attentive. On the contrary, Vasily draws you in, and pulls you toward himself . . . You *open* toward those impressions that come from Vasily. They hit you, and you can't help but notice a multitude of details – some of them please you; others cause you to grow cautious. Internally, your thoughts and feelings are working non-stop . . . you want to speak to him . . . and now you are *truly attentive toward* him.

Notice how complex your attention is: you look, comprehend, compare, and feel . . . Therefore, to tell the actor to "Concentrate, like you do in life," means: 1) *Impressions will stream from a person or a physical object*; 2) *You permit them into your soul*; 3) *When this happens, a reaction will occur*; 4) *Don't interfere with it*.

In other words, "to become attentive" is to *truly begin to live*.

Is it a wonder then that the brief advice to "be attentive" not only doesn't yield any benefit, but usually causes harm? The actor takes it too literally and, most of the time, begins to examine and scrutinize his partner: his wrinkles, hair, the buttons on his clothes . . . Meanwhile, how is it relevant? This just distracts the actor from his circumstances as a character. This procedure casts a chill over him, and nothing else.

Of course, they'll say to me: "The attention you talk about is called *involuntary* – in the sense that we don't control it, but it controls us. And what about the *voluntary* attention?

When we walk out onto the stage, our attention, naturally, will be diverted from what is happening onstage by the audience. This is a powerful and new impression that covers everything else. In the meantime, we need our main focus to be on the stage, and not in the audience.

What can we do?

It's very simple. Everything that is happening in the play has already formed in me, the actor, an entire manifold imaginary life. At this point, a mere thought or recollection of it immediately captures me so strongly that the audience no longer hinders me in the least.

I'm about to go onto the stage . . . What was going on with me, the character, prior to this moment? Where am I coming from? Where am I going? What's on the stage right now? My house? Perhaps, some other place? Why am I going there? What will I run into, when I arrive? All these recollections and thoughts bring me into the life of the play taking place onstage. All this fuels my *involuntary attention*.

With this in mind, we only need voluntary attention for a few moments, and even then – only to recall who we are in the play, and its environment. From that point on, our primary type of attention onstage comes into play – *the involuntary*.

If, on the contrary, everything that is going on in the play and onstage doesn't mean much to me; if it is incomprehensible, unneeded or distant – then my attention, not finding suitable fuel, will come to a halt. If, in these circumstances, someone says to me, "Be attentive to your object (or partner)," that won't help matters a bit. The actor usually fixes his gaze and fakes "attention," to please the director.

It is worth adding that the creative attention of the actor is not just involuntary, but ***involuntary in the presence of the audience***.

However, all these and similar abstract terms distort and obstruct the novice's sound notions of the actor's creative process. We need to teach and direct more simply – closer to life, closer to the everyday language of the actor, and not divert his thoughts with abstract ideas.

It would be *simpler*, of course, only for the student. For the teacher, it would be much more difficult. Here you have to teach these wisdoms, *instilling correct habits in the student*, and at the same time trying not to say a word about these wisdoms . . .

Having gone through such a school, the student knows how to listen, to see, to act, and to generally *live* onstage under any circumstances. For him, it is as easy as it is for a normal person to walk on the earth.

As for the theoretical justifications, it is better if they join in later, once some practical knowledge has been acquired.

How It Happens That Incorrect Methods Lead to Good Results (about Task)

The researcher-inventor [Stanislavsky] once said: we need a task. "Well," a linear-minded director decides, "this means that, first and foremost, the entire role must be broken into tasks. I do the breakdown, I mark it in the script, and my job is as good as done – now it is the actor's job to fulfill the tasks."

However, this leaves us with some unanswered questions. Are these tasks correct? Are they permanent? Maybe it would be worth determining them only in an approximate sense, as their intensity can be affected by the most minor reasons (such as the mood of the partner). "No way!" says the director. "You are splitting hairs."

Meanwhile, to suggest a task to an actor – while it might help him, it also always binds him hand and foot.

You're in love. You're left alone, just the two of you. You don't feel very confident; you don't know what to do. The director prompts you: "When left alone with a person you like so much, what is your task? What do you want? You probably want to be closer to her, to take her by the hand." The actor is eased; he tries to fulfill what the director prompted him to do, he draws closer . . . Meanwhile, in 10 rehearsals his role has grown, and the "helpful" task satisfies him no longer – in fact, it has become annoying. This is natural.

Annoying is half the trouble; it also turns out to be *incorrect*. Is it a given that a person in love, when left alone with his beloved "wants to be closer and take her by the hand"? It certainly happens, it's possible, but . . . it also might not be so. There is a kind of love in which I won't allow myself not only to touch her, but even to get close to her. The fact that I'm looking at her is already an outrage. Forget the "hand"!

Or here is another kind of love: as soon as they see each other, they begin to quarrel. When they are together, they scold and grumble, yet they're bored to death when they are apart. That's how it continues all the way to the marriage . . . No "hands" here either. The task constantly changes, depending on thousands of reasons that can affect a person.

In the eyes of the emotionally willful school, the "task" makes a cornerstone of the actor's inner creative technique. Where do we start? With the task. What do we need to know? The task: what do I want here?

Is that correct?

We'll take the simplest example: there is an ant traveling up and down your spine. What is your task? What do you want? To get rid of the ant. Correct. But did everything really start with the fact that you *wanted to get rid of the ant*?

It started with the ant!

If there hadn't been an ant, would you have wanted to get rid of it? Right now you don't have anything crawling up and down your back – and so you don't have any desire to get rid of an ant.

Let's see how these things occur in life.

You were sitting calmly, doing your own thing. That's the first moment.

The second moment: you sense a tingling on your spine, maybe even a bite . . . in response to it you involuntarily shift your shoulders and shoulder blades; you let go of your task. Then things suddenly quiet down – no task even appeared.

We'll keep going. The ant took a break, and then, once more, it took some initiative.

"What is going on? Again and again – it isn't stopping. An ant! Damn! I have to get rid of it."

This is when the *task appears*. Was it the first thing that happened? God grant that it even was the tenth. The task is not just *not the origin* of life; the task is the **result**. A rather distant result to boot.

Once you learn this, it explains the fiascos of many directors and the failures of even the most capable actors.

However, why is this "task method" so resilient, and why does it often lead to good results?

One of the reasons is this: a talented director, having given a task (having made this mistake) *begins to correct it right then and there*. He compels you to feel and perceive the **circumstances**, he hints at facts, thus instigating your task to *emerge on its own*. More precisely, it is not the task that emerges, but rather – in response to the hinted *circumstances* and facts – you begin to react just as if you had a task (that is, everything happens on its own, without any task or "activity"). That's how a talented director instigates your task.

The second reason: the actor's talent finds its own solution and arrives at the circumstances behind the "task," without any prompts from the director. "Is my task to go for a swim? Aha . . . it means that it's hot . . . I've been walking on foot . . . for many hours . . . I'm tired . . ." At once, the actors' fantasy draws up a noonday sun, dust, a rocky road, and so on. A person of talent steps over the incorrect methods, not even noticing that they are incorrect. (Mediocrity doesn't have the strength to do so; they don't possess the kind of smart "mechanism" that leads them straight to their end goal. They might make the smallest mistake, yet stepping over it is beyond them; they get entrapped at the start of their journey, hopelessly and forever. It's true that talent too can't always escape the trap of the author of the "System," and his premature theorizing. For a talent too, a fair wind would come in handier.)

The third reason is this: the breaking of the role into tasks is a wonderful method for **comprehending** the role.

Let's take the court scene from *The Merchant of Venice* as an example. Generally, the actor playing Shylock, having read the text of his role, immediately begins to search for *the feelings* and for the *intonations* with which to speak the text. Is this the way to work?! He is yet to see or understand the scene as a whole, and he is already looking for its final *details*. The consequences of such a tactic are dire.

This is where a "task" can help him hit the right road.

"What do you want? On the one hand, you want to demand back your money; on the other – to catch him in your snares and avenge all your insults. So, start catching. Your worst enemy is crawling into your snares."

Indeed, it turns out that I didn't pay attention to the main thing, yet it determines everything else. It's all about catching and avenging my worst enemy, who conveniently crawls into my snares. Now I see my way.

Thus, the method of breaking the role into tasks is incredibly helpful for *understanding and interpreting* each scene. This alone, represents a great value. A talented, but inexperienced actor doesn't understand the scene, and gropes his way in the dark. One mistake follows the other. Now he has understood it, and all circumstances and facts, etc. have *emerged* on their own. The actor *comes to life*; now he will succeed with the scene.

This applies to a talented actor. In his moments of discovery, he is in the kind of state when the smallest hint, if it is correct, can decide the successful outcome of the work.

But what is there to do in the absence of this blessed state?

To comprehend the role is one thing – to live it is another.

To know what I *must* want isn't the same as *wanting it*.

Here is where the overestimation of the task method begins. Reliance on an actor's or director's talent doesn't really attest to a definite or permanent validity of a method.

The emotionally willful school categorically forbids suggesting feelings: you can't search for feelings, it says; feelings are the result. It is correct, but so is the task. As every analogy, this one may suffer, yet task is also a result – just to a different degree.

We just saw how suggesting to a talented actor his task has helped him. He reinterpreted it [by translating it into circumstances], and the task lost its poisonous qualities. Similarly, you can suggest a feeling to an equally *talented* actor in his moments of talent. Truly, nothing particularly catastrophic will happen. In the moments of talent, you can suggest anything to an actor – the riskiest, the most anti-pedagogical thing. He'll snatch it up and implement it in his artistic work.

About 20 years ago Stanislavsky was charged with degrading art to a pedestrian level with the help of his "system." If you use his "system," they said, you can act even if you don't have talent – everyone and their uncle will go on the stage, and it will lead to the decline of the actor's art. If memory serves me right, he said something like this: "On the contrary – the system is only for the talented." That's completely true!

"A task" in the hands of a run-of-the-mill, mediocre director who doesn't have the talent to neutralize it is usually just another obstacle in the way.

Moreover, you can only use the majority of the "system's" devices during those moments of the actor's creative readiness and openness. Otherwise the result will be dry – verisimilitude, drudgery, and marionette-like acting. And what is there to do in anticipation of this creative state? And what about those moments when your talent has suddenly gone out the window, as if it has never been there?

More on Task

"The task is assumed consciously and fulfilled unconsciously."[1] This is what Stanislavsky used to say.

This is something similar to the way a person who is intending to get married for convenience assumes the task of courting his bride and appearing to be in love with her.

Of course, this might work out and deceive the bride. Yet, this is just a hoax, a clever double game of a rogue. Can this be our ideal of an actor?

Repetition and Study of Difficult *Passaggi*

When I happened to speak about the murderous cutting into bits with musicians and singers, they were theoretically convinced, but practically still puzzled: "And what about a challenging coloratura or a difficult *passaggio*? Does it mean I should not study and train it separately, as it would destroy my creativity?"

Take a dancer, for example.

He is a gorgeous dancer, but today someone slipped him bad shoes, with huge nails digging into his foot. Can he now be creative in his dancing? Of course not.

But remove the nails, and things will go smoothly.

Now tell me, removing the nails from shoes – what kind of work is it? Does it have anything to do with dancing?

No, it does not. It is not the work of a dancer, but of a shoemaker.

It is the same with mastering difficult *passaggi* or other vocal challenges. This is the process of removing the nails of one's inability, clumsiness, helplessness, and anything else; of overcoming the technical, muscular unpreparedness. Putting it simply – this is a lack of physical technique. Paganini would have probably played it right away.

If, however, this kind of technique is lacking – let's acquire it, at least for this *passaggio*, or for that vocally difficult place. This work, however, lies in an entirely different plane.

A similar phenomenon is present in acting. When an actor's psychological technique is inadequate or incorrect, [Which is even worse, as it requires double work – first, you have to lead an actor away from wrong habits and, secondly, you need to create brand new ones. – *Author's Note*] then willy-nilly you have to break a scene into tiny bits and surmount each of the bits separately. Going forward, you have to carefully fuse it together, bit by bit.

This too, however, is nothing but "removing the nails."

This work is not included in the basic creative laws.

This is a deviation from the chief business.

It is true that in practice, this deviation occurs at every step. Moreover, it takes all of the teacher's and the director's energy and time. Despite all that, this is still just "removing the nails" – the training of ignorant, inept people, who attempt enormous tasks, while not being prepared for them.

Why Does Freedom Have to Be Placed at the Basis of Everything?

Stanislavsky as a director who spent his entire life turning out productions was neither a theoretician, nor a pedagogue who developed the chief properties of talent. He was a pedagogue for a specific role. He didn't achieve good results by discovering the *origins of creativity* in the actor, but by "shaping" the role for him. As far as a sound or correct creative state is concerned, he either simply *demonstrated* it (being a good actor himself), or else he stirred the actor. What is the secret behind this? What are the main springs of this process? He himself didn't know it, thinking that it is either "tasks" or "physical actions." Yet, the latter are suitable only for a specific place of a specific role; they do not *create an actor's talent*. You have to monitor them at every performance, and you have to recover them – otherwise, they quickly fade into nothingness. *This is because the chief properties of talent were never formed into the cornerstone!*

During one of the rehearsals for Ostrovsky's *An Ardent Heart* Stanislavsky told Nikolai Khmelyov [1901–1945]: "You will act well only when you have achieved internal and external freedom."

"*You* have achieved . . ." Why "you," rather than *I will show* you how to achieve this? This is because he himself didn't know "HOW," and didn't know the secret of this state and process called "freedom."

Freedom is a force inherent to life. A force counteractive to freedom (and to the force of life) is the one of necessity (and time).

According to Pavlov, the *reflex of freedom* is one of the unconditioned reflexes.

Give freedom to freedom!

How Did Stanislavsky React to All of These New Things?

First there was a war. It started when he met with a statement that the true reason behind the failures in teaching at the MAT studios and at the MAT school was not that it was rushed, or that students lacked theatrical professionalism or talent. Having received my suggestion to try training the actors in a different, completely new way – he was surprised and dismayed: what does this mean? Does this mean without "tasks?!" Without "objects"?! Without "attention," and without any "elements" at all? How is this possible? Through enormous efforts, we established the basis of the science of the actor's art, and now you suggest scratching it all out? There used to be amateurism; we destroyed it, and now you suggest bringing it back?!

He resisted. He did not want to hear this, was outwardly upset and decisively blocked the idea at all costs.

In short, a "war" had begun. Waxing and waning, it went on for no less than a dozen years. Much blood and nerves were shed on both sides. Considering the unequal strengths, the side that suffered more, of course, was the "non-complying" one.

It went on like this until Stanislavsky was shown one group of students. They were not selected based on their talents. On the contrary, this was just a group of young people who were interested in theatre and chanced to come together. This group, under my supervision, trained with my student Elena Morozova (the one who recorded Stanislavsky's rehearsals and talks with actors in the final years of his life).

They had been training for three or four months, two or three times a week, in the evenings – in their free time. At that point in their work, the young people showed more preparedness to begin working on a play than Stanislavsky had ever seen in theatre schools after a year or more of training.

It forced him to more closely examine his work and to rethink plenty of things.

His book, *An Actor's Work*, was being completed at that moment, and it was time to submit it to the publisher. Meanwhile, these new facts indicated, with ominous certainty, that the book shouldn't be released in its current form, and that there was something missing from it, something essential . . . There were even thoughts of rewriting the entire book. However, firstly, such a task would require a lot of time; secondly, some additional factual materials would need to be collected prior to writing, and that would take even more time . . . In general, the idea of such a fundamental remaking horrified Stanislavsky. Indeed, he'd already spent 20 years on his book!

Having thought about it in depth, he saw that the old "system" and the newly sprung one shared the same ideal – the artistic truth onstage; this put him somewhat at ease, and he even decided that there weren't any fundamental contradictions between the two. He just needed to supplement his book on the "system" with a little something that had been verified by the new search. The old and the new would then peacefully merge, and it would be exactly what was needed.

That's exactly what he ended up trying to do.

And now you shall see the extent to which he was able to achieve these additions and amendments.

The book [the original Russian 1938 ed.] is 575 pages long. Of them, the first 490 are dedicated to well-known principles of teaching his "system;" yet, the final 70 to 80 pages bring something completely different.

Suddenly, at one of the final lessons, the teacher Tortsov (that is to say Stanislavsky [2008: 329–330]) presents his student with "a new element of great importance," without which you cannot come to know the "truth of the character." "If you only knew how very important this new addition is!" he exclaims. This news was the *"pushing to the limit"* of each of the psycho-technical methods.

Pushing to the limit, Stanislavsky [2008: 330] continues, "skillfully involves the actor's own nature and his subconscious in what he is doing. Isn't this something new, isn't that an important addition to what you already know?"

What comes next turns everything upside down:

> In total opposition to some teachers, it is my view that students, beginners, who, like you, are taking their first steps on the stage, should, within the limits of the possible, **be led immediately toward the subconscious**. This should be done **at the earliest stages** . . . Beginners should know **at the very start**, *albeit in isolated moments*, the happiest of moods an actor can have as he is being creative. They should know it not just in words and phrases, not as dead and dry terminology . . . They should come to love this creative mood as part of their work, and really strive for it onstage. [Stanislavsky 2008: 330–331]

What comes from this? A student spends a whole year in school, and in one of the final lessons he is presented with a new method he didn't know until now: "a new element of great importance" that apparently he should have started with.

Question: why didn't they start me, the student, with that? Does it mean that this school is **incorrect**? Without this "greatly important" element – one could even say, *principle* – does this mean that I have learned the most important things "just in words and phrases," by "dead and dry terminology"? Not only did I learn them like that, but I also trained them improperly: I have habituated a mistake!

Such was one of the amendments to the book or, more accurately, one of its additions. Other small changes are dispersed throughout, in order to cover up the contradiction of everything that was written up to this cardinal addition. In the introduction to the book, Stanislavsky [1954: 6] reinforced in italics his suggestion to very seriously consider its "final sixteenth chapter": "*One should pay special attention to this part of the book, as it contains the essence of creativity and of the entire 'system.'*" He was probably racing to rescue the readers from getting too preoccupied with everything in the book without making any distinctions. He called them to be guided chiefly by the final chapters – those describing "the new element of great importance" and the "essential addition." Although he sensed incompleteness in his entire book and in all its practices of teaching "the system," he still thought it was enough to add this "pushing to the limit" to complete and correct the book.

In actuality the "addition" was nothing else but *a denial of the basic principles* that, up to that point, formed the foundation of the entire "system" – starting with the unnatural reduction of the indivisible creative process to its "elements," and many others.

How did this happen? How could Stanislavsky miss this drastic revolution?

There are several reasons. One of them is that the author himself [Demidov] at that time likely did not comprehend the significance of those unique facts he observed in his work, nor was he able to formulate his final conclusions.

★★★

Many will think that the goal of my entire book is to debate Stanislavsky, Diderot, or someone else.

The goal is completely different: to provide guidance, dictated by practice and life.

Note

1 Demidov is slightly paraphrasing Stanislavsky (as quoted in Vinogradskaya 1987: 68): ". . . Creative tasks of the role must be conscious, but the ways they are fulfilled – unconscious."

8

The Embryo

What is the embryo? In a chicken's egg there is a small cloudy speck – it is the embryo of a future chick. An acorn contains the germ of a future oak tree.

If you place an egg in the suitable conditions, the speck will keep growing. After a certain amount of time, a chick will hatch. Plant an acorn in the dirt, give it some time, and a sprout will come out of the ground. In the years to come, people will be able to rest in the shade of this oak.

This is what an embryo is.

The embryo contains everything. In looking at it you won't see anything. Even if you try looking under the strongest microscope, you will see nothing resembling a future chicken or tree. But give it time and the right conditions, things will happen on their own, without any help on our behalf.

How is a work of art created? It all happens in a single moment – the idea of it, its foreshadowing and, moreover, the live sensation of the existing, already-realized artistic creation. This is witnessed by all of the major creators of the great works of art, from all its fields.

Mozart:

> . . . The whole, though it be long, stands almost finished and complete in my mind . . . . Nor do I hear in my imagination the parts successively, but I hear them, as it were, all at once . . . For this reason, the committing to paper is done quickly enough, for everything is, as I said before, already finished" [1891: 20].

Dostoevsky (A letter to Appolon Maikov, from January 12, 1868):

> . . . there are always conceptions of artistic thoughts twinkling in my head and in my soul. But they only twinkle, while I need the complete evocation that occurs instantly and unexpectedly, although you can never calculate exactly when it will happen; [*This still isn't the embryo.–Author's Note*] only then, having received the full image in my heart [*Embryo! – Author's Note*], I can proceed with its artistic implementation. From then on, I can even estimate things without mistakes. [1985: 239]

Tchaikovsky (A letter to von Meck, from February 17, 1878):

> Usually, a **kernel** of a future work appears all of a sudden, and in the most unexpected way. If the soil is fertile, that is if there is a disposition toward work – the kernel, with the most incomprehensible strength and rapidity, roots to the soil, shoots out of the earth, sprouts, grows branches and leaves and, finally, flowers. I can't describe the creative process in any way other than by this comparison. All of the difficulty is in **whether the kernel appears, and whether it falls into the right conditions**. Everything else occurs on its own. It would be useless to try putting into words this immeasurable bliss of a feeling that captures me when the main idea appears, and when it begins to grow into its designated form . . . [1934: 216–217]

Later, Tchaikovsky stopped mentioning the kernel; he spoke of the embryo instead: "an embryo of a song has appeared in me," "an embryo of a symphony," etc. Of course, this comparison is much more precise. It isn't a kernel or an egg that is important, with its husk, shell, white, and yolk. The main thing is the germinal spot, the embryo. It is the center and the beginning of life; all other parts decompose or, in the best case, provide food for this embryo at the very start.

The embryo . . . What is it? A thought? A feeling? A will power? As I've already said, yes: it is all of the above put together – the thought, the feeling, and the will, and hundreds of other unknown forces and phenomena. Where is it? In the mind? Yes . . . in the mind, in the heart, in the blood, in the sympathetic nervous system, and also in dozens and hundreds of others places that are beyond our comprehension – we know too little.

And so, when we are cognizant of this and, mainly, **when we experience this in practice**, then the student [actor] will see his creative process with different eyes.

He would no longer be proud of his habit of cutting the living process into bits and poking at it. He'll understand that his former practices were murderous, and that the first thing he used to do was to kill the nucleus itself – the embryo. Of course, he did not do it on purpose; he meant well – he wanted to uncover the nature's secret and to help it. Instead, he ruined the whole thing. If you keep picking at an embryo with a needle, you will kill it. That's exactly what he did.

The Technique of Treating the Embryo

And so, the embryo is "**the something**" from which the artistic work *develops*. The embryo is the essential condition for art.

How is this "something" conceived?

As with any conception in the natural world, it occurs from the collision and merger of two kindred forces that simultaneously oppose and complete one another.

The first force is the "I" of the actor – the complete content of his personality; all of his abilities and qualities, obvious and hidden; his life experience; his centuries-old ancestral experience; his current state, and his creative readiness, and his predisposition at this very minute.

The second force comes from without. It is the material that finds its way into the actor's soul. In our etudes [or in a play], it is the text, the assigned actions, and the circumstances (predetermined, or originated in the course of an etude [or a scene]). Finally, it is the surrounding environment and the partner.

The contact of all of these materials with the actor's internal content causes a merger and interaction and, finally, the embryo's conception.

Don't think that the actor's embryo can come in the form of some concrete and distinct "image," like the flowering cherry blossom that appeared to Chekhov at his conception of *The Cherry Orchard*. The embryo of the actor comes *already in the form of manifestations* – manifestations and urges that are involuntary and subconscious. The embryo appeared; this means that the life of the role has begun – the life of the artist's ego, creatively merged with the imaginary persona of the character.

However, the presence of the embryo isn't all. You have to know how to take advantage of its appearance and create conditions beneficial for its growth. A second too slow, and the embryo will be irrevocably lost. In nature, many things perish; it isn't afraid of death and murder – indeed, a chicken doesn't come from every egg, nor does an herb or tree grow from every seed.

The artist can't be so wasteful. Not least of all because a man's lifetime and that of nature differ in their longevity. Nature can fling things left and right – life, death, beauty, horror – in the end, through millions of centuries, something will come of it . . . Not so with a man, who only has a short four or five decades at his disposal . . . And even those are filled with illnesses, suffering, and catastrophes . . . Yet, there are so many things to be done, you can't grasp them all.

The ability to completely surrender, without looking back, to that which comes from you, as it was said in the chapters on "green-lighting," is one of the actor's chief qualities. The ability to feel the embryo and give in to it bravely, and whole-heartedly, is the chief quality of the **actor-artist**. The actor-creator.

Our simple little exercises develop this precious quality in actors, in addition to all of the other necessary qualities.

From everything that has just been said, it's obvious that the embryo is something fresh, new, newly conceived; something that is yet to come into the world.

For us, actors and directors, it is the first thing – **what** is conceived upon the reading of the play, or even while reading it. It's something that we can't yet express with words, even something that we don't suspect within ourselves. By the way, there's no point in trying to pull an embryo out into the world before its time. If you do so, you kill it. It will express itself through the process of searching and trying.

How can you determine the moment of its conception? And how can you help its development?

I'll repeat: the embryo of the actor isn't some kind of image that appears in my imagination as something *that is located outside me* (like the image of a character I would need to imitate later); the actor's embryo *is the premonition of a new "I."*

Don't expect this new "I" to seize your entire being. It has *yet to be* fully formed. It is only a premonition: a nucleus, an embryo. At this point, our main care is to help it develop and materialize.

In theory, this question is still unresolved, but in practice, it is solved quite simply.

Give way to all of these sprouts – nothing else is required. Did some thoughts begin to flow? Let them. Did feelings and sensations arise? Don't hinder them; let urges arise, along with some subconscious inclinations. Don't impinge upon them. Do some kinds of small automatic movements break out? Give them complete freedom. Completely surrender yourself to everything that you have inside and everything that is asking to come out.

EVERYTHING is included in the embryo. All of the artistic work with its content and form. This includes all of its established and unestablished "elements": its bits and tasks, supertask and through-action, its rhythms, and anything else you can think of!

If you start to dig into it and cut it to pieces, you'll injure it or entirely destroy it. Give in to it with complete faith, without doubts or hesitations. This is one of the greatest secrets of our "technique."

For that matter, the "technique" at hand seems redundant. This appears to be a repeat of what was already said in the chapters on the *Beginning, Involuntary Movements*, and a few others . . . This is true . . . Except that there, this significant word had yet to be spoken: *embryo*. Now that it's been said, the creative process becomes quite clear. Otherwise, where does this all come from? And how?

Some actors don't require much explanation. They repeat their lines (be it the lines of an etude or those of a play), and the *life* begins on its own. What is there to think of? They just give in to this life.

And then there are those fastidious actors: they have to know everything inside and out. They need to assign a name to everything and to stick a label on it: "So, what is '*this thing*' that suddenly 'appears?' Is it through-action? Or a super task? An idea? Or perhaps an image?"

Ah, these analytic-decomposers! Where do they get it from? Is it acquired, or is it their very nature? Perhaps they are researchers rather than actors? Since you are working with them, however, it is essential to divert them from this decomposing. Of course, it would have been better not to theorize during training. However, as dangerous as it may be, you better tell them: what appears *at once* isn't the through-action, nor is it a super task, etc., *but the* **embryo**.

It contains everything – everything at once.

Organic life onstage, and all its force, is concentrated in the embryo. You have to see to it and ensure that the *embryo appears, and you* **need not hinder** its actions. If it *didn't appear* or didn't awaken, and we are in the throes of anarchy, it means the embryo was destroyed.

All right. Let's suppose that we destroyed the embryo due to ineptitude or from an incorrect school. And what if it never came into existence?

Now we've arrived at what is, strictly speaking, the most essential question – the question of the emergence of the embryo.

It's possible to theorize here to the end of time, but practice answers the question simply.

If you stop reading this book right now and put it aside, giving yourself complete freedom, then your own personal life will begin. If this book has tired you out and hasn't found a resonance in your soul, then you will begin to think about things that genuinely interest you. If, however, the book has touched you to the quick, you will reexamine your personal experience in light of the new ideas that you took from this book. In short, it will nevertheless go on – your *personal, individual life*.

Creativity isn't just your personal individual life. It is the creation of something new.

As it's already been said, in order for the embryo to be conceived, two forces must meet: my personal "I" (with my present and past) and the "material" from the outside (the author's text, the partner, etc.). They meet, merge, interact – and the embryo is conceived.

So, these two forces are necessary for the conception of the embryo. And *these forces are always there*.

". . . And what if, perhaps," you might say, not without malice, "conception *doesn't always* occur!"

"No 'ifs,'" I would answer, "conception *always* occurs! But you miss it. You miss it, because you don't imagine the embryo as it should be. The embryo – it *already* is action, it *already* is manifestation, it *already* is – life. There is no point in repeating it – it has been described more than once and particularly thoroughly in the chapter "On the Beginning," (I direct you back to that chapter that explains "how everything appears on its own").[1]

★★★

It is quite easy to destroy the embryo: in the beginning it doesn't have any defensive power – it's enough to step on any sprout and that's it – everything is over for it. But if you give the sprout time, it will split the cliff in two, if it was peeping through its crevice; as the years pass, it will grow into such a giant that two people – or even 10 – won't be able to budge it.

It's the same in psychological life: a small step, even accidental exposure, can cause a deadly vice. Ideas and passions, obscure from the start, bring people to the stake.

Such is the strength of the embryo at its peak, and such is its weakness at its start.

★★★

The sculptor, architect, or painter creates plenty of preliminary sketches and drafts. Only upon the completion of this preliminary period do they turn to the actual work.

If a dozen missteps are necessary for every artist, they are no less necessary for the actor. To not understand that is to not understand the essence of the actor's art. To immediately require final – "correct" – results of the actor means to require *too little*.

For us, actors, rehearsals serve as drafts and tests. We don't have anything to fear from taking incorrect steps. On the contrary, it is only through these missteps that we can find the correct path.

This might seem contradictory. How can it be? First he claims that the embryo appears, and everything in it is correct – you just have to give in to it. And now he says that anything that happens immediately is never correct. A contradiction!

There is no contradiction. The embryo is the *seed* of the plant, from which, under the right conditions, the plant itself will grow, *its outward appearance never resembling that of its seed*. Nevertheless, it is still the spawn of that seed.

You have to catch the embryo; otherwise, it will disappear.

When you read something and it touches you, the embryo emerges. It emerges and disappears. Moreover, every reaction can be an embryo.

– What do you mean – every reaction? Then why are there so few artistic works?

– Will a chicken necessarily come from every egg? Or a fir or pine grows from every seed in a cone? Or a fish from every roe? Most of them perish. It's the same way with our embryo-ideas.

This is why all writers always carry a notebook with them, where they can record every immediate thought that emerges in their head and every fact that seems to mean something interesting. If you let them slip by just a bit, they will fly away without a trace.

It doesn't happen just because one has a "weak memory": you can remember the thought, but when you try to write it down, having let some time pass, it apparently loses something of its content and becomes bland, boring, and lifeless.

Why? It is very simple: there was an embryo, a nucleus of an entire new creative idea. You should have grabbed the end of its thread and pulled it out. You should have rewound the ball of its hidden feelings and thoughts into a new ball, objective and visible for everyone. You should have given the embryo a chance to develop. If you don't give it way; if you don't let it take shape freely, it will disappear without a trace. Moreover, a partially developed and embodied embryo dies if you let time pass and put off its complete embodiment.

There is another thing: a kind of unconscious chastity. It doesn't allow you to speak about your painting, novel, or role.

Every time you speak about it, it's as if you lose something that was meant for your work. You spoke about it and, by doing so, you released some kind of charge. You spoke about it, and now you neither can nor want to act, write, or paint. This phenomenon has its own laws, and they will be discussed in detail in the coming books.

★★★

Pushkin wrote his poems with inspiration, but later corrected, reworked, re-edited them. Did he search for form?

It's very important to clarify for yourself that the future form is already present in the egg. Just as the future giant tree is already enclosed in the kernel. Pushkin's alterations and revisions of his works were merely the liberation and bringing out into the light the sprout that instantly "shoots from the earth" in the moment of inspiration. The entire content and form pre-exists within it.

The process of altering, revising, and generally *working* on the artistic creation isn't the *pursuit* of some kind of form, but the *liberation* of the form that is anticipated. It is the coming into the world, and the nurturing of a nucleus – *of the embryo* – that already exists. As practice shows, it's not an easy matter, and it is rarely carried out to the end.

(While working on the subject of the Decembrist uprising, Tolstoy [1952: 151] wrote in his diary: "I pray to God that he allows me to do something that is at least approximately close to what I want.")

This process of creative birth and the nurturing of your child (the process of altering, revising and perfecting) obviously isn't simply a process of the refinement of form. Behind every new form, new content is hidden. It means that, in "trying on" this or that form, the poet is trying on content that is more or less different from the original. In other words, when working *as if* on the form, he is essentially working on new content – modifying, bettering, and specifying it.

What is the embryo in its relation to form and content? It is that wondrous *interplay of form and content* that was mentioned a few pages prior.

Note

1 See Book Three, Part Two, Chapter 10 and Part Three, Chapter 27.

9
Synthesis and Grasp

On "Through-action"

Let's take the life of any person: you can view it as a chain of accidents, or else you can see in it one whole.

Take my life for example: my meeting with Sulerzhitsky at wrestling – was that an accident? Or the fact that Stanislavsky needed a gymnast to train his son, and I happened to be there – was that an accident? As for my meeting with Sulerzhitsky, it led to numerous other encounters: with composer Vladimir Pol [1875–1962] and sculptor Sergey Merkurov [1881–1952], spiritual teacher George Gurdjieff and his colleague Thomas de Hartmann, as well as with psychologist Alexei Ukhtomsky. There is no describing what, in its turn, had come out of these encounters.

And if you consider that my meeting with Sulerzhitsky springs back to my athletic pursuits, it is all the more surprising . . .

In the play, too, you need to grasp the inner ties, instead of random accidents; these inner ties create the basic thread – the through-action.

I desire (perhaps even unconsciously). I have my internal charge – my unrecognized aspiration. And so people come my way who, without even knowing it, they "serve" me, obeying my deeply seated designs. (If you prefer, you could say that they obey the designs of my fate). I can feel how people and circumstances turn up as if by magic. Prentice Mulford [1834–1891] explicitly gives us the recipe for how to "wait" in a skillful way. [See "Subconscious Waiting."]

On the other hand, I feel that I myself am a pawn, and that I exist *for* someone else, and speak for someone else. My acquaintance with Boris Grigoriev [1886–1939], the artist – isn't it an example in which I played an entirely passive role as a messenger? Or take Igor [Stanislavsky's son] and many other more or less striking examples.

In the same way, a play features those people who steer it and those who are passive. These latter may be stronger and more interesting than those primary characters, but in this particular chain of events, they are passive; they obey the through-force or the through-action of the play. It binds them together; only through it do they have the right to appear onstage. It alone creates what is known as an ensemble. The ensemble isn't something that was thought-up; it is a necessary force of life.

A single person may propel the play, and be at its center, or else it can be a whole movement – for example, a revolutionary wave. However, it's also true that this whole movement sometimes can only travel arm-in-arm with a person, serving his needs.

Through-Action and Super-Task as a Path to Synthesis

Most people are capable of learning a particular field or subject only within the boundaries of what they can take in. (Some singularly gifted individuals make an exception, but they are rare.)

As for mediocrity, it mostly takes in significantly less of what it is given – it doesn't grasp it in full. Going forward, it uses only what it had acquired, with a greater or lesser degree of success.

A gifted person behaves differently. Firstly, he tries to comprehend the subject *fully*, down to its very essence. He tries to grasp not only what he has been taught, but even further. Secondly, he only recognizes practical comprehension. It is here, in trying to comprehend the subject *completely* – in theory and in practice – that he inevitably crosses over *beyond the border* of what he was taught and what he mastered. Involuntarily, he takes *a step further*.

Thus, a strange, paradoxical phenomenon occurs: wishing to comprehend his field in full, and to gain a foothold in it, the person *steps into a new, unexplored field*, in spite of all of his intentions.

This is how arithmetic crossed into algebra, and chemistry stepped into the field of physics. Similar things happen in art.

In fact, this is exactly what happened in the art of theatre when the so-called "through-action" was developed. The difference is only that here, the artist-inventor himself [Stanislavsky] surpassed his own discovery. Thus, he went beyond the borders that he himself had set.

When Stanislavsky, catering to the weaknesses of emotionally rational actors, ventured upon the path of never-ending analysis, he ultimately (roughly speaking) found himself before a butchered, murdered play and role. Better than anyone, he understood the awkwardness of his situation.

Everything turned into scraps that exist independently of one another. Yet, at the very beginning the role was anticipated as something whole. And so, having reread the play again, he tries to recall his first impression, which has completely faded and become erased. He asks the question – what is the main, fundamental thing in this play? ("How does the task become the super-task, how does action become through-action? I act, but for what purpose?"). Finally, he sees that the play has its own thought and its own task. All other tasks fit into the main one, like the bricks that ultimately make up one building.

Take Pushkin's *Boris Godunov* – what is the main idea of this play?

> . . . naught can give us peace
> Mid worldly cares, nothing save—only conscience!
> Healthy she triumphs over wickedness,
> Over dark slander; but if in her be found
> A single casual stain, then misery.
> With what a deadly sore my soul doth smart;
> My heart, with venom filled, doth like a hammer
> Beat in mine ears reproach; all things revolt me,
> And my head whirls, and in my eyes are children
> Dripping with blood; and gladly would I flee,
> But nowhere can find refuge—horrible!
> Pitiful he whose conscience is unclean!
>
> *[Pushkin 1918: 30]*

This is the main idea of the entire play; the main task of the play; the *task **above all tasks** – the super-task* of the play. As soon as you miss it, the whole construction will sag.

Every role serves in the construction of this complex building, and every role fulfills its own particular task in the construction.

What is a role (if we take it separately from the play)?

The role *is the whole life of the character* – complete, indivisible, beginning on the first day of his life and ending with his final breath.

The author only presents one of its segments – sometimes a year, sometimes a week, a day, and sometimes only an hour. This does not change a thing. Therefore, if we want for the role to be more or less alive and truthful, then we should completely know, feel, and perceive the entire life of the character.

Knowing this, the emotionally rational artist proceeds with the following reasoning: beyond minor desires, tasks, and actions, every person has a main purpose of his whole life – the "super-task," and a main action of his life – "the through-action."

What, for example, was the super-task of Boris Godunov's entire life? To achieve power? Perhaps that is it. It's what he **wants** above all else, and what overshadows everything in his eyes. As if from his earliest years there has been a motor whirring in his depths . . . producing that same energy – a will for power. This energy fuels his entire life, his every step. Invisible, it permeates all of his thoughts and deeds. The main thing that he does in life, his main action, the **through-action** of his whole life: the achievement of power.

How does the emotionally-rational director (and actor) use this discovery?

They suggest the following: let's reexamine the entire role from this point of view – bit by bit. Let us penetrate each bit with this through-action; let's coordinate the task of each of the bits (small, medium, and large) with the main task of the role, with its super-task – "I want power."

This threading together of the disjointed bits of action – into one "through-action" – reminded its inventor of the threading together of beads that have been spilled and scattered across a table. I take one bead at a time, and put them in their appropriate order; I thread them together on one string. Before you know it, a beautiful necklace appears in place a messy pile of beads.

However, this approach to the role failed to produce something essential – the miraculous spark of life hasn't burst through all these bits. The role didn't come to life. It became more meaningful and comprehensible . . . all of its parts began to match up to one another . . . With time, these parts will grind to fit. All together, they will produce an impression *of something that resembles* a "believable" living person.

But . . . this is all!

When the inventor of this method compared it to the stringing together of beads on a thread, he was a great prophet. He didn't even suspect that with this comparison he exposed the **mechanical** nature of this method. You can string dead beads onto a dead thread and you'll get a necklace. Is it dead? Indeed, no one expects for the dead pieces of glass to come to life! [Stanislavsky omitted this example from his book after I pointed out its treacherous mechanicalness. –*Author's Note*]

Wouldn't things entirely change if, instead of an inanimate object, we took a living creature – for example, a bird that has been cut into pieces? It needs to be **revived**. But how? To dovetail the wings, to insert the removed heart, to reattach the dead head, and to sew every part back together . . . Except, this method won't achieve resurrection and life either . . .

Stanislavsky's Searches for a Transition from the Mechanical to the Organic

Upset over these uncomforting results, the inventor of the "through-action" began to search for different paths to merge the divided and disparate bits of the play and the role. He stopped "stringing" together all of the tasks with one "through-action," and began to *merge* several tasks *into one*. This process is brilliantly described on pages 552–559 [of the original Russian 1938 ed.; see Stanislavsky 2008: 332–337] of his book *An Actor's Work*. There, the process is recreated based on the conversation between Othello and Iago.

After the actor has performed all of his minor tasks well, having fulfilled them several times separately, one by one—perhaps at that point all these minor tasks can be replaced with one. When this big task is carried out, it **alone** would remain conscious, while all the minor tasks would become *subconscious*. According to Stanislavsky, they would fulfill *themselves on their own*; there's no need to give them a conscious thought; they would be united by one overarching circumstance. In general, the entire complex scene would transform into a singular piece. You can take care of every scene this way. Finally, you can combine several scenes into one.

And so, combining our tasks and bits, one after another, we ultimately find ourselves with no more than two or three tasks. The other tasks are all included in these.

This method of "merging the tasks" and "converting conscious tasks to subconscious" no longer belongs to analysis. Rather, it belongs to the realm of synthesis.

The thought has probably occurred to you: this is a synthesis, but in order to arrive at this synthesis, we would need to have subjected the role to analysis first. Does this mean that preliminary analysis and dissection are still necessary for the successful fulfillment of synthesis?

For now, I'll answer this only as I have before: all living individual beings, be they plants, animals, or people, were conceived and developed in nature from a nucleus or from an embryo. For the embryo's conception, its coming into the world, and its development—*a dissection isn't required*.

The Living "Through-action" Is Indefinable: Once Defined, It Stops Being Itself, and Becomes Something Different

However, no matter how we merge the tasks, or lessen their number, in the end two, or at least one (super-task) will still remain and be conscious. For as long as even one task is conscious, then it no longer complies with the laws of life and art. How come?!

It is very simple: each one of us has his own "super-task" and "through-action." Do we know them? Let's examine how it happens in practice.

The actress M devotes her entire life entirely to art. She says so herself, and it is obvious to everyone around her – art is the goal of her life! . . . She marries, she has children . . . she leaves the stage of her own volition and gives herself over to a happy family life. What happened? Did her through-action change? If it changed, it means it isn't a *through-action*.

It's just that neither she nor anyone around her got it right. There was a striving toward creativity, toward beauty. Art turned up. A gift for acting was discovered. So, a person began to realize her through-action through art.

Then, something else appeared on her way: true love, a chance to create beauty in life itself – it turned out that she had an even greater gift for creating this kind of beauty, and the person left the stage. It couldn't have been any other way.

Let us be honest and confess: we don't know either our through-action or our super-task. It's more likely that someone on the outside can define them for us.

Let's suppose that I have sensed it, and I have defined: my super-task is not beauty, not truth, not the creation of everlasting things, and not the experience of the world through my art (as it has always been for all great artists), but it is just a career! Praise, stardom, awards, money, public recognition, and resting on my own laurels.

I might not even have suspected it myself: I keep talking of higher art, of eternity, of morals; yet in my soul, I am a climber, and this is the whole point and goal of my ingenuity. I didn't know, I didn't suspect it . . . but now, after an intimate talk with some reader of human nature I have to confess: yes, it is so! I look back at my life, and I see that everything I have been proud of had a completely different motive. It was apparently set in motion by completely different springs than I, or everyone else for that matter, could imagine at the time . . .

And now . . . do I recognize these motives right now? They set me in motion, and cause the mechanism of my heart to beat, yet I don't recognize or sense them. However, as soon as I do recognize them, and get a chance to see them from the outside, I thus put a stop to them.

It would seem that now that we know the main purpose of our lives, we can boldly allow ourselves to take that path. Isn't it so?

In point of fact, something different happens. So long as you and those around you *didn't know* your true super-task, and so long as you and everyone else thought that your life's purpose was art, worship, and other such lofty words, then your hidden careerism was unnoticeably doing its bit in the dark. But as soon as it was exposed, it completely transformed. As soon as I understood that, frankly speaking, deep down I couldn't care less about art – then why should I keep deceiving myself? Deceiving others – perhaps; but myself?

And if I deceive only others (while knowing my own true essence), then my through-action and super-task have already become something different: not just career or "unconscious career," but "career by all means!"

We do a lot of things well only because we do them either unconsciously (submitting to our instincts and reflexes) or half-consciously.

How does this relate to "character?" After all, the knowledge of it is in us, and it doesn't get in the way. Doesn't it mean that knowledge of the through-action also doesn't have to get in the way? The answer is this: the word "knowledge" does not really apply to character. It is more of a half-conscious sensation. To know – let alone wag your tongue about such things – is to lose them. (The question of "point of view on character" will be described later).

And so it turns out that through-action is only genuine when it is unrecognized or, at the very least, merely anticipated. Try "carrying it out," and you can *say goodbye* to it *as a living,* genuinely *real* thing.

"The will to power" of Boris Godunov (just as it was in the aforementioned careerism) is imperceptible and indescribable for Boris himself. As soon as the actor named it for himself, he mixed a spontaneous feeling with *deliberateness.* (Delicate organic matter mixed with crude material chemistry.) This is why, when the actor can elaborate on his role well, he cannot play it genuinely.

People think that by saying "He doesn't even know what he is playing" they debase the actor and wipe him off the face of the earth – while in fact they give him the highest praise. The apple tree also doesn't know the taste of its own apples.

The Path of "Tasks" (To the Intellectually Willful)

If a child bumps his head and begins to cry, an experienced mom will immediately shake a rattle in front of him. She will wave it before the child and say, "look here, look at the toy, look . . . what a pretty toy . . ." The child's eyes will open wide at the rattle; he will reach for it and . . . he will forget about the bump. Perhaps we can borrow something from the mother's methods?

And so, in order to distract the actor's attention from the audience, they suggest the actor busy himself with something, start fulfilling some kind of "actions," begin to do what the character should be (or could be) doing onstage at this point. Occupied by "action," the actor forgets about the audience.

It's the same thing with "tasks" – you have "to want" what the character wants. The action springs from this "want," occupying the actor and distracting him from the audience.

This method is tried and true, if it is carried out correctly. It only has one shortcoming: every two or three minutes (or even more often) you have to think up a new distraction mechanism, a new "task," and a new "action." Otherwise, with one task being just fulfilled (and another yet to come in), an emptiness forms. From this emptiness all kinds of fears attack the defenseless actor: "Ah, they're looking at me; ah, what should I do next?; ah, how do I overcome my fright?, and so on."

It's true that the matter may be mended if all tasks are well identified and follow each other in a believable sequence. If, on top of that, these tasks are connected by one shared task ("the super-task"), then they will fill the actor, and no emptiness will form.

What's more, with frequent repetition, tasks begin to arise automatically, from habit, on their own; the actor no longer needs to evoke them . . .

Similarly, we automatically glance at the clock as we walk, throw off the blanket, stretch, wash, dress, eat breakfast, etc. All of this is habitual and requires no will effort or concentration; on the contrary, these most habitual actions pull us in, and we get carried away by them.

It's exactly the same with those actions that have been performed onstage multiple times, one after the other; they now occur on their own, in their habitual order. If you start one, it will trigger the next, and the third . . . Such action engages the actor; he is ensnared by it. For a few moments, he might even forget himself and begin to feel like his character.

Thus, in several moments of the role he no longer just *depicts* the character, but **he begins to live** as the character.

If a play has been put on many times, then this "living state" becomes all the more habitual. Finally, in several roles – especially those close to his soul – the actor might "come to life" so strongly that everything begins to *happen* on its own (just as it does in life).

Of course, when this occurs, the actor involuntarily steps beyond the bounds of the drilled actions, "tasks" and "adaptations" – life begins for him, and this means freedom and improvisation. Each time, he plays it a little bit differently, depending on his own personal state of being, on his partner, and on random things that happen onstage.

But I must confess that such instances are rare. It is the ideal. It happens only for the very talented. In the majority of cases, from one performance to the next, the acting gradually "turns into clichés," becomes mechanical, its "life" evaporating without a trace.

We need another path. It used to exist (take Yermolova), and it should be rediscovered. This path is the one of synthesis.

Actors with a high dose of intellectualism can come to life only by exceeding their boundaries and crossing over from analysis to synthesis, *from logic to a prelogical mentality*.

This will be discussed in greater detail in the next book.

★★★

The emotionally willful artist-inventor [Stanislavsky] arrived at synthesis ("through-action," "super-task," "I am") when he had learned his techniques "to perfection." Similarly, the emotionally willful actor who is capable of reaching the point of perfection, in one of his favorite roles, steps over the boundaries of will and rationality. Having done so in some of his performances, he becomes the "I am," that is to say that he lives by his circumstances. As long as he lives, it means that he is already beyond the conscious "activity" of the tasks, and so on. In short, the emotionally willful actor, who has *gone beyond his boundaries*, finds himself in the realm of live artistic creativity.

This state already has a lot in common with affectivity: improvisation, freedom, living, the grasp of this person's (the role's) whole life, of his entirety . . . There is only one thing missing – complete liberation from brakes; this "whole life" is mundane, and the grasp is of a small, insignificant person.

This being an act of artistic creation, it does, nevertheless, have philosophical aspects to it. The actor would inspire philosophical thoughts with his role – the grasp of the thinker will be in it. Yet, this does not make the actor an affective type. He has a grasp, but it isn't so much the grasp of passion, but that of ideas.

Comedy has its own grasp and its own philosophy – the grasp and philosophy of the small feelings that belong to small people; they do their work of destruction or creation meticulously, persistently, like a long autumn rain. (Light as it may be, it is capable of drenching the earth down to the roots.) Like earthworms, they slowly but ceaselessly churn the earth and carry out their huge, yet invisible, work.

The Suddenness of the Creative Epiphany: Synthesis

You look at the wall: points, smudges, zigzags, stains . . . lighter, darker . . . Suddenly, you shiver: a face is looking right at you – you can see it clearly . . . all these stains and smudges had suddenly merged, and ceased being stains – there are the eyes, there's the nose, the beard, forehead, wrathful evil eyes, fixed right at you . . .

How did you manage not to notice it before? You kept looking at the wall, studying the stains on it. The old man was looking out at you from the wall then too. How did you miss it? How could you be so indifferent?

The same thing happens with the actor, except that the old man isn't **outside of me, but I myself am the old man**!

This old man, he's alive. Everything is in him, including his through-action, the whole of his difficult life path, and all of the circumstances that made him so evil and scary – all of his misfortunes and grief, his hopes and disappointments, and, ultimately, his complete lack of faith in people and in the truth.

This is the highest point. It is what happens when someone points me to the through-action. What is this pointing about? I look at the wall – and I don't see it. Someone points out to me – there's the nose, there's the forehead . . . Ah! I see it, I see it! I saw it, and my imagination began to work – it created the image.

★★★

This divining; this rise of a living feeling; this instant coming to life is called synthesis (although synthesis, truth be told, isn't necessarily "coming to life." It *is* in organic chemistry; in inorganic chemistry, however, it is not. Isn't our work, however, a living one? If it's such, this means that our synthesis means coming to life).

Perhaps we can find a different name for this moment? The moment of grasp? The moment of creative fantasy? The moment of epiphany of talent? The moment of "breaking one's banks"?

Organic synthesis is instantaneous. It is unconscious. And what is conscious synthesis? Can synthesis, in fact, come from analysis?

And what if it can? At first you look at it and you see a mess; then you begin to examine it in parts and to analyze it – by comparing these parts, you suddenly figure out the common thread. The moment of epiphany follows.

Yet, there is a difference here. Regular *conscious* synthesis is a mosaic. In it, the old man doesn't come to life. In it, the stain would **resemble** an old man. The old man would be "*as if alive.*" This difference is crucial.

The Water of Life

Perhaps it is impossible to get by without analysis?

What, then, could allow the spark of life? What could resurrect the life of the role? There is something (the only thing in the world) – the Water of Life! If you sprinkle something with it, it will come to life.

The Water of Life is talent. Oh, the miracles it can perform! If there is talent – no matter how you cut it and chop it, or even grind it to the dust – it will come through.

Perhaps you imagine it this way: talent comes in, recognizes the through-action, and starts to stitch up your old seams?

Not a bit of it! All the seams begin to burst. Just watch it remake them, while you stand dumbfounded by your own lack of wit. Only now you see what kind of pieces your role used to be made of – dissimilar, eclectic, false and contrived.

With assured unceremonious calm, the talent steps on your most treasured valuables . . . and you see that they were only needed so that you could refuse and discard them . . .

However, perhaps it has to be that way? Perhaps one always needs to go through this thorny path of mistakes? Perhaps, without it, art would be shallow and overly impulsive?

Analysis and Distancing Oneself from the Role

When Yermolova left the stage, the younger actresses who inherited her roles of youthful heroines, naturally, turned to her for advice and assistance. [She later returned and performed almost until the end of her life, but in roles that were more appropriate for her age. –*Author's Note*]

She wanted to help them with all her heart, invited them over and tried to share all of her experience. To the question: "How is this role played?" she would answer something like this: "She loves him, but he doesn't love her . . ." and would become silent.

The sharp young actress, who had heard a lot about new methods for working on the role, of course wasn't satisfied. "Even I know that, Maria Nikolayevna, it's obvious from the play, but what else?" "What else?" Maria Nikolayevna would begin to get worried, "What else? You see . . . he doesn't love her . . . and it's very hard for her . . . because she loves him . . . There . . ." She would become embarrassed and blush, and here the young enlightened actress would begin to assail her with questions about "the inner line of the role," character analysis, about the climax of the role, and finally, about the through-action, bits and tasks . . . Maria Nikolayevna would go hot and cold; she would grab a bottle of smelling salts off of her desk, smell them, and restlessly press her handkerchief to her lips . . . She wouldn't know where to escape, and would whisper, embarrassed: "I don't know . . . I don't know anything . . . We couldn't do this . . . We couldn't do anything. . ." She would feel utterly crushed and destroyed and, in the end she would guiltily say: "My darling . . . it seems that I can't help you with anything . . . if you'd like, I'll act it for you – maybe then you'll notice something . . ."

And . . . she would act. Books could be written about this acting, but they would be useless – you'd have to be Tolstoy to describe how she acted.

I heard these stories from the "students," and I heard them secondhand. Most people would relate it as a curious anecdote. People told it in order to illustrate how our current art has gone so far ahead of the primitive art of our fathers and grandfathers.

Who could blame them? The first actress, the flower and sun of our theatre, and suddenly she has no idea what she is playing . . . And now look at us! We understand everything; we examined the role from all possible points of view; we can give an entire lecture about the role! It's true that we somehow don't produce such a great, overwhelming effect on the audience . . . There we humbly declare that we don't produce it because we aren't genii – we're just ordinary people . . . Or perhaps also because the audience is not the same . . . It is not as spontaneous as it used to be; it is colder and more restrained.

We can only chuckle at this final thought, but as far as the genius part is concerned – that much is true.

Then, perhaps it wouldn't hurt to learn from this genius?

No one can say that Yermolova performed unevenly or sporadically, and was dependent on "rushes of inspiration." The general opinion was that she performed harmoniously. It means that the role was *made*, and made correctly.

So how can we explain that she could act and even demonstrate her role so well, but didn't know and couldn't tell much about the person she was playing?

Now try to answer the question: what do you represent – you, the person reading these lines? Evil? Or kind? A scoundrel perhaps? Honest? Or funny? Which quality dominates in you? What attracts you more than anything in life? What do you not know about yourself? Are you ever puzzled about yourself? What about you attracts other people, and what makes them avoid you?

Questions like this would make any of us put on our thinking cap. Having thought it over, we would then have to confess with amazement: it's true that I don't know myself very well! And what's more, it is quite difficult to talk about yourself. Although, I can talk about someone else all you want. [Of course, there are also people who can *only talk about themselves* – exclusively so. But they don't even know this about themselves, and would be very surprised if someone were to paint them an honest portrait of their own persona. They know themselves only from one side – the side that they like, and they avoid all other sides . . . –*Author's Note*]

That's just the point. Yermolova *became* the character. Therefore, it was difficult for her to talk about herself. As for those who speak about their roles with eloquence and ease, they feel the role *not within, but outside of themselves*. It is a stranger to them – one they could easily dissect from the outside. And that's exactly what they do.

They dissect the play, and each of its characters, and each bit of the role. They sit and split hairs for dozens of hours . . . To be completely honest, almost all of our Moscow theatres practice this. Why do they do this?

This is because a majority of our directors possesses a large dose of rationality and reasoning. And also, because that's how they were taught. After all, there isn't another school. Nothing tangible or solid can be set against the rationality of the imperative "system" (logical and "scientifically justified"). Nothing – except, perhaps, for random flights of inspiration. These flights, however, come for no apparent reason and go when you least expect it (sometimes at the most crucial moment). It's true that there have been some who *had their own system*. They had one, and they employed it successfully. That's how it was for Yermolova. But it didn't even occur to them that it was a *system*. They did not suspect that it was a great discovery, and that future generations would have to *wrack their brains* to come up with it.

And then, there are also those who either received some exciting and powerful methods from their teachers or somehow came up with them on their own. However, they keep those a secret and save them for their own personal use.

What is an affective actor to do in this situation?

There is only one "escape" – to employ the generally accepted methods that have been inscribed into law; otherwise you would gain the reputation of a backward ignoramus . . . And how is he not an ignoramus? He doesn't want to use the latest scientific discoveries, groundbreaking and indisputable! So, the affective actor forces himself to use methods that are completely foreign and harmful to him.

The actively-willful actor loves to scrutinize the subtlest emotions of the role, and the psychological subtleties of the play. Unlike the affective actor, he loves it and he knows how to do it. Why? Now you know – because he sees it somewhat *from the outside.*

Meanwhile, this quality – to see, understand, and scrutinize – comes at a high price. The idea, content, and the character might come to him in all their clarity, complexity, and excitement; yet *they never capture him wholeheartedly, to the full.*

The Tragic Is Outside of the Emotionally Rational Actors' Reach: "My Own Flower Pot": Moscow Art Theatre – Chekhov and Shakespeare

And so, since the emotionally rational actor sees things somewhat from the outside, the feelings of the role **do not** *capture* him fully. (His strongly developed braking system also has a lot to do with this.) This is especially true of those feelings that are heightened, strong, and tempestuous . . . That is, in his imagination he sees them well. But . . . as soon as he tries to approach them (no longer in his imagination; no longer theoretically, but in practice) – nothing comes of it. The only things that do come of it are "effort" and "pushing," fakeness and lies.

As Stanislavsky said so well in his book, to artistically embody what you don't actually feel is impossible. [Demidov is paraphrasing Stanislavsky's (2009: 32) thought that "stock-in-trade . . . is what mostly happens when you take on something . . . you neither know nor feel."]

And how do you "feel" it; how do you give birth to such a grandiose feeling? By all appearances, this is outside the scope of the rational-cerebral actor.

He is smart enough to understand the absurdity of his situation and not to shoulder an intolerable burden. And so he starts to make compromises – at first with pain in this heart; later, having reconciled himself to it . . . Soon it becomes a habit. He passes up the grand image that temptingly flashed in his imagination, and he makes it manageable – he brings the character and his feelings, as described by the author, *closer to himself* and to his everyday persona. (With it, he unintentionally compromises the idea of the play). In some places, he would clip or compress the role . . . More often, he would use simpler means: he would plant the author "in his own flower pot." Have you seen palm trees planted in small flowerpots here in the north?

In their native land, in Africa, where there is an abundance of land and sun – it is a giant tree, taller than a 10-story building. Planted in a flower pot – although it still lives and grows – can it be really called a palm?

A distinctly emotional type, and even more so the affective type, doesn't need to "rouse" his feelings. All he has to do is to barely think about the circumstances of the play, and the feelings burst out of him on their own and overwhelm him. Such is his "mechanism."

The less emotionality an actor possesses, and the more developed his braking system – the more difficult this is. To tell the truth, only the affective actor feels at home in tragedy. As for others, they feel at home in drama – and even more so in comedy. This is their natural environment.

In this natural element they can even "green-light" their freedom. They improvise; they stop constraining themselves to the boundaries of the blocking and psychological patterns. Here they can reach the highest levels – not only of art, but of artistry.

Of course, they also experience heightened emotions and impulses in life, but they are used to stifling them at the very start.

Can one imagine more perfect performances of the Chekhov plays than those done at the Moscow Art Theatre in the first years of its existence? The actors wonderfully grasped *the technique of living onstage, as in life.* Or, more precisely, how *they* were used to living in life. Voynitskys and Prozorovs walked upon the stage boards not as inwardly significant, beautiful people written by Chekhov, but rather as those similar to the actors – an everyday intelligentsia, not very smart and extremely lukewarm. It was not for nothing that prevailing opinion was that it was a good theatre, it's just that there weren't any actors in it. It didn't leave an impression on everyone, but only on the intelligentsia – because Chekhov described their life, their needs, and their people. These performances were full of photographic realism, which is what won the audiences. It passed for truth and artistic insight. This, of course, was a delusion. The performing of Chekhov was naturalistic, without grasp, without grand feelings and big ideas.

And then they took up tragedy – Shakespeare . . . They wanted to do everything as truthfully and realistically . . . and they started to make Shakespeare's text as true to life as they made Chekhov's.

But they misfired.

What happened? Shakespeare doesn't need the truth? Ah, no! Of course not. He needs truth perhaps more than any other playwright.

But this truth isn't our *mundane* truth – filtered, with brakes, with concealment. There, the truth should be to the very end, to the very bottom! There, you must know how to feel grandly, to have a wide grasp and a broad outlook, and to know how to completely give in to your feelings.

> O, that this too too solid flesh would melt
> Thaw and resolve itself into a dew!
> Or that the Everlasting had not fix'd
> His canon 'gainst self-slaughter! O God! God!

What depth and pathos must be needed for a person to speak such language! If we, average people, were to say something similar in moments of despair, we would probably put it much simpler. Something like: "I wish I was dead already!"

Truthful as it may be, this has nothing to do with Shakespearean truth.

However, what is it about this truth that we can't capture? Sure, for some people it will likely forever be a falsehood. Their souls aren't spacious enough.

Imagine that you've got a glass, and you need to pour the contents of a bucket into it. Well, go ahead and pour. The glass will still only hold as much as it has room for; the rest will spill over.

One can object: When did it "misfire"? Was *Julius Caesar* [1903] not an event in the theatrical world? Was *Othello*, put on much later [1930], not an excellent performance?

All the Art Theatre's productions were "events in the theatrical world" and excellent performances, especially in the first fifteen years of its existence. The theatre's fans and enemies heatedly discussed every step, every experiment the MAT had made.

If you are searching for tragedy on the MAT stage, don't look at *Julius Caesar* with its mob scenes and rich, complicated settings done in the spirit of the Meiningen Company. Take a look at Dostoevsky's *Karamazovs* [1902] instead – that was more of a Shakespearean tragedy. However . . . if you take Leonidov's Mitya out of it, you'll have a performance similar to *Nikolai Stavrogin* [1913], which in its own way was an event, although valuable merely as a new experiment and a transitional step.

About the "Head-On" Solution

In the Art Theatre, there is a firm conviction that has been inscribed into *law*: "It is only in the very worst theatres that everything is played straightforwardly: sadness – they perform as sadness; tenderness, as tenderness; passion, as passion; rage, as rage; and so on."

This is the straight or, as they say, "head-on" solution, meaning that it meets every problem "head-on" and is therefore tasteless, primitive and inartistic. Tenderness can be expressed not only with tenderness; it can be expressed with a serious, caring attitude, and then vice versa – it is very often expressed with rudeness. Or rather, it is hiding behind rudeness; a person is ashamed of his tenderness, and he deliberately assumes rudeness to conceal his true attitude. And so on.

This is all very true, very subtle, very psychological . . . But why is there such a persecution of the "head-on solution?" Is it really as tasteless as they say? Is it really not true to life? In my opinion, the matter is extremely simple. The head-on solution is the most difficult; it is the most direct uphill path.

Whenever an actor doesn't have enough open passion, can't display enough unfeigned tenderness, or captivate the viewer with sufficient inner fire, it means that it isn't a suitable solution. True: it isn't suitable, but for whom? For the weak actor and his respective director. That's why today they can't perform the classics, such as Schiller or Shakespeare.

The Art Theatre abandoned backbreaking pathos; unfeasible moments demanding giant strength from the actor, it tried to make feasible, seeking roundabout paths. It found them. Let us thank it for that. All the same, why belie the simplest, most direct, most natural of all paths – the head-on path?

Of course, the head-on path requires the actor's strength and passion. And so what? It's time to search for ways to unlock the temperament. It isn't a bad thing. It's been long overdue.

It's time to put to use all of those methods I have been sweating over these past years.

Is a Person who Has a Low Level of Emotionality and a Significant Dose of Rationality Capable of Being an Affective Actor?

Here's a tortuous and painful question: and what if I'm not affective, but only moderately emotional and possess a good dose of rationality and brakes? Does this mean that, no matter how well I grasp the scope of ideas, the enormity of feelings or the elemental force of my character, I would never fulfill it artistically or in its complete truth?

Practice answers this question categorically: if you don't have the mechanism of the affective creator, then, of course, there won't be any affective creativity.

So does that mean that there's no point in trying?

Of course, it would be better not to try, otherwise you'll find yourself in an awkward position.

Although, the first thing one must clarify is this: **why** doesn't your affective mechanism work?

First of all: do you simply not have it?

One might be able to imagine such a case, even though I, the author of this book, have yet to meet a person – let alone an actor – who is completely devoid of the affective mechanism.

503

Usually it has to do with something else – with the underdevelopment of or damage to this mechanism.

Let us imagine that someone's rational and inhibitory mechanisms (be they hereditary or otherwise) are so strong that they don't allow the affective mechanism to come into play. Deprived of exercise, this mechanism, in the end, freezes and behaves itself as if it were never there at all – edged out, it hides in the corner and languishes.

In other instances the affective quality, being clearly expressed, bursts forth from a person, yet nothing good comes of it. This happens when an actor finds himself in a school that is not suitable for him. I speak of the school of analysis and rationalistic imperativism. His affective mechanism is at first blocked, and later destroyed, by all of these counterintuitive methods and devices.

An even more onerous situation is possible, alas, when life itself (not just the theatre school) has been crippling and breaking a man since childhood, according to its own fashion. His upbringing, life circumstances, the people surrounding him – all of these factors taken together can deprive a person of any traces of spontaneity. When, on top of it all, a school of analysis has been implanted into this soil, to extract a person's affectivity takes sufficient experience, superb pedagogical technique and, most importantly, exceptional tact.

However, practice shows that there is no need to despair. Nature, thank God, is tenacious. You can cut a tree almost down to its base, but, look – there are new shoots growing from its very roots. These are the ones you need to begin with.

The Typical Counterfeit of Affectivity

I hasten to add the caveat that there are many actors who imagine that they are "experiencing" beautifully, and that they have a great temperament. In actuality, they are mistaking their own specific actor's excitement for experiencing and temperament (see Book One, chapters "Pseudo-Experiencing," "Motor Storm," and others).

Speaking from experience, to argue with them is a waste of time.

Unfortunate self-flatterers, they are drunk with their own cheap success; they have set insurmountable obstacles to their own cures, development, and growth. To all those who *don't* belong to this category, I say that the palm, though it is in a flower pot, is still preferable to its stuffed self made of paper, sticks, and cotton, reeking of dust, taxidermy, foul paints, and other chemical ingredients.

It isn't just individual actors who labor under this mistake, but entire theatres do too. Eager to show off strength and the greatness of their souls, they take tragedy after tragedy and put it on. They do so without any regard for truth, but with the help of the simplest, most uncomplicated means: clenched fists, strained necks, and bloodshot eyes. They resort to roaring, wheezing, and screaming until they are hoarse.

As you watch them, in the first minute you think: this is great! Powerful! In the second, you're puzzled: it's more of the same? By the third, you're already tired of it; by the fourth it becomes boring and dreary from the ceaseless howling and shameless affectations.

By the fifth, you are sorry for the actors, and even feel a bit like laughing . . . In the intermission, without even waiting for the end of the play, you're dressing in the coatroom, remembering one of the scenes from the writer Korolenko's [1853–1921] story (I think it is Korolenko). In it, some well-intentioned mom wished to teach one of her children a lesson, as he misbehaved. Having lost her patience, she gave him as big a spanking as she could. "That'll show you! That'll show you! That'll show you! . . ."

She then let go of the kid: "Next time, you won't misbehave!" Her son ran out the door, then peeped his head back through, so as to get away if he had to, and announced: "It doesn't hurt! It's just loud!" And off he went.

It's the same thing here: you watch this great, heartrending tragedy . . . but it doesn't hurt at all . . . it's just loud.

The next day some home-grown critic writes: "The resurrection of tragedy!"; "Genuine pathos!"; "Mind-blowing acting!"; "A profound interpretation!"

How can we blame him? Firstly, he isn't a specialist; secondly, he's never seen any better. And if he'd seen it, he would have regretted lavishing praises for no real reason.

You even feel sympathy for him: it must be that the man is seriously yearning for something good and substantive since he ate and digested such a treat without serious consequences. It must be that he was starved. It must be that he is a good man.

10

Character
Transformation

A Mechanical Understanding of Stanislavsky

The actress Serafima Birman [1890–1976] says that the difference between perceiving a role "from the self" and "from the character" is this: Stanislavsky suggests to begin by building a hearth, and then a house around it – this means to perceive "from the self." She, however, suggests building the house first, and then, at a later date, the oven inside it – this is perceiving "from the character."

Both ways are equally absurd. They are both sheer mechanicalness. The fact of the matter is that nothing needs to be *built*, but rather **birthed**. This is the secret.

If you build your role like an inanimate house from inanimate material – stones and wood – then, ultimately, it doesn't matter what you start with, the oven or the walls. One way might be more convenient to you, the other less so – and that's all. This is all just rhetoric and quarrel. Witty, but quarrel nonetheless.

By the way, a powerful form also gives impulses to inner life. I want something, but what precisely I don't know – a sudden impulse from the back – a powerful form – and I'm off in the right direction.

How the "I" of the Role Is Formed

Who I am exactly is almost impossible to determine. I think I'm good, but those observing me from the outside apparently find me rotten. Therefore, using words to define what I am like (as a character) or how other people see me is simply harmful for the actor. It would lead him to perform a stereotype of a role, without actually being this person. He would be taking the path of depiction and imitation, rather than that of transformation and being.

You should seek character in an opposite way – not inside the self, but outside of it. Take an evil person, for example – he never considers himself evil; on the contrary, he's the nice one, and everyone around him is a scoundrel, a rascal, a fool, and a lout. The actor's attention must then be brought to *what* he sees in his surroundings (as the character). A superficial person sees the superficial (Khlestakov). A profound one sees the profoundness of everything; even in things that are seemingly insignificant he sees great substance and purpose (in a puddle, he would see the reflection of the sky and the sun).

Every fact you encounter in the role, you must see from the point of view of that role – you must turn the fact at such an angle so that to see what the character sees. The facts would then create your individuality as a character. The secret lies in the correct interpretation of the fact (from the point of view of the character's individuality), so that it appears to you just as it would appear to the character.

It's not yourself that you have to create, but rather the facts around you. They must be created and brought to the point *when they become physiologically tangible*.

On the Character in the Context of the Actor's Individuality

Take Mikhail Chekhov as Muromsky (from Sukhovo-Kobylin's *The Case*) – instead of playing the leading man, heroic and noble, he was a touchingly comical and affectionate old man.

Anna Babakhan [1923–1997], who was trying to play the role of Masha Ryzhova as a young enchantress, and was intolerable; I helped her make her Masha into a tomboy, neither a girl nor a boy – and she became disarmingly attractive and charming. [Masha was a character from *Courage*, a 1947 patriotic play by Georgy Beryozko. Anna Babakhan, who rehearsed and studied with Demidov in Sakhalin, proceeded to become a distinguished provincial actress. She is most famous for her role as Anna Karenina at the Moscow Art Theatre.]

This is always the case, if you want to achieve a creative merger between the character and the actor's individuality.

You must lead the actor away from the habit of searching for their favorite path and teach him to green-light "any old way," unfamiliar as it may be, as long as it *arises involuntarily* and of its own volition.

Etudes are a handy way to search for character. In addition to those three "green-lightings" (those of movements, feelings, and thoughts), we discover another: the *green-lighting* of the sensation of self, *of the character*, of the "*I-AM*."

What does it mean to "green-light" character? Above all, it means to green-light *manifestations*, that is, *motions* and *weak currents*.

Instead of calling it a "green-lighting of character," it would be better to refer to it as the "green-lighting of *being*." It is a new and important section. It is discussed in [Book Three, Part Four, Section Two] the chapters on "Character."

Since "green-lighting" is at the heart of the matter, you must exercise special vigilance so as to not miss the *source* of the character, its first sprouts. A mistake or oversight at the start might carry the whole thing off to the side. How could it be otherwise?

Only the first sprouts come from the embryo.

Let us suppose you aren't even chasing after the embryo, but just wish to train the actor in this new type of "line of green-lighting." Even then, you must be particularly vigilant and not miss the *impulse for being*: the impulse for character.

Just as the actors don't dare to make a movement, scared of their own daring, they similarly don't green-light the character.

Once they've failed to give it the green light, they proceed just as in life: I remain myself, I'm only pretending that I'm either very smart, or very busy, or cordial, or playful . . . This is double-cowardice: I didn't dare to give it a green light, and I hid behind a mask.

At such moments, the director and teacher must be especially vigilant. Just as the actor's delicate, barely emerging movements (or mimicry) indicate what he wants ("where he is drawn"), so certain *mannerism*-related motions hint at his character. Having recognized it, we can incite the actor to courageously follow the signals of his creative nature.

A real director with sound instincts does this unconsciously – he demonstrates the character, proceeding from the actor's individuality (as Stanislavsky did for Luzhsky in *Woe from Wit*).

More often than not, the directors demonstrate what they themselves envision, even though it doesn't fit the actor at all.

Is it Possible to Proceed from the External?

For nine tenths of actors, this is perhaps the central question: is it possible to proceed from the external, or is it not? What's more, all nine tenths of them want it to be possible.

Is it actually possible? Of course it is. But, here is the chief thing: from the external, you can receive a mere *impulse*, and that's all. Then you have to green-light all layers of your life, and stop interfering – only then would this impulse touch you to the quick. The main thing is to find the eyes. Otherwise, the first impulse will suffice for a few seconds, and then things will cross over to the mechanical maintaining of the character's exterior. In some exceptional cases – when the internal life of the character has already ripened inside you – a mere final impulse is needed to bring the character into the light. In these instances, one external detail may be enough to complete the work. By the way, the actors' delusions all come from these exceptional cases, and these cases are mostly cited to prove that the character originates from the external.

Another exceptional case exists: an extraordinary imitative giftedness – a genius-imitator.

On Transformation

Our art is the one of creative transformation. The more elements it contains of complete separation from the actor's meddling persona – the greater its artistry, expressivity, brilliance, and naturalness.

Melpomene exists where transformation exists; transformation exists where there is a completely different physical and spiritual "I," where there are completely different circumstances (untested by me), a different understanding of life and worldview.

Ideally: Hamlet, Chatsky, Othello, Carl Moor, Ferdinand, Romeo – these are all people of such different periods, nations, life circumstances, upbringings and so on . . . Can it be that *they all resemble* one another, even in my own imagination? (A single person's imagination?)

Perhaps it is unreasonable to demand complete unrecognizability and the trickery of a quick-change artist. Yet, it's not for nothing that we have costumes that you have to know how to wear and that evoke different postures. It's even more important that you know how to *wear* the makeup. It's not enough to properly paint your face – you have to do it so that the face becomes *yours* or, *rather: so that you become* like it – a different person. Completely *different*. This aspect signifies a deep meaning behind the actor's art.

"I" or "He"?

Since the dawn of time, there has been a heated debate amongst actors: do you need to "experience" onstage or not?

This debate, as can be seen from everything above, is in vain: it is a debate of miscomprehension: everything depends on the **type** of giftedness. The imitator would like to experience, but he can't; the affective would like to remain a cold performer of the external pattern of the role, but he also, likely, doesn't know how.

Although, those actors who can't *not* experience are also far from agreeing with each other on all points; they also debate and can't come to any consensus.

They debate: should your *life* onstage originate from **you** or from the **character**? . . .

Indeed, what good would it do if Ivan Fyodorovich, as we know him, would walk the stage boards, instead of Othello, the Venetian Moor? He may be painted brown, but what's the use, since this did not change him a bit? Ivan Fyodorovich remained the same as he has always been – his habits, his gait, and so on. Yes, you believe him – he is upset, he is agitated . . . it's just that . . . Why is he speaking in rhymes? It would be better if he were speaking in simpler language . . . about simpler, less elaborate things . . .

Is this experiencing? It is. But is it artistic experiencing?

It is the life of Ivan Fyodorovich, only he is in a quite awkward predicament. It isn't the tragic life of Othello – the man of great feelings and mighty passions. No, it is Ivan Fyodorovich's love, jealousy, and real tears, yet watching him is somewhat awkward. Especially when he cries.

By the way, on the subject of tears!

Most people say that real tears onstage are always unpleasant, and that you always feel uneasy seeing these drops of physiological salt solution falling from the actor's eyes.

First of all, it isn't always so; second of all, why is it that you can walk, sit, eat, drink, and laugh onstage, but not cry?

It's true that, for the most part, tears onstage are actually unpleasant, but why?

This is because they usually don't result from great emotional charge or genuine grief, but simply from an actor's *neurasthenia and mental instability*. Of such people they say: he is easily moved to tears. Aren't such tears tiresome and disgusting in life – shed for any reason, at the slightest provocation? Why should we feel any differently about them onstage?

Then again, there are other kinds of tears . . .

I saw Duse's tears onstage . . . But did I really see them? I simply wept, just as the rest of the audience was weeping . . . As soon as those diamonds began to sparkle in her eyes, it was as if someone had stuck a knife into my heart . . . I tried to fight it; I didn't want to weep, but it was beyond my control . . . *It* crumpled and crushed me – the tears burst forth and overflowed . . .

So does this mean that Duse had the right to cry onstage and Ivan Fyodorovich doesn't?

Judge for yourself. I saw Ivan Fyodorovich in a different role. He played a feeble, weak-willed old man. In the final act, when he turned out to have been deceived, robbed, and thrown out onto the street, he just stood there for a long time – bewildered, absent-mindedly looking around. Finally . . . he understood! His whole body sunk; he dropped onto the bottom step of the porch, week, elderly tears dripping from his eyes . . .

It was so touching, so sad, so hopeless . . . People in the audience went for their handkerchiefs. I didn't feel awkward for Ivan Fyodorovich; I pitied this trusting, humble man who had been unjustly crushed by life . . . For me it **wasn't** Ivan Fyodorovich, but **that old man** – somewhat ridiculous, simple-minded, weak-willed, but still completely sympathetic.

"There you go, we caught you at your words!" say proponents of the principle "life onstage proceeds not from the self, but from the character" – "This is precisely it: it isn't personally Ivan Fyodorovich who suffers, but *the old man!*"

Alright, let's imagine that I'm playing the humble old man. And it isn't me who is suffering, but "**HIM**" . . .

However, how can this be? Where is this "*he*"? Frankly speaking, he doesn't exist, *doesn't exist at all*. "*He*" is only in my imagination. "*He*" is only a fiction.

As for me, I do actually exist.

Doesn't it sometimes happen in life that I don't resemble myself and become unrecognizable to people (even to myself)? Aren't we sometimes completely unrecognizable – be it under the influence of strong emotions or alcoholic intoxication?

Nonetheless, it is still the same me.

A similar thing happens onstage: this is nobody else but me – just excellently *tuned up* with the character (like strings that are tuned to each other). It is me, except that it's a new and unknown side of me that was formerly in the shadows; it is me, but put under conditions that have altered me into someone unrecognizable.

If this is not me moving, laughing, and suffering, then who is it? Perhaps they have substituted someone else for me? Perhaps they have extracted the whole of my insides, and put in someone else's? Perhaps they have placed a new brain in my skull?

No matter how you spin it, no matter how you philosophize – if you *live* onstage, then it is *you*. And no one else.

It is you. And you are **he**.

Yet, don't be afraid of remaining "yourself," that is to say of "proceeding from yourself." All the same, if you *merge* (synthesize) with the character's persona, and with all of his circumstances, your personality will change. It can't **not** change – no matter how imaginary this character might be.

It doesn't matter where you begin your change: it will surely restructure you. You can start with your walk or with your pose; with the change in your voice or with a grimace. . .

This ability, to some degree, is inherent in all people – the ability to not only feel, but **to physiologically experience** yourself as someone else, while in a stranger's costume, with makeup, with a "grimace" of the body or face. Doesn't every person feel different when he gets a haircut, changes his hairstyle, or puts on a new suit?

The artist – be he a writer, sculptor, painter, musician or, of course, an actor – is a person with a particularly sensitive and mobile inner constitution: as soon as he fantasizes something and imagines himself as someone else, a complete restructuring takes place within him.

For example, Balzac [1900a: 375] told this about himself (in the story *Facino Cane*):

> . . . I used to watch the manners and customs of the faubourg [suburb], its inhabitants, and their characteristics. As I dressed no better than a working man, and cared nothing for appearances, I did not put them on their guard; I could join a group and look on while they drove bargains or wrangled among themselves on their way home from work . . . . As I listened, I could make their lives mine, I felt their rags on my back, I walked with their gaping shoes on my feet; their cravings, their needs, had all passed into my soul, or my soul had passed into theirs. It was the dream of a waking man. I waxed hot with them over the foreman's tyranny, or the bad customers that made them call again and again for payment. To come out of my own ways of life, **to be someone other than myself** through a kind of intoxication of the intellectual faculties, and to play this game at will, such was my recreation.

If you take a step further and give free rein to that "other person," you would find yourself in the kind of state the tragedian Ernesto Rossi [1827–1896] describes in his letter: his real life begins to feel distant and resembles a dream. He notices, with an inner shiver, how he looks at this torrent of interchanging feelings with a stranger's eyes, and listens to it with a stranger's ears. He feels like an object – some instrument being played by a different creature within him.

Take another step (if you can!), and you would find yourself on the threshold between the normal and the abnormal; you will find yourself in the state of great creative inspiration, where the actor not only feels possessed by "another creature," but also sees everything around him as it appears in his imagination and dreams.

Just a little further, one tiny step and . . . a hallucination, a pathological condition.

However, may this not frighten you. Aristotle himself is believed to have said: "*It seems* that no great mind has ever existed without a touch of madness."

Poets and musicians who have experienced this in person flat out call it delirium and somnambulism.

> In such a somnambulistic condition, it has often happened that I have had a sheet of paper lying before me all on one side, and I did not discover it till all had been written, or I had found no room to write any more. I have possessed many such sheets written crossways, but they have been lost one after another, and I regret that I can no longer show any proofs of such poetic abstraction. (Eckermann. *Conversations with Goethe* [1850: 251])

"All this inventing, this producing, takes place in a pleasing, lively dream (*Schonstarken Traum*)" (Mozart [as quoted in *Musical Times* 1891: 20]).

What about the Art Attracts Us? "The Mask"; "The Confession Beneath the Mask"

The emblem of our art is the mask. How clever this is! The actor puts on a guise, and he thinks that he already *isn't himself*. Now he has the courage to say the most precious and sacred things.

Now it becomes clear why the ancients considered Melpomene – the goddess of transformation – to be the muse and patroness of our art. To put on someone else's costume, to paint your face with makeup, to assume someone else's words, thoughts, and feelings – is this not to clothe yourself in new flesh? . . .

The fact of the matter is they aren't someone else's thoughts or feelings, but they *are all yours*. It's just that they are too deep-seated, unordinary, and hidden from everyone, including yourself.

The flesh might be someone else's, but the life is yours.

How is this possible?

One of the most important attractions of the actor's art is in this loss of personality, in its substitution for another, new persona. One of its chief draws is this imagined life in new circumstances, created by your own imagination.

What is so attractive and tempting about this? This is worth discussing in greater detail.

Have you ever happened, while listening to a song, or while reading a poem or novel (*War and Peace*, Dickens, Balzac, or something else), to suddenly become so deeply touched and agitated that you began to weep bitter tears?

Of course you have.

A similar thing has probably happened to you at the theatre. A full house; you feel joyful and calm; no one's in a rush to be someplace else; everyone has left all of their "business" and worries behind. Today they will relax and live *for themselves*. And so, you too live with this anticipation of relaxing, enjoyable time.

The lights go down. You settle comfortably into your seat. The curtain opens – the play has begun . . .

It's pleasant to sit in the dark and know that nobody can see you, and that you can peacefully watch and listen to everything they are doing onstage, in the light.

The play is excellent. Like in any artistic work, it carries one of the eternally stirring human ideas: love . . .

The author and actors capture your imagination and seize your attention at once . . .

A battle of heaven and earth . . .

An angry scene with the lover . . . the hero's earthly passion spreads like fire . . .

Great, tumultuous passions – do they happen to us in life? Can I experience them? Am I capable of them?

A quick look at yourself, and you begin to feel immensely embarrassed: "How mediocre I have become. It happened unnoticeably, step by step. Could I even feel things like that, want things like that, suffer like that? Everything with me is within the boundaries, restrained, just a touch. Thousands of boundaries: I'm afraid to reach out my hand; to smile at the wrong moment so as not to offend anyone, or betray my feelings . . .

"And then today, this great author, along with this great artist-actor, took me by the hand. They led me, as if I were a small child, across a fallen tree log over an abyss of passions that makes you dizzy if you look down into it. Yet, I came to trust them – my fear disappeared, and I began to lean on that hand. Bravely I went, and in some three hours, I lived (together with the actor) a whole new life . . ."

The hero stands alone on the deck of the ship for a long, long time . . . Gradually, quietly, and barely perceptively, the light dims. Soon everything dives into the abysmal depthless and deadly darkness . . .

You don't want to stand up from your seat. You don't want to tear yourself away from this other life. It would be so nice if you could just sit here in silence and solitude. The final moment with the solitary figure is still before your eyes . . . and so is everything else . . .

Returning to my everyday routine, crushed by this landslide of a life, I feel drained and joyously fatigued. It isn't I who have been crushed, but my pettiness. I myself, on the contrary, feel as if I have been freed from some ridiculous and humiliating weight, and have become more "me," more of myself.

It means that I haven't completely become a content little insect, and my human feelings haven't completely eroded. They may be shoved away, may be clipped, but they are there – my genuine feelings and passions – and they want to be released.

What do we know about ourselves? Nothing! Everything that is significant – the bad and the good – is so deeply hidden that no one, least of all we ourselves, can see it.

Judge for yourself. I'm a quiet, shy and restrained person, and yet I sat there, watching the hero of the play, a fiery Frenchman, and I understood him, and felt, and was all on edge, just like him. It means that this fieriness is in me too!. . .

In life, if someone were to ask me flat: "I heard that you are an ardent, unstoppable man, and that you yearn for some fatal, eternal love – is it true?"

I would be surprised, and wouldn't immediately understand what they were asking me about, and then: "Come on now! Come on!" I would brush the whole matter off, "Who thought up such nonsense?"

It's true that in my childhood I was a dreamer and a fantasizer, and that I imagined myself an invincible conqueror, a noble leader, a champion of truth and justice. In life too, as is just and proper, I tried to be honest, not to tell lies. Yet everyone else considered it their duty to cool my temper in every possible way.

And now . . . my inner temperature has dropped so much that I became . . . totally meek. "I yearn for a fatal eternal love. . ." There is no "yearning" here! It's true that I do possess some sensuality, which I sweep under the carpet. I feast my eyes on every sweet young face, but what does this have in common with eternity and fate?

I still can imagine somebody else's feats. When I looked at the stage, I understood the hero, because I put myself in his place – it was like I was him. This is why it was as if I shared his whole life with him.

This is what our personality thinks, with all of its habits and layers of everyday routine . . . Yet, personality still isn't everything. In our depths lies something even more important – [our] *individuality*. This is our most intimate, most genuine "I." Like a different person, this "I" lives its own life; it searches, it waits, it yearns . . . And we (my small, nearsighted personality) panic at everything that comes from within, from the depths, from our conscience. We fear our frankness and our integrity; we fear our grandeur – and our entire lives are marked by fear.

Yet something possessed you to go to such a play or to set about such a novel. You swallowed the bait, and the all-powerful artist quietly, carefully took you into his hands. He then began to shake you with these hands! "Wake up! Look into the very depths of your soul and finally come to life! Groan, if it hurts! Shout at the top of your lungs if you can no longer be silent; if you are enraged! Don't hold back your tears, if they start to flow!"

The clever mechanism of your mundane life stops, and your "I" begins to speak, along with your conscience, and along with the artist in you . . . He lives! He lives! And you – you're so happy, so joyful to be finally free!

And the man walks away changed; different from whom he was when he arrived. "The spectator walks away refreshed through and through." (Gogol [1913: 64]).

Confession

There are many reasons that draw us to art. One of them is my desire to live my dream life under a mask – a desire to play out my unrealized life resources, to exercise what's inside, overburdening me with its abundance . . . We need to get rid of it one way or another, don't we?

In the time of war, when soldiers were asked what care packages were the closest to their hearts, their faces expanded in blissful smiles. "Of course, the accordion," they all said. There you have it: surrounded by death, wounds, and suffering, they want the accordion!

Why?

Because death runs its course (death is its own funeral, so to speak); and here I am, healthy and strong, so what am I to do with it all?

When the joy of life sits inside a person, no power on earth can scare it away. It keeps overflowing, searching for pretexts to jump out and come into play. If you suppress it, the person becomes depressed.

It's the same thing when playing the role of a villain: doesn't it mean that I myself am a villain if I get pleasure from playing this role?

And why not? Perhaps life has been constantly wearing you out, and people have been offending you a great deal. Over the years, you've nursed one grievance too many. Finally, you've developed a burning desire to seek revenge – to break something, to give vent to your feelings?! . . .

All right. Go ahead then, take the role of Iago, and destroy this "simpleton" Othello. The more cruel and treacherous you become, the more pleasure it will give you. Take it all out on him.

And what pleasure is there in playing a fool? This is the most delicious pleasure, especially for those with the sense of humor.

See for yourself: in life you always have to control yourself – you have to try being smart. Suddenly, you're given complete freedom to be stupid. And the more the better! You feel like those cows that have spent an entire winter standing in the cowshed. Just look at them, as they are let out into the sunshine, onto the grass in the spring – how they lift their tails up, skipping along! They aren't very graceful, but it comes from the depths of their bovine hearts!

There is even a little excuse: supposedly, it isn't I that am stupid, but just some character. I put on a mask, and I can safely be as foolish as my heart desires.

If you look a little closer now, you'll likely say: "What do you know! there *is* stupidity in this person, it's just that he skillfully hides it." You begin to recall one episode after the next, and – it's true. He's an intelligent person, no doubt, but at times he has these fits of strange foolishness. And now, onstage, you can see it in its pure state.

An insidious thing – art. It draws all of a person's secrets out of him, and he doesn't even suspect it. It wasn't for nothing that Goethe [1887–1919 vol. 12: 65] said: "All of my works are fragments of a great confession!"

Facets

A man is like a multi-faceted diamond – it stands before you, the delicate play of its deep violet tones pleasing your eye. It turns a little, and suddenly your eye is hit with such a sharp green – your heart even skips a beat. Another barely perceptible turn, and it strikes you with its radiant red, and then it comes at you with a blue, and then with a yellow. . .

We have many facets, as if there were different people inside of us. They live, play house, converse with one another, and argue . . . Yes, there is much within us: good and bad, human and beastly, intelligent and foolish. We have a hero within us, and next to him – a coward. A saint and a criminal, God and the devil – they all somehow coexist! Just look at this diamond deposit! How much it hides until the time is right, or the opportunity turns up . . . A man would do or say something, and later he won't even believe it: could that be me? Such a rich being is man.

For the actor, this is a genuine fortune. There is no telling what kind of a person he might need to play tomorrow! If not for these deposits, where would he take everything he might need for the role?

As soon as you begin to talk about these diamond deposits amongst theatre students, some-one (one of the adherents of "fast living") will say: "Aha! It means that none of these ascetic sermons on restraint and strict moral life apply to us actors. Moreover, this does us more harm than good!" It's extremely easy to argue against this.

Each of us has a wild animal hidden inside. It is full of dark instincts, and it shows its teeth at the slightest provocation. It takes its beginnings from many thousands or millions of years ago, and it is hereditary. What are our own short lives in comparison with this thousand-century-old experience? Experience, acquired in this life – through carousing, lust, and licentiousness – is a trifling "acquisition" in comparison. Especially if you take into account the immeasurable harm it does to our heart, liver, brain, and nervous system. Its value can be compared to that of a consumptive's hectic flush. When consumption is in its third stage, a deceptive flush appears on a sick person's cheeks. What he wouldn't give to exchange his feverish "beauty" for the ordinary, pale cheeks common to city-dwellers. . .

These issues will be given more place and attention further on. They will be brought to light in several ways: not only philosophically and psychologically, but also technologically – meaning from the standpoint of practical application to the actor's daily work. For now, we will restrict ourselves to what has been said, adding only one more comment. The facets may be numerous, and inner richness bountiful; however, life might break off and grind down the facets. It might scratch the surface of the human crystal so much that, in most cases, it will completely lose its luster and its play of colors. In such a case, drastic measures are needed to make the facets shine again. Sometimes life itself strikes a person unceremoniously and mercilessly, awakening the dreamy passion, and electrifying the burning thoughts. At other times, a man would manage to walk through his forbidden, dangerous inner passages through art. Putting on a mask, he would escape outdoors like a schoolchild, using a clever roundabout path.

★★★

Practically all theoreticians say that the actor's feelings aren't real, but fictional – even though he, in spite of this, still experiences organic emotions. . .

Well, it is precisely because he thinks that these feelings are fictions, that he is experiencing them. If he had thought that they were real, he wouldn't have had courage to green-light them. Moreover, without the mask, they wouldn't have appeared.

In addition to the fictitiousness of feelings, theoreticians also talk about the weakness of feelings onstage – in comparison with regular ordinary feelings.

The degree of feelings depends on the degree of the actor's doubling – it depends on the degree of transformation. A strength of feelings (or their weakness), merely points to a strength of talent (or a lack of such).

Is it Possible to "Play Yourself Onstage"? Is it Feasible?

I play Peter, a high school student. I myself happen to be young. All of Peter's interests are close to mine . . . Nevertheless, I'm not actually Peter, but Sergei, or Vanya, or Alyosha! On top of this, I have a different mother – not like the one in the play; different teachers and friends . . . As a matter of fact, everything is different.

My being familiar with the day-to-day life of the high school, and having a feel for it, young blood running through my veins – these are just further advantages. They help me to properly feel, experience, and artistically embody my role. No more, and no less.

At the end of the day, if I correctly take in all of the circumstances of Peter's life, and I believe that they truly and actually exist for me, then an internal restructuring will inevitably begin within me, as will an external change.

Thus, if you do a good job taking in the circumstances of the play and the role, and if your imagination makes them your own, then no matter how hard you try to stay as *yourself*, you *can't* do it. The circumstances will *remake you*.

Let us suppose that you managed to contrive, in some moments, a way to live with your own personal interests. This would imply that you live with your very own, personal "given circumstances," and therefore have nothing to do with the play.

Even the simplest exercises, such as "How do you like this weather?" already feature a character, instead of my personal "I."

Therefore "I" – *my personal I* – cannot, physiologically cannot, be present onstage.

On the Acquired Persona Onstage

A young actor plays a role that is suitable for him, and he immediately becomes famous – he played it better than anyone else. He was so charming, sweet, so naive, openhearted, bashful and touchingly eccentric . . . There was only one problem: it was said that he "was playing himself," just as he is in life. Although, those interacting with him on a first-name basis, knew that in his intimate life he is actually quite different. It is only in the company of others that he pretends to be so. Using the language of acting, "he plays" such a person in life. Yet, this is only a mask that successfully shields his intimate essence. Since he has been wearing this mask for many years, it has adhered to him well. Behind this familiar habitual mask he appeared in his first role. Is it the true him?

This actor is one-dimensional. In all of his roles, he plays only that childish, simple, pleasant young man. He merely changes his costume and makeup, and perhaps his age, just a bit: he was young; in some roles he got a bit older, but the essence is the same.

Seeing this, everyone around him says: he always plays himself. In actuality, he is merely playing the same role that he plays in life. He plays it well, as in life it has been drilled into him well. Now he has also tested it onstage.

This, of course, is no first-rate accomplishment – to always play the same role as you play in life. Although, we should thank him a lot for small favors!

His truth, while it isn't profound, and is probably one-sided, is still "truth."

The Personal Element in the Actor's Creative Process

There are various methods of making the circumstances *my own* and of ensuring that they excite me genuinely and without fail.

The first, which is all and everything, is the *exposure of the self* and its unveiling through techniques such as "allowing in" of impressions, "breathing," and the "nearest flow of thought" – in general, through everything that was invented for the "*bel canto.*"

By these techniques, the self is brought to a particular state of extreme sensitivity; in such a state, the slightest thought becomes real and creates a tangible material world around me. (". . .Having grasped just one line in a drawing, just one chord and one sound. . .") [An excerpt from A.K.Tolstoy's (1893: 248) 1856 poem "Artist, in vain you imagine yourself a creator of your works. . ." Also see pages 541, 654 and 683.]

The second method is "If."

And the third – the selection of a suitable *affect* from my personal life. I'd like to say a little something about this.

I attempted Hamlet's scene in the graveyard: "Poor Yorick!" What is the main thing here? Yorick's skull. This skull must move me, be dear to me; it must be my friend, my favorite – the person who delighted me every minute. It must be Yorick, and if it's not, then the scene doesn't work.

No matter how hard I tried to deceive myself with all those "Ifs," still nothing came of it; my fantasies weren't concrete, and the thoughts rolled right by me, not touching me, but only passing over.

"Fine then," I said to myself, "we'll leave Hamlet and Yorick alone. Let's have it just be me."

I called to mind those of my relatives who have departed this world long ago; I tried to "take into my hands" the skulls of one or the other, and it became significantly easier – I understood, and I sensed what it means to hold the skull of someone you knew. "I knew him, Horatio" – these weren't just big empty words. It helped, but it was still far from what was needed.

I called to mind my friends who have passed away – no, no one fits the bill . . . and then suddenly it occurred to me: Prokofiev!

Sweet Georgy, he was 26 when he met his untimely death . . . Gloomy at first glance, but gentle and sensitive, with the tender soul of an artist. His selfless devotion to his art, his yearning and suffering eyes – when he had to agree to a compromise in the art that was sacred to him . . . Four years we worked together hand in hand . . . The four best years – my first years in art.

There are some losses . . . where saying "difficult" isn't enough; it is *unbearable* to look at a dead body and to know that something serious, catastrophic, and irreversible had happened. It brought an end to life as we knew it.

We filled in Georgy's grave and stood over it for a long time, astonished. . .

. . ."This skull has lain in the earth for three-and-twenty years. Whose do you think it was?" Nay, I know not. "A pestilence of him for a mad rogue! He poured a flagon of Rhenish on my head once. This same skull was Georgy Prokofiev's skull, the king's jester."

– Georgy? *This?!* – I can't refrain from rushing to it, from seizing it greedily and tenderly, and gripping it lovingly in my hands. Out of me bursts: "Alas, poor Georgy! Poor Yorick! I knew him, Horatio! He was one of the most amazing people in art – a person with ceaseless humor and wondrous imagination.

"How many times did he strengthen me with his faith; how many times did he help me rise, inspired me; he hath borne me on his back a thousand times.

"And now, how abhorred in my imagination it is! my gorge rises at it."

By substituting Yorick for Georgy, I understood and perceived what I should feel during the scene with the skull. Yorick became close and understandable to me. So close that I don't even need to think about Georgy *every time*. The thought of Yorick is already filled with my personal relationship with Georgy, who was so close to me. Georgy begins to vanish, but the feeling (the affective memory) remains. It remained and it merged with Yorick. I somehow grafted Georgy to Yorick, and he came to life for me.

★★★

As an atom, I am one thing, but as a molecule I am completely different. You wouldn't recognize me.

Oxygen and hydrogen are gases. Put together, they produce water with all of its different chemical and physical properties. Try to find oxygen or hydrogen there!

It's the same way with the actor's personality – in joining with the character, it disappears. It's as if it isn't you at all. But it is precisely you. You never disappeared, and at any moment you can be "extracted" from the molecule. While you're part of the molecule, however, you're unrecognizable; you've attained different characteristics and lost your own. This combining of atoms into a molecule is not mechanical, but chemical, with either an absorption or a discharge of energy.

When it comes to the imitator, however, the combining is completely mechanical.

Legitimate and Illegitimate Ways of Acting while Proceeding "from the Self"

How do you become a character when you transform into a stranger, an imagined person?

I was entrusted with the part of Boris Godunov. How do I *become* that Boris just out of the blue? What kind of Boris Godunov am I? So, I begin to primitively depict him: a tsar, which means importance, suspiciousness, imperiousness . . . An actor who hasn't gone through a serious school, who, when left to his own devices, unwittingly searches for the simplest and most direct path: Boris is tormented by his conscience – this means that he ponders a lot, that he broods . . . and so on.

An experienced director would look at such an actor and see how hopelessly far he is from the circumstances of Boris' life. Seeing this, he would tell the actor: "Why don't you hold off on searching for the *tsar* for now. To begin with, let's search for the person. He isn't satisfied with his life, he's summing it up, he's looking for a way out . . . Why don't you, without thinking about Boris at all, just you *personally*, start thinking about your own life."

The actor begins to think and sighs; it's obvious that he's seeing pictures from his life pass before him. He is no longer here, but somewhere far away, in his past . . . Suddenly he tears himself away from his pondering and asks: "He says 'I have attained the highest power' . . . and I haven't achieved any power at all, have I?" [Here, and further in the chapter, *Boris Godunov* is quoted from Pushkin 1918: 28–30.]

"You think so? Is that so? You're already an actor, you're playing major roles – remember when you only dreamt about being an actor – didn't the position you currently occupy seem lofty to you at the time? Well, you've attained it. And doesn't the actor have power over the audience; doesn't he make those sitting there become excited, cry and laugh at his own whim?"

"Yes, that's true!"

"And so you've attained it."

"And so I did. . ."

A shadow of sadness sweeps over the actor's face . . . Apparently, this isn't how he imagined this power back then – it's not even how he imagines it now . . . He once had abilities; they were bursting out of him . . . Apparently, he didn't have enough stamina, diligence, energy, and strength of character . . . His abilities remained unrevealed, his talent – hidden, and his power – unrealized . . .

The actor is lost in thought . . .

"Go ahead . . ." the director whispers to him – carefully, so as not to frighten off the sorrowful thoughts.

"I have attained the highest . . . power . . ." The actor is stung by these words. They are wounding him now; with sadness and pain, he casts his glance at his present, and then speaks about his own (personal) life, having thrown himself into his far-gone past:

> Six years have I reigned in peace; yet comfort
> Lives not within my soul. Just so in youth
> We fall in love and crave its joys, yet when
> We've quenched our heart's thirst with quick possession,
> We grow cold, and bored and sick at heart!

Standing before us isn't a tsar, as we've grown used to seeing one on theatre stages – in a crown and purple mantle – before us is simply a man. A man who, perhaps, for the first time in many years takes a genuine, serious look at his life's path . . . For this man, this is a painful and grim experience . . .

Apparently this is my life! And what next? Live my last years like this? That's all there is to it?

Simply a man . . . not a tsar, but an actor – just an actor . . . Why, then, do these words touch us so? Why do we feel for him? And why, then, doesn't it seem false and bombastic, when he says:

> In vain the wizards promise me the long reign,
> Long days of power, untroubled and secure –
> I find no joy in power, nor in life;
> The wrath of Heaven I forebode, and woes.
> No happiness I see.

Perhaps Boris Godunov wasn't at all a cardboard tsar, but, above all, just a person? Especially now, when he is alone, by himself . . .

The actor is inspired by the right state; he finds himself on the track of organic life, and he runs forward with growing courage . . . He is now *carried away* . . . *Unnoticeably for him, the rails switch*, like at a railroad point, to a different (artistic) track. This does not scare him – he is now comfortable; he doesn't stop his motion, and the locomotive, by all the laws of *nature*, carries him at full steam along the new, unprecedented (personally for him) path.

> I hoped my realm
> To pacify by glory and contentment,
> And gain my people's love by lavish gifts –
> I had to put away that empty hope;
> The power that lives is hateful to the mob, –
> They only love a tsar when he is dead.

His fantasy, placed on the "rails of truth," creates a life that *isn't just his own*, but rather a different, imagined one . . .

When did he pass the railroad point that switched him onto the different rails? He didn't notice. Yet, he is no longer just himself, when he says, "I hoped my realm to pacify by glory and contentment . . ." What realm? And where did he see "his people"? However, the actor doesn't stop:

> Insane we are, if people's approbation,
> Or fierce groans disquiet our heart!

This is how close, apparently, Boris Godunov was to his soul! It doesn't get any closer.

In a few rehearsals, the skillful director transforms all of these *foreign*, obscure moments of the role into *the actor's own*.

As for the unskillful one. . .

He knows that the actor needs to make everything in the role personal and his own. So, he might start with the same thing – by inserting the facts of the actor's personal life behind Boris' text. Perhaps he does this quite fittingly, and the actor draws nearer to Boris' *life*; he begins to perceive things as somewhat tangible. He should have taken it further, and let him transition, unaware, from **his own personal rails** *to those of* **Boris**. . .

Instead, the overly zealous director senses that the actor begins to *depart from himself*, as he transitions to the new rails. In his opinion, this signals falsehood, and therefore the actor must be turned from these new, dangerous rails onto *his own personal truth* – his own private routine, and mundane affairs.

Boris' monologue deals with executions, torture, famine, plague, fires, the foreboding of the wrath of Heaven . . . What an array of human passions!

And what does the unskilled director do? Behind each of these facts, he inserts some fact from the everyday life of the poor actor. By doing so, he keeps pulling him away from Boris's rails, and shaking him out of Boris's shoes.

Just as the actor begins to live and experience, and his imagination transitions from his own personal circumstances to those of Boris the Tsar, the director puts in his two cents of mundane reality. Just as an actor's *creativity* is beginning to take wing, and what he needs most is support and encouragement, the director dispels the magic fog of the imagined life. In the end, the director squeezes all life out of him, decolorizes and degrades him so the crowned tsar of all of Russia turns into Boris-the-office clerk.

This diligent and overly principled director forgot to consider the most important thing. He didn't think through the *chief purpose* of this risky method – *the unnoticeable transition* **onto the other** *rails*. Onto the rails of the **role**.

But . . . it's always been that way, for all time and in all "schools": mediocrity only grasps things that are within its power, that is to say, only those flawed aspects of the method, just its Achilles' heel. It skips over everything that is important, including the very purpose behind the method. Self-satisfied, it plows ahead (where else!), pushing and smashing everything in its way.

★★★

Once the actor is on the right track, the director should slip in such circumstances that would alter the actor, turning him into the object of his "transformation." This should be done carefully, bit by bit, so as not to scare away the actor's proper creative state.

Directors attempt to do just that, but this work isn't simple. Provocative circumstances often cause dislocations. At such moments, the actor yet again distorts his truth. This is why the director keeps returning him back, again and again, to his own "I." To put it more accurately, he brings the actor back to his *personality*, to his habitual life "mask" with its everyday baggage and habits. In the end, this mistake becomes consolidated: on the one hand, the actor becomes used to acting from his own personality; and on the other, everything that doesn't fall within that narrow category, he considers to be a false state. With this, he *blocks his path to artistic transformation* – to the source of his complete self-expression, and to the depths of the character' soul.

"Playing character" is an extremely widespread mistake; almost everyone makes it! It's understandable: I'm playing so and so, and it means that above all I need to portray that "so and so." As soon as I begin to "portray or depict," I thus distance the character from myself. It is not me; I'm only portraying who I am supposed to portray. I don't merge with him, nor transform into him – I depict. Whether my depiction is good or bad is beside the point – inwardly I have distanced this character from myself. The less familiar the character, from my own daily life and mundane routine, the farther away it stands from me.

The Boundaries within which We Can Speak of "Playing the Self" and "Proceeding from the Self"

It is impossible to play the whole role proceeding "from the self" – after all, the circumstances are different. As for individual moments (not even bits, but just moments), it is possible. For this you have to come out of the role, switch over to your own life ("the death of your beloved mother" or something else along those lines). This "patch" in the middle of a role, made from your own everyday life, is a cheap trick. It isn't art at all. This includes methods such as Stanislavsky's "affective memory": think back on an instance when you were happy or unhappy, or something else.

Playing a role while proceeding "from the self' takes tremendous efforts. The character possesses you, and you have to forcefully peel it off. You have to begin anew with each phrase. This isn't an exaggeration: with every new phrase.

To play the role "from the self' and to not be the character is impossible; it can't be done.

If someone uses the death of his own mother to evoke tears onstage, it is because, firstly: he came out of the role and its circumstances, and secondly: it is because he is a shameless interloper, who keeps pestering people with his private grief! It's unpleasant to watch, as it's obvious that he attached *his own circumstances* to the role – *things that have nothing to do with the play*. The other reason why it is unpleasant is that you can't help but feel just how shameless, annoying, and callous a man this is.

Of course, having started "from the self' and "from one's own" (like with "the mother"), *you can be deeply moved and transition to the play and the character*. Similarly, an actor's real rage offstage can "unlock" his temperament for the circumstances of the play. Yet, the purpose of this is to become excited and deeply touched, and to divorce "your own sober-mindedness" so as to ease the **shift** from your own circumstances to those of the play.

To achieve authenticity and truth, you need to begin by "finding yourself" (begin with yourself), to set your eyes, ears, and your whole physiology in motion. *You begin* with this, so as to add the role's circumstances into this physiological machine you've set into motion. These circumstances, *also completely physiological*, would then become augmented by new psychological nuances and by entirely new content.

Then why does this mistaken view on the option of "acting from the self" still exist? It's likely that it isn't for nothing!

Of course, the "I" participates in the process. You might even say that the "I" prevails. What kind of "I" is this, however?

It all has to do with the *very beginning*. Everything begins with my "I": my eyes and my ears – this is where the concreteness of perception comes from. Without this concreteness there can't be anything living. Concreteness is the truth. And then, further on, a shift occurs onto the *truth* of "not I."

Or (the second case), when an actor plays his habitual mask or role.

To live by someone else's feelings (by "his" feelings) is generally impossible. Take laughter – it can't come out of anybody else but myself. This is either one of my special facets laughing, or it is me under a mask.

"Just be yourself" is, by all appearances, no different from: "there's no audience; you're alone." One can hardly be "your own self." The mask will inevitably appear. Similarly, the feeling of the audience can hardly leave the actor. This sense of the audience, however, is rather special; it makes the actor feel even more alone onstage.

Let's return to our question of the participation of "*personality*" in art: how to play (live) "from the self" or "from him" (the character)? How much has been written on this topic by both actors and non-actors! It would be wrong to say that they were all insincere, or said completely wrong things. They keep arguing round and round the truth, but none of them can hit the mark! They just can't come to a consensus.

In the meantime, there is nothing to argue here: *everything from the self and everything from him!* Always and everywhere "I," but just "behind the mask." This is why the actor is unrecognizable. Most importantly, he can't recognize himself – this is what gives him courage to be sincere to his core.

How obvious this is, and how simple!

Patchwork

Patchwork – a disorderly mix of my personal elements, and those emerging from the creative life.

My personal point of view on a partner, and that in the play – my creative act merges and modifies these two; my personal transforms into the imagined.

In the absence of creativity, however, a man lives by his real, mundane life – his personal aspects *keep him out of creativity*. Like a float, they keep him on the very surface.

11

Transformation

Amongst actors, there are many who have become accustomed to filtering their every step onstage through their *consciousness*. They can't imagine how anything could happen on its own. "How could you give yourself full freedom?"

And why not? Surely they *aren't aware* of everything in life?

The difference is only that in life, there is a certain force of their individual being that acts on its own. He is Petrov, and no matter how much his life wears him down, he will remain Petrov and will behave like Petrov. Things are different onstage: he is still Petrov, but in addition to that, he should also manage to become "Stepanov." This fusion between everything in him and "Stepanov's" circumstances leads to the embryo of a certain *new persona*: "Petrov-Stepanov" (or "Stepanov-Petrov"). Now, this new persona, or rather its being, just needs to be given freedom. [For more on transformation, see Book Three, Part Two, Chapter 14, and Book Five, Chapter 4.]

You hear people say: if you "live onstage," you'll forget everything. Not so. The creative state is the simultaneous presence, and the harmonious unity of *all* abilities.

The genuine creative experiencing is always healthy. A person's attention is not distracted; he sees everything. He is playing. He relishes the images his fantasy serves him.

There are also those fearing that "living onstage" would make their acting insignificant and boring. This is the wrong understanding of life and living. Simplicity and nearness to life don't mandate that everything must be done insignificantly, uninterestingly and mundanely – this isn't simplicity, but triviality and callousness. Not truth, but verisimilitude – the portrayal of truth.

Experiencing might not reach the audience because it isn't whole; it is too weak.

How does experiencing onstage differ from that in life? An actor lives onstage and, on top of that, he leads the way for the audience – he lives *singularly*, with such oneness of every feeling, movement or thought that it *alone* reaches the audience. Such experiencing then grows to the size of something significant, and becomes a *singular* phenomenon at this point in time.

Genius is the ability to light your own personal flame.

On Feeling (Perception)

Stanislavsky feels that there are three "drives of the psychical life" – Mind, Will, and Feeling.

To begin with, "psychical life" is the wrong expression, when it comes to creativity.

Second of all, creativity, or at least creativity in art, is entirely based on feeling.

Wouldn't it be more accurate to say that the main thing without which art couldn't exist is *feeling*?

The rest – mind or something else – are only *awakeners* of feeling.

"Admitting," "the eye," "emotional attention," "do you like it or not," "point of view," "perception," and "merging with the object" – these are all methods for awakening feelings.

If we were to assert this principle firmly and unconditionally, it would significantly clarify the aim of the technique.

In any case, it would be correct to take such aim when hunting for the **affective technique**.

This doesn't imply, of course, that you have to constantly chase after grand emotions – it would lead to a distortion of the actor's truth. Yet, our aim should still be fixed on the emotion, or rather on the sensation – on the primitive or primary feeling.

This is exactly how I organized the etudes: do what you want, what you feel like doing. "I feel like moving," "I feel like doing something" – this means that I do it because I *feel*. Therefore – green-light your feeling, and it will arouse movements and actions.

Actors try to fixate feelings and internal states. In the meantime, what can be more important than warming yourself to those circumstances that caused the scene in the first place. These circumstances we must accept in their entirety, with their *exactness* and *inexactness*, with their inherent "surprisingness."

We say: "don't search for feelings." This is too mildly put: for the most part, they search for the peripheral nervous excitement – "Just give me an outburst, give me tears by any means!"

If they were searching for feeling and finding it, what would be the matter with that? In the majority of cases, however, they search and they search, and feeling still does not come; instead they get stupor and convulsions, if not paralysis.

One of the varieties of such a search is *holding onto feeling*.

Let's take a look at what is going on. This actor does not search for feeling: it is a mistake, a definite no-no – he knows that. As a result, feeling comes to him on its own. Alas, the actor still puts too much weight on it; he considers emotionality and explosiveness a chief value in acting. Needless to say, when the feeling appears, he rejoices: here it comes, my precious firebird! And so, he grasps at it, trying to hold onto it, or maybe something even more – to develop, to strengthen, or to green-light it . . . He holds onto it, and the feeling disappears, leaving just tension and spasms behind . . . In a word, he abandons the trail of life and slides down the path of grasping and holding onto something that isn't supposed to be grasped or held – just as we never do in real life. Feeling can't be *held*, for it *flows*. You have to *give in* to it, to this flow. You have to dive "into its waves."

"I saw an actor – what a wonderful performance he gave, just like in real life! . . . His partner was also amazing. What a superb actor – he is completely realistic!"

"Just like in real life," "completely realistic," "couldn't be better," "perfection," – these are all words indicating that this is a lie, a fake, a verisimilitude. The better, the "more amazing" – the falser it is.

When in the presence of **truth**, your jaw drops, and you don't even notice the acting, regardless of whether it's good or bad . . . Art and skillfulness disappear.

How to Start Working on a Role

Incited by directors, actors usually extract climactic moments from the role and try to stir themselves up by squeezing into them.

We'll suppose that this worked out for them. Yet, it only works out once. The actor plays out everything he had inside, and that's it.

Instead of searching for the character through climactic moments, search for it in the uneventful parts of the role. You need to take the calm moments – not only from your present (from the play), but also from everything that happened with your character prior to the start of the play. You have to discover the "I."

The climactic moments are nothing but a catastrophe that happened to the character who thus far has been living a peaceful life.

Take Ivan Kolomiitsev (from Gorky's *The Last Ones*), for instance: he meets nothing but catastrophes in the play. However, they are not the point; they are accidents. The whole point is that, up until now, he generally lived a peaceful life and was satisfied and contented with himself. He isn't accustomed to catastrophes: they are entirely out of his element. This is why he behaves so strangely throughout them.

It's the same way with every role. One shouldn't touch the climaxes. They should come out on their own.

"Taking Hold" of Circumstances

It is impossible to take hold of them; you can only *place yourselves under them*.

At first, they excite you. Then they stop doing so. What should you do?

Don't touch them at all. Start with the *physical truth*. Only then will they come, the circumstances. They'll come on their own, through the *text*. They come because they are already *there*; there's no need to keep picking at them. If you touch them, you'll scare them away.

On Real and Imaginary Objects

It isn't that the stage does not tolerate "real" objects; it's just that things "real" might interfere with the imaginary. Just as the real stew interfered with Stanislavsky's acting. [In Carlo Goldoni's *The Mistress of the Inn*, Stanislavsky played the role of Cavalier di Ripafratta. The real stew, which was given to him onstage, was so delicious that it distracted him and caused him to come out of the role. *–Author's Note*]

Nature should not be feared. (After all, the word "naturalism" comes from "nature." As Maurice Maeterlinck [1862–1949] once told Stanislavsky: "I'm an ultra-naturalist of heightened emotions.") On the contrary, we must fear breaking out of the realm of imagination.

The genuine dagger of Paul I helped Pevtsov in his acting – so, let it! So long as the actor begins to live the real life of Paul through this genuine object. [Pevtsov, who was superb in the role of the Russian Emperor Paul I (and fully transformed into his character), used to hook to his belt the genuine dagger of Paul I he managed to secure. Without this object, he could not play the role, or at least played it worse. The object gave him a vivid feeling that he was the real Paul I. Some would call this entranced naturalism.

However, the audience could not see the dagger of Paul I – it was invisible to them. The dagger was only needed by the actor – as a kind of talisman, or rather, a tuning fork helping the actor to check on the truthfulness of his creative state. *–Author's Note*]

To the "Technique"

Our reflecting machine is at work, and so is the machine of our subtlest feelings. Just as soon as we feel that we "see," we begin to *try* to see – that is to say that we transition over to the plane of conciseness, where we are completely incapable. We just pulled ourselves out of the realm of reflexes and subtler feelings, and into the realm of consciousness. This realm, while strong in other aspects, is powerless here. And so we collapse, we flop.

Consciousness is a gardener. Subconscious is the force of the sun, and that of the kernel. The kernel might die or produce bad fruit if the gardener doesn't help it, doesn't take care of it, doesn't give it enough sun, or doesn't water it properly. The gardener might even propagate a new variety, but it is *Nature* that brings everything to completion.

Affective technique exists! And above all, it consists of "freedom." Not the appearance of freedom, but of the true, genuine freedom – of the ability to involuntarily and spontaneously live onstage.

Truth and freedom: this is what differentiates the behavior of a great actor onstage from a fake.

What's more, one follows the other directly, and they completely depend on each another: if in a moment of truth I don't give it the freedom to emerge, then the truth ceases to be truth – it fades away. And vice versa: I can only give freedom to what is in me at that very second, to what is my truth at that very moment.

In this way, by giving yourself freedom, you inevitably yield the way to truth and thus find it.

What is freedom in our actor's understanding? It isn't too different from *involuntariness*.

When you practice this "freedom" and "involuntariness" often—in short, practice "living" onstage – when you see firsthand a thousand times how mighty it is, then, sitting in almost any theatre, at almost any play, you want to shout, to cry out with all your voice to the actors onstage: "Just stop interfering with yourselves! You don't want to sit, you have an urge to move elsewhere, and yet you break your will and force yourself to sit. Your partner said something; you didn't understand, yet you portray some earlier prescribed feeling." And so on.

The path of "observing" real life is two-fold (three-fold even). Along the lines of the three types of actors. One turns his attention to the psychological side; another toward the physiological (what he does, and what is happening with him physically and physiologically); the third toward the "theatrical" – the imitator.

The embryo has appeared. This means that the life of the role has begun – the life of the artist's personality creatively merged with the imagined personality of the character.

On "Playing One's Point of View on the Character"

There is a movement (it emerged fairly recently) proclaiming that you don't need to "play yourself," nor do you need to "play the character" – instead you need to "play your point of view on the character."

It goes something like this: "Iago is a villain. I, the actor, know that I'm playing a villain, and I should always keep this in mind. When playing him, I should always sense my point of view." This seems logical, and yet, what's all the fuss? Isn't it always like that in art?

A drunk may not sense that he is ridiculous, but the actor playing a drunk knows it perfectly well. One part of him is completely serious, while another part laughs at this seriousness. This other part is located deep down; it isn't visible, but it is there, and without this unique doubling of the consciousness, there is no art. This *doubling* **is** *the nature of creativity*. (For more on this, see Book Five).

Moreover, I cannot act until I've formed my point of view on the character. Thus, my point of view on the character and on all of its actions *can't not exist*.

It's a different matter when the point of view *is incorrect*. For example, playing Iago, I can get confused and believe with all of my soul that I am playing a true angel. If, however, someone *orders* me to change my point of view, it won't do any good. It's obvious that something fundamental escapes me – someone needs to help me make sense of the real state of things. It's essential that I grasp everything well; then my personal point of view on the character will shift *on its own*. Then, things will fall into their place. How is this achieved? This isn't necessarily an easy thing.

After all, what does "point of view" mean? It is my reaction to the given phenomenon or person. Is it even completely conscious? It's tough to decipher how it formed, and what it is like.

In one case, you know a person to be upstanding and spotless; yet something about him still turns you off. Why? You can't tell. Something in him, but it isn't clear what exactly it is.

In a different case, you keep complaining about a man, as if you hate him. Yet, when misfortune strikes . . . where do you go? Go figure, you only go to that person; you pick him out of everyone else.

Point of view is a complicated thing. Therefore, in each separate instance, it is a result of all of my tastes, notions, and habits, and of my entire physical and inner "I."

Therefore, in order to ensure that a correct point of view appears, at times you yourself need to be reborn. Is this possible? Why shouldn't it be?

We learn something new every day; each day makes us older, more experienced, and wiser: today we aren't the same as we were yesterday. In a year we will look back on our current selves, and perhaps even be condescendingly surprised: what were we thinking; what was with those ideas we had?!

And so, with a proper creative state onstage, *there can't not be a point of view on the character that I'm playing*. There's no need to specifically seek it out: it's just there. Playing it deliberately also isn't necessary: it will seep through all on its own – the audience will feel it perfectly well. If, in creative moments, you start thinking things that are dangerous to think (what should be kept as involuntary), then of course you're disrupting your creative process.

A work of art is, above all, absolute unity. The same unity should exist in the actor's creation. The source of it is the complete fusion of the actor and the role – this results in a character.

As for the duality or the doubling of the actor's consciousness – it exists on its own. Moreover, *it* begets the creative unity (for more, see Book Five). You don't have to think about it, or fear forgetting it, just as you don't have to fear that you might forget to breathe. You only need to think about the unity and complete merger with the character.

In playing Iago, I should feel myself *in the right* with all of my being. Otherwise what kind of Iago would this be? A self-doubting one?! A self-reprehending Iago?

Surely a real scoundrel doesn't consider himself a scoundrel? He considers himself to be a capable person.

You just have to give complete freedom to that scoundrel that exists deep down in all of us. Let him emerge; let him act and express himself – that's exactly what all great artists do.

Gogol wrote: "I already disposed of much of my own beastliness by passing it onto my characters; I ridiculed it in them and even made others laugh at it as well." [Demidov summarizes the thoughts expressed by Gogol (1913: 79–80) in his *Selected Passages from Correspondence with Friends*.]

Those advising: "You need to play your point of view on the character," confuse two different processes – the one of **reflecting** on the role and that of **fulfilling** it.

If the role isn't immediately comprehensible, then the process of reflection is definitely needed, in order to clarify what kind of a person you play. However, as soon as you've understood and felt it, then instantly, whether you want it to or not, your point of view on the character will appear.

And now that it exists, it will go about its work. In the process of fulfilling the role (the creative process onstage), I no longer have to go back to the initial process of reflection.

By the way, there are no idyllic roles; there is only a *point of view*, as on an idyllic role.

In general, by shifting our point of view on something this way or that way, we thus predetermine our success.

This goes for our point of view on the play, on the actor, or on something in life. And finally, on our very life.

12

On Several Principles of the Psycho-Technique

On Going back to the Basics

With professional actors, you mostly find yourself having to practice the very first steps: those same steps you take with the beginning students.

This was the only thing Stanislavsky practiced with all of these Moskvins and Kachalovs – these elementary beginner's mistakes: an actor doesn't see, doesn't hear, doesn't talk to his partner; he pushes, spurs himself, performs for the audience, plays results, and so on. [Along with Ivan Moskvin, Vasily Kachalov (1875-1948) was one of Moscow Art Theatre's leading and most experienced actors.]

It's interesting that the more the actor has performed, and the more experienced he has become, the more he makes these primitive, schoolboy mistakes. He is so used to making them that he doesn't even notice it. He even gets offended when they are pointed out to him – "What am I, a schoolboy?! I'm an actor! And you behave with me as if to a student!" Or else, he is surprised: "Impossible! Do I really make these mistakes?"

Yes, it's always a matter of these beginners' errors against the basic principles of creativity.

In this situation, there is no point discussing the role, interpreting character, revealing the essence of the bit, or passing other bits of wisdom an "experienced actor" expects from his director. It's going back to school instead – you have to reawaken in the actor the virginal purity of those early days when he felt even the smallest deviation from his natural state of truth.

It would seem most logical to start with the easiest exercises and then to gradually increase their complexity. This is only partially true, and with serious stipulations.

While performing complicated etudes (mini-plays) does allow actors to spread out their wings, it also spoils them. They begin to make mistakes and not notice them. Why? Because the very plot of the etude – its intriguing content – hides the mistake, and makes it invisible. Invisible as it may be, it still exists. Today one mistake, tomorrow another – and the habit of working *approximately*, with mistakes, begins to develop and grow. Before you know it, the mistakes take root; they begin to spread, and suddenly a teacher is faced with the most unpleasant fact: he was teaching the absolute truth, yet he has taught a more or less clever deception! Or, in the best case, he has taught verisimilitude.

The fact is that, as the exercises become more complicated, new, more complex aspects take up all of the actors' attention. There isn't enough of it left for the old, simpler, basic things. In the meantime, the actor stops believing; he begins to rush, doesn't green-light himself, and so on – in short, he makes those same mistakes that he made on the first day of training.

And the main trouble is that the teacher himself also didn't pay attention to this at the start. He overlooked it, thinking that something new was needed and that the old had worn out its welcome. As a result of this, everything came apart – the actor, feeling that something was off, becomes nervous, and the teacher also loses his calm and begins to rush. In the end, he makes the wrong conclusion: "This exercise is too difficult yet!" This is completely untrue. Now, all of the exercises are difficult, seeing as they've both stumbled.

What to do? Begin again from the beginning?

Yes. Go back to the first lessons. Sit your students in a circle and give them the simplest texts. Suddenly, things that got overlooked from far away (on the "stage") are immediately visible when they are close, face to face. Plus, the simplicity of the text doesn't allow for getting distracted with the plot.

The moral here is to return to the basic exercises as much as possible, almost every day! Then, the more difficult ones will come out on their own. The most rational way is to start each session with the basic exercises. As the class progresses, the teacher should become more and more demanding in respect to the basic issues. Then, in one hour's time, or maybe even later, he can make a transition to those more difficult exercises.

You have to keep returning to the basics for a very long time – maybe even for your whole life. They are like musical scales (or the ballet *barre*).

All of these exercises in "justification of physical movements," simple "questions and answers" about the weather – they should accompany the actor as long as he lives. [On "creative justification," see the Glossary.] Within them and through them, he will keep discovering newer and more profound things.

The entire training should be composed of the easiest and most difficult exercises, and vice versa: from the most difficult and the easiest. This is how it should always be. For your whole life!

Whenever something stops working out – go back immediately to the basics – it simply means that somewhere along the way, you slipped up and violated these elementary principles.

You have to regulate the unhinging of the technique throughout your whole life; you have to sharpen the blade that inevitably dulls with each use. Otherwise, the instrument falls out of tune after every performance.

In the meantime, the actor-artist needs a perfect instrument. It is only on such an instrument that the subtlest and most profound melodies of the human soul can be played.

Absolute precision and flawless correctness are essential. You need 100 percent, not 95 percent; not 99 percent, but 100 percent.

Stanislavsky says that everything onstage needs to be translated into physical tasks – only into physical. I assume that this conviction stems from having to deal with actors who don't practice in the basic aspects of their process, and therefore easily lose these skills. So, let them, at least onstage, proceed from the basics. It's correct and wise, but . . . the lazy-actor often interprets this in his own way (unconsciously): "I need to act 'simpler.'" And so begins this "simplicity that is worse than robbery." It degrades everything.

It would be wiser to move simple things off the stage and into a training studio, backstage . . . wherever you please. As for the stage, it should house something more significant. If you are so trained, simple things will inevitably follow you to the stage.

★★★

We must avoid misunderstandings and dangerously premature conclusions about the technique of the *bel canto*. This includes notions that something supernatural and back-breaking can be achieved immediately, along the lines of Mochalov's "macabre dance" or his face turning dark blue [in the "mousetrap" scene – *Hamlet*]. It must be said that *it's all about the correctness of the very origins* – that is about the simplest things.

Something great can grow only from this. You have to find *nature*. It is hiding in things that seem to be the most insignificant.

★★★

If genius bursts forth from you . . . then you hardly need any advice. Although, even to a genius one might say: hastiness is much more likely to spoil things than caution.

Of course, if the fledgling were to begin to flap its wings, and we were to tie them down and force it to walk like a chicken, then this could hardly be considered the correct path.

Alas, certain educators of a sort that you see far too often don't tie the wings down, but simply clip them and pluck them to the bone.

The Oversimplification of the Technique

Possibly, this is the main reason behind the failures of all knowledgeable teachers and serious students.

They understand everything correctly; things were working out for them; their work met the highest requirements. Later, little by little (or sometimes at once) everything faded; it became false . . . while the truth keeps wandering somewhere nearby – they just can't catch it.

They try to recover (both the director and the actor); they apply what feels like their original methods. Yet, nothing comes of it. It makes them feel dreary and hopeless . . . they want to just give up. What follows is lack of faith in their abilities, in the technique, in the art at large . . .

The cause *is always one and the same* – oversimplification. First, the oversimplification of the technique; then the oversimplification of everything else – everything becomes "approximate." The oversimplification of the technique lies, first and foremost, in the disregard for the "weak currents." In the meantime, they hide the main secret – these miniscule, utterly imperceptible movements, and actions that can only be noticed when they are over. They're so small, so delicate, they are almost *not physical* . . . They are like the waft of the soul. Those are the things you must give in to. They are those "spider webs" by which you can later pull out the rope. In the meantime, actors easily miss them. Yet, without them we are lost – there is no other way onto the unassailable tower of creative inspiration.

If you oversimplify things, make everything overly primitive, and deprive it of its "weak currents," **then there won't be any life onstage. Ever.**

This oversimplification killed the technique of the Maly Theatre, and it is killing and will kill Stanislavsky's "system." It brings death to all great achievements – just as it does in art, so it does in religion, in ethics . . . What is left of early Christianity? It moved forward – look how it has developed: Orthodoxy, Catholicism, Protestantism, and Lutheranism, and what have you! . . . There is only one thing missing – "weak currents." They evaporated. The only thing left is Edison's light bulb and its dependable, convenient wiring in every room.

"Weak Currents"

What characteristics does talent have?

Acute sensitivity. Patience. Tenacity. Faith in yourself. The ability to make associations – remote and close. And so on . . .

Perhaps, the most important of all is the green-lighting of the "weakest currents." What are those? Currents of thoughts and of movements – of the body, mind and soul? They are weak because they are **subtle** and difficult to discern. It seems like they aren't even there. And yet they are the truest. They are invisible, like cosmic rays, but their power is great; *this power* alone is the truth!

Weak currents exist, as do strong, crude ones. The strong ones drown out the weak that can't be heard through them. These crude, strong currents are, above all, our *habits*. This applies to our physical habits, as well as our habits of thought and reaction; it also relates to our traditions.

Our habitual reactions (as contiguous associations) turn up first. This is probably how we miss the call of other reactions (associations that are more remote) – those that are subtler and lie *outside of the circle* of usual reactions. We simply don't hear them over the background noise. When a person falls into a deep sleep, his habitual reactions and "strong currents" go away. Perhaps this is why "prophetic dreams" occur – those are the currents of our reaction to the "unheard" weak currents.

Restructuring

A major thing almost all directors get wrong is "non-restructuring." They all drone on about the truth, but they all force an actor to *restructure* from one state or feeling to another. With this demand, they **kill the main thing:** they don't allow the actor to "finish living," like we finish it in life; they force him to "search for feelings," which we never do in life; they skip from the "process" to the "result."

This heinous act isn't at all what the actor must know how to do. He should learn how to live onstage by the laws of his own nature – to live and to draw the audience into his own life. Meanwhile, what the directors are inciting these actors toward is *distortion*, a criminal perversion. It is exactly what ruins not just the ability, but even talent.

The actor-craftsman probably "should" know to do these malevolent things, but not the actor-artist.

Toward the "Beginning"

The intellectually willful specimens and also those who have been trained in the intellectually willful system always make one and the same mistake at the "beginning." They suspend their own personal lives. (After all, "the life of the character" isn't their life; it is, in their opinion, something completely different – extraneous.) So, the first thing that they do is to inhibit their own lives.

He inhibits the normal process . . . He empties himself . . . Then . . . He begins to catch hold of a feeling or an inner state – happiness or delight, for example. All of this from memory, from scratch . . .

How does he do this? As I said, from memory: with happiness or delight, there should be a smile, a delighted face, and deep breathing . . . Having done all this, he feels some genuine kind of excitement and satisfaction. It encourages him . . . He green-lights this state in himself and, if you look at him from the outside (and if you don't look very closely), it seems that the man is really delightedly happy.

What kind of an actor is considered gifted? The one who is so easily excitable and *seems* so emotional – he can easily feel something similar to happiness when he thinks of happiness, or he can easily experience a feeling akin to grief when he thinks of grief.

Is he really as gifted?

This type of actor is very *convenient* for the incorrect and superficial school – this is undeniable. He won't be at his wits' end if you command him to feel one thing, then another, then a third – all for no apparent reason. This too is undeniable. Yet, it is equally undeniable that these feelings won't be deep; they won't be connected with thought or need. They are more likely fleeting moods than actual feelings . . . Having said that, for the deception of the majority of the audience they are enough. Therefore, the work is done! What else could this school need?

This is neither giftedness nor talent; it is an ability to imitate and to mock.

A genuine actor's gift is *the ability to transform* – the ability to feel that you are the character and to assume responsibility for all of this character's life, and its circumstances.

Restructuring Is also One of the Prescribed, if not Legalized Types of Pushing

Restructuring is a two-step combination: first inhibition, then a "push" toward something that doesn't even exist as of yet (therefore, not even a "push," but the forcing out of "acted" feelings). "This moment requires laughter, or despair, or mockery, and so on. This 'bit' must be played with such and such 'task,' etc." The director's demand to speed up the tempo and rhythm is yet another huge push toward restructuring (like the MAT's Ilya Sudakov [1890–1969] screaming "*Pulse! Pulse!*" to his actors). [See pages 39, 311, 572.]

In life, restructuring happens on its own. Circumstances restructure us. New thoughts and new impressions restructure us.

When do we restructure ourselves in life? When we are fake. Yet, there is always a reason for this (a serious reason, or one that seems serious to us).

Opposition Reflex

This is a very serious phenomenon that completely destroys the actor of the "intellect and will." Any consciously taken task, any restructuring, and any prohibition of a spontaneous reaction, evokes the *opposition reflex*. This is the reason behind the failures of the intellectually willful method.

Letting Go and the Subconscious (The Source of the Creative Process)

On letting go.

"The Poet's dead!, a slave to honor . . . " [Mikhail Lermontov's [1954: 82] 1837 poem "Death of the Poet," dedicated to Pushkin's death.]

Yermolova said these words mournfully, but calmly, and almost coldly. Yet, behind this coldness stood an awareness of irretrievable loss – the kind of loss that would break any pathos of passion and despair. *Following these words, she took a long pause.* It was filled with speechless sorrow: it seemed *that she had nothing else to say.*

Yet, who can grow silent with despair and not be choked by it in the end? And so, again and again, she has to harrow her feelings . . . [Shchepkina-Kupernik 1983: 44]

"Letting go" follows "green-lighting" as a practical device in an actor's work and *as a path to the working of the subconscious.*

There is a certain *effort* that occurs when speaking a line. Perhaps it is unconscious, but it's still effort.

I'm cold, I am freezing . . . I open the booking-office door; I walk in, and there is the counterman, Mitya. I involuntarily feel like speaking, or perhaps I just involuntarily say: "Mitya! Receive unto thyself Liubim Karpych Tortsov, the brother of a wealthy merchant."

In order to say this, you make an involuntary effort. In this case especially – a sickly, exhausted person definitely has to make an effort to overcome his fatigue.

You said it, and the effort ceased; it's no longer needed. I am the "master." I "let go." I now find myself in a certain state of passivity.

What is this state about?

At this time, I might feel "total emptiness" in my head (to put it more precisely – in my consciousness). At the same time, my eyes can involuntarily see an object that had turned up, or a person . . . I see them . . . Some unconscious thoughts float in my mind . . . Let them float.

These thoughts, however, are *superficial.* It is in my depths where the main thing flows: "It's cold . . . This is unbearable . . . I need to get warm . . . I hope to God he doesn't kick me out . . . " This is all deep down – I'm not thinking about this in my conscious mind, yet "it is thought," (and it continues) beyond my conscious horizon.

I keep seeing some random, "irrelevant" objects: a table, paper, an abacus . . . My conscious thoughts are occupied with these things. Despite all that, suddenly (quite unexpectedly in fact), a new effort breaks forth:

"My brother turned me out! And in the street, in a coat like this – one has to dance about a bit! The frost – at Christmas time – brrr! – My hands are frozen, and my feet nipped."

It's over . . . I've said it all . . . the effort is gone – I won't be saying anything else . . . I "let go."

Now I give in to what takes place inside me. I can register a flow of some peripheral thoughts, objects, and sensations . . . These impressions are all on the surface, and they are all I can notice. In the meantime, some significant work keeps happening inside me – as I *finish up living.* This work belongs to my subconscious, so I don't know about it. On the contrary, I feel that I am empty – do nothing and think nothing . . .

The actor fears this state of emptiness and absentmindedness more than anything else. At such times, he thinks that he's got "thrown off." He doesn't allow them. In the meantime, it is the most necessary state. Without it, there can be no normal *subconscious* work. Without it, the need to say the next line doesn't arise – you have to squeeze it out of yourself. If not by squeezing, then it only jumps out as a result of mechanical drill.

★★★

The method of "letting go" and "blurting out words" is an additional technical approach to the implementation of the method of "let it be."

On the Interval between Two Thoughts (See "Stop!," "Culture Of Calm," "Tearing Yourself Away," "On Naiveté" And "Passivity")

This is a period of calm between two storms of thought.

The organic state of our natural "I." (The Upanishads.[1])

The method is this: speak a word; the students hear it (or you can show them an object). Speak a different word. Let them sense the in-between state.

If you take it as far as you should, this produces the sense of fear. Perhaps it is a fear of the abyss, of the eternity.

"I am the lamp; the world of images is the oil; the creative process is the flame. Peace and calm are needed in order to light the lamp."[2]

This condition is underrated. It needs to be blown into a powerful method. It wasn't for nothing that Hindus feature it so prominently in the chapter on *Powers*.[3] *Disruptions in rhythm* − isn't that Laya?[4]

And what about an acute reaction to a completely unexpected impression when your psyche suddenly restructures for no apparent reason?

Today, in bounden duty, I read the piano score of Rimsky-Korsakov's opera *The Snow Maiden*. This style "*a la Russe*" annoys me . . . I can't stand it. I read and I cursed; I cursed and I read. I got to the part where Bobyl takes the Snow Maiden to his place, stupidly bragging all the way in that same "*a la Russe*" style − and I flew into a rage. I read further how the Snow Maiden says farewell to the forest, and the trees, and how the trees and the bushes respond by bowing to her . . . Suddenly, out of the blue, I felt tears coming to my eyes; I could feel my emotions stirring. I remember mechanically reading these words about the trees bowing; suddenly, somewhere from within, from the depth, a wave rose up − and it struck me.

This is an example of how an impression reaches our very, very depths, and how a hot wave of feelings floods up our entire being.

I managed to achieve a similar effect in the chapter on creativity [See pp. 653–654]. In it, following the overly exalted and almost pathetical words about Newton's epiphany − the description of the sense of infinity that fills up a genius at the moment of inspiration, lighting him up like a torch − suddenly come these strange, as if conflicting words − "And all for nothing − for Hecuba! What's Hecuba to him, or he to Hecuba, that he should weep for her??"

There is a great abyss between these two passages, but you fly over it without a moment's hesitation, because the other side of the shore isn't foreign. In essence, it's made out of that same matter. And so, an awesome silence falls between these two storms of thought . . . It swallows everything that is conventional and earthly.

This might be one of the principal methods for the affective actors!!!

Toward Letting Go

The bit is developing soundly . . . I sense an urge . . . I green-light myself . . . Everything works out fine. I hold onto this "fine," and I keep going with it − I do what never happens in life.

You need to *let go*, to not hold onto anything! If I need to finish living this bit, it should "finish up living" beyond me, on its own. Not in my consciousness, mind you, but somewhere on a different plane − in my subconscious. Green-light your internal struggle; green-light your entire complex process of living.

★★★

Acting with a prompter is nothing else but the involuntary letting go. I said my line, and I don't know what will come next. I'll find out what next when they tell me from the prompter's booth.

★★★

The heart doesn't work 24 hours a day, but only 8. The rest of the time it rests (diastolic phase). In the same way, the actor needs to periodically rest (letting go).

If the heart would dwell in the systolic phase for too long, this would lead to a heart seizure and death. This same thing happens when an actor doesn't "let go," i.e. denies himself the necessary rest.

The Full Stop (See "Balls," the Skill of "Cutting Yourself Off," "Restraint")

Putting a full stop *before* a movement and *after* a movement.
    Exercise with an imaginary thread.
    A full stop leads to the economy of gesture.
    Speaking the lines with a full stop. The pause after an exhalation of breath during sleep – also full stop. The full stop is the completion of the bit.
    It's also good to practice this with a ball: you drop a ball and involuntarily follow how it falls; how it rolls; how it stops, and then comes to a rest; how it finally stands still – the full stop.
    "Full stop" exercises provide clarity and artistry, and they prevent you from blurring. They provide sculptural expressiveness. They help with form.
    Sometimes, if you encounter an actor who is restless and nervous, the best way to calm him down is the method of the "full stop." You put a full stop, and it completes the bit. More often than not, the actor is nervous because he hasn't completed it, and this results in a new bit not wanting to begin. As I call it sometime: "he is stepping on his own tail." As soon as you begin to pay attention to the "full stops," then the bits will begin to complete themselves and will "fall off" – giving way to the new bit.
    Before you know it, the actor calms down, since he has stopped "stepping on his own tail." He finds calm and composure and the freedom of creative imagination.
    You can throw a ball – it will roll, or begin to bounce at first, and then roll. It will slowly come to a stop, at last, and then – a full stop will arrive. At times, you can achieve a full stop faster, without waiting for a long time for the ball to come to a stop. For example, you throw a ball with all your might into a down pillow. It will instantly get stuck in it, and a full stop will come right away.

On the Skill of "Cutting Yourself Off" (See "Singularity," "Full Stop," "Blocking the Text")

The director often gets anxious seeing that the actor play an entire monologue, scene, if not the entire role, "piping the same tune," "all in the same register," "in the same key," and so on. The reason behind this anxiety lies in the word "same." It means that there is only one same point of view on everything, or only one same task, or one same agitation (emotion), or in general – "only one thing." And yet somehow in life we easily move from one place to the next – even taking a single step ensures that my foot is no longer in that same place where it was before. It's no longer there – not at all! It is in a different place. It's the same way with psychological movements. You must remember that our entire life is physical; if not roughly physical, then subtly physical. This means that we move and that we can't be in two places at once. This simple truth must be comprehended and trusted in full.
    If I want to take a step, I have to have the courage to tear my foot away from the floor. If that spot on the floor is so dear to you – don't grieve – you can always come back to it. However, right now please tear your foot away, and put in a completely different, although neighboring, place.

Let's take the description of a single landscape, a single fact that would inevitably tempt you to belt it out "in the same key."

> You ask what I contrived to see . . . ? Rich plains, and hills that trees had crowned, woods running riot all around, in whispering clusters, fresh as spring, like brothers dancing in a ring. And frowning cliffs I saw, whose heart cleft by the torrent, beat apart; I guessed their thoughts: diviner's art was given to me from on high! [From Mikhail Lermontov's (1983: 87) narrative poem "Mtsyri."]

"You ask what I contrived to see? Rich plains . . . " Do you see them? There they are: wide and large . . . Now drop them; don't linger on them – do it, as if you were riding on a train and suddenly, outside of your window, a hill appeared after some plains: "hills that trees had crowned, woods running riot all around, in whispering cluster, fresh as spring, like brothers dancing in a ring . . . " Although, is this really one image? " . . . running riot all around, in whispering clusters, fresh as spring, like brothers dancing in a ring" already applies to the trees, and not the hills. Therefore, let go of the hills, and now deal exclusively with the trees.

Now your train has taken you to a completely new place that is unlike any other – namely, to the cliffs beat apart by the torrent. Everything that has come before is now forgotten; there should be no traces of it left. In place of green hills and rich plains come frowning cliffs. How can you lump all of this together? After all, these are completely different phenomena and different impressions; they have nothing in common, and they influence different parts of my "I." They are so dissimilar, in fact, that it is one kind of me that is surveying the rich planes, while the frowning cliffs are being observed by a totally different me. Two different people, to be sure. So, don't be afraid to tear yourself away from one – otherwise, you will never transition to the other.

Moreover, tear yourself away *outwardly*: if the plains are below, then the hills must be higher, and the cliffs, these grand cliffs – there they are ominously pressing down upon you. Previous things were far off, while these cliffs are right here, right next to you.

Giving in to Your Urges

Inventions take time and effort, and they can be quite costly. This is why you're proud of them, you know their worth and keep them a secret.

Sometimes a student-actor, or simply some "guy" continues to pester you. He wants to get some advice, to pry something marvelous out of you, something that would instantly turn him into an actor and help him hit the jackpot.

You give up and toss him one of your inventions. He lets it slip and even says: "This is no big deal; tell me something more significant!"

As far as you are concerned at the moment, this is the most significant thing of all. You say it to him – he turns up his nose, like a stuffed dog who shrinks from bread.

So, you make yourself restructure, and find something different. You toss him another idea – a thought that is very substantial, and deep in content. You roughly sketch it for him – he does not like it either.

You try to explain it, to spoon-feed it to him. This gets him somewhat interested, it seems; he is thinking something like: "Yes, perhaps, this is also interesting, but it's just not it," and he starts pestering you again.

Well, if he didn't pick it up in the first place, or in the second, or when you spoon-fed it to him, then you don't really want to talk to him anymore.

This is exactly how our subconscious behaves. It prompts you: "do this," and yet you won't budge a bit. You don't like the prompt. Instead, you should have listened to it and began to obey. If the prompt isn't clear from the start, it will become clear to you later through the process of doing. Just start obeying the subconscious – you will learn that it has numerous riches in store for you. If you listen, it will behave with you, just like a teacher behaves with a student who suddenly perks up at the first bits of wisdom. Since he is so quick to grasp your ideas and eager to ask questions, you are glad to reveal all of your most cherished secrets to him. You try to make him an accomplice in all of your discoveries, and you let him in on all of the details and amazing nuances.

I see this all the time – in my literary pursuits, as well as in my directing and acting; in life, and in work.

If there is even just the slightest urge, you mustn't stop it – let it run its course; otherwise everything will cease and wither, and nothing will appear again.

Let us say you receive a thought that has nothing to do with what you are doing – take it, and start elaborating upon it in writing. You'll see how, as this thought develops, it becomes richer and richer. Meanwhile, you have stumbled onto your creative state, roused yourself, and raised your game.

Take what turns up. Obey your fate.

Sometimes it so happens that this stray thought blocks you. Even then you won't be able to get rid of it other than by writing it down on paper. The cork is removed, the liquid flows easily – your other long-awaited thought (the one that had been stored deeper in you) now pours out freely.

Sometimes you begin to write, thinking to say one thing, yet something quite different comes out of the blue. And so let it! It will come in handy one day, in due time and place. Therefore, it also has the right to exist. And if you don't let it live, then it will block whatever you are waiting for and so desperately need at this point.

When developing a role, you also can be blocked by something – something you can't get rid of except by "acting" it out of your system.

This method too is related to the "doing what you want" technique. If you keep it inside, it will block your process.

In life too, we often discard our first, barely teething urge. You walk by a store, see something and think: "I guess I should come in and buy it." This thought is immediately chased by the new thought, prompted by laziness or something else: "It won't go anywhere; you will get it another time." You come back the next time, and the thing has been sold. Such instances are numerous – you miss the right moment, and you reproach yourself later: "I did have an inkling to do this, why didn't I?" It's the same thing with first impressions. In retrospect, you would recall: "It was for a reason that I didn't like this guy when I first saw him!" It was obviously some kind of a warning coming from the subconscious, and you ignored it.

You must cultivate this skill of listening keenly to your urges. Instead of obeying your braking system, make sure to *fulfill* your desires *immediately, without fail*. Listen more to the nudges of "Do!" or "Don't do."

One must keep in mind that these nudges of "Do!" can also stem not from the intuition, but from nervousness or inhibitions. Cultivating calm is essential in this regard. We must cultivate *expectant serenity*.

Take Your Time!

It's the end of the 19th century. Moscow. A firehouse's back yard with a watchtower. The alarm bell rings, signaling – fire!

The firemen instantly run out of the barn into the yard, bringing out the horses; their boss swiftly walks out with them – the Fire Chief.

Everything has to be done in just a few seconds. The first command coming from the Fire Chief loudly is:

"Take your time!"

On the Significance of Green-Lighting Small and Miniscule Movements

This is an indispensable attribute of "letting go."

The line has been said. A full stop. I won't be saying anything else . . . The emotional effort has been released . . . Perhaps, some thoughts flow by . . . Perhaps they don't, but the *miniscule movements continue*: those of the eyes, head, hands . . .

Take Irja Viitanen, [who played the title role in Demidov's production of *Nora* (*A Doll's House*)] and her great, inexpressibly enchanting power. In the pauses, her hands, face, and eyes spoke even more than her words; her entire life, which she didn't even suspect in herself, was exposed with these motions – her soul became so naked; her body, which always serves as a shell for the soul, became more than transparent. It conveyed the most subtle and delicate life of the soul. No words can express it. Whatever the words tell, they don't tell it all . . . the body finishes the story in complete silence . . .

Affective Inertia

There is much more to say about the etudes. For example, *about affective inertia*. The etude is done. It's over. A new etude has been assigned. But the inertia from the first etude causes feelings to linger; the first etude still remains inside the actor, continuing to be played out (inwardly) to the end. What comes out as a result is a mix of the second etude with the first.

In such a case, there arises a need to "toss away" and "cleanse" yourself of the first etude.

When training in the technique of "repetition," you also need to master this "tossing away." You do so by revisiting only those *basic* circumstances that immediately precede the etude.

In other words, you go back to those kinds of circumstances that "spring" the etude in motion. And also those that would set your boundaries and wouldn't let you leave the track of the role.

When the student *doesn't green-light himself* and thus *keeps his inner reserves*, then it wouldn't be a bad idea to repeat the etude (or the scene). It would get played through to the end – the form would be found, and the work will unfold.

If the etude or the scene is played well, and the actor *gave it all and acted everything out of his system*, then repetition isn't recommended. Otherwise, forcing the actor would lead to creative depletion harmful for the role, and for the development of the actor's technique. This concerns the careless squandering of one's creative energies at a rehearsal on the brink of an emotionally demanding evening performance. This applies to the harmful repetition of the performance, several nights in a row, on the tails of the opening night. The exhaustion from the first performance doesn't have time to pass, and you already need to play the second, and so on, one after the other for an entire week.

Emptiness

Try to sit for a few seconds without thinking or wanting anything at all; then, a barely noticeable feeling, desire, or need would arise. Or else, these impulses would want to be *manifested* right away through movements or actions. Don't interfere with them; let them develop. The further this goes, the more their inertia will accumulate, making this process grow irreducibly strong.

To know how to not interfere with the development of inertia is to possess an important secret.

We must keep an eye on the issue of inertia and explore it in our intimate practical work. We must catch and extract the phenomenon of inertia and the *state of inertia*. We should try manipulating with it.

★★★

The idea of "emptiness" first came to me randomly in Velsk (in May of 1943). I was explaining to the actors how one shakes the text out of his head after it had been assigned. I spoke of the actor "emptying" himself of the text, and how then suddenly a new *life* and a new *being* (of the character) rush in, trying to fill that void. After I said it, I let the words slip: "Nature abhors a vacuum" [Wisdom attributed to Aristotle].

And from this moment this thought hasn't left me alone.

"Emptiness" is something very serious!

Passivity – is it not a variety of emptiness?

"Letting go" – isn't it also emptiness?

"The disruption in rhythm," which I witnessed with Moissi – isn't it a bold method of emptying yourself at the most heightened moment?

And, finally, what about my technique of etudes with circumstances and, especially, "without circumstances?" They too are based on the factor of "emptiness."

Doesn't the method of physical tasks and physical business also contain the hidden power of "emptiness?"

If this is even partially true, then we are standing on the brink of new discoveries in the creative technique.

The Psychological Cork

The most important thing is to open up. You listen to the music – it's just pleasant, nothing more . . . Suddenly several unexpected chords, or an exciting rhythm, cause you to inwardly restructure. Something in you opens up, and now you listen to it *in a different way* – a different side of you is [doing the] listening.

So, this is it: *the cork*. Pulling it out makes all the difference! You do it with music or words; with paintings or nature's beauty – the means are not as important. What is important to us is to find the technique of popping this cork.

So far, the most powerful aspects of this technique are: "psychological breathing," "liberation from the body," "letting go," and "passivity" in general.

For the most part, it is the "cork" that spoils things.

The cork may be located before the first threshold or before the second. For some people, the cork has not yet been removed – even before the first threshold. When you pull it out, they are shocked, and they feel that they now hold all of the threads to inspiration in their hands. But oh, they still have such a long way to go!

It is highly probable that the most accessible path toward the distraction of this habitual "cork" is *the culture of "green-lighting the first urge."*

The Culture of "Sensitivity"

What is intuition? Isn't it simply *sensitivity*? Extreme sensitivity to very subtle things?

The culture of *sensitivity* being the *root of intuition*, it must find its place next to the culture of *calm* and those other cultures that promise to emerge.

There are probably very few major "cultures": *calm, sensitivity, surrender*, and perhaps one or two others; the rest are all included inside these few.

★★★

The method behind the culture of *intuition* is the development of *sensitivity* to the most subtle urges and processes. This method must *never* be abandoned. Without it you would lose subtlety and sophistication. Things such as subtlety and intangibility are invaluable in art. Not things large and crude, but things minor – the minutest nuances.

★★★

The notorious "attention" that is taught in the most ludicrous way never leads to good results. The very word "attention" creates stress for the actor. It fails to awaken the main thing: passivity.

Furthermore, "attention" in art should certainly be *emotional*; it should have nothing to do with cataloguing. It isn't important to notice the multitude of details, but rather that one detail which would awaken your living, emotional point of view.

The very word *sensitivity* is conducive to openness and to passivity.

Sensitivity comes in different shapes and forms: sensitivity to details and trifles; sensitivity to the overall, greater thing; sensitivity to rhythm, to the musicality of a scene; sensitivity to costume, to the partner, or to yourself (to your own urges and needs, or your involuntary movements). Finally, there is sensitivity to those thoughts that hover near you – to the images and the forms.

"*Admitting to*" and "*Non-Admitting to*" (this is another one of the "cultures") might be one of the major keys to sensitivity.

Every impression provokes a reaction. If the partner speaks, yet an actor has no reaction, then he either missed the first urge, or his "brakes" kicked in way too quickly. (This means that there is a psychological splinter sitting inside this actor.) Sensitivity to the first, *foremost* sensation is one of the essential (the most essential!) conditions for creativity. If you miss the first impression, as in the above example, your habitual reflex won't miss it, and it will automatically slam on the brakes. It happens so quickly that, without enough experience, you won't even notice the workings of this "helpful" mechanism.

On Admitting to Yourself: No. 1

There is always a poorly permeable membrane between the world and us. We don't admit anything to us, to our "I." We admit things only to a certain calculator, which isn't located very deep.

The state of the real "I," of the "I am," can therefore only be experienced when I *admit the object to myself.*

You need to start with something small. Here is a table, on the tabletop plank there is a knot. I calmly look at the knot. Do I admit it to myself? Do my eyes perceive the knot?

You don't have to philosophize or reason, but simply *to look*. You must make your eyes become the passive receivers. And to not search for something in the knot that isn't immediately perceived, *to not search for anything* at all [Meaning not to search for any associations, images, patterns, etc. in the knot] – merely to look, *while admitting it to yourself*. Let something reach you. If it did, then your work is done. What has reached you? Don't try to figure it out; don't think about it. Something did, and what it was exactly is none of your business. It reached not only your usual reasoning apparatus, but even deeper – it reached your subconscious. This is why you can't determine exactly what it was. It is just important to register that something has reached you. Then you can move onto the next knot – admitting it to yourself; let it reach you. And then move onto the third, and so on.

With time, you can arrive at admitting *the whole world* to yourself.

Then you shall achieve the transparency of the *Evangelic Eye*. You shall achieve the enchantment of innocence and serenity, like with Moissi during his successful performances. [See Figure 20.]

"Admitting to" requires remembering the law of singularity: whatever has been admitted is the truth.

It's good to train admitting with a ball – here it is, in my hands; there, I've dropped it – it's in the air; now it fell; it is rolling; it stopped; it stands still – a full stop!

Advice to take risks also helps you to admit things to yourself. Take a risk!

The word "defenselessness" might also help the matter. Give it a try, take the risk of being "defenseless!"

To admit something to ourselves is to open the camera lens – to lift the protective cap off of it. The rays, refracted by the lens (our eyes or ears), enter in, and reach the photosensitive bromine-silver layer. The layer (our soul) reacts to the rays. A photographic negative results from this reaction, and from it – a photo. To allow it in is to not interfere with the photographic process.

On Admitting to Yourself: No. 2

How can you consciously *take* the given circumstances? How can you "appraise" them, [as the Stanislavsky system suggests]? You can't. You must receive a physical sensation from the circumstances, or any kind of *sensation* in fact. Only under such a condition would the circumstances touch and excite you, and cause a reaction with all of its consequences (such as the emerging need, etc.).

The director might talk about them without end, yet the actor is cold – the circumstances don't reach him. No wonder they don't, as they need to be perceived creatively.

You could submerge them into your subconscious.

You could bring them closer to the actor's soul with the help of the "if."

You could, having achieved the state of the "fool," take them without criticism – "idiotically."

Finally, the most interesting thing to do would be to get the circumstances to fall straight into the subconscious – on their own, (without any "submerging").

How is this done? Remove the very membrane separating you from life. Allow whatever you perceived this way to act uncontrollably inside you. Passively give in to whatever happens inside you and to whatever you feel like doing.

Let it all (perception, inner processing of it, and your reaction – your action) take place outside of your conscious mind – this is talent.

" . . . Having grasped just one line in a drawing, just one chord and one sound, pull the entire creation with it into our open-eyed world." (A.K. Tolstoy) [See page 654.]

★★★

The method of Admitting To: No. 2 strikes me as being genuinely remarkable mostly because all of the work is carried out creatively and outside of the conscious mind. It completely lulls our "consciousness," which causes a lot of harm in this situation. This method gives us the opportunity to bypass it, without as much as scratching it.

Admitting To: No. 1 has to be cultivated and trained, starting with the admitting of knots, and so on.

The material obtained via method No. 2 is precious. It remains in the magical, miraculous state – *in statu nascendi*! Its miraculous power is enormous – it reaches down to my very soul. It can possess me in a natural, spontaneous way! Isn't this the dream of every actor – to become possessed by some natural, spontaneous force?

The material obtained *in statu nascendi*! What more can you want?!

Incidentally, this brings to mind the experience of the hypnotist Dahl.[5] He suggested to his somnambulist the idea that he was Macbeth. Dahl himself was greatly confused and horrified when he suddenly met, face to face, with a man who had just committed a murder. It was so horrific and, besides, the somnambulist was so unlike himself that Dahl completely froze. He was barely able to regain control of himself and wake up the somnambulist.

What does a hypnotizer do? He drops material directly into the subconscious of the somnambulist, bypassing his conscious mind; since the material *has just been dropped in*, it exists *in statu nascendi*. With nothing to impede the further workings of this state, the material explodes, and it takes full possession of the somnambulist's body and soul.

You can admit plenty of things to yourself. You should start training it with things small – such as the "knots" – and you must always come back to them as you move forward. Just like an athlete continuously trains with five-pound weights.

But try "admitting" the lump of your own faith! (This lump is also formed by fulfilling elementary tasks.) [See the Glossary for the "lump of faith" exercises.] This would cause a phenomenon very similar to the one I described when writing on talent [see Book One, Chapter 5, "On Art and the Artist"].

When you seek your point of view on an object using ordinary means, the object might capture your entire being: both your consciousness and your subconscious. The technique of admitting is such that it allows you to bypass the consciousness; everything goes straight into the subconscious. What then rises to the surface is the ready result.

Significant outcomes should be received from connecting the "admitting" with the "breathing," [see Book Five, Chapter 12, "On Breathing"]. This is something to experiment with.

A wonderful way to gather material is the "emotionally tactile reading of the text of the role." (This is the further development of the "admitting.") Each word transmits into your soul an entire fragment of the character's life and that of the people around him.

It would be useful if the director too were to try reading the play the same way.

On Sensation

(There is no need to fear sensations because of their primitiveness – here is an example of how the primitive connects with the complex).

Sensation, as defined in psychology, is a very "excitable" phenomenon. An irritation "is sensed." I'm lying down with my eyes closed; something lightly touches my hand – this leads to a primitive irritation – I feel the touch. It is cold, or hot, or dull, or sharp, or dry, or moist . . .

What did I sense? Something touched my hand. Something a bit moist and not too hard.

One doesn't even want to call this a psychological act, not even elementary-psychological. It would seem to be an act that is totally physical; it does not affect the life of my associations (the life of my "soul").

The next moment, I open my eyes and see what touched me. A hand. I quickly look up at the face – it is my friend that I haven't seen for a thousand years. I grasp his hand, and so on.

Here we have two vastly different attitudes towards the same touch: 1. Something warm and soft, perhaps, a human hand; 2. The hand of a dear friend. With the first attitude, the sensation is purely physical; with the second, it is mixed with something psychological, yet it still is a "sensation." There are things such as the "sensation of a friend" and the "sensation of an enemy." They exist. The touch of a friend or an enemy would evoke a specific, almost physical sensation: something warm, slightly moist touched me, and also: something hostile (or friendly) – this too is included in the accord of sensations, and it can even drown out its other (purely physical) tones.

For the most part, actors search for feelings. It doesn't matter how they do it – be it through aggressive pushing, or by the means of the cunning "if." This won't yield us emotions that are real, living and *thrilling* – with ones possessing the concreteness of physical *sensations*. Instead, the emotion would remain as if outside of me, at a great distance. My organism won't sense it, and it would remain somewhat theoretical. Instead of a living feeling – with blood, with physical attraction or repulsion – it will be a dream-like feeling, a ***would be*** feeling. You can start with it, of course. If you've mastered the method of "giving in," you will emotionally evolve and expand.

However, the most proper thing to do would be to search for a *sensation*. "This is the hand of a friend. 'If' it were a friend, then *what kind of a sensation would I receive* from his hand? What kind of a physical 'charge' would penetrate me?" The search for a sensation (instead of a feeling) brings us closer to the life we must live at the moment. It makes everything *physically specific*.

This device includes the effect achieved when working with one of the actors on a role from Gogol's *Evenings on a Farm near Dikanka*. The actor drank his pear kvass, savoring every drop, while describing his drink. This helped us discover everything – the Truth, the character as a whole, and the comedic quality of the piece. [See Book Two, pp. 313–315.]

This also includes the communion and the relationship, discovered by means of sitting next to each other, while embracing or touching shoulders. The relationship conveys through the warmth of the partner's body.

When speaking of the "if," we must consider that the very, very *first moment* (the one the actors usually miss) is the most important. It's so short that it is *elusive*. In the meantime, it is essential to green-light your immediate reaction, instead of green-lighting the speculation: "if it had been like this, I would have felt that way and done that." With such speculations, the most important thing has already been missed. What remains is theoretical psycho-philosophy.

The ability to inwardly mark the primitive irritation, and to give in to the reaction, is *one and the same thing*. To sense and to not give in to the reaction is pointless. A lack of surrender extinguishes the sensation.

Sensation is fluid. It won't form, unless you let it "take its course." There is no other way to allow that, except by giving it freedom to develop. Needless to say, it only develops when you don't interfere with it.

The ability to grasp the sensation and give in to the reaction it inspires – this is the secret of temperament and its very essence. They say: "this actor is emotionally available," or "he's not emotionally available" . . . Wouldn't it be better to say "his emotional availability" is underdeveloped, or hidden, or it has been distorted?"

Tangibility

We encounter three different kinds of tangibility. The first kind is the one that belongs to a stage-director: the ability to initiate an actor into the psychophysical state required for the given scene (at times, for the character as a whole).

The second kind can be compared to *a tuning fork*, which you can use to discover: "So, this is what kind of psychophysical state I need."

And, finally, the third kind of tangibility. While working on it, you can grasp (or rather sense) the very meaning of the physiology in acting. Having done so, you also reach a similar understanding in life: apparently *in life we always speak of things with a varying degree of physiological tangibility.*

You could speak of something abstractly, as if it doesn't directly relate to you at all; or you can speak of it in such a way that you feel it. Moreover, you experience it again, as you speak of it – tangibly and physiologically. (This depends on whether the actor has crossed the Threshold.)

★★★

The sensitivity of the affective actor is of a particular kind – it is tangible, and physiological. He *identifies* himself with the object. Because of this he "gets burned" from it – and even wounded.

It was mentioned that we, in speaking about things, see them at some distance; while the affective type sees them *closely* – they physically *touch him*. With this touch, *a merger* occurs. As the two drops merge, so do the actor and the object he speaks about – they too merge *into one*.

One can see the flame . . . one can imagine how hot it is . . . while the affective actor sticks his hand into the flame . . .

Moreover, the passage of time removes us from our impressions, yet with the affective actor, it is the opposite: time brings impressions closer to him. (A good example of this can be found in Fleury's story of a man who spent all day carrying the wounded away from the barricades. At the end of the day, having returned home and remembering how he could have been killed at any moment, he fainted.) [See Book Five, pages 688-689.]

Is there a technique for this? Yes. The technique of *drawing objects near* (the nearest flow of thought).

★★★

We must add what I call the *primitive* to the list of affective actor's distinctive qualities. He perceives everything through his primitive sensations – through touch, through smell, and emotionally.

Crossing the Threshold of the Mundane Truth (Toward the Primitive)

Not all truths are made equal. Truth can be small or big. It can also be mundane (with brakes) or completely tangible, lying beyond the threshold of everyday truth.

In short, it is the truth of *physical sensations*.

Upon further thought and examination, you can see that the old man [Stanislavsky] didn't think anything through or carry it out to the end. This is what causes the boredom of his theatre's verisimilitude.

Without the "primitive," theatre is modest, "noble," and boring!

Freedom as a Power

Freedom (impulsiveness?) is the most rare quality in an actor. It is completely outside of the willful or intellectual types' reach.

It has to do with the fact that the person, when he is free, completely gives in to the objects of which he speaks. The person doesn't even exist, but just the objects he thinks of or sees.

A free actor ends up reacting completely involuntarily and to the fullest degree. With such an actor, there is no self-observation of any kind in the moment of reaction.

I speak of the involuntariness, of complete obliteration of the self, even of the absence of the self. (What's more, a free reaction proceeds intensely and without inhibitions or control.)

One must do everything in their power to develop this quality.

The initial point is the surrender to involuntary reactions. Complete "cerebral abstinence."

Perhaps this depends on the power of the "facts?"

No. Facts are good things, but I would react to one and same fact in completely different ways, depending on my state and on the flammability of my apparatus.

One's apparatus and temperament can be stiff or mobile.

How do we develop the latter quality?

"Fool": "Headless"

Up until now, I recommended "tossing your head out the window" as a means of freeing yourself from rationality, being able to perceive everything and act "headless." Another method would be to ask yourself: "Am I enough of an idiot?" No, not enough! You need more! Even more!

These methods yielded good results. In the meantime, some new thoughts arise.

What is stupidity? When does it occur in us? Quite often. More often than we think.

Whenever we live under the influence of our emotions, then, immediately, we become a fool.

We are saddened, and we take a dim view of the world – there you go, we are a fool, because we don't see what's really there; we invent things of our own that aren't there at all.

We are happy, and the nastiest autumn day seems beautiful and pleasant to us. Well, once again we are a fool. Again, we see what isn't there.

To give in to sensations and emotions – this is our permanent and natural path to stupidity. It's true that in art this "stupidity" transforms into higher wisdom. And the "wisdom of this world" turns out to be folly and dullness.

The "blurting out" of the text on the tails of "letting go" is also a method for getting around our rationality and, therefore, a path to becoming a "fool."

Toward Training

Sit down and be a fool. Stand up, without rationalizing, and be a fool. Sit down again. Go to the window. Proceed with similar *elementary* physical movements and actions – if you go for more complicated ones, they will trip you.

When this foolish obedience has been established (although it should not be sluggish): sit down and be a fool. Stand up and do whatever your urges prompt you.

When the student begins to do it, you need to remind him again and again: "be a fool, be a fool!"

He won't be able to preserve the needed state through many consecutive actions, which is quite all right. One, two, three actions are already a lot. Moving to expanded improvisation is more than dangerous.

★★★

Fools are lucky. When I think of talent, I realize that an integral part of this condition is *fortunateness*, and that we must seek this condition of *fortunateness*. It would be something along the lines of "the fool in art"; otherwise, it could turn into just a fool – very boring and fruitless.

Ivan-the-Fool of the Russian fairy tales is very fortunate. It is one of his defining characteristics.

Take!

In life, we take things all the time; we can't not take them. However, do we take things in such a way that to give them enough time to reach us in their entirety? We pass things by, we look at them, but do we let them sink down to our very depths?

Look how greedily a child takes from every new object! . . . Then, bit by bit, we grow absentminded; we are no longer surprised by anything, and we merely glimpse at things through our fingers.

A new invention? Ah, that's interesting – and we move on. War?! Damn, I hope it doesn't affect me. And so on. We keep passing by as quickly as we can!

And now, having grown so accustomed to superficiality, try "taking" like you did before, when you were a child. Try taking like Pushkin, Mochalov, and those others, who preserved their "naivety" and temperament. Apparently, your apparatus itself doesn't take, but merely skims upon the surface of things. Someone has put spokes in its wheels (it must have been our blessed self-defense mechanism). You may have been able to take something, but something in you inhibits the process and prevents you from taking.

I can see the gradual resurrection of this ability only through the exercises in the *inhalation (inspiration) of the objects* – at first into your head, and later into your depths.

★★★

You need to take, you do! Then there will be something to give.

You must learn how to take.

1   Take it *now*, in order to give back *now*.
2   Take it *now* and send it somewhere; submerge it into yourself (be it image, object, or thought), so that you have material to give back later, when it is needed.

★★★

I need every detail, every trifle that crosses my sight, or reaches my ear.[6] If it rouses and excites me – how is this a trifle for me? If it were a trifle, then I wouldn't have paid attention to it!

It must be said that analysis is only necessary for the understanding of the entirety of the work and its given circumstances; it is also necessary for the deepening of the text and for making it more concrete. However, the thing to remember (firmly!) is that you must perceive all of these things with absolute freedom, without the shadows of physical nervousness! Otherwise you would only achieve neurasthenia. You would wind up your nerves, and it would lead to the mixture of scattered attention and panic; or to be more precise – just panic.

If this mistake has been made, then let this extreme nervousness settle, and tomorrow you can start to reap the fruits of today's work. However, tomorrow you must begin from a state of calm with its good eye of *asana* and so on. If the mistake hasn't been made yet, then here and now you can achieve a correct result.

Director! Take a good note of this mistake and do not "take" the circumstances with nervousness and physical anxiety, when demonstrating a scene to the actor. You yourself should know how to "take" them soundly. And if you don't know how, then don't be surprised when your actors push and "live" incorrectly.

Chewing over the circumstances is the last thing required for *taking*. *Instant admitting* is required instead. This was how it was with Mochalov's black shawl. In addition to it, arm yourself with *letting go*.

Vakhtangov's Theory on the Unconscious Perception of Material (Admitting)

"The task" is the consequence of the admitted given circumstances. The task is already a manifestation. It results from the material that has been admitted into the soul. This means that the main thing is to have the material; everything else is merely reactions and reflexes.

The best method to acquire the material is *admitting* it. This acquisition is unconscious, first and foremost. Secondly, the material is kept "*in statu nascendi.*" This means that it possesses a miraculous, magical power. [See *Submerging [Text, Circumstances or Tasks] Into the Subconscious.*]

The Nearest Flow of Thought

Circumstances and objects do everything for me. I don't even exist; what does exist is the rain, dampness, and cold slush. So, go ahead and give in to them – let them do their work. You've got nothing to do with this.

The objects and the circumstances are all-powerful; they do what *you* would never be able to do on your own! All power is *in them*. Just give in to the object, or the fact – this will produce "*the nearest flow of thought.*"

I don't think, but the things and the facts think for me. Let the skull of Yorick do the thinking; what am I after all? *Nihil* . . . nothing.

To lose yourself, to disappear into things and facts – this is the important thing. They exist; I don't. Get away from yourself using all possible means! If doing this directly does not work, then do it through action, or through perceptions, and so on.

Notes

1 *The Upanishad*s is Hindu religious-philosophical treatises, and a term of Hindu philosophy, literally meaning "esoteric" or "secret doctrine." The main idea of the Upanishads is the achievement of the "Knowledge of the Self," and of "liberation" – a state analogous to dreamless sleep, and accompanied by a sensation of bliss and happiness. The editors could not locate the actual quote in *The Upanishads*.
2 Demidov is referring to *Bhagavad Gita*, a Hindu scripture, part of the epic *Mahabharata*. Although, Demidov's source may have been Helena Blavatsky's (1909: 78) *The Voice of the Silence*: "'Ere the gold flame can burn with steady light, the lamp must stand well guarded in a spot free from all wind.' [Bhagavad Gita VI, 19] Exposed to shifting breeze, the jet will flicker, and the quivering flame cast shades deceptive, dark and ever-changing, on the Soul's white shrine."

3 Demidov is most likely referring to chapter 3 of *The Yoga Aphorisms of Patanjali* (see Patanjali 1920). This book was originally printed in Bombay in 1885 by Mr. Tookeram Tatya, a Fellow of the Theosophical Society. The brochure had wide circulation in the Theosophical circles, including in Russia.

4 Laya Yoga is one of the yogic practices. Laya means "dissolution" or "extinction" in Sanskrit. Practice of Laya Yoga is aimed at the dissolving of the mind, and obtaining the state of superior conscience, or Samadhi.

5 Among Dahl's patients were Fyodor Chaliapin, Konstantin Stanislavsky, Vasily Kachalov, and Sergei Rachmaninoff.

6 Demidov is referring to the normal, sound creative state of an actor, as described in the subchapter "Letting Go and the Subconscious": "I keep seeing some random, 'irrelevant' objects: a table, paper, an abacus . . . My conscious thoughts are occupied with these things." See page 533.

13

On the Few Principles of Theatre Pedagogy

On Easy, Joyful, and Inspired Teaching

Questions and Answers can be done in such a way that each pair performs the same text, one by one; or they can be done differently – only one or two pairs, and then – a new text. This is more engaging; the other way is a bit boring, especially if there are ten pairs, and you need to repeat some etudes, and you let each of the pairs switch lines. In such a case, the same text ends up being repeated up to 40 times!

You must definitely refresh this flow by injecting new life.

Or else, you could let each pair have their turn quickly, without any major corrections. This method too is based in the kind of ease, freedom, and lack of responsibility.

And what more could you want but *irresponsibility* (excellent word!). Otherwise, responsibility really intimidates the actor. If something worked out well – good for you. If something flopped – well, who cares! What's the big deal? You can just repeat it again. It didn't work again? Well, enough for now, go back to you seat! . . . There, mistakes will get digested on their own.

It should be done so that everyone feels *easy and cheerful*. We should work with a view to "*free creativity,*" rather than exercising "truth," "freedom," "giving in," or even "faith in yourself." When this is done without lightness, it can exhaust or even repel.

Let's say something came out well, one of the bits was successful, and so you should encourage the actor: "Good job! Such and such part was especially good: you perceived such and such thing; you gave it a green-light, and it came out lively. Let's do it again! Livelier, lighter, even freer – everything is going great!"

Keep up a lively, quick tempo through the entire class, and, as they say, go out with a bang.

If the students start getting too loose and begin to fake and overact, then clamp down on them again. However, it would be better to change the text; otherwise the "clamping down" with the same text would be boring and difficult for them.

For the teacher, too, it would not be easy. You have to be very (almost exceedingly) attentive. It is useful, very useful; otherwise the teacher would also start getting too loose, and won't see things properly. But, as I said, it is also difficult. The feeling of difficulty, work and strain, once it sinks in, it begins to gradually permeate you, unnoticed. As a result, you turn into a strict mentor, and not an inspirer. You would lose the main thing – *joyfulness*. You would lose it for them and for yourself.

Another good method: the student did an exercise; now have him go back to his seat and think on his mistakes. In the meantime, two or three other pairs would have their turn, and then he can go again. After his second turn, it would be appropriate to make corrections.

It is important (isn't it more important than anything?) *to be an inspirer*. A teacher who grasps this quality can create miracles.

Towards the Outline

Work on self is divided into different parts: work *visible* and *invisible* – work *with everyone* and with everyone's help, and work *in solitude* – all by yourself. What work do I call "*intimate?*" Work on physical tasks – on the objects and *at the object* (it's a good way of putting it: "working at the object"), as well as work *at the subject* – this means working at your own mechanism, while monitoring it.

In general, you must divide everything not only by the principle of the triad and reflexology [see Glossary], but also by the nature of the work and by its conditions.

Is it possible to do without refining one's human qualities?

Should it not be put forward as training developing "*individuality?*"

This is, of course, correct.

A person who is trained this way will be an individual artist. An artist in and of oneself.

★★★

God forbid that you work or rehearse "anyhow," approximately, just to kill time. This is to sow bad action! It would develop into an obnoxious habit, and then you won't be able to get rid of it!

You can start with something small, something insignificant, but you have to take it through to completion. (See chapter "Energy") [Page 569].

It's the same thing when working by yourself.

You mustn't allow yourself to work half-heartedly: whatever energy you've got, no matter how great or small – just invest *all of it*. Not in the sense of physical exertion or activity, but in the sense of calm and keen emotional attention.

On Intimate Work on Self and on Working without the Exertion of Effort

(See "On the Power of Minor Details (Methodology)," "On the Nearest Flow of Thought, 'What' and 'How.'") [See Glossary.]

In addition to the usual work on self, there should also be another kind of work—intimate, if not *the most intimate*—when you are alone with your own apparatus. During such work, you keep your eye on a thought or sensation, and you observe it in the quiet of your seclusion. Calmly and leisurely, you watch whether it flows close to you, or far; inside or outside of you. You check whether it touches you or just flows by . . . In that same state of complete calm, if not to say contemplation, you carefully try to bring it closer to you or yourself to it. You must only do what doesn't require *any effort*. This is relatively the same as discovering the true "*what*." [See Glossary.]

We have completely the wrong point of view on work: "work is work!"

Far from it!

You can work to goof off; work to contemplate; work to have fun; work to savor every bit; work to rest! The latter is the most productive work.

Thinking about dumbbells is what brought me to this idea of intimate work. Each exercise with the dumbbell is so simple that a child could do it, while the results are astonishing. Exercises, in general, can be of two kinds, and there is no need to confuse them – those performed with effort and those completely without.

★★★

Dumbbell exercises are easy to do, and they can be done at all times. This is how they differ from those other exercises, requiring greater effort. Besides, they aren't complicated; they are elementary.

On top of it all, they are mandatory and daily. Therefore, we should choose our exercises according to these rules. Among them, *"blowing," "whistling,"* and *"breathing on a candle"* should probably be included before anything else.

Additionally, it's important not to forget connecting this with the "intimacy of the exercise."

Green-Lighting Inhibition

An impression has been received; a reaction begins – a manifestation. Without even noticing, the actor inhibits it, thus evoking a peculiar state of reaction – a rather depressing experience. The actor goes ahead and green-lights it.

This reaction seems appropriate when looking at it from the outside. However, a closer look reveals that the actor has green-lighted inhibition. If you don't notice this, you will keep cultivating the inhibition in him. Thus a strange contradiction occurs: *the teacher kept his eye on green-lighting, but developed inhibition instead.*

This type of inhibition comes from *pushing*. It usually happens like this: some intimidating audience member walks in; the performance suddenly becomes *critical*. This causes nervous tension; the actor becomes alarmed; his creative state – forced and distorted, and he ends up green-lighting all that. This can be considered as the green-lighting of *degeneracy*. At the start, the degenerate aspect is very weak, but once the actor gave it a green-light, then it reaches inappropriate dimensions. Meanwhile, the stimuli of such "nervousness" accompany the actor for his entire life: opening nights, showings, critical performances . . .

This excessive stimulation produces scandalous inhibition and failure, and nothing else. The opposite is also true: during an audition, the excitement might cause a person to achieve his maximum, if not his super-maximum. They accept him, based on the audition, and then he returns to his normal condition, and reveals his complete mediocrity. Just once in his lifetime he acted brilliantly, and that's it – nothing good comes out of him again. He "green-lit" himself at the audition – "Ah! Be what may! What do I have to lose!" – from despair, from hopelessness.

Mediocre as his subsequent acting may be, this single flight of inspiration deserves consideration. If he has done it once in his life, it means that he has got something about him. You just have to find your way to it. This can only be done through the techniques of "green-lighting" and freedom.

On the Lightning-Like Zigzag of Feeling

A student-actress was considerably intimidated and spoiled at the Moscow Art Theatre. She gradually started to master the new technique of improvisation, perception, and giving in. Surrendering to it made her feel joyous, and the joy caused her to step on it – to "give out" more than she really wanted to give.

In pushing, she "corrected" the natural trajectory of emotion, making it straight, like a stick. Meanwhile, in life, emotion would follow a zigzag-like path. The lightning bolt must serve as a model here.

The path of a lightning bolt is the one of least resistance – see how it zigzags across the sky!

This is how feeling would sweep in life – in sharp zigzags – if you give it complete freedom. A straight line is the result of forcing.

Toward the Technique of Encouragement

Very young children draw a lot and with ease: they draw a circle or some squiggle, and they joyfully announce that they have drawn their mom. The moment comes, however, when the child begins to understand that his drawing doesn't look at all like what he wanted to draw.

Then comes disappointment and, following it, lack of faith in one's own powers. This doesn't just put an end to all drawing – the prideful child is so humiliated, he won't even pick up a pencil. Doing so would just bring another confirmation of how weak and powerless he is.

You must be able to skillfully lead a person – be it a child or an adult – through this period of disappointment and awareness of one's own insignificance.

1   You need to give easy tasks.
2   You need to ask him to fulfill them sketchily, as a draft – there "isn't enough shot in his locker" to achieve perfection.
3   You need to often repeat how *easy* it is. You need to say: "At such and such moment, you wanted to turn this way; you already began doing it, but then suddenly inhibited yourself. Don't interfere! Just trust yourself! Do whatever you want! Have courage! On the other hand, don't rush yourself; again, believe that everything will come in its own time; just don't urge things."

At the Moscow Art Theatre, and its studios, people usually get stuck in this phase of disillusionment. The exorbitant difference between what they can and what they should be able to do intimidates them.

Talented and free people, they transform into boring marionettes.

In other theatres, however, it is even worse . . .

There is no need to scare the actors with the hidden reefs; you just need to teach them how to *follow the natural clearway.*

Wobbly Doll

There is nothing wrong with an actor or student making mistakes; it's only important that he begins to feel them. If he falls, this is not a big deal; as long as he learns how to get back up on his feet again.

It's essential to train the actor so that this happens on its own, like with a wobbly doll.

552

Teaching Mistakes (Tactics of Teaching)

Mistakes in teaching – a lack of pedagogical tactics; a wrong progression; insensitivity toward the student; inflexibility in handling the living material, and so on and so on – all of this can ruin the most perfect of methods.

Pedagogy is an art. Like any art, it is immensely difficult for people who are devoid of pedagogical sense and unbelievably easy for people who possess this appropriate talent.

Unable pedagogues are the ones who spoiled such things as, for example, the *bel canto*. They know their own subject well, but they teach it more poorly than they know it. As they pass their skills to the next generation of teachers, things gradually get worse and worse . . .

The Actor and Work

Work falls into two categories: the permanent and the temporary.

The permanent is the work on self; the exercises; cultivation; development, and keeping yourself "in shape." Generally speaking, it is the path of progressing further along the way of technique and artistic power (temperament). Physical training, voice, and general development and education all belong to this category.

This work is as *necessary* for the affective type *as the air he breathes.*

The temporary is the work on the role. It is the acquisition of the essential qualities that belong to it, and the maintenance of them within yourself for the period when you play the role.

This work is essential for the emotionally-willful type. For him, everything is built upon it.

★★★

People might be equal in their giftedness, but differ in the strength of their perseverance. The most talented person, when bumping into obstacles (first, second, third) would begin to get bored; for him, things have lost their exciting power; he begins to pay his attention to other things . . . and his work fails.

There are many gifted people. There are few strong, tenacious, stubborn ones.

The task of the leader is, above all, to fight with exhaustion, the loss of interest and boredom. You can uncover a person to his very core, to his genius – only to lose him in the end. And all because of a nuisance, because of boredom. He gets bored; he withers, he becomes interested in some other most unworthy things . . .

It is difficult enough to keep others in a state of interest and persistence; it is even more difficult to keep yourself in this state (see Balzac's thoughts on the importance of work, or, as he put it, "courage")

"Inspiration is a guest who does not willingly visit the lazy." (Tchaikovsky [1934: 372]).

There is a brilliant guitar maker in Moscow by the name of Klimov from the workshop of the world famous Ivan Krasnoshchekov [1798– 1875].

He does wonders. He is a kind of Stradivarius.

When you come to him, oddly enough, you rarely find him repairing or refurbishing guitars. What would you think he is mostly doing?

He is honing his tools.

He sits at a table, sharpening them on his touchstone. Slowly, methodically, and calmly he hones and oils all of his little chisels and knives.

"Vasily, are you sharpening your tools again?"

"Hello, sure I am! This is our job. Can't do without it!"

And so he keeps sharpening, sparing no time. They are all razor sharp, his tools. What an instructive example!

Actors! Do *you* spare no effort honing your instrument? Or do you chop, split, and cut with whichever instrument comes to hand?! By doing so, you damage the material, and do harm to your own hand. Not knowing what kind of tool it squeezes, it has to do its work by guess, losing fine sense and talent and hopelessly destroying its genius.

And what about the directors? Isn't an actor your instrument? Do you hone him and care for him as this 60-year-old uneducated artist does for his tools?

His work is divided into two seemingly separate halves – part of his time he spends working on the guitars; at other times he forgets all about the guitars and sharpens his knives and chisels, or cooks the kind of glue you can't find anywhere else – it spreads in a very thin layer, and it sticks forever.

On Professional Physical Habits

The most important thing is "to go wild," to become a monomaniac, to only think about your passion, and to only do that. For example, you become passionate about writing. Then keep writing without a moment's rest – on paper, on shreds, and if there aren't any, then on chips of wood, in the dirt, and on leaves. On everything . . . You must become possessed. Let it turn into the most genuine writer's itch.

This purely physical habit would make *writing* your second nature; it would penetrate the essence of your inner makeup. It is the same way for an artist – he is drawing all the time.

It is the same for a soccer player, who can't walk by a single splinter without kicking it.

The wrestler grabs at everything – he bends, pulls, and pushes things.

You need to acquire a habit of *physical motion*. According to the law of James, it should move you toward your deeper-seated emotions, ideas, and desires.

What kind of physical motions apply to acting?

On the Necessity of Training in the Basics

I climb into a streetcar, and I overhear a fragment of a conversation. Two young people, around the ages of 25 – 30, are talking.

"Do you love to play scales very much?"

"Yes, I love it a lot; I love it more than anything, but I never get to do it."

"I also love it very much. I think that, in going away this summer, I won't play anything except for scales for two or three months."

"Yes, you know, when you stick to scales as you should, then concerts that were once difficult become so easy. And if you only play pieces, then, in the end, you aren't certain of a single modulation."

By all appearances, these two were violinists finishing up their studies at the musical conservatory.

What an edifying conversation for us actors – we, who hate scales. We appreciate only the roles, and even then only the main parts.

Truly, a school of acting is yet to be created, and the school of the Art Theatre is far from being one.

★★★

Actors' processes of working on a role differ greatly, based on their specific perceptive mechanism and creative type. One perceives superficially (imitator); another deeply (affective); one becomes excited emotionally, and another intellectually and willfully. One brings onstage a copy of what he found in rehearsals or during his solitary tests at home; and another brings his creative state, and his own inspiration (the following chapter is devoted entirely to this). No matter the type, each of them requires *his own* significant preliminary work.

This is work on self, first and foremost – that is work on one's own acting apparatus. During this work, an actor studies his apparatus; he searches for the paths to the creative state; he learns how to acquire and strengthen the necessary habits.

Secondly, the actor has to work on the play and on himself in relation to the play.

The writer has to "build up his writing;" he has to find his own expressive means – those belonging to a *writer*, rather than an actor, for example, or a storyteller. Otherwise, he is not a writer.

The actor has to "build up his acting" – to uncover his particular *acting* abilities through his communion with the audience.

Very few of them – the most gifted – achieve this at once. They walk onto the stage and begin to act beautifully. They sit down at the desk and start writing brilliantly.

However, the first success might be a fluke: the reason for this is the law of maximum. (He played it right away. He burned it all off. And what next? Lack of faith, disappointment, and a change in profession?! Or else, kicking one's heels at a beer bar, waiting for inspiration to descend?)

The tree's roots are deep in the earth; they are invisible. With these roots, the tree sucks lifeblood out of the earth, and its juices. Nourished by them, it grows, and turns into a giant.

If you cut off some of the roots, it will get sick; if you cut off many, it will die . . .

Take an actor who is able, and things come easy to him. Yet, he is lazy, so all of his work is in plain view – at rehearsals. Such an actor is a tree without roots – the first wind will knock it over. Only the watchful director can rescue him. His superhuman patience keeps nourishing the actor – this giant, whose roots are so feeble they are suitable only for goosegrass.

These rescuing measures include the means such as precise stage pattern. One can compare it to a prop meant to prevent the tree from being blown over by the wind. This is how it stands, as if on crutches – fastened and bolted over, it maintains the appearance of standing . . .

The lazy don't have roots.

Only those remain standing in art *who can't not work*, as they've got the roots, and these roots can't not suck the juice out of Mother Earth.

★★★

An ordinary actor is vain, while an artist is ambitious.

Of Irja Viitanen, it was said that she was humble. This isn't true. Every artist knows his worth perfectly well.

When the artist speaks poorly about his work, it is only because his ideal is so high – everything he does fades in comparison.

What is worth learning from Irja is her habit of mastering only one thing – whatever she just received (a method or principle), without trying to connect it with everything else. Or, more accurately: she didn't spread herself thin trying to do several things at once.

The secret lies in the fact that *each* of the methods, if properly understood, has the power to evoke the proper creative state onstage.

14

On Preparing Yourself for Rehearsals and Performance

(See "Selfish Rehearsing" [See Glossary])

"Play" stems from an overabundance of power. Creativity stems from plenitude. To reserve and collect yourself is the main thing.

The German tragedian Ernst von Possart [1841–1921] rested on the day of the performance. He was silent or spoke only in a whisper. He ate one egg and a cup of broth.

Yermolova didn't receive anyone.

Salvini arrived at the theatre many hours in advance.

Look at how athletes prepare for competitions.

Look at the way novices prepare for taking vows or priests for consecration.

Everything requires *specific* preparation.

Persian gymnasts (street performers) always lie on the ground and sleep; as soon as the time comes to "work," they jump up and become unrecognizable with their 20-pound clubs. And then they lie down again and sleep.

The regimen at health resorts: 10 plus 2 hours of sleep.

The "kumis cure" resorts regimen: either moving or lying down – no sitting.[1]

And how do actors spend time after the performance or rehearsal? A successful rehearsal or performance often gets him so worked up, he can't stop the inertia of excitement. So, he goes to have dinner with friends, or to some other theatre, and so on. Beware of this – if the excitement remains, go home and get in bed; this is the right thing to do. Excitement is not power; tomorrow you will suffer the consequences and regret that you wasted the energy you need – tomorrow will be lost.

Although excitement is not power, the thing that evoked the excitement *is*. You received it at a successful or highly unsuccessful performance or rehearsal. This is treasure, so go home and cherish it as the apple of your eye. You don't need to analyze it and "pick at it with your fingers." Just let it ripen all on its own – have faith.

On the day of the performance, avoid all kinds of excitement and distractions. Keep yourself calm and keep anticipating *something joyful and good*. The main thing is calm. Live at 1/4, at 1/10, at 1/100 of your regular life. And don't anticipate *how* you are going to act, and *don't try it out*. For the love of God, don't try it out! Everything will come in its own time – don't rip out the sprout. Peace and quiet, quiet and peace! Keep releasing your muscles and freeing your breath. Keep pacifying yourself! Peace, quiet, and calm! This is Everything!

★★★

Let us say you have an evening rehearsal. You need to start aiming at it, beginning in the morning; but don't rehearse – just keep aiming.

You can go about your day, but somewhere *in the depths of your soul*, let there be a sensation: "tonight I am going to rehearse." You just need to carry this *anticipation* of the rehearsal in you – an inkling of how I am going to rehearse. Or else, spend your day the way Possart, Yermolova, and Chaliapin spent their performance days – economy and accumulation.

Or take your example from athletes and from their preparation: doctor Aleksandr Petrov [1876–1941] – the wrestler at the London Summer Olympics in 1908.[2] Nikolai Sedov [1884–1939] at the World Speed Skating Championship in Helsinki in 1906. The Americans at the Olympics.

Preparation before rehearsal consists of *calming down* or *warming up*.

Exercises that are helpful here are those in "admitting" and cleansing. Eyes (asana), muscular release, exercises in faith, casting yourself aside, the balls, impulses, "I," singularity. Justification (creative), "the fool," the feeling of the audience (the triangle of *deisis*), the merging with the object. The acknowledgement of and giving in to sensations. [See the Glossary on all of these exercises and terms.]

Anticipation and preparation create a special mood; they evoke a sense of solemnity and significance. It is January, and if it were announced that Easter would come tomorrow, as it's been moved, there would be a strange sense of bewilderment, and no solemnity at all. The uplift of the Great Holiday is created by the long expectation of it – by the preparation and by its timeliness. It is essential that everything be ready for its arrival and celebration.

To the Creative State

It is impossible to begin athletic training or vocal exercises, etc., when you are sick or exhausted. This also applies to the important moments in life. Exercising for the stage is no different.

It requires, in general, hygiene, strength, health, and overabundance.

Art always requires *overabundance*.

You need to work on creating this surplus.

You need to know how to spend the day of the performance so as to ensure this overabundance. You should feel like the speed skater Sedov, who was overflowing with energy and couldn't stand still at the starting line in Helsinki.

The great creative state is the splitting of the psyche – there is the *artist*, who leads, urges, and regulates the process, and there is the *executer*, who fulfills the process. On top of it, there is also a sphere from which both of them, at the moment of creativity, draw the material and the impulse for creation. In short, there is some kind of otherworldly "logos." In the presence of inspiration, this would be the "Divine Logos" (this happens infrequently), and then there is simply the "otherworldly logos."

Take the sculptor for example. There are two people in him. One is looking after the image, as it appears in front of his mind's eye; the other is a craftsman, a worker, and a journeyman. He holds a chisel in his hand and pounds it with his hammer. What's more, this second person should be *absolutely* passive and completely submissive to the first. He should listen to his master's slightest desire. In order for him to be able to do this, his hands must be flexible, skillful, and strong; his eye – straight; his attention – sharp.

It is the same with the actor. It's just that he himself is the material.

Although, this is not completely true. It more often than not happens that the ideas are born during work and *from work*. If the sculptor didn't take up his instruments, if he didn't touch the marble, his soul would have remained silent.

If I didn't write a few pages or sentences, then many of my best ideas would never have been born.

On Stretching and Warming Up

This is a science of its own. Hundreds of methods exist. The main thing, however, is to know that the warm-up is essential. When directors and actors fail in performances and rehearsals, this chiefly happens because they underestimate the importance of this process.

When iron has been heated, you can forge it; when it is cold, you would just break your nerves off of it and lose all faith in yourself.

When you've kneaded your wax or your clay, then you can sculpt it, change it, and sculpt it again. Know this, oh master, and don't be upset with the wax if it breaks in your hand, or with the iron when it resists your strikes.

You can't forge cold iron – this is ignorance.

It's the same with the director – he needs to knead and warm up the play if it has lost the temperature of its first reading.

You should also warm yourself up if you lost the temperature before you ask it of others.

On Prayer

Komissarzhevskaya wrote constantly about her insurmountable need to pray. Duse knelt for hours in complete solitude in a humble chapel before a statue of the Madonna. On performance days, Yermolova absolutely refused to see anyone under any circumstances while she prayed for no less than two hours. Only when it was announced that her carriage was ready did she make her final bows and leave for the theatre.

Haydn: "When inspiration abandoned me, I went into the chapel, and I read Hail Marys there until it returned to me again, and then I wrote." [Demidov is slightly paraphrasing Haydn (as quoted in Gruzenberg 1929: 50).]

There is no one common opinion on prayer. "It is a conversation and a communion with the Almighty God or with his saints," say the believers. "Superstition founded on ignorance," says the materialist. We won't discuss who is right and who is mistaken. It would be quite imprudent to ignore facts – it's easy to cast them off, but it's difficult to find them. In the meantime, the facts are obvious.

Interpreting that fact is a different matter. What is it about?

Of course, if it were a fact of communion with some completely otherworldly power – psycho-physiologists like myself should just mind our own business. If this is the case, then things are quite simple – you don't have enough power; you go into a room where "someone" dwells; you request that he give you strength; he does – you go back, and things get moving.

May there be yet another way of looking at this fact? May we be able to foresee some more familiar elements in it?

Figure 18   Vera Komissarzhevskaya as Nina in the Alexandrinsky Theatre's performance of Anton Chekhov's *The Seagull*, 1896. Courtesy of Andrei Malaev-Babel.

I go into a familiar room, to my familiar icon. I stop before it and look into it – it says so much to me. Here, I can open up my soul without fear; I can be utterly passive – nothing bad will touch me. Although I arrived distracted and confused, this place makes all my extraneous thoughts disappear. I return to my "elemental," "natural" state – ideally suitable for the inception of the creative process. (This occurs by force of habit and by the reflex that has been developing for years.) I am visited and possessed by the concentration and calm, and by the reverent readiness to receive something inside.

If I can get no rest from my inner turmoil, then I voice it through my complaints. I vent it in words and moans before this invisible object (fantastic and thus tangibly living).

To voice or to spill out this oppressive worry means to rid myself of it. This is a widely practiced psychotherapeutic method. When it's applied, a patient returns home well-balanced. He has cast off hundreds of troubles that used to dominate his subconscious.

I need to substitute these random thoughts with their turmoil and confusion. I need to exchange them for the mighty flow of my creative river – its images closely knitted, harmonious, and organically merged. I need to restore this flow, and I need for my entire being to submit to it.

When I speak to the icon, when I beg it for help – whom do I implore? With whom do I commune? With some otherworldly and lofty being? I don't know. Perhaps. One thing is certain: my subconscious and my second persona can also hear me.

I have calmed down; I feel concentrated; I have collected myself. I linked my depths with its secret treasure house – with the imagined object; I placed myself on the rails of singularity and truth. Finally, in this concentrated state, I sent myself a series of commands or suggestions.

The prayer, lasting for two whole hours, as it did with Yermolova, you can imagine the kind of state she achieved by the beginning of her creative act – she felt uplifted, concentrated, and free!

Notes

1 Kumis cure resorts were popular in Russia in the 19th, early 20th century. Located chiefly in "middle Asia," these resorts treated patients with *kumis* – fermented mare's milk, considered to be a cure for several illnesses, including tuberculosis.
2 In preparation for the Olympics, Alexander Petrov subscribed to a strict regimen and resisted temptations.

15

Repetition

On the Significance of Repetition in Theatre

In film, you can prepare each scene *ex tempore* (Latin for outside of time, notwithstanding time). In theatre, things are quite different: you have to *prepare* a performance where everything will happen again, as if "for the first time."

Repetition can prove to be dangerous for an actor (cliché acting, mechanization and empty form); or it can strengthen something fundamental in the role – solidify its circumstances and its "I," evoke the new character facets, etc.

Repetition is such a serious aspect of theatre – there is still much to be said about it.

Exact Repetition

At times, the actor feels so connected with his character's condition and its emotional life – they touch him to the quick. Inspired by the role, he wants to play it. He plays it, and he does it well. He is enthralled in his part; everything in it is clear to him – *he is experiencing.*

But here's the question: can he experience it and get so inspired *every* time, at every performance? Practice has shown that the majority cannot. The actor played it once; he was inspired. No matter how hard he tries to do it again, it doesn't work out, and that's all! Perhaps he just "played it out of his system," and there is nothing left in his soul.

In actuality, this is true. A person carried grief inside – he cried it out, and he felt relieved. He carried anger – he vented it, and the anger passed.

Psychology calls this liberation from oppressive thoughts and feelings "catharsis."

In the meantime, this is a catastrophe for the actor! He would have *nothing left* to perform with! There would be no material left in him . . . It would suffice for one time, and that is all!

For the most part, it happens just like that . . . The actor spends the rest of his life remembering that one time (or two) when he played "like a god"; he didn't even recognize himself, and he astonished the audience and his colleagues . . . One or two times . . . and the rest was just mundane mediocrity, tolerable craft . . .

Frankly, this is quite typical of nature: you can experience anything only once. The moment passes; the feeling disappears – it won't be coming back. A different feeling might appear, similar to the first, yet it won't be the same . . . Life flows like a river. The water skips over the rocks, and it isn't there anymore . . . different water comes in its place . . .

If this is so, then how can one talk about experiencing? After all, plays in theatres occasionally run for not just tens of times, but for hundreds!

How can we demand that the actor experiences the same thing hundreds of times, when a person isn't built to experience anything a second time, let alone hundreds?

And so, having become practically convinced that the repetition of feelings does not work, the actor gradually rejects his initial aspirations.

Is it worth giving up so easily? Is there not a kind of misunderstanding or lack of thought here?

We can't bring back yesterday and force it to repeat itself exactly. It's true. But is it even necessary? Do we really need to be *repeating things exactly*?

Inexact Repetition

Hamlet loves his father. He can't be comforted after his death . . . The words *written* by the playwright express Hamlet's grief, sorrow, yearning, and perplexity. You can't change the words.

But how did Shakespeare, this king of playwrights, imagine the actor?

From his point of view, the actor isn't exactly an ordinary person; the actor is someone who . . .

> . . . In a fiction, in a dream of passion,
> Could force his soul so to his own conceit
> That from her working all his visage wanned,
> Tears in his eyes, distraction in his aspect,
> A broken voice, and his whole function suiting
> With forms to his conceit . . .

The actor is a person who is able to fully give in to his imagination – just one thought is enough for him, and his whole body and soul (his "whole function") ignites, completely seized by feelings. The greatest of the playwrights only considered such a person as an actor.

He wrote for such a person and he trusted in him.

Can a person repeat an experienced feeling exactly? Hardly. Yet, Shakespeare didn't think that the actor's chief merit and strength lies in this *exactness of repetition*. He wrote the words for him . . . These words were unchangeable . . . Yet, is there only one way to say the words?

What does it mean – the same words? It means that the *thought* is approximately the same. That's all. As for the *shades* of thoughts and the shades of feelings that accompany the thoughts – they *can't be* the same today, tomorrow, the day after tomorrow, in a year, or whenever.

This is the answer to all of the misunderstandings.

The majority of performers who have a tendency toward representation trip over this stumbling block on the actor's creative path, as described by Shakespeare.

Why is Exact Repetition Impossible in the Art of Experiencing?

"How can we do without precise form? Should we just toss on the waves of experiencing? Should we just cut ourselves adrift? Let's take a painter or a sculptor – does this mean that he should also change his works all the time? Give his statue one pose today, tomorrow another? Otherwise you would say that he isn't creating, and that yesterday's water being gone, he is chasing after the impossible!"

You usually hear objections like this. There's no need to confuse two completely different elements: the *visual* and the *performing* arts. In addition to everything else, the fundamental difference between the two is the *material*. A sculptor works with *lifeless*, immovable marble, granite, or wood; a painter works with canvas and paint, but the actor – he works with a movable *living* organism.

The marble, as you give it some form, only *produces the impression* of something living and movable. The actor is alive from the start; *just take care not to kill him* or turn him into a puppet. (Especially since you couldn't completely kill him even if you tried.)

Having turned the actor into a mechanical automaton, you still don't kill the life in him and, whether you want it to be or not, it is visible. It is visible not least of all because we, people, have a peculiar habit in life. We are not so much interested in the words someone says, but in what he thinks in the process – in what is hidden *behind* the words. It is almost impossible to hide it from us. We can't help but see this . . .

We come to the theatre, and we see some not-quite genuine people walking around the stage . . . They are pretty eloquent, but . . . personally, they aren't here; aren't on the stage. They aren't living with the interest that they should live with, according to their words . . . Simply and crudely put, they are lying; they are deceiving us . . .

In the first moments, this annoys you . . . Then, without even noticing, you begin to listen closer to the words. If the author is good, then the words enthrall you on their own. They distract you a bit from the burdensome impression, produced by the theatre actors' affectations and lies.

And then . . . you gradually *become used to* it all. Engrossed by the author, you are even ready to applaud this bad actor. As for him, he doesn't even hide that he is *lying* – he gets through some "tempestuous" scene and looks triumphantly toward the audience (waiting for his applause) – see what a trick I can pull off? How did you like it?

What are we to do? We can't kill the actor; we can't stop the flow of his life's river; we also can't force him to live by our commands . . .

What can we do?

Let's take a look at those things that force us, as people, to want, act, suffer, and delight . . .

My life is going peacefully, from day to day. Just like a river, it flows along an even path. Suddenly a telegram: "Come immediately! Sasha has died." My dear sister! Her little children are orphaned! A huge stone has smashed crosswise into the river of my life – the river rushes to the side, bumping up against the steep shores; it churns and it roils. It's no longer flowing to the same place it did a month ago: I took the children in; I have turned from a bachelor into a family man, the children get sick all the time . . . Who could now recognize my river bottom or its flow? . . .

Doesn't the author do the same thing? One by one, he drops huge rocks of new facts and circumstances into the river of my character's life. Our hitherto quiet stream suddenly churns, rushing like mad through granite rubble, roaring with waterfalls, and transforming into the terrifying, ravenous Terek [river in Northern Caucasus].

Do you want this Terek to bubble over every time, at every performance? It can. Just don't think about the water or the noise per se. You have to think about the *construction of its bed and the slope of its channel*. Water, if sent down a steep slope – having met along its way obstacles of stone barrages – will boil over by itself; it will whirl, howling and moaning.

In the theatre of the LIVING ACTOR (versus that of a wooden marionette), there also exists a form. It is the form of the *riverbed*, composed of **reasons** that cause the feelings to boil.

Those reasons are the facts of the character's life.

Try putting yourself into your character's shoes, but do it genuinely – with complete trust. What's happening to him has really happened, and it is now happening *to you* . . . Each new event or fact, through no will of your own, would then make you feel hot or cold all over; you would shiver from horror, or you would fall into a rage. In a moment of weakness, you would think of suicide . . . As for the words . . . If you manage to give yourself up to the circumstances of your character's life – completely and without hesitation – then you would just be surprised at how fitting the words have become. Written by the author, they perfectly apply to your situation and truly express the feelings that grip you. You would grasp at these words as at the best and the only words you could speak at the moment.

On "Breaking the Banks" . . .

However, the most exact form of the riverbed doesn't always guarantee the exactness of the river's flow . . . This is especially true when it comes to mountainous rivers that are temperamental and turbulent.

In the personal life of the actor, the sky isn't cloudless at all times, and the sun doesn't always shine . . . Abundant showers can swell up his soul, and violent storms can electrify his will and thoughts. At such times, there is no keeping them within their everyday habitual banks . . .

The actor (especially the affective type) doesn't like to talk about his own misfortunes; he translates them into his art. His Othello used to just get resentful and angry in the jealousy scene. Today, he grew cold with grief from the terrible news; he moaned like a beast, unable to confine his rage. What was left of the established blockings, so convenient for anger and noble resentment? They are hardly suitable for *such an explosion* of sorrow and inhuman rage . . . Today the actor's river broke its banks and smashed the moorings of all its docks. It washed away the peaceful laborers' fences and drowned out their coastal granaries and basements.

Is it necessary to fight back against this act of God?

Let's imagine Mochalov or Yermolova, who were pricked in their very hearts. Should they break their banks or try to "return back" within their shores?

It's likely that you would be able to turn back such an actor – you can try drilling the role into him, but what do we gain from this?

Doesn't this "breaking of the banks" constitute the very essence of the affective type's art?

Wouldn't it be better to try mastering *this kind of internal technique*? After all, it causes the circumstances to *overwhelm and burn* you, so that *it's impossible **not** to break the banks*?

Let this river not even be the Terek, but the humble Klyazma or Yauza – they too, given the opportunity, would not mind breaking their banks!

You are thinking: "Well, you've finally come to anarchy!" This isn't true at all – I have only come to the natural completion of the creative state of the affective type of actor.

Even less so: *to the creative state of any type of actor.* After all, the creative state is always the breaking of the banks of mundane routine; always a daring and over-the-top abundance. How can we not dream about it?!

When, enthralled by such a state, an actor gets *frightened for want of habit* – that's a different matter. If he does not slam on the brakes, then *he will lose his head*. This, of course, is an unpleasant incident. It can get an actor in a lot of trouble. Yet, *his school* alone is to blame for hammering the incorrect point of view into his head and heart. It taught him *the timid creeping technique of flightless verisimilitude* – instead of the proper technique of *free creativity and truth*.

His creativity was nipped in the bud; his faith in himself – killed, along with his daring and ease, essential for his intuition. You might be exceptionally gifted; you might even carry inside a kernel of genius. Yet, all of this might lie within the depths of your soul undiscovered, or even worse – reduced to dust and cast to the winds . . .

Everything depends on the school: *correct* or *incorrect*.

Types of Repetition (Seafarers)

If life can't be repeated exactly, then what is the point of even talking about repetition in the theatre of the "LIVING ACTOR?" Yet, this is precisely what we should be talking about: *repetition* . . .

In the performing arts, everything is based on repetition. Let's begin with the very first steps: the actor reads a play – what does he want? To play this or that role, to embody and realize it. Doesn't it mean to *repeat* what the author has written?

Needless to say, this repetition is not slavish; the actor involuntarily connects the written work (the author's idea) with his own life experience and creative imagination. He *embodies* it, giving life to what has been written on lifeless paper in lifeless ink. However, this is essentially *reproduction* or *repetition*.

What the actor is striving to reproduce and repeat is a different matter. One would be touched to the quick or even inspired by the great philosophical idea of the play. He would want to recreate this idea – to make it tangible and to inflame the audience with it. This is the actor-tribune . . .

Another would be captivated by the personality of one of the characters. He would feel the beauty, power and depths of a human soul – in Hamlet, Horatio, or Othello. He would want to recreate the image of this character, its "I" and its inner content. He would want to live through this character's sufferings, to be overjoyed by its happiness, and to agitate his mind with its thoughts.

A third would want to repeat (reproduce) some details – an effective scene written by the author, an ingenious situation, or some funny catchwords . . .

A fourth, having received an impulse from the author, would be "inspired," in rehearsals, to augment what has been written. He would think up plenty of his own engaging additions (the so-called "tricks" and "gags"), and then want to reproduce and repeat them before the audience.

Where do all these different impulses come from?

They all come from the familiar three types of actors – from the difference in their psychological makeup; from the depth or superficiality of their perception; from the richness or poverty of their inner content, and from their human greatness or smallness . . .

At the top stands the affective type with his gift – like a torch, like a lighthouse in the night, and like the sun at its zenith.

At the very bottom stands the imitator – like a tiny flashlight, like a flicker of a match.

In the middle stands the emotionally willful with his specific gifts; he is like an electrical light bulb we use at home – calm and well tried, convenient and safe.

These might all be actors of experiencing. They all might give themselves over to life onstage, trusting its changeable and fragile nature. They all sail the waters of the unsettled ocean – of the creative life in front of the audience. They are all seafarers . . .

However, just as it is with the seafarers—one (a fearless explorer) launches out across the sea, through the polar night, across the stormy squalls and the thousands of fatal dangers; and the other doesn't sail farther than a few miles offshore; at the first sign of a strong wind, he turns back to the harbor . . .

Repetition as an End and as a Means

Thus, repetition does belong to experiencing (in our case, to the creative experiencing). What's more – repetition is essential and life-giving: without it nothing good would happen onstage. *An artist has only one means to perfect his work* and to bring life to it bit by bit – *repetition*. (This is true of any art.) The loftier the artist – the sharper his eye, the more he demands of himself, and the harder it is for him to rest on his laurels.

All of the so-called "opening nights" feature unfinished and incomplete work. More often than not, they are just sketches. All performers look at "premieres" this way, if they are true artists. They know they will complete their sketch *afterwards*, in the future, when they are free – when the hectic time leading up to the opening is over and its haste has dissipated. In this respect, the actor is the most fortunate of all artists: he can perfect his creation up until the last day of its life. Yet, if desired, a half hour may be enough to restructure the role and make it completely unrecognizable.

Meanwhile, so many audience members prefer to attend a premiere . . . They say that the first performance has the most freshness, and that the actors perform it with such enthusiasm . . . According to these audiences, there is something festive about the first performance.

It's likely that there is some truth to it . . . Except, what does it really mean, if you think about it? It means that future performances are lacking enthusiasm, and that they fade . . . What is going on here? The actors pass the test of the opening night, and "rest on their laurels?" Instead of continuing to get the feel for the nuances and seeking greater truth, they become satisfied with their success? They settle for what they've got and begin to repeat old stuff? Alas, yes! This is exactly how it goes.

For the actor-creator who must strive for perfection, *every repetition* (meaning every rehearsal and every performance) is above all a *vehicle* that can move him further along the path to perfection. As a result of this, his role grows with every performance; it develops and blossoms. For the actor-craftsman, it is the opposite: the performance *is his end goal*. It being achieved, the only thing left is to repeat what you have already found. Why? This is, perhaps, because he considers this *to already be perfection* . . . Or else, this comes from sloth or laziness . . .

The result of such repetitions, no matter the reason for them, inevitably leads to one and the same thing: the role grows deader; it turns into a bunch of clichés; the performance fades; it becomes loose and needs repairs. Not improvement, mind you, but just repairs – it needs fixing.

What a fatal mistake! A fatal incorrectness at work!

They "searched" at rehearsals, but they already "found" it in performance. They should have found this very *state of searching*, instead of its mere consequences. In rehearsals they used to seek and find a *living* person. This person, in his process of living, used to "find" this or that adaptation (speaking approximately). Once they fixated the result, they were left with the adaptation, while *the life was gone*.

★★★

Actors, when met with this seemingly natural demand for ceaseless perfecting – often begin to protest, quite categorically: "Listen, how is this possible?! You demand that the actor give himself up to the role completely, so that he can perfect it time after time. How can he do this? When can he do this!? Surely you know the situation in our theatres. If the play is put on, then it is usually done many times in a row. This requires that I have to perform day after day without any kind of break. How is it possible to give all of myself completely, day after day, if after the first of two performances, I feel drained. And here you want it to get stronger each time! And what's more, you don't take into account that in the mornings I'm already rehearsing a new role. (In the meantime, my evening performances still have to go on.) Under such conditions, where do I find time or strength to continue developing the old role? Just repeating, more or less accurately, what I found and "fixated" at rehearsals is already a heroic deed."

How can you answer this? If the theatre has placed an actor in such conditions, then it is a bad theatre. It is obvious that it isn't in need of an actor's creativity, but it chooses to content itself with the primitive and soulless craft. And that's all.

For the First Time

"The first time" is an indispensable condition of life. In it, everything occurs for the "first," the one and only time. Everything. Up to the daily washing and dressing, not to mention everything else.

How do you make things happen as if "for the first time"?

Oh, it isn't difficult at all. The main thing is to distract yourself from your recollection, and from the repetition of the first, or the previous time.

Plenty of means exists for that, such as "finishing up living" and "non-restructuring," "letting go" and "green-lighting the weak currents."

Use just a single thing from this arsenal – everything else will join in. You will then receive "a first time" impression – the one *of the current moment* and not of yesterday.

Doesn't that explain the power and the effectiveness of "physical businesses" and "physical actions?" Whether you want it or not, they happen "for the first time."

To the Affective Actor

They want him to tame the monsters that burst forth from the abyss – from his subconscious depths. They want him to repeat all their actions and motions. Yet, he himself does not anticipate them, and knows not what they will be. He too can't help but be surprised at what is going on with him.

He doesn't have the power to call forth those exact monsters. As for forcing them to fulfill those exact actions – this is completely absurd.

He can try to call forth other monsters, similar to those, provided he *is armed with correct internal technique.* Under this condition, he can own and govern them in his own way. This, however, doesn't mean that he can rein in and train the monsters of his subconscious.

Such an actor is capable of repeating, although not the details. He has the power to repeat the main thing – the idea, the peak of the idea; the very essence, the very "I" of the role. In chasing after the details, he loses all trace of the main thing. This is because the main thing *doesn't comprise the details – it* **creates** *them.*

On Forgetting the Future

By the way (this is a stunning enough thought), when living truthfully, you never know what awaits you in your future.

This is how it is in life. Do we know our own futures?

Better yet – sometimes we know it (a foreboding), but we brush it off and live only in the present. To be precise, we don't even live in the present, but only in the past.

If the actor knows the future of his role in such a way that it hinders him, then he cannot live truthfully. The state of "truth" includes the ***suppression of the future***.

★★★

Knowing a play is a wrong sensation. You have to know everything "about yourself," and not about "him." Such knowledge will be accumulated gradually and systematically (in reverse). As for "not knowing," this state is achieved by being keen on what happens in the present moment.

Only a few things are known, and even those things are known in rough outline.

To the Afterword

Lesage's [1668–1747] foreword to his novel *Histoire de Gil Blas*:

A tale. Two students travel from Penafiel to Salamanca. They are tired. They come upon a spring, and they have a drink. They see a headstone with fading lettering, ground down by the cattle watering at the spring. The students wash it off and read the inscription: "Here lies the soul of licentiate Pedro Garcia."

One laughs (a sanguine person?): "How can a soul be buried? An odd guy," and so on. And he moves on.

The other is more level-headed, and he is thinking: there must be some kind of a mystery here. When the other is gone, he digs with his knife underneath the headstone, lifts it up and finds a leather purse with a message written in Latin: "You had the good sense to solve the riddle of my inscription, and so you shall be my heir! Perhaps this money shall serve you better than it served me."

The student laid the headstone back in place, took the soul of the licentiate, and went to Salamanca.

Every one of you, readers, will become like one of these students having read this book.

Addendum

Energy

This is extremely significant. They say: "a reliable actor." He planned it – he did it. The original outline got conveyed to the audience . . . A craftsman conveys the ideals of his craft; a magician – the cleanness of his work, the dexterity and agility of his hands, a representational actor conveys the feelings – within his narrow bounds, of course (if he belongs to the emotionally-willful type). Each of them may convey his own thing, yet every school demands that it be done well, reliably, with full confidence – to a T. (As they say nowadays: "at a full 100 percent.")

This explains all the demands for "iron form," clarity, and sharpness.

Although, these demands are quite valid. Otherwise, theatre would be done by dilettante amateurs, or, as Pushkin [1979: 99] put it, by "nervous hands of a schoolmaid."

What is the *affective* actor to do in this case? Perhaps, he also has to search for form, and then try to squeeze his affect into it – or, basically, to follow the willful path?

Wouldn't this signal total capitulation?!

In the meantime – how can one rely on the entire ensemble being inspired? What are the odds that at least one among them, if not the majority, won't be inspired today? This uninspired actor – is he just going to muck about onstage and get in the others' way? Wouldn't it be better, for such an occasion, to create some firm blocking and reliable stage pattern? In other words, wouldn't it be better to have a form just in case – something along the lines of a fire escape, a reserve tank of water, and a fire hose?

Of course you can, and why not – during a fire everything is allowed. The most horrid clichés of a craftsman seem like the saving grace. In any case, it would be better than taking flight – for example, an actor's fleeing from the stage because he got scared . . . In case of dire need, everything is allowed . . . It's just that this, of course, isn't a solution.

In the meantime, the "question-answer" exercises elucidate an actor's particular state – *energy*.

The actor is afraid to overact, and he therefore switches off an entire sphere. Yet, this sphere is the main source of energy. The actor turns helpless, will-less, and irresponsible. Of course, he feels that something is off; he is irritated inside and even gets angry – but the power just isn't there.

The actor must be put in such conditions that his energy comes out on its own and becomes his second nature. At the Art Theatre's studios there is a habit: the actor arrives deflated, and then you have to pump him up and get him going. He won't resist; he won't be capricious – he would allow you to do this to him. You don't have the right to reproach him, yet he won't budge a bit, unless you take some extreme measures – such as Sulerzhitsky's whip.[1] Then he would wake up, and you could work with him.

What kind of conditions can we find for the actor so that to develop his **conditional reflex** – as soon I walk out onstage (or begin to work at the table, or start exercising), I come to life and become full of energy? The following conditions can achieve it:

1   *The give in* to the very psycho-physical state *you are in* at the moment.
2   Keeping plenty of given circumstances unknown.
3   Feeling responsible – both for the details and for the work at large. God forbid that you should do something irresponsibly, or somewhat approximately – by halves!!!
4   Don't fight your sluggishness, but *accept* it, since it is there; arm yourself with it and take advantage of it.

★★★

You're most likely to encounter one of two things: either sluggishness, indifference, and scarceness, or forcing – of the muscles, attention, and one's entire psyche.

Energy has nothing to do with forcing . . .

I wrote somewhere that energy has much in common with restraint – perhaps so.

Energy can be accumulated by purely hygienic means, such as regiment (Sedov in Helsinki).

The most important thing, however, is to learn the path to the kind of energy that arises suddenly, even when one is exhausted – what happens when a person is fond of something; when it is his element (for example, a war horse hearing the sounds of brass), or when one is riding his hobbyhorse.

The Future Book on the Actor's "Ailments" and Errors: Those Provoked by the Audience, Bad Schooling, or Poor Examples (Outline)

All of these errors and "ailments" can be found already at the scene-study level. I must write a book on the typical, vulgar actors' mistakes (something along the lines of the "*Seven deadly sins*").

1   [Clenched] Fists.
2   Not letting go and holding feelings.
3   Restructuring.
4   Not finishing [up] living.
5   Delivery.
6   The absence of thinking onstage.
7   For the audience, and not for the partner.
8   Playing words, playing character, playing emotion.
9   Hastiness in all its forms (not finishing living, patter, etc.).
10 Rationality (meaning not a "fool").

This is probably the right place to feature all of the errors begotten by the "Stanislavsky system": task, attention, and all the other mistakes connected with "activity."

★★★

I must write about those usual, common mistakes committed by actors and storytellers.

1   Standing on the front foot. [The actor's support point should be on his back foot, not his front foot.]
2   Nodding [punctuating lines] with one's chin.
3   Clenching one's fists (muscles in general).
4   Delivering (instead of perceiving).
5   Shaking one's head during the heroic lines.
6   Indication of bits: cheerful tone, sad tone, lyricism, and so on.
7   They speak of it, but they don't see it.
8   To whom are they talking?
9   Is he participating in it personally?
10 Complaining – feeling sorry for themselves.
11 Speaking verse (why rhythm and pathos?).
12 In storytelling, do you need to act as each of the characters in the story, or "act as the author" (which is even worse) – instead of speaking as the person, who tells the story?
13 Reasons behind monotony ("stepping on your own tail" and, chiefly, "not letting go").
14 I already understood, and I want to respond, but my partner still has a line. I wait, and I cool off. The same goes for movements. I stop myself – and I cool off. Yet, it is possible to stop, and begin accumulating (a dam).
15a They speak, but they don't understand what they are saying.
15b Earlier, in the heat of the moment, under the first impression – it worked, but now I lost it. A role, or a scene, used to develop soundly, but now I develop it differently.
16 Playing feeling (without thought).
17 Blabbering of words "under the influence of strong feeling" (Ostuzhev [1874–1953]). In such a case, the feeling is always false.
18 The absence of the "through-action."
19 And why is he telling us this story? What does he personally need? To dazzle the audience? To get applause?
20 The incorrect perception of a scene or a bit.
21 Why certain words get blabbered? Nothing stands behind them.
22 Playing separate words outside of a larger context.
23 They are acting lightheartedness, or grief, or ease, all through direct means. Instead, you should play it "by contradiction." [See Glossary.]
24 *The beginning.* The beginning must not be acted as something new. The beginning is a transition.
    You've got something – whatever is in you at the moment. And then, new circumstances are added to what was there from the start, causing certain changes. That's all there is to it. This is especially important for the book on *the storytellers' mistakes.* In short, you must always begin with what is there now and *fully give in* to it.
    More than often you need to begin with emptiness. You let go. Emptiness. Go out onto the stage. Things will come out of you when you are there – actions and words.
25 Another mistake – *"restructuring."*

The conscious restructuring of self. The actor is in one kind of a state. Yet, in his opinion, he should be in a different state come the next bit, and so he deliberately restructures, forcing himself.

In the meantime, there is decidedly no need for this. Restructuring, if it is necessary, occurs on its own. It does not happen according to a template (feeling, if approached consciously, can only be template-like, rather than individual and concrete). Instead, restructuring will proceed from the given circumstances and the given state; from the given personality and even in the given complex conditions of my today's life.

Two methods cause restructuring: bits and rhythm (or rather tempo, which is commonly mistaken for rhythm). You've broken the role into bits: here, I need this; there, I need something else. You've barely completed a bit (now is your chance to finish living it). Oh no, it is time to start the next bit! And so you restructure.

Rhythm. The scene is acted soundly and fervently; the feeling is choking you, making you grow silent. Your director immediately shouts: "Rhythm! Tempo! No pauses!" And you end up having to force yourself and gallop across the words.

26   On "letting go."

The following mistake is definitely caused by the willful school.

The actor keeps holding himself to a "state," or to a "task," or to whatever you like. He doesn't let go of these things even for a second. At rehearsals Sudakov always shouts: "Pulse! Pulse!" Others shout: "Rhythm! Rhythm!" In general, everything causes the actor to put constant *pressure on himself.*

Yet in life quite the opposite occurs. We say or do what we need (or we think something) and . . . then we *let go.* We allow ourselves to breathe. This isn't a state of emptiness, but the continuation of the work – something in us is finishing thinking, or feeling whatever we just thought, or felt, or said. If we happen to be waiting for an answer to our own question, even then we don't wait, but rather something *is waiting* in us.

This *not letting go* has the same origins as "restructuring" (when the actor consciously restructures his inner life; disconnecting from his actual state, he conducts "restructuring" for the new bit). All of this stems from our well-respected "rationality," "activity," and "action-based process."

Not letting go *is an abnormal, unnatural state.* Therefore, it is false – an actor, when subjected to it, cannot be alive; it wears him out. Everything seems to be correct; it is hard to fault him – yet something just isn't right! This is because he keeps *making things happen,* and nothing **happens on its own.**

The method of "letting go" might not work, if you don't know what comes next.

You spoke. You let go. Emptiness (something within you is finishing living). Suddenly, without a single prior thought – an involuntary inhalation and . . . the new line is spoken! Only as I speak it do I understand the meaning of the line. It might seem strange, but this is how it is. This is precisely how it happens for us in life. We don't think what we are about to say or how, prior to saying it – quite the opposite: the words come ahead of the thoughts.

If you don't know that, a peculiar mistake might happen. Having fallen into "emptiness," you would begin to wait – "The thought should come any moment now . . . it must be on its way . . . almost here" . . . yet it doesn't come, and it won't come. Neither is it supposed to come, because, in life, it doesn't happen like that.

This is a huge secret. Even more so, since it is so unbelievably simple. Simple beyond expression.

27   On mental images.

Do we have to see every detail? Of course not. It should be as it is in life. In life we see only a fragment of an object or fact. It depends on a lot of things: on the type of perception; on the point of view on the object, and so on and so forth.

28 How do you work on entering into circumstances? Not "He," but "*I*."

29 Too much attention to the partner.

30 Too much attention to yourself.

31 *Correct interpretation of the play* that does not collide with the author. 90 percent of Tairov's mistakes come from the fact that he interprets the scene incorrectly.

32 Too superficial.

33 Too deep.

34 *All thoughts are the main ones.* There can only be two to three main thoughts. The others are all ancillary.

35 *On the importance of suggestion.* On preparation for the performance. On dropping [text, circumstances, or tasks] into the subconscious.

36 *On concreteness.* Katerina's key, the skull of Yorick, Joan's helmet.[2] Concreteness (naturalistic and physical) of the imagined. Concreteness allows for letting go. A lack of letting go always results in the lack of concreteness. A search for feeling also results in the lack of concreteness.

Notes

1 A reference to the "device" used by Sulerzhitsky at the rehearsals for the First Studio of MAT's production of Herman Heijermans' *The Wreck of 'Hope'* (1913; Richard Boleslavsky, director). "When they rehearsed Barend's scene, Sulerzhitsky resorted to a whip, and the role began to progress. This helped the actor [Aleksei Dikiy] to find his *I*, and stop being a human machine, who "knew everything" in advance . . . Sulerzhitsky led the actor to discover his true *I*; the actor finally sensed how it felt to be truly saving himself (he was chased [with a whip] under a bed), and the role began to progress" (Fund 59, MAT School Lectures 1924–1925. Notebook 2. p. 40). See the Glossary for "*I am.*"

2 Katerina's key (Ostrovsky's *The Storm*) – the key to the gate that must be unlocked in order to come to a forbidden romantic meeting with Boris; the skull of the jester Yorick in Hamlet's hands in the gravediggers' scene; Joan of Arc's helmet (Schiller's *The Maid of Orleans*).

Book Five

Psycho-Technique of the Affective Actor

Translated by Andrei Malaev-Babel and Alexander Rojavin

Sow the seeds you have been given, sow it in good earth,

sow it in sand, and in stone, and in thorns. Somewhere,

it'll take up and bear fruit, though not very soon.

Seraphim of Sarov

1
Creativity

In the moment of creation, a person buys into the world of his fantasy and lives in it as if in his real life. As an example, take a child who rides on top of a stick, eggs it on, whips it, stops it, and treats it as if it was a horse. Who forces him to do this? Fantasy itself makes him buy into this life, and he gives himself over to it freely, without any reservations . . .

It's the same in the art of the actor – it's not for nothing that we have expressions like "play a part," "play onstage."

If we ponder the expression "to play," then we'll see that we can learn quite a lot from this one word.

This creative life is very different from ordinary life. The most important thing about it is that I live and act in an imaginary world that was created by me, with imaginary people or objects, and I transfigure anything before me as I wish.

It's all fiction, and, knowing that it's fiction, I still live in it as if it was real:

> I'll enter harmony's celestial spheres
> Over mere fiction shed my bitter tears
> *(Pushkin [1959: 299])*

"As if it was real . . . " Is that so? The creative imaginary life is often much more realistic and fulfilling than one's mundane existence.

When we read an interesting and immersing book, and something wakes us from our creative dream – we become annoyed: "Why do they bother me with these trifles!" We want to quickly get rid of the distraction, although it might be important.

We all have dear friends and relatives with whom we became acquainted and to whom we grew so close – characters from works by Tolstoy, Dickens, Chekhov, Cervantes, and whomever else.

Did these people truly exist? Regardless whether they did, it's not important to us – prototypes are the concern of literary scholars. With the help of a great artist, these people were created by our imagination, and they not only existed for us – they still do: we see and feel them – we can almost converse with them.

I know intelligent and quite mature people, who, in difficult times, talk to their favorite, beloved imaginary friends. And they say that they're far more reliable than the advice and friendships you get from real, actual friends.

We don't even have to discuss (it's obvious on its own) that what we imagine in our creative and created lives is not a hallucination, not a manifestation of some sort of illness. A child plays only when he is healthy, and he sees very clearly that the stick is a stick, and not a horse – so what?! At the moment, he wants to play, fantasize, create, live an *unreal* life. He is healthy, and he plays. If he were sick, he'd have priorities other than playing.

And who knows: children's desire for games, this thirst for living in imagined realities – is it not an instinctively right path determined by the organism, which, in following it, nurtures its psychological apparatus.

Who knows – maybe in the midst of the creative process, a person's "radio receiver" is retuned, and he begins to receive something that brings to life and fuels that "part" of him, which is underfed in everyday life?

"Play" in Life

A child plays. He's alone, nobody is getting in his way, which is why he is free to do whatever he wants, to enjoy himself and create to his satisfaction.

Suddenly, he notices that people are watching him! Everything is ruined – he played for himself, not for somebody else; it doesn't matter if it's a mother, father, brother – he can no longer play, and so he leaves upset.

On other occasions, he stays and keeps playing, but he does so quite differently. The whole time, he'll be paying attention to what sort of impression he's leaving with his "audience." He plays in small part for himself, but for the most part, he's playing for them – the audience members. Especially if the child is spoiled, overpraised, and feels that he delights people. In this way, some children learn to fake very quickly and very deftly: it's as if nothing happened, as if he's playing the same way he was before; but, naturally, the greater part crafts falsehoods far more crudely.

Two kinds of play. The first, we can simply call *play*, play for yourself, play-creation, and self-discovery.

The second kind of play can only be called "play" – in quotes. There's nothing left of play! It's nothing but the appearance of play! (In fact, in theatre, there's a term called "play-acting," which denotes this false play in quotes – not play, but play-acting.)

Two kinds of play, neither of which resembles the other; two diametrically opposed states.

But look at how easily one slips into the other! It's enough to catch a single encouraging gaze – you instantly lose it.

By the way, onstage, real *play*, real *acting* occurs very rarely. Acting in public and especially in a large one, made up of 1,000–2,000 people – not many people can do it. Moreover, most people "play" and "act" in quotes – their "acting" is full of falsehoods, given a lack of ability and skills. Some do it more deftly, "realistically," others do it more crudely, primitively. But the point remains the same.

There's no need to think that only children act.

Look at that young mother, look at how adorably she fawns over her baby. But the more you look, the more you see that it's not a mother, but rather a little girl, playing with her doll. No seriousness, no real love – it's mostly just fancy, play.

Look at that young teacher, how he performs before his students and especially the female ones, how he basks in his role of a mentor. Even if he knows his subject, even if his students will learn quite a bit from him, there's still a fairly large part of play on the part of the teacher.

All of these people play and "play," act and "act." Albeit, when they "play," they do it poorly. As they say, not "naturally" enough, not convincingly.

Here's an example of more convincing acting.

An indescribably kind, responsive, wondrous woman. Where people are sick – she's the first one there; where is need, sorrow – she already knows about it – she'll run over, help out, do whatever needs to be done, run whatever errands are necessary, calm them down. A saint!

But at home, everyone's afraid of her, and there isn't much love lost. At home, there's nowhere to hide from her egoism, it's difficult to live with her shrewish personality . . . But it isn't important, the opinion of those at home – what's important to her is that strangers admired her while looking at her saintliness and self-sacrifice, that they said and thought: "What a person, such kindness, such a great heart!"

Practically speaking, do we not try to present ourselves to each person as we want them to see us? We relentlessly present ourselves – we pretend that we're much more sick and tired than we really are, that we're young, fresh, and strong like we were 10, 20 years ago. But even this isn't enough: we want to fool ourselves too – and we act out roles for ourselves quite often too.

We all have a favorite role for our everyday lives; and you get so used to it, and everybody around you gets so used to it, that it's not easy to throw it off. The mask gets stuck, glued to your face – you can't get rid of it, there's no way to tear it off.

Presumably, Napoleon, for example, was a person with just such a glued-on mask. Everything was designed to be as effective as possible, and the design was brilliant. Even the famous pose with the crossed arms before his chest was invented for him by the famous actor, Talma [1763–1826], and it became a habit. Not a single word was simple – he spoke in nothing but aphorisms.

If we are *ourselves* very rarely, if we're constantly playing, "presenting" some role, imitating a person or a feeling, acting not only with others, but with ourselves too – aren't we taking part in a widely spread art form: performance? An art that is in the flesh and blood of each and every one of us.

And people aren't the only ones who have this ingrained: animals have it too.

Take even a cat. It feels that people are talking about it, and it assumes an air of indifference, even turns its head away – as if to say, "there, take that!" But if it's everyone's favorite, and you're adoring it and talking to it too, then what poses *won't* it strike: it'll hang its head off the couch – oh no, it's about to fall! – or it'll lie on its back, paws upraised, but it won't be looking at you, as if her posing isn't for you, but for its own pleasure. It's a cunning coquette!

Dogs will also sometimes try to "act," but they're too spontaneous, to straightforward, they can't do anything as effective.

So, if performance, the desire to "perform" makes up such a huge part in our lives, you would think that there should be a lot of great actors among us! But there aren't!

Why is that?

Maybe because onstage, it isn't enough to perform like that, to "play" and "act" in quotes, to present, imitate feelings. Maybe something else is necessary?

No, that can't be it – after all, there are whole schools of acting that are built around "presenting" and "acting," the *depiction* of feeling. And actors from those schools leave great impressions, they're famous, they've earned their spot in art. But there aren't that many of them either.

Alright, let's assume that what we need onstage isn't mummery or the appearance of emotion, but acting without quotes, authenticity, spontaneity, *involuntariness* – shouldn't a person be more capable in this art form than in any other? After all, it's so intrinsic!

Take children's games as an example. Even animals, especially young ones – look at how they run around, look at the scenes they play with one another!

But, as strange as it may seem, there aren't that many actors like this. Possibly even fewer than the "depictionists."

What's the matter?

Creativity (Reasons and Origins): The Third Basic Instinct

What causes a person to create? What attracts him to art, to science?

Is there really so little content in life that you have to look for it in some imagined world, in daydreams, in fictions?

Isn't that simply glorified and sugarcoated escapism from life? And won't prudent, practical life sooner or later, slam the door right in the absent-minded dreamer's nose?

It happens, it happens . . . and quite often too! Life ridicules escapism, and throws it overboard, and starves it, and ultimately kills it.

As for whether it's right or wrong – is that really such an easy question to answer?

Are you a lazybones or someone who's taken by an artistic idea, who doesn't pay attention to anything else? A parasite or an "inventor of new values"? Are you a good-for-nothing, or have you outgrown life – perhaps you are feeling out the path to some new environment, like a flying fish?

It's not as easy to find an answer to these questions.

And as a result: as long as governments don't look for and take under their wing (possibly even against their will) our genii – scientists, philosophers, poets, artists, inventors – then the majority of them will keep dying, and with them will die what "practical people" believe to be fantasizing from boredom and harmful utopias.

Even if the cause of utopian thoughts is dissatisfaction with reality, even if one's surroundings cause him to plunge into the unknown and even the fantastical, even if the unimaginably brave thought is only the result of human dissatisfaction with a given moment . . . it *inspires and works*; and it does so specifically in the beginning when it simply seems like an unachievable fantasy, utopia.

Has it been a long time since flight through the air departed from the realm of utopia?

Time will pass, and the "utopia" of a brotherhood of nations will be commonly accepted, an everyday given.

Art – isn't that the **sole instinct** that turns a humanlike ape (or an apelike human) **into a human**?

Give it a second, don't rush: things that don't immediately make sense aren't always meaningless.

There are two mighty instincts: *nourishment* and *reproducing*. Without these instincts, life on earth would either freeze or take such forms that we can't even imagine.

Really, how can something live in our physical conditions if it doesn't eat? And won't something that doesn't reproduce die out?

Man is well-armed with these instincts. It's not for nothing that he filled up all the earth.

But who *isn't* well-armed with them? Both plants, and animals, beginning with the single-celled amoeba – all they do is devour everything around them and reproduce, reproduce without end.

However, this doesn't make them what we call the rulers of the earth.

It's not these two, but the third instinct: the instinct of searching beyond the boundaries of the possible, the instinct of creation, study, guessing, the instinct of knowledge and creation, the creation of new values – it's the only thing that singled man out from the other animals.

Could this insatiable thirst for knowledge be our inheritance from Adam and his wife? – after the "fall from grace," after they tasted the forbidden fruit of the tree of knowledge of good and evil?

It's neither here nor there how you interpret this Biblical tale – but isn't the symbol brilliant, ingenious: a creature full of bliss and joy is instantly and forever denied its joy and rest as soon as its lips touched the poison of knowledge!

And isn't it true? Doesn't that poison eat us from within?

But there's no need to grow sad – everything hides within itself an embryo of its antipode: birth hides the embryo of death of within itself, and every death bears with it the embryo of new life.

And this poison, which often makes us unsettled, miserable, suffering, ultimately bears with it liberation, victory, and joy.

Atlantis will drown or some barbarian conqueror will burn down a library, human knowledge will disappear, science and scholarly scrolls, papers will all fall away . . . But *the instinct of striving for enlightenment, self-expression, art* still lives in man – and he creates a new science, unlike the old one: sometimes it's deeper, sometimes not, but it's always selfless, always inquisitive, always youthful . . .

To be able to know, understand, do everything! That's what a person wants. He is fated to it, he can't exist any other way.

Now is the era of discovering and ruling matter, the material world: man, having forgotten about everything else, builds machines by brute force, and they transport him at the speed of the wind, he destroys any mountain that stands before him, unites seas, clothes, warms, illuminates, feeds himself . . .

But just like after playing sports, walking, or physical labor you're drawn towards more cerebral, intellectual work – the time is near when man will hungrily throw himself into a battle against the shortcomings and primitive aspects of his psyche.

If we've come this far from animal to modern human, then why shouldn't we keep blazing the same path onwards? And won't the **humanity** of the future look at us like we currently look at the pithecanthrope?

What are the possibilities that lurk in the human "machine"?

Little by little, one microscopic step at a time, our science is pushing us down this path.

But look at this whole picture?! Science and nothing else? As if we owe everything to science? Then what is art? A greenhouse flower? A whimsy?

Hold on! Does something immediately become science? Isn't the first step always art?

The first hunts and protections of cavemen—clubs, stone axes—aren't they the products of this instinctive resourcefulness and inspired guesswork, i.e. aren't they more art than science?

Has it been a long time since medicine became a science? Time out of mind, medicine was an art. And even today, in the hands of a person who isn't talented or artistically enlightened, doesn't it seem more like a dangerous weapon in the hands of a child?

And has it been long since chemistry became a science? Wasn't it at first "an art of mixing antipathetic and sympathetic matters?"

There's a reason why the family tree of science and art spans many ages, and there's a reason why Apollo was in charge of both at the same time.

The only difference is that science is more patient and sober-minded; it plows on, unconcerned with its slowness, step by step, while art is, as usual, impatient, and, without thinking too much about it, it soars over all obstacles and boldly establishes itself as if at home in the unknown realm of intuition.

The greater, the bigger that art is, then the higher the fields and realms that it pierces; sometimes, they seem miraculous and utterly inaccessible. Although lesser and more modest art doesn't embark on such courageous excursions and only dares to go for modest walks around its house, its natural environment still isn't so much knowledge, contemplation, and conclusions, as much as it is free fantasy, intuition, and guesswork.

Art Is One of an Organism's Reactions

What is this power, this fabled "water of life" that freed us from our eternal animal dream? From eternal animal unconsciousness, from the power of lower nature?

What is this wondrous, salvational instinct?

Can't we take a closer look, couldn't we examine it with a naked human eye to see what it's made of? Could we even change it? Could we perfect the evil stepmother Nature?

An organism nourishes itself, grows, exercises its strength, protects itself from harmful agents, and multiplies. Then it fades, wilts, crumbles, and dies.

Without going in to details, that's what life is. Everything else is only developments of this: in order to eat, you have to find food, and having found it, swallow it . . . In order to defend yourself from harmful agents, you have to flee, fight . . . In order to multiply, you have to find a female and impregnate her, or find a male and be impregnated, then bear the fetus, raise it, teach it some basic lessons . . .

And in order to fade, wilt, and crumble, you don't have to do anything. That process doesn't require your help . . .

An organism reacts to anything that could happen inside or outside of us, and acts accordingly. A reaction is accompanied by a pleasant or unpleasant feeling. This fact is what explains our joy and our sorrow, our delight and our suffering, our victory and our defeat.

When conditions are hard, when there's no way out, a person sighs, moans, cries, tears out his hair – this is a simple, mundane reaction, self-expression that is animalistic.

However, when, instead of giving voice to your suffering in animalistic groans, you do it with verse, song, painting, small acts of heroism – that sort of reaction, that sort of self-expression is intrinsic only to humans.

When nature comes up with obstacles, and man bows in submission, accepts it as it is – adverse, frightening, cunning – this relationship is no different from that of any animal.

However, when the insubordinate two-legs wants to take nature in his hands and, figuring out its secrets and using its own power, forces it to serve *him* – that's the power of a human-creator.

Nourishment

Obeying the instinct to feed itself, a living creature looks for food, fights for it, eats it, and in doing so, gives its body life, warmth, strength . . . Without expending all the energy yet, having only just taken it in, the creature feels hunger again, the instinct for nourishment once again pushes it to look for food . . . etc.

A child doesn't need to fight for food – he gets it already made. Having filled his stomach, he plays, gambols about, rides a stick for a horse, imagines various things . . .

What is this? Why does he do this?

Some will say: it's simple – he's getting rid of excess energy. If an adult has to spend all of his energy getting food and, having consumed it, requires nothing but rest, a child doesn't expend any energy looking for food, but he has to expend it somehow, else the excess will weigh him down: such is the law of equilibrium – he has to expend it.

True.

But isn't there something more here?

A child doesn't just run around – he imagines something, he's living through something the whole time.

Why is there such an attraction to an imaginary life, not the real one? Why the need to give in to the power of dreams and fantasy? Isn't that the instinctive path of the organism, which, under the influence of the creative process "tunes" its "receiver," therefore picks up the proper currents, currents that fuel not his blood or muscles, but the psychological part that starves in everyday life?

We know so little. And what we don't know, we reject – this is considered a good tone, when in reality, it's just narrow-mindedness, nearsightedness, and fear. We can only try to console ourselves with the fact that it has always been this way, and therefore we can do the same thing.

Giordano Bruno is hunted like a wild animal: how dare he come up with the idea that not only the Earth, but our whole solar system is an insignificant grain of sand among endless worlds, a myriad of systems of equal and even greater size! How dare he come up with such heresy? It endangers the very foundations of the widely accepted and accessible "bible"! He is judged, forced to toil away, and is ultimately burned at the stake for the glory of the holy inquisition, in defense of the "truth," and for the edification of all of humanity: don't you dare think something that a pedestrian cannot grasp!

That was a long time ago. But aren't similar things done today?

Our minds do not work so irreproachably, and we are often rather slow on the update, especially when it comes to the new and unfamiliar.

Same thing here: should food only be consumed with the mouth, and should it be only either liquid or solid? It's been discovered that it can also happen via the lungs, which take in oxygen from the air.

And there are other kinds of energy. Let's at least say solar energy. And how many other kinds will we discover?

Lately, for example, there have been some talk about electroreception, i.e. feeding an organism with the electricity that is in the air . . .

What is happening to a child while he is playing? What is happening to a person in the moments of his artistic enlightenments? Why does man experience such joy, delight, and satisfaction in those moments?

We can guess, think, suppose . . .

Maybe in those moments, he truly and factually receives something, some sort of *nutrition*? Some sort of energy enters his system at that time?

But why speak only of enlightenment? Simple, authentic attention makes us happy and satisfied – from a substantive book, from a good, significant show, from prolonged examination of a beautiful painting, from speaking with a great and important person – you experience a feeling that is very akin to satiation. And for a long time afterwards, a few days or a week, you're constantly remembering and chewing it over, like a cow chewing a cud: either the words and thoughts of the writer, or the actor's successful scene, or a musical part of the symphony, or everything that you saw and heard from the person who charmed you with his greatness and depth. You think it over with renewed satisfaction each time, and you don't want new impressions, just like you don't want to eat after you've had a good dinner.

Once you digest it all, and it settles, you'll "want a bite" again. And the person goes in the direction that suits him: one goes to the theatre, another to a concert, a third to a museum, a fourth goes out into nature, a fifth looks for the "wise man" again and gets another conversation, and a sixth opens up a novel or a philosophical treatise or a scientific book.

And he's sated once again, then he digests it, and it starts all over.

And even aestheticism, love for beauty – what is that? Maybe the underlining here is also psychophysiological?

What happens in a person who is gifted with special sensitivity and affinity for beauty? Does he not open himself in the moments of his enlightenment to receive tiny electromagnetic currents or some sort of life-giving thought energy or something else that will soon become common knowledge – after all, they are currently photographing electromagnetic emissions of the living brain.

The acuity of this person's perception of beauty is utterly unfathomable for us. That kind of person will look at a setting sun, and he's not like you or me – we look in order to see the color of the sky. A red sky at sunset means dry weather – but he's looking at it, and he doesn't care about tomorrow, he's just looking at the now. He's simply taking in a simple natural phenomenon, but how!

Have you ever had to suffer from thirst for a whole, hot day during some trek, without a drop of water? And then you get to some clear, cold spring. You drink! And not how you usually drink – there's a certain sweetness, a substance to every sip. It's not life anymore – it's life itself! It's joy! Bliss in liquid form! It's exactly what your body needed and nothing else! Every drop revitalizes, refreshes, and rewards you tenfold for the suffering, the fatigue, the whole day of heat and humidity!

And that's what's happening to this person: he's looking at the sunset, and you see how he's taking it in, sucking it in, greedily absorbing something out of the sunset that usually slips by us, leaving you and me in a state of undisturbed calm – but he's excited, he's sating a burning thirst, he's drinking! Drinking the rapturous life water of witnessing beauty! Beauty is comprehensible to him, close to his heart. He lives and breathes it.

Such is the artist. We aren't so sensitive to beauty, but we require soul food too for our psychological nourishment and for the sake of new impressions and experiences.

In order to get this nourishment, the more courageous, decisive, and uncompromising among us throw themselves without much ado into the rapids of life's most tumultuous straits . . . They're thrown and tossed about, battered all over . . . Some make it out, having received a mass of impressions that changed them for their whole lives, but for most, things end poorly: the daredevils could have their heads burst against rocks, or they'll be torn asunder, but regardless of whether they end up dead, in prison, starved to death, "drowned," or in a "bourgeois happiness," the point remains the same: they're goners!

Being more modest, more "farsighted," we don't mark our foreheads and throw ourselves to the whims of cruel life – we choose a more painless and safe route – we go into art. Here, beneath the mask of another, imagined person, it's like we're in a secure ship – no matter where you set your sights, though you'll be battered and thrown about, you'll not only return alive and healthy, but you'll be renewed, enlightened, and wise.

After a published book, or a finished painting, after an acted role – though you're tired and broken from everything you put into the work, and you're empty, but you're happy, because you're "sated," full. With what? Impressions, knowledge. As if you lived a whole new life and have become many years, a whole life older and more experienced – wiser.

Exercise – Personal Development

This is all about the search for new values from the outside.

But there are also searches inside yourself.

A person is brought into this life with two more or less ready (functioning) systems: digestion and blood circulation. Others, like motor and sensory systems are in such a state that you have to learn to use them by exercising them – they're not suited for life yet.

An infant lies on a pillow, flailing his arms around, waving his feet in the air, deafening everyone with his screams, glaring at his surroundings without seeing anything . . . and screams and laughs again, this time from joy . . . why? What is this pointless activity?

It's the need to move, to exercise your weak body, which is currently unsuited to anything.

The youngling is testing his future weaponry – he's feeling out the potential of his "machine." And gradually, with exercise and experience, his organs strengthen, develop, and begin to function properly.

Let his feet helplessly flail in the air: nature itself ingrained in him this need to exercise – when the time comes, they'll be running and jumping on the earth too. His hands will do any work from the crudest to the most subtle and artistic; his eyes will see everything, he ears will hear.

A poet puts together verse, an actor reads it, a musician makes the string moan and sing . . . The thought of it all makes them "over mere fiction shed their bitter tears," and they forget about everything in the world.

Doesn't that sound like pointless activity?

Let the thought seek refuge among the imaginary, don't get in its way: ultimately, it will conquer everything in the world.

Let new organs be developed; exercise and grow them. We don't know how many new psychological and physical organs will come to light. And what will man transform into with these new ones?

Humanity has a long way ahead of it! Do we dare interfere? And what do we even currently understand in all this?

How?!

That's it!??!

Inspired art, philosophical flights of thought, bold scientific thoughts – that's all just child-like limb flailing?

Is it just instinctively exercising a small bit of flesh?

Well, maybe it's not just that, but, truth be told, if we compare the legs of a month-old infant with those of a young athlete, then we probably shouldn't feel any disappointment.

This is all from a cosmic point of view, after all, where centuries are like seconds, planets are grains of sands, and a person is an electron.

Otherwise, from our point of view, then, of course, it's a "higher product" of our existence.

Is anyone arguing?

Reproduction (the Instinct to Propagate Your Species)

Not too long ago, people considered physics and chemistry to be completely different, independent sciences, and they didn't see anything in common between physical and chemical phenomena.

Now, the boundary between these two fields has smoothed, and we know that chemical processes are entirely subservient to the laws of physics.

Since long ago, human thought has been digging under the hidden roots of hard-to-explain psychological phenomena. We won't speak to whether there's been a lot done in this field, but if we presume for a minute that in the psychological realm, just like in the physical one, we're dealing with some sort of *power*, and this power has to be *appended to something*. Let the substance to which it's appended be so subtle and imperceptible that it would be considered the height of bravery, a bit cavalier, to label it as matter, but since we're dealing with *degrees of subtlety*, then is that really a good enough reason to stop our train of thought? And really: aren't phenomena from both realms subservient to the same laws?

It's difficult to say if psychology and physiology can unconditionally offer each other their hands, but we don't even need to right now. It will be enough if we can come up with certain analogies between physiological and psychological processes.

As for nutrition and all of its possible varieties – we've said enough.

Isn't that also the case for *reproduction* (the instinct to propagate your species)?

Living creatures have a mighty, often insurmountable desire to multiply. Look at how ferociously animals fight for mates – sometimes they fight each other to the death! What happens to the instinct of self-preservation? Seemingly the strongest instinct of all.

The instinct of propagating your species attracts you to the opposite sex. And the instinct to ameliorate your species attracts you to an appropriate and better specimen. And life on earth owes its existence to this attraction. And life owes this attraction's passion and strength the fact that the species is carried on by the strongest and best representatives. The worst and weak kind must cede the path or begin another, weak species, that is destined to die.

Is it not the same with humans?

They fight differently, kill differently, but don't they fight and don't they kill?

Now let's take a step, along with this whole mechanism, into the realm of psychology.

If we are so bold as to discuss psychological nutrition, then why shouldn't we discuss conception?

If brain emissions really are being recorded, and not just recorded, but measured – in a word, if there is something material, something that can move through space and interact with what it encounters, then doesn't it seem like the insurmountable desire to relay your thoughts and delights to another person is an awful lot like the aforementioned instinct to continue your species?

Doesn't it seem like the issue here is that a person has the desire to relate his thoughts or feelings, to infect or even *inject* another with his psychological "I"?

And the other person, once "inseminated" in this fashion, plays host to new internal work, the creation of a new "being," a new thought.

Why does the painter create paintings, why does the sculptor hammer away at his marble, the writer toils over his novel, the philosopher over his treatise, the scientist over his research, and, finally, the actor over his stubborn actor's instrument?

Isn't it easier not to worry, not to suffer for nothing, and just to be satisfied by dreaming and fantasizing to your own heart's content for a bit? Naturally, I'm not talking about craftsmen, but about artists who *cannot* not write, not paint, not sing, not act.

Why does a bird weave a nest, why does it lay eggs, why does it sit on them, why does it feed its chicks, why does it defend them from scary predators, risking its life?

If children aren't just physical, but psychological, then it's not surprising that the artist, the scientist, the thinker, the inventor speak about throes of art, and it's not for nothing that there are expressions like, "*Labor of love*" or "*This is my baby!*"

Don't people suffer for ideas? Don't they die, defending from "wild predators" their flesh and blood?

Galileo is kept in a prison: how dare he insist that the Earth spins! – they persuade him, demand, seduce him to reject his findings. And before all honest people, having forcibly read the prescribed balderdash, the motherly instinct, seeing how her child is perishing, forces him to gather all his last strength and yell out: "And yet it moves!"

And for certain individuals, this instinct is significantly stronger than the instinct of self-preservation. This is the instinct of "reproduction" and "propagating the species" of human thought. And without it . . . what would we have?

Everything that I've called "abandon," "self-expression," "confession," "self-discovery" – aren't these all seeds that are sometimes thrown to a single person, sometimes to hundreds that are sitting in a theatre or auditorium, sometimes simply to the world! Like a book, like a painting, like a statue, like a thought, like my baby – the best part of my psychological "I." A son, born of my labor and joy – it will live when I am gone, and it will continue the work of inseminating other people that come in contact with it.

And so: "I love him who steweth golden words before his deeds and performeth still more than his promise" [Nietzsche (1896: 9)].

On the Desire to Be Inseminated

Reproduction begins with the act of insemination and concludes with the act of birth.

Bringing a work into the world is an act of birth. But is it possible to bear fruit without having been inseminated?

Reading a book, listening to music, steeping ourselves in the depths of scientific of philosophical thought, enthusiastically taking in nature – we're sating ourselves.

But is this always just satiation?

No, not always. Sometimes, it's a much higher, much more wondrous act – an act of insemination. In the depths of our consciousness and even more so in our subconscious, there lie and brew so many thoughts, desires, images, and impressions that we can't even imagine.

What is this life that happens inside us? What are the collisions between our thoughts and feelings? – it's difficult to say, this is a question of investigations far in the future. For now, science gives us only suggestions. Though it's true that, leaning on them, we can, with some certainty, reach certain conclusions.

For example: when something foreign and new – an impression or a thought – gets into the huge anthill of incessant, boiling life that is our brain, then (providing this is a worthy cause) on the inside there is an upheaval, a whole storm, a war . . . And it doesn't quiet down until the battle ends, until the equilibrium is reconfigured. Who will win? – It's impossible to predict.

Generally speaking, of course, the stronger side will win: the newcomer – a thought – could be so powerful that it overturns the whole anthill; the opposite could also be true: despite its power, the anthill's customs and traditions are so mighty that they'll literally eat the poor newcomer alive!

We can also imagine another scenario: at first, a troublemaker, full of vigorous energy, will yell, create a tumult, spread some fear, then will grow tired, quiet down, and will finally become a faithful ant – he'll assimilate.

Sometimes, the anthill greets the random newcomer like a long-awaited guest and sovereign: if only he had come sooner! Everyone will prostrate before him in blissful delight and will subject themselves to him for centuries to come.

Sometimes, however, the wanderer infiltrates the anthill more modestly, quietly, sneakily, without being noticed. He finds himself a mate, creates an offspring as inconspicuously; it grows equally inconspicuously, and then it suddenly appears before our astonished gaze! Unseen, unexpected, unlike anyone else around him.

On the Meeting of Two Thoughts

Observations of the technique of discoveries and inventions show that aside from intended searches in the given field, what also play a significant, decisive role are accidental activities that seemingly have nothing to do with the subject of the investigations.

That which accidently turns up shouldn't be discarded. Who knows – maybe nothing is accidental, nothing ever turns up for no reason.

A person is thinking about bridges, sees a spider on a spider web, and he comes up with a solution to a problem – a hanging bridge.

Another person is considering a problem of the benzene nucleus – he sees five monkeys in a cage, all hanging on to each other – and the scheme of the benzene nucleus is ready.

The *meeting* of two thoughts is very important. Thoughts don't actually meet, they don't bump into each other – they flicker by each other.

And life is constantly tossing seemingly unnecessary, unimportant facts and thoughts in your path. What we usually do is ignore them, walk past them. But let's try to *meet* such a new fact or idea.

In the field of literature, we constantly miss them. We're thinking about one thing, then suddenly, a timid, almost foreign thought or memory or image pops up. You toss it out, thinking that it's just absent-mindedness, a lack of concentration, when you should be grabbing at it, holding on to it! *Force these two thoughts to meet*: your main thought with the wandering one that's timidly passing by the windows of your soul.

And don't just make them meet each other – make them **understand** each other.

Truth be told, the concept of meeting thoughts is underappreciated by me, as Wilde's formula of "green-lighting" was underappreciated for a long time, as the word "play" was thrown about for a long time without giving it enough consideration . . .

However, isn't the most important question whether the thoughts successfully met? Doesn't the "nearest flow of thought" represent the meeting of thoughts, an organic fusion?

If thoughts end up flowing past each other – that's the end – nothing will come of it.

If they unite – a reaction is imminent. If they unite just slightly, the reaction is slight; if they wholly unite, the reaction is whole.

There are several sides to the meeting of thoughts:

1   The *quality* of the thought. Distinct, concrete, charged with power on its own. Or murky, confused, full of doubts and destruction.
2   I thought about discussing the "thought capsule." But I'm not certain that it's right yet. A thought in a capsule is like an egg in a shell. Put an egg next to another egg or even one on top of the other, and they still won't combine. Get rid of the capsule, and the union will occur. Another simile: like a liquid in two bottles.

I just think that a capsule, regardless of how hard it is on its own, dissolves given the nearest possible passing-by between two thoughts. But can this only happen given a *nearest possible passing-by*, i.e. given a certain method, and for all other instances, there's no need to disregard the capsule?

In short, it's vital to tie together the meeting of thoughts with the technique of "*nearest flow.*"

And in general, if we start dealing with "***creative thinking***," we'll have to involve the magnetism of thought, the vivacity of thought, the imagery of thought, the materiality of thought, and its physiological tangibility. And other than that – the laws of motion of thoughts, the position of thoughts, etc.

Receiving and Giving, and Their Symbiosis

We spoke about how a person perceives, how he takes in the "food of life."

(Or how his thoughts become inseminated by taking in the embryos of foreign thoughts, how new thoughts are created, incubated, and born.)

But nourishment consists of four, equally important processes: taking in food, digesting it, transforming it into some kind of energy – heat, mechanical, nervous, i.e. using it – and, finally, removing the remains.

If any one process is disturbed, the whole process of nourishment is disturbed. This, sooner or later, leads to death.

It's the same in the material AND the psychological world.

You can't just consume – you also have to *give*; you can't just breathe in – you have to breathe out as well.

We already discussed the need for giving away when we considered "confession," and the necessity to "live out" what's hidden inside me, while "disguised by a mask" – to rid myself of those emotions and thoughts I don't give much freedom, and which overburden me. We also spoke of "facets," and of the riches that are deeply hidden and undiscovered even by their owner.

How do receiving and giving alternate?

While they do certainly alternate, are they easy to discern from one another? And can we determine whether, at any given moment, there is more of one or the other?

Here, for example: I'm disturbed by some unknown thought that's sitting deep in my soul. A whole clump of thoughts. I feel it and I know, more or less, what it's about, but I don't know what it's about *exactly*. This murky clump of thoughts, feelings, and desires often worries me so much with its presence that I desperately want to remove it. There must be something in the depths of my subconscious itching to get out – it's probably needed to come into the conscious sphere for a long time. Out from the basement and into the light of day, to the mezzanine.

And so I begin to speak, argue, and write about it, and I gradually pull its thread, examine the clump, and ultimately pull the entire thread out: it's outside in its entirety, and it's been respun into completely new skeins. It used to be all bundled up in one huge, indiscernible clump, but now it's been worked-through, it's been sorted. And now I know everything, see everything – I see what goes where; it's reached my consciousness, and I own all of it now.

There's more of what here – receiving or giving? And how can we discern one from the other?

And do we even have to discern these two states from one another, and is it even possible to discern them?

To tell the truth – the heightened state that magnetically pulls the actor to the stage, the musician to the instrument, the writer to the pen, the scientist to the thought, and, finally, the child to his play – it's always complex, it's never *just* giving or *just* receiving.

It's both at once: the exhalation immediately becomes the inhalation, and an inhalation is always followed by an exhalation.

And we can imagine the mechanics of this process approximately like this: when in a state of heightened sensitivity, perception, and clarity of thought – that's when barely perceptible, but precious thoughts that flow through me, close to the threshold of my consciousness, begin to permeate me with greater strength; or when I begin to grasp onto the subtly passing "electro-magnetic" waves – unattainable when I am in my "mundane" state.

In a word – the reception and intake from without and from within becomes more powerful. This is the inhalation.

In order to allow more things to enter you, you grow alert, open the gates to your hidden treasures and depths wider, and at this point, your hidden thoughts, desires, and feelings that have been subdued by life all stream out, yearning for their long-awaited freedom – you give it all out.

And in this moment of giving, I become even more exposed and open. Then, regardless of my desire, the empty space left by the discharged thoughts is filled up by new ones I take in.

The new meets the old, symbiosis takes place, some third thing is born and itself demands release, and then – another release. And so on and so forth: inhale and exhale . . . coupling and uncoupling . . . attraction and repulsion.

And it's difficult to say which is greater in each case: receiving or giving, taking in or giving out.

This is where these endless arguments stem from: each person only notices his own part, and so he advocates it. One notices the leaves and says: the apple tree is green. Another notices the trunk and says: the apple tree is gray A third notices the flowers: the apple tree is white . . . Who's right? Everyone and no one.

Art is complex, multifaceted, and if you really want some sort of formula, then the best one may have been found by the person [Tyutchev (1966: 75)] who said:

The hour of inexpressible longing! . . .

Everything is in me, and I'm in everything...

"Life" in Creativity and in Play: "The Truth of Life" in Creativity, and in Creative Fantasies

When playing, a child becomes immersed; he believes that everything is real. Somebody who doesn't believe, doesn't become immersed, is boring to play with; he doesn't know how to play.

Another, who becomes too immersed, believes too much that he's a warrior, surrounded by deadly enemies, and begins beating and attacking people for real, ignoring reality – he too doesn't know how to play.

How can we work through all this?

At first glance, it doesn't seem like great wisdom: let the child become immersed, let him believe – you can't completely fail to believe or become immersed – only he should do it to a certain point. He should believe to a certain point and not believe to a certain point – then everything will be as it should be.

The tried and true wisdom of mediocrity – searching for the truth in the middle. Always, in every case, this is the path of a dearth of imagination, and is good for nothing in art and creativity.

Searching for truth isn't like weighing potatoes: you put on too little – it's not weighed down; too much – it tips the scale too much; take off five or ten, and that's the right amount.

As always, truth is simple, so simple that it astounds, and disappoints, and frightens, and overwhelms, and makes you laugh. Always, it tries to come to you on its own, and . . . we always search for it where it can never be.

That's how it is with "playing," with "acting."

To become immersed, believe, and live in play to the point of utter self-abandon – that's one extreme. But it's *not "playing"* anymore. It's just: life. What's more, taking my little brother for an enemy, or a pirate, and whacking him on the head with a log with all my strength – that's probably a psychological malfunction, that's a hallucination, that's being "out of your mind"

On the other hand: not believing, being a cold executor of the game's rules, only pretending that you're immersed and that you believe – that's the other extreme.

But the thing is that that's not "play" either.

If the first case is a psychological malfunction, and play slipped into life, then the second case is an "under-transformation," just an attempt without suitable means: *there isn't and can never be any "playing" here* – there was just the depiction of playing, the falsification of playing.

Does the child live in the game?

Of course. But differently than in life.

He lives in a fantastical, *imaginary life*.

Lives in it and creates his own given circumstances, lives and creates himself within those givens, lives in *another* environment – the environment of imagination, fantasy, dreams, an environment that has completely different laws of life.

Life and "play" (i.e. artistic creativity) are two completely opposing worlds, like water and air.

Life is "swimming" in a thick and dense environment of facts, realities, and authenticities (at least, that's how they present themselves).

Play is "flight" on the wings of fantasy; it's a "leap over the logical abyss," it's artistry. Instead of the real, it's imaginary.

But how do these two seemingly irreconcilable environments fit into each other? How do their seemingly adverse laws get along?

A boy sits on a chair and rides his new horse wherever he wants – to his neighbor, to Baghdad, to the North Pole – a chair is instantly turned into a horse to suit the needs of his whims. He is seized in Baghdad and thrown into a dungeon; the adventurer hides under a chair and doesn't dare to move for fear of having his head chopped off: the chair is a dungeon. But later, after dazzling adventures, he frees himself and gallops his chair over unimaginable distances to his home to his kid's room . . .

Whatever happened to the real chair, the kid's room, and, finally, the boy himself?

Before the start of a show, I see made-up colleague-actors, the rags that make up the sets, limelight and stage boards . . .

The show starts, and before me are my father, my beloved, my castle, moonlight or sunlight . . . in a word, it's a new, fantastical life.

Where did the factual, real life that existed before the show started go? It didn't go anywhere – it's still here.

Remember the experiment? A circle was divided into seven sectors, each sector was colored one of the primary colors: red, yellow, green, etc. If the motley disc began to spin very quickly, the colors would disappear, the disc would become blindingly white.

Where did the seven colors go? Red, orange, yellow, green, turquoise, blue, purple?

They didn't go anywhere. They're all there. They make up the white light.

It's the same in the art of the actor – nothing disappears: the partners, the sets, the lights, the stage boards . . .

But fantasy, this sorceress, begins to "spin" them, and it mixes up its own fictitious excitement and desires with the factual reality, thus creating a creative hurricane. It transfigures them with the flames of imagination – and a new reality emerges – the creation of an artist.

The Chief Quality of the Artist-Creator

"Fantasy, this sorceress, begins to 'spin . . . ' and it transfigures everything into the creation of an artist."

But an artist's creation isn't such a common occurrence, and it's not inherent to many, which is why we should delay speaking about it for now; however, isn't there something similar that happens to us in other, more mundane conditions?

"There is a wall before me. An old, brick wall, damp, spotted, stained . . . bluish, yellow, brown, magenta stains . . . I often look at the patterns, deep in thought, awaiting the solution to some difficult problem . . .

"So yesterday, as usual, I was calmly gazing into those familiar spots, and suddenly . . . I nearly became feverish! A horrible old man-vampire is staring right into my eyes . . . His piercing, evil eyes seemed to have been be drinking the blood from my brain.

"I started shaking in horror.

"In two-three seconds, I came to . . . The wall was still covered by the same blotches and spots . . . but they've come together in such peculiar way! There are the eyebrows, the nose, the shoulders. The eyes! It's all frightening, horrifying: phosphoric, irresistible, sorcerous! And yet these are just stains and spots . . . There's a stain, there's some mold . . . And I notice that I am trying to reason with myself, as if saying: 'don't be afraid, it's not alive, it just seemed that way . . .'

"And yet, the eyes are glowing, they make you very uncomfortable . . . That means that no matter how much I try to convince myself that it was just a fancy, I can't do it in full . . . No matter how much I try to rationalize that it's silly, that's it's the accidental interplay of the pattern and the lighting, and maybe my subconscious thoughts in the moment – everything combined, and it caused this deceptive impression – my discomfort wouldn't subside . . .

I had to cover the 'old man' with something.

"Today, I looked at him again. The nose, the eyebrows, the eyes . . . Everything's in place. But the important thing is missing: he's not alive! He *looks* like an old man, but he isn't. No matter how I try to stir myself up, how I try to get myself into yesterday's state of being – it's not there! The living, horrifying old man, the real old man is gone!

"Often, when you look at the clouds, or at the trembling tree shades, you see images, scenes . . . But for the most part, they're like paintings: they *look* alive, they're the *depiction* of life, but it's not life itself . . . But here, it was so real, so indubitable . . . "[1]

Indigenes

The animated spots on the wall . . . What is that? Maybe it's the overly acute reaction of a slightly abnormal mind?

Let's go to a mind that's quite normal, belonging to a person who was brought up in nature.

Here are some fragments from books, letters, and the journals of adventurers and missionaries that could closely observe the life and morals of indigenes in Africa, Australia, America, and Asia.

"We've placed," write Jesuit missionaries, "images of St. Ignatius and St. Xavier on our altar, the indigenes regarded them with surprise. They believed that they were real people. They asked if they were *ondaki* (supernatural beings), they also asked if the shade of the altar was their home, whether the *ondaki* ever wore the decorations that they saw around the altar . . . "

Similarly, in Central Africa, I saw how indigenes refused to enter a shelter that had portraits hanging on the wall out of fear of the *mazoka* (souls) that were present.[2]

American anthropologist and ethnologist Frank Hamilton Cushing [1857–1900], who lived among the Zuni Indians of North Mexico, was adopted by them, and who had an extraordinarily flexible mind that allowed him to think like them, says:

> [The Zuni], no less than primitive peoples generally, conceive of everything made, whether structure, utensil, or weapon, as animistic, as living. They conceive of this life of things as they do of the lives of plants, of hibernating animals, or of sleeping men, as a still sort of life generally, but as potent and aware, nevertheless, and as capable of functioning, not only obdurately and resistingly but also actively and powerfully in occult ways, either for good or for evil. [Cushing 1896: 361–362]

Having read these notes, some might even take offense: what sort of a comparison is this! The undeveloped, primitive minds of barbarians! That's just grand!

However, wait just a moment.

These undeveloped and primitive minds can stand up to ours in quite a few respects.

In preparing tools, in rigging his snares, an indigene often exhibits gumption that bears witness to a very keen perception of cause and effect.

And they are so observant! They can recognize any member of their tribes just by their foot imprints. And they can even tell what occurred on the spot.

And they have such amazing memory! English anthropologist Walter Edmund Roth [1861–1933] writes about the aborigines of northwest Queensland:

> The Corrobboree consists of singing, accompanied by dancing and accompaniments . . . . [It] commences at sunset and may be continued until sunrise, the whole performance being extended sometimes over three, four, or even five nights consecutively. It may . . . come to pass, and almost invariably does, that a tribe will learn and sing by rote whole corrobborees in a language absolutely remote from its own, and not one word of which the audience or performers can understand the meaning of. That the words are very carefully committed to memory, I have obtained ample proof by taking down phonetically the same corrobborees as performed by different-speaking people living at distances of 100 miles apart . . . [Roth 1897: 117]

As for their spiritual level – observers often laud the inherent eloquence of indigenes in many different parts, and the richness of the arguments that they make in various debates and discussions. Their tales and sayings often bear witness to their keen and refined perception, their myths speak of a fruitful, rich, often poetic imagination. Observers who weren't always predisposed to favor the "barbarians" noted it plenty of times.

Emotional Projection

This is all enough to make us rather ashamed of some things.

Why, then, the very strange attitude to portraits, tools, and everything else that was mentioned?

How does it happen that a tribesman that is so reasonable, cunning, adult, and wary, possessed of such sharp perception that we should be jealous, sees obviously dead items and paintings as alive?

Before answering this, let's check to see if we have something similar in our secluded, backwater villages.

Here, we're not dealing with Australian or Asian tribes – we're dealing with people that are essentially no different from ourselves – after all, many outstanding poets, painters and scientists came out of these villages . . .

There, things are as follows: from early childhood, you're taught that all hidden forces, good and evil, live with us, among us: witches, sprites, "Baba Yagas," devils, and other evil spirits flood through our pens, yards, woods, ravines, pools, bogs. But they don't always show themselves, and when they do, it's not when you expect . . .

Just yesterday, a sprite frightened Stepanida, your aunt – it stole her basket of mushrooms. She started screaming, ran full speed off in some random direction, and it stole her scarf from off her head. She looks around, and it's waving at her with the scarf from the top of an old fir, yelling "I'll get you!" The woman completely "lost her mind," ran home more dead than alive.

And you see that it's all true: Stepanida isn't lying, and nobody doubts the veracity of her claim.

And then a neighbor will tell about how not too long ago, a sprite led him all night through the forest. It led him back to the road only in the morning, and some ten kilometers away from home.

And then another guy tells how he saw a mermaid the other week: "She was sitting on a rock, combing her hair. Noticed me, laughed, and jumped into the water – splash!"

And just try to doubt these stories, argue with them, use scientific data – people will look at you with pity, as if to say, "Look at that poor fellow – he studied for so long, but doesn't know elementary things that any little boy knows . . . "

They'll have the same attitude towards your skepticism and sober-mindedness the same way as you regard their skepticism towards your tales about astronomy, the things you could see in a telescope or a microscope, how many kilometers to the sun, how large it is, what it's made of . . . Perplexed, you'll look at their stagnation, at the inflexibility of their beliefs with some pity . . . How can you explain to them these simple and indubitable things?!

They'll regard your "healthy skepticism" of sprites and Baba Yagas with the same perplexity, confusion, and pity.

What can they ask of you if you really haven't seen the subjects of their tales or heard some person of authority explain everything to you? *They've* seen everything! For them, it's not a question of belief or lack thereof – for them, it's a fact.

Then how did they see these creatures? The exact same way that I saw the old vampire in the spots in the wall.

The only difference is that I and others (if this were necessary) would have started convincing myself that it was just an optical illusion, a flight of fantasy. There, in the village, everything is opposite: I myself, as well as everyone around me, would immediately start asserting (and thereby indoctrinating me) that I saw something real, and if nobody else saw it, it was just because it was hidden from them, but *visible* to me.

This would happen to you once, twice, and it would ultimately lead to the creation of an independent psychological mechanism that would cause subjective impressions to appear as objective phenomena.

How and why does this happen? How can you see an old man in the spots of a wall? A sprite in a shaggy, old fir? Elves and gnomes in the distorted, heated air, a salamander in the flames of a campfire?

Is it not because of a sort of prejudice and bias?

Here's one kind of such prejudice. Everybody has felt its touch (in childhood or later).

If you have to walk in the dark of the night down some remote, forest path (especially if you recently heard some scary tales), then it's rather difficult to shake a feeling of disquiet. And if you're easily frightened, then you see a bandit behind every bush, or a bear, or a "Baba Yaga." God forbid if an owl decides to hoot or rotted tree decides to crack and fall – you'll imagine such things you'll run fearing you might never make it out of there alive . . .

Bias can be obvious (like with the night horrors after scary tales), and it can be covert.

For example, where did the old vampire amidst the spots and stains on the wall come from?

Evidently, he appeared because that time was difficult and joyless for me, and it was as if everybody had made a pact to pressure me and tear me to shreds. And it's difficult to imagine something more appropriate, more resonant with my heart's worries, concerns, and suspicions. The old vampire was my own, personal, subjective "creation." He was not an objective phenomenon, indubitable for all – he was visible only to me.

Now let's track by what exact paths and methods the subjective becomes quite objective and real for us.

I have something on my mind that is looking for a way out. Let's say that it's a difficult, disquieted, melancholy condition that I cannot shake off by doing something, by reading, by talking to my friends. The spots on the wall configure themselves in such a way that it looks like the portrait of an old man . . . and instantly, before I can think through anything, I'm seized by a feeling of terror. Where does it come from? From the depths of my soul, evidently; evidently, he's the sum of all my personal fears, humiliations, suspicions from the last, difficult, few years of my life . . .

The spots on the wall are a fact for me; their likeness to some old man is also a fact. But *isn't my terror, my disquiet also a fact*? It's a much more tangible fact, much more real for me! It eclipses everything.

And now, even if I try to calm myself down, as a cultured person is wont, even if I try to work through this "deception" – what will happen? I'll start making out the stains, I'll understand perfectly well were they came from, but the old man . . . he's right there, right in front of me, alive, even angrier, even more dangerous . . . No, I can't look at him. I turn away.

Why is that? Because I'm not looking at the spots with my ordinary, calm, cold eyes – I'm looking at them *through the feeling of terror*, terror that is quite real for me, terror that is inextricably intertwined with the old man – he brings the "spots" to life for me and imbues them with immense power.

Where is this power from? It's from me, from the depths of my psyche.

Like a magic lantern, I project the old man onto the wall, the old man that was instantly evoked in my soul.

And the spots (seeing as they coincide with the contours of "my internal, psychological" old man) stress and accentuate the fact that there is a breathing, real old man that exists outside of me.

And so, the subjective creation, evoked by an insignificant external push, becomes quite objective for me. And even quite corporeal.

★★★

What is the difference between the perception of a tribesman and that of a civilized person?

Why do indigenes possess such subtlety right next to such crudeness and inchoateness? Subtlety is not the fruit of thought and deliberation; it's intuition, a certain practical deftness and artistry that comes as a result of exercise. Sort of like a billiards player that doesn't know geometry and mechanics.

When we see that primitive peoples are physiognomists, moralists, and psychologists that are just as good as us (if not better), we find it very difficult to believe that in other regards, they can be essentially unsolvable mysteries for us.

Similarities can be found in the mental processes that result *action directly evoked by intuition*. Situations that require immediate perception, quick and almost instant understanding of what is perceived. For example, reading the emotions on a person's face, finding the words that will pull the right strings in a person's heart. It's its own kind of sixth sense.

★★★

Primitive people see everything with the same eyes as we do, but they do not perceive things with the same *consciousness*.

The psychophysiological process of perception happens the same way for them as it does for us. But the product of their perception is immediately transformed by certain complex states of consciousness.

A primitive person cannot even imagine that you could discern the nucleus of a fact from the several layers of beliefs and biases.

We can separate them as a result of our mental habits. For him, however, a complex image is indivisible.

What "covers the nucleus" isn't a series of associations. The image that a primitive person gets is an indivisible whole.

Our impressions strive to be as maximally "objective" as possible, and they seek to avoid anything that could be harmful or unhelpful with regards to establishing objectivity. However, not only do the impressions of primitive people not disregard anything that lessens their objectivity (their pathfinding functions), they, in fact, underline the mystical properties, hidden powers, and special abilities of creatures and phenomena, citing elements that *in our mind are purely subjective*, even though in their opinion, *they are no less real* than anything else.

If primitive people perceive an image differently than we do, this happens because *they perceive its **original** differently than we do.*

When approaching this original, we pay attention only to real, objective features – form, size, facial expression. For a primitive person, these features (which he perceives no less than we do) are conducting signs of hidden powers, mystical properties that are, in their understanding, inherent to any being, especially a living being. This is why the image, *which possesses the same conducting signs, seems to be alive to them.*

Their process of thought is more akin to *spontaneous perception or intuition*. In the moment when they perceive what is revealed to their external senses, they also imagine the mystical power that manifests itself in this manner. This operation does not occur in two subsequent sittings – it is instant.

Elements that we do not consider to be objective are the ones that explain and work through everything that happens for a primitive mind. Strictly speaking, everything that happens does not really require explaining, because when an event occurs, not quite logical [prelogical] thinking accounts for the unseen influence of mythological forces that manifest themselves in that manner.

For an indigene, what we consider to be perception is more like **interaction** with spirits, with invisible and hidden forces that surround him on all sides, that determine his fate, and that take up a lot more space in his brain than those constant, visible, tangible elements of what he sees.

For them, what we call objective reality is united, mixed (and often subordinate) to their attunement to mystical elements that we label as *subjective*.

The perception of primitive peoples is oriented in such a way that it is not interested in those signs of creatures and phenomena that we call objective and towards which *our* attention is directed first and foremost. They have no need for experience. After all, *experience,* which is bogged down by what is constant, tangible, visible, and perceptible in physical reality, *misses what is most important to them* – specifically, hidden forces and spirits.

For many of us, there are two worlds: the natural and the supernatural. For them, there is only one world: any reality is mystical, as is any action. Concordantly, any impression is mystical.

We take in experience and passively subject ourselves to the impression we had. On the contrary, the consciousness of a primitive person *is filled, ahead of time,* with an enormous amount of collective beliefs under whose influence, everything appears to have a myriad of mystical properties. This is where the indifference to the objective explanations behind phenomena stems from, as well as a heightened attention to apparent or hidden explanations for these phenomena.

Prelogical thinking is *synthesizing in its very nature,* i.e. unlike ours, the synthesis that makes it up does not assume preliminary analyses whose results are fixated in abstract notions.

In primitive thinking, syntheses *emerge first* and are almost always *undivided and indivisible.*

For this reason, prelogical thinking often finds insensitivity to contradiction and impenetrability with regards to experience.

For primitive thinking, a bare, objective fact can hardly exist.

★★★

Every time certain people (sorcerers) put on the skins of animals (bears, tigers, wolves), they themselves transform into these animals.

The Influence of Emotion on Thought, on Perception

Instances like the one with the old man on the wall do not happen often to us, and . . . is it really worth speaking so much about them? And building entire artistic theories around them?

Very much so. We do not see the world so sober-mindedly, so objectively as we think. Open any collection of poetry:

> Oh, good gigantic smile o' the brown old earth,
> This autumn morning! How he sets his bones
> To bask i' the sun, and thrusts out knees and feet
> For the ripple to run over in its mirth;
> *(Robert Browning [1911: 50])*

Let's try to be "sober-minded" for real – is it possible for the earth, the inanimate earth, to smile? And when does it thrust his bones to bask in the sun? Does it really "thrust" anything at all?

> Storm has set the heavens scowling,
> Whirling gusty blizzards wild,
> Now they are like beasts a-growling,
> Now a-wailing like a child;
> *(Pushkin [1972: 19])*

People will tell me that these are just poetic comparisons, nothing more.

But these poetic comparisons make up the whole language: rain is *falling*, the Volga *rolls* into the Caspian Sea, the table *stands* on four legs, rye *sways*, a thought *popped* into my head, the ham *has a bite* to it, the smoke is *eating* away at my eyes . . .

We don't even notice that we do not speak exactly, properly, but with similes, metaphors – in a word, we speak using "poetic" language.

Evidently, "poetry" isn't such a contradictory way of thought for us.

And there's nothing surprising about this. We're creatures that don't just think, coldly and exactly – we're creatures that *feel*. Sometimes, reason, deliberation, and cold thought win out, but for the most part, it's emotion and feeling that rule us. Emotion is what alters our thought, layers it with so much that it acquires completely new content.

Let's do an experiment.

Let's take anything, whatever you want, it doesn't even have to be poetic – for example, think about dinner. And you'll immediately get a feeling that is inextricable from the thought.

If you're hungry, then it'll be a pleasant feeling of anticipation; if you've just had a good meal, it will be unpleasant: I don't want to, nor can I, eat again right now (or on the contrary: I just had such a good meal! I'd like a second helping!). There could be hundreds of different reactions, depending on the person and the moment.

Let's take something else: "mathematics."

If you do not have a taste for this subject, and you had a bad teacher in school, then, naturally, this word will evoke very unpleasant, maybe even painful, memories. If, however, you enjoy abstract science and always derive pleasure from all the algebras and geometry, then you'll be very happy to transfer your thoughts from something mundane to the world of math. You'll get pleasant memories about the time when you were very interested in the subject and put in a lot of your soul into it.

As you see, almost anything evokes emotion in us.

And emotion, on its own turn, alters the fact for us and makes dinner not just dinner, but makes it either satiating and pleasant or repulsive and painful . . .

And any time you encounter a fact, this complex process takes place: the external fact evokes a response in us; this response is transposed onto the fact and essentially unites, merges with it. Because of this, the fact completely changes in our eyes: it goes from the *objective*, something that exists outside of us, and becomes *subjective*, refined and augmented by our own internal content.

Is Emotionally Synthesizing Thinking a Sign of Backwardness? It Is the Key to Art

Of course, emotion exerts enormous influence on our perception. It's not very strict or objective. There is a great amount of subjectivity in it.

But still, we've gone so far past the tribesmen and even our own countrymen that live in remote villages that we are well within our right to take pride.

We look on the moments spent with the "old vampire" or with the horrors of the night, or whatever else of that sort, to be a deviation from the norm – a decline in our thought processes, and a defect.

But aren't we a little carried away by thinking like this? . . . After all, there are many cases when the "objectivization of the subjective" can be called not a *decline*, but a *flight* of our creative powers. The Russian poet Yevgeny Baratynsky [2002: 278] wrote the following of Goethe:

> He breathed the same air as nature:
> And understood the babbling of the brook,
> He knew the language of the tree leaves,
> He felt the life of the growing grass;
> And the waves of the sea spoke his tongue.
> (Baratynsky, "On the Death of Goethe")

These are moments of "objectivization of the subjective." Is it a defect?

Of course, we owe much to the strength of our intellect, logic, etc. – they are what allowed us to get to the height of civilization at which we are today. But isn't this a bit of an exaggeration? In order to accommodate this train of thought, aren't we disregarding oppression of the power of emotion and "barbarian" ways of perceiving the world. In praising analysis and scientific objectivity to high heavens, aren't we lessening the weight of another, no less important ability of ours?

We loathe stargazing, fantasizing, and unreal trains of thought, while objectivity, or absolutely realistic judgment, is our most ancient quality: lesser animals possess this realistic function and only it.

As for "loathed stargazing" – evidently, it appeared later. And what gives us the right to think that it's a greater boon? The fact that it hasn't yet developed enough doesn't matter: it has time – after all, it's not as old as the boon of realistic thought.

There is no point in debating what is greater and what is lesser. These qualities are incomparable – they act in different spheres, each in its own. We should concern ourselves with something different: how to *develop* in full each quality, and how to *unite* their opposing and contradictory *actions*.

★★★

Up to this point, the main arguments in art concerned the following issue: is an artist's creativity conscious or subconscious?

Some asserted that it is conscious, that everything in art is under the control of one's intellect and willpower.

Others insisted that it is quite subconscious, that a person is seized by a creative state regardless of his will, and, within its grasp, the person (intuitively) writes, paints, sings, acts, and creates works of art.

Knowing from experience that the creative state doesn't always arise when it is needed and often appears when it deigns to, more prudent supporters of subconscious creativity proposed a path: "through the conscious to the subconscious" (Stanislavsky). In other words, you have to find an array of conscious events that cause the subconscious to start working, at which point you enter a creative state.

The significance of the subconscious (or "unconscious," "underconscious," "superconscious" – to each his own) in creativity is enormous.

But is this true only in creativity in art?

What about in life? In our everyday work? And science? Has there been a single great discovery or great invention in the fields of mechanics, chemistry, or mathematics that came to pass without subconscious psychological activity?

The subconscious is not the main and most important thing that differentiates the creativity of an *artist* from any other creativity.

The main and most important that differentiates the creativity of the artist from any other creativity is a special attribute: the attribute that allows one to *perceive and think in an emotionally synthesizing way*, the thing that we have been talking about since the very first pages.

Not a single poet, not a single artist that has experienced this state would call it lesser. Pushkin [1921: 8] describes it as the highest and supernatural:

I dragged my flesh through desert gloom,
Tormented by the spirit's yearning,
And saw a six-winged Seraph loom
Upon the footpath's barren turning.
And as a dream in slumber lies
So light his finger on my eyes,
My wizard eyes grew wide and wary:
An eagle's, startled from her eyrie.
He touched my ears, and lo! a sea

>Of storming voices burst on me.
>I heard the whirling heavens' tremor,
>The angels' flight and soaring sweep,
>The sea-snakes coiling in the deep,
>The sap the vine's green tendrils carry.

Without this attribute, a person cannot be an artist-creator (he can only be more or less a forger of art). If, however, it *is* present – he has a spot among artists.

Synthesis and Analysis

If I juxtapose two thought processes, two impressions, then it's vital to note that one is tightly tethered to *contradiction*, the other to *cooperation*; Analysis for one, synthesis for the other. One involves taking in facts that are independent of each other, the other involves projecting yourself under the exciting influence of an external fact.

At the sight of a chunk of meat, a dog begins to salivate. But if you show it a picture depicting meat, even if it's the most accurately drawn steak in the world, the dog will remain quite apathetic. Evidently, it *doesn't see* what's depicted in the painting.

I knew a very simple and naïve peasant girl, who, at the sight of a painting, oooed and ahhhed – it's so pretty! When she was asked to describe what she was looking at, she said: that's easy! Look at the ladies in beautiful dresses with lace . . . they're dancing . . . There are musicians with horns . . .

It was a seascape – Aivazovsky's painting. [Ivan Aivazovsky (1817–1900) is Russia's most famous marine artist.]

At the sight of Repin's "Zaporozhian Cossacks", she started ooing again – it's so pretty! But what's pretty exactly? It's so simple! Look at the flowers, all the flowers . . . there's a flower, there's one, there and there . . .

She wasn't abnormal, she was just underdeveloped.

What is the difference between our perception of the painting and hers?

We both know that something is always depicted in a painting.

On account of some skill, we take a painting in holistically and interpret it *synthetically*. We're interested not in the individual strokes – we're interested in what the strokes make up, what all the strokes are done for. And if we don't understand from the very first moment what is depicted in a painting, then we immediately ask the question: what *is* this? What is depicted here?

She (Marisha), however, does not have the skill that allows her to take in the painting holistically, and (although she knows that something concrete should be depicted in the painting) her eyes start wandering, and instead of seeing a unifying synthesis that gives meaning and life to the whole image, she perceives it in parts, *analytically*. She sees a board and splotches of different colors. [Marisha tried to guess what it was. The white foam on the crests of the waves struck her eye – it looked like lace. If it's lace then, perhaps, it belongs to ladies' dresses . . . Bright, motley splashes of paint on Repin's painting she mistook for the flowers: this must be a garden . . . or else a bouquet. *–Author's Note*]

We should be fair: such perception is quite realistic and corresponds to authentic reality. And a dog's apathy towards painted meat only proves yet again that for regular, natural perception, meat is meat, and paint is paint.

Perceiving multicolored spots as some *alternate reality* – that's a step in the direction away from simple, natural, so to say, *realistic* perception.

We can hardly call this step a step back – we have to believe that it is a step forward.

In general, reality isn't the greatest thing that humanity bears. Reality is the first thing that arises in a living being.

If emotional synthesis sometimes leads to mistakes, that's because that sort of thinking is still green. At the moment, we know of only one means against its mistakes: intellectual analysis. But further down the road, it might be possible to make do without it.

In art, everything is created specifically with this *ability to think differently, to differently perceive facts of life*. Onstage, everything has to *be realized* for me. If my life and everything about it is not completely realized (and is instead according to Stanislavsky), then the art is rather dubious.

In general, when synthesis begins, that marks the entry into another plane.

Only by a painter – a specialist – can give the ultimate analysis of a painting. He sees both, the *individual colors*, and the *whole* work holistically. He knows the secrets and laws of painting.

Different Steps of Artistic Synthesis

Let's keep going. We are at the Dresden Gallery.

English tourists come with their guides, a family of provincial Germans rolls in with all the family members, with little bags and sandwiches.

But here they go into the room where Raphael's Sistine Madonna is hanging.

They look into the guide and, finding out that it's a famous painting, the one that everybody calls the best, saying that there's nothing like it, that it's the height of painting – they put on triumphant and reverent expressions (they lucked into seeing a wonder of wonders).

To tell the truth, the painting didn't really have an instant effect on them. They just note that the woman is drawn fairly well and is rather attractive. Why is it such a grand and wondrous pinnacle of art? That remains a mystery to them. But in order to demonstrate that they're not fools or a boar, each one tries to express deep thought and delight on their faces.

Here's another kind of impression. [Russian philosopher] Pyotr Engelmeyer [(1855–1942?] in his book *The Theory of Creativity* (1910) insists that understanding of the work of art, and its enjoyment, is in itself an independent creative process.

And a third (Give example).[3]

These are the different steps of synthesis.

Marisha didn't have them at all. She only saw spots on the canvas and nothing more.

These tourists can see that the spots make up a woman.

Engelmeyer feels subconsciously.

An artist (even if he's not a painter – he can just be a person with a sensitive, artistic soul) sees *the very soul* of a work. How does he see it? He notices the subtleties, accents, and, combining, they not only convey to him the likeness of a woman – they fill her with inner meaning. And, to go even further – they bring her to life.

And what should we do with people who see perfection in unskilled scrawling? What, are they artists too? Seriously, why shouldn't we call them that? After all, they synthesize too!

For now, we don't have a proper answer – it's better not to go near these "steps of synthesis!"

Yermolova was amazed and delighted by random trash. Why? Because she added to it from herself. Uneducated audience members do the same thing.

"You Have to Develop Your Fantasy . . . "

It seems that this is a new and heightened stage. As if fantasy is something that we've never had, and now we have to develop it.

But things are completely different. Tribesmen that think prelogically have such a fantasy that we couldn't achieve if given centuries! And not just fantasy – they also have *experiencing*.

In this way, we have to concern ourselves with returning, instead of moving "forward." We won't get very far with such movement.

We have to learn to perceive everything *organically*. If we've lost it, then of course we have to develop it again. But what fantasy, and how? From their earliest days, tribesmen learn to see everything *cooperatively*. This ability functions in *our* childhoods too . . .

Notes

1 This is a fragment from a diary entry made on February 12, 1936 – at the time of Demidov's major disagreement with Stanislavsky. This might explain the hidden circumstances behind the appearance of the "old man" on the wall – "old man" being Stanislavsky's nickname at the MAT. Peculiarly, Demidov's imaginary old man is a vampire, "drinking the blood from my brain." Demidov had supplied Stanislavsky with materials and ideas since 1911, and was the first editor of *An Actor's Work*, "giving away precious inventions, observations and finds," and "negotiating face-saving solutions" [Demidov 2009: 470] for Stanislavsky's inconclusive book. The vampire association, conscious or subconscious, is somewhat justified, especially since at the time of this entry Stanislavsky decided, once more, to sever all creative relations with his closest associate and colleague of 20-some years.

2 Demidov does not specify the exact source, but he is definitely quoting materials related to the 17th century Jesuit missionaries to the Huron people (New France). Similar accounts can be found in Brébeuf 1959.

3 This thought is left unfinished by Demidov, and the example is not featured. From the following discussion, however, it is evident that Demidov was planning to give an example of a true artist's perception of a work of art (Raphael's Sistine Madonna).

2

Emotionally Synthesizing Thinking (*Projecting?*) (*Meta-Logical*)

The Reality of the Imagined

It's raining. A Rembrandt painting is hanging on the wall. There is a photographic card on the table.

These are facts. But facts aren't everything. The most important thing is what a fact means to us, how it appears to us.

It's raining. But you have to go, and you have to go right now, and go far . . . There is nothing pleasant about the fact that you'll be soaked to the bone!

For a farmer or a gardener, things are different – it's a holiday: after a rain this hard, everything will start growing like crazy!

Rembrandt's Prodigal Son. For one person, it's a great discovery, for another, it's a painted rag, because he is blind, deaf to everything, and uncultured.

A photographic card. For everybody else, it's a completely uninteresting and unknown face, but for me it's all that's left of my father. I can look at it for hours . . . and see him alive . . .

But this is not enough. For an overly sober-minded person, a fact is still a fact. But meanwhile, a hypnotized person will eat a lemon, smile blissfully, and assert that he's eating a sweet apple. Native American Indians were tortured, but they still sang their heroic songs.

There is something stronger than a fact.

A man is tied to a "torture post," he knows full well what awaits him, and he begins his swan song. About the glorious "Land of the Dead" where the brave warrior is headed, about successful hunts, great deeds, scores of slain enemies, collected scalps . . . He is stabbed, cut, burned – he feels nothing – he is already there, in that glorious land where he is met by all the braves and heroes of the tribe, where he eats juicy, hot meat, drinks the best drinks, and delights himself with satiating battles . . . he is completely immersed in his hallucinated visions . . . he goes farther and farther away from us, and, finally, having breathed his last, he leaves us forever.

Can something be more realistic than life? than facts? Everything that we smell, see, hear? It would seem that there's no such thing, and yet . . .

Fantasies, daydreams, wishes, visions . . . A person can live in an imagined, self-created world, with imagined realities. He can create life.

And it sometimes happens that the imagined eclipses reality; the imagined becomes more realistic than fact. Doesn't something like this happen to us, not to Native American Indians, but to us, every day, at least something remotely resembling this?

As for more simple and ordinary people – songs and tales have always had enormous meaning for them. In watching the most primitive performance in the world, they would always get carried away like little children.

Now about the artist himself. What does his own fantasy do to him?

Let's begin with the child. His play is his art. Just think about it: he rides a stick, spurs it, whips it, rolls it around, and in general treats it like a horse.

Isn't the art of the actor the same? It's not for nothing that there are expressions like "play a role" and "play onstage."

Aren't decorations, make-up, costumes all the very same wooden stick? Don't I live and act in an imagined, created world, with imagined people and items, in an imagined time, in an imagined place? And me – I'm not me, for I too have been changed by my imagination. Everything is made up, and, knowing that it's all imagined, I still live more or less realistically. I'm not just *"living!"* I'm *"on fire!"* An hour or two is worth ten of my calm, boring years. I love, I hate like I can't in real life. I worry, I suffer . . . My heart thunders – it wants to burst. Is it really me? Why do tears stream out of my eyes, when I'm usually stingy with them?

(This isn't fantasy – it's a special way of perceiving the world – *prelogic*. But for now, let's leave it like this, let it be fantasy, and later we'll see if that fantasy is the *remnant of prelogic*.)

Specific Creativity of the Actor; Bororo-arara: Creativity in Art is a Prelogical Manifestation

A meeting of two thoughts in logical thinking is different from that in prelogical thinking (complicity).

With prelogic it's not similarity – it's equivalence! Similarity is logic and emotional experience; equivalence is prelogical, a certain perception of a kindred element in everything around.

Logic is contradiction.

Prelogic is indubitable fact.

Indigenes aren't "idiots," and in some things, they reason far better than we do. But it's all about the type of perception. Or rather the type of thinking that occurs during perception.

They don't have "concepts" – they have "perceived notions."

Exercising to enhance one's attention (in our logical sense) **destroys** prelogic, when we should be **constructing** it.

This is why children are so good at play, and why they play so easily – because they have not yet been denied prelogic. But adults are logical . . .

Stanislavsky wants to replace prelogic with *naïveté*. This is because he doesn't fully understand the heart of the problem.

Tribesmen see everything as alive, just as I saw the spots on the wall, etc., and they don't *analyze* things, trying to boil a problem down to simple facts – they interpret it as a higher reality. *Birdsong, noise, the rustling of leaves – everything can be perceived with the kind of supplementations I made when I regarded the stains on the stone wall.*

All this concerns the tribesmen's perception of the external world. But the attitude that they have to their internal worlds is equally strange and unclear to us.

You can see a living old man in the spots on a wall, you can hear an entire orchestral symphony in the rumbling of a waterfall, and you can even make out human voices, maybe even individual words and phrases . . . anyone can probably imagine this.

But how should we react to this fact: there is a tribe called "Bororo" among the many tribes of Argentina. And each representative of this tribe, every Bororo insists that he is also an arara (a kind of red parrot).

It's not that he looks like a parrot – he simply *is* a parrot.

He's not a descendant of a parrot, he's not a human manifestation of a parrot's soul – he is factually, legitimately an arara parrot.

How can this be? A Bororo tribesman does not fly, doesn't peck, he has no wings, no tail, no plumage . . . We're astounded, and they're amazed by our confusion and our stupidity . . .

For us, a fact is something unalterable: a piece of paper is only a piece of paper and simply cannot be a pen or an inkwell at the same time. But for them, it can. We have one kind of logic – the logic of facts – they have another.

They don't deny the logic of facts and use it very well: they hunt animals, kill them, skin them, store the meat for future use, build homes, steer their canoes perfectly well, etc., etc . . . And at the same time, they use some kind of logic that isn't the logic of facts.

And as a result of this logic, I (a Bororo tribesman) can easily be a parrot (an arara) at the same time . . .

It's completely unfathomable!

However, isn't there something familiar for us here? I (an actor) am me, and at the same time, I am Liubim Tortsov . . . I am a family man, happy, dressed according to the latest fashion, and at the same time, I'm a hobo, a drunkard, all alone on this earth, unloved and unneeded by anyone in the world – I am Liubim Tortsov, a laughing-stock who has long ago stopped resembling a proper human being. I have a warm apartment, a good coat . . . and here I am, freezing in a torn little woolen coat in negative 30-degree weather.

"Mitya, please take in the merchant's brother, Liubim Tortsov. My brother turned me out! And in the street, in a coat like this – one has to dance about a bit! The frost – at Christmas time – brrr! – My hands are frozen, and my feet nipped."

"Warm yourself, Liubim."

"You won't run me out, Mitya? I'll freeze outside. I'll freeze like a dog."

I am an actor, and at the same time, I am a character.

★★★

A person who hasn't been an actor won't understand this. To him, this might simply sound like an abnormal, unstable psyche.

Though, if he remembers that his childhood games consisted almost entirely of imagining himself as someone else – a mother, a father, a horse, a train – then he might stop being so surprised. But then he'll assert that this is an undeveloped psyche, one fit for children, not for an adult.

However, if we remind him of his dreams, and of the various adventures he experiences every night, and, by the way, how he turns into birds, animals, trees, different items – how he doesn't stop being himself, but transforms into something else at the same time – then he'll better understand the Bororo psychology.

Whether this is a childlike psychology or the psychology of someone who's dreaming, gone far away from the realities of life, whether it's greater or lesser – we won't discuss this.

But one thing is indubitable – that he who doesn't have this ability – to be himself and at the same time be a character – (i.e. he who isn't able to transform) can never be an actor-creator. He can only be an imitator, a "depictor."

People might say: "You're speaking about some highest, absolute state."

The regular state [of an actor onstage] is twofold (according to the accounts of some actors). "Stage emotions" are significantly weaker than the ones you're speaking of.

Weaker . . . well, that depends on how you put it . . . Yermolova's "death." [This is referencing the death of the heroine in the production of *Tatyana Repina*, as performed by Yermolova (see this book, Chapter 5).] This depends on the degree of giftedness and the degree to which one uses technique. Technique? Yes, yes – technique. The only technique that should be dear and near to any actor and the technique that an actor forgets about most of all: *the psychological technique*. The technique that allows him to *feel* any emotion at any given time, and *evoke* any passion.

What does a circus performer or juggler that walks on a tightrope have? A certain technique that we mere mortals do not have. What is an actor? An actor is an acrobat or juggler of his own technique, a person who is able to do things that we mere mortals cannot even dream of. If this technique isn't there, then he is a bad actor. He is a dilettante who is sometimes successful, but for the most part is good for nothing.

You can say that most actors don't have *complete hallucinations* and just have slight shifts – 999 out of 1,000 don't completely give in to complete hallucinations, complete realization of life onstage – they are fully under the control of cold thought.

"The Formula of Life"

First case. A real effect/influence leads to a real response.

Second case. A baggage of memories and combinations between them + real influence = a response that corresponds *not only* to the object of the primitive influence. Because it's perceived not as a real occurrence, but how it was *taken in,* what it *seemed* like to me. What's important isn't that it's objective, but what I subjectively take in. And since reaction always acts quicker than a conscious decision, this leads to one more influence/effect, possibly the strongest one. The spots + the "appearance" of the old man = fear. Fear joins the party and asserts that the old man is alive and that he is indubitably real (because the fear is *real!*).

Third case. The same as in the second case, plus brakes that are put into use earlier and earlier, and, finally, *almost at the very start of the reaction.* This is what turns off the process of subjectivization, and although fact may not be perceived primitively per se, like in the first case, it will still correspond to reality, i.e. it will remain realistically objective.

All actions resulting from this kind of perception (and the kind of reaction it begets) will remain prudent and purposeful; they won't be rush. However, they will always be deprived of involuntariness, and of the intuition.

Play: Its Ephemerality and Effortlessness

A kid-"engineer" plays in his childhood: he builds things out of sticks, planks, little bricks. Then he studies, finishes a university, and builds for real. People don't say that he's "playing" – he's doing real work.

For an actor or a musician, no other word can be used until the end of their days – they *play*. In a manner of speaking, they are still in a childlike position.

Painting, sculpture, poetry – are similar forms of art. Why don't people say anything about them that would imply their worthlessness? Or at least their roots that stem from childlike amusements?

Maybe because:

1   Performing arts are completely subjugated to time: a musician has played, a singer has sung – and everything is gone, faded into eternity. But a painted picture, a sculpture hewed from stone – those will live for very long, long after we're gone, when only murky memories will remain of our time . . .

Poetry is even more resilient.

But actors, musicians, singers – once they've said, sung, played, and danced everything . . . nothing is left, not a trace, it's gone, disappeared, like smoke . . .

Maybe future generations will learn to record our "play" in such a way that the recordings will not only be *like* life and nature, but will *be* life and nature themselves, but for now, they are quite far from being able to convey the most important aspect of performing art – ***the living connection between the artist and the public.***

Along with the ability to render deathless the art of the actor, the musician, the dancer, maybe a new word will come along that will replace ours – "play." Because no matter how much we suffer onstage, how much we worry, how much of ourselves we put into our art, and how much we affect and delight the audience, we're still like children – "playing."

2   But maybe the opposite is true: when people use the word "play," they wish to express not abasement, not loathing, but delight?

Only he who *plays* isn't shackled by difficulties in performing his job.

Only he who *plays* participates in his work with all his soul, like a child.

Only he who *plays* doesn't rely on mere craftsmanship, and does not have to soullessly and forcedly executing what, in the depths of his soul, he doesn't want to do.

Only he who *plays*, who *needs* to play, reveals the depths of his soul in play.

Only he who *plays* creates a new, imagined, maybe even fantastical world, and truly creates, instead of just recycling the old.

A child plays freely, without needing to be coerced. He plays, because he needs to, because it is his joy, his happiness. Forced play evokes only ennui, results in frustration, protest. Play is the first step from the present into the future, into eternity – it's *freedom*, it's his creativity. Willing creativity, joyous creativity, creativity that isn't stymied by life experience, isn't tormented by childhood misfortunes – that's what *play* is.

And if we use this word to call what we do onstage, then there is probably a very small number of people who ***play***.

The only actor or musician who *plays* is the one who doesn't do it forcedly, who creates, invents, lives in play, because he cannot *not* create, not invent, and not live, just like he cannot not breathe, not drink, not eat, and not sleep.

The Mechanics of Play

From nothing to do, I entertain myself: I play with the chain from my pocket watch. I can do this calmly, without worrying, almost mechanically, it doesn't require any effort.

I pick up a ball, get up, and begin to entertain myself with it: I throw it, catch it, throw it again . . . Here, I can no longer say that it doesn't cost me anything: I've no room for yawning, else the ball would constantly fall to the ground or hit something off the table or fall into a vase or, in general, cause some damage.

And so, any play consists of two directly contradictory beginnings. On the one hand, entertainment, relaxation, a fun way to pass the time with calm unconcern. And on the other: interest, excitement, work, mobilization, thrill . . .

The back-and-forth tilting of these scale is what makes up the process of play in its entirety – it's in constant flux, "yes" one moment, "no" the next, victory one second, the next – defeat. It's constant instability, it's balancing on the razor's edge; this ceaseless uncertainty might be the most important thing in play.

I am walking down a path next to a railroad – I walk and I walk. I grow bored . . . and I begin to entertain myself: I jump from crosstie to crosstie, walk on a rail like a balancer, jump from one rail to the other – I walk and mess around, I walk and play. I'm amused by my deftness, I'm overjoyed by my strength, I'm entertained by my mistakes, misses, misfortunes: "yes" one moment, "no" the next; one second, I'm lord of nature, the next it lords over me. But in general, it's all just fun, entertainment, a test of your might – play.

There are games where you need physical dexterity, strength, skill: squares, tag, ball, soccer, tennis, etc.

Then there are games where you need psychological resourcefulness and the ability to reason: cards, chess, checkers, etc.

When play turns into a profession, it stops being play. You and I can play ball – a juggler "works with balls," we amuse ourselves by trying balance on a rail as long as possible, while a circus balancer does "high-wire work."

And in general, as soon as play loses one of its elements, it stops being play.

Many don't care for cards, unless it's gambling. Sometimes the stakes are so high that the game turns into a skirmish, a battle, often a lethal one. Is this play? There are many things missing here that are inherent to play – without which we cannot imagine it. There's no playfulness, no lightheartedness, no levity – none of this is there. If there is something of joy, then it's only in the form of malicious joy. If there is something of roguish playfulness, then it's only in the form of malevolent mischief – to spite everyone, to spite the world, all of nature – a mutiny on the verge of crime. If there is courage, then it's sooner audacity beyond all rational limits, risking everything, maybe even your life, honors, and all that is holy.

What people call "high stakes" – that's not play, that's not well-balanced scales, that's a protest, a mutiny, a challenge to fate, destiny, laws of life and nature. It's shaking something to its very foundations; it's a mad leap over an abyss.

Is this play?

Why shouldn't it be? For the strong, it's play, for the weak, it's a catastrophe, it's affect, it's an accident.

What can be said? – All these "high-stake games" and "playing with fire" aren't for children, they're not radiant, they're not clean: there is a lot of darkness in them, a lot of catastrophes with just fire, the smoke, and the ash that remain after everything else is gone . . .

That's why they are so few tragic actors.

Tragedy is high-stakes play, you have to go "all in," it's when you throw in your last chips, it's when you "go big or go home." It's not lighthearted, delightful, entertaining, and it doesn't lightly tickle your fancy, which is the only thing that the vast majority of actors are capable of, even talented ones, even famous ones. If one of them lucks into playing tragically once in his life, to shake his very core, to pierce his very essence – for him, it's a catastrophe after which he'll be like an empty drum for many years: anything that I play now is pale, weak, and worthless. He had reserves and lived off the interest, but here, he tore through everything in a decisive minute – lost all his capital. And, by the way, between you and me, there wasn't even that much to begin with . . .

On the other hand, only here will a tragedian begin to understand his talent, his power, his calling, his path, and his "technique . . . "

A tragedian . . .

I think it's self-evident that we're not speaking of great thugs with a ringing voice and a bull-thick neck, imagining that they're tragedians by virtue of their animalistic nature; we're also not speaking about hysterics, neurotics, and epileptic people, who bring their unbalanced, pathological souls out onto the stage.

We're also not speaking about directors' ruses and tricks that create an *impression* of intense and deep immersion onstage, when there really isn't and cannot be.

Just like we can speak about real diamonds and fake ones, so can we speak about real and fake tragedians. Let's speak *about the real ones*.

The Substrate of Acting

"My painting is no painting, it is a sentiment, a passion" (Balzac [1900c: 232]).

Mochalov. That was a tragedian. A real one. He was a genius of the stage. He was a "high-stakes player."

What did this "high-stakes player" play for? What did he risk, what did he have riding on his cards? What kinds of riches did he throw onto the tilting scale pan?

And what did he "win"? What did he get from the capricious, deadly, playing field – the stage?

"I" – my precious, my esteemed . . . my one and only "I" . . . the thing that I none of us would ever want to exchange for anything . . . my inimitable . . .

A scale pane . . . Why not throw a modicum of our "I" on it? Similarly – why not I risk three to five rubles when I have hundreds, thousands?

But to let *everything* that I own, present and future, ride on a card – that's madness!

To play, to amuse ourselves a bit – why not? But to put your whole soul with all its secrets, to boldly, daringly throw your hot, pulsating, heart onto the scales?! Is that not an insane thing to do?

What if they don't receive it? What if my heart, my spirit, my soul, so fearlessly exposed and donated to public viewing, rendered vulnerable to ridicule – what if they won't be able to outweigh the apathy, dullness, and crudeness, and my side of the scales will hang in the air, while the opposing one will heavily slam down triumphantly to the ground?

To give away all of yourself . . . It's unusual and scary. The thought of a humiliating, irrevocable defeat is insulting and lethal. It's so scary, so frightening! But, thank god, something happens inside me without my will, some latch snaps shot, and . . . even if I wanted to, even if I tried as hard I could to open up, to give up all of myself, to pour out my heart – nothing would come of it. We all have this locking mechanism, this clever, automatic lock! This saving safeguard! Oh, our reliable, ingenious brakes! They're "Westinghouses" of such herculean strength that if they sense even the slightest bit of a slope – click! – and beyond our will, we proceed in a slow, well-meaning, and highly secure pace.[1]

Just try to slip out from under the oversight of this guardian! No, friend, whether you want it or not, one way or another, you'll be a goody two-shoes – it will instantly calm you down, and you'll get where you have to in a proper, decent manner.

For "high-stakes players," not everything is alright with this "Westinghouse." Either it functions a bit more lazily, or it turns on only in specific moments and doesn't thrust its nose where it's unwanted?

One way or another, we'll have to speak more of these "Westinghouses," and we'll have to speak a lot of them, for they cause great sorrow and harm in our work, more harm than any locust swarm or flu. And we'll speak at greater length about fighting them, about the technique that allows us to turn off the brakes while onstage; but for now, let's get back to the *tragedian*.

So, this is what this high-stakes player throws into the "pot" – first and foremost, **himself**! His whole "I," all of it! His thoughts, desires, passions, misfortunes, his sorrow, his joy, his aspirations, hopes, and dreams.

And just any old hopes and dreams – the dearest, most secret, most deeply hidden, which we wouldn't dare reveal even to our pillow (and "Westinghouses" would help us in this endeavor, and all that is ours would securely stay with us).

What sort of a "weapon" does he use? How does he defend his treasure?

After all, one side of the scales becomes full of fantasy, nothing, imagination, fiction – that which does not exist, fantasies, dreams . . .

And the other! The other side of the scales holds life itself, material, tangible, sensible, juicy, heavy, real life – just try to outweigh it.

And my eyes are mine, and my ears are mine, my hands are mine, everything is still mine, but I see, hear, and feel things like a person should see, hear, and feel . . . And thousands of audience members see, hear, and feel no worse than I do, and they are aware of everything. Against all this I come out even worse-equipped than David against Goliath – without a sword, with nothing other than a dream! And this dream is supposed to replace everything authentic, all reality within me, and in the thousands of audience members that are watching me.

Isn't that a rather bold game?

Because if I don't make my "nothing" more realistic, more powerful than reality itself, if my imagination doesn't create something more real than reality, if the audience remains a cold and calm observer, then it will become clear to everyone, me first of all, that I'm a fraud, a buffoon, a poser, a charlatan, a poor beggar, that I'm showcasing myself for my own goals.

To throw the most precious, invaluable thing that you have and to defend it with your bare hands – that's a game, and it's a high-stakes game.

If, however, a player is co confident that he doesn't have the shadow of doubt in the darkest corners of his soul, than either his might is greater than that of humanity, or his art is unprecedented, unimaginable, and he deserves glory for all eternity!

★★★

I don't know about this thought; maybe it's nothing – do you only put yourself and your "I" on the line?

What about your creation? Your *child*?

I seem to forget that it is valuable on its own? In the meantime, I previously defined it rather incompletely – just as catharsis.

Can we find an answer to this in prelogic?

★★★

It might be that the reader is thinking: my good man, you keep going on about greatness and volcanic passions and Mochalov, but what are you to do with yourself, and what are we supposed to do ourselves?

Firstly, I'll say that conventional wisdom has long ago noted that it is a bad soldier who doesn't want to become a general.

Secondly, it is a rare actor, I probably haven't even met such, who, in the depths of his soul, didn't feel a deeply hidden or maybe even completely untapped, but indubitable, great potential within himself. And sensing them, foreseeing their power, he became an actor. Otherwise, why go to the trouble?

And now, while reading, if his past, nearly-faded excitement, along with his youthful belief in himself – if they start flickering again, if this happens, then I'm not writing for nothing. And it's not for nothing that he's reading. All things considered, you'd think that we should come to some accord.

In art, and especially in theatrical (and musical) art, there is one proper formula that befits human dignity:

> Too low they build
>
> Who build beneath the stars.

Of course, the higher you build, the deeper you need to bury the foundation, the more risk there is: the smallest mistake in the beginning can lead to the collapse of the whole building. Of course, only a boor or a slouch thinks that everything is simple – somebody who's been taught by experience knows that he should rather direct his thoughts to something more modest: to make a small garden next to his home by the sweat of his brow and work and not to "reap where you didn't sow."

Exactly. This plot of land is exactly where we're going to dig deep, artesian wells!

And another reason why it's better to take one's lead not from the lesser or average actors, but from Mochalov, tragedians, and "high-rollers" – because, *in essence*, there's no difference between them: all players – great, medium, or lesser – they all throw something down onto the "green table." But the stakes are smaller and smaller, the risk is smaller, the winnings are smaller, and in case of a loss, there's no resounding sundering of all one's dreams – there is no deadly outcome.

Therein lies the difference between the players. The difference of their gambles. But the *principle* and the essence of things are the same. Regardless of whether you have a sea or a bucket – the water's the same. Except that, of course, you can't really swim too freely in a bucket, and you won't see any storms or waves there either.

In this way, a lesser artist needs *verisimilitude*.

A medium one needs *truth* and *reality* in life.

And a great one needs *truth* itself, *limitless freedom*, and an open window into *eternity*.

Note

1 Westinghouse is an electrotechnical group in the USA, established in 1872. In Imperial Russia, Westinghouse had a factory in St. Petersburg that created parts of the "Westinghouse" air-based automatic brake system.

3

Primitive Sensations and Biologism

"The truth of passions, the verisimilitude of feelings in the assumed circumstances – that's what our minds demand from the dramatic writer." That's Pushkin's [1962: 361] definition – the key not only to dramaturgy, but to all art forms.

Stanislavsky applied it to the art of the actor, and thanks to him, it is now very popular in the world of theatre.

It's created an entire theatrical philosophy and psychology around itself. Theatre theoreticians, as well as the greater part of directors and actors have latched onto the word "verisimilitude" as if it were a life ring.

They say: you see! There shouldn't be truth onstage, there should just be *verisimilitude*. Truth isn't art. And with an easy heart, seemingly endorsed by Pushkin himself, they turn away from truth with loathing and disdain. And they've created a cult following for the proper deity: *verisimilitude* – what resembles truth.

When you read or hear similar discussions, we recall one of Krylov's well-known fables – a man who is used to concern himself with trifles, incapable of lifting his head from the ground, comes to a Kunstkamera [cabinet of curiosities]: he looks everything over, everything amazes him . . . "And have you seen the elephant? Impressive, no? You must of thought you'd met a mountain?" "Is it there?" "There." "My bad, my friend – I didn't see the elephant" [Krylov 1859: 285].

Everybody noticed and latched on to the "verisimilitude of feelings" (regardless of how well they understood it), but where's the most important part? where's the elephant? where's the **truth of passions**, which is what Pushkin wants first and foremost?!

It's as if everyone conspired long ago, and now they're keeping mum about it.

Either they didn't notice this "elephant," because they're not used to lifting their heads, or they did notice it and immediately forgot about it, put it right out of their minds. And really: it's such an "unwieldy" thing, so inconvenient and frightening . . . nothing but troubles and misfortunes stem from it, and there probably aren't even any benefits to having it anyway!

But one way or another – art without the *truth of passions* is the same thing as life without a heart.

In exchange for straightforwardness, openness, sincerity, a certain group of people has developed amiability, courtesy, correctness. It's not a bad trade, but can you really live for so long on just amiability, correctness, and external politeness? Won't you ultimately start pining? Won't you finally start yelling for simple geniality, straightforwardness, and even animosity, as long as it's overt?!

The Truth of Passions

" . . . it isn't skill or a premeditated plan – only the inspiration of passion can be so expressed" (Belinsky [1953: 323]. *'Hamlet,' Shakespeare's drama. Mochalov as Hamlet*).

Where do we search for a source of such passion? Such inspiration, fire, volcanic power?

Any lesser creature, even the single-celled amoeba *senses* – touch, temperature, light, the environment . . . It senses and reacts.

You could say that you and me, we begin our lives by sensing as well.

This sort of sensing is the simplest form of feeling – feeling in its most primitive form.

As our bodies develop, our sensations combine, layer on, unite, and transform into *conceptualization*.

I hold a pen – what sort of senses does it evoke? Something hard, oblong, narrow at the point, light, smooth, dark, the ink is smudged in places . . . the tip is cold, sharp . . . the ink is wet, violet, smelly . . .

All of these sensations, along with a multitude of others, give me the impression: this is my pen.

When I say "my pen," I can *visualize it*, and I immediately recall a whole array of associated sensations, but since it's from memory, it's somewhat theoretical, indirect.

In my "visualizations," the sharpness of the sensations (the physiological response) is significantly lessened.

Next. Aside from my pen, I've seen others: thicker, thinner, rounder, ribbed, lighter, heavier, with metallic points, without points, colored, uncolored, glass, autopens, etc. – and they're all pens. Pens that you can use to write.

I can say: "a pen," and I might **not** get a *visualization* of a certain pen, I will **not** get any *sensations* (even in my memory) – it could just be a pen, any pen, as a *concept*. A concept emerges from repeated visualizations of specific pens that I've seen or held in my life.

The visualizations have been juxtaposed, composed, layered onto one another, united, and finally transformed not into something specific, but an abstract concept: a pen.

And while there is at least a small amount of direct feeling involved in "visualizing" a specific thing, there are no sensations whatsoever associated with a "*concept*" – "pen," pen in general, pen-abstraction.

Human language consists of words. But what is a word? It's a designation of understanding: pen, table, person, winter, sea, cold, heat, wind, hatred, love, beauty – in a word, there is no word that is not an *understanding*. On their own, words do not *mean* and do not evoke specific and exact feelings. Let's say: fatigue: the state that occurs from more or less prolonged activity, and which causes a reaction that ultimately makes further activity more and more difficult. But what feeling does the word "tiredness" evoke? That's utterly indefinite. So indefinite that you could say: no feeling at all.

You're annoyed by your boring conversation partner – you grow tired.

You were at a great show and laughed until you were in tears, until your sides hurt – you grow tired.

You went into the woods, gathering berries, mushrooms . . . you want to sit down, because you grow pleasantly, beneficently, sweetly tiredness.

"Uncle Vanya" rejected personal happiness, spent his whole life doing unpleasant, thankless, dark work, just so that Professor Serebryakov could live and flourish. It turns out that the professor is a fool and an idiot. Vanya's sacrifices have been for naught, his life wasted. And he grows insurmountably tired.

A person climbs snowy mountains, loses his footing, falls, and is now hanging over an abyss, with no one around, and his hands grow . . . tired.

Although the word "tiredness" has a grain of sensation in it, how different and difficult to catch the many sensations are!

A play lies before me, and in that play, dead ink on dead paper, there are words written – designations of concepts. And I have to transform these concepts into visualizations – quite concrete, imagined realities, and I ultimately have to bring them to the point of *sensations* – primitive, simple feelings.

Most often, for an actor, concepts remain concepts – they do not reach visualizations and sensations.

More often, after enough repetitions, words completely lose the ability to excite the actor's thoughts and feelings; he speaks them mechanically, only with his tongue and lips. He trundles through memorized words, with memorized intonations, with memorized gestures and physicality. He trundles through them, and this does not concern him a single bit; moreover, he doesn't even notice it.

King Claudius in *Hamlet* is concerned while he says his prayer:

My words fly up, my thoughts remain below:

Words without thoughts never to heaven go.

But the actor is not concerned a bit; he has turned into a mechanical doll and thinks that that's all his work requires. His words have lost thought, feeling . . .

Every word has a **stinger** that can wound us, every word has **venom** that the artist-creator's soul drank in; without them, it's just a husk.

If we want to get onto the path of the *truth of passions* in the art of the actor, we have to keep this in mind.

And first and foremost, we need to clear the path to *sensation*, the sensation that lies at the fore of any concept (within the given circumstances), to the so-called *primitive sensation*, and we need to resurrect the ability to fully give in to **the first reaction** to such a sensation. The first, not the one that is sifted through ten different sieves and stopped by the hundreds of brakes that we have.

In an accusatory letter to his student, one ancient moralist writes: "you're neither cold nor hot – you're tepid. Oh, if only you were cold or hot!" [Revelation 3:15]

Such well-known tepidity is a bad foundation for developing passion.

The ability to passionately give in to something, forgetting everything in the world – it is gradually corroded in us, from generation to generation. Ignitability seems an ancient holdover. We have turned into "tepid," "cultured" people, behind whose civility lies the same "tepidity," and not fire, not flames, not passion.

Because of this, it's clear that the words about the "truth of passions" in Pushkin's explanations simply pass over us. It's so foreign and incomprehensible to us . . . these words get "lost in translation" . . .

But in the meantime – passion is the fire of life. It burns you and warms you. It creates and destroys.

What causes a person's great victories if not passionate love or passionate hatred?

And all the while, we absent-mindedly want to create high art without this fire, without the *truth of passions*. We plan to play tragedies that are written not by words, but by human passions, we stage pathetical plays in verse, we try our "creative hand" at Dostoevsky!

With what means? With "verisimilar" feelings?!!

★★★

"'A culture of primitive and a culture of direct reactions . . .' but that's just a return to the past, to the animal kingdom? My dog, as soon as it senses a cat, its fur stands up . . . and if it had its way, there'd be nothing left of the cat but tatters. What, you want us to return to that sort of spontaneity?"

"Well, why be afraid?"

This is where Mochalov comes in with his black shawl.

Currently, we put "civility" on a pedestal: this is a cultured theatre, a cultured actor – he acts composedly, modestly . . . "nobly."

Oh, if only we worried less about so-called "civility!"

"Of, if only you were cold or hot!"

(Don't worry that you'll turn into an animal – over the course of many thousands of years, you've left that far behind. Besides, you'll be playing a human! Now, if you were playing a dog, then ideally you would begin to react in a doglike manner. But even in a dog, we play *human attributes!*)

★★★

Michelangelo. She died. He saw how she was dying, and he said the following touching words that showed the chaste restraint that their great love held on to: "Nothing grieves me so much as that when I went to see her after she passed away from this life I did not kiss her on the brow or face, as I did kiss her hand" [Condivi 1903: 85].

"Recalling this, her death," writes Ascanio Condivi [1903: 85], "he often remained dazed as one bereft of sense."

Goethe nearly died when he was rejected.

As for us – we'll be sad a bit, grieve for a bit, and then we'll settle on another "object."

Michelangelo would destroy his statues if he found falsities or mistakes in them, but we – we'll fix it, patch it up, and sell it anyway . . . docking the price slightly.

Pushkin ran out into the December cold almost naked, straight from bed, as soon as he heard the bells of his friend's troika beneath his window.

We'll be overjoyed too, in the very first moment, and we'll have the urge to run *there* too, but the very next instant, we'll be searching for our coat, boots, hat. And if we don't find them, then we'll wait: *he'll* come into the house soon anyway.

But Pushkin . . . imprudently, childishly, even foolishly . . . Fully controlled by his feelings, and where are his adulthood, reason, where's his ability to control himself?

This is all true. All in all, these people are poorly "suited" to their contemporary times, and, for the most part, escape poverty, exile, and death only as a result of their friends or patrons. Why! If they were armed with prudence, they would lose the ability to think so categorically and feel so passionately, and would therefore lose what makes them such giants – inaccessible and unfathomable.

On May 7th, 1824, Vienna witnessed the first performance of Beethoven's Mass in D major [*Missa Solemnis*], and his Ninth Symphony. The audience gave Beethoven five standing ovations, while in this country of etiquette three ovations was considered the limit even for the emperor. Police intervention was necessary in order to put an end to the manifestation. The symphony caused great excitement. Many cried.

After the concert, Beethoven fainted with emotion; they brought him to Anton Schindler's house, where he spent the whole night and all morning in oblivion, fully dressed, without food or drink.

Nikolai Vilde [as quoted in Laskina 2000: 478–479] describes Mochalov's performance of George Moritz in *Countess Clara d'Oberville* the following way:

> . . . when George, who suspected his wife the whole time, sees his friend, Kossad, in the mirror, pouring poison into his medicine . . . something happened to me then that I cannot describe . . . .

> Mochalov's face *contorted so painfully*, he started rising from the armchair, papers started shifting and pharmaceutical vials started clanging beneath his shaking hands on the table, and he yelled out so frightfully: 'Poisoner!' I cannot begin to relay it. I know and remember one thing – that an electrical spark instantly passed from the stage into the audience. I myself involuntarily stood from my chair, as did all the audience members sitting below. No other artist of the stage has ever had such a piercing and sundering effect on me . . . to excite a person's soul, stun it, cause it to forget that in front of him is a stage and not life – not a single artist of the stage could ever do it as well . . .

A Culture of Primitive Sensations: Is This a Return to the Past?

"But wait a second," people might say, "What does this all mean? That art is a return to the past? From reason to blind passion, from culture to barbarianism?"

A counter question. Don't you think that the glorified "reason" and "civility" cost humanity too much?

The caveman had an eagle eye, while we – well, just look around. As a result of our reason, we've lost quite a bit. Where are our senses of smell, hearing, sight? Whereas a Chukchi can find his yaranga tens and even hundreds of kilometers away without a compass.

The conclusion that we can reach from all this: we need to develop *physiology* (or that, which resembles this, and which I pointed to earlier – "sensitivity"). Maybe aided by a sort of "*physiological fantasy, physiological imagination.*"

Second: **all impressions must be made physiological**, and we need to train this ability with specific exercises.

We are looking for how to enrich man, who has been desiccated by reason.

Maybe, with the help of art, we will once again obtain long-lost feelings, and, combined with reason, they might even *harmonize*? That will lead us to new riches.

For the most part, nature is usually blind and hostile, like a storm, like fire, water, and only once it's been harnessed does it become benevolent and man's best friend.

In this way, physiology is *one of the paths* to the sensitivity that is inherent to an affective actor.

★★★

"But wait!" I can already hear a dissident's voice, "How does *biologism* have anything to do with art?!! Could it really be that you think that art obeys the laws of biology?"

Just like in questions of "truth onstage," so here do we have to shed light on the misunderstanding that puts a complete halt to further investigation.

When people speak of art, they suppose the *works of art* themselves, their themes. Who can argue with the fact that a work of art's themes, just like its execution, completely depends on the social nature of the individual?

We're not speaking about this – rather, we're speaking about *the "mechanics" of the creative process as such*.

Seeing as any creativity is a state of doubling, rather than the action of a sole individual, then (just like with willpower) we must first and foremost think of *biological* freedom (in order to find the "I am" of a person, to find him in his moments of "solitude"), after which, having found this freedom, we must put the biologically free subject in social conditions (given circumstances).

What are the sources of life? Biologism or sociologism? Biologism, of course.

But maybe it once existed and doesn't anymore? Now, there is only sociologism?

How can it be gone? Do we not breathe, drink, eat, feel cold, tire, move – in a word, are we not animals?

"Art is social! How dare you speak of biologism! Art is class-specific! And yet you're rambling on about biologism!"

What came first: classes or art? Art, of course. A child's play is already art. When classes a thing of the past, do you think that there won't be art?

Most importantly: *a work of art* is one thing, while *the creative process* is another. And the creative process (which has its origins in the times of the first half-humans, half-apes) is first and foremost biology.

The Sources of Creativity Lie in Absolute Biological Freedom

Only from that moment, when this freedom is established, will the gates of our perception open. In other words: only then can we *tangibly sense* a play's facts and given circumstances. And once we've felt them *tangibly* – that's when we can have involuntary reactions to them.

The paths to this biological freedom are indicated in the chapters on "involuntary movements," "don't interfere with living," "take your time," "carelessness," "let it . . . " [Book Three, Part Two, Chapters 6–9] and some others.

From the point of view of the chapter on "Assignment" [Book Three, Part Three, Chapter 27], you should do the following: first of all, you should passively set yourself to live biologically (or, which is the same thing, to give in to physical and psychological manifestations).

Practically, this can happen as follows: you don't have to pull yourself up or spur yourself on – on the contrary: you should *release* all the screws that are holding you up. Release yourself, relax. And don't get in anything's way: if you want to sit – sit down; if you want to move – move . . . Give in to anything. Don't get in your own way: if you're bored – be bored; if you're frustrated – give that free rein.

Don't push yourself and *don't get in your own way* of living like your whole body wants to live.

Now, if, having fine-tuned this state, you start listening to your partner, and, in this state (even though it might not seem suitable), you start thinking about the play's given circumstances or start speaking the role's words – in no time, your own truth will get mixed with the truth of the play and the role and will ultimately be displaced.

On Entering a Role from Physiological Truth

Having attained a state of "physiological" involuntariness, you now have to make a careful transition to the text of the role (or the lines of the story, if we're talking about a storyteller). Rather, not transitioning to them, but *including the words of the role in this state – on top of what you already have in it.* You have to follow the same plan of action as described in the chapter "Don't Interfere with Living" [Book Three, Part Three, Chapter 18].

You have to do as follows: in a state of physiological freedom, without disrupting anything, you have to say the lines without following some premeditated plan or with some memorized intonation – you have to say them freely: as they *turn out on their own*.

And then – the next line . . . and then the next . . .

If everything is executed soundly, the result will always be the same: in just a few minutes, the truth of the play and the role will mix in with your "physiological" truth – everything will combine, unite forces, and you'll have that creative combination in which you don't know where the "I" is and where "HE"—the character—is.

One should not be flustered if, in the beginning, the actor's personal state doesn't align with the mood of the character. Very soon, the role's lines will fine a living resonance in his soul, and the actor will restructure on his own.

In general, experience shows that such "physiological freedom" can serve as one of the *reliable sources of creative, artistic truth*.

Evidently, many will think that such a path of getting into a role cannot be realized: my personal state as an actor might not even correspond to the state in which the character should be in the scene we're rehearsing right now. The problem, however, isn't in whether the actor's state corresponds to that of the character – it very rarely corresponds – the problem is in *combining my truth, the truth of my entire body with the given circumstances of the role*.

And then, my mood and my state *will change*. They always change from alterations in the facts that surround us: when we hear bad news, we enter one state; when we hear good news, we enter another.

It's important for the role's given circumstances and the lines to *fall onto a truthful soil*. This is what should be established first.

(The correspondence or incorrespondence of an actor's personality with that of a role is resolved not like the congruence of triangles in geometry. A personality is mobile, it can change. Integral identity is a process.)

Physiological Freedom

When does a person behave naturally more than any other time?

When he is completely alone – at home or in nature. In these moments, nothing is tying him down, and he is free. He doesn't stifle his thoughts, his feelings, he doesn't hold back his involuntary actions: it's hot – he unbuttons his shirt, takes off unnecessary layers; if he wants to sing, he sings; if he wants to yawn, he yawns; if he's been sitting for too long and he needs to get up, he'll walk around a bit, do some exercises. In a word, he's free without any limitations. There are no obstructions to his reactions to external and internal stimuli. And we can call this sort of freedom "physiological."

But as soon as a single other person shows up, we begin to observe ourselves, we limit our involuntariness, and we only allow ourselves to do what is *appropriate* in the given circumstances. The freedom ceases to be absolute and becomes relative, limited.

We can best observe a person's absolute freedom in infancy and childhood. Over the years, this spontaneity, this physiological freedom disappears, a person learns to hold himself back, and, adapting to different circumstances, to do only *what is appropriate*.

It also sometimes happens that we adults react spontaneously, without thinking, abruptly. But this happens in exceptional instances. For example, when we're sick, we don't have the strength to hold back our outbursts . . . or we're so frustrated that we're "beside ourselves," or we're so frightened when we hit, burn, or cut our hands – in these cases, we can drop without any hesitation an angry word, scream, make sudden movement . . . maybe even hit something . . .

But these cases are exceptional. Usually, our first reaction is *always automatically repressed* without thinking about it too much, just in case. And seeing as this was repeated minute by minute, day by day, year by year, a self-triggered mechanism was put in place: regardless of what we see or hear – the first thing that happens is that – slam! – the trap door closes shut, burying our response somewhere inside.

In the next moment, once we have already managed to look around and quickly sift through what just happened, we can allow ourselves to have a reaction, but it is, naturally, not as fresh or full-bodied. This won't be the first reaction – it'll be a second, limited one.

This is exactly what we need for life – otherwise, we would be poorly adapted to it and ill-suited to it in general. For a *moment* of *creativity,* however, for the *creative* process, as well as for the *process of experiencing – the most important thing is the* **first** *reaction.*

4

Doubled Consciousness

On Doubled Consciousness and Unity

Is an actor fully under the influence of the power of transformation? Does he feel cold as he does in real life? Is he utterly sure that he really is Liubim Tortsov and none other?

In a word, have his own circumstances fully disappeared, and has he fully become another person?

While onstage before the audience, an actor cannot not see the artificialities of the stage: the sets, makeup, the audience looking at him from the outside; he cannot not acknowledge that the role's words and the circumstances of the play aren't his own, but were instead given to him by the author, and that everything onstage isn't real, and is only "*as if real.*"

But at the same time, our art of artistic realism demands that the actor isn't false, forged, or artificial onstage, but is instead authentic, "realistically" living onstage.

How can we reconcile one with the other? We need the actor to live onstage realistically, but at the same time, it's impossible to live and feel realistically — such life would become a hallucination . . .

Great actors (and even moderate ones in some creative moments) so transform into their role and are so immersed in the play's circumstances that they forget themselves, and they sweep the audience along with them in their stream of artistic imagination.

Doesn't this mean that they lose their normality and are fully under the influence of their imagination, i.e. doesn't this seem like they are hallucinating?

No, judging from witness accounts, as well as a multitude of their own accounts, they somehow *double*: one part of them lives the life of the embodied role (in our case, this would be Liubim Tortsov), while another part exists nearby and, without becoming disoriented, observes the first life and all of its manifestations, and when it needs to, it even directs it, corrects it.

This "sober-minded" part knows full well that there are people sitting in the audience, and that therefore you have to "play" well, "realistically." Otherwise, nobody will believe what happens onstage. This is why you should never try to cool yourself off, but should instead use whatever means necessary to foster the sincerity and truthfulness of your experiencing

How is this? On one hand, you have to live sincerely, spontaneously, but on the other, you have to maintain your sober-mindedness and keep track of yourself and of your surroundings?

Doesn't this require pathological splitting, which has been described at great length by psychiatrists?

A person with this affliction, for a while, is capable of forgetting his own name, his history, and even his own family and friends. And instead imagine himself an entirely different person with a different name and a different personality . . . We even know of such cases when a "newly formed" person runs away from his family and, for a few years, giving off the impression of quite a healthy person, he lives somewhere else, acquires a new family, etc., and suddenly . . . he wakes up!, i.e. he returns to his normal state and doesn't understand how he got there and who this woman is (his wife) and who these children are (his kids) . . .

This affliction paints a picture for us of how a person can be himself and also not himself. But the difference between this state and that of an actor is enormous.

During pathological splitting, a person's sense of self becomes so inhibited that his identity seemingly disappears altogether. In the meantime, another identity rises up in its place – the one created by his imagination.

An actor's identity (his own sense of self), however, doesn't go anywhere – it's with him at all times, and it is constantly living, observing, and directing the life of the "other 'I'" – the assumed new guise – the "character."

What we have is a sort of *doubled consciousness* on the part of the actor: part of his consciousness works normally – he cognizes that he is acting onstage, that he sees and feels the public; the other part lives the life of the play and the character.

For a person who has never experienced this sort of doubling onstage, this would be semi-understandable if only he recalled his childhood games.

The games always involve the child imagining himself as somebody else ("as if" he's someone else); the child gives in to this imaginary character and lives his imaginary life.

However, children do not give in *all the way*, they do not lose their normality and the power of their integral identity, and they can cease their playing at any point.

Framed like this, this duality and the normality of this duality should be comprehensible to anyone.

★★★

There are many methods that are employed to get an actor to the state of *doubled consciousness*, and the "let it" method exists entirely for this purpose. But what other methods are there? At the very least, I could simply transpose all given circumstances into "my personal" key. The second "I personally" find myself in new circumstances – I am no longer "just me."

Two Kinds of Doubling

Yermolova was often surprised why people lauded her. Did she really act so well?

People attributed it to her *modesty*. That was a dreadful confusion on their behalf, and a *deep* misunderstanding of the situation at hand.

There are two kinds of good creative states: one is like that of Pevtsov – see everything, understand everything, be perfectly oriented, and fully sense your doubled consciousness.

Another, when a person becomes so fused with a character that he is no longer capable of any self-awareness. He lives as we live in real life – after all, we don't observe ourselves – we don't have the time for it.

We can observe such cases not only with "Yermolovas" – they occur in rehearsals and shows with regular, moderate actors, when they *forget themselves*. And they don't notice it either and are also surprised when they are complimented – they don't understand what for.

These cases of forgetting oneself are very, *very* serious. What is involved?

This merits some serious, serious thought!

Naturally, there is a doubling – otherwise, there would be a pathological dislocation. But what kind of doubling is it?

Evidently, the identity that lives in character is so great that it fills up *the whole consciousness*. And the actor's personality rests beyond the threshold of consciousness – it departs into the realm of the *automatic*. It executes only automatic functions.

This is all very, *very serious*!!!

In essence, these are *two kinds* of art!

One is *before the threshold* of "abandon," and the other is *beyond the threshold* of "abandon."

This is exactly what separates the genii – the Yermolovas, the Strepetovas, the Mochalovs – from talented masters, like Salvini, Pevtsov, and others.

But what technique is employed here? The first thing that comes to mind is that you have to, if not kill, then exile your consciousness somewhere far away. How? Evidently, at first, the method of the "*Fool*" will be very useful here.

"The Fool"

The "Fool" or "idiot" method is for doubling what the "letting go" method is for the sub-conscious. [For the "Fool" method, as for the meaning of "Letting Go" method for the Subconscious, see Book Four, Chapter 12.]

In order to achieve the phenomenon of doubling, you have to almost *entirely destroy any deliberativeness* and self-awareness. The "fool" and "idiot" take care of that.

Deliberativeness and self-awareness are probably the main pests. They are what lead to "effort" and "activity" and all the worthless contributions of mediocrity.

Doubling and Diderot

People that don't fully get the essence of doubling usually say: yes, yes . . . doubling . . . Diderot spoke of that too!

They haven't understood a thing. Diderot didn't speak about doubling – he said that the actor (as he saw him) "seemingly splits in two" – he lives his own life and observes how his body performs a series of memorized tricks.

This is the *complete lack of* (doubling) a duality!

Alexander Lensky [1894: 82]: " . . . The error in Diderot's view with regard to theatrical art arose, in my opinion, as a result of him mistaking an actor's vast self-control for his inability to feel deeply . . . An absolute lack of emotions, as well as extreme sensitivity without any self-control, makes a person utterly unsuitable for the stage, but **extreme sensitivity with utter self-control makes a great actor**."

On Doubled Consciousness

A common hindrance: an actor is "caught up," he gave himself a green light; his acting becomes interesting and bold – he should have stayed out of his own way and green-lit himself further . . . Instead, he starts admiring *himself*, or maybe laughs at his own funny acting – and the string is severed. Either he "loses it," or, in admiring himself, he stops listening and hearing his partner, and he misses impulses without even noticing it. He doesn't know what the problem is, but "something's stopped working."

He just experienced a doubling of his consciousness, and so he "lost it" as a result of the unexpectedness and unfamiliarity of it all. You have to get used to this "unnatural" state!

These are the first, timid steps of the creative doubling.

You have to develop a *reflex*, like the one that *pikes* have: as soon as you start to "lose it," you have to not just resist looking at it – you have to *hang on to the object even tighter* and "*give in to the feeling*" and "action" even more.

During exercises, a student will be "drawn" to do something remarkably brave: some recklessly bold deed or something insane! He'll get the thought: "I'll jump out of my identity, jump into another, and I won't come back! The horror!" And . . . he won't go through with it.

What is this about? This is the "doubling" of consciousness.

Fearing it is understandable. But with practice, it is possible not only to make this "doubling" completely safe – it will even enable you to take a therapeutic walk into the realm of "not 'I.'"

On Dual State of Being, on the Observing Artist

It seems that nothing that I write concerns itself with the doubling of one's psyche, and the emergence of two "I's" during moments of creativity – an "I" that acts, feels, and thinks, and an "I" that observes, like an artist. I avoid it when I teach, but today I noticed that I am always speaking about it, and that it's impossible to do without it. *It's just necessary to discuss it without confusing the students, or else they'll simply be observing themselves while living mechanically – all their energy will be used to observe.*

In order to demonstrate this process, you usually bring up an example when you're "on fire." It doesn't matter whether you're reciting poetry, singing, delivering a speech, playing a role – what matters is that everything is going so well today that I'm immersed, that I'm moved that I forget everything in the world, and I can cry, weep – God only knows what's happening to me . . . and it feels so good, and I'm so happy – "it's true! true! true!" I can hear myself saying on the inside, "Yes! Yes! Good! More! More! More!" somebody sits inside of me and eggs me on. I make a small mistake – "no worries, no worries, you're good," somebody whispers inside of me, "you'll fix this in a jiffy . . . like that . . . good . . . now green-light it, give yourself a green light!" In the meantime, I remain excited, I play, I live. This hidden well-wisher and observer, some sort of artistic conscience, my director, my artistic "I" – it is an essential prerequisite for a creative process.

If, let's say, someone has to read a book onstage, he starts reading it while observing himself in this matter, and at some point, he becomes immersed in the book and forgets himself – this is a switch to a different set of tracks – the tracks of ordinary life. In art – *a dual life, "dual state of being."*

> Oh, thou, my wizard soul, oh, heart
> That whelming agony immerses
> The threshold of two universes
> In cleaving these, tears thee apart.
> *(Tyutchev [1921: 29])*

There's no need to search for this state of being on the threshold of "two universes," for this dual state of being – it arises on its own. As soon as you have the thought that you're in front of an audience, that somebody is looking at you, you immediately start observing yourself. There's also no need to tell the actor that the audience is there so that he starts thinking about it – the audience is there, that's a fact, and a normal person cannot just ignore it and not see it. This is why if you do have to say something about the audience, say only that it's **not there**. Then there will be exactly as much as you need of it.

But, generally speaking, the reason for the existence of this *artistic conscience* is publicness – the feeling of the audiences' presence. Onstage, during intimate homework, at a writer's desk, in an artist's studio – there is always the feeling that somebody is reading your lines, someone is observing your chisel or paintbrush . . . "I am writing this, and God is reading it over my shoulder " (Knut Hamsun, *Victoria*). [A slight paraphrase of a line from Knut Hamsun's (1908: 98) novel *Victoria*: "It is I, Victoria, who is writing this, and God is reading it over my shoulder."] This triangle always exists: me, my second "I" (the character), and some observer (the audience).

Doubled Consciousness: One of the Main Conditions of an Actor's Art

After everything that's been said, it's evident that a "character" is essentially my "I" or some other part of me that is hidden beneath a "mask."

Listen to Stanislavsky [1931: 428], as he describes his performance in Ibsen's *Doctor Stockmann* (*The Enemy of the People*):

> Wrong! You're animals, you're veritable animals!' I yelled at the crowd during the public lecture in the fourth act, and I yelled it sincerely, for I knew how to get into the point of view of Stockmann. I derived pleasure from saying it, and from recognizing the fact that the audience had fallen in love with Stockmann, was worried for me and angry at the stupidity with which I was pointlessly antagonize the crowd of enemies gone amok. It is well-known that unnecessary straightforwardness and sincerity kill the hero of a play.
>
> The actor and director in me understood full well the effectiveness of such sincerity, so damning for the character, and the charm of his honesty.

A few pages earlier, Stanislavsky [1931: 426] writes:

> When the rot in the souls of Stockmann's friends became gradually more and more evident, it was easy for me to feel the bewilderment of the character. At the moment of his total enlightenment, it was unclear whether I was scared for me or for Stockmann. In this moment, I fused with the role. I clearly understood how gradually, with each act, Stockmann became more and more lonely, and when he finally remains completely alone by the end of the play, the concluding phrase: "The strongest man in the world is the one who ends up alone!" was begging to be said.

Salvini, Rossi, Yermolova, Stanislavsky, and other pillars of stage art (of the sort that "lives onstage") unequivocally speak of a doubled consciousness, and a dual state of being during their creative moments: one lives the life of the character, while the other remains outside of this process and quietly and remotely observes, and sometimes even corrects the first process.

But this doesn't just happen with the "pillars" – good actors who aren't as dazzling or famous similarly experience the process of doubling of their consciousness.

In life, Pevtsov stuttered very badly, but on stage, he spoke without a hitch. But in order to do this, he had to get into the role of the character, and since the character didn't stutter, he didn't stutter either . . . "If I stutter . . . then I'm not Paul I, which means that I left the sphere in which this character existed . . . " "What occurs is a strange duality," – Pevtsov [1935: 43] would later say.

Finally, it should be noted that it's not just famous or good, renowned actors that experience this "strange duality" in the creative moments of their work – it's **all actors without exception**.

An actor's organic artistic creations always involve a doubled consciousness.

What's more: it is the whole essence of the actor's art.

When you understand that the *doubling* is the main factor of an the actor's creativity, multitudes of questions immediately become answered: questions about willpower in artistic creativity, the participation of one's actual persona, the character, the actor's point of view on the character, the significance of the "mask," the authenticity or lack thereof of experiencing, questions about theatrical "convention," and others.

Faith and Truth

What is "truth" in the art of the actor? Stanislavsky explains it like this: "for me (an actor), truth is what I sincerely believe in at a given time."

There are thousands of doubts, misunderstandings, disagreements around this "truth" and this "faith."

After all: how can I, for example, sincerely believe that I'm cold when I'm actually warm? How can I believe that I'm the drunkard Liubim Tortsov when I'm actually some well-intentioned and well-mannered actor?

If I can only think about the matters simply, unpretentiously, believing that I'm only my own persona and none other, then how can I explain to myself the "sincere faith" in nonexistent things? I cannot.

If, however, we account for the *ability to creatively double* your personality, then things become much clearer.

In doubling, my other identity seemingly lives apart from me – it has its own "I" and its own world. I observe it, am amazed by its utterly foreign thoughts and actions, and I can do as I like: either give this new identity free rein, or I can butt in – hold it back or spur it on in its actions . . .

Supporters of depictionism onstage typically like to ask the following "venomous" question: "What do you think, do you have to live onstage as you would in real life or differently? Do you have to believe, hate, and love as in life?"

Some people, like Stanislavsky, respond to these questions categorically and courageously: "Yes, exactly like in life and no other way." [And he would say only to his closest associates, in secret, that: "Naturally, that's not quite true. But we absolutely cannot tell that to anyone. If we do, they'll all stop striving: if it's not like in life, then there's no need to search for truth. Let them search for truth. Their work will send them in the right direction on its own." –*Author's Note*]

Others are instantly put off, and they quail and mumble: "Yes, well, not exactly like in life . . . with some measure of convention that's necessary for the stage . . . " and so on and so forth, saying contradictory things.

You have to believe completely, absolutely! But who is doing the believing? My whole identity? Of course not – otherwise, it would be a case for a psychiatric ward. My other identity that appeared as a result of doubling – it believes. If it completely believes, then it'll act completely; if it believes just a little bit, then it'll act just a little bit.

In the case that it (the other identity), while playing Othello or somebody else, becomes too carried away and tries to choke Desdemona to death for real, then there's a "guard" that keeps track of its double's every action and every thought. This guard is my personal, conscious identity. It sits in the corner, quietly, observing everything, and not getting in the way, but in a dangerous moment, it'll step in . . . and redirect the "criminal" hand.

Where does the inadequacy of an actor's feelings onstage come from (i.e. not truth, but verisimilitude)?

First and foremost from the fact that the actor doesn't fully believe in the character's circumstances. And he doesn't believe in them, because he can't escape from the influence of his personal, conscious identity, he can't let it double.

This also leads to the actor, having been somewhat immersed and agitated onstage, immediately calming down as soon as he leaves the stage. Many actors consider this to be the height of technique. What a mistake! This is *the complete lack of technique.*

Real technique is the following: entering a character and his life so deeply that it becomes stronger than you and refuses to leave you for quite some time. This is exactly how it was with the great actors (not depictionists) – Duse, Yermolova, Mochalov, and others.

If you quickly grow cold, that means that your warmth was only surface-deep. That's not the height of artistic technique – it's just self-deception.

You often hear that it's utterly wrong to expect truth from art, because the very word "art" implies something different: artificiality.

Yes, "art" isn't our mundane truth, the truth of my personal, conscious identity – *it's a much deeper truth* – the truth of the artist's hidden, innermost life, truth that he himself doesn't even suspect or that he cannot bring himself to acknowledge.

And *this* truth is capable, it can be manifested only in certain circumstances – when a "mask" is put on, when there is an artistic transformation, when there is a doubled consciousness.

If the conditions are artificial, then this cannot be brought about. And then we can talk about the "artificiality" of art.

When people say that stage feelings are weaker than everyday feelings (I won't lose my hair from worrying onstage), people fail to take into account 1. The doubled consciousness ("I'm" not feeling anything – "he" is); 2. catharsis (emotion, regardless of what kind, frees me); 3. *most actors interpret their physical excitement as emotion.*

★★★

Theoreticians insist that stage emotions are weaker than everyday emotions.

Is this always the case? Since the issue involves doubling, that means that everything depends on the character of the other identity – the one born as a result of this doubling.

Its emotions can be stronger than the emotions of a personal, conscious identity. Which is understandable: the new identity might not have any brakes.

For example: Stanislavsky said somewhere that he remembers his stage emotions more clearly than things in regular life.

Where there are weaker emotions, there is incomplete doubling.

In general, we could speak of *complete* doubling and of *the first stages* of doubling. This also answers many questions.

"He" Lives

But who is "he?"

It's the *other part* of my doubled identity.

I'm told that "this matchbox is a bird." The degree to which I believe that the matchbox is a bird dictates any further behavior that I exhibit with regards to it.

Leonid Volkov [1893–1976] is afraid to believe – he says: "That's vulgar. You have to believe 'in moderation.'" [Demidov is summarizing Volkov's (1940:69–70) interpretation of Vakhtangov's views on faith.] He considers instability and insufficiency of faith to be great technique. But that wasn't the case for the great actors.

It is "indecent" for the intellectually willful actor.

Improper Interpretations of the Phenomenon of Doubling

As was said earlier, almost all actors know of this strange phenomenon. Some call it "splitting," others call it something else, but everybody knows about it.

However, we can only be bewildered at the observations and especially the conclusions that they make . . .

The actor is immersed, maybe even crying, and at the same time, he's quietly observing himself – that's the phenomenon.

It would seem that this is the most natural way to examine this phenomenon: I'm immersed, something is happening to me . . . I perceive things that don't actually exist as real . . . I consider imaginary circumstances to be my own, real circumstances . . . and along with this "insanity," I still manage to hold on to my reason, and it keeps track of the feelings, thoughts, and actions of the first, "insane" "I."

In other words: the main and new thing here is that something is happening to me and within me, and peripherally, I can observe myself without getting in my own way.

Usually, however, people consider the *observation* of self the main thing, and everything else is peripheral. In other words: the most important thing is the part of the conscious identity that observes, while the other . . . it's as if it doesn't even exist, as if it's just a reflection of the first one.

This sort of observation begs to be made, and so it is – alas.

This leads to a logical conclusion: since I remain myself, and I observe myself during the creative process, that means that the most important thing is not to lose coolness and deliberativeness during it.

All great actors (not depictionists), however, bear witness to something different. (A few pages ago, you could see a few explications on this account, including that of Stanislavsky.) Great actors say that the character (the other part) is stronger than they are, that it lives a full life, that it subordinates their whole body, their whole soul, and they—essentially forced into a corner, holding their breath, careful of not scaring off the whole process—passively and meditatively observe everything that occurs.

They note one more amazing detail, but those who benefit from doing so (i.e. depictionists) take their words and make the opposite conclusions, thereby clouding the minds of actors that are not yet well informed.

The amazing detail is that the stronger a character captivates an actor, the more an actor is within its sphere of influence, the more distinct their consciousness and deliberativeness become.

Pevtsov [1935: 44] writes:

> I insist that the deeper you enter into another life, the more cognizant you become of your artistic possibilities, and of your mastery.

> I don't know to what and how I should compare this. Why is it that when I'm in a bad creative state, when I'm struggling as hard as a swimmer, trying to stay afloat, that's when I don't see the playbill dropping down from the loge? However, when I swim without moving, as people do on their backs, in a state of great calm, when tears come to my

627

eyes – I'm capable of seeing not just the playbill that's falling down onto the bald head of some audience member – I can even laugh [about it] on the inside. It is some sort of *strange duality*. Sometimes, this state happens upon us in real life: during some great revelation, you might notice significantly more details than in a normal state . . . .

Similarly, when you're in a state of creative calm, you, like a swimmer on his back that is carried by the waves themselves, can easily note all the circumstances, you can easily adjust the match-box that is lying uncomfortably in your pocket, move some chair that's gotten in your way, etc.

A hasty glance at this "amazing detail" really does lead to this sort of impression: the better you act, the more you're "in character" and the more you exist within the given circum-stances, the colder you have to be.

When, in reality, it's not so at all. In order to solve this problem, we once again have to turn to doubling – the more you're in character, the more completely doubled you are.

And the more complete your doubling is, the more *distinctly and independently* does *each* of your two parts function.

This is why on one hand, "tears come to my eyes," and on the other, "I'm capable of seeing not just the playbill that's falling down onto the bald head of some audience member – I can even laugh [about it] on the inside."

While in a creative state, do you have to search for this self-awareness and sober-mindedness? Not at all! Seeing as you've doubled, your self-awareness will inevitably increase.

In this way, the question of one's "point of view on the character" is solved on its own.

Should you play your point of view on the character?

When you cognize that the main condition of a proper creative state onstage is the **doubling of your consciousness**, this question is removed from the table. It's not there, and it cannot *be* there. It was there only because you weren't aware of the main spring of the art of the actor.

Seeing as there is such a thing as doubled consciousness, that means that the "life of the character" and "self-awareness" exist simultaneously.

And since "character" and observation exist simultaneously, there cannot be a *point of view*.

If I see that a playbill is falling from a loge onto the bald head of a respectable audience member and I inwardly laugh at it, then, at any rate, I can see the (forgive me) scoundrel or fool or sage that's crawling out of me. At the same time, I cannot not laugh, not be indignant, or not be amazed.

Methods of Doubling

If the most important condition of the art of the actor is doubling, then instead of try-ing to "step into the shoes of the character," [Shchepkin] or instead of trying to "remain yourself within the given circumstances," [Stanislavsky] isn't it better to immediately try to double?

Of course it would be! But how? Tell yourself: "Go! Double!" . . . It won't work.

With hypnosis, it's easy: "Go to sleep!" – and you're asleep. One part of you sleeps, while the other keeps awake.

The sleep of a hypnotized person is a pathological state, akin to that of somnambulatory automatism; here, in art, you have to hold on to your whole consciousness, while simultane-ously giving in without reservations to the power of the imagined character.

A hypnotized sleep state is no good here.

Actors (the more inexperienced and ignorant they are, the more often they do this) do a very simple thing: they draw in their mind's eye (or on paper) the image of Cassio or Iago and then bravely tell themselves: I am Cassio.

For a second (as with the Stanislavskian "if?"), such an actor would feel himself as Cassio, but the character of Cassio didn't take root within him, and – like smoke that is blown away by the wind – it flies away. The actor tries to hold on to . . . what? To whatever he can – the posture, the facial expressions, the rhythm of movements (everything else is gone), and he sincerely believes that he has transformed into Cassio.

Here, not even for a moment can you think of doubling, transforming, or true artistic creation. A duality flared up for a split second, after which it disappeared irrevocably.

A duality exists only when **your other identity lives, lives sincerely and fully within the given circumstances of the play**. Under the guise of Cassio or Iago or whomever you want – it's still *your* other identity. It could be familiar or utterly unexpected, but it's still yours.

How can I make it so that one part of my doubled self became essentially independent and participated in the creative process? How can I find this part? When all is said and done, how can I "zero in on" it?

There's no need to zero in on it – it'll come out on its own.

Behave as if *you yourself were completely* within the circumstances of the play, and when you begin to say words or listen to your partner, you'll start to have thoughts and feel emotions that aren't inherent to you (in your everyday life), as if you stopped being yourself and became someone else. The shift happens **on its own**, without a special command on your part.

And the more you give yourself over to the life of the role, the more (as Pevtsov said) your observing consciousness comes to live. And you begin to see everything around you very clearly, **without interrupting the flow of life of the second identity**.

If, however, you *begin* with a search for sober-mindedness and duality per se, nothing will come of it.

These *doubling processes* **must** take place "in the darkness" of our psyches, just as the processes of digestion happen within the "darkness" of our bodies. Try to interfere with these physiological processes, and you will disrupt them.

But if this is how we should imagine everything: your other identity lives within the "given circumstances," while your conscious, personal self observes and directs the life of the character-self – how then can we explain a case when an actor that is carried away by what is happening onstage forgets himself and considers entire sections of what is happening onstage to be real?

There's nothing to fear here. In the end, he returns to his normal state, doesn't he? There's nothing to be worried about. He's like a swimmer that swims, swims on the surface, then suddenly goes under the water. He'll drop out of your sight for a few seconds, and then he'll resurface.

These cases are easily explained and they are not to be feared.

But how do we explain the following case?

This is happening during one of Stanislavsky's rehearsals. One of the best, strongest actors is rehearsing [Leonidov]. At first, the rehearsal isn't going well, the actors are complaining about not feeling very well, the scene isn't working. But after Stanislavsky's adjustments and after a few repetitions, things have gotten back on track: the actors have begun to live for real, they're gotten into it, they're immersed, and the scene is going along fine.

"Well, how did you feel yourselves now?" Stanislavsky asks the aforementioned actor.

"I don't know how I felt. I wasn't observing myself – I was keeping track of him (my partner), and I can tell you anything about him: where he grew frightened of me, where he was embarrassed by my words, where he wanted to fool me, where he came out of character. But I can't say anything about myself – I didn't have the time to observe myself."

"That's exactly what I need!" Stanislavsky exclaims. "That's the right feeling. You have to completely forget yourself!"

This leads to a completely confusing mess: Salvini and Stanislavsky, and many actors that have entered the annals of theatre, speak of duality, insisting that it's the natural state of an actor onstage.

And then, when one of the MAT's best actors says that he didn't notice anything about himself, that he wasn't observing himself at all, it turns out that he did everything wonderfully onstage, and an infallible authority, Stanislavsky himself, says: that's what you *should* do! That's the right state to be in!

If we trust psychology, then the case is simple: there are people who are very much able to split their consciousness and then there are people that lack this ability.

Might it be that this wonderful actor belonged to the latter group? But then, doesn't that mean that doubling (or splitting) isn't at all the chief and most important quality of an actor?

No, doubling was, is, and will forever be the main quality of any artist, and especially an actor. And this instance only proves *the necessity for the utmost degree of doubling*.

Look: on one hand, the actor identifies with his role and forgets himself; on the other hand, as soon as the rehearsal ends, he begins to discuss the scene he was just in, as well as the behavior of his partners.

If this were complete abandon, a complete shift into somnambulatory automatism, then he would, just like the man who just awoke from a dream, ask: where am I? And what just happened to me?

There certainly was a conscious, personal identity that was playing the observer. But to such a small degree that the actor hardly noticed it. [Earlier Demidov (p. 622) explains that, in such fortunate cases, the actor's consciousness, his integral (observing) identity "departs into the realm of the *automatic*. It executes only automatic functions."] And this minimal dose is the proper one, the most effective one. If it is any bigger, the character becomes weaker, more diluted; if it is any bigger — that's the end: self-awareness, self-observation, and the cessation of any creative process!

Self-Observation

Self-observation: that's the thing that most often hinders an actor in giving himself over onstage and giving himself a green light.

And on the other hand: *green-lighting* is the first and most important weapon we have for combating self-observation.

But what about doubling? You can't have it without self-observation. Self-observation is ingrained in the essence of a creative act; if there is a creative act, there is doubling. Without doubling and unification [of the two parts], there cannot be a creative act.

That means that it's not self-observation that is getting in the way — it's the **kind of self-observation**.

The kind of self-observation that occurs *during doubling* doesn't get in the way. On the contrary, it helps (it doesn't break, but instead unifies). This same kind of self-observation *without doubling* is complete *artistic suicide* — self-destruction.

Towards the Technique of "Green-lighting"

A person "green-lights," and then proceeds to critically observe himself. And nothing happens. You have to green-light yourself *without any observation*!

A person wants to remain himself, he is afraid of losing his critical gaze: what if I end up looking ridiculous, if I let go of my self-observation?! I should keep track of myself.

No observation! This is almost a slogan.

But it's easy to say: "no observation," but how do you achieve it?

Fairly easily. Especially with the help of a perceptive teacher.

A critical gaze is impossible to avoid, and it *shouldn't* be avoided – let it be, but . . . *most importantly*: you have to cultivate *green-lighting*, even of the small automatic movements, even of insignificant trifles. "You wanted to, but for some reason, you didn't do it – the movement was already there, and yet you stopped it."

A critical gaze shouldn't be forbidden – it should be *circumvented*. Slip right by it.

Towards the Technique of Self-Observation

Student: "Nothing is working. I'm constantly observing myself. My consciousness, my head are always in the way."

Teacher: "So go ahead – observe yourself. Observe as much as you want: but don't stop giving in to the spontaneity that is working inside you. Then, gradually, self-observation will assume the place that it is supposed to. It will always be present to a certain degree. Otherwise, you would be in danger of utter abandon and psychological dislocation."

Do not fear self-observation – in general, *don't be afraid of anything* – it's your truth, and there's no need to fight it.

★★★

An actor observes himself and forces himself to do things. In one place, he forces himself to feel and want one thing – this "one thing" ends, and he quickly recalibrates himself.

This self-observation and self-control are possibly the *chief and foremost sins*.

In general, "recalibrating" and "forcing" yourself means consigning any freedom to death, and it heralds the complete destruction of life.

"Don't observe yourself, don't interfere, let it happen as it's happening."

"But how can I not observe?"

"Alright, fine, observe yourself. But do so in order to green-light yourself and not get in your own way. Do so that it keeps on rolling on its own."

"But how? Then I'll just be playing myself."

"We'll see whom you'll be playing. As for now, when you observe and "control" yourself, you're dead and you're playing a statue, a painted doll."

The actor begins to give himself free rein; he stops interfering. He comes to life, and his words lead him into the circumstances, into the character, and everything is put in the right place.

In general, if self-observation is strong, then the whole process is only *surface-deep*.

There is one more way to avoid self-observation – transform entirely into the character. But any advice to transform into a character is naïve, as it is akin to a gem like this: "Be a genius."

In order to transform, one needs all of our tricks. First and foremost, one needs to master a *proper psycho-technique*.

★★★

Regardless of how much we insist that it's not "me," and that it's "him," it's still simply my made-up and costumed and re-costumed "I." Regardless of how much we insist on this, many people that are well-inclined towards imitation will grab on to this idea of doubling, *recalibrate it to suit their own needs*, and will then yell: "This is what we've been saying all along: there's no need to be yourself, you have to be a character!"

It's sad, however, that none of them have *ever been* a character – they've only "played" one, imitated it, depicted it. But they do not understand the difference. In order to be a character, you must always be yourself and not chase after coldness.

★★★

Leonidov asked me: how could he, an actor, do something and simultaneously observe himself? This was after I read to him how I discovered the "Liberation from the Body" [See Book Five, Chapter 10]. He doesn't understand that there are people that are capable of doubling their consciousness and attention, which is why self-observation ("take your time," "green-light yourself") *must* have a place. Everything depends on the type of actor. Leonidov should be led away from doubling – it would kill him, but it can save others.

For example, it's enough to tell Vera Solovyova [1892–1986; MAT and the First Studio of MAT (later MAT the Second) actress] that she should live according to what she feels at a given moments, that she should green-light herself to correspond to what exists, instead of fighting herself, restructuring herself – once she hears that, her self-observation and her doubling will only help her.

Some (like Leonidov) do not have self-observation – their attention and psychology should be directed towards an object (partner) and towards the circumstances.

Others do have self-observation and doubling, regardless of how much you try to lead them away from them. And in this case, it's also a bad idea to fight them on this – you should instead take advantage of it. Turn their self-observation in the right direction. Then, their self-observation will only aid them.

Apparently, this is a very serious discovery.

★★★

It's almost a paradox, but it still has practical value:

"You can't interfere – let it develop *on its own,* let it develop as it's developing." But an actor can't help but interfere – he's grown used to doing so. Well, let him: "Go ahead, interfere, direct yourself, but direct yourself to be quite free and passive. *Interfere and direct yourself towards not interfering.*"

It sounds ridiculous and contradictory, but it leads to great results in practice. Naturally, this is for those who are inclined to double.

★★★

Leonidov said that the most important thing is talent, and not theories, methods, or techniques. But what talent? Those who do not have the ability to double cannot help themselves to fix their own technique. Those, however, who *can* double – only with the help of proper theory and self-direction, they can clamber out onto the heights. And not just clamber out – clamber out into a state of *artistic creativity*.

[Later postscript:]

But what was the case with Leonidov? An inability to double?

If you can imagine it: **No!** Quite the opposite: *it was complete doubling.* After all, he was not only Leonidov – he was also in-role Leonidov. And it wasn't his regular identity—Leonidov—that saw his partner – it was the in-role Leonidov, i.e. Leonidov's other identity – the one that existed in the given circumstances.

And from here, we have to make the most practical of conclusions: there's no need to place an order with yourself – "Go! Double!" – nothing will come of that. On the contrary, you have to *search for unity, think that you're the role or that the role is you. Only then will there be doubling of any kind.*

Small, Automatic Movements as a Path to Doubling

As has already been said, when a person is alone, he is more free and natural. He gives in to all of his spontaneous desires and inclinations. He doesn't observe himself, he doesn't pay attention to what he can and can't do, he gives himself free rein, and every one of his sub-components (if we can use that expression) lives at its own risk: his body does what it wants, his mind thinks whatever thoughts it wants . . . his feelings, sensations, inclinations – they're all free and are all scattered in different directions . . .

Like a herd of animals at a water source: some have gotten into the water and are now standing there, cooling off; others are lying on the shore, focused on digesting; some are roaming, nibbling at grass; some are sleeping with their families, their heads resting on each others' backs . . . And the shepherd is lying under a bush, snoring quietly.

This is the state that is very comfortable for us. More than any other, it can serve as a point of departure for us. There's no need to even think about doubling in this case – *it's essentially already there.* We just have to sustain it. We need to feed the doubled part.

But how? First and foremost, we need to *not get in its way* – let it act as it will, let it strengthen.

We can observe this sort of doubling and involuntariness when a person is alone and in a state of calm and unconcern. But what should we do when we're not alone? During class, at a rehearsal, and ultimately in a show?

All of these pieces of advice, like "calm down," "relax your muscles," "execute your task," "concentrate on the object" – they're attainable only by very experienced people.

Practice shows that the technique of giving complete freedom to small, involuntary, automatic movements is always very effective.

With the help of this seemingly simple technique, we give our involuntariness complete freedom. And where we have powerful involuntariness, out conscious identity weakens, and therefore we can easily achieve a doubled self.

Notes on Creative Doubling

The most important thing is that doubling is at the same time *unity*. It's a creative dialectic.

Having thus provided a simplified interpretation of doubling during an actor's creative process, let's allow ourselves to tentatively say that an actor holds the rivers of two different lives within himself: his own life, and – right next to it – the life of an imagined identity (character). And each of these rivers flows according to its laws and depends on its own circumstances.

Beginning with the fact that upon entering the creative process, although an actor is aware of the theatrical convention and of the audience's presence while onstage, he senses it only as much as he has to. All of these impressions are *restrained* – they don't fill him entirely (like they do an actor who is not capable of entering a creative state, i.e. a bad actor). [It would be even more accurate to say that on one hand, they're restrained (so that they wouldn't distract, interfere, or take up all the actor's attention), and on the other, these sensations stimulate the actor in a person. The audience, the lighting, the stage, the "false" character, another person's words, a premeditated role and play – all of this reminds a person that he is an actor, that his creativity needs to awaken in him, and a new state of being, that he will enthrall the audience only if they believe him, and they'll believe him only if he acts well, full of artistic truth. *–Author's Note*]

And right next to this is the actor's other consciousness, which is dedicated to the embodiment of this imagined character.

Every "character" already contains within him the necessary spiritual qualities and fully cognizes all the given circumstances. They'll all be both stimulators and inhibitors with regards to behaving onstage while in-role. That Don Quixote that you're playing today *won't allow you* to behave as you would if you were playing Othello, and vice versa. This is why you shouldn't stick your nose with all of your stimulation or inhibitions into the life of this "character" – you should instead first concern yourself with green-lighting his ability to live his own life.

Understanding this, you won't argue with whether experiencing is necessary. The only people who will argue are those who aren't acquainted with the doubling that needs to be inherent to the true art of the actor. [Even a depictionist will start speaking of doubling. "You know, I do that too . . . one of my selves observes, while the other acts." It's true that it acts, but it *doesn't live*. It does everything premeditatedly, mechanically, it "works" as a circus performer depicts. That's why he's a depictionist, an imitator, and not an artist of immersion. To be more exact, *there is no doubling to be had with him*. He's the same all the time. *–Author's Note*]

Having understood that doubling inevitably happens when in a true creative state, it's easy to grasp why the aforementioned bit of advice not only doesn't hinder you, but helps you. It's an address to *the actor's observing consciousness*. But there's no need to do it crudely, clashing with the actor's state, else you'll "sober him up" – you'll disrupt his creative doubling.

And it's very easy to disrupt it – everything already does so: the conventions of the stage, the audience, their reactions, the unsatisfactory scene partners, and the knowledge of everything that will happen in the play.

This is why it's especially crucial to try not to disrupt this creative doubling, and why you should instead do everything in your power to strengthen and reinforce it. This is why, when "advising," you should say: "Yes, yes . . . correct, correct . . . Take your time . . . " i.e. don't disrupt yourself, trust the grains of artistic creativity that are trying to break free, don't criticize yourself, don't cool yourself off – everything is going along smoothly. Do not fear the unusual doubled state that you're in.

The state itself is akin to a circus performer walking along a tightrope.

This is one of the reasons why the art of the actor is so difficult.

The circus performer is taught by the dangerous circumstances – the slightest hesitation can lead to disaster. An actor doesn't have such a fine teacher. And he can make mistakes without any comeuppance. And since there's no comeuppance, the mistake is repeated, becomes a habit. And so we get "dislocated" actors that have forever lost their sense of truth, their artistic balance.

5

Unity

On Unity

In discussing doubling, we only concern ourselves with *two* consciousnesses.

But is that enough? Can't our consciousness triple, quadruple, etc.?

As an example, let's look at circus eccentrics that, while playing a role, also play a musical instrument, they run, jump, roll over one another . . .

Or at least a pianist, each of whose fingers does its own job, hitting the keys, his feet pressing the pedals, with greater or lesser force, every musical phrase has its own meaning, and, ultimately, the piece as a whole conveys its musical idea. Doesn't that involve something like *tentupling*? Or is there a limit to the number of parts into you can grow?

Let's recall one the world's finest jugglers, Kara:

> In order to juggle three or four balls, all you really need is simple, well-focused attention. But when you juggle five or more, your consciousness *can no longer keep up*, your eyes don't catch every ball on its own, and only see them *all at once*, as a system, as a sort of living organism moving in the air. And your hands, obeying not your consciousness, but your instinct, enter this living organism, this flying system of balls, on their own. I don't observe the balls from the outside; I insert myself into a single, mobile system with them. I essentially act involuntarily: my hands catch the balls and throw them on their own, without my intellectual interjections. As soon as I interfere with my conscious mind, the system is instantly disrupted, and one of the balls finds itself on the ground.

What does this mean? This means that aside from one wondrous process – *doubling* – there's another, more wondrous one – *unification*.

And they exist in complete harmony, supporting and *evoking* one another.

In our everyday lives, we rely on the harmony of these two processes at every step.

We have before us four different, unconnected words: "wins," "steady," "slow," and "race . . ."

On their own, each of these words carries with it its usual meaning, evoking certain images in our mind. But it's enough to switch up the order (and add some particles): "slow and steady wins the race" – they *become one*, cease to exist independently of each other, and create something new that carries great meaning for us.

While examining individual parts of some complex machine, like an automobile, for example, we'll get hundreds of different impressions. It's possible to throw all the parts together in a heap, and it would just be a pile of unconnected parts. But if you connect them like you're supposed to, pour in some gas, sit, and start driving – don't all the screws, balls, pipes, connectors, etc. all combine into a single whole? They become one and "come to life." All of them will be struck by the same thought: "automobile." All the parts will appear in a new and different light.

Uniting so many different parts into a single whole is called **synthesis**.

This is what we were talking about, and now that we've come full circle, we're back where we started. This was unavoidable, because synthesis represents the foundations of the creative process.

The ability to see *union* amidst thousands of different things *is* a creative ability.

The ability to *step into* this complex "system" *yourself*, to give yourself over and *become a part* of this "system," **as if you lost your own personal "I"** – that's the creative ability of an *artist* – a person who creates works of art.

In particular, this ability is crucial for an actor who gives over not just his body (like the juggler), but his soul, with all its hidden depths, under the influence of a *unified whole*: a work of art.

At every step, we use a unified consciousness just like we use doubling; we go on a walk, we walk around a rock, jump over a fallen log, and at the same time, we're talking – two things simultaneously. Though, all things considered, when the conversation becomes too serious, we stop or sit down and continue the conversation without the distraction of walking.

We look at a painting, and seeing all the details independently, we simultaneously see the unified whole.

We read a book, and understanding each thought and each page on its own, we also comprehend the book as a whole.

At any moment, we're receiving hundreds of impressions that are coming to us both from within and without . . . (Thanks to these impressions, we then get whole arrays of images, thoughts, desires.)

These thousands of impressions either arise in us connected in groups (we see a whole landscape as one: the trees, the bushes, the fields, the hills, the river, the sky, the clouds) or they rise up independently (a mosquito bites my finger, a rabbit blazes across the field, a tree branch lashes my face).

But regardless of how the impressions arise in us – in groups or independently – once they're there, they immediately come in contact with each other, as well as with what's in our souls. They meet and interact, we react to it involuntarily, and it all combines into a single thing: an experiencing. That's typical, everyday synthesis.

Can we speak here of absolute union? Can we speak of how these thousands of impressions harmonize with each other and, like the different parts of an automobile, create a harmonic fruit of human thought – an automobile? Of course not. The impressions combine in random groups, like crowds of people at a fairground, yelling, bubbling, and living in separate parts: one crowd is at the carousel, another is at the show-booth, a third is next to the menagerie, at the shooting range, at the pancake booth, at the stalls, etc., etc . . . This way tens and hundreds of groups of impressions will rise up in our consciousness, living, combining with each other, and again dividing and spreading out.

There *is* union, but it exists only partly. There is no general, absolute, complete union.

In our everyday lives, we don't know what absolute unity is. We only know that the described unity is relative, incomplete.

In order to better understand what unity is, we have to more closely examine instances of pure unity, *absolute unity*.

What we can call a state of absolute unity of consciousness is the state in which our *consciousness embraces only a single phenomenon at any given moment*. In his *L'Automatisme Psychologique*, the neuropsychologist Janet writes that such absolute unity occurs only in extremes: either in a case of extreme pathology (like catalepsy, when an exhausted psyche is incapable of registering multiple sensations at once) and if one is a *genius* ("psychological unity during moments of great intellectual upliftment, when a *perfect* psyche enables a person to fully grasp and synthesize all the images and feelings that he or she is experiencing or that he or she recalls" [Janet 1889: 192]).

In a case of pathological unity, when "an exhausted psyche is incapable of registering multiple sensations at once" [ibid.], it's worth noting that it doesn't involve even a trace of synthesis. In this case, while regarding an object, a person can perceive only that single object and nothing more. For example, he's holding a pen, looking at it, and the pen consumes his full attention. If you focus his attention on a quill, he'll completely transfer his attention to the quill, while the pen will cease to exist for him. However, when he sees the pen again, he has already forgotten about the quill and sees only the pen . . . He looks at a sheet of paper – the paper enthralls him completely and displaces any thought of the pen, ink, quill, etc. That's what pathological unity is, which occurs only with specific illnesses.

"But usually," Janet [ibid.] writes, "one's consciousness isn't so low or so high (as in a case of genius): it stays at a moderate height, that at which one's consciousness contains a multitude of images, but fails to systematize them."

The Actor's Synthesis (Unity)

So, what do I (an actor) "fully unite and synthesize" when I, despite being quite a petty bourgeois, transform into Liubim Tortsov – when I live in his realities, when I experience cold, hunger, and an overwhelming desire for wine?

I'm a normal person who doesn't regularly have hallucinations, so I see full well that this is a theatre and not a street or a booking-office, that there's an audience, that I'm on a stage, that I'm acting today, as are the other actors – my partners in our production of the play, *Poverty is no Vice* . . .

Right next to this rather normal and ordinary attitude towards my surroundings, I experience a psychological shift: looking at my made-up face in the mirror, I suddenly feel myself to be someone completely different – an unshaved, tired, drunk face . . . a torn suit, an old, crumpled cap, and . . . it's as if I am no longer me . . .

. . . It would be nice to go someplace warm, to relax for a bit . . . I'm not ashamed of begging for a few coins for a drink, I perceive my past as real – the debauchery, the nightlife, the poverty . . . The actor that acts alongside me suddenly strikes me as being "Mitya" – my brother's salesclerk, I see the stage as a booking-office . . . Things imaginary – suddenly become real.

My doubled identity has its own realities, its own necessities, and its own ideals. It doesn't have a stage, an audience, actors – it has Tortsov-the-merchant's booking-office, and Mitya the salesclerk.

And the thousands of existing realities all weave together with the thousands of imaginary realities . . . I step into this complex system of facts and fantasies (like the juggler steps into the system of flying balls), and everything begins to live together, not interfering, but assisting each other and contributing to the other's existence . . . This involves the cognizance that I'm an actor, the complete confidence that I'm Liubim Tortsov; this involves reality and fictions . . . thousands of contradictions . . . and they unite into one thing: *a work of art – an artistic transformation – I become Liubim Tortsov.*

Of course, this phenomenon isn't mundane at all – not every performance (even a more or less successful one) will inevitably involve such an artistic transformation, such an organic entry into the "mobile system" of facts. For the most part, the performance will be marked by momentary glimmers: I'm alive! . . . and now I'm not . . . and I haven't been for a long time . . . and suddenly, the truth shines through again . . . and now everything is false and artificial again . . .

There's no need to grieve over this. What the actor *should* do, however, is simply and matter-of-factly tell himself: time to get to work, time to get a new, reliable technique.

Such psychological unity in moments of "great intellectual upliftment, when an *perfect* psyche enables a person to fully grasp and synthesize all the images and feelings that he or she is experiencing or that he or she recalls" – in the opinion of such an expert in psychology like Janet, such unity can be attributed to genius. So, should we really hope to reach such heights so easily and simply?

Among actors, this word isn't venerated very much: at the faintest glimmer of giftedness, everybody instantly yells: "Genius!" Those who throw this word about have "heights" that are far too low . . . they probably don't even know what true height really is. And if they do, if they've seen them, then they've forgotten them. They've forgotten them – it's easier to live that way, otherwise, their consciousness would constantly tug at them: "And what are *you* doing?"

"Heights," "genius" . . . maybe we shouldn't even be discussing this, then?

One really shouldn't be throwing such words about, but it's definitely worth discussing them. Moreover, maybe that's the only thing we *should* be discussing. Because if these glimmers, these instants do exist, then maybe it's possible to extend them . . . Seconds? They can be turned into minutes. Minutes into hours . . .

We just need to apply enough desire, know-how, and decisiveness.

The Highest Degree of the Actor's Unity

"An actor lives, he cries and laughs on stage, but in crying and laughing, he observes his laughter and his tears. And this dual life, this equilibrium between life and acting is what art is made up of" (Tommaso Salvini [1891: 58–60]). If we accept this as true, then how should we interpret an actor's abandon onstage? . . .

One often hears: "I don't remember how I was acting . . . " "I forgot that I was onstage . . . "

Rossi [as quoted in Evreinov 2002: 188], who has been referenced before, wrote after a performance: "I can't tell about all the details of this scene – I only remember that I was brimming with true passion and that I heard the audience's delights and approval and applause as if in a dream . . . I didn't see anyone, I don't know whether I was pleasant enough, I was in some sort of haze . . . "

Or Yermolova [1955: 299]: "Once, I *almost* completely forgot myself – in the scene where Tatyana Repina dies, I tore off my necklace, bit the pillow all over, I don't remember what happened to me."

Could it be that this isn't art, but rather pathology? After all, there's no Salvinian "*equilibrium between life and acting* . . . " True, there is no equilibrium. The "acting" here has expanded so much that it seems as if it has completely displaced "life."

However, it only seems that way.

There is exactly as much "life" (or rather, an actor's conscious identity) as is necessary to safeguard against a catastrophe.

Imagine an automobile that's reached its greatest possible speed . . . It's speeding along so quickly that there's only time to think about one thing: "I hope I don't crash into anything or break my neck!" Everything else isn't even within your power.

It's the same for an actor who's at the highest stage of his creative potential: the car is going at such a high speed, the wheels are spinning so quickly, that it's too late to think about stopping – now, you can only think about blazing past everything in one piece and not crashing into anything.

However, we mustn't ignore Yermolova's little "almost" (I *almost* completely forgot myself). *Almost, but not quite.*

In order to dispel any doubts, I suggest that we read a few lines from a book called *Days of My Life*, written by Tatyana Shchepkina-Kupernik, who knew Yermolova very well:

> Before the staging of *Tatyana Repina*, a weak, though suspenseful play by Suvorin that's intended to be a retelling of the story of Evlaliya Kadmina—a well-known opera singer that poisoned herself during a performance where her character is poisoned onstage and dies – Yermolova couldn't "get" the death scene. Suvorin would get mad and hit the ground with his stick. And suddenly, during the first show, Maria Nikolayevna thought that she was dying. She bit her pillow all over, she tore off her pearl necklace. The people that were standing next to her – the comedian Maksheyev and Aunt Sasha (Alexandra Shchepkina, an actress and colleague), who was playing Repina's jubilant girlfriend – were horribly frightened, truly believing that she was actually poisoned; they forgot everything that they were supposed to say, they ran to her, signaling to bring down the curtain . . . What was happening among the audience is indescribable: hysterics, screams, there were calls for a doctor, women were carried out senseless. Having recovered her breath and come to, Maria Nikolayevna sat up on her pillows and, listening fearfully to the noise in the house, asked: "Sashen'ka, what's going on out there? Is there a fire?"
>
> Realizing that she was alive, and that it was just truly inspired acting, the Aunt and Maksheyev, with tears on their eyes, could only repeat: "Fire? What fire . . . it was you, all you." [Shchepkina-Kupernik 1928: 183–184]

Doesn't this tale tell us that the abandon was far from absolute? Regardless of how far it went, the actress wouldn't stop cognizing that she was onstage and that she was acting.

Of course, there was no celebrated "equilibrium" here (after all, she bit up the pillow and tore off her necklace!), but there was definitely the presence of an observer—the conscious identity—and the actress *almost* forgot herself, but not quite.

In this case, there were both stages of doubling (i.e. doubling, tempered with unity).

An Absolutely Integral Identity

It's worth noting about the above example and others like it that they *are* the surges of an actor's artistic power, and they proudly bear the label of "inspiration."

Here, everything is superlative: the character-identity grows so strong that the actress no longer feels that she is herself – Yermolova – and instead, she is Evlaliya Kadmina, and Yermolova isn't even there. Her imagination is so strong that she experienced real pains – she bit and tore the pillow, she was truly dying . . .

There was precisely the right amount of self-observation so that she wouldn't completely forget herself, so that the case didn't cross into the realm of pathology. If there were more of it, then she would experience just a bit of coldness, just a bit of frost, and it would have destroyed

Figure 19   Maria Yermolova, 1880s. Courtesy of Andrei Malaev-Babel.

her belief in the authenticity of what was transpiring, thereby also putting on the brakes on the whole creative process.

What is this power that so miraculously harmonizes all of our different and contradictory processes during our creative flights? Who is this wisest of "captains?" Who is this perfect artist-director?

Maybe it's our "integral identity" after all? The same one that organizes our everyday, mundane lives? The same whole identity with its life experience and prudence, its habits, passions, sicknesses? . . .

No, this "integral identity" isn't enough in this case – it'll just ruin things. It's too rational, petty, and narrow.

On the contrary, what we need here is vast openness, extraordinary profoundness, as Tyutchev said, "a wizard soul . . . "

Or maybe we don't need to search for anything new, and we just have to return to what has been said for many centuries by scores of philosophers, artists, and poets: that inspiration is something celestial, given from above, and that man has no power over it?

"*Whence* and *hour* they come I know not, nor can I force them" (Mozart [1891: 19]).

"I work, sitting at a piano with closed eyes, and I reproduce what someone is whispering in my ear from the outside" (E.T.A. Hoffman [1971: 53]).

" . . . In an instant the passage was clear. I sat down to the piano and wrote it off as rapidly as if I had known it by heart ever so long" (Richard Wagner [1905: 80]).

" . . . A wonderful sense of pleasure empowers me. I write as one possessed, and fill page after page, without a moment's pause" (Knut Hamsun [1921: 40]).

But should we give up so easily?

Naturally, philosophers, poets, and musicians don't lie: their subjective impression is such: ideas, melodies, and verse – it all comes out of a clear blue sky . . .

Although, in our dreams every night some strange, complex life is also thrust upon us – however, we understand that it's just an echo of our subconscious psychology. And in our dreams, we happen upon many fortunate ideas, the solutions to many difficult questions . . . and why shouldn't they come?

When your active life becomes still, it stops shielding the hidden life of our psyche – we begin to hear and sense thoughts and images that we don't notice during the day; just like in the dark of the night, we begin to hear sounds and odd rustles (during the day, we block them out, and it's as if they don't exist).

An "integral identity," i.e. one's identity as a whole, complete, with all its qualities, abilities, all its experience – in a word, *one's absolute, whole identity* – what is it?

Naturally, it's not just what we observe in life, in our everyday existence. We don't know one's absolute identity – we just know the *relatively whole* identity.

An absolute, integral identity includes decidedly **everything**: everything that's in the consciousness, everything that's without the consciousness (as psychology now calls it, "the sphere"). And what overt and covert powers are nesting in our nerve cells . . .

An integral identity involves not just the qualities and abilities that we already have, but potential ones as well, that are, as of yet, embryonic.

Many boys would sit down in front of a piano in their youth and thumb a song, which wouldn't really lead to anything. But one of them is affected by touching the piano, by the sound that's caused by his finger – he's affected by it as if it were an electric shock. Times passes, and the boy becomes the virtuoso and sorcerer, Hoffman.

What does this mean? That the boy's nerve cells already had the potential for the powers that would later develop and bloom.

And every one of us has the potential for many powers and abilities.

They're not developed, but at the highest stage of one's creative potentials or moments of catastrophe – suddenly, they become clear and astound and dazzle everyone with brilliance that no one was aware of. And what about the powers and abilities that have been handed down to us from generation to generation over the course of hundreds of thousands, and maybe even millions of years, since the time that life on earth began! After all, they haven't disappeared without a trace – nothing does in nature – and all that's necessary is a special, beneficent moment in order for them to manifest.

The contents and reserves of our absolutely integral identity are unlimited. They make up the well that a person draws from in the moments of creative flights, when "*perfect* psyche enables a person to fully grasp and synthesize all the images and feelings that he or she is experiencing or that he or she recalls" (Janet).

On Being in an Artistic Trance and Different Kinds of Equilibrium

It's often been said and written that the state of extreme *excitement* that accompanies a creative flight often poorly reflects on the art.

For example, an actor feels that he's "on fire," he's excited, he's riding a wave of emotions, he's drowning in his excitement, his speech becomes incomprehensible, he moves too much and too quickly, he waves his arms around, comes out of character, out of the circumstances . . .

The act ends, he's delighted – his acting was "inspired."

But to his surprise and disappointment, the general opinion is that he acted poorly, that his inspired acting was good for nothing, that he was simply unbearable onstage.

Many have been in this position . . . Some more timid actors then conclude that "inspired acting" doesn't lead to anything good and that they should insure themselves against it, and in order to do that, they should cool down their superfluous and dangerous passion and not trust their feelings.

Others who are braver, who have a more stalwart character (there aren't many like this, naturally), don't back down: "So it didn't work, so I couldn't do it – I got carried away – so what? I don't know and can't do some things yet – so I blundered . . . But I remember there was something special, something rare there . . . it wasn't for nothing that I felt this rapture and joy!

"No, there's no reason to part ways with this yet – there was something *real* there, something meaningful, I just couldn't handle it. There's nothing surprising about it – I'm completely inexperienced as yet, I'm still wet behind the ears! Given time, once I grow stronger and used to it, I'll be able to handle it, and, with God's help, I'll stay in the saddle."

This is exactly what always happened to our great, almost legendary actors.

For example, in her first appearance in Lessing's *Emilia Galotti*, Yermolova enthralled everyone with her temperament, her wondrous voice, but she also enraged many others – her speech wasn't comprehensible, she fussed around too much. Some critics even found her performance embarrassing and amateur.

It was like this in the beginning, but later on, with time, the hot-tempered stallion was bridled, ridden, and every show was a wonder whose like we can't even imagine today. I can say this safely, because I saw Yermolova, heard her and witnessed her acting, and I was mature enough and well-versed in the art of the actor at the time.

As for Mochalov – nothing even needs to be said: he was all creative flash and inspiration. Without this flash, he wasn't able to act. Without it, he felt like he was out of his element, he would grow mad, he'd try to excite himself, he'd tense up, scream, flail about, and . . . still, nothing would happen.

Only the strongest flashes of inspiration, only the surges of volcanic passion were the natural environment of this actor.

And only when the mundane actorly equilibrium was "disrupted" did he feel like himself right at home and did he create the wonders that his contemporaries, beginning with Russia's most serious critic Belinsky, all wrote about.

★★★

Now let's discuss "*equilibrium*" specifically.

Salvini insists that "dual life, this equilibrium between life and acting is what art is made up of."

Were Mochalov or Yermolova, when she was dying in *Tatyana Repina* experiencing Salvini's version of equilibrium? There certainly was equilibrium. For there was unity, and what is unity if not harmony? And what is harmony if not equilibrium?

But the equilibrium of some actors is akin to the equilibrium of a bartender who's firmly planted behind his bar stand; the equilibrium of others is akin to that of a teen crossing a log over a stream; yet others' equilibrium is like that of a construction worker walking across a beam over an unfinished building; the equilibrium of a fourth group of actors is like that of a balancer that's dancing across a wire tightly strung right under the big top.

This last group is the one in which we should put the risky and rarely attainable equilibrium of the aforementioned and other great tragedians *that truly deserve the title.*

"Big Truths" Always Displace "Small Truths" of the Theatrical Convention

What sort of harmony and equilibrium are we even talking about if an actress tears off her necklace and bites a pillow in abandon while acting?

Let's be sober-minded: is that really such a horrible crime? "She tore off her necklace, she bit on the pillow . . . " So what? Does that mean that you can't tear up a letter that's enraged you? You can't slam your first on the table? You can't throw yourself to your knees – you'll ruin or dirty your pants?

I'll describe another instance with the same Yermolova when the actress didn't tear anything up, didn't bite anything, but she "forgot herself" again, and she committed such sins against all the rules of the stage and against its traditional "truth" that one of our authorities was even stumped by the fact.

In some speech about Yermolova, Vladimir Nemirovich-Danchenko told the following: he was rehearsing Ostrovsky's *Talents and Admirers* where Yermolova played the role of Negina. And in the third act, when a letter is being read, the following mishap happens: the scene has a single lamp. The poor room is lit by a single lamp and doesn't have any other sources of light. Maria Nikolayevna, as she is supposed to, begins reading the letter next to the lamp, seeing as it's dark everywhere else. But as she becomes more and more carried away by what's in the letter, she, unnoticed by herself, moves farther and farther away from the lamp and soon ends up in the farthest possible corner, where (if we take into account that the room has a single, small lamp) it must be very dark and essentially impossible to read. However, this deterred Yermolova not a single bit, and she continued to read the letter and deliver her monologue with fervor.

"What was I to do?" Nemirovich-Danchenko continues the story. "She was acting so well, so infectiously . . . I thought about it, thought about it some more, and decided not to interrupt her, to leave things as they were. Not because she couldn't have done it more naturally, but because it would probably have been worse than what she was doing then."

So what's the issue? It's true, it turned out rather awkward – she read a letter in darkness . . . But why, then, when Yermolova does it, it does not bother me (an audience member)? Why don't I notice this "mistake"?

The issue is very simple. There's a lamp on the table. That means that the letter should be read next to it, next to the light. This is the "truth" of the stage. But this isn't the "truth" at all, it's artificial: there are hundreds of other lights shining onstage: the footlights, the floodlights, the spotlights – it's very bright onstage . . . the lamp is there as a part of the set, it's there for the atmosphere. If the light onstage were limited to this one lamp, it would be so dark, that we, the audience, would only be able to make out the actors' dark silhouettes.

So, first obeying this theatrical convention, this smallest of small truths, Yermolova soon went from everyday truth to the big truth of art, truth that is true for her (and for all of us). She forgot to maintain all the meaningless conventions and started **living**, truly **living**.

It's bright enough, and there's no need to pretend that you can't notice that – there are *significantly more important things to do.*

If she were stopped and directed to execute the small, mundane truth again, the *big* truth would have been put out. Make your choice. And Nemirovich-Danchenko did just so.

This and other instances remind us of the mistakes in the paintings of great masters where some objects are lit from one side, when others are lit from another, but all together, the painting is enthralling – a true *chef d'oeuvre* of beauty.

The Place of Somnambulistic Automatism in Art

During those heightened creative moments, we witness our mundane integral identities become so diminished that it's as if they don't even exist anymore: the character identity achieved through creative doubling—it lords over everything.

How should we interpret the aforementioned somnambulistic automatism when a person completely loses his integral identity? Why shouldn't we put this down as the highest of artistic transformations?

No, this isn't a higher artistic state. It's not even an artistic state. It's pathology. This isn't a flight to the highest spheres of one's consciousness – it's a descent into its darkest depths.

Here, the split part is completely disconnected from the center and begins to behave like an automaton (it's not for nothing that it bears the name of "automatism"). This doesn't involve all of a person's consciousness, but rather just a tiny part of it. This isn't absolute consciousness – it's *narrowed*.

During moments of artistic creation, we witness an expansion of one's consciousness to the very limits.

Tyutchev [1921: 24] wrote a few wonderful lines about this:

> Oh, the hour of wordless longing;
> I in all, and all in me!

This isn't a retreat from one's identity, but rather an expansion of it. In somnambulistic automatism, I lose myself, but here, in a moment of creative flight, I **seemingly** lose myself – in reality, I'm confirming myself more and more.

There can't be any talk of loss here – but rather of doubling. And the same Tyutchev [1921: 29] expressed it better in four lines than anyone could have:

> Oh, thou, my wizard soul, oh, heart
> That whelming agony immerses,
> The threshold of two universes
> In cleaving these, tears thee apart.

Cases where one's consciousness narrows also include when an actor forgets himself to such an extent that he can hit, choke, or stab his partners.

This is no longer an expanded artistic state, when "a *perfect* psyche enables a person to fully grasp and synthesize all the images and feelings that he or she is experiencing or that he or she recalls" (see earlier). On the contrary: the *only* thing that he sees is an enemy. This is self-forgetfulness – it's a shift, but downwards, not upwards – deep into pathology. This isn't a creative flight, but rather a descent in somnambulistic automatism. It's a case of psychological dislocation.

Distribution of Attention

We can observe undistributed attention or a narrowing of one's consciousness (which is the same thing) in primitive people, emotional ones, acutely impulsive ones, and, finally, people in pathological states (epilepsy, atherosclerosis, etc.).

Intellectually willful people have normally distributed attention. This requires some effort on their part, but it's achievable.

On the contrary, people with affectively abstract reactions (outside of their impulsive moments), whose attention bears signs of *diffusion* – they have an *increased distribution of attention*.

If their attention is distributed (rather than narrowed and focused), the quality of the work *increases* and the work itself becomes *easier*.

This can be explained by the fact that people of this type approaching each of their tasks affectively (or with an excess of excitement or disdain) – naturally the rapid changes in focus of attention weaken this affectivity.

This explains the benevolent effect achieved upon the affective type by "physical task" or maybe even by "publicness"!!! After all, the audience is another distracting factor that could somewhat diffuse and weaken a *narrowing* of their consciousness. Which is confirmed by the phenomenon that some people who can't accomplish some difficult experiment in the solitude of their office *can* accomplish it given an audience, in front of their students.

There exists a pathological distribution of attention, when people are restless, unable to spend more than a minute in a single state or concentrating on some one thing ("I lie down, I want to go some other place, I go there, I want to lie down, I don't even know why").

Evidently, weakened by this illness, the psyche constantly shifts the focus of its attention as a defense mechanism, seeing as a more stable dominant would exhaust it even further – it couldn't bear the strain of it.

This sickly instability finds refuge with tasks that dictate a stable and organized *change* of focus, which eases the work of the fatigued psyche.

An interesting experiment on attention distribution was conducted in Moscow in a school for mentally retarded children. For an hour, the children did handwork and simultaneously listened to somebody read.

The results of the experiments were unexpected: all of those students who were usually attentive, under normal circumstances, *couldn't* do this work; and on the contrary, children that were difficult to teach, those with high motor excitability, behaved themselves and did good work.

"Distribution of Attention" and Genius

One could (and under normal circumstances one should) be able to maintain a multitude of constellations in one's mind, like, for example: two interpretations of one notion, parts of one sentence, the many parts of a work of art, etc.; moreover, not only do these parts *not get in each other's way – they even mutually strengthen each other*.

And really, absolute *unity* of consciousness (when one's consciousness has only a single focus at a given moment), just as Janet points out in his *Psychic Automatism*, happens only in extremes. It either occurs on the step of extreme pathology ("like catalepsy, when an exhausted psyche is incapable of registering multiple sensations at once"), or if one is a *genius* ("psychological unity during moments of great intellectual upliftment, when a *perfect psyche enables a person to fully grasp and synthesize all the images and feelings* that he or she is experiencing or that he or she recalls"). "But usually, one's consciousness isn't so low or so high (as in a case of genius): it stays at a moderate height, that at which one's consciousness contains a multitude of images, but fails to systematize them" (Janet).

For example, I see a mass of objects and people around me, but they're individualized, not synthesized into one. *The moment of synthesis is the moment of crossing over the threshold*. Before the threshold, there's a multitude of objects; beyond the threshold – a unity of all objects.

"You must believe . . . " [in Stanislavsky's teaching]. But how can I believe if I'm an integral person? I'm not *insane*!

"Believing" means *doubling*. The *"truth"* of the stage. It's not at all the same thing as mundane truth. But how is it different? It's the truth of one's other identity – that achieved through the process of doubling.

But it's not just the "other identity" – what about the lights? the audience? The truth of the stage isn't just the truth of the other identity – *it's a combination of two truths: that of the character-self* **and** *of the personal self.*

★★★

Creativity in art is the union 1) of everything that exists, that surrounds me, that I perceive with 2) the *personal*, 3) my character–identity and *its realities*, 4) cognizance of the fact that I am creating and 5) the feeling of the audience, 6) the idea [of the play (?)].

★★★

However, we should keep in mind that we don't perceive things in parts, but in *structures*.

This completely contradicts the "synthesis" that was just described.

And what, in essence, *is* synthesis? Isn't it *primitive* **structural** *perception*?

★★★

Unity with a character is, at first, doubling, followed by creative unity. This is just an outline. In reality, doubling and unity occur **simultaneously**. And doubling strengthens unity.

P.S. It's the unity of both the character–identity and the personal, formerly integral identity (or whatever remains of it). This is what explains the seeming artistic *convention*.

★★★

But what is unity? The sum of all of its parts? No.

Individual words: "wins," "steady, "slow," "race" . . . And here they are, put together: "slow and steady wins the race."

This is an example of unification.

Details of a picture (especially in film) and the picture all at once in a single impression.

The parts and the details don't get in each other's way – rather, they strengthen one another and grant life to each part.

This is where different "unities" come from: unity of a single object without its connection to anything else, or unity in a broad synthesis of thousands of objects, facts, and ideas.

A midway point between these two extremes is our usual state: we grasp many objects, there's a lot going on in our head, but it's not systematized, it doesn't obey a single ideal.

On an Integral Identity

What is this?

Complete integration?

Yet "completeness" is a very big issue – it includes all of my potential abilities and knowledge and skills.

When does it happen that a person has reached *all* of his potential?

Wouldn't that be something truly extraordinary?

Our problem is that we live and act partly, *not wholly* (with all our hearts, minds, and other qualities) – you do something, think about it, and then regret it. You make a mistake, and then you see yourself that you've done something foolish.

Maybe we should interpret one's identity as one's *usual*, mundane, *middling identity* or *personality*? It's more well-balanced, sans rises and falls, sans explosions and depressions? It's perfect for everyday use.

Evidently, we'll have to do exactly this – otherwise, we'll get confused. We have to establish the concept of an *integral* identity as *relative*, not absolute.

On Potential

Inside me, there is an animal and a genius, ice and fire. But they don't always manifest themselves. "Inside" Stesha Herzog, there was a brilliant balancer, but she could've remained hidden until the end of her days.

I could carry around some poison with me, but it could rest in my pocket until the end of my life.

I could be a carrier of plague bacilli, but if I don't spread them among others, it's as if they didn't exist.

When we're talking about an integral identity, can we involve our potentials (as parts of an integral identity)? Of course not.

On the Strength of Thought and on One Thought's Capability to Displace Everything Else

Doubling is fine as it is, but a character isn't just me or some additional storey of mine – it's a *whole* identity. A *person*. Polonius, Macbeth . . . He exists somewhere outside me. I either have to "step into his shoes" or "let him in" – at least, according to the best actors in the school of "experiencing."

Yes, it looks like we're dealing with the process of summoning and injecting into ourselves another, foreign person.

What is this "other, foreign person"?

Does he really exist or is it all just self-deception and fiction?

Does the image that is projected onto the wall or screen truly exist? Yes and no.

Factually, there is nothing on the wall – the wall is empty, flat, and cold . . .

But why, then, is the heart of my girlfriend still hammering, why do I still have tears in my eyes?

Similarly, our artistic creativity is just the fleeting shadows cast by our magical *imagination*.

The other, "foreign person" is also a fleeting, elusive shadow. It's all a product of our imagination, fantasy, and, all things considered: *thought*.

The power of our thoughts and our imagination is extraordinarily great. We just have to look around to see it.

How many people stumble about, dragging their feet, ready to die, just because some near-sighted doctor told them that "their heart isn't keeping up?" And how many of them get better after a knowledgeable specialist says two-three words about how, in reality, there's actually "nothing wrong" and that it was just a diagnostic error.

How many intelligent, resourceful, and kind people, when in public, lose their self-control, become inept and silly (this "public" often standing several steps below their gifted and refined selves) – and why? Because they even considered the possibility that they could make a mistake, say something improper, lose their bearing . . .

It won't take much out of you to walk across a plank lying on the ground, even if it's very windy, but if you throw that plank across two roofs, then unless there's no wind whatsoever, you won't take even two steps.

So why is it surprising when an actor with an ardent imagination, with delicate sensitivity, and the responsiveness of a feather to the slightest gust of wind – why is it surprising that *he's entirely under the control of his imagination and his thoughts*?

That's the only kind of person that can be an artist.

Truth be told, this isn't a new idea. It's so old that it's even a bit uncomfortable to linger on it for too long.

More than 300 years ago, Shakespeare used Hamlet to say it best:

> Is it not monstrous that this player here,
> *But in a fiction*, in a dream of passion,
> Could force his soul so to his own *conceit*
> That *from her working* all his visage wann'd,
> Tears in his eyes, distraction in's aspect,
> A broken voice, *and his whole function suiting*
> *With forms to his conceit*? and all for nothing!
> For Hecuba!
> What's Hecuba to him, or he to Hecuba,
> That he should weep for her?

A modest actor will think: oh, so *that's* the kind of sensitivity and responsiveness that you need! I've got no chance! I'm probably not an actor . . . this isn't a profession that I'm suited to.

That might be the case, but it might also be the case that there's no need for his resolve to weaken: after all, *it's possible to awaken and develop* this sensitivity and responsiveness in yourself. Maybe it's just dampened by habit.

Let's look at this in practice: do we heed our thoughts or not?

Right now, you're sitting or lying down with this book in your hands . . . Let it be as is. Now, put the book down and think to yourself: "my right hand is raised up to the ceiling." Do you notice how your shoulder's muscles have almost imperceptibly tightened? As if they're **already** lifting your arm. Feel it? Of course.

Now, do this: you can *green-light* yourself and allow your shoulder's muscles to raise your arm more and more, or you can *shut it down* – halt the begun movement.

Here's more: "something is dripping onto your book from the ceiling." Didn't you immediately begin to turn your head upwards towards the ceiling?

Green-light yourself, *don't resist the already-begun movement*, and you've already done some work today with regards to training you to heed your thoughts.

Usually, we behave like this: we immediately get an impulse, the muscles instantly begin to act, but we reflexively and involuntarily, out of habit, stop ourselves, *we don't green-light ourselves* and, little by little, destroy the involuntariness and responsiveness to our thoughts that we naturally possess and that we manifested when we were children.

Look at them! Look at how easily and unobstructedly they react to everything!

That's exactly the quality that we're looking for. And experience has shown us that it's difficult to develop it.

The most important thing is not to require or expect immediate results from yourself.

You have to begin with what's simplest: the simplest and most primitive exercises that were just described (like "raising your hand" or "drops, dripping from the ceiling").

Then, quantity will become quality: your arms and legs won't be the only things responding to your thoughts – so will your whole psyche.

Soon, you'll be amazed how a single thought can cause you to become another, almost foreign, person – you begin to move, act, perceive your surroundings and react to them completely differently than you are wont to, and instead do it as "him."

6

The Subconscious Nature of Creativity

Different Types, Forms, and Grades of Creativity

There are more than enough glimmers of creativity in our lives. We've grown so used to them that we don't even pay attention to them anymore, or at least, we don't interpret them as such. And in the meantime, a skillful turn of phrase is artistic and creative; a well-timed and instinctive movement without any preparation – a jump, a fall, a blow – is art.

It's as if the word or action was not a result of an association by contiguity, as if it weren't crudely automatic, but were instead brought about by some intelligent idea that I didn't even notice in my haste; either it flickered too quickly in my mind or it didn't even show up there and instead influenced me from my subconscious, which I cannot track.

We are not in control of all of these subconscious processes. Just like we don't control other functions: digestion, circulation, etc. But just like these are quite real, so are our other psychological reserves. They're complex, manifold, almost entirely unstudied, but are way mightier even than internal secretions that caused such a stir.

I hope to discuss the subconscious and the connections between art and reflexes in detail in the next book.

Now, I return again to the *glimmers* of art and the grains that we spill without even thinking about it wherever we go. Astute ideas and observations, witty words that pop up on their own, without any effort or strain, at dinner, while out for a walk, during friendly conversation. Can we not compare them with an artist's drawing, when, in the middle of a conversation, his pencil slides across the paper on its own, and it's almost like the transparent landscapes and delicately etched profiles appear on their own. Sketches, hints, outlines.

In contrast to this, a great work of art (a novel, a painting, a role) or a philosophical or scientific essay (that's supported by research) require long and hard work, massive endurance, patience, continued enthusiasm, and, in general, "work."

There are people that are capable of enduring this prolonged pressure; there are few of them, and the vast majority is satisfied with small, random finds – sparks of art. And they're not even a majority – *everybody* else is like that.

Naturally, someone who is capable of creating something great also has the ability to create lesser works, and someone who is capable of small feats can create something great under the right circumstances: paint a great painting, publish a book, play a difficult role.

With regard to quality, despite its complexity and scope, such work doesn't necessarily have to be very great. Its "greatness" depends on the greatness of the creator himself.

The greater the work, the more original it is, the deeper it is, and more horizons does it discover; it carries us little people away from our mundane lives into the realm of greater truths and, without actually taking us anywhere, it allows us to see the higher truths in our unnoticeable, annoying, and seemingly insignificant and unnecessary everyday existence.

★★★

There are many different kinds of creativity. There are . . . very funny ones.

In terms of mechanics, they're no different from others – the difference stems solely from motivational factors.

At night, you'll see all kinds of horrors in the woods: your fantasy transforms a bush into a horde of lurking bandits; the sound of your own footsteps turns into the clamor of horses . . . and it's all from fear.

What *don't* we get as a result of boredom, idleness, and emptiness of life? So often, we observe various though-out forms of enthusiasm – both in ourselves and others. We suddenly get enthusiastic about whatever: activities, ideas, people . . .

For example, we should put common cases of imagined love in this category . . .

Many fantasies stem from perversion, debauchery and other things of this sort . . .

There are many different kinds of creativity and all sorts of gradations – from the smallest to the largest that astound with their size and scope. From the smallest and tasteless ones to the greatest ones, full of deep intuition.

And despite these differences, they're still all called *creativity* or *art*.

And not just works of different authors – often, a single author's works are such a motley collection that it's difficult to believe: did the same hand create both works?

The explanation is very simple: if the work was hastily done, in one sitting, and wasn't done well as a result of various reasons, then its value and greatness depend entirely on the author's state of being at the moment of creation.

After all, the very same person, at times, can be small and insignificant, even crude, even vulgar, cynical, and tasteless; at others, he is host to a glimmer of great thought and inspiration.

This is where the difference comes from: one moment, it's the primitive and uncomplicated art of a tribal barbarian, and the next – it's that of a refined artist, a paragon of his time. And sometimes, it's even greater: in one swoop, the *artist* intuitively reaches *far beyond the limits of his time*. And there are but a few people among his contemporaries that are able to understand him. True comprehension and acknowledgement comes significantly after his death . . .

The Formula of Life and the Formula of Creativity

It's a hot summer day . . . what's better than sitting under a shady apple tree, listening to the crickets, watching the clouds, breathing in the fragrance of the earth, grass, and flowers? You don't want to move . . . you could just sit and sit and sit . . . Your eyelids begin to droop, your eyes close, and you fall into a sweet sleep . . .

Suddenly, something falls through the branches! . . . Who is it?! . . . What is it?!! . . . Is it a rock?

It's nothing, calm down, everything is fine: an apple fell down. A beautiful, big apple . . . How could you pass it up? It's delicious, juicy, one side warmed by the sun, like blood, the other cold like a mountain stream . . .

651

Such are the psychological mechanics of life: *I* exist with all my habits, with my life experience, tastes, desires, with my physical and psychological state of being in the current moment. (Let's designate this *I* with the letter "a.")

Plus whatever is influencing me from the outside. In the given instance, the apple's fall and the apple itself (let's designate this influence with the letter "b").

This influence evokes a reaction within me.

In this case, the reaction was such: at first, I was scared from the suddenness and was ready to defend myself in case there was an evil plot or a foolish prank. Once I understood what just happened, another reaction arose: I calmed down, I smiled. I looked at the apple, liked it, a third reaction popped up – I picked up the apple, took a bite . . .

Let's designate the reaction (to the influence) with the letter "c."

Having combined all in one, we can derive the following simple formula:

$$a + b = c.$$

In other words, I + influence from without or within (a fact) = my response to the influence (life).

Such is the formula of **life**. The formula of its **mechanics**. Everything that we do, everything that happens on its own – it's all life.

And there's no reason to regard creativity as anything other than one of the manifestations of life. Maybe a higher manifestation than our mundane and everyday ones, but it's still a manifestation of *life*.

Millions of people before Newton saw how apples fell . . . And? If it fell, that means that it was ripe or that a worm loosened it up: Thank god it didn't hit me on the head. Now to pick it up and eat it.

But the hot-blooded head of the 24-year-old philosopher had spent a lot of time lately thinking about the stars, the movement of the planets, the reasons! . . . Why do the worlds move so harmonically? What power moves them, what power holds them in place? What laws do these powers follow? . . .

The apple falls! It's big, beautiful . . . juicy, delicious . . . Why did it fall? what brought it down?.. what pushed it from the top and hit it on the ground?

Or maybe it wasn't pushed, but pulled, as if by a magnet? All across the globe, if you throw something up in the air, it always comes down to the earth . . . Maybe the earth really is one irresistible magnet?

And could it be that the earth pulls not just what's within its atmosphere? Could it be that it pulls other planets? . . . and then the planets and the sun would also be pulling on *it*? . . . This mutual attraction – is it what causes celestial bodies to spin and cycle around each other? . . .

The bold thought tears into the hidden properties of nature and, like lightning, striking the brain, nearly short-circuits the wires in the young mathematician's head.

Every student now knows the law of universal gravitation and follows it . . . with the brave steps of an everyman – apples fall just like they used to, and millions of people continue to pick them up and eat them . . .

As before: a + b = c.

And only for Newton, for people whose "*I*" is built differently – the everyday is consumed by a single great idea, a single drive.

Not one little detail of life will slip by without slamming into this main thing. And even if the detail is insignificant, it holds so much content and richness for the Newtonian "*I*," and it's so burning hot that the tiniest collision results in an explosion. An explosion, a storm, a hurricane.

But this Newtonian "*I*" consists not just of richness and heat that can cause an instant ignition — it also contains unimaginable sensitivity and acuity.

It's like the subtlest electroscope . . . You don't even have to touch it, you just have to walk past it, and the wondrous instrument will already be rustling, its heart beating.

By virtue of these qualities, contrary to the ordinary a + b = c, the life and creativity of Newtons should be designated differently:

A + b = C.

Great creativity in science, art, technology, and life is one and the same: the "*I*" of the creator is always special (richer, restless, searching, more sensitive to some things and indifferent of others); it collides with a fact, and (regardless of whether the fact is great or small) the result is big and unexpected.

For one person, the insignificant fall of an apple reveals the laws of universal motion.

Another witnesses small human interactions, hears ordinary, everyday words, and his eyes open up to the laws of power and the beauty of life, and he writes *War and Peace*, *Othello*, *Faust*.

Another, having read a mediocre play, creates the eternal character of the Lady of the Camellias (Duse).

Mochalov takes an insignificant and falsehood-heavy melodrama by Kotzebue called *Misanthropy and Repentance* and turns it into a tragedy. The role of Meinau turns out to be one of his favorite and best roles. The portrait we have of him is in a costume for this role. And he wanted to be buried in that same costume.

One category of people — the vast majority — do not live — they sleep. They sleep and see dreams of their work and desires. They need a catastrophe or a shattering personal misfortune to wake up . . .

Very few people live. (This is the second category.) Their eyes are open, they see and hear . . . And for them life is . . . clear as an orange. They're the ones for whom the sun rises, clouds bring rain, and nature bears fruit.

The third category contains very few people.

Can it be said about a genius that he "sleeps" or "lives" or something else? He exhibits an inordinately subtle organization that can see all of life at once with all its beauty, greatness, and mystery from a single, tiny occurrence or a barely perceptible reflection.

A single apple falls, and we have the laws of motion for the entire universe.

What ordinary mind can juxtapose and compare these two thoughts of its own accord?

But an extraordinary mind needs but a moment to diffuse all the secrets of eternity, but a single line to draw everything limitless and boundless. It fills up his whole soul. It displaces everything. The person himself even disappears. Only the thought remains, a single, all-encompassing feeling. Just one eternally hungry, unstoppable desire. And the person transforms into a blazing torch.

Is this a dream? Is it life?

While burning up, he enlightens, he warms, he burns . . . While burning up, he takes pleasure, he sacrifices, he suffers, and he dies.

An everyman will look on from the outside, regretfully shake his head in bewilderment, and smile, pleased with his own fortune and wisdom: What shook up that poor fellow? Why couldn't he live like everyone! Why all this? What for?

> After all, it's
> . . . all for nothing!
> For Hecuba!
> What's Hecuba to him, or he to Hecuba,
> That he should weep for her?
>   (Shakespeare, *Hamlet*)

There's nothing to be done – such is their nature: a torch is wont to burn, powder – to ignite, and rotten wood – to decay.

"Kazbek": (The Sphere) [Subconsciousness]

[Instead of using the example of a mountainous peak, of "Kazbek," we should rather think of deep, subterranean springs. The Kazbek mountain is high, and it's difficult to reach. But we have to do the opposite – we need to discover hidden founts. –*Author's Note*] Humanity's life experience, its knowledge, the remnants of ancient abilities that give birth to new ones, and, ultimately, all the material that is collected in one's own life – these are the riches that a person owns, here's our Kazbek.

But that's far from everything.

We've gathered quite a lot over the course of our own existence! And we've gathered a lot more than we think.

We see and hear almost everything that occurs next to us, but we don't notice it, we fail to realize it. This seeing and hearing occurs "without our participation." Our apparatuses function automatically and dedicatedly execute their duties. [See Book One, Chapter 7]

Aside from sight and hearing, we have other senses – they are also constantly working.

Finally, there's a sort of *radio* that catches thoughts.

Who *hasn't* been in such a case: as soon as you think of something, your conversation partner is already saying it. Sometimes, he says the exact thought that was in your head verbatim.

Either he caught it from you or you caught it from him – it doesn't matter. There are many instances of completely identical momentous inventions being created at the same time on opposite ends of the globe.

Now, there is no miracle here – the radio has dissipated the mystery. It will probably uncover even more, but for now, this is enough. Evidently, everybody has their own "radio transmitter" and "radio receiver." And we use this instrument to perceive. How much? Probably, like with other senses – much more than we think.

The foreseer-poet's words, which used to sound like mysticism, now easily make sense in our materialistic worldview:

> Numerous in space are invisible forms and inaudible sounds,
> Numerous wondrous fusions of the letters and lights,
> Yet only he will convey them, who knows how to see them and hear them,
> And, having grasped just one line in a drawing, just one chord and one sound,
> Pulls the entire creation with it into our open-eyed world.
>   (A.K. Tolstoy [1893: 248])

★★★

But there are sometimes droughts . . . a river can become utterly emaciated, barely threading itself over the riverbed, like a silentiary . . . Rarely does it give some sign of life, falling in a thin stream from a high rock.

A frightful horror – a drought in the artist's soul!

Terek is spared from droughts, as it takes its start from Kazbek, covered by eternal snows.

But what are we to do?

★★★

An artist doesn't dare hibernate, he doesn't dare despair from random beneficent storms and tempests; he doesn't dare write anything off as bad luck or as utter futility of life.

Search for things yourself, greedily look for the answer everywhere you can!

Life is so rich. You just have to see and hear it. Look harder, listen harder, tune yourself so that you resonate with life, then you'll catch what usually flies past.

If you're tired of people, go into nature. Listen to the sound of the wind, the rustling of leaves, the singing of birds. Look at the trees, the water, the earth. Take a good look at the starry sky. You've probably forgotten that there's something endless, limitless, eternal . . . Steep yourself in that deep blueness.

You must not sleep! You're not a tree, a rock, or a corpse.

If life and nature aren't enough for you, go to art, science, philosophy – give into a book; there are millions of books written by the best people from all times, that imbued them with the ripest and most perfect thoughts they had. They would spend decades thinking everything over before releasing it to the public. Can't that stir something in you, enrich you, interest you?

You're not in the habit of reading and thinking? You must try to excite your passive, inert soul. And, naturally, to get through a book, you'll have to work quite a bit. You have to put in quite a bit of effort in order to get to the top of Mount Beshtau, but aren't you rewarded in spades once you see the fabled sunrise from the mountain top, and the Caucasus under you, and the wilderness around you?

If you're tired of reading and thinking, go to the museum, look at the sculptures and paintings. There are so many wells, and yet you grow sour and whine!

But the main wellspring is in *you*. There lie the eternal snows of Kazbek; their thawing waters will never dry up, and they will never betray you. The experience of generations doesn't vanish – it is transferred *through living, embryo cells*, and that's how whole mountains of limitless experience are layered onto one another. Which is why each and every one of us carries with him the experience of millions of lives – his ancestors. The only issue is in how to descend into these treasuries and make them talk?

★★★

We perceive more than we realize. Let that be true. But what's the point of that if, on one hand, all of it is lost in some "abyss" that you can't get to, and on the other – it's simply forgotten. Quickly sift through your memory: does it have much left from school science classes that you dedicated 10 years of your life to?!

But it's the same with your memory as it is with perception. We think that we've forgotten something, but it turns out that it's still there.

There is a classic case that was in all the psychiatric journals in its time. [I relay this story from memory. Its essence, at any rate, remains the same. *–Author's Note*]

A common woman ended up in a hospital because of some acute infection.

In a feverish state, she started speaking in some strange language. Soon, everyone in the town knew about it. Spiritualists seized at the opportunity. They concluded that a creature from the beyond was speaking through her – a "spirit." The whole scientific world was dragged out of the hay. The language that she spent hours speaking quite easily and freely wasn't European, Asian, or African – it wasn't any existing language on the planet.

Experts in ancient and dead languages were brought in – they couldn't understand anything either. Evidently, this was a "very, very ancient spirit" – Assyria, Babylon, Egypt!

Extraordinary measures were taken. A very old professor who knew cuneiform was brought in. They wheeled him in a wheelchair, placed him next to the woman's bed . . .

As soon as she started speaking . . . "Huh, your spirit is speaking perfect Chaldean," he said, "Quite freely and without a single mistake!"

The spiritualist's triumph knew no bounds: it was obviously a message "from the other side." The woman couldn't know Chaldean. More than that: she was illiterate!

The professor translated the "spirit's" words, and they turned out to be very wise and wonderful, not at all the nonsense that spirits usually blabbered about during spiritual séances.

Once her fever started abating, the "spirit" visited the woman more and more rarely, until, finally, it left her completely, and she fell silent. She returned to health.

But what turned out! . . . Some five years ago, she worked for the professor a few times as a scrubwoman.

As an erudite man is wont to, the professor had his eccentricities. He would unabashedly walk around his home and speak Chaldean out loud for whole hours. Apparently, he needed that to better grasp the language.

Nobody understood him, and nobody even listened. Least of all, the scrubwoman. But nature did its job: not listening, not understanding, not hearing a thing, she memorized every single thing, "wrote it all down" somewhere in her subconscious, and five years later, it all came out.

There you have the power and accuracy of perception! There you have the power and accuracy of memory!

True, in order for the memory to release from its cellars such old, such aged, imported wines, the woman had to be deathly ill. But that's not the point. Nature itself opened up the book of its secrets. Let's get serious. Let's grow cautious and hold our breath, or else we may let its lesson pass right over us![1]

★★★

Alright, let this be a thing. Let us be able to inherit the riches of centuries of experience. Let us even be able to inherit memories from centuries ago.

Let there be entire waterfalls of riches that are poured into us from the cradle.

Let there be a "radio" that receives thoughts transferred through the air.

Let there be all this and more! . . .

But this is just an amassment of material! We have it all, and it lies there, hidden, and sometimes it rears its head. But so what?

Now, if all the different material collided with each other, and if something practical came out of these collisions, then we'd have some use for it. Otherwise: the material is there, and I can't reach it. Sometimes (not when I need or want it to), some bit of information will pop out. What's the use?

But it turns out that it's not just an amassment of material – it's life, and powerful life!

The mathematician, Henri Poincaré [1854–1912] Poincare tells us:

> One morning, walking on the bluff, the idea came to me, with . . . the characteristics of brevity, suddenness and immediate certainty . . . I made a systematic attack . . . and carried all the outworks, one after another. There was one however that still held out, whose fall would involve that of the whole place. But all my efforts only served at first the better to show me the difficulty . . .
>
> All this work was perfectly conscious. Thereupon I left for Mont-Valérien, where I was to go through my military service; so I was very differently occupied. One day, going along the street, the solution of the difficulty which had stopped me suddenly appeared to me. I did not try to go deep into it immediately, and only after my service did I again take up the question. I had all the elements and had only to arrange them and put them together. So I wrote out my final memoir at a single stroke and without difficulty. [Poincaré 1913: 388]

Later, Poincaré [1913: 389] concludes: "Most striking at first is this appearance of *sudden illumination, a manifest sign of long, unconscious prior work.* The role of this unconscious work in mathematical invention appears to me incontestable, and traces of it would be found in other cases where it is less evident."

We aren't brilliant mathematicians, but who among us hasn't been in a similar situation: you struggle and struggle to come up with the solution to some difficult question, and, without coming up with anything, you go to sleep. In the morning, as soon as you recall yesterday's struggles, the answer flickers through your mind, clear, distinct, simple . . . it's as if the work finished itself during the night.

Folk wisdom came up with the well-known saying: "Sleep brings counsel."

Like chemical ingredients in a solution, thoughts find each other . . . kindred ones fuse, while adverse ones fall apart from collisions. The parts make up new ones that don't resemble their parents . . . Sometimes, they find their way out, sometimes they burrow even deeper and stay there. For how long? . . . Who knows!

Time changes them, and, having descended into the depths as a mere coal, they sometimes return to us in the form of a precious diamond.

And there's nothing surprising about it. Why aren't we surprised that food that slips through our mouths is somehow digested and fuses with our bones, our muscles, our blood, and, indirectly, even into our thoughts and feelings.

Why aren't we surprised that, without our reason, desire, or understanding, after nine months, the body of an inseminated woman gives birth to a living, thinking being?

Is it just because our anatomists and physiologists have gotten involved in these spheres?

Yes, it's true, nobody has gotten to a living mind or heart with either knife or microscope. And it's doubtful that they ever will. Something more suitable needs to be invented. And once they do invent this something and take a good look, they'll laugh quite loudly at our precocious skepticism. Let's not give in to the temptation to create some new theory of psychological mechanics.

What's important for us is to know one thing: for some reason or other, nature has bestowed each of us with an enormous, inexhaustible "Kazbek."

The question is: *how* do we get to it?

Or rather: how do we get it to melt and release to us the eternal snows from its peak? That's a practical question. And a question that wholly involves us.

The answer is direct: a technique of creativity.

We can call it a psychological technique, an internal technique, a spiritual technique – it doesn't matter.

It can be the shallow technique of an imitator.

The slightly deeper technique of the actively-willful.

And, finally, the technique of passion, the technique of affect, the technique of tumultuous stream from our "Kazbek," *the technique of mobilizing and rallying all the forces of a person's soul.*

Note

1 Although Demidov does not provide any sources for this medical case, such cases are certainly known to scientists. As recently as April of 2010, the media around the world reported a case when a teenage Croatian girl, upon waking from a 24-hour coma, was unable to speak her native Croatian, but was able to communicate perfectly in German. *Telegraph* (April 12, 2010) reported that at the time of her illness, "the girl had only just started studying German at school and had been reading German books and watching German TV to become better, but was by no means fluent, according to her parents."

7

Automatisms

We've grown so used to talking about ourselves: "*I*" . . . So confidently do we consider ourselves the masters of our thoughts, desires, and feelings . . .

Few of us have ever gotten the thought: Do I truly, according to my own choice and desire, want this thing or that? Could it be that I 'feel like' this or that without any intervention on my part, and I just simply: 'feel like it,' 'am carried away,' and that I'm not the one doing the wanting?

Am I thinking of one thing or another on my accord? In most situations, I'm "just thinking" . . .

Here, even today . . . and every day – what is it? . . . We're awoken, or we wake up, a few involuntary stretches, and the getting up, the getting dressed, the washing, the breakfast – it's all done on its own, habitually . . . we automatically look at the clock, put on a coat, and then we're outside.

And then, everything is done on its own . . . As if we were wind-up dolls . . .

Any person you meet on the street . . . look closely into his eyes, and what do you see? Is he living in the moment, is his attention focused on what's doing? It's as if **he's** not even there, **he** is "absent," he's off doing his own thing: either in the future or the past . . . What he's doing in the moment is done essentially without his participation, on its own, habitually, automatically, mechanically: it's done, thought, desired, loved, hated.

His life will pass, his final moments will come, he'll look back on his life, and – what a strange feeling! It's as if he never lived through all that . . . Everything that he wanted to do (or at least he thinks that he wanted to do it) – he didn't do any of it . . . It all passed him by: his successes and his misfortunes . . . it all seemed to have happened beyond his will.

I haven't managed to do anything, I haven't *seen* anything – I was in a whirlwind: my surroundings, bodily desires, those of my stomach or my sex, my own ambition was swirling me around, my vanity, traditions that were imbued in me since my childhood.

And where's my life? Evidently, life is something completely different.

For example, "I." Where is my "I"? And what was it doing this whole time?

And even now: am I the one who's pondering all this? Could this work be the work of that same automatic mechanism that looks on at one's past as if it were the life of another, and, like a cunning mechanical calculator, derives mathematical roots from its past?

★★★

Is everything, from the simplest to the most complex things, automatic and mechanical? From the most shallow to the deepest? From the simple reflex of chemotaxis or heliotaxis to the highest artistic intuitions, to prophecy, prediction, and premonition? [Chemotaxis – the drive of simple microorganisms to attractive, external chemical irritants. Heliotaxis – the same for luminous irritations. –*Author's Note*]

There are movements in science that are aiming at this question in the most threatening manner. There are others that do not agree with it. Only the future will show which is right.

Pondering this won't bring anyone any harm. On my side, I purposefully narrow things down to this one assumption: let's assume that *everything is automatic* – I apply that to the creative process, and you'll be more and more convinced that it's not just interesting and entertaining, but most importantly, it's incredibly practical and fruitful.

Associations

We've grown used to hearing certain words together, contiguously, and they are firmly connected to one another. Just as we grow used to seeing a friend of ours always in the same costume, like a military uniform, because this person and his costume are inextricably combined in our mind.

Boris – Godunov. *Leonardo* – da Vinci. *Snow* – White. We've grown so used to that these words are always together, one after the other, that when we hear one, we want to append the other, connected one. In psychology, this connection is known as an *association* (connection, coupling).

There are different kinds of connections: from the simplest, like in this case, to the most complex, ones where you aren't even able to reason out why one is connected to the other.

A simple connection like this one is known as "*association by contiguity*."

The simplest example of association by contiguity, the most elementary and lowest one – the manner of actors to gabble out lines from a play when we hear even one of a line's words. If an actor hears the beginning of a phrase that's been stuck in his ears, he can't restrain himself from gabbling out its ending.

A conversation is happening off to the side. Someone says the familiar combination of words "To be" . . . By doing so, they tug on a thread that's hanging very close. And tied to the thread are very different objects. The order in which they're tied might have at one time made sense, but now there's just the fact: they're tied together. This tied bundle isn't located very deep – it's right on the surface. And it's enough to just barely graze the thread in order to pull one of these things off. It falls down, and the other objects tumble on down after it – after all, they're all tied together. "To be" . . . and instantly, out of nowhere, you get "or not to be . . . that is the question."

What does the flesh have to do with anything? Or the dew? That doesn't matter – it popped out on its own, and now I feel much better!

One word from the phrase is well suited to the moment – there you go – everybody likes it, everybody finds it ingenious, witty . . . the "hero" casts a triumphant gaze on all those present . . .

But, as you see, in this case, there's no trace of cleverness or creativity – it's the lowest form of automatism.

A more complex association is *association by similarity*.

An object that appears in my field of vision evokes in my memory not something that's directly connected to it, but some other object that resembles it. There is a fountain on one of Moscow's squares, and next to it – a marble figure – instantly, without my lifting a finger, the image of another fountain in the gardens of Versailles pops up . . . True, that one is much more grandiose and picturesque, but there's obviously something in common, seeing as I remembered the one from Versailles.

The third kind: association by contrast.

You run into a dwarf on your way somewhere: two, three words about him, and the conversation jumps to the topic of giants.

The thought of giants is evoked automatically, but the automatic mechanism is much more complex than the thread of contiguity that I just described. It's as if there's an unconscious drive to equilibrium: a dwarf appears, it's very unusual, and he's very small . . . Reflexively, the imagination defends itself, desiring to restore the disrupted equilibrium, to balance the scales, and it puts a giant on the other half of the scales, or even a whole group of giants, as many as are necessary to bring about balance.

In this way, associations by similarity and contrast imply some hidden work, some *combination* of materials that have been received earlier in life.

There is never a single, isolated impression or feeling. We perceive our surrounding environment holistically. With all our feelings at once, including those that have been studying by science, as well as those that currently escape us, and which are therefore officially unacknowledged. We cognize some things at the time, but the majority of them smuggle themselves past the guards, ending up in our hidden treasure house, and remaining there until the right time.

Let's think about that fountain in Versailles again.

I lived in Versailles for a week, in the park itself at the end of a hot summer, when the yellow leaves were only just beginning to fall. Along with a very kindhearted youth [Igor Alekseev, Stanislavsky's son] whom I accompanied, spent whole days running from part of the desert park to the other. The sky was clear, the sun was blaring, water gurgled beneath the shade of the giant trees, the air smelled of freshly damp soil. The marble gods wholly fused with the surrounding nature; the trees poked branches through their arms, covered them with falling leaves . . .

Some of the marble was even covered in moss, which made it meld even more closely with the nature.

And in the evening, when there wasn't a soul in the park, we would sneak in, like thieves, felt our way almost blindly to our favorite fountains . . . it was uncanny and exciting . . . we tried to look at them in the almost absolute darkness . . . and in the rustling of the leaves and the gurgling of the water, we heard human whispers, the whooshing of dresses, the scuffling of feet along the ground, and it seemed like we were listening to the life of the old Versailles: somebody was running down the path, music was playing in one of the far-off palaces, sensual perfumes filled the air . . .

Having heard enough and having whispered enough to each other about everything we've dreamed up, the excited, youthful fantasizers would creep back to their room, bury themselves in bed, and, full of poetic thoughts, they would soon be asleep . . .

Many years have passed since then . . .

. . . but if I see a marble figure in a garden, then immediately I see Neptune, erupting from the water, covered with golden leaves, or Apollo's grotto . . .

Walking down a prosaic Moscow boulevard at night, I'll hear the rustling of leaves and the whispers and swishes of Versailles, I'll imagine the elusive, animated marble figures . . . I'll hear an old French waltz or polonaise, and I'm seized by the joyous feeling of evening promenades . . . the smell of the damp earth . . . any trifle evokes memories of the past . . .

One insignificant allusion, and you don't just see images – you sense sounds and smells, as well as the state of being you were in back then, the feeling of your power, youth, and, most likely, joy.

The associations here are complex, multi-level . . .

A flickering thought evokes not only a memory or an image, but the *sensation* that accompanied it at the time, as well as *desires* that commanded me; in a word – it's a whole slice of life.

Regardless of how complex this might be, still – *is anything new being created here*? Something that has already happened is merely being recalled.

You would think that nothing is being created. But is that true?

As time goes on, while lying in our treasuries, facts of the past manage to change significantly: some parts vanish, some details are added, and these facts are presented entirely unlike how they appeared back then – truth be told, they appear how we want them to appear: either too good or too bad. For the most part, they're good: "What has passed we will find endearing" [Pushkin 1959: 96].

And so, this involuntary and unconscious adaptation of one's past, the changes and new coats of paint that are applied to one's memories – if that's not the creation of something completely *new*, if it's not *creativity* – neither is it just *remembering*, or photographic representations of something that has come to pass; there are alterations.

If this isn't *creativity*, then it's at least *transfiguration*.

Usually, things are "transfigured" on their own: facts of past simply become landmarks, one's fantasy is given free rein . . . and wonderful pictures are the result! I like them so much that I get carried away and begin to believe in them myself.

This too is "transfiguration." The only difference is that the memories are *transfigured not entirely unconsciously*. The person *sees* how this process unfolds within him and even *participates* in the work, helps out.

He seems to be overseeing the process of transfiguration.

The Work of Associations, Coordinated by a Single, Main, Idea (Artistic and Scientific Creativity)

Sometimes, a spoken word, a witnessed picture, a heard tale, a sung song – they do not evoke memories, but instead result in new, unseen images: you see new scenes, you hear new melodies . . . your fantasy carries you away into a hitherto unseen world.

It's all new; it is created.

It is creativity.

All of the new is usually a result of the combination of many things that a person saw or heard . . . but the combinations are so unique, unexpected, and, at the same time, convincing, that they appear to be living beings, birthed unto the world.

Looking around the room while waiting for an audience with the governor, Lermontov saw a shabby palm in a wooden tub . . . and suddenly, he got a thought . . . the thought quickly transforms into a fully-fledged image, and right on the spot, he puts down on a piece of paper the famous: *Palm branch of Palestine, oh tell me . . .*

For us average folk, for the most part, these images, ideas, and melodies are sporadic, muddled, and chaotic: something flickers through my mind, and I barely even noticed it . . .

And the thing that flickered past might have even been crucial, valuable . . .

We often see an interesting thought be developed and transformed, and only in hindsight do we realize that that same thought had once flickered through *our* heads . . . It's just that we didn't acknowledge it at the time, we didn't give it safe haven, we sent the timid wanderer away in scorn . . .

A brilliant thought flies into one's mind, like a bird flies into an empty church . . . it zooms around for a bit . . . nobody needs it – somebody even looks at it in disdain: "bah, a bird!" and it flies away . . .

But not all heads are built like this.

There are people with imaginative natures — no bird of passage would ever escape from them. And not just thoughts — not a single allusion, hint, *shadow* of a thought can get past these people. Their consciousness firmly grasps onto them, and creates a whole oasis, a whole new world — all for this barely perceptible fragment of a thought.

In these cases, an idea can so enthrall a person that he cannot oppose it and has to look for a way to express it and breathe real life into it.

Even after its birth, it doesn't leave him right away — which is what happened in Lermontov's case. Thrown off the track of mundane concerns with which he arrived to the governor's office, and still under the influence of creative excitement, he handed the governor the verse instead of the petition.

In Lermontov's story, we have the classic case of an artistic creation being born. When something new is imbued with a single idea, and it manages to fit in a single, harmonic form (while the form and content fuse so much that they transform each other) — then something entirely new is born. This third something has its own personality, its own style, and its own laws — this new thing is an *artistic* creation.

Its emergence into the world is always an event, just like the birth of a new being. And it really is alive, like an organism.

And it instantly dies if it falls into crude, unskilled hands.

Try your hand at the same *Palm Branch of Palestine, oh tell me*: tell it in your own words, i.e. pour the content into another form — that would be the end of it. A new work will appear, and it matters not whether it's worse or better — the point is that it's completely *different*, there won't be anything left of Lermontov.

In an authentic work of art, you cannot separate the form from the content, or else the most important part dies.

★★★

Only men and women of art are called *creators* or *artists*. This is, of course, improper and one-dimensional. A great scientist, a great thinker, a great orator, a great military commander, a great inventor — they are all inevitably great *creators*, great *artists* in their fields. People that lack creativity are copy-machines or, in the best case, simple mathematical tools (like mechanical calculator).

Life won't get very far with only their help.

A Man Is a Creature of Thought

Obviously, everybody believes that they reason — reasoning is like breathing, and there's no need to specially learn it. Reasoning isn't complicated. And this is why everybody believes that they are *smart*.

But *reasoning* isn't simple at all. And very few people know how to do it. And the extent to which we can do so varies.

What is reasoning?

Without getting into a thicket of details, we can say that reasoning is *comparing very different thoughts and leading them to a conclusion*.

As sad as it is to admit, not everybody can juxtapose two different thoughts. And if someone is given three, then they become confused or do something simpler: they only compare two instead of three. Without even noticing it, they throw out the third.

If we give someone *ten* thoughts, then you can imagine what happens . . . In the best case, he'll just take two and subject them to the process, but in the worst: he grabs onto one, the one that's closest to him, and stops. A comical illustration of this – all our meetings and gatherings. Most people are convinced by each and every speaker – whatever the *last speaker* said is correct.

A person who can juxtapose two ideas isn't a fool, but someone who knows how to deal with three at the same time is much smarter. However, one who strives to be considered smart must be able to operate with an unlimited number of ideas.

Where do all of these ideas come from?

Many come externally: ideas that we have to discuss, and many come from within: ideas that we get by association.

The richer that one's associative baggage is, the easier it is for associations to rise up, and ideas come out of one's associative storages more quickly, distinctly, and in greater number; then, a great number of ideas begs to be manifested, perorated, blabbed . . . or, if this process occurs in a smart head, then these ideas are *thought through*.

The process of thinking through can be incredibly quick, almost instantaneous (assuming an advanced "technique" of thinking), or it can be slow and painstaking.

Controlling One's Automatisms

"Take your time!"

Let's take another close look at this wonderful moment. Let's dive into its depths.

An etude is in progress . . . suddenly, a new, unexpected impression!

Before it can even work through it, one's body reacts instantly, and it reacts very primitively: run, jump, grab, scream, blurt something out . . .

What should be done here? The general rule would be – don't get in your own way and *green-light* yourself.

But this will lead to a crude, shallow, motor reflex, akin to a common reaction of the most primitive organisms – a "motor storm."

The received impression results not only in an external, kinetic reflex – internal processes are also triggered, conscious or otherwise.

If you green-light a crude reflex, an external response (movement), you'll block off and even destroy any internal response.

To be more exact, in this case, *rushing* means green-lighting your elementary, external response; i.e. rushing with a *primitive kinetic reflex* means *shutting off the possibility* of a more subtle and complex response. And I'm not talking about "pushing" yourself forwards – I specifically mean *rushing* – what I mean is ripping off an unripe fruit without waiting for it to ripen in full.

It's very subtle work. It's such a subtle difference that you can't immediately comprehend it (immediately "get" it). But in it lies the solution to our seeming contradictions: green-lighting is green-lighting, but . . . not rushing seemingly means impeding. And impeding means not green-lighting, i.e. going against our chief commandment.

Yes, don't green-light, yes, impede. But impede what's crude, primitive, and panicky, in order to let through a deeper and more subtle reaction. This isn't even new – it's just old, but refined. But it's a refinement that opens up a whole new world before us, refinement that allows us to use a *new internal mechanism* and gives us the proper access key.

Don't green-light so that to *green-light* the most important thing: deep *subconscious reactions*.

The described phenomenon carries the good old name of "restraint." This too is a kind of "red-lighting" superfluous impulsivity or impetuosity from overexcitement.

This kind of "red-lighting" – take your time, don't green-light a crude, peripheral reaction – put a break on it – it's no different from being able to *control your automatisms*: I put a stop to one, and others begin to work, unimpeded.

In this way, "red-lighting" is the first attempt to control your automatisms – free one automatism from the harmful influence of other, lesser ones. The lesser ones are constantly trying to break loose – they're ancient.

Perception awakens many different automatisms – currently, we only see two kinds: the old automatism (the *animal, kinetic* one) and, at the same time, a deeper, but younger one – that of *human psychology* . . . a response of the soul . . . Which will triumph? The first, of course – it's stronger.

But we'll take it and put a brake on it ("take your time"). And then, the second will develop – that of the soul.

★★★

"Green-lighting" yourself often leads to muscle spasms: a person is angry, his blood is boiling, and . . . ignoring the calls of subtle psychological and human reactions, he green-lights an animalistic response: he starts punching.

If an actor is so tense that even a fit of punching seems like a brave step on his path of liberation from brakes, then he should follow it, just as long as it's a temporary allowance, a transition to subtler and deeper reactions.

The thing is that there were other reactions, but the actor didn't green-light himself to do them.

This results in a question: why do primitive people (and drunks) so quickly resort to fighting?

Why is this? Do they not green-light subtler reactions? Or are they simply incapable of having subtler reactions?

Probably, they're just incapable of having them (their cerebral cortex is inhibited, after all) – therefore, animals, children, and drunks have but a single step to make from words to fighting, and sometimes even less. People develop subtler reactions gradually, reactions that grow out of imperceptible *traces* of sensations and feelings.

Having undergone many generations of experience, these traces gradually become more and more tangible, and that's when it becomes possible to refer to them as existing, but inhibited by a person (or an actor).

★★★

What about conscious analysis and synthesis? Do they not become superfluous, like the wagon, displaced by the automobile?

Analysis and synthesis were and are one of the greatest achievements of human thought; they are what differentiate the thought process of a person from that of an animal.

And it would be unreasonable to refuse to analyze a role or consider it as a whole, and in its parts. Why shouldn't you divide a role into parts, why shouldn't you work through and assimilate the parts individually if you can't "get" the role as a whole right away?

Or, if we're talking about a complex creative process, why shouldn't you single out some of its obviously noticeable "elements" (like attention, muscular release, etc.)?

Or, after you take the role apart and think through its external and internal qualities, why should you refuse to exercise each of the qualities in yourself; and then, why shouldn't you combine them?

In a word, why shouldn't you employ a rationalistic approach? Why shouldn't you urge yourself on if the work is at a standstill and refuses to go forward?

But there is **another path** to creation and comprehension – the practical path – the path of instincts, the path of automatisms.

You can learn to swim, having first thought through everything that you have to do in advance – how to breathe, how to hold your head, how to move your arms and legs – and only then teaching yourself each step individually. However, you could do it differently: you could do it like animals, tribesmen, and even most "civilized" people do it: go to the water, try your hand at it, and see what comes of it.

The water itself teaches you – your body involuntarily becomes accustomed to its demands, and it tests, verifies, confirms, and quickly becomes used to the new environment.

If we dig around in this process, we can find analysis and synthesis in it too, but the emergence and mutual influence of one on the other are so instantaneous that this process seems entirely unlike thinking through different possibilities, weighing them, and rationally choosing one – in a word, it is unlike most conscious work that we do.

On the contrary, in this case, we find certain automatisms that exist and function beyond the threshold of direct conscious analysis and synthesis.

★★★

The conscious reasoning of a human differs from that of an animal primarily because of analysis and synthesis.

Only analysis and synthesis could have granted humanity precious self-conscience, and with it, the creation of speech, comprehensible language, and ultimately, all kinds of progress: the sciences (like mathematics, physics, chemistry), the arts, and, finally, philosophy.

But regardless of how great human reasoning is when compared with that of animals, we shouldn't forget that it's still very recent, very young: it's still being formed. It's been only a few tens of thousands of years since it came about.

While the reasoning of animals has been formed over millions of years.

And it exists in us, it's also precious: *only in combination with it*, with this formed and tried apparatus, could humanity have grown so quickly.

What is it made up of, this reasoning that has been forming over millions of years?

We don't have the opportunity to witness the incredibly complex path that was treaded from the first, primitive organisms to the human-like ape. And throughout this whole time, all sorts of *automatisms* have been forming in living beings. Thanks to them, living organisms could exist, adapt to their surroundings, orient themselves, and withstand nature's wrath. These automatisms were the primary weapon of living creatures in the fight with their surroundings.

At first, in lesser organisms, automatisms were crudely physiological; after the nervous system became more sophisticated and developed, physiological and kinetic automatisms were joined by emotional, recollective, associational, mental, choice-related, and all kinds of psychological automatisms.

If a living creature has passed through millions of years and myriads of lives and has not only survived, but has even reached the stage of humanity – this is clear evidence that its automatisms are rather well-calibrated.

The job of future progress – not to destroy these automatisms, but combine and harmonically fuse their work with the work of our consciousness. And additionally – create new automatisms, ones that are useful for our lives, work, and art.

★★★

Our work – "the art of living onstage" – is in a very large part, perception, orienting, adapting to circumstances, and, in general – *reacting to the surrounding reality onstage*. Even though the facts and circumstances are, for the most part, imaginary, even though we have to live in the presence of an audience (or even *for an audience* – so that they could see the tiniest nuances of an actor's experiencing), we still have to *live* – react, fight, act. Is this a job for analysis and synthesis? Isn't this, just like life, a job for the hidden *automatisms* that, independently of our will, are tirelessly working every single second?

Conscious analysis and synthesis only *control and direct* (as much as they can) their tireless activity. Sometimes they help, sometimes they hinder, but in general, they try to work with them.

Knowing all this, can we really decline the services of such an ancient and firmly established psychological and physical mechanism?

When we place a rationalistic approach to analysis and synthesis as the *foundation* of our art, what we are doing first and foremost is *halting* the beneficial (and natural) activity of our involuntary automatisms.

To give these automatisms free rein, and to resist ordering yourself to do something ("Here, I must want this and that"), but instead *giving in* to what you want—this device isn't something new, freshly discovered or invented – it precedes humanity.

And although it sometimes makes mistakes that require a conscious effort to fix, we should by no means spurn it.

Taking a close look at different kinds of research, you're led to this thought: isn't the most difficult thing during research throwing away your metaphysical ideas? And, while asking questions of nature, isn't the most difficult thing listening *only to what it's telling you, rather than hinting to it what to answer you*?

Our self-assertive, so-called logical reasoning is wont to jump to conclusions without properly checking all the facts.

Sometimes, these conclusions are correct in their predictions, and sometimes they wind up having a cruel laugh at us.

Towards Automatisms

What we propose [Demidov's School] is a new kind of reasoning. It is reasoning in action. *Reasoning during action – reasoning through action.*

It is awakening your automatisms.

Creativity is a method of reasoning.

Reasoning through creativity is an ancient kind of reasoning, and it shouldn't be discarded, but rather stimulated. It's much stronger than the still green analysis and synthesis.

Automatism as a Foundation of a New School of an Actor's Psycho-Technique

As a result of more than 20 years of work in theatre schools and theatres towards an approach that would bring us closer to *our organic nature*, we developed new principles and methods of an actor's psycho-technique (that can be applied to other forms of art) – methods that are employed by all great artists of the stage (without even noticing it).

Incidentally, two important positions have been cleared up:

1   ***Talent*** – in essence, talent is a series of specific qualities that one has from nature, along with *a predisposition to easily master a corresponding internal technique*. Apparently, this single

correct approach (that obviously needs to be developed further) leads to the cultivation and exercise of both. In this way, if someone isn't very gifted, it's possible to lead them to talent. Of course, if someone is very gifted, then the result is greater. And if someone is naturally talented, then the result is enormous.

2   Is turns out that all this talk of some unspecific and abstract "subconscious" are pretty useless and even harmful for art. It's a fact that creative work and so-called "intuition" exist beyond our conscious field of vision. But words like "subconscious," "superconscious," etc. don't explain anything and don't help advance our work. Twenty years of work have led to an entirely new conviction: *during any creative or artistic work, we employ concrete and specific* **automatisms**. One example of such an automatism that functions quite *autonomously* (like the automatism of a sleepwalker) *is the act of artistically creative* **transformation**.

In the past, I thought that an actor's consciousness splits in two: one part remains as part of the actor's identity, while the other manifests itself as "somebody else," someone who is using the actor's body as a host – Liubim Tortsov, Shylock, Nora, etc. In practice, this isn't "splitting" or "splintering," – it's the *creation of a special automatism* that functions independently according to its own laws. And a person's behavior in these moments is like the flight of an airplane that has been put on autopilot, while the real pilot (the consciousness) merely observes and corrects other, more crucial functions.[1] Actors' automatisms, like "transforming into a character," like the "mutual influence of actor and character," like the "coordination of the condition of the stage and the house," like the "appropriate distribution of physical and psychological power in accordance with the scope of the whole show," etc., etc. All of these automatisms form, evolve, and achieve independence. At the same time, they obey us and become *instruments of our will*.

Up to this point, psychology and medicine have also mentioned automatisms of the human psyche, observing them chiefly among a whole array of pathological processes (splitting of identities, somnambulism, automatic writing). But up to this point, they've concerned themselves with observations, stipulations, and treating these abnormal manifestations of the human psyche. In our school, however, *automatisms are consciously created, consciously exercised, evolved, consciously employed, directed – in a word, there is a completely new relationship between them and their human master.*

Chances are that this can serve as a *new direction* in the study of human psychology.

There's nothing strange or abnormal about the fact that the idea of creating and mastering automatisms was born not in psychological laboratories or the office of a psychiatrist, but in theatre. Naturally, things would be different if the complex and unexplored realm of creativity, and the actor's creativity in particular, was headed and managed by science, but that's not the case. Science has no incentive to jump on this work, whereas theatre, on the other hand, doesn't have the time to wait for proper and reliable scientific help: the curtains always go up, and, if you please – enter a creative state.

Without any concrete, verified, or reliable methods, the actor either has to turn away from creativity onstage as a result of it being capricious, random, and refusing to answer our call, and replace it with the art of craftsmanship – forgery, deft falsification (which is what most actors do), or experiment as they can at their own risk.

This is what the minority that doesn't want to turn into craftsmen does – they want to be *artist-creators* in their field.

Aside from great actors, like Yermolova and the Sadovskys, we had Shchepkin, who tried to unite his ideas and findings that concerned the art of the actor, and closer to our time, we had Stanislavsky. He created a whole "System," a whole school based around evoking a creative state onstage.

But, seeing as he was a great artist of the stage, he wasn't a *thinker* or *researcher*. He became a *"researcher out of necessity."* And he accomplished quite a bit: he explained how to analyze a play so well that it would appear as if there were no better way to go about it. Dividing a play into "bits," external and internal throughactions, breaking a role into "tasks," etc. did so much for our understanding of our work that it's difficult to imagine that it will ever be found useless or flawed. But as for the *psychology of the actor's creative process itself*, it turned out to be slightly different – it didn't obediently follow the directorial thought.

It's possible to divide a play into parts, *but not a person*. This is where a new school rose up. And step by step, it arrived at automatisms.

Just like Leeuwenhoek's glass polishing workshop wound up being the birthplace of a whole new field of science – microbiology – so can a theatre laboratory ultimately be the cradle of a new direction of thought in psychology.

In Leeuwenhoek's workshop, the master kept perfecting his craft, until one day, he saw a new world: he saw some hitherto unseen "beasts" (microorganisms). Meanwhile, in our case, experimenting with their own psyches and mastering them, actors and researchers not only discover new facts of great meaning (medicine stumbles into them too), they most importantly: *try to take automatisms into their own hands and turn them into instruments of their will.*

This can result in new scientific thought on automatisms, on creativity, and on the structure of our so-called "subconscious."

Having stepped onto the path of this new inner technique in theatre (and having been already quite experienced in the realm of theatre pedagogy and modern science), I spent this whole time experimenting with *mastering and utilizing internal automatisms.*

This book series is dedicated to describing, step by step, a new school of actor training, as well as new methods of teaching internal techniques of an actor's art, and the two last books concern themselves with the psychology and theories of the art of the actor.

In order to strengthen and develop what has already been achieved, it is necessary to create not a theatre or a studio, but a new type of a **research institute**: *a studio-theatre, dedicated to the study of creativity and art.*

It would be negligent wastefulness to abandon the thought of doing *further research* on automatisms, research on *mastering and creating automatisms.*

Oh, how I wish that I could pass this work into *reliable* hands!

Note

1 At the time of his death, Demidov was still deliberating on the exact nature of transformation. "The creation of a special automatism that functions independently according to its own laws" is closer to Demidov's concept of "doubling" of the actor's identity. This is why the editors used the term "doubling," instead of "splitting" or "splintering," throughout the book. In addition to that, Demidov strongly considered the concept of "polarization" of the actor's identity, suggested to him by his student and colleague Vladimir Bogachev. The idea of "polarization" appealed to him especially because it excluded the pathological "split." In addition, Demidov deliberated if the "interference theory" (Müller and Pilzecker 1900; McGeoch 1932) might provide another explanation for the actor's process of transformation.

8

Will

Some say: a weak-willed person cannot be an actor. Will in art and creativity is everything. Stanislavsky [1954: 48] himself asserts: "Action, activity – this is what dramatic art, the art of the actor rests on." Further he writes:

> The mistakes of the majority of actors are made, because they think not of action, but only of its result . . . Learn not to play results onstage, and instead execute your tasks via action – authentically, productively, with focus, the whole time you are onstage. [Stanislavsky 1954: 157]

Is there a single person who is familiar with work in theatre that would sincerely assert that an actor should be will-less in his work?

No such person exists, and never will. An actor needs to be able to command himself, he cannot be absent-minded, he must be able to distract himself from the audience, etc.

And alongside this, in his book, *My Life in Art*, in the chapter on Stockmann, the same Stanislavsky [1931: 425–427], that champion of "activity" and "tasks," says:

> My point of departure in my work on a role as a director and actor was the line of *intuition and feeling* . . . From intuition, I *instinctively, on my own*, achieved the inner character, with all its idiosyncrasies, details, nearsightedness . . . From intuition, I also arrived at the outer character: it inevitably grew out of the inner one. The body and soul of Stockmann and Stanislavsky organically fused: I had to simply consider the thoughts and concerns of Doctor Stockmann, and signs of his nearsightedness, his forward-tilted torso, his quick pace – they would rise up on their own; my eyes trustingly gazed into the soul of the object with which Stockmann spoke or communed onstage; my index and middle fingers would stretch forward – as if to better shove my feelings, words, and thoughts into the very soul of my interlocutor. All of these needs and traits appeared instinctively, unconsciously . . .

> Even offstage, all I had to do was assume Stockmann's external mannerisms, and my soul would instantly experience certain corresponding feelings and sensations. The role's characterization and passions organically became my own, or, rather, the other way around: my

own feelings turned into those of Stockmann. At the same time, I felt the highest degree of joy an artist can feel – this joy came from saying another's thoughts onstage, *giving in* to another's passions, *make another's actions*, as if they were my own.

And the following observation comes from Pevtsov [1935: 42]:

I would say that the greatest moments of such self-awareness with regards to your technique, the awareness of *how* you're doing what you're doing and the degree to which you are a master and how you command yourself – these moments occur in instances of affect, when something takes hold of you and plays with you.

Then, you get the feeling that you're crossing some threshold, that you're riding the waves, that you don't have to swim at all, and that you simply stay afloat like a buoy.

Then, you feel joy and fear, wanting this state of being to never leave, wanting it to stay like this forever, and then it begins to creep away . . . it leaves . . . and again you have to toil and sweat, again you have to make an effort of a swimmer.

Some actors insist that in order to act well, they have to get a grip on themselves, concentrate, vanquish their absent-mindedness. Others, on the other hand, will list a few instances when they began to act wanly, absent-mindedly, and suddenly one of their scene partner's words would pierce them, at which point they would become impassioned, and the show would be excellent. However, whenever they would consciously try and concentrate, they couldn't achieve this effect.

Where does the truth lie?

In willpower or the lack thereof?

In "activity" or "passivity?"

In concentration or absent-mindedness, and giving yourself utter freedom?

In order to find an answer to this question, we have to ask another: *what is will?*

Before, empirical psychology said that will was a rather independent function of our psyche, as independent as people used to consider reasoning and emotion. Previously, people thought so: the human psyche consisted of three functions: mind, will, and feeling (emotions).

Now, our views have completely changed, and not a single psychologist believes that will is an independent function.

Today, will is considered to be the coordination of every function of one's personality or "self."

To put it more simply, will is the cooperation of all of our functions: this includes physical desires, habits, the whole brain, reflexive mechanisms; in a word, all of one's life functions, physical and psychological. And the desire or drive that arises as a result of the collisions of every function in one's body (one's whole "self") *is* a manifestation of will.

I'm hungry. I have no money. I walk by a deli, I see a tempting shop-window, I see people walking out of the store with their goods . . . and I want to tear away the food they just bought. But then I would be caught and arrested – and I crush the sudden urge. But I do want to eat . . . should I beg? no, it's shameful! But to die of hunger? so I force myself to extend my hand . . . it's difficult, I feel like everyone is looking at me, judging me, despising me, and I want to hide my hand and run . . . but where? And so I force myself to put my hand out again . . . Nobody gives me anything . . . And so I force myself to say: "Please . . . take pity . . ."

It's such a difficult battle! Everything that I do, my actions are the result of this battle that rages on in my entire body.

And what I *ultimately want*, want I *ultimately do* is the desire of my "self" *as a whole*, and it is my *will*.

Now, let's look at my life circumstances as they are in reality: I'm sated, I'm not cold, but you'll tell me: go outside and beg for scraps.

I – my whole, integral identity – will probably ask: why?! I don't need to. I won't do it.

But you're Liubim Tortsov – put on your torn coat, go to a street corner, and beg.

I – my whole, integral identity – will say: "Not likely! Go out there yourselves. I'm me, thank God, and not Liubim Tortsov, and as long as I'm me, I don't have to take part in this farce."

This would happen if my "I" is harmonically whole. Incapable of doubling.

But if I'm an *actor*, then I'll think, without any internal opposition: "Liubim . . . I'm Liubim Tortsov, a drunkard, an alcoholic . . . hungry, cold . . . You're saying I should put on these rags? Yeah, good point, that'll do . . . Yes, I feel like Liubim even more in them . . . I should go outside? Beg for scraps? Why not? I'll go . . . But I need some other footwear, something worn . . . and I feel like I should be wearing something more suitable for Liubim Tortsov *under* the coat too . . . "

And so, I feel like my other identity (quite powerful, in fact) is starting to feel like Liubim Tortsov. To feel and behave like him.

It's as if this other identity has its own being, its own facts of life, its own freedom, and its own will . . .

My identity has doubled, and my personal integral identity now looks on in surprise as I (my character-identity, Liubim Tortsov) get thoughts and desires that are completely unlike me.

What we get is some sort of dual state of being.

A dual life, a dual consciousness, a dual will.

At this point, it's easy to answer the question: what do we need – will or the lack thereof? Activity or passivity?

Will is the manifestation of **an integral identity**.

And the art of the actor is founded on the *doubling* of one's integral identity.

This means that will, as we understand it (the cooperation of all our physical and psychological functions) is only an impediment during an actor's creative process onstage. Only an obstacle.

And on the contrary, rejecting will and an integral identity gives us the opportunity to double and appear as another character (Liubim Tortsov or someone else).

Here's another example that demonstrates the obvious harmful influence of an integral identity's interference in art.

The actors are calm, free. They become immersed in the lives of the characters, they're affected by the words of their scene partners. In a word, they're living "in the character's shoes" (as Shchepkin would have it), i.e. they're in a state of creative doubling.

In comes Stanislavsky or somebody else whose opinion they all value, and everything flies out the window: they start pushing, applying effort, and everything becomes false.

What's the matter? Their integral identities woke up.

So, the first thing that needs to be fought is the integral identity. And the main purpose behind the technique is to secure yourself against it.

Will in the Actor's Art Is Needed Only to Be Lost

Defenders of will say: alright, an actor's will isn't involved during his creative process per se (since he doesn't have an integral identity at the time, but a doubled one, this excludes the presence or need of will). Alright, an actor doesn't act as his single, integral self – his character-self alone is *sucked into* the action and world of the stage by the character's given circumstances.

But what about the very beginning? How can you get through that without involving your will?

I have an integral identity, which means that my will is in complete order, and I'm me, and not someone else. I'm being suggested to feel like I'm somebody else (like Liubim Tortsov). Why do I need that? To execute this task, I have to apply the power of my will.

So how can you say that one's will isn't involved?

This line of thought is justified: in the first moments, the actor's willpower is necessary just like it would be in order to cross the gangway from the hard ground onto a ship's deck, at which point the ship doesn't need any help from you in order to carry you across the waves.

In a word, you have to exert your willpower in order to double and *deprive yourself of willpower*.

But doesn't this sound absurd – exert your will in order to deny yourself your own will? It's wordplay! Aren't things simpler?

There was collectedness, concentration, and now they're gone . . . Do you really need will-power in order to get rid of them? I hold a pencil in my hand. Do I really need to specially exert my willpower in order to unlock my fingers and drop it? Isn't it the other way around? Don't I need to exert my willpower in order to *hold* the pencil?

Now, imagine that you're lying on a railroad, right between the two rails. It's very comfortable, quiet, the sun is shining. But a linesman comes up to you and tells you that a train is going to be passing by in 10 minutes . . . You can stay there, it's not dangerous, but you have to remain still as a rock. The train will pass some 10 centimeters above you.

Would you really try it?

You hear a noise in the distance. The train is approaching. Just try to maintain the unflappable calm that you had some 15 minutes ago when you were happily looking at the clouds and the butterflies, breathing in the smell of flowers . . .

You *can* force yourself to keep on lying there, gritting your teeth and fearing the beating of your own heart, but that's not what's needed here. Where's the calm, the state of contemplation.

The audience, the show – *they* are the thundering train. You don't even need them to be nearby – all that's necessary is a passing mention, and your insides instantly seize up. You need to exert a massive amount of willpower to placate your involuntary worrying and stress!

However, experience will show you that no amount of willpower will be enough. You won't be able to calm yourself, to release yourself (like you could release a pencil from your grip): all of you has cramped up, including your psyche.

This inability to fix the problem in yourself directly has led actors to the point where they're now coming up with various tricks, various roundabout means.

And the various makeshift inventions have resulted in our psychological (internal) technique.

But what are all the methods of the actor's internal technique (if we're speaking of the successful ones)?

They're none other than means that allow the actor to *slip away* from his normal state of being into a state of artistic doubling. The state in which his integral identity will cease to exist (as an *integral* one, specifically).

Let's begin with Stanislavsky's famous "magic if."

I'm not Liubim Tortsov, I'm some actor. Let that be true – there's no need to try to be Liubim when everything inside me is crying out against such strain. And I'm not even trying. On the contrary, I'll firmly tell myself: I'm such and such, and not somebody else. But I'll allow myself to ask a single question: *but what if I* (I entertain this thought for just a second), what if I really were Liubim Tortsov – a drunkard, a vagabond, run out of the house by my brother . . . and instantly, something extraordinary occurs in me . . . a wondrous **shift** comes to pass from reality into the sphere of imagination and fantasy – a shift in the direction of doubling: I'm still here, I haven't gone anywhere, but at the same time, it's like I'm not just me anymore . . .

This happens instantaneously and without our involvement. But it's gone a second later. *Your integral identity returns to its rightful place*, and it's as if Liubim were never even there. The moment came and went. Alas, the method didn't work. In the first second, it promised us the world, but nothing came of it.

However, is this a good reason to turn away from this method entirely?

Sure, it disappeared, but it was there, I've experienced it being there – isn't that enough? The method isn't perfect yet . . . well, so then we have to think about it and perfect it. It's worth it.

For now, this method is a wonderful tool that demonstrates a *shift* in our identity – towards doubling. Though it wasn't for long – just for a second – with its help, you witnessed this wondrous shift.

And what about an actor's make-up and costume, or generally speaking – the "mask" behind which the actor hides his identity? Is it not a material device, a mechanism that is conducive to the doubling of an actor's integral identity?

They'll make you up, dress you, you'll look at yourself in a mirror . . . Good lord! *This* is how I look!? And you'll immediately feel like someone else, you'll want to walk, speak, laugh, and think like someone else.

Take off the makeup, and once again: here I am!

★★★

When I tell an actor: you're Liubim Tortsov, you want to warm yourself, you might freeze to death, defend yourself, go beg Mitya for a place to stay – I'm addressing his will, but *whose*? The actor's will or Liubim's will? After all, the actor doesn't really need to warm himself.

★★★

What are the methods of "physical tasks" and "physical actions"?

The role isn't progressing, the words feel foreign, all the actor's efforts and the director's explanations are for naught . . . out of confusion and frustration, the actor starts smoking a cigarette, starts rehearsing with the cigarette, and . . . everything is easier and better!

Or real cups with real tea are put on a table, and the actor begins to drink tea for real, and . . . it's as if a load has dropped off his shoulders – everything is easy and comfortable, the words roll off his tongue on their own, it's easy to hear and register the words of his scene partner, and . . . the scene is off!

It's as if some sort of overload has passed, an excess of consciousness has been transferred elsewhere, the actor's identity has been *doubled*, and his imagination is now in full control of *one of these two* identities.

But what is "calm," "muscle freedom," "carelessness," "passivity?" These are states in which it's easier to *slip away* from the oversight of the integral identity.

★★★

When actors try to act well, make an effort, it's awful. But when they are weak, tired, and irresponsible, it's wonderful.

Can an Intellectually Willful Actor Be a Creative Actor Onstage?

That is, can he creatively transform and live onstage as a given character?

Of course not. He has an integral identity that isn't suitable for doubling. A doubled state is "abnormal" for him, and is therefore uncomfortable and unacceptable.

And since he can't sincerely give himself over, or rather, give his other self (a byproduct of doubling) over to the given character's life, he has one way out: use external means to *depict* the character and the "feelings" that it has to experience throughout the play.

Whether he wants it or not – he's a depictionist.

The whole time he is onstage, he is himself. No second identity is formed. And yet, the second identity is crucial. What to do?

Copy it, depict it with external means, while remaining cold and whole internally.

This concerns a purely intellectually willful actor. These do exist, but rarely. For the most part, an intellectually willful actor is made up partly of other qualities as well – emotional, affective, or imitational. And as a result of this, any actor has the ability to double. But regardless of "mix," if an actor is more intellectually willful than anything else, this mix is neutralized: self-awareness, self-control, willpower, and intellectual reasoning – they ultimately get the upper hand; the integral identity reigns supreme, and any involuntary attempt to double hits a brick wall only a few steps in.

★★★

The *extraordinary enthusiasm* with which many premature teachers of the "Stanislavsky System" are approaching *exercises designed to improve an actor's attention* deserves **the sharpest reproof**. What do these exercises accomplish? First of all, they fortify one's will, i.e. the will of one's integral identity. This is useful for supremely distracted and absent-minded individuals, but for the most part, this develops an *inability* to double and be involuntary and free.

By the way, Stanislavsky would sometimes show new students these exercises (memorizing the patterns on a carpet, a painting), but he would never systematically use them for himself or for his students.

An Actor's Creative Moment: The Moment of Doubling

The actor's integral identity hasn't grown cold, but Liubim has. He wants to warm himself, his will is drawing him towards warmth. The actor's identity, however, has no need for this. And it's warm in the theatre anyway . . .

This is why will is necessary, even crucial, but for what? It's necessary in order to extinguish it in yourself, in your integral identity. *In order to achieve the expansion of your integral identity via a state of doubling; from will to a lack of will – to passivity.*

Developing your will for the stage via ordinary means (attention, memorization, etc.) – *this fortifies one's integral identity.* And an integral identity results in an inability to double. These exercises are useful for people with shaky personalities. For people with normal ones, however, they're harmful.

People become overly excited about these exercises and end up *killing one's involuntariness and ability to double.*

On the Intellectually Willful

The main mistake of intellectually willful actors and directors lies in their misunderstanding of will and the concept of an integral identity.

They say: this and that . . . (show examples of what they say)

But it's not necessary to "get a grip on yourself" (as they say), and on the contrary – "to release yourself." To whom? To what? *Involuntariness, the given circumstances, "the impelling meaningfulness of objects."* But since I'm always me (I don't really disappear anywhere), there occurs a wondrous doubling, which is the chief condition of the actor's art.

★★★

Karl Marx [1936: 198]: " . . . The process [or work] demands that, during the whole operation, the workman's will be steadily in consonance with his purpose. This means close attention."

What sort of "attention" and what sort of "will" are manifested during the work process of an actor?

After all, Liubim Tortsov isn't the integral me. He's just one of my identities. *It* lives onstage, not me. Therefore, the actor's will needs to be focused on *giving up his will so as not to have an integral, harmonic identity.*

The "mask" is a mechanism, a tool for doubling. One's will must also be used to this end.

Herein lies one of the intellectually willful actor's main sources of confusion. He doesn't understand this doubling, seeing as he has an "integral identity."

So, one's will doesn't exist as an independent function (like reasoning or emotion). Will is the cooperation of all abilities, instincts, and habits. It's the manifestation of one's integral identity. Developing one's will by ordinary means leads to the strengthening of one's integral identity. And an integral identity means an inability to double.

But what is one's integral identity? Does it involve everything that exists in a person? All of his potential and all of his experience related to his ancestral history, and that of the human species as a whole? If that were the case, then everything would be wonderful, but in reality, an integral identity is a rather limited machine – mundane, common, and restricted.

The "Everyman"

Why bother writing about him? First and foremost, because he exists. Secondly, because he is (alas!) in the majority. Ninety-five percent of all energy is spent specifically on him. After all, it is he who tripped Stanislavsky. Truth be told, his system consists of two paths: one is for the *very talented actor,* who simply needs to be told "what he wants in this bit" – and he's already acting. The other path is *for the everyman* – it turns everything into actions, into small "tasks," "justifications," searches for rhythm instead of feeling. And many other *peripheral tricks* that are seemingly intended to evoke life in an actor, i.e. make his very center live onstage. In reality, *their goal is to circumvent the center – i.e. the truth* – and create verisimilitude.

The imitator – after all, it would appear that he is one such *peripheral* actor whose center (soul) rather successfully keeps quiet.

On the other hand, what's currently happening in the MAT is nothing if not *imitation.* This is unexpected, but it's true.

Looking further down the road, there will be a very serious and exhaustive chapter: "The Center and the Periphery."[1] It will discuss "liberation from the body," "admitting," and "breathing."

"Truth" means that the center is alive. "Physical tasks," "justification," "rhythm" – these are all peripheral tricks that are apparently intended to evoke life in the actor and his center, but are in reality *intended to circumvent them – circumvent the center, i.e. the truth.*

Note

1 Although no such chapter was written by Demidov, these subjects are discussed in the following chapters (9–11). On the concepts of *Center* and *Freedom of the Center*, please consult the Glossary.

9

"Activity" or "Passivity"?

Any reaction is a response to stimulus. The stimulus can be external, internal, and, finally, *the reaction itself can be a stimulus*.

This explains the effect of the device called "action."

When I begin to act, like clean a room, for example, my very actions turn into stimuli and *pull me further* into the action.

In this way, I can begin consciously and out of necessity, but afterwards, the action itself will immerse me – then the *doing becomes involuntary*, and I being to *feel like* fulfilling this action.

This is the very loophole that allows the foolish intellectually willful approach to function properly in practice.

In this way, action isn't the principle itself and is merely one of the ***devices***!!!

This is serious! This clears the way.

Passivity

Passivity is the lightness of a feather: the slightest current of air picks it up and carries it away.

But in the meantime, our actors are like boulders. We couldn't pick them up with our hands, to say nothing of the wind.

There is a danger that people will interpret passivity as inertness and even apathy. I'm passive – that must mean that I don't want anything! Drag me if you want, I won't make a single step myself. This isn't the passivity that I'm talking about. This is stupidity, dullness, heaviness.

★★★

Existing schools require that the actors fulfill assignments, and they never approve of the kind of actor who just gives in to something that *acts for him*. "What do you mean: it just acts on its own?" they'll say. "And why would it do such a thing? With such freedom, can you really guarantee that your Othello won't simply forgive Desdemona instead of choking her?

"'I didn't really *feel like* killing her today,' he'll say . . . No, it's better to stay away from such "free" performance, from the improvisational spirit, involuntariness, and everything like that . . . You must know what you're doing onstage. *Know and actively* strive to fulfill all your *assignments*. In general, onstage, you have to *be active* and *willful*, rather than irresponsible, involuntary, and passive." – Such is their conclusion.

Existing schools employ various exercises to develop *activity*. When they should be developing **passivity**.

Yes, yes, this isn't a typo or a mistake: *passivity*.

For an actor, his salvation onstage isn't activity, but passivity. Only **passivity**.

How can this be? What is this heresy?

This isn't anything special. It's very simple. In life, everything is done involuntarily, as a response to a variety of *influences* and *effects*.

When you're searching for activity directly, it only leads to tension. An example: activity is a result. Demanding activity (attention, etc.) is akin to the demand: "Act well!" (or "Love this person!").

You're walking through a forest, you're in no hurry, you're feeling peaceful and listening to the silence of the woods . . . Suddenly – a snake! Before you can even think, you're ten paces away from it, you somehow have a stick in your hands, and you're ready to do battle.

Did you force yourself to do these things? Of course not. Everything happened on its own. Your activity was a *result*. Stung by a new impression, you "ignited."

Let's take another instance: there's a fire, you're family is there, and you're blazing through the forest in order to reach them . . . A snake . . . You probably don't really notice it, maybe you'll slightly change direction . . . You're preoccupied with the fire: who's there? What's happening? You *have* to get there in time.

In this case, your activity is evoked by this concrete fire. You could say that the fire is rushing you through the woods with lightening speed.

As you see, activity is only the result, only the response to something else.

Truth be told, there's nothing new about this. This is a very simple physiological and psychological fact: a living cell is at rest – touch it, influence it in some way, and it immediately reacts. It's the same with amoebas, ciliates, etc., etc.

We (humans) also react. We respond to the influences that life exerts on us.

If it's cold, we bundle up. If we're hungry, we look for food. If we're sated, calm, tired, and our stomach is pleasantly full, then we go and sleep for an hour or two . . . If nothing is influencing us from without, then we grow calm and plunge into a pleasant, semi-sleeping, semi-meditative state. But it doesn't last long – there are always more influences – internal influences: you are suddenly attached by thoughts, memories, desires . . .

Or, right as soon as you've managed to deal with everything, you suddenly remember that you promised to visit a friend – you jump up, get dressed, and you hurry to make up the lost time.

In a word, it's obvious from these examples that in order to get someone to act, you have to prod them – then they begin to act.

And in order for us to be affected not just by "prods" and "blows," but by light touches too, we have to be *more sensitive*, more **open** [The word "open" deserves its own chapter. This word is **everything**. More so than "passivity." –*Author's Note*] to impressions, more *passive*, i.e. receptive.

An actor, however, needs even greater passivity, because nobody is beating him with a stick, nobody is even touching him. He needs to make do with *a single thought, nothing but fantasy* – just the thought of something wakes him up, causes him to be full of activity, all aflame.

The degree of sensitivity, the degree of passivity determines the power and the depth of the actor's reactions, i.e. the actor's "activity" that people try to catch with their bare hands.

★★★

The director urges an actor towards activity: "be angry at them," etc.

(This needs some examples of psychological actions and tasks to show how he brings an actor to tension, to the *resemblance* of rhythm and action.

In a word: show how this approach creates the majority of our formally "active" performances.)

But some directors manage to use this method to create real, live activity.

However, this is because, without even noticing it themselves, they stop using this method after just a few steps and instantly start using a diametrically opposed one: by saying *activity*, they push an actor towards *passivity*, thereby correcting their mistake, and everything progresses quite well. Why does this happen? Why do they "stop?" Probably because they are talented. They sniff out the right path.

They do approximately the following: first of all, they turn their attention to the physical part of the scene: what can be done physically?

Let's take Ostrovsky's *Family Affair*. Tishka is downstage with a broom. The actor is half-hearted, absent-minded, he says his lines with stale, memorized liveliness, and the director, wanting to make him more "active," starts telling him: "You're saying that as soon as it's light out, you're sweeping the floor — so why aren't you sweeping the floor? You're holding a broom, so get to it."

The actor heeds the advice, pretends that he's "seemingly" sweeping the floor: he waves the broom around in every direction. The director, however, is on his case: "You're sweeping poorly – you missed a cigarette butt, there's a nail over there . . . Sweep the floor, make it clean – your employers will come, and they'll let you have it!"

"Oh, so you want me to sweep for real?"

"Of course. How else are you supposed to do it. Tishka sweeps the floor, and you're Tishka!"

"Huh, well that's easy to do!" The actor looks around and sees a heap of trash, papers, a matchbox . . . he thinks for a second: where should he start from?

He makes his choice, starts sweeping everything into one spot. Now he's not missing anything, even looks under the couch . . .

The actual work makes him involved, piques his interest; he comes to life, starts perceiving everything and reacting to everything for real – he grumbles something under his breath . . .

Seeing that he now has a desire to speak, the director carefully starts feeding him the lines:

"Oh, what a life, what a life! At first light, I'm here, sweeping the floors . . ." It's as if the actor was just waiting to hear these words, at which point the others all follow in a stream: "But is it my job to sweep the floors!" And angrily thrusts the broom into a pile of trash . . . the trash flies around the room . . . he sees that he's just created extra work for himself – he starts cleaning it again . . . The more trash he gathered, the more he became immersed in his simple duty and the more he **opened** himself to it.

Let's take a closer look and see that his activity is the result of his passivity.

Let's start at the beginning: how did the director help him? What did he prompt him to? His task perhaps? No, without even suspecting it, he directed him not towards action, but towards perception. He said: "You're sweeping the floor poorly! – *you missed a cigarette butt, there's a nail over there.*" The actor saw the cigarette butt and the nail, he saw some other trash, and his hands swept the cigarette butt into the pile on their own, automatically. The action began *without his conscious effort* – he's sweeping . . . Now he's doing his own prompting. Why? Because one passivity results in another – he has entered a **stream of passivity** and **perception**. And in response to what he perceived, the action started on its own. "Huh, that's true, there's trash under the couch" – and his hand shoves the broom under there.

Why was the actor "inactive" at first? Because he was attending to something completely different – his personal thoughts, his personal feelings concerned him.

They concerned him, rather than *him being concerned with them*. Therein lies the cardinal difference.

★★★

It's not activity that needs to be cultivated, but *passivity — the ability to place yourself under the circumstances*. Let them twirl and push us around.

That's how things are in life.

If willpower and activity are necessary for something, then only insofar as to make us be passive.

A defender of activity will say: "So does it even matter? It's necessary for a person to live, to see and hear — does it really matter what you call it, what it's called scientifically? Fine, let it be called passivity instead of activity — by all means. Will this make me turn away from an excellent, tried-and-true method? Will I stop saying: 'By active, don't fall asleep?'"

What excellent, tried-and-true method? Ice for heating?

It doesn't matter what we "call" something — what matters is what *happens*. And what happens is that good directors urge their actors towards passivity, and the word "activity" only confuses the actor.

The thing is, though, that the actor (when he turns his attention to the physical part of the scene for the first time), in forcing himself to move brings to life another influential source (the muscles in his arms and legs, faster breathing, etc.). In doing so, he distracts himself from the activity of a performer per se. So, the advice: "By active" is in actually a disguised: "Be passive."

But in practice, "Be active" is most often interpreted as: "put in an effort! tense up! try harder!"

10

The Culture of "Calm"

The Ability to Do what You Want

It's easy to explain things with "questions and answers," especially with the actors' movements in these exercises.

What's important here isn't just *what* somebody wants, but *when* they want it.

For example, you want to say something. You missed the moment – now, you have to wait for another, because if you say the something once you've missed the moment, you've made a mistake, since you didn't want to say it anymore! (You stopped wanting it.)

Also: you can't say something too early. You haven't gotten something yet, but you're already responding; you don't want to, but you're already speaking.

Now, as for the "what." You want to say one thing, but end up saying another. Or the same thing: you pause. You want to say something very badly, but what if you grow scared? What if you don't say everything, i.e. not what you wanted to say?

Or maybe you'll add something: you want to say something simply, but you'll add something, and "step it up." You'll do something you didn't want to. If you want to "step it up," then do it – otherwise, it's neither this nor that.

It's important for things to be done, said, or remain unsaid *on their own*, and not forcedly, on command.

★★★

Freedom, the ability to do what you want – "Isn't all that tasteless!?"

That's because we're not simultaneously giving free rein to *taste*. Taste needs its own freedom – it has its own "sensations."

When a person green-lights himself, wholly gives in to his automatisms – that doesn't yet mean "doing what you want." After all, there's still an *element of choice*, and this choice needs to be made while "*giving free reign to taste*" – then, your artist will inevitably participate.

Training to Give in to Sensation

We either need 1) something that takes over our entire being and displaces everything else – something powerful, like a sickness, or a moan [See exercise in *Giving In To Physiological*

Sounds – exercise 14, in the next sub-chapter]; or 2 we need to cleanse ourselves, prepare a preliminary state of being (a blank sheet,), and evoke perceptions and sensations with the help of notions [See *First Impulse Exercises*].

But there is also a third method: the gradual displacement of the general clutter of images and sensations by fixating simple and proximate images and sensations! [See exercises in *Acknowledgment of and Giving in to Sensations* – exercise 2), in the next sub-chapter.]

There is a state of being in which the soul is *transparent, clear, innocent, and singular* . . . After a tragedy or great sorrow, when life cleanses your soul of all the rubble, and your soul is fatigued, but cleansed, still slightly damp from a passing torrential rain – it sees everything around with the clear eyes, without the tinted glasses.

This occurs after a serious and prolonged illness, when your soul once again steps into life, and all its sins have been suffered through and discarded – a state that can probably be compared to the state experienced by a believer after sincere penance.

And this happens to us every day for a few moments when we *wake* from our dreams.

In all of these cases, our *exposed souls* are receptive to minute sensations, to the tiniest of thoughts.

This is the state of sincerity, authenticity, and *Truth*.

Giving in to Sensations

Write about:

1 The technique of giving in to sensations – see "Towards Wants" [See Glossary].
2 When you stumble upon a sensation and turn it into truth (give in to it entirely), you become singular, at which point it doesn't matter what sensation you give in to, be it even laziness or apathy.
3 Connect "giving in" with "casting away the head," with "the fool," and "the idiot."
4 Connect "what if" with giving in, and with the "fool" again.
5 *Imagination* plus *giving in* equals "transformation," and "a new life."
6 Connect "giving in" with brakes.
7 "Giving in" in life. Pushkin, Mochalov, Byron. A child.
8 The dangers of giving in when it becomes debaucherous.
9 Creative-aesthetic justification is giving in to sensation.
10 The connection between giving in and childishness.
11 The connection with seriousness. [See Glossary]
12 " . . . Having grasped just one line in a drawing, just one chord and one sound . . . "
13 Facsimile exercises. [See Glossary]
14 Let out a moan, and give in to moaning while listening to it; the same with crying and laughter (specific movements of the stomach and the diaphragm), listen and give in. (As Mitrofan Pyatnitsky [1864–1927] used to say: "Sound gives birth to tears.")
15 Giving in to a sensation that was received during an "emotionally tangible" reading of a text.

Towards "Giving in to Sensations"

An exercise: one partner is passive, another is active. The active one touches the passive one. Feeling the touch, receiving the sensation, the first partner reacts involuntarily. As a "receiver," you need to give in to the sensation, and stay out of your own way.

The touch can be felt in two different ways:

1   – something touched me.
2   – my partner touched me.

The first case involves a subtler, finer reaction to the physical sensation itself, which is better from the point of view of training. It's akin to a person practicing giving in to his wants (when an actor is practicing on his own), which is difficult – the sensations are too delicate. Meanwhile, the sharp interference from without helps, as it provides a tangible impulse.

In the second case with a partner, this subtler physical reaction is being crushed by the actual impression from the partner; this results in a "phase jump" – a shock that often leads to false-hoods. This undesirable result occurs because any overload, especially in the very beginning, is already a falsehood (it is not "true").

It also might not lead there. But this occurs only if one green-lights himself towards a living relationship with his partner.

In any case, it's better to begin with the first – without a partner.

A rule for the partner: touch him and sit still! – otherwise, things might lead to scuffling that could even turn into fighting.

A rule for the receiver: don't expect anything extraordinary. See "*Silk Thread.*" [See Glossary and Book Three, Part Three, Chapter 17, *Simplicity and Naturalness.*]

★★★

In order to develop faith in yourself, it's very important to go into exercises *without preparation.*

Everybody always prepares and requires that others always prepare: "don't go onstage with-out a task," "concentrate before beginning an exercise," etc.

It would seem like this is a good plan. But as soon as something goes wrong, and I lose sight of my task – that's the end of it, I'm done.

It's necessary to train faith not in the "rock" on which I'm sitting, but *in my own ability to fly,* and in order to do that, I have to fly through the air, and not while "sitting on a rock" or "hung to a cable."

It's important for a person to know his lines and go onstage *without* predetermining any-thing. This isn't so easy: sometimes, he might sincerely believe that he didn't predetermine anything – as if! You won't even notice how you sometimes predetermine everything. And once you have, then you've put yourself within a frame, you've constrained yourself. Most importantly, you have to develop your freedom. And in order to do this, you have to *throw yourself out into the air,* like a pigeon – there, in the air, the instincts of flight will wake up on their own.

Panic and hastiness might also wake up. In this case, there's only one proper preventative measure: *take your time!* Wait for what you need to come on its own. What you *need* will come *when* you need it.

Feeling, or rather, the state of *intense passivity* of intuitive waiting is brought about only by a *lack* of readiness and a *lack* of predetermination. This can be called "*active passivity.*"

The following method can help in developing this habit: require that an actor fully green-lights himself only *after* his partner has spoken his first words. In other words, have him proceed exclusively from hid partner's first line. As for this partner, he might start something comedic, something dramatic, or something that calls for a physical characterization; or else, the partner might green-light his own first impulse without any regard for the other partner, etc. This puts in actor in the space of uncertainty that inevitably requires passivity, and an utter lack of pre-determination. In a word, the actor needs to be put in a situation in which the only reasonable move is passivity and uncertainty of what might come next.

★★★

As a development tool, this is an interesting method. But we have to remember that in a play the most important thing is *given circumstances*. They have to manipulate me. As well as the "I" – who am I and what am I? Although, my suggestion does not apply to the play, but to exercises. Then it's true. But you also have to develop another habit: how to enter the stage while *wholly living in the circumstances*.

"Trains"

When conducting exercise in "questions and answers," I once stumbled onto a rather vivid comparison.

An actor had an urge of sorts, but he failed to give in to it in time; then, sensing that he missed the moment, he tried to catch up to himself, and he "pushed."

"You've missed it! The train's left the station! You can't catch up to it!" And since then, the "train" has turned into a term.

It's possible to comfortably get onto the train in a timely manner, it's possible to jump onto it as it's leaving the station, it's possible to grab the holding bar of the very last car.

It's possible to miss it and get depressed.

It's possible to miss it, and wait for a minute or two for the next train that is going your way.

It's possible to miss it and enter such a state of panic that you get onto the very next train that you see, regardless of where it's headed, and it will take you somewhere you absolutely do not need to be.

In a state of extreme haste, it's possible to try to force through the closed doors of a train that isn't ready for departure yet. This is called "rushing," when there is no anything to be said or done yet, but the actor can't wait and pushes himself: "Just get it over with. Maybe something will happen!" He tries to break through a closed door, pushes himself, works too hard, but the train isn't and won't be going anywhere yet. This only results in a greater stress for the actor – over the locked railcar.

★★★

Write about *"letting things slip by,"* tell about the pathfinder's flight-shooting, at the first impulse.

On failing during difficult moments and transitioning into hysterics. The reason: a very powerful feeling comes on, I grow scared, I'm afraid of not being able to handle it, I start panicking, I'm afraid of letting the feeling go, I *rush*, and green-light myself to go down the path of nervousness and physical asperity.

Sometimes, a person seeks escape in tension and strain, and doesn't even notice it – he says that he feels good, *relieved* by this, that he finally feels easy. In the meantime, why does he "feel relieved?" Because the incoming feeling was very intense, while our mundane brakes – powerful, and applied in full. This resulted in an internal battle and uneasy feeling. The battle got resolved as soon as he tensed up, i.e. turned himself off with the help of these muscles.

It was difficult to breathe in the depths, but once he swam up, it became easier.

Sometimes, this happens without any strain. A person simply floats up to the surface and keeps swimming up top in perfect comfort, as if with a float, slapping around with his limbs. A perfectly normal state of a trouble-free person.

The Usefulness of Mistakes

It's not good when a student performs all the exercises and rarely makes mistakes.

That means that he doesn't green-light many things that rise up inside him – he keeps himself in the modest valley in which he can calmly walk around with closed eyes, as it has no holes, no ravines, no puddles that he could accidentally trip into.

When you properly give in to what you want to do, you're very quickly drawn into doing something you can't execute – not enough technique yet, enough freedom, enough endurance, and this leads to a crash. Nothing shameful in this – you exercise high jumping, and you try to jump over a height that you can't quite reach yet – wait a bit, you'll manage this one too.

But the fact that you're not getting in the way of your bravery, your faith – that's a much greater achievement and more important habit.

The second advantage is of a different sort. When you make a mistake, you suffer a blow to your ego – this is very educational, kind of like when you bump your head into the top of a doorframe – you'll do it once, twice, and the reflex will form on its own – you'll start automatically bending your head down a bit whenever you walk through that door.

Additionally, a blow to your ego forces you to get angry at yourself, collect yourself, mobilize. Just like any big failure. It is often much more useful than success. Success is often harmful.

Giving In

It's one thing to give in, but it's a completely different thing to surround yourself with conditions that would allow the given circumstances to attach a hook to you and tow you after them. Techniques that allow you to achieve this are "passivity," "admitting," "the nearest flow of though," "breathing," etc.

Concentration, "The Edge" (see "singularity," "attention," "concreteness")

Occultists say that a human has a specific driving force, but that he won't be able to advance [into other spheres] unless he's sharpened: he's too wide and great and multifaceted – he can't squeeze anywhere on his own, like a crudely hewed log, but if he's sharpened, then he'll fit like a wedge.

A wedge needs to be hammered in, while a human's energy, apparently, is all directed into a single spot, and he pushes himself through. So you must only take care of "*sharpening yourself.*" That is, concentrate your attention on a single object. Everything else will happen on its own. In other words, be ready to concentrate on any object – "Let one be like the edge of a razor" [Buddha's aphorism (*The Sutta-Nipata* (1881: 130)].

The "what" method helps you concentrate.

On Slipping Past the Body (see "giving in," "Asana")

Before squeezing into our souls, any impression first hits against our body. This might be the body's reflexive response to the impression's content.

It hits against the body even more so upon leaving us. It trips up in the process, and busts up its edges – anything that is fragile being chipped off. Only a fragment escapes outside, no arms, no legs, no head.

The method: 1) Allow an impression to enter us freely, *without hitting against anything*. "To slip past." 2) Allow a response to exit our souls without any impediments, bypassing the body. As if it were moving through a tube without touching its sides. "To slip past."

Make it through by some lucky fluke, without raising any alarms. Or walk through naively and boldly, as if saying: "It's not me, and over there what you see is not my mare." [This is a literal translation of a Russian idiom, which essentially means that the speaker is pretending not to know anything about what's going on.]

This "slipping past" is very serious. It can be connected with techniques such as "*the sleep of the body*," life "*without a body*," and in general, this device is *very* **much fraught with wonders**.

On Freedom (See Culture of Calm, Muscles, Talent, Sensations, Center, Passivity, Lack of Brakes)

Finding freedom through movements. For example, turn your head in a way that makes it feel as if it's turning on its own. It's easier if you imagine that it's light, has no weight at all (made of air). And it's turned by the wind, by the air, like a weather vane. The same can be applied to arms, legs, etc.

Freedom of whispering, whistling (particularly at a candle), freedom of voice (also by breathing and blowing at a candle), freedom of gaze, freedom while working on your face (the mirror). Freedom of the Center. Freedom of radiation.

Free movement, any movement – justify it creatively, and you'll experience what true freedom of your soul really means. You'll understand the words of Rabindranath Tagore [1916: 68]: "Deliverance is not for me in renunciation. I feel the embrace of freedom in a thousand bonds of delight."

Combine the "weather vane" method with the gymnastics of your joints (according to Marsova) [Varvara Marsova was a movement teacher at the Stanislavsky Opera Theatre and Stanislavsky Studio of Opera and Theatre].

Freedom of Time

It's not worth existing at once in the present, the past, and the future (our usual state).

There is freedom only in the present. "Do not tie yourself down with what was and what will be. Let your heart live in the present and dwell in all places with equal indifference."

Freedom lets you understand the nature of singularity.

The feeling of freedom will let you experience your Higher "Self."

"Though he participates in all things as an ordinary person, either consciously or subconsciously, he soars over all creatures."

"He can call himself free who performs every act without pondering his own personal involvement in it, but rather views it as part of the multifaceted, *spontaneous activity of Nature*" [Editors were unable to locate the sources of these quotes].

Towards Freeing your Muscles and Calm (see also "Physiology" and "Residual Attention")

You can rarely do something useful when advising someone to relax their muscles, to release their tension, etc . . .

In practice, the *opposite* bit of advice often leads to a better result . . . Instead of releasing one's muscles, one must *busy* them, give them something to do.

"Asana" is just such a method.

Physiology is too.

As is physical busyness.

Green-lighting your movements is also. Especially green-lighting *small* movements.

Muscles: Toward the Culture of Calm

If you're in a standard state of absent-mindedness (excess tension), then music is more powerful than you, it can conquer you with its rhythm, but poetry is weaker. Its rhythm will only take over you if you're *very* free. You have to learn to be *very* free. This is one of the foundations of *real* attention.

If something is tensed up, like your shoulder, for example, then that means that there is an unnecessary object – eliminate the tension, and the object will disappear.

Aristocratism is the relaxation of muscles. Raphael's Madonna is the relaxation of muscles. Working on relaxing your muscles in everyday life means getting closer and closer towards the "I" – the aristocratism of the soul – and that means melting our mechanical nature.

Mechanicalness means tensed muscles.

You think or feel something – tense up, and you'll *turn off* the whole realm of feeling, and you'll be left only with the mechanical process of reasoning (the kind of reasoning that is only capable of making a summary of things, or cataloguing them). Go ahead, *justify* your tension (aesthetically, like a creative artist, proceeding not from your head, but from the sensation of tension itself), and you'll once again *turn yourself on **and*** you'll achieve a creative action.

★★★

We are machines; we have no "I," we have no individuality.

Where is the "I"? Where is my conscience? My truth? My honesty?

Here it is, I begin to sense it somewhere deep, under seven locks.

But what happened? As soon as I started "trekking" towards the "I," my muscles started dissipating – my mechanical nature began to melt.

A strained, but artistically unjustified muscle is always a barrier, always an obstacle, always a shutdown.

Relaxation is always a turning on, as well as the beginning of true communion.

Justification is also a turning on – it's an entrance into a creative state, and the attainment of an active task.

★★★

A pretty good way of freeing yourself from tensed muscles is to imagine that you're tossing your arms (or legs or whatever you want) out a window, and that they're not there at all.

I'm a lamp, the world of images is oil; the creative process is fire. In order to light the lamp, we need quiet, we need *calm*. This is where the culture of calm comes from.

Over the course of several hours, a revolutionary rescued the wounded from a fire at the barricades. Over the course of several hours, he could have been killed at any second. Over the course of several hours, he saw blood and suffering. When he finally came home and lay down to rest, he recalled everything and lost consciousness from the horror of it all.

The very presence of tension or movement in one's muscles prevents impressions to reach the depths of one's consciousness and subconsciousness. An impression can reach "the depths" only if one's muscles are absolutely relaxed.

For animals, *rigor nervorum* (general muscle spasms) sets in during moments of danger as a defense mechanism; we can assume that for us, muscle tension is also a kind of shield that doesn't allow traumatizing external stimuli to pierce our consciousness or subconsciousness.

"Releasing your muscles" means releasing your shield. Try to be "*defenseless*" during moments of creativity, and you'll be *inspired*.

Exercises, Suggested by my Brother, Konstantin Demidov

A group of students sit and, in their imagination, follow the slow narration of the teacher; he makes them go on various adventures in their thoughts, even making them climb up on roofs . . .

There have been cases when he would say "you've lost your footing and are falling to the ground" when students would lose consciousness.

★★★

The mistake in Stanislavsky's point of view on muscles: they're cords, while feelings are spider web strands. This is why, in his opinion, in order to tear the cords with the strands, it's necessary to weave the strands into even stronger cords . . . Of course this is wrong. Feelings are light, muscles are cardboard. Cardboard doesn't allow light to go through, but it can reflect it.

Muscles and feelings are different kinds of phenomena.

"Autumnal Meditativeness" (toward the Culture of Calm)

The fall of 1830 was one of the most creatively fruitful for Pushkin. And at the same time, it was one of the more tragic moments in his life:

It was right before his marriage. He thought that the end of his old, difficult and turbulent life was nearing. In reality, he was nearing the final catastrophe. [Pushkin's marriage caused him many humiliations, and it eventually led to his being killed in a duel.]

Pushkin was superstitious; he was also a genius. It's no wonder that the art of a superstitious genius involuntarily foreshadowed his turbulent future and reflected his tempestuous past.

Despite the deep meditative calm that fell upon the poet during that fall in Boldino, his soul was subconsciously drawn to the contemplation of dark and tragic events. *The Small Tragedies,* written in Boldino are dedicated to the manifestation of vices and dark movements of the soul that lead to ruin. *The temporary calm* simply helped the poet bring out and shed light on what lay hidden in the depths of his soul; it helped him transform the personal into the universal; it helped him make the random eternal. (Vladislav Khodasevich [1915: 4])

What an interesting thought! The calm and the meditative state that usually visited Pushkin in the fall helped him bring out and shed light on what was in the depths of his soul. And the depths of his soul weren't calm at all, but rather grim and dark.

And other than this, the meditative calm helped him make the personal universal, and the random (after all, he wasn't grim at all times) eternal.

After this, I think that the culture of calm is the culture of establishing this "autumnal meditativeness."

And the random becomes eternal, and my personal becomes universal.

When I live onstage restlessly, then I can only live personally (i.e. not universally) and can only live off of what piques my interests at a given time (instead of "eternally immovable and eternally beautiful truth"). And this would be trifling and ordinary.

This is how we should understand Pushkin's [1949: 424] line: "The Muses' service brooks no vanity. The beautiful must always be majestic."

★★★

If the audience, the lights, and all conditions of the stage *inevitably* somehow excite the nervous system, can we really speak of *calm*?

Is there any substance to this discussion?

After all, what we're left with is the need to achieve calm in a state of excitement! In other words, combine two mutually exclusive states?

Naturally, such a fantastical combination won't intimidate someone of no great depth or a boor – he can speak on any subject with aplomb – but for a serious man, this could present great difficulties.

★★★

For an actor, these weaknesses [impulsivity, openness] are his greatest strengths. And someone who hasn't been bestowed with this "power" (or is methodically and constantly denied it) is powerless onstage. There is no point in him trying to stick his nose there.

Such a person might be a good researcher or scientist, but never an excitable actor. [We shouldn't conclude from this that the first three types aren't suited to science, and only the rationalist submerges himself in it comfortably. Passion, emotionality – these are some of the most important tools that one uses to happen upon great thoughts. Galileo, Bruno, Lomonosov, Lavoisier – none of them can be called well-balanced, passionless rationalists. On the contrary – the greater the scientist is, the more inner fire is in him. We should make the following conclusion: a rationalist has no place in art, but he can find a rather good niche for himself in science. –*Author's Note*]

In the meantime . . . if he is pleasant to look at, has a good, strong voice, good manners . . . why shouldn't he try his hand at acting?

The audience might miss some things . . . The costume, makeup, magnificent text, a good director, some effective drills . . . As for his "talent" to order himself what to do, he's got enough and to spare . . .

Tell me: do we not know such actors?

Toward the Culture of Calm

William James [1916: 74–75]:

> According as a function receives daily exercise or not, the man becomes a different kind of being in later life. We have lately had a number of accomplished Hindoo visitors at Cambridge, who talked freely of life and philosophy. More than one of them has confided to me that the sight of our faces, all contracted as they are with the habitual American over-intensity and

anxiety of expression, and our ungraceful and distorted attitudes when sitting, made on him a very painful impression. "I do not see," said one, "how it is possible for you to live as you do, without a single minute in your day deliberately given to tranquility and meditation. It is an invariable part of our Hindoo life to retire for at least half an hour daily into silence, to relax our muscles, govern our breathing, and meditate on eternal things. Every Hindoo child is trained to this from a very early age." The good fruits of such a discipline were obvious in the physical repose and lack of tension, and the wonderful smoothness and calmness of facial expression, and imperturbability of manner of these Orientals.

★★★

The freedom of muscles is a means to an end. Otherwise, you could relax and act this relaxation onstage; muscles need to be relaxed *in order not to get in the way* – what's most important is an actor's inner life, the string pulled taut across an actor's soul.

According to James' law, relaxation can lead to emptiness and limpness.

A method: your face is almost always tense (sometimes it even hurts from tension) – take it off, take off your face *like a mask after a masquerade* and put it somewhere, on a table, and exist without the mask, *without your face – exist as the true you.*

(So as not to scream from pain, people bite on their lip, a blanket, etc. Extreme tension, tension and fighting the reflexes that don't allow you to hurt yourself.)

★★★

See "*On Full Stop.*" Anxiety often occurs because an actor "steps on his own tail": before he can finish one bit, he's already tackling the next. In this case, the best way to calm down is to use the "*full stop*" method. The bit finishes itself, and it "falls away" on its own, and it's organically replaced by another bit. This one needs to be finished as well. As a result, anxiety and nervousness disappear and make way for calm, endurance, and the freedom of fantasy.

★★★

I'm a saturated solution. Impressions that enter me are tiny crystals. The reactions that occur as a result of the impressions (the creative process) lead to the formation of crystals in me – after all, I'm a saturated solution.

If I am calm, quiet, unperturbed at this time, then the crystals that form are enormous and beautiful. If something is constantly rocking the vessel (i.e. me), then the crystals will be tiny, possibly as small as dust.

★★★

Take life; some business conversation. You feel nervous and lost, but as soon as it's over, and you calm down, retrospectively you figure everything out: what you said wrong, and what you should have said instead.

★★★

Calm is a preliminary state – "a blank sheet of paper," and when it's there, then the tiniest impression or thought evokes an emotion, which then overcomes your entire being.

"The Threshold of Calm"

When you add drops of a chemical agent to a murky liquid with suspended residual matter, then sometimes, you have to add the drops for a very long time.

For example: the liquid is alkaline, and the residue dissolves in an acidic environment, and so you're adding the drops – it's all alkaline and all murky. Eventually, you'll reach a barely alkaline solution, and finally to a neutral one – still murky! One or two more drops – it quickly begins to grow lighter, until the murkiness disappears.

This is the boundary, the *threshold* in one's internal state.

You keep calming yourself, and at first, it doesn't seem like there's a lot of use out of it; finally, you put in a small amount of effort (or rather a small amount of "rejecting effort"), you step over a threshold—the sea gauge hits the bottom—and everything lightens.

It really is a *crisis* (to use Balzac's words).

As Tarkhanov said: you need to *"calm over."*

That *"over"* implies that you have to get to a certain point and go past it.

This observation is very important. If you know this, then you know what you have to aim for.

Otherwise, an actor relaxes a bit and believes that he's accomplished something.

If you know that you have to reach *a certain threshold and go past it*, and that everything before the threshold won't lead to anything, then things become *clearer*.

The comparison with the neutralization and acidification of the solution helps me a lot.

Even the "drops" are appropriate: when you relax and calm down, you also do it via little pushes, "drop by drop." It's like you're shaking something off of yourself. And you do it with your hands and your whole body.

The expression "meditative state" (which Pushkin experienced in the fall) also implies some sort of threshold.

Once you pass this threshold, only then do you enter another state, another plane (I don't know how else to say it) – another plane of consciousness (that's probably a good way to put it).

It's like you're tossing and turning in bed – you can't fall asleep – nonstop thoughts, you're thinking about life, and then, it's almost instant, like a key thrown into water: plop, it hits the bottom! – and everything is different: you're lying on the bottom and seeing the water, the fish . . . and I'm different . . . life as a whole is different! After all, the laws are different.

And here, while obtaining an actor's real, creative calm, you have to be aiming for another plane of consciousness – ***another state of consciousness***.

If you haven't reached it, then the creative process of artistic perception won't begin – you'll still be a *machine* . . .

Toward the Culture of Calm

Life is complex; you are constantly and reflexively reacting to things. And since your body and mind are executing so many functions simultaneously, and these functions and concerns tear them to pieces, and this state of haste and lunacy and mechanical reactions has already become a norm, I find that it's not enough to tell yourself or an actor: "relax, release your muscles" – you have to act quite decisively and concretely, not "generally."

For example: let your arms (or one arm) drop down, and do it so thoroughly that they begin to weigh down your shoulders, and you shouldn't do this willy-nilly, but quite seriously. Achieve a state in which any individual, independent life in your arms dies out. When this is achieved, check on your eye – how is it looking? – but let it also look quite concretely: at this object or that one or *that* one . . . In the meantime, keep sensing your arms, don't allow them to become numb.

Breathe in and say some phrase; do it with a prelude of an inhalation – and observe your arms, don't let them slip away: their job is to "die"! Keep track of this absolute, almost deathly calm.

Then you truly and concretely become *free* from them.

But the most wonderful thing is that if you've done everything correctly with your arms, your *whole* body follows suit and "dies off."

A Morning State

In the morning, when you've just woken up, you should take advantage of the state in which you are. This state is very appropriate in that your body is still asleep: in essence, I haven't fully woken up yet, I've only *come to*, I've just *regained consciousness*. This is the state that you should try to capture. Say some part from your role, some monologue, in a whisper or even soundlessly.

★★★

"Unbodiliness." A good word that explains and builds on "casting away [the body]."

A good expression: you have to "*release*" all your muscles.

On Genuine and Ostentatious Release (see "Verisimilitude")

A lot has been said about the genuine. We have to keep in mind that, for the most part, an actor, having heard plenty of talk about calm and release, is satisfied with a little – his fists aren't clenched convulsively, his face isn't contorted, his shoulders aren't raised to his ears, he's more or less sitting, more or less standing – everything's fine, everything is released.

Not a bit!

This is the imitation of freedom and calm: it's ostentatious calm, calm for *show* – it's not real, not authentic, not genuine. It's "tepid calm," the calm of verisimilitude. It's the calm of chatty improvisations. The calm of so-called (improperly so) "Chekhovian delicate half-tones" – in a word, the calm of a bad, third-rate Art Theatre.

In essence, this is most frightening of all calms: without great experience, you won't even be able to tell it apart – it seems like everything is right, everything's in order, and yet it's boring, wan, gray

You begin to be angry with the actor, you try to "inspire" him, excitedly describing the given circumstances – nothing comes of it; the actor is cold, he works through everything with his mind, his reason . . .

It would be one thing if there were some obvious error, like a contorted face or tense hands, but here . . . "murkiness" of the actor's soul, which is caused by small tensions, certain discomfort in the positions of his body, etc. – you can easily miss it.

This ostentatious and false calm has poisoned quite a few actors' and directors' lives and has sunk a massive number of shows!

But how can you tell one calm from another – right now, I'm calm, but which calm is it?

For now, this is my answer: "If you're cold, then you're doing it improperly. In a state of true calm, everything reaches your soul and affects you."

Toward the Culture of Calm

The majority of misfortunes occur because of anxiety and rushing. You have to *calm down*.

In your physical state, this means calm down, make yourself at home, get comfortable.

In your psychological state, to calm down means to start living with the true emotion – otherwise you'll "play the emotion."

Calm down in-character, or else you'll start "playing character."

Calm down with regards to your task, or else you'll begin to push.

Another method: doing only things miniscule – what you *truly want* and are capable of doing in the moment." [See *Silk Thread*.] We always overload ourselves.

Another: *full stops* – finish a bit before beginning with the next one.

★★★

Paganini's biographer Julius Schottky [as quoted in Prod'Homme 1911: 15] says:

> When he plays, his right foot is advanced and in brilliant passages marks the time with ludicrous rapidity, the face, however, not losing its stony impassiveness except for the shadow of a smile when thunders of applause greeted him; then his lips moved and his eyes, full of expression, but without kindliness, flashed in all directions.

What does this "stony impassiveness" mean? Not that he's all technique – then, it would be an expression of concern and attention, whereas this is the "impassiveness" of death. The complete "death" and calm of everything that might react to the external world.

There is life only on the inside. Inside, it boils and is transferred into the strings of the violin, and the sounds of the instrument pass through the ears into his heart, where they tear and torment it even more.

What would an "alive" face and inspired eyes mean?

That my soul is not passing through my hands, but through my breath and my gaze. Would there be much left for my hands?

★★★

Swirl your teaspoon around in your cup, and soon, a heap of tea leaves will appear in the center of your cup, slowly swirling around, while the liquid swirls with greater intensity around it.

That's what a tornado looks like. When it swoops down upon us, it tears off roofs, uproots trees, lifts up people, planks, sand, dirt, swirls them all around, carries them farther and farther into the air . . . But at its center, there is *absolute* silence and stillness. Much deeper than it would be in a silent room in which the air is still moving.

This is the *calm of a creative state*, especially of an actor's creative state. There is a flurry of activity, sounds, and forces without, but within, in the center of centers, there is the absolute silence that can form only as a result of *correct vortex* motion.

When a director or a teacher tells an actor: be calm "like in life," then they either don't fully understand what they're talking about or it's a subconscious method with whose help they can distract the actor from the dangerous reefs of thoughts about a "special" state of super-calm, thereby leading him away from tension.

In general, the expression "like in life" is wrong. Just like Diderot's insistence that an actor's soul must be cold. It is only applicable to the school of presentation.

It would be right if we said: *more, significantly more than in life*. This calm is **beyond the threshold** or ordinary calm.

Toward Releasing Muscular Tension

You shouldn't try to *relax* your muscles – this could lead you to limpness, languor, and blankness. What you should do is tell yourself: let *it* (my body) *fly off* of me – let alone not bother me. And then, without it, things become easier and lighter and freer. And your energy doesn't disappear or lessen.

On the Great Sleep of the Body

Physical tension is self-defense. It turns off our depths. Without it, we would suffer far too much from many things.

This random thought is very fruitful.

Our dreams . . . The body is not only resting – it's entirely devoid of tension, and even the muscles of our *vessels* completely relax: the vessels in our legs widen, and our cold legs grow warmer as a result. The face reddens. If you don't bundle up, you'll be cold, seeing as widened surface vessels give off a lot of warmth, etc.

And here, in dreams, every impression is so vivid – such impressions aren't possible in waking life.

The dream state should be investigated very, very seriously. A lunatic is walking along a cornice – watch how his innate sense of balance is released. Poets often spoke of creating art in dreams. Mozart: "in a pleasing, lively dream." Pushkin [1949: 321]: "and strives, as if in sleep, to finally pour out in a free expression." Goethe and Wagner on somnambulism. And what about the appearance of Saints in people's dreams, and not just those of men of faith – recall the appearance of Madonna to Raphael. And what about revelations that come in dreams?

There exists the psychological concept of the "threshold": a stimulus needs to be powerful enough in order to be received; anything that's below the threshold won't register. But this threshold moves: if there are other irritants, then stimuli that are usually received won't get through. For example: in silence, you hear whispering, but if there's noise all about, then you'll have a hard time hearing even a shout, let alone a whisper. Or: at night, you see the stars, while during the day, you have a hard time seeing the moon, to say nothing of the stars.

In dreams, in the absolute silence and darkness of our "bodily night," we see the "sky." Once we awake, the "threshold" skyrockets and situates itself rather high while we're in a waking state.

We need to take this image of the *night* and worm out of it as much as possible. I think that there's much more in it that we'll be able to extract. All those samadhi, seiza, as well as Mochalov "casually half-lounging on the bench" – it's all just the great sleep of the body! [The blocking of Mochalov as Hamlet, in the "mousetrap" scene, when the actor's body was free of any tension, and seemingly absent (see page 747); Samadhi, seiza – supernatural states of consciousness in Hindu and Buddhist meditation techniques.]

A culture of calm isn't enough – for affective art, we need a culture of the *great sleep of the body*!

I've spoken at length about "unbodiliness," about "slipping past the body," about how there is only the "shadow of a soul," but the sleep – the *great sleep* – will be somewhat more comprehensible and practical, just like "asana," for example, is much more practical than simply freeing your muscles. Can the sleep also be asana? Are you asleep? Can you fall asleep better?

And just like in asana, I lie there, while my thoughts are freely and lightly flying about – it's possible to make it so that your body sleeps (in any position), while your spirit is awake – "the spirit is willing" [Matthew 26: 41].

Toward Calm: Creativity Is One Kind of Sleep

When we lie down in bed in the evening trying to fall asleep, we lay ourselves down, our muscles relax on their own . . . A multitude of thoughts, desires, etc. keep our body primed and tense during the day. Now, there is nothing to be ready for other than peace and sleep. Your muscles take off their tension, like you do your clothing; subsequently, thoughts that tend to tear you apart calm down. Only two-three of them remain . . . Finally, one thought remains, and even this one grows thin, like a thread. For some time, your consciousness hangs on this single thought . . . suddenly, it tears, and . . . whoa! – you're flying into a deep abyss, into the realm of subconscious.

Does life in your psyche stop?

On the contrary. In your sleep, nothing distracts you, nothing makes you sober up, and your imagination *wholly* assumes command. Absurd fantasies throw us from fire onto ice, from the underworld into the sky, and there is no stopping the fantasies, the wonders, and the symbolism . . .

Racehorses see the derby, and they are covered all over with sweat from the imagined gallop. Hunting dogs bark while dreaming of chasing down an imaginary animal; they salivate, their hearts beating quickly . . .

Look how easily we fall under the influence of our imagination in a dream, when the rest of the world is shut out.

And look how pale our imagination is during the day. And how weak it is when compared to our nighttime imagination, which fully takes over us.

Our daytime imagination is fleeting, shallow, absent-minded; it doesn't lift us off the ground – it merely skids across our "surface."

At night, however, all we need is the shadow of a thought, and we're instantly under its spell; a barely perceptible physical sensation, and we're in the midst of a storm. It's enough to place your arm in a slightly uncomfortable manner to instantly see a tiger biting it off, or it being cut off by a train. The muted sound of a passing automobile outside turns into a stampeding herd of bulls . . .

Does something similar happen during the great actors' creative flights? Doesn't our "dream state" resemble the state of Yermolova when, in *Richard III*, she saw . . . her beloved dead husband, while the trickster prop master put a toy monkey in the coffin – the monkey Yermolova *didn't see at all*?

Toward a Culture of Calm: Methodology

The ordinary relaxation of muscles almost always leads to the overall limpness. Your will also relaxes. Your impressions become shallow, your voice becomes barely audible – afterwards, you just want to get out of this state – if you had known this would happen, you would never have started!

Naturally, mistakes were made – at some point, you missed the first sprout of apathy, and it grew out, at which point you had no hope of subduing it.

Just like you need attentiveness and vigilance during "questions and answers," so do you need them here. If not more so.

And this attentiveness, vigilance, and pickiness are the *first* thing.

Second: should we perhaps use methods that I suggested for the radio drama? Green-light a *change in the position of your body*. The main secret to this is giving in to barely perceptible movements of the body "as a whole." In order to accurately and clearly observe such barely perceptible movements – or rather, *hints* of movements – you need such silence, caution, and freedom inside you, that everything relaxes inside you essentially on its own. Moreover, this relaxation is absolute.

This same thing would happen with the "questions and answers" if they were brought to the proper level of perfection.

But his method, which excludes mimicry and gesture, and leaves only "position" and "movement," necessitates calming your typically restless body, and this calming gets work done in this case. A lot of attention must be dedicated to this.

The third method.

"Questions and answers" of certain content, of certain conditions, of a certain "I." In this case, gradualness of approach is very important. As the course progresses, you need to gradually and inconspicuously *remove any irritants from the circumstances* and *carefully insert, in proper portions, calm*, quiet, meditativeness (possibly wonder), so that you were drawn not towards movement, but towards immobility, so that you were concentrated on the inside, so that you had greater and greater need of your inner world, rather than your external one.

When teaching methods of relaxation, you need to find a technique that involves calming the body, while simultaneously intensifying inner activity.

"The Perch of Transition"

Physical relaxation is a sorcerer, a wizard with whose help it's possible to reach such levels of creativity that your very soul will begin to sing.

You've achieved physical relaxation – why, then, has the disappearance of tension brought about the death of liveliness? Why has everything wilted and died on the inside?

A precious moment was *skipped*. The *moment of transition* from one set of rails to another. There's a bridge that's two planks wide leading over a very wide river, and there's a small perch that leads to the bridge. You're walking along a wide road, you walk up to the river, and if you don't walk across the perch, you won't reach the bridge, and that means that you need to either stay here or take a dip in the river.

This transitionary perch is what dooms everything – the bridge is ahead, I'm walking toward it, and I see it . . . And I fixate my sight on the bridge so much that I miss the perch – I make a wrong step, and I come to only once I notice that I'm swimming, at which point there's no hope of clambering out – the bridge is high, and there's no way of reaching it.

These are the mechanics behind all failures, when attempting new methods. One small *mistake in the beginning* always results in very confusing results; you have to constantly mind your step. The key is *to not miss a crucial moment*.

The little perch is **the spine and breath**. Release your arms, your legs, release whatever you want, but never release, bend or bow your spine, and *never put your spine to sleep!* – keep it awake upright [even when lying down, preserve the sensation of the spine's uprightness and upwardness].

And never put your breath to sleep – let it be free, but not weak; keep watching it, albeit automatically – "support your sides" [See *Tube*].

And don't let your thought go to sleep – keep it busy; for example, let it oversee all this physical business [see Glossary for details].

11

The Threshold and After-the-Threshold

The Concept of the Physiological Threshold: Before the Threshold, the Threshold, and After-the-Threshold (the First, Second, and Third Thresholds in Creativity)

When I see something, and I still exist "before the threshold," I see it as a dispassionate cataloguer: there stands a flower in a pot. I ask myself: do I like it? I immediately see something in the flower that concerns *me*: this means that a threshold has been crossed.

Same with hearing. "Where are you going?" A cataloguer's response: "home!" – this is before the threshold. Beyond the threshold: "My god – he wants to go with me!"

This *first threshold* is everything: after you cross it, you've entered into life. At that point, whatever new circumstances are given to the actor, they'll come to life too.

The *second threshold* is between the personal, the egoistic, and the social – my family, my relatives; he asks me a question, but it concerns not just me, but everyone with whom I'm connected.

The *third threshold* is the cosmic consciousness: all people, the whole world, all of nature; he asks me a question, and this now concerns the laws of life and nature (truth, goodness?).

Toward the Second Threshold: The Distribution of Attention and Genius

As Janet notes, absolute unity of consciousness (in which one's consciousness holds only a single focus at a time) can occur only in an extreme case: either in a case of extreme pathology (catalepsy, "when a starved psyche is incapable of registering multiple sensations at once") and in a case of *genius*: "psychological unity during moments of great intellectual upliftment, when a *perfect* psyche enables a person to fully grasp and synthesize all the images and feelings that he or she is experiencing or that he or she recalls."

The Second Threshold

When an actor "juggles" a single "ball" successfully, we'll start adding more balls. [See the description of the juggler's process, offered by Kara (Michael Steiner), Book One, Chapter 7, sub-chapter "Talent."] At first, he won't be able to handle two "balls" – he needs to tackle simpler, more primitive circumstances. But the time will come when two "balls" won't be challenging enough for him, and he'll ask for a third on his own.

The farther we go, the more "balls" are tossed at the actor; the farther we go, the closer we get to the *second threshold*, the threshold of heightened *affective creativity* – that of a *tragic actor*.

Hamlet's father died, his mother married a scoundrel . . . Yes, it's hard, yes it's unfortunate, yes, it's painful, but such is life . . . Such is our troposphere.

This might be two, maybe even three, but it's definitely not more than four balls – we can still grasp it, more or less.

But life tosses us a fifth ball: the ghost of Hamlet's murdered father has been seen at midnight wandering around a platform before the palace.

I cannot fathom it – my mortal heart is too small to fit this in, and my human strength is too week to carry the burden. This is an overload – this is five balls. But five isn't enough: life, "with its bountiful hand," tosses us a sixth! At midnight, the ghost appears before Hamlet.

> Angels and ministers of grace defend us!
> Be thou a spirit of health or goblin damn'd,
> Bring with thee airs from heaven or blasts from hell,
> Be thy intents wicked or charitable,
> Thou comest in such a questionable shape
> That I will speak to thee: I'll call thee Hamlet,
> King, father, royal Dane: O, answer me!
> Let me not burst in ignorance; but tell
> Why thy canonized bones, hearsed in death,
> Have burst their cerements; why the sepulchre,
> Whe' we saw thee quietly inurn'd,
> Hath oped his ponderous and marble jaws,
> To cast thee up again. What may this mean,
> That thou, dead corse, again in complete steel
> Revisit'st thus the glimpses of the moon,
> Making night hideous; and we fools of nature
> So horridly to shake our disposition
> With thoughts beyond the reaches of our souls?
> Say, why is this? wherefore? what should we do?

The ghost speaks . . . it says a lot of dreadful things, but beyond this "a lot," we feel that there is something more . . . Something great and frightful . . . A sixth! A seventh! Maybe an eighth ball!

> O all you host of heaven! O earth! what else?
> And shall I couple hell? O, fie! Hold, hold, my heart;
> And you, my sinews, grow not instant old,
> But bear me stiffly up. Remember thee!
> Ay, thou poor ghost, while memory holds a seat
> In this distracted globe. Remember thee!
> Yea, from the table of my memory
> I'll wipe away all trivial fond records,

> All saws of books, all forms, all pressures past,
> That youth and observation copied there;
> And thy commandment all alone shall live
> Within the book and volume of my brain,
> Unmix'd with baser matter: yes, by heaven!

All eight balls swim in a halo through the air, the juggler's hands are flickering with blinding speed, his eyes unable to latch on to anything individually – they see everything all at once, and he, "losing himself" merges as one with the balls and their flight.

This is what we can see in the best moments of a talented affective actor.

It's a rare occurrence. As long as we don't have a school of affective art, it's more than rare. After all, typically, we see how the slightest overload – this doesn't even have to be six or eight balls – it could just be four – results in an actor not even noticing how he drops all of his balls and begins to *wave his empty hands around in the air* because of trying too hard and not having a wide enough grasp. He strains himself, begins to declaim, be full of pathos, pretend that his agitation is tearing him apart, all while his heart and mind are empty, just like his empty hands: all the "balls" have long since been dropped.

There is another path, a path that is exalted by those that do not know how to achieve the affective expansion from an actor and how to keep him in this state.

Yet, the actor recognizes only the "truth" onstage. And he wields the "truth." A small "truth," a truth that consists of only three balls. And he's virtuosic in doing so. But a fourth ball is too cumbersome for him – he avoids it. As for a fifth ball . . . we'll just stay away from a fifth ball.

And so, when Shakespeare tosses a fourth ball to this "virtuosic juggler," the actor takes it, but *artfully* drops one of the previous three . . . And he has only *three* once more: three that he can juggle masterly!

Shakespeare tosses him a fifth, a sixth, a seventh – as many as he wants! – but the actor once again drops one of the invariable three, replaces it with a new one (be it even Shakespeare's *tenth* ball), and keeps on juggling!

I am speaking with my friends – an ordinary event, nothing special: three balls. A fourth ball appears – the Ghost. Something very unnatural . . . Hm . . . Why is it unnatural? It's just a new conversation partner is all . . . It might be a Ghost . . . But I can see it, hear it, converse with it! – that means that all the laws of common communication are still the same!

Father! . . . beloved . . . deceased . . . But it's as if he's alive. We've met up, we're talking . . . I'm the son, he's the father, we're talking . . . The fourth "unnatural" ball, the improbable one, hits the ground, and once again, we have only three balls!

Well, alright, maybe not three balls – maybe they're three glass jugs (a little bit more difficult), but still, just three!

The same mechanics are utilized later on in other scenes and instances.

It looks pretty good, especially if instead of balls and even jugs, there are three torches swirling through the air – this seems like high art.

Though I'm not a fan of such art, I hasten to specify that it, naturally, vastly surpasses *waving empty hands around in the air.*

A Few Thoughts on the Technique of the Second Threshold

Anyone can get to the first threshold and go over it. An experienced pedagogue can teach someone who is absolutely unsuitable to the actor's art to do this much.

As for crossing the second threshold – aside from giftedness and immense assiduousness, you also need to know a few special methods. Without them, it doesn't matter how talented you are – there will inevitably be failures of such magnitude that you won't know what to do with yourself! . . .

In the proper hands, an action-oriented actor's methods of working on a role ("the life of a human body" that is gradually enriched by new circumstances, etc.) can be harmlessly and even beneficially applied to an affective actor. However, the most important thing that needs to be developed is a *certain way of perceiving the world and a certain reaction*, i.e. *a technique of affectivity*, on its own.

1   These methods must grant the ability to *admit external impressions to our depths* (we very rarely admit something into our "most holy place" – it all just skids along our surface).
2   The methods must grant the ability to *green-light such a level of freedom* that would allow us to "exhale" *everything that flared up in our depths* without obstruction. Usually, we keep whatever emerges in our souls buried deep inside. Would we really choose to reveal our bared souls?! Everything seeps out of us through a *filter*. The most dangerous, risky, intimate things (pebbles) remain inside us.

Without knowing the methods of the technique of affectivity, and even knowing them, but not being *trained* in them, nothing good can happen.

The action-oriented school of theatre proposes its own array of methods for this purpose: "activity," "objects," "tasks," "attention," "appraisal of facts," etc. It claims that we have to use these methods to bring an actor to a state of "truth," when an actor begins to perceive all the given circumstances as real, after which the gradually expanding circumstances themselves lead the actor to the point at which he can cross the second threshold and enter a state of "inspiration."

However, experience shows that an actor that's been *trained* by the methods of an action-oriented school is capable of giving himself over to the "truth" *only to a certain degree*. As soon as the circumstances expand, as soon as the situation becomes critical and ordinary life turns into drama (to say nothing of tragedy), the actor cannot handle the overload, and he closes off and grows cold.

So, in practice, these methods do not pull through. Which is unsurprising – such is the careful *nature* of the analyst and the intellectually willful reasoner.

True, there have been cases when, after two-three hours of intense work, a strong and talented director was able to stir up an actor and lead him into a state of great passion – the rehearsal would amaze everyone, but . . . the following day, the same three hours (if not more) were necessary. And the day after that . . . Repeating this kind of work day after day is humanly impossible . . . And so, "inspiration" would cease to exist before it could even reach the performance.

There have been other cases too, when action-oriented methods resulted in authentic internal passion and explosions; this would happen when an *affective* actor was involved. At first, he would follow the regular path of an action-oriented actor – he would search for physical truths, but when the circumstances would grow intense and thick, he would, unnoticeably for the director, *slip away to his own path*, which *his affective nature* hinted at.

The external fire (from "attention," from "appraising the circumstances," from the "tasks" and "bits") suddenly *spread to the actor's inner life*, and this resulted in an explosion. The affective actor's nature hinted to him where to slip away from the action-oriented path to the affective one. Actors of other types are not able to slip away like this.

701

The main difference of the *school of the affective actor* (from the action-oriented school) is that it trains its actors in such a way that they perceive everything **already beyond the second threshold**.

Potential. Five Balls. The Threshold

Let's assume that we all have "Kazbeks" and "depths," that we're all much wider and much deeper than we think ourselves to be.

But, my god, how difficult it is to reach all these Kazbeks, and how little we want to do so!

On our own, we can't dig up anything in ourselves.

You're a wilted, inert, lazy everyman.

But, here comes an artist – he sits you down in the cabin of his airplane, pulls you out of your calm troposphere, and shows you the stars and the sky from a point of view that you could never even imagine.

When we sit in his cabin, we see the world as he sees it – when we sit there, we can fly just as well as he can.

An artist comes and launches an enormous rock drill into your soul, bores all the way to our hearts, to our precious depths, and unleashes the vigorous healing waters, the oil reserves that have been lying in wait up 'til now – a fountain of sorrowful tears . . . golden thoughts will flow forth . . .

This bears witness to the fact that we all have vast potentials.

But if something is *potential* it does not mean that it actually exists.

Potentially, anybody can walk on his or her hands, spin around in the air like a circus acrobat, juggle three-four balls – but do we have the patience and strength to bring ourselves to this point? *You have to learn, train yourself every day for months, years.* The vast majority will only do so for about half an hour.

Two Methods of Entering the "Room of Affect"

1   Break through the door every single time.

Using Stanislavsky's methods (if they're used *perfectly, i.e. only after they've been significantly altered*), it's a very long path to reach a state of inspiration. You have to keep loading up on circumstances until there's an overload, at which point you *beat the door in*, and the way will be clear.

2   Unlock the door with a key.

By the way of *breathing* – without breaking or overloading anything. This method is like opening a door with a *key*.

Toward Tragedy

In drama, do we sometimes involuntarily inhibit our experiencing?

We probably do.

What is drama that has transformed into tragedy? When impressions from objects reach an actor's very depths, and the response also comes from those very depths.

After all, we're not just – how to say this – who we are at the moment; somewhere in our depths we carry a special memory of millions of years of inherited experience.

This immediately results in our inner significance, as well as our connection to eternity and to all of humanity; we can stand up to fate, destiny, and the entire world.

And what about drama? Drama is setting *what is my own* as the limits. But if you "descend" into yourself, only deeper, *beyond the personal* and the mundane, you will inevitably pass beyond the borders of the personal into the realm of the universal and the eternal, a realm that is accessible only to the affective actor.

In this way, *inhibiting the process of perception* is one of the *technical* reasons for departing from tragedy into drama.

Releasing the brakes, however, is a path from drama to tragedy.

If the process is inhibited even further, then we'll be left with comedy – even more, and we'll have vaudeville, in which things are *immensely* serious, but the people themselves are small, lesser, with *no* depth *whatsoever*. Why? After all, the actor has depth – he's not an idiot at all. The reason: the depths are *inhibited*.

★★★

Thin skin, open wounds, and the lack of "protective glass" do not the tragedy make. Tragedy must be *all-encompassing* – it is in things such as "taking upon yourself the sins of the world."

★★★

Tragedy is inevitably deals with greatness. Greek tragedy – battling against fate. A weakling has no hope of fighting fate.

Toward the Threshold

You either have to *pass beyond* the threshold, or you have to demand less of yourself. It's better not to demand that you approach the threshold.

Water that hasn't been boiled well often leads to an upset stomach. Why? Because high temperatures that are close to boiling level develop various malignant substances (perhaps, they stimulate microbes). And this not-quite-boiled water is worse than untreated water.

But it's rather difficult to bring it to boiling (for an actor). Especially because the water grows quiet just before boiling.

All of these "not quites" and "not in fulls" are the worst things that could happen.

★★★

There is a circle. At the very heart of it is a center. If you move from the perimeter to the center, you have to *immediately start moving in the exact direction towards the center*. If you're off by just a degree, then you'll miss it (the center). And once you've passed it, you'll keep getting farther and farther from your goal (the center) with every step, until you get to the other side of the perimeter.

★★★

"Kazbek . . . " "Mashuk . . . " So, if I'm small and insignificant, nothing will come of me? And what about the audience? And what about the Ruhmkorff's coil?[1] or breathing techniques? or physiology? or admitting? or the nearest flow of thought? or dropping [text, circumstances, or tasks] into the subconscious?

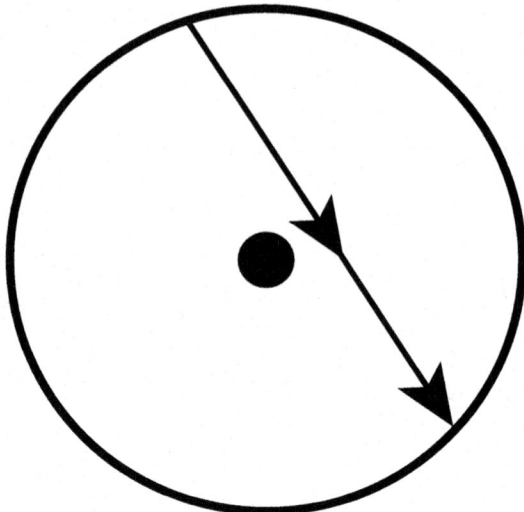

Drawing 1

And finally: training yourself to break the banks?

You can certainly "break" them, but it won't be a "Terek." It'll just be a raging little brook. But this too is *artistry*.

Note

1 Ruhmkorff coil is also known as "induction coil." A German instrument maker Heinrich Daniel Ruhmkorff (1803–1877) patented a coil that utilized long windings of copper wire. A large number of turns results in a voltage pulse of many thousands of volts.

12

On Breathing

When we unexpectedly see someone we know, we inhale, as if we're breathing in the impression we get from the person and maybe even the person himself (as I see, feel, know him, etc.). Without completely holding on to the air, without locking it in, we then exhale his name. We do so, as if we just sucked some air into a ball syringe, and then immediately breathed out the very same air – unaltered, unchanged. And so, our "Ah! Ivan!!!" is let out on its own, without any participation on our behalf. This is the prototype of our inner life when the impression of a given moment is singular.

It would also be good to keep track of all the involuntary "in-breaths" when we sigh about something sad, wistfully, when we sigh in relief (when we sigh out some difficult, or depressing impression). When children sigh, longing for their mothers. And, finally, when dogs, horses, and other animals sigh. Yawning.

In *Hamlet*, Shakespeare says that words are the breath of life.[1]

What we call "preludes" – they are something imaginary, something taken in with breath. Mistakes that can occur while employing this method:

1   People breathe in air, but not an impression, and yet they think that they have also taken in an impression.
2   People breathe in an impression, but they are paying so much attention to whether they've also breathed in air that they breathe in more of it than necessary – this results in untruth – duality.
3   People try too much and simply "floor" the method (as they would a gas pedal) – the result is the same: duality, and too much air leads to choking.
4   People pause after the inhalation, and halt their inner lives, after which they breathe out a completely different thing than they breathe in.
5   People breathe in, don't let the breath get to the right place (the head or the stomach), and they rush to breathe out – this leads to miscarriages, spitting up the words.

When working on a character, it's good to breathe in this person's qualities and attributes – what is he like? When doing so, there's no need to lose your "I." Let the "I" remain the "I." But the role's "qualities" might be very unusual and uncommon for me – these are the qualities that I should take in with the breath.

This is also good in the sense that what is "taken in" immediately drops into our subconscious. [See *Breathing in Character Qualities*]

★★★

On breathing in the lines: naturally, you should be breathing in not the lines themselves, but what's **behind** the lines – not the formal text, but the subtext.

★★★

On breathing in objects, people, and phenomena: the same thing as with lines – don't breathe them in formally; breathe in what the object or person holds for you at the moment, right now.

For Hamlet, in the moment when he's thinking about death, Ophelia isn't just the young girl Ophelia, the nobleman's daughter – she is "his Ophelia," she is "She," and the fact that she showed up at just this moment – it's a miracle! And this miracle is necessary for his distraught soul, and he cries out: "The fair Ophelia! – Nymph (oh, the pure), in thy orisons be all my sins remember'd (deliver me, the Most-Pure)."

For Podkolyosin, marriage isn't just marriage – for him it's "something else, something difficult!" [Gogol 1949: 12].

For Adrienne [Adrienne Lecouvreur, an 18th-century French actress, is a title character of the 1849 drama by Eugene Scribe and Ernest Legouvé], the returned bouquet is the return of all vows, the end of love, and an insult.

But it could be that the truest and most proper impressions that you can take in with your breath are the impressions that you get with the help of "admitting" (see the corresponding chapter), where impressions *must be formal*, unaccompanied by any tangible point of view on the object, line, or circumstance, and in *that* case, once it's reached your subconscious, the stimulation evokes the deepest possible response.

★★★

It's possible to breathe in images that don't concern me, nor my emotions; they flow by me, but leave me cold – they only reach my head.

But it's also possible to breath in images that won't leave me cold, but instead evoke involuntary sensations – emotional reactions. And it should be mentioned that it *depends on me*, not on what's being breathed in.

It's possible to tune yourself so that everything will *only reach your head*, but it's also possible to do it in such a way that everything will reach your emotions, your soul, and, possibly, the Spirit.

What we need here is the Technique.

There are many examples in life: when watching surgeries for the first time, medical students faint at the sight of blood; however, having gotten used to it, they become completely calm and collected – the blood goes no farther than their head.

Executioners. Criminals. Warriors.

At first, when people do not believe the orator (Mark Antony in *Julius Caesar*), they don't admit him to their souls, but as soon as he manages to melt a bit of the ice, every single word assumes a more significant meaning and travels directly to the soul.

"A prayer of the mind" [see Glossary] is one that's admitted with one's breath only as far as their head.

"A prayer of the heart" is admitted, with the breath, all the way to one's soul.

It's possible to tune yourself internally to be conducive to either mode.

First, exercise admitting things, with the breath, only as far as "to the mind." Then, practice the other approach, breathing in impressions all the way to your heart.

Don't rush, don't chase too much after the second kind of admitting – all the way "to the heart." Put in serious and prolonged exercise for both modes. And most importantly: don't mix the two.

★★★

It's often very difficult to listen to the words of your scene partners, but a lot in a scene often hinges on this.

A very good method: *listen to them while breathing in*, and follow this scheme: breathing is a needle, the words are the thread – then they'll get where they have to.

A possible mistake: you might take in your partner's words, listening to him while breathing – everything is right, but then you stop, interrupt the flow, and you lose what you've already taken in. At that point, you'll be breathing out something different, something that's not a reaction to the words you just took in – not the proper result.

It's possible to take in not just your partner's words, but his pauses, his motions, and his silent facial reactions. These often say more than the words themselves.

You can pause after an in-breath, but in this moment – neither the object, nor your attitude towards it should change. [See *Tube*.]

This method is very good for opening up liberating one's temperament. Especially if you learn to "admit" things well and, most importantly, *deeply* (all the way to your solar plexus), and immediately release *everything in its whole* from your depths, without timidity, without interrupting the flow, without correcting it. Then, you'll be able to even release the kind of wailing from your "depths" – your voice will sound as if it's emerging from your very soul.

This is what differentiated our great, old "gut" actors (Ivanov-Kozelsky, Mochalov, Mamont Dalsky) – the mediocre inheritors picked up only on their wailing, only the screams, and now they continue to "howl with the wolfs."

I once had the opportunity to see this in action with Moissi. When, after "To be or not to be," he suddenly and unexpectedly saw Ophelia not too far away, he instantly retreated a few steps, simultaneously breathing in (as if he were breathing *her* in), raised his arm once his breath reached his depths— and immediately, without stopping his breath or internal life, breathed everything back out – the air, and her, and her name: "Ophelia." And he breathed in on a "ghaaa!?" and when this "ghaa," which was full Ophelia, reached his depths, and the air and the feeling of Ophelia filled his chest, then his soul and he breathed out the whole, organically-fused thing. You could hear the fusion even in the sound: he wasn't saying, he was *moaning* her name, and it wasn't "Ophelia," but more like *"ghophelia!!!"* after which he breathed in again (but less so) "gha!" and another out-breath "hnimphe!"

★★★

"A prayer with the mind in the heart:" the in-breath: "Lord Jesus Christ, Son of God . . . " the out-breath: "have mercy on me." Taking in God's Name and then breathing it out, you don't quite exhale all the way out – part of it stays in you and is *digested*.

★★★

There are also subconscious sighs: I don't even know what I breathed in. But I definitely took something in – that's indubitable – there was definitely a psychological inhale. And this "something" shouldn't be delayed, and it shouldn't be let out either, but rather, it should be transformed – you should give in to your subconscious desire and let out a sound, a moan, whatever – it doesn't matter. This moan, etc. will reveal what you just breathed in; you can now follow it with your next line, resting assured that it will pull out, like a needle, the thread of your innermost secret.

Diaphragmatic Breathing

During asana, while in sitting "Tree Pose," in a meditative state, your breathing is restructured: it becomes exclusively diaphragmatic.

This also happens in the state of "liberation form the body," when only the diaphragmatic "tube of breath" feels alive, as well as in accidental creative states, when, all of a sudden, you are "carried by the inspiration."

In general, this *diaphragmatic breathing*, its causes, effects, its mechanics and psycho-mechanics *need our special, undiluted attention*.

It's not for nothing that it is figured so prominently in occultism. Swami Vivekananda [1863–1902] calls it the silk thread with whose help the minister got down from the tower [See Book Three, Part Three, Chapter 17].

It occurs because of psychological reasons, and it can be activated physically – then, we get a psychological restructuring.

It can be achieved by combining it with a few elementary psychological methods (asana, calm, etc.). Finally it can be combined with more serious psychological phenomena: thought, imagination, etc.

However, we must begin establishing its culture, and studying it with the simplest possible steps, else we'll miss what is most essential and relevant, and, by doing so, tear the silk thread right from the start.

There's one thing we shouldn't forget: we have to somehow draw our thought to this act (or else to distract it with something concrete: meditation, rhythm, imagining certain physical states, such as those of "flight" and the "tree" in *asanas*). Otherwise, it will "escape," and inevitably get in our way. It will harm the process, and the whole machine will fall apart. It will inevitably drag the body away with it as well. There's no escaping this – thought is stronger than any other force – it's omnipotent.

★★★

One of the ways to achieve diaphragmatic breathing is the method that I learned about from Pyatnitsky: while speaking some monologue or verse, you follow not so much the words and their meaning, but rather make sure that your stomach rises (on the in-breath) and deflates; and he recommended *not to breathe in until you're entirely out of breath* (until you have expunged all the air out of yourself). But breathe not with your chest, but your *stomach*!

Quite soon, you'll pay less and less attention to the mechanical work and will instead retain some extra attention, which you will then direct at your words. And your words will begin to latch on to you and immerse you.

This method should be combined (though this combination can occur quite naturally) *with liberating your body* (or liberating yourself from your body).

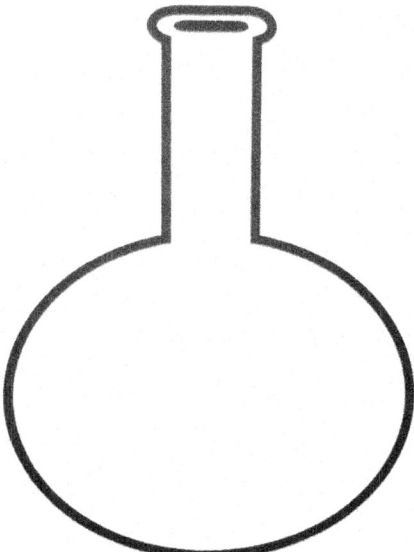

Drawing 2

Then you get the feeling as if the only thing living is this central *tube,* which is shaped like a flask: the top is your throat, and the bottom is the upper part of your stomach.

Everything else merely "exists" – while this tube alone lives.

Toward Breathing: In Life

"Take your models from life" [Stanislavsky's (1958: 403) summary of Shchepkin's teachings]. Not everything that turns up in life can serve as a good model. For example, let's take our current subject – "breathing."

Only the most open-hearted people breathe in everything they encounter. Most importantly, along with their words or actions, they *breathe out* precisely what they perceive with their inhalation. Closed off people do this very rarely, and only with regards to something that truly shakes them to their core.

In the majority of cases, however, you see the following: a person listens to someone speak for awhile, and then suddenly he breathes in loudly and quickly; you expect him to say something deep, something that came from his soul, but no such luck! A pause, some hand gesture, and then some empty, uncharged words – he didn't say a thing of what he took in, of what he wanted to say.

This is the usual turn of events.

Another occurrence – also quite common, yet not as easy to detect – is restricted perception, or *non-admitting.* A person sees a fact or hears words, but doesn't allow all of them inside – he doesn't take them in, and instead sends them through a sieve, which is either a fruit of his cowardice, or, like a conditioned reflex, has been formed by life's hardships.

If you're playing closed off people, then you can use this as your model. Although, these examples are not very precious either – this is our usual state, and we have little to learn from it.

These cases can teach us one thing: what not to do. In life, we very rarely breathe as we are supposed to, so relying on life and recommendations to breathe as you would "in life" are vastly improper.

It would be proper to say: model it after what we *sometimes* do in life. When? When we are *singular*.

★★★

It's possible to breathe in to your head, your stomach, and your soul (spirit). We can only do the latter if we release and cast off our bodies to the maximum possible degree. I.e. achieve complete "bodilessness." Having done so, it's also possible to achieve "the nearest flow of thought," i.e. it's possible to create a very intimate connection between the imagined and my soul. Concordantly, when you breathe in, you will essentially be physically taking in what was happening outside of you just a second ago: "I in all, and all in me . . . "

More on Mistakes

You've breathed in, which caused a psychological impression. However, you don't have the courage to say everything with the same breath you just took in. So you release almost all the air, and use only the leftovers to speak – the effect is extraordinarily unimpressive.

Something significant is taken in with the air, but it's like a harmonica with hole-ridden bellows: part of the air is used to create a sound, but the greater part slips away through the holes. You took in something meaningful – so give it back! Exhume as much meaningful air as you took in! Don't waste it!

What you take in should be, first of all, given back unchanged, and secondly, returned *in full*.

You have to be generous, prodigal. Often, this is the only way to awaken a true temperament. Otherwise, an actor might take in a lot, have a large reserve, and yet he gives back only one tenth, or even one hundredth.

Also, it's necessary to concern yourself with giving back not just the air, but the *state* that you took in with the air – otherwise, you might be breathing like a chugging train, but the state will slip by the air. You have to be prodigal with regards to this *state*. (Also see "*Incomplete-Combustion Products*.")

Sometimes, you take in a lot of air and almost immediately – quickly – but that doesn't always mean that you have to exhume it as quickly. This can happen: I don't know what to say – then, finally, I suddenly understand what to say, take an enormous breath, and I begin a long, measured, and unhurried speech. In this way, a single breath can be enough for even 20 phrases!

★★★

It can happen that the air is inhaled slowly, very slowly, grain by grain, and then it's exhaled momentarily, as if thrown back out. This isn't a mistake, but merely a variation. Just like the previous example is a variation.

★★★

Another variation. When a person says everything, breathes everything out, he can go for a long time without moving or taking a big breath – if "he keeps finishing up his bit." When the bit ends, he'll have a new object, he'll have something new to perceive, and so, after a big pause, there will be a big breath; with this new air, he'll perceive something new. A new bit has begun.

★★★

I said that "it's necessary to concern yourself with giving back not just the air, but the *state* that you took in with the air." So maybe there's no need to discuss the air at all? No, it's crucial to talk about it. The thing is that the air and states of being not only comingle, but are organically fused with each other. It's not just breathing – *it's psychological breathing – the breathing of thoughts.* And so, when an in-breath is a thought (or perhaps a combination of feeling, will and thought), then an out-breath needs to be adequate. And after a few proper in- and out-breaths, you get a reflex that *connects each breath with a state.* They become so connected that a state follows a breath like a thread follows a needle.

So it's necessary, by means of certain manipulations, i.e. proper psychological breathing, to make yourself feel this connection and, once you've felt it, establish it. And once you've established it, become accustomed to it, wield it.

Towards a Pedagogy of Breathing: On Smell

As any delicate thing, it's not always possible to explain the mechanics of psychological breathing in our lives, and, therefore, onstage.

Here's another method (it's good in that it involves not only psychological breathing, but physical as well). This is how it goes:

You're holding in your hands a small bunch of lilies-of-the-valley. You bring it to your nose . . . you smell it . . . "Ahh, it's so good!" The in-breath is crucial, and this is the advantage of this method. And, in order to get the right physiological in-breath, the same method is recommended (smelling a flower).

In this way, using this purely physiological exercise, it's possible to capture the psychological mechanics, especially since the in-breath will be inevitably physiologically correct, and (according to James' law) will therefore result in a state of good passive openness.

In general, we neglect smelling, and neglect the nose . . . But what if we try to employ them more? Smell (combining it with psychological smelling) – smell everything . . . flowers, objects, people, thoughts, present, future . . . this might have a large meaning.

This isn't what dogs do – for them, it's just a highly developed sense – I mean specifically *combining physical breathing with psychological openness.* There's a meaning in it.

It's also good to *listen to some kind of sound* – a tram, a horn, distant music or singing. – This also happens with breathing – it's not hard to notice yourself doing so.

And in general, it's good to treat your five senses and simple sensations as a point of departure.

To peer into the distance, and finally to see; to listen intently and – to hear; to touch and, finally, to discover and guess what kind of object it is.

★★★

Yoga Vasistha. "Yoga is restraining the *breath of life.*"[2] There (seemingly) is psychological breathing, and this breathing should be connected with physical breathing and vice versa: while paying attention to your physical breathing, it's easier to keep track (and influence) your psychological breathing.

★★★

As a method for comprehending the simplest mechanics of proper breathing: breathe powerfully and curtly ("back and forth"), like after a short run that caused some light panting, and then, *immediately* begin speaking your lines. And in general, this method ("panting") should be implemented in quick scenes and especially when an actor stubbornly holds his breath.

This process doesn't involve any psychological perception of an object and merely tunes up the physical apparatus, which, according to James' law, leads an actor to the proper state.

This panting should be done lightly, without straining, without "stepping on it." Let it be a *pleasant* episode of panting that causes everything to be brighter, more jovial, more free.

Evidently, this is one of the reasons behind the enlivening effect of open-air games (aside from increased blood flow, intoxication on your own carbonic gases, etc.) – you enter a light and liberated state.

Toward the Pedagogy of Breathing

In order for an actor to practically understand that in life he is also psychologically breathing in, holding his breath, and breathing out, you often use a simple method: ask him the most common, mundane questions about his day.

"Did you walk or drive here? Did you run into anyone you know?" etc. And you catch him: "There, you breathed! What did you breathe in? Why didn't you breathe out the same thing? Did you change something in yourself?" Once you point this out to him, he'll understand the issue.

But you have to ask him only questions that evoke monosyllabic responses, lest his attention will be solely focused on interesting objects, and he won't have any left to dedicate to the process itself. It would simply be a lively conversation, and an improper one with regards to breathing. And you won't even be able to catch on to why the mechanics are proper or improper. You ask two, three, four, ten questions, and then you get sucked into the conversation yourself, and lose any track at all.

Advice 1: Simple questions, and catch the actor after every one.

Advice 2: Repeat the same question.

Advice 3: Ask questions about visible, audible, smellable, touchable, and other primitive sensations and perceptions – ones that exist for the actor in the present – rather than imaginary ones.

★★★

When we are silent, we breathe physiologically, but when we breathe in (take in air) in order to say something, we begin to breathe psychologically.

★★★

When we breathe in psychologically, the air we take in is accompanied by what we want to say – a picture, an image, a sensation. Ideally, this is the thing that must be given off – since it has been inhaled.

And this is where the difficulties lie. Before exhaling this image, picture, etc., we pause, and we give off not the image in its whole, but rather a cut version.

★★★

When you perceive something, it's not necessary to perceive it clearly and distinctly. After all, do we perceive everything clearly all the time? I might have taken something in indistinctly – so that's the way I'll give it off.

★★★

When perceiving, it's not necessary to understand everything consciously. For the most part, you look at something and deep within yourself, you understand it – therefore, there's no need examining it, or bother transferring it to your conscious mind. And now, whatever you perceived, whatever you sensed – that's what you must give back.

★★★

We can often observe an interesting and traitorous phenomenon among dulled people: they see something (even something unexpected), breathe in, and at the breath's crest, something shuts automatically: bam! and everything stays on the inside – the trapdoor has closed! And there's no way for the impression to get back out.

In this case, we could give some advice that goes against all previous rules – rush. Give off (i.e. speak) before you finish taking something in.

★★★

A similar method: don't "give off" anything – just "take things in"; keep perceiving, but don't give anything back. Don't interrupt the stream of impressions you are receiving. When you speak, it might seem as if you're giving things off, but you just *keep perceiving and taking things in* while you speak.

★★★

Our breathing isn't used to such uncontrolled output. And we don't perceive things too freely either. We're used to impeding these processes, including breathing. In order to combat this, it's quite useful to warm up your breath before you begin. Breathe lightly, without straining, "back and forth." Then do the same with a sound, allowing it to carry some kind of a meaning. Then move on to conversational speech, speaking individual words or phrases. And then furtively sneak up to a scene or monologue.

★★★

It's always necessary to accompany your breathing technique with "*letting go.*"

★★★

How do you give off what you just took in – breathe out what you breathed in? What might help is an advice to green-light the *first* impulse, your first desire – just as you do in the etudes.

"Admitting" and Breathing

In work that has to do with uncovering the secrets of affective creativity, this coupling [of admitting and breathing] is one of the most promising . . .

When you admit things to yourself, your perception is completely formal. The impressions that you get aren't evaluated by your consciousness, and they drop deep inside you, at which point they evoke a reaction.

This requires a lot of thought. A lot of experimenting.

For now, I'll write about something else. So as not to forget it. You'll perceive something and suddenly feel that the impression causes something to happen inside you: your heart contracts, there is a needling sensation in the pit of your stomach . . . And then the impression stays there. Not only did it not find an exit, you don't even know *what* just happed, what exactly pricked you. You try to repeat it: there's nothing exciting or worrying in the vicinity, and there shouldn't even be. Either you missed it when you were taking it in or you formally "admitted" it, and then hit the brakes . . .

★★★

1   It's possible to breathe in an abstract image (it would be better to say: you breathe something *into your head*; see below). It's also possible to receive a tangible sensation from an image (it would be better to say: breathe something *into your stomach*).

2   "Breathing in an image and getting a sensation from it" – so, doesn't this mean that the issue is about the image? Why then do we need the breathing? Isn't it just a complication?

No: *breath clears room for the image*. The image won't materialize inside you if there's no preliminary inhalation. It aids in the appearance of the physical image.

Breathing is the needle that the image follows like a thread. Try to take in an image *with* your breath, and then try to take it in *without* a breath – you won't be able to. Not only does the image not go anywhere near your emotions and sensations, it even has difficulties reaching your head – it'll stay outside of you.

An explanation for 1): an abstract image. When you tell an actor about breathing and then try to get him to feel it for himself like this: "As you were walking here today – what was the weather like?" – he doesn't give in to the sensation and instead cerebrally examines the weather. The image of the weather reaches only as far as his head, or his reason – this image is abstract, and it doesn't evoke a tangible sensation. And so, the actor, who only allowed the image to reach his head, responds in kind: "The weather's fine." You ask him several such questions and try to suddenly shift to a topic that is of greater interest to the actor. When he suddenly takes a breath that coincides with taking in an image, you stop him and say: there, you just breathed in! Can you feel it?

On Mistakes of Breathing In

There's a harmful habit: breathing in without an object, or rather, without a targeted object. For example: an actor says phrase after phrase in one breath and starts choking from the lack of breath (and partly lives with this suffocating sensation – he admits it to himself), after which he breathes in physiologically, rather than psychologically, and suddenly feels that he's internally empty, and starts to strain himself, starts "pushing." What happened? He breathed in, and since he breathed in, he took something in with the breath – what did he take in? He breathed in the very same thing he admitted: that there's no air! There hasn't been anything else!

Conclusion: if you're out of breath, don't breathe in just to breathe in – wait it out until you get the right image, the right picture, the right sensation.

The same, in other words:

You've said everything, exhaled it all, you're out of breath. In the next moment, you breathe in the air without an object. And now you won't be able to take in an object. Once you've exhaled, and run out of air, stay like that until you target a new object.[3]

On Mistakes in Breathing

Non-admitting: Sometimes you see that an impression has started to enter a person, when he suddenly does something to it – it's as if he throws a switch, and instead of going right to his heart, it gets redirected toward the head. This method of throwing a switch is commonly used. A person lets things go only to his head, and upon closer examination, it turns out that, in the most critical moment, he switched the rails. It' as if he suddenly feels that the impression isn't going where he wants it to, and is instead headed for a place that is dangerous for him – he immediately throws a switch – bam! doesn't even notice how he hits it. – And everything is fine – it passed him by!

★★★

What happened with Dante [1911: 222] in Purgatory after Beatrice spoke to him? "The ice that round my heart was fastened, was breath and water made; and lo, with pain, through mouth and eyes from out my breast 'twas shed."

★★★

Everything that's been said about breathing is not "mystic," but "simplistic." In the meantime, *it's possible to breathe into your subconscious.* Then, what has been breathed in ends up dropping deep inside you.

Try to combine this with "tangible," "quiet" speaking of the lines. The result of such breathing can be immediate or not immediate – this will vary. You can see some discussion of this issue in the chapter on "incomplete-combustion products."[4]

It's possible to "permit things in" with the breath – this will be more subconscious and "mystic."

Breathing and Stretching

A yawn: breathing in and taking in a sensation + the involuntary stretching of the jaws and respiratory muscles.

The composer Nikolai Sizov's [1886–1962] tale of how easily he memorized a part for the piano if his hand was stretching while learning the part.

Any stretch is accompanied by an in-breath (possibly several in-breaths with corresponding slight out-breaths). We should recall Sydney B. Flower's [1867–?] "muscle reading method."[5]

When somebody stretches and strains, a "state" falls deep into his subconscious with the breath – this is either the "state" in which he is at the moment or the "state" which he anticipates, or a *thought* that flickered by.

In a word, this is a perfect moment for submerging [something] into your subconscious.

The *desire* drops deep inside, and with it drops in a *suggestion* – unobstructed, through a "direct line."

Breathing and Voice

Breathe in suffering – breathe out a moan.

Breathe in an emotionally imbued word and breathe it out – musically transformed.

Breathe in a musical phrase – breathe it out without a moment's hesitation.

Diction and Breathing

Breathe in a word and it can be *breathed out dictionally.* You can make out every letter if you breathed the word in. If, however, you breathed in clumsily, smudging the word, if you approximately breathed it in, then you'll breathe it back out clumsily, without an end and missing a lot of letters.

It's also possible to breathe in a whole phrase. Let it speak up, breathe itself out on its own. There's no need "stepping on it." Instead, you must breath out everything you've got – disburden your soul with that phrase.

See on "Incomplete-Combustion Products."

Toward the Systematization of the Reflexes

The perception of irritation – in-breath.
The reflex (response) – out-breath.
The body (subject) – retaining.

★★★

It's best *not to try* transforming cerebral perception into heartfelt perception – let it do so on its own – it will.

It's best not to get involved. If, however, you must, then there's a simple method – ask a question with every impression: *do you like it or not?* It's the same thing that I wrote about emotional attention.

On the Audience Mimicking the Actor's Breathing

When a singer strains his voice, the listener's throat hurts too.

When a singer is out of breath, the listener's breathing becomes more difficult too (the same mimicking reflex).

As a result of such a concert, a sensitive audience's voices will be rather hoarse. On the contrary, when you listen to well-trained voices, then when you come home, your own voice will have good tune.

When the "Eisensteins" speak about the audience's mimicking reflex, they don't account for this.[6]

In the meantime, mimicking is very deeply rooted, i.e. the performance itself isn't the only thing that's mimicked – what's "behind" it is too: the breathing is mimicked, as is the straining of the actor's vocal cords, and possibly more . . .

So, when an actor (while performing) breathes like someone who is "pulling off a trick," the trick itself has to be such that you forget about everything and can only pay attention to the trick, else the audience will notice that it's just trickery. Moreover, the mimicking being as deep as said above, when the mesmerizing trick's effect wears off, you'll begin to recall the details – you'll notice your (and the actor's!) unusually calm, unrelated to the moment, breathing.

On the contrary, an actor's proper breathing – "*the tube*" – will gather up the audience, destroy its absent-mindedness, and concentrate their attention.

The same thing will happen with mimicking reflex for seriousness, agitation, tears, and joy.

A good example of the mimicking reflex: if you eat a lemon, then someone who is watching you will also scrunch up their face as if there were something sour in their mouth.

Toward Breathing (Toward Breathing Technique)

You take in an impression and a sensation with your breath . . . and usually, in order to say a *word*, a thought first gets into your head, and this leaves less room for the sensation and air. What you should do – as soon as you take a sensation in with the breath, *immediately give off* not a word, but a *sound*, some inarticulate *moan of sorts*. A word should then follow the sound, in tune with it – like a thread follows a needle (Moissi's "Gh-kaa . . . ").

In general, since this path is intended to awaken some natural power, *primitive* sensations, and the voice of a person's *essence*, it's necessary to pay attention to the reactions of wordless infants and animals. Mimicking them, it's possible to get a hold of this technique – how to *absolutely* give away what you take in, how to give back the air that you took in without any alterations.

In general, it might be possible to begin *only without words*. Words are accompanied by thoughts, reasoning, and, concordantly, brakes.

Breathing: Green-Lighting Your First Impulse

Could this be one of the most important keys to mastery of our automatisms?

Firstly, this is very close to our familiar old "let it . . . " Secondly, this is a direct and simple path to restructuring your braking reflexes.

Thirdly, this involves a complete fusion with the breathing technique. One actor that was learning the technique of psychological breathing understood it only once he came to the conclusion: "Oh, so this must mean to green-light yourself without hesitation, to green-light your first impulse?"

★★★

Yesterday [the summer of 1940], I saw the American film, *The Great Waltz*.

A beautiful film, artistic, deep, poetic, full of Strauss's youthful music, inebriated with beauty and youth and the eternal tragedies of love.

The film is even closer to us, to artists, than to others: it involves something that we intimately understand – the constant battle of the mundane with momentary flights of pretty fantasies and rapturous delight. In the film: Strauss's wife and a beautiful sorceress–singer, his desire, his love 'til the grave. We are all torn apart by these two powers: reality and fantasy, what is and what seems to be, life and dreams.

I was quite affected by the film. It reached my very depths, and cleansed my internal pathways of all the mundane rubbish . . .

And today, *all of my impressions reach me with extraordinary tangibility*, and my perceptions are much more *vivid* and *unimpeded*. Today, I could act and rehearse very well . . .

What does this teach us? The same thing I've been saying many, many times! *Develop your ability to perceive! A faulty* perception mechanism is what gets in our way most of the time! It's our greatest enemy.

How do we develop our perception mechanism? I won't say anything new: ***psychological breathing***.

"***Inspiration*** is the soul's lively disposition ***towards receiving impressions***, as well as towards receiving new concepts, and therefore, explaining them" Pushkin (1962: 268–269).

Notes

1 Gertrude's lines (*Hamlet*, Act III, scene 4): "Be thou assured, if words be made of breath/And breath of life, I have no life to breathe/What thou hast said to me."
2 Demidov is summarizing the teaching of *Yoga Vasistha*, a spiritual Hindi text.
3 It's important to realize that Demidov is not suggesting for actors to hold their breath altogether at such a moment (or at any other moment for that matter). Instead, he refers to "psychological breathing" – the more intense gulps of air an actor takes in before speaking, or prior to making a movement. While such breathing requires a spontaneously "targeted" object, "physical breathing" continues in silences, just as smaller, "auxiliary," or "catch" breaths are permissible when speaking. In fact, breathing onstage must continue at all times – without it, the actor's sound life would freeze and come to a dangerous halt.
4 This chapter was been completed by Demidov. His notes on "incomplete-combustion products" appear in the Glossary.
5 A reference to the method of "mind reading with contact," defined by Sydney Flower as "muscle reading." Demidov must have been familiar with the Russian translation of a collection edited by Flower (see Flower 1907). This was most likely a reprint from *Suggestive Therapeutics*, a journal edited by Flower.
6 A reference to the influential Russian film and theatre director Sergei Eisenstein (1898–1948) – specifically to Eisenstein's unidentified lecture cited in the complete version of Demidov's *The Art of the Actor* . . . Eisenstein (as quoted in Demidov 2004 vol. I: 55) states: "We know how to use reflexes. It is a particular device, a rational calculation based on a certain stimulus. We are not interested in the actor's reflex, bur rather in the audiences' mimicking reflex (Moscow Art Theatre does it the opposite way) . . . we must remember that our business is based entirely in trickery."

13

The Actor and the Audience

The Theatrical Triangle

The actor and the audience – this connection is important, as without it, there is no actor, there is no theatre; but there is a third thing that connects them – the *world of fantasy and imagination* without which the actor and the audience are strangers that have no need for each other.

One corner of the theatrical triangle is the actor; another is what imbues him with life throughout a show: the set, the surrounding characters, the given circumstances – in a word, all of his surroundings (as transformed by his creative mind's eye); and third corner is the audience.

How are these three points connected? What forces bind them together and don't allow them to depart from one another or to mix into one common pile?

Forces of Repulsion

For me, an actor, what can there be that's interesting and attractive in the fact that my scene partner, another actor, is dressed in fantastical armor, has a made-up face, a glued-on beard, is speaking memorized lines about his apparently indescribable suffering, and is calling me his son? How is this attractive to me? Shouldn't it sooner make me laugh, make me angry, and in general repulse me?

And what about the audience? What can there be that's attractive about the fact that I'm made-up just like my partner, have to speak the same predetermined lines, and execute premeditated motions for show, for the entertainment of a few hundred audience members?

There is no more unnatural or more awkward situation – human nature can't help but revolt against this.

What point is there in clowning around, making faces, and posing in front of a crowd of strangers? What point is there in baring your heart, your dreams, your desires, your doubts, sorrows, and joys? To expose your weaknesses and shortcomings?

Or: what point is there in getting excited about nonexistent, imaginary circumstances? I can barely manage my own mundane, everyday circumstances and worries.

My normal human nature won't agree to this strain, to this psychological dislocation, and the three corners of this triangle will decisively bounce away from each other.

Forces of Attraction

It's another thing when I consciously or unconsciously feel my connection with the audience, when all the "strangers" seem spiritually close to me. We're all human. Even though this connection is enshrined in the deepest recesses of our psychological worlds – all things considered: we're all human. Can we be strangers given this?

And so, there are a few hundred or even thousand people sitting in the audience. They've put off their personal concerns, they've come here from all over, maybe even drove from a neighboring city, paid their hard-earned money . . .

Do I as an actor feel what and how much they expect of me? This mass of people is sitting before me and waiting for . . . What? Some have come to gather their strength, to receive new thoughts, to find out something new about life; others have come to relax, yet others have come because of nothing to do with their time, others still have come here to meet up with something . . . so does it even matter? They're all here together – can't I, regardless of whether they want it, get to what is most sacred and important to them?

Let's do it! I'll offer them the best of what I've got in me – I'll reveal to them themselves – humans. Let the sleepy awake, let the tired straighten his back, let him who has already buried himself suddenly burn with the desire to live and learn.

Isn't this a service to humanity? Isn't this work that is worthy of one's life?

A question: if the three points are so irresistibly inching towards one another, then why don't they fuse together?

The forces of repulsion that I spoke about could hardly be at work here, firstly because they've grown weak, and secondly (most importantly), because they're of a different plane – the plane of life and the mundane; here, though everything began with the mundane, it immediately passed *into the realm of fantasy, imagination, and creativity.*

The fact is: for as long as these three points stay out of the realm of the mundane, they won't fuse. As soon as the process slips from the realm of creativity into naturalistic truth, the points all come together, and the process ends. When it comes to expressing myself before people, I can only do it *metaphorically.* Therefore, I need to hold on to this metaphor.

★★★

An inherent quality of theatre is the audience – the audience that is there while the actor creates. After all, only the audience can reveal whether one is an actor, or a vagabond that accidentally ended up on the stage.

For one, the audience is a distraction – they cause them to "break character," they activate all of his brakes – he has to resist them, "overcome" the audience and distract himself with various tricks . . . You have to try to speak louder, because your voice disappeared from worrying; don't turn your back to the audience; in general, keep track of what you're doing to make sure you don't mess up . . .

But for another, it's the contrary: maybe in life, he's awkward, timid, at a loss for words, incomprehensible, but as soon as he gets a whiff of the stage, he throws off all his shackles, his instincts come to life, and he doesn't even have to think about it: it's as if everything gets done on its own – he transforms into his role, he's overcome by a feeling of freedom and power, and his voice has grown strong – his former physical timidity and awkwardness are gone.

I can feel the audience, but they're not getting in my way. On the contrary: I get something from them . . . some strength that I don't have in my everyday life. This many-headed creature – the audience – breathes this strength into me.

Maybe this is self-deception, maybe it's just excitement, but I perceive it as something different: I feel like my own strength isn't involved to a great extent here – most of my strength has come from the audience. It seems like the "strength" inside me, like in a Ruhmkorff coil, is just welling up, and it seems like the more windings there are in the coil, the stronger the current is: the more audience members there are, the greater is an actor's power.

Given a hyper-sensitive apparatus of an actor, the strength of this induction can reach supernatural levels.

Here's what Belinsky [1953: 310] tells about Mochalov:

> Suddenly, like a lion, like lightning, Mochalov leaps from the bench to the center of the stage and, stomping his feet and waving his arms, he deafens the theatre with an eruption of hellish cackling . . .

> No! even if a thousand people started laughing simultaneously as one, it would seem like the weak laughter of a child when compared to his boundless, thunderous, sundering laughter, because in order to laugh like that, you need not a powerful chest with nerves of iron – you need an enormous soul, struck by endless passion . . .

> And the stomping of the feet, the waving of the arms, along with the laughter? – Oh, that was a macabre dance of despair of someone who rejoiced in his suffering, who took delight in his excruciating torture . . .

Where does this strength come from?

Two thousand excited people, transformed by a genius actor into a single, indivisible whole – two thousand people send some unexamined waves of willpower towards the stage, their thoughts, their sympathies (they conjoin their thinking, feeling, and searching apparatus to that of the actor). None of them know about this, but the person onstage gathers all of this power in a single point, sends it all along a single "wire," and what we get is a wonder of induction – a mere mortal becomes a giant.

★★★

People say that actors die young. They dissipate all their energies onstage. This is untrue. The ones that die young do not die from art.

The tragedian Salvini died when he was 87. Yermolova was 74, and yet, didn't she expend a lot of herself?

After a storm like the one that passed through my nervous system, it's usually a good idea to rest, but one's soul, just like nature, only grows stronger and fresher after a torrential downpour, and it is reborn – it's ready for new adventures, for new life. Apparently, this was not *just dissipation* – there was also some *accumulation* here.

But do all actors similarly receive the energy that flows from the audience?

Not all do. Not all, by far.

Almost all are *excited* by the presence of an audience, and they're so excited that they forget about illness and fatigue, but *after* a scene, the majority of actors are tired and even slightly broken. For them, the audience isn't a balm or a charger that fills them with strength – it's just a *whip*.

A poet, a writer, a painter, a sculptor, a composer also work for the audience, but *while* they are creating, there is no actual audience, and there is no exchange of energy.

In a word, though there is an audience in other art forms, the audience is imaginary. But for an actor, the audience is very real, very concrete, very alive.

An Actor's Instincts

1.

There are so many pretty young men, young girls. A pretty face, a pleasant voice, good manners – you would think that they're the ones that should be on a stage, where the stage would stress and underline their features even more . . .

You convince them to participate in some amateur production. You look on – but where has all their beauty gone? They become insignificant, uninteresting, highly unattractive when compared with the other amateurs. And not because they're shy after going onstage for the first time, no – it's the same with subsequent shows.

But then there are others – nothing to look at: shabby, hoarse voice, mumble everything, but once they're made-up and in costume, you can't recognize them! An actor like this, when he gets onstage – he's no longer shorter than everyone, and he suddenly has good posture, and his voice is audible, and all his letters are discernible . . . You don't even pay any attention to the others, you only look at him. And it's impossible not to look at him: he enthralls you, he charms you – *all of his actor's instincts* have awakened.

If they're there – hurray! If not – no amount of beauty, no amount of clarity, no amount of culture, education, or manners *can replace them.*

True, these instincts aren't always inherent – often, they sit quite deeply in someone and come out gradually. But if these actor's instincts aren't there at all, and they refuse to come out no matter how hard you try to tease them out, it's best to try your hand at something else. After all, what point is there in teaching a hen how to swim? Meanwhile, a duck doesn't even have to be taught.

Of course, anything can be learned, but *to what extent?* For better or worse, a person can become accustomed to a strange environment, but he has to *become accustomed,* while an actor with the inherent instincts *lives* in the environment of the stage (which is so foreign to most) like a fish in water, like a bird in the air. And this is the *beginning* of the long path to the heights of his art form.

2. A Neurotic State

I think that if an actor is "constructed" properly, if he gets energy not just from his nervous system, but from the audience as well (not everybody can do this), then not only does he not lose energy – he *gains* energy, he becomes stronger and healthier after every such performance. He doesn't lose his strength, his nervous system doesn't weaken – it only grows stronger and more harmonious.

If, however, an actor "overcomes" the audience, if he endeavors to defeat the audience with his artificial excitement and agitation, if he seeks to subjugate it; if he nearly has a fit while trying to do so, then, naturally, he doesn't walk away scot-free.

But it's worth noting that, in this case, the actor becomes the victim of a sad self-deception: he thinks that excitement brought to the stage of convulsions and spasms and extreme nervous agitation is just powerful, normal, human emotion and evokes sympathy in the audience. In reality – *a neurotic, semi-convulsive cannot evoke anything other than a similar neurotic state,* and even if the audience is emoting, their emotion is by no means harmonious – they're in an unhealthy state of nervous agitation. The actor has infected the audience with his hysterics. *Only if they're grossly misled* will actors interpret their own unhealthy hysterical states as creative flights.

With his acting, Mochalov forced the audience to pale, to grow cold, to moan, but not once did he cause a hysterical fit.

3. On the Hole in the Curtains and the "Volga"

In our ordinary, everyday conversations, we involuntarily speak one way to some, and another way to others – we speak differently to every person we know. Sensitive and well-intentioned people do this subconsciously, because they want to understand the people they speak to and be understandable in return.

Similarly, it's impossible to act the same way for different audiences. Rather, it's possible to do this, but this means that not all is well with one's actor's instincts. [People might argue: but what about film? Nothing changes there! In response, you can only nod your head, and add: not just film, but paintings, and sculptures, and literature. Dead paint, clay, paper – they'll always be dead. Therein lie the advantages and the shortcomings of these art forms. And vice versa – theatre's advantage lies with variability, adaptability, lifelikeness. By its nature, it's not dead. But the tradeoff is that it's not eternal. –*Author's Note.*]

A theatre curtain usually has a hole, and sometimes more than one. Sometimes, the curtain is made this way – with a hole, in order to look at the audience. But usually, the actors themselves poke this hole with their fingers.

Typically, the reasons for making these holes are simple: it's interesting to see how full the house is. Is there anyone I know? Who's sitting where? Who's dressed how? Is there anyone from up high?

But even in my childhood, I saw an actor that used this hole in a completely different fashion. Firstly, he approached the hole when the others' initial curiosity was sated and there were no more peekers. Secondly, he approached the hole very seriously, with great concentration, and he would study the audience for a long time, focusing his attention on a few seemingly uninteresting strangers. Then he would turn around, walk away for a bit, stand there for some time, as if digesting his impressions. Then he would again study the audience with great concentration, after which he would stand for a bit, eyes closed; then, more collected and focused, he would walk away and sit in a dark corner somewhere, awaiting his entrance, carefully listening to the show once it began.

Sometimes, however, time permitting, this actor would go out into the house to a spot where he couldn't be seen, and he would study and "feel out" the audience.

He always knew whom he was acting for, or rather: *with whom* he was acting, seeing as the audience was always *with him*.

Many will probably yell out: "Act for the audience? Stoop to its level? The horror! You shouldn't subjugate yourself to it – you have to carry it to your level, elevate it!"

Exactly. This is why this actor studied them for so long, why he "melded" with it before his entrance.

He had something deep, something elevated, something human to say with his role. But *how* to say it on a particular day? How should he "spin" or "focus" what he had to say to the audience so that the audience wouldn't see it as crude, as philistine, as simple-minded, but rather as something truly human, something hidden deep within?

Where did he get such an attitude towards the audience?

There are people who are completely uninterested by life for themselves. For them, life is people, life is humanity, the whole world. Consciously or subconsciously, they feel that they are builders of the world, responsible for the mistakes of humanity, responsible for its path.

When this kind of psychology is combined with the gift of an actor, we are graced with a very rare kind of actor indeed.

To use more contemporary language – there is no more socially minded person than an artist. His social-mindedness, his feel of humanity, his connection to it, his feelings of responsibility are all imbued in an artistic nature.

This is especially obvious in an actor.

And the actor that performs before an audience just to get them to like him and to get more money out of them isn't an actor. This is . . . I wanted to say a craftsman . . . but no, a craftsman is honest; this is a forger, the worst of all crooks.

It's not enough that he put a ball of dirt into my outstretched hand instead of a piece of bread – he shattered my faith in other artists, in true artists; he caused others to see how easy it is to commit this thievery, paving the way for others to follow in his steps. He's committed sacrilege [onstage], and there is no desire to go out after him with what is most precious and sacred for you.

★★★

But it could be different: I'm not a leader or a preacher or an orator – I'm simply an *actor*.

I love my work, I live for it, I have acting abilities, and I like to use them. I like to use them even more when before an audience, seeing as they expand and grow sharper there (because I'm a natural actor).

And, ultimately, everything leads to the same thing: unnoticeably for me, during one of my performances, I turn into a leader, a preacher, an orator. And here's how easily and naturally one becomes the other: given proper training, my actor's abilities and instincts grow with every day. I can feel the audience as part of myself – I can hear the beating of its heart, I can guess its thoughts as I command it . . .

I get a very heroic or dramatic role. I'm touched by the concerns of the role, they're close to me, and, "under the mask," I bravely bare my "I" – I live. Freely, spontaneously, and . . . after a few seconds, I notice that it's as if someone is feeding me strength from without; with every second, my feelings become greater, deeper and bigger. Soon they break my familiar banks, but this doesn't worry me. New "springs" flow in, my strength is growing, more, more, and more . . .

It's as if my small little river was flowing, and then it took in one, another, a third spring, tens, hundreds, thousands of other rivers – you can't even recognize it anymore: it's transformed from a little river into a mighty queen – the Volga. But it's still the same – the same little river. It's still just me. But it's not just me – it's also everyone who's sitting in the audience; each of them individually, and all at once, in the lofty moment of creative flight.

I can feel the new, hitherto unheard strings resonating inside me: this alone justifies being involved in theatre – without it theatre is a trifle, a mere toy.

In this way, via a proper actor's technique, and via proper channels of communication with the audience, and via the works of an author that is close to my heart, something wonderful has opened up, something that would otherwise have never even seen the light of day.

And it's not just that something of mine has opened up – it's grown, it's become so great that it's impossible to even recognize it: The small "river" has turned into the "Volga!" And every audience member should be lead to such a state when, swept up by me, for a few minutes or hours he'll also become such a "Volga," he'll be a giant just like me, he'll live and feel in doses much greater than the ones that we see in pharmacies – his feelings will weigh hundreds of thousands of tons – he'll be a storm.

This is no longer the call of a simple preacher or orator – this is a fusion of people in a single furnace in ten-thousand-degree heat.

People walk into such a theatre in one state and leave it in another entirely. And they will never, ever forget about these moments.

Mochalov, Yermolova, Duse, the lost Italian bel canto – they weren't great because they "awakened a man's consciousness," addressing his reason and everyday emotions.

All actors do this (with a greater or lesser success), and we should thank them for it. Genii, however, did what others **cannot** – even if I'm still an infant with rather simple demands and needs, if I happen to go into such a monstrous furnace, in one or two hours, I'm completely different; in one or two hours, I've walked a long path from the simple me to the heights of human spirituality.

And so, beginning with the simple satisfaction of his needs as an actor (demonstrating his specific abilities before an audience), a person can, without even noticing it, become a preacher, and an orator, and even a furnace for refining the human essence . . .

If you have an actor's instincts, and if you develop them properly, if an author is close to your most intimate world, then there's no running away from this, for such are the forces tying together the actor with the audience.

★★★

You might get a thought like this: these miracles occur when drama or tragedy are involved . . . as for comedy, vaudeville – you can't really speak about induction in these cases, and certainly not about any sort of "Volga."

Why not? Can merriment, joy, and laughter not be led to their extreme? There's your "Volga."

Tragedy, drama, vaudeville, clowning, opera, operetta, circus – there is always an audience. And where there is an audience, the same laws apply.

4. On the Imaginary Audience

The audience . . . Only in its presence can you tell an actor apart . . . Only in its presence are brilliant creative flights possible . . .

But is the opposite also true? I'm home alone, brilliantly delivering a monologue, I'm immersed, I can feel an enormous well of power inside me: I could drown the world in my emotions! And in front of an audience, I get lost, I tense up and fail.

This happens. And it's not because you're **not** an actor or don't possess one of the chief actor's instincts – the feeling of the audience.

You are an actor, and you have instincts, or else you wouldn't have said: "I could just drown the world with my emotions."

Evidently, when you act, recite, or declaim at home all by yourself, consciously or unconsciously you do this in the presence of an *imaginary audience*, and then, when instead of a comfortable, obedient, imaginary audience, you're given a real one that you don't have enough experience to influence properly, you close up.

But believe me: there is always an impulse to perform in the presence of the audience. The only thing up in the air is an actor's *capacity*. One can "fit inside" the force of an enormous audience, while another would choke up and become derailed from such a massive power. It could happen that, regardless of the amount of practice he puts in, he might never be able to handle more than a couple hundred audience members at a time.

Sometimes, people act and recite very well in a small, intimate setting, but can't manage to do the same onstage.

But still, five, three, or even just one person is still an audience.

5. What to Look for in an Audience and How to Do So

The connection inside the theatre triangle is an organic one. The triangle is a single whole. If a single point is disrupted, the whole triangle is disrupted. If the *connections* between the points are disrupted, the whole triangle is disrupted. The mutuality between all three points is absolute.

An unassuming artist is often wont to go on the following train of thought: an audience is rarely as cultured, refined, and theatrical as it should be. It's incapable of understanding many things, which is why my performance for it should be simpler, more primitive, cruder. Subtlety, elegance – this will all be lost on them, they won't get it. And the cruder the audience, the cruder the performance should be.

It might appear that this train of thought correlates with what we were discussing, but this is an egregious mistake.

People who rarely interact with children in their lives are very bad at speaking with them. They think that they have to adjust themselves somehow, speak in a particular manner to be understood, and so they begin to speak "like a baby," they "play" children. Children, on the other hand, like to be spoken to like adults.

An audience is the same, regardless of audience make-up. Every audience member is first and foremost a *person* – that's whom you need to find, that's whom you have to play for.

It's possible to come to an understanding with anyone. It's possible to shame and convict the crudest animal. You just have to speak cleverly and deftly. And a conversation using the artistic language of theatre is the most comprehensible, most subtle, most piercing, most powerful kind of conversation.

People who believe that art can be used like a maul to beat dear audience upside the head, to simply bludgeon various wise thoughts and elaborate feelings into their heads, as well as to beat various idiocy *out* of their heads – these people are narrow-minded.

Art is not a maul or a whip. Art is **seeds, thrown into the soul**, it's **the sun, bringing life** to the previously sown seeds. It's a **grafting** of a noble, fruit-bearing branch – upon a wild tree.

And unnoticeably, by the forces of nature, the tiny fruit-bearing twig transforms a wilding into a great, fruit-bearing tree.

And if you want to do this work of art, and if you want art in general, rather than a surrogate, then don't forget about the hole in the curtain. Go up to it and look through it. But don't overthink things, don't philosophize, don't deliberate – just look. Without criticizing.

Today you'll act for them. What will you act? Recall what you're supposed to act today. Remember it and observe the audience. Even if it's not the kind that you long for in the quiet of your study, still: calmly, without protesting and criticizing, observe it: you'll be playing for **them** today. And quite soon, inadvertently, you'll get *the proper feeling of* **how** you're going to act, **how you should** act. Act so as to *immerse them, specifically them*, these people. These strangers, who are irrelevant and who knows, maybe they're even unpleasant, maybe they're not that good. Maybe they're even bad. But observe them, and it'll happen on its own that you'll feel them as your *partners*, your co-artists.

And as soon as this happens, everything will become clear, and you'll find your exact, proper place between them and your role. Rather: you won't "find" it – you'll suddenly *feel* that you're in the place you're supposed to be – *creative act has begun*.

6. The Technique of Perceiving the Audience

Tell an actor: "Don't forget about the audience, feel it, live with it, affect it, command it, receive the energy that flows from it, utilize it," – saying this means "killing" an actor, possibly dislocating him, spoiling him.

Yes, exactly so. In practice, you insist the contrary: you insist on completely cutting yourself off from the audience, screening yourself off with an imaginary wall, and then . . . then, you start perceiving the audience *as you're supposed to.*

It's very simple: regardless of how hard you insist that there is no audience, that the actor is alone onstage, that nobody is looking at him, in the depths of his soul – no, even without the depths – it's on the very surface – he knows that people are watching him, seeing and hearing him. And they've come for that reason: to look at to listen.

A task of ignoring the audience, of not seeing or hearing it is a *creative* task. In general, life onstage is a fantastical life, an imaginary life. And if you don't give yourself over to this life as much as you should, if you allow reality, the naturalistic, the material to invade your imagination, if you see that in front of you, it's not a romantic field, but rather the prosaic wooden floor of the stage – your fantasy will abandon you.

He who directly tells the actor: "Remember the audience, think about it" scares off his fantasy and destroys creativity.

In moments of creativity, everything that gives me life is *imaginary*, and only in my depths, regardless of my will, I cognize the real presence of the audience and its attitude towards me, and that I'm onstage, rather than in real life . . . I register all this *unconsciously*; it's almost like it's not me doing the registering, but someone else, sitting in me and observing from the inside. But this observer doesn't interfere, but rather helps, inspires, and regulates. Like a captain of a seafaring ship.

This captain is the artist that is sitting inside me that observes and regulates, leading me through the reefs and shallows, wisely taking advantage of both storm and calm, favorable and oppositional winds. He doesn't make the ship move – he's just the regulator and director.

In this way, the audience is always there for the actor, but it is sensed and felt differently – *it's included in the general flow of creativity.* And thinking about it or remembering it intentionally means disrupting the organic process of the stage. There is no need to think about it consciously. *Any thoughts and concerns will be subconscious, instinctual.*

"Don't think about the audience, forget about it" – this doesn't contradict the advice to look into the hole in the curtain: I am acting today. How can I make it so that what I'm about to act will affect the people in the audience? Let me peer deeper into them, let me permeate their souls . . . Here they are, here are the ones for whom I will act – one, another, a third . . . I enter their lives, I try to sense their humanity, what is best in them . . . Here is a couple . . . They look like they haven't gotten a care in the world; they must be newlyweds . . . Why are they here today? Why do they need *Acosta*? They're happy, they can't stop looking at each other, they don't notice anyone around themselves . . . Why should I lead a storm cloud over their souls with the tragedy of Uriel, of Judith, and the eternal tragedy of any true thinker who cannot simply march to the drum of the wisdom of the horde? . . .

However, I can't sense any crassness or foolishness through their light-mindedness and joy – they're simply young, they love each other, and they are happy.

. . . From the bottom of my soul, I suddenly get memories of moments gone by, moments that looked like this . . . my heart clenches up with melancholic pain . . . I think I've got what I needed . . . I think I can begin . . . I now have something to say to this young couple; I won't could their happiness, I'll simply say that life is much richer, much more beautiful – it's heroic, grand, it's all an adventure . . .

I also know what to tell the tired teacher with the large, sad eyes . . . Maybe she's not a teacher . . . but I feel like she is, so let her be a teacher.

But what should I say to that bearded engineer that is sitting with his 10-year-old daughter and is feeding her an orange? . . . His wife must have died . . . he's alone . . . But why did he bring his child here, today, to see *Acosta?* Maybe he saw this show back when he was young and joyous, like the young couple over there? . . . Very well . . . I know what to say to you, lonely widower, and I know what to say to your little daughter . . .

7. On the Usual Inaccuracies of Communicating with an Audience

For an actor who doesn't have proper actor's instincts, these mechanics act up very badly.

Partners, the circumstances – everything that is supposed to allow him to *live* onstage, and, at least, be of interest to him – when he goes out onstage, when the curtain is raised, all of this doesn't become more saturated or strengthened, but rather retreats to the very far-off background, he starts riding a wave of inertia, and his primary attention goes towards communicating with the audience.

Look closely at the actors; listen to their sometimes disproportionately loud voices. Are they speaking with each other? For the most part, they're not speaking with each other, but with the audience – they're pitching their words to them, their words, which are seemingly intended for their scene partners, but are actually only going in their partners' general vicinity.

This false (uninteresting for the actors) *speaking for the audience* – you can hear it so often (in fact, you rarely hear any other) that, for the most part, you sit in a theatre sad or frustrated: are there really so few actors capable of properly sensing the audience? It seems like most everyone is like a, well, like a deaf conductor or a blind painter – why are they even onstage?

But there are so many bad performances out there that the audience grows used to them (and some have never even seen good performances) – they become accustomed to them and come to believe that they're what theatre should be! Some of these slashing actors even cause delight among the audience with their bravado and self-assuredness.

Oh, it's not easy to see all this!

It's even less easy because you see how some actors think – *this is how it must be done.*

This *speaking for the audience, this landing of the text with the audience* for the most part speaks to the fact that we're dealing with the people why've come to acting due to some self-delusion – they've either never had the most important instinct an actor should have, or they've had it killed or dislocated, or it's been polluted with some professional garbage.

Other mistakes are even less pleasant.

In the case that I just described, the actors don't feel the audience, but they're still doing their jobs – they're trying their best to get the author's text and the director's notes to the audience.

But when an actor finds that the most important thing isn't the author or a show's main theme (even though, formally, he does everything quite loudly and distinctly), but the fact that he *went out onstage in order to please the audience with his own presence* – this is disgusting.

If he is pretty, then he'll pose. If he has a good voice, he'll show it off. If he has good teeth, he'll smile the whole time. If he' s good pretty eyes, he'll be constantly shooting glances at the audience, gazing at the sky, etc., without end, beginning with simple, uncomplicated methods and finishing with more complex, deft, and psychological ones. For example, he could affect the audience *a contrario*: demonstrate a complete lack of attention for it, mumbling the lines barely audibly beneath his breath, and in general not expending too much energy, not "wasting" himself, as if to show how much he is above all of their praise. But the point is the same: for these people, the stage is an opportunity to showcase themselves. They care nothing for art, for striving for perfection, for serving humanity ("it's naïve! it's old-fashioned!"). And I think . . . that you and I should waste no more time discussing them.

8. The Truth and the Audience

Sometimes, life poses exceedingly cunning questions.

At some point in the show, a child must be brought out onstage. He's brought out, and you, sitting in the audience, notice that the child has "upstaged" the actors and that you don't even want to watch them anymore.

The same happens when a dog or a horse is brought out onstage . . .

Do they have an acute instinct of sensing the audience (or publicness)? Do they have a good contact with the audience? Seeing all this, you might begin to doubt: all this discussion of an actor's instincts with regards to the audience — could it just be a bunch of nonsense? Nature has just walked out onto our stage, and it's instantly crushed our art.

That's the point!

The "actors'" acting is usually too false, too artificial, too bad.

Thankfully, however, things are sometimes different.

I remember a show in a provincial theatre that starred Mamont Dalsky, who was on tour, and a cat walked out onstage . . . He walked over to it, picked it up, and then spent half an act performing his role with it in his arms. And if people asked who was freer and more alive – him or the cat – people would probably have said: him. He upstaged her.

There was truth in him and in the cat. This wasn't a clash between truth and lies. This was two truths. His truth – the great truth of human suffering, the truth of a scorned heart, scorned love – and the cat's truth, a small truth: the truth of a cat that had nothing better to do, and accidentally walked out onstage because of the inattentive guard, the truth of a cat that was walking around to whittle away the time. And next to Dalsky's truth, this truth is completely uninteresting to us.

I can imagine how unpleasant it would be to see a cat like this with its minuscule truth next to a tragic creative flight of Mochalov's level!

In such a case, I would either try not to notice it so as to not be distracted from the great to the insignificant; or else, I would be so frustrated that I would want to jump onstage and throw the cat out.

9. How the Audience Causes a Show to Fall Apart

It's sometimes the case that a show that's boring during rehearsals springs to life in the presence of an audience.

The opposite is also sometimes the case. Everything is fine during rehearsals, but once an audience is added to the equation, the show starts falling apart, act by act. Like if a blooming rose were suddenly struck by sub-freezing weather.

There are many possible explanations for such a phenomenon. For example.

A show was rehearsed for a long time, and rehearsed well. The actors have developed their roles, they can easily immerse themselves in the circumstances. But then they get thousands of audience members, and it turns out that their initial measurements were off, that their habitual rehearsal room state does not suffice, but the habit is ingrained – and so everything bursts at the seams.

A show or two will pass, and if the foundation was truthful and full of life, then they'll weather the storm, the actors will acclimate, and everything will be fine. Moreover, they might even go over their rehearsal limits.

Or: a role is constructed in rehearsals, under the persistent tutelage of the director. But once an actor puts on his costume, once he puts on his makeup, once he finds himself in full lights, sees his partners, the set, *and* the audience, suddenly everything shifts: the actor feels himself being pushed in the opposite direction. He can see that he has to act differently, very differently from when he was in rehearsals. If only an actor could take full advantage of this turning point!

But this is not always possible, unfortunately. After all, a director has to be able to sense that the flow of the actor's intuition is correct, you he has to be able to trust it! Sitting in their offices, the majority of directors will think up such a precise and detailed way of staging a show that you won't be able to sway them afterwards – no matter what, you have to do whatever flies into their heads.

And so the actor falls between two stools. With time, he might weather it . . . Maybe . . . But the moment of true, fresh intuition is lost forever. All of your artistic musings are trampled into the ground, there's nothing left from the character you created except for an external counte-nance; your essence as an actor, your psychological apparatus – they might be seriously maimed. And it's possible that they're maimed forever. Nobody even suspects how grievous the situation might be, but often this is exactly how it turns out. But do not retreat! Woe to you if you give up. There are so many maimed actors walking across our stages!

Every artistic bone is fractured inside them, every creative joint is dislocated, and even if some bones grew back together, they did not knit well. The movements of their souls onstage are ugly, exaggerative, and abnormal.

Only the fact that we're accustomed to seeing such dislocation in almost all our theatres, that, for some absurd reason, it has been pounded into our thick sculls that *this is what theatre should be like*, that our "eye" and "ear" has been so mutated – only this fact gives such art the opportunity to exist on our stages.

And we need to exert quite a bit of special effort to make us return to a normal, natural "eye" and "ear." But just think about the energy that flows from the audience when we address not its mutilated senses, but its normal and natural receptors.

10. The Gradual Spoiling of a Show because of the Audience

While examining the audience through the hole in the curtain, it's possible to see a Person in every audience member, and then you'll want to play for this person.

But it's also possible to see something different: crassness, crudeness, primitivity, animalism. It's possible to see this and meet it halfway. This often happens. For example, experience shows that, all things considered, the audience hinders the performance, lessens it.

How does this happen?

Like this: at first, the actors feel responsibility; each of them mobilizes and rallies all of his abilities and instincts. The show enters its peak, its power and significance grow.

The first 10 shows pass, along with the first necessary corrections, seeing as many errors become evident only before an audience, after which there's no real reason to continue seeking perfection like you did at the start of the run.

Besides, the audience begins to "receive" some parts of the show (parts that the actor didn't initially pin much hope on) – it laughs and delights at them. The actor meets this halfway and begins to dedicate more attention to these parts. It, in turn, is received even better, etc. What ends up happening is that the serious parts, the ones on which the whole show was constructed, drown in these over-stressed trifles.

You go see some 50th performance, and you can't recognize the show. Just where has the actors' undemanding attitude towards the audience and themselves *led* them?!

There were whole theatres that took it on themselves as their chief duty to meet such lesser, semi-animalistic instincts halfway; actors and actresses would try to evoke the worst kind of animalism in the audience . . . Even today, there are actors that are all the rage among crude, uncultured crowds, while a more or less cultured person feels shame, awkwardness, disdain . . . These are debauchers and murderers – conscious or unconscious – it does not matter all that much.

11. On the Crudeness and Callousness of the Audience

For the first 10 years of the Art Theatre's existence, applause was forbidden. They weren't forbidden formally – the announcement declared that the actors are grateful for the applause, but that they won't have a curtain call so as not to disrupt the show's impression.

The audience understood that this was a delicate form that required a lack of disruptions, and if someone couldn't hold out and would applaud in the middle of a show, furious hissing would immediately silence him. There was a great wisdom in it.

Naturally, there can be applause that is so heated, so passionate that it will only inflame the actor, carrying him to great heights of truth and power, after which it will quiet down, without hindering him, without stopping him. But it's very difficult to cause the audience to applaud like *this*. Usually, it's different – typically, applause only dilutes a show's atmosphere and scares away an actor's artistic life.

Some 15 years ago, a famous European tragedian (who is now deceased) was on tour in Moscow [Alexander Moissi, who toured USSR in 1924 and 1925]. After a few shows in different theatres with an assembled troupe, he wanted to play parts of his repertoire with the actors from the Art Theatre. He was happily met halfway.

A dress rehearsal was scheduled for the morning. It was attended not only by the whole Art Theatre, but by all of its studios as well – the house was full.

The tragedian, who had limitless respect for the Art Theatre and nearly saw it as the sole source of true high theatre art, could hardly wait for this rehearsal. The show was going to be in the evening – so what? What's so special about a performance in front of an audience? That's so easy and so ordinary! But right now, in the house, there are a thousand and a half of the best actors, the best artists of the stage, and they're all waiting for him . . . This was going to be an exam, an exam for an actor-tragedian: am I a real artist?

This was a collection of people who knew all the secrets of art . . . They were waiting for the "real deal." As if that weren't enough – they want to learn from me; they want what I know and what I don't even suspect in myself to rub off on them . . . If we keep in mind the first thing that the tragedian decided to play was Hamlet's "To be or not to be," and the following scene with Ophelia, then it will become obvious just what kind of thoughts and demands filled this actor while he wondered backstage . . . All of his power, all of his mastery and talent, all the energy of his soul were mobilized and aiming at a single target . . .

We sat and waited . . . One of the theatre's "fathers" walked through the house onstage and backstage . . . In a few minutes, he came back "from him" and whispered to the "family": "He didn't put on a costume, he'll be playing in his jacket . . . " "What a good idea! What a great idea!" I thought. "We don't want a performance. We want the *actor*, we want to look each other in the eyes – no, not the eyes – *past* the eyes, *through* the eyes – submerge ourselves in his heart and see all of his secrets! . . . " I don't know if many were doing this, but I know that some were thinking of this like an exam for the *art form* itself: what is it like in its best iterations? What is it "capable of?"

The curtain was still down . . . It felt like a long time . . . The same person went onto the stage and backstage, but came back immediately. – "He's starting," – he said. "If you greet him with applause, I won't be able to do anything about it," he hinted to us, anticipating our possible lack of hospitality . . . And truly, in our tremulous state, we could very well have forgotten about conventional pleasantries and have met our guest with rude silence.

Slowly, the curtain opened up . . . He was small, in his jacket, standing in the center of the stage, arm extended upwards, hanging onto the draperies. His body was thrust forward, toward us − just slightly. His eyes were seemingly staring off past us; through us, through the walls, into space . . . I was in the sixth row, looking through binoculars: I wasn't expecting such simplicity, such deep eyes gazing "into the other side of life," such demanding eyes, such searing eyes . . . the eyes of a person that was lethally wounded by a thought. He was silent . . . The hosts all came to and burst into applause . . .

I was watching with torturous rapture, greedily looking into his eyes. They didn't tremble; they only grew brighter and clenched my heart even more painfully . . .

The applause continued . . . He kept looking . . . The applause continued . . . He was still looking . . . The applause continued . . . friendly, hospitable, welcoming, tenacious . . .

Something flickered in his eyes . . .

He was walking along a dangerous, mountain path. He had been climbing the steep hill for a painfully long time. He had long ago passed through the part that was accessible to most; now, he was treading the path where few had ever walked. Would he be able to make it through? . . . − there was just a narrow strip of ground beneath his feet; all around − nothing but air and an abyss . . . He was like a tightly coiled spring, with austere gaze peering deeply into something unseen, listening to something within himself . . . A man like that would make it through . . . But suddenly, something flickered before his eyes . . . − it was a passing bird that hit him with the edge of its wing.

But he was strong . . . the bird distracted him only for an instant; now, his gaze was austere and deep again. He would hold on . . .

But the "bird of applause" enjoyed flying around the head of this brave man . . . Again it flies at him and smacks him in the face . . .

He is strong . . . He fights for every sliver of ground, clinging to the mountain . . . He'll make it through! If only the damned bird stopped hitting him in the face. But the bird was growing feisty and took to flying back and forth, hitting him in the eyes . . .

He made a last, desperate effort! . . . But his tired legs are slipping, his hands are unclenching . . .

Self-possession, technique − this can save you up to a relatively low altitude, but up there, just beneath the sky, the air is too thick, the wind is too fierce, and the sun blinds you − there, you have to turn into the eye of a needle, a single point, a . . .

Meanwhile, it continued − this loud burst of applause . . .

Something flickered in his eyes . . . A frightful thought: I'm falling, death! . . . He tried to collect himself, he tried to throw off the insistent and foolish, but not yet disastrous, clapping . . .

But they continued . . . Of course they did! A world-class theatre refused to be outdone − it will welcome that guest, if that's the last thing they do!

That tiresome clapping . . . His eyes showed panic, powerlessness . . . He waved at us a few times: "shut up already!" He wasn't going to thank them, to bow to them, was he?! And for what? For pushing him from the heights? For scaring off a rare moment of inspiration? For almost entering a temple of artists, but instead ending up in a crowd of everymen?

But the theatre was only overjoyed by the wave and took it for a joke; everyone started clapping even louder, bringing their hands together even more passionately . . .

His eyes showed a kaleidoscope of sorrow, fury, the desire to manage, to get a grip on himself, rage, hopelessness, despair . . . Everything was going to hell, it was all falling into an abyss . . . A few more furious waves at the audience that the audience responds to with tireless applause, and finally – he waves at the curtain, signaling someone to close it . . . The curtain stayed closed for a long time . . . I thought, it won't open again . . . And that would have been good, that would have been right. Why would he open it? In order to act before an "audience," a typical audience? Was *that* what he wanted? To act before *co-craftsmen*? There were evidently no artists present . . .

I jumped up to run away from the sorrow, shame, and insult of it all. I jumped up and . . . and I stayed, for some reason. I often kicked myself afterwards: why didn't I leave, why didn't I run away . . . why did I allow myself to keep looking at this actor?! What was initially in his eyes, his pose, his fearsome silence . . . if we hadn't distracted him, if we had understood, if we had *felt* the situation – he could have reached such heights! He could have done miracles onstage! He was ready to take flight! And we let it slip by so odiously!

I had seen this actor before, and I saw him after. I am fond of this actor. I like a lot of things about him, and I learned a lot while watching him. But I have never seen anything like what I saw that day – never again would I see that tragic power worthy of Mochalov, and that greatness. *Sensing a special audience* created this greatness.

Figure 20   Alexander Moissi as Hamlet, The Popular Theatre, Vienna, 1922. Courtesy of Andrei Malaev-Babel.

And the audience *is* special, I swear! It awaited him very faithfully, as it should have. But . . . something happened! Could it have been the inopportune joke about the necessity of greeting him with applause? Could it have ruined everything? But wasn't it possible to greet him, salute him for two-three seconds, and instantly fall silent? We believe in you! We love you. We're listening, waiting, quietly, not even breathing – we're yours! . . .

Is it worth describing what happened next? Nothing out of the ordinary. What would have been worth discussing – it all had vanished. The actor's electrical battery had instantly lost its charge (short-circuited?). Although the actor toiled, although he fought himself, searched himself, tried to animate himself, he couldn't find anything real. And so he relied on "technique," on external tricks and premeditated patterns. Everything that is kept ready in case you can't act on inspiration, when you're tired or sick . . . all the little methods that are intended for deception. In a word, everything that's so prized by actor-craftsmen; everything they steal from each other and reproduce, while the true artists of the stage see no value in it . . .

That night, he performed in front of the regular audience . . . I didn't go. "Such a shame that you weren't there!" people told me. I grew worried: "Why?" "No, it was nothing special, but it was still good – better than at rehearsal." "You poor things . . . " I thought, and I felt pain for the actor and the theatre that didn't quite understand *what* it had destroyed . . . And this is happening now, under *such* managers [Stanislavsky and Nemirovich-Danchenko] – what will things be like later? . . .

This instance tells us a lot: how the mere presence of a keen audience that's close to the actor's heart can fill his soul with great content; how its approval can carry the actor to heights that he would not be able to reach [without an audience]. And how its crudeness and insensitivity can throw an actor off from these heights . . . And how he'll fall headlong, despite his talent and experience . . .

But we don't know everything yet. We don't know how long it takes one to *recover* after such a fall. And we don't know if one's soul ever completely recovers . . .

12. The Audience

In villages, there was a time when grateful audiences would weep at performances of *Tsar Maximilian* . . . [1] It's only possible to watch these performances while dying from laughter, but nevertheless, audiences would weep in delight . . . Why? Are they very foolish? No – they yearn for artistic impressions, and the mere hint of one is enough to bring their fantasies to a flurry, and they create in place of the actors.

Today, it's the same for us.

We should not deceive ourselves and think that the delight of the audience is our due. The opinion of a single expert should be much more valuable to you than that of everyone else. Many years ago, Shakespeare's Hamlet said this, but actors continue to deceive themselves.

I saw how Stanislavsky himself confidently and categorically proved to one actor or another how he was acting incorrectly, poorly, incomprehensibly. You would think that the words of a great expert will carry weight, especially when they're intended to help an actor out, to help him act for real. Alas! "It doesn't matter what the old man says! The audience likes it, so it's good! What else does he want?!"

"But hold on for a minute," people will say to me, "You think that actors should only act for experts? For some Stanislavsky and his posse? And ignore everyone else? You think the audience's opinions don't matter? Just try to make such a theatre – nobody will go to it."

There are different kinds of experts.

Ones like Stanislavsky strive for perfection, and when they attain it, as it would sometimes happen, the theatre's doors would break from the onslaught of audiences.

There are others: experts that believe themselves to be such. There is no time or desire to discuss them.

And the audience . . . there are different audiences.

For example, some two years ago, after a trip to western Europe, an engineer told the following: Out of curiosity, he went to a revue. And a revue, for your information, isn't just a tavern or a café with a stage – the revues over there have seen the best of what the ballet, the circus, the operas, and the stage have to offer . . .

A singer is announced. A beautiful young girl comes out in a gorgeous, though modest dress. She bows with a charming smile, and when the applause dies away, she begins to sing some sort of moralizing romance. Contrary to expectations, it turned out that she didn't have much of a voice, and her singing was quite mediocre, but the audience wasn't disappointed at all – quite the contrary: as soon as the song ends and she tries to go offstage, the audience won't let her, they call her back out. She goes out, bows to the right, to the left, bowing very low. The applause grows stronger, becomes a storm. People peer out from backstage, applauding; she turns her back to the audience and bows to them, lower, and lower, and that's when the "point" of her performance becomes clear: when she bows very low, her dress, cut lengthwise from the waist to the floor, parts, and you see that she has nothing underneath it . . . The applause becomes an ovation . . .

The full house bears witness to the fact that this kind of "art" is highly prized and is preferred to all others.

Are you really going to listen to the opinions of an audience like this? Don't you think that we should create something *so powerful* that's capable of *distracting* these people from this sort of delightful performance?

Serving the public doesn't mean obeying its tastes; serving the public means elevating it, inspiring it, widening its horizons, educating it.

But here is the main obstacle. Educating! Not everybody wants to be educated. The majority of people considers themselves to be quite educated. "Well, if you let me in to your moralizing show for free, I might sit through it, maybe I'll see something interesting, but if you make me pay money for it! . . . I won't go, and I'll tell others not to either!" And that's what happens.

Yes, truth be told, you and I wouldn't go to such a high-minded and highly respected show either if it didn't have *true talent* or at least a grain of *high art*.

If we do go, it would probably be not because of any real desire to go, but because of the *conviction* – we are sometimes led by our indolence and a habit of obeying public opinion. If everyone says that a theatre is good, powerful, old, renowned, that its actors are well-known, as are its directors – that means that we should visit it – the brand doesn't lie.

If it's boring or poorly done, then why should we go? Maybe there once was something worthwhile in this theatre, but it's all gone now – now, there are just portraits hanging on the wall. Why go there? You don't have to yell out on all the town's squares that "the emperor isn't wearing anything at all!" But it's quite within your rights to not go.

And if somebody goes against their will to a theatre that has the highest didactic intentions, then maybe we should look for an explanation not in the person but in the theatre? Maybe the actors *act poorly* in this theatre?

Art educates, art preaches, but how? By means of entertainment, by means of *enthralling the audience's hearts*, by means of captivating with its beauty.

And if people don't go to a certain theatre, then it is probably bad.

Toward Publicness

Being neither an actor, nor a director, the editor of the *Encyclopédie*, Diderot, wrote a book called *The Paradox of the Actor*. The book proves "beyond a shadow of a doubt" that an actor shouldn't feel anything while onstage if he wants to leave a lasting impression, that he should be cold and that he should deftly imitate life, i.e. deftly copy external signs of life. This, he says, is the "paradox" – in order to create the impression of life, you cannot live for real.

The book takes a few *natural-born imitators* and shows what they do onstage. These tales of imitators serve as the foundation for his universal theory of acting.

There is no paradox here – an *imitator* can only imitate – what else is he to do? If he tries to *live* onstage, it wouldn't look good – *it's not his natural environment*.

The real paradox is that a *person* is free and natural when he is alone, by himself, while an actor, *in the presence of a full house* becomes *many, many times freer, more natural, and open*! This really is a paradox. We can always observe this paradox with actors sent to us *dei gratia* – Mochalov, Yermolova, Strepetova, Duse.

The Actor and the Audience

Ostuzhev would tell that Yermolova responded to his question, "How long should you hold a pause and how can you tell?" in the following way: "Hold it for as long as the audience can take it."

This is so perceptive and so wise that you can't come up with anything better. This means that she always senses the audience, that she lives with it the whole time.

Against "Publicness"

When the child-protégé conductor Willy Ferrero's father brought him onstage, he was being naughty. When, however, he was put before the music stand and he took up the conductor's baton, he *suddenly changed* – he grew pale, matured, and it was as if he became possessed.

This is an example of how it isn't the audience that's most important, but the *doing*. In this case, the encounter with the music.

Many doubts rise up because of this . . . Mochalov, Yermolova . . . Maybe the audience matters very little here too . . .

It's another thing that the actor *senses* the audience, that it *enters* his creation, like a part of it . . . but to say that all the power stems from it? . . . Could we be getting a bit carried away here?

It's the same with Pushkin. In Vikenty Veresaev's book [*Pushkin in Life*], there is an instance when, in the middle of a conversation, Pushkin's eyes suddenly became serious and grim, his countenance changed entirely, he became strange . . . he got up and left to write.

> But once Divine and Holly Word
> Reaches the poet's tender ear,
> His soul awakens from its sleep,
> And, like an eagle, it spreads its wings.
> [*Pushkin 1959: 179*]

It's as if the most important thing that "moves" one into the realm of artistic inspiration is the *moment when content and form meet*.

For a poet, when thought meets rhythm, musicality, "denotations" (i.e. words).

For a musician, like Ferrero, when sounds in his imagination meet the sounds of the orchestra.

For an actor, when his own excitement and thoughts meet the "mask" (transformation).

★★★

In general, creativity depends on three conditions:

1   Emotionally synthesizing thinking
2   A splintered [or doubled] identity
3   Non-consciousness [subconsciousness] and for an actor, there is a fourth condition:
4   Publicness.

This is why the first three points can explain the case with Willy Ferrero, while the audience is just a push, it's like a cause that evokes the conditioned reflex of creativity.

★★★

Different actors need to be watched from different distances. Moissi cannot be watched from close-up. The reason: he acts not for the first few rows, but for the whole audience, feeling out its center. This center is the point from which you should watch him.

★★★

We've spoken of the benefits of an audience's influence on an actor – but there is a harmful side as well!

Start with things like "requiring [specific results] of yourself" and "pushing." And what about "compulsive deception masquerading as truth"? These horrible things are all begotten from the audience, after which they bloom and flourish.

The Reflex of Properly Sensing the Audience

The first thing that we need to develop is proper reflexive behavior.

After all, the chief difficulty of the actor's art lies in the fact that an unnatural situation (the audience, somebody else's lines, artificial environment) causes us to reflexively feel *uneasy and cautious*.

How do you calm yourself?

Relaxing your muscles does something to this end, but not everything.

"Tasks" and "activity" distract you from the audience, but only as long as they occupy the actor. As soon as they are gone, then you're unsettled and helpless once more.

True, calm comes on its own with time and experience: there's no task, and I forgot my lines, and I don't get my role, but I'm calm – this is nothing! . . . Experience has shown that nothing catastrophic or fatal will come of it. This is why I'm calm.

Years bring calm, and only if there's nobody in the audience that I'm afraid of – if there's a critic or my boss, then I'll start trembling.

The *reflex of properly sensing the audience* should be fostered from your first days, from your first steps onstage.

This is another reason why my school is true, while the "actively willful" one is improper and harmful.

★★★

A good expression: a good audience galvanizes the actor.

On the Audience and the Actor: Induction

The audience induces me, but how do I control it? After all, *I* lead the way, not the audience – it only gives me the energy. The audience is expectant and passive. However, the audience's passive attention is a kind of energy. It's necessary to perceive this energy while being in the midst of similar "passivity" – it's necessary to receive it, and channel it in the direction necessary for the show and for my creative state (energized by the audience). The passive audience will receive this energy, redirected by me, and it will respond with an even more powerful radiation – just keep receiving it. (But don't become too distracted by this whole process – it should be like breathing, almost automatic – just don't get in its way.)

Resonance

A bad actor apes around. I resonate with him and sense his falsity. I sense it in myself as I transmit it.

Yermolova says a word – a word-moan, a word-sigh – I resonate and . . . I sigh, moan, think in unison with her.

More on the Interplay between the Audience and the Actor

The actor must sense the audience. But how? He needs to **lead** it like the director leads the actor – while demonstrating a role to him.

When you explain something to new listeners, when you teach a new group of students, you light up – it's exciting!

Remember that when you act, you're telling something *to a **new audience*** of 1,000 people *every single time.*

★★★

Before performing, an actor should look at the audience and admit inside the following thoughts and sensations: they've come, they're sitting in anticipation. They're anticipating me. And they want to enjoy my acting. Let's say that I'm acting in a tragedy – and they're anticipating a tragedy. Look at them: how should you act so as to enthrall them? Allow yourself to be charged by them. And look at the obstacles that you have to "overcome" today.

Take aim beforehand.

Most importantly: be able to take in, while looking at these concrete faces, clothes, etc. *a charge of energy* – today's energy. That's how I'm going to act today, that's what I have to do.

And be able to hear this energy, take it in, heed it, and give into it while you act.

Similarly, a person should be able to hear God . . . "*deisis*," standing before God like a *lit candle.*

Who cannot sense the audience in this way is not an actor. Who cannot sense God in life is not a person.

On Filling the Stage (and the Audience Space) with Yourself

One actor might go onstage, and you get the impression that he's filled up the whole stage with himself. The other actors disappear – they're displaced. But a different actor goes onstage – and he's playing a big role – and nothing happens.

Without overthinking it, without analyzing it, try to *"fill the space:"* and not just when entering the stage – try to walk into a room and fill it. Have I filled the room with myself? Go ahead, fill it up!

Then try a street, a forest, a mountain, the whole good earth . . .

Note

1 A primitive popular play, written and performed by amateur peasant-actors. Demidov witnessed such performances in his youth.

14

Advice for Future Researchers of the Actor's Creative Technique

It would like to attract more people to the path of researching and experimenting with regard to the psychological technique of the art of experiencing.

Aside from everything else, this is a very rewarding work, since the researchers have barely touched this realm of knowledge; anywhere you go, there are bound to be discoveries. Just approach it with a fresh mind, give it a little thought – and you will stumble onto a new invention.

But, so that inexperienced experimenters do not make mistakes from the outset, it would be good to give them a few bits of advice.

1 You don't have to try to discover or invent something by any means possible. You just have to *monitor* how and what occurs (in yourself or in others). When you monitor *properly*, your observations will inevitably lead you to discovery (possibly to something that has already been discovered – this is unimportant). An attempt to utilize the discovery will lead you to an invention or closer to perfection.

2 *There's no need to chase after something "special,"* exceptional, extraordinary. It will rise out of the mundane and the ordinary. Otherwise, you will become derailed from the very first steps. A ladder has its own rather severe rule: you have to step on every rung. You have to begin *with the first*, and only once you're sure in your footing can you aim for the second.

3 Search only for the normal, the ordinary. Search only for the simple, something that is by no means complex, something that might be simpler than simple, something you think has long been evident and has even managed to grow stale.

4 *Take your time.* Moving at the speed of a turtle is still going too quickly. If you don't slow down enough, you might miss some *details*. And details are the most important part here. *Ultra slow* steps are the fastest that you're allowed to make.

5 For monitoring, for investigating, you should never bring yourself into a state of some sort of "creative flight." On the contrary, *you need sober-mindedness, calm,* and even cold-bloodedness.

6 Don't do any experiments off the top of your head. There's no need to shoot at the sky, hoping, "Maybe I'll hit something."

740

You should *take the simplest* and smallest of what you have – either in yourself or in others. And you have to decidedly *work with it*.

7   Do not think that you'll find something valuable on your first attempt. The secret lies in *stubborn repetition*.

I'll never forget something I have witnessed:

A man stood atop an enormous stone block the size of a stack of hay and was hitting it with a hammer. "Is it really possible to break such a mound with a simple maul?" I thought. What can non-Herculean, human blows do to a great mound like this? The iron mallet bounced off the stone like a rubber ball bounces off a wall.

"Have you been hitting it for long, dear old man?"

"Not for long, dear. Just since this morning."

"A hard rock, no?"

"Not at all, it's already giving in."

"How do you know that it's giving in?"

"The sound, dear – it's begun to grunt. Some 400–500 more blows – no more."

I was so intrigued that on the way back, I made a detour to this rock again.

The old man was still beating away . . . calmly, methodically, not hurrying. The maul was still bouncing off, ringing, and my ear couldn't pick up on any consolatory "grunting . . . "

I decided to wait it out. Time passed, and the longer I waited, the more hopeless the old man's endeavor seemed. Suddenly, up top where he was hammering away, something really did happen – the rock began to resonate with the blows more dully, softer, and a crack went down the whole mound.

The old man put the maul away and came down.

"Let's have a smoke," he invited me.

Afterwards, I found out that before explosives, this was the usual way of splitting a rock. The secret lay in *guessing* where the crack was more likely to form and accurately choose the place to deliver the blows.

"Cleansing Self-Treatment": The Body Position

In order to illustrate what "monitoring" means, what "searching for the ordinary, simple, and already found" means, what "details" means, and what "sober-mindedness and coldness in observing" means, I'll tell about an instance that included all of these elements.

In the thick of directing and even teaching, you sometimes make mistakes. You inevitably become carried away while working, and you repeat a mistake. Soon, it becomes a habit, and you don't even notice how you've become "derailed" and how you've lost the ability to discern what's right from what's wrong in the actors' work.

This is why, from time to time, I undertake *"cleansing treatment."* It involves me going through various exercises and ensuring the *absolute* soundness of my creative state.

To put it more simply – I work like an actor.

One such approach: having woken up some three hours before I have to get up, while lying in bed, I speak monologues, parts of dialogues, or recite verse.

The morning of interest, I took up a monologue from Tolstoy's play *The Living Corpse* – when Fedya Protasov tells Petushkov the story of his love for Masha.

But things weren't looking good. I was trying my very best . . . but I just couldn't do it right. I knew that I was false, but I couldn't do anything about it. I tried using one method, another, I used an "object," I gave myself "tasks," I did other things – nothing doing!

I got tired of it. I left it alone.

But you let go of something, and yet it stays with you, undulating in your brain on its own . . . I'm lying there while thoughts are flowing around in my brain . . .

Fedya . . . Petushkov . . . the inn . . . Everything seems so clear, so simple! . . . There's Petushkov, there's the inn, there's the table . . . I'm sitting . . . And suddenly, I almost became feverish – I'm not "sitting"!!

Are you sitting? No – you're *lying down*! You're imagining that you're sitting, when in reality, you're lying in your warm bed, beneath the covers, on a soft pillow.

That's where the lie is, where I get derailed!

Alright – you're lying down! What's important about the scene isn't that you're sitting or lying down. After all, couldn't it be in a hospital? Fedya is in a hospital after being too drunk, he's in bed, and Petushkov is lying in the neighboring bed . . . Alright, let's try this out.

I made myself even more comfortable: if I'm going to be lying down, then I'll do it properly. I didn't just lie down, I *placed* myself in bed as best I could. Is my *whole* body lying down? Legs, arms, torso, neck, head? It turns out that I was in a state of some excitement, nothing was *lying down*. I calmed myself, started lying better.

And a wondrous feeling of calm and freedom seized me.

My body was lying down, and my thoughts became clear, transparent, distinct.

Petushkov is next to me . . . And, in my thoughts, I see Masha . . . In my dreams, she is still live . . .

> Yeah, you know, if a girl from our society had feelings like that, if she sacrificed everything for the man that she loved . . . but here, it's a gypsy girl, raised on self-interest, and then this clean, self-sacrificing love! She gives everything away, demanding nothing in return. That's the contrast. [Tolstoy 1952 vol. XLVI: 74]

The delighted surprise, the bright memories of my wondrous past love, the joy that I had once felt it – all of this brought tears to my eyes, and the complex scene in the inn came to life, grew warm, and became heartfelt, overflowing with the truth of life, meaning, and joy.

Hold up, hold up – how did this happen? What did I do that the secret doors of creativity suddenly opened?

Was the act of simply *lying down* the magical key? And from this point, I began to coldly, sober-mindedly, cautiously observe myself and others . . . And what did I find out? Ninety-nine times out of hundred, when we're sitting, we're not actually sitting. We're not sitting or lying down or standing, etc. Technically, I'm sitting, but at the same time, I'm in an hurry to get somewhere, I'm running around somewhere, I'm fidgeting with someone – my legs have already "stood up," my face is full of worry, my shoulders are tense, my neck is tense, etc.

When I came to the theatre with the intention of seeing how people sat, stood, walked across the stage – I was completely astounded and confused. The presence of an audience so affects an actor that the falsity, the duality, triality (I don't even know – innumerability) of positions in which his body wants to be at the same time is just deadly. His body simultaneously exists in ten different positions, and every position tries to pull him into it more and more. Is it possible for a person to be in control of his body when it's being torn in ten different directions?

You're sitting, aren't you? So sit down for real. Let "*it*" be sitting. Let your body be sitting, let your legs be sitting (they keep trying to run away somewhere), let your arms be sitting, let (even if this sounds very silly) everything be sitting – your face, your neck, your fingers . . .

As soon as the actor *sits* himself down, thereby allowing his body to exist in the truth in which it has to exist in a given moment – that's when you truly and completely *free and release your muscles*. Then, your imagination greedily latches on to what your thoughts feed it – your fantasy begins to work, and your creative process commences.

It's enough to grab hold of even the tail end of a string – start pulling on it and winding it, and you won't even notice how you've managed to create a whole ball.

It's the same with this method.

Two Modes of Investigation: Actively Willful and Affective

Depending on his abilities and proclivities, every investigator will take note of the mechanics of the processes that are closer to his heart.

The actively willful researcher will always notice that *activity* solves every problem: my concentration is scattered – I have to make myself "be attentive"; I don't know what to do – I have to pick out a "task" and try to fulfill it; I'm wan and bored – I have to "fulfill actions," as that will excite me and face me in the right direction; I don't care about my partner – I have to figure out my "relationship" with him; I'm not affected by anything that happens to me in the play – I have to "appraise my given circumstances"; I'm senselessly delivering my lines – I have to take it apart, understand it, turn the words into thoughts.

On the other hand, the *affective* researcher sees *passivity* as the main operating force.

Only in a state of *absolute openness, absolute defenselessness, and passivity* can we take in an impression to the very depths of our soul. Complex or simple, it will hit us right in the heart, sting it, wound it, or bind it with deathly frost.

For an affective type, a state of passivity is the alpha and the omega.

Once an impression stings his soul, he doesn't even notice how he begins to functions – he's active, he's more active than the most active emotionally willful type, but his activity is the **result** of an impression, its consequence. After you get an impression, you just have to know how *not to interfere*, how to *green-light yourself*, how *not to get in the way*, i.e. again, be able to be infinitely *passive*.

And Nature, which we've completely chocked up and pushed into a corner in real life (you can't do this! you can't do that!), will grow braver, it'll see that it "*can*" do something, that it won't be beaten, that it has *the right* to do something – it will buck up, take heart, straighten its shoulders, and give us its strength – it will reveal to us its secrets.

Passivity will allow an affective type to transfer his attention to himself, to his own apparatus.

If the surrounding "circumstances" don't concern him, he won't dig around *in them* – he'll inevitably look deeper into *himself*: this bounces off of me, this doesn't excite me . . . that means that something is wrong in my own creative apparatus.

Being closer to nature, he instinctively knows that nature, to be commanded, *must be obeyed*.

Metaphorically speaking, he won't try to pull a sapling out of the ground by force – he'll try to understand what's getting in the way of its growth and will remove the obstacles.

Two Conditions of Research: In Rehearsals and in the Quiet of a Laboratory

Complete Freedom of Muscles

As has already been said, the methods found in Stanislavsky's System are of the actively willful type: "Be attentive," "be interested in an object," or "*what if . . .*" etc.

But, naturally, Stanislavsky's penetrating gaze does not fail to notice an actor's "creative mechanism." From the beginning, he talks about "relaxing your muscles." But the fact that his "system" was developed in the haste of rehearsals, while working on productions, hindered him to investigate this method *in full*.

He has to put on a show – that means that he has to use what already exists in the actor. Does this really give him the time to conduct a lot of research? Naturally, when an actor is tense or closed off, he doesn't see or hear or understand – this can be averted in the thick of it: unclench his fists, release his muscles, calm him down, remind him of his circumstances, imply to him what he should do and what he should "want" in a given moment (i.e. his task), and everything is fine.

But does this really tell us everything we need to know about this method? Has it been pushed to the limit, or brought to its threshold? And more importantly – has it been brought *beyond the threshold*? Of course not.

Meanwhile, it's only once we have crossed *beyond the threshold*, as far as a given method is concerned, that we can utilize it in full force, or experienced its unadulterated effect.

We can throw a log onto a stove and endlessly heat it up there. It will never light on fire – it will smolder, become charred, but it won't catch fire. There will be no flames.

It's not enough to warm it up or even heat it up – you have to push the temperature to the limit, bring it to the *right threshold*, to the point of *ignition*, but even this isn't enough – you have to cross *over* the threshold. Otherwise, it's all for naught.

In order to push a method to the limit, bring it to the *right threshold*, you need time, and there is no such time during rehearsal.

Let me tell you about how "laboratory" work on this this same method [of "relaxing your muscles"] reveals to us all of its secrets and how it can be brought to and beyond the threshold.

In 1924, Moissi was in town on tour.

I quickly chanced to find myself at one of his most successful performances and was completely knocked off my saddle – I was astounded and perplexed. I saw such a degree of "relaxed muscles!" A complete lack of any tension – it seemed like the man simply *did not have a body*!

He [Moissi] didn't move, didn't walk – it seemed like *he was carried* from spot to spot like the wind carries a feather. And when he spoke, it seemed like it wasn't just a creature that could walk on its find legs, a creature that *had* a mind, a heart, a conscience that was speaking . . . but rather that the heart *itself*, the mind *itself*, the conscience *itself* was speaking, and that there was nothing corporeal there at all.

This new, hitherto unseen and unheard of thing unnerved me . . .

Having more or less come to, I grew worried: *how* does he achieve that state?!

I tried to achieve it with my actors in rehearsals – it didn't work, including those actors who heard about it, grew interested, and tried to replicate it.

I was forced to leave it – it would break up rehearsals, lead the actors away from the play, and in general, it's impossible to conduct such experiments during rehearsals.

Some parts of this research *was* useful, but it was so far from what Moissi achieved that it's not even worth mentioning.

So what to do? Give up? That's not in my nature. So what then? Let's "go underground." And so I started trying to get at the essence by experimenting on myself.

I relaxed my muscles . . . More . . . and more . . . and I only managed to make myself incredibly weak and wan. Evidently, that wasn't the right approach. I left it alone.

I began recalling certain poses that were adopted by the enthralling actor; I assumed those poses myself, I recalled *him in full*, including his internal in a given moment and tried to recreate *that* – it seemed that something started coming of it, but I still couldn't grab the beast by the tail – it kept slipping away. I went through every single pose possible until I finally lay down. Lying down, I became even calmer. I kept calming myself down more and more until I fell asleep. Evidently, I slept for a long time – at any rate, I felt thoroughly refreshed when I woke up. I woke up from some random outside noise, and I couldn't understand: where was I, what am I? Is it night, evening, or morning? Why am I fully clothed? I began to remember vaguely that I had nowhere to be, that I had the day free. And what a sleep I had: I couldn't move my arms or my legs – I was still bound by sleep. It was as if my body was dead – only my head was somewhat functioning.

Good god! I had been searching for the secrets of the touring artist! And I fell asleep! Made quite a fool out of myself!

Though, what harm came of it? No big deal! Nothing bad happened: I still wasn't getting anywhere – I had hit a wall. Now at least I'd had some sleep, I was refreshed – I could have at it with renewed vigor. Let's get to it!

(And this still while half-asleep, before I moved a single limb, still half in the world of dreams.) Let's begin!

What was I doing? Right! I was relaxing my muscles. I was looking for complete release; I was trying to completely "*take off my body.*"

Let's keep going.

Stop!!!!.. Hold off . . . hold off! . . . I don't even have to do anything . . . it's right here – total relaxation . . . I just mustn't scare it away . . .

Look at how *it's* lying down, how it's released . . .

It's like there's some sort of duality: *it's* lying down, continuing to sleep, still dreaming, but I'm awake, thinking, reasoning, and even talking to myself in my thoughts . . .

Alright, let me try somebody else's lines . . .

What should I do?

Hm, well, it might be difficult, beyond my reach, but it's very appropriate given the circumstances – Hamlet's conversation with his own body: "O, that this too too solid flesh would melt . . . "

I instantly remember everything that happened to the prince before: his father's death, his mother's marriage, the newlyweds' formal address to the court . . .

I use my mind's eye to investigate my lying, sleeping body . . .

It lies there, giving not a care about what's happening in my mind . . .

O, that this too too solid flesh would melt
Thaw and resolve itself into a dew!

I'm addressing my body as if it were something foreign; I can feel myself, my mind, my consciousness as independent from it . . .

Or that the Everlasting had not fix'd
His canon 'gainst self-slaughter!

I enter a conversation, almost a conspiracy with the heavens against my odious body, against this millstone round my neck.

> . . . Oh God! Oh God!
> How weary, stale, flat and unprofitable,
> Seem to me all the uses of this world!"
> My thoughts span the globe – and now I can see it before my spiritual gaze.
> "Fie on't! ah fie! 'tis an unweeded garden,
> That grows to seed; things rank and gross in nature
> Possess it merely.

Is it really possible, so to say, in the cold light of day, to address *the entire world*? Will it really heed me? Will it want to understand? And is it such a tiny thing that my voice will reach its every corner?

It *is* possible to address it, but you have to be in *such* a state of furor and spiritual openness in order to speak like this and believe that the world is listening and hearing you!

But in sleep, this is possible. In dreams, you completely and whole-heartedly give over to the influence of anything that even flickers through your brain, that exists for just a second before your mind's eye . . .

> A little month, or ere those shoes were old
> With which she follow'd my poor father's body,
> Like Niobe, all tears:

Everything seems so real and tangible – you can even feel the flow of time: one month! You can see her, walking behind the coffin, weeping, inconsolable . . .

But what is this? When I thought of her shoes, my eyes, despite being closed, turned down to look at those ill-fated shoes . . . So that means that a part of me is awake, since my eyes are moving? And forget my eyes – isn't my tongue making small movements when I speak? Soundlessly, but I'm still speaking. Well, let it move, let it do whatever it pleases – I'll just keep paying attention to where this is going.

> O, God!

And I start looking up, searching for someone who hears and sees all up there, somewhere in the ceiling . . . My eyes are open, but I didn't notice when they opened – rather, my state became more comfortable – I now have something with which to see.

> O, God! a beast, that wants discourse of reason,
> Would have mourn'd longer.

I find it difficult to be aware of the closeness of this guilty and shallow woman . . . I turn away and . . . my body follows me and my thoughts. But it has not awoken!

> Ere yet the salt of most unrighteous tears
> Had left the flushing in her galled eyes,
> She married. O, most wicked speed . . .

I sit up; as Pushkin [1960: 272] writes, I am in this "*benign complacent mood when our dreams are clearly drawn before us,*" and my body is obediently following these drawings. It followed, without interfering with my psychological life, as our shadows follow us on a moonlit night, persistently and silently, without giving any sign that it's there, not demanding a thing. I didn't hear it – it became light and flexible, like a shadow; at times, it would run ahead of me, at times, it would walk besides me, and, at times, it would disappear, trailing behind.

I had long ago got up, I had long ago begun to speak out loud without even noticing how I had passed from silence through whispers to full vocalizations . . . And it – it followed my thoughts and feelings like a shadow; I felt like my very soul was speaking, I heard sounds that I had never heard before – my heart was speaking; my thoughts were speaking:

> O, most wicked speed, to post
> With such dexterity to incestuous sheets!
> It is not nor it cannot come to good:
> But break, my heart; for I must hold my tongue.

As in a dream, I saw everything with monstrous clarity – it seized me, twirled me around with wrathful force, dragged me through life, hitting me about its edges – a life that existed only in my mind.

My soul was pained, my chest wanted to tear open, and my body trembled, like leaves in a storm.

Could it have been the same for Moissi during that inspired night?

In his case, the heart and the mind too were alive, while his "absent" body obediently followed them like a shadow. It wasn't sleepy, tired, or heavy; on the contrary – its lightness, freedom, ease, and mobility were much greater than anything one can fathom.

I have seen Moissi in life. He's like everyone else. He doesn't possess any special ease or grace. Why then did he manage it while onstage? Because (I know this now), consciously or subconsciously, in the show, he "***put his body to sleep.***"

A few days in a row, after waking up in the morning, I would tread this whole path, paving and repaving the way. I experimented with very different texts. Finally, when I had gotten a grip on this state of "*liberation from the body,*" I tried to walk along this path in the middle of the day, rather than when I had just woken up. I remember that I was very afraid that I would "lose it." Carefully, slowly, I put my body to sleep, calming it down, but it looked like the work I had done previously wasn't all for naught – the state of "liberation from the body" must have been ingrained in me very well by that time, and I quickly entered it.

Afterwards, I evoked this state of release from my body while sitting, while standing, while walking – in one, two minutes . . .

As a result, people say that what we get is a hitherto unseen person: all of his thoughts, all his feelings, all of his treasuries are open, and he's transparent like the water of a mountain lake.

Have we seen such a thing onstage?

We have. You can see this "sleep of the body" in affective actors' best moments. [See Figure 17.]

There is Mochalov, in the mousetrap scene, "casually half-lounging on the bench"? [See pages 28, 295.]

I will never forget Leonidov's useless, hanging, dangling arms when he was Mitya Karamazov during the interrogation scene. And it wasn't just his arms – his body at large was extraneous, useless; there was life only inside, only in his soul.

And Yermolova! It's like you don't even see her – like she's not even there. There is a candle in the darkness, but you don't see the candle – you see only the flame, only the flame! – it's lighting the grim corners of your life.

That's what it means to push "muscular release" to the limit, *beyond the threshold.*

My first mentor in art [father, Vasily Demidov] would say: "Most importantly, you have to *calm over.*" Only now, in the 50th year of life do I understand this expression: to calm OVER. Not calm ***down*** – calm ***over*** – cross ***over*** the threshold of calm.

Calm isn't enough – you have to go farther, *beyond calm*, i.e. if not strive for death, then at least for *bodily sleep*, for "unconsciousness" of the body. At that point, you'll start doing what you don't even dare dream about.

Did my father understand the accuracy with which he described the technique of calm? I do not know. But he himself would never say: "calm down," and would only say "calm over! calm over!"

And when he acted, I remember that I also *did not see* his body.

★★★

All findings seem *random*; without randomness, there wouldn't be any findings. But the thing is that nature keeps showing us things, but we do not see them, as if we were blind. When we search, we begin to *see*. How many times in life have I similarly woken up and in a state of semi-sleep thought about my concerns or solved abstract problems, but never paid any attention to the complete *liberation from the body*.

★★★

Only in solitude, in a state of complete concentration, without any rushing, when the obligation to keep the play moving isn't looming over your head – only in these circumstances can you *fully* excavate every happy thought that comes into your head and demands your attention.

Such work is too subtle for rehearsal and will hardly lead to anything fruitful in such conditions. Afterwards, once you've passed the first steps, the first stages, once you've managed to pinpoint the most important aspects and confirm the results – then, you can bring your findings to rehearsal.

Naturally, explosions, flights, and "ignitions" can occur not only in "laboratories" – they can happen in rehearsals and during shows. And quite often too. But ***how*** do these explosions occur? The *process* itself, all of its paths, all of its checkpoints, as well as the *main causes* inevitably slip by unnoticed.

This is why it often happens that during rehearsal, you can suddenly "be on fire" and your role comes to life, but afterwards, you can never repeat it . . .

This is understandable – the actors' and director's goal during rehearsal is completely different: they seek to expand the play and the roles, rather than developing the psychological process itself. They hunt other prey.

In a laboratory, however, under investigative circumstances, things are different: you're not very interested in accidental creative successes. You'll see them out of the corner of your eye, but you won't be concerned with *them specifically*. You'll get the thought: "Aha! So everything is going as it should be," – and you'll keep marching on.

It can't be any other way. If I'm a hunter, will raspberries and mushrooms distract me right as the beast I'm seeking steps out into a clearing?

More Advice for Pedagogues

From personal experience and by observing other directors and teachers, I can say one confirmed truth: a pedagogue or a director *also needs to be training and learning at all times*. If you don't act before an audience, then at least do it at home in solitude. Only by doing so will you obtain enough fuel for keeping your quickly exhausting batteries charged. Director or instructor, you have to keep yourself in the realm, in the atmosphere, in the environment of creativity that you teach about.

Otherwise, you quickly lose your good eye – you stop seeing. Maybe because your sight and your actor's instincts disunite. You have to foster their synergy.

★★★

It's the same old story. Especially at the first steps. "I was sitting on a chair, and I could see that I could play the etude like this and like this, but then I went out there and . . . nothing!"

The thing is that these are *essentially two different kinds of fantasy*. One, which sat on the chair – that's the fantasy of the audience, the painter, maybe the writer, but first and foremost, it's that of the *audience*. I can see everything **without me** – I don't act, I just observe.

But when I do begin to act, then I'll have to either: 1) imitate what I see without me – transpose it onto myself, i.e. to double the work or **completely** *reject my audience fantasy* and wait for impulses from within, or 2) give in to my actions: my hands start going, as do my legs and my face – let them all go, let them act. To be an actor means to act, and his fantasy is *active*, rather than observational.

Toward Training

For a teacher, the easiest thing to do is use various terms – "we don't have any communication here," "the task is wrong," etc. For an actor or a student, this only makes things more difficult.

You have to turn his attention to *this concrete situation*. Don't say, "Communicate with the object." Instead, put it more simply: "No, you missed something, he said something different.

"Remember: didn't something flicker in his eyes? Didn't his hand move strangely? – you saw this – you weren't paying good enough attention – you missed it." But if you start speaking about objects and communication, you'll lead his attention away from the details of his scene partner's life and behavior, which, for him, are the only things that matter.

Yesterday, one of the greatest singing instructors said nearly the same thing: "Usually, teachers speak of registers – I consider this to be harmful; the student shouldn't even know that they exist. Let's say he's singing, he hits one note correctly, then the next transitioning one doesn't work out, and then he's fine again. And I simply say: you hear that there's a hole here? – so fix it. There should be no holes. And he instinctively fixes it himself."

How does it go: "With much wisdom comes much sorrow; the more knowledge, the more grief" [Ecclesiastes 1:18].

Although all these words are helpful for systematizing, when using them during work, during rehearsal, they're a superfluous "object," "task," etc., whereas we need simple, singular truths; in this case, you just complicate things – "multiply" them.

★★★

With every year, Stanislavsky keeps simplifying his "system." This is good.

Some 10 years ago, when every action, every word was accompanied by 10–20 various physical and psychological tasks, not to mention supertasks; the actor became a person that was burdened by thousands and hundreds of thousands of distracting things and jobs that kept him from performing his most important job.

Let's say you need to go from Lyubertsy to Malakhovka. But instead of going down the easy path next to the railroad, you decide to walk along the rail. You get on it and walk the 20 kilometers like that. I'd like to see you do that! This is exactly what the "systematizers" would do to actors in their time. The old man quickly understood the folly of his enthusiasm. But many others took to developing this approach even further. They made it so that you would not only have to walk down the rail, but you'd have to do it while hopping on one foot . . .

On the Seeming Absence of a System

In art and creativity, the only true system is that of intuition.

Don't get in your own way. At times, a director suddenly feels like working on the blockings, at times – on acting, at times – working on the space of the stage (on a model), at times – working on psychology. And this apparent lack of a system should be made into law.

The greatest mistake is insisting that you *have* to begin with *this*, that you *have* to continue with *this*, and you *have* to end like *this*.

Everything depends on *what* and *to what extent things are ready inside of me* for a given play. And when you feel like you very much want to do something, this indicates readiness.

True, this readiness might be nothing more than custom. I want to do it because it's familiar – it's a tried-and-true method that I always use in my professional practice.

You *cannot begin with something that is dead*. What is *alive* for me in this show, in this role, or in this bit? What excites me, what draws me in?

Is it true that the first thing you should do when working on a show is search for the "most important thing/theme" in it? After all, this is also just a custom. Sometimes, this might put things to death.

Wouldn't it be better to give yourself over to something that isn't necessarily the most important thing in the play – it might even be a small trifle – but something that is *definitely, indubitably alive*?!

This gives birth to style and organically facilitates the given play's uniqueness.

On Teaching a Psycho-Technique and Training

Take as your foundation: "Mortify our carnal mind, O God, and save us!" [From the Troporation (anthem) of the Ninth Hour of the Christian Orthodox service, based on the Prayer of the Ninth Hour, by St. Basil the Great.]

There is too much knowledge, too much reasoning! This is good for scientists, anatomists, researchers. For culture.

For those who don't have an investigative vein, however, this is very harmful.

Just as after extensive research, doctors prescribe their patients simple pills and don't force them to learn all the ins and outs of the human body – so we too have to come up with several incredibly clever exercises and exercise, exercise, exercise . . . However, *those that have an aptitude for teaching have to go through a separate course of training.*

What sorts of exercises are the most ingenious? This is the main question.

For example: "Questions and Answers." You don't have to explain anything – you don't need to elaborate on truth, communication, objects, "attention," the "I am," and everything else – there's no need to fill up the actors' heads with unnecessary information. Just give them the exercise, and they'll instinctively find their way. In a word, we need to do what physical education instructors now do – they come up with games, manual work, etc. (running, jumping). You have to make things *fun, interesting, and lively*. After all, our work, our art, our creativity, is called "play" and "playing." You have to teach people to sing the same way – don't tell them anything about resonators, breathing, etc. The teacher's job is to make things *easier*, rather than more difficult.

We have to come up with *exercises – games*. We have to develop people's faith in their intuition.

Our motto: "Intuition and intuition!"

1 Exercise: "Questions and Answers."
2 Exercise: "Questions and Answers with Movement."
3 Exercise: "Creative Justification of a Pose," and later, of a word.
4 Exercise: "Questions and Answers" – first making one word important, then another.
5 Exercise: Justify the same pose first one way, then another, and it must all be justified creatively.
6 Exercise: Tell about something you saw; then repeat the story (imagining and forgetting).
7 Exercise: Questions and answers, with props (the feeling of the object).
8 Exercise: Mimicry. Questions and answers.
9 Exercise: "Unpredictability." A question and an answer, or the beginning of an improvised conversation.
10 Ape a voice (a phrase) and green-light yourself towards whatever you want to do next.

★★★

Paganini never played his violin except at concerts. He would pick it up, run his fingers along the strings, but his bow would never emit a single sound.

We need to try to find the *same* thing in the work of an actor. To be able to rehearse not just without words, not just silently – this is the same thing as playing "with a bow" – but to somehow *disunite perception and response* – this is nearly heresy. But we *have* to think about this. Paganini avoided playing for a reason. Nobody *forbade* him to rehearse. And all violinists other than him consider it to be absolutely essential to saw at their instruments six hours a day. There is *something very serious* in this stubborn abstinence. Either he was preserving his [word missing], or he was afraid of turning into a machine. Or could it be something more serious? At any rate: *it wasn't for nothing!*

Towards the Methodology of Training

There have been mistakes in our training – *you cannot skip from one method to another*; you have to stick to one and get a result – whether it's breathing, imagination, seriousness, or activity; *then*, you can start learning a new one. Otherwise, you'll believe more and more that you know a lot, but can't do anything – you just see that everything that you do isn't what you want it to be.

★★★

Everybody makes it so that things are more difficult than they should be. We have to strive to make things *easy*.

This in itself is a method.

We need to bring an actor to this *easiness* gradually, starting with the simplest conversations about the weather (questions and answers in the circle).

Or else, we can keep asking them: "Are things easy enough for you? Make it so that things become easy."

Conclusion

Who among us will deign to ride a horse when we can instead get on a train or an airplane? But after everything great that's been done, after everything that's been discovered, after everything that they've been shown and taught, artists decidedly get down on all fours and crawl like little children – and they even demand amazement and admiration! To live whole centuries after Raphael, Velasquez, millennia after Phidias – and to draw or sculpt like this! It's even a little bit difficult to believe!

Actors, at least, have an excuse: Mochalov, Salvini, Duse, Yermolova – they all existed, but now they're all gone – who can we learn from? They might be gone, but the paintings, the sculptures – they're right here! Stand up and look at them! Use your brains a little bit! No, there is something very serious at work here, and I don't know if it can be fixed . . .

Has humanity really begun going backwards? Has it grown too crude, too foul? In its pursuit of civilization, has it lost all its culture, all of Prometheus's stolen fire?

It's such a frightful thought! . . . We must rescue it! We must yell this out on every street corner!

★★★

Fire . . . Primitive peoples, our ancestors must have regarded it with such confusion and horror! They trembled before it, worshipped it as they would a supreme being, a god!

Centuries have passed, and now it fuels our trains, our ships, carries us through the air, blows up mountains, whirls the flywheels of our motors, lights and warms our cities, our modest apartments, and, finally, lights our cigarettes.

Such is the power of human insight.

Oh, if only we knew as much about our personal fire that sits inside us, stored as an electromagnetic or some other unknown force; if only we knew the force of our thoughts, of our will, or of our subconscious activity, our talent and genius!

We have the same attitude towards this fire as did our ancestors: we don't understand it, we tremble and bow before it. And that's not even the worst of it – some of us just laugh at it stupidly, boldly insisting with the impudence of an ignoramus that it's nothing, rejecting it – and this is easier; this doesn't require any additional effort.

Let's not grab at it or leave it alone; let's not reject it before we even understand what it's all about; let's instead, without much ado, without undue awe, or even with some awe – let's try to catch this secret, unknown, "celestial" fire by the tail.

Sometimes it's small – is there some way to *augment* it? It's weak – let's *expand* it. It shows up whenever it so wills – is there some way to *evoke it at any moment*, whenever we need it? It goes wherever the wind blows – is there some way to *direct it*?

In a word – is there some way that we can wield this tool?

If the mountain doesn't come to Mohammed, then it's necessary to trouble yourself to get up and go to it.

★★★

In order to exhaustively and successfully teach or tell something, you have to know it *in full*, and in order to know it in full, you have to know it *even further*.

Only knowing it further can you step aside and see things from all angles: from behind, from the front, sideways, from the top, from the bottom.

This leads to another conclusion: anyone who knows something *in full* inevitably knows *above and beyond* whatever is involved with the topic.

★★★

It would be so great to tear through this traditional, self-satisfied rigidity – towards the light, *towards freedom, towards a creative fusion with the audience*!

These books of mine are but the first stone of a new building. Either way, sooner or later, this rigidity that bears the name of the art of theatre will die, but there's just no more strength left to wait for this to happen! There's no way to breathe!

On Descending from the Would-Be Mountain and Scaling it Again

When we enter the path of an artist, we think that we know enough and that we can do enough – we stand on the tall *mountain of naiveté* – "**N**." We can see everything from here; other heights seem nearby – there they are – just reach out and grab them! Who among us in his youth didn't stand on this mountain as he learned his first facts about natural science, instantly believing himself to be a sage and instantly declaring himself an atheist?

What soothsayer doesn't believe him or herself to be greater than any doctor?

And the greater that this mountain "N" is, the more ignorant is the person, and the more accessible and achievable he perceives all these other heights.

He wants to instantly jump to them, but, alas, stumbles and breaks his nose on the nearest underfoot rock.

And so, willingly or not, he is forced to descend into the valley in order to approach the hem of a genuine mountain and begin to scale its steep sides, seeking to reach its apex.

As he descends from the mountain "N," he begins to see more clearly his folly and becomes even more aware of his ignorance. He despairs . . .

He curses the minute that he got the idea to descend. He recalls how happy and powerful he was at the top of "N," and how much he "could" do . . .

He's tired now, his feet are tired, and he needs help. Sometimes it comes, sometimes not. You have to *know how to accept it.*

Such is the descent. It's easier to walk along the flatlands, but there are many temptations down here, and things might end with him getting stuck here.

God send him strength for the ascent!

Glossary of Terms
and Exercises

Compiled, translated, and annotated by
Andrei Malaev-Babel

Abilities   pp. 30, 37, 69–70, 132, 133, 435.

Accumulation (of Character, Material and Energy)   See *Incomplete-Combustion Products, Emotionally Tactile Reading of a Text, Theatrical Triangle, Submerging [Text, Circumstances, or Tasks] Into the Subconscious* and *Selfish Rehearsing*.

Acknowledgement of and Giving In to Images, Sensations, or Inner State   See *"What" and "How."*

Absence of the Head   See *Fool, Casting Away the Head*.

Admitting to (Myself)/Non-Admitting   pp. 540–2, 547, 557, 686, 701; "Exercise 1. Sit down, find deep calm – recall a cat or a dog, as they rest in the sun. Do everything without any criticism, fool-like, on the condition of complete passivity. Who is sitting: me or not me? Close your eyes. Find the state of 'I am.' I am receiving some kind of a sound or noise – let it reach you. Look at some part of your clothes – it reached you."

"Now deliberately pick an object – let it reach you. Then another. The simpler the object, the sooner you reach the goal."

"Pick some point above you. Touch it with your finger, at a distance (radiation). Pick another point – 'touch' it with another hand. All this – with absolute calm. Take a partner as your object. Look at the partner, perceive him, reach out to him with your hand."

"Now get up and, without losing what you acquired, take his hand in yours, then come back to your original place."

"Ask something."

"Sort out your sensation. You must have experienced some kind of intercommunion – when you began *admitting* some rays streaming at you from without. You must have experienced some impact from an object, or a living being – his eyes, something behind the eyes. Thus, you arrived at the *perception* of radiation, and you sensed your own ability to radiate. Radiation cannot be tangibly mastered, unless we exercise it with calm and simplicity, and with absolute freedom."

"Exercise 2. Admit an object to you, without giving it a single thought, while preserving the singularity of perception. As soon as the chosen point reached you – get up, walk toward it, and touch it with your finger. 'I and the point.' Then look at a partner – but don't zoom in on his face. Touch your partner, admit yourself to a sensation. Then look at his face, then carefully move to the eye, to the pupil. Then move to something behind the eye. Shake each other's hands, while proceeding from your experience with the eye."

"This experience allows one to physically sense a human being, when your partner becomes someone strongly connected with you." (Fund 59. Lectures and classes delivered at the MAT School in 1924–1925. Recorded by Varvara Sokolova (Zalesskaya). [Further referenced as "Lectures 1924–1925."] Notebook 2. pp. 68–71.) See also *Inhalation (Inspiration) of Objects*.

Affect   pp. 106, 123, 128, 405, 516–17, 608, 658, 671, 702; "Affect is a very complicated state that also involves thought and will. According to Spinoza [1891: 185–186], it consists of pleasant or painful feelings, of desire, and of thought that it causes."

"Let's take an example. On your way here, you met a childhood friend, very dear to you. You haven't seen him in a long while. How do you remember him?"

"You can recall him visually: his height, how he was dressed, how thin he was; you could recall your auditive or tactile impression. You feel pleased, you want to say something . . . A perception that expresses itself via psychological sensation, and immediately transforms into a desire – such is affect. All three elements are at play."

"We create, while drawing from some inner depositories, from our reserves. For example, we want to explain our thoughts. So, we take up some familiar words, in order to express our sensations, or impressions. To express a mathematical thought – a person needs to have a reserve of knowledge. An actor must have a reserve of specific state and sensations – since one creates out of his depositories. Our treasures are our education and culture. These treasures must be accumulated together with an affective component. *I saw something, I read about something – all of it was connected with a certain [emotional] state that got deposited somewhere.* These treasures, as they are served to the actor when he needs them the most – result in the emergence of image. At some point in our life, we took this image in, as we looked at it affectively. The richer a man, as far as life affects are concerned – the more treasures he possesses, and the easier it is for him to create" (Lectures 1924–1925. Notebook 4. pp. 8, 9, 11–13).

"Exercise. Completely clear your mind. I will say some word, and it immediately triggers an image of sorts. Recreate it. 'Peasant woman.' Make sure to catch the creative image – the one that comes unexpectedly, right away and somewhat vividly. 'A crow.' This does not necessarily mean that you will see a bird, but whatever you happen to see associatively, for example: 'A flock of crows cawing, as I take a walk.'"

"You must catch the first impression – be it from a word, from a role, or from a play. Catching *the first* is a precious ability of an artist. Uncreative connections between an association and a word also exist. It is abstract associations, when you don't create anything. A prerequisite is a state that belongs to the realm of creativity. 'Ocean.' 'Pushkin.' If you are in the state of a white sheet of paper, but do not wait for the word – then you will inevitably receive a mundane association, or else you will miss the moment. If, on the contrary, you are waiting, and ready – this begets a creative factor. A skill of waiting is a paramount thing."

"Exercise. Wait. 'Boris Godunov'" (Lectures 1924–1925. Notebook 4. pp. 19–20). For additional exercises in Affects, see *Mimicry*.

Affective Inertia   pp. 538.

Artistic Synthesis   See *Synthesis*.

Asana   pp. 523, 541, 688, 695–6, 708, 771*g*; "Asana is achieved when one can tangibly sense the singularity of one's body position" (Fund 59; Unnumbered Folder titled *Various Notes*; Further referenced as "*Various Notes* folder").

Asana is a body position in yoga recommended for achieving concentration and calm. Demidov does not use this term literally. Instead, he is referring to any *creatively justified* position of an actor's body onstage that is endowed with *singularity*. Demidov offers *asana* exercises fulfilled by justifying an arbitrarily taken body position, or activity (Lectures 1924–1925. Notebook 3. p. 80, reverse side). On this technique, see also **Creative Justification**.

Once an actor's entire being is at one with sitting, standing, leaning, or lying (whatever position actors might find themselves in), then their eyes acquire the kind of *transparency* and *serenity*, associated with creative *passivity* and *perception*. See also **Eyes (of Asana)** and **I am**.

"Exercises. Assume one position, or the other – and speak monologues, verse, or single phrases."

"Don't seek elaborate body positions – our regular positions are in great need of truth and singularity. We must master them. Otherwise – we will keep acting with several objects, tasks, etc. To put it simply – multiplicity."

"Besides speaking, you can do simpler things: look around, see something – in short, *come to life* in this body position. Live in it. Green-light this movement or that, while preserving asana, or asanness (when drastically changing positions)" (*Various Notes* Folder).

"Here is a mistake characteristic of overly zealous students. They assume some kind of an asana, and – while living and speaking in it – they try to preserve it, thus disallowing the slightest movement. Meanwhile, their living state already requires a change of body position. They continue to fight this, thus ruining everything."

"If I lie, then there is no need to fear my head involuntarily turning, or my arm lifting up, or my fingers moving. Otherwise, an actor will go as far as forbidding himself to shift his gaze, to blink an eye, or to breathe! Having assumed an asana, you enter the state of truth, and you find yourself on its rails. Now go full steam ahead – roll! And don't push yourself off these rails."

"If the body position changes on its own (reflexively and involuntarily) – then let it change. As long as you remain in the state of asana of the new movement or body position. As long as you don't lose the 'asanness'" (*Various Notes* Folder).

In addition to the asana of "body position," Demidov worked with "asana of the environment" (tangible perception of the space and surrounding object), of the time (living in the moment, rather than in the past of future), and of a mask (character). Executing an asana over one's character – rather than "playing character" – such was Demidov's device. He also connected the method of asana with the "**Let It Be**" method, and with the singularity of a Center (see **Center**).

Assignment   pp. 231, 321–2, 378, 408, 419, 678.

Attention   pp. 540, 549–50, 477–9, 644–6, 698; "Attention (and its technique)."

"To hear – is already to react."

"The same is true of the attention. To perceive attentively – is to already react to the perceived, to the noted."

"Attention as remembering (according to Stanislavsky). This is what, very likely, is completely unnecessary. What is necessary is attention-reaction, i.e. green-lighting actions and reactions in general" (Fund 59. Folder 7). See also **Emotional Attention**.

Beginning (Technique of the)   pp. 191–8, 283–5, 394, 531–2, 571.

Blocking the Text pp. 535–6; "To block the text means to place the imaginary in different spaces" (*Various Notes* folder). Also see **Full Stop**, **Tearing Yourself Away**, and **Cutting Yourself Off**.

Blowing, Breathing, Whispering, and Whistling At A Candle pp. 429, 551, 687; Demidov considered these exercises as exercises is *faith*. See **Lump of Faith**. Having formed "a lump of faith" by the simple tasks of breathing, whistling and blowing on a candle, Demidov would ask an actor to move to exercising with sounds, and then – words. "A word, charged with true faith can do miracles. If it does not – there is simply not enough faith" (*Various Notes* folder).

Blurting Out Lines (Method of) pp. 533, 545.

Brakes pp. 58, 91, 108, 115–6, 231–2, 238, 251, 374, 380, 498; See also **Lack of Brakes**.

Braking System See **Brakes**.

Breathing See **Psychological Breathing**, **Diaphragmatic Breathing**, and **Tube**.

Breathing in Character Qualities pp. 7; "I think that I am myself, and no one else. However, I carry inside plentitude of inborn characteristics. If I can, even for a second, pick up some feeling, or a characteristic, and then fathom and imagine it – this means that it is present in me, and that it can be developed further. On this basis, one can allow inside some quality needed for the role, and live with this characteristic, while remaining yourself, and only yourself. Yet, give your *I* to it completely."

"It is good to take in these characteristics and qualities with the breath. Creatively justify the inhaled quality. This will result in a process *similar* to transformation (as opposed to real transformation in the form of mystical creativity)."

"Most likely, each quality has its own separate whereabouts ('center')" (*Various Notes* folder). See also **Center** and **"What" and "How."**

Balls/Exercises with Balls pp. 6; See also **Letting Go**, **Full Stop**, **Admitting To**, **Tearing Yourself Away**, **Cutting Yourself Off**, **Calm**, and **Composure**.

In addition to utilizing balls for exercising methods, such as "Full Stop," Demidov also suggested the following ball exercises:

- "Throwing: in front of myself, behind, up, down, to the sides, at myself."
- "Putting down: carefully, swiftly."
- "Letting out of my hand: upward, downward, rolling them "downhill.""
- "Pressing to yourself, pressing to the partner."
- "Taking it from somewhere."
- "Taking it away from the partner."
- "Gathering an armful." (*Various Notes* folder)

Being pp. 319, 355, 367, 378–9, 381–3, 507, 522, 539, 672. See also **Dual State of Being** and **Doubling**

Body Position See **Asana**.

By Contradiction See **Evoking Emtions "By Contradiction."**

Calm See **Culture of Calm**.

Casting Away the Body/Casting Yourself Aside See Book Five, Chapter 10, sub-chapter "Giving in to Sensations," p. 683. See also **Unbodiliness** and **Great Sleep of the Body**.

Casting Away the Head See Book Five, Chapter 10, sub-chapter "Muscles: Toward the Culture of Calm," p. 688; See also **Fool, Idiot, Headless**.

Center pp. 76, 676, 677, 687, 768g; "A piece of paper pierced with a pin rotates easily, if properly centered. The same is true of a person – everything must coincide: will, feeling, etc. As soon as I've got multiple centers, the harmony is lost. I've got one center in the head, another in the chest, yet another in my necktie – and nothing inside. Correct centeredness is the chief thing, when it comes to a person's beauty; center is the point into which everything comes, and from where it all departs."

"I got the idea of center by observing Moissi. One center at a time – and nothing else. He places different things into his center – for example, purity, and thus lives by it alone" (Lectures 1924–1925. Notebook 4. p. 4).

"Moissi . . . lives with one spot; one single point inside him keeps striving, and everything else serves it. This results in calm, in the marvelous singularity of the subject, in one single 'I am,' and tremendous composure" (Lectures 1924–1925. Notebook 2. p. 78).

"Center in the solar plexus – is the secret behind voice, gesture, communication, irresistible charm, and stage presence."

"Inhale (down your spine), then exhale, and accept this sensation as your center. A true artist always lives with this center; with it, he observes the play of a different center."

"Don't attempt to understand – this tends to cool one off, when it comes to the creative realm."

"The most important, and the first link in the chain is the 'I'; if the 'I' is sound – everything else will be too."

"Center conditions the object."

"[Exercise 1.] Having grasped the center, let's try admitting everything to the center. Look at each other – permeate each other with your center. Now speak: 'Once more before you enchanted I stand, and drink in your unclouded gaze.' [Opening line of Vasily Krasov's *Stanzas*.] . . . Keep grasping this sensation, and you will discover a lot – your essence. You will then be able to live with this sensation in a monologue, or a dialogue. True Singularity springs from it – [all impulses stream] from the center into one single point" (Lectures 1924–1925. Notebook 4. p. 5–6).

"A certain part of the body might catch your eye – neck, hand or leg – this means that it lives, and that a person's center is located in it. Out of this principle, one can create a role. One must achieve complete release, when everything streams from the center. The secret behind this release lies in finding the center and using it as a compass. Some roles can be done by shifting center – neck, shoulder, etc." (Lectures 1924–1925. Notebook 3. p. 78).

"So far as I am I – I have my essence, and my center. Therefore, all of my desires must convey from the center – to the periphery. This will ensure that my movements are sound, full of *plasticity* and beauty."

"I sit and slightly observe myself. I chose a point before me, and admit it to my soul. I 'touch' it with my hand [at a distance], and observe my experience. Those who have developed a skill of sound observation, will clearly sense the following. Somewhere inside the center, a desire originates. Something from the center streams – first into the head, then, via thought – into the body, then – into the hand. Finally, I sense a tangible need to touch the object. One can skip all these phases, and simply touch – this will result in a gesture, rather than a movement. The will power passes from the brain to the finger – quick as a lightening; that's why it's hard to notice."

"(In film, the transitional stages are missing.)"

"This is best experienced in slow tempo. The secret lies in singularity. As long as there is only one desire – everything will go well. If, however, you need to simultaneously move your foot, look, and touch – then everything will get mixed up, and nothing will be clear. There must be only *one* center – not 20; *one* action – not 20. Singularity is the secret behind artistry, talent, plasticity – ninety percent of actors lack it."

"Exercise [2]. Chose one point in front of you, get up in a slow rhythm. Keep checking – where is this movement originating? What spot in your body pulls you to stand up?"

"Now call your partner. Catch all the transitional stages – when you catch them, you will discover the correctly placed action; you will acquire singularity, clarity, precision and a task. Often actors lack expressivity onstage – only because they've got twenty tasks at a time, twenty desires, twenty radiations."

"You are all familiar with Stanislavsky's saying 'a movement got stuck in the elbow'; a movement always originates in a center, and it ends in the extremities."

"A cat's movements are full of plasticity, because they are singular; when children play, their games are full of actions – these actions are all singular; the absentmindedness of a great man is explained by an uninterrupted concentration on one single thing. You must develop your skill to instantly move from one thing to the other, to grasp everything *to the end*, and to cut as if with a diamond cutter" (Lectures 1924–1925. Notebook 2. pp. 74–77).

"Exercise [3]. Walk."

"Stand straight. Toss your hands out the window, as if they were gone – walk any way you want, but without the hands. The hands are gone, and the shoulders are also gone – the head and the torso are walking all by themselves. Your legs are also gone – keep walking. Pick yourself up, as if by the waistband, pull the center forward – no arms, no legs – just a single dot is walking. This dot is as light as a feather, and it flies. Don't try to make small steps – let the feather fly. Now let the feather walk, while the head and the feet lag behind."

"Sit down, release all tension – the feather lifts up, and then flies ahead. The feet must be 'scattered,' the walk – uninterrupted, the torso does not sway, the buttocks – correctly placed."

"You must move with the center, rather than with the legs. Now shift your center – walk with your nose alone – everything else has been forgotten. The nose 'goes back to its seat.' Now the lower jaw alone is alive. Then the shoulders are walking, and then the feet alone. The secret lies in being able to take one part of the body, and to toss away the rest – complete singularity. One must have a key to all kinds of walks, and this key lies, of course, in the centers. In a classical posture, the center coincides with the center of gravity; contemporary postures lack this coincidence. Try once more to sense the center any way you wish – as a feather, or as a vessel. The legs are gone, the arms are gone, the head and the chest are also gone – only the center exists. I sense with the center, and all things reach the center. Everything else is soft – as it is gone; it is made of air. When you grasp this secret – you will learn to place your toes, etc. The placement of the feet is as elaborate as playing a violin. (Some violinists play with their shoulders – instead of the inner center. The same is true of actors.) The center is of foremost importance – we must grasp and develop it, by removing everything that gets in the way. Without the center – there is no harmonious walk" (Lectures 1924–1925. Notebook 4. pp. 2–4).

Cleansing See Book Five, Chapter 10, sub-chapter "Training to Give in to Sensation," p. 682–3.

Concentration pp. 477–9, 497, 686, 748.

Concreteness (Physical and Physiological) pp. 185–7, 314–5, 335–6, 343, 346–55, 521, 543, 573, 686; "Concreteness of the imagination, and of the given circumstances alone can evoke true emotions (according to Payot) [Jules Payot (1859–1939), French educationist]. Instead of being generically afraid, I am fear this very concrete thing. Not a generic 'mother,' my mother, this very specific person."

"'I will buy myself a velvet coat.' What kind? I will tell you what kind – the kind I always been dreaming of (describe) – not some generic velvet coat."

"Concreteness draws near (the nearest flow). The opposite is also true: exercises in the nearest flow of thought make everything concrete."

"Here we can compare two opposite ways, and the difference between Stanislavsky's approach and mine. My approach is 'What is that, knowing which, we shall know everything?'" [Chandogya Upanishad 6: 1: 4–6] (*Various Notes* folder).

Creative[-Aesthetic] Justification   pp. 415, 529, 557, 677, 683, 688, 751, 757–8*g*, 763*g*, 766–7*g*, 778–80*g*; Creative Justification, according to Demidov, is the kind of justification achieved by *giving in* to a sensation "behind" the given body position, movement, stage direction, blocking, line from the text, facial expression, makeup, element of costume, prop, and even character.

"Lift up your arm – it feels uncomfortable, the arm is now getting in the way; start 'listening' to it, and green-light yourself toward what the inner experience behind this position of the arm might be. Suddenly, the arm stops getting in the way; moreover, it helps your life to merge into oneness [*singularity*]. As soon as you find a tense muscle – immediately **guess** its preoccupation, and delve into it; the rest of the muscles will then release at once" (Lectures 1924–1925. Notebook 2. pp. 77–78).

"Creative justification of a body position is the guessing of the 'working tension.' When I guess what I am doing, and give in to it singularly – then I give in to the one and only, working tension and annihilate all the extraneous effort. It is blown off by the wind of truth" (Lectures 1924–1925. Notebook 3. p. 79, reverse side).

"Make an arbitrary movement with your arm. 1) Stop it, 2) Listen to it 3) Guess something inside the arm 4) Give in to the feeling and sensation evoked by the arm."

"The moment you make the right guess – you begin to feel truth in the arm. You feel the arm with your entire body. A spasm of truth, so to speak, runs up and down the body. This process is accompanied by pleasure and satisfaction. Such is creative justification."

"At times, I don't know what exactly a given position of the arm might mean, yet all the same – inwardly it feels justified somehow" (*Various Notes* folder).

"When you feel that you've justified the movement – either continue it, or start again with a new movement. When you fail – just start a new movement, but always *without preparation*."

"Start moving, walk – first without giving it a single thought, and then begin to listen to your walk – guess what it is saying to you . . . Make a sound, and listen – a connection is created between you and the sound. When a major director prompts you some "brush stroke" – take it, listen to it closely, and justify it."

"Exercises in justifying a word. 'Oh, my child, if you only knew how miserable I am!' [Chekhov 1916: 71] Speak it, and naively listen to yourself. First say these lines carelessly. The author gives you the lines, speak them and listen – your inner creator will make them truthful for you. If you happen to hear the thought first, then listen to it."

"Start with the text, guess it and keep going – as if speaking these words first as your own prompter – and then actually delivering them."

"Take Chekhov's character descriptions. 'I clearly wrote it – he is wearing a gorgeous tie.' Sense this tie – just as you sense the arm." [Demidov is referring to Chekhov's explanation, to Stanislavsky, on the character of Uncle Vanya: "I clearly wrote it: he is wearing gorgeous ties. Gorgeous!" (Chekhov 1978: 396)].

"Exercise. Lift up your shoulders and lower your chin. Do it at first mechanically, then fully give in to it. Don't settle for a cliché – it will lead to stereotypical acting. Before you develop a habit, move gradually, beat the path – step by step."

"Exercise. Sit straight, thrust your chest forward, lift up your head high, and listen to this posture. Keep checking with yourself – are my eyes transparent, is everything reaching me, can I speak? Perhaps, you perceive a character of a military man. Character description: saggy lower lip" (Lectures 1924–1925. Notebook 3. pp. 35–38).

"I do something. I listen to it. I guess what I am doing – justify it – and give in to it. Such is the path of creative justification."

"Yermolova could not explain anything . . . about the role of Mary Stuart. She said – I can only play it for you – and she did. She felt the truth of the character. To justify a character means to transform" (*Various Notes* folder).

See also Book Five, Chapter 10, pp. 688–9, 691–3, 695–6.

Creative Truth   See **Truth**.

Culture of "Green-Lighting" The First Urge   See **Green–Lighting The First Urge**.

Culture of Calm (and Clarity of Spirit)   pp. 688–97. "Culture of Calm – the kind of calm when the body becomes a mere gas, not even a gas – a shadow, not even a shadow – when *nothing at all* remains! 'The shadow of my soul, overcasting the sun of my spirit' [Source unknown]. When true calm is achieved, the arms weigh down [on] the shoulders. And the shoulders weigh down [on] the neck" (*Various Notes* folder). Demidov lists the following exercises and qualities, connected with the *Culture of Calm and Clarity of Spirit*:

"Liberation from the muscles."
"Liberation of the breath, and sighing."
"Liberation of the eye."
"Body position."
"Retelling something you saw (a description), and then transiting to the author's text."
[See **How to Change the 'Foreign' Words of the Author – Into Your Own Live Sensations**]
"Emotional tactile perception of the author's lines."
"Equilibrium."
"Liberation of the face (taking it off, like a mask after a masquerade, the calming down of the face, and its justification)."
"Talent."
"Passivity."
"Admitting."
"Perception of the body as a shadow of the soul."
"Liberation of the imagination."
"Applying restraint to the culture of calm."
"Simplicity of exercising 'without effort' (psychological 'dumbbells')."
"Concentration (according to the principle of 'the edge of a razor' that permeates on its own)."
"Indirect, or second-order exercises."

Culture of Emptiness   See **Emptiness**.

Culture of Intuition   p. 540; See also **Intuition**.

Culture of Passivity   See **Passivity**.

Culture of Sensitivity   See **Sensitivity**.

Culture of Surrender   See *Giving In*.

Cutting Yourself Off   pp. 535–6.

Desire   See *Wants*.

Diaphragmatic Breathing   pp. 683, 708–9, 789g. See also *Tube*.

Diffusive Transmitting of Character   pp. 381–2; See also *Weak Currents, Surrendering to Character*.

Disruption in Rhythm   p. 534, 539; The technique Demidov observed in Alexander Moissi's acting. "Moissi does the disruption in rhythm – this means that I instantly pick up a certain rhythm; I listen to it and I live by it. You must know how to disrupt rhythm, and organically justify it." (Lectures 1924–1925, Notebook 2, p. 79).

Doubling/Doubled Consciousness   pp. 286–90; 296, 367, 402, 413, 436, 515, 525, 526, 620–34, 617, 639–40, 645–6, 669n1, 672, 675–6.

Dropping [of the Text, Circumstances or Tasks] Into the Subconscious   See *Submerging [Text, Circumstances or Tasks] Into the Subconscious*.

Dual State of Being pp. 289–90, 379, 623–4, 672. See also *Being* and *Doubling*

Duality   See *Doubling*.

Ease and Joy   See *Free Creativity*.

Edge   pp. 686, 762g, 782g; See also *"What" Method, Singularity, Attention, Concreteness*.

Embryo   pp. 322–3, 378, 382, 470, 486–91, 507–8, 525.

Emotional Attention   pp. 523, 550, 716, 764g, 781g.

Emotionally Synthesizing Thinking   pp. 426, 598–9, 603–611, 737.

Emotional Projection   pp. 593–5.

Emotionally Tactile (Imaginative) Reading of a Text   pp. 405, 542; "During such reading, one must not give the text one's full attention, but rather merely 'keep one eye on it.' If you experience it fully, together with the characters, or feel with them – then you will let it all out, and the subconscious will have nothing to do."

"This device is not *only dedicated to tossing* the material into the subconscious; it also takes care of preserving it throughout the reading."

"Your job is to save it up for later!"

"This is yet another reason why you should never begin by speaking the text of the role aloud, or while moving – everything must be first tried out silently, and inwardly. (This will definitely result in a willpower-charge.) The next step. Very carefully, whisper the lines. When transitioning to full voice, you should *never green-light* yourself, but rather *save* the charge. I can feel something ripening in me, and I can feel it living and growing inside."

"When voicing the lines, I restrict myself to speaking bare thoughts."

"Let's now go back to the beginning. When reading the text silently, I must merely 'peep' at it – as if my job is to peep, and eavesdrop on something. And I must do it so that those around me won't notice that I am peeping, and perhaps already oversaw and overheard some things. 'Those around me' - is my conscious mind."

"You must read the text word-by-word, un-expressively, pausing after each word. Speak the text in a neutral tone and fashion, and wait to receive its essence, its true content – as it sinks, reaching down to your subconscious. When you speak a word, some thoughts will inevitably jump out, triggered by the word. This can be compared to electric lights flickering here and there, as the lighting board operator touches a button. Pretend that you don't see them; don't respond to them, and don't let them inside - they flicker, and so let them flicker!"

"All in all, you must peep and eavesdrop without your own knowledge. As the saying goes, 'It's not me, and over there what you see is not my mare'" [Popular Russian proverb, symbolizing denial of guilt].

"Just as there exists 'emotional analysis,' in the same way this device is practically the 'emotionally tactile perception of the role's text.' This is because the words are lowered directly into the realm of feelings – instead of being ushered in through the head, via narrow intellectual mind and reasoning. There they remain – until they blossom, and bare desired fruit. Altogether, this can be called – emotionally tactile perception of everything in the role, accomplished by a special way of reading the text."

"To begin with, you speak the words – as described above. Then, your fantasy beings to work – triggered by the words permeating your soul. You begin to imagine something, and somehow react to what you imagine."

"Thus, life begins to emerge on its own. And now, let's switch to the opposite path. You must grasp this newly born life, give in to it, and proceed by speaking the lines any way you feel. In other words, you are carefully feeling about for the embodiment."

"Here is another possible way – perhaps, it is even more fruitful. Read a section of the text once according to the first method (submerging the words), and then immediately repeat it according to the second method. One way, followed by the other."

"When submerging the words, it might so happen that you will feel something utterly unpredictable – seemingly inappropriate for this role. Do not discard this – after all, this is your intuition speaking. In the end, this may turn out to be the most important and pivotal thing – something our brain cannot work out on its own. So, don't discard it; on the contrary, grasp this feeling at once, and try moving out of it, speaking some words. In general, catch it and strengthen it."

"When you say a word for the third or the fourth time, it ceases to trigger psychological life. This is almost a rule. At times, an actor can't submerge the words inside from the very start. He says that the words leave him cold. In such cases, it helps to remind the actor of the basic given circumstances of the scene. (Prompting them coldly, and in basic terms.) Let's take, for example, Marmeladov's monologue [from *Crime and Punishment*] – an inn, a bar, tables, waiters, I am dressed in rags, etc. In doing so, don't charge yourself, but merely refresh [the basic circumstances], coldly and calmly; avoid stirring your emotions."

"Is this device, in the end – a mere cunning destruction of a thought from the self? Is it not a way to substitute the usual *harmful* self-observation for the basic, yet *helpful* watching of self?"

"When you begin to speak the text of a role in this way, and listen for what it evokes inside, and 'peep' – this calms and balances you in an unusually powerful way. This state of peaceful balance lets the words reach down to the soul, and it allows you to follow what happens there. Thus, this device perfectly develops artistic calm and creative attention; while they enable one to 'see the unseen' . . . In a word, this device must be attributed to the 'culture of calm.'"

"This method is also precious in that you discover calm without seeking it. You find it in action, i.e. by distracting your attention from the very task of seeking calm. Just like a bicyclist, who finds balance on the move – the very balance he could hardly find when he stood still." (*Various Notes* folder.) See also ***Admitting, Submerging [Text, Circumstances or Tasks] Into the Subconscious*** and ***Interval Between Two Thoughts***.

Emotionally Tangible Reading of a Text   See ***Emotionally Tactile Reading of a Text***.

Emptiness   pp. 324, 357, 497, 533, 538–9, 572.

Equilibrium   p. 404, 642–3, 762*g*; "The support of the beam-balance scale is at rest, regardless of how much weight rests on the scale-pans."

"By moving the point of support we can strike a balance – regardless of how uneven the scale-pans' load might be."

"Scale-pans can be located below the support, or above it."

"I am the center, and the foothold; my muscles are the scale-pans."

"Only the support is at work – the weigh beam and the scale-pans are merely hanging, they are idle" (Fund 59. Folder 12).

Etudes   See Index.

Evoking Emotions "by Contradiction"   See Book Four, Chapter 4, sub-chapter "On the Past, Present and Future," p. 460.

Eyes (of Asana)   See pp. 541, 547, 733*f*, 781*g*, 771*g*; "Transparent," "serene" eye is one of the outcomes of the Demidov *asana* exercises aimed at achieving *singularity, openness* and *passivity*.

"Our eye seldom belongs to us. We are not its masters. It does not see well. It is not transparent, it is – foreign."

"Look back at your eye – what do you notice? It does not allow inside everything around, but only the rough outlines of what takes place around you. Release your eye. Let it do what it ought to do – letting things in."

"Occupy yourself with making your eye transparent."

"'The eye is the lamp of the body' [Matthew 6:22]. And it shines the light both inside (into the body) and outside (into life)."

"An eye can be tintless – then everything inside will be clear (Moissi). 'If your eye is full of light, your soul shall be full of light.'" [Demidov seems to be paraphrasing Matthew 6:22. King James' version offers the following translation: "if therefore thine eye be single, thy whole body shall be full of light." Since theologians agree that the bodily eye, in Matthew's version of the gospel, should be taken as the symbol of the outlooking power of the soul, Demidov's interpretation appears to be accurate.]

"An eye can be rosy (when the character is seeing everything through rose-colored spectacles)."

"It can be blue, yellow, and any color you like."

"But it must be transparent without fail."

"Although one has to look at the sun through dark glasses."

"Stanislavsky says that rhythm must be executed not by the hands, or the feet, but by the eyes."

"By the means of the eye, you can master your body – 'The eye is the lamp of the body.' If your eye is cloudy – cleanse it; restless - calm it down; closed (pin hole pupil) – expand it."

"Arrive at the state where the eye is as good as gone, so that an object hits your soul directly, without getting stuck in the eye. Make it disappear, make it intangible – just as a violin should become imperceptible with a good violinist, and voice – with a good singer. If I can hear the voice, then the singing must be bad. A dress - with a good seamstress." . . .

"[Exercise.] Choose an object. Look at it, while releasing all kinds of tension, calming down and cleansing the eye. Catch the truth. The feeling of truth. The more you cleanse and calm your eye, the greater and deeper truth you will catch. The absolute transparency leads to the perception of essence – of Plato's Ideas, and of the object in itself. Cubism." [Plato insisted that every object possesses a non-material abstract (but substantial) Form, or Idea. These ideas, and not the material world as we perceive it through our senses, represent the highest and most fundamental kind of reality.]

"Having mastered this with real objects, you now can easily perceive imaginary objects and circumstances – which is of most importance to us. Or else, you can close your eyes – the sensation of sound eye will persist. This is what happens when we truly see things that we speak of. [A sound] eye aids the discovery of the state of 'I am'".

"Possible mistakes: when looking at an object, associative ideas begin to trigger your thought. This is comparable to a peripheral phenomenon of reflex arc. You must perceive the object itself – and nothing else. You must *sense* it" (*Various Notes* folder). [Reflex arcs help an organism to avoid injury by providing a means for immediate withdrawal from dangerous stimuli. When your finger touches a hot stove, the reflex arc can process the rapid, protective response directly in the spinal cord, bypassing the brain. A response is evoked before the pain is perceived at a conscious level. Demidov suggests that similar reflex arc process is activated when a human being is facing the danger of engaging too deeply. In this instance, an actor is being protected by engaging deeply with an object. A similar phenomenon of instant withdrawal can occur on the brink of a deeper engagement with a partner, a situation (or given circumstances), etc. Such withdrawal is triggered in an actor at the slightest "danger" of becoming psychologically involved. A common symptom of such withdrawals is an actor's smile bursting out in the most inappropriate moments – in the midst of a dramatic situation or encounter, or else, an extremely "comedic" situation that requires maintaining seriousness. In both cases, the "reflex arc" mechanism begins to protect the actor from a deep engagement, just as it does in life.]

Faith pp. 179–80, 232, 291–4, 625–6, 758g; Faith, according to Demidov, is "not the same as naiveté. It is a force. It moves mountains" (*Various Notes* folder).

"Faith is a force, it is already an action, and a manifestation. If we say, 'This is a book, it lies on the table' – everyone believes. 'Today I am going to do this and this' – once again, you feel confident. But as soon as you say: 'This is a table – I will jump over it' – a different state emerges; whenever we face a greater degree of impossible, the situation heightens."

"In these examples, we are dealing with two different phenomena: in one case, everything is evident, and in others – something happens inside of a man, some sort of activity that transforms this table into, let us say, Generalissimo Suvorov's coffin, or into a boat, etc. Therefore, faith is a condition of creativity; it possesses an element of creative attention, and of creativeness."

"Let's try doing this exercise, while observing ourselves. 'I am wearing a scratchy shirt; it irritates my skin.' (In the case you are actually wearing this kind of a shirt, [imagine wearing a silk one]). What do you notice in regards to naiveté and faith? You notice that you 'admitted' the shirt to yourself – this is still a state of naiveté. However, your actions to free yourself from the shirt – this is faith. As soon as you stop acting – toss another portion of naiveté into your creative furnace. It will awaken a state of activity; faith and naiveté keep interchanging. You proceed from an aim – to action; at times, creative justification awakens your faith, and you achieve truth."

"We live in a state of a permanent creative point of view on things – since we continuously believe in something. We create non-stop, we constantly create life, and are responsible for every moment, as every thought is real and carries a definite influence. The force that creates is faith, and faith is *knowing*. 'Faith is confidence in what we hope for and assurance about what we do not see.' [Hebrews 11:1]"

"An acrobat *knows* that he will jump over a bar, he actually *knows* it, rather than thinks he might. Faith is a force that knows what to do, and how. To believe and to think that you believe – is a huge difference. To wait – already means to have an active point of view."

"Each exercise is preceded by a moment of concentration, an ability to choose what you believe."

"[Exercise.] Make an arbitrary movement, justify it and say: 'I feel sad, when you are not around.' Do I really *know* that I felt sad?"

"Choose a sentence, or a verse."

"Now get up, make some kind of a movement, and justify it – having marked which spot in you was in charge. Without losing this lump – speak by it. It is important to sense the inner life, to anticipate it – without naming it for yourself. Knowing everything in advance tends to cool things off. It is important to know the *very basic* essence."

"Learn how to recognize this essence, and how to attune yourself to it."

"No matter where you start – be it with the justification . . . or with the automatic movement – you must manage to catch the sense of the lump, which is faith, knowing and power. As soon as you discovered this center – you must master giving in to this force" (Lectures 1924–1925. Notebook 3. pp. 60–64). Also see **Lump of Faith**.

Facsimile/Facsimile Exercises   pp. 683; "We don't recognize a poet's handwriting, when we see their manuscript printed in facsimile. Their hand thinks, lives, and creates; it hastily tries to record images and feelings, as they sweep past. This hand could care less about eligibility and clarity – just as long as things are taken down. This is how an actor must transmit emotions and images, without much regard for clarity per se. If, to begin with, things get inarticulate, just remind yourself that this is not a problem. You are dealing with the hints of something creative and remarkable."

"As for clarity, articulateness and *pubicness*, in general, there are several ways of dealing with it: 1) train it separately, like a move in wrestling; work on it at home, and then forget all about it 2) as the rehearsal continues, you will become progressively calmer, and therefore won't risk missing the flow of images; so, even if you look back at the clarity and stage worthiness of your work, it won't stop the flow – just like in mastering riding a bicycle, you become freer to look around; or else 3) everything: your creating self, your creative process, and its implementation can be thrust into *publicness*. According to the triangle [of deisis]" (Fund 59. Lectures and classes at the Fourth Studio of MAT, 1921–1922, recorded by Yelena Morozova. Demidov's personal note. Notebook. Pages not numbered. Further referenced as Lectures 1921–1922).

"[Exercise.] When I write, I passively listen to every thought, and immediately take it down – sloppily. Exercises moving [and speaking] the same way, listening to your sensations, facsimile like" (*Various Notes* folder). For further elaboration on this exercise, see **Mimicry**.

Feeling of the Audience   See **Theatrical Triangle**.

Finishing Up Living/Not Finishing Up Living   pp. 227, 531, 533–4, 567, 572; "'Finishing up living' is what ultraviolet light is to the visible spectrum of life, to what we can hear and see. Infrared light – is the prelude."

"This may be a good comparison, but, truth be told, it is not quite accurate":

"Prelude is a cause of speech, movement (action in general), while "finishing up living" is the consequence of a truthful action."

"I think that separate cycles of exercises must be introduced:

1   In Prelude
2   In Finishing up living
3   In Restraint"

"To be brief, finishing up living is this: having collected all of his thoughts, and – pardon my expression – all of his guts, an actor says a line more or less truthfully, and . . . he just drops it all . . . It's as if the job has been done, and nothing else is needed. He does not "finish up living." In order to say the next line, once again, he must collect all of his thoughts, and all of his lost business . . . This is repeated again and again" (Fund 59. Notes toward the books *The Artist's Creative Process Onstage* and *Psycho-technique of the Affective Actor*. Folder number one: 'Part Four. Terminology. "Details" of the psycho-technique. An actor's psycho-technique'. Page titled 'Exercises in "Finishing up Living"').

First Impulse   pp. 182, 188, 290, 294, 297–8, 378, 394, 415, 508, 684–5, 713, 717–18.

First Impulse Exercises   pp. 294–6; Also see Demidov's first impulse exercises with partner, as described in Book Five, sub-chapter "Toward 'Giving in to Sensations,'" pp. 683–4.

Fool   pp. 545–6, 622, 683; See also **Casting Away the Head** and **Naiveté**.

Free Creativity   pp. 56, 549, 564.

Freedom   pp. 6–7, 14, 19, 34, 35, 144, 155–9, 167–72, 232–5, 253–4, 482–3, 419, 475, 525, 545, 618–19, 682.

Freedom of Voice   p. 687; See **Blowing, Whispering, Whistling at a Candle**.

Freedom of Gaze   p. 687; See also **Admitting To, Eyes (of Asana), Transparency, Serenity**, and **Passivity**.

Freedom of/through Movement   p. 687.

Freedom of the Center   pp. 676–7, 687; "An exercise for the freedom of the center. I stand freely, see freely, walk with my center, and do everything with the help of the center [in the solar plexus], and freely."

"I move my center elsewhere, and walk. One must develop freedom *per se*, rather than flexibility of the neck, etc. Moissi plays a pure human being; he plays pure freedom – everything in its pure form; abstracted art" (Lectures 1924–1925. Notebook 3, p. 88). See also **Center**.

Freedom of Radiation   p. 687; "Radiation cannot be tangibly mastered, unless we exercise it with calm and simplicity, and with absolute freedom" (Lectures 1924–1925. Notebook 2, p. 70).

Genius   pp. 79–82, 104–5, 637–8, 645–6, 689.

Giving in to Character   pp. 379–80; See **Being, Weak Currents, Diffusive Transmitting of Character**.

Giving in to One's Urges   pp. 536–7.

Giving in to [Physiological] Sensations   p. 682–4; "Giving in to sensations is, clearly, the *chief* secret of our technique. It's not for nothing that Oscar Wilde said: 'Having the courage to fully give in to sensations – such is the secret of an artist's life'" [The editors could not identify the source of Wilde's quote].

"To give in – would mean to 'inhale' and 'exhale,' to 'take,' 'truth,' 'singularity,' 'naiveté,' and even 'talent.' All these are elements, while the whole is – the surrender to sensations. This means:

1   To perceive an object
2   To take it
3   To let it evoke a sensation
4   To let this sensation flare up
5   To not extinguish this fire
6   To begin acting in this new state
7   To not lose the state of perceiving new sensations

Here, I am only describing intimate exercises in this direction."

"In general, however, this method and this thought – 'to fully give in' – can easily lead to pushing, haste and, therefore, falsehood."

"So, how should one exercise, especially in the absence of a trusted and honest observer?"

"[Exercise.] Let's try starting from the simplest things. One of the most harmful thoughts is that sensations are something *special* – this results in instant pushing."

"The first thing to establish is – ***nothing 'special'***! If, at the moment, I feel sluggish, tired, and even apathetic – so be it. After all, isn't it my actual current 'sensation'? Then, nothing else is needed. We've got a sensation, so let's learn how to handle it."

"And so, I am tired and sluggish – you've perceived it. God spare you from perceiving it in some special way – you will spoil everything. This is because it will cause you to alter your state, to mix it with something else. Once you've done so – the first, original thing will be gone. Therefore, you will have to give in to something else. This something else, however, is yet to establish itself. So, you will start rushing and give in to this feeling of confusion that came over you."

"Let's repeat. I am tired, or sluggish. (Let's take any of these states, for example – the first.) Perceive it, but don't lose the tiredness in the process. Without losing the tiredness – allow this tiredness to live in you for awhile and – without losing the tiredness – express yourself. For example, say any word – whichever you like. Make a movement with your hand, foot, head, eyes, facial muscles, or sigh out a sound – it's all the same. As long as you don't lose your tiredness."

"The part that preceded the expression had to do with accumulation, with charging."

"Expression is a discharge. It's easy to notice, however, that this discharge is incomplete. I hasten to enter the following reservation: when I say 'a charge' – please don't take it in such a way that you are supposed to feel yourself overflowing with energy, or fully charged. Nothing like it, and don't try to imagine yourself as such. All this means is that your tiredness (merely perceptible as it was) emerged from the typical chaos of sensations. And it has gathered, like a cloud, into one single sensation. This perception is now somewhat traceable – that is all we can say about this charge and – please, I implore you – don't worry about receiving anything stronger that this!"

"Now that you've expressed yourself like this, proceed by saying, almost inaudibly, 'I am tired,' or express yourself in some other way. Without losing this state, you will notice how you receive a new thought, a new imagination, or desire."

"Your task is now to take this new thing (without losing, or letting go of the old, or whatever remained of it). You should sense it, as before – as effortlessly as you did the first time, etc."

"You don't have to start with a sensation. Instead, you can begin with some images flashing by in your imagination. If they keep flashing by, are impossible to stop, or simply missing – this means that something is wrong with the asana. You must perform asana over the body position you are in, and your imagination will begin to work in a more harmonious fashion." (Fund 59. Folder 7.) Also see *"Take!," Acknowledgement of and Giving in to Images, Sensations, or Inner State, Giving in to Sounds*, and *"What" and "How."*

Giving in to Emotions   pp. 449, 475; See also **Passivity** and **Lightning–Like Zigzag Of Feeling**.

Giving in to Physiological Sounds (Pyatnitsky Exercises)   p. 683.

Giving in to Thought   p. 90.

Green-Lighting   pp. 279–97.

Green-Lighting the First Urge   pp. 539, 784*g*.

Great Sleep of the Body   pp. 687, 695–7, 744–8.

Habitual Character   pp. 371–3, 375, 378, 382.

Having Grasped Just One Line in a Drawing, Just One Chord and One Sound . . .   pp. 541, 654, 683.

Headless   See **Fool, Idiot, Casting Away the Head**.

Higher "Self"   p. 687; This term is associated with many belief systems, including Christianity and Hinduism. It has also been defined and used by modern teachers, such as Madame Blavatsky and Rudolph Steiner.

How to Change the "Foreign" Words of the Author – Into Your Own Live Sensations   pp. 535–6 This exercise was originally conducted by Demidov together with his brother Konstantin in Ivanovo-Voznesensk around 1910–1912. It is aimed at creating live images for a section of the author's text, and thus breathing life into it. A detailed description of this exercise, recorded by Demidov for Stanislavsky on August 19, 1921, is kept in Moscow, at the Stanislavsky Fund of the Moscow Art Theatre's Archive. (Fund 3, inventory 44, item No. 57.) In the exercise, Demidov is dealing with Mikhail Lermontov's narrative poem *Mtsyri* (see p. 536). The description of nature, offered by the poet, appeared to be foreign and dead in the initial attempt to recite the poem. Then Demidov began to describe to himself, in detail, the sites of nature similar to those mentioned in the poem. He did so *sotto voce*, at the same time ignoring the listener (real or imaginary), and not trying to "interest" the listener with what he was describing. In detail, Demidov would describe the "rich plains," the "hills," the "woods" of the poem, etc. – as if traveling through them, and retelling what he sees. When going back to the poem, Demidov noticed that he now spoke "because these images were alive, and flickered in his consciousness."

I/I am   pp. 219–20, 317, 322–3, 382, 385, 783*g*, 786*g*, 789*g* Stanislavsky borrowed the term *Ya esm'* from the Bible. It has been translated as "I am" by Elizabeth Hapgood, and as "I exist" by Jean Benedetti. The two translations complement each other, revealing the multifaceted meaning of the term. This term is transcribed as "I am character," which is more evident in Hapgood's translation used in this volume. At the same time, it has other meanings, as follows from these explanations by Demidov.

"When the calm state of 'I am' is missing, the actor is unable to grasp or comprehend a single thing, and he is acting not as a human being, but as some mentally incompetent person; he can't say 'this is I,' or sense himself and his own body, and he is deprived of the state of free choice – I give myself over to what I choose . . . A lack of physical freedom leads to apathy, autopilot, and an absence of creative state. The most direct solution is to reach the kind of basic state where an actor can say of himself: 'I am,' 'I exist'" (Lectures 1924–1925, Notebook 2. pp. 38–39).

Among those methods utilized for the achievement of the state of "I am" Demidov suggests 1) calming down, 2) the whip (see pp. 570, 573n1), 3) the eye of *asana*, 5) *asana* (body position), 4) warming up, 5) singularity.

"I sit, but not really; I stand, but not really . . . The same can be said of the 'I'. It's I, but not really I. We must execute an asana over the 'I'. We must live on the roughly physical level – the one we usually ignore. With the asana of a body position, you must organically throw, situate, settle and establish yourself in your actual physical state – then and only then will you come to life. The same is true of your 'I.'"

"To be 'I' on stage (to be yourself) is one thing, while to give yourself, your 'I' – is something different."

"Just 'I' won't suffice; one must be – a creative 'I.' (Although, is it really possible not to be a creative 'I,' as soon as your eye starts perceiving the given circumstances?) (*Various Notes* folder).

"There is a method of listening to a sound, while being merely attentive; the same method exists for the sense of touch, and for any senses. Except that one should perceive [objects] fully, so that the sensation [of the object] is alive. All this is done for one goal alone – for the perception of your *I*" (Lectures 1924–1925. Notebook 1. p. 51).

"The most important link [in the chain of creative perception] is *I*; if the *I* is sound, everything else will be sound. The *center* adjusts the object. . . . Let's try, having caught the sensation of the center, admit everything to the center; let's look at each other, while permeating each other with our center . . . Catch this sensation, and you will discover a lot – your essence – and you will live with it in a monologue, or a dialogue. This leads to true *singularity* – from one single center to one single point" (Lectures 1924–1925. Notebook 4, p. 5).

"What is the secret of a powerful stage presence? . . . Radiation streams out of one spot, into one spot only – without any abstractions. An actor admits everything to himself, freely giving out his *I*. The path toward stage presence – is the radiation of my singular *I*, and receiving radiating with my *I*. Everything in me is open, directly connected with everything around me. My *I* is extremely bare; stage presence is the turning off of the self . . . Seeing and listening with one's essence. The formula is: essence – essentially – with my entire essence" (Lectures 1924–1925. Notebook 2, p. 79).

Also see **Admitting, Asana, Muscles, Interval Between Two Thoughts**.

Idiot   See **Fool**.

Imaginary, The   pp. 153, 184–7, 266, 291, 293, 366, 369, 404–5, 524, 585, 725, 781g.

Imagining and Forgetting Exercise   p. 751; Demidov originally conducted these exercises together with his brother Konstantin in Ivanovo-Voznesensk, around 1910–1912. They consist of telling a story to a partner, then "tossing it out of one's head," and then immediately repeating the story anew. The goal of the exercise is to train keeping the story alive and fresh, despite the fact of its repetition. Demidov identified three important qualities trained by this exercise: 1) Ability to not listen to yourself; 2) Ability to create a live image; 3) Ability to give in to this image. A detailed description of this exercise, recorded by Demidov for Stanislavsky on August 19, 1912, is kept in Moscow, at the Stanislavsky Fund of the Moscow Art Theatre's Archive (Fund 3, inventory 44, item No. 57).

Impulses See *First Impulse*.

Incomplete-Combustion Products pp. 710, 715–6, 718*n*4; "When an impression is taken in (inhaled) – it's as if some combustible material has been tossed inside our psychological furnace. Not all of this material ends up burning – the 'combustion' is 'incomplete.' Some waste remains – smoke. For the most part, a very small fraction of the material burns, while most of it disappears without a trace – just like in our furnaces only 20 percent of the firewood heat is used, while another 80 percent evaporates as smoke."

"In the chapter on breathing, I spoke about an essential skill. Having inhaled an impression, one must learn how to not detain it, to not 'lock it up' inside, but instead – speak it, exhaling the whole volume of the impression in its entirety. In observing ourselves, we will notice the following phenomenon. During the moment immediately following an impression (an inhale) – a particle (a rather large particle too) of it suddenly disappears, falls through, escapes. As a result, the impression is exhaled *incompletely*."

"Here is another thing to keep in mind. As I receive something, I also have something inside. So, one thing added to the other must result in *gain*, not in loss!"

"This is not how it happens in practice, where we deal with leakage, just like in our furnaces."

"Apparently trying to avoid the incomplete-combustion products is a futile undertaking – no matter how 'economical' and resourceful our heating might be. Even the most ingeniously constructed furnaces and engines (diesel) don't allow us to use the entire energy of the combustibles. I already mentioned that regular heating wastes 80 percent. Combustion engines waste 40 percent, if I am not mistaken. These statistics apply to the crude force of heat alone. As for the *entire supply* of energy inside our combustibles – we don't even try to extract it."

"[The French scientist Gustave] Le Bon [1841–1931] insisted on the following. A small copper coin, if disassociated [In chemistry and biochemistry – a process when a larger object, or complex falls apart into its component molecules, or ions], or split down to its original energy, contains enough to drive a fully loaded freight train (40 cars long) around the globe twice [See Le Bon 1907: 41]. If used this way, how much energy would a six-foot stack of firewood contain! And how little we manage to squeeze out of it, despite all our ingenuity."

"The same is true of our psychological life. So far, my methods had been aimed at not wasting the crude heat, and at avoiding leakage – the most basic requirement, to say the least. Somehow or another, we must think of using our impressions 'according to Le Bon.' We must think of it, and experiment. How does one split an impression? A force of thought ? An emotional charge? A volitional charge? A force of faith (a lump of faith – see *Faith*)?" (*Various Notes* folder).

See also **Psychological Breathing, Take!, Imaginary, Restraint, Emotionally Tactile Reading of a Text, Selfish Rehearsing** and **Submerging [Text, Circumstances or Tasks] Into the Subconscious**.

Individuality pp. 463–5, 507–8, 550, 777*g*; Demidov distinguished between a person's "individuality" and "personality." "When walking in a street, and looking people in the eyes, you see that a human being is missing – people are going about their business reflexively. A man, in general, lives like a machine, and does everything reflexively. You hear some words – instantly, some reflexive associations appear. Some people want to achieve great things, while continuing to act merely reflexively – they would dislike a man, simply because they heard something bad said about him. Personality and individuality. There is a difference between the two. Example: In Ibsen's *Peer Gynt*, when Peer Gynt meets with the Button-Moulder. A second birth of a man is when his individuality awakes" (Lectures 1924–1925. Notebook 3. p. 82).

"Take people in life – interesting people stand out by the fact that they constantly live with something singular, definite – something that consumes their entire being. On the contrary, a cultured, well-read and educated person might miss individuality, if his life lines are scattered; you don't trust such a person" (Lectures 1924–1925. Notebook 1. pp. 58–59).

Inertia   See *Affective Inertia*.

Inhalation (Inspiration) of Objects   See *Admitting*.

Inhibition   See *Brakes*.

In Statu Nascendi   pp. 405, 542, 547.

Instinct [Reflex] of [Properly] Sensing the Audience   pp. 557, 736, 728–9, 737–8; See *Theatrical Triangle*.

Integral Identity   pp. 618, 621, 639, 640*f*, 641, 644, 646–7, 672–6.

Interval between Two Thoughts   See *Period of Calm between Two Storms of Thought*.

Intimate Work on Self   pp. 550–1; See also *Power of Minor Details* and *Working without the Exertion of Effort*.

Intuition   pp. 540, 595, 668, 750, 751; Intuition, according to Demidov, is "extreme sensitivity to very subtle things" (p. 540).

Just-Born Character   pp. 375–8, 380–1, 390, 784*g*.

Justification   See *Creative(–Aesthetic) Justification*.

Lack of Brakes   p. 687.

Letting Go/Not Letting Go   pp. 532–9, 534–5, 545–7, 570–2, 713.

Let it (Be)   pp. 177, 286–9, 302, 331, 401, 426, 533, 617, 621, 717, 742–3, 757*g*.

Liberation from the Body   See *Great Sleep of the Body*.

Lightning-Like Zigzag of Feeling/Path of Least Resistance   p. 552.

Literal Pronunciation of Words   p. 18, 780*g*; "Letter" is "*litera*" in Latin, so Demidov's term can be better understood as "letteral" pronunciation of words, or else – "spelling out" of the words by delving into their constituting letters (or sounds).

"Start with 'primitive people' and children: echoism or sound symbolism – sounds imitating thunder, cold, heat."

"Spelling it out literally ('letterally')."

"Spelling it out morphemically, based on the word's roots. Each word then becomes like a whole phrase."

"This type of pronunciation can be called: *active*."

"An important prerequisite is the participation of my true 'I'."

"This will ensure activeness, energy and temperament."

"Temperament is a harmonious combination of emotion (sensation), will (action) and thought (imagination.)"

"We must teach voice according to this method."

"'In the beginning was the Word, and the Word was with God, and the Word was God'" [John 1:1].

"The order in which psychological life emerges:

1	Sensation	_____	_____	_____
2	Sensation +	Image	_____	_____
3	Sensation +	Image +	Concept	_____
4	Sensation +	Image +	Concept +	[Judgment]"

"Thus, with literal pronunciation of words, one should not neglect the *sensation*."

"If our world has been created by the word (not to mention the Word's mystical meaning), then we must practice creating an object – while speaking a corresponding word. Evoking it from the Chaos, creating it out of the Chaos. As it was in the beginning."

"There was Chaos. God decided to create the world, and he began with Light. He said: 'Let there be Light!,' and there was light."

"It is according to this principle that we must try pronouncing words." . . .

"In short, we must pronounce words as if it was a magic act, as a miracle of 'evocation from the darkness,' as an act of Creation."

"The same – with gesture and movement (arms, body, head, eyes). With *prana*. For the most part, there exists one substantial mistake that leads to failure (I am not speaking of magic, but of the creative state). One must remember, and use all the means to achieve an *absolute absence of any effort* – otherwise, no live sensation will come, and you'll get nothing but tension, strain, playacting - and an annoying feeling of failure. *Nothing affects me* – everything goes right past me. This is extremely important! It is difficult to rid yourself of the shield of tension, but no psychic life will ever originate without it. Take risk! Dare to let go of the shield, to slip out of the armor, and to bare your soul. You must be brave and take risk."

"[Exercise.] It helps a lot to form ineligible sounds – as animals and patients with profound mental retardation do, in order to communicate. (These sounds consist almost exclusively of vowels. Depending on the tone and the task, these sounds can plead, implore, or display anger.) Repeat this exercise, but now carefully add any consonant to the vowel."

"This exercise demonstrates without fail that singing is a moan, and that conversation is, therefore – a form of singing. You invest your entire physiological sensation into the sound, and with it – your entire soul."

"Sounds used to be ineligible, then they became eligible, but the formation of sound remained the same."

"The 'What' method aids pronunciation of letters."

"'What' do I convey with this letter?"

"What do I portray?"

"What do I invest in it?"

"What does it mean?"

"The chief thing is to get to the bottom of this 'what.'" (See *'What' and 'How.'*)

"[Exercise.] Here is a good way to receive a strong sensation from a letter. Imagine that there used to be three of such letters in a word, but only one survived. For example: today we say "thunder," while in the old days we used to say "th-th-th-u-under-r-r! . . . For the sake of convenience, these three 'r' are currently spelled by one. Three 'th' – with only one 'th.' In reality, however, you must keep all three letters in mind."

"A vocal coach usually says the very same thing: 'in this word, I want you to sing three 'n,' or 'm'." But why would I do so? A singer must justify it in some way. Otherwise, his diction will become mechanical – well-heard it might be, but it will be lifeless."

"The doctrine on the evolution of the body organs tells us that some of them will gradually become atrophied, which some new organs will develop."

"For example, the function of the reproductive organs will be taken by the speech organs – those producing sound (Steiner) [See Steiner 2000: 147–148]. In conjunction with the breath, these organs will create new beings. This is why the culture of these organs, and the culture of the magic word is destined the most tangible and glorious future."

"In the meantime, speech and sound formation, in our age, are on the downward path. We speak mere thoughts. We lost the music of the word."

"We must most likely move in the following (3?) directions:

1   To utilize the word for the sake of conveying thought. As long as it is a true thought - austere, cold, but extremely precise and complete."

2   To affect with the word – by investing it with will power, and with the force, which is capable of physically moving."

"To invest the Word with feeling and, perhaps, by the use of the word, sound and letter – to draw out those emotions crowding in our soul."

"On the Sonority and Musicality of the Speech"

"It is quite easy to express feeling in singing. Singing also makes acting easier."

"This is, firstly, because it provides melody and rhythm – these alone evoke feeling, as long as you listen and surrender to them. Secondly, there is drawl. In a conversation, we say the words so quickly – the melody of the word is absent, while in music there is time to give each letter and sound a long-drawn-out quality, and even a melody . . . ."

"[Exercise.] I just sang some lines, and then tried to speak them. When spoken, they turned out flat, empty and soundless. Moreover, all of their meaning and content, and all their life was gone."

"Then it tried to speak these lines in a singsong, preserving the musicality and sonority in each letter. Yet, I did not sing them, but spoke them with long-drawn-out quality. I realized that we practically lost this ability to be musical in our conversations. We knock our consonants – as if beating a stone with a wooden mallet."

"Rarely we drawl some letter – we do so when we are surprised, or when describing the beauty of nature, or something else superlative."

"So I began to train the sonority and musicality of the conversational speech. I broke each word into letters, and into roots; I gave each letter, root and word the emotion it carries; I watched for the richness and fullness of sound, and for the resonance of the letters. Soon I became convinced that this is not such a complicated business, after all."

"Apparently, resonant, ductile, musical speech does not have to get into our way, as it does now. On the contrary, it helps inspiring the speaker, as does music, and even the sound of your own voice – in singing."

"'A thought once uttered is untrue' (Tyutchev [1947: 5]) – this is well put, in regard to our customary pronunciation of words."

"[Exercise.] Sonority and musicality can be achieved by the means of the 'What' Method. (See "*What*" and "*How*".) 'Behind a river, on the hill, a green forest rustles; Under the hill, behind the river, a little village stands' [Russian folksong, *Khutorok*, with lyrics by Alexey Koltsov (1839)]. What is behind the river? Do you see it? – I see it. What kind of green? Do you see it? – I see it. Etc" (Fund 59. Folder 12).

Lump of Faith   p. 542; "Get up. Make a few steps forward. Stop. Now return to the exact spot where you stood – walking backwards, but without turning round. And you must make it back there in one move, with certainty, without vagueness or hesitation."

"Before you go, you will feel a sensation of a lump in your stomach – this is faith."

"The same lump appears before a running jump, or before stepping onto a tight rope."

"This is a lump of confidence."

"This power can be developed by the means of simple exercises. Before you do something – be it even as simple as lifting an arm – you must think to yourself: 'I am about to lift my arm. Can I do it? Yes, I can (you will feel the lump). Do it then!' and lift the arm. When all is done, say to yourself: 'I've done what I wanted, and what I believed. My power of faith is growing.'"

"You can grow this power fast and infinitely."

"It grows fast, because we already have faith – it's just that it believes on its own, and it does not believe what we want it to believe, or how. Therefore, all we have to do is to learn how to use this existing material" (*Various Notes* folder).

"Do the following exercises in your existing state. Sit down, and sit 'as it sits.'"

"[Say to yourself:] Can I lift up my head and look at the ceiling? I can. Now try it. Yes, you managed."

"Can I bend down my head and look at the floor? I can. Now do it."

"I look at the chandelier, intending to point my finger at it. Can I do it? Now I am pointing at it. Have I managed to do everything the way I wanted?"

"At some moment, a feeling of satisfaction arrives: I managed to do what I wanted, without a single doubt."

"Say: 'A-a,' remember how it went, and then repeat it. Did you manage?"

"Say the word 'lake,' and repeat it exactly. Can I? I shall give it a try" (Lectures 1924–1925. Notebook 3. p. 55).

"Form two rows, standing in front of each other. Now, I must take the place of my colleague in front of me, approaching it from the left side, memorize my path, and go back to my place – backwards. Would I manage?"

"Remember, with the greatest degree to tangibility, the place where you stood, and the path you took."

"There is a similarity between the experience of the beginning and the end – I grasped something, inside me, green-lit myself with full confidence, and suddenly found myself in my old place – not by accident, mind you, but I knew I would. I had some kind of an inner knowing."

"After a few exercises, you discover a greater trust in yourself – almost the same trust you experienced when you lifted your head, or your hand. You feel that you are governed by some force that resides in your center, and you act, influenced by that force. This confidence that I can do what is needed, is called *faith*."

"Faith is a force – a kind of little lump inside me that urges me to act. Everyone has faith in one thing or another – be it in trifles, or in miraculous things. If such a lump is formed, you would be able to walk across a narrow perch, thrust over some deep water. (Remember what happened with apostle Peter.) Faith is a colossal force, and it is as trainable as attention, memory, or imagination. We are savages: we have tremendous forces hidden inside us – we must realize that they exist, take aim, and shoot like a crack shot. Each of us is an individuality, a talent of their own kind; there is a diamond hidden in each of us. (A Persian legend about a traveling monk, and a rich man, who kept searching for diamonds in other lands; he died, and in his own garden they discovered rich diamond deposits.) Let us say, through this lump inside, you have faith: I am the prince of Denmark, I am – Ophelia. In an instance, everything in you changes: your face, your pulse. Faith is the chief quality to be developed. Faith is power, activity, naiveté – the preliminary state of child-like purity; . . . the combination of these qualities is pure talent."

"Every man has the sensation of this lump; you just need to learn how to find it, and hold on to it. If you start speaking some text, you will feel yourself mobilized, and you will feel the presence of some kind of a center – walk around, but don't lose it. You experience a certain state of your 'I' that says: 'I want and I can; I don't want, and I won't.' Faith enables you to play any role." (Lectures 1924-1925. Notebook 3. Pp. 55–58.)

See also **Center**.

Meditativeness/"Autumnal" Meditativeness   pp. 627, 689–90, 692, 697, 708, 746 , 781*g*; See also **Calm**.

Mimicry   pp. 751, 756*g*, 767*g*; "An actor possesses the natural gift for mimicry, and so he must."

"Exercise. Start [mimicking] one another. One partner approaches the table, picks up a book, and the other repeats."

"Whatever you grasp, it is correct – don't be hesitate, mimic while you are hot on the partner's heels. In order to copy correctly, you must pick up on the partner's emotional life, and perceive it affectively – rather than visually."

"The ability to recreate your creative dream, to enter it immediately, and to begin living it – means to perceive affectively, to affectively grasp and convey what's most important in a role" (Lectures 1924–1925. Notebook 4. p. 13).

"Don't you notice that you are your best director? If you follow the path of your soul, you will follow the path of your creative essence. Learn how to listen to this director of yours. You can approach a role by considering it from a literary standpoint, or you can imagine your character while acting affectively. You see your character in action – how he walks, how he looks. Now act while the scent is still hot – and you will grasp what you want to play in this part. This is called 'active dreaming' – dreaming about your role in action – rather than fanaticizing about the role. Once you see something in your role, translate it into action, and the stage pattern, or the character in your dream. The affect will then pour into action, and merge with you. Such is the wealth of the affective realm" (Lectures 1924–1925. Notebook 4. p. 17–18).

"When a director demonstrates a role, keep watching how he dictates the affect. Don't *copy* him, but rather sift his emotions through your individuality. To be able to grasp the director's hidden affective treasures – is one of the actor's chief qualities. The most important thing, however, is to grasp what *you, the actor, see* in your role. You must develop an organ by which you sense your role, and perceive it affectively – rather than comprehend it."

"Always mimic – be it a passer by, or a cat, a crow, a street lamp, or a chair. An actor's chief quality is to draw sketches, to sketch everything and everyone. When you spontaneously mimic someone – don't be surprised to suddenly experience anguish, or emptiness in your soul. By doing this, you will begin to guess the very essence of a person. The technique of emotional surrender to an affect is a secret behind subconscious creativity . . . Condition your body – does it convey what I see, and do I *actually see*? Embody it without delay – Melpomene is our muse – a goddess of transformation; put on a different flesh, and live in it" (Lectures 1924–1925. Notebook 4. p. 14).

"Recall one of your relatives, and test it in action by aping this person, their entire being." (Lectures 1924-1925. Notebook 4 P. 17)

"Exercise. Split into two rows, standing directly across from each other. At the teacher's first command, each of the actors in the first row does some movement, while the partner across sits still and perceives it affectively. At the second command, actors in the second row mimic their respective partners. It is essential to grasp the very affect of the movement, and to reveal its essence – rather than imitate."

"Exercise. Now the first row repeats the movement again, and the second row mimics. You must guess your partner's intentions, and make their movements realer than they actually were – you must offer the quintessence of the movement, its essence. A skill every director must possess is the ability to guess an actor's intention, and what got in its way."

"In these exercises, one must preserve the clarity of imagination, the affect of perceiving and giving yourself over completely, as well as the singularity of task, object and action" (Lectures 1924–1925. Notebook 4. p. 17).

Muscles pp. 687–9, 692–3, 695, 744–8; "Tense muscles turn off our psychological life; they destroy and extinguish it. Muscular tension is our organism's defense mechanism. (Not unlike catalepsy in animals, when they spot a dangerous predator, is a defense mechanism that saves their life.)"

"If you give way to every psychological experience in life, then it begins to swell, and it reaches down to your depths. Imagine that you are angry, and your anger is swelling. If you don't begin to instinctually tense up, clench your fists and grind your teeth (i.e. extinguish your psychological life) – your anger might turn into such a powerful current, it would burn your wires and cause internal fire. Heightened emotions can cause catastrophes in our nervous system – madness, etc."

"And so, to avoid such catastrophes, we are supplied with protective devices. Like electric fuses that burn out – at the slightest overload."

"As for us, artists – although we know and respect the purpose of this device, nevertheless we have to face its unpleasant, unadvantageous aspect. As soon as we experience an emotion – our muscles come into play, and they stifle it. What shall we do? We must, first and foremost, get used to released muscles. And second, we must learn to release them even further – as our emotions arise. The stronger grows the emotion – the fuller our release must become. We must turn this into a habit."

"'I am the lamp; the world of images is the oil; the creative process is the flame. Peace and calm are needed in order to light the lamp'" (Lectures 1924–1925. Notebook 3. pp. 75–76, reverse sides).

"An exercise. Assume some calm position, and consider yourself. Search for your 'I'. Am I intelligent or not? Discreet or not? Honest or not? As you delve deeper into yourself, your muscular tension decreases, and you gradually become free. Open your arms wide – can you touch your 'I' from such a position? No, it gets in the way. Justify the hands, surrender to this, and then you will be able to hear your 'I'. Thus, tension always gets in the way; one must free himself from it. Mchedelov and Vakhtangov had many exercises in muscular release. Stanislavsky called these exercises – 'a sauna.' Tension per se is not the issue, but whether this tension is to the point, or not."

"Observe yourself. Where is tension? Let's suppose it is in the shoulders. What stands behind this tension? Some thought keeps weighing on you. My left foot, my toes – yet another thought. I try to let this thought take its free course, and then notice that the foot too was tense, [as this tension gets released]."

"When noticing tension – immediately guess what kind of thought occupies this part of the body. You then will be able to release your tension. Any partial tension points to the fact that your 'I' is preoccupied with something inessential. If you check with your entire self, you will notice that a major part of you is absent. It is elsewhere, and only a small fraction of you lives in this space. When you release the muscles, however, some kind of an [extra] object goes away. Even in a state of heightened concentration, we still unconsciously retain some cares and thoughts – they all find their expression in partial tension. This tension is fraught with worries. We have some 'signature' tense spots. They distort our faces, bodies, and they make everything look 'peculiar.'"

"Certain muscles are in charge of certain psychological life; when you delete extraneous tension, you remove the unnecessary object. A person is doing something, but nothing works. Remove his arm, and things will go smoothly. Apparently an extraneous object was connected with the arm. At times, everything depends on this, as this person's entire subconscious is focused on this object. It turns him off, and he is incapable of doing a thing. To detect what is getting in the actor's way is extremely important. Remove the distraction, and everything will be just fine. In addition to physical knots, there are mental ones – they too get in the way."

"When you detect tension, you must also detect what kind of an extraneous object the actor has. Remove this object – tension will also disappear, and vice versa."

"We must have working tension – life is impossible without it. Every other kind of tension is non-working. It belongs to our psyche, and it ties a person in a knot. Letting go of tension means a lot for our psyche – it is like brushing a horse. Little by little, you will reach the center, and comb out all extraneous thoughts and centers – except for one."

"Many thoughts battle in us at once. As a result, you only give away one hundredths of your I. Often, this is just a mechanical fraction of you, and you give it away for the sake of protocol. To remove everything that gets in the way, to give life to only one center – this is a must in art. Take our most significant actors, at their best moments – they always coincide with muscular release. Skillful release leads to singularity of the object, and of the subject, and it leads to being able to fathom everything. Otherwise, we are tied into knots, with up to 20 objects of concentration. Remember the silent sitting of the Japanese – 'seiza.' They are completely free, their spine is a straight line; everything is free, and they are all meditation on what subject they've been preparing for. The state of scattered attention is, alas, our normal state, while the state of collectedness is rare. One of the reasons why we are drawn to the stage – is the state of concentration, deprived of our mundane habits-knots. In life, we simultaneously have many objects, and everything is non-artistic and non-creative. Stage, however, only tolerates justified, working tension."

"Exercise. Lift up your hand – it's not a pleasant feeling; the hand is in the way. Now begin 'listening' to it, and green-light what you heard – now the hand is no longer in the way. On the contrary, it contributes to the overall fusion. As soon as you discover a tense muscle, guess its object and delve into it – the other muscles will immediately release" (Lectures 1924–1925. Notebook 3. pp. 73–78).

"The freedom of muscles is a section of a larger chapter on freedom. When you are on the stage – you are not as free as at home, alone with a loved one. Something constrains you onstage. Muscles are the silk thread in the Indian legend – the very thread the minister's wife tied to the leg of a cockroach. We must hold on to it tight" (Lectures 1924–1925. Notebook 3. p. 85).

See also **Casting Away the Body**, **Great Sleep of the Body**, **Singularity**, **Center**, and **Creative Justification**.

Muscular Release   See **Muscles**.

Naiveté   pp. 293–4, 533, 604, 766g, 769g, 777g. "Balzac. *Honorine.* 'My poor uncle, a heart consumed by charity, a child of seventy years, as clear-sighted as God, as guileless as a man of genius, not doubt read the tumult of my soul; . . .'" [Balzac 1900a: 299].

"The following words have something in common":
Spontaneous
Unconstrained – pronounce them literally [see **Literal Pronunciation of Words**]
Trusting"

"Connection with fantasy: I am naïve, because I immediately find a justification, having fantasized it."

"The opposite is also true: I fantasies are so free and unconstrained, as I am naïve" (*Various Notes* folder). See also **Fool** and **Idiot**.

Nearest Flow of Thought   pp. 516, 544, 547, 550, 588, 686, 703, 710, 761g; "What is necessary in order to evoke the attractive force of a magnet, or to create an electric spark between two electrodes? They must be brought close to each other. Otherwise no magnetic power, nor electric charge will occur."

"Similarly, the imagined must closely touch our consciousness, in order to become real and tangible."

"The 'what' method is yet another way of making the imagined real and tangible. When answering the question 'what' – you gradually move away from the external and formal [perception] – to genuine and internal, from distant – to the near, from foreign – to tangible."

"Perhaps, the thought must not flow near the body, but near the soul instead, and take the soul in tow."

"It would seem that the objects of our thoughts (the thinkable) differ from those of our imagination (from the imagined). Nevertheless, when 'speaking your thought,' you also can draw the 'thinkable' near."

"Exercise: try thinking your thoughts and then, when they become clear and tangible, try drawing them nearer."

"The 'literal' pronunciation as the means to convert words and thoughts into physical tasks, and to achieve the nearest contact with the soul."

"This *'nearestness'* removes all possible obstacles and begets *unobstructedness.*"

"*Unobstructedness* begets talent."

"One must 'tangibly sense' and 'touch.'"

"The absorbability of a sponge – absorbing the word greedily. To become soaked through, to achieve complete saturation."

"The flow of thought can be drawn so near, it begins to merge with me and, therefore, flow inside me (not just near me)."

"We must establish: the stream, the 'flow' of thought, and draw this stream near."

"This does not mean trying to draw near the 'thinkable,' or the 'imaginary' (that is the objects of our mental attention – in the case with the 'thinkable,' or emotional attention – in the case with the 'imaginary'). No, we should not try to draw near those objects, but rather the thought *process* itself. So, my first formula was precise: 'The nearest flow of thought.' Later, having lost the secret, in my search for the loss I strayed off the right path. I began to draw near those objects carried by the thought (the 'thinkable'), rather than *thought* itself" (*Various Notes* folder). See also **Intimate Work on Self, Point of View, "What" Method, Emotionally Tactile Reading of a Text**, and **Literal Pronunciation**.

Object See *"What" And "How."*

Oneness p. 63.

Passivity, Culture of Passivity pp. 96, 217, 286, 381, 401, 421n1, 434, 436, 533, 539–41, 616, 627, 632, 671–2, 674–5, 678–81, 684, 686, 738, 743, 786g; Passivity is connected with many other aspects of the Demidov School. Similarly, exercises in Passivity and Freedom can be conducted by seeking the state of meditativeness: "*transparent, clear, innocent, and singular*" (p. 683). One should also train the transparency of the gaze – this state of "*expectant serenity*," which will result in the transparency or the asana of the "*Evangelic Eye.*" Demidov calls the actor to "achieve the enchantment of innocence and serenity, like with Moissi during his successful performances" (p. 541). Similarly, these kinds of exercises are aimed at training one's thoughts to become "clear, transparent, and distinct." The state of passivity equals psychological transparency, when all of the actor's "thoughts, all his feelings, all of his treasures are open, and he's transparent like the water of a mountain lake" (p. 747). Truly passive actors, according to Demidov, are "so transparent that their inner life is visible in their face and body, in every word and movement" (p. 294).

Perch of Transition p. 697; In the experience of the editors, having the thought *relentlessly* control the process of putting the body to sleep, as recommended by Demidov, is the best way of "keeping it busy." If the thought wanders off, even for a second, this puts the spinal chord to sleep, thus producing the effect opposite to the one intended by the technique of the sleep. Not letting the thought "escape" is one of the chief skills an actor must master while moving across "the perch of transition." It is also beneficial to bringing one's attention to the inwardness and ease of the spine, awakeness of the eye and the freedom of breath – prior to "exhaling" the body. Inhaling "prana" into the spinal cord, vertebra by vertebra (while using exhalations to keep putting the body to sleep) also can yield positive results. Outsourcing to the subconscious the monitoring of the spinal cord's awakeness (see **Submerging [a Task] into Subconscious**) is yet another technique practiced by the editors.

Period of Calm between Two Storms of Thought pp. 533–4, 771g, 787–8g; In addition to this writing, Demidov also quotes *The Upanishads* in his Moscow Art Theatre School 1924–1925 lectures (Notebook 3, p. 66), where he says: "An interval between one image and the other, or between the two storms of thoughts, is the state of our true 'I.'" Sri Ramana Maharshi (1989: 53), one of the most influential Hindu gurus, says: "The 'I' in its purity is experienced in intervals between the two states or two thoughts. Ego is like that caterpillar which leaves its hold only after catching another. Its true nature can be found when it is out of contact with objects or thoughts." See also **Culture of Calm, Stop!**

Perception See Index for "creative perception/perceiving."

Personality See **Individuality**.

Physiology   pp. 313–20, 382, 397, 436, 521, 544, 586, 616, 687–8, 703.

Play   pp. 577–83, 588–91, 603–11.

Power of Minor Details   pp. 473, 540, 550–51; "In monasteries, the circle of one's interests becomes strangely narrow."

"The monks confess to their ghostly father of all their thoughts – not just those connected with things major, but also things such as 'I thought of eating an extra spoon of peas, of going for a walk, of climbing a tree' etc. – everything, inside and out."

"What mediocrity!, I used to think."

"But things are not as simple. What is the monks' occupation? They are reorganizing their apparatus, making an exact chronoscope out of a bad watch. They are turning their crude mechanism into the most refined and finest one, which is why they must only pay attention to minor details. After all, chronoscope is held in place by minor details alone."

"Thus, the monks make singular 'truth' a tool of their cultivation."

"They refine and sharpen themselves 'like the edge of a razor.'"

"Actors should similarly narrow their circle of interests and occupations, if they want to perfect their own apparatus. Minding one's ability to see and hear everything isn't enough. One must mind *how* he is seeing. Just imagining isn't enough; one must mind *how* his thought flows – is it near enough?"

"A chronoscope calibrated down to one hundredths of a second will surely always show the right hour" (*Various Notes* folder).

The "power of minor details" is described in Book Four, Chapter 6 (sub-chapter "The Minor Details of Form Are Stronger Than Major Things"), Chapter 12 ("The Culture Of Sensitivity") and 13 ("On Intimate Work on Self and on Working without the Exertion of Effort"). In the Demidov technique, "intimate" exercises are meant to achieve the complete merger with the given circumstances of the role, when the actor becomes infiltrated by the circumstances, and vice versa. Most of these techniques are described in Book Five, Chapter 14, dedicated to the "methodology" of the creative research. (Specific sub-chapters to pay attention to are "Advice For Future Researchers of the Actor's Creative Technique," "Cleansing Self-Treatment," "Toward Training," and "Concentration, 'The Edge.'" See also *Intimate Work on Self*, *Culture of Calm (and Clarity of Spirit)*.

Prayer of the Heart/Prayer of the Mind   p. 707; "Prayer of the mind" (Prayer with the mind) and "Prayer of the Heart" ("Prayer with/from the heart" or "with the mind in the heart") are the terms of Eastern Orthodox Christian Doctrine, often referred to as Hesychasm or Christian Yoga. Some of these concepts appear in *The Art of Prayer* by St. Theophan the Recluse (1815–1894), a Bishop in nineteenth-century Russia, known in the world as George Govorov (see Chariton 1997). Other important sources on prayer, studied and utilized by Demidov are the writings on "three methods of attention and prayer," attributed to St. Simeon the New Theologian (11th century; see *Writings From the Philokalia* 1992). These writings speak of physical (body position, or "*asana*") and breathing exercises connected with prayer. As early as 1911, Demidov supplied Stanislavsky with the descriptions of his own experiments connected with the working of the subconscious, with deep relaxation and meditation, as well as excerpts from *Philokalia* and other early Christians' writings on prayer and superconscious. Demidov's notes are kept in the Stanislavsky section of the Moscow Art Theatre Archive (Fund 3, inventory 44, item No. 59). See also *Admitting* and *Psychological Breathing*.

Prelude   See *Finishing Up Living*.

Primitive (Sensations, Irritation, Impressions) pp. 542–4, 616.

Principle of the Triad See *Reflexology*.

Prelogic, Prelogical Thinking pp. 497, 596–7, 602, 604–6, 610.

Psychological Breathing pp. 16, 539, 707, 711–12, 717–18, 718n3.

Publicness See *Theatrical Triangle*.

Pyatnitsky Exercises See *Giving in to Physiological Sounds* and *Diaphragmatic Breathing*.

Questions and Answers See *Etudes*.

Questioning Method pp. 271–3, 343–5, 384.

Radiation pp. 687, 738, 755*g*, 760*g*, 768*g*, 771*g*, 786*g*; "One's ability to radiate, and receive radiations, equals one's ability to fulfill actions onstage, or to live along the line of your radiation. As soon as one grasps this within himself, he will grasp the singularity of action, singularity of the object, the *I am*, muscular freedom – all while proceeding from this radiation" (Lectures 1924–1925. Notebook 2. p. 71). The opposite is also true: establishing one's singularity, the state of *I am*, and one's muscular freedom and center – leads to powerful radiation. Also see *Freedom of Radiation* and *Center*.

Reflexology pp. 15, 550; "According to the latest psychological thought – an organism's behavior is a reflex response to a stimulus coming from within, or without."

"Thereby, the entire psycho-technique can be divided into three major sections: 1) Organism (the subject); 2) The process of perceiving stimulus; and 3) Reflex (free, delayed, or regulated).

1 Organism (the subject). Correct, or incorrect state of the organism itself during the creative act onstage, or during the study of the role.
2 The technique of perceiving stimulus in a form conducive for triggering the required secondary reflex.
3 The technique of free surrender to the reflex, or its delay, or its transformation." (Fund 59. Folder titled *Part II. Role and Reflexology*).

Residual Attention pp. 687–8; Physical business, or even audience, attract the "residual attention" of the actor – attention that otherwise would have been spent on harmful self-observation, thus preventing the benevolent "doubling."

Restraint pp. 415, 535, 570, 762*g*, 768*g*; "The actors give in to their wants, and they begin to jump from one thing to the other . . ."

"They do so, instead of steadily walking their path, once they've stepped onto it the moment they sensed the first urge."

"*A talent possesses this grip, a mediocrity – does not.*"

"One must develop this quality. One must learn to maintain the balance on the tight rope for a long period of time – not just for a second or two.

1 A lack of grip is the reason why the actors take so long to start, and abuse pauses. I usually say: this is because of the 'missing trains.' This is true, but why do they miss these trains? No grip, and a weak hook.
2 A lack of grip causes them to jump from character to character, and eventually play several roles in the course of one etude."

3   Long hesitations, endless deliberation – this is also a lack of grip. How do I begin to explain this? A talented actress is onstage. She grabbed the line, and kept developing it, while climbing higher and higher. How did she do it? I can't explain. Now a talentless actress is onstage – it's all so sluggish, uninteresting and just long. She seems to be "truthful," but then why is it so boring? Or else it is uneven. We analyze it, and discover that she kept falling off, coming off and sliding off the etude's axle. We apply restraint. We introduce the "restraint machine," or the buildup machine (the "temperament machine" [The "machine" should be featured in the *Scene Study* section. *–Author's Note*]), . . . and we get the etude on the right track . . .

4   A student usually plays one and the same character in all etudes – two at the most. "How does this happen? Here is how. In the first moment, he gets the impulse for something new and unexpected. This lasts for a short moment. Fearing this new experience, he. . .slightly delays his life. . . In the meantime, deprived of fuel, the newborn life goes away, and everything slides down, onto the well-trodden path – into his usual, habitual, well-tried 'character.' The rest of the etude goes smoothly, without any surprises."

"This goes to prove that the sameness of character is fully determined by the fact that an actor does not grip the first urge (or does not give in to it). If the actor only had the courage to give in to this new, unexperienced character – then it would develop and grow stronger."

"This [just-born] character arrives without fail, but so does the delaying of it – out of fear of everything new and unexperienced."

"The reader should consult the chapter on 'Character' [Book 3. Chapter 34]. There, I speak of two kinds of 'grip' – an active kind (with a push), and a passive kind (with waiting and taking time)" [See pp. 379–82] Fund 59. Folder titled Book 2. # 3. *SCENE STUDY. Circumstances. Repetition. Assigning.* See also ***Just–Born Character***.

Restructuring/Non-Restructuring   p. 191, 217, 283, 354, 426, 510, 515, 531–3, 567, 570–2, 632; See also ***Beginning (Technique of)***.

Roughly Physical Sensations   See ***Subtly Physical Sensations / Roughly Physical Sensations***.

Selfish Rehearsing   p. 556; "Maly Theatre's major actors (and especially actresses) used to rehearse like this. They were offered a chair; they sat down and whispered their lines, or spoke them *sotto voce*, giving nothing to the partner. The partners, on the other hand, were required to act full force. When, in their estimation, they needed to change location – their chair was moved into a different spot."

"They did not act, but merely studied the conditions in which they will have to act. They researched them – practically on the sly. Their inner charge was saved up for the performance. Perhaps, it is even a bit premature to speak of the charge. Perhaps, they had no charge as of yet. Most likely, their charge was accumulated while they were held themselves back and exercised restraint – while accumulating the material for this charge during such rehearsals. All this material went directly into the subconscious, as it found no other exit. When it was most needed, however, it was served to the audience in a ready state" (*Various Notes* folder).

Selfish rehearsing can be defined as a means of accumulating character, as well as energy and material for the performance. Other examples of "selfish rehearsing" are featured in Demidov's books. Among them, "the communion, and the relationship, discovered by the means of sitting next to each other, while embracing or touching shoulders. The relationship conveys through the warmth of the partner's body" (p. 543). See also ***Incomplete-Combustion Products***, ***Submerging [Text, Circumstances or Tasks] into the Subconscious***, and ***Emotionally Tactile Reading of a Text***.

Sensations pp. 85–6, 186–7, 542–3, 612–13, 682–6, 760–70g, 788g, 790g. See also ***Giving in to Sensations***, **Subtly Physical Sensations / Roughly Physical Sensations**, and ***Primitive Sensations***.

Sensitivity pp. 235, 438–40, 449, 540, 544, 584, 616, 648, 679.

Seriousness pp. 683, 751, 766g; "Etudes and improvisations, for the most part, turn into chatter – and only for the lack of seriousness. The actors assume their character – lightly, for fun, superficially."

"Here is the method that can aid this. Keep repeating to yourself: is this in earnest? Is this for real? And what 'if' it was in earnest, how would it go then? Can it be even more serious?"

"The same applies to comedy."

"Things are only funny if we perceive them seriously, really and truly. As for the laughter, it is triggered by the fact that we play a certain kind of people [shallow, egotistical], or by the coincidence of circumstances. . . ."

"One more thought on comedic seriousness. It should be complete, and proceed from a specific place. Not from the depth, but from some superficial part of me. Folly is, first and foremost - narrow-mindedness and depthlessness."

"Yes and No"

"We rarely say: yes! or now! For the most part, it is "neither yes, or no." We must watch for this in a role, and grasp singularity, as well as the task, and the thoughts, and the *I*."

"'You rise at break of day!

And I fall at your feet.'" [Griboyedov 1969: 139]

"Am I really at your feet? Yes or no? Now say it so that it really becomes: 'Yes! At your feet!'"

"We must also learn to do this in life: to seriously ask, seriously affirm, seriously deny, command, or tell our opinion. In short, we must learn to execute these three things: question, affirmation and negation. Everything else is a mere variety of these three."

"In life, we can not do this – even despite a great level of intellectual development. Everything is a half-question, half-affirmation, or half-negation. Why so?"

"Most likely, fear is the main factor. Our fright leads to indecision, uncertainty of thought and vagueness of desires. Energetic people, Napoleons in life, the men of action – they are distinguished, first and foremost, by this property of definiteness. It chooses its way and goes without looking back. Even if it does look back – it does so not to weigh everything anew and breed doubts. It only does so in order to get even a stronger impetus, and dash forward even bolder."

"Every work, and every action – in short, everything that cultivates definiteness – develops this precious property, and consequently – begets great deeds."

"Every deliberation, calculation, endless weighing of pros and cons – cultivates speculativeness and inaction. It breeds tons of books and articles, and it serves as a necessary manure, without which the men of action, perhaps, would be unable to realize their projects."

"When I was young, energetic, and believed in my star – I had a favorite formula: I wanted everything to be 'clear, definite and complete!' How splendid this is! How business like!"

"We must be certain to avoid 'merely-conversations,' 'speculations,' etc. We need to have 'conversations-deeds.' This thought has a deep meaning – much deeper than it seems."

"When working on 'yes' and 'no,' it will help being categorical: categorically yes! categorically no! I categorically want!" (Fund 59. Folder 12).

Shadows (of Thought and Emotion) Flickering Across the Face pp. 48, 91, 448, 469; See also **Weak Currents**.

Silk Thread pp. 241–2, 684, 694, 708, 780g; "One of the amazing secrets of the technique of calm, singularity, creative passivity and complete freedom is":

"Doing only what you feel like – what you truly want and are capable of doing."

"This means – without the slightest, most miniscule effort."

"As soon as we start practicing, the fist thing we do is force ourselves. Moreover, we don't force ourselves to do what we feel like doing, but rather to do something on top of that."

"We must take off this entire load – all of it. We must drop it all, and keep only the miniscule, barely noticeable automatic want. Not even a want, but an inclination. Let it alone remain, without any rough tasks, without responsibility."

"By doing so, you will strike upon your immediate truth and freedom. Other wants will then come on their own – you won't have to even think of them. They will come – singular, unpolluted, and they will fulfill themselves. On their own!"

"This is so clear to me now, that I am inclined to think that, perhaps, the main reason why you can't find your true self in the maze of falsehood and constraint - is that you always – always - overload your exercises. You think that you don't, but in actuality you overload them all the same. This is why this device – to 'find the silk thread' – is, perhaps, one of the very, very best."

"Perhaps, one should always think only the silk thread, instead of pulling at a rope, as we usually do."

"We must do *only miniscule things* – this will pull things big out of our subconscious . . ."

"[Exercise.] Here I sit in absolute calm . . . In two to three seconds, I barely sense that my leg has become uncomfortable – there is an urge to change its position, and to make the subtlest shift. It has emerged, this minuscule need, and I give it freedom – but only as much freedom as it wants. I don't shift my leg any more than I need, I don't 'overload.'"

"Having shifted like this, I wait for the new inclinations – as microscopically small and barely perceptible as the polar attraction for the compass' magnetic arm."

"Concentrating this way – by the power of my *live* attention, *live* feeling, and *live* act – I place myself on the path of *live*, active truth, with all ensuing consequences."

"Such exercises often put one to sleep. This is because they are done incorrectly" (Fund 59. Folder 7). See also **Culture of Calm**.

Singularity pp. 462, 522, 535, 541, 557, 560, 683, 686–7, 705, 710, 755, 757g, 759–61g, 765g, 769g, 771g, 773g, 778–9g, 786g, 781–3g, 785–6g, 789g, 791g; "Singularity of the object – we always have several at once."

"Singularity of the task."

"Singularity of radiation – a lack of it leads to excess tension."

"Of desire."

"Of communication."

"Of the truth (falsehood is several truths at once; they tear a person apart, dragging him in different directions. One must have one, singular truth, and that will rid him of falsehood.)"

"One can have several truths, as long as they drag you in one and the same direction."

"Of the rhythm."

"Of 'I am' – otherwise one would have several 'Is.'"

"Of the time – present, past and future. Present being the most important of all."

"Of the center – otherwise one will lack freedom, and be subjected to his brakes."

"Of the body position (if you sit, then sense yourself sitting; otherwise, no pose will ever be singular, at this given moment)."

"Singularity is a key to artistry."

"Aristocratism in life is nothing but singularity."

"Singularity is not the same as being attentive and having an object [of attention]."

"Only *through* singularity can one experience what attention and object are."

"For example: I listen to a sound; sound is my object; I am attentive to the sound. Such is the usual path."

"And what about my cheek? It should also be listening. And what about my nose, eye, shoulder, arm, hand, fingers, chest, stomach, feet, thought and heart? When all of those listen, and have a single object and a single task of hearing – only then do you understand the true nature of attention, of the object, etc. Saving clause – it can be so, but it can be even better. Imagine that your body is sitting or lying (in short, it died off), while the ear alone! lives a doubled life."

"Attention, object, etc. – these are (alas!) mere results of singularity."

"'No one can serve two masters'" [Matthew 6:24] (Fund 59. Folder 12). See also *"What" and "How,"* **Body Position**, and **Concreteness**.

Slipping Past the Body pp. 686–7, 695.

Small Automatic Movements pp. 202, 236–43, 242–3, 245–6, 253, 288, 295, 323, 411, 488, 631, 633.

Splitting, Splintering See **Doubling**.

Stepping On It pp. 277, 306–12, 401, 552, 712, 716.

Stop! p. 533; "To fulfill the stop – is to immediately stop every action or movement (except breathing) upon hearing the command 'Stop!' and to remain in this state until you hear the releasing command 'Enough.'"

"This exercise has three levels:

1st All physical activities stop, while thought keeps working, occupied by self-observation.
2nd Thought also comes to a stop; emotions alone continue to swell, like water in a dammed creek. On the brink of 'Enough,' it begins to break its banks, and as soon as the dam gates of 'Stop' have been lifted, it continues to flow, but now as a mighty, deep river.
3rd The highest stage – when everything comes to a stop. It signifies an 'interval, a period of calm between two storms of thought – the state of our true 'I.' (*The Upanishads*)
This is the state of the abyss. Of the *seiza*" (*Various Notes* folder).

"*The first* level is good for verifying truth, publicness and stage intelligence."
"*The second* – for restraint and accumulation."
"*The third* – for inspiration and for the practice of superconscious."
When describing the second level of "Stop!" exercise at the MAT School, Demidov said: "If your eyes, or your feet feel uncomfortable, heavy, this means that the stop did not really happen, and something in you is still 'pressing.' If, having heard 'proceed,' you don't want to continue the original movement, it also means that 'stop' did not happen, but instead you

just changed your objective . . ." Another exercise: "Look at the mirror, then at the window, while observing yourself deep inside. In between these two actions, you will grasp the interval – the state of our true *I*, silence, and calm of thought. The trick is to grasp this borderline state. . . In these exercises ('Stop!' and 'interval between the two thoughts'), a person remains alone with his own *I*; he senses his *I*; during the stop, the work of our desire continues, while our temperament grows" (Fund 59. Lectures 1924–1925. Notebook 3. pp. 65–68). See also ***"I," Restraint, Period of Calm between Two Storms of Thought***, and ***Culture of Calm***.

Subconscious Waiting p. 492; When it comes to *subconscious waiting*, Demidov offers the following advice from Prentice Mulford: "When you don't know what to do in any matter of business, in anything – wait. Do nothing about it. Dismiss it as much as you can from your mind. Your purpose will be as strong as ever. You are then receiving and accumulating force to put on that purpose. It comes from the Supreme Power. It will come in the shape of an idea, an inspiration, an event, an opportunity. You have not stopped while you waited. You have all that time been carried to the idea, the inspiration, the event, the opportunity, and it also has been carried or attracted to you" (Mulford 2007: 69). See also ***Submerging [Text, Circumstances, or Tasks] into the Subconscious***.

Submerging [Text, Circumstances, or Tasks] into the Subconscious pp. 18, 541, 547, 715, 764g; "When something isn't working, be it a problem with diction, voice, or else you lose emotion in a given scene, or don't know how to play it; immediately sense this problem in a [subtly] physical way, and submerge it into your subconscious . . . Imagine a trap door in the floor. Toss [the *physically felt sensation* of the problem, or desired result] down into the subconscious, while saying: 'subconscious, work on this.' Not a single thought of the problem must remain in me; everything must be delegated to the subconscious, and its work. . . . Don't expect to receive the answer in word or in thought – it will always come practically [in the next rehearsal] . . . The very moment of submerging is very important. You must have a very tangible sensation that you've ***submerged***. If you don't have such a sensation, but just thought of it instead, the material will slip away, and the answer received will be imprecise. After the submerging one must remain trustingly expectant: I believe that the answer will be supplied" (Lectures 1921–1922. Pages not numbered). See also ***Admitting, Subtly Physical Sensations / Roughly Physical Sensations, Emotionally Tactile Reading of a Text***, and ***Subconscious Waiting***.

Subtly Physical Sensations/Roughly Physical Sensations p. 535; "Let's take this table, for example; touch it, and sense it physically. Now close your eyes, or turn away, and sense this table standing over there. In your mind, touch it, in a subtly physical way. But exactly as if your hand was touching it."

"If I touch something with my hand, I will sense it roughly physically . . . . I could come outside, and make a snowball; or I could sense how I went, took some snow, and I can sense the snowball in my hands. In this case, I fulfilled this task in a subtly physical way" (Lectures 1921–1922. Pages not numbered).

Superconscious pp. 599, 668, 782g, 787g; "Our creative state is the perception of influences from elsewhere. While in it, we exist onstage in an unconscious state; our *I* does not participate. It is subjected to its super-conscious, to its instinct of beauty" (Lectures 1924–1925. Notebook 2. p. 62).

Surrender See ***Giving In***.

Synthesis See Index for "synthesis and grasp."

Take! pp. 546–7.

"Exercises in the 'courage of giving in to one's sensations,' i.e. in doing what I feel like doing at the moment."

"Sometimes, the students interpret it in such way that they begin to tear around – they flutter, imagining that they are doing what they feel like.

1 You must grasp the flickering want
2 Determine it (this can be done instantly)
3 Give yourself a green-light in its direction; having done that you
4 Carry it to the end
5 Make a full stop, and
6 A new want will arise

Several wants might arise at once; you must choose the one you need – 'grasp' it, 'determine' it, and give yourself a green-light in its direction."

"This constitutes the freedom of choice. My choice is sound only when it isn't dictated by my head, but by my artist, my creativity, and my higher consciousness. When I am 'led by the spirit.'"

"When the role is underdeveloped, then you have to choose among many urges and wants. Not so, if it is well founded, correctly sent into the subconscious, and draws on the abundance of affective material. In such a case, only the correct wants will arise – there will be no reflex garbage."

"Not to forget that the psychology is defined thus:

First – impression – these goods are always in plentiful supply.
Second – wishes – these are fewer.
Third – wants – these are fewer yet."

"When working on a role, you often achieve less by seeking 'what I want', and more by seeking 'what I don't want' – the latter easier. For example: 'I want beauty' is difficult; 'I don't want vulgarity, pettiness, mundaneness' – this is easier. Etc. (Stanislavsky's advice.)" See also *Admitting*.

Weak Currents   pp. 380–1, 507, 530–1, 567.

"What" and "How"   pp. 686, 776g; "In a role, one should never look for *how* one does something, but only *what* he is doing, at this instance, or in general."

"*How* – is a result. It is a result of *how* he is as a person. Or, to be more precise – 'what kind' of a person he is!"

"In a role, one should look for two things:

1 What kind of a person
2 What is he doing"

"In seeking correct answers to both questions, one should not neglect the 'object' method: both subject and action are derived from the correct perception of the objects, and of the given circumstances."

"As for *how* he is as a person (a subject), that can be achieved by one's point of view on his environment – by one's objects. To put it differently – by what one sees in the surrounding objects. When seeing a giant, Gulliver feels himself as small; and faced with a Lilliputian, he feels himself a giant. As for Gulliver himself, he does not change. Therefore, *everything* must be translated into *what*."

"'What' should never be understood peripherally, as a mere cataloguing. For example: what am I doing now? Writing. Is that all? No, I am writing down what I consider important. That's all? No, not just anything important, but what I consider important in art. Perhaps I am writing my book? Or perhaps, after a long break, I finally forced my lazy self to sit down at my desk and commit to paper some important thought that would have perished otherwise? Or perhaps, through the very process of writing, I clarify something for myself? Or else, I am fancying myself an author, and feed my ego by writing?"

"Thus, to answer the question 'what' am I doing now? as primitively as 'I am writing' – is to say nothing, and to confuse yourself altogether. On the contrary, if one properly operates with this question ('what'), and keeps asking it to the end – the results will be most alive and emotionally exciting."

"Moreover, 'what' must be applied to a subject ('what' am I, and what do I presently live by?), and to an object (who, or what is before me? what kind of a person, or object, and what do I see in him?), as well as to action."

"Finally, it can be applied to perception and breathing (what exactly am I perceiving in this particular fact, or line?)."

"The correct use of this method begets the correctness of task, its precision, the correctness of given circumstances, of the psychological states, and of the 'I.' Such correctness, in its turn, leads to specificity, clarity, and singularity" (*Various Notes* folder). See also *"What" Method*, *Seriousness*, *Singularity*, *Concentration*, *Weak Currents* and *Concreteness*.

"What" Method pp. 686, 776g; "To say 'What' means to give in to one's sensation. In essence, it means to do what I feel like doing. After all, *this is* what you want to say now, so – go ahead. In life, as well as onstage – we typically don't say what we want."

"Breathing will lend decisive support in this matter. What you feel like – you end up taking it in with breath. One must learn to give it away unchanged, without substitution, and exhale it – be it in a form of a word, or a movement, or an action" (*Various Notes* folder).

The "What" method is connected with "singularity" and deep, involuntary (effortless) concentration. One of the method's variations is based in the non-intellectual and completely effortless "discovery," or rather acknowledgement of one's immediate inner state or content (and/or that of an object of attention) – the acknowledgement of the true "what." As all of Demidov's "heightened" exercises and techniques, the "what" method requires for an actor to be "in that same state of complete calm, if not to say contemplation" (p. 550). Having fully surrendered to one's inner truth (to one's "what"), the actor achieves singularity and inner attention (contemplation). In a similar way, an actor can discover the "what" of an object – by surrendering to one's singular inner impression from the object. This would result in deep "emotional concentration" on the object – possibly even in a *merger* with the object. See also *"What" and "How."*

Working without the Exertion of Effort pp. 550–1; See also *Power of Minor Details* and *Intimate Work on Self*.

Bibliography

Arber, Agnes (1954) *The Mind and the Eye*. Cambridge: Cambridge University Press.

Balzac, Honore de (1900a) *Modeste Mignon and Other Stories*. Translated by Clara Bell. With a preface by George Saintsbury. Philadelphia: The Gebbie Publishing Co.

Balzac, Honore de (1900b) *The Works of Balzac*. Centenary Edition. Volume XXXIV. Cambridge: Little, Brown and Company.

Balzac, Honore de (1900c) *The Works of Balzac*. Centenary Edition. Volume I–II. Boston: Little, Brown and Company.

Baratynsky, Yevgeny (2002) *Polnoye sobranie sochineniy i pisem* [*Complete Works and Letters*]. Volume II. Part 1. Moscow: Yazyki slavyanskoi kul'tury.

Belinsky, Vissarion (1953) *Polnoye sobraniye sochineniy v trinadtsati tomakh* [*Complete Works* in Thirteen Volumes]. Volume II. Moscow: Izdatelstvo Akademii nauk SSSR.

Blavatsky, Helena Petrovna (1909) *The Voice of the Silence: And Other Chosen Fragments from the "Book of the Golden Precepts."* Point Loma, California: The Aryan Theosophical Press.

Brébeuf, Jean de (1959) 'Relation de ce qui s'est passé aux Hurons en l'année 1635. Envoyée à Kebec au P. le Jeune, parle P. Brébeuf [*Relation of what occurred among the Hurons in the year 1635*].' In Volume 8 of *The Jesuit Relations and Allied Documents: Travels and Explorations of the Jesuit Missionaries in New France, 1610–1791*. Edited by Reuben Gold Thwaites. New York: Pageant Book Company. pp. 67–154.

Browning, Robert (1911) '*Oh, good gigantic smile o' the brown old earth. . .*' In *The Pageant of English Poetry*. Robert Maynard Leonard, compiler. London: Oxford University Press.

Chariton, Igumen, ed. (1997) *The Art of Prayer: An Orthodox Anthology*. London: Faber & Faber.

Chekhov, Anton (1916) *Plays by Anton Tchekoff*. Translated from the Russian by Marian Fell, New York: Charles Scribner's Sons.

Chekhov, Anton (1978) *Complete Works and Letters in 30 volumes*. Volume XIII. Plays 1895–1904. Moscow: Nauka.

Condivi, Ascanio (1903) *The Life of Michael Angelo Buonarroti*. Translated by Charles Holroyd. In Holroyd, Charles. *Michael Angelo Buonarroti* (with Translations of the *Life of the Master by His Scholar*, Ascanio Condivi, and *Three Dialogues* from the Portuguese by Francisco d'Ollanda), London: Duckworth and Company; New York: Charles Scribner's Sons.

Cushing, Frank Hamilton (1896) *Outlines of Zuni Creation Myths*. Extract from the Thirteenth Annual Report to the Bureau of Ethnology. Washington, DC: Government Printing Office.

Dante Alighieri (1911) *The Divine Comedy*. Translated by C. E. Wheeler. Volume II. London: J.M. Dent & Sons; New York: E.P. Dutton & CO.

Davydov, Vladimir (1962) *Rasskazy o proshlom* [*Tales About the Past*]. Moscow-Leningrad: Iskusstvo.

Demidov, Nikolai (2004) *Tvorcheskoye naslediye v 4 tomakh* [*Creative Heritage in 4 volumes*]. Margarita Laskina, ed. Volume II. St. Petersburg: Giperion.

Demidov, Nikolai (2009) *Tvorcheskoye naslediye v 4 tomakh* [*Creative Heritage in 4 volumes*]. Margarita Laskina, ed. Volume IV. St. Petersburg: Baltiiskiye Sezony.

d'Ollanda, Francisco (1903) *Three Dialogues*. In Holroyd, Charles. *Michael Angelo Buonarroti* (with Translations of the *Life of the Master by His Scholar*, Ascanio Condivi, and *Three Dialogues* from the Portuguese by Francisco d'Ollanda), London: Duckworth and Company; New York: Charles Scribner's Sons.

Dostoyevsky, Fyodor (1985) *Polnoye sobraniye sochineniy v tridtsati tomakh* [*Complete Works in 30 volumes*]. Vol. XXVIII. Books 1 and 2. Leningrad: Nauka.

Efros, Natan (2007) 'Moliere v Khudozhestvennom teatre [Moliere at the Art Theatre].' Rech Newspaper. March 29, 2013. Reprinted in *Moscow Art Theatre in Russian Theatre Criticism*: 1906–1918. Olga Radischeva and Elena Shingareva, eds. Moscow: Artist. Rezhissyor. Teatr.

Engelmeyer, Pyotr (1910) *Teoria tvorchestva* [*The Theory of Creativity*]. St. Petersburg: Obrazovaniye.

Erberg, Konstantin (1913) *Tsel' tvorchestva. Opyty po teorii tvorchestva i estetike* [*The Aim of Creative Work. Experience in Creativity Theory and Aesthetics*]. Moscow: Russkaia mysl'.

Evreinov, Nikolai (2002) *Demon teatral'nosti* [*The Demon of Theatricality*]. Moscow-St. Petersburg: Letniy sad.

Fet, Afanasy (1949) 'I come again.' In *A Treasury of Russian Verse*, translated by Frances Cornford and E. Polianowsky Salaman. Edited by Avrahm Yarmolinsky. New York: The Macmillan.

Filshtinsky, Veniamin (2006) *Otkrytaya pedagogika* [Open Pedagogy]. St Petersburg: Baltiyskiye Sezony.

Flower, Sydney B., ed. (1907) *Chteniye myslei* [Mind Reading]. Translated from English [into Russian] by V. Sing. St. Petersburg: Leontiev Printing Workshop.

Gellershtein, Solomon (1968) 'Nauka o tvorchestve [The Science of Creativity].' In TEATR Magazine. 1968. Issue 7.

Goethe, Johann Wolfgang von (1850) *Conversations of Goethe with Eckermann and Soret*. Translated from German by John Oxenford. In 2 volumes. Vol. II. London: Smith, Elder and Co.

Goethe, Johann Wolfgang von (1892) *Goethes Werke* [Goethe's Works]. Part 1. Volume XII. Weimar: H.Bohlau.

Gogol. Nikolai (1926) *Evenings on a Farm Near Dikanka*. In *The Collected Works of Nikolay Gogol*. Translated By Constance Garnett. New York: Alfred A. Knopf.

Gogol, Nikolai (1940) *Polnoye sobraniye sichineniy v 14 tomakh* [*Complete Works in 14 volumes*]. Volume X. Moscow-Leningrad: Izdatel'stvo Akademii Nauk/Pushkinskiy Dom.

Gogol, Nikolai (1949) *Polnoye sobraniye sichineniy v 14 tomakh* [*Complete Works in 14 volumes*]. Volume V. Moscow-Leningrad: Izdatel'stvo Akademii Nauk/Pushkinskiy Dom.

Gogol, Nikolai (1913) *Illustrirovannoye sobraniye sochineniy v vosmi tomakh* [*Illustrated Collected Works in Eight Volumes*]. Volume VIII. Moscow: Pechatnik.

Griboedov, Alexander (1969) *Gore ot uma* [*Woe From Wit*]. Moscow: Nauka.

Grigoriev, Apollon (1985) *Teatral'naya kritika* [*Theater Criticism*]. Leningrad: Iskusstvo.

Gruzenberg, Semyon (1923) *Psikhologiya tvorchestva* [*The Psychology of Creativity*]. Volume I. Minsk: Beltrestpechyat'.

Gruzenberg, Semyon (1929) *Geniy i tvorchestvo* [*Genius and Creativity*]. Leningrad: Soikin.

Hoffmann, E.T.A. (1971) *Tagebucher* [*Diary*]. Friedrich Schnapp, ed. München: Winkler Verlag.

Humsun, Knut (1908). *Victoria*. Kristiania: Gyldendalske Boghandel.

Humsun, Knut (1921). *Hunger*. Translated from the Norwegian by George Egerton. New York: Alfred Knopf.

James, William (1893) *Psychology*. New York: Henry Holt and Company

James, William (1916) *Talks To Teachers On Psychology: And To Students On Some Of Life's Ideals*. New York: Henry Holt And Company.

Janet, Pierre (1889) *L'automatisme psychologique* [*On Psychic Automatism*]. Paris: Felix Elcan.

Khodasevich, Vladislav (1915) 'Predisloviye [Preface].' In Pushkin, Alexander. *Dramaticheskiye stseny* [*Dramatic Scenes*]. Vladislav Khodasevich, ed. Moscow: Pol'za.

Kizevetter, Alexander (1925) 'Geroicheskoye i budnichnoye v tvorchestve Yermolovoi [Heroic and Mundane in Yermolova's Creative Work].' In *Maria Yermolova*. Moscow: Svetozar.

Koenigsberger, Leo (1906) *Hermann von Helmholtz*. Translated by Frances A. Welby. Oxford: Clarendon Press.

Kretschmer, Ernst (1960) *Hysteria, Reflex, and Instinct*. New York: Philosophical Library.

Krylov, Ivan (1859) *Sobraniye sochineniy I. Krylova* [*Collected Works by Ivan Krylov*]. Volume II. St. Petersburg: Veimar.

Laskina, Margarita, Ed. (2000) *Mochalov. Letopis' zhizni i tvorchestva* [*Mochalov. The Chronicle of Life and Creative Work*]. Moscow: Yazyki russkoi kul'tury.

Lapshin, Ivan (1923) *Khudozhestvennoye tvorchestvo* [*Artistic Creativity*]. Moscow: Mysl'.

Le Bon, Gustave (1907) *The Evolution of Matter*. London: The Walter Scott Publishing, New York: Charles Scribner's Sons.

Lensky, Alexander (1894) 'Zapiski aktyora [An Actor's Notes].' In *Artist* Magazine. 1893. Issue 43.

Leonidov, Leonid (1960) 'Mitia Karamazov.' In *Leonid Mironovich Leonidov: Vospominaniya, statyi, besedy, perepiska, zapisnye knizhki* [*Leonid Leonidov: Memoires, Articles, Talks, Letters, Notebooks*]. Moscow: Iskusstvo.

Lermontov, Mikhail (1954) *Sobraniye sohineniy v 6 tomakh* [*Collected Works in 6 volumes*]. Volume II. Moscow: Izdatel'stvo Akademii Nauk SSSR.

Lermontov, Mikhail (1983) *Narrative Poems by Alexander Pushkin and Mikhail Lermontov*. Translated by Charles Johnston. New York: Random House.

Marden, Orison Swett (1894) *Rising in the World: Or, Architects of Fate*, New York: Thomas Y Crowell & CO.

Marx, Karl (1936) *Capital*. Translated by Samuel Moore and Edward Avering. New York: The Modern Library.

McGeoch, John (1932). 'Forgetting and the law of disuse'. *Psychological Review* 39 (4): 352–370.

Merejkowski, Dmitri (1905) *The Romance of Leonardo da Vinci*. Translation by Herbert Trench. New York and London: G.P. Putman's Sons.

Mulford, Prentice (2007) *The God in You*. Radford, VA: Wilder Publications.

Mochalov, Pavel (2000) 'Neokonhennaya statya ob iskysstve aktyora [Unfinished Article On the Art of the Actor].' In Mochalov, Pavel. 'Khronika zhizni i tvorchestva' [*Chronicle of Life and Art*]. Margarita Laskina, ed. Moscow: Yazyki russkoi kul'tury.

Müller, Georg; Pilzecker, Alfons. (1900).'Experimentelle beiträge zur lehre von gedächtnis [*Experimental Contributions to the Science of Memory*]'. *Zeitschrift für Psychologie* 1: 1–300.

Murphy, Althur (1801) *The Life of David Garrick*. Dublin: Brett Smith.

Mozart, Wolfgang Amadeus (1891) 'From a Letter of the Composer to Baron F-'. In *The Musical Times*. 1891. No. 585. Vol. XXXII. *Mozart Supplement*. London and New York: Novello, Ewer and Co. pp. 19–20.

Nietzche, Friedrich (1896) *The Works of Friedrich Nietzche*. Volume VIII. *Thus Spake Zarathustra*. Translated by Alexander Tille. London: The Macmillan Company.

Nemirovich-Danchenko, Vladimir (2009) 'Pismo v TSEKUBU [Letter to TSEKUBU].' In Demidov, Nikolai. Tvorcheskoye naslediye v 4 tomakh [Creative Heritage in 4 volumes]. Margarita Laskina, ed. Volume IV. St. Petersburg: Baltiiskiye Sezony.

Orlova-Savina, Praskovya (1994) *Avtobiografiya* [*Autobiography*]. Moscow: Khudozhestvennaya literatura.

Ostrovsky, Alexander (1899) *The Storm*. Translated by Constance Garnett. London: Duckworth & Co.

Ostrovsky, Alexander (1917) *Plays by Alexander Ostrovsky*. A translation from the Russian, edited by George Rapall Noyes. New York: Charles Scribner's Sons.

Patanjali (1920) *The Yoga Aphorisms of Patanjali*, An Interpretation by William Q. Judge. Los Angeles, California: United Lodge of Theosophists.

Pavis, Patrice (1998) *Dictionary of Theatre*. Toronto: University of Toronto Press.

Pavlov, Ivan (1949) *Pavlosvkiye sredy* [*Pavlov's Wednesdays*]. Volume I. Moscow-Leningrad: Isdatelstvo AN SSSR.

Pavlov, Ivan (1951) *Izbrannye proizvedeniya* [*Selected Works*]. Moscow: Gosydarstvennoye izdatel'stvo politicheskoy literatury.

Pevtsov, Illarion (1935) *Beseda ob aktyore* [*Conversation About Acting*]. In Illarion Nikolayevich Pevtsov 1879–1934. Leningrad: Gosudarstvennyi teatr dramy.

Pevtsov, Illarion (1978) *Literaturno-teatral'noe nasledie* [*Literary and Theatrical Heritage*]. Moscow: VTO.

Poincaré, Henri (1913) *The Foundations Of Science*. Authorized translation by George Bruce Halsted. New York and Garrison, NY: The Science Press.

Prod'Homme, J. G. (1911) *Nicolo Paganini: A Biography*. Translated from the original French by Alice Mattullath. New York: C. Fischer.

Prokofiev, Vladimir (1948) 'K. Stanislavsky o tvercheskom protsesse aktyra' (ocherk 2) [Stanislavsky on the Actor's Creative Process (essay 2)]. In TEATR Magazine. 1948. Issue 3. pp. 34–43.

Pushkin, Alexander (1888) *Poems by Alexander Pushkin*. Translated from Russian, with Introduction and Notes by Ivan Panin. Boston: Cupples and Hurd.

Pushkin, Alexander. (1918) *Boris Godunov*. Rendered into English verse by Alfred Hayes. Preface by C. Nabokoff. New York: Dutton.

Pushkin, Alexander (1936) *The Poems, Prose and Plays of Alexander Pushkin*. Translated by Avrahm Yarmolinsky. New York: Modern Library.

Pushkin, Alexander (1949) *Polnoye sobraniye sochineniy v 16 tomakh* [*Complete Works in 16 volumes*]. Volume III. Moscow: Izdatel'stvo akademii nauk.

Pushkin, Alexander (1959) *Sobraniye sochineniy v 10 tomakh* [*Collected Works in 10 volumes*]. Volume II. Moscow: Khudozhestvennaya literatura.

Pushkin, Alexander (1960) *Sobraniye sochineniy v 10 tomakh* [*Collected Works in 10 volumes*]. Volume V. Moscow: Khudozhestvennaya literatura.

Pushkin, Alexander (1962) *Sobraniye sochineniy v 10 tomakh* [*Collected Works in 10 volumes*]. Volume VI. Moscow: Khudozhestvennaya literatura.

Pushkin, Alexander (1972) 'Winter Evening.' In *Pushkin Threefold*. Translated by Walter Arndt. New York: Dutton.

Pushkin, Alexander (1979) *Eugene Onegin*. Translated by Charles Johnston. Middlesex: Penguin.

Pushkin, Alexander (2009) *Eugene Onegin*. Translated by James E. Falen. Oxford: Oxford University Press.

Roth, Walter E. (1897) Ethnological Studies Among The North-West-Central Queensland Aborigines. Brisbane: Government Printer.

Rousseau, Jean-Jacques (1920) *Selections from the Works of Jean-Jacques Rousseau*. Christian Gauss, ed. Princeton: Princeton University Press.

Rosanoff, M.A. (1932) 'Edison in His Laboratory.' In *Harper's* Magazine, September 1932. Volume 165. New York: Harper & Brothers.

S. (1891) 'Obschestvo iskusstva i literatury [Society of Art and Literature].' In *Artist* Magazine. 1891. Issue 12.

Sadovsky, Prov (1889) '*Fyodor Semyonovich Potanchikov*.' In *Artist* Magazine. 1889. No. 3.

Salvini, Tommaso (1891) 'Neskol'ko myslei o stseniheskom iskusstve [A Few Thoughts on the Art of the Stage.' In *Artist* magazine. No. 14.

Schiller, Friedrich (1802) *Die Räuber*, C.F. Schwan und G.C. Götz, Mannheim.

Schiller, Friedrich (1883) *Schiller's Works*. Edited by J.G. Fischer. Volume II. Philadelphia: George Barrie, Publisher.

Sechenov, Ivan (1965) *Reflexes of the Brain*. Russian text edited by K. Koshtoyants. Translated from the Russian by S. Belsky. Edited by G. Gibbons. Notes by S. Cellerstein. Cambridge, MA: M.I.T. Press

Shchepkin, Mikhail (1984) *Mikhail Semyonovich Shchepkin. Zhizn i tvorchestvo* [Life and Art]. In 2 volumes. Volume I. Moscow: Iskusstvo.

Shchepkina-Kupernik, Tatyana (1924) *Dni moyei zhizni* [*Days of My Life*]. Moscow: Federatsiya.

Shchepkina-Kupernik, Tatyana (1940) *O M.N. Yermolovoi (Iz vospominanyi)* [*On Yermolova. (From Memoirs)*]. Moscow-Leningrad: VTO.

Shchepkina-Kupernik, Tatyana (1983) *Yermolova*. Moscow: Iskusstvo.

Sibiryakov, Nikita (1974) *Mirovoye znacheniye Stanislavskogo* [*Stanislavsky's Significance in the World*]. Moscow: Iskusstvo.

Sobolev, Yuri (1937) *Pavel Mochalov*. Moscow: Zhurnal'no-gazetnoye obyedinenie.

Spinoza, Benedict De (1891) *The Chief Works of Benedict De Spinoza*. Translated from the Latin, with an Introduction by R.H.M. Elwes. Vol. II, London: George Bell and Sons.

Sri Ramana Maharshi (1989) *Be as You Are: The Teachings of Sri Ramana Maharshi*. David Godman, Ed. London: Penguin Books.

Stanislavsky, Konstantin (1931) *Moya zhizn' v iskusstve* [*My Life in Art*]. Leningrad-Moscow: Academia.

Stanislavsky, Konstantin (1938) *Rabota aktyora nad soboi* [*An Actor's Work on Self*]. Moscow: Khudozhestvennaya literatura.

Stanislavsky, Konstantin (1954) *Sobraniye Sochineniy v 8 tomakh* [*Collected Works in 8 volumes*]. Volume II. Moscow: Iskusstvo.

Stanislavsky, Konstantin (1958) *Sobraniye Sochineniy v 8 tomakh* [*Collected Works in 8 volumes*]. Volume V. Moscow: Iskusstvo.

Stanislavsky, Konstantin (1961) *Sobraniye Sochineniy v 8 tomakh* [*Collected Works in 8 volumes*]. Volume VIII. Moscow: Iskusstvo.

Stanislavsky, Konstantin (1988) *Sobraniye Sochineniy* [*Collected Works*]. In 9 vols. Volume I. Moscow: Iskusstvo.

Stanislavsky, Konstantin (1999) *Sobraniye Sochineniy* [*Collected Works*]. In 9 vols. Volume IX. Moscow: Iskusstvo.

Stanislavski, Konstantin (2008) *An Actor's Work: A Student's Diary*. Jean Benedetti, translator and editor. London and New York: Routledge.

Stanislavsky, Konstantin (2009a) Kharakteristika Nikolaya Demidov [Reference on Nikolai Demidov.] In *Demidov, Nikolai. Tvorcheskoye naslediye v 4 tomakh* [*Creative Heritage in 4 volumes*]. Margarita Laskina, ed. Volume IV. St. Petersburg: Baltiiskiye Sezony.

Stanislavsky, Konstantin (2009b) Pismo predsedateliu Mossoveta, I.I. Sidorovu [Letter to the Chairman of Mossoviet, I.I. Sidorov]. In *Demidov, Nikolai. Tvorcheskoye naslediye v 4 tomakh* [*Creative Heritage in 4 volumes*]. Margarita Laskina, ed. Volume IV. St. Petersburg: Baltiiskiye Sezony.

Steiner, Rudolf (2000) *Rosicrucian Wisdom* [*Theosophy of the Rosicrucian*]. East Sussex: Rudolf Steiner Press.

Sutta-Nipata, The (1881) In *The Sacred Books of the East*. Volume X. Part II. Edited by F. Max Muller. Translated by V. Fausboll. Oxford: Clarendon Press.

Tagore, Rabindranath (1916) *Gitanjali, Song Offering*. New York: The Macmillan Company.

Tairov, Alexander (2009) Pis'mo v Moskovskuiu Kvalifikatsionnuiu Komissiyu pri GubProse [Letter to the Moscow GubPros Qualifying Committee]. In *Demidov, Nikolai. Tvorcheskoye naslediye v 4 tomakh* (*Creative Heritage in 4 volumes*). Margarita Laskina, ed. Volume IV. St. Petersburg: Baltiiskiye Sezony.

Tchaikovsky, Pyotr (1934) *Perepiska s N. F. fon-Meck v 3 tomakh* [*Correspondence with Nadezhda von-Meck in 3 volumes*]. Vol I. Moscow-Leningrad: Akademia.

Tcherkassky, S. (2013) *Stanislavsky i yoga* [*Stanislavsky and Yoga*]. St Petersburg: Izdatelstvo Sankt-Peterburgskoy gosudarstvennoy akademii teatralnogo iskusstva.

Tolstoy, Count A.K. (1893) *Polnoye sobraniye sochineniy v 2 tomakh* [*Complete Works in 2 volumes*]. Volume I. St. Petersburg.

Tolstoy, Lev (1952) *Polnoye sobraniye sochineniy v 90 tomakh* [*Complete Works in Ninety Volumes*]. Volume XLVI. Moscow: Khudozhestvennaya literarura.

Tolstoy, Lev (1984) *Sobraniye sochineniy v 22 tomakh* [*Collected Works in Twenty-Two Volumes*]. Volume XXII. Moscow: Khudozhestvennaya literarura.

Tyutchev, Fyodor (1947) *Silentium. In Three Russian Poets: Selections from Pushkin, Lermontov and Tyutchev*. Translated by Vladimir Nabokov. London: Lindsay Drummond.

Tyutchev, Fyodor (1966) *Lirika: v dvukh tomakh* [*Lyric Poems, in 2 volumes*]. Volume I. Moscow: Nauka.

Tyutchev, Fyodor (1921) 'Oh, thou, my wizard soul. . .' In *Modern Russian Poetry: An Anthology* Translated by Babette Deutsch and Avrahm Yarmolinsky, New York: Harcourt, Brace and Company.

Ukhromaky, Alexei (2002) *Dominanta. Statyi raznykh let. 1887–1939* [Dominant. Articles From Various Periods.] St. Petersburg: Piter.

Vakhtangov, Yevgeny (2011) '*Lectures on the Stanislavsky System.*' In *The Vakhtangov Sourcebook*. Andrei Malaev-Babel, ed. Routledge: London and New York.

Vinogradskaya, Irina ed. (1987) *Stanislavsky repetiruet* [*Stanislavsky Rehearses*]. Moscow: STD.

Volkov, Leonid (1940) 'Interview.' In *Besedy o Vakhtangove* [*Conversations About Vakhtangov*], Khersonsky, Khrisanf (ed.) (1940) Moscow-Leningrad: VTO.

Wagner, Richard (1905) *Richard Wagner to Mathilde Wesendonck*. Translated, prefaced, etc. by William Ashton Ellis. New York: Charles Scribner's Sons.

Wilde, Oscar (1909) *The Complete Writings of Oscar Wilde*. New York: The Pearson Publishing.

Writings From The Philokalia On Prayer Of the Heart (1992) Translated from the Russian Text 'Dobrotolubiyhe' by E. Kadloubovsky and G. E. H. Palmer. London: Faber & Faber.

Yermolova, Maria (1955) 'Otvety M.N. Yermolovoy na ankety teatral'noi sektsii Akademii khudozhest-vennykh nauk po psikhologii aktyorskogo tvorhestva [Maria Yermolova's Answers to the Questionnaire on the Psychology of Acting of the Theatre Division of the Academy of Creative Sciences]'. In *Maria Nikolayevna Yermolova*. Moscow: Iskusstvo.

Young, Edward (1854) *The Complete Works, Poetry and Prose of the Rev. Edward Young, LL.D.*, in Two Volumes. Volume I. London: William Tegg and Co.

Yuzhin-Sumbatov, Alexander (1941) 'Maria Yermolova.' In *A.I. Yuzhin-Sumbatov. Vospominaniya. Zapiski. Statyi. Pis'ma.* [*Yuzhin-Sumbatov. Memoirs. Notes. Articles. Letters*]. Moscow-Leningrad: Iskusstvo.

Index

Note: The following abbreviations have been used — *f* = figure; *g* = glossary term; *n* = note

Taylor & Francis eBooks

Helping you to choose the right eBooks for your Library

Add Routledge titles to your library's digital collection today. Taylor and Francis ebooks contains over 50,000 titles in the Humanities, Social Sciences, Behavioural Sciences, Built Environment and Law.

Choose from a range of subject packages or create your own!

Benefits for you

>> Free MARC records
>> COUNTER-compliant usage statistics
>> Flexible purchase and pricing options
>> All titles DRM-free.

Benefits for your user

>> Off-site, anytime access via Athens or referring URL
>> Print or copy pages or chapters
>> Full content search
>> Bookmark, highlight and annotate text
>> Access to thousands of pages of quality research at the click of a button.

REQUEST YOUR **FREE** INSTITUTIONAL TRIAL TODAY

Free Trials Available
We offer free trials to qualifying academic, corporate and government customers.

eCollections – Choose from over 30 subject eCollections, including:

Archaeology	Language Learning
Architecture	Law
Asian Studies	Literature
Business & Management	Media & Communication
Classical Studies	Middle East Studies
Construction	Music
Creative & Media Arts	Philosophy
Criminology & Criminal Justice	Planning
Economics	Politics
Education	Psychology & Mental Health
Energy	Religion
Engineering	Security
English Language & Linguistics	Social Work
Environment & Sustainability	Sociology
Geography	Sport
Health Studies	Theatre & Performance
History	Tourism, Hospitality & Events

For more information, pricing enquiries or to order a free trial, please contact your local sales team:
www.tandfebooks.com/page/sales

 **Routledge**
Taylor & Francis Group

The home of
Routledge books

www.tandfebooks.com